MITCHELL BEAZLEY

# The [illegible] Schoo[illegible]e 2004



The ***ONLY*** guide you need to choose your child's **secondary school** in London

EDITOR JOEL WOLCHOVER

## Joel Wolchover

Joel Wolchover was educated at Latymer Upper School in Hammersmith and Sidney Sussex College, Cambridge. He has worked at the *Richmond and Twickenham Times, Cambridge Evening News, The Times* and was Education Correspondent of the *Evening Standard* from 1997–2000, where he helped to establish the London School Awards. He now co-owns Catchline News, a London-based news and features agency.

## Specialist writers

Jane Wharton, Joel Wolchover

## Contributors

Shirin Aguiar, David Brown, Robert Campion, Lindsay Coulson, Jo Dixon, Alexis Dite, William Dixon, Rachel Doeg, Nicholas Holebrook, Marie Jackson, Patrick Lambelet, Nicholas Hull-Malham, Beth Miller, Joanna Norris, Christina Park, Mike Parkinson, Clare Peel, Oliver Roberts, Lesley Saunders, Deryn Summers, Kristian Triggle, Patrick Wheaton, Jenny Vereker, Alice Whitehead and Danielle Wrate

## Future editions

This book is as accurate as the combined efforts of a large number of people could make it. We would be grateful to receive news from readers about changes to any schools and any other comments they might have.

**The London Schools Guide 2004**

Published in 2003 by Mitchell Beazley,
an imprint of Octopus Publishing Group Ltd
2–4 Heron Quays, London E14 4JP



ISBN 1 84000 783 4

A CIP record for this book is available from the British Library.

At Mitchell Beazley

| | |
|---|---|
| Executive Editor | Kate John |
| Executive Art Editor | Christine Keilty |
| Project Editor | Peter Taylor |
| Editor | Maxine McCaghy |
| Designer | Alexa Brommer |
| Production | Alexis Coogan |
| Proofreader | Andy Hilliard |
| Indexer | Sandra Shotter |

Set in Clearface Gothic, Franklin Gothic and Helvetica Neue
Printed by Mackays of Chatham

# Contents



## London schools in 2004



## The local education authorities



## League tables

# Introduction

'I start from the belief that every child is capable of attaining high standards. All children should leave school having achieved their potential. They should all acquire the knowledge, qualifications and life skills they need to succeed in the adult world.' Charles Clarke, Secretary of State for Education and Skills, February 2003

London parents have long suspected that they get a raw deal when it comes to finding school places for their children, and since the *London Schools Guide* was first published in 2001, new research has come along that proves them right.

The Office of National Statistics has found that parents in the capital are less likely to be offered a place at their first choice of school than parents elsewhere in the country – 70 per cent get their favourite school compared with 85 per cent nationwide – and the latest figures show that the number of appeals against admissions decisions made by schools and Local Education Authorities has soared.

Choosing a school in London has many parallels with buying property in the capital. You will almost certainly be struck by the immense diversity of options, the often shocking gap between the best and the worst schools, the huge number of different factors that you have to consider and balance against one another and, most frustrating of all, the sheer complexity of the whole process.

Just as you would be foolish to rush into buying a house or a flat without having first found out something about the general market, the area in which you plan to buy and the state of the properties you have in mind, these same considerations should come into play when choosing a school for your child.

For a long time the world of education had the reputation of being something of a 'secret garden', in which teachers and schools operated largely away from the prying eyes of parents and the wider community. It seemed at times that even the government and the Whitehall civil servants who were in charge of the education system had little idea what was going on behind the gates of most schools.

Changes in recent years have done much to open up this closed world. The establishment of the schools inspectorate Ofsted in 1992, the publication of academic results, from which newspapers produce their league tables, and the present government's introduction of targets for raising exam performance, have all contributed to a new culture of openness and greater disclosure.

This book aims to help further the cause of openness. Aimed at parents living in or moving to London, it is designed to be as detailed, comprehensive and up-to-date as possible, while at the same time offering a simple and accessible guide to all of the capital's secondary schools.

Sources of information that are already in the public domain, such as Ofsted reports and exam results, are an invaluable resource but they can just as often baffle as enlighten parents seeking answers to questions about their children's education.

The fanfare which accompanied the publication of the first league tables has been replaced by almost complete indifference, as parents come to realize what many education experts said all along – that the information contained in the tables is virtually useless unless it is put into context.

It is this context that the journalists and writers who have contributed to this book are able to offer. Drawing on all the information available and combining it with their personal knowledge of each school and the community it serves, they are able to give insights that no isolated official report or league table can hope to provide.

Unlike other books on the market this is not a guide to the 'best' secondary schools in London. It is a guide to all secondary schools in London, from the most successful to those that are struggling – and every shade in between. We believe that every school has something to offer and only by covering every option can we give a comprehensive picture of what is available.

From Barking to Westminster, all 33 education authorities in the Greater London area are covered along with all mainstream secondary schools, with the exception of special needs schools.

That means that state schools and private schools, grammar schools and comprehensives, religious and non-religious schools all rub shoulders in this book. For each school you will find all the basic information you would expect: the address and telephone number, as well as e-mail addresses and web sites where applicable. We also provide the name of the current head teacher and chairman of the school's governors, along with a brief description of the school uniform. Practical information is also given about school hours, public transport that serves the school and the type of food available, as well as information on the admissions process, including the deadline for submitting application forms and an indication of how heavy demand for places has been in previous years.

Our writers have also profiled each school in-depth, with a detailed explanation of the academic standards and extra-curricular activities on offer, from school sports, music and drama to trips abroad and organized voluntary work.

The latest league tables are included in the appendices, so that you can see at a glance how the schools have performed academically, both in relation to other schools in their area and across London.

Tips on how to interpret these tables can be found in the first part of the book, along with chapters that aim to explain the whole process of choosing a secondary school in London and applying for a place. They include hints on how to choose a school that is right for your child, an explanation of the many different types of school and the various bodies responsible for them, and advice on tackling the inevitable red tape you will encounter along the way.

As you start your research, it is worth bearing in mind that there is no such thing as a school that will suit all young people. Secondary schools tend to develop their own distinctive character and it is for you to decide, knowing your child's temperament, whether or not he or she will fit in. What's more, no school, however highly regarded, can offer a cast-iron guarantee of academic success.

Having said that, there are certain characteristics that good schools have in common. Certainly good resources help. It is no coincidence that private schools, where annual fees are typically three times the amount of money that is spent on each child in the state sector, consistently perform better academically. Their other major advantage is that most of them select pupils for their academic ability, insisting that applicants take competitive entrance exams. This is a practice also maintained by the handful of state-funded grammar schools that remain in London, which also tend to have equally impressive exam results. However, the mark of a good school is not to be found in its facilities or the social environment in which it operates but in that indefinable and often over-used word 'ethos'. Good schools are those which, to use the current jargon, 'add value' to your child's education. Above all, they are schools that have high expectations of all the children in their care and not just the high achievers.

Conversely, there are clearly schools that are not doing as well as they could. The government has set a minimum requirement that all secondary schools should ensure that at least 15 per cent of their pupils achieve five good GCSE passes, at grade C or above. Although this is not particularly ambitious – the national average is 51.5 per cent – there were nine state secondary schools in London that failed to achieve even this low target in 2002.

Parents who have been successful in securing a place at the school of their choice have said it feels like winning the lottery. Certainly, as competition for the most sought-after schools increases, it can feel as if the odds are stacked against you. However, it is still the case that with careful planning and a realistic attitude, your search should ultimately prove successful. Good luck.

Joel Wolchover, London, March 2003

# How to use this book

The first part of this book contains the analysis and reference chapters: a guide to London's secondary schools. Look here for information on how to choose a school for your child, how London's secondary schools work, the different types of school, admissions policies, who runs London's schools, and an explanation of league tables.

At the core of this book is a survey of London's secondary schools, borough by borough. At the beginning of the description of each borough is a handy factfile, with details of the LEA and relevant statistics, including borough admissions procedure and a general overview of the borough itself and its education statistics. School league table positions and borough positions are for 2002.

Each section contains descriptions of all the secondary schools in the borough plus a general introduction to the borough itself. A list of the schools covered appears in the index.

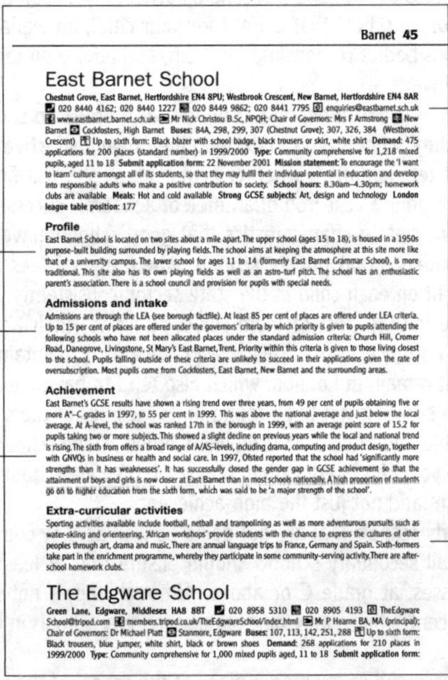

Barnet 45

## East Barnet School

**Chestnut Grove, East Barnet, Hertfordshire EN4 8PU; Westbrook Crescent, New Barnet, Hertfordshire EN4 8AR** 020 8440 4162; 020 8440 1227 020 8449 9862; 020 8441 7795 enquiries@eastbarnet.sch.uk www.eastbarnet.barnet.sch.uk Mr Nick Christou B.Sc, NPQH; Chair of Governors: Mrs F Armstrong New Barnet Cockfosters, High Barnet **Buses**: 84A, 298, 299, 307 (Chestnut Grove); 307, 326, 384 (Westbrook Crescent) Up to sixth form: Black blazer with school badge, black trousers or skirt, white shirt **Demand**: 475 applications for 200 places (standard number) in 1999/2000 **Type**: Community comprehensive for 1,218 mixed pupils, aged 11 to 18 **Submit application form**: 22 November 2001 **Mission statement**: To encourage the 'I want to learn' culture amongst all of its students, so that they may fulfil their individual potential in education and develop into responsible adults who make a positive contribution to society. **School hours**: 8.30am–4.30pm; homework clubs are available **Meals**: Hot and cold available **Strong GCSE subjects**: Art, design and technology **London league table position**: 177

### Profile

East Barnet School is located on two sites about a mile apart. The upper school (ages 15 to 18), is housed in a 1950s purpose-built building surrounded by playing fields. The school aims at keeping the atmosphere at this site more like that of a university campus. The lower school for ages 11 to 14 (formerly East Barnet Grammar School), is more traditional. This site also has its own playing fields as well as an astro-turf pitch. The school has an enthusiastic parent's association. There is a school council and provision for pupils with special needs.

### Admissions and intake

Admissions are through the LEA (see borough factfile). At least 85 per cent of places are offered under LEA criteria. Up to 15 per cent of places are offered under the governors' criteria by which priority is given to pupils attending the following schools who have not been allocated places under the standard admission criteria: Church Hill, Cromer Road, Danegrove, Livingstone, St Mary's East Barnet, Trent. Priority within this criteria is given to those living closest to the school. Pupils falling outside of these criteria are unlikely to succeed in their applications given the rate of oversubscription. Most pupils come from Cockfosters, East Barnet, New Barnet and the surrounding areas.

### Achievement

East Barnet's GCSE results have shown a rising trend over three years, from 49 per cent of pupils obtaining five or more A*–C grades in 1997, to 55 per cent in 1999. This was above the national average and just below the local average. At A-level, the school was ranked 17th in the borough in 1999, with an average point score of 15.2 for pupils taking two or more subjects. This showed a slight decline on previous years while the local and national trend is rising. The sixth from offers a broad range of A/AS-levels, including drama, computing and product design, together with GNVQs in business or health and social care. In 1997, Ofsted reported that the school had 'significantly more strengths than it has weaknesses'. It has successfully closed the gender gap in GCSE achievement so that the attainment of boys and girls is now closer at East Barnet than in most schools nationally. A high proportion of students go on to higher education from the sixth form, which was said to be 'a major strength of the school'.

### Extra-curricular activities

Sporting activities available include football, netball and trampolining as well as more adventurous pursuits such as water-skiing and orienteering. 'African workshops' provide students with the chance to express the cultures of other peoples through art, drama and music. There are annual language trips to France, Germany and Spain. Sixth-formers take part in the enrichment programme, whereby they participate in some community-serving activity. There are after-school homework clubs.

## The Edgware School

**Green Lane, Edgware, Middlesex HA8 8BT** 020 8958 5310 020 8905 4193 TheEdgwareSchool@tripod.com members.tripod.co.uk/TheEdgwareSchool/index.html Mr P Hearne BA, MA (principal); Chair of Governors: Dr Michael Platt Stanmore, Edgware **Buses**: 107, 113, 142, 251, 288 Up to sixth form: Black trousers, blue jumper, white shirt, black or brown shoes **Demand**: 268 applications for 210 places in 1999/2000 **Type**: Community comprehensive for 1,000 mixed pupils aged, 11 to 18 **Submit application form**:

See key for icons below

The profile includes a brief description of the school and its facilities.

Admissions procedure

In Achievement, GCSE and A-level results are surveyed, also noting if pupils can take GNVQs.

Extra-curricular activities gives details of which sports are on offer, how pupils get involved with the local community, music and drama provisions and details of school trips.

**Key to Icons in Factfiles**

| | | | |
|---|---|---|---|
| | Telephone number | | Overground rail station |
| | Fax number | | London Underground station |
| | E-mail address | | Head teacher |
| | Website address | | Uniform |

# School map information

**Each borough starts with a map, which shows the locations of the schools, transport links and major road names. Every school is listed by name in the key under each map.**

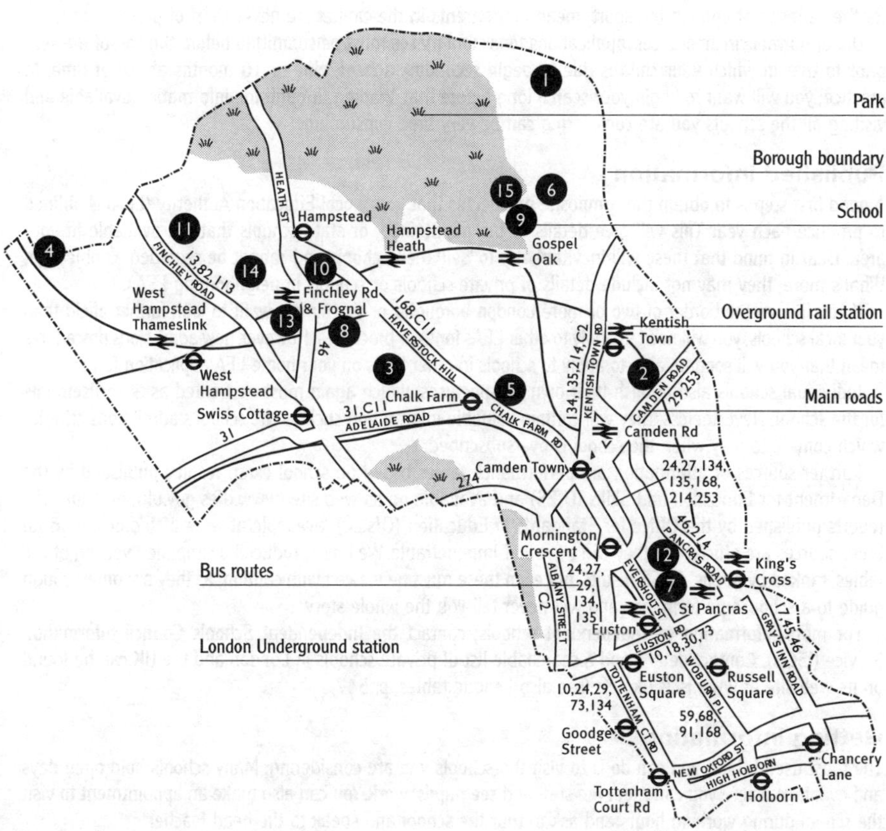


### Tables

**The appendices contain useful tables, including the year 2002 league table results, organized by borough and also by a London-wide ranking.**

# How to choose a school

**The most stressful events in anyone's life are said to be marriage, divorce and moving home. For parents living in London, the list could also include finding a secondary school place for your child. In theory there should be enough to go around. Within the Greater London area there are around 400 state secondary schools to choose from and almost half as many again in the independent sector.**

The present government has maintained the Conservative doctrine of 'parental choice', which empowered parents to be more demanding about the sort of school they will accept for their children. Recent legistlation has refined the principle in recognition of the fact that, where demand outstrips supply, the admissions process will inevitably bring disappointment for those parents whose application to a particular school is rejected.

Everyone wants the best for their children and, although that will mean different things for different children, good schools will always attract more applications for places than they can accept. In the most extreme cases, a school may be 10 times oversubscribed, with 1000 applications for just 100 places.

More positively, the diversity of schools in London and the abundance of transport links, even accounting for the vagaries of London transport, mean that parents in the capital are never short of possible options.

Under normal circumstances, applications for school places must be submitted before the end of the year prior to that in which your child is due to begin secondary school, nine or 10 months ahead of time. In practice, you will want to begin your search long before that. Wading through the information available and visiting all the schools you are considering can be very time consuming.

## Published information

A good first step is to obtain the composite prospectus that your Local Education Authority (LEA) is obliged to produce each year. This will give details of the maintained, or state schools that are available in your area. Bear in mind that these will inevitably try to 'sell' their schools and cannot be regarded as objective. What's more, they may not include details of private schools or schools in neighbouring LEAs.

If you live on the border of two or more London boroughs, or you simply want to look further afield than your local schools, you will need to apply to other LEAs for their brochures. However, new admissions procedures mean that you will soon be able to apply to schools in other LEAs on your home LEA application form.

Individual schools also publish their own prospectuses, which again must be treated as advertisements for the school. Nevertheless, they will contain valuable information such as the school's admissions criteria, which come into play when the school is oversubscribed.

Further sources of information are performance tables based on school exam results, published by the Department for Education and Skills (DfES) and available on its web site (www.dfes.gov.uk), or inspection reports published by the Office for Standards in Education (Ofsted), available at www.ofsted.gov.uk. Both these sources are official but they can be rather impenetrable. We have produced a simplified version of the tables, ranked by pupils' GCSE results, but even these must be viewed with caution, as they are only a rough guide to a school's performance and will never tell you the whole story.

For more information on independent schools, contact the Independent Schools Council Information Service (ISCis). Contact details and a searchable list of private schools in London and the UK can be found on its web site at www.iscis.uk.net; (see also League tables, p. 547).

## Getting information

The most useful thing you can do is to visit the schools you are considering. Many schools hold open days and evenings where you can meet the staff and see pupils' work. You can also make an appointment to visit the school during working hours and ask to tour the school and speak to the head teacher.

Academic results are important to many parents but you should also be aware of the curriculum that is offered. A school full of academic high-fliers may not offer a wide range of subjects, particularly the vocational options that your child may eventually wish to pursue.

If your child is entering the school at age 11 (or 13 in the case of some independent schools), you should ask if the school has a sixth form and if children can automatically transfer from the lower school, or whether this transfer is dependent on their final GCSE results.

Most schools have a parent-teacher association (PTA), which may be able to give you extra information and offer advice on the admissions process. Again, ask the school for further details.

## Streaming

The way that children of different abilities are grouped within a school is a hotly debated issue. On one side of the debate is the practice of mixed ability teaching, which means that gifted children, those of average ability and those who are less able are taught alongside one another in the same classroom. The theory is that the interaction of children of varying abilities works to the benefit of all. The bright children, supporters of mixed ability teaching argue, will help their less gifted peers and also benefit themselves. Critics allege that mixed ability teaching is a form of political correctness, which does not work in practice. They argue that by trying to be all things to all pupils, teachers are unable to tailor lessons to the children's real needs. Fashions change and, while mixed ability teaching was all the rage in the 1960s and 1970s, it is now frowned upon by official bodies such as the Department for Education and Ofsted. Instead, streaming or setting, which involves separating children into different classes according to their ability, is the order of the day in most secondary schools.

Nevertheless, schools retain a wide discretion over how they arrange their classes, and head teachers would strongly oppose any diktat from central government or Ofsted over how precisely to organize streaming. Some schools operate streaming for each subject, or just for core subjects such as English and maths. Others have a fast stream of pupils who take all their subjects together. Some schools are also experimenting with separate classes for boys and girls in key subjects.

It is worth checking what sort of streaming, if any, is practised in each school that you are considering, and what sort of tests your child will be required to take to determine which class they are put in.

### Application forms and admissions criteria

Once you have narrowed your choices, you must start the application process. To help you, all state schools and Local Education Authorities must, by law, publish their admissions criteria. This is a checklist of the points which will be considered when assessing your application and, equally importantly, the order in which each factor will be considered (see Admissions procedures, p. 18).

Typically, the criteria will include the distance you live from the school, whether you already have children at the school and, for a church school, whether you can demonstrate religious commitment, for instance with a recommendation from a local vicar or priest. In a comprehensive school, your child's academic ability will not be taken into account, except where a school routinely tests applicants to ensure they have an equal spread of children across the ability range, known as banding.

In the relatively small number of grammar schools and partially selective schools left in London, a proportion of places (all of them in the case of grammar schools), are allocated on academic ability. If you apply to a selective school, your child will be expected to sit an 11-plus style entrance exam. Unless schools share test results, as they do in Wandsworth, your child will face a fresh test at each school you apply to (see Types of school, p. 12).

# Who runs London's schools?

Following the Thatcher government's abolition of the Inner London Education Authority (ILEA) in 1990, there has been no single authority in charge of London's schools.

The creation of the Greater London Assembly (GLA) and the election of Ken Livingstone as London's first elected Mayor has done nothing to change this situation. Neither of them have any formal influence over education policy in the capital. This may come to be seen as a wasted opportunity, as there is a pressing need for the London-wide coordination of strategic decisions, such as the building of new schools and the allocation of school places across LEA borders.

### Local Education Authorities (LEAs)

There are 33 LEAs in London and each London borough has an LEA, including the Corporation of London. The Local Education Authorities are responsible for running all central services, such as school transport and facilities for children with special needs, as well as administering admissions for those schools that come directly under their control.

You do not have to choose a school in the borough in which you live. State schools are paid by the number of pupils that they admit, regardless of where the pupils live. A legal ruling in 1989, known as the Greenwich Judgement, established the right of parents to apply to any school they want. In London, where the sheer density of population means that local authorities are close to one another, it is common to send your child to a school outside the borough in which you live. Around 14 per cent of children in London travel every day to schools outside their 'home' borough.

The right to apply to any school you choose is not the same as the right to a place. Legally, only your own borough has a duty to find a school place for your child. Otherwise it is up to you to find a school and to persuade the relevant admissions authority that your child meets the entry criteria. These admissions criteria must, as the law states, be clear, objective and published openly.

The inner London LEAs are: the Corporation of London, Camden, Greenwich, Hackney, Hammersmith and Fulham, Islington, Kensington and Chelsea, Lambeth, Lewisham, Southwark, Tower Hamlets, Wandsworth and Westminster.

The outer London LEAs are: Barking and Dagenham, Barnet, Bexley, Brent, Bromley, Croydon, Ealing, Enfield, Haringey, Harrow, Havering, Hillingdon, Hounslow, Kingston upon Thames, Merton, Newham, Redbridge, Richmond upon Thames, Sutton and Waltham Forest.

## Governing bodies

Individual schools are run by their governing body. It is the governors who set the school's internal policies, hire teachers and decide whether or not to permanently exclude pupils. The composition of the governing body is important to the way the school is run, in particular the proportion of governors who are appointed by the LEA.

In schools where the majority of governors are appointed by the LEA, community and voluntary controlled schools, the LEA is the admissions authority. In voluntary aided and foundation schools, and now Academies, the LEA has some representatives on the governing body but they are not in the majority and the governing body is the admissions authority. However, new government rules mean that LEAs will co-ordinate admissions arrangements for all maintained secondary schools and Academies. Although schools where the governing body is the admissions authority will still decide which pupils to admit, parents will enjoy a much simpler application process. There will be just one form for applications to all state schools – even schools in other LEAs – and all parents will find out on the same day which school their child has won a place at. The new application system will be examined in detail below.

## Maintained schools

Maintained schools are state schools that are funded by the government out of public funds, as opposed to independent schools, referred to variously as private or fee-paying, where parents have to foot the bill.

If you feel schools in your area are being under-funded, contact your local council as it is the job of councillors to set the education budget, which is then distributed to local schools. However, they are constrained by limits that the government places on the amount they can spend above the Standard Spending Assessment (SSA) – a restriction which is known as capping. The amount schools receive is dictated by a complex series of formulae devised by Whitehall. There is extra money for children with special needs, children for whom English is not their first language and children who are refugees. But changes in the funding system mean that some London schools received less money in 2003 than in previous years, leading to well-publicized cutbacks.

In education, as in most public services, however much money is provided it is never enough. Some maintained schools have begun asking parents for donations towards their running costs. This is a relatively recent and controversial phenomenon. Parents of children at maintained schools are not obliged to pay anything towards the cost of their children's education, and many feel that being asked for a donation places them in an uncomfortable position and believe, wrongly, that not contributing might affect their children's treatment at the school.

## Community schools

Community schools are those schools that are run by the LEA. Representatives of the LEA will have a majority on the governing body of a community school and the LEA is the admissions authority, responsible for admissions to all community schools within its boundaries. Community schools usually accept a comprehensive intake (see Types of school, p12) and are unlikely to be affiliated with a church or religious group, as those schools usually have voluntary controlled or voluntary aided status.

### Voluntary controlled

For admissions, a voluntary controlled school should be thought of in the same way as a community school. Although a foundation, usually a church or religious group will be involved in the running of the school. It does not have a majority on the governing body and the LEA is the admissions authority.

### Voluntary aided

The majority of church schools are voluntary aided, which means they are funded by the LEA but not controlled by it. This means that the foundation which runs the school, for example, the Church of England or the local Roman Catholic diocese, maintains a majority on the governing body which, in turn, is the admissions authority for the school.

### Foundation schools

Foundation schools are, with very few exceptions, schools which opted out of local authority control and became grant-maintained under the Conservative government's policy. This was designed to give schools complete control of their own admissions and budgets. The present government ended the policy of allowing schools to opt out shortly after coming to power, but they created foundation status as a halfway house between complete autonomy and town hall control.

Foundation schools have had to accept local authority representatives onto their governing bodies but not so many as to give them a majority. The schools can, if they wish, surrender control of admissions to their local authority, but most prefer to retain their own control over admissions. They must, however, comply with the new co-ordinated applications process that will come into force nationwide by 2004.

### Independent schools

Independent schools are free from most interference from local or central government. They must, however, be registered with the DfES and meet certain basic rules governing the quality of their facilities and the education on offer. LEAs may include details of independent schools in their school admissions literature but applications must be made direct to the school and arrangements for admission are decided independently. Some schools may, for the convenience of parents, follow the same timetable for applications as local state schools.

Although they operate as separate admissions authorities, most independent schools belong to one or more representative bodies. The most useful point of contact for parents is the Independent Schools Council Information Service (ISCis), which provides impartial information on behalf of those independent schools that subscribe to it. In addition to ISCis, there are other organisations that function as representative bodies and provide a forum for discussion for independent school heads. The Head Masters' and Head Mistresses' Conference (HMC), for example, or the Girls' Schools Association (GSA).

There are foundations which run a number of independent schools; sometimes this may just be a pair of schools or they may be a larger group. The largest is the Girls' Day School Trust (formerly known as the Girls' Public Day School Trust), which runs 25 schools in England and Wales, including 12 in London, 11 of which are secondary schools and are included in this guide.

### Useful organizations

**Independent Schools Council Information Service (ISCis) London and South-East:** Umbrella body offering information and advice about the majority of independent schools in this country. Grosvenor Gardens House, 35–37 Grosvenor Gardens, PO Box 29141, London SW1W 0BS 020 7798 1560 020 7798 1501 info@.iscis.uk.net www.iscis.uk.net

**Head MastersÕ and Head MistressesÕ Conference (HMC)**represents the heads of those private schools traditionally referred to as public schools. 130 Regent Road, Leicester LE1 7PG 0116 255 1567 0116 255 6972 hmc@hmc.org.uk www.hmc.org.uk

**The GirlsÕ Schools Association (GSA)**Represents more than 200 leading independent secondary schools for girls in the UK. 130 Regent Road, Leicester LE1 7PG ☎ 0116 254 1619 📠 0116 255 3792 ⓔ office@girls-schools.org.uk 🌐 www.girls-schools.org.uk
**GirlsÕ Day School Trust (GDST)**A group of 25 girls' day schools, 12 in London, the remainder in major towns and cities in England and Wales. 100 Rochester Row, London SW1P 1JP ☎ 020 7393 6666 📠 020 7393 6789 For queries about fees, scholarships and bursaries ⓔ r.nichols@wes.gdst.net For all other enquiries complete the online form 🌐 www.gdst.net
**The Choir Schools Association:** A group of 44 schools attached to cathedrals, churches and college chapels around the country. The Minster School, Deangate, York YO1 2JA ☎ 01904 624900 🌐 www.choirschools.org.uk
**The Woodard Corporation:** 1 The Sanctuary, London SW1P 3JT ☎ 020 7222 5381 📠 020 7799 2781 🌐 www.woodard.co.uk
**The Allied Schools:** 42 South Bar Street, Banbury, Oxon OX16 9XL ☎ 01295 256441
**The Church Schools Company:** Church Schools House, Titchmarsh, Kettering, Northants NN14 3DA ☎ 01832 735105 📠 01832 734760 ⓔ admin@church-schools.com 🌐 www.church-schools.com
**Methodist Colleges and Schools:** 25 Marylebone Road, London NW1 5JP ☎ 020 7935 3723 📠 020 7224 0702 ⓔ grussell@methodisteducation.co.uk
**The Catholic Education Service for England and Wales:** 39 Eccleston Square, London SW1V 1BX ☎ 020 7901 4880 📠 020 7901 4893 ⓔ general@cesew.org.uk 🌐 www.cesew.org.uk
**Quaker Social Responsibility and Education Department:** Friends House, 173–177 Euston Road, London NW1 2BJ ☎ 020 7663 1000 📠 020 7663 1001 🌐 www.quaker.org.uk
**Jewish Board of Deputies:** 6 Bloomsbury Square, London WC1A 2LP ☎ 020 7543 5400 📠 020 7543 0010 ⓔ info@bod.org.uk 🌐 www.bod.org.uk

# Types of school

## Comprehensive schools

Comprehensive schools are open to children of all abilities. Their admissions criteria must not give preferential treatment to children who are more academically able. However, applying to a comprehensive does not mean that your child will not have to sit an entrance test. In many areas, all children are asked to sit tests and the results are used to divide applicants into 'bands' of ability. Schools argue that this 'banding' allows them to ensure that their intake has an even spread of children of all abilities. What it means for parents is that a school may decide that a particular ability band is oversubscribed, even if there are places left which have been earmarked for children with a different level of ability.

## Grammar schools

There are 19 remaining grammar schools in London. A grammar school is a state school that selects all of its pupils on the basis of their academic ability, as determined by an entrance exam. It is a controversial topic, and opinion is sharply divided between those parents whose children attend a grammar school and those who live nearby, who claim that other local schools are denied the talents of pupils 'creamed off' by the grammar schools. Most of London's grammar schools produce GCSE and A-Level results that would be the envy of all but the very best independent schools. What's more, since entry is decided on academic merit, you do not need to move house to stand a better chance of securing a place.

Grammar schools attracted renewed attention in 1998 when new rules were introduced which, theoretically, allowed local parents to decide whether they should remain academically selective or become comprehensives. The legislation infuriated parents on both sides of the debate. Grammar school supporters claimed it left grammar schools open to attack. Anti-grammar school campaigners believed the rules were stacked against any chance of holding a successful ballot to end selection at a school, a view which has proved to be the more accurate. The only ballot held so far, in Ripon in North Yorkshire, showed parents to be two to one in favour of keeping the town's grammar school selective. If you are thinking of applying for a place at a grammar school, the slim risk from a future ballot should not concern you too much, though a group of Labour MPs and the Institute for Public Policy Research think-tank have recently re-opened the debate by calling for London's grammar schools to be abolished.

## London's 19 remaining grammar schools:

**Barnet:** Queen Elizabeth's School (boys), St Michael's Catholic Grammar School (girls), The Henrietta Barnett School (girls)
**Bexley:** Beth's Grammar School (boys), Bexley Grammar School (mixed), Chislehurst and Sidcup Grammar School (girls), Townley Grammar School (girls)
**Bromley:** Newstead Wood School (girls), St Olave's and St Saviour's School (boys)
**Enfield:** Latymer School (mixed)
**Kingston upon Thames:** Tiffin Girls' School, Tiffin School (boys)
**Redbridge:** Ilford County High School (boys), Woodford County High School (girls)
**Sutton:** Nonsuch High School (girls), Sutton Grammar School (boys), Wallington County Grammar (boys), Wallington High School (girls), Wilson's School (boys)

## Partially selective schools

The handful of partially selective schools that can still be found in London are a throwback to a Conservative policy, which allowed head teachers to select up to 50 per cent of their pupils on the basis of their academic ability. The present government came to power with a commitment not to allow any more schools to become selective, so only those that adopted partial selection before the start of the 1997 school year are able to continue the practice.

The Office of the Schools Adjudicator (see Admissions procedures, p. 18) has the authority to order a partially selective school to reduce or abandon altogether its policy if other local schools or parents can prove that children are being disadvantaged by the presence of a partially selective school. The most common grounds for objection are that the partially selective schools are 'creaming off' the brightest children in an area. This issue led to a very public High Court battle between the DfES and Wandsworth council, who were acting on behalf of three secondary schools in the borough; Burntwood School, Ernest Bevin College and Graveney School. The council and the schools won the first round on a technicality but two of the schools, Ernest Bevin and Graveney, were later ordered to cut the proportion of children that they select from half to a third of the intake each year (the same proportion selected at Burntwood), although they were not forced to abandon partial selection altogether.

## Mixed or single-sex schools

There has been a lot of talk about the advantages of single-sex teaching. It is argued that girls are intimidated by the presence of boys in the classroom, while boys feel the need to act in a typically 'laddish' way if there are girls around. Where concern was once focused on the underachievement of girls, boys are now perceived as the more problematic gender and attention has switched to ways of encouraging them to take more interest in school. Some mixed schools have already experimented with single-sex teaching and even setting up separate playgrounds for boys and girls. This may catch on, but single-sex schools will always remain a popular option for many parents. One of the main reasons is that they have traditionally performed well academically, perpetuating the idea that segregated schooling for boys and girls is inherently better. It is worth highlighting that single-sex schools often share other ingredients that contribute to a school's performance, so their academic success may not be solely attributable to single-sex teaching.

You may want to do some investigating of your own. Raw exam results will show a school's overall results but most schools will have these broken down for girls and boys. If the school will not provide them, then they will be in the school's most recent Ofsted report, but only for the year in which the report was written.

## Specialist schools

There are now 121 specialist schools in London and their number is growing. They are an extension of the City Technology College (CTC) programme begun by the last Conservative government, which was intended to bring private firms closer to the running of state schools. The present government first expanded the programme to allow schools to specialize in the arts, languages or sports. More recently, schools have been allowed to specialize in Business and Enterprise, Maths and Computing and Science. Education secretary Charles Clarke has announced that all secondary schools can apply to specialize, and to allow them to focus on even more areas of the curriculum including, from October 2003, Humanities (based around history, geography or English) and Music.

To achieve specialist status, schools must demonstrate they have the ability to develop their facilities and staff to teach the specialist subjects to a higher than average level. In return, they receive extra government money to develop their specialism. They may also select 10 per cent of their pupils on the basis of their 'aptitude' for the subject in which the school specializes. In fact, under the law, any school may do this, as long as the test used to decide aptitude is used only for that purpose and not to determine general academic ability or aptitude for another, unspecified, subject.

There is much controversy over the use of aptitude tests. Critics claim it is contrary for the government to oppose selection by academic ability but promote selection by aptitude. They fear that there is little to stop schools using the aptitude tests as tests of all-round academic ability. However, very few schools take advantage of the aptitude quota that they are allowed, either because the head teachers are opposed to selection or because they think the advantages of being able to recruit a handful of students talented in one area of the curriculum are not sufficient to outweigh the practical implications of testing the aptitude of every applicant.

New schools are being awarded specialist status all the time. Below is a list of London's specialist schools in each category, correct at the time of publication.

### Arts

Acland Burghley School, Camden
Bishopshalt School, Hillingdon
Brentside High School, Ealing
Central Foundation Girls' School, Tower Hamlets
Chadwell Heath Foundation School, Redbridge
Charles Darwin School, Bromley
Charles Edward Brooke High School, Lambeth
Chestnut Grove School, Wandsworth
Claremont High School, Brent
Dagenham Priory Comprehensive, Barking & Dagenham
Glenthorne High School, Sutton
Hatch End High School, Harrow
Highgate Wood School, Haringey
Hornsey School for Girls, Haringey
Hurlingham and Chelsea School, Hammersmith & Fulham
Kidbrooke School, Greenwich
Lister Community School, Newham
Nower Hill High School, Harrow
Plumstead Manor School, Greenwich
Sion Manning RC Girls School, Kensington & Chelsea
St Marylebone School, Westminster
St Paul's Way Community School, Tower Hamlets
Stoke Newington School, Hackney
Thomas Tallis School, Greenwich
Warwick Park School, Southwark
Welling School, Bexley

### Business

Copthall School, Barnet
Finchley Catholic High School, Barnet
St Michael's School, Southwark
Swanlea School, Tower Hamlets

### Language

Bexley Grammar School, Bexley
Bullers Wood School, Bromley
Connaught School for Girls, Waltham Forest
Convent of J & M High, Brent
Coombe Girls' Schools, Kingston upon Thames
Cranford Community High School, Hounslow
Elizabeth Garrett Anderson School, Islington
Elliott School, Wandsworth
Gaynes School, Havering
Greenford High School, Ealing
Grey Coat Hospital, Westminster
Haydon School, Hillingdon
Hendon School, Barnet
Our Lady's Convent High School, Hackney
Shene School, Richmond upon Thames
Sir John Cass's Foundation Redcoat School, Tower Hamlets
Westwood High School, Croydon
William Ellis School, Camden
Woodbridge High School, Redbridge

### Maths and Computing

Tiffin Girls' School, Kingston upon Thames
Virgo Fidelis Senior Convent School, Croydon
Wilson's School, Sutton

### Sports

Ashmole School, Barnet
Ellen Wilkinson School for Girls, Ealing
Preston Manor High, Brent
Trinity Catholic High School, Redbridge
Barking Abbey School, Barking & Dagenham
Compton High School and Sports College, Ealing
Coopers' Company and Coborn School, Havering
Eltham Green School, Greenwich
Ernest Bevin School, Wandsworth
Featherstone High School, Ealing
Hackney Free and Parochial CE School, Hackney
Harrow High School, Harrow
Langdon School, Newham
Lea Valley High School, Enfield
Southfields Community College, Wandsworth
St Thomas More RC School, Haringey
Whitefield School, Barnet
Whitton School, Richmond upon Thames
Woodcote High School, Croydon

### Technology

All Saints Catholic School, Barking & Dagenham
Archbishop Michael Ramsey, Southwark
Beaverwood School for Girls, Bromley
Beths Grammar School for Boys, Bexley
Brittons School, Havering
Canons High School, Harrow
Cardinal Wiseman RC High School, Ealing
Chiswick Community School, Hounslow
Clapton Girls' Technology College, Hackney
Compton School, Barnet
Coopers School, Bromley
Coulsdon High School, Croydon
Dunraven School, Lambeth
Eastlea Community School, Newham
Edenham High School, Croydon
Eltham Hill School, Greenwich
Fortismere School, Haringey
Geoffrey Chaucer Community School, Southwark
Graveney School, Wandsworth
Haggerston School, Hackney
Hall Mead School, Havering
Hampstead School, Camden
Highams Park School, Waltham Forest
Holy Family College, Waltham Forest
Homerton College of Technology, Hackney
John Kelly Boys Community School, Brent
John Kelly Girls Community School, Brent
Kemnal Technology College, Bromley
King Solomon High School, Redbridge
Langley Park School for Girls, Bromley
Loxford School of Science and Technology, Redbridge
Mill Hill County High School, Barnet
Mount Carmel RC Girls' School, Islington
Northolt High School, Ealing
Park High School, Harrow
Parliament Hill School, Camden
Queensmead School, Hillingdon
Quintin Kynaston School, Westminster
Ravens Wood School for Boys, Bromley
Raynes Park High School, Merton
Seven Kings High School, Redbridge
St Angela's Ursuline Convent School, Newham
St Bonaventure's School, Newham
St Mark's Catholic School, Hounslow
St Martin-in-the-Fields High School for Girls, Lambeth
St Philomenas Catholic High School, Sutton
Uxbridge High School, Hillingdon
Valentines High School, Redbridge
Wembley High School, Brent
Woolwich Polytechnic Boys School, Greenwich

## Religious schools

London's church schools are among the most popular and successful in the capital. Supporters of religious schools argue that the success stems from an ethos that is founded on a set of moral principles. Cynics argue that their popularity means that church schools are often massively oversubscribed and have their pick of bright youngsters. Although their day-to-day funding comes from the LEA, most church schools own their buildings and have to pay 15 per cent of the costs of any refurbishment or new building work.

The other major distinction is that, except in the case of the small number of voluntary controlled schools, the church, and not the LEA, has a majority on the school's governing body and they can be distant from local educational politics and bureaucracy. However, they may have a local diocese or church board that supervises their activities and the local vicar or other religious leader is often involved in the admissions process, as he or she may be asked to vouch for the religious commitment of applicants to the school.

The problem with trying to secure a place at a church secondary school is that there are not enough of them. There are fewer than 200 church secondary schools in England, five per cent of the total and far fewer than would be needed to accommodate all the children who leave church primary schools each year.

The school should tell you in its prospectus what proof of religious observance is required. A letter from a member of the clergy may be enough, but they are no longer allowed to interview children or parents, even to determine religious commitment.

For historical reasons most religious schools are either Church of England or Roman Catholic, but other religions have their own primary and secondary schools, both in the maintained and independent sectors. There is a Sikh secondary school, the Guru Nanak College in Hillingdon, which operated for many years as an independent school, supported by the local community before securing state funding in 1999, and The John Loughborough School in Haringey, run by Seventh-day Adventists, which opened as an independent school in 1980 but became a state school in 1998.

## Independent schools

Private schools, or independent schools as they prefer to be known, are independent of the state education system and they control their own admissions arrangements. Many, though not all, are highly selective, and have huge waiting lists and intense competition for places.

For most parents, the significant barrier to entry is the fees, which can reach many thousands of pounds a term for boarding schools. However, in London more parents send their children to be educated privately than the national average (around 10 per cent, compared with 7 per cent nationally) and surveys show that around half of all parents would send their children to independent schools if they could afford to.

Most children at independent schools are day pupils, but some of London's most famous public schools also take boarders, including Westminster School and St Paul's Boys' School. Many of London's independent schools have had close links with the maintained sector. Some were direct grant schools, a now-abandoned system of funding which meant that schools could operate independently but receive government funding for pupils whose parents could not afford to pay the fees. More recently, many independent schools participated in the Conservative government's Assisted Places Scheme, which also subsidized places for pupils from less well-off homes. This scheme has now been phased out.

Many independent schools are trying to replace some of the subsidized places lost with their own scholarships. These places are usually reserved for highly gifted children who perform exceptionally well at the entrance exam and whose family background warrants financial assistance. It is worth asking individual schools if they have such a scheme.

## Beacon schools

Beacon schools are chosen by the government as an example for others to follow. It is an honour bestowed on schools which have done very well generally or in a particular field, or have managed to successfully overcome difficulties. They are given the title and extra money to use to spread their good practice, by sending teachers out or inviting staff from other schools to come in and see what it is they do so well. Since 1998 around 1000 schools in England have earned Beacon status, including 250 secondary schools. The Beacon secondary schools in London are as follows:

Barking Abbey Comprehensive, Barking and Dagenham
Blackfen School for Girls, Bexley
Bullers Wood School, Bromley
Burntwood Foundation School for Girls, Wandsworth
Camden School for Girls, Camden
Compton School, Barnet
Connaught School for Girls, Waltham Forest
Convent of Jesus and Mary Language College, Brent
Coombe Girls' School, Kingston upon Thames
Copland Community School and Technology Centre, Brent
Douay Martyrs Roman Catholic School, Hillingdon
Drayton Manor High School, Ealing
Dunraven School, Lambeth
Ellen Wilkinson School for Girls, Ealing
Elliott School, Wandsworth
Enfield County School, Enfield

Graveney School, Wandsworth
Green School, Hounslow
Grey Coat Hospital, Westminster
Grey Court School, Richmond
Haggerston School, Hackney
Hall Mead School, Havering
Heston Community School, Hounslow
Highbury Fields School, Islington
Hornsey School for Girls, Haringey
Jews Free School, Camden
John Roan School, Greenwich
Kingsbury High School, Brent
La Retraite RC Girls' School, Lambeth
La Sainte Union Convent School, Camden
Lampton School, Hounslow
Langdon School, Newham
Langley Park School for Girls, Bromley
Mulberry School for Girls, Tower Hamlets
Nonsuch High School for Girls, Sutton
Norbury Manor High School for Girls, Croydon
Notre Dame School, Southwark
Nower Hill High School, Harrow
Our Lady's Convent High School, Hackney
Park High School, Harrow
Parliament Hill School, Camden
Plashet School, Newham
Prendergast School, Lewisham
Queen Elizabeth's Girls' School, Barnet
Queen Elizabeth's School, Barnet
Ricards Lodge High School, Merton
Sacred Heart High School, Hammersmith & Fulham
Sarah Bonnell School, Newham
Seven Kings High School, Redbridge
Sion-Manning School, Kensington and Chelsea
Southgate School, Enfield
St Angela's Ursuline Convent School, Newham
St Bonaventure's Roman Catholic School, Newham
St Marylebone CofE School, Westminster
St Michael's RC School, Southwark
St Paul's RC Comprehensive School, Greenwich
St Saviour's & St Olave's School, Southwark
St Ursula's Convent School, Greenwich
Sydenham School, Lewisham
Thomas Tallis School, Greenwich
Tiffin Girls' School, Kingston upon Thames
Tolworth Girls' School, Kingston upon Thames
Trinity Catholic High School, Redbridge
Valentines High School, Redbridge
Waldegrave School for Girls, Richmond
Wallington High School for Girls, Sutton
Walthamstow School for Girls, Waltham Forest
Winchmore School, Enfield

### Fresh start schools

Four secondary schools in London that were declared to be failing by the education watchdog Ofsted, have been closed and re-opened under the Government's 'fresh start' programme. One – Telegraph Hill in Lewisham – has now closed for good. Each school receives a new name and a new head teacher and often substantial re-building work. They also appear in performance tables under their new names. The list below gives the new names of the schools, their borough and (in brackets) their previous name. But the programme has itself come under criticism for not raising standards sufficiently and there are no plans for any further 'fresh starts' in London.

Bishopsford Community School, Merton (Watermeads High School)
Islington Arts and Media School, Islington (George Orwell School)
Park View Academy, Haringey (The Langham School)

### Academies

The most recent attempt to turn around the most seriously failing secondary schools has been to turn them into Academies, formerly known as City Academies, which are funded by the taxpayer but run by a 'sponsor', which can be a charity, a religious groups or even a private firm. New schools can also be created as City Academies and a number are planned in London between now and 2006 (see below).

Each sponsor must pay 20 per cent of the costs of refurbishing a run-down school, or building a new one, up to £2 million (the government will pay the rest). In return the sponsors are able to nominate members of the governing body, to sit alongside staff, parents and a local authority representative. They will also have much greater flexibility than other schools to reorganize the curriculum and staff pay and conditions.

More than half of the proposed new academies are in London. They are listed below with (in brackets) the name of any schools they will replace and the planned opening date.

Open
The Academy at Peckham, Southwark (Warwick Park), 2003
The Business Academy Bexley, Bexley (Thamesmead Community College), 2002
Capital City Academy, Brent (Willesden High School), 2003
City of London (Southwark) Academy, Southwark (new school), 2003
Greig City Academy, Haringey (St David and St Katherine's CE High School), 2002

Implementation
Lambeth Academy, Lambeth (new school), 2004
Mossbourne Community Academy, Hackney (new school), 2004
West London Academy, Ealing (Compton High School and Sports College), 2003

Feasibility
Harefield Academy, Hillingdon (John Penrose), 2005
London Academy, Barnet (Edgware School), 2004
Name to be confirmed, Croydon (Stanley Technical High School for Boys), 2005
Name to be confirmed, Kensington and Chelsea (New school), 2005
Name to be confirmed, Lewisham (St Josephs Academy), 2005
Name to be confirmed, Lewisham (Malory School and Haberdashers' Aske's Hatcham College), 2005
Name to be confirmed, Westminster (new school), 2006

# Admissions procedures

Under the principle of parental choice, the admissions authority, whether it is an LEA or the governing body of the school you are applying to, has a duty to meet your wishes as far as possible. However, they have an equal duty to meet the wishes of every other parent who applies for a school place for their child.

When choosing a school, it is important to know your rights. Schools and LEAs have to observe a complex series of rules, many of which are legally binding, that control the way in which they consider your application and allocate places. Understanding these rules will make the applications process easier. It will also enable you to decide, if you are unhappy with the decision made, whether you have reasonable grounds to appeal.

## Published information

Each admissions authority must publish details of its admissions arrangements before the start of the applications process. Other schools that may feel adversely affected by these arrangements can appeal to the Office of the Schools Adjudicator, a watchdog that mediates in disputes between schools. Parents can refer a complaint to the adjudicator only if it is about a school that practises partial academic selection, or if they feel that the school has room for more children than the number of places on offer. For more information visit the website www.schoolsadjudicator.gov.uk or write to the Office of the Schools Adjudicator, 3rd Floor, Vincent House, 2 Woodland Road, Darlington DL3 7PJ Tel: 0870 0012468 Fax: 01325 391313 E-mail: offschl.adj@dfee.gov.uk.

LEAs must publish details of admission arrangements for all the maintained schools in their area. This can also include schools maintained by a neighbouring LEA and private schools. The prospectus must include the name and address of each school and details of who to contact. It will also indicate the type of school and a summary of the school's admission policy, including, if necessary, a statement of the school's religious affiliation.

The admission policy must include details of the criteria used to decide which pupils to admit if it is oversubscribed. These admission criteria must be ranked in the order of priority. For example, it must be made clear whether having a child already at the school, often described as the sibling rule, is taken into account before considering whether a child attended a nearby primary school or the distance that a child lives from the school. For secondary schools, the prospectus must also say how many places there are available in the first year and how many applications there were in the previous year. It must also explain how parents can express a preference for a particular school.

## Application forms

A 1997 legal ruling, known as the Rotherham Judgement, established that admission authorities are obliged to consider pupils whose parents express a preference for a particular school over those who did not. This does not mean that your child will be left without a secondary school place if you do not apply. The local authority in which you live is obliged to find a place at a school that is a reasonable distance from your home. But if you do not apply for a particular school, then it is inevitable that the place you are offered will be at a school that is less popular than others.

The Education Act 2002 has introduced considerable changes to the way applications for places at maintained secondary schools will be made in future. These changes will be compulsory from 2004.

Parents who wish to apply to maintained schools will in future submit just one application form, to their home LEA. They will be asked to list a minimum of three and a maximum of seven schools, in order of preference, together with relevant information to support their application. This list can include schools that control their own admissions (Voluntary Aided and Foundation schools and Academies) and even other LEAs, as any information relevant to an application will be passed on to those schools and LEAs.

There is no national deadline for submitting an application form, though the government has suggested October 24 (whatever the deadline, admission authorities are not supposed to give priority to parents who get their application forms in early. As long as you meet the deadline, you should not be disadvantaged). There is however a new national 'offer date' of March 1 (in the year in which a child is due to start secondary school). On that date all parents who submitted an application form for a place at a maintained school should be told which school their child has won a place at. This is a significant change from the present system, in which some parents receive multiple offers of school places and others receive no offers at all and have to hope for spare places that other parents have turned down.

Applicants may be offered a place at more than one school if they applied, through their home LEA, for places at schools in one or more other authority areas. But there are plans to co-ordinate arrangements between LEAs so that each applicant will receive just one offer of a place, no matter how many they put on their application form or where in the country the schools are located.

This does not mean the end of parental choice. School places will be allocated according to how high up each parents' list of preferences they come, but that does not mean that all parents will get their first choice. If the school at the top of your list is full then the published over-subscription criteria apply and the school can turn down your child. The school you will be allocated a place at is the school nearest to the top of your list that accepts your child.

## Admissions criteria

We have already mentioned some of the criteria that are used to decide which pupils are accepted if a school is oversubscribed. If a school is not oversubscribed, then these do not come into play. If a school has a spare place, it is obliged to take any child who applies, except in extremely limited circumstances. A fully selective grammar school can refuse to accept a child who does not pass the entrance exam, but a school which bands pupils according to ability cannot leave spaces unfilled because there are not enough applicants of a certain ability band.

Schools are also bound by law not to promote discrimination on the basis of race, colour, sex, nationality or ethnic origin. Their admissions criteria must be carefully worded to avoid doing so, even inadvertently. For example, giving preference to children whose parents attended the school or have a particular occupation could disadvantage children from ethnic minorities or refugee families who recently moved into the area.

It is acceptable, and common, for schools to give preference when allocating places to children who already have brothers or sisters at the school. The reasoning is that children from the same family should have the chance to be educated together and there are practical benefits for parents. Often the sibling rule is the first of the criteria that are applied when a school is oversubscribed.

Other common criteria are based around the distance that a child lives from the school. This may be based on a catchment area, the ease of access by public transport or simply the distance as the crow flies. The right of schools to operate a catchment area was established by the Rotherham Judgement, but preference is given to parents who express a preference, whether or not they live inside the catchment area. An earlier legal ruling, the 1989 Greenwich Judgement, established that a local authority cannot refuse a place at one of their schools simply because a child's parents live outside of their administrative area. This is particularly important in London where there are 33 different LEAs and your nearest school may not be in the authority in which you live.

Children coming from certain named 'feeder' primary schools and parents' ranking of preference for a school on their LEA application form may also be used as admission criteria, but they must be published so that parents can judge in advance what their chances of securing a place at a given school are. Admission authorities should also make clear how any 'tie-break' decisions are made.

## Interviews and tests

State schools or LEAs should not interview parents as any part of the application or admission process. There has been an exception that allows church schools to assess religious or denominational commitment, but the Education Act 2002 ended this. Now the only maintained schools that may interview parents or children are boarding schools, to assess a child's suitability for a boarding place.

Maintained schools are not allowed to charge for the application or admission process. Schools are strongly advised not to invite parents to make a financial contribution to the school prior to their child being accepted. This could be seen as a disguised fee and offers strong grounds for potential appeals.

## Waiting lists

Many admission authorities maintain waiting lists, although they are not obliged to. Where a waiting list is used, the school must make clear how children will be ranked so that, if spare places become available, parents know where they stand. The same admission criteria should be used when picking children from the waiting list as are used to decide other applications. In other words, priority should not be given simply on the basis of the date on which parents were added to the list. Placing your child's name on a waiting list does not affect your right of appeal against an unsuccessful application.

## Being offered a place

Once your child has been offered a place at a school, you should respond within a reasonable time. The letter of confirmation from the school or LEA should state the date by which you have to reply, otherwise the offer may legitimately be withdrawn.

The only other circumstances in which an offer can be withdrawn once it has been made is if a parent lied to secure a place at a school, for example by giving a false address that lies within a school's catchment area, or falsely claiming religious convictions when applying for a place at a church school. Even in these circumstances, if the child has started at the school, they will not normally be thrown out.

## Appeals

If you do not secure a place at a school and feel you have been unfairly treated, you have the right to appeal. If you applied to several schools unsucessfully, you have the right to make separate appeals for each school. The fact that you are making multiple appeals should not be used against you.

Appeals will be heard by the admission authority handling your application. So, if you applied for places at more than one school through the LEA, your appeals will be heard together by an appeals panel appointed by the LEA. Appeals against decisions by foundation or voluntary aided schools will be heard by a panel constituted by the school. The appeal panel should be independent. It will have three or five members and parents must have the right to appear before the panel accompanied by a friend, family member or legal representative. The child may attend but is not expected to.

The panel must include at least one lay member, someone who does not have personal experience of the management or provision of education in any school, as well as someone familiar with the situation faced by schools in the area. They could be a local parent but if they have children at the school in question, or a school that might have to take the child in question if the appeal fails, they should probably not sit on the panel. Teachers who work at the school in question and employees of the LEA are banned from sitting on appeal panels.

You must submit your appeal within 14 days of being refused a place at a school (although late appeals will be considered if there is a good reason). You will be given at least 14 days' notice of the date on which the appeal is to be heard, and you should confirm whether or not you intend to be there. Parents are encouraged to attend but cases can be determined on written evidence alone. Panels aim to come to a decision within a week of the appeal.

You cannot re-appeal once a decision is made, but if you feel that the appeal was handled badly, you can make a complaint to the Local Government Ombudsman (its website is www.lgo.org.uk).

For London boroughs north of the Thames (including Richmond but not Harrow or Tower Hamlets) contact Tony Redmond, 21 Queen Anne's Gate, London SW1H 9BU ☎ 020 7915 3210 📠 020 7233 0396.

For Tower Hamlets contact Patricia Thomas, Beverley House, 17 Shipton Road, York YO30 5FZ ☎ 01904 663200 📠 01904 663269

For London boroughs south of the Thames (except Richmond) and Harrow contact Jerry White, The Oaks No 2, Westwood Way, Westwood Business Park, Coventry CV4 8JB ☎ 024 7669 5999 📠 024 7669 5902.

The Ombudsman will not look at the merits of your case again but may investigate whether there has been 'maladministration', if procedures were not followed correctly. However, even if this is proved, the Ombudsman can only order compensation to be paid and a fresh appeal to be held but cannot force a school to take your child.

In the last instance, you may want to contact the Secretary of State for Education, currently Charles Clarke. He cannot review the decision of an individual appeal panel but he can consider whether the LEA or governing body has correctly constituted the appeal panel and whether they acted reasonably. Once again, the best that you can hope for is that a fresh appeal is ordered but there is no guarantee that a different outcome will be reached.

If you are thinking of bringing a case under the Human Rights Act, which incorporates the European Convention on Human Rights into English law, bear in mind that the present government believes that, under the Human Rights Act, all children have a right to an education but not necessarily to a place at a particular school – although that opinion has yet to be tested by the courts.

## Exclusions

A school cannot refuse to admit a child just because they fear that they will be disruptive, or because they believe that a child should first be assessed for a statement of special needs. Statementing, as it is known, can be undertaken once a child is at the school.

Certain schools may refuse to take children that they fear will 'prejudice the provision of efficient education or the efficient use of resources'. These are schools that the education inspectorate Ofsted has put under a regime of special measures within the past two years or identified as having serious weaknesses, Fresh Start schools or Academies that have been open for less than two years, and schools where fewer than25 per cent of pupils achieved 5 GCSEs at grades A*–C in the previous year. Such schools can only invoke this rule outside the normal year of entry, so if you are applying for the first year and a school has places, they are obliged to take your child. However, a child applying in later years, especially if they were permanently excluded from their previous school, may be refused a place.

If a child has been permanently excluded, that is expelled, from two or more schools, since September 1997 their chances of getting back into mainstream education are drastically reduced, as the next school they apply to – whether or not it is on special measures or has serious weaknesses or spare places – is within its rights to refuse to accept them. This penalty lasts for up to two years after the most recent permanent exclusion and has serious consequences for the child, who will most likely be forced to attend a Pupil Referral Unit (PRU). This is a unit designed for youngsters who cannot handle school. Despite more money being ploughed into PRUs and similar facilities within schools for pupils on the verge of exclusion (officially described as Learning Support Units but widely referred to as 'sin bins'), they are rarely an adequate substitute for full-time mainstream schooling.

There is no way to appeal against a school's refusal to take a child if they have been permanently excluded twice, but parents can appeal against the decision of the previous school to permanently exclude their child. In the first instance, they should approach the school's governing body, although governors will be unwilling to countermand the orders of the head teacher who will have sanctioned the permanent exclusion in the first place, and are unlikely to reverse the decision. Further appeals must be made to an independent appeals panel, which you can arrange through your LEA.

Following head teachers' concern that panels have been reinstating too many pupils, they have been issued with new guidelines that make it much harder to do this. Schools were also concerned that government targets to reduce the number of permanent exclusions had put them under pressure not to expel difficult pupils. Ministers pledged to reduce the 1997 figure of 12,700 permanent exclusions by a third by 2002. That figure was achieved and there are no plans to set a new target.

## Disciplinary procedures

New legislation means that head teachers now have a specific duty to draw up measures to prevent all forms of bullying among pupils. Strategies to combat bullying should form part of a school's discipline and behaviour policy, ideally with a separate written anti-bullying policy. The attitude that a school takes towards pastoral care of pupils is one of the most important things to look for and you can ask to see the school's discipline and anti-bullying policies in addition to information you collect on other aspects of the school, such as academic results. Bullying behaviour is generally defined to include name-calling and teasing, physical violence, threats or isolating individuals from group activities.

If you think that your child has been bullied, the first thing to do is to calmly talk with the child about the experience. Make a written note of what he or she says, getting as many details as you can of what happened, where it happened, who was involved and whether the incident has been repeated. Reassure your child that they have done the right thing by telling you about the bullying and advise them to tell a teacher or form tutor if it happens again. You should then make an appointment to visit the school and explain the problems your child is having.

When you meet the teacher, try to stay calm and bear in mind that they may not know that your child has been bullied or may have heard a different version of events. Make a note of what action the school intends to take and ask if there is anything you can do to help. Stay in touch with the school and let them know if things improve as well as if problems continue. If you are still not satisfied, you can make an appointment to discuss the matter with the head teacher.

Remember, however strongly worded the school's discipline policy, there can be no blanket rules covering all cases. Children accused of bullying or other wrongdoing have certain rights. They cannot be excluded, temporarily or permanently, unless the head teacher can justify that the punishment is warranted. The head's decision can be overturned by the governing body, or by an independent appeal panel, which sits to hear disputed cases. However, recent advice to these panels from the Secretary of State for Education makes clear that violence or threats of violence will normally justify the expulsion of a child from school. If you are unhappy with the way a bullying incident has been dealt with, you might consider writing to the school's governors, explaining your concerns and what you would like to see happen. As a last resort, you can contact the LEA or the DfES. There are also a number of charities and support groups which may be able to offer more advice and practical help.

## Charities and support groups for anti-bullying

**ChildLine:** 0800 1111 www.childline.co.uk
**Anti-Bullying Campaign:** 185 Tower Bridge Road, London SE1 2UF 020 7378 1446 help@bullying.co.uk www.bullying.co.uk
**Advisory Centre for Education (ACE):** 1c Aberdeen Studios, 22 Highbury Grove, London N5 2DQ 0808 800 5793 020 7704 9822 020 7354 9069 ace-ed@easynet.org.uk www.ace-ed.org.uk

**Careline:** ☎ 020 8514 1177
**Kidscape:** 2 Grosvenor Gardens, London SW1W 0DH ☎ 020 7730 3300 📠 020 7730 7081
✉ webinfo@kidscape.org.uk 🌐 www.kidscape.org.uk
**Parentline Plus:** 520 Highgate Studios, 53–79 Highgate Road, London NW51TL ☎ 020 7284 5500
🌐 www.parentlineplus.org.uk

## The National Curriculum

The National Curriculum is divided into four key stages taught to children in maintained schools between the ages of 5 and 16. At each stage there are compulsory subjects, although pupils may study other subjects as well, such as personal, social and health education. The key stages are as follows:

Key Stages 1 (ages 5–7) and 2 (ages 7–11): Art and design, English, design and technology, geography, history, information and communication technology (ICT), maths, music, physical education, religious education, science

Key Stage 3 (ages 11–14): Art and design, citizenship, English, design and technology, geography, history, ICT, maths, a modern foreign language, music, PE, science

Key Stage 4 (ages 14–16): Citizenship, English, design and technology, ICT, maths, a modern foreign language, PE, science (religious education, careers education and sex education are compulsory but are not national curriculum subjects)

However, proposed changes to the curriculum for pupils aged 14 to 16 will mean that only maths, English and science will remain compulsory GCSE subjects. Pupils will be able to drop languages and design and technology. They will also learn about 'work and enterprise' through work experience.

## League tables

Where once there was little or no information available to parents about the quality of the schools available to them and their children, there is now the danger of being deluged by baffling statistics.

League tables caused a storm of controversy when they were first introduced in 1992, but now they are an established feature of the educational landscape. They are acknowledged to have done much good in exposing truly awful schools to public scrutiny but they are not an unqualified success.

The most common criticism of league tables is that they have distorted the whole system of education so that schools teach to the tests and concentrate their efforts on borderline pupils. Although it is good to know which schools are doing well and which are struggling, you should be wary of those schools who seem unduly proud of their league table placing.

Selective schools always tend to do well in league tables and single-sex schools also have a good record, although critics argue that this is because many of them are former grammar schools that have retained their cachet and are able to attract a higher proportion of bright children from 'good' homes.

Most league tables are compiled from figures published late in the year by the DfES – be wary of any which originate from any other source, with the exception of the independent schools' own league tables put out by the ISCis. The information, as presented by the DfES in what they term 'performance tables', is available on the Internet at www.dfes.gov.uk. Schools are listed alphabetically and, while this is useful up to a point, most parents also want an indication of how schools compare to one another, and this is what league tables such as those published in newspapers and the one published here can offer.

Following a pilot scheme in 2001, the government has now published the first nationwide 'value added' performance measures for secondary schools. Unlike traditional league tables, which show only 'raw' exam scores, the new measures are designed to highlight those secondary schools that do well with pupils of all abilities. Two tables were published in 2002, showing separately the improvement made by pupils between the ages of 11 to 14 and from 14 to 16. It is the second of these measures that is included in this edition of the London Schools Guide. From 2003 just one value added measure will be produced, measuring improvement between the ages of 11 to 16. Another innovation is the national publication of schools' Key Stage 3 results - the tests that children take at the age of 14.

## GCSE results

General Certificate of Secondary Education (GCSE) results are a good indicator of a secondary school's performance, but pupils also take a range of vocational qualifications, including General National Vocational Qualifications (GNVQ), as well as GCSE short courses (worth half a full GCSE) and Entry Level Qualifications (previously known as Certificates of Educational Achievement) for those pupils unlikely to pass a full GCSE.

GCSE league tables commonly use one of two measures of a school's performance: the proportion of pupils who achieve five passes at grades A*–C, and the average number of points scored by each pupil. The first measure is the benchmark that was used when GCSE league tables were first published, and the government still uses it to set both local and national targets for school performance, although pass grades at GCSE run from A*–G. Many school sixth forms and sixth-form colleges require C grade passes or above for admission to A-Level courses.

It is easy to compare schools using the five A*–C measure but, at the top end of the performance scale, it is rendered meaningless as several hundred of the country's best state schools manage to score 100 per cent. Critics also point out that the measure ignores the achievements of pupils with fewer than five passes or grades below C.

A new GCSE points score has been introduced in recent years, and it is increasingly being used in preference to the five A*–C benchmark, as it is gives a more precise indication of pupils' performance. Under this system, each pupil's best eight GCSE and GNVQ grades are given a points value, from eight points for an A* down to one for a G. Each pupil's score is added together and divided by the total number of pupils, producing an average score for the school. The benefit to schools and pupils of using this measure is that every child is regarded as contributing to the school's success, so there is no temptation for teachers to concentrate on any one group of pupils.

## A-Level and AS results

Since September 2000, sixth-formers have had the opportunity to take a number of AS (Advanced Subsidiary) courses in their first year. These are designed to both stand alone, as qualifications, and to represent the first year of a full two-year A-Level course. The change was designed to broaden the curriculum, so pupils can continue with subjects they might otherwise have dropped after GCSE.

Following complaints that schools and pupils were overwhelmed by the new work required of them, there will now be just one three-hour exam for each AS subject, plus coursework.

The new system allows universities to consider applicants' AS grades, as well as their predicted A-Level grades, at the time they apply to university. This is at the end of the year before they intend to start their course (unless they defer for a 'gap' year).

The changes, sometimes described by their official title of Curriculum 2000, hit the headlines when a number of schools – mainly independent schools – reported that some students had received much lower final marks than they had been predicted.

An inquiry headed by the former Chief Inspector of Schools Mike Tomlinson discovered that OCR – one of the three main exam boards – had changed the grade boundaries (the number of marks needed to obtain a particular grade) of a number of course options. In total 1945 pupils at 839 schools had at least one AS or A-level grade changed. The A-level tables printed in this guide reflect these changes.

The Universities and Colleges Admissions Service (UCAS) introduced a new 'tariff' system for applications to higher education institutions from September 2002. It replaces the old A-level and AS points score. It gives numerical values to different grades in a range of qualifications, including AS, A-Level, Advanced General National Vocational Qualifications (AGNVQ), Scottish qualifications and, eventually, the International Baccalaureate that is being offered in a growing number of state and independent sixth forms.

Some universities and colleges will ask for a minimum number of points as the condition for entry to a course, although others will specify particular A-level grades, especially in the subject which applicants want to study.

### Truancy rates

Performance tables do not just measure exam results, they also detail the absence of pupils, both authorized and unauthorized. This information is available for each school alongside the results for GCSE, A-level and vocational qualifications and also as a separate National Pupil Absence Table. Schools take a register twice a day, in the morning and after lunch, and so absence is counted in half days. The absence tables list the number of half days missed by pupils of compulsory school age, the average number of half days missed by each pupil (which is calculated in much the same way as the GCSE points score: by adding up the number of half days missed and dividing by the total number of pupils), followed by the proportion of half days this represents (excluding weekends and school holidays).

Tables also make a distinction between authorized absence, verified by a note from a parent or guardian or sanctioned by the school, and unauthorized absence – truancy in the traditional sense. These figures are all averages and can be badly skewed by a small number of persistent truants.

Having failed to meet a self-imposed target to cut truancy by a third by 2002, the government has now agreed a less ambitious target to cut unauthorized absence by 10 per cent by 2004. It appears to be a tough nut to crack, the average number of half days missed each year through unauthorized absence by state school pupils has remained constant at around 1 per cent of total school time.

## Special educational needs

Some children seem to sail through childhood; they feed well, sleep well, talk and crawl at all the normal times. Going to school is a natural extension of this development and the challenge of academic and social learning is a valuable and satisfying experience.

Unfortunately, for some children growing up poses a variety of difficulties. Perhaps most obvious are the physical problems that can be identified at birth or during early infancy. Long before formal education is being considered, parents will usually be involved with medical professionals who will offer advice regarding appropriate steps to be taken. A large number of associated professionals, including speech and language therapists, physiotherapists and others may be involved from the very first year of a child's life.

For some children, problems are less obvious to detect. You may have nagging feelings that all is not well but it may be as vague as noting that concentration is a problem. A variety of conditions from dyslexia to depression may be the cause and only thoughtful investigation will illuminate where the problem lies.

The question of what is an appropriate educational environment is likely to result from what is considered to be suitable to the child's needs and what is locally available. The government jargon for children needing special consideration is special educational needs (SEN). This term has a legal framework and a host of powers and entitlements that can procure a multitude of resources (including financial ones), to support a child's education.

There are specific issues, particularly in respect to segregated schooling, that are making an impact on the kinds of schools being supported by the DfES. Twenty years ago, there were a considerable number of schools established for children with what were termed 'handicaps' that were deemed to impede the children's educational progress. Nowadays, the thinking is to enable as many children as possible to be educated alongside each other in mainstream schools. The provision of special needs education in London has been profoundly affected by these ideas. The 1981 Education Act opened the way for the closure of specialist schools in the capital and the alternative move towards 'integrated education'. Many of these schools were small, expensive and relied on local authority funding to make their numbers viable, and so several have closed. However, there is now a dearth of separate provision that is well established and easy to recommend.

### Choosing the right school for a special-needs child

How do you judge if it is important for your child to go to a specialist school in preference to a mainstream school, be it maintained or independent? The answer to this question depends on a variety of factors. Firstly, the nature of your child's special need. Secondly, the quality of the provision available. Thirdly, your child's view of him/herself and the difficulty he/she experiences.

By the time your child is ready for secondary school, many special needs will already have been addressed during the primary school years. Some children with the most severe difficulties may already be in specialist schools. Others, with some physical difficulties, may have been well catered for in a primary school. The questions may now be about whether the chosen secondary school has the requisite facilities – ramps, lifts and others necessary – to include your child.

Some children with severe physical difficulties have a great desire to lead a life alongside their peers. If this is the case, you should not be discouraged from pressing for the school of your choice. The law is on your side and the government is particularly committed to inclusive education for all. The SEN and Disability Act 2001 was implemented in September 2002. This extends the same rights to schools as exist in the workplace. The main effect is to strengthen a parent's right to obtain a mainstream school place for their child, if it is seen to be in the interests of the child and is not incompatible with the provision of efficient education for others. Schools and local authorities will need to step up moves to adapt buildings to include children who would previously have been turned down.

However, physical resources are not the only consideration to be explored in the placement of children with special needs in ordinary schools. Secondary schools are larger than primary schools, and discipline is often more difficult to maintain. It is important to be assured that the school has a good atmosphere and that the pupils are not overly at risk of bullying or other forms of intimidation. Ask about pastoral or tutorial support and check that the school has a good discipline policy. If possible, try to spend a little time at the school and talk to pupils.

Academic achievement can be seen through the published league tables. It may be useful to enquire about the inclusion of other pupils with special needs and their progress.

## Determining if your child has special needs

What if your child does not have a medically diagnosed condition that automatically entitles him/her to specialist resources and support before he/she has reached secondary school? What if you just have a feeling that your child is not learning at school or at home? How do you discover if your child has a special need? The law says that a child has special needs if he/she has: a learning difficulty (ie. a significantly greater difficulty in learning than the majority of children of the same age, or a disability that makes it difficult to use the educational facilities generally provided locally); and if that learning difficulty calls for: special educational provision (ie. provision additional to, or different from, that made generally for children of the same age in local schools).

Whether or not a child has special needs will depend on the individual and on local circumstances. It may be entirely consistent with the law for a child to be said to have special needs in one school, but not in another.

This shows the nub of the problem in assessing special needs. How are you to know if your child's difficulty reflects his/her innate need or results from less than satisfactory schooling? In the late 1980s, one London borough had about 50 per cent of its children unable to read at a level commensurate with their chronological age at secondary transfer. Did this indicate fifty per cent having special needs? What was perfectly clear was that the local primary schools were failing dismally. With ever-closer scrutiny and published results, it is at least easier now to spot obviously failing schools. Consequently, it should be easier to recognize which children are having difficulty learning.

In the state sector, schools are required to consider the assessment of special needs through a published code of practice. This was revised in 2001, and thanks to intense lobbying by parents' groups, the new code offers more direct help to parents. As well as setting up parent partnerships, LEAs are obliged to make arrangements for solving disputes about provision. A specific guide for parents is available through DFES publications ☎ 0845 6022260 or 🌐 www.dfes.gov.uk/sen. This should help parents find their way through the maze of SEN provision. The main tenets of its philosophy are a staged assessment process, involving parents as well as a variety of professionals. Varying degrees of support are provided at each stage of the code, culminating in a formal statement of special needs. This statement is a legal entitlement. It may require the LEA to fund specialist equipment such as a braille computer. It may also require extra support in the classroom such as a learning assistant or helper to assist the child. It may consider that a specialist school placement is the preferred option. This could mean that the LEA will pay the full cost of school fees in either a maintained or independent school.

Unfortunately, LEAs rely on their own educational psychologists for the assessment of special needs, who may not always have an independent view. Much has been reported in the press recently about court cases involving LEAs not having fulfilled their statutory duties with regard to support for dyslexic children. This is a grey area, as is the whole field of children with emotional and behavioural difficulties. It is also evident that many professionals, educationalists as well as doctors and psychologists, cannot agree about the precise nature of these conditions. The most recent additions to this field are the classifications of attention deficit disorder (ADD) and attention deficit or hyperactivity disorder (ADHD).

## Factors to look for

The period of secondary school education coincides with adolescence, and it is often hard to differentiate what is normal, if frustrating, behaviour from what is a learning difficulty. How are you to distinguish between normal healthy behaviour and that which indicates a level of difficulty likely to impede educational progress? There are several indicators which may alert you to a problem that needs to be addressed:

Is your child attending school on a regular basis?
Is your child reluctant to go to school?
Does your child complain of feeling unwell on a regular basis?
Is your child withdrawn or unhappy?
Is your child finding it difficult to make or keep friends?
Is your child constantly reporting that he/she is being treated unfairly by the teachers?
Is your child unable to concentrate on his/her work?
Is your child performing below his/her or your expectations?
If any, but especially two or more, of these indicators seem to be a recurring problem, you should be discussing them with your child's school.

## Taking action

The importance of the role of parents in education is being given a higher profile by this government. Therefore, it is paramount that you make your concerns known to those responsible for your child's education. You should not be satisfied by answers such as 'it's a phase she's going through'. Press for a meeting with the class tutor or year head or, if necessary, the head of the school.

It is not unheard of for children (particularly adolescents) to be permanently excluded from school for bad behaviour, when in fact they have special needs. If your child is getting into trouble at school, it may be that he/she is confused and frustrated with what he/she is expected to do. Do not wait for a crisis to occur or for your child to be excluded. Contact the school as soon as possible and try to speak with those concerned. With large class sizes, individual children can sometimes be perceived as troublemakers when their real problems are not recognized.

A consequence of the government's commitment to inclusive schooling has led to a new structure being set up in many schools, called a Learning Support Unit. Most units are situated within the main school building but they offer children in difficulty a chance to attend the unit rather than their regular classes.

These units are aimed at keeping difficult children in school by removing them from the classes they are finding too difficult and having them taught seperately from their peers. One of the problems with this kind of development is the confusion of aim. Although called Learning Support Units, they are not set up under the SEN umbrella and may serve the purpose of masking the identification of pupils with SEN.

Given that most schools are dealing with groups rather than individuals, it is quite possible that these units may become a holding bay for children who exhibit various difficulties, rather than a specific resource for those with specific learning difficulties.

If your child is sent to the learning support unit for part of the week (most of the units do not offer full-time education), make sure that you are aware of the purpose of the placement. Check for how long it is being suggested and make sure that you monitor what your child will be doing whilst he or she is at the unit. Placement at a unit is not intended to last more than one to two terms and should not be for the majority of the week. Without care, some children may lose the opportunity to study for some GCSE courses as they will not be with their specialist teachers.

Permanent exclusion can significantly reduce the chances of a child finding a new school. Figures show that fewer than a third of those pupils excluded permanently are re-integrated into another school. Many are placed in Pupil Referral Units, which are likely to have a modified curriculum with the emphasis on literacy, numeracy and vocational courses. It is therefore essential that if you feel anxious or dissatisfied with your child's progress, you raise your concerns.

On a more legalistic note, unless a step-by-step approach to the assessment of special needs is embarked upon, the chance of proper resources being made available is probably small. In the public sector, where aspiration is high and political rhetoric plentiful, words come easily, but provision less so.

## Independent schools and special needs

The London private sector's provision for children with special needs at secondary level is scant. What little there is focuses on two main areas: specialist support for dyslexic children and coaching in specific subject areas, including tuition in English as a foreign language. There are also a handful of schools supporting children who have moderate learning difficulties. There is practically no day school provision for secondary age children who are perceived to have emotional and/or behavioural difficulties. Boarding provision offers a little more choice in this field.

## Useful organizations

Other areas of need – autism, Asperger's Syndrome, as well as areas of physical difficulty and vulnerability – are not well catered for in the capital. However, there is an enormous number of support groups, and nationally established organizations that offer advice, such as the Royal National Institute for Deaf People and the Royal National Institute for the Blind. For children who need to remain in hospital for some time, it is worth enquiring about the availability of a hospital school. Most large teaching hospitals have them.

Recently the DfES have made considerable steps to help parents who have children with SEN. Their web site www.dfes.gov.uk/sen is particularly informative. It covers the step-by-step approach for assessing SEN and has a host of articles on topics such as 'How do I tell if a child is dyslexic?' It provides a 'SEN toolkit' and has information about the workings of the SEN tribunal, which is set up to enable parents to challenge local authority and/or school decisions about children's needs.

## Useful contact addresses

**DfES (Department for Education and Skills)**: Provides publications on special needs, eg code of practice. Sanctuary Buildings, Great Smith Street, London SW1P 3BT ☎ 020 7925 5000 📠 020 7510 0151

**Independent Coalition Service**: This is DfES funded through the Shaftesbury Society. The Shaftesbury Society, 16 Kingston Road, London SW19 1JZ. ☎ 020 8239 5555.

**IPSEA (Independent Panel for Special Education Advice)**: Helps parents obtain a second professional opinion about their child's needs. Offers a free representation service for parents at special needs tribunals. 6 Carlow Mews, Suffolk 1P12 1EA ☎ 01394 382814

**ISCis** Provides lists of independently run, registered special schools with information regarding their specialisms, such as dyslexia, teaching English as a foreign language and support for specific learning difficulties. Also has information about a myriad of support groups for children with rare medical conditions and their families.

# Map of boroughs

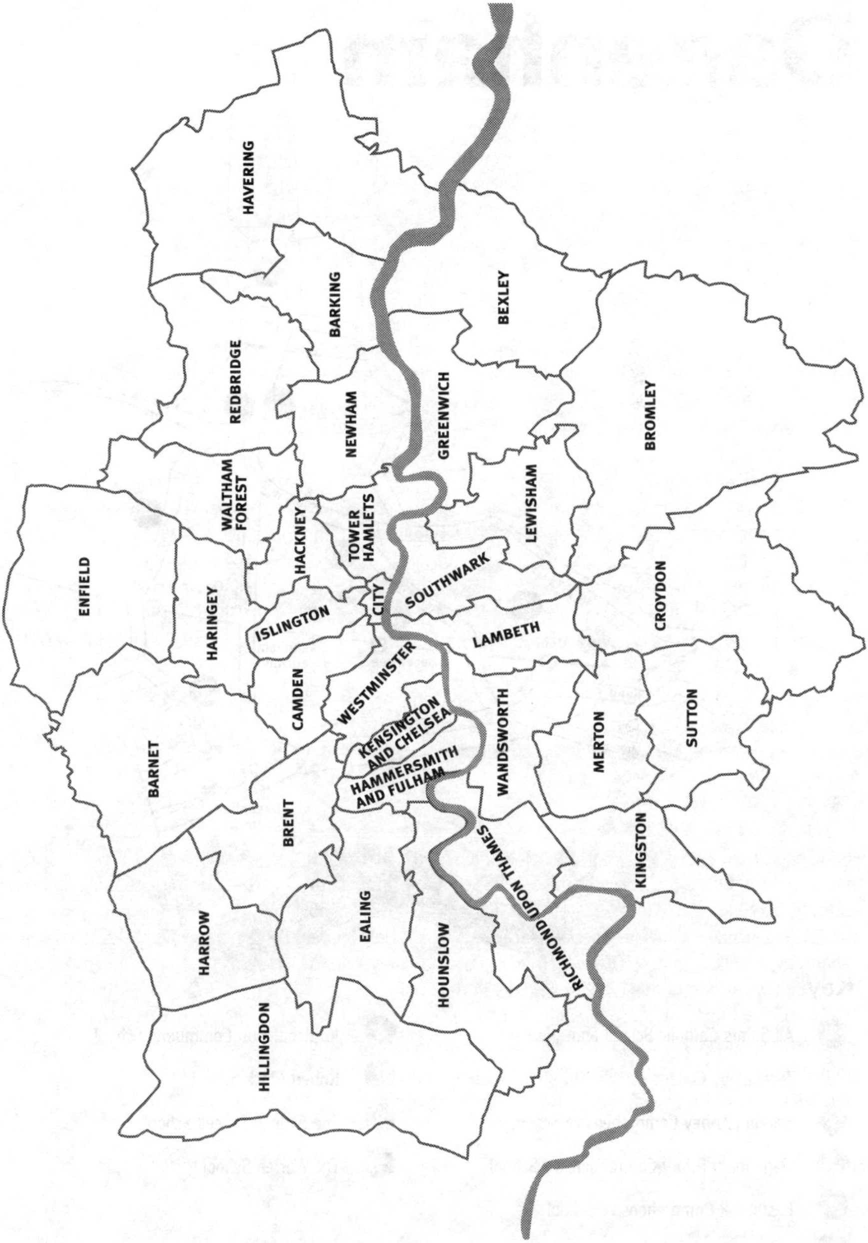

# Barking and Dagenham

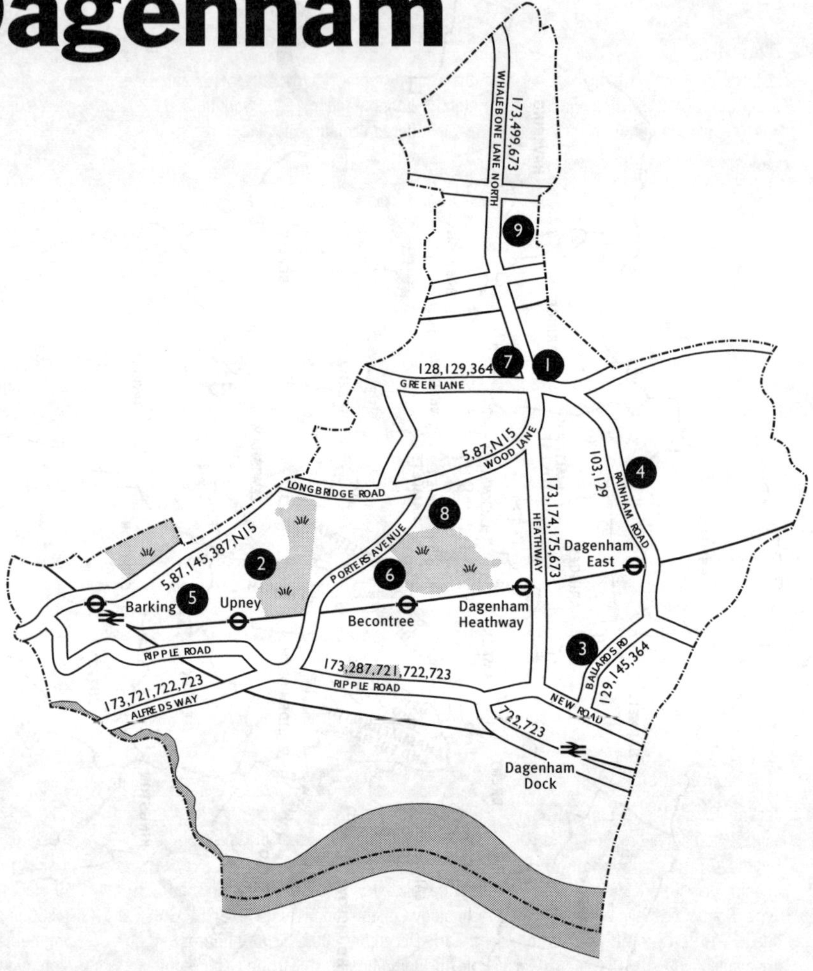


## Key

1. All Saints Catholic School and Technology College
2. Barking Abbey Comprehensive School
3. Dagenham Priory Comprehensive School
4. Eastbrook Comprehensive School
5. Eastbury Comprehensive School
6. Jo Richardson Community School
7. Robert Clack School
8. The Sydney Russell School
9. The Warren School

# Factfile

**LEA: Town Hall, Barking, Essex 1G11 7LU** ☎ 020 8592 4500 🌐 www.barking-dagenham.gov.uk **Director of Education:** Roger Luxton **Political control of council:** Labour **Percentage of pupils from outside the borough:** 6.5 per cent **Percentage of pupils educated outside the borough:** 8.9 per cent **London league table position (out of 32 boroughs):** 23rd

## Profile

Located east of Newham and north of the Thames from Woolwich, Barking and Dagenham is home to around 155,000 people. Unemployment is fairly high for London and in 1991, Barking and Dagenham was ranked the 18th most deprived borough in the country. Having suffered economic decline in recent times, large sums of government money are being poured into regenerating the area, focusing on social, economic and environmental improvement. Around £7 million is being invested in the Artscape Project, aimed at enhancing the environment around the A13. Funds have also been awarded from the Millennium Commission for a variety of redevelopment projects.

A large proportion of the borough is covered by the Becontree estate. The slightly smarter end of the borough is Chadwell Heath, characterized by 1930s semi-detached housing. Around 50 per cent of houses are now owner-occupied and the area is starting to attract people wishing to buy affordable housing with accessibility to central London. There are plans afoot to build new homes along the riverside, which should bring more money into the area.

Although the borough's exam results are relatively low compared with the national picture, progress is being made and most schools serve their pupils well. Since 1996, Barking and Dagenham has proven to be the 11th fastest improving LEA in the country for pupils gaining five or more GCSEs at A*–C grades. In 2002, the Barking average for pupils with five or more GCSEs at A*–C grades was 42.3 per cent, below the national average of 51.6 per cent. It is one of the only boroughs in the country that has had its secondary schools invited to take part in two new programmes for improving standards and attainment: the Key Stage 3 and Excellence in Cities programmes. The LEA was one of the first in England to be inspected by Ofsted and was subsequently described as a 'model of LEA activity'.

## Policy

Parents should contact Barking and Dagenham council for application forms for secondary schools, apart from All Saints Catholic School and Technology College, where they must apply directly to the school. Criteria for allocating places, in order of priority, are: children with a sibling at the school; children attending a nearby junior or primary school, included in an approved linking arrangement with specific secondary schools; and children who live closest to a particular school.

# All Saints Catholic School and Technology College

**Terling Road, Wood Lane, Dagenham, Essex RM8 1DS** ☎ 020 8270 4242 📠 020 8270 4024 ✉ all-saints@bardaglea.org.uk Mr DPM Smith MA, BA, Ac.Dip; Chair of Governors: Mr D Savage OBE Chadwell Heath ⊖ Dagenham Heathway, Dagenham East **Buses:** 5, 87, 173, 175 Grey trousers or skirt, white blouse or shirt, grey V-neck sweater with school badge, blazer with school badge **Demand:** 303 for 180 places in 2001/2 **Type:** Roman Catholic voluntary-aided Technology College comprehensive for 1103 mixed pupils (166 in sixth form), aged 11 to 18 **Submit application form:** Early December 2003 **School hours:** 8.45am–3.25pm; homework clubs are available **Meals:** Hot and cold available, including breakfast **Strong GCSE subjects:** Art, design and technology, geography and PE **London league table position:** 203

## Profile

All Saints provides a Christian, caring and supportive environment in which its pupils flourish. It promotes technical and vocational education according to its Technology College status, granted in 1994 and now in Phase III. The school has high-quality facilities for sport, technology, vocational subjects and a sixth form. In 1999, the DfES awarded the school £1.5 million for new science labs which opened in 2001. Organized into tutor groups, all pupils have equal access to the curriculum. Work experience takes place in Year 10 and some pupils in Year 11 can become prefects. There is a school council. Parents are kept informed through annual parents' evenings and reports. The school also produces a review, grading performance, behaviour and attendance. The Friends of All Saints help with fund-raising.

### Admissions and intake

Applications are made direct to the school. If oversubscribed, places are awarded according to the following criteria: baptized practising Catholics in Barking and Dagenham Deanery; baptized practising Catholics from other parishes with sibling at the school; non-baptized children of Catholic parents, with application endorsed by a parish priest; and other baptized children. Over 80 per cent of pupils are from a Catholic background and 60 per cent are boys.

### Achievement

All Saints' academic performance has vastly improved since the school's establishment and this upward trend looks set to continue. Although attainment on entry is below the national average, overall attainment is close to the national average at GCSE. In 2002, 68 per cent of pupils gained five or more A*–C grades, a dramatic rise from 9.9 per cent in 1990 and well above the national average. The school ranks top out of eight in the borough. Pupils can choose from impressive science, design and technology options and attainment is at or above national expectations in design and technology, PE, geography and art. At A-level, while a significant minority of students attain higher grades, the overall performance is below the national average. In 2002, the average point score for A-levels was 203.5, above the borough average, placing the school fifth out of eight in the borough. The sixth form is part of the consortium with Eastbrook, Robert Clack and Warren, which means there is a wide range of sixth form courses available and GNVQ programmes are particularly well structured. In 1997, Ofsted found that teachers provided 'sensitive but firm support' to children with emotional and behavioural difficulties.

### Extra-curricular activities

All Saints offers homework clubs and the traditional range of sports. Religious activities include retreat days and voluntary Masses. A justice and peace group also provides an opportunity for pupils to explore moral and social issues. The school runs drama and music clubs and trips abroad. Some pupils undertake charity work.

## Barking Abbey Comprehensive School

**Sandringham Road, Barking, Essex IG11 9AG; Longbridge Road, Barking, Essex, IG11 8UF** ☎ 020 8270 4100; 020 8270 4140 📠 020 8270 4090 ⓔ office@babbey.bardaglea.org.uk Mr Mark Lloyd BA (Hons); Chair of Governors: Mr Peter Burch ⇄ Barking ⊖ Upney, Barking **Buses:** 62, 287, 367 and all other buses to Barking station Up to sixth form: Black blazer, black trousers or skirt, school tie **Demand:** 450 for 270 places in 2000/1 **Type:** Community comprehensive Sport College for 1615 mixed pupils (283 in sixth form), aged 11 to 18 **Submit application form:** Early December 2003 **Motto:** *Laborare et servire* (Work and Serve) **School hours:** 8.45am–3pm; homework clubs are available **Meals:** Hot and cold available **Strong GCSE subjects:** Art, German, PE and science **London league table position:** 282

### Profile

Barking Abbey was one of the first six schools to be named a specialist Sport College in recognition of its outstanding reputation for sport, and it now has the prestigious Sport England Award. The school is divided between two sites and set in extensive grounds. It has a new leisure centre including 12 floodlit, all-weather netball and tennis courts, weights and fitness room, gym, sports hall and crèche. The Technology for Schools initiative paid for over £200,000 worth of equipment for the design and food department. Pupils are organized into tutor groups and form tutors, who stay with their groups from Years 7 to 11, are responsible for pastoral care. Sixth-formers help younger pupils with special needs. Pupils can be elected to a school council or can become form monitors, librarians and sports captains. The school elects sixth-formers as prefects and there is a head girl and boy. Work experience takes place in Year 10. There is a record of attainment along with annual parents' evenings, an active PTA, written reports and an 'open house' policy. Attendance is above the national average.

### Admissions and intake

Induction days are held for all Year 6 pupils and 'link evenings' are held for the parents of new pupils. Admission is through the council's education department. If oversubscribed, the following criteria applies: sibling at the school; a linked primary (St Margaret's, Manor and Northbury); and proximity to home.

### Achievement

Barking Abbey was named as one of the 41 most improved secondary schools in the chief inspector's last report and has an Investor in People Award, a Basic Skills Agency Quality Mark and Schools Curriculum Award 2000. Although on entry pupils achieve well below average results, GCSE results are now above national averages. In 2002, 54 per cent of pupils gained five or more A*–C grades at GCSE, giving the school the second best result in the borough. The average point score for pupils taking two or more A/AS-levels was 218.3, below the national average but above the borough's average. In 1997, Ofsted noted that pupils make 'exceptionally good progress' in vocational subjects, attaining results well above the national average. The large sixth form offers 24 A-level options along with GNVQ and BTEC courses. Ofsted found that pupils were diligent and well behaved and special needs pupils make good progress at all stages.

### Extra-curricular activities

Barking Abbey excels at sport on county and national levels. Sports on offer are as diverse as rugby, trampolining, basketball, aerobics, dance, cross country and table tennis. After-school clubs are also held in drama, chess and science. Many subjects offer homework clubs. Many students take part in concerts, trips to the theatre, art galleries and historical or geological sites at home and abroad. Sixth-formers can take part in community work.

## Dagenham Priory Comprehensive School

**School Road, Dagenham, Essex RM10 9QH** ☎ 020 8270 4400 📠 020 8270 4409 ⓔ kwiley@dag-priory.bardaglea.org.uk 🌐 www.priory.bardaglea.org.uk Mr J Torrie M.Ed, Adv Dip.Ed; Chair of Governors: Mr Ray Descombes ⇄ Dagenham Dock ⊖ Dagenham East, Dagenham Heathway **Buses:** 145, 364 Up to sixth form: Black blazer, trousers or skirt, white shirt **Demand:** 89 first-choice applications for 240 places in 2000/1; 240 second- and third-choice applications **Type:** Community comprehensive Arts College for 890 mixed pupils (61 in sixth form), aged 11 to 18 **Submit application form:** Early December 2003 **Motto:** Achievement for All **School hours:** 8.45am–3.15pm; homework clubs are available **Meals:** Hot and cold available, including breakfast **Strong GCSE subjects:** Arts subjects, geography **London league table position:** 481

### Profile

Dagenham Priory recently achieved specialist Arts College status and will receive more than half a million pounds over the next four years to transform its art department into a centre for artistic excellence. It has its own sports hall, sports fields and a special needs centre. Recent improvements include new arts rooms, science labs, a motor vehicle studies area, a sixth-form block and a £1-million extension for English, maths and humanities. In 2001, a purpose-built dining facility, offering breakfast, lunch and snacks to pupils opened. The school is a key member of the Comenius Project, linking five schools across Europe in various arts projects. It was also involved in dance and art projects at the Millennium Dome and with Ford. Work experience is undertaken in Year 10. Form tutors are responsible for pastoral care and there are annual parents' evenings and written reports. In 1999, the school's curriculum was criticized by Ofsted as 'unsatisfactory' since it is not in line with national requirements in modern languages, RE and IT. Although it is working hard to improve its attendance record, truancy remains a problem. There is a student council.

### Admissions and intake

Open mornings and evenings are held for prospective pupils and they are invited to spend a few days at the school. Admission is through the LEA. If oversubscribed, the following criteria apply: sibling at the school; a linked primary (Beam, Godwin, John Perry, The Leys, Marsh Green, Thomas Arnold and William Ford); and proximity to home. The majority of pupils come from disadvantaged backgrounds.

### Achievement

The school's GCSE results in 2002 were below the borough's average, with 20 per cent of pupils gaining five or more A*–C grades, nine per cent down on 2001. The average point score at GCSE was 24.8, below the borough average of 31.3. However, pupils do make 'satisfactory progress' according to Ofsted, thanks to good teaching and a supportive environment. The school's strengths lie in geography and art whilst weaker subjects include design and technology, modern languages and science. Progress in the sixth form was described by Ofsted as 'never less than satisfactory', although overall results are poor. A-level students had an average point score of 114.1, well below the borough average, placing the school bottom in the borough. The sixth form is operated in consortium with The Sydney Russell School to widen the range of subjects available. Most pupils choose to study three subjects. Ofsted found that behaviour is 'broadly satisfactory' but the school ethos was criticized as 'unsatisfactory', mainly owing to a lack of a long-term planning within the school.

## Extra-curricular activities

Ofsted highlighted the extra-curricular activities as one of Dagenham Priory's strengths. A key focus is dance and drama and the arts, with an annual school play performed at a local theatre and the school choir performing Christmas carols in central London hotels. In addition the school offers a wide selection of homework clubs. Around 40 per cent of pupils take part in sports. Pupils can take part in the Young Enterprise scheme and community and charity work. The school has also 'adopted' a child in the Philippines and has links with schools abroad. The school also has girls' football and rugby teams.

# Eastbrook Comprehensive School

**Dagenham Road, Dagenham, Essex, RM10 7UR** 020 8270 4567/4568 020 8270 4545 office@eastbrook.bardaglea.org.uk Mr K Drury BA, B.Ed, FRSA; Chair of Governors: Mr JR Fryer Dagenham Dock Dagenham East **Bus**: 364 Up to sixth form: Navy or black trousers or skirt, white shirt or blouse, school tie, black blazer with school badge, black shoes **Demand**: 425 for 300 places (306 accommodated) in 2000/1 **Type**: Community comprehensive for 1498 mixed pupils (150 in sixth form), aged 11 to 18 **Submit application form**: Early December 2003 **Motto**: Commitment to Excellence **School hours**: 8.50am–2.40pm; homework clubs are available **Meals**: Hot and cold available **Strong GCSE subjects**: Art, business education, design and technology, economics, history, PE **London league table position**: 375

## Profile

Established in 1934, Eastbrook is the third largest school in the borough and is located on the busy Dagenham Road. A recent £6.5 million development programme resulted in many improved facilities and the science facilities and sports hall are notably good. The school also has a new performing arts centre, housing a dance studio, drama studio, two music rooms, three practise rooms and a recording studio. The learning resource base houses good computer facilities. All pupils follow a broad, balanced curriculum and homework is set regularly. A Personal and Social Development (PSD) programme aims to further pupils' social development. Various personal development courses are also on offer. Pupils are organized into mixed-ability forms, with form tutors responsible for pastoral care, along with year heads. All pupils undertake work experience, which is organized in conjunction with Project Trident, a borough-wide scheme to place pupils in work placements across the borough. There is a record of achievement, which may be presented to future admissions tutors or employers. Parents are kept informed through termly updates and annual reports, and are also given a parents' handbook. The Friends of Eastbrook society involves parents in the running of the school. There is a prefect system.

## Admissions and intake

This is a highly regarded, oversubscribed school. Open days and evenings are held for prospective pupils and admission is through the LEA. If oversubscribed, the following criteria apply: sibling at the school, a linked primary (Hunters Hall, John Perry, Parsloes, Richard Albion and Rush Green), and proximity to home. Significant numbers of pupils have parents who attended Eastbrook. Around 39 pupils (mainly boys), have statements of special needs.

## Achievement

Many pupils have low levels of attainment on entry to the school. Attainment at GCSE is below the national average in the majority of subjects and, in line with national trends, boys usually perform less well than girls. In 2002, 38 per cent of pupils gained five or more A*–C grades, up on 29 per cent in 2001, and the school came fifth in the borough. Attainment in core subjects is broadly in line with national averages and standards in history, art, PE, design and technology, business education and economics is good or better than national expectations. In 2002, the average point score for pupils taking two or more A/AS-levels was 200, below the national average but above the borough's average. The GNVQ pass rate is very good. Ofsted visited Eastbrook in 2000 and found that 'teaching is good overall'. The sixth form is part of the consortium with All Saints, Robert Clack and Warren which allows a wide choice of subjects. Ofsted commented that it is a 'well run school' with 'good management of pupils' behaviour'. Eastbrook's performance at GCSE was described as 'better than that of similar schools'.

## Extra-curricular activities

A reasonable range of activities are on offer including sports, music, drama and academic subjects. Various fund-raising charity events are also organized. There are trips abroad to France and Holland and local field trips.

# Eastbury Comprehensive School

**Dawson Avenue, Barking, Essex IG11 9QQ (lower school); Rosslyn Road, Barking, Essex IG11 9UH (upper school)** 020 8270 4001 (lower school); 020 8270 4000 (upper school) 020 8270 4051 (lower school); 020 8270 4041 (upper school) headteacher@eastbury.bardaglea.org.uk; Mr Nicholas Weller MBA; Chair of Governors: Cllr Raj Patient Barking Upney, Barking **Buses**: 62, 287, 367 and all other buses to Barking (lower school) or Upney (upper school) stations Black blazer, white shirt or blouse, black trousers or skirt, black shoes **Demand**: 300 for 300 places in 2000/1 **Type**: Community comprehensive for 1500 mixed pupils (166 in sixth form), aged 11 to 18 **Submit application form**: Early December 2003 **Motto**: To Thine Own Self Be True **School hours**: 9am–3.10pm; homework clubs are available **Meals**: Hot and cold available **Strong GCSE subjects**: History **London league table position**: 432

## Profile

Eastbury School aims to provide a solid academic grounding within a caring and stimulating environment and the majority of pupils respond well. The school is split between two well-maintained sites about a mile apart: the Dawson Avenue site for Years 7 to 9 and the Rosslyn Road site for all other years. There is a multimedia library, sports and leisure centre, dining area, administration block, a hall with good performing arts facilities, and a state-of-the-art technology block. Construction of a new sixth-form centre and Internet café is in progress. Pupils are initially taught in mixed-ability groups but are streamed in later years. Work experience is undertaken in Year 11. The school's Personal and Social Education (PSE) programme incorporates careers advice, and the school has its own careers library. From Years 7 to 11, pupils are divided into form groups, and form tutors are responsible for pastoral care. Parents receive annual reports, regular progress sheets and attend consultation evenings. Homework is monitored in homework diaries.

## Admissions and intake

Admission is through the LEA. If oversubscribed, the following criteria apply: sibling at the school; a linked primary (Gascoigne, Monteagle, Ripple and Thames View); and proximity to home. The school has a base for hearing-impaired pupils and therefore the proportion of pupils with a statement of special needs is higher than the borough average.

## Achievement

In 2002, 38 per cent of pupils gained five or more A*–C grades at GCSE, below the borough average of 42 per cent and below the national average of 31.6 per cent. The average point score was 28.1, just below the borough average of 31.3. This placed the school sixth in the borough. For pupils taking A/AS-levels, the average point score was 216.7, above the borough average, placing the school third in the borough league table. English, maths, science, modern languages and music are the weaker subjects whilst history is the strongest. Ofsted found that a high level of absence and exclusions was having a detrimental effect on attainment when they visited in 1997. At A/AS-level, overall attainment is above the national average in all subjects, with many pupils gaining higher grades. The sixth form offers around 13 A/AS-levels plus a variety of GNVQ courses. All sixth-formers are encouraged to take part in performing arts or sports courses. Ofsted found that 'almost all teachers establish good classroom relationships' and the development made by pupils with special needs is good.

## Extra-curricular activities

A wide range of activities is on offer, including football and rugby (for both sexes), netball and martial arts. There are clubs for art, vocal and instrumental music, drama and current affairs. Study support is provided in the form of homework clubs, extra lessons before school, revision classes in the Easter holidays and paired reading. Pupils take part in charity work.

# Jo Richardson Community School

**Cannington Road, Dagenham, Essex RM9 4BL** 020 8270 6222 020 8270 6223 headteacher@jrcs.bardaglea.org.uk www.jrcs.bardaglea.org.uk Andy Buck; Chair of Governors: Graham Bramley Barking Becontree Buses: 62,145,368 plus a school bus service from Thames View Estate Grey polo shirt, navy blue sweatshirt, fleece, coat and baseball cap, all with JRCS logo, black trousers or skirt, black trainers or low-heeled shoes; plain navy hijab may also be worn **Demand**: 248 applications for 180 places in September 2002 **Type**: Community comprehensive for 1500 mixed pupils, aged 11 to 19 **Submit application form**: Early December

2003 **Motto**: Success for All **School hours**: 8.45am–3.30pm; **Meals**: Hot and cold available including breakfast from 8am **Strong GCSE subjects**: Not yet known **London league table position**: Not yet known

## Profile

JRCS opened in September 2002 on a temporary site in Cannington Road. In 2005, the school will move to brand new facilities being built at Castle Green. From the outset the school has established clear procedures for promoting academic achievement and maintaining discipline. All students are regularly monitored to see if they are falling behind with their studies and the dedicated Student Development Department has a team of staff who can offer one to one or small group tutorials to help children overcome specific problems. There is also a special programme of 'masterclasses' for particularly gifted or talented students, and a school counsellor to provide confidential support.

## Admissions and intake

Admission is through the LEA. If oversubscribed, children who already have a sibling at the school will be given priority, as long as their parents or carers named JRCS as their first preference. However, these criteria may change.

## Achievement

With only one year of admissions so far, pupils have not yet sat any national tests or exams and the school does not appear in the London league table. The first results, for Key Stage 3 tests, will not be recorded until 2005.

## Extra-curricular activities

The brand new purpose built facilities that JRCS will occupy from 2005 have been designed to be used by both pupils and members of the local community. They will include a major library and extensive sports facilities.

# Robert Clack School

**Green Lane, Dagenham (lower school); Gosfield Road, Dagenham, Essex RM8 1JU (upper school)** ☎ 020 8270 4200 📠 020 8270 4210 ✉ office@robert-clack.bardaglea.org.uk Mr P Grant MA, BA; Chair of Governors: Mr D Cane Chadwell Heath Dagenham Heathway, Dagenham East **Buses**: 5, 87, 173, 175, 367 Up to sixth form: Black trousers or skirt, white shirt, black blazer with school badge, red-black-and-white school tie **Demand**: 394 for 300 places in 2001/2 **Type**: Community comprehensive for 1493 mixed pupils, aged 11 to 18 **Submit application form**: Eary December 2003 **Motto**: *Forti difficile nihil* (With Strength Nothing Is Difficult) **School hours**: 8.55am–3pm; homework clubs are available **Meals**: Hot and cold available **Strong GCSE subjects**: Art, English literature, maths, PE, RE, science **London league table position**: 302

## Profile

One of the borough's largest schools, Robert Clack is located in an area of high social and economic deprivation. Despite this, it is currently one of the most improving schools in Barking and Dagenham and it recently won an Investor in People Award. The school is divided between two sites, located about a mile apart. Year 7 to 9 pupils are based at the Green Lane site, which has a new £1.5 million science and technology block. Older pupils are based at the Gosfield Road site. This site is fully linked up to a computer network and the Internet and the building of a new sports centre is also underway. Pupils are streamed in most classes and follow a balanced curriculum. Special needs pupils are well integrated and have good provision. Pastoral teams monitor pupils' progress and there is an active school council. Parents are kept informed through reports, and parents' and presentation evenings.

## Admissions and intake

Open evenings are held for prospective pupils and parents. Admission is through the LEA. If oversubscribed, the following criteria apply: a sibling at the school; a linked primary (Becontree, Five Elms, Grafton, Henry Green, Rush Green, Valence and William Bellamy); and proximity to home. There is a higher than average percentage of pupils with special needs.

## Achievement

In 1999, Ofsted inspectors commented that the new head, appointed in 1997, has 'transformed' the school and this is reflected in recent exam results. The percentage of pupils earning five or more GCSEs at grades A*–C was 47 per cent in 2002, its highest ever level and up from 39 per cent in 2001. The school came third in the borough in 2002.

Achievement is considerably higher than in similar schools. Attainment in art, PE and RE is above the national average and standards in design and technology and history are in line with national expectations. Teaching is now one of the school's strengths, with 95 per cent of classes described by Ofsted as 'satisfactory or better' and 65 per cent classed as 'good or very good'. The sixth form is part of the consortium with All Saints, Eastbrook and Warren, that offers students a broad range of around 26 A/AS-levels and 8 GNVQs. Ofsted concluded that Robert Clack 'provides a welcoming, calm and orderly learning environment'. Standards of behaviour and attendance are also improving, owing to a code of behaviour being introduced.

### Extra-curricular activities

Ofsted reported that 'this aspect of the school...is a major strength'. The music department runs a school choir and produces well-reputed school productions. Departmental visits include trips to museums, galleries and the theatre. Past excursions abroad include visits to Barcelona, Florence and Paris. Some sixth-formers take part in the Young Enterprise scheme and many participate in first aid, music and sports activities. There are regular homework and catch-up clubs, and holiday clubs for Year 11 pupils.

# The Sydney Russell School

**Parsloes Avenue, Dagenham, Essex RM9 5QT** ☎ 020 8270 4333 📠 020 8270 4377 ✉ office@sydney-r.bardaglea.org.uk Mr Roger Leighton BA; Chair of Governors: Mr I Rowley ⇌ Barking ⊖ Becontree, Dagenham Heathway, Barking **Buses:** 129, 145, 364 Green blazer, school tie, black skirt or trousers; Sixth form: Office-style dress **Demand:** 220 first-choice applications; 300 first-, second- and third-choice applications for 270 places in 2001/2 **Type:** Community comprehensive for 1405 mixed pupils (120 in sixth form), aged 11 to 18 **Submit application form:** Early December 2003 **Motto:** Learning Together **School hours:** 8.50am–3.15pm; homework clubs are available **Meals:** Hot and cold available, including breakfast **Strong GCSE subjects:** Art, humanities, science **London league table position:** 451

### Profile

Sydney Russell was born out of what the 1998 Ofsted report termed a 'complex amalgamation' in the early 1990s, which gave rise to many weaknesses across the school. In 1996, a new head was appointed and his leadership has had a positive effect. The school has 12 well-equipped science labs, a state-of-the-art dance and drama studio, a leisure centre and a well-stocked library. Pupils are streamed in each subject and follow a curriculum in line with national recommendations. Sixth-formers can participate in the school council. Careers education is provided for Years 7 to 11 and is part of the sixth-form tutorial programme. Work experience is arranged in Year 10 or 11. Homework is recorded in a diary. There is a thriving PTA along with annual parents' evenings, reports and frequent summary cards. Authorized and unauthorized absence rates are both above the national averages.

### Admissions and intake

Applicants are recommended to attend open days or evenings held in the autumn term. Admission is through the council's education department. If oversubscribed, the following criteria apply: a sibling at the school; a linked primary (Becontree, Cambell, Dorothy Barley, Roding and Southwood); and proximity to home. Parents and children must also attend an interview at the school. Levels of literacy and numeracy on entry are poor for the borough. There is a large number of pupils with special needs, and the number of pupils with statements is above average.

### Achievement

Attainment has improved considerably in recent years, although pupils still perform well below the national average in many areas. In 2002, 27 per cent of pupils gained five or more GCSEs at A*–C grades, three per cent up on 2001's results. This was below the national and borough averages, and the school came seventh in the borough. In 2001, Ofsted visited Sydney Russell and found it to be providing 'an effective education for the majority of pupils'. The school's strong subjects were seen to be science, PE, dance, business education and RE. Inspectors praised the leadership and management of the school and found the level of teaching to be 'satisfactory'. Pupils' entitlement to modern languages and the use of computers across the curriculum needed to be improved. The school's A/AS-level results have been improving. In 2002, the average point score per pupil gaining two or more subjects was 162.8, below the borough average. The sixth form is part of the consortium with Dagenham Priory and offers a range of A-levels and vocational courses. The progress of pupils with special educational needs is good. Most students work hard and are rewarded with merits and prizes. The school takes a strong stand against poor discipline and has a high number of exclusions.

## Extra-curricular activities

Frequent visits are made to museums, theatres, art galleries and concert halls. Pupils also attend field trips and have visited French watersports centres and Austrian ski resorts. Lunchtime and after-school clubs include homework clubs, chess, languages and sports. Pupils take part in several major drama productions each year. They also contribute to community activities such as environmental improvement programmes.

# The Warren School

**Whalebone Lane North, Chadwell Heath, Romford, Essex RM6 6SB** ☎ 020 8270 4500 📠 020 8270 4484 ⓔ abuck@warren.bardaglea.org; Mr Andy Buck B.Sc; Chair of Governors: Rev R Gayler ⇌ Chadwell Heath **Buses**: 86, 296, 367, 551 Black blazer with school badge, school tie, black V-neck jumper, white shirt or blouse, black trousers or skirt, school PE kit; Sixth form: Office-style dress **Demand**: 305 for 240 places in 2001/2 **Type**: Community comprehensive for 1271 mixed pupils (c. 150 in sixth form), aged 11 to 18 **Submit application form**: Eary December 2003 **Motto**: Achievement for All **School hours**: 8.30am–3.10pm; homework clubs are available **Meals**: Hot and cold available **Strong GCSE subjects**: Art **London league table position**: 344

## Profile

The Warren Comprehensive has an intelligent and imaginative vision, a clear dedication to attainment and a good overall standard of teaching. It was awarded first prize in a DfES competition to identify good management and administration practice in schools. A new building for history and modern languages was opened in 1994, and the school also boasts a new canteen, sixth-form centre and improved sports facilities. Plans are afoot to improve the facilities for music and special needs, which were criticized by Ofsted in 1999 as the only areas in the school that were inadequately housed. The school has a well-managed learning resources centre. The curriculum was described by Ofsted as broad and balanced. The sixth form is part of the consortium with All Saints, Eastbrook and Robert Clack. Form teachers are responsible for pastoral care and monitor pupils' progress. There is a school council and each form has a form representative. Parents are kept informed through the *Warren Weekly* newspaper, parents' evenings, annual reports and homework planners. New parents are cared for through induction evenings and a Help Your Child Succeed course.

## Admissions and intake

Admission is through the LEA. If oversubscribed, the following criteria apply: sibling at the school; linked primary (Henry Green, Marks Gate and Warren); and proximity to home.

## Achievement

Ofsted praised the head teacher's 'vigorous, intelligent and high-quality leadership' under which the school is thriving. GCSE results in 1999, however, did not reflect the progress made since the previous Ofsted inspection in 1994 but Inspectors did not believe that these results were indicative of a future downward trend. They were right as results in 2000 were greatly improved with 40 per cent of pupils gaining five or more GCSEs at grades A*–C. This rose to 44 per cent in 2002 and the school came fourth in the borough. This was above the borough average of 42 per cent but just below the national average of 51.6 per cent. Recent results have been close to the national average in English language and literature, design, technology, food studies, catering, geography, history, modern languages and PE. Attainment is higher than the national average in art, below average in maths, drama, music and RE, and very low in science. At GCSE, 91 per cent of teaching is described by Ofsted as 'satisfactory' or 'good', and much sixth-form teaching is described as 'good'. At A-level, 205.3 was the average score for pupils taking two or more A/AS-levels in 2002. This was above the borough's average but below the national average. Journalism, media studies, Spanish and IT are among the 24 A- and A/S-levels on offer, besides GNVQs. Special needs care was also complimented by Ofsted.

## Extra-curricular activities

Many pupils take part in extra-curricular sport, drama and music clubs. Cultural trips include visits to the theatre, art galleries and concert halls, and the school also organizes trips to France. Some pupils take part in the Duke of Edinburgh's Award. The school is active within the community, collecting money through presentations and funded non-uniform days. There are after-school homework clubs.

# Barnet

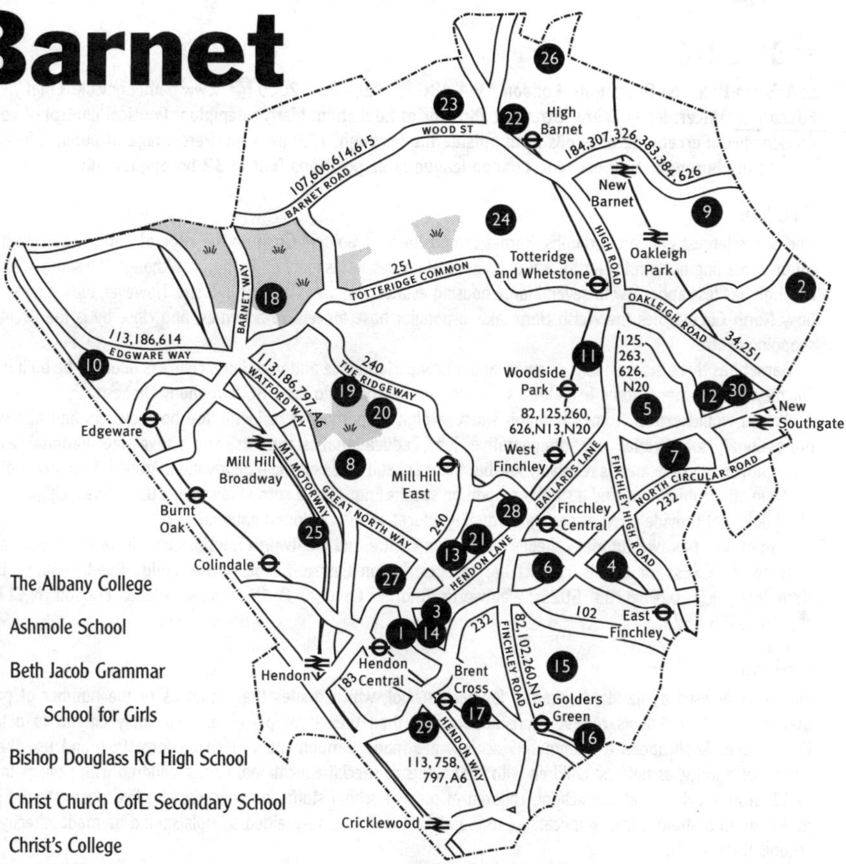


**Key**

1. The Albany College
2. Ashmole School
3. Beth Jacob Grammar School for Girls
4. Bishop Douglass RC High School
5. Christ Church CofE Secondary School
6. Christ's College
7. The Compton School
8. Copthall School
9. East Barnet School
10. The Edgware School
11. Finchley Catholic High School
12. Friern Barnet School
13. Hasmonean High School
14. Hendon School
15. The Henrietta Barnett School
16. King Alfred School
17. Menorah Grammar School
18. Mill Hill High School
19. Mill Hill School Foundation
20. The Mount School
21. Pardes House Grammar School
22. Queen Elizabeth's Girls' School
23. Queen Elizabeth's School
24. The Ravenscroft School
25. St James' Catholic High School
26. St Martha's Senior School
27. St Mary's CofE High School
28. St Michael's Catholic Grammar School
29. Whitefield School
30. Woodside Park International School

# Factfile

**LEA: Town Hall, The Burroughs, London NW4 4BG** ☎ 020 8359-2000 🌐 www.barnet.gov.uk **Chief Education Officer**: Jenny Cairns **Strategic Director of Education:** Martyn Kempton **Political control of council:** Conservative **Percentage of pupils from outside the borough**: 17.9 per cent **Percentage of pupils educated outside the borough:** 12.9 per cent **London league table positions (out of 32 boroughs)**: 4th

## Profile

One of the largest London boroughs, Barnet extends beyond Golders Green to the edge of Hampstead Heath in the south, spreading north into Hertfordshire. Its general impression is leafy and affluent, although the south-west of the borough has less appeal, with several large housing estates and areas of light industry. However, tucked away by the busy North Circular lies the Welsh Harp lake, a popular base for leisure activities, and close by is the Brent Cross shopping centre.

Barnet has three independent cinemas, and a new performance and visual arts centre is about to be built in North Finchley. The old hippodrome in Golders Green is currently home to the BBC Symphony Orchestra.

As you would expect from a borough where a high proportion of residents are homeowners and half work in professional, managerial or administrative jobs, educational standards are above the national average. Unemployment in the area is relatively low but there are still areas of social deprivation. Around 30 per cent of pupils are from ethnic minorities and a similar proportion speaks English as a second language. Barnet has a higher number of schools that provide good or very good quality education than is found nationally.

Barnet also has two tutorial colleges: the Tuition Centre and Wentworth Tutorial College, where pupils can take a range of GCSEs. For details, contact the colleges: Tuition Centre, Lodge House, Lodge Road, Hendon, London NW4 4DQ ☎ 020 8203 5025; Wentworth Tutorial College, 8 Brentmead Place, London NW11 9LH ☎ 020 8458 8524.

## Policy

The DfES devises a 'standard number' for each school, which guides the school as to the number of pupils it may admit. Most schools receive more applications than they have places and so apply criteria to determine their intake. Applications to community schools are made through the council on form PS1 and use the LEA's criteria of priority, as follows: children with statements of special educational needs; children with siblings in Year 7 to 11 at or previously at the school; children of present school staff; and children who live closest to the school, measured in a straight line. Applications to foundation and voluntary-aided schools should be made directly to the schools themselves.

# The Albany College

**21–24 Queen's Road, Hendon, London NW4 2TL; Hendry House, 413 Hendon Way, London NW4 3LJ** ☎ 020 8202 5965; 020 8202 0822 📠 020 8202 8460 ✉ admin@albany-college.co.uk 🌐 www. albany-college.co.uk 👤 Mr Bob Arthy (principal) ⊖ Hendon Central **Buses**: 83, 183, 240 (to Queen's Road); 113, 143, 186, 326 (Hendon Way) 👔 None **Demand:** No figures available but generally fully subscribed **Type**: Selective independent for 203 mixed pupils, aged 14 to 19 **Fees:** GCSE one-year courses – £9,600 (6+ subjects), £1,750 (per subject); GCSE resits – £750 (per subject); A-level one-year courses – £9,600 (3 subjects) or £4,400 (1 subject); A-level resits – £4,800 (3 subjects) or £2,200 (1 subject) **Submit application form**: No cut-off date **School hours**: 8.30am–5.30pm; also depends on pupil's timetable; homework clubs are available **Meals**: Hot and cold available **Strong GCSE subjects**: All relatively strong **London league table position**: 394

## Profile

Albany College is an independent fifth- and sixth-form college. It was established in 1974 and now occupies two main sites: the central site on Queen's Road accommodating arts, social science, biology and chemistry, and Hendry House on Hendon Way housing maths, economics, physics and computing. Other departments are spread across three sites nearby. The college has its own library and science labs, a student common room and canteen, with a spacious garden at Queen's Road. It offers full-time one-year GCSE courses, November resit GCSE courses, one- and two-year A-level courses and A-level resit courses. Learning at the college aims to be as well monitored and assessed as at any school, with regular homework and weekly tests. Regular attendance is demanded and registers are taken twice daily. A full range of university prospectuses are at the students' disposal as well as access to their own personal counsellor to help with applications. Parents are expected to play a key role in their child's attainment, and there are open evenings and termly reports.

### Admissions and intake

The large majority of pupils are from north-west London. Pupils based overseas are assisted in finding accommodation. Pupils choose to come to Albany from a wide range of schools to better their chances of obtaining the qualifications they need. The school has sometimes seen students go on to Oxbridge.

### Achievement

With a low number of Year 11 pupils (13 in 2000), aggregated GCSE results may not provide the most useful measure of performance. In 2002, 56 per cent of pupils gained five or more GCSEs at grades A*–C, down 11 per cent on the previous year. This was above national but below borough averages. The average point score was 29.6 and the college was ranked 27th in the borough league table. The college offers all the mainstream subjects at GCSE as well as Jewish studies and modern Hebrew, with pupils able to take up to eight subjects. The college was ranked 19th in the borough league tables in 2002 for A-level results, with an average point score for pupils taking two or more subjects of 221.4. An article in the *Daily Telegraph* in September 1999, ranked Albany first in a table of tutorial colleges based on A-level grade improvements. It compared pupils' resit results with their original results, with grades going up on average by over two points. Film studies and classical civilization are some of the options available to study at A-level. In 1999, 70 per cent of pupils went on to 'red-brick' universities.

### Extra-curricular activities

Some sports are offered at the school such as table tennis and football. Trips to France are regularly arranged, as well as local trips. After-school homework clubs are available.

## Ashmole School

**Cecil Road, Southgate, London N14 5RJ** ☎ 020 8361 2703 📠 020 8368 0315 ⓔ office@ashmole.barnet.sch.uk 🌐 members.aol.com/ashmole ➡ Mr Derrick Brown MA, MBA, Dip.Ed; Chair of Governors: Mr Don Goodman ⊖ Southgate **Buses:** W8, 84A, 121, 125 👔 Up to sixth form: Dark trousers or skirt, white shirt or blouse, school pullover **Demand:** 602 applications for 180 places (standard number) in 2001/2 **Type:** Comprehensive foundation school for 1290 mixed pupils, aged 11 to 18 **Submit application form:** 24 October 2003 **School hours:** 8.40am–3.25pm; homework clubs are available **Meals:** Hot and cold meals available **Strong GCSE subject:** Art **London league table position:** 162

### Profile

Ashmole School is a large school, serving a culturally diverse community. It is located within an expansive, wooded 28-acre site that offers good opportunities for pupils to participate in a range of sporting activities. The school's facilities include a sports hall, gym, drama studio, sixth-form centre, IT area and a refurbished library. There are also 17 mobile classrooms, which is less than ideal in bad weather with students having to move around classes outdoors. In 2000, Ofsted commented on the 'dilapidated' buildings and leaking gymnasium, and stated: 'It is a tribute both to pupils and to staff that the school achieves good standards in difficult circumstances.' There is a large sixth form with over 226 pupils. A sixth-former chairs the school council and others help younger pupils with reading. The parents' association raises money for school projects.

### Admissions and intake

Application is made direct to the school. Admission is not selective, but if oversubscribed priority is given, in order, to: siblings of present or past pupils, children of staff; pupils from Osidge and Walker primary schools; and those living closest to the school. About 30 per cent of pupils are on the register of special needs, which is above average. The attainment of pupils on entry is not dissimilar to that nationally in comprehensives.

### Achievement

In 2002, 69 per cent of pupils earned five or more A*–C grades at GCSE. This was well above the national and borough averages. The school was placed 13th in the borough. Performance in GCSE exams is 'well above what is achieved both nationally and in similar schools', according to Ofsted, and has improved over the last five years for boys and girls alike. Overall GCSE performance is well above average for similar schools. There has been a particular improvement in A-level results, which were below average five years ago. In 2002, the average point score for pupils taking two or more subjects at A-level was 252.3, just below the national average, ranking Ashmole 14th in the borough. Ofsted found that 98 per cent of teaching at Ashmole was at least satisfactory, 76 per cent was good or better, of which 19 per cent was very good, and 6 per cent was excellent. Ashmole has for many years had an excellent reputation for art, and this was highlighted as 'outstanding' by Ofsted. Performance in all core subjects is high, particularly in science. The inspectors also noted the very good behaviour of pupils as a particular strength. Ashmole has a close, caring atmosphere.

### Extra-curricular activities

The school has a wide variety of sports teams. Pupils also have the opportunity to organize charitable and social activities. The school arranges annual trips to France and Germany, with past visits to Switzerland, China, Romania and Russia. There are after-school homework clubs, local field trips and fund-raising for local charities.

## Beth Jacob Grammar School for Girls

**Stratford Road, Hendon, London NW4 2AT** 020 8203 4322 Mrs D Steinberg; Chair of Governors: Mr Benzian Freshwater Hendon Central **Buses:** 83, 183, 240 Contact the school for details **Demand:** Contact the school for details **Type:** Non-selective Orthodox Jewish independent for 324 girls, aged 11 to 17 **Fees:** Contact the school for details **Submit application form:** Contact the school for details **School hours:** Contact the school for details **Meals:** Contact the school for details **Strong GCSE subjects:** Contact the school for details **London league table position:** 100

### Profile

Beth Jacob is the sister school of Pardes House Grammar, a boys' school. There is a small sixth form with fewer than 40 students. There are 38 pupils recognized as having special needs, which is not far below average for all schools but higher than for most local independents; this is because the school's intake is non-selective.

### Admissions and intake

The school should be contacted directly with regard to admissions.

### Achievement

Based on exam results at Key Stage 4, Beth Jacob is providing a high quality of education for its pupils. In 2002, 83 per cent of pupils gained five or more A*–C grades at GCSE. This was much higher than the local average of 59.1 per cent and national average of 51.6 per cent for all schools, though a decrease on 87 per cent in 2001. The average point score was 48.0 and the school was ranked ninth in the borough league table. In 2002, the average point score for pupils taking two or more subjects at A-level was 229.6, placing the school 17th in the borough league table.

### Extra-curricular activities

Contact the school for details.

## Bishop Douglass RC High School

**Hamilton Road, East Finchley, London N2 0SQ** 020 8444 5213 020 8444 0416 schooladmin@bishopdouglass.barnet.sch.uk www.bishopdouglass.barnet.sch.uk Michael Kelly B.Sc (Hons), M.Sc; Chair of Governors: Mr Paddy Costello East Finchley, Finchley Central **Buses:** 143, 232, 263 Dark trousers, white shirt, blazer, school tie (boys); dark skirt, white blouse, pullover or cardigan, jacket (girls) **Demand:** 233 applications for 180 places in 2001/2 **Type:** Voluntary aided Roman Catholic comprehensive for 1017 mixed pupils, aged 11 to 18 **Submit application form:** 24th October 2003 **Mission statement:** To provide every student with the opportunities to realize their potential. **School hours**: 8.45am–3.30pm; homework clubs are available **Meals**: Hot and cold meals available **Strong GCSE subject**: Science **London league table position**: 388

## Profile

Since its amalgamation with a local grammar in 1969 to become Barnet's first comprehensive, Bishop Douglass's original accommodation has been extended. Some buildings are less up-to-date than others, but new facilities include a fitness centre and drama studio. Sixth-formers elect a council and take part in the 'buddy' reading scheme to help younger pupils. The school has well-established links with industry, which contribute to the success of work-experience activities. It also has a good relationship with parents, with an active home school association organizing social and fund-raising activities. Past pupils have the opportunity to join the Old Hamiltonians. Attendance has been a problem at the school, with a relatively high unauthorized absence rate of 2.9 per cent in 2000. There is a PTA, a school council and provision for pupils with special needs.

## Admissions and intake

Application forms are available from the school. All applicants are interviewed and the intake represents the full cross-section of prior attainment, with admission making no reference to ability or aptitude. Preference is given to baptized Roman Catholics, whose application is supported by the parish priest. No more than 10 per cent of the intake are non-Catholic. When applicants exceed the number of places available, the following criteria apply: Catholicism; sibling at the school; sibling previously at the school; proximity of home to the school; and membership of other Christian churches.

## Achievement

The number of pupils achieving five or more A*–C grades at GCSE hovered around 50 per cent for some time, with a jump to 54 per cent in 1999. In 2002, results dropped to 37 per cent. This was below the borough and national averages, and placed the school 26th in the borough league table. A-level results have risen closer to the local average and in 2002 the school was ranked 22nd in the borough, with an average point score of 199.1 for pupils taking two or more subjects. The school operates an 'open sixth form', catering for a wide range of abilities, and GNVQs are offered in addition to A-levels. In 1998, Ofsted reported that the school's strengths outweighed its weaknesses. Inspectors noted that GCSE results in science are significantly better than the national average. 'Teaching is never poor ... In nearly one half of all lessons, the standard ... is good or better ... In the very best, pupils are highly motivated, fully involved and work productively.' Also highlighted was the good provision made for the social development of pupils and the good attainment in the sixth form. The school also provides well for those with special needs.

## Extra-curricular activities

Clubs available include those for astronomers and science-fiction fans, and there is also a school orchestra and choir. The drama department organizes regular productions. The library is open to pupils after school to do homework. Sixth-formers run their own magazine and senior pupils can take part in exchange visits to Spain. There are also many local trips. A wide range of sports is on offer and pupils do fund-raising for local charities.

# Christ Church CofE Secondary School

**Hilton Avenue, North Finchley, London N12 9HB** 020 8445 3249 020 8343 9368 Mr Peter Haigh, BA (Hons), Ad Dip Ed, (acting); Chair of Governors: Cllr Brian Coleman New Southgate Woodside Park, Arnos Grove **Buses**: 43, 82, 125, 134, 221, 234, 260, 263 Navy blue sweater and blazer, dark trousers, white or pale blue shirt **Demand**: 108 applications for 150 places in 2001/2 **Type**: Voluntary aided Church of England comprehensive for 605 mixed pupils, aged 11 to 16 **Submit application form**: 24th October 2003 **Motto**: Onward **School hours**: 8.40am–3.25pm; homework clubs are available **Meals**: Hot meals available **Strong GCSE subjects**: Art, English, history **London league table position**: 342

## Profile

Christ Church School is housed in pleasant and welcoming surroundings, with new accommodation for science, music and drama. Its computer facilities are not as good as at other schools in the area and indoor space for PE is limited. However, the school is well maintained and in good condition, generally unvandalized and free from graffiti. German and Latin are sometimes offered in Years 8 and 9. There is no sixth form but pupils have preferential access to Woodhouse College. Children with special needs are catered for by the learning support department, which is well organized and gives good support to pupils and parents. In 2000, Ofsted inspectors found the partnership between the school and parents to be weak, although parental surveys revealed that they feel comfortable approaching the school. Truancy is a problem at the school and in 1999 the unauthorized absence rate of 2 per cent was fairly high. There is a PTA, a school council and a prefects system.

### Admissions and intake

Applications are made direct to the school. Priority is given to those pupils living in the Deanery of Central Barnet in the following order: children of active Christian families; children from the same home as (past) pupils; and children who attended a CofE primary school. Attainment on entry is generally below average.

### Achievement

The Ofsted report in 2000 noted: 'In comparison to similar schools, GCSE results last year were well above average.' In 2002, 38 per cent of pupils gained five or more A*–C grades. This was up on 34 per cent in 2001 but below the borough and national averages. This placed the school 23rd in the borough league table. However, Ofsted commented that 'events over the past year, including the early retirement of the head teacher, considerable changes to the senior management team and the governing body, as well as excessive harmful publicity, have had a profound detrimental impact from which the school is starting to recover.' The report claimed that 'a very high proportion of the teaching, particularly of the younger pupils in the school, is unsatisfactory and results in underachievement.' Ofsted found that 'results since 1997 indicate a significant downward trend in attainment of both boys and girls in maths, English and science over the past three years.' This was said to be partly a consequence of the 'high proportion of unsatisfactory teaching'.

### Extra-curricular activities

Lunchtime and after-school homework clubs are held by many subject teachers, and those waiting to sit exams can attend revision classes. The school arranges visits to West End theatres and pupils can go on skiing trips to Andorra and overnight camping expeditions. They participate in raising money for charity. A wide range of sports is on offer.

# Christ's College

**East End Road, Finchley, London N2 OSE** 020 8349 3581 020 8349 8972 sgh@ccfitsch.demon.co.uk www.ccfitsch.demon.co.uk Mr Paul O'Shea MA, FRSA; Chair of Governors: Mr M Cohen East Finchley **Buses**: 143, 232, 643 Up to sixth form: Navy blazer, black trousers, white shirt, school tie **Demand**: 433 applications for 150 places (standard number) in 2001/2 **Type**: County comprehensive for 926 boys, aged 11 to 18 **Submit application form**: 24 October 2003 **Motto**: *Usque proficiens* (Advancing Every Moment) **School hours**: 8.35am–3.30pm **Meals**: Hot and cold meals available **Strong GCSE subjects**: Maths, science **London league table position**: 219

### Profile

Christ's College can trace its roots back to a tiny private boarding school known as Finchley Hall School, which was established by The Reverend TR White in 1857. The school moved to its current site in 1991. Facilities include a sixth-form suite with a computer room, drama studio, sports hall, fitness room and gymnasium. It also has its own animal house and aviary. There are school parliaments to encourage pupils to take on more responsibility. There is provision for pupils with special needs. Parents are also invited to play an active role in school life. Unauthorized absence has been effectively stamped out at the school and was down to 0.1 per cent in 2000 from a rate of 2.3 per cent in 1998. Charles and Maurice Saatchi and Harvey Goldsmith are former pupils.

### Admissions and intake

Admission is through the LEA (see borough factfile). At least 85 per cent of places are offered under LEA criteria and up to 25 per cent of places are offered under the governors' criteria to sons of former pupils and staff. The school has established long-standing links with many of its feeder primaries to ease the transition to secondary school, although close curriculum arrangements have not been forged. The intake is mixed and almost half of all pupils come from homes where English is an additional language.

## Achievement

GCSE results have often been well above the national average, which is particularly pleasing for a boys' school. In 2002, 55 per cent of pupils achieved five or more A*–C grades, above the national average and placing the school 17th in Barnet. Performances at Key Stage 3 have been just as promising, with results in core subjects far exceeding the national average. However, this success is yet to move through to the sixth form. In 2001, the average point score for those entered for two or more subjects at A-level was 213.7, below the national and borough averages. The school has an 'open' policy with regard to entry to the sixth form and GNVQ in business studies has recently been introduced. In 1999, Ofsted reported that 93 per cent of teaching was satisfactory or better, with most at least good and some excellent. Especially encouraging were the performances of pupils in maths and science, where attainment is above average. Ofsted also praised pupils' vocational opportunities and stated: 'Provision for careers education and work experience, including a European dimension, is outstanding.' The inspectors were impressed by sixth-form students, who were found to show 'a commitment and loyalty to the school...frequently providing very good role models for younger pupils and...(keenly supporting) classes and groups'.

## Extra-curricular activities

Boys play a full range of sports, with some teams achieving local success. Other pursuits include the Cadet Corps, drama and a film club, with some pupils engaged in photography. A popular debating society participates in competitions with other schools. A magazine, *Young Enterprise*, is published regularly by pupils. There are regular trips both at home and abroad. Pupils are involved with fund-raising for the local community. There are lunchtime homework clubs.

# The Compton School

**Summers Lane, London N12 0QG** ☎ 020 8368 1783 Fax 020 8368 2097 Teresa Tunnadine, B.Sc, NPQH; Chair of Governors: Mrs Mel Parker ⇌ New Southgate ⊖ West Finchley **Buses:** 43, 134, 221, 234 Black blazer with school badge, mid-grey trousers or school kilt, black V-neck jumper with school crest, white shirt, school tie, black shoes **Demand:** 500 applications for 150 places in 2001/2 **Type:** County comprehensive Technology College for 750 mixed pupils, aged 11 to 16 **Submit application form:** 24 October 2003 **Mission statement:** To provide a secure, well ordered and happy environment at the core of which is the learning process. **School hours:** 8.35am–3.30pm; homework clubs are available **Meals:** Hot and cold available **Strong GCSE subjects:** History, geography **London league table position:** 236

## Profile

The Compton School opened in September 1992 on the site of Finchley Manorhill School, which closed in 1991. It is situated on compact premises in a residential area between Finchley and Friern Barnet. The post-war buildings provide a pleasant working environment. The school recently achieved Beacon School status. Notable facilities at the school include a separate music block, drama studio, large purpose-built art rooms and two fully equipped ICT rooms. The site is clean and well maintained. Compton places a strong emphasis on creative arts. There are a large number of pupils with special needs – over 300 in 1999 – who are given considered support, with lessons well structured to cope with different needs and abilities. Pupils can sit on a year council and participate in making financial decisions. The school has excellent links with local primaries and with the parents of pupils. It is generally held in high regard within the community. There is no sixth form but pupils have preferential access to Woodhouse College. An Ofsted report in 2002 found attendance to be 'broadly average by national standards' but unauthorized absence was 'still the main hindrance to progress for a minority of pupils'.

## Admissions and intake

Admission is through the LEA (see borough factfile). About 41 per cent of pupils are on the special needs register.

## Achievement

In 2002, 57 per cent of pupils gained five or more A*–C grades at GCSE. This was a slight increase on 53 per cent in 2001, continuing an upward trend. These results were just below the borough average but above the national average. Compton was placed 19th in the borough league table. Ofsted was highly complimentary of Compton. It was said to be a 'an excellent school, in which very good teaching and first-rate leadership and management enable pupils to progress.' Inspectors found pupils' behaviour to be 'very good and frequently excellent'. Praise was also given to standards of teaching and learning in English, mathematics and science. However, standards in modern languages were reported to be below the national average but an improving trend was being established.

## Extra-curricular activities

Musical and dramatic productions at the school have a high reputation. There is a band, two choirs, a string group, brass group, rock groups and a keyboard club. Instrumental tuition is also provided and pupils have the opportunity to work with professional artists. Clubs on offer include Amnesty International and a homework club. Off-site facilities enable pupils to participate in canoeing, body-conditioning and squash. Pupils go on regular trips abroad, including skiing, and there are residential trips to Wales and Norfolk as well as visits to London museums.

# Copthall School

**Pursley Road, Mill Hill, London NW7 2EP** 020 8959 1937 020 8959 8736 enquiries@easymail.copthall.barnet.sch.uk www.copthall.barnet.sch.uk Mrs Lynn Gadd, BEd, MA; Chair of Governors: Mr Graham Slyper Mill Hill Broadway, then 211 bus Mill Hill East, then 221 bus **Buses**: 113, 211, 221, 240 Black Watch tartan kilt or trousers, mint green shirt, navy blue V-neck jumper, white or navy socks, and white, navy or black tights and black shoes **Demand**: 553 applications for 180 places in 2001/2 **Type**: Community comprehensive for 1118 girls, aged 11 to 18 **Submit application form**: 24 October 2003 **Motto**: A Celebration of Excellence **School hours**: 8.35am–3.30pm; homework clubs are available **Meals**: Hot and cold meals available, including breakfast **Strong GCSE subjects**: History, science **London league table position**: 160

## Profile

Copthall school was established in 1936 and gained its current identity as a girls' secondary school in 1973. After a fire in 1996, the school was re-housed and refurbished onto one attractive site. Purpose-built accommodation now exists for some departments including science and design and technology, with the PE department making use of a new sports hall and extensive playing fields. The library was extended and completely refurbished in 1999 and includes a CD-ROM resource and a suite of Internet-linked computers. There is a school council and provision for pupils with special needs. Every attempt is made to respond to the concerns of parents, who in turn are supportive of the school and regularly attend consultation evenings and school events. Parents can also add their name to a 'skills register'. The school association arranges social and fund-raising events.

## Admissions and intake

Admissions are through the LEA (see borough factfile).

## Achievement

In 2002, 71 per cent of pupils achieved five or more A*–C grades at GCSE, up from 66 per cent in 2001 and continuing a rising trend. The school came 12th in the borough. GCSE subjects on offer at Copthall include Information and Communication Technology (ICT), art, dance, PE and technology. Science, art and dance are strong subjects, with history and science gaining a very high percentage of A*s in 2000. The average point score for pupils taking two or more A/AS-levels in 2002 was 308, above the national average, placing the school ninth in Barnet. Most girls stay on to the sixth form, where around 220 pupils study A-levels and intermediate level GNVQs. Options available include theatre studies, dance and media studies. In 1999, Ofsted noted that 'results in Key Stage 3 tests are well above national averages in English, maths and science and very high in comparison with similar schools. Overall, the results are similar to those in the highest 5 per cent of comparable schools.' Inspectors were particularly enthusiastic about 'the automatic assumption by teachers that pupils will reach a high standard'. Inspectors also commented positively on the pastoral system, teaching, behaviour and attitudes of pupils.

## Extra-curricular activities

An impressive range of activities is on offer, including sports teams, an orchestra, choir and clubs ranging from homework clubs to electronics to trampolining. There are summer trips to Austria, France, Germany, the Netherlands and Spain, where the girls participate in special projects such as film and photography. There are also trips to theatres and museums. Sixth-formers can take part in schemes to help local primary school children with their reading.

# East Barnet School

**Chestnut Grove, East Barnet, Hertfordshire EN4 8PU; Westbrook Crescent, New Barnet, Hertfordshire EN4 8AR** 020 8440 4162; 020 8440 1227 020 8449 9862; 020 8441 7795 enquiries@eastbarnet.sch.uk www.eastbarnet.barnet.sch.uk Mr Nick Christou B.Sc, NPQH; Chair of Governors: Mrs F Armstrong New Barnet Cockfosters, High Barnet **Buses**: 84A, 298, 299, 307 (Chestnut Grove); 307, 326, 384 (Westbrook Crescent) Up to sixth form: Black blazer with school badge, black trousers or skirt, white shirt **Demand**: 544 applications for 200 places (standard number) in 2001/2 **Type**: Community comprehensive for 1239 mixed pupils, aged 11 to 18 **Submit application form**: 24 October 2003 **Mission statement**: To encourage the 'I want to learn' culture amongst all of its students, so that they may fulfil their individual potential in education and develop into responsible adults who make a positive contribution to society. **School hours**: 8.45am–3.35pm; homework clubs are available **Meals**: Hot and cold available **Strong GCSE subjects**: Art, design and technology **London league table position**: 242

## Profile

East Barnet School is located on two sites about a mile apart. The upper school (ages 15 to 18), is housed in a 1950s purpose-built building surrounded by playing fields. The school aims at keeping the atmosphere at this site more like that of a university campus. The lower school for ages 11 to 14 (formerly East Barnet Grammar School), is more traditional. This site also has its own playing fields as well as an astro-turf pitch. The school has an enthusiastic parents' association. There is a school council and provision for pupils with special needs.

## Admissions and intake

Admissions are through the LEA (see borough factfile). At least 85 per cent of places are offered under LEA criteria. Up to 15 per cent of places are offered under the governors' criteria by which priority is given to pupils attending the following schools who have not been allocated places under the standard admission criteria: Church Hill, Cromer Road, Danegrove, Livingstone, St Mary's East Barnet, Trent. Priority within this criteria is given to those living closest to the school. Pupils falling outside of these criteria are unlikely to succeed in their applications given the rate of oversubscription. Most pupils come from Cockfosters, East Barnet, New Barnet and the surrounding areas.

## Achievement

East Barnet's GCSE results have shown a rising trend over five years, from 49 per cent of pupils obtaining five or more A*–C grades in 1997 to 58 per cent in 2002, ranking it just above the national average and below the local average. At A-level, the school was ranked 18th in the borough in 2002, with an average point score of 225.3. for pupils taking two or more subjects. The sixth from offers a broad range of A/AS-levels, including drama, computing and product design, together with GNVQs in business or health and social care. In 1997, Ofsted reported that the school had 'significantly more strengths than it has weaknesses'. It has successfully closed the gender gap in GCSE achievement so that the attainment of boys and girls is now closer at East Barnet than in most schools nationally. A high proportion of students go on to higher education from the sixth form, which was said to be 'a major strength of the school'.

## Extra-curricular activities

Sporting activities available include football, netball and trampolining as well as more adventurous pursuits such as water-skiing and orienteering. 'African workshops' provide students with the chance to express the cultures of other peoples through art, drama and music. There are annual language trips to France, Germany and Spain. Sixth-formers take part in the enrichment programme, whereby they participate in some community-serving activity. There are after-school homework clubs.

# The Edgware School

**Green Lane, Edgware, Middlesex HA8 8BT** 020 8958 5310 020 8905 4193 principal@theedgwareschool.com members.tripod.co.uk/TheEdgwareSchool/index.html Mr P Hearne BA, MA (principal); Chair of Governors: Dr Michael Platt Stanmore, Edgware **Buses**: 107, 113, 142, 251, 288 Up to sixth form: Black trousers, blue jumper, white shirt, black or brown shoes **Demand**: 320 applications for 180 places in 2001/2 **Type**: Community comprehensive for 1113 mixed pupils, aged 11 to 18 **Submit application**

**form**: 24 October 2003 **Mission statement**: To help each other succeed. This includes ensuring that students gain the highest possible examination results, providing opportunities to develop students' talents, and developing a sense of pride in and commitment to the community both inside and outside the school. **School hours**: 8.45am–3.25pm; homework clubs are available **Meals**: Hot and cold available **Strong GCSE subjects**: English, maths **London league table position**: 441

## Profile

Edgware School has undergone much refurbishment and redecoration over the past few years, from classrooms to playing areas. Parents are encouraged to play an active role in the school and to discuss any problems openly. The school has good links with industry and has enterprise projects, an industry day and work-experience placements. Vocational and business education courses are available in Years 10 and 11. There is a prefect system and pupils can be form representatives. Unauthorized absence in 2000 was higher than the national average at 4.2 per cent.

## Admissions and intake

Admission is through the LEA (see borough factfile). The school's catchment areas suffer from relative economic deprivation. About 39 per cent of pupils are from ethnic minorities and 8 per cent of these are refugees. A very high proportion of pupils, 45 per cent, are on the school register of special needs.

## Achievement

Ofsted inspected the school in 1995 and 1999. Radical changes were implemented from 1997 following a decline in standards since the 1995 inspection. A new management structure was put in place and a new head, renamed principal, was appointed. Since then standards have improved remarkably, with GCSE results improving 100 per cent by 1999, a trend continued by 28 per cent of pupils gaining five or more A*–C grades at GCSE in 2002. The average point score of pupils taking two or more A/AS-levels was 150, placing the school 24th in the borough league table. The sixth form has grown in size to around 150 pupils and was described by Ofsted as a 'credit to and strength of the school'. It offers a range of A/AS-levels and GNVQs at foundation, intermediate and advanced levels. Ofsted found that: 'Much of the teaching throughout the curriculum and the school is good and often very good', with special reference made to standards in art, drama, design and technology, history, modern languages, PE, vocational courses and business education. The report highlighted the excellent provision made for pupils with special needs.

## Extra-curricular activities

The school stages an annual dramatic production employing pupils in a range of roles. Pupils are also involved in producing a magazine and in debating clubs. Sixth-formers appoint their own social committee, which organizes a variety of activities, including the school's annual charity week. The school's premises are used most days by the local community for a range of events, including sports. A wide range of sports is on offer to pupils. Ofsted praised Edgware's role in the wider community, calling it 'a valuable extension of the normal curriculum (which) helps pupils appreciate a wider horizon'. Edgware also has after-school homework clubs and regular trips, both at home and abroad.

# Finchley Catholic High School

**Woodside Lane, London N12 8TA** 020 8445 0105 020 8446 0691 admin@fchs.demon.co.uk www.finchleycatholic.org.uk Mr Kevin Hoare B.Ed (Hons); Chair of Governors: Mr Michael Bolger Woodside Park **Buses**: 125, 221, 263 Black blazer with school badge, black trousers, white shirt, school tie; Sixth form: Smart dress code **Demand**: 273 applications for 150 places (standard number) in 2001/2 **Type**: Voluntary aided Roman Catholic comprehensive for 1003 boys, aged 11 to 18 **Submit application form**: 24 October 2003 **Motto**: *Danobis Recta Sapere* (Allow Us to Be Truly Brave) **School hours**: 8.40am–3.20pm; homework clubs are available **Meals**: Hot and cold available **Strong GCSE subjects**: Information not available **London league table position**: 211

## Profile

Founded in 1926, this school has a mixture of attractive old buildings and newer purpose-built classrooms. It recently gained Business and Enterprise College status. Teaching classes are set by ability from Year 8 for English, science, languages and classics, and maths from Year 7. RE, considered to be central to the school's aims, is a core subject at Key Stage 4. The comprehensive principle is extended to the special needs policy, whereby all pupils are provided with equal access to the full curriculum and to the sixth form. Nearly 200 pupils study A/AS-levels and GNVQs as well as GCSE resits. Sixth-formers can become prefects or stand for election to the executive committee. There is a PTA.

### Admissions and intake

Application is made directly to the school. The governors allocate places in order of priority to: boys of practising Roman Catholic families; those with a family connection with the school; boys with special pastoral or medical needs; and sons of parents who work in Catholic schools in the diocese, or who are governors in diocesan schools. No more than 10 per cent of the intake is non-Roman Catholic.

### Achievement

Finchley Roman Catholic High School was included as one of 63 outstanding secondary schools in the Chief Inspector of Schools' annual report for 1996/7. In 2002, 68 per cent of pupils gained five or more A*–C grades at GCSE, up on 60 per cent in 2001 and above the national average. The school came 16th in the borough league table. At A-level, the school attained an average point score of 200 for pupils taking two or more subjects. This placed the school 21st in the borough. Ofsted visited the school in 2000 and noted: 'Good teaching results in good learning and pupils achieve well, especially by the end of Key Stage 4.' Praise was given to the 'strong, clear-sighted leadership, particularly by the head teacher'. The report challenged the idea behind the open sixth-form policy, claiming that 'allowing pupils to embark on A-level programmes even when their prior GCSE results are discouraging means that too many do not even achieve the lowest passing grade...(the) wide range of A-level courses (offered are not) necessarily appropriate for the needs of some who are not academically inclined'. Teaching was found to be consistently good on GNVQ programmes.

### Extra-curricular activities

Clubs available include RSPCA, gardening and drama, as well as the Duke of Edinburgh's Award scheme. Music is given a high status. There are lunchtime homework clubs. A link with the Royal Opera House allows some boys to appear in professional productions. Sport plays a central role at the school and links exist with local clubs such as Saracens RFC and Shaftesbury Harriers Athletics Club. A number of foreign visits are arranged, including a foreign language exchange, skiing trips, visits to Rome and Greece and a religious trip to Lourdes. Pupils are involved with fund-raising for local charities.

# Friern Barnet School

**Hemington Avenue, London N11 3LS** ☎ 020 8368 2777 📠 020 8368 3208 ⓔ school@ friern-barnet.sch.uk 🌐 members.tripod.co.uk/fbsfriends Mr Geoffrey Gosling BA, B.Sc; Chair of Governors: Ms Laura Lassman New Southgate Arnos Grove **Buses**: 43, 134, 221, 234 Navy blazer, grey trousers or kilt or navy trousers, white shirt **Demand**: 284 applications for 150 places in 2001/2 **Type**: Community comprehensive for 750 mixed pupils, aged 11 to 16 **Submit application form**: 24 October 2003 **Mission statement**: Through challenge and commitment we: enjoy learning; will attain the highest standards; will develop respect and integrity; will create a responsible and caring community; enjoy and excel. **School hours**: 8.45am–3.30pm; homework clubs are available **Meals**: Hot and cold available **Strong GCSE subjects**: English, languages **London league table position**: 387

### Profile

This school is situated on a compact site in Friern Barnet. The design and food technology, textiles, IT, drama and music facilities are well housed in new accommodation. Hard surface outdoor areas are available in the vicinity, and pupils have use of the grass pitches at nearby Bethune Park. Unusually, the school operates a 10-day timetable for subjects. There is no sixth form, but pupils have preferential right of access to Woodhouse College, which over 30 per cent of leavers took up in 1998. A further 40 per cent went on to further education elsewhere, the majority of the rest entering work or training. The school has a good range of links with business and is a member of the North London Chamber of Commerce. The 1998 Ofsted report found that 'tutors and heads of year get to know the pupils and their families well', while the school encourages parents to become involved in their children's education. Pupils of all ages have access to a counselling service. There is a school council, prefects system and provision for pupils with special needs.

## Admissions and intake

Admission is through the LEA (see borough factfile). Due to a large number of selective schools in the area, pupils coming to Friern Barnet have slightly below the national average level of attainment, although overall pupils represent the full range of prior attainment.

## Achievement

In 2002, 37 per cent of pupils gained five or more A*–C grades at GCSE. This was slightly up on 36 per cent in 2001, continuing an upward trend. This result was below the borough and national averages. The average point score for pupils at GCSE was 30.1, below the borough average of 39.7 and just below the national average of 34.7. This placed Frien Barnet 25th in the borough. Results have fluctuated over the past four years, with a previous high of 41 per cent gaining five or more A*–Cs in 1996. Ofsted reported that: 'The school provides a good range of opportunities for pupils' social, moral and personal development... A high proportion of teaching (nearly one half of lessons) is good or very good... The climate for learning in the school is frequently good, and often very good... Based on a number of indicators, the school is achieving above average educational standards in comparison with similar schools.' Results at Key Stage 3 compare well with those achieved in similar schools, and at GCSE they compare very well.

## Extra-curricular activities

Activities on offer include a wide variety of sports, a choir, drama productions and field trips. Foreign exchange visits take place to Germany, Sweden and the Czech Republic. Homework groups are run for the lower years of the school and older pupils can do their GCSE coursework in supervised clubs. Pupils are involved with fund-raising for local charities.

# Hasmonean High School

**2–4 Page Street, London NW7 2EU (girls); Holders Hill Road, London NW4 1NA (boys)** 020 8203 4294 (girls); 020 8203 1411 (boys) 020 8202 4527 (girls); 020 8202 4526 (boys) Rabbi Radomsky; Chair of Governors: Judge M Zimmels and Sonny Baunerfreund Mill Hill Broadway (girls) Mill Hill East (girls); Hendon Central (boys) **Buses**: 113, 186, 221, 240 Up to sixth form: Grey skirt, grey and white striped shirt, grey jumper (girls); Black trousers, white shirt, school tie, skullcap in school colours (boys) **Demand**: 217 applications for 150 places (standard number) in 2001/2 **Type**: Voluntary aided Orthodox Jewish school for 1094 mixed pupils, aged 11 to 18 **Submit application form**: 24 October 2003 **School hours**: 9am–4.05pm (girls), 8.40am–4.05pm (boys), (Fri: time varies in winter months according to Jewish calendar); homework clubs are available **Meals**: Hot and cold available **Strong GCSE subjects**: Art, languages, maths, modern Hebrew, RE **London league table position**: 83

## Profile

Hasmonean High is an Orthodox Jewish school with two separate sites located about two miles apart. The boys' school is a mixture of modern and 19th-century buildings, and is on a busy main road. The girls' school has more modern buildings and is a few minutes from the A1, set into Copthall Playing Fields. Both sites have extended libraries. Vocational courses are available in Years 10 and 11. Senior pupils have the opportunity to become prefects and there is a school council. The school enjoys good relations with parents, who participate in the careers and work-experience programmes. In 1999, levels of authorized absence were high at over 10 per cent.

## Admissions and intake

Application is made directly to the school. All candidates must be Jewish according to Jewish religious law, or Halachah, observe the Sabbath and holy days, adhere to the Jewish dietary laws and maintain active membership of, or participation in, an Orthodox synagogue. Having a religiously selective intake means that the pupils come from a wide area, and not solely from the affluent immediate vicinity. The proportion of pupils on the special needs register is high at over 20 per cent. The typical Year 7 intake is of very mixed ability, with above average overall attainment.

## Achievement

In 2002, 87 per cent of pupils achieved five or more A*–C grades at GCSE, slightly up on 84 per cent in 2001, and the school came fifth in the borough. In 2000, the school was placed 34th in *The Guardian*'s table of the top national comprehensive schools. The large sixth form has over 200 pupils. A/AS-levels and advanced and intermediate GNVQs are on offer. In 2002, the average point score for pupils taking two or more subjects at A-level was 311.1, placing the school seventh in the borough. Ofsted visited the school in 1999 and reported that the school is successful in ensuring pupils of all abilities can make good progress, so that exam results are well above national averages. Key stage 3, GCSE and A-level results are well above average for all schools and for similar schools. Inspectors commented that the school 'helps pupils to develop into confident and articulate young adults who are caring and reflective of their traditions and role in society'.

## Extra-curricular activities

The school organizes a wide range of visits to London museums, theatres and other places of interest, and also some residential trips. Pupils are involved in successful fund-raising activities for many charities and sixth-formers can take part in community work. A wide range of sports is on offer. Pupils can also participate in the Duke of Edinburgh's Award scheme. A Jewish studies programme runs on weekdays after school and on Sunday mornings. There are after-school homework clubs.

# Hendon School

**Golders Rise, Hendon, London NW4 2HP** 020 8202 9004 020 8202 3341 info@hendon.barnet.sch.uk Mr Peter Boursnell BA (Hons), NPQH; Chair of Governors: Mrs J Foster Hendon Central **Buses**: 83, 113, 143, 183, 186, 240, 326 Up to sixth form: Navy blue blazer, black trousers or black or navy blue skirt, white shirt, school tie **Demand**: 650 applications for 200 places in 2001/2 **Type**: Comprehensive foundation school Language College for 1231 mixed pupils, aged 11 to 18 **Submit application form**: 24 October 2003 **Motto**: Learning Together Across the World **School hours**: 8.40am–3.25pm; homework clubs are available **Meals**: Hot and cold available **Strong GCSE subjects**: English **London league table position**: 235

## Profile

This school is situated close to Hendon Central tube station. Its facilities include eight science labs, two new drama studios, a new music suite, six technology workshops and five computer rooms. Sports facilities include a large sports hall, gymnasium and fitness area, and off-site, all-weather pitches. Hendon achieved Language College status in 1995, now extended for a further three years. It has also received a Sportsmark Award and an Investors in People Award. In Year 12, pupils help their younger counterparts with reading skills. Famous ex-pupils include Rabbi Lionel Blue and Peter Mandelson.

## Admissions and intake

Application forms are available from the school. To maintain an intake that represents the full ability range, all Year 7 applicants are subject to a standardized test at the beginning of the calendar year of proposed entry. Pupils are then placed into one of three ability bands and are admitted from each band according to a variety of criteria.

## Achievement

Hendon was recently listed in *The Observer's* top 100 state schools in the country. In 2002, 58 per cent of pupils gained five or more A*–C grades at GCSE, below the local but above the national averages. This placed the school 18th in the borough league table. Hendon offers French, German and Japanese at Key Stage 3, and Spanish is an additional option at GCSE. Other options available include business studies, sociology and child development. The average point score for pupils taking two or more A/AS-levels was 247.7, very slightly above the borough average, placing the school 15th in the borough. The expanding sixth form has a growing number of A-level groups and GNVQs at advanced and intermediate level are well established and popular. The GNVQ programme has a close relationship with industry, with community work being particularly strong in the sixth form. Two-thirds of sixth-formers go into higher education. In the latest report, Ofsted praised the standard of English teaching at Hendon. 'It overcame the problems presented by the high number of pupils for whom it [English] is an additional language, so that attainment at the end of each key stage is above the national average'. The report noted that: 'Pupils make good progress during their time at the school and emerge confident and well-educated young people...'.

### Extra-curricular activities

A high number of pupils participate in competitive sports and have achieved success individually and in teams at local and county levels. The girls' football team reached the Middlesex County semi-finals. There is a school choir, orchestras and a jazz band. Drama productions are regularly staged. Pupils can participate in the Duke of Edinburgh's Award scheme and World Challenge expeditions. Trips are organized abroad, in addition to field trips, skiing trips to Andorra and a residential outdoor activities week for Year 9. The school also runs a Saturday Languages School.

# The Henrietta Barnett School

**Central Square, Hampstead Garden Suburb, London NW11 7BN** 020 8458 8999 020 8455 8900 hbs_school@btconnect.com http://members.aol.com/hbsschool Ms J Pain; Chair of Governors: Mrs E Miller Golders Green (then H2 bus) **Buses:** H2, 82, 102, 260 Up to sixth form: Navy skirt, blue or white shirt and knitwear **Demand:** 1034 applications for 93 places in 2001/2 **Type:** Voluntary aided selective for 696 girls, aged 11 to 18 **Submit application form:** 24 October 2003 **Mission statement:** To provide the highest level of achievement regardless of social, economic, cultural or ethnic background. **School hours:** 8.30am–3.55pm **Meals:** Hot and cold available **Strong GCSE subjects:** All relatively strong **London league table position:** 15

### Profile

Founded in 1911, Henrietta Barnett School is housed in a beautiful building in an attractive environment close to Hampstead Heath, shared with the Hampstead Garden Suburb Institute. This can be restrictive, especially in PE and for extra-curricular activities, while many of the classrooms are small. The school's eponymous founder sought to ensure that women had equal access to educational opportunities, and it has succeeded in maintaining an envious reputation for high standards. Latin is taught to all girls in Years 8 to 9. The sixth form is very popular among girls leaving other schools in the area at 16, a third of the entire school population being in Years 12 to 13. The parents' association plays an active role in the school, contributing over £30,000 annually to funds. There is a school council. Henrietta Barnett is one of London's 19 remaining grammar schools.

### Admissions and intake

Application forms are available from the school. All candidates must sit a reasoning test in November, and are placed in rank order according to the results. Girls ranked up to and including 275 are asked to take a further exam in maths and English, then ranked according to the combined test scores. When girls are ranked equally, the following criteria are used to decide the final placings: a sister currently or previously at the school; local residents; and geographical distance from the school.

### Achievement

Henrietta Barnett was the winner of the *Evening Standard* London School Award for Academic Excellence in 1999, and it was also selected for a special mention in the Chief Inspector of Schools' annual report. On top of the school's established success at Key Stage 4, the average total GCSE points have been rising at a faster rate than the national trend over the past three years. In 2002, 100 per cent of pupils gained five or more A*–C grades at GCSE, equalling the result for 2001. The school was ranked second in the borough. Results are very high in relation to the average for selective schools. Pupils taking two or more A/AS-levels averaged 371.9 points, way above the national average. Ofsted visited the school in 1998 and stated: 'The Henrietta Barnett School provides an excellent standard of education... Examination results are extremely high, and attitudes to work are first rate... Behaviour, relationships and the ethos of the school are also excellent... 97 per cent of teaching is satisfactory or better.'

### Extra-curricular activities

Ofsted reported that the extra-curricular activities at the school were unusually rich. Pupils organize their own clubs, social events, magazines and arts festivals, and have the chance to use a residential study centre in Wiltshire. Music concerts are regularly held and there is an annual drama festival. Debating is a popular activity, with the school frequently pitted against other schools. However, given the pressure on accommodation, some rooms for extra-curricular activities need to be booked as much as 18 months in advance. Pupils are involved with fund-raising for local charities.

# King Alfred School

**149 North End Road, London NW11 7HY** ☎ 020 8457 5200 Fax 020 8457 5249 e kas@kingalfred.barnet.sch.uk www.kingalfred.barnet.sch.uk Sue Boulton; Chair of Council: Peter Palliser Cricklewood Golders Green, Hampstead **Buses**: 210, 268 None **Demand**: Oversubscribed **Type**: Non-selective independent for 507 mixed pupils, aged 4 to 19 **Fees**: from £2,300–£3,120 per term **Submit application form**: No cut-off date **Motto**: *Ex corde vita* (From the Heart Springs Life) **School hours**: 8.55am–4pm **Meals**: Hot and cold available **Strong GCSE subjects**: All relatively strong **London league table position**: 99

## Profile

King Alfred's was established in 1897 in Hampstead, moving to its present site at Manor Wood in 1921. It is situated close to Golders Hill Park and Hampstead Heath on a wonderful six-acre wooded site, incorporating tennis courts and an amphitheatre. Raymond Unwin and Charles Voysey designed the school buildings. It is notable for its open and informal ethos. There is no homework timetable, with children encouraged to plan time for work themselves. Teachers are called by their first names. Pupils are split into the lower (ages 4 to 10), middle (ages 11 to 14), and upper (ages 14 to 18) sections of the school. Year groups are small, with the total number purposely limited to 500 pupils. There is a dyslexia unit and the school is also equipped to teach pupils with physical disabilities. Sixth-formers take younger pupils on visits or supervise lunchtime football. There is an annual 'sixth-form teaching day', when older pupils take over the middle and upper schools. Senior pupils annually elect six sixth-formers onto the 'school six', which liaises with senior bodies of the school, and every year group from age 10 sends a representative onto the school council. Each class also has a 'parent representative' who sits on the parent/staff committee. Home-school links are very good, with the school selecting the children of parents who it feels will fit with its unique ethos.

## Admissions and intake

Application forms are available from the school. Entrants at age 7 are tested in English and maths. At age 11, pupils feed into one of two parallel classes of only 20 or so pupils each. Parents wishing to gain a place for their child at age 11 are interviewed and their children are tested by the school's own exams in maths and English. Candidates then visit the school for two days, after which any offer of a place may be made. For entry to the sixth form, candidates visit the school for a day. Applications are considered in order of registration, so early application is advised.

## Achievement

In 2002, 87 per cent of pupils gained five or more A*–C grades at GCSE. This was up from 81 per cent in 2001, continuing an upward trend. The average point score was 47.2 and the school was ranked 11th in the borough. GCSE options available include drama, photography and technology. The school was ranked fourth at A-level with an average point score of 345.7 for pupils taking two or more subjects, up on previous years and well above the borough and national averages. A-level options available include photography and Spanish, with graphical/technical communication, life skills and singing as non-exam options.

## Extra-curricular activities

There is a wide range of activities available including a choir, an orchestra and drama group. All pupils enjoy a 'choice afternoon' once a week when they can choose from a range of pursuits including self-defence, pottery and sport. Ballet, dance and photography are also on offer. The school organizes a skiing trip and teaches sailing. There is involvement with the local community, including carol concerts in an old people's home.

# Menorah Grammar School

**Abbots Road, Edgware, Middlesex, HA8 0QS** ☎ 020 8906 9756 Fax 020 8959 1557 e menorahgrammar@hotmail.com Rabbi AM Goldblatt; Chair of Governors: Joseph Pearlman Brent Cross **Buses**: 83, 183, 210, 240 Charcoal grey trousers, plain navy blue blazer, plain white or light blue shirt, plain V-neck navy blue jumper, plain black shoes **Demand**: Heavily subscribed **Type**: Selective independent for 185 boys, aged 11 to 18 **Fees**: Contact the school for details. **Submit application form**: October 2003 **School hours**: 8.50am–5.35pm **Meals**: None **London league table position**: 103

## Profile

Menorah Grammar School moved to its new site in Edgware in September 2000. It is an Orthodox Jewish school, which is three-times oversubscribed by the north London Jewish community, among whom it is well known. Pupils come from Orthodox Jewish primary schools. Hebrew studies are taught for three to four hours daily. The sixth form is small with only around 30 pupils in Years 12 and 13, but is growing each year. There is a PTA, a prefects system and a department for pupils with special needs.

## Admissions and intake

The school should be contacted with regard to admissions. Parents fill out an application form and children sit an entrance exam.

## Achievement

With small year groups, the school has earned a pattern of high GCSE results. In 2002, 89 per cent of pupils gained five or more A*–C grades, up on 71 in 2001, continuing a generally high trend. The school was ranked 10th in the borough league table. Pupils taking two or more subjects at A-level in 2001 averaged 331.7 points. This was above the national and borough averages. The school was ranked sixth in the borough, a huge improvement on 2001.

## Extra-curricular activities

Boys play a wide range of sports. There is a school choir and pupils can go on a five-day walking trip in the UK.

# Mill Hill High School

Worcester Crescent, Mill Hill, London NW7 4LL ☎ 020 8959 0017 Fax 020 8959 6514 e Suer@mhchs.org.uk www www.mhchs.org.uk Dr Alan Davison MBA, FIMgt, Ed.D; Chair of Governors: Mr M Dannell Rail Mill Hill Broadway Tube Mill Hill East **Buses**: 113, 186, 221, 240, 251, 292 Uniform Up to sixth form: Black trousers or skirt, white shirt, school tie, black V-neck pullover, maroon school blazer with black stripe, black shoes **Demand**: 1,265 applications for 240 places in 2001/2 **Type**: Comprehensive foundation school Technology College for 1510 mixed pupils, aged 11 to 18 **Submit application form**: 24th October 2003 **Mission statement**: Innovation and initiative within the context of traditional values **School hours**: 8.30am–3.20pm; homework clubs are available **Meals**: Hot meals available **Strong GCSE subjects**: English, maths, science **London league table position**: 94

## Profile

Mill Hill High's popularity has meant it has grown within a site which is now almost too small for the number of pupils, although recent redevelopment has attempted to address this issue. The buildings are modern, clean and well maintained. Additional funding to improve accommodation and resources for science, technology and maths is provided through the Technology College status. An increased availability of IT has benefited all areas of the school. Classes are set by ability. Parents can join a Friends' association, which has raised significant funds for the school. There is a school council.

## Admissions and intake

Applications are made direct to the school. Places are allocated according to the following criteria: siblings of current pupils at the school; 10 per cent of places for pupils with proven musical ability; 5 per cent of places for pupils with ability in dance (auditions take place); 30 per cent of places for pupils with technological aptitude; pupils whose parent works at the school; pupils with a statement of special educational needs that can be supported by staff at the school; and remaining places allocated according to proximity to the school.

## Achievement

In 2002, 84 per cent of pupils gained five or more A*–C grades at GCSE. This was a rise on 71 per cent in 2001, reversing a downward trend. The results were well above the national and borough averages, placing the school sixth in the borough. Performance at A-level was good, with the school ranked 11th in the borough. The average point score of 296.7 for pupils taking two or more subjects was well above local and national averages. The sixth form is popular and successful, with over 300 students taking A-level and vocational courses, including a one-year combined studies vocational course leading to an NVQ level 2 in business administration. Options available in this course include health and social care, engineering, construction and business services. A City and Guilds Diploma is also offered at Key Stage 4. A wide range of subjects is on offer at A-level, including dance, psychology and IT. In 1997, Ofsted visited the school and found attainment and progress in relation to prior attainment to be generally above average in English, maths and science. Overall the report claimed Mill Hill High to be 'a very good school... (which) enables its pupils to attain excellent standards in many areas', with 'very hard working and dedicated' staff.

## Extra-curricular activities

The school organizes evening computer classes for children and ICT classes for parents. There are also after-school homework clubs. Pupils practise a wide range of sports. There are Easter holiday fun camps and an exchange to Germany takes place annually. Year 10 food technology students can go on a trip to France. A skiing trip is arranged to Prato Nevoso in Italy, and there has even been an expedition to Nepal. Pupils undertake fund-raising for a number of local charities.

# Mill Hill School Foundation

**The Ridgeway, Mill Hill, London NW7 1QS** 020 8959 1176 020 8201 0663 headmaster@millhill.org.uk www.millhill.org.uk Mr WR Winfield; Chair of Governors: Rt Hon Dame Angela Rumbold DBE, PC Mill Hill Broadway Mill Hill East **Buses:** 240 Black blazer with school badge, black trousers or skirt, white shirt or blouse, house tie **Demand:** A new form of 20 pupils is created at age 11 for newcomers, with around 80 to 100 candidates sitting the exam annually **Type:** Selective independent for 1118 mixed pupils (538 pupils aged 13 to 18: 363 day, 175 boarders), aged 3 to 19 **Fees** (per term): £3,715 (day), £5,724 (boarding) **Submit application form:** Contact school for details **Mission statement:** To provide excellence in education; support pupils in the passage from childhood towards responsibility; develop in every pupil self discipline, responsibility, spiritual and moral values, leading to the highest possible standards of behaviour, consideration for others and a pride in oneself and one's achievements. **School hours:** 8.20am–5.30pm **Meals:** Hot and cold available **Strong GCSE subjects:** All relatively strong **London league table position:** 178

## Profile

Mill Hill Foundation was founded in 1807 and comprises of a pre-prep, junior and senior school/sixth form, the latter being Mill Hill School, located in a semi-rural area not far from the M1. The main building is a beautiful, two-storey construction of neo-classical design set within 120 acres of mature parkland. The school has an artificial hockey pitch and a new 200-seat studio and library. Sporting facilities include an all-weather pitch, athletics track, two swimming pools, a sports hall and squash courts. Pupils are placed into houses when they come up from the Foundation's prep school, Belmont, or transfer from other schools. This increases their chances of playing representative team sports or holding positions of responsibility, such as head of house. There is also a school council and a prefects system. Mill Hill Foundation offers provision for pupils with special needs.

## Admissions and intake

Applicants sit the Scholarship Exam and take an interview in the January preceding their admittance. Boys greatly outnumber girls, as the school has only recently begun the transition to co-education.

## Achievement

In 2002, 81 per cent of pupils gained five or more A*–C grades at GCSE, compared with the local average of 59.1 per cent, and the school was placed 14th in the borough. This was one per cent up on 2001's results and the average point score was 40.4. In 2000, the proportion of students failing to gain any GCSEs, 13 per cent, was high compared with other independent schools in Barnet. The school was also ranked 10th in the borough at A-level in 2002, with an average point score of 307.9 for pupils taking two or more subjects, above the national average. All pupils are expected to continue into the 200-strong sixth form (subject to GCSE results), which teaches a full range of A-levels, including music, classical civilization and Latin.

## Extra-curricular activities

Pupils can participate in a wide range of sports including table tennis, Eton fives, golf, martial arts, canoeing, fencing, shooting and sailing. Other activities include the Combined Cadet Force (CCF) and Air Cadet Force (ACF) for militarily minded pupils, a choir and orchestra, debating society, film club, pottery and Duke of Edinburgh's Award scheme. The school offers lessons in singing and nearly all instruments. All pupils in the senior school spend four days in a major European city as part of the school's 'European initiative'. Many pupils also go on European exchange visits. Pupils participate in local community schemes.

# The Mount School

**Milespit Hill, London NW7 2RX** 020 8959 3403 020 8959 1503 mountscl@rmplc.co.uk www.mountschool.com Mrs J Kirsten Jackson; Chair of Governors: Mr Norman Freegard Mill Hill Broadway Mill Hill East **Buses**: 221, 240 Up to sixth form: White blouse with maroon stripes, maroon pullover, brown skirt, shoes **Demand**: 38 places in Year 7 for outside applicants; c. 160 children sat the entrance exam in 1999 **Type**: Selective independent for 383 girls, aged 4 to 19 **Fees**: £2,090 per term **Submit application form**: Contact school directly **Motto**: *Esse Quam Videre* (To Be Rather Than to Seem to Be) **Mission statement**: To send out girls with integrity and solid efficiency for their chosen careers. **School hours**: 8.50am–4pm; homework clubs are available **Meals**: Hot and cold available **Strong GCSE subjects**: French, maths **London league table position**: 140

## Profile

Having originally been established in 1925, and located at its present Mill Hill site since 1932, The Mount School is housed in Grade II-listed buildings with immediate views out to open countryside. Despite its rustic setting, there is convenient access to London transport, with the Northern Line of the Underground within walking distance. The school grounds contain tennis and netball courts and playing fields incorporating a hockey pitch. There is a school parliament and most sixth-formers are made prefects. Parents are encouraged to join Friends of the Mount, which arranges social and fund-raising activities.

## Admissions and intake

Applications for admission must be made on a printed form available from the school and returned with a registration fee of £45. Entry to the school is based on the result of an exam, usually held in January and at other times throughout the year. The main entry ages are 5, 7, 11, 14 and 16. Some places may be available at other age groups. The school's intake is selective and a greater number of pupils come from socio-economically advantaged backgrounds than is average for the borough.

## Achievement

In 2002, 84 per cent of girls at The Mount obtained five or more A*–C grades at GCSE. This was down from 97 per cent in 2001 and the average point score was 42.8. The school was placed 11th in the borough league table. These results are well above the borough and national averages. Results at the school have fluctuated greatly in recent years, between 70 per cent and 97 per cent, due to the small number of pupils in each year, which makes aggregation less useful. In 2002, the average point score for pupils taking two or more subjects at A-level was 308.5, above local and national averages, and placing the school eighth in the borough league table. Results are around average for girls' schools in the borough, of which there are many. The Mount School offers a wide range of languages at both GCSE and A-level, including German, Italian, Spanish, Japanese, Latin and ancient Greek. There is provision made for pupils with special needs.

## Extra-curricular activities

There is a high degree of participation in musical activities at the school, with choirs, an orchestra, wind band and string and flute ensembles. Musical productions and concerts are frequently held. Other clubs and activities include homework clubs, debating, chess, drama and Indian dance. In the sporting field the school is proud to run the North London Tennis and Badminton Leagues for local schools. Pupils also take part in a Mathematics Challenge. For an ecology project, some students visited the Isle of Wight, while classicists have the opportunity to go on trips to Italy or Greece. Frequent trips are arranged to theatres and museums. Pupils in the sixth form work with local charities such as MENCAP and Breast Cancer Awareness.

# Pardes House Grammar School

**Hendon Lane, Finchley, London N3 1SA** ☎ 020 8349 4222 📠 020 8349 4777 Rabbi Dunner ⊖ Finchley Central **Buses:** 143, 326 Black trousers, white shirt, grey V-neck jumper, black skullcap **Demand:** No figures available but highly subscribed **Type:** Non-selective independent for 178 boys, aged 10 to 16 **Fees:** Contact school directly **Submit application form:** Contact school directly **School hours:** 8.45am–5.20pm **Meals:** Sandwiches available **Strong GCSE subjects:** Maths, sciences **London league table position:** 1

## Profile

Pardes House is an Orthodox Jewish school, well known within the Jewish community from which it draws its intake. It is the sister school of Beth Jacob Grammar, a girls' school. Unauthorized absence is very low at 0.1 per cent and attendance is high at over 95 per cent. There is provision for pupils with special needs.

## Admissions and intake

The school should be contacted with regard to admissions. Parents complete an application form, available from the school, and pupils sit an entrance exam.

## Achievement

The school's GCSE results suggest an extremely high quality of teaching with 100 per cent of pupils regularly attaining five or more A*–C grades and this continued in 2002. The average point score per pupil in 2002 was 64. The school ranks number one on London's schools performance table for 2002.

## Extra-curricular activities

Pupils are involved in working with the local Jewish community.

# Queen Elizabeth's Girls' School

**High Street, Barnet, Hertfordshire EN5 5RR** ☎ 020 8449 2984 📠 020 8441 2322 qegs@talk21.com Ms K Webster; Chair of Governors: Mrs Dorothy Wilkinson ⊖ High Barnet **Buses:** 34, 84, 107, 184, 234, 263, 307, 326, 385 Up to sixth form: Pale blue checked kilt, navy sweatshirt, blue blouse (Years 7 to 9); navy blue kilt, blue blouse (Years 10 to 11) **Demand:** 627 applications for 180 places in 2001/2 **Type:** Community comprehensive for 1074 girls, aged 11 to 18 **Submit application form:** 24 October 2003 **Motto:** Forward Thinking **School hours:** 8.40am–3.15pm; homework clubs are available **Meals:** Hot and cold available **Strong GCSE subjects:** English, English literature, sciences **London league table position:** 195

## Profile

Queen Elizabeth's Girls' was originally established in 1888 as a grammar school and has been comprehensive since the 1970s. The numerous buildings set in attractive, extensive grounds are notable for the range of periods they illustrate. Facilities for drama and music are very good and a learning resources centre has recently been built. There is provision for pupils with special needs. The newer buildings provide a very good teaching environment, especially for PE, which makes use of a swimming pool, gymnasium and sports hall. Although the school provides a sixth-form education, many of its highest-attaining pupils choose to transfer to a local sixth-form college or a selective school at 16. The vocational courses offered by the school have a good success rate. Some students take up foreign work-experience placements. Local companies help to organize management simulation exercises for sixth-formers. The school is an associate of the Cambridge Institute of Education and as such engages in research projects, such as that designed to improve classroom practice. There is an active parents' association that raises funds for school resources and a school council.

## Applications and intake

Admission is through the LEA (see borough factfile). Over 40 primary schools feed into the school. The intake is generally of broadly average ability with a slight upward skew.

## Achievement

In 2002, 66 per cent of pupils gained five or more A*–C grades at GCSE, placing the school 15th in the borough league table. These results were down on 75 per cent in 2001. The school was also ranked 13th in the borough at A-level. The average point score for pupils taking two or more subjects was 266.8, above both the local and national averages. In 1997, Ofsted described QE Girls' as 'a good school, with some excellent features'. It has 'a positive ethos (and) is focusing on raising achievement...providing an effective learning environment'. The report noted that: 'Pupils have a positive attitude to learning. They are generally attentive and well motivated', with teaching found to be at least satisfactory in more than nine-tenths of lessons and very good or excellent in just over one-tenth.

## Extra-curricular activities

There are trips abroad to Belgium, France and Germany, with pupils also able to take part in exchanges with Swedish and American children. Pupils have the opportunity to go on educational trips to museums, galleries and theatres. The school is involved with many local charities, for instance collecting goods for a homeless centre, and pupils also hold musical shows for the elderly. Pupils practise a wide range of sports. There are after-school homework clubs.

# Queen Elizabeth's School

Queen's Road, Barnet, Hertfordshire EN5 4DQ ☎ 020 8441 4646 📠 020 8440 7500 ✉ admissions@qebarnet.co.uk 🌐 www.qeb.barnet.sch.uk Dr John Marincowitz BA, Ph.D, FRSA; Chair of Governors: Mr Barrie Martin ⊖ High Barnet **Buses**: 84A, 107, 234, 263, 307, 384, 385; also private coach scheme House uniforms up to fifth form **Demand**: 1145 applications for 180 places in 2001/2 **Type**: Selective foundation school for 1163 boys, aged 11 to 18 **Submit application form**: 24 October 2003 **Mission statement**: The training of boys in manners and learning. **School hours**: 8.45am–3.35pm; homework clubs are available **Meals**: Hot and cold available **Strong GCSE subjects**: All relatively strong **London league table position**: 41

## Profile

This school was founded in 1573 by Queen Elizabeth I. Accommodation includes four new labs, a sixth-form centre, a specialist music room, a multimedia lecture room and an electronic reference library. Boys are divided into houses and there is a prefect system. Parents are actively involved in the school through the Friends of Queen Elizabeth's School Association. Writers Will Self and Edward Blishen are former pupils. Queen Elizabeth's is one of London's 19 remaining grammar schools.

## Admissions and intake

Application is made direct to the school. Pupils are admitted at age 11 with regard to ability and aptitude for the nature of the education offered by the school. Of the 180 places available, up to 160 places are allocated on the basis of academic ability, established by tests set by the school. Up to 20 places may be allocated on the basis of musical ability, established by audition. Pupils come from over 100 primary schools, with many travelling a considerable distance. Some feeder primaries are Radlett, Garden Suburb, St Paul's, Stanburn and Broadfields. The number of pupils with special needs was low at 64 in 2000.

## Achievement

In 2002, 99 per cent of pupils achieved five or more A*–C grades at GCSE and Queen Elizabeth was ranked third in the borough league table. This result was equal to that of 2001 and the school's results are rising faster than the national trend. Pupils gained an average point score of 55.2 at GCSE. As well as the usual subjects offered at GCSE, pupils also have the opportunity to study photography and Russian. The school was the best performer in the borough at A-level in 2002, with an average point score for pupils taking two or more subjects of 387.8. In 2000, the school was ranked 12th in The *Guardian*'s national table of selective schools in 2000, and the *Daily Telegraph* ranked it first in its league based on its 83 per cent A or B grade pass rate at A-level. The sixth form offers A/AS levels and GNVQs, with provision for the latter judged by Ofsted to be 'of the highest quality'. In general, around three-quarters of pupils go on to higher education. Ofsted visited the school in 1998 and found it to be 'a harmonious community (that) meets its aims of producing young men who are confident and responsible...The school provides an excellent standard of education for its children in all aspects of its life... An outstanding feature is the very high standards of teaching which produce exceptional publication results.' A high percentage of pupils at Queen Elizabeth's go on to study at Oxbridge.

### Extra-curricular activities

Boys play a wide range of sports at competitive and other levels, with pupils having represented county or country at some sports. The school regularly organizes trips to residential geographical field centres in Dorset and Somerset. Some pupils join the Combined Cadet Force. Individual departments organize extra sessions in their subjects and there are also after-school homework clubs. Pupils have the opportunity to go on exchange visits with French and German schools and some sixth-formers take up foreign work-experience placements. The school ski club also organizes overseas trips. There are regular visits to London theatres, galleries and museums. Pupils work with local charities and hospitals.

## The Ravenscroft School

**Barnet Lane, London N20 8AZ** 020 8445 9205 020 8343 5437 ravenscroft@ravenscroft.barnet.sch.uk Mary Karaolis B.Ed, MA, NPQH; Chair of Governors: Cllr Mr A Hardy High Barnet, Totteridge (with school coach service) **Buses**: 251; 606 (school days only) Up to sixth form: Black blazer with school badge, white shirt, red V-neck pullover – optional, black trousers (boys); black blazer with school badge, black skirt or trousers, white blouse (girls) **Demand**: 179 applications for 180 places in 2001/2 **Type**: Community comprehensive for 789 mixed pupils, aged 11 to 18 **Submit application form**: 24 October 2003 **Mission statement**: To provide high-quality education in a safe, caring and disciplined environment, so that all pupils are able to reach their full potential and go on to become educated, responsible, independent members of society. **School hours**: 8.40am–3.30pm **Meals**: Hot and cold available **Strong GCSE subjects**: PE **London league table position**: 402

### Profile

Ravenscroft School is housed in a modern complex set in an attractive 29-acre site on the borders of Totteridge. PE is well resourced with a fully equipped sports hall and newly erected fitness centre. Other recent additions include a technology centre, two drama studios and a television and video recording studio. The school is well equipped with computers. The Centre for Pupils with Specific Learning Difficulties, an on-site local authority facility, provides tuition and curriculum support for a number of pupils with learning difficulties. Both A-levels and GNVQs (advanced and intermediate) are on offer in the sixth form. The school operates a house system, with captains elected from Year 11, and a school council is run by the sixth form. There is a PTA. Truancy is a problem the school has sought to rectify, but the rate of unauthorized absence was at 3.5 per cent in 2000, down on 1999 but still above the national average.

### Admissions and intake

At least 85 per cent of places are offered under LEA criteria (see borough factfile). Up to 15 per cent of places are awarded under the governors' following criteria: children whose parents have named the school as a sole choice; pupils from the main feeder schools (Barnet Hill, Foulds, Queenswell, Underhill and Whitings Hill), who would therefore expect to gain a place; and children of former pupils. Pupils tend to have lower than average prior attainment on entry.

### Achievement

In 2002, 34 per cent of pupils gained five or more A*–C grades at GCSE, this was up from 20 per cent gained in 2001. The average point score was 29.4 and this ranked the school 28th in the borough. In 2002, results at A-level had an average point score of 116.7 for pupils taking two or more subjects. This placed the school 25th in the borough league table. In 2000, the school was put on special measures but Ofsted revisted Ravenscroft in 2002 and recommended that the special measures be removed. Inspectors found the quailty of pupils' learning to be 'satisfactory overall' and special needs pupils to be 'well supported'. Praise was given to the good leadership of senior managers and the curriculum was 'suitably broad and balanced'. However, some staff were criticised for having low expectations of pupils'attainment and progress.

### Extra-curricular activities

Charities supported by pupils have included those for the homeless and for leprosy sufferers, while musically minded students put on a concert for senior citizens. The school jazz band has a high reputation. Ravenscroft is well known locally for its dramatic productions and enjoys a link with the National Theatre. Pupils practise a range of sports.

# St James' Catholic High School

**Great Strand, Colindale, London NW5 5PE** 020 8358 2800 020 8358 2801 admin@st-james.barnet.sch.uk Kevin McSharry BA, MCollP, FRSA; Chair of Governors: Anthony J Burke Colindale **Buses**: 204, 303, 632 Up to sixth form: Black blazer with school badge, black trousers or school kilt, white shirt, school tie **Demand**: 333 applications for 180 places in 2001/2 **Type**: Voluntary aided Roman Catholic comprehensive for 1047 mixed pupils, aged 11 to 18 **Submit application form**: 24 October 2003 **Motto**: *Veritas* (Truth) **Mission statement**: 'I have come that they may have life and live life to the full.' (John 10:10) **School hours**: 8.35am–3pm; homework clubs are available **Meals**: Hot and cold available **Strong GCSE subjects**: Drama, English **London league table position**: 292

## Profile

Founded in 1934, St James' carries on the Catholic principles of the Sisters of the Order of St Dominic. In 1996, the school moved to its present site, which boasts excellent specialist accommodation for technology, art and science, including 10 new, fully equipped and networked labs and a new six-room music centre. Sports facilities at the school include outdoor pitches, sports hall and multi-gym. Many pupils participate in the school council, provide peer-to-peer support in class and are trained to act as 'buddies' to younger pupils. The school has links with a number of feeder schools, and some pupils carry out their work-experience placements in these primaries. There is a department for pupils with special needs. Many parents join the Friends of St James', which organizes social and fund-raising events. Famous ex-pupils include newsreader Moira Stuart.

## Admissions and intake

Applications are made direct to the school. Priority is given to first-choice applicants who have shown a firm family commitment to the Roman Catholic faith and its practice, as supported by a priest's reference, and who will support the school's Roman Catholic ethos. In the case of oversubscription, the following criteria applies, in order of priority: presence of a brother or sister in the school, previous family connections, and exceptional compassionate and pastoral consideration supported by written confirmation. Children who are not from families of practising Catholics will be considered if vacancies remain and parents support the school's Catholic principles. In 2001, a quarter of pupils were identified as having special needs and 39 had statements, above the national average.

## Achievement

In 2002, 48 per cent of pupils gained five or more A*–C grades at GCSE. This was below both the local and national average, ranking the school 22nd in the borough. This was also slightly down on 52 per cent in 2001, continuing a downward trend. A special effort to reduce the gap between boys' and girls' results has shown considerable success. Pupils can study drama and music at GCSE as well as the usual subjects. At A-level the school was ranked 12th in the borough, with an average point score of 269.4 for pupils taking two or more subjects. St James' offers a range of A-levels and GNVQs to its large sixth form. In 2001, Ofsted described St James as '... a good school with a very strong Catholic ethos. It is very committed to the care and education of all its students. It has many strengths.' However, provision for pupils with special needs was found to be 'unsatisfactory'.

## Extra-curricular activities

Clubs available include art, music, drama, rugby, hockey and basketball, in addition to homework clubs. The school organizes regular music and drama productions as well as visits to London museums and galleries. Pupils can also participate in the Duke of Edinburgh's Award scheme. The history, geography, science and modern languages departments organize regular trips, some overseas. An annual skiing trip is arranged. Pupils work with local charities.

# St Martha's Senior School

**Camlet Way, Hadley, Barnet, Hertfordshire EN5 ONJ** 020 8449 6889 020 8441 5632 Constance Burke; Chair of Governors: Rev Bernard Boylan Hadley Wood High Barnet **Buses**: 399 Up to sixth form: Black blazer with school badge, black skirt, white blouse **Demand**: Figures unavailable; oversubscribed **Type**: Selective Roman Catholic independent for 297 girls, aged 11 to 19 **Fees**: £1,825 per term (basic) **Submit application form**: December 2003 **Motto**: *Servite domino in laetitia* (Serve the Lord with Joy) **School hours**:

8.45am–3.35pm **Meals**: Hot and cold available **Strong GCSE subjects**: Modern languages **London league table position**: 97

## Profile

In 1903 two French sisters fled their homeland because of anti-clericalism and began a small school in Wood Street, Barnet, which today houses the junior school. After World War II, a new building, Manor House, was purchased, which is the site of the senior school. Manor School lies a few minutes' walk from Barnet High Street in the attractive rural enclave of Hadley Wood. It is a beautiful building with a central clocktower and weather vane. The well-resourced library also has attractive architectural features. The school relates its welcoming and open principles back to its patron, Martha of the Gospels, Martha of Bethany. Its stated aims are the promotion of the spiritual, aesthetic, intellectual and physical well-being of every girl put into its care, in the spirit of the Gospel. The school chaplain holds a regular Mass, attendance at which is voluntary. The small number of pupils allows individual needs to be easily met. The small sixth form has only 29 pupils, from which prefects and a head girl are nominated. Work experience is organized for girls in Year 11. From Year 8 onwards, pupils are set by ability for French, maths and science. Parents are invited to join the parent-staff committee, which fosters social contact between parents and links between home and school. There is provision for pupils with special needs.

## Admissions and intake

The intake is not restricted to Catholics. Girls are selected through an entrance exam, which is held in the spring term preceding entry in September, subsequent to which they are placed in one of two parallel forms.

## Achievement

In 2002, 94 per cent of pupils gained five or more A*–C grades at GCSE and the school was ranked seventh in the borough. This was up from 91 per cent in 2001 and the school's results have remained at least 30 per cent higher than the national average for all schools over recent years. The average point score was 47.1 in 2001. St Martha's teaches German, Latin and classics at Key Stage 3 and IT throughout the school, as well as at GCSE. At A-level, the school was placed fifth in the borough in 2001, with an average point score of 337.1 for pupils taking two or more subjects. The school offers subjects at A/AS-level only, including IT and business studies.

## Extra-curricular activities

The school runs a chamber orchestra and choir, as well as providing individual instrumental tuition. It is also associated with the Youth and Music Organization and the Ernest Read Music Association. Visits are regularly made to concerts, ballets and operas, while art and design students visit galleries and exhibitions. The school participates in competitive netball and tennis fixtures with other schools, and offers pupils the chance to learn a number of sports and activities, including athletics, dance, self-defence and Pilates. Drama productions are frequently staged, and pupils can take a speech and communication exam. The school also arranges vacations abroad and foreign language exchanges. Pupils work with local charities.

# St Mary's CofE High School

**Downage, Hendon, London NW4 1AB** ☎ 020 8203 2827 📠 020 8202 5510 ⓔ StMarys01@aol.com Mr R Hannon B.Sc; Chair of Governors: Cllr J Hedge JP ⊖ Hendon Central **Buses**: 83, 143, 183, 226, 240, 326 Up to sixth form: Royal blue blazer, white shirt, navy skirt, grey trousers **Demand**: 350 applications for 210 places (standard number) in 2001/2 **Type**: Voluntary aided Church of England comprehensive for 1105 mixed pupils, aged 11 to 18 **Submit application form**: 24 October 2003 **School hours**: 8.40am–3.15pm (Mon–Thurs), 8.40am–2.45pm (Fri) **Meals**: Hot and cold available **Strong GCSE subjects**: Information not available **London league table position**: 360

## Profile

St Mary's can trace its history back to 1707, serving the Anglican community and families of other faiths who share its moral framework. It operates on split sites 150 metres apart. The buildings and grounds are clean and well maintained. The school does not have its own playing fields or sports hall, which proves rather restrictive in PE. Teaching classes are designed to reflect the comprehensive make-up of the school.

## Admissions and intake

Application forms are available from the school. A total of 25 places are given to pupils selected on the basis of their performance in the school's exam. Applicants who sit the tests and do not secure a place will automatically be offered an interview under the Foundation Criteria. A total of 185 pupils are admitted through these interviews, which gives priority, in order, to: children of committed members of the Church of England; those of committed members of other Christian denominations; those with siblings at the school; those with parents of other faiths benefiting from a CofE school education; and those with the shortest travelling time to the school. There are 19 pupils with statements of special need, below average for similar schools, and 192 have some measure of special need. English is an additional language for more than a third of pupils.

## Achievement

On entry, pupils' attainment is at levels that reflect its comprehensive status, with a downwards skew. However, by Key Stage 4 pupils are attaining well above expected levels. In 2002, 39 per cent of pupils achieved five or more A*–C grades at GCSE. This was down on 40 per cent in 2001 and the school came 24th in the borough. Attainment at GCSE has risen steadily in most subjects but at a slightly slower rate than nationally. In 2002, the average point score of pupils taking two or more A/AS-levels was 185.7, ranking the school 23rd in the borough. The sixth form has a high rate of sending pupils into higher education – 98 per cent in 1998. The Ofsted report in 1998 found that: 'St Mary's is a good school with a wide range of strengths, the most outstanding of which is its positive Christian ethos. 'Teaching was found to be good to excellent in two-thirds of lessons. The report also highlighted 'the support most parents give the school (which is) reflected in the high level of pupils' attendance...well above the national average.'

## Extra-curricular activities

There is a wide range of lunchtime and after-school clubs on offer, including language clubs. Inter-school competitions are organized for many sports. Year 8 pupils have set up and now run a school shop, providing pupils with cheap stationery and developing their business acumen. There are visits to London art galleries as well as local and residential field trips. Many pupils are taught to play musical instruments.

# St Michael's Catholic Grammar School

**Nether Street, North Finchley, London N12 7NJ** 020 8446 2256 020 8343 9598 stmichael@rmplc.co.uk Ursula Morrissey BA; Chair of Governors: Mr B Hartigan Finchley Central, West Finchley, Woodside Park **Buses:** 82, 125, 134, 260, 263 Blazer, purple kilt, mauve blouse; Sixth form: Appropriate clothes for school **Demand:** 328 applications for 96 places in 2001/2 **Type:** Voluntary aided Roman Catholic school for 732 girls, aged 11 to 18 **Submit application form:** 24 October 2003 **Motto:** 'Love one another as I have loved you.' (John 15:12) **School hours:** 8.40am–4pm; homework clubs are available **Meals:** Hot and cold available **Strong GCSE subjects:** English, English literature **London league table position:** 47

## Profile

St Michael's was founded in 1908 by the Sisters of the Poor Child Jesus, in whose trusteeship the school remains. It is one of London's 19 remaining grammar schools. The school's stated aim is the formation of responsible and committed Catholic citizens. The grounds are compact, which means accommodation for PE is limited. All classes are of mixed ability. Pupils with learning difficulties are not admitted, although disabled pupils are admitted to the school. Some pupils take up foreign work-experience placements. There is a school council and pupils keep homework diaries. The parents' association holds fund-raising events. The author Jill Paton-Walsh and journalist Analise Macalfie are former pupils.

## Admissions and intake

Applications are made directly to the school. Priority is given to baptized girls who have made their first Holy Communion, with a reference from the parish priest of their commitment to the Roman Catholic Church. Candidates are asked to sit written tests in verbal and non-verbal reasoning, English and maths. The top 130 are invited to take oral tests and attend with their parents for an interview. Family links are taken into account when girls tie for places. Non-Catholic girls are only considered when there are less than 150 Catholic candidates, with preference given, in order, to: children of staff; members of other Christian churches; and proximity to the school. No more than five per cent of pupils are non-Catholic. Each year there are a limited number of places available in the sixth form for outside applicants.

### Achievement

St Michael's is in the top five per cent of grammar schools nationally for GCSEs. In 2002, an impressive 96 per cent of pupils gained five or more A*–C grades at GCSE, slightly down on the school's 100 per cent success in 2001. The average point score at GCSE was 54.8, ranking the school fourth in the borough. As well as the usual subjects, French, Spanish, Latin and German are on offer at GCSE. The school was the third best performing at A-level in the borough in 2002, with an average point score of 347.3 for pupils taking two or more subjects. A-level options available include Christian theology, classical civilization, food science, psychology, PE, performing arts and politics. For the year preceding the 1998 Ofsted inspection, almost all pupils achieved A*–B grades in GCSE English. In English literature over 90 per cent of pupils achieved A* and A grades. The report noted that: 'Teaching is exceptionally strong in the sixth form'. Around 90 per cent of pupils go on to higher education. Ofsted drew the rare conclusion that, with the exception of already planned improvements in accommodation, 'there are no key issues for the school to address'.

### Extra-curricular activities

An outstanding range of activities includes a debating and drama club, plus a variety of sports. Homework clubs are also run for Year 7 and Key Stage 4 pupils. There are choirs and an orchestra, with many pupils taking part in an annual concert at St John Smith's Square. Regular visits are made to theatres, museums and galleries. Sixth-formers are involved in community work. There are exchange trips and work experience trips to France and Germany and a skiing trip to Canada.

# Whitefield School

**Claremont Road, Cricklewood, London NW2 1TR** ☎ 020 8455 4114 📠 020 8455 4382 ⓔ admin@whitefield.barnet.sch.uk ✉ Mr P Blenkinsop M.Ed, M.Sc; Chair of Governors: Dr Eva Jacobs ⊖ Brent Cross **Buses**: C11, 102, 113, 189, 226 (to school); 112, 142, 143, 182, 210, 266, 326 (to Brent Cross) 👔 Up to sixth form: Navy skirt or trousers, navy sweatshirt, white shirt or polo shirt, school tie **Demand**: 197 applications for 150 places in 2001/2 **Type**: Community comprehensive Sport College for 781 mixed pupils (120 in sixth form), aged 11 to 18 **Submit application form**: 24 October 2003 **Motto**: For Respect and a Quality Education **School hours**: 8.45am–3.15pm (Mon–Thurs), 8.45am–3pm (Fri); homework clubs are available **Meals**: Hot and cold available **Strong GCSE subjects**: Art, PE, photography **London league table position**: 516

### Profile

Whitefield School is situated on a large site close to the M1. It's upgraded facilities include a new technology and creative arts building and refurbished science labs. The school is a designated Sport College, with enhanced opportunities for PE and a capital grant for extending facilities. The existing facilities include an all-weather playing surface and use of an adjacent sports centre. There is also an excellent dance studio. The LEA has designated Whitefield for pupils with physical disability, and it is fully adapted for wheelchair users. Disabled pupils are well integrated, with provision in a special unit for 20 pupils. There is a sixth-form council.

### Admissions and intake

Places are offered under LEA criteria (see borough factfile), but application is made directly to the school. Those pupils living locally typically come from the most deprived areas of Barnet. More than 50 different languages are spoken at the school. A high proportion have special needs. There is a high rate of casual admissions, sometimes almost 50 per cent of a given year group, with many having limited English or behavioural problems. There is a school council and a parents' association, Friends of Whitefield.

### Achievement

In 20021, 24 per cent of pupils obtained five or more A*–C GCSE passes, an improvement on 21 per cent in 2001. This continues a rising trend in results at Whitefield School. The school offers GNVQ part 1 in business at Key Stage 4, alongside GCSEs. At A-level, pupils achieved an average point score of 86.5. In the sixth form, GNVQs at three levels are offered in addition to A/AS-levels and a BTEC National Diploma in sports studies. Each GNVQ area is linked to relevant local businesses. The latest Ofsted report in 1999 recognized the challenging circumstances of the school's intake, but noted that: 'From this low base almost all students make sound progress throughout the school.' It commented further that: 'Some students achieve good GCSE results in Year 12, particularly if they have had only part of their secondary education at the school. These results reflect the delayed success of these students, but are not taken into account in comparative figures.' Teachers were found to respond 'exceptionally well to the individual needs of a very wide range of students'.

## Extra-curricular activities

A wide range of sports are available at the school, including the chance for pupils to take advantage of the Hendon Youth Sports Centre organization. An annual residential trip for outward-bound activities and team-building is available to all sixth-formers. Pupils are also involved in fund-raising and charity events. Homework clubs are run every day, and the learning resource centre is open out of school hours.

# Woodside Park International School

**Friern Barnet Road, London N11 3DR** 020 8368 3777 020 8368 3220 director@ipis.org.uk www.ipis.org.uk Christopher Platford (director); Managing Director: Mr Jonathan Evans New Southgate (senior department), Woodside Park (sixth form/junior department) Arnos Grove (senior department) **Buses**: Transport provided for day pupils None **Demand**: No figures available but 40 places in Year 7 **Type**: Selective independent for 531 mixed pupils, aged 2 to 19 **Fees (per term)**: Senior department – £2,724 sixth form (International Baccalaureate) – £4,000; **Submit application form**: No cut-off date **Mission statement**: Woodside Park International School aims to create a secure, well-ordered and happy environment at the core of which is the learning process. It offers the finest possible education for all students in order that they may achieve their full potential. **School hours**: 8.30am–3.30pm; homework clubs are available **Meals**: Hot and cold available **Strong GCSE subjects**: All relatively strong **London league table position**: 268

## Profile

Woodside Park refers to itself as an international school and it certainly has a cosmopolitan community, with over 35 nationalities on its student body. The school is spread across various sites, with its senior (11 to 16) accommodation located on Friern Barnet Road with the sixth-form centre situated on nearby Woodside Avenue. The school playing fields are just a short bus ride away, offering facilities for athletics, basketball, cricket, football, hockey, softball and tennis. The senior department benefits from a sports hall, theatre and Craft, Design and Technology centre (CDT). In the sixth form, international students have the opportunity to take up 'home stay' accommodation and be housed with local families. The school operates a Quest programme. This is a programme designed to support those students who are having problems with reading, writing, maths or organization, but it does not help those pupils with behavioural problems. The programme has specialist staff to help pupils with special needs operate in a mainstream setting. Sixth-form students study the International Baccalaureate (IB) for which they select one course from each of six subject groups. The IB diploma is recognized by all UK universities as equivalent to A-level.

## Admissions and intake

Application forms, which are available from the school, should be returned with an application fee of £100 (which will only be refunded if a place is not available). Candidates will be given a straightforward test and interview prior to consideration of the application. Successful candidates will receive a formal acceptance form. A registration fee of £750 is payable on acceptance. This is carried forward during the pupil's stay at the school and credited against the final term's fees.

## Achievement

In 2002, 53 per cent of pupils obtained five or more A*–C grades at GCSE. This result was a rise on 50 per cent in 2001 and reversed a downward trend in Woodside's results over five years. The average point score at GCSE was 36.1 and the school was ranked 21st in the borough league table. Having so few pupils in each year means that results tend to fluctuate, but they do tend to be high compared with all schools, although the school does recruit from a largely privileged, if internationally and linguistically diverse, pool of children. Woodside Park offers a number of languages at GCSE such as Spanish, German, Italian, Chinese and Turkish. English can also be studied by pupils as an alternative language. There were two entries for the IB diploma in 1999, both achieving a 100 per cent pass rate.

## Extra-curricular activities

Students participate each year in the Model United Nations Conference held in The Hague. Year 6, 7 and 8 students spend five days at the school's European Studies Language Centre in Normandy to complement their French, geography, history and science studies. Activities available at the school include astronomy, ballet and dance, choir, a film/video club, an orchestra and a skiing trip. Internal house matches take place in sport. Pupils work with local charities.

# Bexley

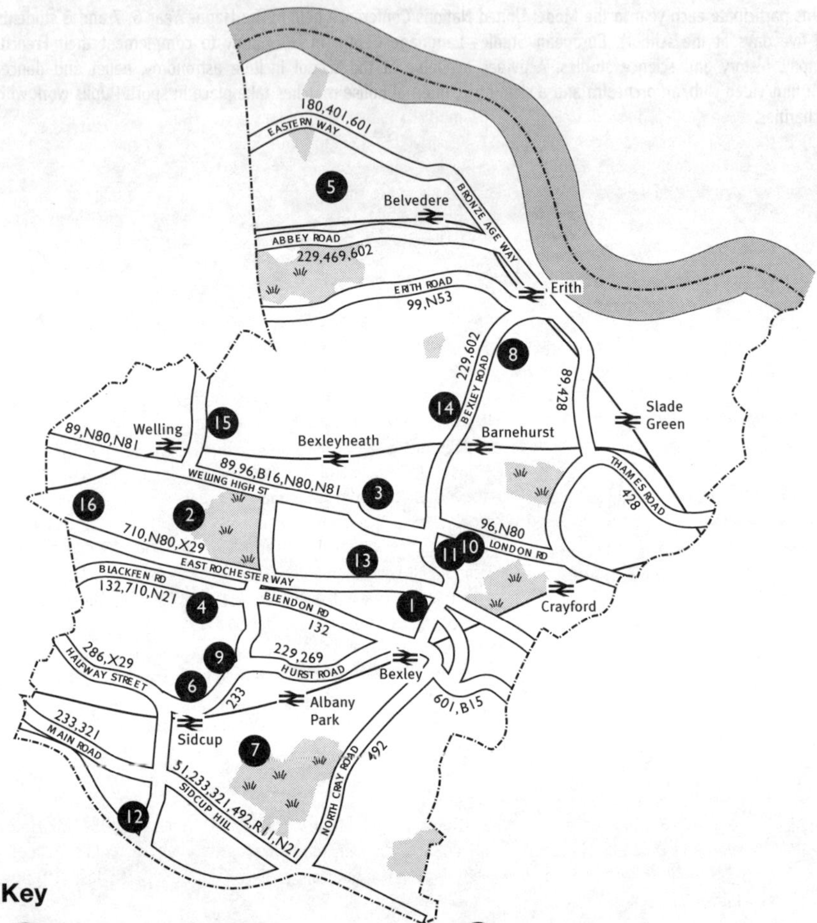


## Key

1. Beths Grammar School for Boys
2. Bexley Grammar School
3. Bexleyheath School
4. Blackfen School for Girls
5. The Business Academy
6. Chislehurst and Sidcup Grammar School
7. Cleeve Park School
8. Erith School
9. Hurstmere Foundation School for Boys
10. St Catherine's RC School for Girls
11. St Columba's Catholic Boys' School
12. St Mary and St Joseph's Catholic School
13. Townley Grammar School for Girls
14. Trinity School, Belvedere
15. Welling School
16. Westwood College

# Fact File

**LEA: Hill View, Hillview Drive, Welling DA16 3RY** 020 8303 7777 www.bexley.gov.uk **Director of Education**: Paul McGee **Political control of council**: Labour **Percentage of pupils from outside the borough**: 13.1 per cent **Percentage of pupils educated outside the borough**: 10 per cent **London league table positions (out of 32 boroughs)**: 9th

## Profile

Bexley has often been portrayed as an oasis to which commuters retreat after the daily City grind. Extensive residential development means that much of the borough does have a surfeit of suburban semis and many of its population do make the daily trip to central London to earn their living. But Bexley is more than a middle-class housing estate. To the north of the borough lies Thamesmead, a Greater London council development. The area is as near Bexley comes to inner-city but it does contain attractive canalside properties alongside the tower blocks. It has recently received several million pounds in government grants for regeneration, targeted at schemes to revitalize its community and bring in new businesses.

## Policy

Selective education has been under the national spotlight in recent years as bands of protesters launch challenges to grammar school status. However, there has been no such revolt in Bexley, where the system is considered a firm asset. The tests are held in August each year and it is not obligatory for children to sit Bexley's four selection tests in English, maths and verbal and non-verbal reasoning. In fact, some of the Christian schools positively discourage it. Bexley's real strength is that the standards of education offered at grammar level are matched in all-ability schools. This explains why almost all of its schools are routinely oversubscribed. Since the landmark 'Greenwich judgement', Bexley cannot prioritize applications inside its boundaries so there can be a scramble for places. Most applicants need to live within a couple of miles of their chosen school to have a chance of admission and it has been known for officials to physically measure the distance from doorstep to school gate to decide who the final places go to.

Bexley's standard admissions criteria, in order of priority, are: children with a formal statement of special educational needs; naming the school; children with a medical condition, which could cause hardship at another school (with professional evidence); children with a sibling or half-sibling living at the same address at the school; exceptional cases of social or domestic hardship and distance from the school measured by the shortest walking route.

# Beths Grammar School for Boys

**Hartford Road, Bexley, Kent DA5 1NEA** 01322 556538 01322 526224 admin@beths.bexley.sch.uk www.beths.bexley.sch.uk Mr James Skinner MA; Chair of Governors: Mr David Blake Bexley **Buses**: B13, B15, 89, 132, 229, 269, 492, 601 Blue blazer with Kent Invicta badge, grey trousers, white shirt, brown or black shoes; Sixth form: Suits **Demand**: 237 applications for 155 places in 2001/2 **Type**: Selective foundation school Technology College for 823 boys, aged 11 to 18 **Submit application form**: 12 December 2003 **Mission statement**: To maximize the potential of every boy within a supportive environment. **Motto**: Learning for Life **School hours**: 8.40am–3.40pm; homework clubs are available **Meals**: Hot and cold available, including breakfast **Strong GCSE subjects**: Maths and science **London league table position**: 92

## Profile

Beths became Bexley's only City Technology College in 1995. A new sports hall, conference rooms, classrooms and a music and drama centre were unveiled in September 1999. The library has been converted into a learning resource centre with video-conferencing. There is a heavy emphasis on science and technology and the school's technology centre has been extended and refurbished with its workshops generously equipped. There are two specialized music areas and a sports field on site. Beths is part of the Sportsmark Gold Award scheme, and is an interactive learning resource centre and a National Grid For Learning school. Pupils receive individual support from form tutors and assist in the organization of the school. There is a sixth-form school council and the school has prefects. A work-experience programme runs in Years 10 and 12 with some boys travelling around the country and abroad. There is provision for pupils with special needs. Parents receive termly progress reports and a regular newsletter. Truancy is at 0.1 per cent and is below local and national averages. Famous ex-pupils include Olympic javelin thrower, Steve Backley, and county cricketer Graham Kersey.

### Admissions and intake

Beths shares the same initial application process as other Bexley schools (see borough factfile), but as a foundation school with special status, it has individual criteria. Pupils, who must have passed the borough's selection tests, are then assessed by the following criteria: if they had a father attending Beths; if a sibling attends Beths; and finally on distance from home to the school. Successful applicants generally live within five or six miles of the school.

### Achievement

The number of pupils passing five-plus A*–Cs at GCSE has enjoyed an upward trend with results soaring from 24 per cent in 1998 to 93 per cent in 2000 and 100 per cent in 2001, although this has dipped to 95 per cent in 2002. This result placed the school fourth in the borough league table. Boys are expected to take 11 GCSEs. In 2002, there was a 337.9 average point score per student at A-level. This placed Beths third in Bexley. Ofsted visited the school in 2002 and noted that: 'Pupils receive a very good education which has many very good and outstanding features. The quality of teaching is very good overall'. Inspectors praised the 'outstanding' leadership of the school and found results to be well above national averages and well above average in comparison with similar schools. However, the teaching of chemistry in Years 10 and 11 needed to be improved. Strong GCSE subjects were English, mathematics, biology and science. Beths pupils have earned a haul of accolades, including the Young Engineer of the Year Award, finalists in the Nationwide UK Awards for Voluntary Endeavour and Contiboard Young Designer of the Year.

### Extra-curricular activities

Beths sports teams are successful up to international level and activities such as canoeing, karting, skiing, mountaineering and golf are available. The school orchestra, brass ensemble, string quartet, big band and choirs perform at termly concerts and at outside venues. There are regular drama productions and a community service programme. Boys also put together a school newsletter. The school organizes trips, both local and abroad, to a variety of destinations. There is a wide range of homework clubs available at the school.

## Bexley Grammar School

**Danson Lane, Welling, Kent DA16 2BL** ☎ 020 8304 8538 📠 020 8304 0248 ✉ Mr Roderick MacKinnon B.Sc; Chair of Governors: Mr Alan Overton ⇄ Welling **Buses**: B15, B16, 51, 89, 96, 624 👔 Navy blazer, tie, dark-grey trousers or skirt; Sixth form: Suits with a sixth-form tie for boys **Demand**: 264 applications for 224 places in 2001/2 **Type**: Selective country grammar for 1120 mixed pupils, aged 11 to 18 **Submit application form**: 12 December 2003 **Motto**: *Praestantiae studere* (Striving to Excellence) **School hours**: 8.35am–3.40pm; homework clubs are available **Meals**: Hot and cold available **Strong GCSE subjects**: Art, geography, history **London league table position**: 68

### Profile

Bexley Grammar opened in 1955, and in 1995 the Le Feuvre Building was created to house a new library and information technology facilities. The latest project comprises a new sports hall and specialist facilities for music, art, technology and science. Pupils use a nearby sports hall and there are plans to develop the library into a resource centre. Teaching is in form groups until Year 10 with setting in mathematics, modern languages, sciences and technology, until they choose their GCSE options from 14 subjects. Parents are kept informed through regular reports and annual meetings and the parents' association is said to be 'flourishing'. The school has a prefects system. Truancy is only half that of the borough and national averages at 0.6 per cent. Bexley Grammar is one of London's 19 remaining grammar schools. Famous ex-pupils include Chris Ball, Mayor of Bexley; Gavin Peacock, footballer; and Matthew Rose, footballer.

### Admissions and intake

Pupils must first apply to sit Bexley's selection tests and, if successful, they can apply to the school. After special needs and sibling priorities, distance is the major factor and it is usually necessary to live within a two-mile radius. The main feeder schools are Danson, East Wickham, Fosters, Eastcote and Deansfield. There is a roughly 60:40 boy-to-girl ratio. Bexley Grammar pupils come from a broad social spectrum.

### Achievement

The school's GCSE results are among the highest in the borough. In 2002, 100 per cent of pupils achieved five or more A*–C grades. This was five per cent up on 95 per cent in 2001. The average points score is the second best in

Bexley and well above national average, as is expected for selected schools. Ofsted visited the school in 1998 and noted that the intake included fewer very high achieving students than average, particularly in English. Pupils do best in art, history and geography but not so well in IT. Latin and a second foreign language are available at GCSE. A-level results are among the best in Bexley, with students averaging 371.1 points in 2002, putting the school top of the borough league table. These results have always remained above the national average. Sixth-formers can take three or four A-levels from 20 subjects. Ofsted asked the school to look at ways of improving its methods of monitoring teaching and to improve the provision and teaching of IT. It concluded: 'Bexley Grammar has many strengths. The most apparent are the behaviour and demeanour of the students who, with their parents, like the school and value highly the opportunities it provides.'

### Extra-curricular activities

Games fixtures include basketball and tennis, and teams enter tournaments up to international level. Cultural and charity activities include debating, recycling, music and toy-making. Clubs on offer range from ancient Greek and chess to technology and fishing, as well as homework clubs. Pupils enjoy theatre visits, croquet, orchestra and jazz and can join the Christian Union or Duke of Edinburgh's Award and Mayor of Bexley Award schemes. There is a programme of drama and dance productions and environmental events. Trips organized by the school have included skiing in Italy and Germany.

## Bexleyheath School

**Graham Road, Bexleyheath, Kent DA6 7DA** ☎ 020 8303 5696 📠 020 8303 9151 ⓔ info@bexleyheath.bexley.sch.uk 🌐 http://schoolsite.edex.net.uk/736 Malcolm Noble MA; Chair of Governors: Rev Dick Johnson ⇌ Barnehurst, Bexleyheath **Buses:** B11, B12, B13, B15, B16, 89, 96, 132, 229, 401, 422, 469, 492 Blue blazer, white shirt, grey trousers or skirt; Sixth form: Business wear **Demand:** 400 applications for 390 places in 2001/2 **Type:** Community comprehensive for 1201 mixed pupils, aged 11 to 18 **Submit application form:** 12 December 2003 **Mission statement:** We value and support learning, instilling pride in self, school and community, recognizing the worth of each individual. **Motto:** Pride Through Achievement **School hours:** 8.40am–3.40pm **Meals:** Hot and cold available **Strong GCSE subjects:** Art, business studies, music, PE, personal and social education **London league table position:** 380

### Profile

Bexleyheath is the borough's largest school. It has Technology College status and ICT is central to its learning. The school's facilities include seven computer suites, an Internet link and video-conferencing. The lower school is separated from the upper school by playing fields. A new library block, IT centre and sixth-form centre have been added to the upper school. There is also a new classroom and performing arts block and an all-weather sports facility is planned. Pupils are streamed on arrival but constantly assessed, and there is an accelerated learning scheme for top-ability pupils. Work experience and careers advice are available in Years 10 and 11 and some students take on a weekly work placement. Social and personal education tackles challenging issues such as drugs. There are regular parents' evenings and two reports a year, and an active parents' association. There is a school council and a prefects system. Truancy is at 1.0 per cent, below the local norm and in line with the national average. Famous cookery personality Delia Smith is an ex-pupil.

### Admissions and intake

Standard Bexley admissions criteria apply (see borough factfile). Most pupils come from Bexley but around 15 per cent are out-of-borough pupils. There is a good gender balance and 10 per cent of students have English as a foreign language. Attainment on entry varies. A low number of students have special needs but the proportion with full statements is above local and national averages.

### Achievement

In 2002, 34 per cent of Bexleyheath pupils won five or more A*–C grades at GCSE, a figure well below the national and borough average, though up from 28 per cent in 2001. Results have fluctuated since 1996. Attainment is sound in art, music, PE, business studies and personal and social education. In 1998, Ofsted noted that performance in science, geography and RE was cause for concern. Motivation is high on the fast-track scheme for the most able although there is concern about its effect on lower streams. Attainment is higher in the sixth form but some students struggle at A-level, and GNVQ results are better at intermediate than advanced level. The average A-level point score per student was 162.5 in 2002. These results are below national and borough averages, ranking the school 11th in the borough. Sixth-formers can choose from 13 A-levels and a number of GNVQs. Ofsted concluded that Bexleyheath 'is a calm and orderly institution with an emphasis on learning' and that it is 'well able to address the key issues for improvement which remain.' Since the report, punctuality and attendance have improved.

## Extra-curricular activities

Pupils play regular matches in football, hockey, cricket and tennis. Individual music tuition is available, as are choirs, ensembles and a school orchestra. New pupils can join a residential course in Surrey and there are French and German exchanges, an annual ski trip and theatre visits. There is a summer arts festival and a science and technology week. Pupils can also join the Interact group, the youth section of Bexley Rotary Club. Work experience encompasses a wide range of businesses and the school attempts to match each pupil's needs.

# Blackfen School for Girls

**Blackfen Road, Sidcup, Kent DA15 9NU** 020 8303 1887 020 8298 1656 blackfen.tbr@btinternet.com Louise Sharples BA, MA; Chair of Governors: Carol Townsend Sidcup, Falconwood **Buses:** B13, 51, 132, 494, 710 Red or blue sweatshirt, navy skirt, white blouse; Sixth form: Office wear **Demand:** 373 applications for 210 places in 2001/2 **Type:** Community secondary modern for 1143 girls, aged 11 to 18 **Submit application form:** 12 December 2003 **School hours:** 8.45am–3.30pm; homework clubs are available **Meals:** Hot and cold available **Strong GCSE subjects:** Childcare, English literature, French, home economics, music, RE, textiles **London league table position:** 199

## Profile

Opened in 1935, Blackfen School for Girls is a large secondary modern school in a residential area. In 1993, a new art and technology block was opened and since then a new sports hall and accommodation for science and music have been added. The library and resources centre and two networked IT suites were completed in 1997 alongside accommodation for the sixth form. Further science and maths teaching areas have also been added. However, there are still cramped conditions and the school is seeking finance for further improvements. Girls are initially taught in tutor groups with setting in maths, English and science, until they take their options in Year 10. There is a work experience programme in Year 10 and for some sixth-formers that involves businesses, parents and ex-pupils. Sixth-formers can become prefects or take part in 'listening ears' to help the social development of younger students. There is a 'life skills' programme to aid personal and social development. Each pupil has a contact book that provides parents with an insight into the school day. There are regular consultation evenings, written reports and a parents' and friends' association. The school has provisions for pupils with special needs and a school council.

## Admissions and intake

Standard Bexley admissions criteria apply (see borough factfile). Few Blackfen pupils have passed Bexley's selection tests. Pupils generally live within two miles of the school.

## Achievement

With 61 per cent of girls gaining five or more A*–C grades at GCSE in 2002, Blackfen is one of the most successful secondary moderns in Bexley. These results equalled results from the previous years, and are better than the other non-grammar Bexley schools, and sometimes above average for all borough pupils. Over the years, strong results have been achieved in English literature, French, home economics, textiles, childcare, music and RE. NVQ and GNVQ results are good and A-level grades are improving. At A-level, the average point score of 198.4 is below the national and borough averages because most candidates sit two rather than three A-levels. This placed the school eighth in the borough. In 1999, Ofsted found that Blackfen's strong ethos based on working hard and enjoying learning achieved high standards. They noted that: 'Blackfen School for Girls is a very good school with some outstanding features', and concluded: 'the many strengths of the school outweigh the few weaknesses, which have all already been identified by the school.'

## Extra-curricular activities

Pupils can join clubs in sport, keep fit, dance, trampoline, computers, choir, music and drama and academic study. There are journeys abroad for French and art, outdoor pursuits weekends and the Duke of Edinburgh's Award scheme. The school also receives visitors from local charities, organizations and residents and there are business studies links with the Bluewater shopping centre. Homework clubs are available.

# The Business Academy

**Yarnton Way, Erith DA18 4DW** 020 8312 4938 020 8312 3287 Mr TE Widdows; Chair of Governors: Sir David Garrard Abbeywood and Belvedere **Buses:** B11, 180, 401, 229 Purple blazer, purple tie, white shirt, grey trousers or skirt **Demand:** Unknown as new school **Type:** City academy for 606 mixed pupils, aged 11 to 19 **Submit application form:** 12 December 2003 **Motto:** No goal is beyond our reach **School hours:** 8.25am–3.25pm **Meals:** Hot and cold available **Strong GCSE subjects:** Not yet known **London league table position:** Not yet known

## Profile

The Business Academy is a new school that was established in September 2002. The failing Thamesmead Community College closed in 2002 and all pupils have transferred to the Business Academy. The new school is housed in purpose-built facilities on a 33-acre site, and aims to provide pupils with access to the most advanced Information Technology including video-conferencing, Internet and e-mail. The Academy has a special partnership with business and industry and aims to establish a Centre of Excellence for Business and Industrial Development. This will enable pupils to gain a real insight into the economy and the world of work. All pupils will be eligible for the Business Academy Award.

## Admissions and intake

Applications should be made direct to the school.

## Achievement

No exams have been taken yet

## Extra-curricular activities

A wide range of sports including volleyball, football, rugby and cricket. Other activities will be made available during the course of the year.

# Chislehurst and Sidcup Grammar School

**Hurst Road, Sidcup, Kent DA15 9AG** 020 8302 6511 020 8309 6596 doruss@csgrammar.bexley.sch.uk www.csgrammar.bexley.sch.uk Mr Jim Rouncefield B.Sc, MA, FRGS; Chair of Governors: Cllr Graham Holland Sidcup **Buses:** 51, 160, 229, 233, 269, 286, 494, 726 Purple blazer, white shirt, grey trousers or skirt, purple and silver tie for boys; Sixth form: Formal office wear **Demand:** 1302 applications for 192 places in 2001/2 **Type:** Selective county grammar for 1320 mixed pupils, aged 11 to 18. **Submit application form:** 12 December 2003 **Motto:** *Abeunt studia in mores* (Character Grows Through Study) **School hours:** 8.45am–3.40pm; homework clubs are available **Meals:** Hot and cold available **Strong GCSE subjects:** All relatively strong **London league table position:** 73

## Profile

Chislehurst and Sidcup Grammar School was founded in 1954. It is one of London's 19 remaining grammar schools. It is a 17-acre site bordered by parkland, a golf club and an avenue of detached housing. It is a school that aims for excellence in all fields – academic, cultural, aesthetic and sporting. The school's computer facilities have been enhanced and a music centre was completed in 2001. There are two gymnasia, a multi-gym and hard tennis and netball courts. However, in 1999, Ofsted noted that increasing numbers are beginning to put pressure on the 'just adequate accommodation'. Pupils are split into six tutor groups on entry. Initially streaming only takes place in maths, but from Year 10 onwards, pupils are taught in ability and options groups. The school has a Young Enterprise group, where pupils run their own company. IT core skills are considered a basic entitlement for all students. In Year 11 pupils go to local employers and into the City for work experience. Sixth-formers act as prefects or provide supervision and support to younger pupils at tutor groups. Regular meetings are held with parents and the head has an open-door policy. Parents take part in concerts and drama productions and there is a parents' association. Famous ex-pupils include Children's Laureate Quentin Blake and the journalist and author Will Hutton.

## Admissions and intake

All applicants must have passed the Bexley selection test and apply through the local authority (see borough factfile). The principal feeder schools are Dulverton, Hurst, Holy Trinity and Burnt Oak. Most successful applicants live within 2.5 miles of the school. The pupils are creamed from the top 30 per cent by Bexley's selection system. Only 2 per cent are deemed to have special needs and their attainment on entry is well above average.

## Achievement

Chislehurst and Sidcup's consistently high GCSE results earned it a place in the borough's top three schools in 2002. Five or more A*–C grades were earned by 96 per cent of pupils, above national and borough averages. Pupils follow the national curriculum, but study three separate sciences and two modern languages, with the addition of Latin in Year 8. At A-level, the average point score per entry was 300.6 in 2002, the fourth highest in the borough. A-level success is particularly strong in IT and government and politics. Sixth-formers can choose from more than 20 A-levels and all take an AS-level in general studies. Ofsted observed that while pupils are high-attainers at GCSE and A-level, their performance still falls below expectations for selective schools. Inspectors felt students should have more chance to use IT in their work and should make greater use of the library as a resource. They concluded that 'Chislehurst and Sidcup Grammar School is a very successful and high achieving school with a great many strengths and few weaknesses'.

## Extra-curricular activities

The school has a full symphony orchestra, a chamber orchestra and a thriving jazz tradition. On any winter Saturday up to 20 sporting teams may be competing for Chislehurst and Sidcup. There are regular drama productions and regular visits and field trips. The sixth form writes a school magazine and there are good links with the community. After-school homework clubs are available.

# Cleeve Park School

**Bexley Lane, Sidcup, Kent DA14 4J** ☎ 020 8302 6418 📠 020 8308 1571 🌐 www.cleevepark.kentsch.uk ✉ Mrs L Karmock-Golds BEd, MA; Chair of Governors: John Gray ⇌ Albany Park, Sidcup **Buses**: B14, 21, 51, 229, 233, 269, 492 👔 Pale blue shirt, dark blue school tie; Sixth form: Dress 'as for business' **Demand**: 234 applications for 240 places in 2001/2 **Type**: County secondary modern for 1200 mixed pupils, aged 11 to 18 **Submit application form**: 12 December 2003 **Motto**: Learning for Life **School hours**: 8.45am–3.35pm, 8.45am–3pm (Tues and Thurs for Years 7 to 9), 8.45am–3pm (Fri); homework clubs are available **Meals:** Hot and cold available **Strong GCSE subjects**: History, maths **London league table position:** 356

## Profile

Cleeve Park School formed in 1985 and occupies an open suburban site with trees, lawns and playing fields. Facilities include eight laboratories, workshops, studios, computer and home economics suites. A new sports hall and drama and music suite opened in 1998 and a purpose-built art block, refurbished science laboratories, technology room and six classrooms were added in 1999. Cleeve Park was one of the first schools to try out government initiatives for technical and vocational education and pupils embrace all aspects of technology. ICT facilities have had a major upgrade. Children are divided into form groups on entry but streamed academically. A programme of personal, social and careers education begins in Year seven, and sex and drugs education is built into the curriculum. All pupils undertake work experience in Year 10. Pupils can take on extra responsibilities such as form prefect and monitor whilst sixth-formers can help the anti-bullying initiative by befriending younger pupils or they can assist in the library or organize the school council. There is a contact book, review meetings with parents and an active PTA. Truancy is was at 1.5 per cent in 2000, above the Bexley and national norms.

## Admissions and intake

Standard Bexley admissions criteria apply (see borough factfile). The numbers of students with English as a second language and with a statement of special needs is below average for a secondary modern.

### Achievement

In 2002, 42 per cent of pupils gained five-plus A*–C grades. This represented a return to the impressive upward trend of 1999 when results soared by nearly 50 per cent to 39 per cent and 41 per cent in 2000. This result remains below borough and national averages and the school came 10th in the borough. Pupils can choose from 20 GCSE subjects, with many taking advantage of Cleeve Park's business and technology bias. At AS and A-level, the average point score per pupil was 142.2, below the borough and national averages. The sixth form is open to students from other schools and offers a range of A-level subjects and vocational courses. Cleeve Park's exam results are below average for all types of school, but are above the standards set by secondary modern schools nationally, particularly in maths and English literature. In 1996, Ofsted noted that pupils make notable progress in history and mathematics and the drama course was successful. Science attainment is below average, particularly among girls, but some pupils do achieve top grades. Pupils are well behaved and have good relationships with each other, and pupils with special needs are well taught and make good progress. The school teaches GNVQ courses in tourism and leisure and childcare, and there is a Young Enterprise group who run their own company.

### Extra-curricular activities

School journeys on offer include a skiing trip, geography field trip and Year 8 camp. Pupils perform concerts at elderly people's homes and raise money for charity. There are public speaking competitions, an annual drama production and theatre trips. The school has homework clubs available after school hours.

## Erith School

**Avenue Road, Erith, Kent DA8 3BN** ☎ 01322 348231 📠 01322 351528 ⓔ info@erith.kent.sch.uk 🌐 www.erith.kent.sch.uk Mr Toby Hufford B.Ed (Hons), M.Phil (Cantab), FBIM; Chair of Governors: Mr David Friend 🚆 Barnehurst, Erith **Buses**: 89, 99, 229, 428, 469, 602 Blue blazer, pale blue shirt, school tie; Sixth form: Smart dress code **Demand**: 604 applications for 360 places in 2001/2 (60 selective/300 non-selective) **Type**: Bilateral community comprehensive for 1858 mixed pupils, aged 11 to 18 **Submit application form**: 12 December 2003 **Mission statement**: Our main purpose at Erith School is to provide a high quality learning experience appropriate to the needs of each and every child. To achieve this objective we will promote a stimulating learning environment and constantly seek to improve the quality of teaching and learning. We will pursue these objectives within a caring and challenging school. **Motto**: Working Together **School hours**: 8.30am–3.05pm; homework clubs are available **Meals**: Hot and cold available **Strong GCSE subjects**: Sciences **London league table position**: 379

### Profile

Erith is Bexley's second largest school and the only bilateral school in the borough, i.e. combining selective with comprehensive entry. It is one of London's 19 remaining grammar schools. All-ability pupils can transfer to the grammar stream if they improve. A £6 million investment has developed six labs, six technology rooms and 16 classrooms including a humanities centre, a maths centre, a new hall, dining room and library. There is also a new creative arts complex and sports complex with fitness room, all-weather pitches and tennis courts. Another £4 million has been spent on a new technology and mathematics centre. Pupils are set according to their ability in key subjects and pushed to obtain the best grades possible. There is extra provision for high-fliers and those with special needs. Work experience is provided with local employers. Sixth-formers look after Year 7 and 8 tutor groups. The school has a prefects system. There is a daily contact book, termly and yearly reports, regular newsletters, parents' evenings and an active PTA. The truancy rate of 0.4 per cent is better than the local and national levels.

### Admissions and intake

Applications must be made through Bexley LEA. Selective places are allocated first. After special education, medical or social needs and sibling priorities are considered, and priority is given to pupils within the closest walking distance, currently within one mile. About 15 per cent of pupils have English as an additional language. More than half of a recent intake was of below average ability, although this varies from year to year.

### Achievement

Erith School's rapid progress over the last six years saw Ofsted name it as one of the 41 most improved schools in the country in 1999. At GCSE, 28 per cent of pupils scored five or more A*–C grades in 2002, and Erith came 13th in the borough. This was below the borough and national average, and one per cent below results in 2001. Generally GCSE results have slowly improved while the national picture remains static despite increasing numbers of pupils with special needs and fewer selective students. All pupils take English language, maths, double science and at least five more subjects in their GCSE year. GNVQs are on offer in a range of subjects. At A-level pupils scored an average 155.2 points in 2002, slightly down on 10 points in 2000 and placing the school twelfth in the borough. In 1998, Ofsted observed that 'Erith School has made considerable progress since the last inspection and is totally committed to sustaining this progress and raising standards.' Teaching is now a 'major strength' at Erith.

## Extra-curricular activities

There is a varied programme of music, drama, dance, sport, trips and other clubs, homework clubs and societies. Sports teams compete at borough and county level and the new leisure centre is shared with the community. Pupils can take a residential visit or work with the community during Erith's activities week. The Air Training Corps has a base in the school grounds.

# Hurstmere Foundation School for Boys

**Hurst Road, Sidcup, Kent DA15 9AW** ☎ 020 8300 5665 Fax 020 8300 2039 @ info@hurstmere.kent.sch.uk www.schoolsite.edex.net.uk/334 Mr I G Sharp BA; Chair of Governors: Mrs V Hughes-Narborough Albany Park, Sidcup **Buses:** B13, B14, 51, 132, 229, 233, 269, 286 Black blazer with pocket badge, black or dark grey trousers and V-neck jumper, white or grey shirt, school tie, dark socks, black shoes **Demand:** 340 applications for 195 places in 2001/2 **Type:** Comprehensive foundation school for 879 boys, aged 11 to 19 **Submit application form:** 12 December 2003 **School hours:** 8.45am–3.15pm; homework clubs are available **Meals:** Hot and cold available **Strong GCSE subjects:** Art, PE, technology **London league table position:** 298

## Profile

Hurstmere is set on a leafy site next to Sidcup Golf Course and near to Lamorbey Park. A secondary modern until 1994, it now seeks pupils from across the ability spectrum but is hampered by Bexley's selective system. The extensive grounds provide excellent facilities for outdoor sports and a recent expansion of the sience and technology facilities has resulted in seven specialist teaching rooms. A new sports hall and two new classrooms are to be completed this year. The school is committed to fulfilling individual potential and welcomes pupils' displays of initiative. Pupils are set by ability on arrival in classes usually sized well under 30. Further setting takes place in mathematics and English for GCSE, but tutor groups remain the same throughout their school life. ICT is taught from Year 7. The school runs a reading programme and a Success Maker programme that provides extra opportunities for less able pupils. Hurstmere follows the national curriculum with the addition of religious education and a personal and social education programme until pupils take their options. Local businesses provide work experience for all boys in Year 10. Pastoral care and guidance is a strength of the school and is lead by form tutors. There are regular progress evenings for parents, reports are issued four times a year, and there is a homework timetable and an active PTA. The school has provision for pupils with special needs, including classes and a special-needs coordinator.

## Admissions and intake

Hurstmere uses Bexley's admissions process (see borough factfile) but as a Foundation School, it can introduce its own criteria so check with the school first. Pupils are drawn from about 60 primaries in south-east London and Kent.

## Achievement

In 2002, 52 per cent of Hurstmere pupils scored five or more A*–C GCSEs. This was up on 35 per cent in 2001 and continued an upward trend. These results were just above the borough and national average, and Hurstmere was placed 11th in the borough league table for GCSEs. The sixth form is open to outside applicants including girls. It offers two-year advanced and one-year intermediate GNVQ courses in art, business studies, ICT, manufacturing and leisure and sports management. A-levels are run in English and mathematics, but further options are planned. In 1996, Ofsted observed that Hurstmere compared soundly with other similar schools. Results in art, PE and technology were above average for all maintained schools but results were well below in science. They noted that 'Hurstmere is a well-ordered community where pupils and staff work together with much mutual respect' and concluded 'High priority is given to producing polite, conscientious and responsible members of society. The quality of learning is generally sound.'

### Extra curricular activities

Homework clubs are available after school hours. There are regular cultural visits to London, including art galleries and theatres, as well as residential and field work centres. A skiing trip is organized annually. Pupils participate in the Duke of Edinburgh's Award scheme and other competitions and challenges, including sporting fixtures.

# St Catherine's RC School for Girls

**Watling Street, Bexleyheath, Kent DA6 7QJ** ☎ 01322 556333 📠 01322 555919 Ms Susan Powell MA (Oxon); Chair of Governors: Mrs Betty Denyer ⇄ Barnehurst, Bexley **Buses:** B15, 89, 96, 132, 229, 401, 492, 494, 601, 726 Tartan kilt, yellow blouse, navy blue jumper **Demand:** 230 applications for 140 places in 2001/2 **Type:** Voluntary aided comprehensive for 810 girls, aged 11 to 18 **Submit application form:** 12 December 2003 **Mission statement:** The predominant aim of St Catherine's is to provide a genuine Christian education through which all may come to recognize the dignity of the person and the basic equality of all people. We aim to achieve this within the atmosphere of a caring Christian community, supported by the ideals and practices of our Catholic faith. The uniqueness of each girl is acknowledged and her ability, aptitude and gifts developed to the full. **School hours:** 8.45am–3.35pm; homework clubs are available **Meals:** Hot and cold available **Strong GCSE subjects:** English literature, history **London league table position:** 171

### Profile

St Catherine's site boasts trees, playing fields and views across the Kent countryside. Modern extensions to the building include science and technology and IT blocks, and three newly fitted ICT rooms. The Millennium Building provides 14 classrooms and a base for English, mathematics and humanities. The large grounds allow for a variety of sporting activities. The school aims to provide a genuine Christian education within a caring community, supported by the ideals of its Catholic faith, inspired by its patron, St Catherine of Siena. Students are divided into mixed-ability groups on entry but are set in English, mathematics, science, ICT and modern languages including Spanish. A head of year oversees their personal development. There is work experience in Year 11 and a sixth-form programme is tailored to career interests. There is a school council and prefect system. Parents receive a copy of the homework timetable and a regular newsletter and are invited to consultation evenings at key points in their child's career. There is an active parents' association. Truancy is below national and local averages at 0.1 per cent. Pupils with special needs are helped by the school's special needs coordinator.

### Admissions and intake

Applications should be made directly to the school and rules are designed to highlight those applicants who genuinely want a Catholic education. First preference is given to practising Catholics who have not sat Bexley's selection tests, followed by more sporadic attenders at Catholic churches. Most places are filled by this stage, but any remaining places go to children practising other Christian denominations. Potential pupils undergo a short interview about their faith and need their priest to sign their application form. The school has a prefects system and a coordinator for pupils with special needs.

### Achievement

In 2002, 66 per cent of girls at St Catherine's achieved five-plus A*–C grades at GCSE. This was up on 64 per cent in 2001 and the school's results are consistently above the national and borough averages for state schools. St Catherine's was ranked fifth in the borough league table. Ofsted inspectors visited the school in 2000 and concluded: 'St Catherine's is a sucessful school which is working hard to improve both the quality of education and the pupils' standards'. The school was also seen to provide 'very good opportunities for pupils' spiritual, moral and social development'. St Catherine's A-level results are below national averages with only a few higher grades obtained. In 2002, the average point score per pupil was 244.5. This was below the borough and national averages. The sixth form is a consortium with St Columba's Boys School. Ofsted praised the school's 'good quality of teaching' which 'enables pupils to achieve well'. There was found to be a high standard in English throughout the school. Ofsted commented on the need to improve the use of ICT by other subjects and the need for higher attainment in French and Spanish.

### Extra-curricular activities

Concerts and dramatic productions are the school's strengths as is sport, which includes football, trampoline, tennis and athletics. GNVQ students travel to Paris and there is an annual skiing trip. There are also visits to the theatre, museums and academic lectures. A flourishing chemistry club has won competitions. Many pupils are involved in voluntary work, and there are after-school homework clubs available.

# St Columba's Catholic Boys' School

**Halcot Avenue, Bexleyheath, Kent DA6 7QB** 01322 553236 01322 522471 Mr Stephen Foster BA (Hons), PGCE, M.Sc; Chair of Governors: Mr Philip Clemas Barnehurst, Bexley **Buses**: B15, 89, 96, 132, 229, 401, 492, 494, 601 Charcoal trousers, white shirt, black blazer; Sixth form: Smart, formal dress **Demand**: 216 applications for 150 places in 2001/2 **Type**: Voluntary aided comprehensive for 764 boys, aged 11 to 18 **Submit application form**: 12 December 2003 **Mission statement**: Sharing a commitment to quality and care **Motto**: *Tenui nec dimittam* (To hold fast) **School hours**: 8.50am–3.35pm; homework clubs are available **Meals**: Hot and cold available **Strong GCSE subjects**: Art, English, geography, history **London league table position**: 313

## Profile

St Columba's is small for a school of its type and work has been underway to ease some cramped school buildings. There are now seven new classrooms for maths and foreign languages and a new hall. The IT suite has been refurbished and the library is furnished with computers. Money provided by the New Deal for Schools has provided an additional science lab. The school aims to provide a Christian community with strong links between home, school and parish. New boys are taught in a mixed attainment group then set in English, maths and science. Pupils with special needs are taught in smaller groups. A pastoral care system is run by form tutors and work experience is available in Year 11. There is a form council and a buddy system that allows students to befriend younger pupils. Parents are kept informed through a monitored journal, twice-yearly reports and consultation evenings. There is a PTA and a home-school agreement where parents are contacted on the first day of an unauthorized absence. The school has both a school council and prefects system.

## Admissions and intake

Priority is first given to the sons of practising Catholics being educated at a Catholic school or at home. Priority then goes to the sons of practising Catholic families at other schools, sons of practising Christians at Catholic schools, sons of other practising Christians, sons of those practising other faiths who attend Catholic school, sons of those practising other faiths at other schools and sons of other applicants. Applicants need to fill in a form and have it signed by their priest. Bexley's selective system means some Catholic boys go to grammar schools, reducing the school's share of the highest attainers.

## Achievement

St Columba's GCSE results fall mid-table for Bexley. In 2002, 57 per cent of pupils gained five or more A*–C grades. These results were above the national average, and the school was placed eighth in the borough. Such results are about average for a school of its type, according to Ofsted inspectors who visited in 1998. They found that the strongest subjects were English, art, geography and history and the weakest were RE and foreign languages. At A-level, grades fall below national expectations, but there are good performances in design and technology and science while mathematics and history do less well. In 2002, the average A-level point score per student was 195.9, falling well below national and borough averages. The school runs GNVQ courses, covering business and leisure and tourism. The joint sixth form is run with St Catherine's RC School for Girls. Ofsted praised the school's special needs provision but noted that pupils did not use IT in all curriculum areas. The school has acted on these comments and improved resources for IT, design, technology, science and the library.

## Extra-curricular activities

Activities available include lunchtime and after-school clubs, including homework clubs. There are enrichment classes for gifted pupils as well as chess, library, computers, science, art, drama, music, weight-lifting and a tradition of success at sport. Pupils are encouraged to perform charitable work.

# St Mary and St Joseph's Catholic School

**Chislehurst Road, Sidcup, Kent DA14 6BP** 020 8309 7700 020 8300 6815 info@stmary-stjoseph.bexley.sch.uk www.stmary-stjoseph.org.uk Mr JJ Flannery MA, B.Ed; Chair of Governors: Mr C Avery

Sidcup **Buses:** 51, 160, 229, 233, 269, 286, 494, 726 Black blazers and maroon sweatshirts compulsory for Years 7 to 11 **Demand:** 263 applications for 150 places in 2001/2 **Type:** Voluntary aided comprehensive for 800 mixed pupils, aged 11 to 18 **Submit application form:** End of October 2003 **Motto:** Growing by Learning Together in a Catholic Community **School hours:** 8.40am–3.10pm; homework clubs available **Meals:** Hot and cold available **Strong GCSE subjects:** Business studies, English, geography, history, IT, PE **London league table position:** 367

## Profile

A new head teacher and the attentions of Ofsted have seen a drastic turnaround in the fortunes of St Mary and St Joseph's. It was removed from 'special measures' in October 1999 after 18 months, thanks to clear leadership and improving results. It is located on a spacious green belt site. ICT provision includes a new 15-station network installed to support literacy and numeracy skills. Students are divided into mixed attainment tutor groups and set in English, maths and science, and later in French. Careers guidance is available and includes a two-week work placement. A behaviour charter lists the school's expectations. Sanctions for bad behaviour include a three-hour Saturday school, that is also open to those wanting to do extra work. Pupils can take part in the school council, a paired readers scheme or voluntary work. There is a daily journal and termly reports for parents as well as a PTA. There are also regular newsletters and a school magazine. Truancy levels are low at 0.2 per cent.

## Admissions and intake

Applications should be made to the school. Around 80 per cent of pupils come from Catholic families and 12 pupils have a statement of special needs. A quarter of pupils have a reading age one or two years below their own on admittance.

## Achievement

Ofsted visited the school in 2001 and described it as '... an improving school, which in many respects offers an effective education to its pupils'. GCSE standards were seen to be improving with 'satisfactory' teaching overall. Inspectors praised the head teacher's 'excellent' leadership. Strong subjects were found to be geography and PE. However, standards in mathematics needed to be improved. In 2002, the number of pupils gaining five or more A*–C GCSE grades fell to 38 per cent. This was below both local and national averages. The school ranked 11th in the borough. At GCSE, students must add a modern language, technology, humanities and creative arts options to their core subjects. At A-level, the average point score for pupils taking two or more subjects was 170.8, also below the national average. A-level options include theology, sports science and media studies or a one-year GNVQ in retail and distribution.

## Extra-curricular activities

Sporting fixtures available include athletics, netball, hockey, soccer, rugby, cricket and tennis with some students representing their district, county and country. There is a school choir and instrument groups, and some pupils attend the borough's music school. School trips include a French exchange, Disneyland Paris and visits to Ireland and Scotland. The school involves itself with the local community. After-school homework clubs are available.

# Townley Grammar School for Girls

**Townley Road, Bexleyheath, Kent DA6 7AB** 020 8304 8311 020 8298 7421 admin@townleygrammar.org.uk www.townleygrammar.org.uk Mrs Linda Hutchinson BA, M.Ed; Chair of Governors: Mr John Patterson Bexley, Bexleyheath **Buses:** B11, B12, B13, B15, B16, 89, 96, 132, 229, 269, 401, 422, 492, 494 Grey blazer, grey skirt, grey cardigan or jumper, blue shirt (Years 7 to 8); White shirt (Years 9 to 11); Sixth form: School colours and tailored black jackets **Demand:** 278 applications for 210 places in 2001/2 **Type:** Selective community for 1170 girls, aged 11 to 18 **Submit application form:** 12 December 2003 **School hours:** 8.35am–3.35pm; homework clubs available **Meals:** Hot and cold available **Strong GCSE subjects:** Music, maths **London league table position:** 60

## Profile

Townley Grammar School was founded in the 1930s as a technical school for girls and moved to its current green-field site in 1937. It is one of London's 19 remaining grammar schools. Its spacious 17-acre site has undergone a major building programme to provide extra specialist teaching rooms. There are provisions for pupils with special needs. A new performing arts block opened in 2000 for music, drama and dance. Science, computer, technology and art facilities have recently been enhanced. The school has a tradition of excellence in music. Girls are taught in tutor groups for the first two years before being streamed in subjects such as maths, science and modern languages. All girls undergo work experience. Pastoral care is provided by form tutors under the auspices of the year head. Parents receive twice-yearly form reports followed by consultation evenings and there is a PTA. The school has a sixth-form school council. There is a prefects system. Famous ex-pupils include Baroness Valerie Amos.

## Admissions and intake

Applicants must have passed Bexley's selection tests, then the borough's standard admissions criteria apply (see borough factfile). Townley recruits from more than 50 primary schools, including those in Greenwich, Bromley, Southwark and Kent. The large catchment area means pupils come from a variety of backgrounds.

## Achievement

Townley's excellent exam results regularly top the borough's league tables. In 2002, 100 per cent of girls passed five subjects with A*–C grades. All girls take nine or 10 GCSEs and the curriculum includes IT and environmental awareness in the first three years. At A-level, girls gained average points of 354.8, well above the borough average and national mean. Results at both A-level and GCSE are consistently good but have shown gradual improvement over the last six years. In the sixth form, AS- or A-levels are available in subjects such as economics, Italian and law. A GNVQ is offered in business studies. Ofsted visited the school in 2002 and concluded that attainment is well above national averages at all Key Stages. Inspectors described Townley as 'a very good school with very many outstanding features'. High standards were seen to be achieved by all pupils, whatever their ability. Particular strengths lie in English language and literature, art business studies and ICT. Provision for pupils' moral and social development was found to be excellent. However, Inspectors found the school's buildings needed improving to accommodate a recent increase in pupil numbers.

## Extra-curricular activities

The varied programme of lunchtime and after-school clubs include homework, science, Christian Union, drama, CDT, environment, debating and the Duke of Edinburgh's Award scheme. The award-winning PE department coaches teams in hockey, swimming, athletics, rounders and football. Music is represented by two choirs, two orchestras, a concert band and string and woodwind ensembles. There are field trips to the theatre, conferences, museums, art galleries and home stays in France and Germany. Holidays include skiing and watersports, as well as trips to Egypt, Austria and Germany. The school is involved in local charity fund-raising.

# Trinity School, Belvedere

**Erith Road, Belvedere, Kent DA17 6HT** 01322 441371 01322 436723 staff@trinity-school.demon.co.uk Mr I Collins BEd; Chair of Governors: Canon DAS Herbert Belvedere, Erith **Buses:** B12, B13, 89, 99, 401, 428, 469, 602 Electric blue sweatshirt, light blue polo neck, black trousers or navy skirt; Sixth form: Smart-casual dress code **Demand:** 300 applications for 180 places in 2001/2 **Type:** Voluntary aided comprehensive for 850 mixed pupils, aged 11 to 18 **Submit application form:** 12 December 2003 **School hours:** 8.45am–3.30pm; homework clubs available **Meals:** Hot and cold available **Strong GCSE subjects:** History, maths **London league table position:** 328

## Profile

Trinity school opened in 1994, and is the borough's only Church of England School. It aims to provide an excellent education for pupils of all abilities within a Christian environment. Trinity has a new library, learning support areas, technology and food technology rooms and science labs, business studies and ICT facilities. There is a fitness training area, multi-gym, sports field, tennis courts and all-weather area for games. Pupils also have access to local swimming and sports provision. A new technology block and sports hall opened last year. New pupils are grouped by ability for most subjects with additional support provided where necessary. Each year group undergoes a programme of personal, social and health education. Pupils receive work experience and careers counselling. It is the only Bexley school to operate a unit supporting students with emotional and behavioural difficulties. Pastoral support includes clerical counselling. Pupils can join the school council and help write the school's code of conduct. There is a Friday bulletin and homework book for parents as well as reports, consultations and an active Trinity School Association. Truancy is low at 0.5 per cent, below the national and borough averages.

## Admissions and intake

As a Church of England school, Trinity has its own admissions criteria. They are, in order of priority: children with a parent or guardian on the electoral roll of a Church of England parish; children with a parent or guardian who is a frequent worshipper at a church eligible for membership of Churches Together in England, and who can provide written evidence from their priest or minister; children with a parent who practises a faith other than Christianity and have a written testament from their religious leader; children who already attend a church school; children with siblings on school roll; children whose parents can provide evidence of a strong wish for a Christian education; and distance from the school. About 18 per cent of pupils are on the special needs register and about half of those require outside specialist help.

## Achievement

Improving exam results has become a major feature of Trinity School. In 2002, 43 per cent of pupils achieved five or more GCSEs at A*–C grades. This is below the national and borough averages, but is a fair attainment for the school's intake and an increase on 33 per cent in 2001. Results have remained steady over the last six years. The broad curriculum is supported by lessons to develop library and study skills, keyboarding and ICT in Years 7 to 9. In 2002, the average point score for pupils taking two or more A-levels was 220, below the borough average and placing the school sixth in the borough. Students do particularly well at GNVQ. The sixth form provides a range of A-levels and is a centre for GNVQ training. In 1997, Ofsted found that Trinity's positive and Christian ethos has been the cornerstone of its 'outstanding' improvement. Some very good teaching was notable in art, business studies and modern languages. Success in vocational subjects was well above average with art and business studies particularly strong. Ofsted wanted to see the school maintain its attainment levels and ensure IT was available for all national curriculum subjects.

## Extra-curricular activities

The school runs numerous clubs and sports groups, organizes dance, musical and drama productions and runs a choir. Lessons are supported by field trips and local visits and students take part in foreign activity holidays, local and national competitions and charity fund-raising events. There are after-school homework clubs.

# Welling School

**Elsa Road, Welling, Kent DA16 1LB** ☎ 020 8304 8531 📠 020 8301 6414 ✉ postmaster@welling-school.freeserve.co.uk 🌐 www.welling-school@freeserve.co.uk Mr Bryant Ambrose B.Ed (Hons), M.Sc, FCP, MI.Mgt FRSA; Chair of Governors: Mr Martin Johnson ⇌ Welling **Buses:** B11, B12, B15, 89, 96, 422 Black skirt and tights or black trousers, red jumper, white shirt and black blazer with badge and school tie for boys; Sixth form: Smart-casual dress code **Demand:** 357 applicaations for 300 places in 2001/2 **Type:** Community secondary modern Arts College for 1322 mixed pupils, aged 11 to 18 **Submit application form:** 12 December 2003 **Mission statement:** Our principle aim is to provide quality education which enables all our students to achieve their maximum potential and grasp the opportunities presented to them in the future. **School hours:** 8.45am–2.50pm; homework clubs are available **Meals:** Hot and cold available, including breakfast **Strong GCSE subjects:** art and design, drama and PE **London league table position:** 377

## Profile

A major development programme has helped boost morale at Welling School. More than £4 million has been pumped into a range of general and specialist accommodation. A science and technology block opened in 1995 and a learning resources centre with ICT facilities followed in 1998. The latest addition is a centre for performing, visual and media arts that is among the most advanced in the country. Its facilities include video production, animation and a recording studio. The performing arts are a particular strength of the school and it recently gained Arts College status. This means Welling will receive extra funding to spend on additional arts facilities, IT and digital equipment. The school will also receive around £12 million as part of a successful PFI bid to the government. This will be spent on new accommodation and sports facilities. Pupils are allocated to mixed-ability tutor groups but are later streamed. A careers programme is introduced in Year 9 and work experience takes place during Years 10 and 11. The school's caring philosophy starts with staff visits to prospective pupils at primary schools and form tutors stay with their groups for five years. Parents are involved with the disciplinary procedures and are kept in touch through a home/school diary, two parents' evenings a year and termly reports. There is an active PTA. Attendance of pupils is below the national average. There is a school council.

### Admissions and intake

Standard Bexley admissions criteria apply (see borough factfile). Pupils' attainment has dropped in recent years. Around 17 per cent have special needs and 1.3 per cent have a statement. The gender balance is generally even.

### Achievement

In 2002, 42 per cent of pupils achieved five or more A*–C grades. This was below the borough and national averages, but a rise from 30 per cent in 2001. The school was placed 12th in the borough. Pupils take eight or nine GCSEs. At A-level, pupils' performance averaged 200.3 points each. Pupils can choose from 15 A-level subjects and a number of GNVQs. In 2001, Ofsted reported that: 'Welling School is an effective school. Although the standards achieved by pupils are generally below the national averages for all schools, they are in line with pupils in similar secondary modern schools'. Inspectors found pupils to make 'satisfactory progress' with teaching being 'good in almost two out of five lessons and very good or excellent in a further one in five lessons'. However, the quality of teaching is hampered by a shortage of permanent teachers as the school has had 'serious difficulties in recruiting and retaining appropriately qualified staff'. Strongest GCSE subjects include art and design, drama and PE.

### Extra-curricular activities

Students enjoy a range of sports clubs, instrumental and choral groups, drama workshops and dance. They go on trips to the theatre and art galleries, and industrial and commercial visits. Clubs on offer include gardening at local parks, homework and IT support groups. There are extra classes, outdoor pursuits, journeys to Europe and skiing trips. In 2000 the dance class went to New York. There are annual concerts, drama productions and an art exhibition. The 'XL' club organizes fund-raising and other events for charities within the community.

## Westwood College

**The Green, Welling, Kent DA16 2PE** 020 8304 4916 020 8298 7121 Mrs KWL Clements B.Sc (Econ); Chair of Governors: Mrs Geraldine Hennessey Falconwood, Welling **Buses**: B16, 51, 89, 624 Dress Gordon kilt, navy blue jumper and white blouse (girls); blazer with badge, grey trousers, white or blue shirt and college tie (boys); no trainers, boots, denim, suede, leather or sheepskin coats and jackets **Demand**: 153 applications for 180 places in 2001/2 **Type**: Secondary modern community for 818 mixed pupils, aged 11 to 16 **Submit application form**: 12 December 2003 **Motto**: Under the Badge **School hours**: 8.25am–3pm **Meals**: Hot and cold available, including breakfast in winter **Strong GCSE subjects**: English literature, science **London league table position**: 431

### Profile

Westwood has suffered mixed fortunes over the years. A disastrous merger in the 1980s sent pupil numbers spiralling downwards and the school was threatened with closure. The current head took over in 1988 and Ofsted saw it as a tribute to her that Westwood then prospered. In 1993, it became an LEA-maintained Technology College. However, the school is again in difficulties following a recent Ofsted inspection. Westwood has a new science block, enhanced technology facilities, music room, ICT centre, expressive arts suite, sports hall, business and information studies suite and sixth-form centre. The college also has a purpose-built stage with specialist lighting and sound systems. Pupils are streamed in English, maths, French and science. Between Years 7 and 9, pupils take part in an enrichment programme that includes activities such as chess and t'ai chi. Pastoral care is overseen by form tutors and discipline includes sanctions and a system of merits. Parents receive regular reports, attend meetings and can make contact through a day book. There is a flourishing Home College Association. Famous ex-pupils include professional footballer Neil Carey.

### Admissions and intake

Standard Bexley admissions criteria apply (see borough factfile). The proportion of families containing someone with a further education qualification is about half the national average and an unusually high proportion of students go into employment at 16. A small number of pupils come from homes where English is not the first language and about 35 per cent have special needs.

## Achievement

Westwood's GCSE results in 2002 reversed a slump since 1999 after three years of increasing achievement. A total of 29 per cent of pupils gained five or more A*–C grades at GCSE. This was well below the borough average and the school was placed 15th in the borough. GCSE pupils take English language and literature, French, design technology and double science and choose from a range of other options. All students take a life skills exam. Ofsted inspectors visited in 2002 and found Westwood to be in decline, recommending that the school be put on special measures. Inspectors reported that the school fails to 'provide a satisfactory standard of education for its students due to many factors outside of its direct control'. The overall quality of teaching was seen to be poor, leading to pupils underachieving and leaving school with results that are well below the national average. However, Inspectors noted that 'standards are average in comparison with similar secondary schools'. The good leadership and management of Westwood was praised and pupils were seen to do well in art and design and PE. However, the rate of attendance was found to be very low, provision for special needs pupils 'unsatisfactory' and there were not enough 'suitably qualified and experienced teachers'.

## Extra-curricular activities

Activities available include sports, technology, drama and music with regular college productions. School trips take place with visits both at home and abroad.

# Brent

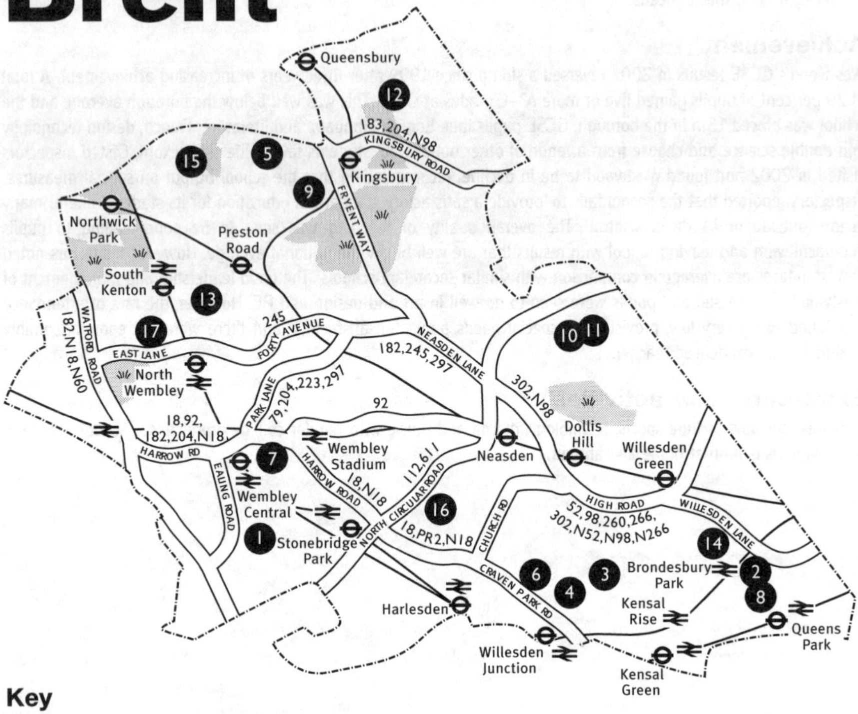


## Key

1. Alperton Community School
2. Al-Sadiq and Al-Zahra Schools
3. Capital City Academy
4. Cardinal Hinsley High School
5. Claremont High School
6. Convent of Jesus and Mary Language College
7. Copland Community School and Technology Centre
8. Islamia Girls' High School
9. JFS
10. John Kelly Boys' Technology College
11. John Kelly Girls' Technology College
12. Kingsbury High School
13. Preston Manor High School
14. Queens Park Community School
15. St Gregory's RC High School
16. The Swaminarayan School
17. Wembley High School

# Factfile

**LEA: Chesterfield House, 9 Park Lane, Wembley HA9 7RW** ☎ 020 8937 1234 🌐 www.brent.gov.uk **Director of Education, Arts and Libraries: John Crispie Political control of council:** Labour **Percentage of pupils from outside the borough:** 12.8 per cent **Percentage of pupils educated outside the borough:** 19.8 per cent **London league table positions (out of 32 boroughs):** 15

## Profile

Brent is a borough of two halves, with a prosperous suburban north and an inner-city south. Unsurprisingly, the more successful schools tend to be in the north of the borough and the weaker schools are often in areas of deprivation.

The borough is one of the most ethnically diverse areas in Europe, and 121 languages are spoken in its classrooms, the most common being Gujarati, Urdu, Somali and Arabic.

All but two of the state secondary schools opted out of LEA control and took grant-maintained status in the early 1990s. Many of the schools have built up good reputations and exam results in the last decade.

The rehabilitation of education in Brent was highlighted in a favourable Ofsted report on the LEA published in 1999. It said that the LEA worked well with schools to improve quality and was good at implementing the national literacy and numeracy strategies.

Brent has been successful at seeking extra additional government and private funding and is usually at the forefront of new innovations. It has three technology colleges, a language college and an arts college. A new City Academy opened in September 2003 to replace the failing Willesden High School. There is a relatively small independent secondary sector, with two schools catering for Brent's large Muslim community and another school for north-west London's Hindu community. The JFS School moved to Brent from Camden in 2002.

Exam results are improving, with the number of students gaining five or more GCSEs at grades A*–C increasing from 35.7 per cent in 1996 to 45.6 per cent in 2001, and 49.6 per cent in 2002. These figures are now only just below the national average.

There is no general admissions policy for Brent. Pupils and parents at Brent primary schools must fill out an AS2 form which is sent to the LEA and lists the applicants' top three choices. Parents then apply individually to the schools.

# Alperton Community School

**Stanley Avenue, Wembley, Middlesex HA0 4JE; Annex at Ealing Road, Wembley, Middlesex HA0 4PW** 020 8902 2293 020 8900 2720 admin@alperton.brent.sch.uk Alexander Wills B.Sc, NPQH; Chair of Governors: Vinod Mehta Alperton **Buses**: 79, 83, 224, 297 Black blazer, black trousers or skirt, white shirt, black school tie with red and white strips and school logo **Demand**: 235 applications for 217 places in 2001/2; waiting list of 50–60 for each year **Type**: Comprehensive foundation school for 1420 mixed pupils, aged 11 to 18 **Submit application form**: 21 November 2003 **Motto**: Through Learning Together with Care and Respect for Ourselves and Each Other We Shall Achieve and Grow **School hours**: 8.40am–3.15pm; homework clubs are available **Meals**: Hot and cold available **Strong GCSE subjects**: All relatively strong **London league table position**: 345

## Profile

Alperton is Brent's second largest secondary school, based on two sites located half a mile apart. The lower school is set in spacious grounds backing on to park land. The upper school, which includes the sixth-form centre and facilities for drama, technology and art, occupies an older building. Gujarati is included in the national curriculum for Years 7 to 9 and can be taken at GCSE. A-levels on offer include economics, law and psychology. There is a school council and pupils can act as counsellors to their peers. Each group of pupils run their own common room within a set budget. Alperton has a faculty for pupils with special needs but it is not fully accessible to wheelchair users. There is an active parents, teachers and friends association. Ofsted inspectors have found the behaviour of pupils to be good.

## Admissions and intake

Preference is given, in order of priority, to: siblings, if Alperton is their first choice; applicants living closest to the school; those with exceptional medical or special educational needs; and the children of staff.

## Achievement

In 2002, 43 per cent of pupils obtained five or more A*–C grades at GCSE. This was up from 38 per cent in 2001 and the school came 11th in the borough. The average point score for pupils taking two or more A-levels was 183.9, below national and borough averages, and ranking the school 11th in the borough. Alperton has 'a positive ethos which provides good behaviour, relationships and attitudes to learning', according to Ofsted inspectors following an inspection in 1998, and it has considerably more strengths than weaknesses. They reported: 'The staff are a strength of the school. They are hard working, appropriately qualified and experienced.' Attainment of pupils on entry was below national levels, particularly in language and literacy, but results in exams were close to the national average. The school is approachable and enables pupils to reach high standards. Weaknesses identified by Ofsted included limited access and use of IT, accommodation that required improvement and the need for a wider range of qualifications, including vocational options at Key Stage 4. Attendance was above the national average, although punctuality gave cause for concern.

## Extra-curricular activities

Ofsted inspectors praised the 'teachers who work hard and contribute particularly well to a good range of extra curricular activities'. Computer learning resource centres are open until the early evening and there are after-school homework clubs. The school has its own youth club and activities include chess, science, computing, arts, drama and music.

# Al-Sadiq and Al-Zahra Schools

**134 Salusbury Road, London NW6 6PF** 020 7372 7706/6760 020 7372 2752 alsadiq@btconnect.com Dr Manteu Movahedi (principal) Brondesbury Park, Queen's Park Queen's Park **Buses:** 36, 98, 187, 206 Navy blue blazer, grey trousers, light blue shirt, navy tie (boys); girls are expected to observe the Islamic Hijab from Year 3 onwards and are required to wear a navy blue manteau, white headscarf and black shoes **Demand**: 20 places available; pupils from the primary school take all places in first year of senior school, but there is a waiting list for free spaces **Type**: Non-selective independent for 390 mixed pupils, aged 4 to 16 **Fees:** £1,050 per term for secondary pupils **Submit application form**: March 2004 **Motto**: In the name of Allah, the all-merciful, the all-compassionate **School hours**: 8.50am–3.45pm **Meals**: Hot and cold available **Strong GCSE subjects**: Arabic, biology, chemistry, IT, maths, Persian **London league table position**: 70

## Profile

Both schools were established in 1991 under the guidance of the Al-Khoei Foundation and occupy the site of the former Brondesbury and Kilburn High School. The Al-Zahra School for Girls is named after the daughter of the Prophet Muhammad. The Al-Sadiq School for Boys is named after her son. Each school has its own teaching staff and head teacher with a single principal coordinating the running of both schools. The school aims to provide education in accordance with the Islamic faith, which 'stresses the virtues such as discipline, dedication, family values, community spirit, respect and tolerance towards others'.

Facilities include a computer room, a video room with audio-visual facilities and equipment for learning foreign languages, and a purpose-built gymnasium. The core subjects of the national curriculum, English, maths and science, are studied by all years. In addition, pupils attend classes in Islamic studies and Arabic for 10 per cent of the school day. In the secondary school, pupils also study IT, craft and design technology and art. In Years 7 to 9, they attend classes in geography, history and French. In Years 10 and 11, pupils take a second language and a choice of humanities and art subjects. Truancy is a problem and the school has the worst unauthorized absence record of Brent's three independent schools, at 3.2 per cent.

## Admissions and intake

Pupils automatically move from the primary into the secondary school. Any new pupils must sit an entrance exam and undergo an interview. However, places only become available if a pupil leaves, and there is a waiting list.

## Achievement

In 2002, the school was the second best performing in the borough with 86 per cent of pupils gaining five or more GCSEs at grades A*–C. This was an increase on 82 per cent in 2001. The school says: 'In a fast-changing secular environment, which often manifests itself in a declining trend in moral and social behaviour, the need for an education based upon academic excellence coupled with principles of morality, tolerance and spiritual understanding is of utmost importance.'

### Extra-curricular activities

The school offers the normal range of sports and stages an annual drama production, which parents can attend. Day trips are organized to museums and places of local, historical, cultural and national interest.

# Capital City Academy

**Doyle Gardens, Willesden, London NW10 3ST** 020 8965 0409 020 8838 3680 info@capitalcityacademy.org www.captialcityacademy.org Frank Thomas BA, PGCE, DMS(Ed); Chair of Governors: Sir Frank Lowe Willesden Junction Willesden Junction, Dollis Hill **Buses:** 206, 226 The uniform has been designed by students of the London School of Fashion – navy blue suit (choice of skirt or trousers for girls) and a shirt in different shades of blue depending on the year the child is in. Specially designed headscarf and long skirt for Muslim girls. **Demand:** 196 places available in 2001/2 **Type:** City Academy for 1200 mixed pupils, aged 11 to 18 **Submit application form:** 21 November 2003 **Motto:** Success Breads Success **School hours:** 8.30am–4.30pm, 8.30am–2.45pm (Fri); **Meals:** Hot and cold meals **Strong GCSE subject:** None taken **London league table position:** Not applicable

### Profile

Capital City Academy is a brand new school that opened in September 2003 to replace the failing Willesden High School. A £7.5 million redevelopment includes school buildings designed by Foster and Partners, a purpose built theatre, three performance/exhibition spaces and a specialist art, drama and music suite. The Academy is the first of a new type of state school which aims to raise the academic standards of all pupils including those with disabilities or special educational needs. It also places a strong emphasis on sport for building team spirit. A fifth of the Academy's money will come from advertising tycoon Frank Lowe, who will effectively be given control of the school. The Academy will have state of the art ICT facilities with at least six PCs in every classroom. It will also have disabled access. All subjects will be taught in the curriculum with special emphasis on the arts, sport, ICT and Citizenship. The school aims to have five terms and a longer school week, with enrichment activities on most afternoons.

### Admissions and intake

Preference is given, in order of priority, to: applicants with statements of special educational needs who give the Academy as their first preference; applicants who show an aptitude in sport using specified tests (up to 10 per cent admitted); children in the care of Brent LEA; significant medical or social need; siblings currently at school; distance from school.

### Achievement

No exams taken yet.

### Extra-curricular activities

The school has an internet café that opens at 8am every morning with a snack bar serving breakfast. Every Wednesday afternoon the school runs an Enrichment and Enhancement programme, when pupils will have a chance to pursue a learning activity such as lessons in time management, go on a theatre visit or take part in a sport.

# Cardinal Hinsley High School

**Harlesden Road, London NW10 3RN** 020 8965 3947/8947 020 8965 3430 admin@cahins.brent.uk George Benham; Chair of Governors: John Fox / Willesden Junction **Buses:** PR1, 18, 187, 206, 220, 224, 226 Black blazer, black trousers, black school tie with red stripes **Demand:** 109 applications for 180 places in 2001/2 **Type:** Voluntary aided Roman Catholic for 725 boys (mixed in sixth form), aged 11 to 19 **Submit application form:** 21 November 2003 **Motto:** *Tales Ambio Defensores* (With Champions Such As These) **School hours:** 8.45am–3.20pm (Mon–Wed), 8.45am–2.45pm (Thurs–Fri); homework clubs are available **Meals:** Hot and cold meals available, including breakfast **Strong GCSE subject:** Mathematics **London league table position:** 483

## Profile

Cardinal Hinsley was founded in 1958 to serve Catholic families in Brent, but it now attracts pupils from about 60 junior schools across North London. It is situated in one of the most deprived parts of the borough. The school is generally well maintained and has a new sixth-form area, including a library. There is a large sports hall and gym. The head, George Benham, appointed in September 1999, is Brent Council's former director of education. More than half of Cardinal Hinsley's staff left during the year 2000 summer holidays, with trade unions blaming the school for failing to deal effectively with pupils' violent or disruptive behaviour. Pupils are generally taught in banded ability groups with extra teacher support provided for those with special needs. RE plays a key role in school life and includes many activities with local Catholic parishes. There is a school council and all parents and teachers are members of the Cardinal Hinsley Association, which organizes social and fund-raising activities. There is provision for pupils with special needs. The footballer Cyril Regis is a former pupil.

## Admissions and intake

The school is open to boys attending local primary schools or living within access of the school. Preference is given, in order of priority, to: practising Roman Catholics with a priest's reference; those with a brother at the school; those with a previous sibling connection; the sons of staff; those with medical grounds; and those living closest to the school.

## Achievement

In 2002, 21 per cent of pupils gained five or more GCSEs at A*–C grades. This was down on 25 per cent the previous year and continued the downward trend of the previous year. The school was placed 17th in the borough league table. The average point score for pupils taking two or more A-levels was 138.7. This ranked the school 14th in the borough. Pupils can also take GNVQs.

In 2002, Ofsted visited the school and recommended it be put on special measures. Pupils were seen to be underachieving and 'teaching does not equip the students with the basic skills to learn, including literacy; weaknesses are evident in many subjects'. However, the proportion of pupils gaining at least one graded GCSE result in 2001 matched the national average. Inspectors found that the number of pupils with special educational needs was well above the national average.

## Extra-curricular activities

These include competitive football, cross-country, athletics and basketball clubs. There are links with local sports clubs for football, hurling, volleyball and table tennis. Pupils are involved in Lent charity fund-raising that raises about £4,000 a year. There are after-school homework clubs. Trips are held both at home and abroad, including a skiing trip. Pupils can also engage in community work with the elderly and the homeless.

# Claremont High School

**Claremont Avenue, Kenton, Harrow, Middlesex HA3 0UH** ☎ 020 8204 4442 Fax 020 8204 3548 e claremont-high.btinternet.com Terry Molloy; Chair of Governors: Steven Brunswick ⊖ Kingsbury, Kenton **Buses:** 79, 183, 204, 305 Navy blazer, navy blue skirt or trousers, white shirt, bright blue school tie with yellow stripes; Sixth form: Smart casual wear **Demand:** Not available but oversubscribed **Type:** Comprehensive foundation school Arts College for 1334 mixed pupils, aged 11 to 18 **Submit application form:** 21 November 2003 **Mission statement:** To prepare our students to realize their full potential **School hours:** 8.40am–3.20pm; homework clubs are available **Meals:** Hot and cold available, including breakfast **Strong GCSE subjects:** All relatively strong **London league table position:** 159

## Profile

Claremont High is set in a pleasant suburban area with its own playing fields. Most of the buildings date from the 1930s, with later additions providing specialist facilities for science, music, technology and the sixth form. During 1999/2000, a £104,000 conversion of the main stage into a TV studio and performance area was completed. The school recently achieved Art College status. From Year 7, one half of the year group begins a five-year French course while the other half studies a five-year German course. Pupils are streamed according to their ability in maths and languages. Parents receive a detailed report on educational progress each year and a newsletter is published every two weeks. There is also at least one annual consultation evening as well as review days. The PTA was resurrected in

1999/2000. There is a school council and provision for pupils with special needs. Notable ex-pupils include England footballer Stuart Pearce and cross-Channel swimmer Kevin Murphy.

### Admissions and intake

Preference is given to siblings of current pupils, then those living closest to the school. Special medical and social reasons may be given priority in exceptional cases.

### Achievement

In 2002, 69 per cent of pupils achieved five or more A*–C grades at GCSE, above both the borough and national averages and an increase on 62 per cent in 2001. Claremont was the best performing state school in the borough. Claremont came second in the state school borough league table in A-level results, with an average point score of 257.2 for pupils taking two or more. Pupils can also take GNVQs. In 2001, Ofsted inspectors reported: 'Claremont High School is a good and improving school', where 'almost no teaching is unsatisfactory and on occasions it is of the highest quality'. Pupils achieve good results in Key Stage 3 tests and at GCSE where results are above the national average and are particularly high in mathematics. The use of assessment and provision for personal, social and health education needs to improve.

### Extra-curricular activities

Claremont offers a wide range of extra-curricular music and drama groups. It also has a number of societies including chess, skiing, ornithology, squash and canoeing. There are after-school homework clubs. Over the last 15 years, an outdoor pursuits group has arranged trips to Snowdonia, the Peak and Lake districts, Scotland and the Alps. Activities include rock climbing, orienteering, rafting and abseiling. A skiing trip is held each February half term. In Year 8, all pupils are expected to attend a residential multi-activity trip. Pupils in Year 9 and above may participate in the Duke of Edinburgh's Award scheme.

## Convent of Jesus and Mary Language College

**Crown Hill Road, London NW10 4EP** 020 8955 2986 020 8838 0071 cjmhs@cjmhs. rmplc.co.uk www.cjmhs.brent.sch.uk Mrs G Frear Willesden Junction Harlesden, Willesden Junction **Buses:** PR1, 18, 187, 206, 220, 224, 226, 260, 266, 487 Blue jumper, blue skirt, white blouse, blue school tie with yellow stripes **Demand:** Information unavailable but regularly oversubscribed **Type:** Voluntary aided Roman Catholic comprehensive Language College for 1101 girls, aged 11 to 18 **Submit application form:** First Friday in November 2003 **Motto:** With God's Grace, to Excel and Lead **School hours:** 8.45am–3.05pm; homework clubs are available **Meals:** Hot and cold available **Strong GCSE subjects:** Drama, English, food technology, geography, maths, science **London league table position:** 209

### Profile

Founded by the Sisters of the Congregation of Jesus and Mary in 1888, this school is surrounded by attractive grounds in one of Brent's most deprived areas. It was granted Language College status in 1996 and awarded Beacon status in September 2000. A £710,000 technology wing was opened in 1996 and five new labs and prep rooms were completed the following year. The sixth form offers 21 A-levels, with video conference teaching used for accountancy and psychology. Daily assemblies, Masses, liturgical prayer groups, pilgrimages and days set aside for quiet reflection are considered an essential part of the curriculum in order to help the spiritual formation of pupils. Gifted and talented pupils are supported through specialist classes after school whilst those at risk of underachieving are given extra tuition after school and on Saturday mornings. There is provision for pupils with special needs. There is an active Jesus and Mary Association, which provides a link between staff and parents.

### Admissions and intake

Only applicants who make the school their first choice are interviewed. Preference is given, in order of priority, to: practising Roman Catholics; applicants with a sibling at the school; and those with an aptitude for foreign languages.

### Achievement

In 2002, 65 per cent of pupils gained five or more A*–C grades at GCSE, continuing an upward trend and the school came ninth in the borough league table. Surprisingly for a Language College, standards are not considered high enough in mainstream foreign languages, except in the sixth form. The average point score for pupils taking two or more A-levels in 2002, was 205.8, placing the school eighth in the borough league table. The 'outstanding' leadership of the head was praised by Ofsted inspectors following a visit in 2000. Inspectors noted that 'the great majority of pupils make very good progress'.

The quality of teaching was described as 'generally good' and the school was described as having 'a strong spiritual and moral ethos'. Standards have been above average over the past four years in comparison with other schools and very high in comparison with results attained in similar schools.

### Extra-curricular activities

Clubs include computer, film, basketball and training for altar service. The Saturday school offers classes in French, Italian, Arabic, Portuguese, Polish and Tagalog. These languages are taught in state-of the-art language labs to pupils from other schools in addition to its own. Several educational visits are arranged throughout the year, including trips for Years 8 and 10 to France and Spain.

## Copland Community School and Technology Centre

**Cecil Avenue, Wembley, Middlesex HA9 7DX** 020 8902 6362/020 8903 3323 020 8903 1943 copland@copland.brent.sch.uk Sir Alan Davies; Chair of Governors: Eva Davidson MBE Wembley Complex Wembley Central **Buses**: 18, 79, 83, 92, 182, 224 Black blazer with school badge, black trousers or skirt, black jumper with school badge, white shirt or blouse, school tie, black shoes **Demand**: Information unavailable; waiting lists of 70–130 for every academic year **Type**: Comprehensive foundation school for 1593 mixed pupils, aged 11 to 18 **Submit application form**: 21 November 2003 **Motto**: *E libertate virtus* (Freedom of Truth) **School hours**: 8.45am–3.05pm; homework clubs are available **Meals**: Hot and cold available **Strong GCSE subjects**: Gujarati, RE **London league table position**: 357

### Profile

This school is situated close to Wembley town centre on a 22-acre campus. The site includes a large area of playing fields, which are a possible location for an athletics warm-up track for the redeveloped Wembley Stadium. There is also a large technology centre with three computer rooms. Head Sir Alan Davies and four of his deputies also took over management of the failing Harlesden Primary School in September 2000, following a request by Brent council. In the lower school, emphasis is placed on independent study and the use of IT. Some sixth-formers are attached to tutor groups and help tutors, while Year 10 and 11 pupils are involved in clubs where they assist younger pupils. Each tutorial group elects two pupils to be representatives on the year and school councils. There is a large special-needs department. A weekly newsletter is sent home to parents, and there is a thriving Friends of Copland Association.

### Admissions and intake

All applicants are required to take a standardized national test to ensure that the intake is across the range of ability. Teachers speak Arabic, German, Gujarati, Russian and Somali.

### Achievement

In 2002, 41 per cent of pupils gained five or more A*–C grades. This was down on 42 per cent in 2001 and continued a downward trend. The school came 13th in the borough league table. The average point score for pupils taking two or more A-levels was 232.3, placing the school fourth in the borough. Following an inspection in 2000, Ofsted inspectors commented: 'Copland is a good school which has successfully gained the support of its parents and local cosmopolitan community in seeking to raise the achievement of all students.' They added: 'the school provides a very good learning environment and standards are improving'. Two-thirds of teaching was at least good, 15 per cent was very good and just three per cent was classified as unsatisfactory. Pupils' results in tests on entry show their standard is well below the average for comprehensive schools. However, by the age of 16 they are in line with the national average. Ofsted found the pupils' behaviour around the school and in lessons to be very good.

## Extra-curricular activities

There is a popular Saturday school and an annual enrichment week which gives pupils a chance to take part in a range of activities. Basketball is particularly popular. Clubs include homework clubs, video, debating, languages, electronics, self-defence and swimming. The school also supports a wide range of international and national charities.

# Islamia Girls' High School

**129 Salusbury Road, London NW6 6PE** 020 7372 3472 020 7604 4061 Parin Kassam; Chair of Governors: Yusuf Islam (formerly known as the singer Cat Stevens) Brondesbury Park, Queen's Park Queen's Park **Buses**: 36, 187, 206 Islamic head scarves, long brown skirt, white long-sleeved blouse **Demand**: 30 places; waiting list of c. 60 for each year group **Type**: Selective independent for 126 girls, aged 11 to 16 **Fees**: £4,200 per year **Submit application form**: Up to January 2004 **Mission statement**: To strive to provide the best education in a secure Islamic environment through the knowledge and application of the Koran and the Sunnah **School hours**: 8.30am–3.30pm **Meals**: Hot and cold available **Strong GCSE subjects**: Chemistry, English and English literature, information studies, Islamic studies, physics **London league table position**: 77

## Profile

This school was founded in the early 1980s and occupies the site of a former grammar school. Its facilities have been extensively modernized. The school provides an Islamic education and pupils pray five times a day. The school is linked to Islamia Primary, which was one of the first Islamic schools to be granted voluntary aided status. All pupils follow the standard national curriculum and in addition have lessons in Islamic studies, Arabic and the Koran. Music is not studied in the secondary school as it is not considered an appropriate subject for a girl's Islamic education. The school says its aim is to 'produce total Muslim personalities through the training of children's spirit, intellect, feelings and bodily senses. The ultimate aim of Islamic education is the realization of complete submission to Allah on the level of the individual, the community and humanity at large.' Two parents are elected onto the Shura Council, which governs the school. There is no formal PTA.

## Admissions and intake

Applicants have to fill out a questionnaire and points are awarded for the answers given. The highest scoring applicants are offered a place. Priority is given, in order, to: those applicants who practise and have an active commitment to the Islamic faith; those with social and welfare needs; siblings of current pupils; those living closest to the school; and non-Muslims who support the high moral values of the Islamic faith.

## Achievement

GCSE results are high compared with state schools in Brent. In 2002, 95 per cent of pupils achieved five or more A*–C grades, continuing an upward trend and the school came third in the borough league overall. In 2000, there was not a single unauthorized absence by a pupil.

## Extra-curricular activities

In the past, the school offered extra classes in French, Italian and Urdu, and these may be restarted. Pupils are involved in fund-raising for charities. The normal range of sports is on offer.

# JFS (Jews' Free School)

**The Mall, Kenton HA3 9UA** 020 7485 9416 020 7284 3948 jfs@mcmail.com Miss Ruth Robins BA, TTHD; Chair of Governors: Mr Arnold Wagner Queensbury Kingsbury Blue blazer, grey trousers or skirt, blue shirt or blouse, tie for boys **Demand**: 300 places available in 2003; regularly oversubscribed **Type**: Voluntary aided comprehensive for 1486 mixed pupils aged 11 to 18 **Submit application form**: Second Friday of December 2003 **Motto**: Light and Honour **School hours**: 8.35am–3.35pm (juniors); 8.35am–3.45pm (seniors);

8.35am–1.30pm (Fri); homework clubs are available **Meals**: Hot and cold available **Strong GCSE subjects**: English **London league table position**: 118

### Profile

JFS (Jew's Free School) is a school that is going from strength to strength. It moved to Brent in 2002. It was founded in the 19th century to provide free schooling for Jewish children. It aims to build a strong sense of identity with Judaism and Israel while offering an excellent all-round education. JFS sees itself as a 'family school' and works closely with parents. Its pupils live throughout London and the active parents-teacher association runs local liaison groups. There are also very good links with the Jewish community in the UK and abroad. Sixth-formers can become student officers and are given responsibility in the running of the school. Truancy was 0.1 per cent in 2000.

### Admissions and intake

The school's pupils come from 18 London boroughs. Applicants must all be recognized as Jewish by the Office of the Chief Rabbi. They are placed in one of four ability bands after sitting an assessment and equal numbers are taken from each. Priority is given, in order, to: siblings of pupils; current attendance at a Jewish primary school; siblings of former pupils; and distance from the school, proportionate to the numbers from each borough. There is a mix of Jewish denominations and practice. Around 10 per cent of pupils are Israelis.

### Achievement

After some disappointing years, the school's reputation has vastly improved. It has been awarded Beacon status and, in 2000, won an *Evening Standard* Award for Academic Excellence. In 2002, 75 per cent of pupils achieved five or more A*–C grades at GCSE, maintaining the standard of the previous year. JFS was placed fifth in the Camden borough league table. JFS is 'a very successful and continually improving school with a range of distinctive and outstanding features', according to an Ofsted report from 1998. The inspectors found that three-quarters of the teaching was good, very good or outstanding. Nearly all subjects are very strong, particularly English. All younger pupils take Jewish studies and Hebrew to study for GCSE. JFS was top in the A-level borough league table in 2002, with an 299.2 average point score for pupils taking two or more A-levels, continuing an upwards trend since 1998. Most groups are of mixed ability, but in every year there are 'accelerated' tutor groups. Spiritual, moral, social and cultural development was especially praised by Ofsted who commented: 'The school very successfully achieves its aim of producing caring and responsible young people who have a strong sense of identity.'

### Extra-curricular activities

Special interest clubs include astronomy and Jewish art. Musical groups include choirs and a big band. The school participates in the Duke of Edinburgh's Award scheme and Young Enterprise. Its 14-year-old pupils can spend five months in Israel. Other foreign trips include a sixth-form memorial visit to Poland.

## John Kelly Boys' Technology College

**Crest Road, Neasden, London NW2 7SN** ☎ 020 8452 8700 Fax 020 8208 2281 e jkboys@aol.com www.jkbtc.co.uk Alexander Young MA (RCA); Chair of Governors: Liz Goodenough ⊖ Neasden, Dollis Hill **Buses**: 112, 182, 232, 245, 316 Black blazer, black sweatshirt, black trousers, black school tie with yellow, pink, blue and green stripes **Demand**: 117 places in 2001/2; oversubscribed **Type**: Comprehensive foundation school Technology College for 625 boys, aged 11 to 18 **Submit application form**: 21 November 2003 **School hours**: 8.35am–3.20pm; homework clubs are available **Meals**: Hot and cold meals, including breakfast **Strong GCSE subjects**: English, design and technology **London league table position**: 455

### Profile

The college was founded in 1958 and is set in extensive grounds just south of the North Circular Road. A £1 million building project in 1997 provided new science labs, a learning resource centre, technology workshop areas and music and art rooms. As a technology college, the school places special emphasis on maths, science and technology. Pupils in Year 7 use the Success Maker integrated learning system daily to improve their literacy and numeracy. The college has received funding for a link with schools in Germany and Sweden, to compare their work and to allow exchanges for teachers and possibly pupils. Members of the sixth form can become prefects and there is a school council. England cricketer Mike Gatting is a former pupil.

### Admissions and intake

Priority is given, in order, to: pupils with sibling or other family connections; those with a sister at John Kelly Girls' Technology College; those living within a three-mile radius of the college; those with religious, social or medical reasons; and those who attend a Brent primary schools. Of those pupils who joined in Year 7 in 1998, 80 per cent read at a level below the average for their age.

### Achievement

In 2002, 31 per cent of pupils gained five or more A*–C grades. This was up on 24 per cent in 2001 and the college was placed 16th in the borough league table. The average point score for pupils taking two or more subjects was 26.4, below the national average. Following an inspection in 1999, Ofsted reported: 'The college has some important strengths but also some significant weaknesses.' Teaching was at least satisfactory in 79 per cent of lessons, and in 11 per cent it was very good. Results in Key Stage 3 tests for English, maths and science were well below the national average. Overall, these results are also well below those achieved in similar schools, although the results for maths are average. Overall, the college has improved its GCSE results, and they tend to be in line with the national average and above those for similar schools. Ofsted reported that pupils' attitudes to learning were at least satisfactory and often good. However, in a significant minority of lessons, pupils' behaviour was poor and this was clearly linked to weak teaching.

### Extra-curricular activities

Each year group has a football, cricket and basketball team, and there is a volleyball club. There is also a homework club and a Saturday music school, providing three and a half hours of tuition. All pupils have the chance to visit France and Spain, and join residential weekends in Britain.

## John Kelly Girls' Technology College

**Crest Road, Neasden, London NW2 7SN** 020 8452 4842 020 8452 6024 admin@jkgtc.brent.sch.uk www.jkgtc.brent.sch.uk Mrs Kathryn Heaps; Chair of Governors: Cllr Tom Taylor Neasden, Dollis Hill **Buses**: 112, 182, 232, 245, 316 Grey college sweatshirt, black trousers or skirt, white shirt, black school tie with yellow, pink, blue and green stripes (Years 7 to 9); Black college sweatshirt, black trousers or skirt, white shirt, optional school tie (Years 10 to 11); all girls must wear black shoes **Demand**: No figures available but 155 places in 2001/2 oversubscribed **Type**: Comprehensive foundation school Technology College for 880 girls, aged 11 to 18 **Submit application form**: 21 November 2003 **Motto**: Working Together, Building Tomorrow **School hours**: 8.35am–4.10pm (Mon), 8.35am–3.20pm (Tues to Fri), 8.35am–4.10pm (Tues, Year 10); homework clubs are available **Meals**: Breakfast and halal meals are available **Strong GCSE subjects**: French, German, history **London league table position**: 369

### Profile

This school was founded in 1958 and is set within extensive grounds close to the North Circular Road. An extensive building programme has been completed to provide specialist accommodation in the main building, and new humanities, languages and sixth-form facilities. As a technology college, John Kelly devotes more time to maths, science, technology and ICT. Sixth-form studies are shared with pupils from John Kelly Boys' Technology College. The college has a nationally respected learning development department. Pupils are placed in mixed-attainment groups in Year 7 and have a form tutor and year manager assigned to them until Year 11. There is a school council and prefects. Gifted arts pupils or linguists can take an additional GCSE in French, art, music or PE. Former senior European MP Pauline Green is an ex-pupil.

### Admissions and intake

Priority is given, in order, to: sisters of current pupils; those with a brother at John Kelly Boys' Technology College; those with medical grounds; the daughters of staff at the John Kelly Girls' or Boys' Technology Colleges; and those living closest to the school. In 2000, 35 per cent of pupils were on the special needs register.

## Achievement

Following an inspection in 1998, Ofsted reported that the college had some important strengths but also some significant weaknesses. About 38 per cent of pupils joining in Year 7 had a reading age two or more years below their age, while 6 per cent had a reading age four years or more below their age. Attainment at the end of Key Stage 3 rose sharply to the national average in 1998, although it remained below this level for Key Stage 4. The inspectors found that 17 per cent of teaching was very good, 89 per cent was satisfactory or better and 11 per cent was less than satisfactory. In 2002, 41 per cent of pupils obtained five or more A*–C grades at GCSE. This was down from 46 per cent in 2001 and below the borough average. The college was placed 14th in the borough league table. The average GCSE point score was 30.8. At A-level, the average point score for pupils taking two or more was 203.9, ranking it ninth in the borough. Pupils can also take GNVQs. Behaviour in classrooms was found to be invariably good, although in some lessons the behaviour of a small minority of pupils had a detrimental effect on their learning.

## Extra-curricular activities

A Saturday music school is on offer and a literacy and numeracy summer school is provided for pupils preparing to join the school. There is also an Easter revision school for those pupils taking GCSEs and after-school homework clubs. Extra studies in maths, science and technology are provided for Year 10. Clubs include dance, drama and regular sports training. A drama production is staged annually with concerts every term, and there are trips to France, Italy and a skiing trip. Pupils in the sixth form are involved in fund-raising for local charities.

# Kingsbury High School

**Princes Avenue, Kingsbury, London NW9 3JR** ☎ 020 8204 9814/17 Fax 020 8206 3040 e school@kingsbury.brent.sch.uk www www.kingsburyhigh.org.uk (under development) Head CR Chung BA, MA, NPQH; Chair of Governors: Roger Stone MBE ⊖ Kingsbury **Buses**: 183, 204, 302 Uniform Black blazer, black trousers, white shirt or skirt, grey school tie with blue stripes **Demand**: No figures available but regularly oversubscribed **Type**: Comprehensive foundation school for 1914 mixed pupils, aged 11 to 18 **Submit application form**: 21 November 2003 **Motto**: *Spectemur agendo* (Let Us Be Judged by Our Actions) **School hours**: 8.40am–3.30pm **Meals**: Hot and cold available **Strong GCSE subjects**: Art and design, double science, maths **London league table position**: 198

## Profile

Kingsbury High is one of the largest secondary schools in the country, with a sixth form of about 300 pupils. It is located on two neighbouring sites, one for Years 7 to 9 and the other for Years 10 to 11 and the sixth form. The school is set within park land and has its own extensive playing fields. It was the setting for the television drama *Grange Hill*. The original building is about 75 years old but extensive modernization has taken place and there are new facilities for art and IT. There is a unit for pupils with sensory impairments and the buildings have wheelchair access. Kingsbury High also has prefects, a school council and a parents' guild.

## Admissions and intake

About 10 per cent of places are allocated on the basis of ability. Priority for the other places is given, in order, to: siblings; children of staff at Kingsbury High, Kingsbury Green, Roe Green or Fryent primary schools; those with social or medical reasons; and those living closest to the school. There are 24 places in the sensory support unit for children with a statement of special needs or those with hearing or vision loss. These places are available though Brent Council's Special Needs Assessment and Pupils Services. About 250 pupils have special learning needs, a lower proportion than the national average.

## Achievement

Following an inspection in 2000, Ofsted reported: 'Kingsbury High School is a very effective school which achieves high standards in all that it does.' The school's GCSE results are above average, although the rate of improvement is slightly lower than the national trend. In 2002, 63 per cent gained five or more A*–C grades at GCSE and Kingsbury High School came eighth in the borough league table. This was above the local and national averages. Results at A-level are improving faster than nationally. Pupils taking two or more subjects in 2002 gained an average point score of 230, placing the school fifth in the borough. Pupils can also take GNVQs. Pupils' attainment on entry is broadly average. During Years 10 to 11 and in the sixth form, they make good progress so that by the ages of 16 and 18 they achieve standards that are above national averages overall. Teachers are enthusiastic and knowledgeable about their subjects and teaching was found to be good or very good in eight out of 10 lessons, and very good or excellent in more than a quarter. Pupils are keen to succeed and are well behaved, but in a small number of lessons there was too little variety, or the teaching methods used led to a slow pace of learning.

### Extra-curricular activities

A full range of sports, music, dance and drama activities are on offer after school. Concerts regularly feature the school's bands, orchestras and choirs. There are trips to France, Italy and a skiing trip.

# Preston Manor High School

**Carlton Avenue East, Wembley, Middlesex HA9 8NA** 020 8385 4040 info@pmanor.brent.sch.uk www.pmanor.brent.sch.uk Mrs Andrea Berkley BA, FRSA; Chair of Governors: Rob Maclachlam Preston Road, Wembley Park **Buses**: 223, 245 Navy trousers or skirt, navy jumper, white shirt, blue school tie with pale blue stripes **Demand**: 628 applications for 216 places in 2001/2 **Type**: Comprehensive foundation school for 1348 mixed pupils, aged 11 to 18 **Submit application form**: 21 November 2003 **Motto**: Duty Before Rights **School hours**: 8.45am–3.20pm; homework clubs are available **Meals**: Hot and cold available **Strong GCSE subjects**: Art, English literature, maths, science **London league table position**: 182

### Profile

Preston Manor was founded in 1938 and is situated in a quiet residential area. There are plans to sell part of its extensive playing fields for housing development in order to help fund new teaching accommodation. A five-year development programme will provide new design and technology workshops, a food technology room, two special needs suites, art studios and a learning resource centre. Security cameras monitor the school and all visitors carry security passes. Sports facilities include three football pitches, six tennis courts, a full-size athletics track and two indoor gymnasia. The speech and language resource centre has 12 places for pupils – a maximum of four in any one year – with speech and language difficulties. Pupils are initially streamed for maths and then for science and modern languages in Years 10 to 11. The school has a part-time professional counsellor and uses local counselling services. There is a school council and a prefects system.

### Admissions and intake

Priority is given, in order, to: siblings of current pupils; those with a medical condition, social needs or special educational needs; and children of staff at Preston Manor High. Admission to the speech and language resource centre depends on a review of the child's statement of special needs.

### Achievement

In 2002, Preston Manor won the London *Evening Standard* Award for outstanding performance. It also won the Government School Achievement Award for Excellence in 2001 and 2002. Ofsted inspectors visited the school in 1995 and concluded that it is a 'rapidly improving and effective school'. Since the arrival of the present head 18 months earlier, the school had been taking a new direction. The leadership style was positive, up-beat and ambitious. Many of the weaknesses identified by Ofsted have since been tackled. At that time, teaching was found to be satisfactory or better in two-thirds of Key Stage 3 lessons and three-quarters of Key Stage 4 classes. Eight out of ten lessons were satisfactory in the sixth form, with A-level results sound overall. Vocational qualifications were also reported as good. The school's GCSE results in 2002 continued a general upward trend with 65 per cent of pupils achieving five or more A*–C grades. The school came seventh in the borough league table. The average point score at GCSE was 40.2, above the borough and national averages. The average point score of pupils taking two or more A-levels was 238.5, placing the school third in the borough.

### Extra-curricular activities

Music activities are strong, with full and string orchestras, gospel singers, choir, rock bands and 'Asian sounds'. Sports include boys' and girls' basketball clubs, badminton, bowling and sailing. There are after-school homework clubs. Pupils also have the opportunity to take trips to places of interest in Britain and abroad.

# Queens Park Community School

**Aylestone Avenue, Kilburn, London NW6 7AD** 020 8438 1700 020 8459 1895 admin@qpcs.brent.sch.uk Miss Mary Norton MA; Chair of Governors: Ms Amanda Bowman Brondesbury Park, Queen's Park, Kensal Green Kensal Green, Queen's Park, Willesden Green **Buses**: 6, 52, 187, 206, 302 Black tracksuit with logo and T-shirt or polo shirt **Demand**: 394 applications for 200 places in 2001/2 **Type**: Comprehensive foundation school for 1177 mixed pupils, aged 11 to 19 **Submit application form**: 21 November 2003 **School hours**: 8.45am–3.25pm; homework clubs are available **Meals**: Hot and cold meals, including breakfast **Strong GCSE subject**: English **London league table position**: 349

## Profile

Queens Park celebrated its 10th anniversary in 2000. It was recently awarded £6.8 million by the government to replace two-thirds of its teaching accommodation. This provided new art, technology, drama and science rooms and a library and resource centre that includes computer suites and multi-media workshops. It is currently applying to become a specialist Business and Enterprise School. The school buildings are accessible to wheelchair users and are monitored by security cameras. There is an active school council. Extra tutorials are provided for sixth-formers applying to university.

## Admissions and intake

Priority is given, in order, to: those applicants with siblings at the school; the children of staff; those with a medical reason; and those living closest to the school. About a third of pupils have special needs, which is well above average. The school primarily serves an area outside of its immediate, affluent neighbourhood. A fifth of pupils come from outside Brent and many come from disadvantaged areas.

## Achievement

In 2002, 42 per cent of pupils achieved A*–C grades at GCSE, below the borough average of 49.6. This continued an upward trend and the school was placed 12th in the borough league table. The average point score for pupils taking two or more A-levels was 172.7, placing the school 12th in the borough. Pupils can take a GNVQ in art and design in the sixth form. Ofsted visited the school in 1998 and commented: 'This is a good school with many strengths and an excellent capacity to improve still further.' The head was found to provide very strong leadership by promoting high standards with a caring ethos. Attainment of pupils on entry had been substantially below the national averages for all schools. However, a third of pupils in Year 7 were above their expected reading age and 19 per cent significantly above it. Results at the end of Key Stage 3 had been well below the national average for all schools but above the national average for similar schools. Attainment in English was close to the national average and well above for similar schools, while maths results were well below the national average and below the average for similar schools. Teaching was satisfactory in 93 per cent of lessons and very good or better in a fifth. The school was very well staffed and teachers were well qualified. Ofsted found that pupils' behaviour in classes was of a good standard and there were few inappropriate incidents.

## Extra-curricular activities

Sports clubs available include soccer, rugby, basketball, badminton, netball and running. There are also clubs for homework, technology, art, dance, drama and steel bands, as well as a choir and wind group. There is an annual skiing trip and visits to Europe for language students.

# St Gregory's RC High School

**Donnington Road, Kenton, Harrow, Middlesex HA3 0NB** 020 8907 8828 020 8909 1161 schooloffice@stgregorys.harrow.sch.uk www.SchoolOffice@stgregory.harrow.sch.uk Martin Earley BA, MA, M.Sc; Chair of Governors: Michael Daley Kenton, Northwick Park **Buses**: H10, H18, 114, 183, 223 Navy blazer, white shirt, navy trousers or navy skirt and tights, navy school tie with red and orange stripe (lower school); navy school tie with orange stripe (upper school) **Demand**: 255 applications for 176 places in 2001/2

**Type:** Voluntary aided Roman Catholic comprehensive for 1000 mixed pupils, aged 11 to 18 **Submit application form:** 21 November 2003 **Motto:** Love God and love thy neighbour as thyself. I am the Way, the Truth and the Life **School hours:** 8.50am–3.30pm **Meals:** Hot and cold available **Strong GCSE subjects:** All relatively strong **London league table position:** 251

## Profile

St Gregory's is situated in a leafy suburb and serves Catholic families in Brent, Harrow and surrounding boroughs. The original school building was constructed in 1956 and was substantially extended during the 1970s. The science rooms were refurbished in 1994. A new sixth-form centre has recently been completed. Security CCTV cameras monitor the premises. When the school became grant-maintained in 1993, it decided to invest a proportion of its budget in employing more teachers. This means that no class contains more than 25 pupils. St Gregory's has a head boy and girl, and a school council. There is an active PTA and a coordinator for pupils with special needs.

## Admissions and intake

Preference is given, in order, to: practising Roman Catholics with a priest's reference; applicants with siblings at the school; those with a proven family connection to the school; those with medical or social needs; and those living closest to the school.

## Achievement

Following a visit in 2001, Ofsted inspectors reported that St Gregory's was an 'effective school' and that: 'standards of attainment are above the nationally expected levels and the quality of teaching is satisfactory with many strengths'. Inspectors praised the 'strong leadership' of the head teacher and noted that children with special educational needs, gifted children and those learning English as an additional language all made 'good and often very good progress'. There were good procedures for monitoring attainment and progress of pupils. Ofsted also noted the 'good partnership' between the school and parents. The school has gone on to perform well, with 61 per cent of pupils in 2002 achieving A*–C grades. This was above the national average of 51.6 per cent and up on 55 per cent in 2001. St Gregory's was ranked the 10th best performing school in the borough. The average point score for pupils taking two or more A-levels was 214, placing the school seventh in the borough league table. Pupils can also take GNVQs.

## Extra-curricular activities

Latin classes are held before school. Several foreign trips are organized each year. Pupils are involved in charity fund-raising, particularly during Lent, and provide entertainment at old people's homes. The normal range of sports is on offer.

# The Swaminarayan School

**260 Brentfield Road, Neasden, London NW10 8HE** 020 8965 8381 020 8961 4042 admin@swaminarayan.brent.sch.uk www.swaminarayanschool.co.uk Mahendra Savjani; Chair of Governors: Piyush Amin Stonebridge Park Neasden, Stonebridge Park **Buses:** PR2, 18, 112, 206 Blue blazer, charcoal grey trousers or tartan check skirt, white shirt, gold and blue striped school tie **Demand:** Contact school for details **Type:** Selective independent for 442 mixed pupils, aged 2 to 18 (senior school 11 to 18) **Fees (per term):** £1,440 (Year 7); £1,870 (Year 12) **Submit application form:** No cut-off date **Motto:** Education Is That Which Liberates **School hours:** 8.30am–4.05pm (senior school) **Meals:** Vegetarian Indian and Western dishes **Strong GCSE subjects:** English, maths, sciences **London league table position:** 79

## Profile

This school was founded in 1991 by His Divine Holiness Shree Pramukh Swami Maharaj to provide a Hindu-based education for its pupils. The school is based in the buildings of a former state school opposite the beautiful Swaminarayan Temple, the largest Hindu temple outside of India. It has extensive sports facilities, including two indoor cricket nets, a netball court, a gym and shared grounds. Pupils follow the national curriculum with French and Gujarati as compulsory languages. The head, Mr Savjani, said: 'We are first and foremost an English school, preparing children for the English workplace. We, however, have a reputation of combining the best of both Eastern and Western education to bring out the best in our students in a caring and tolerant Hindu environment.'The school also runs an extensive cultural programme, which includes all aspects of Indian culture. Children may learn classical and folk Indian dance, flute, tabla, harmonium, singing, piano, violin, drums and drama. There is an active parents, teachers and friends association, which raises funds for the school and helps organize celebrations of major religious festivals. There is also a school prefects system.

## Admissions and intake

Entrance is by exam, interview and a reference from the candidate's previous head. Those applicants applying to enter the sixth form require a minimum of six GCSE passes at A*–B grades. Although most pupils are practising Hindus, the school is open to children of all religions.

## Achievements

In 2002, 92 per cent of pupils achieved five or more A*–C grades at GCSE. and the school was placed fourth in the borough and independent schools league tables. These results were well above the borough and national averages and up from 2001's 81 per cent. The average point score for pupils taking two or more A-levels was 216.9, ranking it sixth in the borough. The school won fame in August 2000 when one student passed 12 GCSEs all with A* grades. There were no unauthorized absences in 2000, and authorized absence was the lowest in the borough at 3.7 per cent.

## Extra-curricular activities

The usual range of music and sport clubs are on offer as well as activities such as dry-slope skiing, canoeing and wall climbing. Pupils can take part in the Duke of Edinburgh's Award scheme from the age of 14.

# Wembley High School

**East Lane, North Wembley, Middlesex HA0 3NT** ☎ 020 8904 5066 📠 020 8908 6826 ⓔ admin@wembleyhigh.brent.sch.uk 🌐 www.wembley-high.brent.sch.uk Mr G Bal BS.c (Hons), NPQH; Chair of Governors: Ms Helen Pollendine ⊖ North Wembley, Wembley Park **Buses**: 79, 204, 245 Black blazer, black trousers or skirt, white shirt, red school tie with logo (lower school); black school tie with logo (upper school) **Demand**: 210 places in 2003; waiting lists of up to 25 for each year group **Type**: Community comprehensive Technology College for 892 mixed pupils, aged 11 to 18 **Submit application form**: 21 November 2003 **Motto**: Achievement for All **School hours**: 8.40am–3.20pm; homework clubs are available **Meals**: Hot and cold available **Strong GCSE subjects**: Arts, English, geography **London league table position**: 420

## Profile

Wembley High is situated in a residential area of North Wembley. Built in the 1920s, it has several new buildings including a maths block which was completed in 1999. CCTV cameras monitor the school and sixth-formers have to use security swipe cards. Wembley High was one of two secondary schools not to opt for grant-maintained status in Brent and many of its difficulties were due to a major budget deficit. This deficit has since been tackled and the problems appear to be improving. The school gained Technology College status in 2002 which will provide extra funding for science, mathematics, technology and IT facilities. Wembley High also receives government Excellence in Cities funding to help talented pupils. Those pupils in the sixth form for two years can study for A-levels or for GNVQ advanced courses in art and design, business and science. Pupils spending just one year in the sixth form can take GNVQs in art and design, business, health and social care or science, with GCSEs in English, maths or one other subject. There are school and year councils and a coordinator for pupils with special needs. Former pupils include comedian Brian Conley.

## Admissions and intake

Application forms should be sent to the school and the LEA. Priority is given to: children in local authority care; those with medical, social and educational needs; siblings of pupils at the school for at least a year; children living in the catchment area (three-mile radius); and the children of council staff working in the catchment area. In 1999, the reading age of 48 per cent of pupils of the Year 7 intake was at least two years behind their actual age.

## Achievement

In 2002, 34 per cent of pupils gained five or more A*–C grades at GCSE. This was up on 32 per cent in 2001 and reinstated an upward trend. The school was ranked 15th in the borough league table. Pupils taking two or more A-levels had an average score of 192.2, ranking the school tenth in the borough. Pupils can also take GNVQs. Ofsted visited the school in 1999, and found that significant improvements had been made since the appointment of a new head in 1998. The low standard of pupils on entry presents a challenge but most pupils made satisfactory progress in most subjects. Standards were well below average in Key Stage 3 and below average in Key Stage 4. Teaching was satisfactory or better in 86 per cent of lessons, good or better in 46 per cent and very good in 12 per cent. Ofsted also noted that most teachers had sound subject knowledge but too many had low expectations of their pupils. Less than half of parents believed the school achieved high standards of behaviour. Although Ofsted found behaviour in the classroom was usually satisfactory or good, it was not always satisfactory around the school.

## Extra-curricular activities

After-school practice sessions are held for football, hockey, volleyball, rugby, trampolining, swimming and gymnastics. There are also after-school homework clubs. Music activities available include African drumming. An annual visit to Yorkshire is organized for outdoor activities.

# Bromley

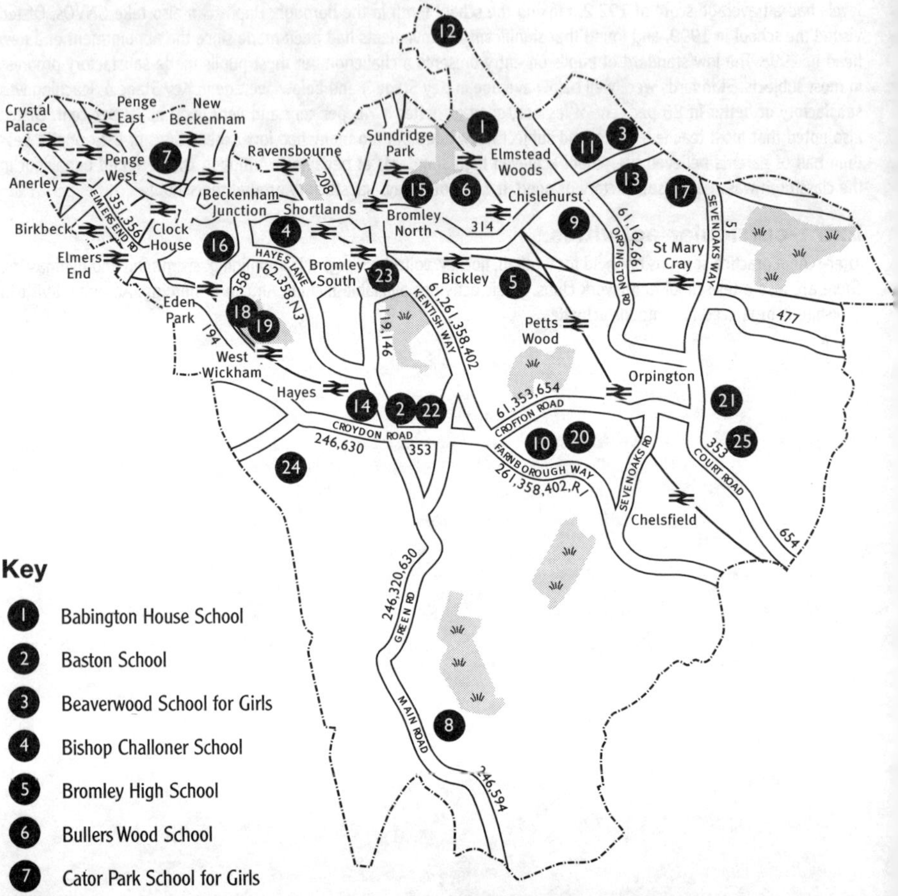


## Key

1. Babington House School
2. Baston School
3. Beaverwood School for Girls
4. Bishop Challoner School
5. Bromley High School
6. Bullers Wood School
7. Cator Park School for Girls
8. Charles Darwin School
9. Coopers School
10. Darrick Wood School
11. Darul Uloom London
12. Eltham College
13. Farringtons and Stratford House School
14. Hayes School
15. Holy Trinity College
16. Kelsey Park School
17. Kemnal Technology College
18. Langley Park School for Boys
19. Langley Park School for Girls
20. Newstead Wood School for Girls
21. The Priory School
22. Ravens Wood School
23. The Ravensbourne School
24. St John Rigby Catholic College
25. St Olave's and St Saviour's Grammar School

# Factfile

**LEA: Civic Centre, Stockwell Close, Bromley BR1 3UH** ☎ 020 8464 3333 🌐 www.bromley.gov.uk **Director of Education:** Ken Davis **Political control of council:** Conservative **Percentage of pupils from outside the borough:** 14.9 per cent **Percentage of pupils educated outside the borough:** 7.5 per cent **London league table positions (out of 32 boroughs):** 5th

## Profile

In terms of area, Bromley is London's largest borough and has a population of roughly 300,000. It incorporates Biggin Hill, Chislehurst, Orpington, Beckenham and Penge as well as Bromley itself. It is a suburban borough with the southern half remaining mostly open countryside. It is one of London's most affluent boroughs, although it still contains areas of social deprivation. These include the regeneration areas at Crystal Palace and the Crays, as well as Bromley Common and Mottingham. In fact, the Crays area is home to the largest settled traveller community in the UK. As a whole, the borough has one of the lowest unemployment rates in London. Beckenham has many business and finance institutions while Orpington town centre is a retailing hub, with Bromley town centre being a combination of the two.

The borough is served by mainline train services from Victoria, London Bridge, Waterloo and Charing Cross as well as to towns outside London such as Maidstone, Canterbury and Tunbridge Wells. The new Tramlink service from Croydon also stops at stations such as Beckenham Junction.

There is only one LEA-run school in the borough with the rest being foundation (formerly grant-maintained), voluntary aided or independent. There are a large number of independent schools. GCSE results are above the national average: 67 per cent of pupils in state schools achieved five or more A*–C grades in 2002 compared to the national figure of 51.6 per cent. A significantly large number of pupils in the borough continue into further education. The average point score for students entered for two or more A-levels for state schools was 233.6. For the purpose of assisting pupils' residential fieldwork, necessary for such subjects as biology and geography, the borough has developed a nationally recognized Field Studies Centre at Scadbury Park.

## Policy

Parents should contact the Bromley LEA for details of admissions to state schools. All schools, except St John Rigby Roman Catholic College, which will interview applicants to establish a family's religious commitment, will be allocating places first to siblings and then on the basis of proximity of the home to the school. Open days are in September/October and completed application forms should be sent to the schools by Mid-November 2003. Closing dates for selective schools are in October. Schools' individual details can be found in the Bromley LEA's brochure *Admission to Secondary School in Bromley*.

# Babington House School

**Grange Drive, Elmstead Lane, Chislehurst, Kent BR7 5ES** ☎ 020 8467 5537 📠 020 8295 1175 ✉ babingtonhouse@compuserve.com 🌐 www.babingtonhouse.com Miss D Odysseas BA (Hons), PGCE; Chair of Governors: TN Guise ⇄ Elmstead Wood **Buses:** 161, 314 Up to sixth form: Navy blue skirt, blue blouse, blue school tie **Demand:** No figures available but variable **Type:** Non-selective independent for 213 girls, aged 3 to 16 **Fees:** £2,327 per term **Submit application form:** No cut-off date **Motto:** *Semper fidelis* (Always Be True to Yourself) **School hours:** 8.40am–3.40pm (seniors) **Meals:** Not provided **Strong GCSE subjects:** All relatively strong **London league table position:** 78

## Profile

Babington House is an independent day school located in the suburban area of west Chislehurst. A Belgian lady, Madame Rossell, founded the school in 1887 in Eltham to foster arts for 'young ladies and small boys'. Hence, the school educates boys up to the age of 8 and girls up to 16. It has been administered as an educational trust since 1959 when it moved to Chislehurst. Its present listed building, known as Elmstead Grange, was built in 1876 in the Jacobean style. A new building project has been launched in order to provide new facilities for the school. Existing facilities include an all-weather pitch and a sports hall. There is good provision for IT with video conferencing facilities enabling pupils to link up with other countries. The school's diminutive size allows pupils' timetables to be individually designed. Girls usually study eight GCSEs with choices available including creative textiles and theatre arts. Elocution lessons are also offered with girls able to take LAMDA exams. In addition, pupils can also take ISTD exams for dance and Associated Board exams for singing. Upon entry to Babington House, girls join one of four houses and the older pupils are issued with the responsibility for younger children within the house framework. There are also many inter-house events.

### Admissions and intake

An application form is available from the school. Parents and child will then be interviewed. A date is arranged for the child to spend a session with their intended class, after which a place may be offered. Academic scholarships are available and a scholarship exam is held in the spring term.

### Achievement

In 2002, 100 per cent of pupils in Year 11 achieved five or more grades A*–C at GCSE. This result was well above both national and borough averages, and maintained the standard of the previous year. The school was ranked fifth place in the borough league table. In 1999, Ofsted commented on the 'excellent quality of teaching' and 'caring and committed staff'. The senior and junior schools were the winners of the Independent Schools Association National Drama Award in 1999, and the school has also received an Investors in People Award.

### Extra-curricular activities

Individual instrumental tuition is available at the school and there are many musical groups including an orchestra, a choir which is successful in regional competitions and a rock band. The school holds regular dramatic productions and organizes theatre visits. The Opera Club, in conjunction with The Royal Opera House, has created two original operas since 1994. Among the sports on offer are trampolining, football and netball. There are many inter-house sporting competitions including an annual swimming gala and sports day. There is an annual skiing trip for which girls can have preparatory dry-slope skiing lessons. There are also regular German and French exchanges.

## Baston School

**Baston Road, Hayes, Bromley BR2 7AB** 020 8462 1010 020 8462 0438 head@bastonschool.org.uk www.bastonschool.org.uk Mr CRC Wimble Hayes **Buses**: 146, 353 Tartan skirt, white blouse, dark V-neck pullover with school crest; available from the school shop; Sixth form: Smart clothes **Demand**: No figures available but variable **Type**: Non-selective independent for 148 girls, aged 2 to 18 **Fees** (per term): £2,780 **Submit application form**: No cut-off date **Motto**: *In minimis fidelis* (Be Faithful in Small Things) **School hours**: 8.40am–4pm (Mon, Tues, Thurs); 8.40am–3.30pm (Wed, Fri); homework clubs are available **Meals**: Hot and cold available **Strong GCSE subjects**: All relatively strong **London league table position**: 311

### Profile

Surrounded by 14 acres of playing fields, gardens and orchard, Baston School is situated on the outskirts of Bromley. The school was founded in 1933. It has expanded and improved its facilities to include libraries, computer, art and textile rooms and a pottery centre. In 1998, a new teaching and music block was opened. The extensive grounds include a large sports pavilion, an open-air heated swimming pool, three lacrosse pitches and four netball courts in winter, and seven tennis courts and an athletics track in summer. Girls have the opportunity to study speech and drama as an extra subject and work in small groups to prepare for the English Speaking Board Exams. The sixth form offers a wide range of arts, humanities and sciences. In addition to A-level subjects, pupils take a general studies course, which includes word processing, typewriting, 'understanding industry' and a 'pre-driver' course. The small school population means that class sizes are accordingly small. Pupils' progress is carefully monitored through a contact book, and reports are sent home at the end of every term. Four visiting teachers run a special needs unit to support those girls with dyslexia or other special needs. The school is organized into three houses for pastoral care, and girls set up house assemblies and competitions. Parents automatically join the parents' association, which organizes social events as well as fund-raising activities.

### Admissions and intake

Application forms are available from the school. Offers of places are conditional upon a test/exam, interview and recommendation from the pupil's present head.

## Achievement

In relation to similar schools in the borough, Baston has performed well at GCSE, though results have declined since 200; in 2002 60 per cent of pupils achieved five or more A*–C grades. This was still above the national average, and the school was placed 19th in Bromley. The average point score for students entered for two or more A-levels in 2000 was 15.6. This was up on 1999 and just below the borough average. This placed the school 14th in the borough. The small number of pupils in each year group means that the results are prone to fluctuation and in 2001 and 2002 no A-levels were taken.

## Extra-curricular activities

Visiting speakers are invited as part of the PSHE courses. From Year 10 onwards, girls are able to participate in the Duke of Edinburgh's Award scheme and are actively involved in the *Baston Banter*, the school newsletter. There are after-school homework clubs. The school arranges skiing trips and placements with foreign families. Other recent trips have included visits to the US, Mediterranean cruises and activity holidays in the South of France, Spain and Greece. Instrumental tuition is available for a variety of instruments and in solo singing. There are three choirs, two orchestras and woodwind and percussion groups. There is also a thriving drama club and productions are regularly staged. Sporting activities include lacrosse, synchronized swimming and tennis.

# Beaverwood School for Girls

**Beaverwood Road, Chislehurst, Kent BR7 6HE** 020 8300 3156 020 8300 3251 info@beaverwood.bromley.sch.uk www.beaverwood.bromley.sch.uk Mrs KJ Raven; Chair of Governors: Mr David Cooper Chislehurst, Sidcup **Buses**: R3, 51, 227, 338 Tartan skirt, blue blouse, navy pullover with school crest; Sixth form: Smart dress **Demand**: 726 applications for 224 places in 2001/2 **Type**: Comprehensive foundation school for 1237 girls, aged 11 to 18 **Submit application form**: Mid-November 2003 **Motto**: *Altiora sequamur* (Reach for the Heights) **School hours**: 8.30am–3.15pm; homework clubs are available **Meals**: Hot and cold available **Strong GCSE subjects**: All relatively strong **London league table position**: 207

## Profile

A popular and expanding school, Beaverwood is situated in a semi-rural setting on the borders of Chislehurst and Sidcup. Established in 1896 as Sidcup High School, the school developed into Chislehurst and Sidcup County Grammar School for Girls and became all-ability in 1982. Recent additions to the main 1930s building include a science and refurbished music block, modern foreign languages block and an all-purpose dining hall. The learning resources centre contains computers, video machines, interactive video, teletext and listening equipment. There are also fully equipped drama and music suites, a traditional gymnasium, modern sports hall and spacious outdoor facilities. A choice of French, German, and Spanish is on offer at GCSE. The school also offers a wide range of A-levels including media studies, theatre studies and sociology as well as GNVQs in business and health and social care. Girls can take a Community Sports Leadership Award. Pupils are placed in one of three houses and have the opportunity to become a prefect, a librarian, join the school council, run a school club and assist younger pupils. All parents are members of the parents' and friends' association, which organizes fund-raising events. Communication with parents is made through contact books, newsletters and written reports.

## Admissions and intake

Application forms are available from the school. The entrance criteria, in order of priority, are: siblings (i.e. if a sister, half sister or step-sister is living with the child and is currently being educated at the school); and proximity, measured in a straight line from the school to the home address. A significant number of pupils travel from Greenwich and Bexley. Due to the number of selective grammar schools in the area, the majority of pupils are of average ability on entry.

## Achievement

In 2002, 64 per cent of pupils achieved five or more grades A*–C at GCSE, above with the borough average, and Beaverwood was 15th in the borough. This was up on 55 per cent in 2001. The average point score for students entered for two or more A-levels in 2002 was 191.7, below the borough average, placing the school 17th in the borough. In 1997, Ofsted stated: 'The school has high expectations of pupils, their achievements and their behaviour and makes good provision for developing these. Pupils' attitudes to learning are overwhelmingly positive. The school is an orderly and friendly place in which to learn with very good relationships between pupils and teachers.' Pupils with special needs were said to make 'sound progress'.

## Extra-curricular activities

Beaverwood won the Education Extra Distinction Award for Outstanding Extra-Curricular Activities in 1999. Among those activities on offer are badminton, aerobics, running, trampolining, language clubs, engineering, orchestras, choirs, homework clubs and debating clubs. School events include dance, music and drama productions, technology and public-speaking competitions and sports trips. Recent trips abroad were to Germany, Belgium, Israel, France, Austria and Spain. There is also a popular Duke of Edinburgh's Award scheme. Pupils raise funds for charities in the sixth form.

# Bishop Challoner School

**228 Bromley Road, Shortlands, Bromley BR2 0BS** ☎ 020 8460 3546 📠 020 8466 8885 ✉ office@bishopchallonerschool.com 🌐 www.bishopchallonerschool.com J A de Waal; Chair of Governors: Rev Canon J Madden ⇌ Shortlands, Ravensbourne **Buses**: 227, 358, 367, 726 Navy blue blazer with badge, light blue blouse or shirt, charcoal grey trousers or navy skirt, navy striped school tie; Sixth form: Smart business attire **Demand**: No figures available but 40 places (max) regularly oversubscribed **Type**: Non-selective independent for 421 mixed pupils, aged 2 to 18 **Fees**: £1,925 per term **Submit application form**: February 2004 **Motto**: *Quantum potes tantum aude* (Do the Best of Your Ability) **School hours**: 8.50am–3.35pm **Meals**: Hot and cold available **Strong GCSE subject**: English **London league table position**: 101

## Profile

Bishop Challoner is a small Catholic school owned by the Trustees of the Roman Catholic Archdiocese of Southwark. The Archbishop of Southwark is the principal trustee and president of the school. It was founded in 1950, in the historic building known as Shortlands House. Several additions to the original building include an art block and gymnasium built during the 1960s. The usual Key Stage 3 curriculum is followed, along with lessons in Latin. All pupils take RE at GCSE, with an option to take Latin. The sixth form is a popular choice for Year 11 pupils and offers a wide range of A-levels. Sixth-formers run the house system, organize the school council and run the tuck shop. The visiting chaplain is available for the pastoral care of both Catholic and non-Catholic pupils. There is a school chapel and Mass is celebrated every week. With only 30 pupils in Year 11, class sizes are small, allowing pupils to receive individual attention. Parents are kept informed of their child's progress via quarterly progress cards and twice-yearly full written reports. There is widespread support for the PTA, which has raised funds for the purchase of a new school minibus, musical instruments, computers and the refurbishment of the library. There is a coordinator for pupils with special needs.

## Admissions and intake

Application forms are available from the school, to be completed and returned as early as possible before the date of proposed entry, along with a £25 registration fee. An interview will then be arranged, and the candidate will be required to sit an entrance exam (held in November and March). Scholarships are available to academically able pupils. The intake is broadly Catholic, although children of all faiths are welcomed.

## Achievement

In 2002, 89 per cent of pupils achieved five or more grades A*–C, a significant rise from 46 per cent in 2001. This was well above the national and borough averages and the school was ranked seventh in the borough. The average point score for pupils entered for two or more A-levels was 266, placing the school ninth in the borough. The small number of pupils in each year means that the results are prone to fluctuation.

## Extra-curricular activities

Individual tuition on a variety of musical instruments is available from visiting music teachers. The school hosts many concerts and theatrical productions. Sports available include rugby, gymnastics, athletics, swimming and fencing. Past pupils have gone on to represent the borough, county and country at fencing. Recent visits abroad have included trips to Israel, Turkey, Spain and Italy. There are many after-school clubs, notably a homework club and a successful chess club. Pupils are involved in fund-raising for local charities.

# Bromley High School

**Blackbrook Lane, Bickley, Bromley BR1 2TW** 020 8468 7981 020 8295 1062 bhs@bro.gdst.net www.gdst.net/bromleyhigh Mrs L Duggleby; Chair of Governors: Mr B Dance Bickley, Chislehurst **Buses:** 208; coaches organized by parents run from Beckenham, Hayes and Shortlands Up to sixth form: Grey skirt, white shirt, maroon jumper **Demand:** No figures available but variable demand for 108 places **Type:** Selective independent girls' day school trust for 899 girls, aged 4 to 18 **Fees:** £2,385 per term **Submit application form:** No cut-off date **Motto:** *Fides et opera* (Loyalty and Work) **School hours:** 8.35am–3.45pm; homework clubs are available **Meals:** Hot and cold available **Strong GCSE subjects:** All relatively strong **London league table position:** 22

## Profile

Bromley High is among the highest achieving schools in the borough. It is housed in modern attractive buildings, with recent improvements including a new arts studio and a drama studio. The school is set in 24 acres of parkland and has excellent sporting facilities such as an athletics track, three hockey pitches, one of which is all-weather, and eight netball courts, as well as a gymnasium, sports hall and indoor swimming pool. A-level subjects include German, French, Spanish, government and politics, economics, business studies and music, with a music technology option which makes use of the school's high-tech software. Work experience in France or Germany can be organized through the school. There is a school council, a PTA and a coordinator for pupils with special needs.

## Admissions and intake

Application forms are available from the school. Admission is determined by an entrance exam and an interview. Girls will first be interviewed and must then take the exam in mid-January. There is a £40 registration fee. Scholarships are available for those applicants with academic merit.

## Achievement

Bromley High achieves consistently excellent results. In 2002, 100 per cent of girls achieved five or more A*–C grades at GCSE, with an average point score of 57, placing the school second in the borough. This repeated the 100 per cent success of 1999, 2000 and 2001, and results have consistently reached between 97 or 100 per cent since 1997. The average point score for students entered for two or more A-levels was 350.3, well above the national average of 254.5, placing the school fourth in the borough. The school is also very successful at sport, with the under-12s netball team recently becoming Kent Champions. The tennis team won the Plate Competition in the national Aberdare Cup competition, and out of over 46,000 candidates, a pupil at Bromley High gained the highest mark in PE at GCSE. At the Young Enterprise Bromley borough finals, a Bromley High pupil was selected as the Young Achiever of the Year.

## Extra-curricular activities

A huge number of activities is available. Individual instrumental tuition is on offer from the harp to the piano. There are musical groups and recent concerts have been held at Southwark Cathedral and St-Martin-in-the-Fields. Tours are organized each year to countries such as Australia, South Africa, Belgium and Italy. There was also a World Challenge expedition to Ecuador. Annual productions are staged by both the drama and music departments. There is also a popular annual art exhibition, which included a fashion show in 2000. Another production held each year is the annual dance production. More unusual sports available include archery, fencing, health-related fitness, rowing, self-defence, short tennis and skiing. The school regularly holds a series of free, public lectures, known as the Oakdene Lectures. Speakers at these lectures have included Virginia Bottomley and David Helfand, American Visiting Professor of Astronomy at Cambridge. Exchanges are arranged with schools in Germany, France and Spain. There are after-school homework clubs.

# Bullers Wood School

**St Nicolas Lane, Logs Hill, Chislehurst, Kent BR7 5LJ** 020 8467 2280 020 8295 1425 office@bullerswood.bromley.sch.uk www.bullerswood.bromley.sch.uk Ms Kathleen Clarke MA, FRSA; Chair of Governors: Mrs S Ladd Elmstead Woods, Chislehurst **Buses:** 162, 269 ; Up to sixth form: Tartan kilt, cream blouse, navy jumper or cardigan with the school rose emblem **Demand:** 740 applications for 220 places in 2001/2 **Type:** Comprehensive Language College foundation school for 1253 girls (mixed in sixth form), aged 11 to

18 **Submit application form**: Mid-November 2003 **Motto**: Strive to Your Utmost **School hours**: 8.50am–3.35pm; homework clubs are available **Meals**: Hot and cold available **Strong GCSE subjects**: Art and design, English, French, German, history **London league table position**: 105

## Profile

In a borough with many independent and selective schools Bullers Wood performs extremely well. It has had Language College status since 1996. The school consists of purpose-built modern language, science and technology blocks together with Bullers Wood House, a Victorian mansion, and Inglewood House, an Edwardian house. The buildings are set in extensive, well-landscaped grounds. In 1999, Ofsted praised the school's 'unusually broad' curriculum, with facilities for learning French, German, Spanish, Italian and Japanese. Alongside the traditional A-levels, a range of vocational courses are offered, including a national diploma in catering, for which the accommodation is 'near professional standard' (Ofsted) with its own restaurant. Several networked computer suites cater for the computing needs of pupils. Bullers Wood has strong European ties, with visits and exchanges organized throughout the year. Year 12 pupils are able to take part in work experience abroad and the school has its own house, *La Serronnerie* in Normandy, where pupils have residential stays during their school career. There is an active parents' association.

## Admissions and intake

Application forms are available from the school. The entrance criteria, in order of priority, are: siblings (i.e. a sister or brother in the sixth form who will be in attendance at Bullers Wood in the September of entry or has attended the school within the last five years); and proximity, measured in a straight line from the school to the home address.

## Achievement

In 2002, 84 per cent of pupils achieved five or more grades A*–C at GCSE. This was well above the national average, and the school was ranked eighth in the borough. The average point score for pupils entered for two or more A-levels was 341.2, again well above the national average, placing the school fifth in the borough. Ofsted commented that the school 'achieves excellent examination results and high standards in virtually all subjects'. Teaching was described as 'very good' with a 'significant proportion excellent'. The school was described as a 'centre of excellence for languages'. GCSE results were 'very high compared with schools with pupils from similar backgrounds'. Results overall have seen a steady improvement over the past few years. Ofsted also noted a high success rate in vocational qualifications, with 'many students gaining merits and distinctions', notably in hospitality, catering and photography. Pupils with special needs were said to make 'good or very good progress'. Ofsted found pupils' behaviour 'very good' with 'very good attitudes to learning'.

## Extra-curricular activities

There are excellent provisions available for music, drama and sport. Pupils are encouraged to become involved in helping the community, with many taking part in fund-raising activities. Pupils can also participate in Young Enterprise and the Duke of Edinburgh's Award scheme. There are trips both at home and abroad.

# Cator Park School for Girls

**Lennard Road, Beckenham, Kent BR3 1QR** ☎ 020 8778 5917 📠 020 8778 2043 ⓔ office@catorpark.kent.sch.uk 🌐 www.catorpark.kent.sch.uk Mrs M Davies BA (Hons); Chair of Governors: Mr M Blazey ⇌ New Beckenham, Kent House **Buses**: 351, 352 Up to sixth form: Red or blue pullover with school crest, white blouse, dark skirt **Demand**: 387 applications for 210 places in 2001/2 **Type**: Community comprehensive for 1233 girls, aged 11 to 18 **Submit application form**: Mid-November 2003 **Mission statement**: We are committed to providing a caring, well-disciplined environment where girls, whatever their ability, learn to enjoy working hard in order to fulfil their potential. **School hours**: 9.25am–3.30m; homework clubs are available **Meals**: Hot and cold available **Strong GCSE subjects**: Modern languages **London league table position**: 444

## Profile

Cator Park School is on the borders of Beckenham and Penge, one of the least prosperous areas of Bromley. A new block has been built, providing 16 new classrooms for maths and humanities, a special educational needs suite and a large area for the sixth form. There is a large library, a computer design area, several computer network rooms, a purpose-built theatre, a pottery room, a fully equipped darkroom and a media education studio. Girls are placed in one of eight houses on entry, and many activities are organized on a house basis. The school is notable for teaching five foreign languages – French, Spanish, Italian, German and Russian – through to A-level. Extension classes are provided for more able pupils. The sixth form offers GNVQs in art and design, business, health and social care, hospitality and catering, IT and leisure and tourism, along with a wide range of A-levels. Pupils can become a form representative on the school council or a prefect. There is a parent-teacher association.

### Admissions and intake

Application forms are available from the school. The entrance criteria, in order of priority, are: siblings (i.e. a sister at the school at the beginning of the first term); and proximity, measured in a straight line from the school to the home address. Overall ability of the intake is below average.

### Achievement

Following their inspection in 1999, Ofsted stated: 'The GCSE results overall were well above those of similar schools, though still below the national average.' In 2002, 31 per cent of pupils achieved five or more grades A*–C, consistent with the previous two years. The school was placed 24th in the borough. The average point score for pupils entered for two or more A-levels was 189.3, below the borough average. This placed the school 18th in the borough. Progress in English was said by Ofsted to be 'good'. The school is also strong in design and technology. However, 'attainment and progress in science and maths are not as good as in English'. Overall, 92 per cent of the teaching was judged 'satisfactory or better' with examples of very good teaching in English, history, RE, maths, art, science, geography, IT, design and technology, PE, Russian and careers. The provision for special educational needs was also said to be good.

### Extra-curricular activities

Girls have the opportunity to take part in the Youth Award scheme as part of their 'learning for life'. The pastoral programme receives visiting speakers. There are a number of school journeys, including recent skiing trips, watersports holidays, a Russian exchange and a world challenge visit to Venezuela. Most subject areas offer lunchtime or after-school clubs, including homework clubs, a variety of music groups and choirs, drama, computing and gardening.

## Charles Darwin School

**Jail Lane, Biggin Hill, Westerham, Kent TN16 3AU** ☎ 01959 574043 📠 01959 540036 ✉ enquiries@cdarwin.com 🌐 www.cdarwin.com Mr Robert Higgins MA; Chair of Governors: Mr MP Sharp Bus from Bromley South **Buses**: 320 Up to sixth form: Blue blazer, grey trousers or navy skirt, white shirt or blouse, school tie **Demand**: 480 applications for 224 places in 2001/2 **Type**: Comprehensive foundation school for 1196 mixed pupils, aged 11 to 18 **Submit application form**: Mid-November 2003 **School hours**: Years 7 to 9: 8.25am–2.55pm (Mon), 8.25am–2.45pm (Tues), 8.25am–3.30pm (Wed), 8.25am–2.30pm (Thurs–Fri); Year 10: 8.25am–3.10pm (Mon), 8.25am–2.30pm (Tues, Fri), 8.25am–3.30pm (Wed–Thurs) **Meals**: Hot and cold available **Strong GCSE subjects**: Business studies, drama, music **London league table position**: 279

### Profile

Founded in 1973, Charles Darwin was the first ever purpose-built comprehensive in Bromley. Located near the border with Surrey, it has a quiet country setting. The school is currently undergoing expansion; a new teaching block is due to be followed by a new science and technology wing and new music and drama development. The school has a purpose-built sports hall and an all-weather pitch. Provision for IT is particularly good, with industry-standard equipment providing Internet access at school and, for those pupils with computers, at home. Pupils also have their own e-mail accounts and there are video conferencing facilities. A wide range of GCSEs are on offer at Key Stage 4, including sports science and graphic products, as well as GNVQs in leisure and tourism, and health and social care. The sixth form offers both A-levels and GNVQs. Pupils are able to become prefects and to take part in the school council. There is a parent-teacher association.

### Admissions and intake

Application forms are available from the school. The entrance criteria, in order of priority, are: siblings (i.e. those who have a brother or sister at the school); and proximity, measured in a straight line from the school to the home address.

### Achievement

In 2002, 58 per cent of pupils gained five or more grades A*–C at GCSE. This was below the borough average and the school was ranked 17th in the borough. The average point score for pupils entered for two or more A-levels was 220.3, placing the school 17th in Bromley. Ofsted inspected the school in 1997 and stated: 'The quality of teaching is a particular strength with 95 per cent of lessons judged as satisfactory or better...The ethos of the school reflects its stated commitment to raising pupil achievement, providing a good learning environment and fostering good relationships...Pupils, parents, staff and governors all demonstrate a firm commitment to the work of the school.' When pupils' ability on intake is taken into account the report said 'the majority of pupils make sound progress'. High levels of attainment were achieved in music, drama and business studies. Attainment was also said to be well above average for pupils taking vocational qualifications. 'Careful attention' was given to pupils with special needs.

### Extra-curricular activities

There is a wide range of sport, music and drama activities on offer. A number of visits to concerts, performances, exhibitions and the theatre within the UK are organized, as well as regular residential visits to many European countries. The sixth form has a community service programme.

## Coopers School

**Hawkwood Lane, Chislehurst, Kent BR7 5PS** 020 8467 3263 020 8295 0342 cwiles@btconnect.com www.coopers.bromley.sch.uk Mr Robert Dilley BA (Hons); Chair of Governors: Mrs Ros Allen Chislehurst **Buses**: 61, 161, 162, 269, 638 Blue blazer, trousers or skirt, white shirt or blue checked blouse, school tie; Sixth form: Smart casual wear **Demand**: 1132 applications for 258 places in 2001/2 **Type**: Comprehensive foundation school Technology College for 1551 mixed pupils, aged 11 to 18 **Submit application form**: Mid-November 2003 **Motto**: *Haec tibi consecro* (Dedicating These Things to You) **School hours**: 8.30am–3.30pm; homework clubs are available **Meals**: Hot and cold available **Strong GCSE subjects**: English, maths, sciences **London league table position**: 265

### Profile

Coopers School is located near London's green belt on an attractive and well-maintained site. A major building programme has recently been completed at the school, providing new facilities for science and technology. It also has a new learning and information centre, which provides excellent facilities, including a large electronic reference library. Coopers shares its site with the Marjorie McClure School, a special school for pupils with physical disabilities, and some of its pupils attend lessons at Coopers. The school has a large, growing sixth form which offers a range of A-levels and advanced and intermediate GNVQs, as well as other vocational qualifications. Optional courses include computer-aided design, sports leadership award, foreign languages, community service and pre-driving skills. The majority of pupils go on to higher education. For the remainder, the school offers a two-day 'preparation for employment' course. Older pupils are able to become prefects and there is a school council. There is a PTA.

### Admissions and intake

Application forms are available from the school. The entrance criteria, in order of priority, are: siblings (i.e. a brother or sister who attends or has attended the school); and proximity, measured in a straight line, from home to school.

### Achievement

In 2002, 53 per cent of pupils achieved five or more grades A*–C at GCSE. This was above the national average but slightly down on 55 per cent in 2001. The school was placed 16th in the borough league table. The average point score for pupils entered for two or more A-levels was 234.5, above the borough average but below the national average. This placed Coopers 16th in the borough. Ofsted visited the school in 1997 and stated: 'Coopers is a good school with many strengths including a commitment to innovative development and clear vision for the future'. It praised the ethos of the school and the staff, commenting that 'the quality of teaching is satisfactory or better in 96 per cent of lessons and good in more than two-thirds'. Pupils were said to be both 'courteous' and 'friendly'. Those pupils with special educational needs were said to make 'effective progress' throughout the school. A 'major strength' was said to be the 'attainment of pupils in extra-curricular drama and music'.

### Extra-curricular activities

Coopers has a school choir and other musical groups, regular musical and dramatic productions and a great range of sports. Pupils are also able to participate in the Duke of Edinburgh's Award scheme. There are a number of theatre trips and many opportunities for overseas travel. Pupils are active in charity work and entertain residents at a local elderly people's home, as well as pupils from the Marjorie McClure special school. There are after-school homework clubs.

## Darrick Wood School

**Lovibonds Avenue, Orpington, Kent BR6 8ER** 01689 850271 01689 857257 office@darrick-wood.bromley.sch.uk www.darrick-wood.bromley.sch.uk Mr B Rhymaun B.Sc, MA; Chair of Governors: Mr M Hewitt Orpington **Buses**: 208 Brown blazers, trousers, yellow shirt, brown tie (boys); brown pullover with school crest, brown skirt, yellow blouse (girls); Sixth form: Smart dress **Demand**: 800+ applications for 240 places in 2001/2 **Type**: Comprehensive foundation school for 1573 mixed pupils, aged 11 to 18 **Submit application form**: Mid-November 2003 **Mission statement**: Darrick Wood School seeks to provide the highest quality of teaching and learning. **School hours**: 8.35am–3.20pm; homework clubs are available **Meals**: Hot and cold available **Strong GCSE subjects**: Business, history, IT **London league table position**: 181

### Profile

Darrick Wood is housed in modern buildings on an attractive site, surrounded by playing fields and tennis courts. A huge £6.7 million building project was completed in March 1996 and includes an impressive assembly hall and dance studio. In June 1998, an all-weather pitch was added to the grounds. The school has five IT rooms, a flexible learning room, a business and office technology room fully fitted with modern computer equipment, a sound recording studio and a computer network that extends to every main teaching room. Darrick Wood contains a special unit for pupils whose hearing is impaired. These pupils are full members of the school but are taught many lessons by specialist teachers of the deaf. The school has a strong tradition of performing arts; dance, drama and music can be studied to GCSE and in the sixth form. Vocational GNVQs are offered in addition to A-levels. Sixth-formers can be active in school life as prefects and in the sixth form council, and there is a parent-teacher association.

### Admissions and intake

Application forms are available from the school. The entrance criteria, in order of priority, are: siblings (i.e. an elder brother or sister in attendance at the school in the September of entry); and proximity, measured in a straight line, from home to school.

### Achievement

Darrick Wood is a good school and the results it achieves reflect this, especially when the number of selective schools in its vicinity is taken into account. In 2000, Ofsted also noted that: 'Darrick Wood is a well led school which within a well planned curriculum and good teaching leads to very high standards and very good exam results'. In 2002, 66 per cent of pupils achieved five or more grades A*–C at GCSE. This was above average for the borough and up on 63 per cent in 2001. The school came 12th in the borough. The average point score for pupils entered for two or more A-levels was 240.5, above the borough but below the national average, placing the school 11th in the borough.

### Extra-curricular activities

The PE department offers the usual school sports as well as weight training, volleyball, swimming, dry-slope skiing and trampolining. The school has had many sporting successes at county and national level. Music activities include orchestras, a jazz band and choirs, and among the many clubs are dance, drama, science, animals, chess and Christian Union. Pupils are also involved with the production of a school newspaper. Several major music, dance and drama productions are held annually, as well as a music festival and drama festival. Out of school visits include geography and biology field trips as well as trips abroad.

## Darul Uloom London

**Foxbury Avenue, Chislehurst, Kent BR7 6SD** 020 8295 0637 020 8467 0655 Mr MM Musa (principal) Chislehurst, Sidcup **Buses**: 160, 269 **Demand**: No figures available **Type**: Selective independent for 132 boys, aged 10 to 19 **Fees**: £1,800 per year (variable) **Submit application form**: No cut-off date **Mission statement**: To familiarize the young generation with the teaching of The Holy Qur'an and Sunnah so that they can practice Islam and serve the 'Deen' of 'Allah' **School hours**: 8am–4.30pm (winter), 8.30am–5pm (summer) **Meals**: Hot and cold available **Strong GCSE subjects**: Information not available **London league table position**: 504

## Profile

Darul Uloom is a full-time residential school situated in Chislehurst, Kent. It is housed in modern rectangular buildings. One of the aims of the institution is to help children develop an Islamic identity. Accordingly, Darul Uloom offers extensive Islamic studies as well as the optional languages of Arabic, Urdu and Bengali. The national curriculum subjects of English, maths, science, geography, IT, business studies and accounts are also offered up to GCSE level. A-levels are not offered. There is a parent-teacher association.

## Admissions and intake

The school should be contacted with regard to any applications. The intake is solely Islamic.

## Achievement

The school emphasizes the study of Islam and pupils do not sit exams in the standard way. As such, with the exception of 2001, no pupil has gained five or more grades A*–C for the past four years. A high proportion of pupils do not achieve any passes at GCSE as they are not entered for them, which further explains the school's position in the London league table.

## Extra-curricular activities

Pupils participate in the normal range of sports and there are local trips.

# Eltham College

**Grove Park Road, Mottingham, London SE9 4QF** 020 8857 1455 020 8857 1913 mail@eltham-college.org.uk www.eltham-college.org.uk Paul Henderson; Chair of Governors: Mr D Norris Mottingham Station, Grove Park **Buses**: 124, 126, 161; school bus services from Blackheath, Orpington and Beckenham Dark blazer, white shirt, dark trousers, school tie **Demand**: c. 35 places available for external candidates at 11+; waiting list for entry at 13+ **Type**: Selective independent for 778 boys (mixed in sixth form), aged 7 to 18 **Fees**: £2,900 per term (day); boarders pay an extra £3,080 **Submit application form**: Early January 2004 **Motto**: *Gloria filiorum patres* (The Fathers Are the Glory of the Sons) **School hours**: 8.30am–3.50pm **Meals**: Hot and cold available **Strong GCSE subjects**: Drama, English, modern languages **London league table position**: 30

## Profile

Eltham College is situated on a 34-acre site and housed in attractive buildings centred on an 18th-century mansion. There is boarding provision for a small number of boys in Turberville House. The college's Antony Barnard Hall is a modern, in-the-round theatre with a high-quality sound system and professional computerized lighting. In January 2000, the Mervyn Peake library opened, housing books and computer equipment. Sports facilities include a swimming pool, galleried sports hall and physiotherapy clinic based in the Eric Lidell Sports Centre. The college has been designated a Centre of Excellence for Cricket. Latin and scripture are offered at GCSE and a wide range of A-level subjects are also available. Pupils in the lower sixth follow a life skills course and in the upper sixth, they take a general studies course. The college has a house system, and 20 members of the upper sixth are appointed prefects each year. There is an active PTA as well as The Old Elthamians. Former pupils include the author Mervyn Peake, Olympic gold medallist Eric Lidell and Scottish rugby captain Leslie Gracie.

## Admissions and intake

Pupils are admitted at 11+, 13+ and 16+. Registration for entry can be made at any time. The registration form, available from the school, should be completed and returned along with a £60 fee. Candidates must sit several exams that are held in January (February for the sixth form), as well as undergo an interview. Scholarships are available to more able applicants.

## Achievement

2002 was a highly successful year for Eltham College, with 99 per cent of pupils gaining an A*–C grade at GCSE, a dip of only one per cent on 2001. The school's average GCSE point score was 55.9, which placed it fourth in the borough league table. The average point score for pupils taking two or more A-levels in 2002 was 404.6, above the borough and national averages. This placed the college first in the borough. Each year approximately 15 per cent of sixth-form leavers at Eltham College go on to study at either Oxford or Cambridge universities.

## Extra-curricular activities

Eltham College holds a number of theatrical productions. There is individual tuition in musical instruments, including masterclasses at the highest levels, and a wide range of musical groups. The best musicians are invited to join the Eltham College Community Orchestra, which performs under the direction of distinguished guest conductors and regularly tours abroad. Rugby and cricket are the major sports, with the U14 cricket team winning the Kent Cup. The College Meeting is the college's pre-eminent society and arranges guest speakers to visit, including university professors and celebrities. There is also a successful debating society, whose team reached the London finals of the Observer Mace Debating Competition. The school takes part in exchanges with 11 schools in Europe and beyond.

# Farringtons and Stratford House School

**Perry Street, Chislehurst, Kent BR7 6LR** 020 8467 0256 020 8467 5442 head@farringtons.kent.sch.uk www.farringtons.org.uk Mrs CE James MA; Chair of Governors: Mr BC Drury MA Chislehurst **Buses:** 160, 269 Green tartan skirt, green striped blouse, green school pullover; Sixth form: Appropriate dress **Demand:** No figures available but regularly oversubscribed **Type:** Non-selective independent for 499 girls, aged 2 to 18 **Fees** (per term): £2,580 (day), £4,620 (boarder) **Submit application form:** January 2004 **Motto:** *Posside sapientiam* (To Have Wisdom) **School hours:** 8.30am–4.05pm; homework clubs are available **Meals:** Hot and cold available **Strong GCSE subjects:** All relatively strong **London league table position:** 169

## Profile

Farringtons and Stratford House is a medium-sized day and boarding school for girls. It is situated on an attractive 25-acre site in a Kent village on the outskirts of the borough. The school has a Methodist tradition and its stated aim is 'to provide the best in education for every pupil here within a happy, safe, supportive Christian environment'. The school is housed in pleasant buildings with modern facilities, which are continually updated and which include a new computer suite, an extensive sports hall with dance studio and weights room, and a new technology centre. The school also has its own chapel. The grounds include tennis courts and an open-air swimming pool. The school's relatively small size allows it to limit class sizes accordingly. The usual range of GCSEs are on offer, with modern languages options of French, German and Spanish. The sixth form has its own common room, games room, kitchen and library. Girls are able to take A-levels and GNVQs. Sixth-formers can become prefects, sit on the school council or become the head of one of the three houses. Teachers provide supervised study sessions after school. There is a coordinator for pupils with special needs and a parent-teacher association.

## Admissions and intake

Application forms are available from the school and must be returned along with a £50 registration fee. Girls must sit an entrance exam which is held each January before the September of entry. Academic scholarships are awarded on the basis of this exam. Music scholarships are also available.

## Achievement

In 2002, 69 per cent of pupils gained five or more grades A*–C at GCSE. This was a rise on 62 per cent in 2001 and above the borough and national averages. The average point score was 40.6 and the school was placed 11th in the borough. Small year groups mean that results tend to fluctuate. The average point score for pupils taking two or more A-levels was 257.6, above both the borough and national averages. This placed the school 10th in the borough league table. Over 90 per cent of sixth-form leavers go on to some form of higher education.

## Extra-curricular activities

Visiting music teachers enable girls to learn various musical instruments and the school's two choirs, orchestra and concert band regularly take part in local festivals and competitions. Drama is a strong feature of the school, with recent annual productions of *The Little Shop of Horrors* and *My Fair Lady*. It is also possible for girls to take LAMDA exams. There are regular supervised outings to the theatre, cinema, ice-rink and museums. Trips abroad have included lacrosse tours of the US, annual skiing trips to the Alps and language trips to Germany, France and Spain. Other activities available include homework clubs, a chess club, a debating club, trampolining, fencing and photography. Pupils raise funds for local charities.

# Hayes School

**West Common Road, Hayes, Bromley Kent BR2 7DB** 020 8462 2767 020 8462 0329 info@hayes.kent.sch.uk www.hayes.demon.co.uk Mr John Catmull B.Sc; Chair of Governors: Mrs B Hoppé Hayes **Buses**: 119, 138, 146, 314, 353 Dark navy blue school blazer; white shirt or blue striped blouse, dark trousers or navy blue skirt, dark school tie; Sixth form: Office attire **Demand**: 1015 applications for 240 places in 2001/2 **Type**: Comprehensive foundation school for 1367 mixed pupils, aged 11 to 18 **Submit application form**: Mid-November 2003 **Motto**: Always to Excel and to Be Distinguished from Others **School hours**: 8.30am–3.20pm; homework clubs are available **Meals**: Hot and cold available **Strong GCSE subjects**: Sciences **London league table position**: 205

## Profile

Hayes is a popular school with a reputation for high standards and academic success. The main school building is an imposing red-brick Victorian Gothic-style mansion. The school was extended in 1973 and a major rebuilding programme has begun due to the high demand for places. It has an attractive learning resources centre and there are excellent computer facilities. All pupils study two modern languages in the first three years and are able to take GCSEs in both. Most pupils carry on into the sixth form. A wide range of A-levels are on offer, including psychology and philosophy and ethics, as well as intermediate and advanced level GNVQs. Prefects, chosen from the sixth form, play an important role in the school. There is also a school council. The parent-teacher association is very active, organizing social events and raising considerable funds. There is provision for pupils with special needs.

## Admissions and intake

Application forms are available from the school. The entrance criteria, in order of priority, are: siblings (i.e. a brother or sister at the school; or an older brother or sister who has completed their compulsory secondary education at the school); and proximity, measured in a straight line, from home to school. The ability of pupils is above average on entry.

## Achievement

In 2002, 62 per cent of pupils achieved five or more grades A*–C at GCSE, above the borough average. The average point score was 39, placing the school 14th in the borough. Results over recent years have remained consistently good. The average point score for students entered for two or more A-levels was 237.9. This was above the borough but below the national average, placing the school 13th in the borough league table. In 1997, Ofsted commented: 'This is a good school with many strong features. There is a very positive ethos and most pupils demonstrate very good attitudes towards their learning'. Teaching was also praised: 'Across all subjects there are examples of good or very good teaching. However, there is a consistently high standard of teaching to be found in English, maths, PE and art lessons'.

## Extra-curricular activities

A wide range of sports is available including athletics, fencing, golf, hockey, chess, rugby, squash and softball. There are also after-school homework clubs. There is an Air Training Corps Squadron and a Duke of Edinburgh's Award scheme. School teams have recently been county champions in basketball at six age levels. Cricket and rounders teams have also been Bromley champions. Interested pupils have also worked with professional local artists. There is a school choir and orchestra, and concert tours are often made to European countries. Trips abroad include language trips to France, Germany and Spain, skiing in the Alps and a watersports week in France.

# Holy Trinity College

**81 Plaistow Lane, Bromley BR1 3LL** 020 8313 0399 (head), 020 8313 8106 (admissions) 020 8466 0151 info@htc-bromley.co.uk www.holytrinitycollegebromley.co.uk Mrs Janet Dunn BD (Hons) PGCE; Chair of Governors: Mrs S Clarke Sundridge Park **Buses**: 314 White blouse, grey skirt, school tie; Sixth form: Black blazer, black skirt, white blouse, red school tie **Demand**: No figures available but oversubscribed **Type**: Non-selective independent for 526 girls, aged 2 to 18 **Fees**: £2,288–£2,358 per term **Submit application form**: By end of Autumn term 2003 **Motto**: *Acceuil et écoute* (Welcome and Listen) **School hours**: 8.40am–3.40pm; homework clubs are available **Meals**: Hot and cold available **Strong GCSE subjects**: All relatively strong **London league table position**: 96

## Profile

Holy Trinity College is a successful independent day school for girls, founded in 1888 by French Trinitarians. It is a member of the worldwide Trinitarian community and prides itself on its 'caring Christian ethos'. It is housed in a grade II listed building set in 15 acres of gardens and parkland, with playing fields extending back to a wooded area. The building has been developed and extended, and the excellent facilities include an extensive computer network throughout the school, a drama studio, a pottery kiln, a heated outdoor pool, an all-weather hockey pitch and six tennis courts. The sixth form has its own common room with a kitchen. At GCSE, French and German are the main foreign languages on offer. The choice of A-levels includes psychology, computer studies and theatre studies. Mock interviews are held to help pupils gain places at university. Sixth-formers can become prefects or run clubs. Sixth-formers are also involved with community service including the holding of a regular Christmas party for the local elderly community. There is a house system to aid pastoral care and a parent-teacher association.

## Admissions and intake

The college welcomes pupils from all faiths and cultures who are sympathetic to its Christian ethos. Application forms are available from the school. Pupils wishing to enter at 11+ must sit an entrance exam held in January. Scholarships and bursaries are available to more academically able girls, as well as to those who are gifted musically. Music scholarship auditions are also held in January.

## Achievement

In 2001, 88 per cent of pupils at Holy Trinity achieved five or more A*–C grades at GCSE. Results are consistently high and these results were up from 81 per cent in 2000. The school was placed fifth in the borough with an average point score of 58.8. At A-level, the average point score for pupils entered for two or more subjects was 270, above both national and borough averages, placing the school ninth in the borough. However, small year groups mean results do tend to fluctuate. The college is also proud of the number of its pupils who successfully find university placements.

## Extra-curricular activities

There is a wide range of clubs on offer at the school, including those for sport, music, art, IT, homework, public speaking and debating. The college organizes visits to museums, galleries and theatres. There are regular trips abroad for language work, as well as watersports and skiing trips. Sixth-formers are able to take part in a Young Enterprise scheme, aided by members of the local business community. They can also participate in a community service scheme, which enables girls to help out in places such as local hospitals. At the Bromley Schools Achievement in Sports Award evening, several pupils received awards, including one for county tennis champion. The college also won the Bromley school skiing competition, and the Senior Choir won the WW Bell Baton for the fifth year in succession at the Beckenham Festival.

# Kelsey Park School

**Manor Way, Beckenham, Kent BR3 3SJ** 020 8650 8694 020 8658 5527 rah@kelseypark.bromley.sch.uk www.kelseypark.bromley.sch.uk Mr Richard Harknett B.Sc; Chair of Governors: Mr J Getgood Beckenham Junction, Eden Park, Clock House **Buses**: 54, 162, 194, 227, 351, 352, 358, 361, 367, 726 Black school blazer with badge, black trousers, house tie, white shirt, navy blue jumper; Sixth form: Smart dress

**Demand**: 272 applications for 200 places in 2001/2 **Type**: Comprehensive foundation school for 806 boys, aged 11 to 18 **Submit application form**: Mid-November 2003 **Motto**: Celebrate Achievement **School hours**: 8.40am–3.30pm; homework clubs are available **Meals**: Hot and cold available **Strong GCSE subjects**: Modern languages, performing arts **London league table position**: 437

## Profile

Kelsey Park is situated in Beckenham and its main school building dates from 1968. The school offers French and Spanish at GCSE as well as the usual core subjects. The majority of pupils continue into the sixth form, which offers a range of A-levels, including photography, as well as GNVQs at advanced and intermediate level in product design and business studies. The school is organized into four faculties (languages, universal sciences, creative and performing arts, and humanities), each linked to a particular 'house'. The house system is used to foster loyalty, belonging and stability. Senior pupils can become house captains, sports captains and prefects. Truancy was a problem in 2000, with the unauthorized absence rate at 1.1 per cent of pupils, above the national average. There is a PTA.

## Admissions and intake

Application forms are available from the school. The entrance criteria, in order of priority, are: siblings (i.e. a brother who attends or has attended the school); and proximity, measured in a straight line, from home to school. The number of pupils has fallen from 865 in 1995 to 806. The ability of the intake covers the full range, although Ofsted stated that 'many pupils arrive at the school with low levels of language skills'. Roughly one-third transfer from four neighbouring local authorities. In 2000, 19 per cent of pupils had special needs.

## Achievement

Kelsey Park was inspected by Ofsted in 1998 when the Chief Inspector of Schools was 'of the opinion that the school no longer requires special measures, since it is now providing an acceptable standard of education for its pupils'. The school has continued this improvement and was praised by Ofsted in 2001 as '...substantial improvements have taken place in quality of teaching since the last inspection'. Inspectors noted the 'strong leadership' of the head teacher and there is 'good care and guidance for students'. The school now provides a 'much better learning environment'. Ofsted commented that: 'standards are improving and overall, most students make satisfactory progress.' They also said that: 'there is an effective focus on raising the academic standards and on the personal development of all groups of students in the school'. In 2002, 30 per cent of pupils achieved five or more A*–C grades at GCSE and the school was placed 23rd in the borough. This was below the borough and national averages, but a rise from 23 per cent in 2001. The average point score for pupils entered for two or more A-levels was 125. This was below the borough and national averages. This placed the school 22nd in the borough.

## Extra-curricular activities

There are many clubs and societies available including those for chess, homework, model railway, Islam, computer, drama and debating, plus a choir, school magazine and Duke of Edinburgh's Award scheme. Drama productions are staged annually. Regular visits are arranged to theatres as well as canal trips, visits to France and skiing holidays.

# Kemnal Technology College

**Sevenoaks Way, Sidcup, Kent DA14 5AA** ☎ 020 8300 7112 📠 020 8300 5619 ✉ admin@ktc.bromley. sch.uk 🌐 www.schoolsite.edex.net.uk/290/index.html Mr John Atkins Bed Adv Dip.Ed, FRSA (principal); Chair of Governors: Mrs L Alexander 🚉 Sidcup **Buses**: 51, 68 Black blazer, black trousers, white shirt, black and red school tie; Sixth form: Suits **Demand**: 407 applications for 270 places in 2001/2 **Type**: Technology College foundation school for 963 boys (mixed in sixth form), aged 11 to 18 **Submit application form**: Mid November 2003 **Mission statement**: Learning for life: Respect; Excellence; Industry **School hours**: 8am–4.30pm **Meals**: Hot and cold available **Strong GCSE subjects**: IT, technology **London league table position**: 300

## Profile

Kemnal Technology College is located on an attractive, spacious site in St Paul's Cray. The main building is Grade II listed, dating from 1930. The school has Technology College status. A total of £700,000 has been spent on refurbishing science labs and £2.5 million on two new teaching blocks. The Harris Wing includes an up-to-date art technology room and The Sims Wing has an IT room, two technology rooms and a new library resources area.

A further £1.2 million will be spent to cater for the school's rising roll, and a darkroom, two drama studios, new classrooms and a small sports hall are to be built. IT facilities, which include access to the Internet and e-mail, are open to pupils and parents in the evenings and during holidays. In 1999 the college gained the Investors in People Award. At Key Stage 4, all pupils take a GCSE in IT and the more able pupils can take GCSE statistics a year early. There is also a GNVQ part 1 course available at this stage. The school has a small mixed sixth form offering both A-levels and GNVQs. Setting is used in almost all subjects. A numeracy and literacy summer school is run for new Year 7 pupils. There is a college council and pupils can become prefects and library monitors. There is a coordinator for pupils with special needs.

## Admissions and intake

Application forms are available from the school. The entrance criteria, in order of priority, are: siblings (i.e. a brother currently attending or who has attended the school), and proximity, measured in a straight line, from home to school.

## Achievement

In 2002, 56 per cent of boys achieved five or more grades A*–C at GCSE. This was an increase on 37 per cent in 2001 but below the national average. The school was placed 18th in the borough. The average point score for pupils entered for two or more A-levels was 151. This was well below the borough and national averages, placing the school 20th in the borough. The report following the inspection by Ofsted in 2001 praised the 'very good leadership' of the head teacher and noted that pupils were making 'satisfactory progress'. Inspectors commented on '...significant improvements in the quality of teaching' since their last inspection. The school is seen to implement an 'imaginative policy to meet academic and social needs of pupils'. In 2000, unauthorized absence was below the national level at 0.7 per cent.

## Extra-curricular activities

Among the activities on offer are drama and music. Instrumental tuition is available, including for steel bands. Sport is particularly strong, with inter-school and internal competitions. The college offers football, rugby, tennis, cricket, basketball, volleyball and athletics. Activities such as climbing and orienteering are also available.

# Langley Park School for Boys

**Hawksbrook Lane, South Eden Park Road, Beckenham Kent BR3 3BP** ☎ 020 8650 9253 📠 020 8650 5823 ⓔ office@lpbs.kent.sch.uk 🌐 www.lpbs.kent.sch.uk Mr Robert Northcott MA; Chair of Governors: Mr Charles Grimble 🚆 Eden Park **Buses**: 194, 358 Maroon school blazer and school tie, white shirt, dark grey trousers (Years 7 to 10); dark grey trousers, black school blazer and tie (Year 11); Sixth form: Formal dress **Demand**: 675 applications for 210 places in 2001/2 **Type**: Comprehensive foundation school for 1296 boys, aged 11 to 18 **Submit application form**: Mid-November 2003 **Motto**: *Mores et studia* (Character and Good Learning) **School hours**: 8.20am–3pm; homework clubs are available **Meals**: Hot and cold available **Strong GCSE subjects**: English, history, sciences **London league table position**: 135

## Profile

Formerly Beckenham and Penge Grammar School, Langley Park School for Boys is now a very good comprehensive. It is situated next door to Langley Park School for Girls, south of Beckenham. The modern buildings include a new two-storey teaching suite, providing classrooms for English and art, as well as a fully equipped library. The school has its own tennis courts, sports pitches and an astro-turf hockey pitch, which is shared with the girls' school. The new computer network provides boys with access to the Internet and e-mail. A GNVQ course in leisure and tourism is offered in addition to the usual GCSEs. The majority of boys stay on in the sixth form and study for A-levels, although GNVQs at advanced and intermediate level are also available. All of Year 12 are given the responsibility of being prefects. Progress cards are sent home to parents and the Friends of Langley Park are actively involved with school life. There is a coordinator for pupils with special needs.

## Admissions and intake

Application forms are available from the school. The entrance criteria, in order of priority, are: siblings (i.e. an elder brother in attendance at the school); and proximity, measured in a straight line, from home to school. Ability on entry is usually above average.

### Achievement

In 2002, Ofsted reported: 'this is a very good school with many outstanding features'. Inspectors noted that: 'Standards are well above average and pupils at all levels achieve very well'. The level of teaching was 'very good' with 'excellent leadership' by the head teacher. In 2002, 81 per cent of pupils gained five or more grades A*–C at GCSE, a rise from 68 per cent in 2001. This was well above the national average and the school was ranked 10th in the borough league table. In 2002, the average point score for pupils entered for two or more A-levels was 282.8, well above the borough and national averages. This placed the school sixth in the borough league table. The school has established a reputation for sporting excellence and in 1999 achieved the prestigious Sportsmark Gold Award. It has produced international players in five of its major sports of rugby, hockey, basketball, cricket, tennis and athletics.

### Extra-curricular activities

Ofsted praised the 'excellent' range of activities on offer. In addition to sport, the school is noted for its musical achievement; there are numerous bands and orchestras. Each year, boys take part in a camp at the school's own outdoor centre in Derbyshire; one group made the first recorded European ascent of a Himalayan peak. There are regular skiing trips, French and German exchanges and sporting tours. Other activities include voluntary service, a debating society, an Air Training Corps, homework clubs and a chess club.

# Langley Park School for Girls

**Hawksbrook Lane, South Eden Park Road, Beckenham, Kent BR3 3BE** 020 8650 7207 020 8663 6578 jsage@lpgs.bromley.sch.uk www.lpgs.bromley.sch.uk Miss Jan Sage MA; Chair of Governors: Mr GA Miles Eden Park **Buses**: 194, 358 Grey or blue tartan pleated skirt, white shirt, navy V-neck jumper with trim at neck, dark blue blazer with piping; dark blue socks, tights (Years 7 to 8); Sixth form: Smart casual wear **Demand**: 601 applications for 240 places in 2001/2 **Type**: Comprehensive Technology College foundation school for 1392 girls, aged 11 to 18 **Submit application form**: Mid-November 2003 **Motto**: Respect for the Individual, Pursuit of Excellence, Equality of Opportunity **School hours**: 8.20am–3pm **Meals**: Hot and cold available **Strong GCSE subjects**: English, maths, science **London league table position**: 120

### Profile

Langley Park School for Girls is a very successful comprehensive in a borough that offers strong competition from selective schools. It is housed in modern buildings in a pleasant residential area. An attractive new science block, IT business suite and library were recently completed. The school has extensive playing fields, including an astro-turf hockey pitch shared with the boys' school, as well as a sports centre. In 1999, the school received a Charter Mark, a government award that recognizes and encourages excellence in public service. It has also received an Investors in People Award and a health-promoting schools award. As a reflection of its Technology College status, the school offers A-levels in design and technology as well as an advanced level GNVQ in science. It also offers a wide range of other courses including A-level theatre studies and a GNVQ in leisure and tourism. The school employs a computerized monitoring system of pupils which assists teachers in setting targets. There is an active parents' association which raises funds for the school, a school council and the Adremian Association for old girls. There is a coordinator for pupils with special needs.

### Admissions and intake

Application forms are available from the school. The entrance criteria, in order of priority, are: siblings (a sister already at the school at the time of proposed entry or within the last five years); and proximity, measured in a straight line, from home to school. The ability of pupils on entry is usually average or above.

### Achievement

The most recent Ofsted report in 2000 stated: 'This is a very good and effective school. Pupils attain high standards in academic work because of very good teaching and their hard work'. The care and support provided to pupils was seen to be of a 'very high quality'. The provision for pupils with special educational needs is very good and the leadership of the head teacher is 'excellent'. In 2002, 79 per cent of pupils achieved five or more grades A*–C at GCSE, well above the borough average. These results were slightly down on 81 per cent in 2001, with an average point score of 44.6, placing the school ninth in the borough. The average point score for pupils entered for two or more A-levels was 239.9, above the borough average of 233.6 and the national average of 254.5, placing the school 12th in the borough league table.

## Extra-curricular activities

A wide range of activities is on offer, including drama clubs, school productions and theatre visits, as well as workshops with professional actors. The school holds an annual Christmas music night. It is very successful at sport and pupils have represented the county at hockey, netball, rugby, cricket and cross-country. Many trips abroad are organized, which has included a New Year skiing trip to Verbier in Switzerland.

# Newstead Wood School for Girls

**Avebury Road, Orpington, Kent BR6 9SA** ☎ 01689 853626 📠 01689 853315 ⓔ office@newsteadwood.bromley.sch.uk 🌐 www.newsteadwood.bromley.sch.uk Mrs E Allen; Chair of Governors: Mr A Brakefield ⇄ Orpington **Buses:** R4, 61, 208, 353, 357 Green kilt, white and green blouse, green pullover **Demand:** 766 applications for 130 places in 2001/2 **Type:** Selective foundation school for 882 girls, aged 11 to 18 **Submit application form:** Early October 2003 **Mission statement:** To offer a high standard of education through freedom, opportunity and choice **Motto:** *Fortitudine Crescamus* (May We Grow in Strength) **School hours:** 8.25am–3.35pm **Meals:** Hot and cold available **Strong GCSE subjects:** All relatively strong **London league table position:** 16

## Profile

Newstead Wood is consistently one of the top state schools in the country. It is one of London's 19 remaining grammar schools. Founded in 1958, it is situated in a pleasant eight-acre site overlooking the Kent Downs. There are extensive playing fields, along with tennis and netball courts, a sports hall and gymnasium. Recently improved facilities include science and language labs, additional classrooms, specialist drama provision and expanded computer facilities. The sixth form enjoys its own facilities. A broad curriculum is offered, with all girls studying Latin in the first two years. The majority of pupils stay on in the sixth form and choose from a wide range of A-levels. Girls are introduced to university life through visits, conferences and a residential course at Oxford University. The school council is headed by sixth-formers, who also take on roles as form leaders and house captains. Pastoral care is aided by the house system. There is an active parents' association. Former pupils include Christine Hancock, general secretary of the Royal College of Nursing; Barbara Harriss-White, director of graduate studies in development, Queen Elizabeth House, Oxford; Emma Johnson, clarinetist; Lorraine McAslan, violinist; and Susan Tebby, sculptress.

## Admissions and intake

Application forms are available from the school. A selective test is held in November. Girls who live in a nine-mile radius of the school and who have been ranked as one of the top 130 scorers in the test will be offered a place. If places remain, girls who live further away will be invited to sit the test and places will be offered in rank order.

## Achievement

Ofsted last inspected Newstead in 1996 and the report commented: 'This is a first-class girls' grammar school. The pupils, all of high ability, respond very well to the high quality of teaching provided....' The report added: 'Overall, the high quality of teaching in all subjects is the single most important factor in enabling the girls at Newstead Wood to reach such high levels of achievement.' In 2002, 100 per cent of girls achieved five or more grades A*–C at GCSE, replicating the achievement of 2000. An average point score of 58.4 placed the school top of the borough league table. The average point score for students entered for two or more A-levels was 383, which was the third highest in the borough. Over 95 per cent of girls at Newstead Wood go on to higher education, with 10 per cent usually going to Oxford or Cambridge universities.

## Extra-curricular activities

An outstanding range of activities includes clubs for chess, computing, creative writing, photography and the environment. Sports include fencing and golf in the sixth form, and girls regularly compete at national level. Each year, an established writer joins the school to give a creative writing course. A composer in residence is also an annual feature. The music society gives regular concerts. Art trips are organized to Amsterdam and Paris, and language exchanges to France, Germany and Spain. There is also an annual enrichment week.

# The Priory School

**Tintagel Road, Orpington, Kent BR5 4LG** ☎ 01689 819219 (head); 01689 600841 (office) 📠 01689 600842 Mr Nicholas Ware MA; Chair of Governors: Mrs J Prior 🚉 Orpington **Buses**: 654 Up to sixth form: Burgundy blazer with school badge; white shirt or blouse, grey trousers or tartan skirt, tartan tie or cravat **Demand**: 619 applications for 270 places in 2001/2 **Type**: Comprehensive foundation school for 1326 mixed pupils, aged 11 to 18 **Submit application form**: Mid-November 2003 **Mission statement**: To enable all pupils to make a useful contribution to society **School hours**: 8.40am–3.20pm **Meals**: Hot and cold available **Strong GCSE subjects**: Art, English, maths **London league table position**: 354

## Profile

The Priory School was opened in September 1990 after two schools were amalgamated. It is located on an estate in an area of relatively high unemployment. The main school buildings date from 1986 with a £4 million expansion being completed in 1994. In 1999, a new dance studio, art and design building, and reception and entrance area were added. Currently, £1.5 million of grants are being used to further enhance the accommodation. Sports facilities include a gym, sports hall, fitness room and a floodlit all-weather pitch. The sixth form has a purpose-built common room, library and IT suite. More able pupils are able to study German as well as the mandatory French. A total of 19 subjects are offered at A-level along with advanced and intermediate GNVQs, and a vocational nursery nursing qualification. Prefects are drawn from the sixth form, and senior pupils also take part in a 'big brother, big sister' programme giving support to Year 7 pupils. The academic progress of pupils is monitored via individual termly profiling sessions. There is a school council and an active PTA. There is a coordinator for pupils with special needs.

## Admissions and intake

Application forms are available from the school. The entrance criteria, in order of priority, are: siblings who attend or have attended the school within the last five years; and proximity, measured in a straight line, from home to school. Priory attracts pupils with the full range of abilities, although many high performers attend the local selective schools.

## Achievement

In 2002, 39 per cent of pupils achieved five or more A*–C grades at GCSE, in line with 2001's results. This was below the national average and the school was ranked 22nd in the borough. The average point score for pupils entered for two or more A-levels in 2002 was 211.9. This was below average for the borough, placing the school 16th. In 2001, Ofsted reported: 'Students achieve well in comparison with students in similar schools'. Inspectors praised the 'good moral, social and cultural development' of pupils and noted that 'the quality of teaching across the school is good'. The majority of students are 'proud of their school' and there is good behaviour amongst the vast majority of pupils. Ofsted commented that the range and variety of teaching styles could be improved.

## Extra-curricular activities

All pupils visit the school's own Outdoor Pursuits and Field Study Centre in South Wales at least once during their school career. Many sports teams utilize the school's excellent facilities. Plays and concerts are regularly staged and the school's concert band and choir often undertake weekend tours. Other recent trips have included a golf and tennis trip to France, a German exchange and history visits to Berlin and Prague. There is a thriving Christian Union.

# Ravens Wood School

**Oakley Road, Bromley, Kent BR2 8HP** ☎ 01689 856050 📠 01689 850452 office@ravenswood.bromley.sch.uk; gtberwick@ravenswood.bromley.sch.uk Dr George Berwick MA; Chair of Governors: Mr C Hillier 🚉 Orpington, Hayes **Buses**: 320 Dark blazer with school badge, white shirt, dark school tie, dark trousers; Sixth form: Office attire **Demand**: 760 applications for 199 places in 2001/2 **Type**: Comprehensive Technology College foundation school for 1236 boys (mixed in sixth form), aged 11 to 18 **Submit application form**: Mid-November 2003 **Mission statement**: To be an outstanding community for teaching and learning, at the forefront of innovation, ensuring that all exceed their expectations **School hours**: 8.40am–1.25pm (Mon–Tues), 8.40am–4pm (Wed–Fri); homework clubs are available **Meals**: Hot and cold available **Strong GCSE subjects**: English, maths, sciences **London league table position**: 194

### Profile

Ravens Wood School is housed in modern buildings and situated in extensive grounds. One of the first Technology College initiative schools, it has retained that status for a further four years by meeting targets for improving pupils' performance in technology, maths and science. It has also achieved Investor in Careers status for the work carried out by its careers department through their multimedia careers computer system, work shadowing, industry links and work experience. The modern languages department also organizes work experience abroad. The school has sister schools in Sweden and France and pupils maintain video conferencing links with them. Ravens Wood offers the usual range of GCSE and A-level subjects as well as statistics and photography, and the option of foundation level GNVQs in Year 10, and intermediate and advanced GNVQs in the sixth form. It has an outstanding parent-teacher association which brings in additional funding of over £10,000 per year. There is a coordinator for pupils with special needs.

### Admissions and intake

Application forms are available from the school. The entrance criteria, in order of priority, are: siblings (i.e. a brother or sister who previously attended or is currently attending the school); and proximity, measured in a straight line, from home to school.

### Achievement

In 2002, 72 per cent of pupils achieved five or more grades A*–C at GCSE. This was up on 56 per cent in 2001, reinstating an upward trend. The school was placed 13th in the borough. This result was above the local and national average. The average point score for pupils entered for two or more A-levels was 270.8. This was above the borough and national averages, placing the school seventh in the borough. In 1998, Ofsted reported: 'This is an outstanding school, which has made substantial improvements since the last Ofsted inspection. It has a deservedly high reputation and is popular with both pupils and parents.' The report highlighted the 'outstanding' quality of teaching in English (in Key Stage 4 and post 16), art (post 16), design and technology (in Key Stage 4 and post 16), drama (in Key Stage 4 and post 16), geography (at all ages), history (in Key Stage 4 and post 16), media studies (at all ages), PE (at all ages) and RE (post 16)'. However, Ofsted also noted that the organization for special education needed to improve and the school is now addressing this problem.

### Extra-curricular activities

Activities available include maths competitions, an astronomy club, a rocket makers club, homework clubs and a mileage marathon club. There is also an environmental survey undertaken in liaison with a Swedish school, which has received a national award from the Living Earth organization. Drama and music are strong, as is sport with the U19 football team being recently invited to compete in the English Schools Invitation Cup. There is an annual skiing trip and an annual 'summer adventure in the Mediterranean'.

## The Ravensbourne School

**Hayes Lane, Bromley, Kent BR2 9EH** ☎ 020 8460 0083 📠 020 8460 7525 ✉ rick@ravensbourne.bromley.sch.uk (ICT Manager) 🌐 www.ravensbourne.bromley.sch.uk Mr P Murphy; Chair of Governors: Mrs A Clements 🚉 Bromley South **Buses:** 119, 146, 314 Navy blazer, dark trousers, red and white striped school tie (Years 7 to 9); Navy blazer, dark trousers, plain red tie with school crest (Years 10 to 11); Sixth form: Smart attire **Demand:** 728 applications for 227 places in 2001/2 **Type:** Comprehensive foundation school for 1209 mixed pupils, aged 11 to 18 **Submit application form:** Mid-November 2003 **Motto:** *Dum cresco spero* (While I Grow I Hope) **School hours:** 8.30am–3.25pm; homework clubs are available **Meals:** Hot and cold available **Strong GCSE subjects:** All comparable **London league table position:** 336

### Profile

The Ravensbourne School is an improving comprehensive housed in excellent accommodation, with many of its buildings Grade II-listed. The school has invested heavily in refurbishment and extension, and there are immediate plans to expand the science facilities and to build an improved sports complex. Ravensbourne was formed in 1989 from the amalgamation of three schools, leaving it with a gender imbalance towards boys. The school has particularly good provision for music, art, PE and technology. Beyond the national curriculum, it offers Latin, media studies, a Sports Leadership Award, computing and, in the sixth form, a range of GNVQs. Pupils can become representatives on the school council, while sixth-formers can become prefects and receive training to act as counsellors for younger pupils. A range of fund-raising and social activities are organized by the school's parents' association. Sir George Martin, Sir Michael York, Tibor Fischer and Billy Idol are all ex-pupils. Truancy is a problem and in 2000 the percentage of unauthorized absence was high at 1.5 per cent, although this was down on 1999 and not significantly higher than the 1.0 per cent national level.

### Admissions and intake

Application forms are available from the school. The entrance criteria, in order of priority, are: siblings (i.e. a blood relative living at the same address in attendance at the school or who will be in the September of entry); and proximity, measured in a straight line, from home to school. Pupils' ability on intake is roughly average although it covers the whole range. At the time of the Ofsted report in 1997, about one-fifth of pupils had reading difficulties on entry.

### Achievement

Ofsted reported that Ravensbourne was a 'well-ordered school' which 'has been successful in creating a harmonious community for pupils from a variety of backgrounds'. Those pupils with special educational needs were said to make 'sound progress'. In 2002, 43 per cent of pupils gained five or more A*–C grades at GCSE. This was below the national average but an increase on 39 per cent in 2001. The average point score was 32.4, placing the school 21st in the borough. The average point score for pupils entered for two or more A-levels was 174.9. This result was below the borough and national averages, placing the school 19th in the borough league table.

### Extra-curricular activities

The school achieves great success at local and county level in team sports. There is a large Road Running Squad, which is extremely successful in local races and the London Marathon. Staff organize numerous visits to museums, music festivals and galleries as well as residential stays in European countries. Pupils participate in the library committee, homework clubs and the garden club run a Peace Garden. Musical links are maintained with the Bromley Youth and Music Trust. Pupils also take part in various community activities.

## St John Rigby Catholic College

**Wickham Court, Layhams Road, West Wickham Kent BR4 9HN** ☎ 020 8777 8383 📠 020 8777 2231 Mr John Stanley B.Ed, MA Ed; Chair of Governors: Mr MC Hedger 🚉 Hayes, West Wickham **Buses**: 119 Up to sixth form: Blue blazer, shirt, kilt or trousers **Demand**: 234 applications for 210 places in 2001/2 **Type**: Voluntary aided Roman Catholic comprehensive for 1156 mixed pupils, aged 11 to 18 **Submit application form**: Mid-November 2003 **School hours**: 8.45am–3.45pm; homework clubs are available **Meals**: Hot and cold available **Strong GCSE subjects**: French **London league table position**: 335

### Profile

This school is under the trusteeship of the Archdiocese of Southwark and as such has a strong Catholic ethos. The college has a complex arrangement of buildings, all dating from various periods. A £2 million building programme was completed in 1996 and includes new faculty and specialist rooms. There is a house system with older pupils able to take responsibility for younger pupils. Students can also become delegates on the college council. Social and fund-raising events are organized by the college's parent-teacher association.

### Admissions and intake

Application forms are available from the school. The admissions criteria, in order of priority, are: baptised Roman Catholic children with at least one parent and themselves who are active and committed to the Faith; other baptized Roman Catholics; children with at least one parent and themselves who are active and committed members of other Christian denominations; and children of Christians or other religious faiths whose parents accept and support the ethos of a Roman Catholic school. The intake of children in the last two categories will not exceed 20 per cent. In the event of subscription, places will be allocated according to: a brother or sister at the college at the time of admission, and medical or social reasons, which make the college particularly suitable for the child. There is a wide catchment area, with about half the pupils coming from Bromley and half from Croydon. The presence of selective schools in the borough has some affect on the intake though the ability of pupils on entry covers the whole spectrum.

### Achievement

In 2002, 39 per cent of pupils achieved five or more A*–C grades at GCSE. This was below the national average and the school was ranked 20th in the borough. Results over recent years have varied but this reinstated a slight upward trend. The average point score for pupils entered for two or more A-levels was 138.8, well below average for the borough, placing the school 21st in the borough league table. Pupils can also take GNVQs. In 2001, Ofsted commented that: 'The college has had a very troubled twelve months, owing to serious mismanagement and financial irregularities under the previous senior management and governors'. However, under the 'good leadership' of the new head teacher, the college is now '...operating effectively in most areas of its work'. All staff are seen to be committed to the success of the college.

### Extra-curricular activities

Ofsted commented that 'enrichment through extra-curricular provision is a strength' of the college. Numerous clubs are on offer, including homework clubs, biology and maths clubs. The college often invites visiting speakers and organizes regular theatre trips and other trips both at home and abroad. Many sports are available and there are a number of inter-house and inter-school competitions. Several pupils have gone on to represent the county at various sports. There is a popular choir and orchestra, and regular musical productions. There is also a community service programme.

# St Olave's and St Saviour's Grammar School

**Goddington Lane, Orpington, Kent BR6 9SH** 01689 820101 01689 897943 office@saintolaves.net www.saintolaves.net Mr Anthony Jarvis B.Ed, MA, FRSA; Chair of Governors: Dr M Elvines Orpington **Buses**: R1, R2, R5, R11, 358 Black blazer, white shirt, black trousers, black school tie; Sixth form: Office attire **Demand**: 762 applications for 112 places in 2001/2 **Type**: Voluntary aided selective for 803 boys (mixed in sixth form), aged 11 to 18 **Submit application form**: Mid-October 2003 **Mission statement**: To provide a secure, happy, stimulating and disciplined environment in which young people can achieve high academic, social and moral standards **School hours**: 8.40am–3.30pm; homework clubs are available **Meals**: Hot and cold available **Strong GCSE subjects**: English, maths, science **London league table position**: 28

### Profile

St Olave's was described by *The Sunday Times* as being 'among the best schools in the UK' and by *The Independent* as 'one of the state schools elite'. It is one of London's 19 remaining grammar schools and is an Anglican school with a multicultural intake. There is a school chapel, although attendance is voluntary. Founded in 1571, it moved to its present location in 1968. The school has 20 acres of tree-lined playing fields. Extensive rebuilding and refurbishment include a new science block and three newly equipped computer suites. The school also boasts squash and Eton fives courts, a large indoor heated swimming pool, five rugby pitches and a cricket square with two all-weather cricket strips. In the first two years, all pupils study Latin. A wide range of GCSEs and A-levels are on offer, including Arabic and Japanese studies in the sixth form, which is now co-educational. Work experience placements in Europe are available. There is an active parents' association as well as the Old Olavians' Association for former pupils. There is a coordinator for pupils with special needs.

### Admissions and intake

Application forms are available from the school. Selective tests are held in early November and the first 112 in rank order are offered places. Boys may sit the tests if their 11th birthday falls between 1 September and 31 August inclusive of the academic year in which the November test is set. If their 10th birthday falls within this period, boys may take the test for entry one academic year early, provided a letter of recommendation is received from the head of their primary school (entry for these boys will be at the Governors' discretion).

## Achievement

In 2002, Ofsted reported: 'St Olave's is an extremely successful and effective school which achieves exceptionally high standards'. Teaching was found to be 'very good' and results are very high in national tests and examinations in all years. Inspectors also praised the 'thriviing sixth form'. In 2002, 98 per cent of boys gained five or more A*–C grades at GCSE, slightly down on 100 per cent in 2001. The average point score of 56.2 ranked the school third in the borough. At A-level, the average point score for pupils entered for two or more was 385, well above the national average, placing the schooll second in the borough league table. The vast majority of pupils go on to higher education, with a dozen or so each year going to Oxford or Cambridge.

## Extra-curricular activities

There are a number of musical groups, and some regularly appear in the National Schools' Chamber Music Competition and the National Festival of Music for Youth on the South Bank. Drama productions are also staged. Teams have been in competition at national level in rugby, basketball, athletics, swimming, chess and Eton fives. The *Le Chavetois* society carries out voluntary work in the local community. Pupils can take advantage of after-school homework clubs. Pupils also enter for the Duke of Edinburgh's Award scheme. St Olave's provides the trebles for the Queen's Chapel of the Savoy, who sometimes appear before the Queen. There are trips both at home and abroad.

# Camden

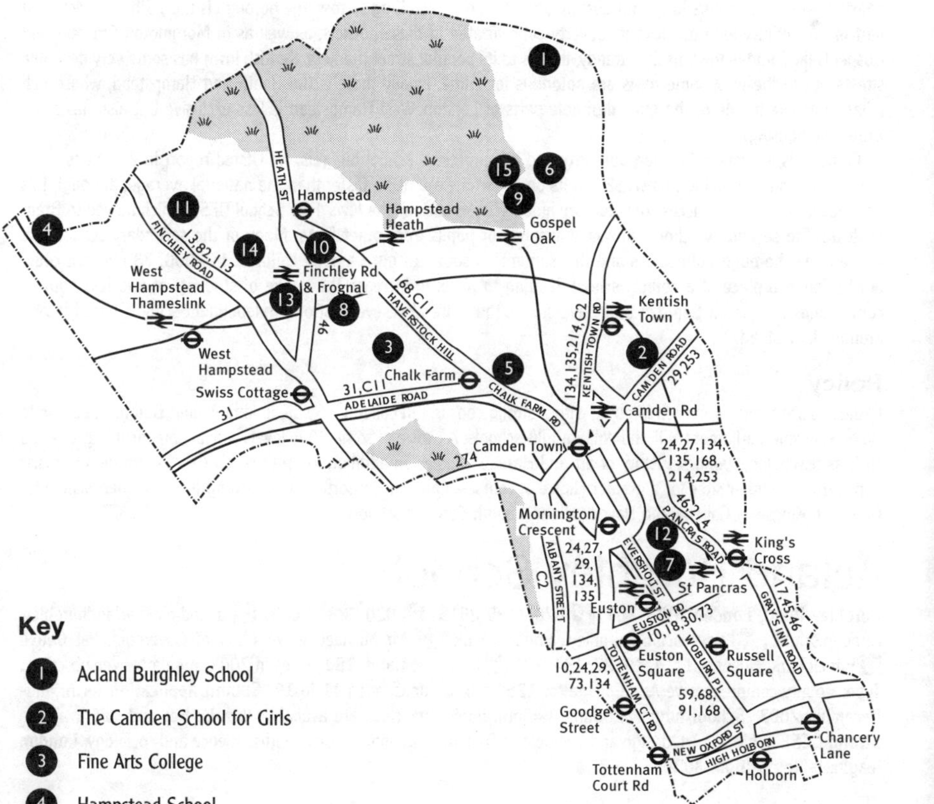


## Key

1. Acland Burghley School
2. The Camden School for Girls
3. Fine Arts College
4. Hampstead School
5. Haverstock School
6. La Sainte Union Catholic Secondary School
7. Maria Fidelis RC Convent School
8. North Bridge House School
9. Parliament Hill School
10. Royal School Hampstead
11. St Margaret's School
12. South Camden Community School
13. South Hampstead High School
14. University College School
15. William Ellis School

# Factfile

**LEA: Crowndale Centre, 218–220 Eversholt Street, London NW1 1BD** 020 7974 1525 www.camden.gov.uk. **Director of Education**: Bob Litchfield **Political control of council**: Labour **Percentage of pupils from outside the borough**: 31 per cent **Percentage of pupils educated outside the borough**: 21.4 per cent **London league table positions (out of 32 boroughs)**: 16th

The borough of Camden is packed with contrast and character. To the south lies Bloomsbury, home to the British Museum. Primrose Hill is upmarket and Belsize Park is also well-heeled. Yet Camden also includes the deprived housing estates of Somers Town and Euston, as well as rundown King's Cross. The borough is the 16th most deprived part of the country with much of its poverty concentrated in these pockets, as well as in Mornington Crescent and Gospel Oak. Camden Town itself is trendy, thanks to its popular street markets. Kentish Town has some very desirable streets but to the west some parts are notorious for crime. Finally there is the Heath and Hampstead, whose rich inhabitants live in one of the most desirable parts of London. West Hampstead is less exclusive but also has some expensive housing.

Camden is a strong education authority and has protected school budgets. An Ofsted report in 2000 described it as 'good' and 'improving'. Its GCSE results on the whole are rising faster than the national average, although this depends largely on the success of voluntary aided schools such as the Jews' Free School (JFS), which moved to Brent in 2002. The secondary schools attract thousands of pupils from other LEAs. Many of the secondary schools are located near borough boundaries and this sometimes squeezes out Camden children. In 2000, 73 children could not be found a place at a council school, leading to plans to increase the intake of students at two less popular comprehensives (South Camden and Haverstock). There are also several strong independent schools based in and around Hampstead.

## Policy

Camden's sixth-form provision is good, with a strong consortium called La Swap, linking Acland Burghley, La Sainte Union Convent, Parliament Hill and William Ellis schools. A choice of some 30 A-levels is available including subjects such as psychology, politics, history of art and classical studies, in addition to up to seven GNVQs. Where necessary, pupils travel to other sites for a greater choice of courses. Camden Consortium (sixth-form) links Camden School for Girls with Kingsway College and Haverstock and South Camden schools.

# Acland Burghley School

**Burghley Road, London NW5 1UJ** 020 7485 8515 020 7284 3462 genadmin@aclandburghley.camden.sch.uk www.aclandburghley.camden.sch.uk Mr Michael Shaw; Chair of Governors: Pat Cattell Tufnell Park **Buses**: C11, 4, 19, 27, 134, 135 None **Demand**: 180 places in 2003; regularly oversubscribed **Type**: County comprehensive Arts College for 1250 mixed pupils, aged 11 to 19 **Submit application form**: Mid-December 2003 **School hours**: 8.55am–3.40pm; homework clubs are available **Meals**: Hot and cold available **Strong GCSE subjects**: Art, design and technology, French, geography, history, maths, science and sociology **London league table position**: 308

## Profile

Acland Burghley school has an outstanding art department and in 2000 was awarded Arts College status. This new status brings a grant of over £200,000 that will be used to upgrade the arts facilities. A new library is also planned. The school has well-organized pastoral care and there are school and year councils. Parents can see the head each day from 8–8.30am and there is an active parents' association. Pupils are encouraged to become '21st century citizens in control of their own destiny'. Girls are outnumbered by two to one. Two problems were highlighted by an Ofsted visit in 1999: the relatively poor showing of girls and the need to improve the performance of high achievers. The school is now tackling these problems. Truancy has improved and has gone down from 2.4 per cent to 1.9 per cent in 2000. However, this is still above the national average. Famous ex-pupils include Suggs, singer from the group Madness, and Ross Boatman, actor.

### Admissions and intake

Admission is through the council. Once special needs applicants have been taken into account, priority is given first to the siblings of pupils and then to those living closest to the school's main entrance measured 'as the crow flies'. In 2000, this was within 0.427 of a mile.

### Achievement

Acland Burghley is a 'turnaround' school, its once bad reputation now greatly improved. In 2002, 48 per cent of pupils gained five or more A*-C grades at GCSE, just down on 49 per cent in 2001.The school was placed 11th in the borough. The art results tend to be outstanding, and design technology, French, geography, history, maths, science and sociology are also good.The quality of teaching impressed Ofsted inspectors who visited in 1999.They commented on 'the unusually high representation of very good or excellent teaching, 21 per cent of the total'. Art, drama, dance and PE were judged to be especially good. Only 4 per cent of lessons were found to be unsatisfactory. Maths was weaker but is now improving according to Ofsted. IT was also weak. Overall, the inspectors found the GCSE grades were above average for similar schools nationally, although they dipped in 2000. Art was equally impressive at A-level and chemistry, DT and English were also very good. Students taking two or more subjects scored an average 251 points in 2002, in line with the borough average, placing the school sixth in the borough. The sixth form is part of the La Swap consortium (see borough factfile). GNVQs are also available.

### Extra-curricular activities

These are helped by an on-site youth centre. Field trips and homework clubs are available. Clubs include chess, gymnastics and drama. Musical tuition is on offer along with an orchestra, ensembles, rock bands and jazz groups. Sport is especially strong, with the boys' and girls' junior athletic teams enjoying great success in the 2000 Camden Athletics Championships. The school has strong links with the community and employers, and it offers work experience.

## The Camden School for Girls

**Sandall Road, London NW5 2DB** 020 7485 3414 020 7284 3361 csg@rcamdengirls.camden.sch.uk www.camdengirls.camden.sch.uk Anne Canning; Chair of Governors: Penny Wild Kentish Town Camden Town, Kentish Town **Buses**: 29, 253 None **Demand**: 112 places in 2003; oversubscribed **Type**: Voluntary aided for 840 girls (mixed 16 to 19), aged 11 to 19 **Submit application form**: Mid-December 2003 **Motto**: Onwards and Upwards **School hours**: 8.45am–3.35pm **Meals**: Hot and cold available **Strong GCSE subjects**: All good in comparison to similar schools **London league table position**: 168

### Profile

Founded in 1871 by Frances Mary Buss, Camden School for Girls promotes high-quality women's education for girls from all backgrounds. Its classrooms and labs are sometimes poorly resourced but refurbishment is planned, helped by £350,000 of government money. There will also be a new science wing and library. The girls are involved in a school council and the 'SOS counselling' project. There is a prefects system in the sixth form. The school's pastoral care is excellent. There is a strong parents' association and a weekly newsletter. Truancy has improved and at 1.2 per cent it is just above the national average. Famous ex-pupils include the actresses Emma Thompson and Jodhi May, writer Gillian Slovo, TV and film director Beeban Kidron, and journalist and writer Kate Saunders.

### Admission and intake

The school has an assessment test to ensure it has a balanced intake. After sitting the test, candidates are put into one of four ability bands. Priority goes first to special needs applicants and then up to five applicants with musical aptitude and commitment (they complete a questionnaire and then audition). Priority is then given to those with siblings at the school, and then to those living nearest to the school's main entrance 'as the crow flies'. In 1999, successful applicants lived within 0.35–1.5 miles of the school depending on their assessment band.

### Achievement

In 1999, Ofsted described Camden School for Girls as 'unique and very effective'. It came seventh in the GCSE borough league table in 2002. A total of 61 per cent of pupils obtained five or more A*–C grades, reversing an upward trend from 1996. This was above the national average. The average GCSE point score was 40.7. Of the lessons observed by the inspectors, 80 per cent were deemed to be good, with only a handful unsatisfactory. Latin, art, science and maths were especially impressive. All pupils are taught classical studies in Year 8. Besides the usual core subjects available at GCSE, there is also child development, design and technology, drama, food technology, German, Latin and textiles technology. At A-level, maths, Spanish, music, art, Latin and modern languages were especially strong. In 2002, the school was fourth in the A-level table, with students taking two or more subjects scoring an average 282 points. This was above the borough and national averages. GNVQs are also offered. The sixth form has taken boys since 1990 and is part of the Camden Consortium (see borough factfile). Ofsted found that the school has 'a very positive...strong and vibrant ethos'. It is 'racially harmonious' with 'courteous and trustworthy' pupils.

### Extra-curricular activities

Musical activities on offer include chamber music ensembles, choirs, a wind band and a recorder group. The orchestras tour internationally. Homework clubs are popular. There are several special interest groups, including one for Asian girls. A variety of sports are available from basketball to trampolining. International visits have included an art trip to Barcelona. Pupils are involved with the local community and take part in fund-raising for charity.

# Fine Arts College

**85 Belsize Park Gardens, London NW3 4NJ** 020 7586 0312 020 7483 0355 Fine_arts.college@virgin.net Candida Cave CFA (Oxon); Co-Principal: Mr Nicholas Cochrane CFA (Oxon) Belsize Park, Swiss Cottage **Buses**: C11, 143 None **Demand**: Figures not available, but there is a high demand for places **Type**: Non-selective independent for 99 mixed pupils, aged 14 to 19 **Fees**: £3,975 per term **Submit application form**: Closing date depends upon where pupil is applying from **School hours**: 9am–6pm **Strong GCSE subjects**: Art **London league table position**: 486

### Profile

Fine Arts is a private college specializing in arts and humanities. It is particularly popular with students hoping to go on to art school. Founded by a playwright and an artist in 1978, it has a pleasant setting in Belsize Park. The main academic building is a 19th-century house with a garden, situated at the end of a Blue Plaque-studded avenue. As well as classrooms, there is a studio for each of painting, printmaking, sculpture and photography. Each subject has a specialist library. There are video and film-editing facilities on site and sculpture and photographic studios at the YMCA in Great Russell Street. Students are given reports on their progress every two weeks (weekly for GCSE pupils), and have regular meetings with their personal tutors. The staff combine teaching with practical involvement in the arts and humanities, and the staff includes a playwright and actress, a portrait artist, a practising archaeologist and a published poet. A close relationship between the school and parents is encouraged. There is provision for students with special needs.

### Admissions and intake

Admission is based on an interview and a previous school's reference. A-level applicants are expected to have 'satisfactory' GCSE results. A few scholarships and bursaries are given to students previously educated in the state system or those unable to afford private education.

### Achievement

The college's main strength is in visual arts and it has an excellent record in helping candidates get into art school. The majority of students attend the school for the sixth form, and 26 A-level subjects are offered including sculpture, film studies and classical archaeology. In 1999, 11 of 16 students achieved an A grade at A-level art, and 5 out of 7 in printmaking. Photography, history of art and English also made strong showings but theatre studies was the weakest subject. In 2002, 55 per cent of pupils gained five or more A*–C grades at GCSE. This was a drop on 83 per cent in 2001, and the school was placed 15th in the borough. The college came fifth in the Camden A-level tables, with those pupils taking two or more achieving an average point score of 261.8. This was above the borough and national averages. A-level class sizes average between six and seven pupils. The college also helps with university and art school applications. Since 1993, the college has offered a one-year intensive GCSE programme of up to eight subjects, including drama and design. However, numbers for these classes are usually small and this explains the wide variations in results. In previous years, results have ranged from 25 to 83 per cent of pupils with five or more A*–C grades. The college runs an introductory study skills week for GCSE pupils and they attend a supervised study period each day. It also runs Easter revision courses.

### Extra-curricular activities

Extra-curricular activities are strongly slanted towards the arts and include trips to the world's artistic centres. Pupils also take part in a range of sports, including aerobics, tennis and cricket, using facilities at Swiss College Sports Centre and the London Central YMCA. A recently established football team has had several successes.

## Hampstead School

**Westbere Road, Hampstead, London NW2 3RT** 020 7794 8133/020 7435 8927 (information line) 020 7435 8260 inquiries@hampsteadschool.org.uk www.hampsteadschool.org.uk Mr Andy Knowles (acting); Chair of Governors: Mr Geoff Berridge Cricklewood, Brondesbury Kilburn **Buses:** C11, 16, 28, 32, 159,226, 245, 260 None **Demand:** 210 places in 2003; oversubscribed **Type:** County comprehensive Technology College for 1294 mixed pupils, aged 11 to 19 **Submit application form:** Mid-December 2003 **School hours:** 8.40am–3.20pm; homework clubs are available **Meals:** Hot and cold available **Strong GCSE subjects:** Art, drama, English, history **London league table position:** 295

### Profile

Now a Technology College, Hampstead school has spent £500,000 on a new library with state-of-the-art multimedia facilities. It also has extra money to help talented children. Pupils are encouraged to take responsibility through a school council and peer counselling. There is excellent pastoral care, including the school's Children of the Storm charity, established to support its many refugee pupils. The school has integrated Down's Syndrome children successfully and undertaken considerable building work to accommodate a pupil with severe physical disabilities. There is a home-school association. Truancy is in line with the national average. One famous ex-pupil is author Zadie Smith.

### Admissions and intake

Once special needs applicants have been taken into account, priority is given first to the siblings of pupils and then to those living closest to the school's main entrance, measured 'as the crow flies'. In 1999, applicants needed to live within 1.053 miles of the school in order to be admitted.

### Achievement

Hampstead is proof that an inner-city comprehensive can be a well-ordered school where pupils make good progress. Its GCSE results are well above average for similar schools, and the slight fall in recent years is mostly due to an increased number of special needs children. In 2002, 50 per cent of pupils obtained five or more A*–C grades at GCSE. This was up on 44 per cent in 2001 and the school was ranked 10th in the borough. It was below the national average of 51.6 per cent. The sixth form's 'open door' policy means that its results tend not to be as good as previously. Pupils taking two or more subjects scored an average 234 points, placing the school 10th in the borough league table. There are 19 A-level subjects on offer, along with nine GNVQs. An Ofsted report in 2000 noted that Hampstead provides 'a very good quality of education for the diverse community it serves' and 'a positive atmosphere in which all pupils can give of their best'. It found that 70 per cent of the teaching is good. The inspectors commented: 'Teachers' enthusiasm and energy create a stimulating environment for learning.' However, the girls' performance seemed to be declining compared to the boys, going against the national trend. Some low achievers were also doing less well than nationally. Generally the atmosphere was considered to be 'harmonious'.

### Extra-curricular activities

The quality of Hampstead's extra-curricular activities has won it an Education Extra Award. The school is well known for its musical and dramatic productions. There are several choirs, orchestras and other groups, some of which have toured internationally. Hampstead is linked to the National, Tricycle, Globe and Hampstead Theatres and the coordinator of the National Playwright Commissioning Group. Regular exchanges take place with schools in Moscow and Spain. There are day trips to museums, theatres and galleries. There are also opportunities to try outdoor pursuits such as camping, water skiing and snowboarding. Community work is available and the school also runs homework clubs.

# Haverstock School

**Crogsland Road, Chalk Farm, London NW1 8AS** 020 7267 0975 020 7267 3807 haverstock@haverstock.camden.sch.uk www.haverstock.camden.sch.uk John Dowd; Chair of Governors: Dave Moulson Kentish Town West Chalk Farm **Buses:** 24, 31, 46, 168 None **Demand:** 180 places in 2003 **Type:** County comprehensive for 1040 mixed pupils, aged 11 to 19 **Submit application form:** Mid-December 2003 **Mission statement:** High standards, challenge and support for every student **School hours:** 8.45am–3.30pm **Meals:** Hot and cold available **Strong GCSE subjects:** Art, business studies, English, history **London league table position:** 482

## Profile

Haverstock school struggles with mixed success to overcome a mosaic of problems, including the social deprivation faced by its pupils and a very mobile population. It provides well-organized pastoral care that includes a school counsellor. There is a school council and all sixth-formers do voluntary work. Parents regularly receive a newsletter and the school runs English classes for mothers. There is also a home-school association. The school's Victorian buildings are set to be redeveloped into modern, purpose-built premises in the summer of 2003. Behaviour and truancy are continuing problems. In 1998, Ofsted observed 'too much bad behaviour in some classes and over boisterousness outside them' and heard reports of violence and bullying. The school is trying to tackle this but bullying continues to be a problem. Truancy was two times the national average at 2.2 per cent in 2000. Famous ex-pupils include John Barnes, ex-England footballer; Oonagh King, local Labour MP; and Paul Bradley, actor.

## Admissions and intake

Admission is through the council. Any candidate putting Haverstock as a first preference will be admitted. The school's turnover runs at 50 per cent between Year 7 and 11 and those joining include about 30 refugees each year. The percentage of pupils with special needs is high at 18 per cent. Girls are outnumbered by two to one.

## Achievement

In 2002, 28 per cent of pupils obtained five or more A*–C grades at GCSE. This was up on 27 per cent in 2001 and continued an upward trend. The average point score at GCSE was 24.7 and this placed the school at the bottom of the borough league table. It was also below the national average. The GCSE results are about average for similar schools. At GCSE, languages on offer include French, Spanish and German and optional subjects include business studies, dance and IT. Ofsted praised the school's excellent support for special needs children. They found some teaching to be very good, especially in English, art, history and business studies. These subjects also tended to achieve better exam results. However, Ofsted inspectors were concerned at the level of unsatisfactory teaching, especially in maths, and that more able pupils were unchallenged. Girls generally underperformed. Teaching in the sixth form is generally good and A-level results are improving. Pupils taking two or more subjects at A-level scored an average 180 points in 2002, placing the school 14th in the borough. The sixth form is part of Camden Consortium (see borough factfile) and offers 22 A-levels, including history of art, politics, photography and Latin. It also offers three foundation courses based on BTEC Kingsway College.

## Extra-curricular activities

Sport, especially football, is strong at Haverstock along with volleyball, basketball, trampolining and climbing. Clubs available include the Refugee Support Group and Girls' Group. The drama group is also strong, having performed plays at the Almeida and Shaw Theatres. Overseas trips are arranged for all ages with residential stays in Britain for younger pupils. An activities week at the end of the summer term offers pupils the chance to sample a range of activities, such as sports, drama and music. Haverstock has good links with employers, including major retailers. Under the 'business associate' programme, representatives of large firms, such as banks, come in to help the school. Pupils also work with local charities.

# La Sainte Union Catholic Secondary School

**Highgate Road, London NW5 1RP** 020 7428 4600 020 7267 7647 lsu@l+j25camden.sch.uk Sister Theresa Finn; Chair of Governors: Sister Margaret O'Reilly Kentish Town, Gospel Oak Kentish Town, Archway **Buses:** C2, C11, 214 Green blazer and kilt, white blouse **Demand:**180 places in 2003; heavily oversubscribed **Type:** Voluntary aided Roman Catholic comprehensive for 900 girls plus 260 in sixth-form consortium (boys admitted in sixth form), aged 11 to 19 **Submit application form**: Mid-December 2003 **School hours**: 8.45am–3.40pm, 8.45am–2.45pm (Thurs) **Meals**: Hot and cold available **Strong GCSE subjects**: English, science **London league table position**: 142

## Profile

La Sainte Union is housed in elegant buildings beside Hampstead Heath. It is very popular and escapes many of the problems of its neighbouring schools. The Sisters of La Sainte Union founded the school in 1861 and continue to run it. The school has extra funding for able and gifted children. Links with parents are promoted through the school journal and regular newsletters, as well as the parent-teacher association. Truancy is very low at 0.3 per cent.

## Admissions and intake

Admission is only given to baptized Roman Catholic girls with one or more parents who are practising and can produce a written reference from their parish priest. Priority is given to: sisters of pupils; those with special social or medical needs; those with musical aptitude (up to 18 places); and those with the shortest reasonable travelling time. The pupils tend to have above-average ability when they join the school.

## Achievement

La Sainte Union is an excellent school that continues to improve. Its GCSE results are very good and should improve further, following the excellent SAT results lower down the school. In 2002, 79 per cent of pupils achieved five or more A*–C grades, which was up from 70 per cent in 2001. The average point score was 42.8 and this placed the school fifth in the borough. English is exceptional and science is also good, putting La Sainte in the top five per cent of similar schools. Apart from the usual curriculum, pupils can opt for drama, PE, business studies, ICT and sociology. In 2002, pupils who took more than two A-levels scored 248.8 points on average, continuing a steady upward trend and placing the school seventh in the borough. However, the A-level results are better than the league table suggests – La Sainte pupils get better grades than average but tend to spread their subjects over three years. GNVQs are also offered. The sixth form takes boys and is part of the La Swap consortium (see borough factfile). In 1999, the school was awarded Beacon status for its work in music and PE. An Ofsted report in 2000 praised the school's rising academic standards and its 'well-structured and caring environment where pupils feel secure and happy'. Ofsted was especially impressed by the 'outstanding' way the school promoted the girls' personal development, helping them acquire 'a strong belief in Christian morality...tempered by common sense and humour'.

## Extra-curricular activities

At least five clubs or activities are offered every lunchtime and after school, with a good range of arts, dance and drama available. There are regular field trips. Music activities include an a capella group as well as choirs and an orchestra. There is a sixth-form Amnesty International group and much charity work is undertaken. Each Thursday there is an annual day of retreat and voluntary Mass.

# Maria Fidelis RC Convent School

**34 Phoenix Road, London NW1 ITA (main office and upper school); North Gower Street, London NW1 1HR (lower school)** ☎ 020 7387 3856 📠 020 7388 9558 ✉ admin@mariafidelis.camden.sch.uk Mrs Maria Williams; Chair of Governors: Father Malcolm Euston, Kings Cross, St Pancras Euston, King's Cross, St Pancras, Euston Square, Warren Street **Buses**: 10, 14, 18, 24, 27, 29, 68, 73, 77, 137, 168, 188 Up to sixth form: Dark blazer and kilt, blue or red jumper, white blouse **Demand**: No figures available but oversubscribed for 156 places annually **Type:** Voluntary aided Roman Catholic comprehensive for 885 girls, aged 11 to 18 **Submit application form**: Mid-December 2003 **School hours**: 8.45am–3.30pm; homework clubs are available **Meals**: Hot and cold available **Strong GCSE subjects**: Art, English literature, science, Spanish **London league table position**: 330

## Profile

Maria Fidelis' lower school is perched just above Tottenham Court Road. The upper school is 10 minutes walk away in a Mornington Crescent street. The split site has given the upper and lower schools distinctive atmospheres. Only a few of the older girls have to use both sites. However, the city location means that space is limited – pupils have to travel by coach to a sports centre and the upper school playground is small. There is a school council, a prefects system, a parents' association and a good library. Pastoral care includes professional counselling. Maria Fidelis has a strong Christian ethos and has good links with the Anglican as well as Roman Catholic church, plus good links with the Bangladeshi population. There is provision for special needs pupils. Truancy levels are above the national average.

## Admissions and intake

Priority is given to girls from practising Roman Catholic families, confirmed by a priest's reference. If further priority is needed it is given to: Roman Catholic girls with a sister, mother, aunt or grandmother who attended the school; and Roman Catholic girls who would derive particular religious, medical or pastoral benefit from the school. The remaining places are allocated according to walking distance from the school, or travel by public transport.

## Achievement

Maria Fidelis' exam results fluctuated during the 1990s but were reasonably good. In 2002, 43 per cent of pupils obtained five or more A*–C grades and the school was placed 12th in the borough. Results in art at GCSE have been outstanding as have art and design at A-level. GCSE science, English literature and Spanish have also been strong. Religious studies and PE are compulsory at GCSE. Other GCSE options available include child development, and drama and dance. The small sixth form offers 14 A-levels, including communication studies, performing arts and politics and GNVQs in leisure and tourism (intermediate), health and social care (intermediate) and business (advanced and intermediate). Students taking two or more subjects at A-level scored an average 197.9 points in 2002, placing the school 11th in the borough. An Ofsted inspection in 1996 found standards to be 'sound' and teaching 'a strength'. Inspectors described 'a lively and vibrant community...(where) pupils are encouraged...to develop as confident and independent young women'. They were impressed by the sensitive support for ethnic minority girls.

## Extra-curricular activities

There are regular trips, both at home and abroad. Drama activities and PE are on offer, and there are music and religious groups and homework clubs. The school raises funds for charity and has good relations with the local community.

# North Bridge House School

**1 Gloucester Avenue, London NW1 7AB** 020 7267 6266 020 7284 2508 Mr Richardson Camden Town **Buses**: 31, 46, 134, 135, 253, 274 Navy blazer, grey trousers or skirt, white shirt or blouse, grey pullover, school tie for boys **Demand**: Figures not available but entry at age 11 is competitive; most pupils enter lower down the school **Type**: Selective independent for 482 mixed pupils, aged 2 to 16 **Fees**: £2,650 per term, plus lunch (£156) **Submit application form**: No cut-off date **School hours**: 8.40am–4.05pm; homework clubs are available **Meals**: Hot and cold available **Strong GCSE subjects**: Art, CDT, English, Russian **London league table position**: 84

## Profile

Originally a successful prep school aimed at getting children into private secondary schools, North Bridge House established its senior branch in 1987. Many children still leave at age 13 and the senior school is quite small with about 25 children in each year. However, the school is now coming into its own academically. Its turn-of-the-19th-century premises are housed behind a tall brick wall located on the edge of Regents Park. Pupils benefit from the many facilities the park offers, including several sports pitches, tennis and netball courts and athletics track. A gym is on site as well as science and art facilities, a darkroom and media suite. There are two recently equipped computer rooms. A coach system and a minibus pickup service are available. Help for dyslexia is an important feature of the school and has been extended. Withdrawal lessons provide individual attention, and in severe cases pupils are offered a course at the school's recently opened specialist facility, Willoughby Hall in Hampstead. Parents' involvement is welcomed. There is a prefects system. One famous ex-pupil is Gavin Rossdale, singer with pop/rock group Bush.

## Admissions and intake

Candidates spend a morning in class and are tested in English and maths in the course of lessons. Following an interview, applicants are asked for a current school report.

## Achievement

Results at GCSE at North Bridge House tend to be very high. In 2002, 92 per cent of pupils obtained five or more A*–C grades, a rise on 85 per cent in 2001, reversing a downward trend. The average point score was 44.8, above the borough and national averages, placing the school third in the borough. The school is keen to stress that it is not just an academic hothouse and it prides itself on its 'happy, civilized' atmosphere. Its deliberately co-educational nature is important to this. Pupils go on to a range of sixth forms, including many of those of the top private schools, such as Westminster, South Hampstead and Mill Hill, but also the state consortium La Swap (see borough factfile).

## Extra-curricular activities

The senior school is very strong at chess and two clubs continue the outstanding record of the junior school, who are longtime National Junior Champions. Athletics is another area of strength, with some pupils competing at national level. Other sports available include fencing. Music is also well-established with a choir and several ensembles who perform regularly. There are school trips both within England and abroad. There are homework clubs. Pupils do fund-raising for charities such as the NSPCC.

# Parliament Hill School

**Highgate Road, London NW5 1RL** ☎ 020 7485 7077 Fax 020 7485 9524 e enquiries@parliamenthill.camden.sch.uk Head Christine Peters; Chair of Governors: Dr John Clarke Rail Kentish Town, Gospel Oak Underground Kentish Town, Archway **Buses:** C2, C11, 214 Uniform None **Demand:** 180 places in 2003; oversubscribed **Type:** County comprehensive Technology College for 1650 girls, aged 11 to 19 **Submit application form:** Mid-December 2003 **Mission statement:** The school is a workplace and the work is learning. **School hours:** 8.45am–3.20pm; homework clubs are available **School meals:** Hot and cold available **Strong GCSE subjects:** Art, drama, English, history, music **London league table position:** 264

## Profile

Parliament Hill has won Technology College status along with more than £100,000 extra funding, and it hopes to become a centre for female excellence in science, maths and ICT. The school has an enviable site on the edge of Hampstead Heath and attractive grounds including a sculpture garden. There is a good gym, tennis courts and a playing field. There is a school council and a regular, well-produced newsletter for parents. Truancy remains a problem and has slightly worsened since 1998 to 1.7 per cent, above the national average. In 2000, a few disturbing incidents of violence by pupils outside the school gates were well handled by the head. There is a parent-teacher association.

## Admissions and intake

Admission is through the council. Once special needs applicants have been taken into account, priority is given first to the siblings of pupils and then to those living closest to the school, measured 'as the crow flies'. In 1999, this was within 1.468 of a mile. The girls come from 60 primary schools. The school has quite a wide social mix.

## Achievement

Parliament Hill has improved greatly since the early 1990s. Its success in overcoming inner-city problems was recognized in 2000 when it also became a Beacon school. In 2002, 53 per cent of pupils obtained five or more A*–C grades at GCSE, a rise from 47 per cent in 2001. This was above the borough and national averages and the school was ranked eighth in the borough. GCSE subjects available include performing arts, dance, drama, business studies and IT. A 1998 Ofsted report found Parliament Hill 'impressive...a lively and positive school in which pupils feel valued and supported'. Its GCSE exam results put it in the top 5 per cent of similar schools and the inspectors felt these were not as good as the quality of teaching might suggest. They found only 5 per cent of lessons unsatisfactory and 57 per cent to be good or better. Teaching in the sixth form was also good, with above national average results in A-level English, music, history, French and chemistry. In 2002, pupils taking two or more A-level subjects scored an average 282.8 points, above the national average of 254.4. These results placed Parliament Hill third in the borough league table. GNVQs are available. The sixth form is run jointly with nearby William Ellis Boys' School and is part of the La Swap consortium (see borough factfile). Ofsted praised the head for creating a revitalized school which now provides a 'stable, supportive and caring environment for learning'.

## Extra-curricular activities

Musical activities on offer include two orchestras and an excellent choir. After-school clubs range from homework clubs and trampolining to computing. There are plenty of school trips, including many abroad and an exchange with a Spanish school. There is also a creative-writing club and school and science magazines. There are various activities involving pupils with the local community.

# Royal School Hampstead

65 Rosslyn Hill, London NW3 5UD ☎ 020 7794 7707/8 📠 020 7431 6741 ✉ royschham@aol.com 🌐 www.royalschoolhampstead.net Mrs Carol Sibbson; Chair of Governing Body: Major General PJ Sheppard CB, CBE ⊖ Hampstead **Buses:** C11, C12, 13, 46, 82, 268 Grey blazer and skirt, white shirt or blouse, red pullover, red-and-white school tie, boaters in summer **Demand:** Figures not available, but always fully subscribed **Type:** Selective independent for 241 girls, aged 4 to 18 **Fees:** £2,060 per term, plus lunch (£1.95 a day) (non-boarders); £4,093 per term (full boarders) £3,403 (weekly boarders) **Submit application form:** No cut-off date **School hours:** 8.30am–4pm (seniors), 8.30am–3.45pm (middle school), 8.30am–3.30pm (juniors); homework clubs are available **Meals:** Hot and cold available **Strong GCSE subjects:** All relatively strong **London league table position:** 110

## Profile

Originally known as the Royal Soldiers' Daughters School, Royal School Hampstead was opened in 1858 'to nurse, board, clothe and educate the female children...of soldiers...killed in the Crimean War'. Now open to all families, it still has something of a period feel – pupils wear boaters and the governing body includes several titled members. HRH Princess Alexandra is the school's patron, and the Archbishops of Canterbury, York and London are vice-presidents. The military connection also remains strong. The Ministry of Defence allowance, available through the ranks, enables many army families to take advantage of the only girls' boarding school in London. It is a small school, still on its original site near some of the most picturesque parts of Hampstead. Its present purpose-built buildings are, however, modern and characterless. Boarding arrangements are flexible, with weekly boarding possible. The school welcomes family and friends to visit and encourages frequent contact. The school's small size enables individual attention and a family feel. However, the small number of pupils also means that some areas of school life are less extensively developed than at bigger schools. Class sizes are small. Boarders share bedrooms, and housemistresses live on the same floor. There is a prefect system. Parents report a caring if slightly old-fashioned atmosphere.

## Admissions and intake

Junior girls transfer automatically. Admission to the senior school is by interview and written test, with school reports given consideration. The number of girls from army families means there is an ethnic and social mix.

## Achievement

The school is not especially academic but many girls do well. The exam results partly reflect that the school's selection is less rigorously based on academic potential than in many private schools. In 2002, 74 per cent of girls gained five or more GCSEs at grades A*–C, a drop from 92 per cent in 2001. The school came fourth in the borough league table. The sixth form has only about 16 pupils in total, and not all of them sit two or more A-levels. The standard of A-level results tends to fluctuate. Pupils taking two or more subjects averaged 243 points in 2002, placing the school ninth in the borough A-level league table. The sixth form offers 10 subjects at A-level.

## Extra-curricular activities

Sports available include netball, hockey, rounders, gymnastics and athletics. There is a choir and instrumental tuition on offer. Ballet and speech lessons are also available. There are regular dramatic productions, and clubs include art and computer clubs. There is a range of homework clubs and after-school workshops for specific subjects. The school uses its own minibus to make regular trips to London museums, galleries and theatres. Pupils are encouraged to become involved with the local community through working with charities, including the Camden soup kitchen, among others.

# St Margaret's School

**18 Kidderpore Gardens, London NW3 7SR** 020 7435 2439 020 7431 1308 suzannemeaden@infinnet.co.uk www.st-margarets.co.uk Mrs SJ Meaden, BA (Hons), MBA; Chair of Governors: Lady Smith-Gordon Euston, King's Cross Euston, King's Cross, Mornington Crescent **Buses**: 24, 27, 29, 46, 134, 135, 168, 214 Grey blazer and red sweatshirt, grey skirt, white blouse **Demand**: About three applicants for every place **Type**: Selective independent for 148 girls, aged 5 to 16 **Fees**: £2,200 per term, plus books and extra lessons **Submit application form**: Beginning of December 2003 **Motto**: *Devoir fait loi* (Duty Makes Law) **School hours**: 8.40am–3.20pm (juniors), 8.40am–4pm (seniors); after-school homework provision available **Meals**: Not provided **Strong GCSE subjects**: Art, history, maths, modern languages **London league table position**: 154

## Profile

St Margaret's is a small private school that was founded in 1884. Since 1943 it has been situated in a large red-brick house in a prosperous Hampstead street. The Heath is nearby, and so is the less lovely Finchley Road. The school prides itself on not pressuring girls and on its caring approach. There is one form in each year and class sizes usually number about 20. There is a school council and prefects. The girls walk to a gym for PE and dance and use a nearby playing field for tennis, netball, hockey and rounders. They use the Royal Free Hospital pool for swimming. A mini-bus service, provided by an independent company, can help with transport to and from the school. There is parental involvement through the Friends of St Margaret's.

## Admissions and intake

Applicants sit the school's entrance exam. About half of the pupils aged 11 come from the junior school. Transfer from the junior to the senior school is usual although not automatic.

## Achievement

The school's exam results are good despite its deliberate 'not pushy' approach. Numbers are small and in 2002, 85 per cent of pupils gained five or more A*–C grades at GCSE. This result was well above the borough and national averages and an increase on 83 per cent in 2001. The average point score was 41.8 and this score ranked the school sixth in the borough league table. All girls are taught music and drama. Lots of individual attention is possible, thanks to the school's small size, and the school deliberately cultivates a 'family feel'. Pupils go on to a range of local sixth forms, including those of South Hampstead High School, Channing, Henrietta Barnett and La Swap (see borough factfile).

## Extra-curricular activities

St Margaret's extra-curricular activities are somewhat limited by nature of the school's small size. They are also charged-for in addition to the school fees. The activities include gym clubs, canoeing, sailing and dry slope skiing. Horse riding is also popular. Self-defence is offered as well as speech and drama. There are two choirs and music ensembles and tuition is available in several instruments. There is provision to do homework on the premises after school. School trips include science lectures at the Royal Institution and visits to theatres and concerts.

# South Camden Community School

**Charrington Street, London NW1 1RG** 020 7387 0126 020 7387 0739 Mr Huw Salisbury; Chair of Governors: Mr Alan Chesters Euston, King's Cross Mornington Crescent, Euston, King's Cross **Buses**: 24, 27, 29, 46, 134, 135, 168, 214 Up to Year 9: Navy jumper, sweatshirt or cardigan and black or grey trousers or skirt **Demand**: 180 places in 2003 **Type**: County comprehensive for 910 mixed pupils, aged 11 to 19 **Submit application form**: Mid-December 2003 **Motto**: Skills, cooperation, commitment and success **School hours**: 8.50am–3.25pm; homework clubs are available **Meals**: Hot and cold available **Strong GCSE subjects**: Art, Bengali, drama, photography **London league table position**: 383

## Profile

South Camden Community School serves one of the most deprived areas of Britain. Yet the school, far from being overwhelmed, has many positive features. A committed staff and head work well to provide a mostly orderly environment. There is a refugee coordinator and special provision for helping children who do not speak English. The school has a strong SEN department and works with several outside agencies to help special needs children. There is a prayer room for Muslims. A special unit helps any disabled pupils, of which there are currently nine, become fully integrated members of the school and there is wheelchair access throughout. A brand new technology and ICT block recently opened and there are plans to construct a modern suite of language classes. There is a school council and a parent-teacher association. Truancy remains a problem at 5.1 per cent, five times the national average. However, some of this is accounted for by the high turnover of pupils who leave the area without informing the school. Girls are outnumbered by two to one in some classes.

## Admissions and intake

Admission is through the council. Anyone putting the school as a first choice will be admitted. Many pupils come from the local Bangladeshi population and more than 20 per cent are from refugee families, predominantly Somalian. Many pupils have little or no English and about 80 per cent speak English as an additional language. There is a high number of pupils with learning or other difficulties. The turnover of pupils is high, nearly 50 per cent over five years.

## Achievement

South Camden is a good school, which tries hard to help often disadvantaged pupils. Its exam results represent progress. In 2002, 32 per cent of pupils obtained five or more A*–C grades, and the school was ranked 13th in the Camden. This continues an upward trend over the past seven years. Ofsted visited the school in 2001 and found that it had 'many more strengths than weaknesses'. South Camden was seen to 'meet the diverse needs of all its pupils very effectively'. Teaching is good and the school is led and managed well. Good GCSE results are achieved in art and design, drama and modern foreign languages. In 2002, students taking two or more subjects at A-level scored an average 165.7 points, placing the school 13th in the borough. This was again part of an upward trend. The sixth form is run in partnership with four other schools (see borough factfile). Ofsted found the sixth form to be 'satisfactory' but 'not flourishing as well as it could'. GNVQs are available. Inspectors praised the 'ethos of tolerance and respect' but expressed concern at the low levels of attendance.

## Extra-curricular activities

Football is a popular activity and there are art, music, science, IT, reading and drama clubs. Homework clubs are popular. Weekend residential trips and day visits are arranged. Special activity days in the summer term allow pupils to try out different sports. There is a teacher assigned to involving pupils with the local community and pupils work with various charities.

# South Hampstead High School

**3 Maresfield Gardens, London NW3 5SS** ☎ 020 7435 2899 📠 020 7431 8022 Ⓔ senior@shhs.gdst.net 🌐 www.gdst.net/shhs Mrs V Ainley; Chair of Governors: C Avent Finchley, Frognal, South Hampstead Finchley Road, Swiss Cottage **Buses**: C11, C12, 13, 31, 82, 113, 268 Up to sixth form: Gold blouse, navy skirt or trousers, navy or black coat **Demand**: Figures unavailable but oversubscribed **Type**: Selective independent for 932 girls, aged 4 to 19 **Fees**: £2,385 per term, lunch and extra music excluded **Submit application form**: End of November 2003 **Motto**: *Mehr Licht* (More Light) **School hours**: 8.35am–3.55pm (Mon–Wed), 8.35am–3.30pm (Thurs–Fri); homework clubs are available **Meals**: Hot and cold available, including breakfast **Strong GCSE subjects**: Biology, chemistry, English, French, Latin, physics, religious studies **London league table position**: 11

## Profile

South Hampstead is one of London's most prestigious private schools with a reputation as an academic hothouse. The school shares its otherwise residential street with the Freud Museum and overlooks the busy Finchley Road. It moved to its mainly Victorian red-brick buildings in 1882. With a modern addition, they house excellent facilities, including a large sports hall, theatre and a nearby four-acre sports ground. Careers guidance continues after the girls leave school, with the Minerva Network helping ex-pupils find contacts in the workplace. There is a parent-teacher association, a school council and provision for special needs pupils. The school is not a religious foundation. Famous ex-pupils include the writer Fay Weldon, the actress Helena Bonham-Carter, and Rabbi Julia Neuberger.

## Admissions and intake

Admission is by interview and the North London Consortium examination. South Hampstead is in group one, setting common papers with seven other schools. Music scholarships are available.

## Achievement

The school is 'unashamedly academic' with very high expectations, but it also has what it calls 'a real buzz', with lots of extra-curricular activities going on. Standards are high and results are very good. At GCSE in 2002, five or more A*–C passes were achieved by 100 per cent of girls. This was up on 99 per cent in 2001 and consistent with results over the previous three years. It was well above the borough and local averages and South Hampstead came first in the borough league table. Generally, English, French, Latin, religious studies, biology, chemistry and physics tend to be strong subjects. Greek, Chinese, Japanese, Hebrew and Polish were offered in 1999 at GCSE, as well as French, German, Spanish and Latin. The large sixth form has its own centre within the main site offering 20 A-level subjects, including Latin, Chinese, pure and further maths and politics. Girls are usually expected to have achieved an A grade at GCSE in A-level subjects. In 2002, those pupils taking two or more subjects at A-level averaged 382.3 points. This result was well above the borough and national averages of 251.3 and 254.5. This placed South Hampstead at the top of the borough league table. In previous results, English literature has been outstanding and art and design, biology, French and history have also been very good. There is no subject at the school that could be described as weak.

## Extra-curricular activities

There are extra-curricular activities every morning. There are lots of clubs, including homework clubs and Chocoholics! The school features three orchestras, choirs, chamber groups, big band and sax and salsa groups. The school holds at least two dramatic productions a year. Art visits take place to Rome, Venice, Greece and Turkey. Sport includes netball, football, trampolining and hockey. Pupils can partake in the Duke of Edinburgh's Award scheme and Pensioners' Link as well as charity fund-raising. Foreign expeditions include trips to Peru and Sinai.

# University College School

**Frognal, Hampstead, London NW3 6XH** ☎ 020 7435 2215 📠 020 7431 4385 ⓔ seniorschool@ucsonline.demon.co.uk 🌐 www.ucs.org.uk ➡ Mr Kenneth Durham MA ⇆ Finchley Road and Frognal ⊖ Hampstead, Finchley Road **Buses**: C11, C12, 13, 46, 82, 268 👔 Red and black blazer, white or light blue shirt, black trousers, school tie **Demand**: c. 200 outside applicants for c. 25 places at age 11 **Type**: Selective independent for 714 boys, aged 3 to 19 **Fees**: £3,475 per term, including lunch **Submit application form**: November 2003 **Motto**: *Paulatim* (Slowly But Surely) **School hours**: 8.50am–3.35pm (juniors), 8.50am–4pm; after-school homework provision available **Meals**: Hot and cold available **Strong GCSE subjects**: History, Latin, modern languages **London league table position**: 45

## Profile

Founded in 1830, UCS is a private boys' school with a strong reputation. The school's elegant buildings house a new swimming pool and amphitheatre. It is especially proud of its modern library, which has good IT facilities, and a new sports hall is planned. The school owns 27 acres of playing fields, about 10 minutes away across the Finchley Road. The school also has a field centre in County Durham. Classes normally consist of 22 boys in the first few years, falling to 20 for GCSE courses. Older boys are grouped into one of four 'demes', or houses based on their form class. Pastoral care includes a school counsellor. There is a school council, prefects system and an active parents' guild. There is provision for special needs pupils. Famous ex-pupils include the poets Stephen Spender and Thom Gunn, and the mountaineer Chris Bonington.

## Admissions and intake

Boys at the junior school automatically transfer. Other applicants sit English and Maths exams and are interviewed. For entry at 13, boys must have been registered at least a year in advance and must sit preliminary assessment tests as well as the Common Entrance Exam. They then spend a morning participating in a school activity. A current school report is considered at both 11 and 13.

### Achievement

UCS offers excellent resources combined with high academic standards. In 2002, 98 per cent of pupils obtained five or more A*–C grades, matching the results of 2001. There are a very high number of As or A* grades, which in 1998 accounted for 64 per cent of exams taken. Modern languages, Latin and history tend to be strong, with maths, English and physics also doing well. IT and design have been weaker but the UCS has recently overhauled its IT teaching. In addition to core subjects, economics is an option at GCSE and language choices are French, German, Spanish, Greek and Latin. UCS was second in the GCSE borough tables in 2002. At A-level, the school was placed second in the borough league table with an average point score of 383.3 for pupils taking two or more A-levels. A fail or even a D grade is rare at A-level and in 1998, nearly half of all papers were graded A. Modern languages, Latin and history perform very well at this level along with art, English and maths. The sixth form offers 20 subjects at A-level and allows sciences and arts to be mixed. Classes are usually between eight and 10 pupils. Over 20 per cent of pupils go on to Oxbridge.

### Extra-curricular activities

Clubs at UCS included magic, bee-keeping, roller-blading, debating, film and literature. Hockey, Eton fives, fencing and sailing are among the sports offered. There have been expeditions to Indonesia and India, as well as European visits. A range of musical activity is on offer, with orchestras, choirs and chamber ensembles regularly touring Europe. An annual oratorio is held with a professional orchestra. Several dramatic productions are staged, often in conjunction with girls from South Hampstead High School. There is provision for pupils to do homework after school on the premises. Pupils are involved with the local community by raising money for charities and visiting old people's homes. There is an annual concert for the old people's homes.

## William Ellis School

**Highgate Road, London NW5 1RN** 020 7267 9346 020 7284 1274 info@williamellis.camden.sch.uk www.wellis.camden.sch.uk Mr Richard Tanton BA; Chair of Governors: Mr Martin Hayman Gospel Oak, Kentish Town Kentish Town **Buses**: C2, C11, 214 Up to sixth form: Blue blazer, school tie, white and blue shirt, black trousers **Demand**: 123 places in 2001/2; oversubscribed **Type**: Voluntary aided comprehensive Language College for 887 boys, aged 11 to 19 **Submit application form**: Mid-December 2003 **Motto**: Rather Use Than Fame **School hours**: 8.40am–3.25pm **Meals**: Hot and cold available **Strong GCSE subjects**: Art, maths, sciences **London league table position**: 281

### Profile

Founded in the 19th century by Utilitarians, William Ellis remains proud of its traditions of independent thinking. It is situated on the edge of Hampstead Heath with Parliament Hill Girls' school next door. The school's main hall has been remodelled and several brand-new facilities added, including an excellent library. In 1997, the school became a Language College and all boys study two modern languages in Years 8 and 9. There is a school council and a parent-teacher association. Pastoral care is good, as is pupils' behaviour in general. However, in 1999, Ofsted inspectors were concerned by a disruptive minority who, when unsupervised, were rowdy and aggressive. Famous ex-pupils include Mark Bedford, musician (Madness); Hugh Cornwell, singer (The Stranglers); and Hank Wangford, musician.

### Admissions and intake

Pupils come from around 40 primary schools. The criteria for priority are: brothers of pupils; attainment and commitment to music (up to 12 places); social or medical needs; a strong family connection with the school; and closeness to the school. Where this is broadly equal, nearness of other schools and ease of travel is taken into account. Applicants living more than half a mile away are unlikely to be successful. The intake is of lower attainment than the national average, but the school also attracts significant numbers of boys from a range of abilities.

### Achievement

William Ellis is in the top 5 per cent of similar schools in the country. It takes a below average intake and helps them progress to and above national standards. In 2002, 51 per cent of pupils achieved five or more

A*–C passes at GCSE. This was up on 47 per cent in 2001 and the school was placed ninth in the borough league table. Ofsted found in 1999, that 'standards are rising for pupils of all abilities...and shows pupils (are) making substantial progress'. Maths, sciences and art are especially strong subjects. Modern languages are also good and the school aims that half of all students should take two language GCSEs. One of the few weaknesses was the teaching of music in the younger years. ICT was also criticized but the school has recently overhauled its multi-media facilities. Sixth-form results reflect the fact that many pupils join and leave at this stage, but the teaching and choice of subject are good. Results are very good in art and good in modern languages, design technology, music and geography. Pupils taking two or more A-levels scored an average of 245.7 per cent in 2002, placing the school eighth in the borough. GNVQs are available. The sixth form is run in partnership with Parliament Hill and as part of La Swap consortium (see borough factfile). Ofsted praised the staff's expertise and their committed caring approach – the school 'successfully builds a sense of belonging'.

## Extra-curricular activities

William Ellis has a strong emphasis on music. There is an orchestra, choirs, ensembles and a jazz band. There is a sixth-form trip to China and exchanges with Russian and Spanish schools. The Community Service Volunteers (CSV) learning programme gives pupils community experience and training. The school has excellent links with business, including an ongoing relationship with British Airways.

# Corporation of London

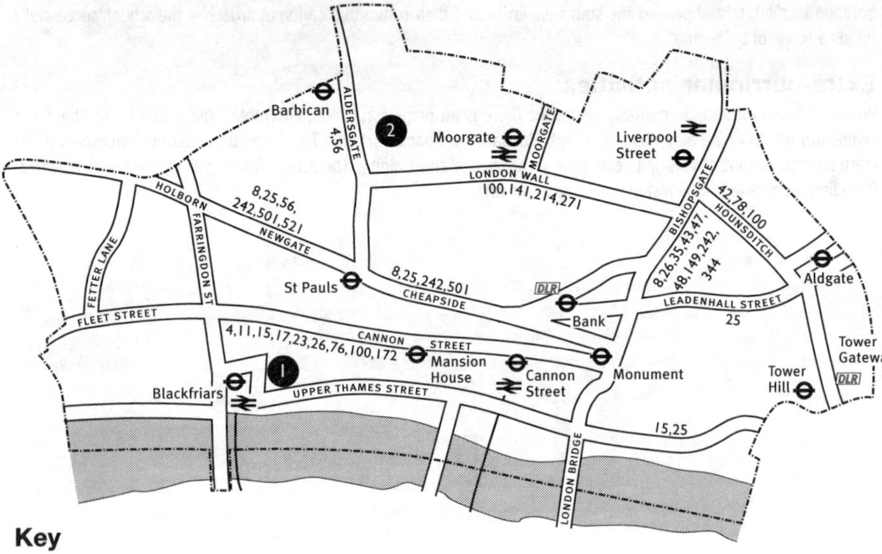


**Key**

1 City of London School

2 City of London School for Girls

# Fact File

**LEA: Guildhall, PO Box 270, London EC2P 2EJ** ☎ 020 7332 1750, Fax 020 7332 1621 🌐 www.cityoflondon.gov.uk **City Education Officer:** David Smith **Political control of the council:** Works on a non-political basis **Percentage of pupils from outside the local authority:** More than 50 per cent of pupils are from North London **Percentage of pupils educated outside the local authority:** 100 per cent of pupils attending maintained schools are educated outside the authority's area as there are no maintained secondary schools in the City.

## Profile

The Corporation of London covers the square mile of the city of London and is the oldest local authority in England, dating back to medieval times. It is like an island in the middle of the capital with its own police force and Lord Mayor. One fifth of the nation's wealth is created in the office blocks of the City by some 28,000 commuting workers, while most of the 8000 residents live in the four post-war residential estates, including the Barbican. The medieval guildhall still remains, alongside many Wren churches and the majestic St Paul's Cathedral, with Tower Bridge as the gateway from the Pool of London to the sea.

The City of London Schools are situated in the heart of the financial district, including the stock exchange and the Bank of England, providing a range of enviable links with business and communication giants. These companies are likely to give pupils assistance with work experience and provide school leavers with valuable career opportunities.

The City supports a vast arts culture, in the internationally renowned Barbican Centre and elsewhere, and the Museum of London is situated along the original London Wall.

## Policy

The Corporation of London assists City residents in finding places in state secondary schools outside the Corporation.

# City of London School

**Queen Victoria Street, London EC4V 3AL** ☎ 020 7489 0291 📠 020 7329 6887 ⓔ information@cls.city-of-london.sch.uk 🌐 www.clsb.org.uk David Levin Becon MA, FRSA; Chairman of Governors: Mrs MWF Kellett JP ⇌ Cannon Street, Blackfriars, City Thameslink ⊖ Bank, St Paul's, Barbican, Mansion House, Monument **Buses:** 45 Black school blazer, black or dark grey trousers, white shirt, school tie **Type:** Independent day school for 900 boys, aged 9 to 19 **Fees:** £2,979 per term **Submit application form:** End of November 2003 **School hours:** 8.45am–4pm **Meals:** Hot and cold available **Strong GCSE subjects:** Drama, English, history, maths **London league table position:** 51

## Profile

City of London School was founded by John Carpenter, Town Clerk of London, in the 15th century. In 1883, the school moved from its original building in Milk Street to the Embankment, and in the summer of 1986, it moved to newly built premises in between Queen Victoria Street and the banks of the river. A path leads from the school's forecourt to the Millennium Bridge, which connects the school with the Globe Theatre and Tate Modern.

The school has a vast playing field and pavilion situated at Grove Park in South-East London. There is computer access for all boys, which includes Internet, CD-ROMs and e-mail. The music technology studio is equipped with 14 multi-media stations with keyboards, specialist software and recording facilities. Other facilities include a 200-seat theatre, drama studio, a Meteosat satellite link, greenhouse and vivarium. The school also boasts an extensive library which stocks more than 20,000 books. Sports facilities include a gym, 25-metre swimming pool, tennis courts and a climbing wall. The sixth form offers the usual range of curriculum-based subjects, with particular emphasis on art, music and drama. Each boy has a homework diary, which both tutors and parents sign. There is a school council, a prefects system and a PTA.

## Admissions and intake

Entrance exams are held in January each year for entry the following September. These include tests in English and mathematics. There are 22 places available for entry at age 10, 70 places for entry at age 11 and 45 places for age 13. Potential candidates are invited for an interview.

## Achievements

The school's GCSE results fluctuate from year to year but remain very high. In 1996, 98 per cent of pupils gained five A*–C grades, which improved to 100 per cent in 1997 but dropped to 98 per cent in 1999 and 2000. In 2001 and 2002, this dropped slightly further to 96 per cent. When Ofsted visited the school in 1999, they found that the boys had a positive approach to their work and achieved very good results. Inspectors noted that there was an excellent atmosphere in the art classes and that the pupils' work was of a high quality. The boys were found to have a very good understanding of most subjects, with the drama, English, maths and music departments described as being 'very strong' with boys achieving 'very high results' in each. The inspectors also found that pastoral care was good.

## Extra-curricular activities

There are a large number of school societies available including political, musical and scientific clubs. Regular field trips and an annual skiing trip take place. The language department organizes an exchange programme each year. Pupils can also take part in the Duke of Edinburgh's Award scheme. A wide range of sports are on offer, including fives, canoeing, sailing and fencing. Pupils work with charities in the local community.

# City of London School for Girls

**St Giles' Terrace, Barbican, London EC2Y 8BB** 020 7628 0841 020 7638 3212 info@clsg.org.uk www.clsg.org.uk Dr Yvonne Burne BA Hons, Ph.D; Chairman of Governors: Edward Lord Cannon Street, Blackfriars, City Thameslink Barbican, St Paul's, Moorgate, Bank **Buses:** 4, 56 Red blazer with school badge, red skirt and white shirt, white socks and black shoes **Type:** Non-Denominational independent day school for 682 girls, aged 7 to 18 **Fees:** £2,787 per term (excl. lunches) **Submit application form:** Contact school for details **School hours:** 8.15am–4pm for juniors and seniors, 8.15am–3.45pm for preparatory department; homework clubs are available **Meals:** Hot and cold available **Strong GCSE subjects:** English, languages, science **London league table position:** 8

## Profile

The school is set within the heart of the City of London, nestling amongst the futuristic glass and concrete towers of the business district, the Barbican cultural centre, and the ancient spires of St Paul's. It was created by William Ward in the late 19th century, after he left a third of his fortune to the Corporation of London to fund the foundation of a girls' school. A £4-million building and redevelopment programme has given the school a 21st-century boost. The school has a preparatory department for 7 to 11 year olds, a senior school and a sixth form. It has a broad curriculum with particular emphasis on art, drama and music. There are extremely good sport facilities, including a 23-metre indoor pool, gym, and two netball and tennis courts. The school has good information technology equipment with more than 200 machines with e-mail, Internet and special science facilities. Sixth-form pupils can organize a peer support group to help the younger girls. There is a good communication between home and school with parents receiving regular reports, and each girl keeping a homework diary. There is a PTA and a school council. There is also provision for special needs pupils.

## Admissions and intake

The admissions procedure is rigorous for both preparatory and senior years. There is an entrance exam for the preparatory department and also for the senior school. These exams are held during spring term with papers in English and mathematics. Selected candidates are then called for an interview.

## Achievements

GCSE results at the school fluctuate from year to year but remain very high. In 1996, 97 per cent of pupils gained five A*–C grades, which improved to 100 per cent in 1998 but dropped to 97 per cent in 1999 and 2000. This improved to 100 per cent in 2001 and 2002. There has not been an Ofsted report for six years.

## Extra-curricular activities

There is a wide range of clubs available, including homework clubs, subject-based clubs, computing, drama, play-reading, French cine club, and junior and senior debating societies. One major drama production is staged each year. There are also regular school visits around the UK and abroad. Music is also central to the school's philosophy and there are four choirs, three orchestras, a wind band, a madrigal group and several chamber groups. Sixth-formers can take part in community work. Pupils can also take part in the Duke of Edinburgh's Award scheme and a Young Enterprise business initiative.

# Croydon

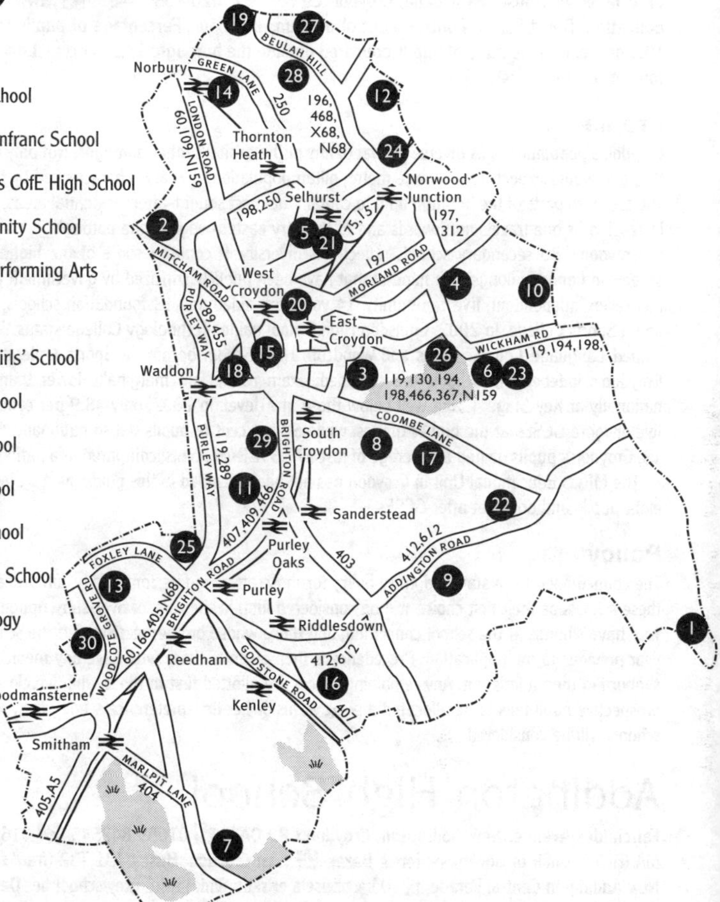


## Key

1. Addington High School
2. The Archbishop Lanfranc School
3. Archbishop Tenison's CofE High School
4. Ashburton Community School
5. BRIT School for Performing Arts and Technology
6. Coloma Convent Girls' School
7. Coulsdon High School
8. Croham Hurst School
9. Croydon High School
10. Edenham High School
11. Haling Manor High School
12. Harris City Technology College
13. Lodge School
14. Norbury Manor High School for Girls
15. Old Palace School of John Whitgift
16. Riddlesdown High School
17. Royal Russell School
18. St Andrew's CofE Voluntary Aided High School
19. St Joseph's College
20. St Mary's High School
21. The Selhurst High School for Boys
22. Selsdon High School
23. Shirley High School
24. Stanley Technical School for Boys
25. Thomas More School
26. Trinity School
27. Virgo Fidelis Convent Senior School
28. Westwood High School
29. Whitgift School
30. Woodcote High School

# Factfile

**LEA: Taberner House, Park Lane, Croydon C9 3JS** ☎ 020 8686 4433 🌐 www.croydon.gov.uk **Director of Education:** David Sands **Political control of council:** Labour **Percentage of pupils from outside the borough:** 10.1 per cent **Percentage of pupils educated outside the borough:** 13.2 per cent **London league table positions (out of 32 boroughs):** 13th

## Profile

Croydon's population is as diverse as that of any of the capital's other boroughs. Not only does it show the ethnic mix that one would expect from a large metropolitan population, it is also characterized by huge income discrepancies. The southern parts of the borough tend to contain the most sought-after residential areas, with levels of disadvantage increasing as one travels northwards and to the very eastern edge of the borough.

Croydon's 30 secondary schools reflect this diversity. It contains some of the highest-performing independent schools in London, alongside a handful that have been publicly criticized by government education officials. Croydon has seven independent, five community, 14 voluntary aided and 13 foundation schools, two city Technical Colleges and a Sports College. In 2002, Coulsdon High School gained Technology College status, Westwood Girls' High School gained Language College status and Woodcote High School became a Sports College. When the performance of Croydon's independent schools are excluded, exam results are marginally lower than the average expectations nationally at Key Stage 4, and well below those at A-level. In 2002, only 48.9 per cent of Croydon's pupils gained five or more GCSEs at the higher grades, while 50 per cent of pupils did so nationally. Similarly, by the end of Year 13, Croydon's pupils gained an average of just 172.5 A-level points, compared to a national average of 254.5 points.

The MRCS Educational Unit in Croydon has not been included in this guide, as it an independent school with only eight pupils and does not offer GCSEs.

## Policy

The council operates a standard entry policy for those attending its community comprehensives. Pupils who place these schools as their first choice will be considered first. In the case of over-subscription, priority is given to those who have siblings at the school concerned, and those whose brother or sister left the school not more than one year previous to the application. Precedence is then given to those who have any medical or special reason supporting their admission. Any remaining places are allotted first to those who live closest to the school. If the prospective pupil fails to be allocated a place at his or her first-preference school, then second- and third-choice schools will be considered.

# Addington High School

**Fairchildes Avenue, New Addington, Croydon CR9 0AA** ☎ 01689 842545 📠 01689 843504 Tim Davies MA (Hons); Chair of Governors: Mrs A Baker 🚆 East Croydon **Buses:** T31, T32 (from tram), X30, 130, 464 Trams: New Addington Central Parade 👔 Dark trousers or skirt, white shirt, grey school tie **Demand:** 416 applications for 180 places in 2001/2 **Type:** Community comprehensive for 803 mixed pupils, aged 11 to 16 **Submit application form:** October 2003 **Motto:** Ambition, Harmony, Success **School hours:** 8.45am–3.15pm; homework clubs are available **Meals:** Hot and cold available **Strong GCSE subject:** Art **London league table position:** 492

## Profile

Addington High has extensive playing fields covering approximately 32 acres of grounds. It has also benefited from the construction of a new library and a computer suite in recent years. The school buildings are quite generous for the size of the school, although a small number of them remain shabby in appearance. In 2002, Ofsted inspectors criticized the 'dilapidated' condition of the buildings. Beyond the core subjects at Key Stage 4, pupils have a choice of two further subjects, including media studies, business studies and information studies. One strength of the school is its commitment to the personal development of its pupils. It has worked hard to develop links with the local community and now has an admirable work experience programme for all Year 10 pupils. Since February 2000, Addington High has also been participating in the Heartstone project to raise multi-cultural awareness. Pupils are encouraged to assume responsibility through involvement in the school council and the prefect system for those in the upper years. Year 11 pupils are given specific training as anti-bully counsellors. There is a coordinator for pupils with special needs. Most pupils go on to John Ruskin sixth form, although Croydon College is also popular. Truancy is a problem at the school and in 2000 it had the highest rate of unauthorized absence in the borough at 3.7 per cent, three times the national average.

### Admissions and intake

Admissions are through the council (see borough factfile). Most pupils are drawn from the immediate area of New Addington.

### Achievement

The area of New Addington is marked by relatively high levels of social disadvantage, which has not helped the school in its search for high results. To combat the school's low standards, Addington High was incorporated in an Education Action Zone in 1998. Although this has allowed new funding to be channelled into the school, the results have yet to show a corresponding improvement. In 2002, 18 per cent of pupils obtained five or more GCSEs at grades A*–C. This was up on 10 per cent in 2001, but still behind 22 per cent in 2000, and the school was ranked 27th in Croydon's league table. Ofsted inspected the school in 2002 and praised the 'very good' leadership of the head teacher. Inspectors noted that all the staff 'are making great efforts to bring about improvements' and that some of the teaching 'reaches high standards'. However, there were still 'serious weaknesses' owing to a shortage of teachers, a 'significant proportion' of unsatisfactory teaching and 'very poor' attendance levels.

### Extra-curricular activities

Ofsted praised the range of activities available and the school boasts over 40 clubs ranging from computers to netball, drama and fishing. Sports include football, athletics, cricket, basketball and tennis. There is an after-school homework club and Saturday morning homework classes. Occasional trips are organized to theatres, museums and other places of interest. Pupils work with local charities.

## The Archbishop Lanfranc School

**Mitcham Road, Croydon CR9 3AS** ☎ 020 8689 1255 ℻ 020 8683 3113 ✉ admin@lanfranc.com ☞ Mr DC Clark BA; Chair of Governors: Cllr D Loughborough **Buses:** 264, 289 👔 Navy blue school blazer, dark grey trousers or skirt, white shirt or blouse, school tie **Demand:** 523 applications for 200 places in 2001/2 **Type:** Foundation school for 1035 mixed pupils, aged 11 to 16 **Submit application form:** October 2003 **School hours:** 8.50am–3.20pm; homework clubs are available **Meals:** Hot and cold available **Strong GCSE subjects:** Art, IT, modern languages, sociology **London league table position:** 347

### Profile

Archbishop Lanfranc School opened its doors in 1931 as a separate girls' and boys' school, and remained so until they were merged in 1970. Four years later, the school moved to its current, purpose-built site. Although this is far from being Croydon's most attractive school, it does have a 12-acre site with its own playing fields, and its buildings are well equipped to deliver all national curriculum subjects. All pupils also follow a PSE course and Year 11 participate in a work experience programme. There is a school council and a parent-teacher association. There is provision for pupils with special needs.

### Admissions and intake

The school admits up to 15 per cent of its annual intake on the basis of academic performance in standard tests administered by the school. The remaining 170 places are allotted in accordance with the Council's standard entry formula (see borough factfile). It mainly draws pupils from the immediate locality, an area of significant social disadvantage.

### Achievement

In 2002, 37 per cent of pupils gained five or more GCSEs at grades A*–C and the school was placed 22nd in Croydon. Although this was below the national average, this result does compare favourably against the levels of attainment witnessed in similar schools and those on entry to the school. The school has been slowly improving its results over recent years and this was four per cent up on 2001. The average point score at GCSE was 32.1, below the borough average of 34.3. Archbishop Lanfranc's success at ensuring that 95 per cent of its pupils left with five or more passes at grades A*–G in 2000, a figure that far exceeds national expectations, is a credit to the school. The best results have generally been seen in IT, art, sociology and modern languages. In 2000, Ofsted was complimentary of the education that Archbishop Lanfranc's offers. It claimed that 'this is a very effective, and improving, school. The good quality teaching, combined with the pupils' very good attitudes, ensures that pupils' levels of attainment are improved significantly whilst they are at the school'. They judged that 'pupils are enthusiastic about school and learning' and that they 'are attentive and many show real interest in their subject'. Ofsted added that 'pupils take pride in their school and speak highly of their teachers'. However, like all schools, it does have a difficult minority, which led to 54 fixed-term and three permanent exclusions in 1998–9.

### Extra-curricular activities

All pupils are encouraged to take part in the school's busy sporting calendar, which features competitive and non-competitive activities such as football, rugby, netball, hockey, basketball, badminton, table tennis and trampolining. There is also a popular Duke of Edinburgh's Award scheme, which many students choose to follow to gold standard, and a large selection of lunchtime and after-school clubs to suit most interests, including homework clubs. There are trips both at home and abroad.

# Archbishop Tenison's CofE High School

**Selborne Road Croydon, CR0 5JQ** ☎ 020 8688 4014 Fax 020 8681 6336 ✉ archten@rmplc.co.uk 🌐 www.archten.croydon.sch.uk Head: Mr RT Ford BA, FRSA; Chair of Governors: Mr T Godfrey Rail: East Croydon **Buses**: X30, 54, 64, 119, 130, 194, 198, 353, 354, 367, 466 Uniform: Navy school blazer, grey trousers or skirt, white shirt or blouse, house tie; Sixth form: Business-like dress **Demand**: 256 applications for 96 places in 2001/2 **Type**: Voluntary aided Church of England comprehensive for 700 mixed pupils, aged 11 to 18 **Submit application form**: October 2003 **Motto**: *Tenaciter* (Tenaciously) **School hours**: 8.25am–3.20pm **Meals**: Hot and cold available **Strong GCSE subjects**: English, PE **London league table position**: 125

### Profile

The school was founded in 1714 by its namesake to provide education for 10 boys and 10 girls from Croydon. It moved twice before settling in its current location in 1959. It is built on a fairly constricted site, with a limited provision of playground and playing fields. The buildings themselves are dominated by the original 1959 structure, along with further additions. The school is to benefit from a long-awaited extension, providing additional teaching space. All pupils study English, maths, French, the three sciences and technology, and opt for two further subjects from art, geography, German, history, music and RE. Pupils can also take GCSE PE. The majority of pupils remain at the school and study A-levels at the sixth-form centre, which is run with St Andrew's and based at the Tenison's site. A total of 17 A-levels are on offer, including government and politics, PE and sociology. A business GNVQ at both intermediate and advanced levels is also available. All pupils have career lessons in Year 9 and then have a two-week work placement in Year 10 or 11. Senior pupils can become prefects. Special needs pupils may be taught in smaller groups. The strong PTA raised money for a school minibus in recent years.

### Admissions and intake

The school operates a joint admissions process with St Andrew's. A minimum of 70 per cent of places are reserved for families who are practising members of the Church of England and who live within the Archdeaconry of Croydon. Any remaining places are granted first to members of other Christian denominations that are specified in the school prospectus. The school remains comparatively small, making the application process highly competitive.

### Achievement

Tenison's may not be one of Croydon's most attractive schools, but it is certainly one of its most academically successful. It consistently comes towards the top of Croydon's league tables, performing well when compared to both borough and national averages. In 2002, it was eighth in the borough. A total of 80 per cent of pupils gained five or more GCSEs at grades A*–C. This was down up on 68 per cent in 2001 and reversed a downward trend. The average point score of pupils taking two or more A/AS-levels was 280.5, above the national average, placing the school sixth in the borough league table.

### Extra-curricular activities

A great range of activities include a thriving science society, which helped three students in 2000 to win the Charles Darwin prize in the finals of the Royal Society's British Youth Science Fair. The debating society has also had recent success in the London Oratory Group public speaking competition. There are frequent sporting fixtures for cricket, football, netball and tennis. The senior netball team has been successful, winning the national schools championship in 1992. Regular trips to London's theatres, museums and places of interest are arranged, as well as annual French and German exchanges. Pupils are involved with local charities.

## Ashburton Community School

**Shirley Road, Croydon CR9 7AL** 020 8656 0222 020 8656 1474 admin@ashburton.croydon.sch.uk Mr R Warne B.Sc, MA; Chair of Governors: Mr D Wada Woodside **Buses**: 54, 312, 726 Dark navy school blazer, dark grey or black trousers or skirt, white shirt or blouse, school tie **Demand**: 1071 applications for 240 places in 2001/2 **Type**: Community comprehensive for 1110 mixed pupils, aged 11 to 16 **Submit application form**: October 2003 **School hours**: 8.40am–3.15pm; homework clubs are available **Meals**: Hot and cold available **Strong GCSE subjects**: Art, double-award science, drama, history, media studies, RE **London league table position**: 398

### Profile

Having been criticized as one of the worst 18 schools in England in 1997, Ashburton was released from 'special measures' two years later. Since 1999, improvements have continued to be made, with the result that the school was given special recognition in the annual report of Her Majesty's Chief Inspector of Schools in February 2000. Plans have been floated to launch it as a centre for sporting and educational excellence. Purpose-built in the 1960s in concrete and located in a largely residential area, the school uses its 22 acres of grounds and sports fields to develop a broad and popular PE curriculum. It boasts the national Sportsmark Award for its provision of sport and has achieved much recent success, such as reaching the national finals of the Sun Alliance Pentathlon in 2000. It also has a reasonable stock of adequately maintained rooms, with specialist facilities for all subjects. Changes have been introduced to make the curriculum more accessible and relevant to its pupils, most significantly through the introduction of GNVQs. Subjects on offer include health and social care, and business. Ashburton runs a strong system of prefects and a school council, allowing pupils of all ages to become involved in the running of the school. There is a parent-teacher association and provision for pupils with special needs.

### Admissions and intake

Admissions are through the council (see borough factfile). The school roll had fallen over recent years from around 1000 in 1995 to about 600 in 2000. However, this trend has now been reversed, with places being significantly oversubscribed since 1999. Most pupils come from the immediate locality, but some come from Lewisham, Southwark and Lambeth.

### Achievement

There has been a huge improvement in exam results at Ashburton. In 2000, 25 per cent of pupils gained five or more GCSEs at grades A*–C, compared to just 17 per cent in 1997. Results dipped in 2001 to 22 per cent but rose again to 31 per cent in 2002. This was below the local and national averages and the school was ranked 25th in Croydon. Perhaps the most dramatic transformation has occurred in the attitudes of pupils. There now appears to be a positive attitude towards learning, and although the 1999 Ofsted inspection claimed that 'standards of behaviour remain uneven', behaviour has improved. The fact that the incidence of permanent exclusion has dropped from 14 pupils in 1997–8 to just one student in 1999–2000, speaks volumes about the school's turnaround However, authorized absence is high at 8.8 per cent, but unauthorized absence is below the national average at 0.8 per cent.

### Extra-curricular activities

Sporting clubs include badminton, table tennis, trampolining, athletics, cycling, weight-training, orienteering and rugby. There is an increasing number of non-sporting clubs, including a rocket club, a flourishing drama club and numerous music groups, including an orchestra, a band and several choirs.

# BRIT School for Performing Arts and Technology

**60 The Crescent, Croydon CR0 2HN** ☎ 020 8665 5242 📠 020 8665 8676 ✉ admin@brit.croydon.sch.uk 🌐 www.brit.croydon.sch.uk 🧑 Nick Williams; Chair of Governors: Mr John Deacon 🚉 Selhurst **Buses:** 50, 75, 157, 468 👔 None **Demand:** 110 to 120 places available **Type:** Comprehensive City Technology College for 761 mixed pupils, aged 14 to 19 **Submit application form:** Contact school for details **School hours:** 9am–7pm **Meals:** Hot and cold available **Strong GCSE subjects:** Drama, IT, music **London league table position:** 126

## Profile

Britain's only free performing-arts school opened amid much publicity in September 1991. The modern concrete, glass and steel buildings have a light, airy feel. The school's excellent specialist facilities include a 350-seat theatre, a radio broadcasting suite, TV studio, video-editing suite and music-recording studio, and dance and drama studios. There are also two gymnasiums. At Key Stage 4, pupils opt for a major and minor arts specialism, in addition to the core national curriculum subjects. In the upper years, pupils undertake a BTEC National Diploma or an advanced GNVQ qualification, plus additional A-levels if preferred. This emphasis means that the school appears to perform poorly in performance tables, when in fact its standards of achievement are quite commendable. All Year 11 pupils have the opportunity to do work experience, and for pupils who are 16 and above, the school also organizes work experience related to pupils' specialist course choices. School days are long and the system of five terms of about eight weeks can be unsettling. However, most pupils seem to thrive in the unconventional, flexible and friendly atmosphere. There is a parent-teacher association, a school council and provision for pupils with special needs. In 2000, 44.5 per cent of leavers went on to further or higher education, many taking up entertainment-related courses. It is a reflection of BRIT's success that it has already produced some famous faces, notably members of pop group Another Level. Many more ex-pupils can be found performing in London's West End or working in production for television, radio and theatres across the country.

## Admissions and intake

Applications should be made directly to the school. Applicants must show a commitment to the performing arts and a willingness and an aptitude to meet the demands of the curriculum, but there is no academic selection. All candidates and their families are interviewed. The school is heavily oversubscribed, drawing pupils from across Greater London and occasionally beyond.

## Achievement

The 2002 results were very good, with 87 per cent of students gaining five or more GCSEs at grades A*–C, This reversed the trend of the past few years when figures have been well below borough and national averages, ranking the school ninth in the borough. Pupils taking two or more A/AS-levels scored an average of 118.6 points, well below the national average, but this figure represents a minority of the school's students. The A-level results were up on 1999's results and placed the school bottom of the borough league table. Ofsted found pupils' behaviour and attendance to be 'excellent'. They continued, 'It is clear from their very positive attitudes that students across all year groups want to come to the BRIT school to learn and, in many cases, have to be persuaded to go home at the end of the day.'

## Extra-curricular activities

Unsurprisingly, strong emphasis is placed on the performing arts, with drama and music productions frequently staged to a very high standard. The school also has popular radio and TV production groups. There are trips to the theatre and also trips abroad.

# Coloma Convent Girls' School

**Upper Shirley Road, Croydon CR9 5AS** ☎ 020 8654 6228 📠 020 8656 6485, 020 8654 4550 🧑 Mrs M Martin BA; Chair of Governors: Mrs A Jackson **Buses:** 54, 119, 130, 166, 194 👔 Blue school blazer, navy skirt, blue blouse **Demand:** 328 applications for 150 places in 2001/2 **Type:** Voluntary aided Roman Catholic comprehensive for 924 girls, aged 11 to 18 **Submit application form:** October 2003 **Motto:** *Laborare est orare*

(To Work is to Pray) **School hours**: 8.20am–3pm; homework clubs are available **Meals**: Hot and cold available **Strong GCSE subjects**: All relatively strong **London league table position**: 80

### Profile

Originally founded in 1869 by the Daughters of Mary and Joseph, Coloma moved to its current location in 1965. It is situated in a residential area set in spacious grounds, which include tennis and netball courts and a lacrosse and athletics field. Other notable facilities are a purpose-built sixth-form centre, a music studio, art and pottery rooms, technology workshops, three computer rooms and two gymnasiums. All girls take RE to GCSE besides English language and literature, maths, double-award science, technology and French or German and geography or history. An optional subject is then chosen from art and design, drama, music, business studies and GNVQ IT. In the sixth form, 20 A-levels and GNVQs in health and social care, IT and business studies are on offer. Sixth-formers can also become prefects or participate in the school council. All Year 11 pupils have a two-week work experience placement. There is a PTA. A member of Croydon's Education Psychology Department visits each half term to help girls with specific learning needs, and support is also offered by Croydon's Hearing and Visually Impaired Service.

### Admissions and intake

Preference is given to practising Catholics, and although the school claims to welcome applications from other faiths, given its popularity, there is little chance that they will meet with success. The chance of admission if Coloma is not given as a first choice is also slim. Priority in admissions is given to those applicants who show the greatest degree of commitment to the Catholic church and a Catholic education, followed by those who have either a sister at the school or have a direct family link to Coloma. Those with medical reasons supporting their application are also given high consideration. Any remaining places are given to those living closest to the school.

### Achievement

Coloma was singled out for praise in 1999 by the then Chief Inspector of Schools, Chris Woodhead. The school has since improved standards still further to retain its position at the top of Croydon's state schools league table for GCSE results. In 2002, 89 per cent of pupils gained five or more GCSEs at grades A*–C, considerably higher than the national average. The average point score for those pupils who studied two or more A-levels was 305.8, above the national average, placing the school first in the borough's state schools league table. In 2001, Ofsted described Coloma as 'a very effective school, in many respects excellent'. Inspectors praised the 'outstanding' ethos of the school and its 'consistently good teaching'.

### Extra-curricular activities

Ofsted inspectors found that the range of activities on offer was 'very good' and that 'performances in music are excellent'. The choir has a very good reputation, having regularly recorded for the BBC, and the school has a commendable sporting record in netball, rounders, lacrosse, tennis and athletics. There are numerous clubs and pupils can participate in the Young Enterprise scheme. Among the many trips organized, there are skiing expeditions, sports and music tours and language courses abroad, as well as a religious retreat. Pupils raise funds for local charities.

## Coulsdon High School

**Homefield Road, Old Coulsdon, Coulsdon, Surrey CR5 1ES** ☎ 01737 551161 📠 01737 557410 ⓔ admin@coulsdonhigh.net 🌐 www.coulsdonhigh.croydon.sch.uk Mr C Mackinlay MA, Cert.Ed; Chair of Governors: Mr D Howard **Buses**: 404, 409, 466 Dark school blazer (boys); green school jumper (girls), dark trousers or skirt, white shirt or blouse, school tie **Demand**: 423 applications for c.180 places in 2001/2 **Type**: Comprehensive Techonolgy College foundation school for 849 mixed pupils, aged 11 to 16 **Submit application form**: October 2003 **School hours**: 8.40am–3.30pm **Meals**: Hot and cold available **Strong GCSE subjects**: All relatively strong **London league table position**: 326

### Profile

Coulsdon High is set in 19 acres of grounds on the edge of Coulsdon Common, giving it a very rural atmosphere. Most of the buildings date from the school's opening in 1964, but have been supplemented by modern additions to provide the school with up-to-date facilities. It has well-resourced science labs, technology rooms and a specialist drama studio. A new learning-resources centre was opened in 1998 and two new design technology laboratories are to open in summer 2003. The school gained Technology College status in 2002. It is the policy of the school to enter all pupils for nine GCSEs, unless deemed inappropriate. All pupils study a broad curriculum that includes English literature and language, maths, double-award science, technology, a foreign language, geography and/or history or business studies and one of the creative arts. More gifted pupils can also take GCSE statistics and AS-level English. All pupils participate in a work experience programme and can become prefects in the upper year. There is a school council and a parent-teacher association. There is provision for pupils with special needs. Over 80 per cent of leavers continue their education after the age of 16, with the nearby Coulsdon College being the most popular choice.

### Admissions and intake

The school generally draws pupils from a wide catchment area, with priority being given to the pupils of the local village schools of Keston and Byron, and to Coulsdon CofE Primary. Any remaining places are given first to pupils with siblings at the school, then to those who have medical reasons for wanting to attend Coulsdon High. Finally, places are allocated to those applicants who live within the shortest distance, measured in a straight line from the school.

### Achievement

In 2002, 44 per cent of pupils gained five or more GCSEs at A*–C grades, below the national average of 51.6 per cent. This result was up on 42 per cent in 2001 and the school was ranked 20th in the borough league table. In 2001, Ofsted reported that Coulsdon High is a 'good school', with '...skilful leadership, a committed teaching staff and a strong governing body'.

### Extra-curricular activities

The school's size affords it an ample choice of sporting and creative extra-curricular activities. There are regular competitive football, cricket, basketball, swimming, athletics, netball, hockey and tennis fixtures. During lunchtimes and after school, pupils can engage in activities such as trampolining and aerobics, or join the chess, computer, and photography clubs, or even the juggling society. The school also participates in the Duke of Edinburgh's Award scheme. Visits are organized to local theatres, museums and places of interest. In recent years, trips have been arranged to Greece, Germany, Belgium and the US for educational and recreational purposes. The school also has use of a cottage in Snowdonia, which is enjoyed annually by groups in Years 7 and 10.

## Croham Hurst School

**79 Croham Road, South Croydon, Surrey CR2 7YN** ☎ 020 8680 3064 Fax 020 8681 2490 ✉ headcroham@aol.com 🌐 www.croham.surrey.sch.uk Head: Miss SC Budgen; Chair of Governors: Mr David Simmons ⇄ South Croydon **Buses:** 64 Uniform: Royal blue school jumper, blue skirt, blue blouse; Sixth form: Smart casual clothes **Demand:** No figures available but 50 places available **Type:** Selective independent for 547 girls, aged 3 to 19 **Fees:** £2,425 per term **Submit application form:** No cut-off date **Motto:** *Finis Coranate Opus* (The End Crowns the Work) **School hours:** 8.30am–3.45pm **Meals:** Hot and cold available **Strong GCSE subjects:** Art, English, maths **London league table position:** 71

### Profile

Since its foundation in 1899, Croham Hurst has occupied an attractive, open site on the edge of Lloyd Park. The school itself is a pleasing mixture of Edwardian and later 20th-century buildings, surrounded by gardens and playing fields. It has an extensive array of facilities, including a modern science block, art and drama studio, appropriate technology facilities and an outdoor heated swimming pool. The relatively small size of the school helps to give it a friendly, welcoming atmosphere. Pupils are offered a wide choice of GCSEs, with most girls selecting 10 subjects from a possible 24. Beyond the national curriculum subjects, classical studies, Latin, Spanish and textiles are available as additional options. Sixth-formers can choose from a total of 20 A- and AS-levels. Croham Hurst does not have prefects, but there is a school council and sixth-form committee for those pupils keen to assume responsibility around the school. There is a parent-teacher association.

### Admissions and intake

The school's proven record of exam success at both Key Stage 4 and beyond makes it an appealing option for parents and ensures that it is regularly oversubscribed. Admissions are based upon the results of the school's own entrance exam held in the January preceding the September intake. A small number of scholarships are available for the very academically able, and the school is also able to offer financial bursaries. Pupils come from all over Croydon and beyond.

### Achievement

In 2002, 95 per cent of pupils gained five or more GCSEs at grades A*–C. This result delivered the high standards that parents and pupils have come to expect of Croham, improving on 91 per cent in 2001. The results of 2002 were well above the national average and the school was ranked fifth in the borough league table. Given these results, it is not surprising that most girls choose to remain in education beyond 16, with the majority continuing at Croham Hurst. Again, pupils in the sixth form achieve impressive results. The 2002 A/AS-level results saw pupils taking two or more subjects gaining an average of 266.8 points. This was above the borough average and placed the school seventh in the borough. Pupils can also take GNVQs. Over 80 per cent of pupils decide to continue their education at university level, many going to some of the country's best-known and respected institutions.

### Extra-curricular activities

The school offers a wide range of recreational and curriculum-enriching activities. Music is a particularly popular choice, with girls playing in a variety of orchestras, wind bands, jazz bands and choirs. Sport is dominated by lacrosse and netball, with tennis, athletics, basketball, cricket and swimming also on offer. There is a wide variety of lunchtime and after-school clubs, including computer and debating groups, as well as Christian Union and drama societies. The school organizes residential visits to field centres for biology and geography, and there are also skiing trips. Charity activities are a regular feature. In the academic year 1999–2000, the school raised money for a number of charities, including the Association of Children's Hospices and The Teenage Cancer Trust.

## Croydon High School

**Old Farleigh Road, Selsdon, South Croydon, Surrey CR2 8YB** ☎ 020 8651 5020 📠 020 8657 5413 ⓔ info@cry.gdst.net ✉ Miss LM Ogilvie; Chair of Governors: Mr AC Carey ⇄ East Croydon **Buses:** 64, 354, 412, 612 👔 Navy skirt, blue blouse, navy school jumper with green and white trim; Sixth form: Smart casual clothes **Demand:** No figures available but 100 places available **Type:** Selective independent, part of the Girls' Day School Trust for 929 girls, aged 4 to 18 **Fees:** £2,385 per term **Submit application form:** No cut-off date **School hours:** 8.30am–3.30pm (Mon and Fri); 8.30am–4pm (Tues, Wed, Thurs) **Meals:** Hot and cold available **Strong GCSE subjects:** All relatively strong **London league table position:** 34

### Profile

Croydon High was founded in 1874 and moved to its present purpose-built site in 1966. Set amongst large, spacious grounds, the landscaped site does much to soften the otherwise harsh appearance of many of the buildings. There is an ample provision of well-maintained classrooms, as well as a number of specialist facilities of the highest quality. The school makes a concerted effort to ensure that its facilities are constantly improved to keep up with demand and it now has a new computer suite and dance studio. The sports centre is only a few years old and comprises a large sports hall, a well-equipped gymnasium, a swimming pool and fitness studio. Most pupils take at least nine GCSEs, with textiles, classics and options for a second or even third modern foreign language on offer. In the sixth form, pupils can choose from among 20 A-levels and 12 AS-level options. Pupils can become prefects or members of the school council. There is a parent-teacher association and provision for pupils with special needs.

### Admissions and intake

Croydon High is a prominent member of the Girls' Day School Trust, which has been providing affordable independent education of a high quality since it was founded in the 19th century. Entry is based on a competitive exam held in early January. In line with the GDSTs founding aims, the school offers a wide range of scholarships based on academic performance in the entrance tests and a generous system of bursaries according to financial need.

### Achievement

Described in the last Ofsted report as 'an excellent and highly successful school', Croydon High's previous results have consistently placed it among Croydon's very best. The 2002 results were no exception, with 100 per cent of pupils gaining at least five GCSE passes at the higher grades. The average point score was 55.6 and this placed the school second in Croydon. These excellent standards are maintained in the sixth form, with an average point score of 366.8. This was well above the national average. Croydon High was placed second in the borough league table results. An impressive 95 per cent of pupils choose to continue in higher education, many going to the country's most prestigious universities.

## Extra-curricular activities

The school has a successful range of extra-curricular activities. For sporting types, options include netball, hockey, dance, tennis, table tennis, swimming, rounders, volleyball, badminton, basketball and aerobics. Every year for the past three decades has seen at least one of the school's netball teams reaching the National Finals, winning the title a staggering 14 times in total. Given that the school's alumni includes Jacqueline du Pré, the world-famous cellist, it has a suitably flourishing musical life, with three orchestras, a wind band, brass ensemble and three choirs. The school also runs Croydon's largest centre for the Duke of Edinburgh's Award scheme. Regular trips include geography and biology field trips as well as skiing and adventure holidays.

# Edenham High School

**Orchard Way, Shirley, Croydon CR0 7NJ** ☎ 020 8776 0220 📠 020 8777 3904 ⓔ admin@edenham.croydon.sch.uk 🌐 www.edenhamhigh.croydon.sch.uk Mr J Parker BS.c; Chair of Governors: Mrs J Pay East Croydon **Buses**: 54, 119, 194, 198, 289, 367, 466, 729 Dark trousers or skirt, white shirt or blouse, school tie **Demand**: 665 applications for 240 places in 2001/2 **Type**: Comprehensive foundation school Technology College for 1095 mixed pupils, aged 11 to 16 **Submit application form**: Late October the year preceding that of entry **Motto**: Raising and Rewarding Achievement **School hours**: 8.30am–7.15pm; homework clubs are available **Meals**: Hot and cold available **Strong GCSE subjects**: Art, geography, PE, science **London league table position**: 284

## Profile

Edenham High was opened as a purpose-built comprehensive with on-site playing fields in 1977. In July 1998, it became the first school in Croydon to be granted specialist Technology College status, giving it access to additional funding specifically to improve its technology and IT resources. This funding has already had a visible effect on the fabric of Edenham High. The Edenham Learning for Life Centre, for example, contains up-to-date computer facilities and a new, well-stocked library was opened in July 1999. The school has also been allocated a £1.25-million grant to upgrade its facilities and rectify the problems of some of its shabbier buildings. Pupils study a broad and balanced curriculum, which is set according to the student's academic ability gradually from Year 7 onwards. All Year 10 pupils are offered a two-week work placement to complement the compulsory careers course that all pupils must follow. Those pupils with learning difficulties are given support within the class. There is a parent-teacher association and a school council. Most pupils seem to favour John Ruskin College or Croydon College for further studies.

## Admissions and intake

Edenham High is regularly oversubscribed. Priority in admissions is given first to siblings of current pupils at the school, and then to those applicants who may have medical or social reasons supporting their application. Those applicants attending local primary schools are also given high consideration. The school may also admit up to 15 per cent of its annual intake based on academic performance in standard tests. Any remaining places are decided by the distance that prospective pupils live from the school. All applicants must also complete the school's own application form.

## Achievement

Edenham High is generally a successful and happy community. In 1998, Ofsted inspectors found that 'the school successfully promotes positive attitudes to work on the part of pupils, good behaviour and sound personal and social development'. They also noted that 'high standards of behaviour are set' by all but a small minority of pupils. The school has gained some encouraging exam results in the past few years. In 2002, 52 per cent of pupils gained five or more GCSEs at grades A*–C. This was down on 60 per cent in 2001 but still well above the national average. Edenham was placed 18th in Croydon's league table.

## Extra-curricular activities

The school places particular emphasis on sport. Edenham High's Year 11 netball team has been especially strong in recent years, becoming Croydon champions in 2000. The school also has strong musical groups, including an orchestra and choir, as well as drama groups. These clubs put on regular performances. The Duke of Edinburgh's Award scheme has recently been introduced. The school organizes annual exchanges to France and Germany. Pupils raise funds for local charities and there are after-school homework clubs.

# Haling Manor High School

**Kendra Hall Road, South Croydon Surrey CR2 6DT** 020 8681 1141 020 8681 1144 enquiries@hmhs.croydon.sch.uk www.enquiries@hmhs.croydon.sch.uk Mr DJ Troake B.Ed, MA Cert.Ed (Adv), FRSA; Chair of Governors: Mr N Graves Purley Oaks **Buses**: 50, 60, 68A, 109, 166, 312, 403, 405, 407, 409, 455, 498 Black school blazer, dark trousers or skirt, white shirt or blouse, school tie **Demand**: 545 applications for c.180 places in 2001/2 **Type**: Community comprehensive for 675 mixed pupils, aged 11 to 16 **Submit application form**: October 2003 **Motto**: *Virtus Mille Scuta* (Virtue Is Worth a Thousand Swords) **School hours**: 8.20am–3pm; homework clubs are available **Meals**: Hot and cold available **Strong GCSE subjects**: Art **London league table position**: 508

## Profile

Haling Manor was formed in 1970 and until 1990 it suffered from dwindling numbers and declining standards. Indeed, exam results reached such a nadir in the early 1990s that there was even talk of closing the school. However, the school has undergone a remarkable turnaround in subsequent years, and has become a thriving, vibrant community which is increasingly popular with local parents and children alike. The school has 12 acres of grounds which provide its own playing fields. It is also next to the council-owned Purley Way playing fields, offering a further 98 acres of pitches. Until recently, the school suffered from a lack of both general teaching areas and specialist art, music and design facilities, but the completion of a new three-storey block and a separate two-storey building has redressed this problem. These new buildings provide six additional classrooms, two science labs and two rooms dedicated to technology. A second phase of development has provided a new sports hall, a much-improved library, music rooms, a drama workshop, dance studio and art classrooms. The school has also made important strides in devising a curriculum that is both broad and relevant to its pupils' interests. GCSEs are offered in food technology, business studies, double-entry human physiology and statistics, and double-entry drama with theatrical and expressive arts. Haling Manor also runs an NVQ course in building construction which is particularly popular. There is a parent-teacher association, a prefects system and a coordinator for pupils with special needs.

## Admissions and intake

Admissions are through the council (see borough factfile).

## Achievement

For all the upgrading of facilities, it remains the case that Haling Manor's academic standards are not particularly high. The most recent Ofsted inspection in 1998 found that 'basic standards of reading and writing are generally adequate to meet subject demands but are not necessarily good enough to enable many pupils to gain higher grades'. In the school's defence, about three-quarters of pupils have a reading age below their chronological age on entry. Standards are also depressed by the only recently dropped policy of encouraging applications from pupils who had been excluded from elsewhere. As a result, the school experienced a substantial casual intake across year groups. Standards amongst those pupils educated at the school throughout their secondary school years have always been higher, and now that this policy has ended, Haling Manor is witnessing commendable advances in its GCSE results. In 2002, 16 per cent gained five or more GCSEs at the higher grades. This was a slight rise from 15 per cent in 2001 and the school was ranked 30th in the borough league table.

## Extra-curricular activities

There is a wide range of clubs and societies on offer, including after-school homework clubs. There is an energetic sporting calendar, fielding teams for football, rugby, basketball, hockey, netball, tennis and cricket. Regular music and drama performances are also staged at the school. There are trips both at home and abroad.

# Harris City Technology College

**Maberley Road, Upper Norwood, London SE19 2JH** ☎ 020 8771 2261 📠 020 8771 7531 ✉ inof@harrisctc.org.uk 🌐 www.harrisctc.org.uk Mrs C Bates; Chair of Governors: Mr A Bull Crystal Palace, Penge West **Buses:** 49, 68, 157, 196, 249, 358, 361 Dark grey trousers or skirt, green school jumper, white shirt or blouse, school tie; Sixth form: Office-style clothes **Demand:** 1222 applications for 180 places in 2001/2 **Type:** Comprehensive city Technology College for 1030 mixed pupils, aged 11 to 18 **Submit application form:** October 2003 **Motto:** All Can Achieve **School hours:** 8.30am–3.20pm; homework clubs are available **Meals:** Hot and cold available **Strong GCSE subjects:** English, maths, sciences **London league table position:** 111

## Profile

Harris City Technical College was opened in 1990 on the site of the former Sylvan High School with the aid of funding from its namesake, carpet retailer Lord Harris. Over the past decade, the school has been raising its standards, and was named as one of the country's most improving schools in 1997. It is well resourced all round, but its provision for technology and science is particularly noteworthy. The school claims to have more computers per pupil than any other college or school in the local area. It also has full use of the Lewis Sports and Leisure Centre, which has been built on the site to provide sporting facilities both for the school and the local community. Harris places special emphasis on maths, science and technology, with pupils having the option to drop some national curriculum subjects and combine their remaining GCSE options with GNVQ courses. Approximately two-thirds of pupils remain at Harris beyond Key Stage 4. In the sixth form, pupils have a choice from 14 A/AS-levels, as well as GNVQs in art and design, leisure and tourism, leisure and recreation, travel and tourism, business and engineering. Relations within the school are based on mutual respect. Staff encourage pupils to assume responsibility through an established prefect system and the school council, which represents all year groups. There is a PTA and provision for pupils with special needs.

## Admissions and intake

Applications are only accepted from residents of the school's catchment area, consisting of various electoral wards in Croydon, Bromley, Lambeth, Lewisham and Southwark. The final admissions list is then drawn up following interviews with applicants to determine the commitment of prospective pupils to a city technical college-style of education, with its emphasis on maths, science and technology.

## Achievement

The school's results have fluctuated in the past, but standards have always been considerably higher than both borough and national expectations. Results in 2002 were no exception with 91 per cent of pupils gaining five or more GCSEs at grades A*–C, an increase on 88 per cent in 2001. The school was ranked seventh in the borough. Performance in the sixth form again tends to be subject to wide variations, but as the results from 1997, 2000 and 2001 have illustrated, Harris has the potential to perform very well. In 2002, the pupils who sat two or more A/AS-levels gained an average of 208 points, placing the school 10th in the borough's performance table. In 2001, Ofsted noted that: 'The teaching is good and the students' attitudes and behaviour are positive.' Attainment levels were seen to be above average. It is also to the school's credit that over 60 per cent of those pupils who left Harris in 1998 continued their education at university level.

## Extra-curricular activities

Pupils are encouraged to assume responsibility for the wide variety of clubs on offer at the school, which range from music to drama, and include homework clubs and all the usual sports. There are trips both at home and abroad.

# Lodge School

**Woodcote Lane, Purley, Surrey CR8 3HB** ☎ 020 8660 3179 📠 020 8660 1385 ✉ principal@lodge.croydon.sch.uk 🌐 www.lodgeschool.co.uk Miss PA Maynard; Chair of Governors: Mrs A Stranack Purley **Buses:** 127, 463 School blazer, green skirt, white shirt, school tie; Sixth form: Smart clothes **Demand:** No figures available but variable **Type:** Non-selective independent for 275 girls, aged 3 to 18 **Fees:** £2,190–£2,290 per term **Submit application form:** No cut-off date **Motto:** Keep Truth **School hours:** 8.30am–3.30pm **Meals:** Hot and cold available **Strong GCSE subjects:** Sciences **London league table position:** 206

### Profile

Lodge School is a small independent situated on an eight-acre site in the middle of the exclusive Webb Estate. It comprises three schools. Silverdene Lodge and Downside are respectively the primary and junior sections, providing a mixed education for pupils aged three to 11. The senior section, also known as Commonweal Lodge, caters for girls only. All three sections are housed in period buildings along Woodcote Lane. Newer additions provide the school with more modern facilities. The school has its own heated swimming pool and in the past few years has opened three new science labs. The buildings are surrounded by well-maintained playing fields. Class sizes are generally small, with a strong emphasis on individual care and attention. Pupils study three sciences, English literature and language and maths. The school also offers French, German, Spanish, history, geography, RE, business and information studies and PE to GCSE. Beyond Key Stage 4, the curriculum is as wide as one might expect at a far larger school. For those in their final year, the school runs a strong system of prefects, who assume significant responsibility lower down the school. There is a parent-teacher association and pupils can join the school council in the sixth form.

### Admissions and intake

Most pupils come directly from the junior school Downside, although they are also joined by a small number of girls from other local state and independent junior schools. A limited number of music and academic scholarships are available from the Lodge Educational Trust, which are awarded strictly on the basis of ability.

### Achievement

Despite its wider than average ability intake than typical independent schools, Lodge usually produces a healthy set of exam results. In 2002, 72 per cent of pupils gained five or more GCSEs at grades A*–C, placing the school 14th in the borough. This figure was down on 85 per cent in 2001. Results are subject to wide variations because of the small year groups. It is more significant that the school has consistently performed at a level far higher than national expectations. In particular, the school is justifiably proud of its science results, with almost all girls gaining grades A*–C in biology, physics and chemistry over the past few years. Results at A-level are again subject to significant fluctuations. In 2002, the average point score for those pupils who sat two or more A/AS-levels was 238.3, below the national but above the local average, placing the school ninth in the borough.

### Extra-curricular activities

Given its relatively small size, Lodge School offers a wide selection of activities. Sports include lacrosse, netball, tennis, rounders and swimming. More senior girls also have the opportunity to try badminton, volleyball and aerobics, as well as windsurfing and sailing. The school also has a popular Duke of Edinburgh's Award group and frequently participates in the Young Enterprise scheme. Educational visits are organized in the London area, in addition to popular sailing weekends, skiing trips and foreign exchanges.

## Norbury Manor High School for Girls

**Kensington Avenue, Thornton Heath, Surrey CR7 8BT** ☎ 020 8679 0062 📠 020 8679 8007 ⓔ admin@nmhs.org.uk 🌐 www.nmhs.org.uk Miss C Nicholls MA; Chair of Governors: Mrs B Washington ⇄ Norbury **Buses:** 50, 59, 109, 159, 250 Dark skirt, red school jumper, white blouse **Demand:** 600 applications for 180 places in 2001/2 **Type:** Comprehensive foundation school for 850 girls, aged 11 to 16 **Submit application form:** October 2003 **Motto:** Progress to Excellence **School hours:** 8.50am–3.30pm; homework clubs are available **Meals:** Hot and cold available **Strong GCSE subjects:** Art, business studies, drama, English literature, IT, RE **London league table position:** 191

### Profile

Norbury Manor High School for Girls is situated in spacious grounds next to Norbury Park, giving it an attractive setting. It recently acquired Beacon School status. The school has a relatively new two-storey maths and design technology building that provides good facilities, but which also means that technology departments occupy three different parts of the school. It has a wide curriculum that offers some unusual options, including GCSEs in child development, drama, food technology, graphic art, office technology, resistant materials, textiles and a GNVQ in leisure and tourism. It is compulsory for all girls in Year 10 to participate in the school's work experience programme. In general, the school tries to provide in-class support for those pupils with special educational needs, but it will also withdraw pupils where appropriate. Provision for those pupils with English as a second language is good. An ESL teacher works with pupils in lessons and prepares suitable material to support their language development and give access to the subject area. There is also a bilingual Home Support Teacher, who works with bilingual pupils and their parents in order to remove barriers of culture and language. There is a PTA and a school council.

### Admissions and intake

Norbury Manor is a consistently popular choice for pupils and parents. Most pupils come from the north of the borough, or from the feeder schools which are located close at hand – Kensington Avenue Junior, Norbury Manor Junior and Winterbourne Girls' Junior. Priority in admissions is given to those applicants with siblings at the school or those with medical reasons supporting their applications, followed by pupils from the above local junior schools. Any remaining places are awarded on the basis of proximity of the child's home to the school.

### Achievement

When it was inspected by Ofsted in 2001, officials reported that Norbury is 'a very good school with many excellent features'. Standards were found to be above average and pupils 'achieve very well'. The quality of teaching had 'risen significantly' and is well supported by the school's 'very good ethos'. However, Inspectors wanted more accurate school targets to be set and assessment to be linked to national standards. Results have been consistently high over the last five years. In 2002, 53 per cent of pupils gained five or more GCSEs at grades A*–C. This was above the national average, placing the school 12th in the borough.

### Extra-curricular activities

Sports available include hockey, netball, trampolining, gymnastics, cross-country, athletics, tennis and rounders. There are also drama, choir and computing groups, as well as the Duke of Edinburgh's Award scheme. A number of trips are organized annually to theatres, art galleries and places of historical, geographical and scientific interest. There are after-school homework clubs. Residential trips include a weekend at an adventure centre and a visit to Crete.

## Old Palace School of John Whitgift

**Old Palace Road, Croydon CR0 1AX** 020 8688 2027 020 8680 5877 info@oldpalace.croydon.sch.uk Mrs J Hancock; Chair of Governors: Mr North East Croydon, West Croydon, Church Street Tramlink Brown skirt, brown school jumper, school blouse; Sixth form: Smart clothes **Demand**: No figures available but c. 80 places **Type**: Selective independent day school for 827 girls, aged 3 to 19 **Fees**: £2,283 per term **Submit application form**: Contact school for details **School hours**: 8.35am–3.40pm; homework clubs are available **Meals**: Hot and cold available **Strong GCSE subjects**: All relatively strong **London league table position**: 24

### Profile

Old Palace is one of the jewels of Croydon's educational system. It was founded in 1889, but only became fully Independent in 1974. Since 1993, it has been a member of the Whitgift Foundation, which is also responsible for Trinity and Whitgift schools. The Old Palace, from which the school takes its name, was a former residence of the Archbishop of Canterbury, and some of the original buildings remain and have been incorporated into the school. The chapel, great hall and library all date from the 15th century. The older buildings have been improved by modern extensions to give the school outstanding facilities. The school also has a new technology and arts block and a new swimming pool. There are plans to extensively remodel the preparatory section of the school. Old Palace's central location, however, means that the grounds available for outdoor sports are limited. At Key Stage 4, all students learn French and can choose from Latin, Greek, German, Spanish, Italian and Russian. Most girls stay into the sixth form and are joined by a small number of pupils from neighbouring schools. There is a choice of 26 A-levels, with all pupils choosing three or four options. Girls are encouraged to take personal responsibility for the maintenance of their environment through the strong sixth-form prefect system. There is a PTA and provision for pupils with special needs.

### Admissions and intake

Admissions are based on success at the school's own selective exam, designed to test the child's aptitude for English comprehension and composition, maths and verbal reasoning. This is held in the January preceding the September intake. Most pupils will also be interviewed before any place is offered. There is a generous system of scholarships and bursaries available from the school.

## Achievement

In 2002, 97 per cent of pupils gained five or more GCSEs at grades A*–C. This was almost twice the national average, and the school came top in the borough. Success at A-level is outstanding, with an average score of 403.5 in 2002, almost twice the national average. This result once again put the school at the top of Croydon's A-level league table. The most recently available figures, those from 1998, show that 87 per cent of leavers chose to continue their education at university, including a number at Oxford and Cambridge.

## Extra-curricular activities

Old Palace prides itself on turning out well-balanced individuals and places great emphasis on the importance of extra-curricular activities. The school's reputation for music and drama is especially strong, with several flourishing choirs, orchestras and a chamber music ensemble. In sport, netball, hockey, swimming and tennis all enjoy a high profile. A wide range of clubs includes dance, keep-fit, debating and chess, with pupils also participating in the Young Enterprise scheme and the Duke of Edinburgh's Award scheme. There are regular exchanges with German, French and Italian schools.

# Riddlesdown High School

**Honister Heights, Purley, Surrey CR8 1EX** 020 8668 5136 020 8660 9025 admin@riddlesdown.croydon.sch.uk www.riddlesdown.croydon.sch.uk Dr DR Dibbs BA, B.Sc, ACP, MI.Biol, FLS; Chair of Governors: Mr A Carter Riddlesdown, Kenley **Buses:** 412 Black school blazer, dark trousers or skirt, white shirt or blouse, grey school tie; Sixth form: Smart clothes **Demand:** 750 applications for c300 places in 2001/2 **Type:** Voluntary aided comprehensive for 1500 mixed pupils, aged 11 to 16 **Submit application form:** November 2003 **School hours:** 8.50am–3.20pm; homework clubs are available **Meals:** Hot and cold available **Strong GCSE subjects:** History, PE **London league table position:** 197

## Profile

With well over 1000 pupils, Riddlesdown is Croydon's largest school, and one which is justifiably popular amongst local parents. The school stands in 25 acres of grounds, almost entirely surrounded by fields and woodlands, giving Riddlesdown an unusually rural outlook for London. The buildings mainly date from 1957, when the school moved to its current purpose-built location, but they also include modern, well-equipped facilities. Barely a year passed during the 1990s without Riddlesdown witnessing some major building work. All the classrooms have been refurbished and 1993 saw the construction of a new sports hall. In 1994 there was a new arts centre, followed by a new technology block in 1995. New classrooms were added in 1996 and a new library and gymnasium in 1997. This extensive development has allowed Riddlesdown to cater comfortably for its rising numbers. There is a parent-teacher association, a school council and provision for pupils with special needs. The sixth-form centre was opened in conjunction with the Stafford College of Technology and the Arts. Pupils have a wide choice of 18 A/AS-levels, in addition to GNVQs in business studies and health and social care.

## Admissions and intake

Priority in admissions is given to those applicants with a family connection with the school, those with medical reasons supporting their application and pupils of local primary schools. The latter are numerous and are generally located in Sandersted, Selsdon, South Croydon, Purley and Tandridge. A total of 15 per cent may also be admitted on the basis of academic ability. Any remaining places are given to those applicants living closest to the school.

## Achievement

Over the past few years, the school has been improved greatly, a fact that was recognized and highly praised in Riddlesdown's Ofsted inspection in 2000. Inspectors noted: 'Riddlesdown High School is an excellent school', and that it 'has many major strengths and only a few areas for further improvement'. They observed that 'pupils are highly motivated, with a real thirst for learning'. Behaviour around the school is generally good, with pupils of both sexes displaying high levels of tolerance and courtesy. Conditions such as these allow both motivated and talented pupils to fulfil their potential. Riddlesdown finished in 13th place in Croydon's league table in 2002, with 65 per cent of pupils gaining five or more GCSEs at grades A*–C. This was an increase on 60 per cent in 2001 and well above the borough and national averages.

### Extra-curricular activities

Riddlesdown's large size allows it to support a whole host of extra-curricular activities, catering for almost all interests. Sport, drama and music are particularly strong. The school boasts several choirs, orchestras and ensembles, including recorder and handbell groups. There are after-school homework clubs. Outside visits are regularly organized, and make full use of the opportunities that the capital has to offer.

# Royal Russell School

**Coombe Lane, Croydon CR9 5BX** 020 8657 3669 020 8657 9555 admissions@royalrussell.co.uk www.royalrussell.co.uk Dr JR Jennings; South Croydon **Buses**: 130, 254, 353; Tramlink Coombe Lane Red school blazer, dark trousers or skirt; white shirt and house tie (boys); white striped blouse (girls); Sixth form: Smart clothes **Demand**: No figures available but 80 places available **Type**: Selective independent for 535 mixed pupils, aged 3 to 19 **Fees** (per term): £2,750 (day), £5,300 (boarder) **Submit application form**: No cut-off date **Motto**: It's Not for Self but for Others **School hours**: 8.30am–3.50pm **Meals**: Hot and cold available **Strong GCSE subjects**: All relatively strong **London league table position**: 291

### Profile

Royal Russell was founded in 1853, and moved to its present site in 1924. The school is situated in a beautifully landscaped, 100-acre wooded estate. Royal Russell recently opened a new, large sixth-form centre and school library, and the upgrading of the boarding facilities has recently been completed. The school has a welcoming atmosphere, which has been described as being more like a university campus than a secondary school. There is a parent-teacher association and a prefects system. There is provision for pupils with special needs. Arrangements for boarders at weekends are flexible, with those who choose to stay at school enjoying full use of the facilities. Pupils have a choice of 22 GCSEs, including drama, theatre arts and Spanish. In addition, a City and Guilds qualification in professional cookery is available, and all pupils participate in a career education programme. There are a total of 19 options at A-level, including business studies, geology and media studies.

### Admission and intake

The school has traditional links with the Church of England but is keen to welcome pupils of all faiths and denominations. Admissions are based on the results of the school's own entrance exam held in November. A number of scholarships are awarded according to academic potential, and a limited number of awards are also available for drama and music. About half the pupils come from the school's own junior section, with the rest coming from neighbouring junior schools, both state and independent. About a quarter of pupils choose to board.

### Achievement

Over the past few years, academic standards have gradually been rising, with 64 per cent of pupils gaining five or more GCSEs at A*–C grades in 2002. This was five per cent up on 2001 and above both the national and borough averages. However, ranked 19th in Croydon's league table, the school lags some way behind other selective schools. The average point score for those pupils who sat two or more A/AS-levels in 2002 was 259.3, well above the borough average of 271 and above the national average, placing the school in eighth place in Croydon's A-level league table. Approximately 85 per cent of pupils continue their education at university, with the school building up a good reputation among some of the country's most prestigious institutions, including Oxford and Cambridge.

### Extra-curricular activities

Pupils from Year 9 upwards have the chance to assume responsible leadership roles in the school's flourishing Combined Cadet Force, which has both Army and RAF wings. The school also makes good use of its large sports hall, swimming pool and extensive playing fields to cater for most sporting interests. The main competitive sports are athletics, cricket, football, netball and tennis, but pupils can also participate in aerobics, badminton, fencing, judo, sub-aqua and trampolining. Royal Russell is heavily involved in the Model UN programme and Young Enterprise scheme. It commands a good reputation for its various orchestras, chapel and chamber choirs, and its drama productions are very popular. There are trips both at home and abroad and pupils raise funds for local charities.

# St Andrew's CofE Voluntary Aided High School

**Warrington Road, Croydon CR0 4BJ** ☎ 020 8686 8306 Fax 020 8681 6320 Dr M Martin; Chair of Governors: Rev P Hendry East Croydon **Buses**: 154, 157, 407, 410, 455, 726; Tramlink 1 Dark school blazer, grey or black trousers or skirt, white shirt or blouse, school tie **Demand**: 282 applications for 110 places in 2001/2 **Type**: Voluntary aided Church of England comprehensive for 534 mixed pupils, aged 11 to 18 **Submit application form**: October 2003 **Motto**: *Per cruem ad coronam* (Through the Cross to the Crown) **School hours**: 8.25am–3.25pm **Meals**: Hot and cold available **Strong GCSE subjects**: English language, English literature, French, home economics, maths, music, RE **London league table position**: 128

## Profile

Established by St Andrew's Church in 1857, the school moved to its current location in 1964. The school has an elevated site, commanding views over much of Croydon. The school itself is quite small, but enjoys a fairly extensive and well-maintained range of facilities. These have been greatly expanded over the past few years, following the completion of a £1.4 million technology building during the winter of 1999–2000. Classrooms, a drama room, an extra science lab and a learning resources centre have also been constructed over the past few years. Over 90 per cent of St Andrew's pupils regularly stay on in education after Key Stage 4, with most pupils deciding to go into the sixth form that the school runs in conjunction with Archbishop Tenison's. Although this is a joint project, the sixth form is based exclusively at the Tenison's site, located in Selbourne Road. Pupils have the choice of 17 A-levels, including government and politics, PE and sociology. A business GNVQ at both intermediate and advanced levels is also available. There is a school council and a PTA.

## Admissions and intake

The school operates a joint admissions procedure with Archbishop Tenison's, which requires prospective parents to complete the school's own application forms. Both are regularly oversubscribed. A minimum of 70 per cent of places are reserved for families who are practising members of the Church of England and who live within the Archdeaconry of Croydon, with priority going to those who can display the highest levels of Christian commitment. Any remaining places are granted first to members of other Christian denominations that are specified in the school prospectus. All applicants are interviewed before a firm place is offered.

## Achievement

The most recent Ofsted report in 1998 was largely complimentary, declaring that the school 'provides an education of good quality'. It also noted that 'pupils have very positive attitudes to their work and to each other'. GCSE results have steadily improved over recent years, with 75 per cent of pupils gaining five or more A*–C grades in 2002, up from 64 per cent in 2001. The school came 10th in the borough. In 1999, the school was ranked seventh in the borough for A/AS-levels, with pupils taking two or more subjects achieving an average point score of 16.7 (under the old scoring system). This was below the national average but significantly higher than the local average. Figures for 2002 are not available. Approximately 65 per cent of pupils go on to university, with many others attending institutions of further education.

## Extra-curricular activities

Sport is strong at the school and good use is made of its on-site pitches. Visits are organized to cultural sites in London, including theatre trips and visits to museums. French and German exchanges are regularly arranged. Pupils raise funds for local charities.

# St Joseph's College

**Beulah Hill, London SE19 3HL** ☎ 020 8761 1426 Fax 020 8761 7667 Mr E Connolly B.Ed; Chair of Governors: Mr B O'Donohoe West Norwood, Streatham Common North **Buses**: 137A, 68A, 196, 137, 249 Maroon school blazer, dark grey trousers, white shirt, school tie; Sixth form: Office-style clothes **Demand**: 700 applications for 180 places in 2001/2 **Type**: Voluntary aided Roman Catholic comprehensive for 1050 boys (mixed in sixth form), aged 11 to 18 **Submit application form**: October 2003 **Motto**: *Fides intrepida* (Undaunted Loyalty)

**School hours**: 8.15am–3pm; homework clubs are available **Meals**: Hot and cold available **Strong GCSE subjects**: Art, maths **London league table position**: 232

## Profile

St Joseph's College was founded as a Roman Catholic school by the De La Salle Brothers in 1855 and continues under the guidance of their trustees. Originally established in Clapham as an independent school, St Joseph's moved to its current location in 1904 and came under state funding in 1973. The school is dominated by the original imposing building, dating from the turn of the century and adorned with the school's characteristic eagle statues above the entrance. It also has a somewhat less attractive, more modern extension, but one which provides St Joseph's with a range of up-to-date facilities. The school has its own chapel, modern science labs and technology rooms, a large sports hall and swimming pool, with one rugby and two football pitches on site. In 1999, Ofsted criticized some of the classrooms for being cramped, but the school does have more extensive resources than many others in Croydon. Pupils in the mixed sixth form have a wide choice of 23 A/AS-level options and a GNVQ in business. There is a school council, a parent-teacher association and provision for pupils with special needs.

## Admissions and intake

St Joseph's is an increasingly popular school. Priority is given to applicants who are practising Catholics and who can provide a statement detailing their religious practice, supported by their local church. If not enough Catholics apply to fill the annual intake, priority is then given to those applicants who have a family link with the school. Any remaining places will then be offered to Christians from practising families, those with special medical or social circumstances supporting the application and finally to families who are in sympathy with the school's ethos.

## Achievement

In general, Ofsted inspectors were complimentary about the school. They found that 'pupils generally concentrate very well, listen intently; they are keen to learn and succeed'. Academic standards have, however, been variable over the past few years. In 2002, 58 per cent of pupils gained five or more GCSEs at the higher grades, continuing an upward trend. St Joseph's was placed 17th in the borough league table. The average point score for those pupils who sat two or more A/AS-levels was 177.7 in 2002. This was below the national but above the borough average, ranking the school 11th in the borough.

## Extra-curricular activities

St Joseph's offers a full range of sports, including competitive matches in football, rugby, cricket, swimming and basketball. It also offers pupils opportunities to participate in personal fitness training, gymnastics, hockey, tennis, badminton and volleyball. The school is the champion in diving for Croydon. There are after-school homework clubs. Pupils can gain the Duke of Edinburgh's Award and first-aid awards. St Joseph's also runs a popular Combined Cadet Force. Pupils raise funds for local charities.

# St Mary's High School

**Woburn Road, Croydon CR0 2AB** ☎ 020 8686 3837 📠 020 8781 1264 ✉ office@stmaryshigh.croydon.sch.uk Stephen Harding; Chair of Governors: Mr W McVicker East Croydon, West Croydon **Buses**: 68, 75, 157, 289 Navy school blazer, dark trousers or skirt, white shirt or blue blouse, school tie **Demand**: 200 applications for 180 places in 2001/2 **Type**: Voluntary aided Roman Catholic comprehensive for 716 mixed pupils aged 11 to 16 **Submit application form**: October 2003 **Motto**: *Fidem serva* (Faithful Servant) **School hours**: 8.35am–3.15pm; homework clubs are available **Meals**: Hot and cold available **Strong GCSE subjects**: English, maths, science **London league table position**: 361

## Profile

St Mary's was founded in 1851, but its current buildings primarily date from 1955, with a major extension added in 1972. The site, near the centre of Croydon, is quite restricted. The school does, however, enjoy access to fields at Coombe Lodge, and the lack of immediate facilities does not seem to have had a detrimental effect on the school's sporting achievements. The school has four science labs, an art suite with facilities for drawing, pottery, plasterwork, fabric printing and photography, two music rooms and two practice rooms. A broad curriculum is offered, including GCSEs in food technology, textiles, child development and tourism and travel. The school has a strong religious ethos.

Parents receive regular communications from teachers, and there is an annual meeting with the governors in November. There is a prefects system and provision for pupils with special needs.

## Admission and intake

St Mary's faces stiff competition from neighbouring Catholic schools and the roll had declined in recent years but has now risen. Priority is given to applications from practising Catholics who can provide written support from their parish priest. Any remaining places are given to children who are practising members of other recognized religious denominations. Again, such applications must be substantiated by the written support of their religious leader. Almost half of the school's current roll of 625 come from homes where English is not the first language. The majority of pupils have a below-average level of attainment before they begin their secondary education.

## Achievement

The disadvantaged nature of the school's intake is reflected in its exam results. In 2002, 37 per cent of pupils obtained five or more GCSEs at grades A*–C. This was significantly lower than the national average, and the school came 24th in the borough league table, though this was a marked rise from 30 per cent in 2001, and reinstated the upward trend of recent years. Ofsted inspectors in 1997 found St Mary's to be 'a harmonious multi-cultural community where relationships are good, behaviour is orderly and the Catholic ethos is clear'. The school appears to instill its pupils with an enthusiasm for learning, with approximately 85 per cent continuing in education beyond Key Stage 4.

## Extra-curricular activities

The school enjoys a tradition of success in competitive football, basketball, netball, cricket, rounders and athletics. An array of clubs and societies is on offer, including debating, drama, science, art, badminton, aerobics and homework clubs. Pupils can also participate in the Duke of Edinburgh's Award scheme. The school organizes watersports activities near Rochester in Kent, geography and biology field trips, and visits to theatres, cinemas, museums and exhibitions. In recent years there have been excursions to France, Spain and Belgium.

# The Selhurst High School for Boys

**The Crescent, Croydon CR0 2HN** ☎ 020 8665 7989 📠 020 8665 0119 ⓔ selhurst-boys.croydon.sch.uk Mrs Joan Pickering; Chair of Governors: Mr J Kuipers ⇄ Selhurst **Buses**: X68, 50, 75, 157, 198, 468 Black trousers, grey school sweatshirt, white school polo shirt **Demand**: 393 applications for 150 places in 2001/2 **Type**: Community comprehensive for 640 boys, aged 11 to 16 **Submit application form**: October 2002 **Motto**: Putting Learning First **School hours**: 8.30am–3.15pm; homework clubs are available **Meals**: Hot and cold available **Strong GCSE subjects**: Art, PE **London league table position**: 497

## Profile

Pupils and staff alike have been working very hard to try and rectify the problems which have hampered Selhurst High in the past, and it recently won an Excellence in the City award. Although a number of advances have been made, there is still some way to go before the school fully answers all of its critics. Following an Ofsted inspection in 1995, inspectors concluded that Selhurst 'is failing to give its pupils an acceptable standard of education'. Following this, the school was branded as one of the worst in the country and placed on 'special measures' in an attempt to improve standards. Over the past five years, the school's academic success has risen and it was removed from 'special measures' in 1998. An Ofsted inspection in 2000 judged the school to provide 'an acceptable standard of education' and that 'most pupils make satisfactory progress'. Selhurst High has also benefited from a move to a new location in 1997, to the former site of Selhurst Grammar School. The council has spent £3.5 million refurbishing and upgrading the existing facilities to a fairly high quality. There are now two new science labs with plans for a third ICT suite. Even so, the school remains less popular than its immediate neighbours. In 1999 a new head, Joan Pickering, was appointed to make further improvements. Since then, the gradual process of improvement has continued. Behaviour has changed for the better, and the school has been more successful in attracting specialist teachers than it had been in the past. Selhurst High offers a very popular programme of work-related courses in catering and construction. It also offers a work experience course to all of its Year 10 pupils. There is a school council and a prefects system.

## Admissions and intake

Admissions are through the council (see borough factfile). Located in a residential ward with above-average levels of socio-economic disadvantage, pupils are drawn from the immediate locality. About 29 per cent of pupils have English as a second language.

## Achievement

In 2002, 25 per cent of pupils gained five or more GCSEs at grades A*–C. This was up on 12 per cent in 2001 and more akin to results of recent years, with the school peaking at 26 per cent in 1997. The average point score was 23.4 and Selhurst High was ranked bottom of Croydon's league table at Key Stage 4. A total of 70 per cent of pupils continue on to further education when they leave the school. One of the school's more traditional strengths has been its broad and relevant curriculum. It currently offers a total of 19 GCSEs, including courses in graphics, integrated humanities, leisure and tourism, and business studies.

## Extra-curricular activities

The school offers a wide range of extra-curricular activities. There is an extensive fixture list for most competitive sports, with additional opportunities for pupils to develop their interests in activities including basketball, rugby, diving and orienteering. There are also a number of curriculum-related clubs, as well as others not directly related to school courses, such as motor maintenance and the Duke of Edinburgh's Award scheme.

# Selsdon High School

**Farnborough Avenue, South Croydon, Surrey CR2 8HD** 020 8657 8935 020 8651 6065 selsdon-high@dialnet.com Mr GH Smith; Chair of Governors: Mrs L Martin East Croydon. Tramlink: Gravel Hill **Buses:** 64, 359 Navy school jumper, dark grey trousers or navy blue skirt, white shirt or blouse **Demand:** 953 applications for 210 places in 12001/2 **Type:** Community comprehensive for 1050 mixed pupils, aged 11 to 16 **Submit application form:** October 2003 **Motto:** Everyone Counts **School hours:** 8.45am–3.30pm; homework clubs are available **Meals:** Hot and cold available **Strong GCSE subjects:** Art, DT, IT, music, PE **London league table position:** 467

## Profile

The school is located on the edge of two large housing estates – Monks Hill and New Addington. Sports facilities are very good and Selsdon High also has specialist facilities for teaching visually impaired children. A £250,000 refurbishment programme was recently completed. In addition to GCSEs, the school offers Associated Examining Board Basic Tests and the Diploma of Vocational Education, in which some pupils succeed where they have failed in GCSEs. All pupils in Year 10 engage in a work experience programme. Those in the upper years have the opportunity to become prefects. There is a parent-teacher association. Truancy was a problem in the past but the unauthorized absence rate is now 0.6 per cent, below the borough and national averages.

## Admissions and intake

Admissions are through the council (see borough factfile). Selsdon High draws most of its pupils from the immediate locality, but also opens its doors to a comparatively large number of children who have been excluded from other schools.

## Achievement

The school's levels of attainment have fluctuated but have been consistently poor. In 2002, 28 per cent of pupils gained five or more GCSEs at the higher grades, an increase on 22 per cent in 2001. This reversed a downward trend following a low of just 13 per cent in 1998. Selsdon High was ranked 26th in the borough. However, the fact that the majority of pupils have already displayed low levels of attainment before entering the school needs to be taken into account, and that standards are further depressed by the large casual intake of pupils across all year groups. Pupils who remain at the school throughout their secondary education generally make satisfactory progress. These figures also fail to reflect the real advancements that have been made to ensure that few pupils leave Selsdon High with no qualifications. As recently as 1998 some 28 per cent of pupils left with no exam passes, whereas in 2000 this figure was reduced to 14 per cent. Approximately 60 per cent of pupils go on to further education. The behaviour of the majority of pupils, who are courteous and keen to learn, is often overshadowed by an unruly minority.

### Extra-curricular activities

Selsdon High offers a wide variety of sports to appeal to almost all interests. The curriculum is also enriched by a host of lunchtime and after-school clubs, ranging from the Duke of Edinburgh's Award scheme to an environment club, and homework clubs and societies for chess, sculpture and climbing. Many Year 10 and 11 pupils participate in voluntary work for Selsdon Contact, visiting elderly local residents and performing various tasks of community service. There are trips both at home and abroad.

# Shirley High School

**Shirley Church Road, Croydon CR0 5EF** 020 8656 9755 020 8654 8507 headteacher@shirley.croydon.sch.uk www.shirley.croydon.sch.uk Mr JG Harker B.Sc, M.Sc, DMS; Chair of Governors: Cllr M Horden **Buses:** 119, 194, 198, 367, 466 Navy school blazer, mid-grey trousers or skirt, navy school jumper, white shirt or blouse, school tie **Demand:** 775 applications for 180 places in 2001/2 **Type:** Comprehensive foundation school for 900 mixed pupils, aged 11 to 16 **Submit application form:** October 2003 **School hours:** 8.30am–3.05pm; **Meals:** Hot and cold available **Strong GCSE subjects:** Business studies, English literature, information studies, music **London league table position:** 227

### Profile

Shirley High is a modestly successful secondary school situated on a 13-acre site in Upper Shirley. The original school buildings dating from the 1950s are fairly drab and there is a large concrete playground which greets approaching visitors. However, the playing fields are located beyond these buildings, and from here, the school borders open countryside. A major extension programme was begun in 1986, giving the school specialist science facilities. A new sports hall was constructed in 1991, and three years later, the school added a new learning-resources centre and classroom block. A new music centre opened in 2002. Pupils are placed into sets in Year 7 for English and maths, and then progressively in other subjects from Year 8. Pupils can study up to 11 GCSEs, although most students choose to do less. Relations within the school are based on mutual trust and respect. Shirley High's staff are happy to give their pupils responsibility as prefects and members of the school council. There is a parent-teacher association.

### Admissions and intake

Priority in admissions is given first to those applicants with a family connection with the school – either to those who have a sibling at the schoo,l or to those who have had a sibling attending within the past five years. Consideration is then given to those seeking admission on medical grounds, supported by medical evidence. Up to 15 per cent of places may then be given on the basis of academic performance in the school's ability test. Any remaining places are given to those applicants who reside closest to the school. Pupils are drawn mainly from the local area.

### Achievement

Standards at the school are reasonably high compared to similar schools, and most pupils seem to enjoy their experience at Shirley High. In 2002, 56 per cent of pupils gained five or more GCSEs at grades A*–C. The school was placed 16th in Croydon's league table. Results have shown improvement over recent years. In 2001, Ofsted noted that: 'The school achieves average standards in GCSE and pupils achieve well when compared to similar schools'. Teaching was found to be 'good or better in two-thirds of lessons' although the number of very good or excellent lessons is 'comparatively low'.

### Extra-curricular activities

The school offers a wide range of competitive and non-competitive sporting opportunities including aerobics, cricket, judo, rugby, athletics, football, netball, softball, tennis, badminton, hockey, orienteering, squash and weight-training. Shirley High is also renowned for its lively music and drama productions. The school arranges annual foreign exchanges to Koblenz in Germany and Charlieu in France, in addition to other overseas trips, and a variety of cultural and educational visits in and around London.

# Stanley Technical High School for Boys

**South Norwood Hill, London SE25 6AD** 020 8771 9961 020 8771 7588 Patricia Mennie; Chair of Governors: Mrs S Lewington Norwood Junction **Buses:** 75, 157, 197, 312, 361 Black school blazer, dark grey trousers, white shirt, school tie **Demand**: 320 applications for 180 places in 2001/2 **Type**: Voluntary aided comprehensive for 708 boys, aged 11 to 16 **Submit application form**: October 2002 **School hours**: 8.45am–3.15pm; homework clubs are available **Meals**: Hot and cold available **Strong GCSE subjects**: All relatively strong **London league table position**: 496

### Profile

Stanley High was founded in 1906 by the local philanthropist WF Stanley, and the main building dates back to this time. It has long had ambitions for expansion, and began to take extra pupils in 1996 on the understanding that it could purchase a former office block next to the school. These plans, however, suffered a series of delays resulting in overcrowding. Ofsted strongly criticized the overcrowding in its inspections of 1994 and 1998. The required £2 million has now been set aside, and the school's extension became a reality in 2001. There are now 14 new classrooms, a learning-resource centre and canteen. Stanley High offers its pupils some interesting GCSE options beyond the requirements of the national curriculum, and these include drama, media studies, archaeology and sociology. There is a school council, provision for pupils with special needs and a parents association: the Friends of Stanley.

### Admission and intake

Parents who wish to apply to the school must visit the school and register an interest by the end of November in the preceding year to entry. An automatic place will be given to children who have a brother either at the school, or whose brother left not more than one year previously. Priority will then be given to those applicants who show a commitment to education, and to those who name the school as their first choice. Each year, Stanley High takes boys from a wide area covering Croydon, Lambeth, Bromley and Lewisham.

### Achievement

Over the past few years, standards have been rising sharply so that the school now enjoys a modest amount of success at Key Stage 4. However, in 2002, it finished 28th in the borough's league table, with only 14 per cent of pupils gaining five or more GCSEs at A*–C grades. This was a fall on 16 per cent in 2001, and continues a downward trend over the past three years. The average point score was 23.5, below the borough and national averages. In 2000, Ofsted visited Stanley High and found teaching to be 'sound' and 'often good', but Inspectors judged the school to have 'serious weaknesses' in attainment, behaviour and the quality and range of the curriculum.

### Extra-curricular activities

Although the school has limited sports grounds on site, it makes good use of playing fields located about one mile from the school, in order to offer its pupils a full range of sporting activities. Similarly, over the past few years, the school has been struggling with poor music facilities, but still manages to sustain a lively music scene. Regular visits to London's cultural sites are arranged, including theatres, museums and exhibitions. In recent years, there have been geography trips to study the Sussex coast as well as overseas trips to Italy, France, Spain and Austria. A camp is also organized annually, offering pupils the chance to develop outdoor skills.

# Thomas More School

**Russell Hill Road, Purley, Surrey CR8 2XP** 020 8668 6251 020 8660 9003 Ms M Kotalawela; Chair of Governors: Cannon J Pannett Purle **Buses**: 127, 289, 412 Dark green school blazer, dark trousers or skirt, white shirt or blouse, school tie **Demand**: 280 applications for c.150 places in 2001/2 **Type**: Voluntary aided Roman Catholic comprehensive for 710 mixed pupils, aged 11 to 16 **Submit application form**: October 2003 **Motto**: To Care, to Learn, to Achieve **School hours**: 8.40am–3.30pm; homework clubs are available **Meals**: Hot and cold available **Strong GCSE subjects**: English, IT, maths, PE, RE **London league table position**: 338

### Profile

Approaching the school from its wooded driveway, Thomas More is imposing and stately, built in a Gothic style. It has a good range of facilities that are well-utilized to produce some good exam results. In addition to the five specialist science and seven technology rooms, the school has a well-equipped music wing, two computer suites, a drama studio and a large number of general teaching rooms. A new careers facility was opened in 1998 and a new learning resources centre opened in 1999. Thomas More also has an indoor swimming pool and on-site football and hockey pitches, tennis courts and athletics facilities. However, the school would benefit from the much-anticipated new sports hall, but as yet this has not advanced beyond the planning stage. The school is keen to emphasize that teaching takes place within the context of a strong Catholic ethos. Most classes are mixed-ability, with all pupils following a core of English literature and language, maths, science, a foreign language, technology and RE. Pupils can then choose two additional courses from a list of nine options. However, pupils are unable to study two foreign languages. All pupils also follow a PSE course and participate in a compulsory careers placement in Year 11. The school is keen to encourage its pupils to assume responsibilities both around and outside school. It therefore operates a prefect system for those pupils in the upper years. Senior students are also responsible for organizing an annual Christmas party for local senior citizens. There are at least two parents' meetings every year, with additional interviews arranged at key times in the pupils' school career. The school has a strong PTA, there is a school council and there is provision for pupils with special needs.

## Admissions and intake

Priority in admissions is given first to practising Roman Catholics. Any remaining places are then given to those applicants who have siblings at the school, followed by practising members of other Christian denominations affiliated to Churches Together in Britain. Finally, practising members of other faiths are considered.

## Achievement

Levels of attainment at the school have tended to lack consistency over the past four years. In 1999, they reached a new high with 44 per cent of pupils gaining five or more GCSEs at grades A*–C . After less-satisfactory years, standards are again rising, to 36 per cent in 2002. The average point score was 32.4 and the school was ranked 21st in the borough league table. Ofsted inspectors in 1999 generally found that 'pupils are well motivated, responsible and cooperative, and respond well to stimulating teaching'. Thomas More has a relatively high level of fixed-term and permanent exclusions, but this reflects the school's determination to maintain high standards of behaviour rather than any specific problems.

## Extra-curricular activities

A wide range of sports is available including football, swimming, athletics, tennis and dance. The school also has an orchestra and choir. There are a variety of curriculum-enriching societies on offer and a thriving Duke of Edinburgh's Award group. Pupils raise funds for local charities. There are trips both at home and abroad.

# Trinity School

**Shirley Park, Croydon CR9 7AT** ☎ 020 8656 9541 📠 020 8655 0522 ✉ adm@trinity.croydon.sch.uk 🌐 www.trinity.croydon.sch.uk Mr CJ Tarrant; Chair of Governors: Sir Douglas Lovelock East Croydon **Buses:** X30, 54, 119, 130, 194, 198, 367, 466 Black school blazer, dark trousers, white shirt, school tie; Sixth form: Suit **Demand:** No figures available but c. 120 places **Type:** Selective independent day school for 876 boys, aged 10 to 18 **Fees:** £8,400 per annum **Submit application form:** Contact school directly **Motto:** He Who Perseveres Conquers **School hours:** 8.30am–3.45pm **Meals:** Hot and cold available **Strong GCSE subjects:** All relatively strong **London league table position:** 44

## Profile

Trinity School was founded in 1596 as part of the Whitgift Foundation, to which it still belongs. The Foundation is also responsible for the running of neighbouring Whitgift and Old Palace schools. The school moved from central Croydon to its current 27-acre site in 1965. It is set in landscaped grounds, with playing fields available at Sandilands, a short walk away. Trinity has an outstanding range of facilities, including specialist science labs and IT resources. With the completion of the Shaw building in the past few years, the school has gained up-to-date art and design rooms, two impressive sports halls and a fully equipped fitness centre. These additions, together with the swimming pool, five squash courts and new all-weather hockey pitch, mean that Trinity offers some of the finest sporting facilities to be found at any school. All boys follow a core curriculum of English literature and language, the three sciences and a modern language, with an additional three GCSEs from a list of 10. Virtually all boys stay into the sixth form, where they choose three or four A-levels from 19 options. Additional GCSEs are also available in electronics, geology, economics, business studies and music technology. All Year 11 pupils engage in a work experience programme. Boys can become prefects in their final year and there is a school council. There is an active parent-teacher association.

### Admissions and intake

Although the school has traditional links with the Church of England, admissions are based purely on academic ability, as determined by the school's own entrance exam held in late January. Successful candidates are interviewed before the final offer of a place is made. Currently about 40 per cent of the intake comes from independent preparatory schools, with the remainder from state junior schools. A substantial system of academic, sport, music, design and technology and arts scholarships are available to help with fees, and the Whitgift Foundation offers a generous system of bursaries to those applicants who may need financial assistance.

### Achievement

In 2002, Trinity came fourth in the borough's GCSE league table, with 100 per cent of pupils gaining at least five or more GCSEs at A*–C grades. This was in line with 2001's results. At A-level, the average score of 355.8 points for pupils taking two or more subjects, ranked the school fourth in the borough in 2002. Around 95 per cent go on to university, with many going to Oxford and Cambridge.

### Extra-curricular activities

Rugby, hockey and cricket are the most prominent sports available, but swimming, water polo, tennis and squash are also on offer. After-school clubs include shooting, sailing, sub-aqua and jogging. Trinity excels at music, with more than 20 groups for all interests and instruments. The choir has appeared at Glyndebourne, the Royal Opera House, Covent Garden and the National Theatre. As one would expect from a school with two theatres and a specialist drama studio, drama is also thriving. There are regular trips to Europe as well as music and sporting tours. The school also arranges activity weekends in the UK in addition to trips overseas. Pupils raise funds for local charities.

# Virgo Fidelis Convent Senior School

**Central Hill, Upper Norwood, London SE19 1RS** ☎ 020 8670 6917 📠 020 8761 4455 Sister Bernadette B.Ed, C.Biol, MI.Biol; Chair of Governors: Sister F De Reviers de Mauny 🚉 Gypsy Hill **Buses**: 2, 3, 63, 122, 137A, 157, 202, 306, 355, 391, & 450 Grey school blazer, grey skirt, blue school jumper, blue blouse, school tie; Sixth form: Smart clothes **Demand**: 483 applications for 90 places in 2001/2 **Type**: Voluntary aided Roman Catholic comprehensive for 598 girls, aged 11 to 18 **Submit application form**: October 2003 **Motto**: *Credo Spiro Eno* (We will have gained everything when we have taught the children) **School hours**: 8.30am–3.30pm; homework clubs are available **Meals**: Hot and cold available **Strong GCSE subjects**: English **London league table position**: 166

### Profile

Since it was founded in 1848, Virgo Fidelis Convent School has gone through many changes. Most notably, it transformed from an independent school to grant-maintained status in September 1997, then finally to a voluntary aided school in 1999. When the school was inspected by Ofsted in 2000, inspectors found that it was managing this transition well, and continued to be 'a good and effective school'. The oldest part of the school is the imposing Gothic structure which, along with later additions, provides all the classrooms and specialist facilities needed to provide a high standard of education. The school also benefits from a large sports hall and spacious grounds. In addition to national curriculum subjects, the school offers Greek, Latin, food technology, dance, theatre studies, psychology and media studies. All subjects are taught within a framework of traditional Christian values and a strong Catholic ethos. There are 20 A- and AS-levels available in the small sixth form, including accounting, philosophy, Latin, classical studies, Greek, dance and media studies. GNVQs are also available. Work experience is offered to all Year 10 pupils and again in the sixth form. Sixth-formers can become prefects and participate in the sixth-form council. There is a parent-teacher association and provision for pupils with special needs.

### Admissions and intake

Admission is determined primarily by the degree of commitment to the Catholic Church, and all applications must be supported by written evidence of family involvement in the church. Any remaining places are given first to girls who are active in other Christian denominations, followed by those who have siblings at the school, those whose parents work at the school, and those whose application is supported by medical reasons. In the last resort, the distance that girls live from the school is used to determine the intake. All applicants must, however, agree to participate fully in Virgo Fidelis' acts of collective worship and its religious studies programme.

### Achievement

The school performs well in all subjects, with standards being particularly high in English at Key Stage 4. In 2002, 66 per cent of pupils gained five or more GCSEs at the higher grades. This was well above the national average and reversed a modest decline over the previous five years. The school was ranked 11th in the borough league table. A-level results in 2002 saw an average point score of 164.4 for pupils taking two or more subjects, a level well below the national and borough averages, ranking the school 12th in the borough. Despite a relatively high rate of fixed-period exclusions, with a total of 60 suspensions in 1999, pupils are generally very well behaved. Ofsted found that 'pupils' attitudes to school are very good; they are keen to learn and are responsive'.

### Extra-curricular activities

Virgo Fidelis has a wide range of sports teams. It also offers music and drama groups as well as a variety of lunchtime and after-school clubs and activities, such as homework clubs, chess and an animal club. There are trips both at home and abroad.

## Westwood High School

**Spurgeon Road, Upper Norwood, London SE19 3UG** 020 8653 1661 020 8771 6573 mail-ww@westwood.croydon.gov.uk www.westwood.croydon.gov.uk Margaret Hedley; Chair of Governors: Dr J Gooding Crystal Palace **Buses:** X68, 196, 249, 468, Light grey trousers or skirt, scarlet school jumper, white blouse, school tie **Demand:** 750 applications for 180 places in 2001/2 **Type:** Community comprehensive Language College for 900 girls, aged 11 to 16 **Submit application form:** October 2003 **School hours:** 8.40am–3.35pm; homework clubs are available **Meals:** Hot and cold available **Strong GCSE subjects:** All relatively strong **London league table position:** 359

### Profile

Westwood School was built in 1958 in 10 acres of grounds, commanding impressive views over large areas of South London. Since then, a number of additions to the original structure have been needed to keep the school in line with changing educational requirements and to keep pace with its increasing rolls. The most significant addition was completed in 1985, providing the school with a full range of specialist facilities for the first time. In 1998, there was the construction of a new sports hall and teaching block, furnishing the school with a new library and both art and music studios. The school became a Language College in 2002. All pupils follow a core curriculum of English literature and language, maths, a modern language, PE, science, technology, PSE and religious studies. These are supplemented by a further choice of two subjects from a list of 11, including such unusual options as classical studies, Spanish, Modern Greek, travel and tourism, Japanese and media studies. Westwood has a particularly praiseworthy careers programme. All students follow a general careers course in Year 10, and then undertake specific placements in Year 11. The school also has a school council, encouraging its pupils to assume responsibility by playing an active role in determining how the school is run. There is a parent-teacher association and provision for pupils with special needs.

### Admissions and intake

Admissions are through the council (see borough factfile). The school remains popular, especially with local parents. Most pupils are drawn from the surrounding area.

### Achievement

The faith of the local community in the school is justified, since Westwood has a proven record of exam success. It also compares favourably to other institutions whose pupils come predominantly from similar, disadvantaged backgrounds. Results at GCSE have consistently been above the borough average, and have often matched national expectations for all schools. However results have been a little disappointing over the last four years, with 32 per cent of pupils gaining five or more GCSEs at the higher grades in 2002. This continues a downward trend following a high of 45 per cent in 1998. The results in 2002 were also below the local and borough averages, and the school was ranked 23rd in the borough's league table. The average point score was 31.3. When Ofsted inspected the school in 1999, its findings were generally positive, commenting that Westwood 'fosters very good attitudes to learning'. Ofsted also described it as a 'harmonious multi-cultural community' in which 'the majority are well motivated and keen to succeed in their work'.

## Extra-curricular activities

Westwood has a flourishing extra-curricular life with regular drama and music productions and numerous clubs and societies, including homework clubs and a Duke of Edinburgh's Award scheme. It also has a strong sporting reputation, with its hockey and athletics teams achieving particular success in the past. Trips are organized to places of cultural interest.

# Whitgift School

**Haling Park, South Croydon, Surrey CR2 6YT** 020 8688 9222 020 8760 0682 hmspa@whitgift.co.uk www.whitgift.co.uk Dr CA Barnett; Chair of Governors: Mr MA Fowler South Croydon **Buses:** 60, 166, 312, 403, 405, 407, 409, 412, 466, 468 Dark navy school blazer, dark grey trousers, school tie, grey shirt (Years 7 to 8); white shirt (Years 9 to 11); Sixth form: Dark suit **Demand:** No figures available but 150 places **Type:** Selective independent day school for 1099 boys, aged 10 to 18 **Fees:** £9,975 per annum **Submit application form:** Contact school for details **School hours:** 8.25am–3.45pm; homework clubs are available **Meals:** Hot and cold available, including breakfast **Strong GCSE subjects:** Languages **London league table position:** 39

## Profile

Founded in 1596 by John Whitgift, the Archbishop of Canterbury, and opened in 1600, Whitgift is Croydon's oldest school. It is also one of the most beautiful, set in 45 acres of wooded parkland with peacocks wandering the grounds. The current site has been occupied by the school since 1931 but was formerly the estate of Lord Howard of Effingham, who commanded the British fleet against the Spanish Armada in 1588. Although the walled swimming pool gardens are the only surviving elements of the previous buildings, any new additions continue to give the school a stately feel. A new extension built in 1990 houses state-of-the-art technology and IT facilities, a new library, art studios and science labs. These are all pleasantly offset by Haling Park, which offers a number of fine sports pitches. All Year 11 pupils undertake a work experience programme, which includes a placement. The school also has an extensive careers department. There is a strong sixth-form prefects system and a parent-teacher association.

## Admissions and intake

Although the school has obvious links with the Church of England – the Archbishop of Canterbury retains the title of Visitor – the school welcomes pupils from all faiths and backgrounds. Entry is based on the school's own competitive exam held in early January. All applicants will also be interviewed. There is a very generous system of both academic scholarships and bursaries.

## Achievement

In 2002, 96 per cent of pupils gained five or more GCSEs at grades A*–C, and the school was ranked third in Croydon's league table and among the best-performing schools in London. Standards in the sixth form have gradually been rising from their already high mark, and in 2002 there was an average point score of 378.3 for pupils taking two or more A-levels, ranking the school second in the borough. Whitgift has an exceptional choice of subjects and offers 21 GCSEs. It is particularly proud of its languages provision, offering French, German, Italian, Japanese, Mandarin Chinese, Russian and Spanish in addition to the classical languages. The choice of A-levels is also outstanding, including further maths, government and politics, Greek, Japanese, Spanish, classical civilization and photography, with all pupils starting a minimum of three courses.

## Extra-curricular activities

Whitgift has a tradition of rugby, hockey and cricket success. In 1999, the under 15s won the *Daily Mail* National Championship, and the school boasts many players representing their county, or even country, at all three sports. Other competitive sports include athletics, cross-country, swimming and squash. Pupils can also engage in climbing on the school's own climbing wall, judo, shooting in the firing range and canoeing. Lunchtime clubs range from debating to bridge and model railways, and there are after-school homework clubs. The school has also staged successful music and drama productions. There are frequent theatre and museum trips, and exchanges are arranged to France, Germany and Japan. Pupils participate in activities at Whitgift House, the Whitgift Foundation's own complex of accommodation for the elderly.

# Woodcote High School

**Meadow Rise, Coulsdon, Surrey CR5 2EH** 020 8668 6464 020 8660 9038 enquiries@whs.woodcote.croydon.sch.uk www.woodcote.croydon.sch.uk Mr D Peaple; Chair of Governors: Mr J Speller East Croydon **Buses:** 60, 166, 463, 466 Royal blue school blazer, grey trousers or skirt, white shirt or blouse, school tie **Demand:** 1175 applications for 210 places in 2001/2 **Type:** Community comprehensive Sports College for 970 mixed pupils, aged 11 to 16 **Submit application form:** October 2003 **Motto:** A Learning Community **School hours:** 8.25am–3.10pm **Meals:** Hot and cold available **Strong GCSE subjects:** Biology, chemistry, English, history, maths, physics **London league table position:** 223

## Profile

Woodcote is a pleasant and largely successful school. It is set in 47 acres of well-tended grounds in one of Croydon's more wealthy, leafy suburbs, situated on the edge of the green belt. The most prominent buildings date from the mid-1950s, but a substantial extension was added in 1988. The construction of a new music and arts block was completed in 1995. The school acquired Sports College status in 2002. Woodcote offers ample facilities of a reasonable standard. Students are set in most subjects from Year 8, allowing more able children to thrive. However, all pupils follow the same broad curriculum, encompassing all of the national curriculum subjects. In addition, the school offers Latin and a second foreign language. Approximately 80 per cent of leavers continue their education at a local college, with most going to either Croydon, Coulsdon or John Ruskin colleges. Woodcote is also keen to nurture a sense of responsibility amongst its pupils. All members of Year 10 undertake community service, while those pupils in the following year participate in a work-placement programme. There is a parent-teacher association, a school council and provision for pupils with special needs.

## Admissions and intake

Admissions are through the council (see borough factfile). The school is heavily oversubscribed, with most pupils coming from nearby south of Croydon and parts of Surrey.

## Achievement

Woodcote's GCSE results have fluctuated over recent years, with the percentage of pupils gaining five or more GCSEs at A*–C grades falling to 41 per cent in 1998 from a high of 59 per cent in 1996. However, results have recovered in recent years, reaching 57 per cent in 2002, above the national average. The school was ranked 15th in the borough. Woodcote benefits from a vibrant and generally well-behaved community of hard-working students. In 1996, Ofsted found that pupils exhibited 'sustained concentration, enjoyment, great commitment and enthusiasm' both for their work and the school.

## Extra-curricular activities

The school has a good reputation for competitive sports and offers a packed fixture list for most of the usual team and individual games. It also provides opportunities for pupils to develop their interests in dance, lacrosse and volleyball, among other activities. The non-sporting extra-curricular life of the school is equally lively, with regular meetings of the chess, art and chef's clubs. There are also Amnesty International, environmental and Duke of Edinburgh's Award groups on offer, as well as a number of orchestras and bands. There are trips both at home and abroad.

# Ealing

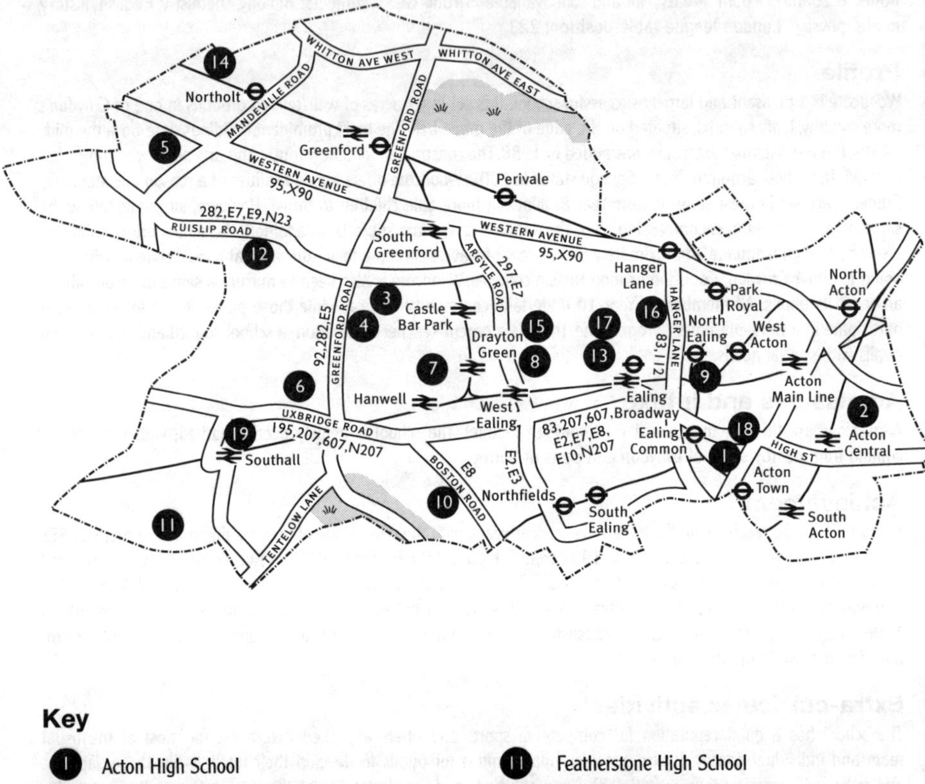


**Key**

1 Acton High School
2 Barbara Speake Stage School
3 Brentside High School
4 The Cardinal Wiseman RC School
5 The Compton High School & Sports College
6 Dormers Wells High School
7 Drayton Manor High School
8 Ealing College Upper School
9 The Ellen Wilkinson School for Girls
10 Elthorne Park High School
11 Featherstone High School
12 Greenford High School
13 Harvington School
14 Northolt High School
15 Notting Hill and Ealing High School
16 St Augustine's Priory
17 St Benedict's School
18 Twyford CofE High School
19 Villiers High School

# Factfile

**LEA: Perceval House, 14–16 Uxbridge Road, London W5 2HL** ☎ 020 8825 5000 🌐 www.ealing.gov.uk **Director of Education:** Caroline Whalley **Political control of council:** Labour **Percentage of pupils from outside the borough:** 8.4 per cent **Percentage of pupils educated outside the borough:** 4.2 per cent **London league table positions (out of 32 boroughs):** 12th

Ealing borough is made up of four distinct areas, each with their own economic, cultural and social characteristics. These are Southall, Greenford and Northolt, Acton and Ealing itself. Ealing is a prosperous area with many good independent schools. It is famous for Ealing Studios and continues to be called the 'Queen of the Boroughs' because of the large number of green spaces. Acton is moving increasingly upmarket in some areas, mixed with poorer housing estates. Greenford and Northolt are mainly suburban with some industrial parks and large council estates. Southall is perhaps the most colourful and distinctive corner of the borough; it is also the poorest. Whilst many of those who settled there in the 1960s and 70s are becoming prosperous, newer arrivals, mainly from Somalia, Sri Lanka and Eastern Europe, often endure poor housing, high unemployment and poverty. The borough is one of the most culturally diverse in London. Dozens of languages are spoken, from Urdu and Gujarati to Polish and French. It also has the largest Polish community in Britain and one of the biggest Sikh communities.

Ealing's schools cater for many children with English as an additional language and many schools have support teachers to assist with this. Seven schools have college status: Brentside High was granted Art College status in 2000; Walford High School is now The Compton Enterprise & Sports Academy, Cardinal Wiseman is a Technology College, Brentside High is an Art College, Greenford High is a Language College, Northolt College is a Technology College and Acton High has IT College status. Compton High is now a City Academy. Many schools have Beacon status and others have received the Investor in People Award. Ealing Council and Ealing National Union of Teachers (NUT) are at the forefront of a campaign for better pay for teachers. The borough boasts one of the top-performing independent schools in St Augustine's and, according to Ofsted, one of the most improved secondary schools in Cardinal Wiseman. Elthorne Park's innovative design and curriculum structure is also seen as a benchmark for future schools.

Ealing also includes the Greek School of London, the Japanese School and King Fahad Academy. As these schools do not teach a GCSE curriculum in English, they have not been included here.

## Policy

Parents should contact the LEA to get a copy of the brochure *High Schools*. Applications for Cardinal Wiseman RC High School or Twyford Church of England School must be made directly to the schools. The criteria for admission for children to oversubscribed state schools are: if the child has a sibling at the school; medical or social circumstances; and how close the child lives to the school.

# Acton High School

**Gunnersbury Lane, Acton W3 8EY** ☎ 020 8752 0005 📠 020 8993 7236 🌐 www.actonhigh.cjb.net Ms L Hall; Chair of Governors: Mr G Fiegehen 🚆 Acton Central ⊖ Ealing Common, Acton Town **Buses:** E3 and all buses along Uxbridge Road Navy blue, black or grey trousers or skirt, navy sweatshirt and white or blue polo shirt. **Demand:** 510 applications for 240 places in 2001/2 **Type:** Comprehensive for 1158 mixed pupils, aged 11 to 16 **Submit application form:** Early November 2003 **Motto:** Achieving for All **School hours:** 8.40am–3.25pm; 8.40am–3.05pm (Wed) **Meals:** Hot and cold available, including breakfast **Strong GCSE subjects:** Art, English **London league table position:** 480

## Profile

Acton High was built in the 1920s and the school recently underwent a million-pound facelift, including repainting, a new roof and an information technology block, which was completed in autumn 2001. A new humanities block and expressive-arts block was also recently built. There are sports fields on-site. The school offers the usual curriculum but pupils can also choose one of three pathways up to their GCSEs. This means they can take all GCSEs or mix GCSEs with a small number of vocational subjects, or with a greater number of vocational subjects. Acton High was one of the first schools to pilot a government literacy and numeracy project, and there is a learning support unit for pupils with special needs. Pastoral care is very effective with counsellors, a mentoring system and the South Acton Pupil-Parent Project. Work experience is offered to Year 11 pupils and there is an opportunity to serve on the school council.

The school has a special-needs coordinator. There is a very active Acton High School Association made up of current and past parents. Ex-pupils include musician Pete Townshend from The Who.

## Admissions and intake

Admission is through the LEA. The principal feeder primary schools are: Berrymeade, Derwent Water, Montpelier, Little Ealing and West Acton. Pupils are also drawn from a number of primary schools in Hammersmith.

## Achievement

Acton High is in the bottom five of the borough league tables but it has been improving. In 2002, 26 per cent of pupils gained five or more A*–C grades at GCSE, a fall on 28 per cent in 2001. In 2002, Ofsted stated that: 'The school is providing a satisfactory education for its students'. Inspectors praised the school's 'good leadership and management' and found 'good quality' teaching in Years 10 and 11. Pupils with English as an additional language were seen to 'make satisfactory progress', and the standard of pastoral care was 'high'. However, Inspectors found the quality of science teaching in Years 7 to 9 unsatisfactory, with a lack of support staff for those pupils at an early stage of learning English. Attendance is well below the national average and this was seen to have an adverse effect on learning and progress.

## Extra-curricular activities

There is a wide variety of after-school clubs, including public speaking, a steel band, the Chinese Culture Club, potholing and other outdoor pursuits. The school offers exchange trips to Europe and America, skiing trips and an activity weekend in the Isle of Wight. There are also theatre trips and visiting speakers such as Neville Lawrence (father of Stephen Lawrence), who spoke of the consequences of racism. The BBC, based nearby in White City, often uses pupils for comment. Pupils do community work, including helping out at Acton Hospital and making up Christmas parcels to send abroad. Sports on offer at the school follow the national curriculum.

# Barbara Speake Stage School

**East Acton Lane, Acton W3 7EG** 020 8743 1306 Same as telephone, but call first to say you are sending a fax. cpuk@aol.com David R Speake Acton Central, Acton Mainline East Acton **Buses:** 70, 266, 207 Red blazer, red and black tie, black trousers, red skirt, white shirt **Demand:** There is a lot of demand at Year 11 but space for younger pupils. On the whole, however, pupils can join throughout the year. **Type:** Independent for 142 mixed pupils, aged 4 to 16 **Fees:** £1,025 a term junior (nursery to Year 6), £1,125 a term senior (Year 7 to Year 11) **Submit application form:** No cut-off date **Mission statement:** We aim to develop the artistic and academic talents of the individual. **School hours:** 9.30am–4pm **Meals:** Hot and cold available **Strong GCSE subjects:** English, maths **London league table position:** 216

## Profile

This school was opened in 1945 by Barbara Speake as a dance school with only eight pupils. In 1961, it became an academy and numbers have increased ever since. Ms Speake is still very much involved with the school and her nephew is the head teacher. The school building has an imposing hall surrounded by classrooms. There are some temporary buildings outside but there are plans to replace them with a block of eight classrooms. During the day, most lessons are academic but there is also one lesson a day in the performing arts, for example, ballet, dance or drama. Pupils also study dance rather than sports. The GCSE curriculum offers 10 GCSEs covering a broad spectrum. The school does not offer A-levels. The Barbara Speake Agency is attached to the school and pupils have the opportunity to find work through it. One pupil filmed *The Emperor's New Clothes* in Italy, while other pupils have had parts in the musicals *Whistle Down the Wind* and *The King and I*. The agency will also help pupils to find employment in modelling, voice-overs and commercials. There is a fund-raising committee rather than a PTA, although parents are welcome to come into the school at any time, and homework books help to keep them informed. Ex-pupils include actress and singer Michelle Gayle, entertainer and comedian Brian Conelly, TV presenter Keith Chegwin, and film director David Parfitt.

## Admissions and intake

Applications should be made directly to the school. Entry criteria is based on an interview, and the school looks for a good attitude. There is no catchment area as such and the school takes pupils from across London.

## Achievement

The school's exam results vary have been in decline for the past three years, with 43 per cent of pupils gaining five or more A*–C grades at GCSE in 2002, down from 69 per cent in 2001. The school was last inspected in 1993. The report noted that it was a happy school with confident pupils. However, a number of academic areas were highlighted as requiring improvement. These problems were the lack of variety in the curriculum, the number of hours spent on each subject and the need for teaching in IT, French and science. The school has been revisited and inspectors are satisfied that these problems have now been addressed.

## Extra-curricular activities

The school has a drama club and Saturday morning dance workshop. There are a number of stage productions held each year. Trips to theatres are also organized and pupils are involved in fund-raising for the Variety Club.

# Brentside High School

**Greenford Avenue, Hanwell W7 1JJ** ☎ 020 8575 9162 ℻ 020 8578 8905 ⓔ head_teacher_bhs@btconnect.com 🌐 www.brentsidehigh.ealing.sch.uk ✉ Avril Phillips; Chair of Governors: John James ⇄ Greenford, South Greenford ⊖ Perivale **Buses:** E1, E3, E7, E9 👔 Up to sixth form: Black skirt or trousers, black V-neck jumper, blazer, white shirt **Demand:** 329 applications for 200 places in 2001/2 **Type:** Comprehensive Arts College foundation school for 1134 mixed pupils, aged 11 to 19 **Submit application form:** Early November 2003 **Motto:** Learning and Achieving Together **School hours:** 8.45am–3.20pm; homework clubs are available **Meals:** Hot and cold available **Strong GCSE subjects:** English **London league table position:** 422

## Profile

Brentside opened in 1937 as a boys' school. It became a comprehensive in 1974 and a grant-maintained school in 1992. It has since become a foundation school and recently gained Arts College status. The school has new dance, drama and music studios; a large, well-equipped art, craft and design suite including a multimedia suite, sculpture studio and recording studio. A new IT centre opened in 2001. The curriculum offers the usual broad range of subjects but also includes Latin, which can be studied from Year 7 until A-level. Brentside has a strong art department, especially in the expressive arts. The sixth form offers a general range of subjects, including GNVQs in business, health and social care and others, and an A-level in classical civilization. Work experience is offered to Year 10 and sixth-form pupils. The school has good provision for pupils with special needs. There is a school council and sixth-formers can be trained as peer listeners by 'Relate' to listen to the problems of younger pupils. Pastoral care is good, with a student link worker and student welfare officer. There is no PTA but parents meet regularly with the school and keep in touch via pupils' contact books. Ex-pupils include the Norwich City Footballer Adrian Forbes.

## Admissions and intake

Applications should be made directly to the school. The main entry criteria are: whether a sibling is at the school; proximity of home to the school; and medical grounds supported by evidence. The main feeder primary schools are: Brentside, Hobbayne and Mayfield.

## Achievement

Compared to other similar schools in the borough, Brentside performs well above-average in most areas, with Ofsted giving it an 'A' in its last inspection in 1999. In 2002, 32 per cent of pupils gained five or more A*–C grades at GCSE, a fall on 38 per cent in 2001. The school was ranked in the bottom three of the borough league table for 2002. At A-level, the average points score for pupils taking two or more was 202.7, placing the school 13th in the borough league table. The academic standard of pupils entering the school is often low and the school does well to improve them. In 1999, Ofsted reported that the school had good sixth-form teaching and strong leadership. However, attendance was deemed unsatisfactory and inspectors asked for standards in IT to be raised.

## Extra curricular activities

The school offers after-school clubs in most sports, arts and drama, science and information technology and Move, a board game club. There are visits to Italy, France, Spain and Germany each year to support languages, along with Latin, geography and history trips, and a residential trip to Wales.

# The Cardinal Wiseman RC School

**Greenford Road, Greenford UB6 9AW** 020 8575 8222 020 8575 9963 info@wiseman.org.uk Paul Patrick; Chair of Governors: Mr L Misquitta Greenford Station Perivale **Buses:** 95, 105 Blue blazer, grey trousers or skirt, white shirt, striped tie **Demand:** 803 applications for 270 places in 2001/2 **Type:** Voluntary aided comprehensive Technology and Arts College for 1568 mixed pupils, aged 11 to 18 **Submit application form:** Early November 2003 **Motto:** All things for Christ **School hours:** 9am–3.20pm **Meals:** Hot and cold available **Strong GCSE subjects:** Art, English **London league table position:** 143

## Profile

Cardinal Wiseman recently gained Arts College status and has a strong art department, particularly in the expressive arts. It has a new specialist arts centre, gymnasium, IT centre and a refurbished suite of rooms for pupils with special needs. The curriculum includes Latin, which can be taught from Year 7 until A-level. The sixth form offers a general range of subjects, including GNVQs in business, health and social care and others, and an A-level in classical civilization. Work experience is offered to Year 10 and to sixth-formers. The school is willing to take disabled pupils and has good provision for pupils with special needs. There is a school council and sixth-formers can be trained as peer listeners by helping younger pupils with problems. Pastoral care is good, with a student link worker and student welfare officer. There is no PTA but parents meet regularly with the school and keep in touch via pupils' contact books.

## Admissions and intake

Applications should be made directly to the school. Entry criteria are: whether a sibling is at the school; proximity of home to the school; and medical grounds supported by evidence. Pupils come from 54 primary schools, with the main ones being Brentside, Hobbayne and Mayfield.

## Achievement

Cardinal Wiseman performs well above average in most areas, with Ofsted giving it an 'A' in comparative assessments. In 2002, 76 per cent of pupils gained five or more A*–C grades at GCSE, a rise from 60 per cent in 2001. The average point score was 42.7, placing the school sixth in the borough league table. At A-level, the average point score for pupils taking two or more was 214.6, ranking the school 11th in the borough. The academic standard of pupils entering the school is often low and the school significantly improves them. In 2000, the school received a glowing Ofsted report which named it as one of the 'top 50 most improved schools nationally'. Inspectors judged the school to have made 'outstanding progress under the inspirational leadership' of the head teacher and said that the school has 'many strengths'. Teaching was deemed to be of a 'very good quality' and there was 'very good provision for students with special needs'.

## Extra-curricular activities

The school offers after-school clubs in most sports, arts and drama, science and information technology. There are visits to Italy, France, Spain and Germany each year to support languages, Latin, geography and history and also a residential trip to Wales. The school is raising money for Arts College status and organizes several charitable events where half the money raised goes to charity.

# The Compton Enterprise and Sports Academy

**Bengarth Road, Northolt UB5 5LQ** 020 8841 4511 020 8841 4480 Mrs Monica Cotterell; Chair of Governors: Cllr Fred Dunkley Northolt **Buses:** 90, 120, 140, 282 Black skirt or trousers, white blouse, black blazer, black sweater **Demand:** 362 appications for 180 places in 2001/2 **Type:** Comprehensive City Academy for 866 mixed pupils, aged 11 to 19 **Submit application form:** Early November 2003 **Motto:** Education for Life **School hours:** 8.40am–3.15pm **Meals:** Hot and cold available, including breakfast **Strong GCSE subjects:** Drama, PE **London league table position:** 506

## Profile

Formerly The Compton High School and Sports College, the school is now a City Academy and will receive around £19 million to be spent on new IT suites, a new library and resource centre and a range of sports facilities. Its Sport College status means that it also gets extra money, equipment and sponsorship for teaching sports. The school is also home to Northolt Primary School and John Chilton Special School, meaning it integrates disabled pupils and is fully accessible to wheelchairs. With the primary school on-site, it also means pupils can go through the same school from age five to 18. The school has a 22-acre site with playing fields. It offers the general curriculum plus a variety of pupils' first languages including Turkish. There is a strong emphasis on sports with special coaching in all areas. The sixth form covers most A-level curriculum subjects as well as GNVQs. Pastoral care is strong, with a head of year for each year group and a mentoring scheme. Parents can become involved through parents' evenings and workshops.

## Admissions and intake

Principal feeder schools are Northolt Primary and other Northolt primary schools, plus schools in Harrow and Hillingdon. If there is excessive demand for places, then the school will give priority to pupils living nearest or those with siblings at the school. Of the 866 pupils, over 300 are on the special-needs register.

## Achievement

The school is bottom of the borough for GCSE results, with 13 per cent of pupils gaining five or more A*–C grades in 2002, compared to 20 per cent in 2001. A-levels only began in 1999 and in 2002 the average point score was 164.2, placing the school bottom of the borough. The majority of pupils arrive at the school with their standards of learning well below national levels. In 1998, Ofsted reported: 'Walford has considerable potential for development. Much progress has been made during the last year and the school has several strengths'. The report praised the good relations between teachers and pupils. However, the school was asked to develop its learning support, improve its information technology and monitor pupils more satisfactorily. Since then, a consultant has been brought in to improve special needs, and computers have been added to two new computer suites.

## Extra-curricular activities

There are lots of sports clubs, coaching and training available, including coaching from premier basketball team the Ealing Tornados. The football and basketball teams consistently do well. There is also a drama club, annual panto and plays staged by drama students. There are trips abroad, including a skiing trip. The school is very involved in fund-raising, and pupils help out at the on-site special school.

# Dormers Wells High School

**Dormers Wells Lane, Southall UB1 3HZ** ☎ 020 8813 8671 📠 020 8813 8816 ✉ Mrs Janet Leigh BA; Chair of Governors: Vladimir Kopecky ⇄ Southall **Buses:** 207, 607 👔 Black blazer, grey trousers or skirt, white shirt, striped tie **Demand:** 686 applications for 120 places in 2001/2 **Type:** Comprehensive for 852 mixed pupils, aged 11 to 16 **Submit application form:** Early November 2003 **School hours:** 8.45am–3.25pm; homework clubs are available **Meals:** Hot and cold available **Strong GCSE subjects:** Business studies, economics, English, maths **London league table position:** 393

## Profile

Dormers Wells faces many challenges, identified by Ofsted in 1995 as a higher than average percentage of pupils with English as an additional language, a higher than average number of pupils with special needs, and an intake of pupils of whom a high proportion are below the national average in test results at Year 7. Since then the school has dealt with these initial disadvantages very well, and was commended by Ofsted in its 2000 inspection as one of the 29 most-improved secondary schools in the country. It was judged to have made outstanding progress, to be racially harmonious and to give children a sense of pride. Dormers Wells also has a good personal development programme, with pupils in the final year training as mentors. There is also an anti-bullying provision. Pupils can become class monitors, receptionists and librarians. Computers are available at lunchtime and break times for homework. The school also has a special-needs coordinator and an active PTA.

### Admissions and intake

Admission is through the LEA (see borough factfile for details).

### Achievement

The school's exam results place it in the bottom half of the borough league table in 2002, with 36 per cent gaining five or more A*–C grades at GCSE, a rise from 31 per cent in 2001. The last Ofsted report from 1999 commended teaching in English, maths, Urdu, business studies and economics. Areas said to be in need of improvement were the teaching of pupils with English as an additional language and the design curriculum, areas which the school is addressing.

### Extra-curricular activities

Dormers Wells has a wide range of clubs available, including the Duke of Edinburgh's Award scheme. Year 9 pupils make an annual residential visit to the New Forest. A summer activities week is held along with drama and dance performances, which recognize the different cultures of the pupils in the school. There are also theatre visits and an art group visit to Paris. After-school homework clubs are available in many subjects.

# Drayton Manor High School

**Drayton Bridge Road, Hanwell W7 1EU** 020 8357 1900 020 8566 1918 Pritpal Singh; Chair of Governors: Mr R Elliott Hanwell, Drayton Green Ealing Broadway **Buses:** E1, E3 Navy blazer, grey trousers, white shirt, navy V-neck jumper **Demand:** 700 applications for c.200 places in 2001/2 **Type:** Comprehensive for 1540 mixed pupils, aged 11 to 19 **Submit application form:** Early November 2003 **School hours:** 8.30am–4.30pm; homework clubs are available **Meals:** Hot and cold available **Strong GCSE subjects:** Maths, science **London league table position:** 200

### Profile

Drayton Manor is a 'good school' according to the last Ofsted report in 1996, and it recently became a Beacon School. Although the school's accommodation was criticized by Ofsted as being 'insufficient in some areas', there are plans to extend the school facilities. There are seven tennis/netball courts in addition to both on-site and off-site playing fields. The sixth form offers 25 A-levels, including business and finance. Work experience placements are offered to all pupils. There is a programme for personal and social education, a year and school council, and a house system. Ofsted saw the 'multi-ethnic and multi-cultural mix [as] a strength of the school, which 'the school exploits to the full in order to promote a sense of fascination across racial, cultural and religious boundaries'. The school promotes this sense of harmony with a firm anti-bullying and anti-racism policy. The PTA is very committed.

### Admissions and intake

Admission is through the LEA. As the school is often oversubscribed, the criteria for entry include preference given to siblings and those living closest to the school. The main feeder primaries are Drayton Manor, Fielding, Grange, Little Ealing, Montpelier, North Ealing and Selcombe primary schools. The school's intake has average attainment on entry. A total of 14 per cent of all pupils are on the special-needs register.

### Achievement

Drayton Manor is usually in the upper half of the borough GCSE and A-level league tables. In 2002, 65 per cent of pupils gained five or more A*–C grades at GCSE, an increase on 55 per cent in 2001. The last Ofsted report was carried out in 1996 and stated that attainment is consistently sound, with good teaching and good leadership. Reading and writing, and maths and science were picked out by the inspector as being particularly good. However, it also stated that there was insufficient use of computers in the sixth form.

### Extra-curricular activities

The school offers after-school clubs in most sports, arts and drama. There is a very active Amnesty International group and a successful debating society. The school takes part in Young Enterprise schemes and organizes visiting speakers, visits to the theatre and trips abroad. Pupils raise money for charity from a variety of fund-raising events such as non-uniform day, a pantomime and washing cars.

# Ealing College Upper School

**83 The Avenue, Ealing W13 8JS** 020 8248 2312 020 8248 3765 Barrington Webb West Ealing, Ealing Broadway Ealing Broadway **Buses:** 83, 207 Black blazer, tie, grey or black trousers, white or grey shirt **Demand:** Varies for up to 20 places **Type:** Non-selective independent for 128 boys, aged 11 to 19 **Fees:** £5,440 per annum **Submit application form:** Contact school for details **Motto:** *Cona Bor* (I Shall Endeavour) **School hours:** 8.50am–3.40pm **Meals:** Hot and cold available **Strong GCSE subjects:** All relatively strong **London league table position:** 208

## Profile

The school was founded in 1820 in Acton and moved to in Ealing in 1925. It is housed in a Victorian building which has had many additions over the years. In 1983 a new library and IT centre were added. The school adheres mainly to the national curriculum, with a slight emphasis on science, in which all pupils must take at least one GCSE. All pupils must take nine or 10 GCSEs and there is the facility for early entry. Government and politics and computing are also offered at A-level. Work experience is offered in Year 11 to pupils who are thought likely to benefit. The school has provision for pupils with dyslexia and will take physical disabilities, although wheelchair access can be a problem because of the nature of the building. Pastoral care is considered to be good under a house system, and pupils are watched over very carefully. There is a PTA, which is responsible for organizing social activities.

## Admissions and intake

Applicants are admitted only after taking a diagnostic test to find out what they have been taught already and an interview with the head teacher. The intake is from across all ability ranges.

## Achievement

In 2002, 65 per cent of pupils gained five or more A*–C grades at GCSE, a slight rise from 63 per cent in 2001. The school was placed 11th in the borough. At A-level, the average point score was 219 points in 2002, ranking the school 10th in the borough. The school was last inspected two years ago and inspectors found it to be quite satisfactory. The school was praised for its science teaching and for its ability to bring out the best in pupils. Behaviour and attitude to learning was also praised.

## Extra-curricular activities

The school offers the usual after-school clubs in sports, and football is particularly popular. It also enters pupils in independent school competitions such as cross country running. There is a film/video club, pottery, Duke of Edinburgh's Award scheme and chess. There are many opportunities for trips abroad, including three-day trips to France and an annual skiing trip. Many visits to the theatre and exhibitions are organized to support the curriculum. The school has a long-standing relationship with Northwick Park Hospital and the children's ward at Ealing Hospital and raises funds for both.

# The Ellen Wilkinson School for Girls

**Queens Drive, Acton W3 0HW** 020 8752 1525 020 8993 6632 ewsoffice@AOL.com www.ellen_wilkinson_school.co.uk Sue Parrott; Chair of Governors: Mrs S Pocock Ealing Broadway North Ealing, West Acton **Buses:** 207, 607 Navy blue skirt or trousers, white blouse, navy blue jumper or cardigan **Demand:** At least two applicants for every place **Type:** Comprehensive foundation for 1311 girls, aged 11 to 19 **Submit application form:** Early November 2003 **Mission statement:** All have an infinite potential for learning regardless of age and a capacity to change **School hours:** 8.40am–3.30pm **Meals:** Hot and cold available **Strong GCSE subjects:** Art, business studies, English, RE, sociology **London league table position:** 156

## Profile

This school was the Ealing Girls Grammar School until 1974, when it became Ellen Wilkinson School. The school is in good condition following a five-year modernization plan. A new art block, media studies block and learning support room have been added, and a science lab has been refurbished. It recently became a specialist school for science and mathematics. It is the only non fee-paying girls' school in the borough and tries to offer a broad curriculum with equal emphasis on all subjects. The sixth form offers A-levels in sociology and media studies among others. There are also

GNVQs in a variety of subjects. Work experience is available. There is a school council system and head girl and house system. The school provides a good range of pastoral care. There is no PTA but many of the governors are parents, and parents are kept in touch by pupil/parent handbooks. Ex-pupils include newsreader Gargi Patel.

### Admissions and intake

Pupils are taken from over 60 primary schools across the borough, mainly Horsenden, Perivale, West Acton, East Acton, Montpelier, Derwentwater and West Twyford. The entry criteria are: having a sibling at the school; daughters of members of staff; and pupils from Perivale and Horsenden who are beyond the distance criteria for other schools. The majority of pupils do not have English as their first language. At the time of writing, there were 339 pupils on the special needs register and 12 were statemented.

### Achievement

The school is better than most similar schools and above average for the borough. In 2002, 70 per cent of pupils gained five or more A*–C grades at GCSE, up from 63 per cent in 2001. The school was ranked eighth in the borough league table. The average point score for pupils taking two or more A-levels was 231.3 in 2002, placing the school seventh in the borough. Ofsted visited the school in 2001 and the strong subjects were found to be art, media studies and ICT. Weaker subjects were music and PE. The school was judged to be 'a good school with several excellent features'. Teaching was seen to be 'consistently good' and 'relationships and students' personal development are good'. Help given to pupils learning English as an additional language was described as 'outstanding'. The school has a 'very positive ethos of success'. However, cramped accommodation was criticized again, despite the school having completed a five-year modernization plan.

### Extra-curricular activities

The school has a wide range of clubs, including a gardening group, called the Quad Squad, which was responsible for a centrepiece in a courtyard outside the school. There are trips abroad – in recent years there has been a survival course to Malaysia – visits to galleries and theatres and visits by guest speakers. The school also does charity work in the community, holds book weeks and other fund-raising events and supports Amnesty International.

## Elthorne Park High School

**Westlea Road, Hanwell W7 2AH** 020 8566 1166 020 8566 1177 elthorne@EPHS.ealing.sch.uk www.ephs.co.uk Mohamed Sabur; Chair of Governors: Cllr Margaret Majundar West Ealing **Buses:** E8 Burgundy or white polo shirt, burgundy sweatshirt, black trousers or skirt, school bag **Demand:** 813 applicants for 180 places in 2001/2 **Type:** Comprehensive for 900 mixed pupils, aged 11 to 16 **Submit application form:** Early November 2003 **Motto:** Individual Achievement in a Learning Community **School hours:** 8.40am–3.30pm; homework clubs are available **Meals:** Hot and cold available, including breakfast **Strong GCSE subjects:** All relatively strong **London league table position:** Not available

### Profile

Elthorne Park was opened in September 1998, following a long campaign by local parents who wanted their children to go to a school nearer to home. The school has been built on the site of a Victorian school previously converted into offices. The building has been completely refurbished and modernized. There is a brand new expressive arts building which includes practice rooms and a drama studio, plus a newly resourced library/learning resource centre. The sports centre onsite won a Sportsmark Award for its high standard of equipment. The timetable offers a broad curriculum plus a highly praised enrichment programme, which gives pupils the chance to take four to five modules a year in a huge variety of subjects, from touch rugby and astrology to first aid and orienteering. There is a strong emphasis on IT. Three languages are taught in Year 7 – French, German and Spanish. Plans are being drawn up to offer pupils work experience for two weeks in Year 10. The school's pastoral care is good, with tutor groups, counselling and a mentoring scheme. There is also good provision for special-needs pupils. The school has a home-school association that is extremely active, organizing both social and fund-raising events. Pupils can join the school council.

### Admissions and intake

Admission is through the LEA. When oversubscribed preference is given to those with a sibling at the school, those living closest to the school, and relevant medical grounds supported by evidence.

### Achievement

There are no exam results yet as pupils have not reached Year 11. However, the school says it plans to adopt a policy of early entries.

### Extra-curricular activities

The school offers a range of after-school clubs, including everything from drama to football and dance. There is a strong leaning towards environmental teaching and the school won a national award for its promotion of safe cycling. Elthorne Park also won an award from Groundwork environmental charity to design tiles to brighten up the towpath of the Grand Union Canal. There is a residential trip for pupils in Year 7, an outdoor pursuit trip for Year 8 and French and German trips for Year 9 pupils. Pupils work with elderly people and hold tea parties for senior citizens. The learning-resource centre opens at 8am, lunchtime and after school, when a teacher is available to help with homework.

## Featherstone High School

**11 Montague Way, Southall UB2 5HF** 020 8843 0984 020 8574 3405 enquiries@featherstone.schoolzone.co.uk Thelma Cox; Chair of Governors: Cllr Paothak Southall Black blazer, black trousers, white shirt, school tie **Demand:** 479 applications for 240 places in 2001/2 **Type:** Comprehensive for 1105 mixed pupils, aged 11 to 16 **Submit application form:** Early November 2003 **School hours:** 8.50am–3.25pm **Meals:** Hot and cold available **Strong GCSE subjects:** Art, English, history **London league table position:** 337

### Profile

Featherstone High is located in the south-west corner of Ealing in the Featherstone area of Southall. This area of Southall has poor housing and much temporary accommodation. As a result, there is a large transient population, which includes a significant number of asylum seekers. The school was formed in 1975 by the amalgamation of two single-sex modern schools. The school's accommodation has improved significantly with the completion of the community sports hall and a new teaching block that enabled the move to a single site. It now has two brand new science labs, a drama suite and movement studio. In 2001, the school won a DfES Award for Excellence. Spiritual development is fostered in several subjects and pupils attend two assemblies each week. Pupils are encouraged to celebrate their own cultural heritage. The school's pastoral support is generally strong. The school has council and a special-needs coordinator. There is a strong PTA.

### Admissions and intake

Admission is through the LEA (see borough factfile).

### Achievement

In 2002, 39 per cent of pupils gained five or more A*–C grades at GCSE, a drop from 39 per cent in 2001, which had been the highest result for five years. In 2001, Ofsted visited the school and found it to be 'a very effective school with many strengths'. GCSE results were seen to be 'much higher than might be expected given pupils' attainment on entry'. Inspectors noted that 'teaching is good and often very good' and they praised the head teacher's 'excellent' leadership. Pupils were seen to do well in French, community languages and PE. However, Inspectors criticized the school for lacking a consistent approach to teaching literacy and numeracy, and noted poor achievement in design and technology due to 'unsatisfactory' teaching.

### Extra-curricular activities

There is a variety of sports available, as well as music and drama clubs. Theatre trips are organized along with visits to complement history and RE.

## Greenford High School

**Ruislip Road, Greenford UB6 9RX** 020 8578 9152 020 8578 8963 kategriffin@greenfordhighschool.co.uk www.greenfordhighschool.uk.org Kate Griffin; Chair of Governors: Mr G Smith Greenford Greenford **Buses:** E6, E7, E9, (E7 and E9 from Ealing Broadway), E10, 282 Up to sixth form: Black blazer, white shirt or blouse, school tie, black sweater, black trousers, skirt, dark shoes **Demand:** 507 applications for 210 places in 2001/2 **Type:** Comprehensive foundation Language College for 1500 mixed pupils, aged 11 to 19 **Submit**

**application form:** Early November 2003 **Mission statement:** Everyone to achieve the best possible results and enjoy the process **School hours:** 8.35am–3.25pm; homework clubs are available **Meals:** Hot and cold available **Strong GCSE subjects:** English, maths **London league table position:** 231

## Profile

The school opened in 1939 as a grammar school and became a comprehensive in the early 1970s. The school has been described as a mini Hoover building and is a classic example of the art deco style of the 1930s. The amount of space was criticized by Ofsted at the last inspection, but since then a new dining hall has been built and the sixth form has been completely refurbished. The curriculum is very wide-ranging, with an emphasis on languages and the school gained Language College status in 2001. Greenwood has had a lot of success in sports, especially cricket, tennis, football and athletics. Cricketers reached the semi-finals of the Middlesex County Championships in 2000. The school offers GNVQ and advanced vocational A-levels in business studies, engineering, health and social care and travel and tourism, as well as the usual curriculum. Work experience is offered to Year 11 pupils. There is a school council and mentoring scheme as well as strong pastoral care. There is no official PTA but the school organizes 'Raising Achievement' days. Ex-pupils include theatre director Karen Peters and the footballer Paul Merson.

## Admissions and intake

The principal feeder primary schools are Ravenor, Lady Margaret, Stanhope and Durden Parks. Entry criteria are siblings in the school and proximity of home to the school. Parents should apply in writing or by phoning the school.

## Achievement

In 2002, the school was rated 13th for GCSE results in the borough. A total of 56 per cent of pupils gained five or more A*–C grades at GCSE, a slight drop on 60 per cent in 2001. The average point score for pupils taking two or more A-levels was 223, placing the school ninth in the borough. Ofsted visited the school in 1999 and found that standards in GCSEs had been raised at a rate much faster than nationally. The report also praised the good leadership of the head teacher and found that pupils had a good attitude to learning and above-average behaviour. English and maths teaching were also praised. The school compares well with similar schools and since its last inspection was named as one of the top 25 improved schools, with one of the most-improved sixth forms.

## Extra curricular activities

The school offers a wide variety of clubs and sports at lunchtime and after school in everything from drama to football. It also holds its own sports day. The school took part in the National Playwrights Competition in 2000 and holds its own summer festival of drama and music each year. There is an after-school homework club and revision classes before exams. Sixth-form pupils can take part in the Young Enterprise scheme. The school organizes trips to Spain, France and Germany and all Year 9 pupils go on a residential trip to Dorset. Pupils get the chance to work with the community by organizing a Christmas party for the elderly and helping at nearby Mandeville Special School. Pupils also raise money for the elderly with a Diwali disco and send Christmas parcels to Albania and Romania every year.

# Harvington School

**20 Castlebar Road, Ealing W5 2DS** 020 8997 1583 020 8810 4756 admin@harvington.school.com Dr Fay Meek; Chair of Governors: Alan Gillett Ealing Broadway Ealing Broadway **Buses:** E2, E8 E9, 83, 297 plus all buses calling at Ealing Broadway Station Black skirts, black and yellow blazers, school tie **Demand:** Demand varies for up to six places each year **Type:** Selective independent for 218 girls, aged 3 to 16 **Fees:** £1,500–1,660 (lower school), £1,950 (upper school) **Submit application form:** No cut-off date **Mission statement:** Harvington is a school with a happy, creative environment providing the conditions for learning, individual fulfilment, achieving excellence and social responsibility. **School hours:** 8.30am–3.20pm (Year 7), 8.30am–4pm (others) **Meals:** Hot and cold available **Strong GCSE subjects:** All relatively strong **London league table position:** 123

## Profile

Harvington was built in the 1890s as a school for girls and was a boarding school until World War II. The nursery school for three to five year olds takes boys and is oversubscribed. The school nestles amongst large Victorian terraced houses. The grounds at the back house a gym block but sports lessons are taken at Baths and Ealing Cricket Club. The school is fully equipped with science labs, art rooms and IT facilities. There are plans to build a new gym block with changing facilities. The curriculum is broad and balanced with strong results in all areas and opportunities for pupils to study drama, arts and music. There is no sixth form and most pupils go on to St Paul's, Godolphin, St Benedict's or St Augustine's. Work experience is offered to Year 11 pupils. Children with minor disabilities are welcome at the school but the layout means severely disabled pupils cannot be catered for. The school has a head girl, deputy head girl, games captain and house captains. Pastoral care is particularly strong as classes are small. The parents' association is very active.

### Admissions and intake

Prospective pupils must take an exam if they want to join the school from Year 11 onwards. For pupils in the lower school, there is an informal interview. Pupils are drawn from across west London.

### Achievement

In 2002, 83 per cent of pupils gained five or more A*–C grades at GCSE, a fall from an impressive 100 per cent in 2000. The school was ranked fifth in the borough league table. The school is a member of the Independent Schools Association and was inspected in 1998. Its findings were very positive, saying the school had a good attitude and excellent exam results. One area of concern, however, was the lack of space in the school, although this would be addressed with the creation of a new games block.

### Extra-curricular activities

The school offers a whole range of after-school and lunchtime clubs from sports, dance, arts and music. There is an after-school club until 6pm for pupils whose parents are at work and a Camp Harvington in the summer holidays between 8am–6pm each day. The school has a strong debating society and pupils do well at the annual Ealing festival of arts. There is a number of trips abroad each year, including a biology field trip, skiing and an outdoor activity trip for Year 7 pupils. Years 4 and 5 get the chance to go on a creative writing course on the Isle of Wight. Pupils are involved in a lot of charity work, including organizing a harvest festival each year in which all the proceeds go to a local homeless charity. They have raised £2,500 for the National Asthma Campaign and regularly raise money for the Great Ormond Street Hospital for Sick Children.

## Northolt High School

**Eastcote Lane, Northolt UB5 4HW** 020 8864 8544 020 8426 9207 admin@northolt_dialnet.com www.northolt-high.ealing.sch.uk John Parry; Chair of Governors: Cllr Brenda Hall Northolt Park Station Northolt **Buses:** 92, 140, 141, 282 Navy blue blazer, white shirt, dark trousers or skirt, school tie **Demand:** 430 applications for 210 places in 2001/2 **Type:** Comprehensive foundation Technology College for 1286 mixed pupils, aged 11 to 18 **Submit application form:** Early November 2003 **Motto:** A Community Learning and Achieving Together **School hours:** 8.40am–3.15pm; homework clubs are available from the end of November **Meals:** Hot and cold available **Strong GCSE subjects:** English, ICT, maths, science **London league table position:** 323

### Profile

Northolt High was formed in 1974 when a secondary school was amalgamated with the grammar school. A new sixth form was built in 1998. The school has an Investors in People Award and a Football Association Quality Standard, and now has Technology College status. It has a good personal and social education programme, plus a range of traditional A-levels and GNVQ courses. Work experience is available and career talks are given by local firms. There is a good PTA and the sixth form organises open evenings. A coordinator is also available for special-needs pupils.

### Admissions and intake

A total of 210 pupils a year come from local Ealing primary schools. Parents should contact the school for application forms.

### Achievement

Compared to other schools nationally, Northolt performs below average, but in relation to similar schools, it performs well above average in most areas, with Ofsted giving it an 'A'. 47 per cent of pupils achieved five A*–C grades at

GCSE in 2002, up from 38 per cent in 2001. The school was ranked 15th in the borough league table in 2002. At A-level, the average point score for pupils taking two or more was 229.2, placing the school eighth in the borough. Overall, GCSEs have improved considerably, for example, in 1996, the school scored only 21 per cent A*–C grades in English. In 2000, the percentage was 50 per cent. The academic standard of pupils entering the school is often very low and the school does well to improve them. In 1998, Ofsted reported that the school: 'provides an atmosphere where pupils value and enjoy learning' and 'has considerably more strengths than weaknesses'. Pupils were found to be well behaved and under strong leadership. However, standards in IT could be further improved and punctuality was criticized; these have now been addressed.

### Extra curricular activities

The school offers a broad range of clubs, including homework clubs, a combined cadet force for boys and girls, the chance to participate in the Duke of Edinburgh's Award scheme, and educational visits to the theatre, museums and exhibitions. There are also field trips, exchange trips abroad, skiing trips, a choir and rock band. The school also teaches jazz. Pupils are involved with the community through fund-raising activities for local charities. Pupils also take part in a range of sports.

## Notting Hill and Ealing High School

**2 Cleveland Road, Ealing W13 8AX** 020 8799 8400 020 8810 6891 inquiries@NHEHS.gdst.net www.nhehs.gdst.net Susan Whitfield; Chair of Governors: Prof Sue Malcolm Drayton Green, West Ealing Perivale, Ealing Broadway **Buses:** 297 Up to sixth form: Navy blue V-neck jumper with red trim, navy blue skirt, red and white striped blouse **Demand:** Oversubscribed **Type:** Selective independent, part of the Girls' Day School Trust, for 832 girls, aged 5 to 18 **Fees:** £1,835 per term junior, £2,355 per term senior **Submit application form:** Contact school directly **Motto:** Excellent Education in All Fields **School hours:** 8.45am–3.45pm **Meals:** Hot and cold available **Strong GCSE subjects:** All relatively strong **London league table position:** 49

### Profile

The school began life in Notting Hill in 1837 and moved to Ealing in 1931. The original 1930s building has been added to in the 1950s, 1970s and 1990s. There are future building plans but they are under wraps until planning permission has been granted. There are good IT resources and good facilities for drama, art and sport. The school offers the basic curriculum plus dual award science, so all pupils take three sciences up to GCSE level with a moderated curriculum. If they pass, they gain two GCSEs. They must also take two modern languages and Latin from Years 7 to 9. In the sixth form, pupils can take A-levels in history of art and government and politics. There is a head girl and three deputies, and sixth formers can become department secretaries. The parents' guild is very active and organizes a careers fair for pupils each year. The school is part of the Girls' Day School Trust, which is centrally run and provides support for staff and a forum for the exchange of ideas and information. Ex-pupils include the *Blue Peter* presenter Connie Huq and politician Dame Angela Rumbold.

### Admissions and intake

Pupils are generally selected on academic ability and enter the school mainly at the ages of 5, 7, 11, 14 and 16. If pupils have similar academic ability, priority is given to those living closest to the school. If a sibling is at the school, then an applicant's case might be given priority. Some pupils have assisted places and others are given bursaries.

### Achievement

The school's academic achievements make it one of the best schools in London. In 2002, 98 per cent of pupils gained five or more A*–C grades at GCSE, up from 96 per cent in 2001. The school came first in the borough league tables. The average point score for pupils taking two or more A-levels in 2002 was 373.5, again ranking the school top of the borough league table. In 2000 at GCSE level, 82 per cent got grades A or A*. At A-level, 72 per cent got As and Bs.

### Extra-curricular activities

The school provides a large number of after-school clubs in sports, music and drama. There is also a school choir, orchestra and wind band. One pupil made the England rounders team and the school has produced some very good tennis players. Pupils who recently entered an art competition won a weekend in Paris. Each form in the school has a fund-raising week and Year 10 pupils organize a tea party for children from a disabled youth centre. There are also visits abroad and some exchange trips.

# St Augustine's Priory

**Hillcrest Road, Ealing W5 2JL** 020 8997 2022 020 8810 6501 admin@saintaug.demon.co.uk www.saintaug.demon.co.uk FJ Gumley Mason Ealing Broadway North Ealing, Ealing Broadway **Buses:** E2, 83, 206 Full uniform compulsory except in sixth form, dark blue jumper, navy skirt and white blouse **Demand:** 100 girls compete annually for 24 places at age 11 **Type:** Catholic independent day school for 465 girls, aged 4 to 18 **Fees:** £2,115 per term **Submit application form:** Contact school directly **Mission statement:** We will continue to strive to equip our girls with the confidence and common sense to face the challenges of our changing world drawing on nearly 2000 years of religious traditions and on all that is best in developing educational practice **School hours:** 8.30am–3.40pm **Meals:** Hot and cold available **Strong GCSE subjects:** All relatively strong **London league table position:** 63

## Profile

St Augustine's Priory was founded in France in 1634 by Lady Mary Tredway. It moved to Ealing in 1914–15 and follows the philosophy of its patron that children learn better with smiles and encouragement than with threats and scorn. The school is situated on 13 acres in a leafy part of Ealing. Its facilities are constantly being updated. The sixth form was refurbished in 1999 and a new state-of-the-art IT suite was installed in 2000. The school boasts floodlit netball courts and an astroturf hockey pitch. There is plenty of space for future building work and lots of space for the pupils to spend time outdoors. St Augustine's offers a full academic curriculum plus an excellent drama, music and public speaking department. Over 30 per cent of its pupils learn a musical instrument. All pupils get the opportunity to study three sciences at GCSE. Work experience is offered to Year 11 pupils. Pupils with disabilities are individually assessed to see whether they can join the school. There is also a coordinator for special-needs pupils. There is a school council and an active PTA, and the school chaplain helps to provide pastoral care.

## Admissions and intake

Four-year-old applicants are interviewed for entry. At age 11, entry is based on a school entrance examination and interview. Entry to the sixth form is based on five GCSEs at grades A*–C. There are waiting lists at all levels. Pupils come from all parts of West London.

## Achievement

The school's GCSE and A-level results are excellent, and it is one of the top schools in the borough. In 2002, 100 per cent of pupils gained five or more A*–C grades at GCSE, a rise from 92 per cent in 2001. The average point score for pupils taking two or more A-levels was 300.3, placing the school third in the borough. St Augustine's came 24th for GCSE results in *The Times'* list of independent schools. It was the only Ealing school to make the top 50.

## Extra-curricular activities

Pupils can participate in the Duke of Edinburgh's Award scheme, compete in music festivals and take part in the Youth Speaks Out public-speaking competition. There are two orchestras, music groups and choirs. There is also an IT club. The school offers clubs at both lunchtime and after school. There are numerous sports groups available and pupils have represented the county and regional level at hockey. Pupils are very active in raising money for the local community.

# St Benedict's School

**54 Eaton Rise, Ealing W5 2ES** 020 8862 2010 020 8862 2199 headmaster@stbenedicts.org.uk www.stbenedicts.org.uk Mr CJ Cleugh Ealing Broadway Ealing Broadway **Buses:** E1, E2 Green blazer and grey trousers; Sixth form: Black blazer and dark green trousers (boys); dark skirts and sweaters (girls) **Demand:** 80 places available **Type:** Selective independent for 782 boys (mixed in sixth form), aged 11 to 19 **Fees:** £2,580 per term **Submit application form:** Contact school directly **Motto:** Start from Little Things **School hours:**

8.50am–4.10pm **Meals:** Hot and cold available, including breakfast **Strong GCSE subjects:** Arts, English, sports **London league table position:** 81

## Profile

St Benedict's was opened in 1902 by Benedictine monks to teach Catholic children. There are several modern blocks containing a design, technology and arts centre and a mini theatre. The school's sports facilities and playing fields are a couple of miles away in Perivale Lane but are well equipped. The curriculum offers the usual broad range of subjects and is particularly strong in arts and music. Sports science is offered at A-level. The pastoral care is very strong, some of the teachers are priests and the responsibility for pastoral care is the domain of the head teacher, also a priest. There is a prefect system and head boy and deputy, as well as a school council. There is also a coordinator at hand for any special needs pupils. A very active society of parents and friends raises money for the school and organizes social events.

## Admissions and intake

Pupils come from a variety of local prep schools and primary schools. Entry at Year 11 is based on passing the 11-plus exam; at age 13, pupils must pass a common entrance exam and at age 16, entry is based on exam results. To enter the sixth form, pupils must have five or more GCSEs and a grade B in the subjects they wish to study. The head teacher interviews all pupils and their parents.

## Achievement

The school's GCSE and A-level results are above average for London. In 2002, 92 per cent of pupils gained five or more A*–C grades at GCSE, a rise from 87 per cent in 2001. This placed the school in the borough's top four. At A-level, the average point score for pupils taking two or more was 303.3, ranking second in the borough. The last Ofsted report was carried out in 1998; it praised the academic success of the school, which is predominantly strong in arts, English and sports. Pastoral care was particularly praised for the warm and caring atmosphere in the school.

## Extra-curricular activities

The school offers a variety of clubs from football, cricket, tennis and rowing to chess, maths, photography and a debating society. The school has produced some particularly good rugby players. Skiing trips and a visit to Italy are organized each year, as are visits to the theatre. In 2000, pupils performed at the Edinburgh Festival to excellent reviews. The school has a task force that serves the local community by working with the elderly and handicapped.

# Twyford CofE High School

**Twyford Crescent, Acton W3 9PP** ☎ 020 8752 0141 Fax 020 8993 7627 e davidbates@twyfordhigh.freeserve.co.uk Head: Alice Hudson MA; Chair of Governors: Brian Hardey Rail: Acton Central, Acton Mainline Tube: Acton Town **Buses:** 207 Uniform: Black skirt or black trousers, plain white shirt, school tie, black or royal blue V-neck pullover, black blazer **Demand:** 630 pupils applied for 180 places in 2001/2 **Type:** Voluntary aided comprehensive for 1146 mixed pupils, aged 11 to 18 **Submit application form:** Early November 2003 **School hours:** 8.45am–3.15pm **Meals:** Hot and cold available **Strong GCSE subjects:** Maths, science **London league table position:** 150

## Profile

Twyford High opened as a church school in 1980 and celebrated its 21st birthday in 2001. The sixth-form building called The Elms was built in 1740. It was used as a county hospital and toy factory before opening as a school in 1945. Twyford High has Beacon status. The chapel was refurbished last summer and there is a rolling programme of refurbishment. There is a new sports hall and modern languages building. The curriculum is studied although pupils can take RE and English a year early. The school offers leisure and tourism and business studies at GNVQ. It is particularly strong in the arts and pupils can take exams in drama and photography. Work experience is offered at the end of Year 10. The school does take disabled pupils but each case is looked at individually. There is a student leadership team and peer mentoring. A learning mentor is employed by the school to help underachievers and high-achievers. The PTA is very active and pupils attend assembly every day, where a minute's silence is held to reflect and worship. Ex-pupils include the athlete Julian Golley and the Brentford footballer Mark Williams.

### Admissions and intake

A total of 150 of the 180 Year 7 places go to pupils from the Church of England. Priority is given to those who worship in Ealing first, then Brent and Harrow, then the Willesden Episcopal area. Pupils must also have a reference from their church. The other 30 places are allocated to pupils from other faiths. The school has a mixed intake and takes pupils chiefly from the Ealing area but also from other parts of London.

### Achievements

Twyford is the best non fee-paying school in Ealing for exam results. In 2002, 72 per cent of pupils gained five or more A*–C grades at GCSE, compared to 68 per cent in 2001. At A-level, the average point score for pupils taking two or more was 296.2, placing the school fourth in the borough. In 1997, Ofsted stated that standards of attainment at the end of all stages are mostly satisfactory and often good. Standards of English are broadly similar to the national average, science and maths are well above. Pupils' attitudes are described as positive. However, the school was asked to improve its longer term strategy and improve IT provision. The attendance rate is described as above the national average and overall quality of teaching was also seen as good.

### Extra-curricular activities

The school boasts a variety of clubs, including a Young Enterprise group and most sports clubs. Several pupils play for Middlesex county at hockey and netball. Visits to theatres are organized as well as links between students and an art gallery. Pupils won a public speaking cup in 2000's Youth Speaks Out competition. The school is also taking part in a European Dimension project – a three-year programme involving science, maths and geography. It will mean exchange trips to schools in Italy, Malta and Spain. The pupils are also involved with the community through various fund-raising projects for local charities.

## Villiers High School

**Boyd Avenue, Southall UB1 3BT** 020 8813 8001 020 8574 3071 vhorne@ACHTER.co.uk www.villiers.ealing.school.uk Juliet Strang; Chair of Governors: Mr H Duhra Southall **Buses:** E3, 105, 120, 207, 607 Black blazer, black trousers and black skirt, white shirt and tie **Demand:** 569 applications for 240 places in 2001/2 **Type:** Comprehensive for 1200 mixed pupils, aged 11 to 16 **Submit application form:** Early November 2003 **Motto:** Work Conquers All **School hours:** 8.40am–3.30pm; homework clubs are available **Meals:** Hot and cold available **Strong GCSE subjects:** Art, history **London league table position:** 255

### Profile

Villiers High is the oldest school in Southall. It was founded as a county school in 1907, became a grammar school in 1944 and a comprehensive in 1974. A recently added arts, design and technology department has won plaudits. The school is a Comenius School, a status granted by the European Union, which means it has partner schools all over Europe, including in Norway, France, Belgium, Germany and Italy. Exchange visits and exchange of information and projects takes place regularly. The curriculum offers the usual broad range of subjects at GCSE but also includes media studies. There is no A-level provision and students usually go on to Ealing Tertiary College and Uxbridge and Richmond colleges. Work experience is offered to all pupils. The school is willing to take disabled pupils and has good provision for pupils with special needs. There is a school council and house system and pupils can become prefects and student librarians. The PTA is active and parents are kept in touch with the school via a diary system and reading project. Ex-pupils include the economist Lord Roberts and the actor Barry Foster.

### Admissions and intake

This is a community school which takes most of its pupils from the surrounding 16 streets. Pupils come from 14 primary schools, the main ones being Tudor and North. Priority of entry is given to those with a sibling at the school and those applicants that live closest to the school.

### Achievement

In 2002, 54 per cent of pupils achieved five or more A*–C grades at GCSE, compared with 48 per cent in 2001. The school was placed 14th in the borough league table. The last Ofsted report was done in 1997 and stated: 'The school makes very good progress from a weak base. Many pupils enter well below the norm and yet GCSE results are respectable'. The report also praised pupils' behaviour saying, they show 'respect and tolerance'. History and art were praised as being above average. The inspector asked for better IT provision and a better focus on languages and both have been achieved. The school now has a new IT department and pupils can study Spanish, French, Punjabi and Urdu. The head teacher arrived after the last report and has brought even more vision and leadership to the school.

## Extra-curricular activities

The school offers after-school clubs in everything from chess to football and film-making, and homework clubs. It does particularly well at girls' basketball and football, and cricket is very popular. There is a link with the Royal Opera House and in 2000 pupils performed their own version of *Turandot*. The school also holds its own sports day every year and raises money for charity with a variety of events, including a cycle ride to Brighton, and concerts.

# Enfield

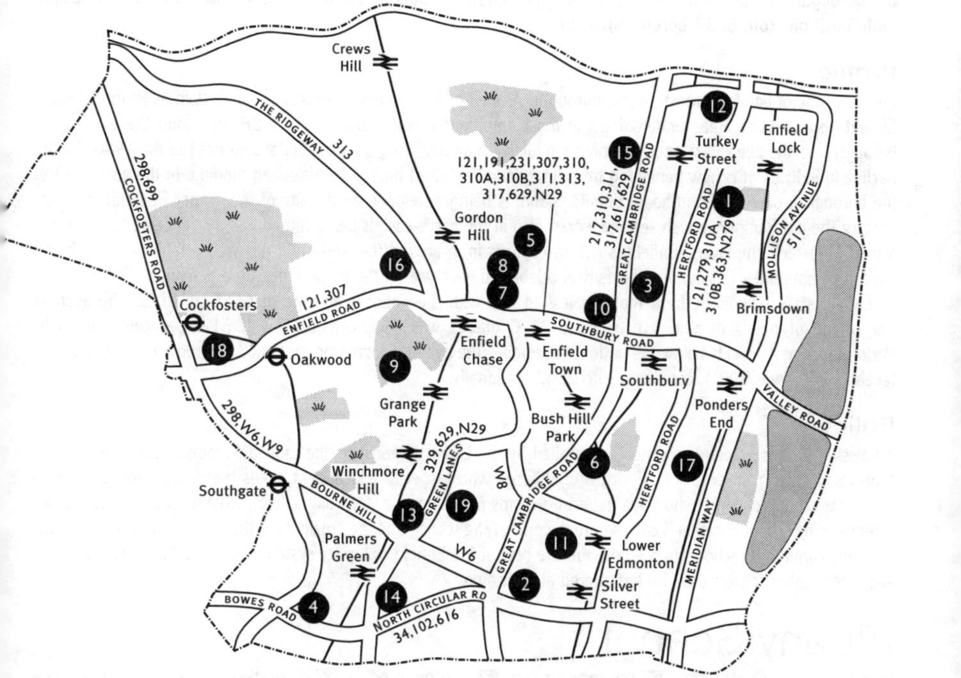


## Key

1 Albany School
2 Aylward School
3 Bishop Stopford's School
4 Broomfield School
5 Chace Community School
6 Edmonton County School
7 Enfield County School
8 Enfield Grammar School
9 Highlands School
10 Kingsmead School
11 The Latymer School
12 Lea Valley High School & Sports College
13 Palmers Green High School
14 St Anne's Catholic High School for Girls
15 St Ignatius College
16 St John's Senior School
17 Salisbury School
18 Southgate School
19 Winchmore School

# Factfile

**LEA: PO Box 52, Civic Centre, Silver Street, Enfield, EN1 3XQ** 020 8366 6565 www.enfield.gov.uk **Director of Education:** Liz Graham **Political control of council:** Conservative **Percentage of pupils from outside the borough:** 10.5 per cent **Percentage of pupils educated outside the borough:** 9.8 per cent **London league table positions (out of 32 boroughs):** 17th

## Profile

Enfield is one of London's most diverse boroughs. As well as the residential streets of places such as Palmers Green, Enfield also contains areas undergoing the most ambitious urban regeneration in Britain. Along the east of the borough runs the Lea Valley, once the most productive manufacturing area in London. Hit hard in the 1980s by the decline in industry, it is now benefiting from a regeneration effort backed by European funding. In the north-east of the borough a new neighbourhood, Enfield Island, is being developed on the site of the former Royal Small Arms Factory. The old Rammey Marsh sewage works, also in the north-east, is being turned into a science park in order to attract high-tech employers. Enfield is rich in cultures from around the world and has well-established Greek and Turkish communities. This cultural diversity is celebrated each year in the Under One Sun arts festival.

Enfield state schools perform more or less in line with the national average at GCSE. In 2002, the average percentage of pupils gaining five or more A*–C grades was 46.2 compared with 51.6 per cent nationally. Performance at A-level is below the national average – the average point score per pupil entered for two or more A-levels in 2002 was 209.4, compared with 254.5 nationally.

## Policy

Admission to those secondary schools controlled by the LEA is handled by the Enfield Schools Admissions Service. Placement criteria, in order of priority, are: children whose special educational needs mean they are suited to a particular school; children who have medical grounds for going to a particular school; whether a child has siblings attending the school; whether a child's parent works at the school; and the proximity of the school to the child's home.

Many community schools in the borough are part of the Enfield collegiate system, which enables pupils to study subjects at other schools that are not offered at their own.

# Albany School

**Bell Lane, Enfield EN3 5PA** 020 8804 1648 020 8805 9949 www.albany.enfield.sch.uk/home.htm Mr A Milward MA; Chair of Governors: Mrs M Weadick Enfield Lock, Turkey Street **Buses:** 121, 191, 279 Black blazer with school badge, black trousers, white shirt, school tie (boys); tartan kilt or black trousers, white blouse, black V-neck jumper with school logo (girls); Sixth form: Smart attire **Demand:** 270 places regularly oversubscribed **Type:** Comprehensive foundation school for 1294 mixed pupils, aged 11 to 18 **Submit application form:** 1st week of November 2003 **Motto:** Learning and Growing Together Successfully **School hours:** 9am–3.15pm; homework clubs are available **Meals:** Hot and cold available **Strong GCSE subjects:** Drama, Turkish **London league table position:** 459

## Profile

Albany school is located on the north-eastern edge of Enfield and is housed in modern buildings. It has recently benefited from financial investment and there are now six new classrooms, a technology block, four new IT rooms, a well-equipped business education suite and a refurbished learning resources centre. It has also been awarded the Charter Mark, which recognizes and encourages excellence in public service. There is both an active PTA and school council. The school has a head boy and girl chosen from the sixth form.

## Admissions and intake

Application forms are available from the school. When oversubscribed, places are allocated in order of priority to: those with a sibling at the school; those with a sibling who has attended the school; medical grounds; and proximity of the applicant's home to the school.

### Achievement

In 2002, 28 per cent of pupils gained five or more A*–C grades at GCSE with an average point score of 26.1. The school was ranked 16th out of 18 in the borough league table. This was up on 22 per cent in 2001 and below the borough average. The average point score for students entered for two or more A/AS-levels was 137.2, placing the school 14th in the borough. This was up on 1999's results but below the borough average. However, there has been a general slight rise in results over the past few years. The sixth form is very small (61 pupils in 1999), and offers A-level courses as well as successful GNVQs in business at advanced and intermediate level. Ofsted visited the school in 1997 and described the overall quality of teaching as 'good'. It commented: 'The head teacher's strong, purposeful and committed leadership has given the school a clear direction and focus. This has had a significant impact on the school's ability to make progress and on the commitment of everyone to raise standards and improve the quality of education.' It also praised the learning support department for helping pupils with learning difficulties and the support given by the LEA's language support service to pupils for whom English is an additional language.

### Extra-curricular activities

Albany school has a strong sporting tradition and there are many clubs and activities run during lunchtimes and after school, including homework clubs. Music and drama productions are regularly staged. The modern languages department arranges annual trips to France and Germany, and there are many other opportunities for pupils to travel abroad. The sixth form has acquired a reputation for its community work and at the time of the Ofsted report in 1997, a large number of sixth-formers were actively involved in the Enfield Youth Services Project.

## Aylward School

**Windmill Road, Edmonton, London N18 1NB** ☎ 020 8803 1738 📠 020 8807 6285 ✉ aylward-school@btconnect.com 🌐 aylward-school@btconnect.com 👤 Mr JR Salisbury BA (Hons); Chair of Governors: Mrs Anne Lindsay 🚆 Silver Street **Buses:** W6, 34, 102, 144A, 217, 231, 444 👔 Black trousers or black skirt, white shirt, blue pullover **Demand:** Oversubscribed for 255 places in 2001/2 **Type:** Community comprehensive for 1447 mixed pupils, aged 11 to 18 **Submit application form:** 1st week of November 2003 **Mission statement:** To cater for the needs of each individual through our carefully structured curriculum and pastoral system, and to help our pupils achieve their full potential whilst at the same time acquiring the knowledge and skills which are relevant to adult life and the world of work. **School hours:** 8.35am–3.30pm; homework clubs are available **Meals:** Hot and cold available **Strong GCSE subjects:** Art, drama and media studies **London league table position:** 484

### Profile

Aylward School is housed in attractive buildings, a product of the major building programme completed in 1991, which provides purpose-built facilities of a very high standard. A new theatre complex was opened in 1994 and specialist facilities include a kiln room for pottery and a photographic darkroom. Every classroom is linked to the computer network. With a large proportion of pupils coming from homes where English is not the first language, the school offers alternative accreditation in English for pupils unable to sit for English GCSE. There is also an induction programme for those starting to learn English, and targeted support in class to assist with English acquisition. Many vocational courses are available to pupils in Years 10 and 11 (aged 14–16), including catering and building studies. Pupils can sit on the school and year councils and act as pupil librarians. Truancy remains a problem: in 2000 unauthorized absence was at 3.1 per cent, above the borough and national averages. There is a PTA.

### Admissions and intake

Admission is through Enfield schools admission service (see borough factfile). In 1997, 36 per cent of pupils came from homes where English was not the mother tongue. Among the 50 or so first languages represented, the main ones were Turkish and Greek.

### Achievement

In 2002, 19 per cent of pupils achieved five or more A*–C grades at GCSE and the school was placed 17th in the borough. As well as the usual range of GCSEs, pupils can also study for a qualification under the Youth Award scheme. The average point score for pupils entered for two or more A/AS-levels in 2002 was 182.9, below the national average. This placed the school 11th in the borough. A range of academic, practical and vocational courses are taught in the sixth form and through the borough's collegiate system. On entry at Aylward, most pupils have a lower than average attainment. An Ofsted report in 2000 described Alyward as 'an effective school no longer showing serious weaknesses'. The head teacher and senior staff were praised for their 'clear educational direction' and teaching was 'good overall' with strengths at Key Stage 4 and sixth form. The teaching and learning of art, drama, media studies, Turkish and sociology was particularly strong. Inspectors believed standards of literacy and numeracy could be improved along with the use of ICT in subjects offered at Key Stages 3 and 4.

## Extra-curricular activities

Football is particularly strong and the school's steel band is also a great success. There are cultural visits to theatres and galleries as well as foreign visits and skiing holidays. Community links are good, with pupils raising money for charity. There are after-school homework clubs.

# Bishop Stopford's School

**Brick Lane, Enfield EN1 3PU** 020 8804 1906 020 8805 9434 admin@bishop-stopfords-school.co.uk www.bishopstopfords.enfield.sch.uk Mrs B Evans; **Chair of Governors:** Mr Derek Woodward Southbury **Buses:** 121, 279, 307 Dark grey trousers or navy-blue skirt, white shirt or blouse, navy-blue V-neck jumper, navy-blue school tie; Sixth form: Smart dress on normal days; uniform on major school occasions **Demand:** Figures vary but 180 places regularly oversubscribed **Type:** Voluntary aided Church of England comprehensive for 1062 mixed pupils, aged 11 to 18 **Submit application form:** 1st week of November 2003 **Motto:** *Animus noster dei gloria* (The Reason, the Purpose, the Strength and the End of Our Existence Is the Glory of God) **School hours:** 8.35am–3.15pm; homework clubs are available **Meals:** Hot and cold available **Strong GCSE subjects:** Sciences **London league table position:** 324

## Profile

As a Church of England foundation, Bishop Stopford's has a strong Anglican ethos and all pupils must attend daily worship and divinity lessons. The school was opened in 1967 but the large main buildings date from 1934, and are set in well-maintained spacious grounds with good outdoor facilities. In 1995, a new science wing and a lift giving disabled pupils access to the upper floor were completed. The house system is used to aid pastoral care and the head and his deputies run a well-regarded weekly surgery for parents. The school has a prefects system.

## Admissions and intake

As well as the general Enfield schools admissions service form, prospective parents must complete the school's form. Places are allocated, in order of priority, to pupils and their family who have regularly worshipped in an Anglican church within the Deanery of Enfield for at least two years, and who have an active family connection to the school; then to pupils who fulfil the religious criteria but have no family connection; pupils and their family who have worshipped for less than two years in an Anglican church in the Deanery of Enfield or those who worship outside of the deanery; pupils and family who worship at another Christian church; and pupils who can benefit from the school's way of life.

## Achievement

In 2002, 45 per cent of pupils gained five or more A*–C grades at GCSE. This was just below the borough average and the school was placed 12th in the borough. The average point score for pupils entered for two or more A/AS-levels was 185, below average for the borough, placing the school ninth. The sixth form offers GNVQs in business and art and design as well as A-levels. A unique aspect of the school's post-16 curriculum is the opportunity for pupils taking maths and science A-levels to gain accreditation against the BTEC science course. Ofsted visited the school in 1997, and described it as 'a stable and caring community to which pupils have great loyalty and form a strong affection'. The standard of teaching was praised, as was pupils' 'positive attitude' to learning. Attainment was said to be above average at ages 14 and 16, although below at 18. Weaknesses were found in the monitoring and evaluation of special needs and in the difference between girls' and boys' attainments.

## Extra-curricular activities

The choir is a central feature of the school and is accompanied by the school's pipe organ. There are many musical groups and the school stages an annual production of light opera. There is a strong tradition of giving to charity. As well as geography and biology field trips, there are skiing trips to Italy and visits to France. Among the many sports on offer are football, athletics, golf, rugby and cricket. Homework clubs are available.

# Broomfield School

**Wilmer Way, Southgate, London N14 7HY** ☎ 020 8368 4710 📠 020 8368 1287 ⓔ suttonp@broomfield.enfield.sch.uk 🌐 www.broomfield.enfield.sch.uk ✉ Mr P Sutton B.Sc, MA; Chair of Governors: Mrs G Cole ⇄ Palmers Green, Bowes Park ⊖ Arnos Grove, Bounds Green **Buses:** 43, 84A, 112, 102, 299 👔 Up to sixth form: Black blazer with school badge, white shirt or blouse, black trousers or tartan skirt, black school tie **Demand:** Figures vary but 200 places regularly oversubscribed **Type:** Comprehensive foundation school for 1246 mixed pupils, aged 11 to 18 **Submit application form:** 1st week of November 2003 **Mission statement:** Our overall aim is to provide the broadest possible range of children with the highest quality education supported by excellent staff and facilities. **School hours:** 8.50am–3.30pm; homework clubs are available **Meals:** Hot and cold available **Strong GCSE subjects:** English, history, science **London league table position:** 301

## Profile

Broomfield is a rapidly improving comprehensive in the suburb of Southgate. Recently completed facilities include new classrooms and rooms for science, technology and art. A total of £120,000 has been invested in a new computer network. There is a fully equipped gym and an all-weather astroturf pitch. Pupils can be representatives on the school council. Broomfield has recently become a member of the North London Chamber of Commerce, forging good links with local contractors. There is a PTA.

## Admissions and intake

An admissions form is available directly from the school. The admissions criteria take into account the presence of a sibling at the school, any medical grounds on which the school is particularly suitable, and proximity of home to the school. The majority of pupils come from homes within a two-mile radius.

## Achievement

In 1999, Broomfield was one of the most improved schools in the country, having more than doubled the percentage of pupils gaining five or more A*–C grades at GCSE since 1995, at 63 per cent. However, this dipped in 2000 to 52 per cent and again in to 2002 to 50 per cent. A total of 24 languages is spoken at Broomfield, with no single culture dominating, and pupils are encouraged to take these languages at GCSE. The average point score for pupils entered for two or more A/AS-levels in 2002 was 191.8, below average for the borough, placing the school eighth. A-level options available include business studies, economics, theatre studies and sports studies, as well as advanced and intermediate level GNVQs. Ofsted last visited Broomfield in 1999 and noted: 'The school is strongly led by a head teacher who has been the main influence in transforming its reputation.' It was said to be 'now in the top quarter of schools nationally'. A high proportion of teaching was found to be 'good or very good' and most pupils had 'good attitudes in lessons'. However, Ofsted noted that not every Year 11 pupil was entered for examination in a modern language. The sixth form has not been doing as well as the rest of the school but 'it is now receiving strong direction'. Provision for special needs pupils and those with English as a second language was said to be 'good'.

## Extra-curricular activities

Broomfield has an annual sports day where all pupils are given the opportunity of competing in a local stadium. Another annual event is the school concert, with many musical groups participating, including the 120-strong choir. There is the Duke of Edinburgh's Award scheme and Year 7 pupils take part in outdoor pursuits at the Cheshunt Water Sports Centre. As well as exchange trips there is also an annual trip to Paris. There are after-school homework clubs.

# Chace Community School

**Churchbury Lane, Enfield EN1 3HQ** ☎ 020 8363 7321 📠 020 8342 1241 ⓔ Chace@chace-school.demon.co.uk 🌐 www.chace.enfield.sch.uk ✉ Ms S Warrington B.Ed (Hons), MBA, NPQH; Chair of Governors: Mr Huw Jones-Owen ⇄ Enfield Town, Gordon Hill **Buses:** W8, W10, 191, 610 👔 Up to sixth form: Black blazer, trousers, school tie **Demand:** 210 places available each year; oversubscribed **Type:** Community comprehensive for 1213 mixed pupils, aged 11 to 18 **Submit application form:** 1st week of November 2003 **Motto:** Aiming to Be the Best We Can **School hours:** 8.40am–3.25pm; homework clubs are available **Meals:** Hot and cold available **Strong GCSE subjects:** Art, drama, technology **London league table position:** 412

## Profile

Chace is located on a nine-acre site close to the centre of Enfield town and is housed in modern buildings with some prefabricated classrooms. The on-site playing fields include tennis and netball courts. There is a gymnasium, a weight-training room and a large sports hall. Pupils are able to take part in the student council and sixth-formers can become prefects. The school also operates a house system. There is a weekly open afternoon for parents to see the head. The Chace Association, which includes staff, parents and friends, is very active and organizes fund-raising and social events. Truancy is a problem and in 2000 the proportion of unauthorized absence was 3.5 per cent, above the national average.

## Admissions and intake

Admission is through the Enfield schools admissions service (see borough factfile).

## Achievement

In 2002, 33 per cent of pupils achieved five or more A*–C grades at GCSE. This was below the borough and national averages and the school was ranked 14th in the borough. Alongside GCSEs, as part of a national pilot, the school also offers a GNVQ business course. The average point score for pupils entered for two or more A/AS-levels was 208.4, close to the borough average, placing the school sixth in the borough. However, attainment in vocational qualifications is in line with national averages. A range of A-levels is on offer in the sixth form and as part of the Enfield collegiate system. Vocational courses available include intermediate GNVQs, NVQs and a Community Sports Leadership award. In 1997, Ofsted reported that Chace provides 'a sound education for its pupils and is regarded well by the local community'. However, the deficit in comparison between boys' and girls' GCSE results 'was amongst the highest in the country'. Literacy on intake may be an issue and the school is now addressing the problem. Ofsted also found that punctuality was 'unsatisfactory'. Some pupils were said to 'present difficult and demanding problems' and it was to 'the credit of the pastoral system' that most of these were resolved. Provision for special needs pupils was said to be 'a strength of the school'.

## Extra-curricular activities

The school offers a range of sports, including football, athletics, basketball, cricket, tennis and netball. An 'athletics championship' is held each summer in the local Queen Elizabeth Stadium. There are a number of musical groups that perform regularly at school concerts. Drama productions are also held. All Year 7 pupils participate in a residential trip to Fairplay House in Witham, Essex, and take part in team-building activities. Pupils are also able to participate in skiing trips, annual school exchanges and visits to France and Germany. After-school homework clubs are available.

# Edmonton County School

**Great Cambridge Road, Enfield, Middlesex EN1 1HQ (upper school); Little Bury Street, London N9 9HZ (lower school)** ☎ 020 8360 3158 (upper); 020 8360 7228 (lower) 📠 020 8364 2218 (upper); 020 8360 8253 (lower) ✉ edmontoncs@sol.co.uk 🌐 www.pftp.org.uk/edmontoncs Ms L Robinson; Chair of Governors: Mr Gordon Thongs-George 🚆 Bush Hill Park, Edmonton Green **Buses:** W8, 192, 217, 231 👔 Navy blue blazer, dark trousers or skirt, royal blue school tie; Sixth form: Appropriate dress **Demand:** 270 places available each year; oversubscribed **Type:** Community comprehensive for 1586 mixed pupils, aged 11 to 18 **Submit application form:** 1st week of November 2003 **Mission statement:** To be a centre of learning and achievement for all **School hours:** 8.30am–4.30pm; homework clubs are available **Meals:** Hot and cold available **Strong GCSE subjects:** History **London league table position:** 306

## Profile

Two schools were amalgamated in 1967 to form Edmonton County. The present upper school (Years 10 to 11 and sixth form) was originally known as Edmonton County Grammar and was built in 1931. The lower school (Years 7 to 9) was built in 1960 as the Rowantree Secondary Modern. The sites are located about a mile away from each other and have attached playing fields and gardens. New wings for music, English, drama and maths have been added to the lower school and further development is planned for both sites. Pupils who are not fluent in English receive assistance in lessons from specialist teachers. The Edmonton School Association encompasses parents, staff and friends and is well supported. In 2000, the percentage of unauthorized absence was 1.1, below the borough average. Pupils can join the school council and the prefects system. Norman Tebbit and Sir Roy Strong are former pupils.

### Admissions and intake

Admission is through the Enfield Schools Admissions Service (see borough factfile). The catchment area comprises some of the more affluent parts of Enfield along with areas less advantaged. A range of cultures are represented, though mainly Greek and Turkish.

### Achievement

In 2002, 45 per cent of pupils gained five or more A*–C grades at GCSE, below the borough and national averages but up on 40 per cent in 2001. The school was placed 11th out of 18 in the borough. Pupils can take the usual range of GCSEs, as well as economics, child development and community languages such as Greek. The average point score for pupils entered for two or more A/AS-levels was 178.7, below the borough average. This placed the school 12th in the borough. Sixth-formers can take either the traditional A-levels, with a wider choice available through the borough's collegiate system, or vocational GNVQs at intermediate or advanced level, including business, media and leisure, and tourism. In 1996, Ofsted reported: 'Edmonton County School provides a sound education for its pupils.... Staff work hard and are committed to the success of their pupils.' Attainment was best in the sixth form. The standards of the team sports and performing arts were also commended. Weaknesses were highlighted in modern languages, RE and science, as well as in the progress of more able pupils. The school has been addressing these issues, however, and extension work is now available for the more able.

### Extra-curricular activities

Numerous activities are on offer including team sports, music and drama groups. There are also various subject clubs, a computing club, a karting club and homework clubs. Pupils often have the chance to visit foreign countries and the most recent trip was to Barcelona.

## Enfield County School

**Holly Walk, Enfield EN2 6QG (upper school); Rosemary Avenue, Enfield EN2 0SP (lower school)** ☎ 020 8363 3030 (upper); 020 8363 9934 (lower) 📠 020 8367 6569 ⓔ office@enfieldcs.enfield.sch.uk 🌐 www.enfieldcs.enfield.sch.uk ✉ Miss IA Byard BA (Hons); Chair of Governors: Mr L Farraway 🚉 Enfield Chase, Enfield Town (upper school); Gordon Hill (lower school) **Buses**: 192, 317, 329 (upper school); W8, 191 (lower school) ▣ Up to sixth form (no details available) **Demand**: 190 places available each year; oversubscribed **Type**: Community comprehensive for 1107 girls, aged 11 to 18 **Submit application form**: 1st week of November 2003 **Motto**: Onward Ever **School hours**: 8.40am–3.20pm **Meals**: Hot and cold available **Strong GCSE subjects**: English, design and technology, science **London league table position**: 175

### Profile

Enfield County School is situated in the north of Enfield. The upper and lower schools are located on separate sites about a mile apart and both sites are well maintained. The older part of the upper school dates from 1909 and is Grade II-listed. A new block has been built in the upper school, providing accommodation for music, dance, drama and PE. There is an active parents' association. The school has both a school council and a prefects system. Pupils with special needs are provided for by a special needs coordinator. In 2000, the rate of unauthorized absence was low at 0.2 per cent.

### Admissions and intake

Admission is through the Enfield schools admission service (see borough factfile). Application forms are available from primary schools and the LEA. Pupils are drawn from across the borough and some come from neighbouring LEAs. Ability on entry covers the full range.

### Achievement

In 2000, Ofsted stated that Enfield County was a 'good school' which turns out 'confident and well educated young women'. The 'strong leadership' of the head teacher was praised and teachers were seen to have 'excellent relationships' with the pupils. The school created a 'positive culture of success'. Strong subjects were seen to be English, science and design and technology but results were good in nearly every subject. Inspectors praised the girls' 'excellent attitude to learning and the expectation of hard work'. Since 1995, results at GCSE level have greatly improved at Enfield County. In 2002, 68 per cent of pupils achieved five or more A*–C grades. This was down on 77 per cent in 2001, though well above the borough and national average. The school was ranked fourth in the borough. The average point score for pupils taking two or more A-levels was 219.4 in 2002, above the borough average, placing the school fifth in the borough league table. A range of A-level subjects and GNVQs are on offer in the sixth form. Pupils wishing to take subjects that are not available at Enfield County can study these subjects at other schools via the Enfield collegiate system.

## Extra-curricular activities

Music, sport and drama are all represented at the school, with many groups for girls to join. As well as the normal range of sports, pupils can also learn self-defence. After-school homework clubs are available. Pupils support a variety of causes through extensive fund-raising activities. Many educational visits and residential field trips are organized both at home and abroad.

# Enfield Grammar School

**Market Place, Enfield EN2 6LN (upper school); Enfield Court, Baker Street, Enfield EN1 3EX (lower school)** 020 8363 1095 020 8342 1805 enfgrammar@aol.com Mr M Weeks B.Sc, MA; Chair of Governors: Rev MM Edge Enfield Town, Enfield Chase **Buses:** W8, W9, 121, 191 Black blazer, trousers, white shirt, school tie; Sixth form: Same uniform but with a special badge **Demand:** 700 to 1000 applications regularly received for 180 places **Type:** Comprehensive foundation school for 1124 boys, aged 11 to 18 **Submit application form:** 1st week of November 2003 **Motto:** *Tíant que je puif* (As Much As I Can) **School hours:** 9am–3.45pm; homework clubs are available **Meals:** Hot and cold available **Strong GCSE subjects:** Art, English, maths, PE, science **London league table position:** 220

## Profile

Enfield Grammar School has a long tradition going back over 400 years. Located in the centre of Enfield Town, it occupies two sites separated by an eight-minute walk. It is housed in imposing Grade II-listed buildings whose maintenance poses challenges for the school. Older pupils can become prefects and can also help younger pupils with their reading, and pupils are involved in the school council. The school benefits from strong support from parents and has a new colour-coded 'traffic light' report system to aid communication. Pupils with special needs are under the guidance of the school's special needs coordinator. Former pupils include the writer Norman Lewis; the 19th-century art critic Walter Pater; and Hugh Jenkins, a minister in the Harold Wilson government.

## Admissions and intake

An application form is available from the school. Places are allocated according to the following criteria: boys with brothers attending the school; 10 per cent on music or sporting ability; boys with parents who are members of staff; boys with medical grounds for attending the school; and the distance of a boy's home to the school. The school serves a wide catchment area and pupils of all abilities attend, with slightly more average or above-average pupils.

## Achievement

In 2002, 60 per cent of pupils achieved five or more A*–C grades at GCSE, seven per cent up on 2001's results and above the borough average. The school was ranked seventh in the borough. As well as the usual GCSEs on offer, pupils can also take French and Spanish. The average point score for pupils entered for two or more A/AS-levels was 227.1, below the national average, placing the school fourth in the borough. The school offers a wide choice of A-levels as well as intermediate and advanced-level GNVQs in business. About 85 per cent of sixth-form leavers go on to further education and this is above the national level. In their report of 1999, Ofsted praised the effort of teachers in overcoming shortcomings in accommodation: 'It is of considerable credit to them that the overall quality of teaching is of such a high standard.' Attainment was above average in maths and English and 'very high' in art. Standards were also high in science and PE. IT was an area of weakness, as were A-level results. The school has since raised its entry requirement for A-level courses. 'Small groups and effective teaching' aided the progress of pupils with special needs. Pupils were described as 'well-behaved' and 'courteous'.

## Extra-curricular activities

Ofsted commented that extra-curricular sport was a 'strength of the school' and one at which it excelled. Cultural visits to theatres, art galleries and museums are organized and there are also opportunities for pupils to travel abroad. There are regular dramatic and musical productions. Pupils help to raise money for charity and have recently donated a large sum to the Enfield Toy Library. There are also homework and other clubs available during and after school hours.

# Highlands School

**148 Worlds End Lane, Winchmore Hill N21 1QQ** 020 8370 1100 020 8370 1110 Mrs Monica Cross; Chair of Governors: Cllr Dale Goddard Oakwood, Southgate **Buses:** W9, 125 Green blazer and black trousers or green skirt, white shirt, school tie for boys, black shoes, black long socks for girls **Demand:** 1000 applications for 200 first year places in 2000; 240 places available in 2002 **Type:** Community comprehensive for 1300 mixed pupils, aged 11 to 18 **Submit application form:** 1st week of November 2003 **School hours:** 8.45am–3.25pm **Meals:** Hot and cold available **Strong GCSE subjects:** Not applicable – no pupils will sit GCSEs unitl 2005 **London league table position:** Not applicable

## Profile

Highlands School opened in September 2000 in the north of Enfield to cater for a growing demand for secondary school places in the borough. It is sited in the new housing development of Highlands Village and serves a relatively affluent population that is ethnically diverse, with significant populations of Greek, Turkish, Jewish and Asian pupils. To build and equip the school cost £25 million, which the council raised through the Governments Private Finance Initiative (PFI), in partnership with a company called Equion Plc. It has state-of-the-art facilities and has recently installed an advanced computer server that will allow students to access terminals throughout the school. It also has a technology suite with a large number of computer operated machines.

## Admissions and intake

The school was deluged with applications when it first opened in 2000, with 1000 applications for just over 200 places. The demand was such that 100 parents who were not given places appealed against the decision. To help cope Enfield council asked the school to increase its intake in 2001 to 240, which is likely to remain the figure for future years. Applications are made via the LEA, which applies the standard criteria to deciding who gets places if, as seems inevitable, there are more applications than places.

## Achievement

Pupils at the school will not sit GCSEs until summer 2005. They will sit Key Stage 3 tests in 2003, and the government has pledged to publish these results nationally. The school is not eligible to become a specialist college until it has GCSE results, but it is likely to be particularly strong in technology subject as it is so well-equipped.

## Extra-curricular activities

The school has a large sports hall and astroturf pitch and is able to run a number of sports activities, including a boys rugby team, a girls netball team, boys and girls soccer teams and cross-country running. There is a homework club every night except Tuesdays and separate clubs after school for art, science, French and Spanish. There is also a wind band, string ensemble, and regular drama productions.

# Kingsmead School

**Southbury Road, Enfield EN1 1YQ** 020 8363 3037 020 8366 3709 Mr GRC Bird BA; Chair of Governors: Mr Ken Gregory Southbury **Buses:** 121, 191, 217, 307, 317 Grey jacket, grey trousers or skirt, white shirt or blouse, burgundy tie; Sixth form: Dress in a 'sensible manner' **Demand:** 250 places available; oversubscribed **Type:** Community comprehensive for 1284 mixed pupils, aged 11 to 18 **Submit application form:** 1st week of November 2003 **Mission statement:** To create a caring community where all members are valued and have an equal chance to realize their full potential and to learn how to make the most of life. **School hours:** 8.35am–3.45pm; homework clubs are available **Meals:** Hot and cold available **Strong GCSE subjects:** History **London league table position:** 371

## Profile

Kingsmead School is situated near a junction with the A10, less than a mile from Enfield town centre, and a footbridge allows children to cross the road safely. The modern teaching buildings are grouped around an attractive garden. A recent building development programme has introduced new play areas as well as a new maths and English building. The library, technology building and many other rooms have also been refurbished. Pupils who speak another language at home are encouraged to take exams in their mother tongue, and specialist staff are available to support those children learning English for the first time. The school has excellent facilities for those pupils with special needs, including a special needs department and an in-school support centre. Pupils are able to sit on year and school councils. Truancy is a continuing problem, with the percentage of unauthorized absence at 1.2 in 2000, above the national average.

## Admissions and intake

Admission is through the Enfield schools admission service (see borough factfile). Forms are available from primary schools and the LEA. At the time of the Ofsted report in 1998, over a third of pupils came from homes where English was an additional language.

## Achievement

In 2002, 38 per cent of pupils achieved five or more A*–C grades at GCSE. This was up on 33 per cent in 2001 but well below both the borough and national averages. The school was ranked 13th in the borough league table. The average point score for pupils entered for two or more A/AS-levels was 157, also below the borough and national averages. The school was ranked 13th in the borough league table. Many pupils stay on into the sixth form where the main requirement is a willingness to learn. Some pupils follow one- or two-year vocational courses whilst others take A-levels. GNVQ courses in subjects such as business education and leisure and tourism are available. The most recent Ofsted inspection reported that: 'Kingsmead School has made some big improvements since the last inspection in 1994 whilst maintaining the strengths noted at that time.' The ethos of the school was described as 'positive and supportive' and 'support for pupils with English as a second language is very good'. Standards of behaviour were described as 'good', but at the time there were a high number of exclusions.

## Extra-curricular activities

Kingsmead has good links with neighbouring Enfield Football Club and the many sports on offer include football, basketball, athletics and gymnastics. Pupils can also compete in inter-school and borough competitions. Musical tuition is available through the borough scheme and pupils can take part in many musical activities, such as the choir. Drama performances and musicals are also staged. Pupils take part in charity fund-raising and assist staff in the library, at the school's reception and help run a tuck shop. There is also a Duke of Edinburgh's Award group. Year 8 pupils are taken on a field trip to the Lake District. After-school homework clubs are available.

# The Latymer School

**Haselbury Road, Edmonton, London N9 9TN** 020 8807 4037 020 8807 4125 office@latymer.co.uk www.latymer.co.uk Mr MJ Cooper OBE, BA, Mi Biol, FRSA; Chair of Governors: Mr I Pilsworth Edmonton Green **Buses:** W8, 34, 102, 279, 444 Dark school blazer, white shirt, black trousers or dark skirt, dark school tie **Demand:** 180 places available; heavily oversubscribed **Type:** Voluntary aided selective for 1344 mixed pupils, aged 11 to 18 **Submit application form:** Late September 2003 **Motto:** *Qui patitur bincit* (He Who Endures Will Win in the End) **School hours:** 8.30am–3.45pm; homework clubs are available **Meals:** Hot and cold available **Strong GCSE subjects:** All relatively strong **London league table position:** 17

## Profile

The Latymer School is extremely popular and is among the top state schools in the country. It was established in 1624 by Edward Latymer and has been at its present location since 1910. It is one of London's 19 remaining grammar schools. The main school buildings date from this period, with substantial additions in 1928 and 1966. A new £1-million performing arts centre was opened in June 2000, adding to the already impressive array of facilities. A number of science and technology rooms have been modernized within the last five years and there are excellent facilities for IT, with access to the Internet and a comprehensive school Intranet. All assemblies are held in the imposing Great Hall. The school site also encompasses 12 acres of playing fields. The parents' and friends' association is very hard-working and organizes fund-raising and social events. The school has form year councils. There is a special needs coordinator. Former pupils include actress Eileen Atkins and *Sunday Times* jazz critic Derek Jewell.

## Admissions and intake

Latymer is hugely oversubscribed. Application forms are available from the school during its open days in September. It requires that all pupils are able to travel to the school via public transport in an hour or less. All candidates must take a non-verbal reasoning test, and if they achieve a sufficient standard they will then be required to sit a verbal reasoning test. Places are awarded with reference to performance in these tests, as well as to musical ability.

## Achievement

Results at Latymer are consistently excellent. In 2002, 99 per cent of pupils gained five or more A*–C grades at GCSE. The average point score was 58.4 and this placed the school at the top of the borough league table. The average point score of pupils entered for two or more A/AS-levels was 25.0, the best in the borough. The school has a large, very successful sixth form, with a high percentage of pupils going on to Oxbridge. The most recent Ofsted report in 1999 was extremely positive. A high proportion of teaching was described as 'good, very good or excellent'. The business studies and economics departments were said to be 'outstanding'. Results at GCSE were said to compare 'favourably with those for similar schools'. The selective nature of the school means that high results are expected, but Ofsted noted that the school also enables pupils to enjoy the experience of learning.

## Extra-curricular activities

Activities on offer were described by Ofsted as 'outstanding, particularly in music'. As well as an array of sports clubs, there are also numerous other clubs including after-school homework clubs, one for chess with tuition given by an international master, and another teaching martial arts. There are also high-quality music and drama performances. The school owns an outdoor education centre in Wales, which all Year 7 pupils visit. There are many opportunities for pupils to visit foreign countries. A biennial visit to Iceland is organized by the geography and science departments. The chamber orchestra regularly tours European cities and exchange visits take place with schools in France, Germany and Russia. The sixth form does community service.

# Lea Valley High School

**Bullsmoor Lane, Enfield EN3 6TW** 01992 763666 01992 653854 www.lvhs.enfield.sch.uk Mrs J Cullen-Cornelius MA, MBA; Chair of Governors: Mrs Sheila Grayston Turkey Street **Buses:** 217, 327 Up to sixth form: Colours are green and tartan; pupils wear a sweatshirt, shirt, trousers **Demand:** No figures available but 150 places **Type:** Community comprehensive Sports College for 931 mixed pupils, aged 11 to 18 **Submit application form:** 1st week of November 2003 **Motto:** Creating Opportunities to Achieve, Develop and Excel in a Challenging World **School hours:** 8.40am–3.30pm; homework clubs are available **Meals:** Hot and cold available **Strong GCSE subjects:** English literature, history **London league table position:** 488

## Profile

Lea Valley High is housed in modern buildings but the site suffers from litter. The learning resource centre is well equipped with dual-language texts and books in several languages, as well as access to the Internet. As part of a government programme, the school has been designated an IT-for-all learning centre and provides access to computers for the community with free tuition given on some evenings. There is an induction programme for asylum seekers and refugees and support via specialist staff for children who do not have English as their mother tongue. Pupils take a 'life skills' course to help them become responsible adults and are able to take part in the school council. The transitory nature of the school population means that parental groups are difficult to establish. Truancy is a serious problem and in 2000, Lea Valley's unauthorized absence levels of 3.1 per cent were three times the national average. The school has an active PTA and provisions for pupils with special needs.

## Admissions and intake

Admission is through the Enfield schools admission service (see borough factfile). Application forms are available from local primary schools and the LEA. Nearly half the pupils have English as an additional language. Refugees and asylum-seekers make up a quarter of the school population and about 20 per cent arrive or leave the school outside of the usual term times. Thus attainment on entry is also generally very low.

## Achievement

In 2002, 25 per cent of pupils gained A*–C grades at GCSE. This was a fall on 26 per cent in 2001 and the school was ranked bottom out of 18 in the borough league table. The average point score at GCSE was 24.1. At A-level, results tend to be in the lowest 5 per cent nationally. The average point score for pupils entered for two or more A-levels in 2002 was 115.7. The small sixth form offers A-levels, GNVQs and other vocational qualifications. Ofsted visited Lea Valley in 2000 and stated: 'The school has overcome many difficulties and has several good features. Strong leadership has brought about improvement in several areas, but the standard of the pupils' work is still low. There is a high turnover of staff and much pupil mobility.' Inspectors praised the induction procedures for asylum-seeking and refugee pupils. However, there was an 'unacceptably high proportion' of unsatisfactory teaching at Key Stage 3. Weak language and numeracy skills of pupils were said to 'impede learning', although the work of the speech and language unit was 'good'. The proportion of pupils who achieve five or more A*–G grades at GCSE was seen to have 'risen impressively in recent years' and is now 'well above similar schools'. Pupils' behaviour was 'satisfactory, although boisterous'.

## Extra-curricular activities

There are many sporting opportunities on offer, including a panathlon competition. The school holds regular dramatic productions and recently there has been a performance of *Oliver*. Workshops are held with professional musicians. The school also has a popular cheerleaders' squad. There are after-school homework clubs. The school organizes trips both abroad and in the UK. Pupils have a teacher who liaises between themselves and the community.

# Palmers Green High School

**104 Hoppers Road, London N21 3LJ** ☎ 020 8886 1135 📠 020 8882 9473 ⓔ head@palmersgreen.enfield.sch.uk Mrs Christine Edmundson; Chair of Governors: Mrs EM Smith Winchmore Hill, Palmers Green Southgate **Buses**: W9; the school also provides transport for some girls Green blazer, green skirt, pink blouse **Demand**: 12 places are available in Year 7; 90 girls were tested in 1999/2000 **Type**: Selective independent for 343 girls, aged 3 to 17 **Fees**: £2,250 per term **Submit application form**: Depends upon age of applicant, check with school **Motto**: By Love, Serve One Another **School hours**: 8.30am–3.50pm **Meals**: Hot and cold available **Strong GCSE subjects**: Art, science **London league table position**: 64

## Profile

Palmers Green High School is a small independent day school for girls. Alice N Hum, a member of the Society of Friends, founded the school in 1905. A vital part of the school's ethos is derived from the ideals, integrity and care implicit in that philosophy. The school is housed in modern buildings and is continually updating its resources. In 1995, a multi-purpose hall/theatre/gymnasium, dining room, kitchen, workshop and dance studio were completed. All teaching rooms are equipped with computer and video facilities. Owing to its small size, typical class sizes in exam years are 12 to 14 pupils. Internal exams are set either annually or biannually to monitor progress. Girls can become form or school prefects and be involved with the pupil council. During their last year, girls are prepared by the head for sixth-form interviews for entry into other schools, if desired. The majority of pupils move into sixth forms when they leave, with girls recently gaining places at Westminster School, North London Collegiate, City of London and Woodhouse Sixth Form College. There is a parents' association and all pupils become lifelong members of the Old Girls' Association. Former pupils include actress Dame Flora Robson and Marion Tait, a principal dancer of the Birmingham Royal Ballet.

## Admissions and intake

An admissions form is available from the school. This should be completed and returned along with a £40 registration fee. A senior school entrance and scholarship examination is held in January. A shortlist of candidates will then be interviewed in February. A limited number of scholarships is available.

## Achievement

Palmers Green is a high-performing selective school and results are consistently excellent. In 2002, 100 per cent of girls gained five or more A*–C passes at GCSE, matching 2001's results. The average point score was 52.5 and this placed the school third in the borough league tables. As well as the usual range of subjects on offer, all girls work towards an RSA Certificate of Computer Literacy. All pupils take courses in the core subjects along with French, and options that include environmental studies, music and German.

## Extra-curricular activities

From the age of 14, girls are able to take part in the Duke of Edinburgh's Award scheme. Sports on offer include aerobics, badminton, lacrosse, racketball and squash. There is enthusiastic involvement in the choir, orchestra and chamber music ensembles. Tuition is available for musical instruments, speech, drama and ballet. In memory of Dame Flora Robson, there is an annual speech and drama competition. Marion Tait maintains links with the school by encouraging girls to attend ballet workshops and performances. Pupils regularly visit museums, theatres and concerts and have recently travelled to Scandinavia and Russia.

# St Anne's Catholic High School for Girls

**Oakthorpe Road, Palmers Green, London N13 5TY (upper school); London Road, Enfield EN2 6EN (lower school)** 020 8886 2165 (upper school); 020 8366 0514 (lower school) 020 8886 6552 (upper school); 020 8366 1168 (lower school) Mrs C Byamuka Adv.Dip.Ed; Chair of Governors: Mrs M Baker Palmers Green (upper school): Enfield Town (lower school). **Buses**: 121, 329 (upper school); W8, 329 (lower school) Burgundy school blazer, skirt, blouse; Sixth form: Normal trousers, navy blue school sweatshirt **Demand:** Figures vary but 180 places usually oversubscribed **Type:** Voluntary aided Roman Catholic comprehensive for 971 girls, aged 11 to 18 **Submit application form:** 1st week of November 2003 **School hours:** 8.45am–3.25pm; homework clubs are available **Meals:** Hot and cold available **Strong GCSE subjects:** Drama, history **London league table position:** 226

## Profile

St Anne's is a smaller than average voluntary aided comprehensive that performs comparably well in relation to other schools in the borough. A recent amalgamation of two older schools, it is split into an upper and lower school separated by about three and a half miles. The upper school is located in the mainly residential area of Palmers Green. The lower school is near Enfield Town, with the school's playing fields situated alongside it. The school has a strong Catholic ethos. There is a school chaplain and days begin with a short prayer. Pupils can assume responsibility as prefects and serve on the school council. There is an active friends' association and PTA. Pupils with special needs are helped by in-house counsellors and a coordinator.

## Admissions and intake

Application forms are available from the school. Admissions criteria place priority on baptized members of the Roman Catholic Church and then on girls from other Christian denominations whose parents are sympathetic to the aims of the school. The intake includes pupils from neighbouring London boroughs as well as from Hertfordshire.

## Achievement

In 2002, 63 per cent of girls achieved five or more A*–C grades at GCSE, well above average for the borough. This was up on 58 per cent in 2001, reinstating an upward trend. The school was ranked eighth in the borough league table. The average point score for pupils entered for two or more A/AS-levels was 252.7, above the borough average, placing the school second in the borough league table. The sixth form is small and in 1999 it had only 88 pupils. A range of A-levels is available, including French, German and Italian, as well as GNVQs. Ofsted's last inspection was in 2000, where it described the school as an 'effective school' where 'standards are improving as the quality of teaching is getting better'.

## Extra-curricular activities

Various sports are on offer, with many inter-form and inter-school competitions. There is a school choir and orchestra, as well as a gospel choir. After-school homework clubs in most subjects are available. Pupils are able to visit a retreat in order to aid spiritual development and there are also trips to the theatre and annual ski trips to Europe.

# St Ignatius College

**Turkey Street, Enfield EN1 4NP** ☎ 01992 717835; 760520 📠 01992 652070 Mr MJ Blundell MA; Chair of Governors: Mr Patrick Bolger ⇄ Turkey Street **Buses**: 217, 310, 311, 317; special buses run for the college in the mornings and evenings Black blazer with college badge, dark grey trousers, white shirt, light grey pullover, school tie; Sixth form: Special tie, optional striped shirt **Demand**: 180 places available; oversubscribed **Type**: Voluntary aided Roman Catholic for 1124 boys, aged 11 to 18 **Submit application form**: Beginning of December of year before entry **Motto**: *Ad Maiorem Dei Gloriam* (To the Greater Glory of God) **School hours**: 8.50 am–3.15pm/3.50pm (split system) **Meals**: Hot and cold available **Strong GCSE subjects**: History **London league table position**: 192

## Profile

The trustees of St Ignatius College are members of the Society of Jesus. The school was founded by the Jesuit community in 1894 at Stamford Hill and moved to its present location in 1968. The college has many excellent additional resources, including a chapel, swimming pool and a new gym. In 1998 it took possession of the octagon building that houses the library and a new IT suite. Jesuit principles shape every aspect of school life. Mass is held every day and there is a strong tradition of charitable work. There are good relationships with parents and an active PTA. There is a school council.

## Admissions and intake

Application forms are available from the college. Two forms must be completed, one by the parents of the applicant and one by a Roman Catholic priest. The following criteria in order of priority are applied when places are oversubscribed: evidence that the child comes from a family with a parent who is a practising member of the Roman Catholic Church, plus evidence of additional Christian commitment or activity of the child or parents; a brother at the school, or a brother who has previously attended the school; special medical or social needs; and distance between the child's home and the school. Applicants may be called for an interview. Pupils on entry represent the whole ability range, with most pupils just above average.

## Achievement

In 2002, 63 per cent of pupils achieved five or more A*–C grades at GCSE, above the national average. The school was ranked sixth in the borough league table. Pupils can take classical studies and Latin at GCSE besides the usual subjects. The average point score for pupils entered for two or more A/AS-levels was 246.5, above the borough average. This placed the school third in the borough. Sixth-formers may study either for A-levels, with options including Latin, RE and classical civilization, or for a one-year GNVQ course in business studies or information studies. In 1998 Ofsted reported; 'Teaching is at least satisfactory in 92 per cent of lessons and is good or better in 47 per cent of lessons. In 11 per cent of lessons teaching is very good or better. Teaching is particularly effective in Key Stage 3 and the sixth form.' It also commented: 'At GCSE the results show that the school is well above the national average and in comparison with schools with a similar intake they are also well above average.' Ofsted found pupils 'very polite' and 'keen to learn'.

## Extra-curricular activities

The school has a Combined Cadet Force, with 130 pupils split between the RAF and army sections. There are excellent drama facilities. Instrumental tuition is available and there are many successful musical groups, including a chamber choir and orchestra. Sports on offer include cricket, golf, rugby, football and athletics, with teams for the latter three having competed at national level. The school also organizes skiing trips to Europe.

# St John's Senior School

**The Ridgeway, Enfield, EN2 8BE** ☎ 020 8366 0035 📠 020 8363 4439 stjohnssc@aol.com Mr Tardios ⇄ Gordon Hill **Buses**: 313 Blue blazer, grey trousers, white shirt **Demand**: No figures available **Type**: Selective independent for 430 boys, aged 4 to 18 **Fees**: £2,050 per term **Submit application form**: No cut-off date **Motto**: *Res Ipsa Loquitur* (The Thing Speaks for Itself) **School hours**: 8.30am–4.45pm; homework clubs are available **Meals**: Hot and cold available **Strong GCSE subjects**: Arts, law **London league table position**: 59

### Profile

St John's Senior School is a co-educational independent school. In September 2003 there will be over 400 boys and girls, in roughly equal numbers. Attendance levels are excellent at the school and in 2002, there was zero per cent unauthorized absence. There is a prefects system and a school council. Parents meet regularly with staff at coffee evenings.

### Admissions and intake

The school should be contacted with regard to admissions. Applicants are required to sit an entrance exam.

### Achievement

St John's consistently achieves excellent results, with its pupils enjoying success at both GCSE and A-level. Between 1996–2002, 100 per cent of pupils have gained five or more A*–C grades at GCSE. In 2002, the average point score at GCSE was 53.2; this placed the school second in the borough league table. The average point score for pupils entered for two or more A/AS-levels in 2001 was 18.0, above the national average, placing the school fourth in the borough. Figures for 2002 were unavailable.

### Extra-curricular activities

St John's has a wide range of extra-curricular activities. There is a complete range of sports and clubs, including chess, geography, and an after-school homework hour. There are trips both at home and abroad. Pupils work with the local community and are involved with the Great Ormond Street Hospital for Sick Children.

## Salisbury School

**Nightingale Road, London N9 8DR (upper school); Turin Road, Edmonton N9 8DQ (lower school)** 020 8372 5678 020 8372 0303 headteacher.salisbury_school@virgin.net Mr M Rainsford; Chair of Governors: Mr I Wigget Lower Edmonton **Buses:** 149, 191, 279 Navy blue blazer with school badge, black trousers or grey skirt, white shirt, school tie in year colour; Sixth form: Office attire **Demand:** Figures vary for 270 places available **Type:** Community comprehensive for 1324 mixed pupils, aged 11 to 18 **Submit application form:** 1st week of November 2003 **Motto:** A School That Works for Everyone **School hours:** 8.40am–3.30pm, 8.40am–3.45pm (Wed); homework clubs are available **Meals:** Hot and cold available **Strong GCSE subjects:** Art, English **London league table position:** 450

### Profile

Salisbury is a large school, occupying two sites about a third of a mile apart. The lower school (Years 7 to 9) has recently been expanded with 27 new classrooms and a new hall. The upper school site is shared with a primary school. Playing fields are located next to the lower school and include tennis courts. Salisbury is a multicultural school, second language support is available and there are some multilingual signs and displays located throughout the school. There is a learning support centre for pupils with behavioural difficulties, and Salisbury is the borough centre for specific learning difficulties. There are both school and year councils and a prefect system. The school has an active PTA.

### Admissions and intake

Admission is through the Enfield schools admission service (see borough factfile). Application forms are available from local primary schools and the LEA. Nearly 39 per cent of pupils are on the special needs register. Literacy levels are generally low on intake.

### Achievement

Salisbury School is on special measures. In 2002, 22 per cent of pupils achieved five or more A*–C grades at GCSE, slightly up on 2001. The school came 15th out of 17 in the borough league table. Pupils are able to take Turkish at GCSE and A-level, and Salisbury is one of a few pilot schools that offer a full GNVQ part 1 alongside GCSEs. The average point score for pupils entered for two or more A/AS-levels was 81.3, placing the school 16th. The sixth form offers A-levels, GNVQs and other vocational qualifications, and options are enhanced by the Enfield collegiate system. Ofsted visited Salisbury in 1999 and reported: '...Her Majesty's Chief Inspector of Schools is of the opinion that the school requires special measures since it is failing to give its pupils an acceptable standard of education'. It noted:

'In too many classrooms, disruptive behaviour undermines learning' and the punctuality of some pupils was 'unacceptable'. Achievement was said to be limited, with a significant number of pupils failing to achieve a pass at GCSE in English, maths and science. A new head has since been brought in, and the school has bid into funding allocated for the Single Regeneration Budget, enabling the school to run schemes such as a literacy project for Year 7.

### Extra-curricular activities

The popular Salisbury Steel Band is in great demand for local events. There is a homework club at the lower school, and the upper school has a study centre open at lunchtimes and after school. Sports available include athletics, basketball, rugby, netball and football. Salisbury was the first school in the borough to form 'Clampdown', a youth action group that looks at 'student safety'. This group won a Metropolitan Police Award for its effectiveness. There are regular day trips to France and pupils have been skiing in Andorra. Pupils on both sites run a branch of the Yorkshire Bank.

# Southgate School

**Sussex Way, Cockfosters, Hertfordshire EN4 0BL** 020 8449 9583 020 8441 6424 Mr Anthony Wilde; Chair of Governors: Mr Peter Leedham New Barnet Cockfosters, Oakwood **Buses**: 121, 298, 299, 307 Up to sixth form: Black trousers or skirt, black pullover, white shirt, school tie **Demand**: Figures vary for 240 places available **Type**: Community comprehensive for 1622 mixed pupils, aged 11 to 18 **Submit application form**: 1st week of November 2003 **Mission statement**: To provide a secure, happy, caring and well-ordered environment in which pupils, staff and parents can work confidently together. **School hours**: 8.50am–2.45pm (Mon), 8.50am–3.35pm (Tues to Thurs), 8.50am–3.20pm (Fri); homework clubs are available **Meals**: Hot and cold available **Strong GCSE subjects**: Drama, English and history **London league table position**: 179

### Profile

Situated at the western edge of the borough near the green belt, Southgate is a good comprehensive. The upper and lower schools were amalgamated after the completion of major building work, leaving the school with extensive new buildings alongside the original buildings dating from 1961. A large sports hall was added which, along with the school's all-weather pitch, provides good facilities for sport. Over £100,000 has been invested in computers, with a school-wide network. A television recording studio enables media studies students to create their own programmes. Two lifts, ramps, a physiotherapy room and other specialized equipment mean that Southgate caters well for pupils with physical disabilities. The school considers each child's individual special needs and there is support for the pupil from a coordinator. The large sixth form has a self-contained unit. Pupils are able to join year councils. Parents are kept informed of events via a weekly newsletter and there is an active friends' association. Former pupils include actor Warren Mitchell and local MP Stephen Twigg.

### Admissions and intake

Admission is through the Enfield schools admission service (see borough factfile). Application forms are available from local primary schools and the LEA. The school also draws pupils from neighbouring Barnet as well as from the relatively affluent area surrounding the school.

### Achievement

Results at Southgate are consistently good. In 2001, 64 per cent of pupils gained five or more A*–C grades at GCSE. This was an dip on 69 per cent in 2001 but above the borough average. The school was ranked fifth in the borough league table. The average point score for pupils taking two or more A/AS-levels was 205.9, just below the borough average. This placed the school seventh in the borough. Both advanced and intermediate GNVQs are offered at Southgate, and courses available in the sixth form are supplemented by the Enfield Collegiate system. Ofsted visited the school in 2000 and reported that it was 'a very good and very effective school'. They added: 'The high quality of the head teacher's leadership and the way all staff work as a team to teach pupils, helps to create a civilized school where there is a commitment to high achievement.' Standards are particularly strong in English, drama and history with some strengths in mathematics, science and design and technology. Weaker subjects were found to be French and ICT.

## Extra-curricular activities

Southgate encourages all pupils who are keen to 'have a go' and to take part in the many sports and homework clubs on offer. Pupils can also become involved in the choir, wind band, orchestra or recorder group, and a festival of music is held annually.There is a well-established ATC squadron at the school. Each year has a charity committee that plans fund-raising activities. Pupils are able to travel abroad on an annual skiing trip as well as on established exchanges to France, Germany or Spain.

# Winchmore School

**Laburnum Grove, London N21 3HS** 020 8360 7773 020 8360 8409 Mrs L Mansbridge: Chair of Governors: Mr P Cox Winchmore Hill **Buses**: 125, 329 Navy blue blazer, grey trousers, light blue shirt, school tie (boys); navy blue skirt or trousers, light blue blouse, V-neck school jumper (girls); Sixth form: Appropriate dress **Demand**: 240 places available; oversubscribed **Type**: Community comprehensive for 1413 mixed pupils, aged 11 to 18 **Submit application form**: 1st week of November 2003 **Motto**: Together We Work **School hours**: 8.40am–3.35pm; homework clubs are available **Meals**: Hot and cold available **Strong GCSE subjects**: English language, art and history **London league table position**: 299

## Profile

Winchmore School is a larger than average secondary school, situated in a mixed residential area.The main building was opened in 1956 and since then the school has extended its accommodation. High student numbers have put pressure on facilities in recent years. The buildings and grounds are well cared for. There is a house system that provides pupils with competition and rewards. Pupils can also become prefects and participate in the school council. Parents are kept informed via regular newsletters and progress reports. The PTA helps raise funds to purchase additional equipment. Winchmore also has a special-needs coordinator.

## Admissions and intake

Admission is through the Enfield Schools Admission Service (see borough factfile). Application forms are available from the LEA and primary schools. Pupils' ability on entry is relatively low, although the assessment of some is affected by their initial lack of English language skills. A large number of pupils come from the local, well established Greek and Turkish communities.

## Achievement

A high proportion of Winchmore's pupils have English as an additional language, which the school serves well – there was a 100 per cent pass rate for English language in 1999. Pupils are allowed to take exams in their mother tongue. In 2002, 47 per cent of pupils achieved five or more A*–C grades at GCSE. This was down on 48 per cent in 2001 and the school was ranked ninth in the borough league table. This result was in line with the borough but below the national average. Foundation level GNVQs in business and finance are available along with the usual range of GCSE subjects. The average point score for pupils entered for two or more A/AS-levels was 184, placing the school 10th in the borough. The sixth form offers a wide range of A-levels, including film studies and psychology. Some subjects are taught in partnership with other collegiate schools in Enfield. In 2001, Ofsted reported: 'This is a good school that is full of very pleasant pupils'. Inspectors praised the 'very good' leadership of the school and observed that 'teaching is good across the school'. Pupils make good progress up the the age of 16 and 'satisfactory progress' is made in the sixth form. GCSE results were seen to be average in 2001 with strengths in English language, art and history. Ofsted found 'significant weaknesses' in science and design and technology.

## Extra-curricular activities

The school offers many lunchtime clubs, including the Christian Union, a computing club and a homework club, which is also available after school. There are numerous team sports available as well as aerobics and keep-fit in the multi-gym. Language trips are made to France and Germany, and there is an annual skiing trip and a regular music tour. Residential fieldwork takes place in geography and biology and there is an annual week's camping expedition for Year 7. Pupils work within the local community.

# Greenwich

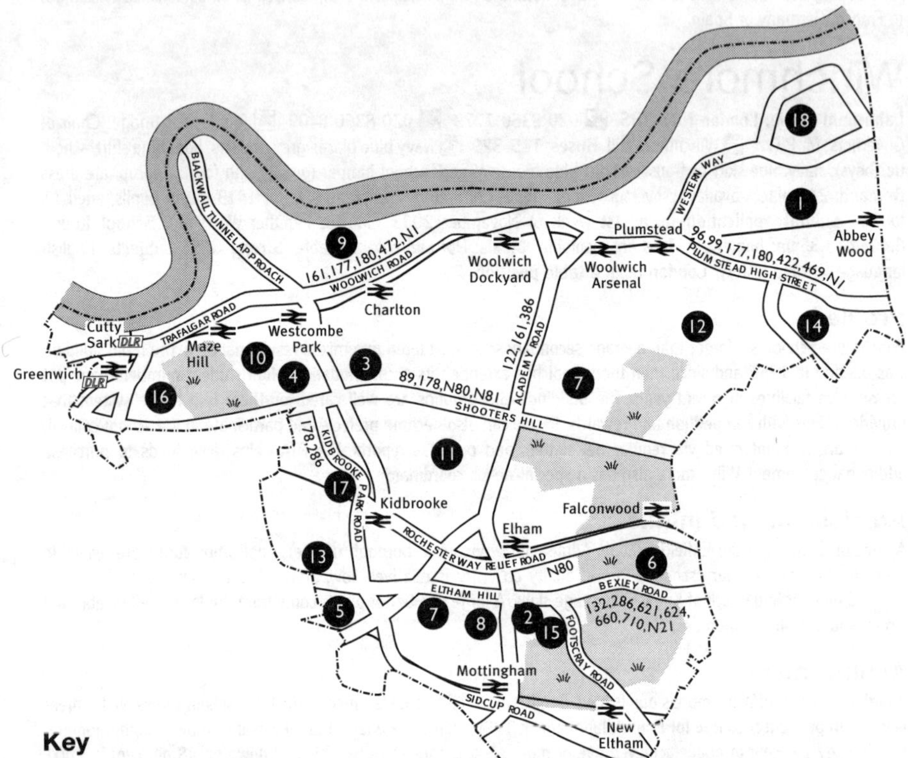


## Key

1. Abbey Wood School
2. BLA Theatre School
3. Blackheath Bluecoat CofE Secondary School
4. Blackheath High School
5. Colfes School
6. Crown Woods School
7. Eltham Green School
8. Eltham Hill Technology College for Girls
9. Holborn College
10. The John Roan School
11. Kidbrooke School
12. Plumstead Manor School
13. Riverston School
14. St Paul's Catholic School
15. St Thomas More RC Comprehensive School
16. St Ursula's Convent School
17. Thomas Tallis School
18. Woolwich Polytechnic School for Boys

# Fact File

**LEA: Riverside House, Woolwich High Street, London SE18 6DF** 020 8854 8888 www.greenwich.gov.uk **Director of Education:** Paul Burnett **Political control of council:** Labour **Percentage of pupils from outside the borough:** 23.3 per cent **Percentage of pupils educated outside the borough:** 6.4 per cent **London league table positions (out of 32 boroughs):** 29th

## Profile

The little town of Greenwich is undoubtedly the most famous part of South-East London. This quaint little corner of the capital has always been a magnet for tourists from all over the world, with its great maritime tradition, resplendent architecture and the Greenwich Meridian, to which the whole world once looked to set its clocks. The Millennium Dome, located between Greenwich and Charlton, attracted many visitors in 2000, and the long-awaited London Underground has finally arrived, along with a new road network.

However, what the casual visitor will not see in the leafy walkways of Greenwich Park, once the hunting playground of Henry VIII, are the depths of social deprivation that afflict a good proportion of the borough's population. While the beautiful vistas of Blackheath are enjoyed by the wealthy professionals living on its borders, a vast number of people living in Greenwich live in some of the country's most deprived council estates.

Most Greenwich schools, like those in many inner-city boroughs, do not enjoy great academic success. Apart from one or two beacon schools, whose glowing Ofsted reports and enviable exam results are usually the result of a strict selection policy, most schools GCSE and A-level results are well below the national average. Ofsted inspectors put these failings down to a number of factors, including the high level of social deprivation. Truancy levels are high in many schools, and poor punctuality and behaviour on the part of the pupils has not helped the situation. However, on the brighter side, many of the schools are slowly improving, with the new literacy strategy at primary level placing a greater emphasis on improving basic skills. Holborn College recently moved from Hammersmith and Fulham to Greenwich; Eaglesfield School is to close so it has not been included. Greenwich has two EAZ's operating in the borough: the Greenwich EAZ that includes Plumstead Manor and the Plumstead EAZ that includes both Eltham Green and Eltham Hill schools – all are recent government initatives to improve standards.

## Policy

To apply to any of the state schools in Greenwich and John Roan School, parents must contact the Greenwich LEA. Visits to prospective schools are in October 2003, when parents are given an application form to fill out for the school of their choice. Parents should contact voluntary aided schools direct. If there are more applicants than places available at the state schools, priority will be given to pupils in the following order: children who attend a nearby primary school; children with siblings at the school; and children who live nearest to the school. Priority is given to pupils for whom a specific school is named on a statement of special educational needs.

# Abbey Wood School

**Eynsham Bridge, Abbey Wood, London SE2 9AJ** 020 8310 9175 020 8312 1866 admin@abbeywood.greenwich.sch.uk Ms Susan Harry B.Sc; Chair of Governors: Olwyn Bond Abbey Wood **Buses:** B11, 99, 177, 180, 229, 422, 469 Black trousers or skirt, white polo shirt (winter), white polo shirt with school motif (summer), turquoise school sweatshirt, black shoes, white or black socks or black tights; make-up and nail varnish are strictly forbidden, small items of jewellery permissible **Demand:** 103 applications for 180 places in 2001/2 **Type:** Community comprehensive for 870 mixed pupils, aged 11 to 16 **Submit application form:** October 2003 **Motto:** Take Up and Read **School hours:** 8.45am–3pm; homework clubs are available **Meals:** Hot and cold available **Strong GCSE subjects:** Art, drama **London league table position:** 509

## Profile

Abbey Wood School is a collection of concrete buildings situated in the middle of a well-kept housing estate. There are ample sports facilities in the school's 12.5-acre site, including six tennis courts, three gyms, a fitness training room, a multi-purpose floodlit area, football and hockey pitches, and full athletics facilities in the summer. In 2002, a City Learning Centre was opened. The school has a learning resources centre and a library with over 100 computers, providing controlled Internet access for students. It was the first school in Greenwich to acquire the SuccessMaker system, which enables children to work on literacy and numeracy at their own pace. At Key Stage 4, pupils can opt for GNVQ part 1 as well as GCSE options, such as Spanish, drama and graphics. Pupils can also become library assistants or sit on the school council. Those pupils with above average ability are offered academic tutoring to enhance their skills. The learning support department works closely with primary schools to assess children transferring to the school. Those pupils who need extra support in literacy are given at least one lesson in a small group every week, with each child having an individual education plan. There is a department to help pupils with special needs. Hope Powell, coach to the England women's football team, is a former pupil.

### Admissions and intake

Admission is through the council. The main feeder schools are Alexander McLeod, Boxgrove and De Lucy schools. However, there is no restricted catchment area and children come from all over the borough.

### Achievement

In 2001, Ofsted inspectors described Abbey Wood as a 'school with significant strengths', but it was noted that GCSE results are well below average. Pupils were seen to make 'at least satisfactory progress' and the school was seen to have made 'good overall progress' since its last inspection in 1998. In 2002, only 12 per cent of pupils gained five GCSEs at grades A*–C, down on 19 per cent in 2001. Ofsted praised the quality of the leadership and management of the school but commented that standards need to be raised in education and test results. They also suggested a re-decoration programme to make the school building 'more attractive and welcoming'.

### Extra-curricular activities

A variety of clubs are on offer, including languages, arts, computers, homework, trampolining and girls' football. There are outings to museums and concerts, and trips to Inverliever Lodge in Scotland as well as language trips to France and Spain. Pupils take part in charity fund-raisers and can help in producing the school newsletter, the *Abbey Times*.

## BLA Theatre School

**Performance House, 20 Passey Place, Eltham, London SE9 5DQ** ☎ 020 8850 9888 📠 020 8850 9944 ⓔ bla@dircon.co.uk ✉ Susan Prendergast (principal); Chair of Governors: Mr Daniel Hussey ⇌ Eltham **Buses:** B16, 124, 126, 132, 160, 321 👔 For academic teaching sessions: Kilt, green jumper and blazer with gold trim, cream blouse or shirt, school tie; For performing arts lessons: Tracksuit **Demand:** No figures available but oversubscribed for 10 places in 2000/1 **Type:** Selective independent for 44 mixed pupils, aged 7 to 16 **Fees:** £1,350 per term, excluding exam fees, £100 academic exercise book fee payable yearly, plus meals **Submit application form:** No cut-off date **Motto:** Believe and Succeed **School hours:** 8.45am–4.30pm; homework clubs are available **Meals:** Not provided **Strong GCSE subjects:** Art, drama **London league table position:** 439

### Profile

This bohemian little school was established three years ago with 19 pupils, and is gradually building up a reputation in the local area. As the school is growing rapidly, the staff are looking for a new building. New accommodation will be used to improve facilities and the school plans to move within the next two years. Pupils spend the equivalent of two days per week on drama, dance and other vocational subjects. The other three days are spent following the national curriculum. Vocational subjects on offer include tap, ballet, jazz, acting, musical theatre and production. Other show-business skills, such as camera technique and audition skills, are also taught. Pupils are also encouraged to sit dance and modern theatre exams run by the Imperial Society of Teachers of Dance (ISTD) and the London Academy of Music and Dramatic Art (LAMDA). Pupils audition for parts in television adverts or stage productions so that their work experience resumé is as impressive as possible. Parents are kept informed through open evenings, and children carry a contact book in which key information is kept. There is a PTA. The school prides itself on its discipline record and encourages pupils to develop pleasant manners and to be confident. There is a prefect system.

### Admissions and intake

Pupils travel from as far away as Greenwich, Lewisham, Beckenham and even Streatham. Although most pupils join at age 11, the school also provides evening classes and Sunday sessions, and children may elect to join the school full-time at any age. Candidates need to be artistically inclined but also sure they want to pursue a career in show business, and staff will only accept those who show determination to succeed. During the interview, the pupil must read an excerpt of the interviewer's choice, perform a short acting audition and sing a song. Candidates must also provide a recent school report and may have to sit a short academic test.

## Achievement

Owing to the small pupil intake at this school, it is difficult to compare it academically with other schools. Three pupils sat GCSEs in 2000 and gained a 67 per cent pass rate at A*–C grades. In 2002 the average point score had risen to 27.7, ranking the school 10th out of 18 in the borough. Since BLA has only been open for three years, it has not yet received an inspection report. Pupils have taken part in television adverts and shows, including *The Bill* and *Holby City*. One pupil, Billy Smith, played the lead part in *The Ghost of Greville Lodge*, which was broadcast on television in December 2000. Another two pupils have worked on a film starring Helen Mirren and Sir Michael Caine.

## Extra-curricular activities

The school has its own production company, Little Star Productions, which stages a variety of shows and musicals at different venues. Theatre excursions and educational trips are provided. There is also a casting agency, which pupils can opt to stay with once they have left the school. After-school homework clubs are available.

# Blackheath Bluecoat CofE Secondary School

**Old Dover Road, London SE3 8SY** 020 8269 4300 020 8853 5978 BBCSADMIN@aol.com Mrs Kay Bickley; Chair of Governors: Rev Mike Marshall Blackheath **Buses**: 53, 54, 89, 178, 386 Navy blue sweatshirt, grey trousers or navy skirt or trousers, white shirt, school tie **Demand**: No figures available but oversubscribed for 85 foundation places for Christians and 81 open places on offer each year **Type**: Voluntary aided Church of England foundation school for 917 mixed pupils, aged 11 to 18 **Submit application form**: October 2003 **School hours**: 8.50am–3.20pm **Meals**: Hot and cold available **Strong GCSE subjects**: All relatively strong **London league table position**: 453

## Profile

Blackheath Bluecoat dates from 1700 and enjoyed a good reputation in the 1960s and 1970s. Notable facilities include a comprehensive library resources centre, a sports hall and gym, two hard outside playing areas, one with floodlighting, and a sports field within walking distance. The school has a strong religious ethos and has good links with local churches, including St John the Evangelist in Blackheath, whose vicar is the chair of governors. There is a daily morning act of worship. The sixth form is run in conjunction with the nearby John Roan School. There is good provision for special needs and extra literacy and numeracy lessons are available. The school is noted for its sporting excellence, England footballer Rio Ferdinand was a pupil here, and its continuing success in football, basketball, softball and volleyball has resulted in a Sportsmark Award for excellence. There is a school council and a PTA.

## Admissions and intake

The school reserves a large number of places for pupils who are practising Christians. Those applicants who have a long-term commitment to the Anglican faith and can support this with a letter from their parish priest, stand a better chance of obtaining a place for their child. Intake consists of 25 per cent above average pupils, 50 per cent average and 25 per cent below average pupils.

## Achievement

The school's standards in achievement and teaching have improved between the two latest Ofsted inspections in 1998 and 2000. However, the standard of work at Key Stages 3 and 4 is still below average in most subjects. The percentage of pupils passing five GCSEs at grades A*–C was 27 per cent in 2002, halting a downward trend since 1998. The school was ranked 13th in the borough. Sixth-formers are well-motivated and their achievements are deemed 'satisfactory', although A-level point scores are below the local average and in decline. In 2002, the average point score for pupils taking two or more A-levels was 115.4. About half the sixth form opt for vocational qualifications and 35 per cent passed in 1995. Ofsted inspectors noted that pupils have 'negative attitudes' and are unpunctual and difficult to manage at times.

### Extra-curricular activities

Activities available include a computer and drama club, sports teams and Christian Union. Skiing and watersports holidays are arranged and pupils can participate in the Duke of Edinburgh's Award scheme from Year 10. Pupils can use the library resources centre and the IT suite after school.

## Blackheath High School

**Vanbrugh Park, London SE3 7AG** 020 8853 2929 020 8853 3663 info@bla.gdst.net www.gdst.net/bromleyhigh Mrs Elizabeth Laws; Chair of Governors: Rev Henry Burgin Blackheath, Westcombe Park, Maze Hill **Buses**: 53, 54, 108, 202, 286, 306, 380 Navy skirt, navy pullover, maroon and white striped blouse, navy tights, black shoes; Sixth form: Smart outfits **Demand**: No figures available but 67 places in 2001/2 **Type**: Selective independent Girls' Day School Trust for 588 girls, aged 11 to 18 **Fees**: £7,155 per annum, excluding meals **Submit application form**: No cut-off date **Motto**: A Place to Grow, a Place to Excel **School hours**: 8.40am–4pm **Meals**: Hot and cold available **Strong GCSE subjects**: All relatively strong **London league table position**: 82

### Profile

This elegant school opened in 1880 in Weymuss Road and moved to its new premises in 1994 after being taken over by the Girls' Day School Trust. The junior school now occupies the Weymuss Road premises. A Grade II-listed army chapel serves as a performance area and there is a range of practice rooms for music. Science labs and a technology room are equipped to a high standard, and there is a new purpose-built resources centre, including computers for private study, sports pavilion and fitness studio. Subjects on offer include art and design, dance, drama, French, German, Latin, science and technology. Although lessons finish at 4pm, girls can stay on until 6pm if necessary. There is a school council, prefects system and PTA.

### Admission and intake

The selection process is fairly rigorous. English and maths exams and a general paper are all sat in one afternoon in January of the entry year. Girls may also join in the sixth form, subject to an entry exam. As a member of the Girls' Day School Trust, the school strives to admit girls from all cultural and social backgrounds. Pupils mainly come from the local area, with some travelling further afield from Docklands. A scholarship scheme is available for academically gifted girls, consisting of one art and three music scholarships. The maximum remission is 50 per cent of the fees.

### Achievement

The school's exam results are impressive, with 92 per cent of pupils gaining five or more GCSEs at A*–C grades in 2001. This was two per cent down on 2001's results, and the school was placed at the top of the borough league table. A-level results are equally good, with pupils achieving an average point score of 294.6, well above the local and national average. This placed the school second in the borough. During its last independent inspection in 1995, Blackheath was commended for its exam results, which put the school 'in the front rank of independent schools'. Inspectors also praised its 'charismatic leadership'. Most sixth-formers go on to university.

### Extra-curricular activities

Pupils are encouraged to take part in music, art or drama and there are various orchestras, bands and choirs. These cooperated to produce a CD, *Music 2000 – Blackheath High School.* Sports available include gymnastics, trampolining, netball and hockey. After-school clubs include public speaking, creative writing and a storytelling club. There are also annual music tours. Other school trips include a language and history of art tour of Spain. All pupils take part in charity fund-raising events and older girls are encouraged to do voluntary work.

## Colfes School

**Horn Park Lane, Lee, London SE12 8AW** 020 8852 2283 020 8297 1216 AH Chicken; Chair of Governors: David Curtis Lee **Buses**: 122, 160, 202, 261, 278, 306, 321 Navy blazer, grey pullover, black trousers, blue and yellow school tie, black shoes **Demand**: No figures available but oversubscribed for 109 places in 2001/2 **Type**: Selective independent for 694 mixed pupils, aged 3 to 19 **Fees**: £2,748 per term, excluding meals

**Submit application form**: No cut-off date **Mottoes**: To God Alone, Honour and Glory/Through Striving to the Stars **School hours**: 8.30am–3.30pm **Meals**: Hot and cold available **Strong GCSE subjects**: Economics, geography, history **London league table position**: 86

## Profile

Colfes is one of London's oldest schools, dating from 1494. It was re-founded by Abraham Colfe, one of the governors, in 1652. He invited the Leathersellers' Company, a well-established City livery company, to be trustee of his will and there is still a link between the company and the school today. It moved to its present site at the end of World War II. It opted to become independent in 1977 and has gradually made the transition to a fully co-educational school. Famous ex-pupils include author Eric Ambler. The senior school has acquired a new classroom block for economics, business studies and modern languages, and the science labs have been modernized. There is also a new sixth-form study centre and library and the Bearwood Arts Centre for drama and music productions. Colfes boasts 30 acres of playing fields, a modern sports complex with swimming pool and fitness suites and three new tennis courts. Class sizes are relatively small, and GCSE classes usually average 17 pupils. The school is a Christian foundation and pupils attend assembly every morning, although children from other faiths are welcome. Parents are expected to ensure children do their homework and have a good attendance record. Regular parents' evenings are held. There is a school council and a prefects system.

## Admissions and intake

Children can join the senior school at age 11, when they take a school entrance exam and attend an interview, or at 13, where again they take an exam. Scholarships are offered to outstanding pupils at age 13. Pupils from other schools can join at sixth-form level, subject to an interview and a reference provided by their senior school. However, children can join at any age, subject to the headmaster's discretion.

## Achievement

Colfes' GCSE results are good, with 92 per cent of pupils passing five or more at grades A*–C in 2002. At A-level, the point scores are well above average, with an average score of 380.2. Colfes was placed second in the borough for GCSEs and first for A-levels. Colfes offers pupils an impressively wide range of subjects at GCSE, including Spanish, business studies, PE, art, design and technology, music, religious studies, IT, Latin and French. Sixth-formers can also study a variety of subjects, including ancient history, computing, economics, media studies and Latin. Subjects in which pupils excel include history, economics and geography.

## Extra-curricular activities

Sporting activities available include squash, badminton, rugby and cricket. Clubs include bridge, meteorology, forensic science, radio, chess and IT. All pupils in their first two years spend a week in the Lake District and in North Wales, and other foreign excursions can be taken up in later years. Some pupils took part in the Greenwich *Passion Play* in 2000, which was broadcast on television to celebrate the millennium. Children are encouraged to learn a musical instrument, and the school holds a number of concerts each year. Some pupils have travelled to the US and South Africa on musical tours.

# Crown Woods School

**Riefield Road, Eltham, London SE9 2QN** ☎ 020 8850 7678 Fax 020 8294 1921 ⓔ crownwoods@cix.co.uk Michael Murphy; Chair of Governors: Mr S Offord Falcon Wood **Buses**: B16, 132, 286, 621, 624, 660 Up to sixth form: Black trousers or skirt, white shirt or blouse, school tie, black shoes, black or white socks, plain-coloured raincoat, duffel coat or anorak **Demand**: 419 applications for 369 in 2001/2 **Type**: Community comprehensive for 2000 mixed pupils, aged 11 to 18 **Submit application form**: October 2003 **School hours**: 8.50am–3.35pm, 8.50am–3pm (Wed); homework clubs are available **Meals**: Hot and cold available, including breakfast **Strong GCSE subjects**: Art, drama, French, music, Spanish **London league table position**: 415

## Profile

Crown Woods is situated in a leafy suburban street in Eltham. The school has received local authority grants to improve the buildings, including £200,000 for new lighting. It has four purpose-built studios with sound and lighting facilities, specialist art rooms for pottery, photography, painting and drawing, sixth-form common rooms, IT rooms, a library, which is open until 4.30pm each day for research or homework, Internet access and a coffee bar. Languages are a strength of the school, with GCSEs available in French, German, Spanish and Latin. Italian and classics (ancient Greek) are also offered at sixth-form level. Crown Woods is part of Dialogue 2000, a scheme that funds A-level students for a month's study stay in Europe. Extra support is given for pupils with learning difficulties or for gifted pupils. There is a unit for pupils who are visually impaired, a school council, a prefects system and a PTA.

## Admissions and intake

Admission is through the council. Upon entry, about a quarter of the children have a reading age two years below the national average.

## Achievement

In 2002, 39 per cent of pupils passed five or more GCSEs at grades A*–C. This result was up six per cent from the previous year, continuing an upward trend. It was above the borough state school average and the school was placed ninth in the borough. Crown Woods holds the national record for educating the pupil with the best ever A-level results. Back in 1978, Stephen Murrell obtained seven A grades. A-level scores are still reasonably high, competing well against other Greenwich schools. In 2002, pupils scored an average of 166.8 points. This was below the local average, placing the school seventh in the borough. Results have been consistent over the past six years. During the last Ofsted inspection in 1999, inspectors noted that 'the school has failed to raise attainment significantly over recent years'. Inspectors also felt that many pupils' behaviour and attitudes were disruptive, and teachers had low expectations. They advised that behaviour could be improved by implementing a more consistent approach to discipline throughout the school. Crown Woods successfully challenged Ofsted's decision to add the school to its list of failing schools. The inspectors backed down before the case was heard in court.

## Extra-curricular activities

There are a number of clubs available, including an Amnesty International group, horse riding and chess, and pupils can attend the Pelican Club, an after-school homework club funded by the Prince's Trust. Regular trips are run to Inverliever Lodge in Scotland, which was bought by the school trust many years ago. These feature outdoor activities such as rock climbing, mountaineering and watersports. A trip to Italy or Greece is organized each year. All students are encouraged to contribute to house charities.

# Eltham Green School

**Queenscroft Road, Eltham, London SE9 5EQ** 020 8859 0133 020 8294 1890 admin@eltham_green_school.dialnet.com Anne Barton; Chair of Governors: Mrs Betty Weston Eltham **Buses:** B16, 21, 122, 126, 132, 160, 228, 328, 386 Up to sixth form: Green school sweatshirt, white polo shirt with school logo, black trousers or skirt, black shoes, plain-coloured coat; make-up not permitted, jewellery confined to small studs or sleeper earrings **Demand:** 231 applications for 210 places in 2001/2 **Type:** Community comprehensive Sports College for 835 mixed pupils, aged 11 to 18 **Submit application form:** October 2003 **Mission statement:** Aiming for Excellence **School hours:** 8.45am–3.15pm; homework clubs are available **Meals:** Hot and cold available **Strong GCSE subjects:** History, maths, RE **London league table position:** 456

## Profile

Established in 1957, Eltham Green was one of London's first comprehensives. A major programme of redecoration has improved the school's previous shabby exterior. The playing fields are well-maintained and the school recently gained Sports College status. Eltham Green has its own theatre, which is hired out to local opera and theatre groups. Although science facilities are good, the computer system was found to be in poor condition by Ofsted in 1999. Since then, a new ICT centre has opened. GCSE options include creative arts and media studies. An Eltham Green literacy summer school deals with poor standards in literacy. Gifted pupils can receive extra help, including different tasks in lessons, 'fast-track' GCSE classes in Year 10, lunchtime and after-school study sessions and by joining competitive sports teams and activities. Pupils with learning difficulties are put on the special-needs register and the school receives extra funding to provide help. Parents sign a home-school agreement to ensure that their child's punctuality and attendance is good, that they read and check homework and also attend parents' evenings. There is a prefects system. Pupils can also join the school council. Famous ex-pupils include Boy George and the singer Grace Kennedy.

## Admissions and intake

Admission is through Greenwich council. A large number of pupils – 256 at the last count – have individual education plans.

## Achievement

In 2002, only 17 per cent of pupils passed five or more GCSEs at grades A*–C. This was up on 16 per cent in 2001 and continued an upward trend. The school was ranked 14th in the borough. Ofsted inspectors noted that pupils are not achieving high enough standards by the age of 16. This is partly due to the fact that children in Year 7 are already disadvantaged, with only half gaining the expected levels in English, maths and science, and 10–30 per cent have a reading age four years below the norm. Results of Key Stage 3 tests were very low, and GCSE results are well below average in the core subjects of English, maths and science. However, the school has improved since its previous inspection in 1996, and teaching is deemed satisfactory – especially in the sixth form – with the best teaching in music and English. No A- levels were taken in 2002. Pupils are still disruptive at times, but attendance has improved with unauthorized absence down to 1.7 per cent in 2000.

## Extra-curricular activities

There is a study and homework-support centre and pupils can use the library for homework during lunchtime and after school. Clubs include astronomy and the impossible puzzle group, as well as opportunities to develop public speaking and debating skills through the Greenwich Young People's Council. School trips include a visit to Inverliever Lodge in the Scottish Highlands and Snowdonia in Wales. The school celebrates International Women's Week by inviting women speakers from various traditionally male-dominated professions, such as firefighting and cricket.

# Eltham Hill Technology College for Girls

**Eltham Hill, London SE9 5EE** 020 8859 2843 020 8294 2365 info@elthamhill.greenwich.sch.uk www.elthamhill.greenwich.sch.uk Mrs M Findlay Stone BA; Chair of Governors: Mark Payne Eltham **Buses**: 161, 314, 321 Navy blue skirt or trousers, blue and white checked blouse, school sweatshirt, navy or white socks or black tights **Demand**: 258 applications for 180 places in 2001/2 **Type**: Community comprehensive Technology College for 921 girls, aged 11 to 18 **Submit application form**: October 2003 **School hours**: 8.35am–3.10pm, 8.35am–2.30pm (Wed); homework clubs are available **Meals**: Hot and cold available **Strong GCSE subjects**: Business studies, drama, IT, PE **London league table position**: 329

## Profile

This school is situated off the busy trunk road leading out of Eltham. The school's attractive bright blue fence and gates give an aura of orderliness and good maintenance. The modern brick buildings are surrounded by playing fields and tennis courts, and there is an intercom entry system. Eltham Hill has a developing ethos, which encourages high achievement for young women, and it now has Technology College status. Pupils can take up to 10 GCSEs, including art, music, textiles, general technology and two modern languages including German, French, Turkish and Gujarati. The sixth form is small but A-level options include art, biology, business studies, French, geography, physics, psychology and sociology. GNVQ courses are available in art and design, business, health and social care and science at foundation and intermediate level, and business studies is available at advanced level. Famous ex-pupils include the actress Trudie Goodwin, who stars in the television series *The Bill*.

## Admissions and intake

Admission is through the council. When pupils join the school they are generally six months behind national expectations in their core subjects, but they tend to make fairly good progress.

## Achievement

In a 1997 Ofsted report the school was deemed to provide an effective education with vocational education seen as one of its strengths. The head was described as 'perceptive and hard-working'. Teaching was found to be satisfactory and sometimes very good, while teaching in English was consistently good. Some of the teachers were singled out as being 'very good', showing a 'very high standard' in their classroom performance. However, at Key Stage 3, standards in English, maths and science were below the national average and the standard in numeracy was poor. In 2002, 42 per cent of pupils passed five or more GCSEs at grades A*–C. This was above the borough average and the school was ranked seventh in the borough. The average A-level score for pupils taking two or more subjects was 172.2 in 2002. This placed the school fifth in the borough. At age 16, most pupils transfer to other schools or colleges to complete their education, and a campaign is running to boost the sixth form and keep it open. According to Ofsted, standards of behaviour can be poor and need more rigorous attention, whilst discipline was not consistently applied to improve behaviour or sanction disruptive pupils.

## Extra-curricular activities

A large number of lunchtime and after-school clubs include art, computing, chess, debating, gardening, maths, science, a wide range of sports and homework clubs. There is a band and a choir, and a number of concerts and drama productions are staged. A variety of school trips are organized, as well as visits to museums and galleries.

# Holborn College

**Woolwich Road, London SE7 8LN** 020 7385 3377 020 7381 3377 hlt@holborncollege.ac.uk www.holborncollege.ac.uk Mr Philip Moere Charlton **Buses:** N1, 161, 177, 180, 472 None **Demand:** Places available **Type:** Independent college of higher education, including GCSEs for 14–16 year olds **Fees:** Contact school for details **Submit application form:** No cut-off date **Motto:** *Potes tas ex valente* (Power through will) **School hours:** 8.50am–4.40pm **Meals:** Hot and cold available **Strong GCSE subjects:** Business, languages, law **London league table position:** Not available

## Profile

Holborn College recently moved from Fulham to the borough of Greenwich. It is an independent college of higher education, specializing in law, accounting and business. The college was set up in 1969 and runs a modest independent school, currently with about 20 pupils, studying GCSEs and A-levels. GCSE candidates study maths, English and science, plus options including business and law. A-level students are offered subjects that include maths, English and foreign languages. Three quarters of the college's students are from outside the European Union. Many live with host families while studying. There is provision for pupils with special needs.

## Admissions and intake

Applications should include a £500, non-refundable deposit.

## Achievement

In 2002, 70 per cent of pupils achieved five or more A*–C grades at GCSE. This was above the local and national averages and up from 50 per cent in 2001. However, the small number of pupils means results tend to fluctuate.

## Extra-curricular activities

Not applicable.

# The John Roan School

**Maze Hill, Blackheath, London SE3 7UD** 020 8516 7555 020 8516 7594 Christopher Deane MA; Chair of Governors: Ms Christine Smith Maze Hill, Westcombe Park **Buses:** 53, 54, 108, 177, 180, 202, 286, 386 Green sweatshirt, grey skirt or trousers, white polo shirt **Demand:** 300 applications for 210 places in 2001/2 **Type:** Voluntary controlled comprehensive for 1040 mixed pupils, aged 11 to 18 **Submit application form:** October 2003 **Motto:** *Honore et labore* (Through Work and Honour) **School hours:** 8.45am–3.25pm, 8.45am–2.25pm (Wed); homework clubs are available **Meals:** Hot and cold available **Strong GCSE subjects:** English, history, maths **London league table position:** 386

## Profile

Established in 1677, John Roan School is one of the borough's oldest schools. It is named after its founder, a 17th-century landowner who served at the court of King Charles I. He left his land 'to bring up so many poor town-born children of Greenwich at school'. Although the Roan trustees still administer the funds, the modern-day school is controlled by Greenwich LEA. The school is divided into two sites. The lower school is situated in Westcombe Park Road and the upper school is located in Maze Hill. The split site rather hampers the school's progress and doubles manpower and other expenditure, which means the school's budget has suffered. Consequently, many of the classes are large and games lessons have had to be reduced. However, there is a computer network linking the two schools. The school has also recently acquired two new science labs, and both libraries have been refurbished. The sixth form is run with Blackheath Bluecoat School, allowing students access to a wide range of subjects. Some pupils with special needs are withdrawn from the national curriculum lessons. However, they are still deemed by Ofsted to receive good support, particularly with reading and numeracy. The John Roan Association arranges social and fund-raising events and there is a school council.

## Admissions and intake

Admission is through the LEA.

## Achievement

The school has a good reputation as a caring environment but academically it is struggling. In 2002, 37 per cent of pupils passed five GCSEs at grades A*–C. This was up on 35 per cent in 2001, continuing an upward trend. The school was ranked eighth out of 18 in Greenwich. The joint sixth form has produced good A-level results in maths, art, photography, media studies, psychology and biology. However, these results had fallen in the last couple of years, with the average point score only 147.6 in 2002. This ranked the school ninth in the borough league table. In 1998, Ofsted found pupils to be polite, courteous and trustworthy. They also praised the racial harmony in the school. Pupils with special physical and behavioural problems are well integrated.

## Extra-curricular activities

The school has an outdoor pursuits centre in the Lake District called The Hope Memorial Camp. Built in 1989, it is a 40-acre purpose-built centre. It is used for field trips for geography and biology, outdoor activities such as walking and camping, and drama and music workshops. The school also organizes exchanges to California, Denmark and Ghana in West Africa. There is also a lively music department, where a range of instruments are taught. The school's high profile choirs have toured Europe and the US. In 1997, a group travelled to Ghana where they took part in a production with some Ghanaian students. After-school clubs include a homework and study club.

# Kidbrooke School

**Corelli Road, Shooters Hill, London SE3 8EP** 020 8516 7977 020 8516 7980 admin@kidbrooke.greenwich.sch.uk Trisha Jaffe; Chair of Governors: Dick Quibell Kidbrooke **Buses:** 89, 122, 161, 178, 386 Plain grey or black skirt or trousers, blue school sweatshirt, polo shirt with school badge **Demand:** 187 applications for 210 places in 2001/2 **Type:** Community comprehensive Arts College for 1222 mixed pupils, aged 11 to 19 **Submit application form:** October 2003 **Motto:** Learning to Succeed **School hours:** 8.45am–3.30pm **Meals:** Hot and cold available **Strong GCSE subjects:** Art, English, dance, design and technology, drama, music **London league table position:** 466

## Profile

Kidbrooke School opened as a girls' school in 1954 and became co-educational in 1981. Today it is an Arts College and liaises with nearby Thomas Tallis School. Specialist facilities include a hall with concert-standard acoustics and full lighting rig for productions. Kidbrooke focuses on the performing arts, including drama, dance, music and media studies at GCSE, in addition to the core subjects. It also offers advanced level GNVQ in performing arts, besides other vocational choices including IT at foundation level and BTEC engineering at intermediate and advanced level. A-level in media studies is also on offer. Truancy is a problem with unauthorized absence rates at 4.4 per cent in 2000. Former pupils include the opera singer Alison Hagley and actor Jude Law.

### Admissions and intake

Admission is through the LEA. Attainment level on entry is 'well below average', according to Ofsted in 1998.

### Achievement

In 2002, 29 per cent of pupils passed five or more GCSEs at grades A*–C. This was below the borough and national averages and on a par with the results of 2001. The school was ranked 15th in the borough league table. The best results at GCSE tend to be in English, design and technology, art, music, drama and dance. Although GCSE results are not very good, the school has made a lot of progress in improving pupils' literacy skills. Ofsted inspectors commended staff for their commitment to raising standards, particularly in English, art and music. However, attainment is not high enough in maths and science and too little use is made of computers, according to inspectors. A-level results have been low at Kidbrooke for some time, and in 2002 the average point score was 157.9. This was below the local average, placing the school eighth in the borough.

### Extra-curricular activities

After-school clubs include drama, music, French, dance and chess. Pupils take part in many school productions, including a whole school play each term, plus a number of other smaller drama productions and shows. Music is also a strong point, and pupils in the orchestra have practised and performed with the London Symphony Orchestra and the English National Opera. French exchange trips to Tours are arranged every year and sixth-formers have travelled to northern France as part of their leisure and tourism GNVQ work.

# Plumstead Manor School

**Old Mill Road, London SE18 1QF** ☎ 020 8855 5011 📠 020 8317 9743 ✉ Ms J Harding; Chair of Governors: Mr Frank Lerner ⇌ Plumstead, Woolwich Arsenal **Buses**: 51, 53, 96, 99, 122, 180, 272, 653 👔 Red sweatshirt and polo shirt with school badge, white shirt, grey skirt or black trousers (Years 7 to 10); the same except sweatshirt and polo shirt is jade green (Year 11) **Demand**: 405 applications for 240 places in 2001/2 **Type**: Community comprehensive Arts College for 1540 girls (mixed in sixth form), aged 11 to 19 **Submit application form**: October 2003 **Motto**: Success and Harmony **School hours**: 8.50am–3.35pm; homework clubs are available **Meals**: Hot and cold available **Strong GCSE subjects**: Art and design, business, drama, English, music **London league table position**: 446

### Profile

The Victorian facade of this school overlooks Plumstead Common. This building housed the original grammar school, King's Warren, established in 1913, which amalgamated with other schools in the mid-1970s to become the present-day comprehensive. The school gained Arts College status in 2000 and will be developing its facilities and curriculum to provide a wide choice of performing arts subjects. A new, fully equipped dance studio opened in 2001 and a theatre, complete with separate rooms for workshops and classes, is also planned. Sixth-formers are housed in the separate Negus Centre. At GCSE all students study English, maths, PE, RE, science, technology and a modern language, and select two further subjects. There is a PTA, and a system of form captains. Pupils can choose from a wide range of A-levels, including computing studies, dance, media studies, law, Punjabi, Spanish and sports studies. A wide range of work experience placements are available.

### Admissions and intake

Admissions are through the council. The average ability of pupils on entry is below average, and the school has 30 per cent of pupils with special needs, above the national average. The sixth form has 400 pupils.

### Achievement

Ofsted reported in 1999 that attainment at Key Stage 3 was below average in English, maths and science. By the end of Key Stage 4, standards were still below the national average but well above the average for similar schools. However, in national comparisons with similar schools, attainment was well above average for English. There has been a clear upward trend since the last inspection. GCSE results are below the borough average with 26 per cent of pupils passing five or more GCSEs at grades A*–C in 2002. This was nine per cent down from the previous year and the school was placed 12th in the borough. A-level point scores averaged at 168.5, below the borough and national averages. However, these results reflect the fact that the school supports students who wish to take English and maths exams, rather than restricting entry to those who are likely to score well. GNVQ results are in line with expectations. Ofsted found that pupils' behaviour is overall quite good, and they approach certain lessons – including art, drama, dance and PE – with a 'buzz of excitement'.

### Extra-curricular activities

As well as studying dance and drama as part of the curriculum, the after-school activities also lean heavily towards the arts. Pupils can learn an instrument free of charge, including the guitar, sitar, piano and clarinet, and there is a steel band and several string ensembles. After-school clubs include gardening and video as well as a homework club. There are plenty of overseas trips, including a watersports holiday in France. Pupils work with local charities.

# Riverston School

**63-69 Eltham Road, Lee Green, London SE12 8UF** 020 8318 4327 020 8297 0514 riverston@fastpo.st www.riverstonschool.ik.org Mrs S Salathiel Lee **Buses:** 122, 160, 202, 261, 278, 306, 321 Navy blue blazer, school tie, white shirt, grey skirt or trousers **Demand:** No figures available but 46 places in 2000/1 **Type:** Non-selective independent for 422 mixed pupils, aged 2 to 17 **Fees:** £2,070 per term, excluding meals (seniors) **Submit application form:** No cut off date. **Motto:** *Ut Prosim* (That I May Be of Service) **School hours:** 8.40am–3.15pm (infants), 8.40am–3.30pm (juniors), 8.40am–3.40pm (seniors) **Meals:** Not provided **Strong GCSE subjects:** All relatively strong **London league table position:** 473

### Profile

This school was founded in 1926 by two spinsters, and a year later it moved from Blackheath to its present site in Lee Green. Riverston has been owned by the Lewis family since 1956. It caters for over 450 children, including 60 pupils in the early years department, which starts at the age of 12 months, 275 pupils in the infants and juniors (ages 4 to 11), and 130 pupils in the senior school. It is an attractive collection of Victorian brick houses interspersed with more modern additions. A new expressive arts faculty was developed in 1988 for drama, music and art. Sports facilities include a fully equipped sports hall, large playing fields and tennis courts. In the senior school, pupils study art and design, English, French, geography, history, IT, maths, science, music and PE. At GCSE, all pupils are expected to gain their minimum five subjects at grades A*–C. The school prides itself on its drama department and pupils can study a GCSE in theatre arts as well as in music. There is also a student council, which liaises between students and teachers. A learning support unit helps children with learning difficulties such as dyslexia. The school aims for these children to be fully integrated into the main school community. There is a PTA.

### Admissions and intake

Pupils travel far and wide to the school. Most come from south and east London but some travel from Kent. The school takes children of all abilities and is not selective.

### Achievement

Riverston has a good reputation for helping pupils to reach their full academic potential. However, in 2002, 42 per cent of pupils passed five or more GCSEs at grades A*–C, a slight rise on 39 per cent the previous year but below the national average. The school was placed 16th in the borough league table for GCSE. Truancy is very low at 0.2 per cent.

### Extra-curricular activities

There is an after-school club until 6pm so that pupils with busy working parents can have afternoon tea, do their homework or take part in activities. A holiday club is available during the Easter and summer breaks. Pupils have regular swimming lessons and take part in football, netball, gymnastics, cricket and athletics. Sports clubs include football for both girls and boys. Pupils excel in athletics and each year a number of children represent south London in the Independent Schools Athletics Championships in Birmingham. Most pupils visit the Chateau de la Baudonniere in France, a European language centre, and during the summer holidays pupils can also visit with their families and friends. The school has a sister-school relationship with The Steward School in Richmond, Virginia, in the US and exchange trips are arranged between the two. The school is also establishing further links with Spain, Kuwait, India and Russia.

# St Paul's Catholic School

**Wickham Lane, Abbey Wood, London SE2 0XX** 020 8311 3868 020 8312 1642 headteacher@St.Pauls.greenwich.sch.uk Patrick Winston; Chair of Governors: David Prior Abbey Wood, Plumstead **Buses**: 96, 422 White shirt, blue and black striped school tie, grey trousers, black blazer (boys); White blouse, black blazer, grey skirt (girls in Years 10 to 11); Light blue blouse, navy skirt, blazer (girls in Years 7 to 9) **Demand**: Oversubscribed for 98 places in 2001/2 **Type**: Voluntary aided Roman Catholic comprehensive for 550 mixed pupils, aged 11 to 16 **Submit application form**: October 2003 **Motto**: *Labore Est Orare* (To Work Is to Pray) **School hours**: 8.45am–3.10pm; homework clubs are available **Meals**: Hot and cold available **Strong GCSE subjects**: Art, English, maths, science **London league table position**: 260

## Profile

This imposing, four-storey Victorian building overlooking the busy Wickham Lane is a very traditional looking school complete with school yard. Accommodation is fairly tight but in a good state of repair, and the school is surrounded by high security fencing. The 19th-century building previously housed a county school but there has been a Catholic school here for about 50 years. Most pupils going on to further education transfer to the Christ the King sixth-form college in nearby Charlton, another Catholic institution, for A-levels and GNVQs. Others opt to go to Bexley College or Woolwich College. There is school council and a PTA.

## Admissions and intake

The school is selective on the grounds of religion, and 94 per cent of pupils are baptized Catholics. Prospective pupils must supply a supporting letter from their parish priest when applying to school. The other 6 per cent of the school population is made up of different faiths. Four pupils have special education needs statements.

## Achievement

St Paul's GCSE scores are well above the borough average, and generally in line with the national average. In 2002, 46 per cent of pupils gained the benchmark five GCSEs at grades A*–C, a fall from 52 per cent in 2001. The school was ranked fifth in the borough league table for GCSE results. St Paul's was last inspected by Ofsted in 1995. Inspectors commented that the school 'is an orderly, caring, supportive, Christian community with a distinctive Roman Catholic ethos'. They were impressed by the pupils' good behaviour and the quality of education, noting that 'overall educational standards achieved by pupils in GCSE have been rising for some years'. Attendance is high, exclusions are rare and teaching standards are good. A particular strength of the school is the strong relationship between pupils and teachers.

## Extra-curricular activities

Given the strong Irish contingent, the school runs a Gaelic football team that draws its team members from all the different ethnic groups. The team is linked to the Dulwich Harps Gaelic football team, and 12 boys currently represent their under-14 team. School trips include an annual visit to Inverliever Lodge in Scotland for Year 7 pupils, while Years 8 to 9 visit the Arethusa centre in Kent where they take part in outdoor pursuits such as orienteering and climbing. Other school trips include skiing in Italy. Pupils are involved with fund-raising for local charities.

# St Thomas More RC Comprehensive School

**Footscray Road, London SE9 2SU** 020 8850 6700 020 8294 1855 Mr PG Murray; Chair of Governors: Mr G Peters Eltham **Buses**: B16, 21, 124, 126, 132, 160, 233, 286, 314, 321 Maroon blazer, grey trousers or skirt, white shirt, school tie **Demand**: 120 applications for 120 places in 2001/2 **Type**: Voluntary aided Roman Catholic comprehensive for 600 mixed pupils, aged 11 to 16 **Submit application form**: October 2003 **Motto**: Christ commands us 'Love one another as I have loved you' (John 13:34) **School hours**: 8.50am–3.30pm; homework clubs are available **Meals**: Hot and cold available **Strong GCSE subjects**: English, maths, science **London league table position**: 157

## Profile

This beautifully kept Roman Catholic school is one of Greenwich borough's shining stars and Ofsted inspectors gave it a glowing report in 2001. The school received over £1 million for an expansion plan and new facilities include a much-enlarged block for design technology. The food technology room was also enlarged and refurbished and a textile technology room was set up, with a joint computer area. Two new large science labs were built, as well as a drama studio and modern languages and geography classrooms. Sports facilities include the school's own gym and outdoor playing areas, but pupils can also use local playing fields and leisure facilities. The school has close links with Meadowside Leisure Centre, Footscray Rugby Club, Blackheath School FA, Cambridge Harriers, the Lawn Tennis Association and the Greenwich Basketball Association. It also maintains strong connections with parents and the community and there is a supportive parents' association. There is a school council and a designated teacher for pupils with special needs.

## Admissions and intake

The school is vastly oversubscribed. Priority is given to children with at least one Catholic parent or guardian and the family must prove that they are regular churchgoers, backed up with a letter from their parish priest. Pupils come from a catchment area encompassing a number of London Catholic parishes, but most pupils come from a three-mile radius of the school.

## Achievement

Described by inspectors as 'a very effective school with many excellent features', St Thomas More is deemed to provide a very good quality of education. Academic achievement is not only high compared with national standards, but GCSE results have been improving faster than the national average for several years. In 2002, 67 per cent of pupils gained five GCSEs at grades A*–C, well above the borough and national averages. This level of success has been consistently high over the past few years. Pupils do particularly well in English, mathematics, science, art, drama and food technology amongst others. Ofsted praised the 'excellent leadership and very effective teaching' of the school. They commented that: 'Pupils' attitudes and motivations are exceptionally strong and contribute significantly to their very good learning'. Attendance rates are excellent and truancy is virtually non-existent. A large proportion of pupils go on to further education.

## Extra-curricular activities

Pupils have the opportunity to learn a wide range of instruments, including euphonium, clarinet, flute and trumpet. The school has a band and choir, as well as a chamber choir, string ensemble, brass group, flute ensemble and recorder group. There are after-school homework clubs. Pupils can participate in a drama festival and can also enter public-speaking exams. Ofsted commented: 'Pupils are very generous in their support of charities and participate enthusiastically in local initiatives.' There are school trips both at home and abroad.

# St Ursula's Convent School

**Crooms Hill, Greenwich, London SE10 8HN** 020 8858 4613 020 8305 0560 Mrs Geraldine Scanlan; Chair of Governors: Sister E Campbell OSU Greenwich **Buses:** 53 Navy blazer, skirt, pullover, white shirt, school tie **Demand:** Oversubscribed **Type:** Voluntary aided Roman Catholic comprehensive for 600 girls, aged 11 to 16 **Submit application form:** 30 August 2003 **Motto:** *Serviam* (We Serve) **School hours:** 8.45am–3.45pm; homework clubs are available **Meals:** Hot and cold available **Strong GCSE subjects:** English, maths **London league table position:** 224

## Profile

This quiet little school has long had a reputation for academic excellence and was singled out by Chris Woodhead, former Chief Inspector of Schools, as one which is 'providing a good-quality education and achieving high standards' back in 1998. The school was a grammar school for girls, established in 1877 by Ursuline nuns. It became a comprehensive in 1977 and is now a voluntary aided school. The building is adjoined by a small convent where a community of Ursuline nuns, many of whom are teachers, live. The school has specialist rooms for science, music, art and technology and a purpose-built activities and sports hall. It has recently acquired a parish hall to provide a Year 11 common room and dining area. The school's mission statement states: 'As a Catholic school, St Ursula's has a commitment to fostering a particular ethos in the school. We aim to develop in the pupils the qualities and attitudes of a Christian way of life and an awareness of belonging to both a particular local and international Christian community.' Every class begins with a prayer. There is an active PTA that raises funds for the school. A school journal acts as a message book between school and home. There is a school council and a prefects system.

### Admissions and intake

The school is oversubscribed and girls who come from a committed Catholic family are given preference. Only a quarter of the girls come from Greenwich borough itself. In 2000, only eight pupils had statements of special needs.

### Achievement

The school's GCSE results have been amongst the highest in the borough (excluding private schools) over the past few years. In 2002, 50 per cent of pupils gained five or more GCSEs at grades A*–C, 16 per cent down from 2001 but still above the borough average. The school was ranked second of the borough for state schools and fourth in the borough overall. Results have been consistently high over the past six years. Ofsted inspectors, who last visited in 2001, deemed it a 'very effective school in which pupils make very good progress and attain high standards'. English and maths results are good, while achievement in the sciences is in line with national expectations. Teaching is 'good overall and much is very good or excellent'. Inspectors also found St Ursula's provision for the social and moral development of its pupils to be good.

### Extra-curricular activities

Exchange visits are organized to France and Spain, and Year 11 pupils have the opportunity to travel to places such as Turkey, Egypt and Italy. In 1999 pupils travelled to Prague. Visits take place to theatres, museums and concerts, and there are trips to France and Spain as well as residential field trips. The school makes good use of local facilities, such as the National Maritime Museum and the Greenwich Observatory. The school also has links with local charities.

## Thomas Tallis School

**Kidbrooke Park Road, Blackheath, London SE3 9PX** ☎ 020 8856 0115 📠 020 8319 4715 ⓔ Admin@ThomasTallis.Greenwich.sch.uk 🌐 http://members.aol.com/ttallisit R Thomas; Chair of Governors: Margery Nzerem ⇄ Kidbrooke **Buses:** B16, 21, 178, 286, 386 Dark grey trousers or skirt, light blue sweatshirt **Demand:** 470 applications for 240 places in 2001/2 **Type:** Community comprehensive Arts College for 1330 mixed pupils, aged 11 to 18 **Submit application form:** October 2003 **School hours:** 8.40am–3.20pm (A week), 8.40am–2.30pm (B week) **Meals:** Hot and cold available **Strong GCSE subjects:** All relatively strong **London league table position:** 296

### Profile

This school was established in 1971 and moved to its present site two years later. It is not the most attractive of establishments and the grounds are strewn with litter. However, brightly painted murals have been added to cheer up the exterior. Thomas Tallis took on Arts College status in 1998 and works in collaboration with Kidbrooke School. It has also been singled out as a Beacon School by the Department of Education. While Thomas Tallis concentrates on visual arts, Kidbrooke specializes in the performing arts. As an Arts College, all pupils study art, dance, drama and music during their first three years at the school. Pupils also have the opportunity to study German or Italian as well as French. There is a special language unit and a unit for the hearing impaired, a school council and a PTA.

### Admissions and intake

This is a popular school and has to turn away more pupils than it accepts every year. Recent grand aid has allowed the school to expand from 120 to 240 places in Year 7. Most of the pupils come from within a two-mile radius of the school. About 34 pupils have a statement of special needs, but 297 pupils are on the school's special needs register.

### Achievement

Pupils make good progress at Key Stage 4, especially in English, maths, history, art, business studies, drama and design and technology. Ofsted inspectors, who last visited in 1997, claimed it was 'a good school with many outstanding features' and 'an outstanding ethos'. The school has a good GCSE pass rate compared with similar schools in Greenwich, at 41 per cent in 2002. This standard has been fairly stable over recent years and just a little down on a full 50 per cent in 1996. A-level students scored an average 233.6 points, above the local but below the national average.

## Extra-curricular activities

The school prides itself on its variety of clubs and activities and has won the Education Extra Mark of Excellence four years running for its after-school clubs. These include sports clubs, breakfast clubs, photography and astronomy clubs. There is a lunchtime reading club and a homework club for younger pupils. A summer arts festival is held and lavish drama productions, such as *Romeo and Juliet* are staged. In 1999, the choir performed at St Paul's Cathedral and at the Greenwich Festival with the Township Choir of South Africa. Pupils in Years 7 to 9 can visit the residential centre at Inverliever in Scotland. There are also trips to France, Germany and Italy. Pupils raise funds for local charities.

# Woolwich Polytechnic School for Boys

**Hutchins Road, Thamesmead, London SE28 8AT** ☎ 020 8310 7000 📠 020 8310 6464 ⓔ enquiries@woolwichpoly.greenwich.sch.uk B Parker BSC, (Econ) MA; Chair of Governors: Mr Chris Jefferies ⇄ Abbey Wood, Woolwich Arsenal **Buses:** 244 Navy blue trousers, school blazer and tie, white shirt **Demand:** 251 applications for 170 places in 2001/2 **Type:** Community comprehensive Technology College for 996 boys (mixed in sixth form), aged 11 to 18 **Submit application form:** October 2003 **School hours:** 8.30am–3.15pm; homework clubs are available **Meals:** Hot and cold available **Strong GCSE subjects:** All relatively strong **London league table position:** 442

## Profile

This school was established in 1912 for boys aged 13 to 15 who were trained in vocational studies, with many of them going on to apprenticeships at nearby Woolwich Arsenal or continued studies at Woolwich College. The school has a long association with Thames Polytechnic, now called Greenwich University, and many students take degrees there. It became a comprehensive in 1975. The school was once situated in nearby Woolwich, but in 1997 it was fully integrated on to its present site in Thamesmead. It also received a £3.5-million grant for development and became a Technology College. The new building is a space-age concrete jumble of buildings with some bizarre features, including a glass-and-steel panelled roof. A new block of 10 teaching rooms was completed in 2002 along with an all-weather playing surface. It has been identified as a lead school in striking up links with several European countries and has been endorsed by the University of Greenwich for its European business course. The school has also been named as a centre of excellence for ICT. Sixth-formers can choose from a range of A-levels in addition to GNVQs in business and finance. There is a department to assist pupils with special needs.

## Admissions and intake

Admissions are through the LEA and the school is oversubscribed, with boys travelling from Woolwich, Plumstead, Charlton and Abbey Wood to attend. Many pupils start the school in Year 7 at a lower-than-average level of attainment, but their standards improve as they progress through the school.

## Achievement

Ofsted inspectors were impressed with the school's improvement during their last inspection in 1999 and stated that it is a 'successful and improving school', which has 'many more strengths than weaknesses'. At Key Stages 3 and 4, results are below the national average in English and maths but compare well with similar schools. However, standards are improving and the school is commended for its 'positive learning ethos'. GCSE and A-level results have been improving at a faster rate than nationally, although still below average, and teaching is considered to be good. In 2002, 27 per cent of pupils passed GCSEs at grades A*–C, and this level has been fairly consistent over the past six years. This was below the Greenwich average, placing the school 11th in the borough. At A-level, the average point score in 2002 was 200, above the borough average but below the national average. This placed the school fourth in the borough. Ofsted inspectors noted that behaviour in and around the school is good and that boys are 'courteous and respectful to each other and to adults'.

## Extra-curricular activities

Pupils enjoy weekend trips to Europe and several study trips per year are organized to Spain and France. A skiing trip to Switzerland is also arranged. There are outdoor activities trips to Tyn-Y-Berth in Wales, as well as field trips to Dorset and a residential PE week in Shropshire. Clubs include drama and chess, as well as sports activities.

# Hackney

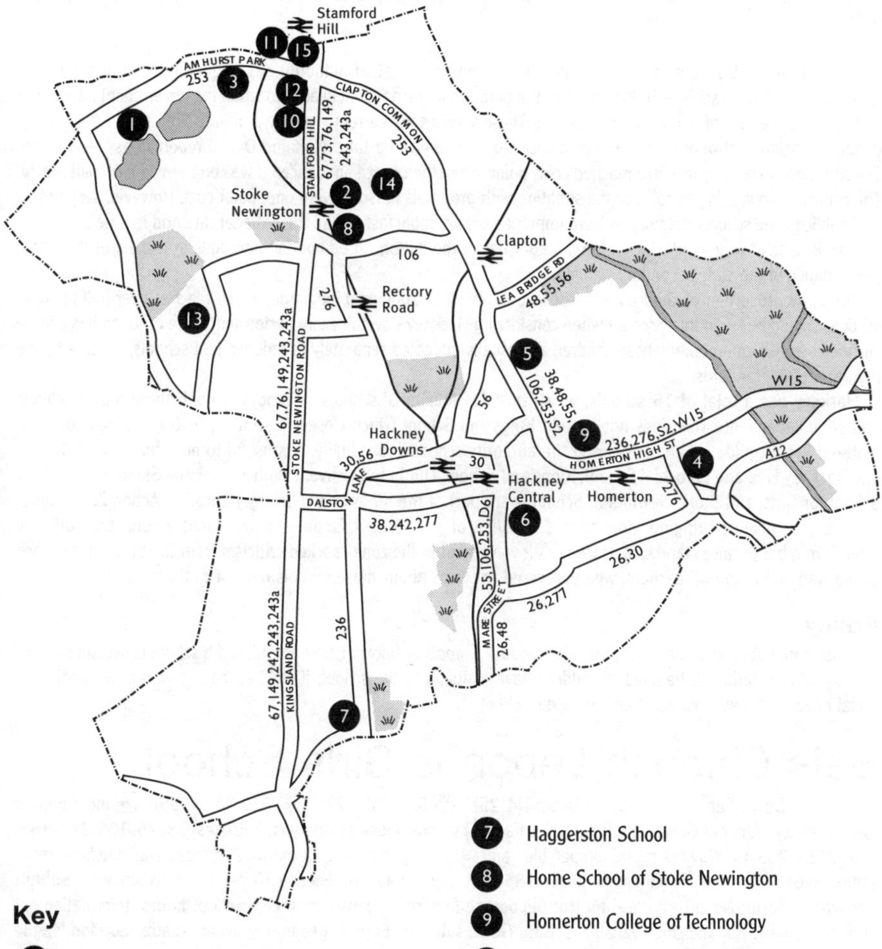


## Key

1. Beis Chinuch Lebonos Girls School
2. Beis Malka Girls' School
3. Beis Rochel d'Satmar Girls' School
4. Cardinal Pole RC School
5. Clapton Girls' Technology College
6. Hackney Free and Parochial CofE Secondary School
7. Haggerston School
8. Home School of Stoke Newington
9. Homerton College of Technology
10. Lubavitch House Senior School
11. Our Lady's Convent RC High School
12. The Skinners' Company's School for Girls
13. Stoke Newington School Media Arts College
14. Tayyibah Girls' School
15. Yesodey Hatorah School

# Factfile

**LEA: Edith Cavell Building, Enfield Road, London N1** ☎ 020 8356 5000 🌐 www.hackney.gov.uk **Director of Education:** Alan Wood **Political Control of council:** Labour **Percentage of pupils from outside the borough:** 8.3 per cent **Percentage of pupils educated outside the borough per cent:** 22.4 per cent **London league table position (out of 32 boroughs):** 31st

Hackney is one of the poorest boroughs in London and its education authority has frequently been in the media spotlight for failing its schools. In March 1999 the borough made national headlines when the government intervened and stripped the LEA of two of its five services. These services are currently run by a private firm. The LEA is now in danger of losing control of its remaining services after it received a third damning Ofsted report in as many years. The situation in Hackney in 2000 reached crisis point, when the council announced it was on the verge of bankruptcy. The council is now trying to salvage the situation with proposals for some very unpopular cuts. However, despite this bad publicity, the schools themselves have improved considerably faster than the national rate and morale within the schools is usually very good. Hackney still languishes in the bottom three London boroughs in respect of the GCSE performance of the state secondary schools.

The large proportion of children who speak English as an additional language, which reaches over half in some schools, should be taken into account when considering Hackney's overall exam performance. The borough has a large Orthodox Jewish community whose children are usually educated separately in independent schools, which all have high academic standards.

Hackney has a total of 15 schools, which includes four girls' schools, one boys' school, three mixed schools and six independents. This does not include Kingsland School which closed in summer 2003 and has not been featured in this guide. When considering the authority schools individually, it is useful to note that five of them – The Hackney Free and Parochial School, Kingsland School, Our lady's Convent High School, The Skinners' Company School for Girls, and Stoke Newington School – are part of the Kingsland Highway Education Action Zone. This is a three-year scheme bringing more than £1 million of government funding to be shared among the authority schools in a bid to raise standards. Hackney's involvement in the zone sparked criticism from the borough's branch of the National Union of Teachers, who expressed concerns about those schools left out of the zone.

## Policy

Parents should get a copy of the brochure *Secondary Schools in Hackney* from the LEA. If a school is oversubscribed, the following criteria will be used: if children have a sibling at the school; if children have a particular medical or social need; and how close children live to the school.

# Beis Chinuch Lebonos Girls School

**Woodberry Down Centre, Woodberry Down N4 2SH** ☎ 020 8809 7737 📠 020 8802 7996 Mrs Springer (senior school); Chair of Governors: Rabbi Friedman ⊖ Manor House, Finsbury Park **Buses:** 73, 76, 106, 141, 149, 243, 243A, 253 Navy skirt and jumper, blue and white striped blouse **Demand:** 27 places available September 2000 **Type:** Non-selective independent for 385 girls, aged 2 to 16 **Fees:** £20 per week (voluntary) **Submit application form:** No cut-off date **Motto:** Supporting Tomorrow's Jewish Mothers **School hours:** Information not provided **Meals:** Hot and cold available **Strong GCSE subjects:** English, geography, history, maths **London league table position:** 391

## Profile

Beis Chinuch Lebonos Girls School opened in 1989 and is a small school catering for Orthodox Jewish girls only. Mornings are dedicated to Jewish subjects such as Hebrew and Yiddish, for which the school has its own internal exams. Pupils spend the mornings studying Jewish subjects, such as Jewish law, religion, history, Hebrew and Yiddish. GCSEs are offered in English, maths, geography and history, although the girls do not study science because it conflicts with some Jewish beliefs. The school is quite small, with only five classrooms and there are no IT facilities. However, the school has a strong community feel and parents can phone the head teacher at any time. Prayers are held every morning and there is a main assembly every Friday. The head teacher is in charge of pastoral care. There is a school council and a PTA.

### Admissions and intake

As the school takes children from the age of two, it is rare that there are places available in the secondary school for children who have not already attended at primary level. Parents who are interested in sending their child to the school must contact the administrator to arrange a meeting with the school governor. Children are interviewed for places and are usually given an entrance exam. Pupils usually come from Hackney, its neighbouring borough, Haringey, and sometimes Golders Green in North London.

### Achievement

Pupils perform exceptionally well at this school. In 2002, Beis had 68 per cent of pupils achieving five grades A*–C or more at GCSE. This was an increase on 67 per cent in 2001 and only the third year that GCSEs had been taken. In 2000, 14 out of the 15 pupils who took English and maths gained a grade C or above. Similarly, 13 out of the 15 pupils who took geography gained a grade A*–C, as did 12 out of the 15 pupils who took history.

### Extra-curricular activities

The school maintains strong links with the Beth Jacob Club in nearby Amhurst Park, which is specially for Orthodox Jewish children. There are regular day trips to museums and parks and Year 11 students can take part in a three-day hike. Although pupils do not study music, there is a school choir. There are after-school homework clubs.

## Beis Malka Girls' School

**93 Alkham Road, London N16 6XD** 020 8806 2070 020 8806 1719 Mrs Wind Stoke Newington **Buses:** 67, 149, 243 Navy, green or grey uniforms, contact school for details **Demand:** Fully subscribed **Type:** Independent school for 307 girls, aged 2 to 16 **Submit application form:** No cut-off date **School hours:** 9am–4pm **Meals:** Not provided **Strong GCSE subjects:** Information not available **London league table position:** 266

### Profile

Beis Malka Girls' School caters for Orthodox Jewish girls only. Please contact the school for further information.

### Admissions and intake

Parents should apply directly to the school.

### Achievement

In the secondary school performance tables for 2002, Beis Malka had 65 per cent of pupils who achieved five grades A*–C or more at GCSE. This was an increase from 58 per cent in 2001 and the school was ranked fourth in the borough league table.

### Extra-curricular activities

Please contact the school for details of extra-curricular activities.

## Beis Rochel d'Satmar Girls' School

**51–57 Amhurst Park, London N16 5DL** 020 8800 9060 Mrs Smus None **Demand:** Heavily oversubscribed **Type:** Independent school for 675 girls **Submit application form:** No cut-off date **Meals:** Hot meals available **Strong GCSE subjects:** Art, maths **London league table position:** 522

### Profile

Beis Rochel d'Satmar caters for Orthodox Jewish girls only. Mornings are dedicated to Jewish subjects and secular subjects are studied in the afternoons.

### Admissions and intake

Parents should apply directly to the school.

### Achievement

In the secondary school performance tables for 2002, eight per cent of pupils gained five A*–C grades at GCSE.

## Extra curricular activities

There is a youth club where girls take part in sports. The girls also put on an annual show and there is a drama club.

# Cardinal Pole RC School

**Kenworthy Road, Homerton, London E9 5RB (upper school); Victoria Park Road, London E9 7HE (annexe)** ☎ 020 8985 5150 📠 020 9533 7325 Tom Mannion BA (Hon), MA; Chair of Governors: Philippa Toomey ⇌ Homerton (upper school) **Buses:** S2, W15, 236, 242, 276 Black blazer and trousers, white or grey shirt, grey pullover, school tie, black shoes (boys); navy skirt, white blouse, navy sweatshirt, black shoes (girls) **Demand:** 340 applications for 180 places in 2001/2 **Type:** Voluntary aided Roman Catholic comprehensive for 1005 mixed pupils, aged 11 to 18 **Submit application form:** Late November 2003 **Mission statement:** Cardinal Pole is a Roman Catholic school with a Christian commitment to building community through the individual care of children and staff. **School hours:** 8.45am–3.30pm, 8.45am–2.30pm (Fri) **Meals:** Hot and cold available **Strong GCSE subjects:** Double science, English, geography, IT, RE **London league table position:** 304

## Profile

Cardinal Pole is split over two sites, with the older children going to the main school in Kenworthy Road. Built in the mid-1960s, it is spacious, with a large playground area and chapel. The 11 to 14 year-old students attend an annexe set in a Victorian building close to Victoria Park. Both sites have a gym and there are four computer suites. At GCSE, child development, economics and business, German and graphic products are among the subjects on offer. GNVQs available include advanced-level leisure and tourism and intermediate-level business. Emphasis is placed on pupils' spiritual development and there is an assembly four days a week. Year 11 have work placements with city banks and local councils. Pastoral care is the responsibility of year heads. The head is strict about standards of school uniform and does not tolerate tardiness. All children are given homework diaries, which are monitored. Parents can join the Friends of Cardinal Pole. There is provision for pupils with special needs.

## Admissions and intake

Parents apply through Hackney Council, but places will only be offered to those families for whom Cardinal Pole is their first choice on the secondary transfer form. Children are admitted in the following order of priority: children from practising Roman Catholic families whose applications are supported by the parish priest; baptized children from Roman Catholic families who can show evidence of current religious practice; and children from families of non-Christian faiths whose parents or guardians are aware of, and support the religious ethos of the school. If oversubscribed, priority is given to children for whom the Kenworthy site is the nearest secondary school to their home.

## Achievement

The school's results have been in decline over the last three years. In 2002, 40 per cent of pupils achieved at least five GCSEs at grades A*–C. This was a fall from 46 per cent in 2001. This result was above the borough but below the national average. The school was ranked sixth in the borough league table. Pupils perform particularly well in English, geography, double science and RE, with more than six out of 10 pupils earning a grade A*–C in 2000. At A-level, pupils taking two or more A/AS-levels in 2002 achieved an average point score of 163.2, again above the borough but below the national average, placing the school third in the borough league table. The best results were in drama in 2000, where all pupils gained grades A–C. Pupils can also take GNVQs. Ofsted visited the school in 2001 and reported that Cardinal Pole is 'a very effective' school where 'pupils achieve very well'. Standards at GCSE were seen to be at the national average and teaching is 'good'. However, the management of special educational needs needs to be improved as does the use of ICT in lessons.

## Extra-curricular activities

Clubs available include those for pottery, trampolining, science and IT, plus exam revision and a homework club. Encouraging sportsmanship is a high priority and the school also has a band. Students go on day trips to France and take part in exchanges with Cardinal Pole's twin school in Germany. Pupils raise funds for local charities.

# Clapton Girls' Technology College

**Laura Place, Lower Clapton Road, London E5 ORB** 020 8985 6641 020 8986 4686 claptongtc@aol.con Cheryl Day B.Ed, MA (Educ); Chair of Governors: John Williams Clapton, Hackney Central **Buses:** S2, 38, 48, 52, 55, 106, 253 Lavender polo shirt or blouse, black trousers or skirt, black shoes **Demand:** 136 applications for 180 places in 2001/2 **Type:** Community comprehensive Technology College for 865 girls, aged 11 to 16 **Submit application form:** Late November 2003 **Mission statement:** Learning together, working together and welcoming the community **School hours:** 9am–3.05pm; homework clubs are available **Meals:** Hot and cold available **Strong GCSE subjects:** English literature, maths, science **London league table position:** 364

## Profile

Opened in 1916, Clapton now has five main blocks, four of which were built in the 1970s. All are equipped with their own computer suite and three of the eight science labs are brand new. The school was granted Technology College status in September 1999, bringing with it funding in excess of £200,000. A City Learning Centre opened on the site in September 2001 and is also used by other Hackney schools and the community. GCSE options available include Turkish and Bengali. Pupils can participate in the school council, which has an anti-bullying committee. Assemblies are held once a week for each year group and the whole school meets on the last day of each term and on International Women's Day. A student support centre opened in 2000 for children with special needs. Pupils are encouraged to enter into a home-school agreement, which establishes a set of ground rules for the school, the girls and their parents to follow. The Parents and Friends of Clapton School successfully campaigned against plans to turn Clapton into a mixed school.

## Admissions and intake

Parents can apply through Hackney Council while their child is still at primary school, and children are selected from all ability groups. Interviews are held to provide applicants with an opportunity to find out more about the school itself. The school is open to parents throughout October, when a main open evening is also held.

## Achievement

The social deprivation of the area it serves and the number of pupils who speak English as an additional language have to be taken into account when considering Clapton's academic achievements. Ofsted praised the school in light of these challenges, noting that 'girls make good progress in this school; the average attainment on entry is low but by the age of 16, the average GCSE point record is high for similar schools and particularly good in English, maths and science'. In 2002, 34 per cent of pupils gained five or more GCSEs at A*–C grades, up from 29 per cent in 2001. This was below the borough average and the school was placed eighth in the borough. Ofsted commented: 'The behaviour of the majority of students is satisfactory in most lessons and good or very good in some, although in too many lessons there is a low level of disruption throughout'.

## Extra-curricular activities

A vast array of activities take place after school, including clubs for homework, music, drama, sport and the arts. Sports available include trampolining, dance and football. There are Saturday morning and holiday revision clubs. The school hosts a technology conference each year. As well as science and geography trips in Britain, there are also annual trips to France and Germany.

# Hackney Free and Parochial CofE Secondary School

**Paragon Road, Hackney, London E9 6NR** 020 8985 2430 020 8533 5441 Joan Barnes; Chair of Governors: Mr R Jenkins Hackney Central Bethnal Green **Buses:** D6, 26, 38, 42, 48, 55, 106, 253, 276, 277 Dark blue sweatshirt or blazer, blue or white shirt, blue trousers or skirt **Demand:** 250 applications for 151 places in 2001/2 **Type:** Voluntary aided Church of England comprehensive Sports College for 750 mixed pupils, aged 11 to 16 **Submit application form:** Late November 2003 **Motto:** Striving for Excellence **School hours:** 8.50am–3.30pm; homework clubs are available **Meals:** Hot and cold available, including breakfast **Strong GCSE subjects:** English **London league table position:** 517

## Profile

Hackney Free is the only CofE school in the borough and is one of the oldest state schools in the country, dating back to 1520. A commitment to sport underpins the school's ethos, which encourages children to work together. Facilities include two gyms and a dance studio.The school was awarded with a Sportsmark for its commitment to PE. It receives extra funding as part of Hackney's Education Action Zone. Turkish is on offer at GCSE. The school has a strong programme for the protection of the environment. Assemblies are held twice a week and bring together two year groups at a time. Pupils can participate in the school council and become prefects, with head boys and girls appointed every year. There is a very successful peer mentoring scheme in which senior pupils counsel younger ones who are experiencing problems such as bullying.

## Admissions and intake

Parents must supply written evidence from the parish of their child's regular attendance at a CofE school. Alternatively, they must supply written evidence of regular attendance at another Christian church or proof of being a practising member of another world faith. Governors will look at whether the child has a brother or sister at the school and consider the distance between the child's home and the school. They will also take into account documented medical needs which deserve special attention. If oversubscribed, governors also follow the banding arrangements of the LEA. More than 300 pupils have special educational needs and 43 pupils have statements – well above the national average.

## Achievement

In 2002, 18 per cent of pupils gained five or more GCSEs at grades A*–C. This was well below the borough average but halted an upward trend. The high proportion of students with special needs should also be taken into account when considering the results. Ofsted visited the school in 2002 and reported that the school 'provides a sound education with clear signs of improvement'. Pupils' achievements were seen to be 'satisfactory' with 'much good teaching' although teachers were criticized for inconsistency in their expectations of pupils. GCSE results were found to be well below average but in line with similar schools, with pupils achieving well in English. However, the number of pupils gaining GCSEs needs to be improved as does levels of punctuality and attendance in Years 10 and 11. For the last three years, the school has represented Hackney in the Greater London Panathlon Championship and has reached the finals in 10 separate events, from chess to football.

## Extra-curricular activities

The school introduced an activities week in 1999 which has proved very popular. This includes trips to France and Germany, day excursions and workshops based at the school. A range of after-school clubs is also on offer, including homework clubs, and a breakfast club allowing children to make use of the library before school officially starts. Pupils raise funds for local charities.

# Haggerston School

**Weymouth Terrace E2 8LS** 020 7739 7324 020 739 8603 haggerstonschool@haggerston.hackney.sch.uk Ann Shapiro MA, NPQH; Chair of Governors: Barry Cox Liverpool Street, Old Street **Buses:** 26, 48, 55 Blue jumper, skirt, trousers **Demand:** Oversubscribed, 208 applicants for 180 places in 2001/2 **Type:** Comprehensive Technology College for 900 girls, aged 11 to 16 **Submit application form:** Late November 2003 **Mission statement:** High standards, high expectations and high achievements **School Hours:** 8.50am–3.35pm, 8.40am–3.45pm (Tues); homework clubs are available **Meals:** Hot and cold available **Strong GCSE subjects:** Drama, music, RE **London league table position:** 286

## Profile

Haggerston School was established in 1966. The school has its own ethos called the Haggerston Way, the main points of which are defined in its mission statement. In 1998, it was given Technology College status and now has outstanding ICT facilities, including a computer network system, which allows students to access their work from any school building. Haggerston has also become a Beacon School. Strong links have been formed with businesses and industry, providing pupils with the opportunity for work experience and to gain feedback from employers. Pupils can become involved in the running of the school through the pupil council. As well as having good on-site PE facilities, including a sports hall and two gymnasia, the school is close to a swimming pool and leisure centre. Assemblies are held regularly and are planned to encourage pupil participation and promote spiritual and moral development. Parents can join the Haggerston School Association. There is a provision for pupils with special needs.

### Admissions and intake

Parents apply through Hackney council while their child is still at primary school. If oversubscribed, a number of factors are considered, including whether the child has a medical need, whether she has a sister at the school and the distance she lives from the school. Students are also drawn from a range of abilities in accordance with the banding system of the LEA. As soon as a child is offered a place, they are interviewed and both parents and pupils are invited to enter into a home-school agreement, which is a list of rules for both them and the school to adhere to.

### Achievement

GCSE results have improved at Haggerston school in recent years and are higher than average for the borough. In 2002, 41 per cent of pupils achieved five GCSE passes at grades A*–C, the same as in 2001. This result was above the borough but below the national average, and the average point score was 35.2. The school was ranked fifth in the borough league table. Ofsted Inspectors visited the school in 2000 and described Haggerston as 'a very good school that succeeds in encouraging pupils to achieve the best of their ability'. Inspectors praised the 'very good leadership' and the school's 'vibrant community with learning as its focus'. Pupils were seen to be 'lively and committed learners'. There were '...rising levels of achievement across the school and particularly in Key Stage 4'. However, Inspectors commented that there were '...still some weaknesses in quality of teaching as well as the curriculum'.

### Extra-curricular activities

Activities include regular homework and study clubs, as well as a breakfast club and music tuition. Pupils go on a range of educational visits, including trips to theatres, art galleries and the Science Museum. There are also annual trips to France and Spain. Pupils participate in the normal range of sports and raise funds for local charities.

## Home School of Stoke Newington

**46 Alkham Road, Stoke Newington, London N16 7AA** ☎ 020 8806 6965 Catherine Allen BA (Hon), PGCE Stoke Newington, Stamford Hill **Buses:** 67, 73, 76, 106, 149, 243, 243A None **Demand:** 14 applications for 7 places in 2000/1 **Type:** Selective independent for 14 boys, aged 11 to 16 **Fees:** £2,937 per term **Submit application form:** No cut-off date **Motto:** I Can and I Will **School hours:** 9am–4pm, 9am–5pm (Tues–Wed, depending on teacher commitments), 9am–12pm (alternate Sats) **Meals:** Hot and cold available **Strong GCSE subjects:** All relatively strong **London league table position:** Not available

### Profile

This is a tiny school based in a 130-year-old Victorian house. It is one of the few secondary schools in London that specifically teach pupils suffering from learning difficulties such as dyslexia, Asperger's Syndrome and dyspraxia. These difficulties usually affect boys. Class sizes are small, with a maximum of eight pupils in each class, and there is one teacher for every four children. The school is equipped with textbooks that are designed for children with learning difficulties and there is an emphasis on one-to-one tuition. Pupils tend to have good spatial awareness and visual memory, so much emphasis is placed on art. Maths and IT are also strong because they rely relatively little on writing. For those pupils who are unlikely to pass their GCSEs, the alternative Certificate of Achievement is offered in English and maths. Borderline pupils are entered for both. The head encourages the development of pupils' individuality, so there is no set uniform, although pupils have been known to develop their own in the past. Pupils and staff meet every morning to discuss the business of the day.

### Admissions and intake

The school accepts children from across north-east London and sometimes beyond. Interested parents contact the school and make an appointment to view. Children are then invited to spend a week at the school on a trial basis, when they are assessed both socially and academically. Pupils tend to be of average intelligence or above and the school does not take on children with behavioural difficulties.

## Achievement

In 2001, 50 per cent of pupils passed five or more GCSEs at grades A*–C, an increase from 33 per cent the previous year. In 2000, a child who could not read or write on entering the school, achieved five GCSEs at Grade C or above.

## Extra-curricular activities

There is little demand for after-school clubs. However, there are annual trips to the coast and an activity holiday in Wales, as well as days out to art galleries and museums. Pupils participate in the normal range of sports.

# Homerton College of Technology

**Homerton Row, London E9 6EB** ☎ 020 8986 8144 📠 020 8533 1356 Mr Neil McDonough MA; Chair of Governors: Ms June Pipe ⇄ Homerton, Hackney Central **Buses:** S2, W15, 30, 38, 48, 55, 106, 236, 242, 256, 276, 277 Black blazer and trousers, blue or white shirt, school tie, black shoes **Demand:** 113 applications for 210 places in 2001/2 **Type:** Community comprehensive Technology College for 1050 boys, aged 11 to 16 **Submit application form:** Late November 2003 **Motto:** Access, Entitlement and Opportunity **School hours:** 8.40am–3pm; homework clubs are available **Meals:** Hot and cold available **Strong GCSE subjects:** Business, IT, PE **London league table position:** 474

## Profile

Homerton is the only boys' school in Hackney and it was awarded Technology College status in 1997. The extra funding from this status meant that in 1999 the school could entirely refurbish the technology block. It has good ICT facilities and there is one computer for every four students. The sporting life of the school is also very strong and Homerton won the British Schools Team Championship in 1999 for Olympic free-style wrestling. There is also a successful basketball team, and again in 1999 the school team won the national championships in both the under-15 and under-14 categories. Pupils are represented by a school council and there are plans to introduce prefects. Year groups meet every week for assembly and both form tutors and heads of year are responsible for pastoral care. There is a learning support centre for the high proportion of children with special needs.

## Admissions and intake

Parents can apply through Hackney Council when their child is at primary school. Students are interviewed but this is merely a fact-finding exercise for parents and their child. Pupils are drawn from a cross section of abilities and some travel from outside the borough to attend. Parents can find out more about Homerton at an open day for all the borough's secondary schools at Hackney Town Hall in the autumn term. Forty-nine per cent of pupils in the school have special needs.

## Achievements

In 2002, 22 per cent of pupils gained five or more GCSEs at grades A*–C. This was a fall on 27 per cent in 2001 and above average compared to similar schools, but well below the national average. The disadvantaged nature of the school's intake and the fact that a number of children join it midway in the curriculum clearly has an effect on performance. In 2000, Ofsted remarked that when 14 year-olds took their national curriculum tests that year, 40 per cent of them had only recently joined the college. The quality of teaching was praised and the attitudes and behaviour of pupils was considered generally good, with lessons being conducted mainly in a 'purposeful atmosphere'. The college as a whole was said to have a 'positive spirit' and a 'growing reputation in the community'.

## Extra-curricular activities

A wide range of activities is available outside school hours, including an early morning maths club and after-school homework clubs. For drama enthusiasts, the school has developed links with the Hackney Empire, and there is also a football club. An activities week is held towards the end of the summer term and children can go on day trips to France.

# Lubavitch House Senior School

**107–115 Stamford Hill, London N16 5RP (girls); 133–135 Clapton Common, London E5 9AE (boys)** 020 8800 0022 020 8809 7324 Rabbi Shmuel Lew Stamford Hill BR, Stoke Newington BR Manor House **Buses:** 67, 76, 149, 243, 253 Grey skirt, light blue shirt and a navy jumper or cardigan (girls); grey trousers, navy jumper (boys) **Demand:** Some spaces usually available **Type:** Non-selective independent for 228 mixed pupils, aged 2 to 17 **Fees:** Contact school for details **Submit application form:** No cut-off date **School Hours:** 9am–4.30pm **Meals:** Hot and cold available **Strong GCSE subjects:** Art, English, religious study **London league table position:** Not available

## Profile

This is a small school that caters for the Orthodox Jewish community. Boys and girls are separated and children can start at the age of two and stay until they have finished their GCSEs. Much like other Jewish schools in Hackney, part of the pupils' day is dedicated to studying Jewish law, religion and language. At midday each day, the senior school say prayers together and there is an assembly for the whole school every Friday. Both the class teachers and head teachers are in charge of pastoral care, and because children tend to start at a young age, by the time they get to senior school, the teachers know them well. There is no school council but each class has a captain, whom the pupils vote in. They are given certain responsibilities, including collecting work at the end of each lesson. The school is equipped with 30 computers and IT training is a high priority. There is provision for pupils with special needs.

## Admissions and intake

The school is strictly for Orthodox Jewish children only. There are more applications than places and pupils tend to start at an earlier age than 11. Interested parents should contact the school and arrange an interview with the head teacher. Pupils are given an exam, although acceptance into the school is not based on academic ability alone. The pupils come from Hackney and other areas across London.

## Achievement

The school sets high academic goals for the children, which they usually reach. In the GCSE league tables for 2001, Lubavitch was the fourth best performing school in Hackney, with 73 per cent of its pupils achieving five grades A*–C or more. This was down from 78 per cent in 2000. The school has a strong community feel, where children can flourish both socially and academically.

## Extra-curricular activities

After-school lectures and activities are regularly organized around Jewish festivals. There are some educational trips to museums and older children have the opportunity to go on a weekend trip away in Britain. Pupils raise funds for local charities.

# Our Lady's Convent RC High School

**6–16 Amhurst Park, Stamford Hill, London N16 5AF** 020 8800 2158 020 8809 8898 Margaret Dixon MA (Oxon); Chair of Governors: Gerald Murphy Stamford Hill, Stoke Newington Manor House **Buses:** 67, 73, 76, 149, 243, 253, 318 Royal blue blazer, blue sweater, blue skirt, blue and white checked shirt; Sixth form: Blue or white shirt, navy sweater, grey or blue trousers (boys); blue skirt, white or blue polo shirt, blue sweater (girls) **Demand:** 250 applications for 120 places in 2001/2 **Type:** Comprehensive voluntary aided Roman Catholic Language College for 670 girls, aged 11–18 (mixed in sixth form) **Submit application form:** Late November 2003 **Mission statement:** To meet the needs of all Our Lady's pupils by providing high quality comprehensive education, incorporating Servite values, within a secure and caring environment. **School hours:** 9am–3.45pm; homework clubs are available **Meals:** Hot and cold available **Strong GCSE subjects:** English, music **London league table position:** 215

## Profile

Our Lady's was the best-performing comprehensive in Hackney in 2001, repeating its success of 2000. It was established in 1904 by the Servite Sisters and has twin schools in both France and Italy. The school boasts a modern language suite, video-conferencing room and three IT rooms. A new wing, housing a department for music, design and technology, and art was completed in 2001. Pupils use the sports facilities at the Michael Sobell Sports Centre, including the ice rink and netball courts. In 1999, the school was awarded specialist Language College status, receiving funding in excess of £200,000. In 2000, it gained Beacon status. It is also included within Hackney's Education Action Zone. Pupils can study for A-levels in Japanese, Portuguese and Italian, as well as a range of other subjects. There is a strong school council, chaired by sixth-formers, and each form is given a hand in the decision-making process. The school caters well for children with special needs, especially those suffering from sight or hearing impairments. Parents can join the Friends of Our Lady's Association.

## Admissions and intake

Parents can apply directly to the school or through their child's current primary school via the LEA. Applicants are expected to supply a reference from the parish where the family worship and evidence of the child's membership of either a Roman Catholic or Christian church must also be provided, usually in the form of a Certificate of Baptism. All children are interviewed and parents are welcome to attend either of the two open evenings or any of the six open mornings.

## Achievement

Achievement at the school is usually high, with 54 per cent of pupils gaining five or more GCSEs at A*–C grades in 2002, a slight fall from 63 per cent in 2001 Pupils perform particularly well in English, and in 2000, 76 per cent gained grades A or above while 86 per cent earned one of the top three grades in music. Ofsted inspected in 2000 and praised the school's strong Christian ethos along with its success in teaching pupils about the richness of different cultures in society. Pupils can also take GNVQs in the sixth form.

## Extra-curricular activities

A wide range of lunchtime and after-school clubs include netball, maths, design and technology, reading and debating. There is also a homework club. The school holds regular extra-curriculum classes in Japanese, Portuguese and Italian for children aged 13 and over. There is a highly regarded choir, which has been invited to sing in both France and Italy. There are regular visits to partner schools in France and Italy. Pupils can participate in the Duke of Edinburgh's Award scheme and raise funds for local charities.

# The Skinners' Company's School for Girls

**117 Stamford Hill, London N16 5RS (upper school); Mount Pleasant Lane, London E5 9JG (lower school)** 020 8800 7411 (upper school); 020 8806 3128 (lower school) 020 8806 0609 (upper school); 020 8809 1382 (lower school) skinners@Campus.bt.com Jenny Wilkins M.Ed, B.Ed Hons (Exeter), FRSA; Chair of Governors: Sir Richard Butler Stamford Hill, Stoke Newington Manor House **Buses:** 67, 76, 73, 149, 243, 243A Black skirt or trousers, white shirt, black or red sweatshirt with school badge, black shoes **Demand:** 100 applications for 150 places in 2001/2 **Type:** Voluntary aided comprehensive for 850 girls, aged 11 to 19 **Submit application form:** Late November 2003 **Mission statement:** Excellence for the 21st Century **School hours:** 8.45am–3.30pm; homework clubs are available **Meals:** Hot and cold available **Strong GCSE subjects:** Art **London league table position:** 425

## Profile

Skinners' was established in 1890 by the Skinners' Company, which still has a role in the running of the school and provides funding. Girls aged 14 and upwards are based at the Stamford Hill site, where parts of the original Victorian buildings are still in use. The lower school was built in the 1920s, with a new science and technology block erected in 1995. Both sites are well-equipped with ICT facilities. The school is part of Hackney's Education Action Zone. The main feature of the Skinners' is the wide range of vocational training it offers. From age 14, pupils are able to take GNVQs alongside traditional GCSEs. At 16, pupils can study for a GNVQ at intermediate level, equivalent to four GCSEs, or at advanced level, equivalent to two A-levels. The courses available are business studies, health and social care, and art and design. A-levels are offered in English, history, maths, sociology, media studies, chemistry, biology, art, religious studies and business studies. Year 11 pupils can spend a trial week at a university.

Prefects are appointed on both sites and there is a school council. Pupils attend at least four assemblies a week, and form tutors and heads of year are responsible for pastoral care. Parents can join the Friends of Skinners', and the Skinners' Old Girls' Association holds regular reunions. There is provision for pupils with special needs.

### Admissions and intake

Parents can apply directly to the school or through Hackney Council while their child is at primary school. There are no interviews and applicants are not chosen on their level of ability. Pupils come from around 45 different primary schools, some travelling from Islington and Tower Hamlets. Open days are held in the autumn term. In 1997, Ofsted noted that six out of 10 pupils spoke English as an additional language and 'the average reading age of pupils coming to the school is consistently less than nine years [old]'.

### Achievement

In 2000, Ofsted commented: 'Whilst standards are well below the national average, the school is enabling many pupils to make good progress.' In 2002, 34 per cent of pupils gained five or more A*–C grades at GCSE, a rise from 30 per cent in 2001. The school was ranked 10th in the borough. At A-level, the average point score was 116.6, ranking the school fourth in the borough league table. Ofsted noted: 'Relationships in the school are good and the school promotes well its pupils' spiritual, moral, social and cultural development.'

### Extra-curricular activities

A range of after-school activities includes coursework clubs to help pupils with their studies. There is also a PE club, after-school homework clubs and a theatre group. The lower school has been on trips to France and Germany and the upper school has travelled to Spain and the US. Pupils raise funds for local charities.

## Stoke Newington School Media Arts College

**Clissold Road, Hackney, London N16 9EY** ☎ 020 7254 0548 Fax 020 7923 2451 e admin@sns.hackney.sch.uk Head: Mark Emmerson; Chair of Governors: Bill Sheafgreen Rail: Stoke Newington Tube: Manor House **Buses**: 73, 106, 141 Uniform: None **Demand:** 480 applications for 240 places in 2001/2 **Type:** Community comprehensive Arts College for 1170 mixed pupils, aged 11 to 16 **Submit application form:** Late November 2003 **Mission statement:** To be a successful comprehensive community school working together to inspire and empower all students to achieve their full potential. **School hours:** 8.55am–3.40pm; homework clubs are available **Meals:** Hot and cold available **Strong GCSE subjects:** Art **London league table position:** 341

### Profile

Stoke Newington School was designed in the late 1960s and emulates an American campus. It recently gained Arts College status and has a 240-seat theatre built to professional standards with lift access for disabled children. The school has received extra funding for its membership in the borough's Education Action Zone, and the LEA approved a £500,000 refurbishment of the science block. There is an emphasis on IT, with work on a £40,000 Internet suite currently underway. A new sports centre was completed in late 2001. This gives pupils access to a swimming pool, astroturf, basketball courts and a grass playing area – a rare advantage for an inner-city school. Eton fives is a popular sport and the under-15s national champion is a pupil at the school. Although there is no official school motto, pupils are taught to respect themselves, each other and their environment. If children do experience bullying, they are provided with plenty of opportunities to tell a member of staff. Pupils are also represented on a school council. The parent group SNAPS has regular meetings and organizes school fairs. Year groups meet for assembly. Support is provided for children with learning difficulties.

### Admissions and intake

There is a tight catchment area and children have to live close to the school to be accepted. Applications are made through the LEA when the child is still at primary school. Admissions are drawn evenly from all abilities and at least a quarter of pupils are in the top band. Parents interested in sending their child to the school are invited to attend open mornings or evenings.

### Achievement

In 2002, 40 per cent of pupils achieved five GCSE passes at grade C or above, down from 49 per cent in 2001, above the borough but below the national average. The school was ranked seventh in the borough league table. Ofsted inspectors last visited the school in 1998 and praised the relationships between pupils, who tended to make friends easily and treat each other with respect. Bullying is not seen as a significant problem and pupils enjoy the multicultural nature of the school. Strengths were noted in the 'extent of teachers' knowledge of what they teach' and the way 'lessons are presented in an interesting way and usually sustain the interest and enthusiasm of pupils at all levels'. Weaknesses were identified in the teaching of higher attaining pupils who are occasionally left 'marking time' and making limited progress because they are not challenged enough. Ofsted inspectors also criticized the lack of support for pupils who speak English as an additional language.

### Extra-curricular activities

There is a range of lunchtime and after-school clubs. Exchanges are organized to France and the school band has toured in Germany and Holland. Pupils also participate in the normal range of sports.

## Tayyibah Girls' School

**88 Filey Avenue, Stamford Hill, London N16 6JJ** 020 8880 0085 020 8880 0085 Mrs Nahida Qureshi Stamford Hill, Stoke Newington Manor House **Buses:** 67, 73, 76, 149, 243, 243A White and green dress, white scarf, black cardigan or green and white checked shirt, green trousers **Demand:** 30 places available in September 2000 **Type:** Non-selective independent for 228 girls, aged 4 to 16 **Fees:** Contact school **Submit application form:** No cut-off date **School hours:** 8.30am–2.15pm (Mon–Thurs), 8.30am–11.45am (Fri); homework clubs are available **Meals:** Hot and cold available **Strong GCSE subjects:** All relatively strong **London league table position:** 2

### Profile

Most pupils who attend Tayyibah are Muslim and although it does cater for pupils of other religions, the children spend a lot of time studying Islam. The school was established eight years ago and is situated in a quiet street. Space and funding is limited. This means that older children are not given PE lessons; instead they are taken to the nearby park for exercise. An extension is planned, but in the meantime there are only 13 classrooms, so pupils tend to stay in one classroom and teachers go to them. Assemblies are held every morning and class teachers are responsible for pastoral care. Pupils are given extra responsibilities by becoming class monitors. There are no computers at the school and there are no facilities for disabled children.

### Admissions and intake

Very few pupils are admitted to this school at senior level who have not already been attending at junior level. There are no entrance exams. The school has a long waiting list and children are awarded a place on a first come, first served basis. Interested parents should contact the school for an application form.

### Achievement

Tayyibah is the best performing school in Hackney. In the GCSE school league tables for 2002, all pupils who took exams at the school achieved five grades at grades C or above. At A-Level, the average point score was 325, again the best in the borough. Pupils are taught to aim high and aspire towards higher education.

### Extra-curricular activities

There are no set activities for after school. However, if children need extra help with their school work, teachers will stay behind with them or see them at lunchtimes. There are trips both at home and abroad.

## Yesodey Hatorah School

**2-4 Amhurst Park, London N16 5AE** 020 8800 8612 020 8802 2479 yeshatorah.@at.aol.com Rabbi Abraham Pinter (principal) Stamford Hill, Stoke Newington Manor House **Buses:** 67, 76, 149, 243, 253 Blue trousers or skirt, white shirt **Demand:** No figures available but 75 places (50 girls and 25 boys) in 2000/1 **Type:** Non-selective independent for 973 mixed pupils, aged 3 to 16 **Submit application form:** No cut-off date **Fees:** A voluntary contribution of £32 per week **Motto:** From the Mouths of Children You Establish Strength and Foundation **School hours:** 9am–4pm, 9am–5pm (senior boys) **Meals:** Hot and cold available **Strong GCSE subjects:** French **London league table position:** 32

## Profile

Yesodey is the largest school for Orthodox Jewish children in Hackney, and children who attend the school's primary school are given priority for places at secondary level. The two sexes are separated and girls go to a site in nearby Stamford Hill. In addition to studying for GCSEs, pupils are taught about Jewish history, law and religion. Children with disabilities or learning difficulties are welcome, and pupils are not streamlined with regards to their ability, except for certain GCSE subjects such as maths. There tends to be 25 pupils to a class and pupils usually move on to Jewish finishing school to continue their education. Mothers can get involved in the running of the school through the Ladies Guild. Assemblies are held once a week and all important events on the Jewish calendar are adhered to.

## Admissions and intake

Yesodey is strictly for Orthodox Jewish children. It is very rare that there are any places available for children who have not already attended the school at primary level. Most pupils who attend Yesodey live within 1.5 miles of the school. Application forms are available on request from the school. Parents and children are interviewed, although success is not based on academic ability but rather a sign that the prospective pupil is willing to work to the best of their ability.

## Achievement

Yesodey's pupils perform well above the national average in their GCSEs and in 2002, 84 per cent of pupils gained five GCSE passes at grade C or above. This was an increase on 80 per cent in 2001 and the school was ranked second in the borough league table. The average point score at GCSE was 55.9. Children work hard and there are no problems with discipline. Underpinning the whole activity of the school is a need to instill in pupils a strong sense of their Jewish identity. Teachers aim that they should leave with good moral and community values and have a clear idea of their career path.

## Extra-curricular activities

The school has strong connections with a Jewish youth club that arranges camping expeditions and residential educational weekends in the UK. Pupils participate in the usual range of sports.

# Hammersmith and Fulham

### Key

1. Burlington Danes CofE School
2. Fulham Cross Secondary School
3. The Godolphin and Latymer School
4. Henry Compton Secondary School
5. Hurlingham and Chelsea Secondary School
6. Lady Margaret School
7. Latymer Upper School
8. The London Oratory School
9. Parayhouse School
10. Phoenix High School
11. Ravenscourt Theatre School
12. Sacred Heart High School
13. St James Independent School for Girls
14. St Paul's Girls School

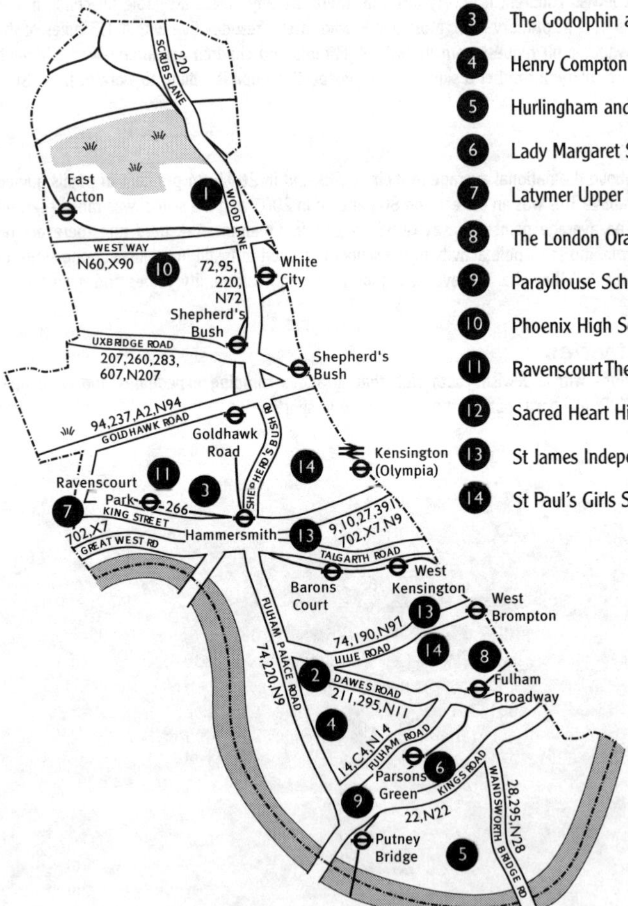

# Factfile

**LEA: Town Hall, King Street, London W6 9JU** ☎ 020 8748 3020 🌐 www.lbhf.gov.uk **Director of Education:** Sandy Adamson **Political control of council:** Labour **Percentage of pupils from outside the borough:** 28.7 per cent **Percentage of pupils educated outside the borough:** 23 per cent **London league table positions (out of 32 boroughs):** 11th

## Profile

Hammersmith and Fulham is a borough of contrasts, with some of the most expensive areas in the capital rubbing shoulders with poorer housing estates. In 2000, Hammersmith and Fulham slipped back from 16th place to 88th place in the government's index of deprivation. In the future, this may affect the council's ability to secure European Union and government grants, which poured into the borough in the four years leading up to 2000. For example, a £20–50 million New Deal for Communities grant will soon be improving north Fulham.

The borough's contrasts are reflected in its secondary schools. It has three girls' state schools, two boys' state schools, three mixed state schools, three girls' private schools, one boys' private school, one mixed theatre school and one sixth-form centre. Holborn College, an FE college in the borough, has recently moved to Greenwich while St James Independent School for Girls has relocated from Kensington and Chelsea. The private sector schools achieve consistently high results, while the state sector provides a very mixed picture. At the top end of the state sector, schools such as Lady Margaret continue to dominate, amid accusations that they are creaming off the most able pupils. At the other end of the state sector, academic achievements have been very poor, but there has been improvement in GCSE results. The government has set up the Fulham EAZ, which consists of three primary schools and one secondary school (Fulham Cross Secondary School), which aims to improve standards. Most of the state schools cater for pupils up to the age of 16. Many then transfer to the William Morris Academy, the council's sixth-form centre in Barons Court. The alternative, for many pupils, is the Hammersmith and West London College, also in Barons Court.

The borough also has Twynholm School, which is listed in the DfES secondary school performance table (but does not offer a GCSE curriculum, so is not included here). It provides the Christian ACE curriculum, leading to the National Christian Education Certificate. The borough's schools are supported by an LEA, which received a glowing Ofsted report in 2000. The inspectors wrote: 'the LEA has played a key part in helping to improve the management and quality of teaching in schools'. The LEA was found to have many strengths.

## Policy

Parents should get a copy of the brochure *Making the Right Choice* from the LEA. Criteria for admission to community schools when oversubscribed are: children with a sibling at the school; children with a medical and/or social need for that school; and children who live closest to the school. Applications for voluntary aided schools should be made directly to the schools themselves.

# Burlington Danes CofE School

**Wood Lane, Shepherd's Bush, London W12 OHR** ☎ 020 8743 4950 📠 020 8740 5659 Margaret Craig B.Sc, MA; Chair of Governors: Father Paul Andrew ⊖ White City **Buses:** 94, 95, 105, 260, 283 Grey or white shirt, navy trousers, jumper (boys); green blazer for younger pupils; navy skirt and jumper, blue striped shirt (girls) **Demand:** 310 applications for 181 places in 2001/2 **Type:** Voluntary controlled Church of England comprehensive for 1085 mixed pupils, aged 11 to 16 **Submit application form:** Mid-November 2003 **Motto:** Three Hundred Years of Educational Excellence **School hours:** 8.30am–3.15pm; Homework clubs are available **Meals:** Hot and cold available **Strong GCSE subjects:** English, geography, history **London league table position:** 433

## Profile

Burlington Danes was originally two separate schools: Burlington Girls' Grammar and St Clement Danes Boys' Grammar. Both schools moved to Shepherd's Bush in the 1930s, and in 1976 they merged to form Burlington Danes. Until 1999, the school's two main buildings were on split sites. However, following the sale of the Danes building, £5 million has been ploughed into a new teaching block and improvements to the Burlington building. The school has extensive, 10-acre grounds and offers football, rugby, netball and track and field activities. Non-swimmers travel to the nearby Janet Adegoke Centre for lessons. The library has been developed into a Learning Resource Centre and there is a new IT suite. All parents are automatically members of the parents' association and there is a school council. There are homework diaries, and newsletters are sent home. After GCSEs, 95 per cent of pupils transfer to sixth-form colleges to continue their studies. The school is partnered with the William Morris Academy. There are good links with 150 employers, including the BBC, hospitals and schools. Famous ex-pupils include Frank Field MP.

### Admissions and intake

Applications should be made jointly to the school and the borough's education department. Children of any faith are welcome, but all pupils are expected to uphold the school's Christian ethos. Twenty-nine per cent of pupils are on the special needs register.

### Achievement

Burlington Danes is mid-table compared to the borough's other seven state schools. In recent years, the school's GCSE results have varied from a high of 40 per cent of pupils achieving five or more A*–C grades at GCSE in 2001, to only 26 per cent in 2002. This was below the borough and national averages and the school was ranked 10th in the borough league table. Key stage 3 results for the last two years have been encouraging, suggesting GCSE results are likely to improve. In 1997, Ofsted found attainment was mainly average or below average. The weakest core subject was maths, where results were found to be well below average, although results are now improving. The best taught subjects were found to include English, history and geography. Ofsted found the attainment of pupils on admission to the school was mainly average or below average. A substantial number of pupils entered the school with very low levels of literacy. Inspectors praised the school's caring environment and strong sense of community.

### Extra-curricular activities

Lunchtime and after-school clubs available include homework clubs, sports, drama, music and information technology. In 1999, the Year 7 football team won the West London and Inner London championships. Girls' football is also popular. Music and drama are among the school's strongest subjects. In 1999, the school's 300th anniversary was marked by *The History Play*, written by pupils and teachers. The school also has its own steel band, orchestra, choir and gospel choir, and in 1999 pupils recorded a CD of original songs. Pupils take part in a number of fund-raising activities, including Red Nose Day and *Blue Peter* appeals. There are trips both at home and abroad.

# Fulham Cross Secondary School

**Munster Road, Fulham, London SW6 6BP** ☎ 020 7381 0861 📠 020 7386 5978 ⓔ admin@fulham_cross_secondary_school.dialnet.com Jan Cartwright MA; Chair of Governors: V Carter ⊖ Hammersmith, Barons Court **Buses:** 74, 211, 220, 295 Grey skirt or trousers, white blouse, royal blue jumper or cardigan **Demand:** 120 places available in 2001/2 **Type:** Community comprehensive for 735 girls, aged 11 to 16 **Submit application form:** Mid-November 2003 **Mission statement:** The philosophers, in their different ways, used simply to explain the world, but changing it is what it's all about. **School hours:** 8.30am–2.50pm; 8.30am–3.30pm (Tues–Fri); homework clubs are available **Meals:** Hot and cold available **Strong GCSE subjects:** Art, drama, history, textiles **London league table position:** 366

### Profile

Fulham Cross has a large, well-equipped gym and uses hard-surfaced areas, in front of and behind its Victorian school buildings, for sports. New pupils are taught in mixed ability classes until Year 8, when they are assigned to sets for English, maths, science, music and French. Sex education, including sexually transmitted diseases, assertiveness in relationships and the law, are taught as part of the school's Personal, Health and Social Education programme. Parents and guardians can choose to withdraw pupils from these lessons. All pupils undertake two weeks of work experience in Year 10. The top 10 per cent of pupils take part in an Excellence in the Cities initiative. This can involve extra exams, early entry to exams and University Summer School placements. A system of return slips for parents is used to ensure homework is completed. Pupils are also issued with school journals and parents are asked to sign the journals weekly. There is a school council, a parent-teacher association and provision for pupils with special needs. The majority of pupils go on to further education.

### Admissions and intake

Admission is by application to the school and the LEA. The main feeder schools are Fulham Primary, Melcombe Primary and Sir John Lillie Primary. The school draws its pupils from Hammersmith and Fulham and the surrounding boroughs.

### Achievement

In 2002, 43 per cent of pupils achieved five or more A*–C grades at GCSE. This matched 2001's results and the school was placed ninth in the borough league table. In 1998, Ofsted found Fulham Cross had more strengths than weaknesses. Praise was offered for the school's effective leadership, the quality of teaching and its systems for monitoring pupils progress. Standards in English at Key Stage 3 were found to have improved at a faster rate than the national average. Unsatisfactory standards were found in maths, geography and ICT at Key Stage 4 but the school is working to address these concerns. Since Ofsted's visit, academic standards have improved significantly. In 1999/2000, the strongest subjects were art, drama, history and textiles. Attendance was generally good, although a very small minority of pupils had problems of persistent truancy and/or lack of punctuality. The school is also addressing these problems, and in 1999/2000, the unauthorized absence rate was 1.4 per cent.

### Extra-curricular activities

The school's wide range of extra-curricular activities was praised by Ofsted. Drama is a particular strength of the school, with regular performances taking place. Visits to the school by the Rambert Ballet Company are also a regular feature. Good links with Fulham FC and the London Towers allow pupils to develop their soccer and basketball skills. The Duke of Edinburgh's Award scheme is offered for girls in Years 10 and 11. There are trips both at home and abroad.

## The Godolphin and Latymer School

**Iffley Road, Hammersmith, London W6 0PG** ☎ 020 8741 1936 📠 020 8746 3352 ✉ Registrar@godolphinandlatymer.com 🌐 www.godolphinandlaytmer.com ✎ Miss Margaret Rudland B.Sc; Chair of Governors: Mrs L Patten ⊖ Hammersmith Broadway, Ravenscourt Park **Buses:** 9, 10, 27, 33, 72, 190, 211, 220, 266, 267, 283, 295, 391 👕 Up to sixth form: Grey skirt, pink and white striped blouse, grey sweatshirt **Demand:** Five applications for every place **Type:** Selective independent for 705 girls, aged 11 to 18 **Fees:** £3,115 per term, plus £147 per term for music lessons **Submit application form:** End of November 2003 **Motto:** Free and Loyal Thou Art **School hours:** 8.35am–3.50pm **Meals:** Hot and cold available **Strong GCSE subjects:** French **London league table position:** 12

### Profile

Godolphin and Latymer was built in 1861 as the Godolphin School, a boarding establishment for boys. It became an independent day school for girls in 1905 with the help of the Latymer Foundation. From 1951 it held voluntary aided status, reverting to full independent status in 1977. Recently the school opened up a new block, which provides many new classrooms, technology labs, a pottery room, a new sixth-form common room and a food service area. Hockey and tennis are played on an all-weather surface and pupils travel to nearby Latymer Upper School for swimming lessons. The art facilities include three studios, a graphics room and a photography dark room. There is a school-wide network, two computer rooms and multimedia machines in the library. For the first three years, pupils study 16 subjects including English, French, history, maths, physics and drama. In the second year, they can add Latin or German, with Spanish and Russian available in the fourth year. A wide choice of subjects is also on offer at A-level. There is a school council and parent-teacher association. An annual parents' meeting is held and there are two annual reports. Famous ex-pupils include television presenter Davina McCall, singer Sophie Ellis-Bexter, actress Kate Beckinsale and Professor Susan Greenfield, president of the Royal Institution.

### Admissions and intake

The school takes pupils from across the UK and abroad, on a competitive basis. Application forms must be submitted with a £50 fee by November for admission the following September. Written exams in English and maths take place in January, followed by two interviews. Offers are made in March. Five or six bursaries are available each year.

## Achievement

The school's exam results at GCSE and A-level are outstanding in all subjects. In 2002, 100 per cent of pupils gained five or more A*–C grades at GCSE, one per cent up on 2001's results. The average point score was 59.7, placing the school second in the borough. In 1999, of the 100 pupils who sat GCSE French, 71 achieved an A* grade and the remaining 29, an A grade. A-level results are also excellent, with an average point score of 401.4 for pupils taking two or more A/AS-levels in 2002. A high proportion of girls go on to the leading universities, many first taking a year out to travel to countries such as India, Nepal and South America.

## Extra-curricular activities

An impressive range of clubs and societies is offered. Chess, computing and the Classics are available along with music, sport and drama activities. There are three choirs, an orchestra and several ensembles. Formal evening concerts are staged both by pupils and with the Latymer Upper School. Day trips to exhibitions, galleries and concerts are arranged, as well as geography and biology field courses. Foreign exchanges include visits to Germany, France and Russia. Large numbers of girls take part in the Duke of Edinburgh's Award scheme. The school provides a Christmas party for the elderly people in Hammersmith.

# Henry Compton Secondary School

**Kingwood Road, Fulham, London SW6 6SN** 020 7381 3606 020 7386 9645 admin@henrycompton.dialnet.com Dinesh Ramjee B.Sc, PGCE; Chair of Governors: Joan Christmas Putney Bridge, Parsons Green **Buses**: 74, 211, 220, 295 Black blazer, black trousers, white shirt, navy V-neck jumper, black shoes **Demand**: 120 places in 2001/2; demand has been growing year on year **Type**: Community comprehensive for 531 boys, aged 11 to 16 **Submit application form**: Mid-November 2003 **Mission statement**: Henry Compton is a multicultural community of learners whose sights are set on personal and group achievement. It supports its members' endeavours to take charge of their own learning and draws on all of the resources of the community that it serves to enrich and legitimize that learning. It is the entitlement of all its members that they should experience success within a community which values their efforts and celebrates their diversity. **School hours**: 8.30am–3pm; homework clubs are available **Meals**: Hot and cold available **Strong GCSE subjects**: Art, PE **London league table position**: 478

## Profile

Henry Compton School is on a four-acre site near Fulham Palace Road. It consists of two buildings dating from the early 1900s, with later additions. There are newly refurbished science laboratories and a library with computers. A £2.2-million high-tech and City Learning Centre recently opened, bringing an extra 60 computers to the school, plus food technology, graphics and fabrics facilities. The school also has music facilities and a state-of-the-art recording studio. For sport, pupils use nearby Bishops Park or the Lillie Road Recreation Centre or travel to Barn Elms. All pupils follow the core subjects of English, maths and science, plus foundation subjects including history, geography, Spanish, music and art. Parents are required to sign homework diaries. Year 10 pupils spend two weeks on a work experience programme. Each spring term, the school allows employers to hold mock interviews with pupils and run workshops. Employers represented include theatre companies, the fire brigade, the Metropolitan Police and hospitals. There is a school council and a prefect system. Provision is made for pupils with special needs. Famous ex-pupils include Olympic athlete Linford Christie.

## Admissions and intake

Pupils are drawn from across west and central London. The procedure involves submitting forms to the school and the LEA. There is an entrance test for setting purposes.

## Achievement

In 1996, Henry Compton was put on 'special measures'. The LEA appointed a new head teacher, John Hayes, who successfully turned the school around, improving pupils' behaviour, attendance and GCSE results. The school came off special measures in 1998 and in 2001, Ofsted judged it to have made 'much improvement' with 'good teaching' and GCSE results well above those of similar schools. In 2002, 29 per cent of pupils achieved five or more A*–C grades, maintaining the standard of 2001. The school was ranked 14th in the borough.

### Extra-curricular activities

All year groups have their own football teams, which compete at the highest level in London. Pupils also have a solid record in athletics. In 2000, 27 pupils were chosen to represent the borough in a London-wide athletics competition. Good links with Fulham FC and Chelsea FC have helped develop pupils' soccer skills. The art department offers ceramic and clay work, printmaking and photography. The music department runs an orchestra and a choir, and individual tuition is also available. Pupils can take advantage of after-school homework clubs.

## Hurlingham and Chelsea Secondary School

**Peterborough Road, Fulham, London SW6 3ED** 020 7731 2581 020 7736 7455 Miss V Gerber; Chair of Governors: Rosemary Radcliffe Parsons Green **Buses:** 74, 211, 220, 295 Royal blue jacket, black trousers, black skirt, white shirt or blouse, royal blue jumper, black anorak **Demand:** 240 places in 2001/2; oversubscribed **Type:** Community comprehensive for 1002 mixed pupils, aged 11 to 16 **Submit application form:** Mid-November 2003 **School hours:** 8.10am–2.10pm (plus one optional hour of enrichment from 2.30pm, Mon–Thurs); homework clubs are available **Meals:** Hot and cold available **Strong GCSE subjects:** Art, design and technology, drama, English, French, music **London league table position:** 463

### Profile

After a decade in the doldrums, Hurlingham and Chelsea School appointed former head teacher Michael Murphy in 1994. Under his leadership, the school went from strength to strength and is now oversubscribed. Former Chief Inspector of Schools, Chris Woodhead, named it as one of the most improved schools in the UK. The school has been awarded specialist status to concentrate on music, drama, art and textiles. It is also taking part in the Excellence in Cities scheme, focusing on improving attendance, punctuality and behaviour. Its modern facilities have been upgraded with a £750,000 arts centre and a £400,000 maths block. Other facilities include a video editing centre and a well-stocked library with Internet access. The school is unique in the borough in offering a continental school day. From Monday to Thursday at 2.30pm there is an extra enrichment hour of teaching, with staff working unpaid to provide 90 supplementary lessons. In addition to the core subjects, pupils can study dance, ceramics and media studies. Year 10 pupils have two-week work experience placements. There are also talks by trade unionists and career discussions in the Personal and Social Education Programme. Parents are asked to check homework diaries and there is a parent-teacher association. Hurlingham and Chelsea is partnered with the William Morris Academy, where many pupils continue their studies.

### Admissions and intake

Applications are submitted jointly to the school and the LEA. Staff visit feeder primary schools to help ensure the transition is smooth. More than 20 per cent of pupils are on the special needs register.

### Achievement

In 1997, Ofsted inspectors praised the improvements following their visit in 1994, which had led to the school being placed on special measures. The head teacher was found to have transformed the school and responded to the last Ofsted report with 'vigour and determination'. The school's results seen improvement over the last four years but it is still towards the bottom of the borough's state schools table. In 2002, 23 per cent of pupils achieved five or more A*–C grades at GCSE, a fall from 32 per cent in 2001. Ofsted found the strongest GCSE subjects to be music, art, English, French, drama and design and technology. Inspectors reported the teaching to be satisfactory or better in 92 per cent of lessons. They also said the moral, social and cultural development of pupils was sound.

### Extra-curricular activities

Sport is actively pursued, especially football, rugby, netball, tennis and cricket. The IT rooms are open at breaktimes and lunchtimes for pupils to do homework and coursework. There are also after-school homework clubs. Saturday morning music classes are open to all pupils, and there are termly concerts. Drama clubs at Key Stages 3 and 4 offer the chance to explore the technical side of theatre as well as performance. There are trips both at home and abroad.

# Lady Margaret School

**Parsons Green, Fulham, London SW6 4UN** ☎ 020 7736 7138 📠 020 7384 2553 🌐 www.ladymargaret.hammersmith-fulham.sch.uk ✉ Mrs Joan Olivier BA; Chair of Governors: Mr Richard Waterhouse ⊖ Parsons Green **Buses:** 14, 22, 28, 239, 295 👔 Up to sixth form: Black blazer with red pin-stripe, red pin-striped shirt, black sweatshirt with school logo, kilt-style skirt, low-heeled shoes, red pin-stripe dress. Sixth formers wear their own clothes. **Demand:** 651 applications for 90 places in 2001/2 **Type:** Voluntary aided comprehensive for 560 girls, aged 11 to 18 **Submit application form:** Mid-November 2003 **School hours:** 8.30am-3.30pm **Meals:** Hot and cold available **Strong GCSE subjects:** Art, English, modern languages, RE **London league table position:** 74

## Profile

Lady Margaret School was named after Lady Margaret Beaufort, mother of Henry VII and an educational benefactor. A new technology building was opened in 1994, and a 10-classroom block opened in 1997. The school has launched a £150,000 renovation appeal. Parents are also expected to pay £75 per year towards repairs. Lady Margaret lacks its own sports grounds, with just three netball courts, a gym and a hall on site. Tennis is played at Hurlingham Park. Years 10 and 11 go to a recreation centre in Barnes for rowing on the Thames and hockey. There is a well-equipped library and a computer network allows filtered access to the Internet. The curriculum's emphasis is on a balanced mix of arts, sciences and other subjects. A total of 16 courses are offered at A-level, including fine art, sociology and sport studies. One-week work experience placements are organized for Year 10 pupils. Under the Excellence in Cities scheme, extra tuition is provided for the top 10 per cent of pupils. The PTA is very active and parents receive a weekly newsletter. Famous ex-pupils include Janet Street-Porter. There is provision for pupils with special needs and also a school council.

## Admissions and intake

Candidates sit assessment tests in December to determine banding. Each year, the school looks for 24 pupils of above average ability, 50 of average ability and 16 of below average ability. The school does not prioritize siblings or applicants from church primary schools. A total of 45 places of the 90-strong intake are reserved for children from church-going families. References from vicars are required. There are 35 places that go to open place applicants – children from families who are not necessarily church-going, but who respect the school's Anglican ethos. Ten places go to 'World Faith' applicants, who need references from their priest, mullah or other religious teacher. In all cases, primary school references are also required.

## Achievement

Lady Margaret is the top achieving girls' state school in Hammersmith and Fulham. Ofsted visted the school in 2001 and found it to be 'very effective' with 'many outstanding features'. Pupils were seen to receive 'a high quality education'. In 2002, 90 per cent of pupils achieved five or more A*–C grades at GCSE and the school was ranked fifth in the borough league table. Lady Margaret is also the top-performing state school for A-levels, with a point score of 330.2 for pupils taking two or more A/AS-levels. Over the years, results have been good in English, modern foreign languages, art and religious education, and only slightly less impressive in maths and science. Ofsted wrote: 'staff know pupils well and the ethos of the school is one of care and concern for individuals'.

## Extra-curricular activities

Activities available include bridge lessons and lateral thinking classes. The school boasts three choirs, an orchestra, a swing band, a string ensemble and wind and brass groups. In 2001, there was a trip to America. Year 9 pupils take part in a French exchange programme, and A-level art pupils visit Florence and Sienna. Grants are available for school trips. Pupils do the normal range of sports.

# Latymer Upper School

**King Street, Hammersmith, London W6 9LR** ☎ 020 8741 1851 📠 020 8748 5212 ✉ registrar@latymer-upper.org 🌐 www.latymer-upper.org ✉ P Winter; Chair of Governors: John Bullock ⊖ Ravenscourt Park, Hammersmith Broadway **Buses:** 9, 33, 72, 237, 267, 290 **Uniform:** Compulsory up to sixth form: black blazer with badge, white shirt, black trousers **Demand:** Six applications for every place **Type:** Independent for 967 boys (mixed in sixth-form), aged 11 to 18 **Fees:** £3,160 per term Music lessons £139 per term. **Submit application form:** No cut-off date **Motto:** *Paulatim ergo certe* (Slowly Therefore Surely) **School hours:** 8.40am–3.20pm **Meals:** Hot and cold available **Strong GCSE subjects:** Chemistry, English, English literature, geography, maths, Spanish **London League table position:** 53

### Profile
Latymer Upper is an excellent school that prides itself on its impressive academic results but also stresses the importance of social development. Founded in 1624, the school moved to its present site in Hammersmith in 1895. Part of the site is shared with the Latymer Preparatory School, which admits pupils from the age of seven. A new arts centre was added four years ago and offers pupils the chance to perform on stage in a 300-seat theatre or work in a large art studio. A total of 27 A-level subjects is offered, including classical civilization, history of art and Spanish. Pupils can take several AS-level subjects, and up to four to A-levels. There is an active PTA that raises funds to subsidize the cost of school trips for children from less well-off families. Famous ex-pupils include Hugh Grant, Mel Smith, Alan Rickman, Keith Vaz, Larry Whitty and Dan Luger.

### Admissions and intake
Entry to Latymer Upper can be to the prep school at the age of seven or to the upper school at 11, 13, or 16. Exams in English, maths and verbal reasoning are set for 11-year-olds, 13-year-olds sit the Common Entrance Exam, and 16-year-olds are admitted by interview and reference. Girls are admitted to the sixth form. Open days are held in October and November. The school is run by the Latymer Foundation, which offers bursaries and scholarships for academic subjects, music, sport, drama and art. A range of scholarships paying up to half of the fees are available and currently one third of the pupils benefit from these. There are also foundation places awarded on academic merit and means-testing.

### Achievement
Latymer Upper has an excellent academic record. In 2002, 97 per cent of pupils achieved five or more A*–C grades at GCSE. This was two per cent down on 2001 and the school was ranked third in the borough. At A-level, the average point score was 360.1 for those pupils taking two or more A/AS-levels, again ranking the school third in the borough league table. In 1999, out of a total of 1343 GCSE entries, only 13 results were below grade C. The strongest subjects were English Language, English Literature, chemistry, maths, Spanish and geography. In that same year, A-level results showed high achievements in English, maths and physics, with more than half of the candidates achieving A and B grades. Pupils fared slightly worse in business studies and French, but the overall pass rate was 99 per cent. Over the last three years, one in 10 sixth-formers has gone on to Oxford or Cambridge.

### Extra-curricular activities
Sport, performing arts and music feature strongly in the school's extra-curricular activities. Soccer and rugby are popular, and there is the chance to row on the River Thames. The new arts centre offers a fantastic facility for budding actors and technical crew, and in addition the school has its own orchestras and choirs. MPs regularly visit the school to take part in question-and-answer sessions with pupils. Pupils engage in fund-raising for local charities.

## The London Oratory School

**Seagrave Road, Fulham, London SW6 1RX** ☎ 020 7385 0102 Fax 020 7381 7676 ✉ admin@london-oratory.org 🌐 www.london-oratory.org Mr John McIntosh OBE, MA, FRSA; Chair of Governors: Rev Ignatius Harrison 🚆 West Brompton ⊖ West Brompton, Fulham Broadway **Buses:** C1, C3, C4, 11, 14, 28, 74, 190, 211, 295, 328, 391 Black blazer, grey trousers, white shirt, black and red school tie, black shoes **Demand:** 160 places in 2001/2; heavily oversubscribed **Type:** Voluntary aided Roman Catholic comprehensive for 1360 boys (354 in mixed sixth form), aged 7 to 18 **Submit application form:** Mid-November 2003 **Motto:** *Respice finem* (Keep the End in Mind) **School hours:** 8.40am–2.45pm **Meals:** Hot and cold available **Strong GCSE subjects:** Art, German, history, Latin, physics, RE, Spanish **London league table position:** 95

### Profile

The Fathers of the London Oratory in Brompton, Knightsbridge, opened their first school in the City in 1852. A school for boys was established in Chelsea in 1863, and after a series of mergers, the school moved to its present site in 1970. New additions to the school buildings have included an arts centre, a chapel and Junior House. On-site sports facilities include a large gym, an indoor swimming pool and a fitness centre. Pupils travel to sports fields in Barnes for rugby, hockey, cricket and athletics. The school's impressive academic results and its strong Christian ethos have led to intense competition for places. Prime Minister Tony Blair's eldest son was a pupil at the school and his youngest son is still there. RE is obligatory. Music is especially important, and for the first three years there are two music lessons a week; it only becomes optional in the fourth form. There is a school council. There is provision for pupils with special needs.

### Admissions and intake

Pupils and their parents are expected to be practising Roman Catholics and parish priests are asked to endorse applications. Candidates with siblings at the school, with a parent employed at the school, and who are involved in the work of the Oratory Parish are favoured. Applications should be returned to the school by November for entry the following September. Interviews are held between October and December and places offered in January. There are 100 pupils on the special needs register and 16 of these have statements, which is below the national average.

### Achievement

The London Oratory is one of the top performing state schools in Hammersmith and Fulham, and indeed, in the UK. In 2002, 88 per cent of pupils achieved five or more A*–C grades at GCSE. This placed the school seventh in the borough. At A-level, the average point score was 305.8 for those pupils taking two or more A/AS-levels, again ranking the school seventh in the borough. In 2000, Ofsted commented: 'the London Oratory School is a very good school with many strengths and few weaknesses. Pupils and students are keen to learn and they achieve very high standards in most of their work.' The best GCSE results in 1999 were in Latin, physics, art, Spanish, religious education, German and history. All other subjects received grades that were well above the national average. No significant weaknesses were seen in any subject.

### Extra-curricular activities

The school has four choirs, an orchestra, a chamber orchestra, junior strings, a concert band and several chamber groups. There is also a range of societies, the cadet force and modern language clubs. School journeys, visits and cultural activities have included tours of the First World War and American Civil War battlefields. Pupils can also take part in retreats and raise funds for local charities. The normal range of sports is on offer.

## Parayhouse School

**New Kings School Annexe, New Kings Road, London SW16 4LY** 020 8740 6333 020 8740 6333 Sarah Jackson **Buses:** N22,22 Navy trousers, jumper and tie, white shirt **Demand:** Information unavailable **Type:** Special school for up to 30 children with speech, language and communication difficulties, aged 8 to 16 **Submit application form:** No cut-off date **School hours:** 9am–3.30pm **Meals:** Hot and cold available **Strong GCSE subjects:** All relatively strong **London league table position:** Not available

### Profile

Parayhouse Special School transferred to the site of the defunct Ellerslie Primary School in September 1999 from its previous home, a church in Kensington and Chelsea. Links have been established with nearby Queens Park Rangers FC, and pupils visit the Janet Adegoke Leisure Centre for swimming classes. There is a parent-teacher association. Pupils with moderate learning difficulties attend the school.

### Admissions and intake

Pupils attend the school from 12 local authorities across London.

### Achievement

All pupils sit GCSE subjects.

### Extra-curricular activities

Pupils take part in the regular range of sports and there are school trips both at home and abroad.

# Phoenix High School

**The Curve, Shepherd's Bush, London W12 0RQ** 020 8749 1141 020 8740 0393 admin@the_phoenix_school.dialnet.com William Atkinson MA, FRSA; Chair of Governors: Mrs Viv Bird White City, Shepherd's Bush **Buses:** 94, 95, 105, 260, 283 Black blazer, burgundy jumper or sweatshirt, black trousers or skirt, white shirt, school tie **Demand:** 180 places available in 2001/2 **Type:** Community comprehensive for 913 mixed pupils, aged 11 to 16 **Submit application form:** Mid-November 2003 **Motto:** Strength through Knowledge **School hours:** 8.40am–3.30pm **Meals:** Hot and cold meals including breakfast **Strong GCSE subjects:** Art **London league table position:** 458

### Profile

Phoenix High rose from the ashes of The Hammersmith School, which received a damning Ofsted report in 1995, pointing to high levels of truancy, bad behaviour and dismal exam results. New head teacher William Atkinson was appointed to turn the school around. He renamed it, replaced a quarter of the teaching staff and introduced 'tough but fair' policies. His efforts are paying off, with lower truancy and expulsion rates, but there is still some way to go. Mr Atkinson's popularity with parents has resulted in a more balanced school population, and academic achievements are climbing as a consequence. Facilities on the spacious, 10-acre site include a theatre, a technology suite, six gymnasia, an extensive new library and a newly refurbished music suite. On joining the school, all pupils follow the core subjects of English, maths and science, plus foundation subjects including art, history, geography and drama. The modern languages offered are French or Spanish. In Year 9, pupils select their GCSE subjects, with careful guidance from teachers. There is a school council and provision for pupils with special needs. Famous ex-pupils include footballers Les Ferdinand and Dennis Wise, and millionaire businessman Ram Gidoomal.

### Admissions and intake

Parents and pupils attend an informal interview with Mr Atkinson, followed by a meeting with teachers at which the school's philosophy, expectations and code of conduct are explained. As with all county schools, priority is given to those applicants with siblings already at the school, those with medical and social needs, and those nearest the school. The principle feeder primary schools are in Shepherd's Bush and White City but Phoenix High draws pupils from across the borough.

### Achievement

In 2002, 25 per cent of pupils achieved five or more A*–C grades at GCSE. This placed the school 11th in the borough league table and was 14 per cent up on the results of 2001. In the past, the school has accepted large numbers of refugee children, many of them with a limited grasp of English. In these circumstances, it is hardly surprising that its GCSE results are low. After visiting the school in 2001, Ofsted found that the school '..has improved in the last five years but standards are still too low'. They praised the 'dynamic leadership' of the head teacher and commented that '...assessment and target setting to raise standards are good'. Pupils with special needs make good progress. However, there are 'serious weaknesses in recruitment and retention of teaching staff' and the school's achievement is hampered by low attendance rates.

### Extra-curricular activities

There are after-school exam revision classes, maths club, chess club and numerous sports clubs. Pupils also take part in the Duke of Edinburgh's Award scheme. Residential trips in recent years have been to Devon and Paris.

# Ravenscourt Theatre School

**Tandy House, 30–40 Dalling Road, Hammersmith, London W6 0JB** 020 8741 0707 020 8741 1786 Ravenscourttheatreschool@hotmail.com www.ravenscourttheatreschool.co.uk John Roper; Chair of Governors: Sir Robin Philips Ravenscourt Park **Buses:** 9, 10, 27, 33, 72, 190, 211, 220, 266, 267, 283, 295, 391 Green and yellow blazer, black or grey trousers, green pinafore, pale yellow shirt or blouse **Demand:** In September 2000, there were 85 pupils at the school **Type:** Theatre school for 84 mixed pupils, aged 7 to 16 **Fees:**

£1,550 per term **Submit application form:** No cut-off date **School hours:** 8.45am–4pm **Meals:** Hot and cold available **Strong GCSE subjects:** Arts, drama, music **London league table position:** 465

## Profile

Sir Robin Phillips, who founded the school in 1989, previously ran the Corona Academy. Many of the traditions of Corona, including the structure of academic studies in the morning, followed by drama, dance and singing in the afternoon, were built into Ravenscourt. The school aims to develop its pupils' talents to help them launch a career in theatre, television and film. All pupils are exclusively contracted to the school's own agency, which seeks work in BBC and independent television, the West End, feature films and commercials. The school has extensive digital post-production facilities to create drama, documentary and music videos. Sports facilities are limited, with supervised groups of pupils taken to nearby Ravenscourt Park to play football and cricket. Producers and casting directors are encouraged to visit the school to see the pupils training. Eight subjects are taken to GCSE level on a compulsory basis: English language and literature, maths, history, French, art, media studies and drama. Pupils can also take computer studies, RE and general knowledge. Pupils are regularly tested by examiners from the London Academy of Music and Dramatic Art (LAMDA). The parent-teacher association meets regularly and there are homework diaries. Pupils can join the school council. Famous ex-pupils include Susan George, Denis Waterman and Danielle Denby-Ashe.

## Admissions and intake

The school draws pupils from across the UK and abroad. Entrance is by interview and audition. Demonstrations of prepared work are welcome, but prospective pupils will also be expected to improvise.

## Achievement

In 2002, 14 per cent of pupils achieved five or more A*–C grades at GCSE. This was down from 33 per cent in 2001 and the school was ranked 13th in the borough league table. However, the school's primary aim is to prepare children for a career in show business, and that is what it does well. After completing their GCSEs, pupils move on to other performance arts institutions such as Rada, Lamda and the Arts Educational School in Chiswick. Some go directly into work from the school. As well as the UK, pupils have worked in Hollywood, Russia and Zimbabwe.

## Extra-curricular activities

Ravenscourt runs a Saturday School, evening classes and a summer course. Private tuition is also available in all subjects. School trips are arranged to places of interest, for example the Globe Theatre and the Science Museum. The normal range of sports is on offer.

# Sacred Heart High School

**212 Hammersmith Road, Hammersmith, London W6 7DG** ☎ 020 8748 7600 Fax 020 8748 0382 e admin@_heart_high.dialnet.com www.sacredhearthighschool.org.uk Dr Christine Carpenter; Chair of Governors: Sister Elizabeth Smith ⊖ Hammersmith Broadway **Buses:** 9, 10, 11, 27, 72, 266, 295 Blue blazer, skirt, jumper, sweatshirt, white blouse **Demand:** Figures unavailable; oversubscribed **Type:** Voluntary aided Roman Catholic comprehensive for 777 girls, aged 11 to 16 **Submit application form:** Mid-November 2003 **Mission statement:** Above all else, this community works together to bring one another to an awareness of the fullness and meaning of their life, rooted in the love of God. **School hours:** 8.45am-3.15pm **Meals:** Hot and cold available **Strong GCSE subjects:** History, science, Spanish **London league table position:** 93

## Profile

Sacred Heart was built on a site whose Catholic traditions date from 1609, when a convent was set up with the help of Catherine of Braganza, wife of Charles II, who introduced the first in a series of four different orders of teaching nuns. The present buildings date from 1884 and were designed by John Francis Bentley, the architect of Westminster Cathedral. It became a grammar school in 1948, and a comprehensive in 1976. In 1999, Sacred Heart was made a Beacon School, setting an example of good practice for the borough's other schools. It now works to develop the skills of newly qualified teachers across Hammersmith and Fulham. The school failed to secure lottery funding for a sports hall in 1998, and its sports facilities are limited. There is a dance studio/gym and four netball courts. A science and technology wing opened in 1993. The school offers a broad range of GCSE subjects, including French, Spanish and dance. After GCSEs, most pupils transfer to the St Charles Sixth Form College in Kensington. Some also go to the

London Oratory and Cardinal Vaughan Schools in Kensington. There is a very active PTA, which meets regularly and there is provision for pupils with special needs. Famous ex-pupils include actresses Pauline Collins and Patricia Hayes. Cherie and Tony Blair's daughter is a current pupil.

### Admissions and intake

Interviews take place in November and December. Places are offered in January. Priority is given to Roman Catholic applicants. Baptismal certificates are required as proof, supported by a priest's reference. Other considerations are: siblings already at the school, medical and social needs, accessibility, and attendance at Catholic primary schools. Sacred Heart draws its pupils from Hammersmith and Fulham and neighbouring boroughs.

### Achievement

The school is in the top five per cent of schools nationally in terms of pupils achieving five or more A–C grades at GCSE. In terms of girls' state schools, only Lady Margaret in Fulham gets better results. In 2002, 88 per cent of pupils gained five or more A*–C grades at GCSE. This was up from 84 per cent in 2001. Overall, Sacred Heart came sixth out of all the borough's schools. An Ofsted inspection in 2000 was very positive. Inspectors commented that 'Sacred Heart High is a school of excellence, with many outstanding features. Excellent leadership has created a positive and supportive ethos, in which pupils show a thirst and enthusiasm for learning. High expectations lead to unusually high standards.'

### Extra-curricular activities

Sessions are on offer for pupils to consolidate their regular work. School trips have recently included visits to Boulogne, Kew Gardens and the Science Museum. There is also the chance to look behind the scenes at the Lyric Theatre and a circus skills workshop. Every year, an activities week offers a further opportunity to develop pupils' non-academic skills. The normal range of sports is on offer.

## St James Independent School for Girls

**Earsby Street, London W14 8SH** 020 7348 1748 020 7348 1749 enquiries@ stjamesgirlsschool.org.uk www.stjamesschools.co.uk Mrs Laura Hyde; Chair of Governors: Roger Pincham CBE Kensington Olympia Kensington (Olympia), West Kensington **Buses:** 9, 10 Up to sixth form: Royal blue blazer, grey skirt **Demand:** No figures available, some places were available in 2000 **Type:** Non-selective independent for 192 girls, aged 10 to 18 **Fees:** £2,225–2,295 per term **Submit application form:** No cut-off date **Mission statement:** To give children information of the simple principles of spiritual knowledge, knowledge of the universe, mankind and the individual's relationship thereto, and to remind the child of the essential human duties; to remember the Creator, to live according to the fine laws of the universe, and to find the way back to God. To give disciplined practice in spiritual, mental and physical fields, including training in appropriate skills. **School hours:** 7.55am–4.15pm **Meals:** Hot and cold available **Strong GCSE subjects:** Maths, sciences **London league table position:** 67

### Profile

The school was founded in 1975 by Leon MacLaren, senior tutor at the School of Economic Science, with the aim of providing for the spiritual, mental and physical development of children (the boys' school is in Twickenham). There are now affiliated schools in Leeds, Dublin, Amsterdam, New York, Australia and South Africa. They combine a spiritual tradition, which values all faiths, a grounding in classical languages and service to the community and nation. The school recently moved from the borough of Kensington and Chelsea to Hammersmith and Fulham. A special feature of the curriculum is that Sanskrit, considered by the school to be the root of all European languages, is taught early on. Latin and Greek are taught in the senior schools, while French is taught from age 10. The school also offers pupils the opportunity to participate in meditation sessions. Special needs provision is available according to the individual's requirements. The school has a lift for disabled access. There is a PTA.

### Admissions and intake

Applicants are accepted on the basis of being in sympathy with the school's aims. The school also sets its own entrance tests in English, maths and verbal and non-verbal reasoning. Entry to the sixth form requires five good GCSE passes, with A or B grades, in subjects to be taken at A-level.

### Achievement

In 2002, an impressive 100 per cent of pupils gained five or more A*–C grades at GCSE, equalling the results of 2001.The average point score for pupils taking two or more A/AS-levels was 387.7 and this was above the national average.The varied curriculum is a strength of the school and it offers a good range of science, maths and humanities A-levels. Philosophy, IT and drama are also available, and in the sixth form, current affairs, rhetoric and debating can also be taken.

### Extra-curricular activities

The upper sixth spend a week in a stately home to learn fine hospitality skills, including make-up and good dress sense. Other visits take place to the ancient sites of Greece and the art treasures of Florence.There is also a tour of US schools to play competitive lacrosse. Other outdoor activities include cross-country running and adventure training. Each year the school chooses a different charity to support.The school also holds an annual concert in aid of UNICEF.

## St Paul's Girls School

**Brook Green, Hammersmith, London W6 7BS** 020 7603 2288 020 7602 9932 admissions@spgs.org www.spgs.org Elizabeth Diggory; Chair of governors: The Hon Henry William Palmer Hammersmith Broadway **Buses:** 9, 9A, 10, 27, 28, 33, 72, 91, 220, 283, 295 **Uniform:** None **Demand:** Three applicants for every place **Type:** Independent girls school for 670 girls, aged 11 to 18 **Fees:** £3,161 per term including lunch **Submit application form:** End of November 2003 **School hours:** 8.30am–4pm **Meals:** Hot and cold available **Strong GCSE subjects:** Chinese, English language, Greek, Russian **London league table position:** 5

### Profile

St Paul's is located in a quiet part of Brook Green, perhaps the most exclusive area in Hammersmith. In the 16th century, John Colet founded a school 'for the children of all nations and countries'. At the end of the 19th century, the Mercers' Company, guardians of the Colet Estate, used part of that endowment to establish a new day school for girls, which opened in 1904.The school aimed to develop 'independent, clear-thinking and informed minds'.The original school building was designed by Gerald Horsley and contains a long corridor, known as the Marble, leading to an oak-panelled hall with a vaulted ceiling. New additions include a science block, a swimming pool, a theatre and extra classrooms. Sports facilities include tennis courts, lacrosse pitches, an athletics field, and basketball and volleyball courts.The school's 'Big Sister' scheme pairs new entrants with members of the final year. Pupils study 15 subjects in their first three years and take at least 10 subjects at GCSE. Famous ex-pupils include actress Dame Celia Johnson and scientist Rosalind Franklin.

### Admissions and intake

Application forms must be completed by November of the preceding year, and entry is by competitive exam.There is a £55 registration fee, plus a £50 exam fee. About 40 London prep schools provide three-quarters of successful candidates; the rest come from state primaries.The school offers four Ogden Bursaries and five music scholarships, two at 11+ and three at 16+.

### Achievement

In 2002, 99 per cent of pupils achieved five or more A*–C grades at GCSE and the school was ranked top of the borough.The average point score at A-level was 438.7, again placing the school top of the borough. In 2000, St Paul's became the first school to achieve the UK's top A-level and GCSE results in the same year. An impressive 100 per cent of pupils gained five or more A*–C grades at GCSE. All of the candidates achieved A* or A grades in English language, Greek, Russian and Chinese. Overall, 93.3 per cent of candidates achieved A* and A grades, and 99.1 per cent got A* to B grades. Similarly, the pass rate for A-levels, was a high 99 per cent. All of the candidates achieved A grades in geography, German, Greek, Russian, music, statistics, AS mathematics and AS photography. In 1996, the *Daily Telegraph* called St Paul's 'The best school in Britain'. More than 90 per cent of sixth-formers go on to university, and 30–40 per cent win places at Oxford or Cambridge.

### Extra-curricular activities

The school has a wide range of clubs and societies. There is a strong emphasis on music – composer Gustav Holst was the school's first director of music. About 80 per cent of pupils take music lessons and perform at concerts, operas, musicals and jazz recitals. There are two orchestras, two choirs, two madrigal groups and many smaller ensembles. There are also clubs for philosophy, the French Revolution, plate tectonics and chess. The Economics Society attracts senior politicians for lectures and question-and-answer sessions. Each year, the school's drama clubs stage seven or eight studio productions and two or three productions in the Celia Johnson Theatre.

# Haringey

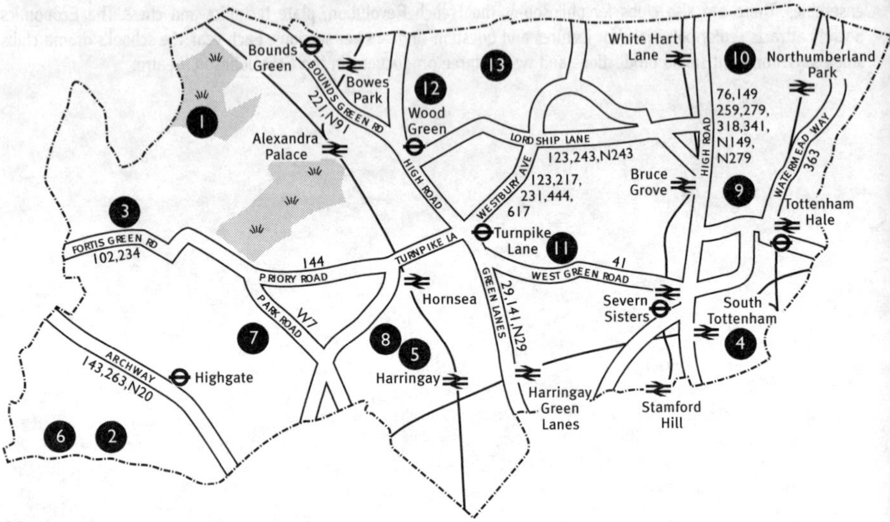


## Key

1. Alexandra Park School
2. Channing School
3. Fortismere School
4. Gladesmore Community School
5. Greig City Academy
6. Highgate School
7. Highgate Wood Secondary School`
8. Hornsey Secondary School for Girls
9. The John Loughborough School
10. Northumberland Park Community School
11. Park View Academy
12. St Thomas More RC School
13. White Hart Lane Secondary School

# Factfile

**LEA: 48 Station Road, London N22 4SG** ☎ 020 8489 0000 🌐 www.haringey.gov.uk **Director of Education:** Paul Roberts **Political control of council:** Labour **Percentage of pupils from outside the borough:** 13.4 per cent **Percentage of pupils educated outside the borough:** 26.5 per cent **League table positions (out of 32 boroughs):** 30th

## Profile

Few people describe themselves as living in Haringey; the borough has been created out of neighbourhoods that contrast as strongly as any in London. At the Camden boundary, Highgate is very affluent, containing some high-priced property. To the east lies Tottenham, parts of which are among the most poverty-stricken in the country. Finsbury Park is also run down, but some parts have become popular due to good transport. Wood Green has a large shopping centre that is quite downmarket. Hornsey is more mixed socially with some expensive houses. Crouch End is popular with media types and is now increasingly expensive. Solid, sought-after Muswell Hill is often portrayed as the archetypal North London middle-class suburb. Neighbouring Alexandra Park, which surrounds one of London's most spectacular green spaces, tends to be less expensive. Despite the concentration of wealth in some pockets, Haringey is the ninth most deprived borough in the country, with the capital's fourth worst unemployment rate. Although officially 'outer London', it suffers all the inner-city problems of social disadvantage and a changing school population. Even taking this into account, the record of the education authority is still poor and it was slated in a 1999 Ofsted report. There have been improvements recently in reorganization but spending per pupil still tends to be below that in similar boroughs. Most secondary schools struggle to improve on performances, with the gap widening between national exam results. One school was closed and relaunched under the government's 'fresh start' scheme as Park View Academy, and Greig City Academy has replaced the School of St David St Katherine. Fortismere in Muswell Hill is very popular, Alexandra Park School opened in 1999 and has proved to be popular whilst Hornsey School for Girls is well liked. There are two independent schools with good reputations situated in Highgate.

## Policy

The Nexus sixth-form consortium linking Gladesmore, Northumberland Park, Park View Academy and White Hart Lane schools is a recent innovation, aimed at rescuing languishing A-level results. It offers a choice of up to 11 A-levels and eight GNVQs.

# Alexandra Park School

**Bidwell Gardens, London N11 2AZ** ☎ 020 8826 4880 📠 020 8888 2236 ✉ Admin@alexandrapark.haringey.sch.uk Rosslyn Hudson; Chair of Governors: Clive Boutle ⇌ Alexandra Park ⊖ Bounds Green **Buses:** 102, 184, 221, 299 Black blazer with school badge, black trousers or skirt, red pullover, white blouse or shirt, school tie optional for girls, compulsory for boys **Demand:** 162 places in 2001/2; oversubscribed **Type:** Community comprehensive for 653 mixed pupils, aged 11 to 16 **Submit application form:** 24 October 2003 **School hours:** 8.45am–3.30pm; homework clubs available **Meals:** Hot and cold available **Strong GCSEs:** Not yet known **London league table position:** Not yet known

## Profile

Alexandra Park opened in September 1999 in order to ease the increasing demand for secondary schools within the borough. It was immediately oversubscribed and looks to become even more popular in the future. Although at present no sixth form is planned, it intended to have 810 pupils by 2003. The school is housed on the site of the old Alexandra Park school, which ironically was amalgamated to form Fortismere in 1983. The premises were taken over by Haringey College and then the College of North London, which added an excellent learning resources centre. The school's well-landscaped grounds include allotments, playing fields and ball courts. A new dance and drama studio opened in September 2002. It is next door to the well-regarded Rhodes Avenue primary school. Alexandra Park is especially proud of its ICT facilities, which students have access to before and after school and at lunchtime. In addition to the standard curriculum, French and Spanish are compulsory in Years 8 and 9. There is a school council and pupils are encouraged to think of themselves as role models for future years. The Alexandra Park School Association is already proving active in fund-raising and arranging for parents to help in school. Regular newsletters are sent to parents and there is a home-school agreement.

## Admission and intake

Admission is through the LEA. After special-needs applicants have been considered, priority is given to those with siblings at the school and then to those living nearest the school, measured in a straight line.

## Achievement

Too early to make a judgement but the school is 'confident that the quality of education...will be excellent'.

## Extra-curricular activities

The after-school activities include computers, art, drama and team games. A homework club is run four days a week. The music department is setting up an orchestra, a band and ensembles. There will be a major school journey or activity holiday offered each year, with overseas trips and exchanges for older pupils.

# Channing School

**Highgate, London N6 5HF** 020 8340 2328 020 8341 5698 admin@channing.co.uk www.channing.co.uk Elizabeth Radice; Chair of Governors: Mr GA Auger FCCA Highgate, Archway **Buses:** 143, 210, 271 Up to sixth form: Brown school sweatshirt, white blouse, dark skirt **Demand:** c.3 pupils per place available **Type:** Selective independent for 531 girls, aged 4 to 18 **Fees:** £2,785 per term, plus lunch **Submit application form:** Early November 2003 **Motto:** *Conabor* (I Shall Try) **School hours:** 8.40am–3.45pm **Meals:** Hot and cold available **Strong GCSE subjects:** Art and design, double science, English, French **London league table position:** 29

## Profile

The 19th-century buildings of Channing school are blessed with panoramic views across London. The school has seven acres of grounds containing playing fields, ball courts, a gym and an arts centre. The facilities are good, and include an audio-visual lecture theatre and well-stocked libraries. The school was founded by Unitarians in 1885 and encourages all faiths equally. Class sizes are small, usually less than 20 in Years 10 and 11. The school's small size means there is a friendly atmosphere, with girls receiving individual attention. There is a prefect-like school officer system and a school council. Pastoral care is also good. There is an active parents' association and an annual founder's day at the end of the summer term. Ex-pupils include Baroness Cox.

## Admissions and intake

Entry is through an interview and the North London Consortium entrance exam at age 11. Channing School is in group two of the consortium, setting common papers with six other schools, including North London Collegiate, Queen's Gate, City of London School for Girls and Godolphin and Latymer. Academic and musical scholarships are available. Entrance to the sixth form is subject to an interview and candidates must sit entrance papers in English and two of their chosen A-level subjects.

## Achievement

Channing's academic standards are excellent. In 2002, 98 per cent of pupils obtained five or more A*–C grades. This was more or less on a par with results of the last five years, and the same as those of 2001. The average point score was 56.1 and Channing came first in the borough league table. English, French, double science and art and design are particularly strong subjects. There is an emphasis on classics and modern languages with all girls studying French, Latin, German and Spanish until Year 9, when Ancient Greek is also offered. ICT is compulsory in Years 7 to 9 with good networked computers available. Academic standards are just as high in the sixth form. In 2002, the average point score for pupils taking two or more A-level subects was 372.4. This placed Channing top of the A-level borough league table. Economics, English, maths, classical and modern languages and physics tend to perform strongly. The sixth form is relatively small, but of a very high standard. At least 10 per cent of pupils go to Oxbridge.

## Extra-curricular activities

There is a wide range of clubs on offer including pottery, chess and photography, and girls have the opportunity to work on a web site. Music is very popular, with half of all pupils playing an instrument, and orchestras, choirs and wind and jazz bands available. Sports include football, self-defence, table tennis and trampolining. Girls can also take part in the Duke of Edinburgh's Award scheme, Young Enterprise, charity work and community service. There are overseas visits and an annual skiing holiday. A number of joint extra-curricular activities take place with Highgate, the local independent boys' school.

# Fortismere School

**South Wing, Tetherdown, Muswell Hill, London N10 1NE; North Wing, Creighton Avenue, Muswell Hill N10 1NS** 020 8365 4400 020 8444 7822 (South Wing), 020 8883 5583 (North Wing) Mspencer@fortismere.haringey.sch.uk www.fortismere.haringey.sch.uk Mr Andrew M Nixon MA, Dip.Ed; Chair of Governors: Ms A Janssen MA, B.Sc East Finchley **Buses:** W7, 43, 102, 134, 144 None **Demand:** 422 applications for 246 places in 2001/2 **Type:** Community comprehensive Technology College for 1600 mixed pupils, aged 11 to 19 **Submit application form:** 24 October 2003 **School hours:** 8.40am–3.30pm; homework clubs are available **School meals:** Hot and cold available **Strong GCSE subjects:** Art, maths, physics **London league table position:** 170

### Profile

Fortismere is one of Haringey's most popular schools. It opened in 1983 and became a Technology College in 1997. It is a big school on a 20-acre site. The grounds include an all-weather pitch, a heated outdoor pool and two gyms. The science labs were rebuilt in 1998 and the music rooms have been upgraded. The school has recently completed an extensive re-equipping of its IT and design technology facilities. The Blanche Nevile School for the hearing impaired shares the site and many of its pupils are integrated into Fortismere. Pupils can participate in a school council and community service. There is a strong parent-teacher association and a weekly newsletter. The pupils' behaviour is generally orderly, and strong attendance policies succeed in keeping truancy in line with the national average. Ex-pupils include *Big Brother* contestant Melanie Hill.

### Admissions and intake

After special-needs candidates have been considered, priority is given to those with siblings at the school and then to those living nearest to the school, measured in a straight line from the tennis courts. In 2000, some successful applicants lived as much as a mile and a quarter away, but families are advised that they probably need to be closer to secure a place. There are slightly more girls than boys.

### Achievement

Fortismere combines a relaxed informal atmosphere with good behaviour and improving academic standards. In 2002, 67 per cent of pupils obtained five or more A*–C grades at GCSE. This was down from 69 per cent in 2001 and the school was ranked third in the borough league table. The average point score at GCSE was 40.6, above the borough average. In 2001, Ofsted reported that Fortismere has 'many strengths'. Inspectors praised the school's 'vibrant community' and noted that: 'pupils make good progress, achieve well and attain well above average standards at GCSE'. Strong GCSE subjects were found to be mathematics, English and Science. Standards at GCSE are improving at a faster rate than nationally. GCSE subjects on offer include business studies, expressive arts and home economics. The large sixth form offers more than 24 A-levels along with nine GNVQs. Students taking two or more A-level subjects averaged 275.8 points in 2002. Ofsted praised the 'good teaching' in the school and the 'rich range of learning opportunities' available to pupils. However, Inspectors noted that the provision for the teaching of ICT and modern languages needed to be improved.

### Extra-curricular activities

Fortismere offers a wide choice of excellent activities, clubs and charity work. It also has a good sporting tradition, with regional and sometimes national success in soccer, athletics, road running and cross country. More than 30 sports were on offer in 2001/2. There is a varied musical programme, together with regular dramatic and dance performances. There are homework clubs. Residential field courses and outdoor-pursuit holidays are on offer. There are also regular exchange visits to France, Germany and Spain. The school also has good business and community links and also supports local charities.

## Gladesmore Community School

**Gladesmore Road, London N15 6JT** 020 8800 0884 020 8800 1947 gladesmore@yahoo.co.uk Mr T Hartney; Chair of Governors: Ms Liz Singleton South Tottenham, Seven Sisters Seven Sisters **Buses:** 41, 49, 67, 76, 230, 243, 279 Up to sixth form: Navy cardigan or pullover, dark navy trousers or skirt, light blue shirt or blouse; school tie, badge and sweatshirt available from school **Demand:** 243 places available; oversubscribed **Type:** Community comprehensive for 1246 mixed pupils, aged 11 to 16 **Submit application form:** 24 October 2003 **School hours:** 8.45am–3.20pm (Mon–Wed), 8.45am–2.45pm (Thurs–Fri); homework clubs are available **School meals:** Hot and cold available **Strong GCSE subjects:** Art, drama, maths, Turkish **London league table position:** 475

### Profile

Gladesmore makes a good job of serving a socially disadvantaged population. Much of the school was rebuilt in the late 1980s, including the science block and sports centre. A new City Learning Centre with state of the art information technology facilities opened in 2002, along with new facilties for design and technology, art, music and drama. The school works closely with Middlesex University, where all pupils spend a day each week. There is an active PTA, a prefects system and a school council. In 1998, Ofsted found behaviour was mostly good, but observed disruptive incidents in and out of class, which not all teachers handled well. Truancy remains a problem at 3.7 per cent, three times the national average.

## Admissions and intake

Admission is through the LEA. After special-needs applicants have been considered, priority is given to those with siblings at the school and then to those living nearest the school, measured in a straight line. Approximately 80 per cent of new pupils are at least two years behind in literacy, and 25 per cent have English as an additional language. There is a turnover of 25 per cent between Year 7 and 11. Girls are outnumbered by three to two.

## Achievement

Gladesmore's pupils make 'sound progress from a low starting point', according to Ofsted. In 2002, 30 per cent of pupils obtained five or more A*–C grades at GCSE. This reversed the downward trend over the previous two years. The school was ranked eighth in the GCSE borough league table. Drama, art, Turkish and maths all perform strongly. Ofsted found that the teaching was satisfactory overall. It is strongest in English, where teachers face a challenge. IT was weak, something the school is addressing by overhauling its facilities. The sixth form is part of the Nexus consortium (see borough factfile). Pupils must have passed their subjects with at least a C at GCSE to study at A-level. Vocational education in particular is well taught. In 2002, pupils taking two or more A-levels scored an average 80 points. This was well below the borough average. This placed Gladesmore 10th in the borough for A-level results. The fluctuating results reflect the sharply changing school population.

## Extra-curricular activities

A full programme of activities is run for an hour three days a week, after school and at lunchtimes. It includes homework clubs, GCSE help sessions and learning support. The usual range of sports is offered, including basketball and American football, coached by professionals from London clubs. The soccer teams do well at borough and all-London level. The steel band has also won several London competitions. School journeys include Outward Bound holidays, field trips and exchange visits with a French school. There are also youth clubs. There are good links with the local community, and the school offers health clinics, young mothers classes and senior citizens groups.

# Greig City Academy

**Hillfield Avenue, Hornsey, London N8 7DT** 020 8348 6292 020 8341 3290 Graham Horsewood (principal) MA, NPQH; Chair of Governors: Thomas Peryer MBA, MA Hornsey Turnpike Lane **Buses:** W3, W5, 41, 144 Up to sixth form: royal blue blazer or pullover with school badge, white shirt or blouse, school tie, black skirt (girls) or trousers (boys), black low-heeled shoes (no trainers) **Demand:** 180 applications for 215 places in 2002 **Type:** City Academy for 900 mixed pupils, aged 11 to 18 **Submit application form:** November 2003 **School hours:** 8.25am–3.10pm (Mon, Fri); 8.25am–3.40pm (Tues–Thurs) **Meals:** Hot and cold available **Strong GCSE subjects:** Not yet known **London league table position:** Not yet known

## Profile

Greig City Academy opened in September 2002 on the site of the former St David and St Katharine Church of England High School. The old buildings have been refurbished and new facilities added. The sponsors, the Greig Trust and the Diocese of London, have pledged support of £2 million. As an Academy, the school is funded by the state but largely free from Department for Education control. The head teacher and governing body have wide powers to modify the National Curriculum, change the structure of the school day and change teachers' pay and conditions. The school's stated aim is to build a genuinely comprehensive City Academy with a strong Christian ethos, catering for pupils of all abilities and aptitudes drawn from all parts of Haringey.

## Admissions and intake

If more than 215 applications are received in any year, 38 per cent of places will be allocated to children from practising Church of England families, 28 per cent to children of other Christian denominations, 10 per cent to children of other faiths and 24 per cent to children who live within Haringey. Although they are independent, Academies must comply with the official School Admissions Code of Practice.

### Achievement

St David and St Katherine was an undersubscribed and underachieving school where only a quarter of pupils achieved five GCSEs at grades A*–C in 2000. As Greig City Academy is a new school it has no results yet to report and does not appear in the London league table.

### Extra-curricular activities

The Academy promises to continue the impressive tradition of high level performance in sports, music and drama achieved by St David and St Katharine pupils. England sprint star Dwain Chambers is a former pupil and current pupils play football, basketball and athletics at international level. Outdoor pursuits are available including hiking, sailing and skiing and pupils can take part in the Duke of Edinburgh's Award Scheme. The school's steel band have performed at the Royal Festival Hall and the gospel choir took part in the Millennium celebrations at St Paul's Cathedral. The school production of Romeo and Juliet was part of an international drama festival in Edinburgh.

## Highgate School

**North Road, London N6 4AY** 020 8340 1524 020 8340 7674 Office@highgateschool.org.uk www.highgateschool.org.uk Richard Kennedy MA; Chair of Governors: Mr JF Mills Highgate **Buses:** 143, 210, 271 Black trousers and blazer with red braid, white shirt and school tie **Demand:** 90 for 30 places not taken by boys from the junior school **Type:** Selective independent for 1055 boys, aged 11 to 19 **Fees:** £3,475 per term, including lunch, books and stationery **Submit application form:** 2 December 2003 **Motto:** *Altiora in Votis* (Strive for Excellence) **School hours:** 8.45am–4pm **Meals:** Hot and cold available **Strong GCSE subjects:** Art and design, English literature, French, maths, sciences **London league table position:** 56

### Profile

Highgate offers the advantages of a well-established and generously resourced independent school. It was founded in 1565 at the top of a hill, near Hampstead Heath. The school has excellent facilities, including satellite-receiving equipment. The modern sports centre houses a large swimming pool and a weight-training suite. There are 20 acres of playing fields. Despite recent expansion, class sizes are small – in the low 20s or less. Highgate is a Christian foundation and most boys attend Church of England chapel once a week. Other faiths are welcome and well represented. There is provision for special-needs pupils. The house system is based on the areas that the boys live in, and prefects are elected by pupils and staff. There is also a student committee and a parents' association. Famous ex-pupils include poets Gerard Manley Hopkins and John Betjeman, composer John Tavener, film critic Barry Norman, cricketer Phil Tufnel, and fashion designer Hussein Chalayan.

### Admissions and intake

Entry is possible at age 11 but is more usual at 13. Applications must be made no later than December 1 of the year preceding entry and earlier if lists close. The school has its own entrance examination, but an interview and current school report are also taken into consideration. Boys sit the Common Entrance Exam to determine what sets they are put into. Academic and music scholarships are available.

### Achievement

Highgate's academic results are very good. A recent breakdown showed a quarter of all boys taking GCSEs scored all As or A*s and half scored five or more A grades. In 2002, 96 per cent of pupils obtained five or more A*–C grades, which was slightly up from 95 per cent in 2001. The school was ranked second in the GCSE borough league table. Maths, French, English literature, sciences and art and design tend to do especially well. Greek, Latin, Russian and Spanish, as well as French and German, are offered at GCSE. The sixth form offers 20 subjects at A-level. In 2002, pupils sitting two or more A-levels scored an average 348.5 points, placing the school second in the A-level borough league table. It is very rare for any boy to fail an A-level at Highgate; on average they get an A and two Bs with just under a quarter getting three A grades. Virtually all pupils go onto university and nearly 20 per cent go to Oxbridge.

### Extra-curricular activities

There is a wide programme of activities aimed at enriching school life. Sports available include Eton fives, water polo, fencing and karate. Music is strong, with orchestras, choirs, a concert band, barbershop quartet and rock groups on offer. The jazz quartet reached the final of the National Festival of Music for Youth and the chapel choir has appeared on professional recordings. There are also regular drama productions. Clubs include car restoration, debating and 'vinyl and philosophy'. Overseas visits on offer include a diving trip to the Red Sea and a football tour of Prague. Pupils can also take part in the Duke of Edinburgh's Award scheme, the Combined Cadet Force, Young Enterprise and charity work. Higher up the school, many activities take place with nearby Channing School.

# Highgate Wood Secondary School

**Montenotte Road, London N8 8RN** ☎ 020 8342 7970 📠 020 8340 8072 ✉ hws.haringey.sch.uk 🌐 www.hws.uk.com Pauline Ashbee; Chair of Governors: Mr C Menzies ⊖ Highgate **Buses:** W5, W7, 43, 134 : None **Demand:** 243 places in 2001/2; oversubscribed **Type:** Community comprehensive Performing Arts College for 1326 mixed pupils, aged 11 to 18 **Motto:** Striving for Excellence **Submit application form:** 24 October 2003 **School hours:** 8.35am–3.20pm **Meals:** Hot and cold available **Strong GCSE subjects:** PE, science **London league table position:** 418

## Profile

Highgate Wood lies near well-heeled Highgate and trendy middle-class Crouch End. It was built in 1961, and design faults combined with neglect have led to problems such as leaky roofs. The site is also crowded, taking more pupils than was originally intended. However, some facilities are good, including the science labs, sports hall and the all-weather playing surfaces. A £6 million project is underway to provide more specialist accommodation and to refurbish existing accommodation. Parental involvement is encouraged through a weekly newsletter and an active PTA. There is a school council and older pupils act as mentors to younger ones. In 1999, Ofsted was impressed with the school's racial harmony and found the attitudes of most pupils satisfactory. However, inspectors noted: 'a small number are disruptive and their unchecked behaviour also impedes the learning of others'. Some boys were also badly behaved outside of class. Truancy continues to be a serious problem, and at 2.6 per cent it is twice the national average.

## Admissions and intake

Admission is through the LEA. After special-needs candidates have been considered, priority is given to those with siblings at the school and then to those living nearest to the school, measured in a straight line. There are a large number of pupils with English as an additional language, including many of Turkish descent.

## Achievement

The school's results at GCSE are above average for similar schools, and even better in Key Stage 3 tests. In 2002, 41 per cent of pupils obtained five or more A*–C grades, equalling the results of 2001. The school was ranked sixth in the borough. In 1999, Ofsted inspectors found that the teaching had 'much improved', judging only 8 per cent of lessons to be unsatisfactory. Maths was weak but had still improved. Art was also disappointing. High-attainers progressed well in general, but they 'sometimes have progress impaired by the poor behaviour of a few individuals'. Overall, girls were found to perform better than boys. Inspectors also found teaching in the sixth form to be good. The sixth form runs in conjunction with Hornsey School for Girls, with a choice of more than 20 subjects at A-level, alongside GNVQs. Pupils taking two or more subjects averaged 139.1 points in 2002, placing the school sixth in the A-level borough league table.

## Extra-curricular activities

There is plenty of sports coaching available, in addition to a range of clubs. The school has a good reputation for team games. Athletics is also strong, with some pupils competing at national level. Musical activities include an orchestra and ensembles. Dramatic productions are regularly staged. There are also school trips and exchanges both in the UK and abroad. All sixth-formers are involved in community service.

# Hornsey Secondary School for Girls

**Inderwick Road, London N8 9JF** ☎ 020 8348 6191 📠 020 8340 1214 Jean Lebrecht; Chair of Governors: Lucy Moy-Thomas ⇌ Hornsey, Haringey West **Buses:** W3, W5, 41 Up to sixth form: Plain red, white, grey or black skirt or trousers, plain-coloured blouses, jumpers, cardigans and sweatshirts **Demand:** 243 places in 2001/2; oversubscribed **Type:** Community comprehensive Performing Arts College for 1384 girls, aged 11 to 18 **Submit application form:** 24 October 2003 **School hours:** 8.30am–3.10pm; homework clubs are available **School meals:** Hot and cold available **Strong GCSE subjects:** English, modern languages, music, science **London league table position:** 283

## Profile

Haringey's only girls' school is a popular, well-run institution. A new block housing maths rooms and an IT suite has eased the problem of overcrowding. There is a sports hall, gym and dance studio, all-weather pitches and other outside sports facilities. A new drama and music block opens in 2003. The school recently gained Performing Arts College status. An 'open door' policy towards parents includes mornings when they can look round, a weekly newsletter, a parents' room and an active association. A well-attended International Day is run each year. There are also junior and senior school councils. In 1996, Ofsted found behaviour to be very positive, but a minority of girls were disruptive, in and beyond lessons – a problem the school has since tackled. Truancy is low at 0.7 per cent.

## Admissions and intake

After special needs applicants have been considered, priority is given to those with sisters at the school, then places are allocated according to the primary school the girls attended. All primary schools from which girls apply will be given at least one place, then places are allocated according to the number of applicants from each school. If there are more applicants than places from a primary, priority goes to those girls living closest to Hornsey school, measured in a straight line. Pupils come from across and beyond the borough.

## Achievement

Hornsey's achievements are good compared to similar schools. Pupils enter the school with lower than average attainment but their GCSE results are near the national level. In 2002, 52 per cent of pupils obtained five or more A*–C grades, up from 33 per cent in 2001 and reinstating an upward trend. The school was ranked fourth in the borough. An Ofsted report in 2002 described Hornsey as 'a good school with some very good features'. The leadership of the school was found to be 'good' and examination results were found to be above average in comparison with similar schools, and well above average in English. Pupils with special educational needs or English as an additional language make 'very good' progress. In 2001, pupils taking two or more subjects at A-level scored on average 164.9 points, in line with the borough state school average. These results placed Hornsey fifth in the borough. The sixth form works with Highgate Wood School and offers 23 A-level subjects and five GNVQs. Ofsted praised the school's 'very good' atmosphere but noted that poor attendance hampers the progress of some pupils and that provision for teaching ICT needs to be improved.

## Extra-curricular activities

Music clubs are popular at Hornsey, with a choir, instrumental groups and tuition on offer. There are homework, drama and computing clubs. The school offers geography and biology field trips and overseas visits. There are also plenty of sporting activities, including ice skating and aerobics. Pupils can take part in the Duke of Edinburgh's Award scheme.

# The John Loughborough School

**Holcombe Road, Tottenham, London N17 9AD** 020 8808 7837 020 8801 6719 loughsch@aol.com Ms Edwena McFarquhar; Chair of Governors: Pastor D MacFarlane Bowes Park **Buses:** 102, 184, 221, 299 School tie, white shirt or blouse, burgundy jumper, burgundy skirt or black trousers, conventional hair **Demand:** 56 places available in 2001/2; oversubscribed **Type:** Voluntary aided Seventh-day Adventist comprehensive for 308 mixed pupils, aged 11 to 16 **Submit application form:** 24 October 2003 **Motto:** *Spiritus, Mens, Corpus* (Spirit, Mind, Body) **School hours:** 8.45am–3.40pm; homework clubs are available **School meals:** Hot and cold available **Strong GCSE subjects:** English, Maths **London league table position:** 498

## Profile

The John Loughborough opened in 1980 as an independent school. It was originally established by members of the Seventh-day Adventist church who were unhappy about the education offered to their children. Many of its pupils came from families who had to struggle to find fees, and a lack of finance was a real problem limiting the school's resources. The dedication of parents, teachers and other church members prevailed, and in 1998, it became a state school. Bible studies and Seventh-day Adventist beliefs are an important part of the education offered, but other non-creationist views are considered in these teachings. Lessons begin and end with prayers, frequently led by pupils. Numbers are small and there is a strong community feel. There is also a good gym on site. The special-needs of school pupils are answered through a special needs coordinator and department. There is a prefects system and a PTA.

## Admissions and intake

The school has a strong Seventh-day Adventist ethos and, although it accepts pupils of other faiths, nearly all are of Afro-Caribbean or African descent. Applications are made directly to the school, and parents must attend an interview and provide a current school report. They must complete a form, expressing willingness to support the school's Christian ideals. Priority is given to those pupils from practising Seventh-day Adventist homes, supported by a pastor's reference, in the following order: to those with siblings at the school; those with parents employed by the church; those with special medical needs; those whose parents or siblings attended the school; and nearness to the school, as measured by the shortest safe route. At age 16 pupils go on to a variety of sixth forms.

## Achievement

The school's Christian ethos and its teaching of Seventh-day Adventist beliefs make it unique. Many parents are also attracted by its tradition of providing a disciplined and dedicated environment in which teachers hold high expectations of black pupils. Pupils tend to start the school with lower than average attainment levels and the small numbers taking GCSEs mean fluctuations in grades are likely. In 2002, 24 per cent of pupils obtained five or more A*–C grades at GCSE. This equalled the results of 2001 and the school was placed ninth in the borough. The school will need to take strong action to return to the more promising trend it set in the mid- and late-1990s. Ofsted visited the school in 2002 and noted that it 'provides a sound education for its pupils in most subjects'. Inspectors praised the 'strong' leadership of the head teacher and the school's success in raising pupils' self confidence and aspirations. Standards at GCSE are low but the majority of pupils make better progress than statistics suggest. Achievement in English and mathematics is good. The quality of teaching and achievement in French and aspects of design and technology needs to be improved.

## Extra-curricular activities

There are several homework clubs at the school. National and overseas trips take place to destinations such as the US, France, Italy and Spain. The school is currently reviving its previously good musical tradition, including a gospel choir. The art club is well attended and has had several successful exhibitions.

# Northumberland Park Community School

**Trulock Road, Tottenham, London N17 0PG** ☎ 020 8801 0091 Fax 020 8801 9022 ⓔ admin@northumberlandpark.haringey.sch.uk Head: Mr John Coughlan BA; Chair of Governors: Councillor Reg Rice ⇄ Northumberland Park, White Hart Lane **Buses:** W3, 76, 149, 171A, 259, 279 Uniform: Up to sixth form: Black or grey trousers or skirt, white or purple shirt or blouse, purple jumper or sweater, school tie (optional) **Demand:** 210 places available in 2001/2; oversubscribed **Type:** Community comprehensive for 1048 mixed pupils, aged 11 to 18 **Submit application form:** 24 October 2003 **Motto:** *Curamus* (We Care) **School hours:** 8.45am–3.20pm; homework clubs are available **School meals:** Hot and cold available **Strong GCSE subjects:** English, Science **London league table position:** 430

## Profile

Northumberland Park school opened in the early 1970s and is based in one of the most deprived areas in the country. The site is overcrowded but facilities available include a full-size astroturf pitch and swimming pool plus a new arts and media block. The school recently joined the Excellence in Cities initiative, aimed at offering funding to help gifted and talented children. There is a fortnightly newsletter and a scheme in Year 7 asks families to help children with maths each week. There is an active school council. In 1998, Ofsted inspectors found behaviour was improving but they were worried by some pupils who did not have positive attitudes to work. Truancy has worsened slightly since the report, but at 1.9 per cent it is accountable considering the school's challenges.

## Admissions and intake

After special needs applicants have been considered, priority is given to those with siblings at the school and then to those living nearest the school, measured in a straight line. About half of the pupils speak English as an additional language, with many refugee children among them. Approximately 45 per cent were in the lowest band assessed by ability tests, compared to 16 per cent nationally. There are about 10 boys to every eight girls.

## Achievement

Northumberland Park does well in providing a relatively orderly and harmonious environment and it has had some success in improving academic standards. However, its exam results are low, even compared to other inner-city comprehensives. In 2002, 19 per cent of pupils obtained five or more A*–C grades. This was one per cent up from 18 per cent in 2001. The school was ranked seventh in the borough. Ofsted inspectors visited in 2002 and noted that 'The school provides a satisfactory education for students up to Year 11 and standards are improving'. GCSE results are below the national average but better than in similar schools. Virtually all pupils achieved a GCSE grade in English and science, and the majority achieve a grade in maths. Teaching was found to be good in many lessons especially Years 10 and 11. However, Inspectors noted that pupils' attitudes to learning in Years 7 to 9 needs to be improved. The school has the Successmaker computer programme, designed to boost literacy and numeracy in Year 7. The sixth form is part of the Nexus consortium (see borough factfile). In 20021, pupils taking two or more subjects at A-level scored an average of 108 points. Since 1994, a compact agreement with Middlesex University has guaranteed places for up to 15 pupils who meet the minimum entrance requirements. GNVQs are available. One impressive feature of the school is its integration of pupils with physical disabilities. Up to 16 students, many severely disabled, take a full part in school life, supported by The Vale School that shares Northumberland's site.

## Extra-curricular activities

The activities on offer include singing clubs, drama, swimming, science and maths. The school has a good sporting reputation that includes cross-country, road running, basketball and gymnastics. The sports facilities are open in the evenings and at weekends. There is also a youth club on site. It has good links with local employers, who offer work placements. There are local field trips, as well as trips abroad.

# Park View Academy

**Langham Road, London N15 3RB** 020 8888 1722 020 8881 8143 knicola@parkview. haringey.sch.uk www.parkview.haringey.sch.uk Mr Peter Walker; Chair of Governors: Dr Edgar Neufield Seven Sisters Turnpike Lane **Buses:** 1, 41, 67, 84, 171A, 221, 230 Up to sixth form: Black blazer with school badge, black or grey trousers or skirt, white shirt or blouse, school tie **Demand:** 243 places in 2001/2 **Type:** Community comprehensive for 1050 mixed pupils, aged 11 to 18 **Submit application form:** 24 October 2003 **Motto:** Learning to excel **School hours:** 8.30am–3.15pm; homework clubs are available **School meals:** Hot and cold available **Strong GCSE subjects:** Not yet known **London league table position:** 512

## Profile

Park View Academy opened in 1999 under the government's 'fresh start' scheme. It replaces the failing Langham School. Although the academy inherits both the old school's site and its pupils, it is promising a new identity based on radical changes. A committed head and staff are trying hard to make the school work, despite the problems facing its socially disadvantaged intake and the scepticism of some local parents. There are signs it may be working – those applicants putting it as a first preference more than doubled in the school's second year. Brand new gates and security cameras protect the school's site. The buildings have been extensively overhauled using 'fresh start' money and there are now 150 networked computers and an upgraded library. As well as their own sports hall, pupils can also use the national standard New River Sports Centre. The school's aim is be 'at the cutting edge of teaching and learning' and much use of ICT is planned. It is applying for Language College status. Literacy will also be a central focus. The school is hoping to build a strong partnership with the local community and is opening its facilities for wider use. The small sixth form works with other Haringey schools in the Nexus consortium (see borough factfile). This should increase the range of A-level and GNVQ subjects on offer. There are year and school councils. Special provisions for exceptionally able pupils include masterclasses at local universities and accelerated entry to GCSEs and A-levels. A parents' association is being organized.

### Admission and intake

Admission is through the LEA. Anyone putting the school as a first choice has been admitted so far, but the school is becoming more popular. If it becomes oversubscribed, special-needs applicants will be given priority, followed by those with siblings at the school, and then those living nearest the school, measured in a straight line.

### Achievement

In 2002, 16 per cent of pupils achieved five or more A*–C grades at GCSE, up on 15 per cent in 2001. The school was ranked 10th in the borough table. However, It is still too early to make a fair assessment of Park View.

### Extra-curricular activities

A session is run four days a week after school that gives pupils additional support with work or allows them to study new subjects, as well as offering extra-curricular sport and arts. It is known as the 'additional session', and is seen as an integral part of the school's work. It gives access to ICT suites, homework clubs, sports and arts workshops and masterclasses in a range of subjects. Professionals from outside the school are encouraged to take part and Spurs football club runs weekly coaching. Work experience is offered to all Year 10 students. There are lots of field trips.

## St Thomas More RC School

**Glendale Avenue, Wood Green, London N22 5HN** ☎ 020 8888 7122 Fax 020 8886 9370 Email SaintThomasMore.School@haringey.gov.uk Head Mr CJ Cahill B.Sc, Dip.Ed; Chair of Governors: Mrs S Berkery-Smith OBE, JP, DHS Rail Bowes Park Underground Wood Green **Buses:** W3, 9, 329 Uniform Navy pleated or flared skirt, pale blue blouse, navy blazer and cardigan (girls); dark grey trousers, pale shirt, navy pullover and blazer, school tie (boys) **Demand:** 289 applications for 192 places in 2001/2 **Type:** Voluntary aided Roman Catholic comprehensive Sports College for 1147 mixed pupils, aged 11 to 18 **Submit application form:** 24 October 2003 **Mission statement:** To lead those in our care to grow in their faith and to benefit from an enriching education **Motto:** The King's Good Servant but God's First **School hours:** 8.50am–3.40pm (Mon, Tues, Thurs), 8.40am–3.15pm (Wed), 8.40am–2.55pm (Fri); homework clubs are available **School meals:** Hot and cold available **Strong GCSE subjects:** Design and technology, history **London league table position:** 400

### Profile

St Thomas More serves pupils with high levels of social disadvantage. The school has a strong Catholic ethos, with parents expected to set children an example of regular religious practice. A chaplain assists with pastoral care. Parental involvement is encouraged and many families take part in the school's community services. There is a parents' association and the school offers English lessons to parents. The school recently gained Sports College status. In 1999, Ofsted found that some less able 14- and 15-year-olds were causing disruption. Truancy was high at 2.4 per cent in 1999 but the school has implemented policies to tackle this and it has now fallen to 1.1 per cent in 2000.

### Admissions and intake

Application is made directly to the school. Priority is given, in order, to: practising Roman Catholic families, supported by a priest's reference; baptized Roman Catholics; Greek Orthodox families with a priest's supportive reference; Christians in sympathy with the school's aims and with a minister's reference; and those of other faiths with similar sympathy and a reference. Within each category, having a sibling at the school will increase priority. Many pupils come from Enfield and Barnet and 47 per cent speak English as an additional language. There are almost three boys for every one girl. There is provision for special-needs pupils.

### Achievement

St Thomas More has made good progress in improving standards. In 2002, 33 per cent of pupils obtained five or more A*–C grades. This was below the borough average, and the school was ranked fifth in the borough. Ofsted found that 'the school does very well by its pupils'. Inspectors judged teaching to be good overall, and most effective in art and history. Modern languages and geography were found to be weaker. Standards at age 14 were well above average compared to similar schools, especially in English. The trend continued at GCSE with results in history and design technology particularly good. Geography was the weakest subject. The school was seventh in the A-level table in 2002, with pupils taking two or more subjects scoring an average 130.9 points. A-level art, history and music are strong. GNVQs are available. Inspectors felt the school was improving, crediting 'the effective management of pupils' behaviour and the creation of a positive climate for learning'. They highlighted the school's contribution to its pupils' social development, praising its 'impressive' programme of community service and a mentoring system where sixth-formers help children in Years 7 and 8.

### Extra-curricular activities

The Sports Council has given the school its Sportsmark Award in recognition of its wide range of high-quality sports. Pupils have competed nationally at athletics and have achieved county success at football. The school has also received the Football Association's Charter Standard. The school has after-school homework clubs. There is a strong musical tradition, with choirs, an orchestra and several groups. The Duke of Edinburgh's Award scheme is popular and community service, often linked to the church, is well supported. There are school trips, both local and abroad.

## White Hart Lane Secondary School

**White Hart Lane, London N22 5QJ** 020 8889 6761 020 8365 8164 WhiteHartLane.School@haringey.gov.uk David Daniels; Chair of Governors: Mrs B Beutel Wood Green **Buses:** W3, W5, 144, 230 Up to sixth form: Royal blue school sweatshirt or blue or white polo shirt with school motif, black or navy blue trousers or skirt **Demand:** 243 places in 2001/2 **Type:** Community comprehensive for 1140 mixed pupils, aged 11 to 18 **Submit application form:** 24 October 2003 **School hours:** 8.40am–3.10pm; homework clubs are available **School meals:** Hot and cold available, including breakfast **Strong GCSE subjects:** Art, Turkish **London league table position:** 511

### Profile

Even by inner-city standards, the problems facing White Hart Lane are formidable. Its pupils are some of the most socially disadvantaged in the country. The school has good access to the New River Sports Centre, and it also has the unique training restaurant 'Foodles', which is run by pupils as part of their catering courses. A recent grant of £200,000 has been used to upgrade the business technology facilities and the library. Total redecoration of the school will be completed in 2003. The spacious grounds include an all-weather pitch and a gym. The school has also joined the Excellence in Cities project. Two trained counsellors assist with pastoral care. The Friends of White Hart Lane School encourages parents and staff to run activities together. The school offers English lessons to adults and runs special parents' evenings, where interpreters are available. An Ofsted report in 2000 found some disruption in class and around the school, as well as 'some undercurrents of racial tension'. Truancy is a serious problem at 3.9 per cent, although some of this is accounted for by the transitory school population. There is provision for special-needs pupils.

### Admissions and intake

Admission is through the LEA. Anyone putting the school as a first or second choice will be admitted. Around 40 per cent of pupils are refugees, many Kurdish, and 35 per cent are beginners at English. Many live in temporary accommodation and there is a high turnover from one year to the next.

### Achievement

In 2002, 24 per cent of pupils obtained five or more A*–C grades, up from 10 per cent in 2001. The school was ranked one place above bottom of the borough table. Inspectors visited the school in 2002 and reported that: 'White Hart Lane is an improving school that is providing a satisfactory education for its pupils'. Ofsted praised the 'effective leadership' of the head teacher and noted that punctuality and attendance is improving. Pupils do well at art and Turkish but standards of attainment in English, maths and science need improving. In Years 7 and 8 a literacy programme – Talking Text – is run to help develop language and writing skills. The sixth form is part of the Nexus consortium (see borough factfile). It has a compact agreement with Middlesex University. Pupils taking two or more subjects at A-level scored an average of 94.2 points, placing the school ninth in the borough. Very few pupils sit A-levels. Results in the vocational courses were above average. Staff turnover is high, but teachers try hard to support pupils, and many are generous with their own time.

### Extra-curricular activities

There are homework clubs in every subject, and Easter and summer schools. Sports and arts activities are on offer, along with trips to Wales. The school runs an artist-in-residence scheme. There are also links with the local Turkish radio station. Pupils are involved with the local community, visiting local nurseries and businesses.

# Harrow

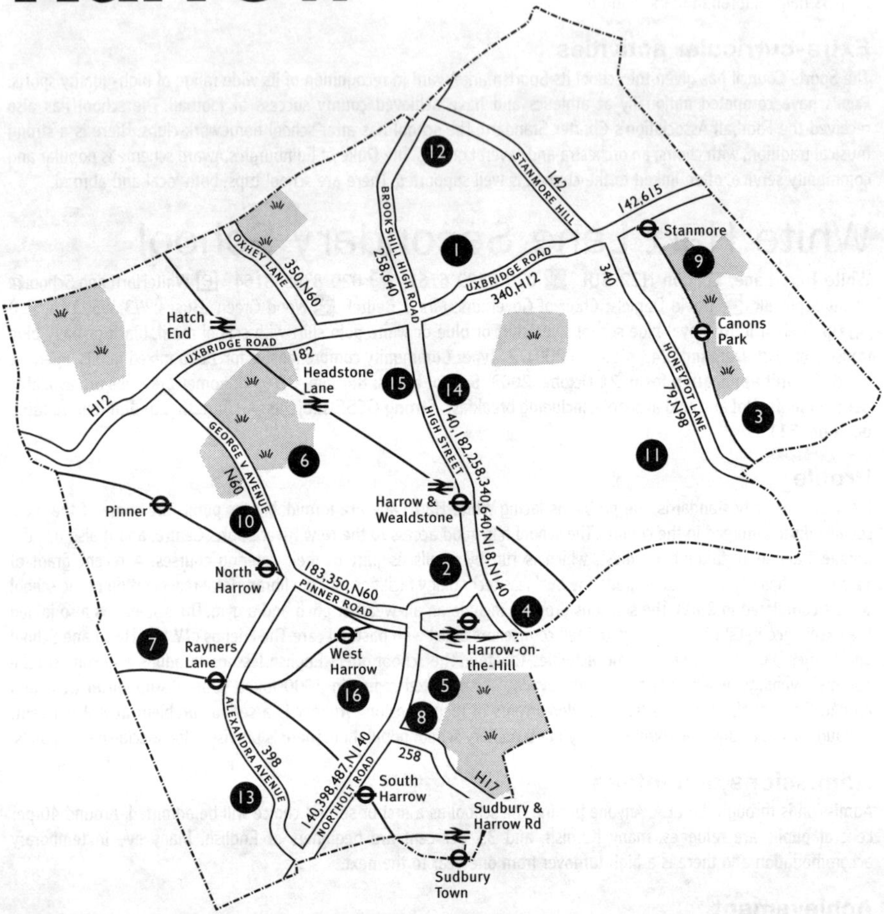


**Key**

1. Bentley Wood High School
2. Buckingham College School
3. Canons High School
4. Harrow High School
5. Harrow School
6. Hatch End High School
7. Heathfield School Pinner
8. The John Lyon School
9. North London Collegiate School
10. Nower Hill High School
11. Park High School
12. Peterborough and St Margaret's School
13. Rooks Heath High School
14. The Sacred Heart RC High School
15. Salvatorian RC College
16. Whitmore High School

# Factfile

**LEA: PO Box 22, Civic Centre, Station Road, Harrow HA1 2JU** ☎ **020 8863 5611** 🌐 **www.harrow.gov.uk** **Director of Education:** Paul Osburn **Political control of council:** No overall control **Percentage of pupils from outside the borough:** 10.5 per cent **Percentage of pupils educated outside the borough:** 8 per cent **League table positions (out of 32 boroughs):** 6th

## Profile

Harrow is fairly homogeneous – the epitome of suburban metroland – although the north-west of the borough is more affluent than the south-east. Harrow Hill, with its famous public school at the summit, can be seen from across the borough and seems to act as a beacon for good education. This world-famous institution has made Harrow synonymous with education. However, the borough's state secondary school system should also be given its due in adding to the borough's reputation in the field, since it is one of the most successful in the country.

Over recent years there has been an extensive building programme to enlarge the capacity of the borough's state schools, but more than half are oversubscribed by first-choice applications and there are just 56 excess places in the system. Since none of the state schools are selective, none of them appear at the top of the individual exam league tables, but as a whole they are invariably in the top 10 and in some years in first place. Families frequently move to Harrow so that their children can obtain a secondary school place, but since they are only available to pupils at 'linked' primary schools, the moves have to be planned well in advance. Unusually, Harrow's state secondary schools start at Year 8 (ages 12 to 13), a year after most other areas. None of the state secondary schools has a sixth form, with post-16 education provided by two tertiary colleges and a Roman Catholic sixth-form college.

Besides Harrow School, there are several other highly regarded schools in the Independent sector. North London Collegiate, Peterborough and St Margaret's and Heathfield are all highly regarded girls' schools with outstanding exam results that attract pupils from across north London.

## Policy

None of the non-denominational state schools opted out of council control by taking grant-maintained status, so the LEA remains relatively influential in formulating cross-borough policy, including the admissions policy. Parents should contact Harrow LEA for a copy of the brochure *A Guide to Secondary Schools in Harrow*. If a state school is oversubscribed, the criteria in order of importance, for places are: pupils with statements of special educational needs which are met best by a particular school; applications made on medical grounds; pupils with a sibling at the school; and pupils attending a linked primary school and with a sibling at the school. Applications for Sacred Heart or Salvatorian need to be made directly to the schools.

# Bentley Wood High School

**Bridges Road, Stanmore, Middlesex HA7 3NA** ☎ 020 8954 3623 📠 020 8954 0427 Annette Ford; Chair of Governors: Gwen Day ⊖ Stanmore **Buses:** 340, H12 Bottle green blazer or sweatshirt, bottle green skirt or trousers and white blouse **Demand:** 185 first-choice applications for 180 places in 2001/2 **Type:** Community comprehensive for 713 girls aged 12 to 16 **Submit application form:** 5 December 2003 **School hours:** 8.40am–3.05pm; homework clubs are available **Meals:** Hot and cold available **Strong GCSE subjects:** English, history **London league table position:** 278

## Profile

Bentley Wood is Harrow's only non-denominational single-sex school for girls. It is located on the edge of Stanmore's green belt off a quiet side road. The buildings are modern and well equipped, with a large library, a purpose-built drama studio and expanding computer facilities. The school is set in 27 acres of woodland, and has its own tennis courts, hockey fields and athletics track. In addition to the National Curriculum, Year 8 and 9 pupils study two modern foreign languages, and there is an emphasis on drama and music. The school provides year-based pastoral support for pupils and has an induction for new girls. Pupils can become members of the school council and a head girl and deputy are appointed each year. There is an active parents, teachers and friends association. There is provision for special-needs pupils.

## Admissions and intake

Admission is through the LEA. Priority is given to applicants with approved medical reasons and those with a sister at the school. If there are still more applicants than places, a random selection is made by computer.

## Achievement

In 2002, 56 per cent of pupils achieved five or more A*–C grades at GCSE. This was down on the previous year and below the borough average. A cooperative and stimulating environment that enabled pupils to learn happily was reported by Ofsted inspectors who visited Bentley Wood in 1996. The extent of racial harmony at the school was exceptional. The inspectors also noted: 'Teaching is a major strength of the school'. The quality of teaching was at least satisfactory in nine out of 10 of the lessons, good or better in over half, and in one lesson in 10 it was very good. Unsatisfactory teaching was relatively unusual and the incidence of poor teaching was negligible. Attainment of pupils on entry appeared to be average. Results were good in English, average in maths and science, above average in languages, high in history and satisfactory in geography. Inspectors concluded: 'Standards of attainment are good and compare well with attainment nationally'. Ofsted found overall standards of behaviour in and around the school were very good, often excellent, and pupils' attitude to the school was a significant factor in the academic standards achieved.

## Extra-curricular activities

After-school clubs include homework clubs, IT, music, maths, chess and Spanish. Regular visits are organized to Spain, France and Germany. The school provides an extensive range of sporting activities, including hockey, tennis, trampolining, football, aerobics, athletics, netball and dance. There are two drama productions a year and concerts of music and dance. Pupils visit art galleries, museums and theatres, and also have the chance to take part in the Duke of Edinburgh's Award scheme.

# Buckingham College School

**15–17 Hindes Road, Harrow, Middlesex HA1 1SH** 020 8427 1220 020 8863 0816 enquiries@buckcoll.org David Bell; Managing Governor: Malcolm Leach Harrow-on-the-Hill Harrow-on-the-Hill **Buses:** H10, H11, H14, H17, H18, 114, 140, 182, 183, 186, 223, 258, 340, 350, 640 Navy blazer, grey trousers and red and gold striped school tie **Demand:** c.60 applications for 30 places in 2000/1 **Type:** Selective independent for 176 boys (mixed in sixth form), aged 10 to 19 **Fees:** (per term): Year 7 – £1,980, Year 8 to 11 – £2,210, sixth form – £2,295 **Submit application form:** No cut-off date **Motto:** Man Know Thyself **School hours:** 8.45am–3.55pm **Meals:** Hot and cold available **Strong GCSE subjects:** English, English literature, maths, modern languages, sciences **London league table position:** 117

## Profile

Buckingham College was founded in 1936 and is part of the E Ivor Hughes Educational Foundation, which includes Peterborough and St Margaret's School in Harrow. The college occupies a row of late 19th-century buildings close to Harrow town centre. The lower school is based about a mile away. It has the use of two public playing fields in Harrow and Kenton as well as the facilities of a nearby sports club for badminton, squash and table tennis and the local authority sports centre for swimming. At Key Stage 3 all pupils follow the national curriculum, in the second year they start a second modern language, usually German, and in the third year they take separate sciences – biology, chemistry and physics. At Key Stage 4, economics and business studies are added to the curriculum. Pupils are expected to take nine GCSEs. In the sixth form, those seeking entrance to Oxbridge or medical school are expected to take four A-levels and all others take three, or two A-levels with two AS-levels. Class sizes are under 20 and the pupil-to-teacher ratio is 10:1. Pupils can become monitors and prefects. There is a house system, that fosters a competitive spirit, culminating in annual awards for achievements in sport as well as shields for academic achievement. Individual awards, including house colours, are also given to pupils. There is an active society of parents and friends. Former pupils can become members of the Old Buckinghamians Association.

## Admissions and intake

Candidates are required to sit an entrance test and undergo an interview.

## Achievement

In the 2002 GCSE results, a substantial 73 per cent of pupils gained five or more A*–C grades. This figure was down from 75 per cent in 2001. It was however above the borough and national averages, and the school was ranked sixth n the borough league table. The average point score for pupils taking two or more A/AS-levels was 277.9 in 2002. These results were above the national average and borough averages. The school was placed fifth in the borough league table. The school itself says: 'Preparing pupils for the pressures of a competitive world is an important part of school life. Competition is not only a reality, in its rightful place it is healthy.'

## Extra-curricular activities

A range of musical activities is offered, as well as sports such as horse riding, dry-slope skiing and golf. There is an annual skiing trip to the Alps. All pupils are encouraged to take part in the Duke of Edinburgh's Award scheme from the age of 14. The school organizes an annual speech day and a music and drama festival.

# Canons High School

**Shaldon Road, Edgware, Middlesex HA8 6AN** 020 8951 5780 020 8951 2333 info@canons.harrow.sch.uk Bruce Goddard; Chair of Governors: Mr P Younger Queensbury, Canons Park, Burnt Oak **Buses:** 79, 114 Black blazer, black skirt or trousers, white shirt and maroon school tie with grey stripes **Demand:** 83 first-choice applications for 180 places in 2000/1 **Type:** Community comprehensive Technology College for 720 mixed pupils, aged 12 to 16 **Submit application form:** 5 December 2003 **Mission statement:** Canons is working hard to raise educational standards and good citizens of the future – like your children **School hours:** 8.45am–3.30pm; homework clubs are available **Meals:** Hot and cold available **Strong GCSE subjects:** Music **London league table position:** 294

## Profile

Canons High is set within its own playing fields in the heart of a residential area. The area is less prosperous compared with much of Harrow. The school was built in the 1950s and there is a five-year plan to improve facilities for science, art, textiles and performing arts. It recently gained Technology College status and was awarded the School Achievement Award for Excellence in 2001. There is a special unit for pupils with specific learning difficulties, and there are proposals to open a new facility for pupils with severe learning disabilities. Two pupils from each year become members of the school council. There is a prefects system and a parents association, the Friends of Canons.

## Admissions and intake

Admission is through the LEA. Priority is given to pupils from linked primary schools, namely Aylward, Glebe, Little Stanmore, St Bernadette's and Stag Lane. If the school is oversubscribed by first-choice preferences, priority is given to applicants living the shortest safe walking distance from the school. Pupils come from a wide range of ethnic backgrounds. Just over half of them are of Indian origin and there is a significant number of pupils from Black-African and Black-Caribbean backgrounds. A total of 64 per cent of pupils have English as an additional language.

## Achievement

In 2002, 48 per cent of pupils gained five or more A*–C grades at GCSE, a rise from 43 per cent in 2001 but below the borough and national averages. The school was ranked 14th in the borough league table. Canons High is in the top 5 per cent in the country for improving pupils' standards between National Curriculum tests at the end of Key Stage 3 and GCSE. It is placed in the top 10 per cent when compared with similar schools by the government. *The Guardian* newspaper reported that Canons' exam results were the most improved in North London. Ofsted visited the school in 2002 and commented: 'Canons High School is a very good school. Pupils make good progress in their time at the school and their performance in the GCSE examinations is well above that of pupils in similar schools'. The quality of teaching was found to have 'improved considerably' and Inspectors noted that the school was 'well led'. The school's provision for pupils' cultural development was seen to be 'excellent'. However, pupils' skills in literacy needs to be improved along with attainment in the core subjects of English, maths and science by the end of Year 9. Inspectors also wanted to see a reduction in the school's 'above average' level of fixed term exclusions.

## Extra-curricular activities

A variety of sports, drama and musical activities are on offer, and pupils are actively encouraged to become a member of at least one club or team. There is a variety of clubs, including homework clubs, Gujarati and Greek. There is involvement with the local community.

# Harrow High School

**Gayton Road, Harrow, Middlesex HA1 2JG** 020 8861 7300 020 8861 4024 inquires@harrow-high.harrow.sch.uk Christine Lenihan; Chair of Governors: Linda Heggie Harrow-on-the-Hill Harrow-on-the-Hill **Buses:** H10, H11, H17, H18, 223, 340, 350 Navy blazer, grey trousers or pleated skirt, white shirt, blue and gold striped school tie **Demand:** 180 places available in 2001/2 **Type:** Community comprehensive Sports College for 535 mixed pupils, aged 12 to 16 **Submit application form:** 5 December 2003 **Mission statement:** Our purpose is to ensure education which promises excellence and provides all our students with the confidence and skills to meet the challenges of the 21st century. **School hours:** 8.45am–3.35pm, 8.45am–3.15pm (Thurs); homework clubs are available **Meals:** Hot and cold available **Strong GCSE subjects:** Art, business studies, drama, English, geography **London league table position:** 395

## Profile

Although Harrow High only opened in September 1998, there has been a school on the site since 1911. As Harrow County Grammar, it was the most prestigious boys' state school in the area. It was renamed Gayton High when it became a boys-only comprehensive and its reputation and popularity waned. It recently gained Sports College status. The school is situated on the outskirts of Harrow's town centre. Many facilities in the original main building have been modernized in recent years and the school has a new sports hall, classroom block, drama suite, dance/fitness studios, a music suite, textiles room and media studies area. The school has just started to offer GNVQ in business studies. Former pupils include politician Michael Portillo, chat-show host Clive Anderson, comedian Cardew Robinson and England test cricketers Mark Ramprakash and Angus Fraser. There is a school council and a PTA.

## Admissions and intake

Admission is through the LEA. Priority is given to pupils from linked primary schools, namely Belmont, Elmgrove, Norbury and Whitefriars. If the school is oversubscribed by first-choice preferences, priority is given to applicants living the shortest safe walking distance from the school. Two-thirds of pupils in 1998 came from homes where English was not the first language and a quarter were on the special-needs register.

## Achievement

In 2002, 37 per cent of pupils achieved five or more A*–C grades at GCSE, well below the national average and the lowest results in the borough. However, these results were an improvement on 33 per cent in 2001. Ofsted visited the school in 1998 and commented: 'Pupil attainment is high when compared to schools with similar characteristics, but shows no improvement since the last inspection and overall remains below national averages.' It was still a boys' school at that time but preparing to become co-educational. Results of pupils aged 14 put the school in the top quarter when compared with similar schools nationally and for boys aged 16 it was in the top 10 per cent. At both ages 14 and 16, results in English and science were below national standards, and in maths they were below national standards for 14-year-old children but at national standards by age 16. The quality of teaching was at least satisfactory in more than eight lessons in 10, and in over half the lessons it was good or very good. Ofsted found that pupils had a positive attitude to learning, and behaviour in lessons and around the school was good.

## Extra-curricular activities

In addition to sporting activities and music and drama groups, clubs are organized in art, chess, information, science and technology and homework. Pupils can take part in Young Enterprise and the Duke of Edinburgh's Award scheme. There are school trips both at home and abroad.

# Harrow School

**15 High Street, Harrow-on-the-Hill, Middlesex HA1 3HW** 020 8872 8000 020 8872 8012 hm@harrowschool.org.uk www.harrowschool.org.uk Barnaby J Lenon Harrow-on-the-Hill Harrow-on-the-Hill, South Harrow **Buses:** H17, 258 Dark blue jacket, grey flannels, white shirt, black tie, distinctive Harrow hat; on Sunday mornings and for special functions in the Speech Room, tailcoats are worn **Demand:** No figures available but high school's 160 places fully subscribed in 2000/1 **Type:** Selective independent for 795 boys, aged 13 to 19 **Fees:** £6,375 per term **Submit application form:** No cut-off date; best to apply two years in advance **Motto:** *Stet fortuna domus donorum dei distensatio fidelis* (May the Fortune of the House Stand.

The Faithful Stewardship of the Gifts of God) **School hours:** 8.35am–4.30pm plus Saturday mornings, but hours variable; homework clubs are available **Meals:** Hot and cold available **Strong GCSE subjects:** Art, French, maths, sciences **London league table position:** 76

## Profile

Harrow is one of the most famous public boarding schools in the country and has taught seven prime ministers, including Winston Churchill. Founded in the 16th century, it occupies much of the top of Harrow Hill. The school consists of a series of beautiful old buildings, although there are a number of newer buildings and a constant modernization programme. The school is surrounded by about 300 acres of its own land, including its own working farm. Harrow remains proud of its traditions and the boys wear a distinctive uniform. There is a strong house system and the school timetable is full of reminders of the past. It even has its own sport – Harrow football – which is played with a rugby-type ball in deep mud. The head appoints a head of school, heads of houses and senior boys who together make up the school monitors responsible for the welfare and good order of the school. In addition, each house has its own body of house monitors appointed by the house master. Sports and games are administered by the group of senior boys known as 'the Phil' (the Philathletic Club). When boys first arrive, all lessons are taught in school, but later some are given as private study. The average class size is about 20. Weekday and Saturday mornings are devoted to academic work. After supper boys can go to clubs, societies or extra tuition or remain in their houses for prep time. There is a prefect system and provision for special-needs pupils.

## Admissions and intake

Registrations are accepted from birth onwards but there is no particular advantage to be gained from a very early application. Registration should be completed before the age of 11, however, since late applications may limit the choice of house. Admission is via the Common Entrance Examination, Harrow Scholarship Examination or the Harrow Test. Most successful applicants achieve an average score of 55–80 per cent in the Common Entrance, but a small number are accepted who score 50–55 per cent but have ability in some other area such as sport, art or drama.

## Achievement

Academic results are not outstanding, and certainly for the money, higher grades are more likely at other schools. In 2002, 88 per cent of pupils gained five or more A*–C grades at GCSE. Harrow was ranked fourth in the borough. The average point score of pupils taking two or more A/AS-levels was 379.6, the second-best results in the borough. However, Harrow maintains that it provides an all-round education and preparation for life in a caring environment.

## Extra-curricular activities

Half-holiday afternoons and spare time at weekends are available for extra-curricular activities and personal interests. Harrow has an unrivalled choice of activities – from bagpipe lessons to Eton fives. There are also regular trips abroad. Boys spend Wednesday afternoons serving the community. There are after-school homework clubs.

# Hatch End High School

**Headstone Lane, Harrow, Middlesex HA3 6NR** ☎ 020 8428 4330 ℻ 020 8420 1932 ✉ admin@email.hatchend.harrow.sch.uk 🌐 www.hatchend.harrow.sch.uk D Allan Jones; Chair of Governors: Dr Clem Lewis ⇌ Headstone Lane ⊖ North Harrow **Buses:** H12, H14, H18, 350 Black blazer, black skirt or trousers, white shirt, black school tie with red and white stripes (lower school); black school tie with a pattern of the school's crest (upper school) **Demand:** 339 first-choice applications for 300 places in 2001/2 **Type:** Community comprehensive for 1215 mixed pupils, aged 12 to 16 **Submit application form:** 5 December 2003 **Motto:** Committed to Excellence **School hours:** 8.55am–3.25pm; homework clubs are available **Meals:** Hot and cold available, including breakfast **Strong GCSE subjects:** Music **London league table position:** 189

## Profile

Hatch End is the largest school in Harrow and is situated on the edge of the green belt in a quiet residential area. It was built in the 1950s and recent modifications include new workshops, science labs and a school-wide computer network. The buildings are accessible to wheelchair users and a deaf resource base provides places for 13 pupils with severe hearing impairments. The school has its own heated swimming pool, two gymnasia and tennis courts, and offers a wide range of sporting activities, for which it has received a Sportsmark Award. The school is a member of the National Association for Able Children in Education (NAACE). Pupils in Year 11 can become prefects and there is a school council. There is also an active parent-teacher association. Former pupils include the MP for Harrow West, Gareth Thomas.

## Admissions and intake

Admission is through the LEA. Priority is given to pupils from linked primary schools, namely Cedars, Grimsdyke, Marlborough, Pinner Park, St John's, Weald and Whitefriars. If the school is oversubscribed by first-choice preferences, priority is given to applicants living the shortest safe walking distance from the school. A total of 19.3 per cent of pupils have special needs, which is broadly average.

## Achievement

In 2002, 68 per cent of pupils pupils gained five or more A*–C grades. This was an increase on 63 per cent in 2001 and above the national and borough averages. Pupils who are exceptional at maths can take the GCSE a year early. When inspected in 2000, Ofsted found Hatch End 'a very effective school which enables pupils of a wide range of abilities to make good and often very good progress to reach above average standards'. Attainment on entry ranges from well below average to very able and gifted pupils. Although the majority of pupils achieved the levels expected in national tests taken at age 11, a significant number were below that level. Behaviour is very good in the great majority of lessons and there is orderly conduct around the school.

## Extra-curricular activities

Hatch End has 'an unusually wide variety of ensembles and bands' according to Ofsted. These include senior and junior wind bands, string orchestra, sinfonia, brass ensemble, clarinet ensemble, saxophone ensemble, flute ensemble, string quartet, percussion ensemble, classical guitar ensemble, recorder ensemble, Indian ensemble, steel bands and Dixie, rhythm and blues and salsa bands. There are after-school homework clubs, and pupils can participate in the Duke of Edinburgh's Award scheme, the Society of Young Scientists and Young Enterprise. Sports include basketball and girls' football, as well as the other regular sports. There are trips both at home and abroad.

# Heathfield School Pinner

**Beaulieu Drive, Pinner, Middlesex HA5 1NB** ☎ 020 8868 2346 ⎙ 020 8868 4405 ⓔ enquiries@hea.gdst.net 🌐 www.heathfield.gdst.net ✉ Miss Christine Juett; Chair of Governors: Andrew Lee ⊖ Eastcote, Rayners Lane **Buses:** H12, 398; school's coach service covers Wembley, Kingsbury, Kenton and Harrow 👔 Navy jersey skirt, burgundy and white pinstripe blouse; regulation dark navy coat, gaberdine raincoat or navy waxed jacket (winter), cherry red blazer (summer) **Demand:** No figures available but 80 places oversubscribed in 2001/2 **Type:** Selective independent Girls' Day School Trust for 598 girls, aged 3 to 18 **Fees:** £2,385 per term **Submit application form:** 5 December 2003 **Motto:** *Vincit qui se vincit* (She Who Conquers Must First Conquer Herself) **School hours:** 8.30am–3.50pm (Mon–Thurs), 8.30am–3.30pm (Fri) **Meals:** Hot and cold available **Strong GCSE subjects:** All relatively strong **London league table position:** 69

## Profile

Heathfield is 100 years old but has only been at its current location since 1982. The school joined the Girls' Day School Trust (GDST) in 1987. The nine-acre site dates from the 1920s and recent upgrading of facilities includes a new library, sports hall and swimming pool. An ongoing four-year modernization programme will add a new music and performing arts centre. The school has its own playing fields with six tennis courts, two lacrosse pitches, an athletics track and netball courts. 'Heathfield provides a well-balanced education, meeting individual needs, providing support and developing every girl's different abilities through the provision of a wide range of opportunities both within and beyond the curriculum,' according to the head, Christine Juett. Girls transfer from the junior school at the end of Year 6. There are 300 girls in the senior school and 80 in the sixth form, which is housed in a separate wing. All pupils follow a 'way of life' course run jointly with the boys at Harrow School, which explores current issues on the environment, society and personal relationships. Drama is popular, with many girls choosing to take private tuition in speech and drama. A variety of performances are held annually, ranging from Shakespeare to musicals. Pupils can become form captains and members of the school council and older girls can become prefects. There is a thriving friends association open to parents, which organizes social events to raise funds for school amenities. Former pupils can become members of the Heathfield Old Girls' Association and the Minerva Network run by the GDST.

### Admissions and intake

The senior school takes pupils from 11+. Applicants are assessed by exam and an interview. Pupils are drawn from across Harrow and also from Brent, Barnet, Hillingdon and south Hertfordshire.

### Achievement

In 2002, 91 per cent of pupils gained five or more A*–C grades at GCSE. This result was down from from 93 per cent in 2001 and the school was ranked third in the borough league table. Pupils follow the core requirements of the National Curriculum and are expected to take nine GCSEs. The average point score of pupils taking two or more subjects at A/AS level was 342.1 in 2002. This was above the national but below the borough averages. These results placed the school third in the borough league table. The sixth form offers just under 20 A-levels. Almost all pupils go on to university.

### Extra-curricular activities

Activities available include sports, music, drama, chess, debating, ballet and gymnastics. Pupils can also take part in the Duke of Edinburgh's Award scheme. Many trips are organized by the school and recent destinations have ranged from York and Chester to Athens and Madrid.

## The John Lyon School

**Middle Road, Harrow-on-the-Hill, Middlesex HA2 OHN** 020 8872 8400 020 8872 8018 johnlyon@dial.pipex.com www.johnlyon.cc Dr Christopher Ray; Chair of Governors: Professor M Edwards Harrow-on-the-Hill Harrow-on-the-Hill, South Harrow **Buses:** H10, H17, 258 Navy blazer, white or grey trousers, maroon and navy striped school tie, plus house tie **Demand:** Twice as many applications for 66 places at 11+ and 22 places at 13+ **Type:** Selective independent for 547 boys, aged 10 to 19 **Fees:** £2,820 per term **Submit application form:** End of November 2003 **Motto:** *Stet fortuna domus* (May the Good Fortune of This House Stand) **School hours:** 8.30am–3.10pm (junior), 8.30am–3.50pm (senior) **Meals:** Hot and cold available **Strong GCSE subjects:** Biology, English language and literature, maths **London league table position:** 58

### Profile

John Lyon School was founded in 1853 by Dr Charles Vaughan, headmaster of Harrow School, to provide for the education of the sons of Harrow townsmen. It opened on its present site in 1876 and is under the management of a committee appointed by the Governors of Harrow School. The head is an elected member of the Headmasters' Conference. The school has its own playing fields, including a new pavilion. Most boys join Oldfield, the junior school, at 11+, which is housed in a separate modern building, where they spend the first two years. They then move to the middle school together with new boys who join at 13+. A total of 15 subjects are taught prior to GCSEs. The parents' association runs social events to raise funds for charity or for the school. There is also an active Old Lyonian Association. There is a school council and a prefects system in the sixth form. There is provision for special needs pupils, with an appointed head of learning strategies.

### Admissions and intake

Boys must sit the school's entrance exam and undergo an interview. Pupils are drawn from north-west London and south Hertfordshire.

### Achievement

'John Lyon has often been compared to a traditional grammar school, and academic excellence is certainly our first priority,' commented the current head, Dr Christopher Ray. In 2000, all entrants passed the maths GCSE with a grade A*–B and all passed English with grade C or above. In 2002, 98 per cent of pupils gained grades A*–C in at least five subjects at GCSE. This was slightly up from 98 per cent in 2001 and the school came second in the borough. The average point score for pupils taking two or more A/AS-levels was 323, ranking the school fourth in the borough. The school offers a choice of 17 subjects at GCSE from which pupils must select a minimum of nine GCSEs. Many boys take maths GCSE a year early. All pupils take science to GCSE level and many take one or more at A-level. Design and technology, including computer-aided design and computer-aided manufacturing, is a growth area. Sixth-formers study three or four A-levels from the 16 on offer. The head concluded: 'Firm discipline is at the heart of a good school as it is at the heart of family life, yet it is always tempered by the deepest respect for the individual character of each and every boy.'

### Extra-curricular activities

Clubs available include chess, bridge, art, fish and stamps, while for music there is a school choir and orchestra, a wind band and chamber groups. Sports teams include karate, volleyball, golf and squash as well as the more traditional activities. Trips and expeditions feature watersports in the south of France, cricket tours to Norfolk and Barbados, skiing holidays and sailing. Pupils can also take part in the Duke of Edinburgh's Award scheme. The school sponsors every lower sixth-former to go on a week's course run by the Outward Bound Trust in Scotland.

# North London Collegiate School

**Canons Drive, Edgware, Middlesex HA8 7RJ** ☎ 020 8952 0912 Fax 020 8951 1391 e office@nlcs.harrow.sch.uk www.nlcs.org.uk Mrs Bernice McCabe; Chair of Governors: Ian McGregor ⊖ Canons Park, Stanmore, Edgware **Buses:** 79, 186, 340; the school also operates a number of coaches to collect and return pupils from across north London Brown blazer, blue shirt, brown skirt **Demand:** No figures available but 104 places in 2001/2 **Type:** Selective independent for 1008 girls, aged 11 to 18 **Fees:** £2,764 per term (senior school) plus £250 for lunches **Submit application form:** End of November for up to GCSE level; end of October for sixth form **Motto:** We Work in Hope **School hours:** 8.40am–4pm **Meals:** Hot and cold available **Strong GCSE subjects:** All relatively strong **London league table position:** 10

### Profile

North London Collegiate is one of the oldest girls' day schools in the country. It was founded by Mary Buss in 1850 and is set within 30 acres of its own landscaped parkland, which was once occupied by the palace of the Duke of Chandos. The main building dates from 1760 and the school moved to the site in 1926. There is a recently opened performing arts centre, medical centre and library. The school has its own lacrosse pitches, an athletics track, tennis courts and new sports centre with indoor swimming pool and fitness suite. Girls follow the national curriculum to Key Stage 3. At Key Stage 4 English language and literature, maths and dual science (taught as three separate subjects) are compulsory. Greek and Russian can be started at this stage and between nine and 10 subjects may be selected from a range of 18. In the sixth form there are 22 subjects on offer. Sixth-formers can become prefects and in Year 13 are expected to assume at least one official responsibility, such as form assistant, librarian or chair of a society. There is an active parents' guild, which also organizes social evenings. Britain's first qualified female dentist, Lilian Lindsay, and women's rights campaigner, Marie Stopes, were pupils at the school. There is a school council.

### Admissions and intake

Applicants must sit an entrance exam and undergo an interview. Most pupils are drawn from the borough and Barnet, Brent and Hillingdon, while a few come from overseas and stay with relatives or friends.

### Achievement

The school invariably appears at or towards the top of the exam league tables for Britain, and it was voted *The Sunday Times* Independent School of the Year in 1999. In 2002, 100 per cent of pupils gained five or more A*–C grades at GCSE and the school came top of the borough league table. The average point score of pupils taking two or more A/AS-levels was 419.1, the top results in the borough 'We want all our pupils to value academic excellence and to realize that it is attainable; we aim to encourage a love of learning, a spirit of enquiry and an independence of mind,' stated the head teacher, Bernice McCabe. In sport, the junior, intermediate and senior teams came first in the Harrow Athletics Championships in 2000.

### Extra-curricular activities

A huge number of clubs and societies exist. The Duke of Edinburgh's Award scheme is open to Year 10 and above, and the debating and model United Nations societies provide the opportunity to develop public speaking skills. There is a wide range of sports on offer, including lacrosse. An annual skiing trip and holiday in the Ardeche is organized by the PE department. Classics trips take place to the Bay of Naples and history pupils can visit the battlefields of World

War I. There is an active programme of community service for sixth-formers, including work in local schools, hospitals, nursing homes and conservation schemes.

# Nower Hill High School

**George V Avenue, Pinner, Middlesex HA5 5RP** ☎ 020 8863 0877/8 📠 020 8424 0762 ⓔ lwhittington@nowerhill.org 🌐 www.nowerhill.org ✉ Howard Freed; Chair of Governors: Mr Peter Daffon ⊖ North Harrow **Buses:** 183, 350 👔 Black blazer, black or grey skirt or trousers, white shirt or blouse and navy school tie with silver stripes **Demand:** 300 places available in 2001/2 **Type:** Community comprehensive for 1204 mixed pupils, aged 12 to 16 **Submit application form:** 5 December 2003 **Motto:** Service Not Self **School hours:** 8.45am–3.15pm; homework clubs are available **Meals:** Hot and cold available **Strong GCSE subjects:** English, arts, maths **London league table position:** 185

## Profile

Nower Hill is the second largest school in Harrow. It is situated on a busy road in one of the most affluent parts of the borough. A recent £2.75-million building programme has provided an IT centre, business studies suite, modern science labs, a technology centre, studios for music, drama and dance, a sports hall, a library and learning resource centre and two new arts rooms. However, the school has had some financial difficulties, followed by the resignation of the previous long-serving head and concern about reductions in the budget for staff. The new head joined in 1999/2000. There is a head boy and girl, prefects and a school council. There is a PTA. Nower Hill has Beacon School status.

## Admissions and intake

Admission is through the LEA. Priority is given to pupils from linked primary schools, namely Canon Lane, Pinner Park, Pinner Wood, St John Fisher and West Lodge. If the school is oversubscribed by first-choice preferences, priority is given to applicants living the shortest safe walking distance from the school. In 2001, about 50 per cent of pupils came from ethnic minority groups, mainly Asian. The proportion of pupils with special educational needs and statements of special needs was in line with the national average.

## Achievement

In 2002, 66 per cent of pupils gained five or more A*–C grades at GCSE and the school was ranked eighth in the borough. Following an inspection in 2001, Ofsted reported: 'Nower Hill High School is a good school, very ably led and managed by the head teacher'. Inspectors praised the school's 'good teaching' particularly in English, maths, art, drama and music. Results in the National Curriculum tests and at GCSE were seen to be well above average. The school's strongest subjects are English, art and maths. Pupils who are exceptional at maths can take the GCSE a year early. Inspectors found pupils 'friendly, enthusiastic and keen to learn'. Those pupils with special educational needs or those learning to speak English were seen to progress well. However, Ofsted wanted to see improvements in pupils' progress in science in Years 8 and 9, and for all pupils' ICT skills to be improved. Nower Hill has won the Toyota Science and Technology Award six times, the Barclays New Futures Award in 1997 and the Quality Work Experience Pan-London Standard Award in 1998.

## Extra-curricular activities

The school has thriving clubs in music and drama, as well as a homework club. It has teams for most major sports and has had local and national success in athletics, cricket, cross-country, gymnastics, hockey, netball, rounders, rugby, soccer, swimming, tennis and trampolining. Pupils can also take part in the Duke of Edinburgh's Award scheme. Recent school visits have included exchanges to Germany, France, Italy and Greece with classical studies and skiing trips to France. The Parents and Friends of Nower Hill High arrange social and fund-raising activities.

# Park High School

**Thistlecroft Gardens, Stanmore, Middlesex HA7 1PL** ☎ 020 8952 2803 📠 020 8952 6975 ⓔ phsharrow2@aol.com 🌐 www.parkhighstanmore.org.uk ✉ Tony Barnes; Chair of Governors: Elizabeth Clery ⊖ Canons Park, Queensbury **Buses:** 79, 114, 186 👔 Navy blue blazer, navy blue trousers or skirt and white shirt; burgundy school tie for prefects, otherwise blue with light blue and burgundy stripes **Demand:** 280 places available in 2001/2; oversubscribed **Type:** Community comprehensive Technology College for 1137 mixed pupils, aged 12 to 16 **Submit application form:** 5 December 2003 **School hours:** 8.40am–3.35pm; homework clubs are available **Meals:** Hot and cold available **Strong GCSE subjects:** Art, business studies, geography, IT, maths, PE, science **London league table position:** 146

## Profile

Park High was formed before the Second World War but has seen widespread modernization, including a large sports hall that was built a few years ago. The site is on a quiet residential road beside a park. The school obtained some notoriety as the subject of the Park High fly-on-the-wall television documentary in the mid 1990s. However, since the arrival of head Tony Barnes, it has become hugely popular and is the most oversubscribed state school in Harrow. It recently gained Technology College status. Each pupil has a personal tutor who sees them at least three times a day, including scheduled one-to-one review sessions to discuss progress and future plans. There is an active PTA, a pupils' committee and a prefects system.

## Admissions and intake

Admission is through the LEA. Priority is given to pupils from linked primary schools, namely Belmont, Kenmore Park, Priestmead, Stanburn and Whitchurch. If the school is oversubscribed by first-choice preferences, priority is given to applicants living the shortest safe walking distance from the school. There are 118 pupils on the special-needs register, which is close to the national average.

## Achievement

In 2002, 74 per cent of pupils gained five or more A*–C grades at GCSE, the best results for a state school in the league table. In the past, results have been particularly good in maths, science, art, business studies, geography, IT and PE. Results in drama, French, German and history were not as good. In 2000, Ofsted reported that Park High 'is a very effective school and the number of strengths far outweigh its weaknesses'. Pupils' attainment on entry is slightly above the national average. Results gained in the national curriculum tests at the end of Key Stage 3 are above national figures. At this stage, pupils' achievement is better than might be expected. During Years 10 and 11, pupils make good progress and achieve GCSE results that are significantly better than expected in relation to their attainment on entry. Boys achieve similar results to girls. The quality of teaching was satisfactory or better in 97 per cent of lessons and was good or better in 76 per cent. Very good teaching was seen in a quarter of lessons. The quality of teaching is better at Key Stage 3 than at Key Stage 4. The use of IT to support learning in all subjects was considered weak and there was a lack of consistency in the quality of marking. Inspectors found that: 'Pupils' attitudes towards their learning are very good. They come to school to learn and they are intolerant of pupils who misbehave.'

## Extra-curricular activities

The school provides the usual range of sports, music and drama activities. There are after-school homework clubs. Pupils have also been involved in supporting a number of charities. There are trips both at home and abroad.

# Peterborough and St Margaret's School

**Common Road, Stanmore, Middlesex HA7 3JB** 020 8950 3600 020 8421 8964 psm@psmschool.org www.psmschool.org Davina Tomlinson; Managing Governor: Malcolm Leach Stanmore **Buses:** 142, 258; the school also operates its own bus service to Radlett/Elstree and to Harrow White blouse, blue jumper, tartan skirt **Demand:** 34 places available; oversubscribed **Type:** Selective independent for 238 girls, aged 4 to 16 **Fees:** £2,210 per term (senior school) **Submit application form:** No cut-off date **Motto:** *Sic itur ad astra* (Reach for the Stars) **School hours:** 8.40am–3.45pm **Meals:** Hot and cold available **Strong GCSE subjects:** All relatively strong **London league table position:** 90

## Profile

Peterborough College and St Margaret's School were both founded about 100 years ago and were amalgamated in 1941. The school forms part of the E Ivor Hughes Educational Foundation, which also runs the Buckingham

College in Central Harrow. Peterborough and St Margaret's was based in central Harrow until 1993, when it moved to its current 3.5-acre site within the green belt on the border of Middlesex and Hertfordshire. Pupils transfer to the senior department at the end of Year 6. During the first three years there, pupils receive a broadly based education and many lessons are divided into groups of 10 to enable girls to gain confidence. Pupils choose their GCSE courses before entering Year 10. Separate courses are offered for GCSE biology, physics and chemistry, as well as the single-award combined science. French is taught from the school's reception classes and German is introduced as a second language in Year 8. A home economics department provides basic skills in textiles and food and nutrition. After GCSEs, pupils are able to transfer to the mixed sixth form of Buckingham College. Girls receive music and singing lessons, with individual tuition also available, and are entered for the Association Board of the Royal School of Music Examinations. Pupils can become prefects and members of the school council. There is an active society of parents and friends, provision for special-needs pupils, and the school is accredited by the Independent Schools Council.

## Admissions and intake

Candidates are required to sit the school's entrance exam and undergo an interview. Most pupils come from Harrow and south Hertfordshire, with some from Barnet and Hillingdon.

## Achievement

The school has an enviable reputation for its GCSE results, placing it towards the top of the league table for independent schools in Britain. It also has an excellent record for the lack of unauthorized absences. The school says: 'As well as ensuring that each girl reaches her full potential academically, we aim to prepare her in every possible way for the life that lies ahead.' The head Davina Tomlinson added: 'Academic qualifications are vital these days and we achieve excellent results.' In 2002, results improved slightly with 89 per cent of pupils gaining five or more A*–C grades at GCSE, up on 88 per cent in 2001. The school was ranked fifth in the borough.

## Extra-curricular activities

The school has a comprehensive choice of clubs, including drama, ballet and tap dancing, which meet during breaks and before and after school. It also has orchestras, choirs and various ensemble groups, which are regular winners at local festivals. A Social Action Society run by a committee of Year 10 pupils supervised by staff is responsible for organizing fund-raising events for charity. Residential trips include a biannual educational visit to Devon for pupils in Years 5 and 6. There are also field studies, visits to the Continent and skiing trips to Europe or Canada in the February half term.

# Rooks Heath High School

**Eastcote Lane, South Harrow, Middlesex HA2 9AG** 020 8422 4675 020 8422 4407 rooks.heath.high.sch@harrow.gov.uk John Reaveley; Chair of Governors: Catherine Woods Northolt Park South Harrow, Rayners Lane **Buses:** H10, 114 Navy blue blazer, navy blue skirt or trousers, white shirt, blue school tie with white stripes (lower school); black school tie with school crest (upper school) **Demand:** 260 places available in 2001/2 **Type:** Community comprehensive for 990 mixed pupils, aged 12 to 16 **Submit application form:** 5 December 2003 **Motto:** Loyalty, Truth and Service **School hours:** 8.50am–3.15pm; homework clubs are available **Meals:** Hot and cold available **Strong GCSE subjects:** Art, business studies, design and technology, drama, English, sociology **London league table position:** 312

## Profile

Rooks Heath was founded in the 1930s and is situated in a neighbourhood classified by the local health authority as an area of economic and social deprivation. Recent modernization work to the school has provided new IT rooms, science labs, library, humanities block, dance studio, music rooms, a drama studio and an outdoor games area. There are CCTV security cameras and an entry buzzer and telephone for visitors. In addition to the National Curriculum, all pupils study Latin and French in Year 8. Each pupil is assigned a personal tutor. There is a school council and pupils in Year 11 can become prefects. The school has a PTA, which actively raises funds for the school. Truancy is a problem and in 1999 Ofsted reported that the the most pressing area for action was the need to improve attendance in Years 10 and 11. In 2000, the truancy rate was 2.0 per cent, twice the national average.

## Admissions and intake

Admission is through the LEA. Priority is given to pupils from linked primary schools, namely Earlsmead, Newton Farm, Roxbourne, Roxeth Manor and Welldon Park. If the school is oversubscribed by first-choice preferences, priority is given to applicants living the shortest walking distance from the school. Pupils come from across four London boroughs: Harrow, Ealing, Brent and Hillingdon. Almost 40 per cent of pupils have special needs, well above the national average.

## Achievement

Rooks Heath was one of 52 schools singled out for praise by the former Chief Inspector of Schools. Ofsted reported that 'There are many more strengths than weaknesses because teachers are strongly committed to the school and the pupils.' When they join the school pupils are average at maths and numeracy skills and below average in English and literacy skills. But results in GCSE exams are generally in line with the average for secondary schools nationally and above average for those schools serving pupils from similar backgrounds. In 2002, 49 per cent of pupils gained five or more GCSEs at A*–C grades. Ofsted commented: 'Attainment is better than in schools of a similar type because pupils make good progress over the whole four years of study.' Teaching was good overall and was at least satisfactory in 95 per cent of lessons; in 17 per cent it was very good or excellent. The behaviour of pupils was also considered good.

## Extra-curricular activities

There is a range of competitive sports teams available for both boys and girls, and the school has been particularly successful at soccer, basketball and cricket. Music groups include an orchestra, wind band, jazz group, choir, chamber choir and steel band, and there are upper and lower school drama clubs. There is also a breakfast club which provides access to the Internet and library and an after-school homework club. There are trips both at home and abroad.

# The Sacred Heart RC High School

**186 High Street, Wealdstone, Middlesex HA3 7AY** 020 8863 9922 020 8861 5051 sacred.heart.high.sch@harrow.gov.uk Mary Waplington; Chair of Governors: Mark Murphy Harrow and Wealdstone Harrow and Wealdstone **Buses:** H12, H18, 140, 182, 258, 340 Blue blazer, navy kilt, navy or red jumper, white shirt **Demand:** Twice the number of applications for 150 places in 2001/2 **Type:** Voluntary aided Roman Catholic comprehensive for 508 girls, aged 11 to 16 **Submit application form:** November 2003 **Mission statement:** We strive to live, proclaim and promote the message of the gospel of Christ in this school. **School hours:** 8.45am–3.30pm, 8.45am–3pm (Fri); homework clubs are available **Meals:** Hot and cold available **Strong GCSE subjects:** Double science, music **London league table position:** 212

## Profile

Sacred Heart was founded in 1911 and had been a grammar school until the 1970s. It is situated just north of the Wealdstone shopping centre and is almost opposite Salvatorian College. There is a new study centre and IT suite and plans for a new technology building. CCTV cameras monitor the school. Music is a particular strength of the school and every girl is encouraged to learn to play a wide range of instruments. RE is central to the curriculum, with Masses, retreats, the rosary and daily prayer being key aspects of school life. The school has a head girl, two deputies, prefects and a school council. There is a PTA, the Friends of Sacred Heart.

## Admissions and intake

Priority is given to practising Roman Catholic girls, drawn from Harrow and the surrounding boroughs. Some join at Year 7, while others, particularly those from Harrow primary schools, are admitted at Year 8. It has the lowest number of pupils for a state secondary school in Harrow. About 10 per cent of pupils have special needs.

## Achievement

In 2002, 64 per cent of pupils achieved five or more A*–C grades at GCSE. This was slightly up on 56 per cent in 2001 and above the borough and national averages. The school was placed 11th in the borough league table. Following an inspection in 1999, Ofsted inspectors commented: 'When compared with similar schools, Sacred Heart High School pupils perform very well indeed.' Over the previous three years the performance of pupils had been close to the national averages in all three core subjects and had shown a rising trend. The attainment of pupils on entry broadly reflected national averages. Across both Key Stages 3 and 4, 96 per cent of teaching was satisfactory or better, with over 60 per cent good or very good. The quality of teaching had a significant impact on the progress pupils made in lessons. Figures published by the DfES in 1998 showed that pupils at the school had made much greater progress than the national average between the 1996 Key Stage 3 test results and the 1998 GCSE results. In 2000, 100 per cent of pupils gained A*–C GCSE grades for music. All pupils, including those with special needs, had very good attitudes to learning, and their behaviour in the classroom and around the school was also considered very good. Ofsted found that 'Pupils display maturity and older pupils show great care for younger ones.' There were good relationships between pupils and between pupils and their teachers, although pupil relationships with some teachers sometimes lacked warmth.

## Extra-curricular activities

There is an annual pilgrimage to Lourdes. Charity work is also important and pupils raised about £1,000 in 2000. An active Friends of the Sacred Heart High School association organizes functions and social events. There is a choir, many different bands, madrigal and gospel choirs and ensembles. A wide range of sports is on offer, including trampolining. There are trips to Germany and France, as well as local trips. There are after-school homework clubs.

# Salvatorian RC College

**High Road, Harrow Weald, Middlesex HA3 5DY** ☎ 020 8863 2706 Fax 020 8863 3435 Head Andrew Graham; Chair of Governors: Father Peter Preston ⇌ Harrow and Wealdstone ⊖ Harrow and Wealdstone **Buses:** H12, H18, 140, 182, 258, 340 Uniform Emerald green blazer, grey trousers, white shirt, green, red and black striped school tie **Demand:** 150 places available in 2001/2; oversubscribed **Type:** Voluntary aided Roman Catholic comprehensive for 624 boys, aged 11 to 16 **Submit application form:** November 2003 **Motto:** *Deo duce* (God Leads) **Mission statement:** To build a Christ-centred community helping the individual on his/her faith journey; to assist every individual in realizing his/her full potential academically, physically and socially; to strengthen bonds between home, parish and school, providing a preparation for the pupil's entry into the wider community. **School hours:** 8.45am–3.35pm; homework clubs are available **Meals:** Hot and cold available **Strong GCSE subjects:** English language and literature, geography **London league table position:** 254

## Profile

The Salvatorian Fathers founded the college in 1926 as an independent grammar school. It is situated just to the north of Wealdstone town centre and almost opposite Sacred Heart High School for Girls. A new £300,000 technology block has recently been completed. Gospel values are central to the school's teaching principles and there is daily worship, class retreats, school missions days of recollection and residential courses in Years 10 and 11. The school has applied for Language College status. IT is taught across all subjects and a qualification in IT can be taken at the end of Year 9. Pupils can become prefects or members of the school council. A weekly 'open house' session is held for parents. Former pupils include the Harrow East MP, Tony McNulty.

## Admissions and intake

Admissions criteria are detailed but priority is given to practising Catholic boys, drawn from Harrow and the surrounding boroughs. Some join the school at Year 7 and others, particularly those from Harrow primary schools, are admitted at Year 8.

## Achievement

Salvatorian College 'promotes high standards', according an Ofsted inspection in 1997. Pupils' attainments were broadly average on entry and in some years a few pupils were of above-average ability. In 2002, 51 per cent of pupils gained five or more A*–C grades at GCSE. This was slightly down from 58 per cent in 2001 and below the borough and national averages. The school was ranked 12th in the borough league table. Ofsted found progress in lessons to be generally good throughout the college and standards improved from broadly average in lessons in earlier years to above average in well over one-third of lessons in later years. Key Stage 3 results in English, maths and science were usually well above average, reflecting good progress relative to pupils' attainment on entry. Overall, GCSE results at the time were above national averages, well above average for boys' schools and improving steadily. Ofsted found that teachers had good knowledge of their subjects, high expectations of work and behaviour and used time effectively in most lessons. The inspectors reported: 'Priority is given to the creation within the college of an extension of traditional Christian family value. Staff promoted a well disciplined, orderly, respectful and forgiving framework. Pupils develop a good sense of values and this is appreciated by parents.'

### Extra-curricular activities

The school is renowned for its sporting achievements and has a number of thriving music and drama groups. Recent educational visits have taken place to France, Spain and Italy. An active Friends of the Salvatorian College organizes functions and social events. There are after-school homework clubs.

# Whitmore High School

**Porlock Avenue, Harrow, Middlesex HA2 0AD** 020 8864 7688 020 8422 3449 whitmore.high.sch@harrow.gov.uk Peter Allan; Chair of Governors: Mary Ling Harrow-on-the-Hill West Harrow, Rayners Lane, Harrow-on-the-Hill, South Harrow **Buses:** H11, 114, 140 Black blazer, black trousers or skirt, white shirt, silver and black striped school tie **Demand:** 260 places available in 2001/2; oversubscribed **Type:** Community comprehensive for 1046 mixed pupils, aged 12 to 16 **Submit application form:** 5 December 2003 **School hours:** 8.45am–3.15pm, 8.45am–3.35pm (Tues and Wed) **Meals:** Hot and cold available **Strong GCSE subjects:** English, maths **London league table position:** 204

### Profile

Whitmore dates from the 1940s and occupies a large site in a residential area. A recent building programme has provided a new IT suite, new equipment for design and technology, five science labs, two new food technology rooms, a music/dance studio, new departmental areas for history and RE, an extended and refurbished dining hall and a floodlit sports area. On entry pupils are placed in form groups of varying abilities and backgrounds. Pupils are taught in classes of 26 for most subjects in Years 8 and 9. GCSE subjects include Gujarati and media studies. In Year 11, a large number of pupils have an adult mentor to provide additional guidance and support. The head holds a 'surgery' each Monday evening for parents to raise issues of concern. There is a school council. Former pupils include Olympic athlete Andre Whitcombe-Jackson; Olympic boxing gold medalist Audley Harrison; footballers Marvin Bryant and Derek Payne, and cricketer David Goodchild.

### Admissions and intake

Admission is through the LEA. Priority is given to pupils from linked primary schools, namely Elmgrove, Grange, Longfield, Roxeth and Vaughan. If the school is oversubscribed by first-choice preferences, priority is given to applicants living the shortest walking distance from the school. In 2002, over one third of pupils came from homes where English was not the first language spoken, the largest racial group being of Indian origin. The number of pupils with special educational needs is above the national average.

### Achievement

In 2002, 66 per cent of pupils gained five or more A*–C grades at GCSE. This was slightly up on 57 per cent in 2001, continuing an upward trend. The school was ranked 10th in the borough league table. Ofsted visited the school in 2002 and described Whitmore High as a 'good school' with an 'inclusive and multicultural ethos within which it achieves high standards for its students'. The school was seen to be 'led with commitment and integrity'. The overall average score at GCSE is above the national average and has improved faster than the national rate over the last five years. Inspectors found the quality of teaching to be 'predominantly good' and 'excellent' in art, music and religious education. Whitmore High was also seen to provide well for those pupils who are physically disabled or have significant learning difficulties. However, Inspectors wanted to see improvements in the co-ordination of the school's pastoral programme and expressed concern over the quality of the school environment, including the toilet facilities.

### Extra-curricular activities

The school has a wide range of extra-curricular activities. Music activities available include brass, wind and string ensembles, pop and jazz groups, samba and concert bands, steel bands and two choirs. A wide range of sporting activities is offered and pupils have been particularly successful in competitions for football, trampolining, netball, gymnastics, athletics and basketball. Drama productions are staged annually. There are many educational visits available, including language trips to France and Germany, a watersports holiday in Spain and skiing in northern Italy and Bulgaria. There are also many local cultural and educational trips on offer.

# Havering

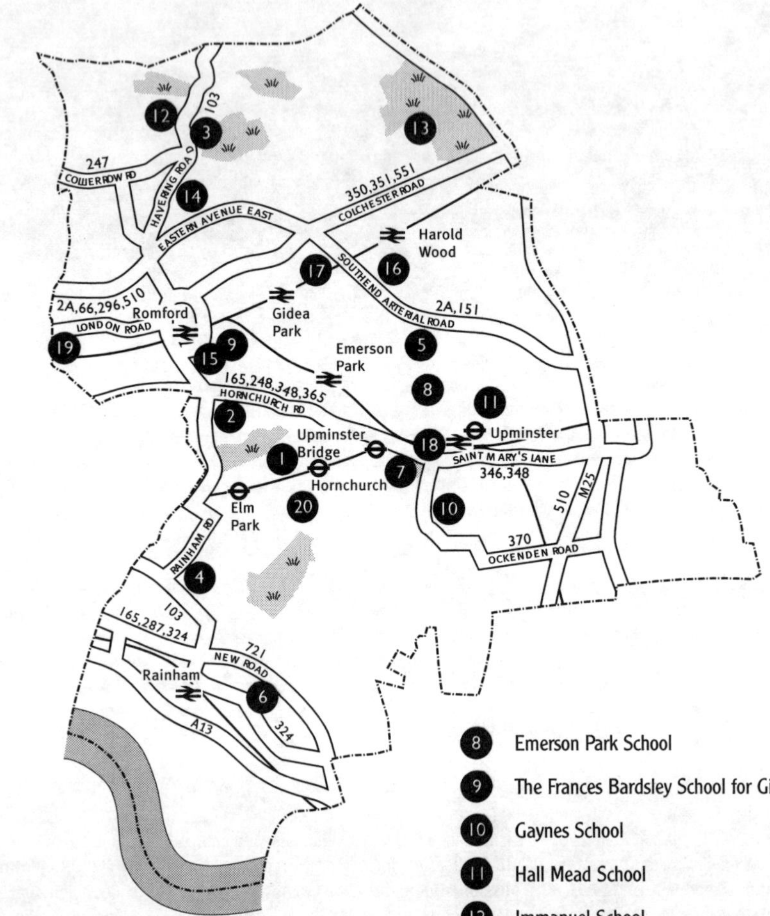


## Key

1. Abbs Cross School
2. The Albany School
3. Bower Park School
4. Brittons School and Technology College
5. The Campion School
6. The Chafford School
7. The Coopers' Company and Coburn School
8. Emerson Park School
9. The Frances Bardsley School for Girls
10. Gaynes School
11. Hall Mead School
12. Immanuel School
13. King's Wood School
14. Marshalls Park School
15. Raphael Independent School
16. Redden Court School
17. The Royal Liberty School
18. Sacred Heart of Mary Girls' School
19. St Edwards CofE Comprehensive School
20. The Sanders Draper School

# Factfile

**LEA: Town Hall, Main Road, Romford RM1 3BD** ☎ 01708 434343 🌐 www.havering.gov.uk **Executive Director of Children and Lifelong Learning:** Stephen Evans **Political control of council:** No overall control **Percentage of pupils from outside the borough:** 9.7 per cent **Percentage of pupils educated outside the borough:** 8 per cent **London league table positions (out of 32 boroughs):** 7th

## Profile

Havering is a new borough, which was formed in 1965 from the merger of Romford borough and Hornchurch urban district councils. It is the second largest borough in London and is nearly 40 square miles in area, of which half is green belt. Its population is around 230,000 and unemployment is low. Though the neighbouring boroughs of Redbridge and Barking and Dagenham have some large employers, most businesses in Havering are small. Romford's history dates back to a Roman staging post, which grew in the Middle Ages to become a market town. The town's growth, however, dates mainly from the railway era, which from 1839 enabled people to commute into London.

Rainham and Wennington are rich in archeological finds that date back to the time of the mammoths. Cranham and Bishop's Ockenden were substantial manors before 1086 and Upminster had 39 inhabitants as recorded in the Domesday Book. Gidea Park was opened as a garden suburb, thanks to the generosity of Sir Herbert Raphael, who donated part of his estate and hired leading architects to design the houses.

Havering has 22 schools. Its high-grade GCSE achievements were above the national average of 51.6 per cent in 2002. The league table averages for the borough in 2002 for pupils achieving five or more A*–C grades was 57.3 per cent. The average point score for A/AS-levels was 259.7. In 1995, the LEA took the decision to remove the sixth forms from its schools and to set up a sixth form college. Both the Havering Sixth Form College and Havering College of Further and Higher Education offer A-level courses. Of the two, the sixth form college students have a higher average point score. Havering LEA was inspected by Ofsted in 2001.

## Policy

Parents should contact the Havering LEA for a copy of the brochure *Changing Schools at Eleven in Havering.* Criteria for admission to a community school when it is oversubscribed are as follows: medical or social grounds; attendance of a sibling at the school; and children who live closest to the school. Applications to Royal Liberty School should be made directly to the school.

# Abbs Cross School

**Abbs Cross Lane, Hornchurch RM12 4YQ** ☎ 01708 440304 📠 01708 620360 ✉ enquiries@abbscross.havering.sch.uk 🌐 www.atschool.eduweb.co.uk/abbscross Mr G Mayoh; Chair of Governors: Mrs Gill Murkin ⇌ Romford, Upminster ⊖ Elm Park and Hornchurch **Buses:** 165, 365 Black blazer, black or grey trousers or grey skirt **Demand:** 168 places in 2002; oversubscribed **Type:** LEA maintained comprehensive foundation school for 806 mixed pupils, aged 11 to 16 **Submit application form:** End November/early December 2003 **Motto:** Commitment to Opportunity and Excellence **Mission statement:** Abbs Cross will continue to provide a high quality of education, striving for increasingly high standards, for the benefit of its pupils, staff governors and local community, in a caring, supportive and disciplined environment. **School hours:** 8.45am–3.30pm; homework clubs are available; library and learning resource centre open till 5pm each day **Meals:** Hot and cold available, including breakfast and vegetarian options **Strong GCSE subjects:** Business studies, English, French, maths, science **London league table position:** 270

## Profile

Abbs Cross School was opened as a post-war technical school and was expanded and reorganized as a comprehensive in 1973. Facilities include a hall with theatre lighting, six science laboratories, four language rooms with computers and visual aids, an ICT centre, two home economics and two arts and crafts rooms, a music suite, a drama workshop, three modern technology rooms and a library. There are 17 acres of playing fields, including a concrete cricket strip. Local sports centres supplement the on-site gym and fitness centre. It recently gained the Artsmark and Sportsmark awards. Subjects such as design and technology, electronics, food, textiles and graphics are on offer. Years 10 and 11 have careers lessons and can use computerized careers guidance programmes. Pupils in Year 11 undertake two weeks' work experience. Pupils can become prefects, and there is a school council. Younger pupils take turns to staff the school's stationery shop. A support team provides help for special-needs pupils both in class and through withdrawal. The Friends of Abbs Cross School are active in bringing parents, community, staff and pupils together, and in fund-raising. The school has achieved an Investors in People Award through its staff development work.

## Admissions and intake

Applications should be made directly to the school. There is no testing, except for 10 pupils who are chosen for their ability and aptitude in music, for whom Royal Schools of Music graded test results, previous school reports and an audition are required. The school is oversubscribed, and priority is given for exceptional need, having a sibling already at the school and proximity of home to the school. Ofsted remarked that the level of attainment was 'broadly average' on entry. In 2000, there were 144 pupils with special needs, of whom 32 had statements.

## Achievement

Abbs Cross is consistently near or very near the borough average for GCSEs. In 2002, 49 per cent of pupils achieved five or more grades A*–C, down from 60 per cent in 2001. This was just below the national average. English, French, mathematics and science tend to be the best subjects. In 1999, Ofsted noted with approval the improvements made since its last inspection in 1995, along with the governors' plans to reduce weaknesses. Teaching was satisfactory or better in 94 per cent of all classes. Unauthorized absence was in line with the borough average at 0.1 per cent in 2000. Unauthorized absence for 1999 was 0.5 per cent. Pupils go to Havering sixth-form colleges.

## Extra-curricular activities

Various sports are played at the school. There are non-sporting clubs such as chess, art and computer clubs. Trampolining is also on offer. The school visits France and Germany, has a skiing trip to Austria and the dance band tours Europe. The school has a tradition of fund-raising for charities. Homework clubs after school are available.

# The Albany School

**Broadstone Road, off Albany Road, Hornchurch RM12 4AJ** ☎ 01708 441537 Fax 01708 437157 Head Mrs M Johnson M.Ed, B.Ed (Hons); Chair of Governors: Mrs J Hardy Rail Chadwell Heath **Buses:** 165, 248, 252 Uniform Navy blazer, navy trousers or skirt, white shirt **Demand:** 423 applications for 186 places in 2001/2 **Type:** Community comprehensive for 827 mixed pupils, aged 11 to 16 **Submit application form:** End November/early December 2003 **Mission statement:** We aim to encourage and enable pupils to be confident and successful individuals. **School hours:** 8.35am–3.20pm (Mon and Tues), 8.35am–3pm (Wed–Fri); homework clubs are available **Meals:** Hot and cold available, including vegetarian options **Strong GCSE subjects:** Information unavailable **London league table position:** 246

## Profile

The Albany School dates from 1982 when Havering Lodge and Mayland School were amalgamated. The school has good facilities and it has had a computer/IT department for some years, which it updates regularly. There is also excellent provision for a range of sports, track events and fitness, and the Harrow Lodge sports centre can also be used. The school recenty won an Investors in People Award. Form representatives are listened to constructively and they meet the head and deputy heads regularly. The school is part of the Havering Business and Education Partnership and has a nationally recognized work experience programme and an annual careers convention. Special-needs pupils are looked after by a special-needs department and in-class support. The parents' and friends' association is open to all parents, and is active in supporting the school with fund-raising and events.

## Admissions and intake

The school is over-subscribed, and the LEA applies the standard criteria of: exceptional need; having a sibling at the school; and proximity of home to the school. Pupils have average or below average attainment on entry. In 2001, 13.7 per cent of pupils had special needs, of whom 27 had statements, and this is above average.

## Achievement

In 2002, the number of pupils gaining five or more grades A*–C at GCSE rose to 59 per cent from 54 per cent in 2001. This was above the national and borough averages and the school was placed 10th in the borough league table. Overall, GCSE performance has substantially improved over the past six years. Ofsted visited the school in 2001 and commented that Albany 'has a number of strengths'. Inspectors praised the school's 'positive ethos' and 'caring community'. Pupils' attitudes were found to be 'very positive' and the quality of teaching was 'good overall', although there is a high staff turnover. Unauthorized absence is low at 0.4 per cent.

### Extra-curricular activities

The school holds the Education Extra Distinction Award for extra-curricular activities, which include the Duke of Edinburgh's Award scheme, maths, chess, IT and science clubs, the Albany Soapbox (debating and public speaking) and creative arts evenings, as well as an annual talent show. Field trips and visits are arranged to Stubbers Outdoor Pursuits Centre, the Isle of Wight, France, Italy and Austria. The school has held the Excellence in Public Service to the Community Charter Mark since 1996 for its participation in fund-raising and charity work. After-school homework clubs are available.

## Bower Park School

**Havering Road North, Romford RM1 4YY** 01708 730244 01708 741748 www.sch.softinv.co.uk/havering/bowerpark/ Mr PR Davies M.Sc, BA, Ad.Dip, Em.ACP, MBIM; Chair of Governors: Mr Norman Kemble Romford **Buses:** 500, 502, 510 Black blazer with badge, black trousers or skirt, white shirt or blouse with school tie, V-neck black jumper **Demand:** 144 applications for 180 places in 2001/2 **Type:** Community comprehensive for 645 mixed pupils, aged 11 to 16 **Submit application form:** End November/early December 2003 **Mission statement:** Bower Park will continue to be an establishment where every pupil is happy and secure, and where each is challenged to reach their true potential in every aspect. **School hours:** 8.55am–3.20pm **Meals:** Hot and cold available, including vegetarian options **Strong GCSE subjects:** Art, science **London League table position:** 410

### Profile

This school opened in 1990 after the amalgamation of Chase Cross and Forest Lodge Schools. It has a good, well-used library with computers and CD-ROMs, which also functions as a homework centre. The music rooms have recently been upgraded with electronic keyboards, and there is a large hall with lighting and sound equipment. The school has upgraded its IT/computer provision since the last Ofsted report criticized it. There is also an enclosed hard court area and a full-sized gym. Vocational subjects on offer include business studies, information studies, food technology, and design technology. Year 10 undertakes two weeks of work experience. Pupils are placed in tutor groups, and these are part of the pastoral care system. There is a school council and prefects. In 1998, Ofsted commented that the requirements of special-needs pupils were not always met in standard lessons, but the school now has a system to ensure all staff know and follow the new code for special needs. The school association meets regularly and raises funds enthusiastically. Parents are kept informed through regular meetings and the head sends weekly newsletters.

### Admissions and intake

The school is slightly over-subscribed and the LEA applies the criteria of: exceptional need, having a sibling at the school, and proximity of the home to the school. In 2000, there were 156 pupils with special needs, of whom 44 had statements.

### Achievement

Bower Park is improving its performance achievement, although it is still well below the borough and national averages. The percentage of pupils gaining five or more A*–C grades has risen steadily since 1998, reaching 39 per cent in 2002. This was still below the local and national averages and the school was ranked 17th in the borough league table in 2002. The average point score at GCSE was 29.2. Science was found to be good, but French was poor. Ofsted noted that in some classes more able pupils were bored and dissatisfied. Pupils go on to Ardleigh Green College and sixth- form college in Havering.

### Extra-curricular activities

A youth club on the school premises is well used, and the Duke of Edinburgh's Award scheme, annual theatre production, visits to art galleries and theatres and language trips to France and Germany are all available. The school is working towards being a community school. It has links with a local church, which runs a weekly Christian Union club, attended by pupils. Favourite charities have included Children in Need, the annual Poppy Appeal and two local hospices. Sports available at Bower Park cover the usual range and include basketball and netball.

# Brittons School and Technology College

**Ford Lane, Rainham RM13 7BB** 01708 630002 01708 630325 principal@brittons.havering.sch.uk www.brittons.havering.sch.uk Mr R Sheffield; Chair of Governors: Mr C Saunders Rainham **Buses:** 103, 165, 365; also a privately contracted daily bus between Barking and Dagenham and the school Maroon blazer with badge, maroon jumper or cardigan, white shirt or blouse, black trousers, skirt or culottes **Demand:** 329 applications for 225 places in 2001/2 **Type:** Community comprehensive Technology College for 1106 mixed pupils, aged 11 to 16 **Submit application form:** End November/early December 2003 **Mission statement:** The school aims to provide a secure and stimulating environment. Every student is seen as an individual and encouraged to develop his or her intellectual, creative, moral and social abilities to the full as part of a caring community. The school provides a broad and varied curriculum, which offers opportunities for each student to achieve his or her potential. **School hours:** 8.40am–3.40pm (3pm, Thurs and Fri); homework clubs are available **Meals:** Hot and cold available **Strong GCSE subjects:** No statistics available **London league table position:** 285

## Profile

Brittons School opened in 1952 as a mixed secondary modern school, was extended in 1964, and is now a comprehensive. Its learning centre has 20,000 books in two libraries, plus access to the Internet and a reference section. There are also seven science labs, four workshops, two arts and crafts rooms, two food technology and four language rooms. An IT coordinator was appointed in 1999 and there are four IT rooms with 120 computers. The school recently gained Technology College status. Sports facilities include 19 acres of playing fields, a new hard surface area and two gyms. Vocational subjects offered include business studies, food handling, health, hygiene and safety. Project Trident organizes two weeks' work experience for pupils. There is a house system with house captains, elected head boy and head girl, school council and prefects. With regard to special needs pupils, Ofsted noted that the school noticeably improves their attainments and the examination results are generally good. There is one parents' evening a year and parents appreciate the contact made through the year book and newsletters. Both a PTA and the Friends of Britton School arrange events and raise funds.

## Admissions and intake

The application procedure is standard LEA. If oversubscribed, the LEA follow the criteria of: exceptional need; having a sibling at the school; and proximity of home to the school. Due to demand, the school roll has risen from 675 in 1995 to 1106 in 2001. There were 245 special-needs pupils in 2000, of whom 23 had statements.

## Achievement

The school's exams performance has been improving. At GCSE the percentage of pupils gaining five or more grades A*–C reached 49 per cent in 2002, up from 48 per cent in 2001. Core subjects are found to be generally good, but the school's poor performance in RE and spiritual development is being addressed. In 1999, Ofsted noted approvingly that the school had made faster progress than average, and continued to have more strengths than weaknesses.

## Extra-curricular activities

Clubs available include maths, IT, art, geography, history, languages and sports. There are regular field trips and visits to the local Hindu temple, churches and theatres and galleries. Good use is made of the borough's European centre. The school participates in regular charity days, which are primarily for local groups but also for specific needs, such as raising funds for an electric wheelchair for the Motor Neurone Disease Society. The school lets its facilities to local groups as part of its community liaison. Homework clubs are available after school hours.

# The Campion School

**Wingletye Lane, Hornchurch RM11 3BX** 01708 452332 01708 456995 www.sch.softinv.co.uk/havering/campion/default.htm Mr JA Johnson MA Cantab; Chair of Governors: Mr R Townsend Upminster Upminster **Buses:** 193 Charcoal grey blazer with badge, charcoal grey trousers, white shirt, school tie **Demand:** 150 places available in 2002; oversubscribed **Type:** Voluntary aided Roman Catholic comprehensive for 933 boys (mixed in sixth form), aged 11 to 18 **Submit application form:** November 2003 **Mission statement:** To develop enquiring minds, self-discipline and application in the pursuit of excellence, encourage individuals towards personal development through academic studies and the school's extra-curricular activities, and to lead young people to faith in Christ and a mature understanding of the Catholic faith. **School hours:** 9am–3.45pm, homework clubs are available **Meals:** Hot and cold available, including breakfast **Strong GCSE subjects:** All relatively strong **London league table position:** 151

## Profile

Built as a Jesuit grammar school in 1962, Campion School was taken over by the diocese of Brentwood in 1965 and became a comprehensive in the 1970s. The school has four technology rooms, music and art rooms and a chapel. There are four IT rooms with 100 computers and more in subject classrooms. The school also has 20 acres of playing fields, a multi-purpose sports hall and indoor swimming pool. The standard range of A-level subjects is offered, plus classical civilization, Latin, economics, computing, business studies and PE. Local businesses support the two weeks' work experience undertaken by Year 10. There is a school council and prefects have the power to deal with minor transgressions. There is a tradition of pupils offering help to any pupil returning to school after a period of sickness. Special-needs provision has been improved over the past few years. There is an active parents' association, which raises substantial funds and organizes social functions. Parents receive regular reports and attend parents' evenings. Famous ex-pupils include Anthony Diprose, England rugby captain.

## Admissions and intake

Preference is given to pupils who are recommended by their parish priest as practising Roman Catholics. A total of 140 boys are taken from the Catholic deaneries of Havering and Brentwood and the parishes of Aveley and Grays, and 10 from other areas of the Brentwood diocese. The school is slightly oversubscribed, and selection will also be made according to exceptional need, having a sibling at the school and proximity of home to the school. Applicants and their parents are interviewed. Pupils' attainment level on entry is above the national average. In 2001, the school had 36 special needs pupils, of whom six had statements.

## Achievement

The number of pupils achieving five or more grades A*–C at GCSE reached 73 per cent in 2002, down 10 per cent from the previous year. The school was ranked fifth in the borough league table. A-level point scores are above the national averages and it was 280.3 in 2002. All subjects achieve good results. In 2002, Ofsted described Campion as 'a very good school in which consistently high standards are promoted by good teaching'. Inspectors praised the school's 'climate of good relationships and behaviour' in which pupils achieve well.

## Extra-curricular activities

Rugby is pre-eminent in sports with the U18 rugby team winning the national final in 2001, but fencing, golf and judo are also popular. A barber shop group is one of a number of musical ensembles. There is a public speaking team, an active justice and peace group, video camera and technology clubs, and an Air Training Corps squadron. Places of cultural and academic interest are visited and there are exchanges with France, Outward Bound courses, skiing trips and performance tours. The sixth form undertakes community service projects.

# The Chafford School

**Lambs Lane, Rainham RM13 9XD** 01708 552811 01708 522098 info@thechafford.havering.sch.uk www.thechafford.havering.sch.uk Mrs C Hassell; Chair of Governors: Cllr R Emmett Rainham **Buses:** 324, 721 Black blazer with red school badge, white shirt, black V-neck sweater, black trousers or skirt **Demand:** 239 applications for 170 places in 2001/2 **Type:** Community comprehensive for 899 mixed pupils, aged 11 to 16 **Submit application form:** End November/early December 2003 **Motto:** Achievement for All Through the Pursuit of Excellence **School hours:** 8.40am–3.15pm **Meals:** Hot and cold available, including breakfast **Strong GCSE subjects:** Art, maths **London league table position:** 277

## Profile

Established in 1928 as Rainham Senior Mixed Public Elementary School, this school became comprehensive in 1973. Facilities include a science suite with a weather satellite, a library with professional staff and networked to the other resource areas, technology and arts rooms, and four ICT suites. The extensive sports facilities, including a 25m indoor pool, are used by the local community out of school hours. The school recently received the Sportsmark award. Business studies is on offer along with design and technology. There is good careers guidance and worthwhile work experience available. Chafford promotes good spelling and literacy, setting higher targets than average in secondary schools. Good behaviour is rewarded and there is an effective internal exclusion unit, which takes disruptive pupils out of the normal classroom and provides a disciplined learning environment for them, with counselling and support. All year groups are represented on an assembly committee. There is an active school council and a prefects system. Parents are kept informed through newsletters and regular reports. The PTA is active.

## Admissions and intake

Admission is according to standard LEA procedures. Chafford is over-subscribed and the LEA applies the criteria of exceptional need, having a sibling at the school and proximity to the school. Pupils' entry attainment is average. In 2000, there were 129 pupils with special needs, of whom 36 had statements.

## Achievement

The school's performance is slightly below the borough but above the national average. Whilst the LEA's average for gaining five or more grades A*–C rose steadily from 1996 to 2000, the school's average has been erratic and was 53 per cent in 2002, up from 42 the previous year. Ofsted noted in 2000 that more pupils than average were not entered by the school for examination in subjects they had studied, which made comparison with national data unreliable. Ofsted also reported that improvement has been steady since the last inspection but IT is 'still not used sufficiently in most subjects'. The school's modern language teaching is not universally good, and in general the ablest students are insufficiently challenged and resent this. Inspectors also noted that the assessment is not always translated into appropriate and measurable targets in some lessons.

## Extra-curricular activities

There is a club for the most able students, which arranges a variety of activities, and there are also science, chess and other challenging clubs. Orienteering and dance are also available. Trips abroad are gradually increasing and there are new pen-friend schemes with France and Germany. The school has an artists-in-residence scheme. There are particularly good links with the local community in environmental areas, with pupils helping with landscaping and recycling projects in the school grounds and the grounds of a local retirement home. Together with a local employer, Tilda, the school arranges the annual Havering half-marathon and fun run, which has raised substantial sums for charity. The local curate and his wife have arranged a link between the school and Gambia, and pupils have raised funds for refugees.

# The Coopers' Company and Coburn School

**St Mary's Lane, Upminster RM14 3HS** ☎ 01708 250500 📠 01708 226109 ✉ info@cooperscoborn.org.uk 🌐 www.cooperscoborn.org.uk Dr D Lloyd; Chair of Governors: Mr MJV Housley ACII ⇄ Upminster ⊖ Upminster **Buses:** 346, 348 Dark navy blazer with badge, dark navy V-neck sweatshirt, light blue shirt with tie, dark grey trousers (boys); dark navy knife-pleated skirt, light blue blouse (girls); Sixth form: Black blazer, charcoal grey or black trousers (boys); black skirts, white shirt or blouse (girls) **Demand:** 180 places in 2001/2; oversubscribed **Type:** Voluntary aided comprehensive Sports College for 1252 mixed pupils, aged 11 to 18 **Submit application form:** End November/early December 2003 **Mission statement:** Our aim is to provide a liberal education, which recognizes and develops the potential of every pupil, within a caring, supporting and friendly environment, thus helping our pupils in their preparation to become full and effective citizens. **School hours:** 8.40am–3.40pm, library is open after school **Meals:** Hot and cold available, including breakfast and vegetarian options **Strong GCSE subjects:** English, mathematics, science **London league table position:** 61

## Profile

The school resulted from the amalgamation of two schools dating from the 16th and 19th centuries, Coopers' Company and Coburn. The two schools were joined as a mixed comprehensive, but with the intention of preserving and developing the two original foundations' Christian character. The science centre has eight laboratories. IT is extensively used and there are two language laboratories, a recording studio, theatre, dance studio and exhibition area. The sports facilities cover team games, athletics and swimming, and the school recently gained Sports College status. The standard A-level subjects are offered, plus music, arts, theatre studies and design, with IT and industrial society available at GCSE. Career choice begins in Year 8 and work experience, work shadowing and workplace visits are arranged. There are sports captains and school captains. There is a special-needs coordinator, and a governor has special responsibility to ensure support is available. Parents are kept informed through parents' meetings, reports, and pupils' homework and academic target organizers. The parents association works closely with the school.

## Admissions and intake

Parents should apply to the school for details of the admission criteria. Further criteria are: exceptional need; having a sibling at the school; and proximity to the school. Applicants and parents are interviewed. The school is over-subscribed and can choose pupils of above average ability. In 2000, there were 21 special-needs pupils, of whom only one had a statement.

## Achievement

In 1996, this school was the highest performing mixed comprehensive in the country at GCSE level. In 2001, the school came second in the borough league table with an impressive 99 per cent of pupils achieving five or more grades A*–C, down from 100 per cent in 2001. The average A-level point score was 372, again placing the school top of the borough. Ofsted last inspected in 1997, after the school had come top of the GCSE tables in the country. Inspectors commented that 'the whole school community deserves praise for these excellent achievements'. There is no unauthorized absence.

## Extra-curricular activities

There are sports teams and music groups available, and clubs ranging from Irish dance and fishing to the Duke of Edinburgh's Award scheme and martial arts. There are around 12 residential trips each year, abroad and in the UK. There are also many day trips, arranged by individual departments. The school supports an overseas charity and also a charity of the year in the UK.

# Emerson Park School

**Wych Elm Road, Wingletye Lane, Hornchurch RM11 3AD** 01708 475285 01708 620963 Mr S Berwitz BA; Chair of Governors: Ms P Brown Upminster Upminster Bridge **Buses:** 193, 248, 256, 649, 656 : Navy blue or black blazer with badge, school tie, grey or black trousers, white shirt (boys); grey skirt, blue shirt (girls); navy blue V-neck pullover or school sweatshirt **Demand:** 574 applications for 192 places in 2001/2 **Type:** Community comprehensive for 905 mixed pupils, aged 11 to 16 **Submit application form:** End November/early December 2003 **Motto:** A Good Name Endureth **Mission statement:** The school: a) endeavours to ensure that each and every pupil achieves the highest academic standards of which they are capable, b) places great emphasis on the importance of pupils learning how to learn, c) encourages mutual respect and tolerance for other people's beliefs and d) endeavours to develop an ordered community with shared values of behaviour and morality. **School hours:** 8.50am–3.30pm; homework clubs are available **Meals:** Hot and cold available, including snacks for breakfast **Strong GCSE subjects:** English language and literature **London league table position:** 348

## Profile

Emerson Park School claims the distinction of being the only grammar school to be established in the country during World War II, in 1943. It became a comprehensive in 1973. It has six science laboratories, six design and technology rooms, three networked IT laboratories, a fully computerized business studies room, a media studies suite, a drama studio and music studio, together with a sports hall, gymnasium, outdoor pitches, tennis courts and field events areas. The school recently won a Sportsmark award. A total of £100,000 is to be invested in upgrading and updating the school's computers. A range of vocational subjects is offered, with work experience available through Project Trident. A well-staffed and resourced special-needs department supports younger pupils in the classroom and runs a vocational education group for older pupils. There is a school council with elected representatives. Reports are issued twice yearly or on request, and parents are encouraged to contact the school if they have any concerns. There is a termly parents' forum with the head teacher. There is also a flourishing parent-teacher association.

## Admissions and intake

Admission is according to standard LEA process and practice, with over-subscription dealt with through exceptional need, having a sibling at the school and proximity of home to the school. There were approximately 157 special needs pupils in 2000, of whom 17 had statements.

## Achievement

The achievement of five or more grades A*–C has varied fairly widely. It was 41 per cent in 1997, immediately before the last Ofsted inspection, which raised questions about serious weaknesses in the school, but it was 51 per cent in the year of the inspection, 1998. Since then it has fluctuated, reaching 39 per cent in 2002, down from 45 per cent in 2001, and below national and borough averages. The school commits itself to making every effort 'to eliminate the ignorance and distrust which can lead to prejudice and discrimination'. In 2000, Ofsted found the school to be 'effective' with 'pupils making steady progress in almost all subjects'. The school has gained the confidence of parents. Inspectors praised the 'outstanding' leadership of the new head teacher who has done much to remedy weaknesses found in earlier reports.

## Extra-curricular activities

Sports are encouraged, and the school has facilities for all the major sports. Chess is popular, and there are several clubs to pursue curriculum subjects outside the classroom. Music and dance are well supported and exhibitions of pupils' artwork are held. There are geography and science field trips, plus history visits to Normandy. Local and national charities are well supported. After-school homework clubs are available.

# The Frances Bardsley School for Girls

**Brentwood Road, Romford RM1 2RR (upper school); Heath Park Road, Romford RM2 5UJ (lower school)** ☎ 01708 447368 (upper school); 01708 446470 (lower school) 📠 01708 442729 (upper school); 01708 442735 (lower school) Mrs SE Philipps M.Sc; Chair of Governors: Mr J Hewitt 🚉 Romford **Buses:** 193, 294, 324, 374 Bottle green blazer and skirt, white blouse and school tie **Demand:** 315 applications for 210 places in 1999 **Type:** Comprehensive foundation school for 1209 girls, aged 11 to 18 **Submit application form:** End November/early December 2003 **Motto:** Gladly Lerne, Gladly Teche **Mission statement:** The school's overall aim is to encourage excellence through intellectual curiosity, independence of mind, self-awareness and consideration of others. It seeks to do this through providing a caring, friendly and exciting community where individual abilities and talents are fostered and the highest possible standards can be achieved. In addition, the school encourages pupils to take corporate responsibility and to have a pride in the school and its traditions. **School hours:** 8.35am–3.25pm; homework clubs are available **Meals:** Hot and cold available **Strong GCSE subjects:** English, mathematics **London league table position:** 230

## Profile

When Havering opted to remove sixth forms, Frances Bardsley School became a grant maintained school in order to keep its sixth form and it then became a foundation school. Both the upper and lower school buildings have their own science laboratories, design and technology rooms, libraries and halls. There is also a large gymnasium and 12 acres of grounds. The school is currently negotiating a private-public partnership to combine the schools on one site, with extensive rebuilding and expansion. In addition to the standard A-level subjects, dance, economics, home economics, law, psychology and sociology are on offer. Vocational GCSEs are available in design and technology and IT. Work experience is also available. Pupils can become prefects or form captains and join the year and school councils. The special-needs coordinator was praised by Ofsted in 1999 for strong leadership, and the support department modifies tasks to enable success and increase pupils' confidence. The Abacus Club for abler pupils was successful in the regional mock trials organized by the Magistrates Organization, and in 1999 it was coached for the national final. There is an active parent-teacher association.

## Admissions and intake

The school is responsible for its own admissions, the closing date being set by the LEA. Pupils with sisters at the school, then those who live closest, form the first 110 of the 210 intake. The remaining 100 places are filled according to the strength of an applicant's commitment to single sex education. In 2000, there were 116 special-needs pupils, of whom 17 had statements.

## Achievement

Frances Bardsley was deemed 'a very good school' by Ofsted in 1999, with above average attainment in several areas. Results have been consistently high. In 2002, 58 per cent of pupils gained five or more grades A*–C. This was down from 64 per cent in 2001 and the school was ranked ninth in the borough. For A-levels, the average point score was 263.9, above borough and national averages. Skills in design and technology are higher than average but French is poor. Ofsted noted that the use of IT to support the curriculum and the lack of religious education in the sixth form had not been sufficiently improved since their previous inspection in 1994. The school is recognized for outstanding creative arts, and three pupils had works exhibited in the exhibition *Alive* at the Royal Academy in 2000. Homework clubs are available after school.

## Extra-curricular activities

School sports teams regularly compete successfully outside the school. In addition to the internationally touring choir, there are jazz and tin whistle ensembles. Exchange programmes are organized with Germany and Sweden. The school supports the Meningitis Trust and the Sargent Cancer Care Fund.

# Gaynes School

**Brackendale Gardens, Upminster RM14 3UX** ☎ 01708 502900 📠 01708 502901 ⓔ admin@gaynes.havering.sch.uk 🌐 www.gaynes.havering.sch.uk Mr R Ayling MA, BA, NPQH, MI.Mgt; Chair of Governors: Cllr Owen Ware ⇄ Upminster ⊖ Upminster **Buses:** 370, 373 Bottle green blazer with badge, bottle green pullover, white shirt or blouse, tie, dark grey or black trousers or bottle green skirt **Demand:** 526 applications for 192 places in 2001/2 **Type:** Community comprehensive Language College for 969 mixed pupils, aged 11 to 16 **Submit application form:** End November/early December 2003 **Motto:** Learning and Dignity **School hours:** 8.50am–3.25pm **Meals:** Hot and cold available, including vegetarian options **Strong GCSE subjects:** English mathematics, ICT and PE **London league table position:** 222

## Profile

Founded in the 1940s as a secondary modern, Gaynes School became a comprehensive in 1973. The original school and its later additions are well maintained and very tidy, surrounded by extensive, well kept playing fields. There are CCTV cameras in place. Facilities on-site include three science laboratories, three CDT workshops, a graphics room with technology area, two technology laboratories, IT rooms and workshops, two art studios, a drama room, a recording studio and an audio-visual room. A brand new music and drama block opened in 2002. The library is staffed by a professional librarian and a library assistant. Computers are also in subject classrooms. Sports facilities include a gymnasium, sports hall, covered heated swimming pool, tennis and netball courts and sports pavilion. Careers education makes full use of the borough's computer-assisted programme, and work experience provision is good. The school is part of the Havering Business and Education Partnership. The school has started a reading recovery scheme to help the increasing number of new pupils with too low a standard of reading. There is a school council with representatives from each year. The parents' association is very active and in 1999–2000 it raised funds for a minibus for the school. Parents are extensively involved in both educational and administrative work in and for the school. There are reports and regular newsletters, as well as individual contacts about pupils' progress.

## Admissions and intake

The school is heavily oversubscribed, and the LEA applies the criteria of: exceptional need; having a sibling at the school; and proximity. In 2001, two per cent of pupils had statements of special needs, which is about average.

## Achievement

Gaynes' GCSE achievement has risen sharply since 1996. In 2001, 60 per cent of pupils gained five or more grades A*–C, and in 2002 this dropped to 59 per cent. This was still above the borough average. Ofsted visited the school in 2002 and noted that it had made 'significant progress' with 'unmistakeable improvements' since their last visit in 1996. The school was seen to be 'led with passion and vision' with good teaching and learning. The best GCSE results were in English, mathematics, ICT and PE, while the weakest results were in German and design and technology.

## Extra-curricular activities

The school arranges language trips abroad and to the borough's Europa Centre. There are also theatre, gallery and museum visits, skiing trips and summer camps. Pupils can participate in the Duke of Edinburgh's Award scheme. Music ensembles available include an orchestra and brass band. There is an annual music festival. All pupils take part in the annual sponsored walk, with older pupils allowed to wear fancy dress. The money raised is divided between the school and charities. The school offers the usual range of sports, such as rugby, netball and hockey.

# Hall Mead School

**Marlborough Gardens, Cranham, Upminster RM14 1SF** 01708 225684 01708 220232 hallmead@btinternet.com.uk www.upminster.com/upminster/hallmead Mr A Wunderly B.Sc (Hons); Chair of Governors: Mrs D Jenkin Upminster Upminster **Buses:** 248, 346 Navy blazer and badge, dark grey or black trousers or navy skirt, white shirt or blouse, school tie, school pullover **Demand:** 558 applications for 192 places in 2001/2 **Type:** Community comprehensive Technology College for 1010 mixed pupils, aged 11 to 16 **Submit application form:** End November/early December 2003 **Mission statement:** To provide and maintain a disciplined, caring environment in which teachers can teach and pupils can learn. To provide the highest standard of teaching and ensure the highest standard of learning for all pupils, and the highest standards in personal care, support and individual development. To challenge each pupil to achieve the best of which he or she is capable. To enable pupils to understand and be part of the wider world, and to take their places with confidence in a rapidly changing technological environment. **School hours:** 8.50am–3.35pm; homework clubs are available **Meals:** Hot and cold available, including vegetarian **Strong GCSE subjects:** Information studies, science **London league table position:** 141

## Profile

Hall Mead was designated a Technology College in 1997, and after meeting its targets faster than predicted in its first three years, this status was confirmed in 2000 for a further three years. The school was also awarded Beacon School status. Facilities include six science laboratories, four design and technology workshops, an ICT and business studies suite and a library with multi-media, audio-visual and reprographics resources. A sports hall, gymnasium, tennis courts and playing fields are on-site, and the school uses Central Park swimming pool at Harold Hill. All four design and technology subjects, electronics, food, graphics and resistant materials are offered. Careers guidance begins in Year 9, with personal counselling, a careers fair and a college taster experience. All Year 10 pupils have two weeks' work experience. There is a prefect system and a school council. A learning support department is available for pupils who have fallen behind and for pupils with special needs. In 1999, Ofsted praised the French and science teaching for special needs pupils. Fast track schemes enable pupils to take examinations early. The Hall Mead Friends' Association includes parents of present and past pupils. Parents are encouraged to contact the school with queries and concerns.

## Admissions and intake

Admissions are dealt with by standard LEA procedure. The criteria for dealing with oversubscription are: exceptional need; having a sibling at the school; and proximity of home to the school. There are 166 pupils with special needs, of whom 23 have statements.

## Achievement

The school's performance is excellent. The percentage of pupils achieving five or more grades A*–C has climbed steadily, from 58 per cent in 1996 to 80 per cent in 2002. The school was ranked fourth in the borough. Science and information technology are good, but in some other subjects, for example geography, achievement ranges from A* to fail. In 1999, Ofsted commented 'there is no doubt that the school's excellent ethos promotes a very good learning environment. Working relationships amongst staff and between staff and pupils are extremely productive and there is good equality of opportunity'. Unauthorized absence was low at 0.1 per cent. Pupils go on to Ardleigh Green and Havering sixth-form colleges.

## Extra-curricular activities

There are 16 PE activities, nine music activities and 20 other clubs available, including drama, art, technology and magic. Some highlights include a cricket tour of Barbados, skiing, at least one major drama production a year and exchange visits with Berlin. Fund-raising for charity is actively pursued, and music groups play at a range of venues.

# Immanuel School

**Havering Grange Centre, Havering Road North, Romford RM1 4HR** 01708 764449 01708 736292 Miss F Norcross; Chair of Management Team: The school is part of the Christian Schools Trust and the management team of the school is chaired by a member of the Leadership Team of Immanuel Church. Romford **Buses:** 103, 500, 501 Navy blue skirt, blazer, jumper, black trousers **Demand:** Applications matched the number of places available **Type:** Non-selective independent for 97 mixed pupils, aged 3 to 16 **Fees:** £242 to £525 per month **Submit application form:** No cut-off date **Mission statement:** We provide, in partnership with parents, good quality education in a secure environment which enables children to know and understand God, the world and each other from a Christian perspective. **School hours:** 9am–3.35pm **Meals:** Not provided **Strong GCSE subjects:** All relatively strong **London league table position:** 263

## Profile

Acorn primary school was founded in 1980, by members of the Romford Christian Fellowship. In 1986, Covenant School was opened as a Christian secondary school. In 1993, the schools were joined to form Immanuel School, with a reception year and nursery education class added in 1994. Immanuel School is now run by Immanuel Church as an alternative to the present education system. It is one of 40 schools belonging to the Christian Schools Trust. Facilities on-site include a science room, IT room, hall with stage and gymnasium facilities, library and kitchen. There are computers in all classrooms. Sports facilities include a large playground with netball court and playing field for football and athletics. The school also uses a local sports centre. The national curriculum is taught from a Christian perspective and biblical world-view. Vocational subjects offered include art and craft and computer studies, but work experience is not offered. All teachers are committed Christians and most are members of Immanuel Church. Pupils and parents are offered pastoral and prayer support by the staff. The school is too small to require prefects, but all pupils are expected to take an active part in the life of the school. One teacher has a diploma in special needs education. Many parents offer voluntary support, including covering for teachers' absence. They are kept informed through regular reports, parents' evenings and training days.

## Admissions and intake

Applications can be made at any time. The criteria for acceptance into the school is full support for the school's aims and parents are asked to visit the school informally. A formal interview takes place after application. A decision is made after prayerful consideration and consultation with the management team. There are 18 pupils with special needs, three of whom have a statement.

## Achievement

As a non-selective and very small school, its performance will inevitably vary, but achievement of good grades at GCSE has been consistently higher than both the national and borough averages. The percentage of pupils gaining five or more GCSE grades A*–C in 1999 was 82 per cent, dropping to 50 per cent in 2000. However, it rose again to 58 per cent in 2002 and the school was ranked 11th in the borough.

## Extra-curricular activities

There are educational trips organized but no trips abroad. No sport is played after school.

# King's Wood School

**Settle Road, Harold Hill, Romford RM3 9XX** 01708 371331/4 01708 347515 Mr C Rudge; Chair of Governors: Mr Mike Davis Harold Wood **Buses:** 296 Black blazer with badge, black trousers or skirt, white shirt or blouse, school tie, black V-neck pullover or cardigan **Demand:** 188 applications for 180 places in 2001/2 **Type:** Community comprehensive for 852 mixed pupils, aged 11 to 16 **Submit application form:** End November/early December 2003 **Mission statement:** To equip young women and young men to make their way in adult life as responsible citizens. **School hours:** 8.50am–3.20 or 3.40pm; library open after school **Meals:** Hot and cold available, including breakfast **Strong GCSE subjects:** Business studies, information studies, PE **London league table position:** 493

## Profile

In 1993, the amalgamation of four different schools on Harold Hill was completed to form Harold Hill Community School. When the present head took office, he decided that the new image of the school required a change of name, and asked the pupils to join in the search for a replacement. King's Wood emerged the victor from the democratic elections. Facilities are good, with six science laboratories and four technology workshops. There are specialist rooms for all other subjects. The school also has its own recording studio. There are two computer rooms, with 50 computers, and at least 40 more computers elsewhere in the school. The school has two gymnasia and extensive playing fields. All pupils have two weeks' work experience and there is good liaison with the careers service and the two FE colleges. Pupils are active in the school council, help as school receptionists and visit local primary schools as teacher assistants. These opportunities are much sought after, and training is given and the work is evaluated with the Havering Business and Education Partnership. In-class support and withdrawal classes are provided for special-needs pupils. An active PTA organizes events. Parents can visit or contact the school if they have problems. Each pupil has a personal organizer and there are regular reports and an open evening.

## Admissions and intake

The standard LEA procedure for applications is followed. Pupils often have low levels of attainment on entry, particularly in reading. Ofsted, however, noted that the school does very well in raising reading levels. In 2000, there were 250 pupils with special needs, of whom 68 had statements.

## Achievement

The school is making great efforts to improve its image, and achievement levels are slowly rising, though still well below the national and borough averages. The number of pupils gaining five or more grades A*–C rose from 10 per cent in 1998 to 16 per cent in 1999, 2000, 2001 and 2002. The school was ranked one above the bottom of the borough league table.

## Extra-curricular activities

The school organizes any club requested, with the arts well in evidence. The school has had considerable success in sports competitions. Field trips and visits support the curriculum. A member of staff runs a scheme to help Romanian schools with AIDS education, giving pupils responsibilities and a chance to learn what it means to be part of an emerging nation. Pupils also help with riding at a local school for children with moderate learning difficulties. The library is open after school hours for further study.

# Marshalls Park School

**Pettits Lane, Romford RM1 4EH** ☎ 01708 724134 Fax: 01708 746021 Head: Mr CG Hendricks; Chair of Governors: Mr B Gilley Rail: Romford **Buses:** 66, 103, 175, 247, 294, 296, 365, 500 Uniform: Black blazer with badge, dark grey or black trousers or dark grey skirt, white formal shirt and school tie (alternative tie for Year 11) **Demand:** 504 applications for 180 places in 2001/2 **Type:** Community comprehensive for 777 mixed pupils, aged 11 to 16 **Submit application form:** End November/early December 2003 **Mission statement:** High academic standards, self-discipline, self-motivation, understanding, respect and care for others, attainment of individuals' full potential **School hours:** 8.40am–3.15pm; homework clubs are available **Meals:** Hot and cold available **Strong GCSE subjects:** Drama, mathematics, music, RE **London league table position:** 332

## Profile

Established in the 1920s as the Intermediate School for Romford, as a comprehensive it combined two schools and two sites, but in 1999 it was consolidated onto one site to which had been added extensive new buildings. There are five science laboratories, a satellite dish for geography and science support, 10 language rooms, a well equipped hall and a drama studio, a music laboratory for traditional and electronic music and an art complex. There is one computer for every seven pupils. There is also a sports hall and floodlit all-weather playing areas. As well as ICT and design and technology, environmental education and citizenship are taught, and pupils are well prepared for their two weeks' work experience through careers education. There is satisfactory assistance for pupils with special needs. Higher achievers are taught together for certain subjects as they move up the school. Prefects assist in the summer term induction class for joiners, and mentor pupils in Year 7. There are year councils and a school council. In 1999, Ofsted remarked on the 'strong and constructive relationship between staff and pupils'. Parents receive reports each term and there are regular newsletters.

### Admissions and intake

The LEA operates its standard procedure for applications. The criteria for choice when oversubscribed are: exceptional need; having a sibling at the school; and proximity to the school. Pupils' attainment on entry is below average. In 2000, there were 99 special needs pupils, of whom 31 had statements.

### Achievement

The school has been improving steadily, with GCSE results now above the national average, though still below the borough average. In 2002, 53 per cent of pupils achieved five or more grades A*–C, up from 29 per cent in 2001. Unfortunately, results fell again to 29 per cent in 2001. Maths, drama, music and religious education tend to be good, history and geography less so. Ofsted noted that 'the school is well placed to make further improvements. It has very successfully moved onto one site and now has accommodation of high quality in most areas'. Pupils go to Havering Sixth Form College.

### Extra-curricular activities

The school arranges theatre trips, geography and science field trips, along with language trips to France and Spain. There are schoolwork clubs and the computer clubs are very popular. The school has links with the local newspaper and Rotary Club, and pupils are encouraged to take part in fund-raising activities. They arrange a Christmas party for senior citizens, and the PE department arranges an annual games tournament for primary school children. There is a wide range of sports on offer, including trampolining and gymnastics.

## Raphael Independent School

**Park Lane, Hornchurch RM11 1XY** 01708 744735 01708 722432 Mr Nick Malicka BA (Hons); Chair of Governors: Paul Gilbert Romford **Buses:** 193, 294, 324, 374 Maroon blazers, dark grey trousers or skirts, white shirt and school tie **Demand:** 30 per cent up for entry in September 2000 **Type:** Selective independent for 147 mixed pupils, aged 4 to16 **Fees:** £895–£1,930 per term **Submit application form:** No cut-off date **Motto:** *Resurgam* (I Will Arise and Go Forward ) **School hours:** 8.40am–3.25pm **Meals:** Hot and cold available **Strong GCSE subjects:** French, IT **London league table position:** 4

### Profile

Raphael was formed in 1935 and named after Sir Herbert Raphael MP, a barrister and a benefactor in Gidea Park. The present head teacher moved the school to its present site in 1994. Facilities on-site include a science laboratory, a music room, an art room, classrooms and an ICT room. The school has 16 computers. A new library opened in September 2001. For sports there is a small hall, two hard surface areas, and two leased rugby/football fields within 300m of the school. Pupils also use Harold Hill swimming baths, Romford YMCA for multi-sports and Hylands tennis club courts. Vocational subjects offered include business studies (NVQ level 2) and a strong Young Enterprise initiative. One week's work experience is offered after GCSEs. The school has prefects and a head boy and head girl. There are two houses, each with captains, and there is a student council. There is a member of staff designated with responsibility for special-needs pupils. Friends of Raphael raise funds and organize social events for parents, staff and pupils. There are regular consultations and reports, and parents are encouraged to contact the school and staff with any problems.

### Admissions and intake

To apply, contact the school to arrange a visit and submit a registration form. No formal interview with pupils or parents is required, but the school sets its own entrance tests in English, maths and science in November, and again (but with a different set of papers) in March. A report is requested from applicants' previous school. Some pupils are above average for their age group. At the time of writing, there were 20 pupils with special needs, none of whom had a statement.

### Achievement

The school's GCSE performance has fluctuated widely over recent years, from a low of 27 per cent of pupils achieving 5 A*–C grades at GCSE in 2000, to 55 per cent in 2001, and 100 per cent in 2002. This placed the school at the top of the borough league. Information technology tends to be a good subject but art is poor. The last independent school inspection date was in 2000.

## Extra-curricular activities

Extra-curricular activities range from visits to WWI historical sites in Belgium and France, and Barcelona for Spanish culture, to outdoor activities on the Isle of Wight. There are theatre, opera and ballet visits and trips to Alton Towers. Members of the police education liaison team, Nat West Bank and QUIT (on the dangers of smoking) are among the visitors who talk to the school. The school also encourages membership of its own provision of activities, which range from chess and desktop publishing to cookery. A school charity is chosen each year, and in 1999 it was the RNLI. The school won first prize for Best Presentation in the Havering final of the Young Enterprise scheme. The normal range of sports is on offer.

# Redden Court School

**Cotswold Road, Harold Wood, Romford RM3 0TS** ☎ 01708 342293 📠 01708 386550 ✉ info@reddencourt.org.uk 🌐 www.reddencourt.org.uk Mr P Townrow B.Sc; Chair of Governors: Mr John Hooper 🚆 Harold Wood **Buses:** 256, 265, 294 Navy blazer and badge, navy trousers or grey skirt, white shirt, school tie **Demand:** 224 applications for 120 places in 2001/2. **Type:** Community comprehensive for 600 mixed pupils, aged 11 to 16 **Submit application form:** End November/early December 2002 **Motto:** Committed to Success **School hours:** 8.45am–3.30pm; homework clubs are available three nights a week **Meals:** Hot and cold available, including breakfast **Strong GCSE subjects:** Art **London league table position:** 495

## Profile

Established on its present site in 1938, Redden Court took its first comprehensive intake in 1970. Facilities on-site include four science laboratories, two home economics rooms, three art and craft rooms, two technology workshops, a drama studio and a music suite. As well as the three networked computer rooms, many classrooms also have computers. There is a large sports hall and sports fields, which enable all the major sports to be played, plus athletics, short tennis, softball and gymnastics. Design and technology can be taken in resistant materials, food and textiles and health and social care. Two weeks' work experience is offered and there is a close liaison with the borough careers guidance service. The prefect, year and class representatives system enables pupils to take on responsibilities. The specia-needs centre is open for use before and after school and during breaks. Ofsted noted that while special needs pupils are mainstreamed, other pupils accept their needs and there is no apparent discrimination. There is a 'stalwart core' of parents in the Friends of Redden Court who raise funds. The school has a delayed start on the first day of the autumn term so that the new intake has the school to themselves, with prefects and teachers on duty to help them settle in before having to cope with their seniors. The school has twice been awarded Investors in People status.

## Admissions and intake

The procedure for application is standard LEA procedure. Oversubscription is dealt with by applying the criteria of: exceptional need; having a sibling at the school; and proximity of home to the school. In 2000, 32 special-needs pupils had statements.

## Achievement

The school's achievement of five or more grades A*–C has been creeping up, from 11 per cent in 1996 to 24 per cent in 1999 and 2000, and to 28 per cent in 2001, though it dipped again in 2002, to 26 per cent. The best subject is art, while history, geography, languages and music are poor. In 1998, Ofsted noted that the head teacher had only been in the post for one term, and that 'Redden Court is a caring school which provides a welcoming and positive learning environment... There is an upward trend [in academic achievement] at a rate faster than the national average.' Inspectors also remarked that expectations were too low, but the current prospectus claims that the school's policy of grouping pupils according to ability enables the more able pupils to move faster than the less able, who are 'taught at a pace which is more appropriate to their needs in order that they too can achieve to their maximum potential.'

## Extra-curricular activities

There are clubs for chess, dance, outdoor pursuits and drama. Geography and science field trips are organized, along with visits to France, Chessington World of Adventures and the Imperial War Museum. The school helps local disabled youngsters, and pupils help produce and sell local history guides through Redden School Enterprises. They put on an annual pantomime, and the music department gives concerts in local churches. Homework clubs are available. The sports on offer follow the National Curriculum.

# The Royal Liberty School

**Upper Brentwood Road, Gidea Park, Romford RM2 6HJ** 01708 730141 01708 723950 Mr M Morrall MA Med; Chair of Governors:Mr Garry Woodman Gidea Park **Buses:** 296, 374, 551 Black blazer with badge, black trousers, white or blue shirt, school tie **Demand:** 186 applications for 120 places in 2001/2 **Type:** Community comprehensive for 511 boys, aged 11 to 16 **Submit application form:** End November/early December 2003 **Motto:** *Semper Procedens* (Forever Forward) **School hours:** 8.40am–3pm; homework clubs are available **Meals:** Hot and cold available, including breakfast **Strong GCSE subjects:** Drama **London league table position:** 427

## Profile

Essex County Council took over Hare Hall in 1921 and converted it into the Romford County High School for Boys; the first head teacher changed the name to The Royal Liberty School. In 1996, Ofsted recommended special measures for the school. This was later followed by an inspection in 1997, and six in 1998 and 1999, followed by one in 2000, which recommended that the school be taken out of special measures, although there were still serious weaknesses. A positive Ofsted report in 2002 described the school as having 'many strengths' and it said 'no longer has serious weaknesses'. The present head teacher took over in September 1997. Facilities include five science laboratories, three technology rooms, a new food technology department, a drama studio and a media studies recording studio. The library has 12,000 books, four daily newspapers and various magazines, along with part of the school's computer network, and multi-media computers for CD-ROMs. Sport is important in the school. Past pupils have represented Essex and England in football, cricket, basketball, swimming and athletics, and the facilities reflect this. Work experience is offered through the Havering Education and Business Partnership. The school recently won a Sportsmark award and an Artsmark award. The school is divided into houses and each form group elects a representative to serve on the school council. There is a head boy with deputies and prefects. Special needs pupils receive in-class support, which Ofsted noted to be good in 2002. The Parents, Teachers, Pupils Association is a forum for discussion of curriculum, head teacher's reports and fund-raising events.

## Admissions and intake

Admission is by standard LEA procedure. Oversubscriptions are dealt with by applying the following criteria: exceptional need; having a sibling at the school; and proximity of home to the school. Pupils' attainment level on entry is average. In 2001, the number of pupils with special educational needs was about average.

## Achievement

The school's GCSE achievement rose to nearly national average in 1997 but has since slumped, with only 32 per cent of pupils gaining five or more A*–C grades in 2002, up from 25 per cent in 2001. This placed the school 18th out of 20 in the borough. Ofsted described the school as 'having moved from a period of decline to one of significant improvement and now offers its students a good standard of education'. Teaching was seen to be on the whole 'consistently good' with very good teaching in mathematics, design and technology, drama, geography and media studies. Inspectors praised the head teacher as a 'good leader'. However, GCSE results are below average compared to similar schools with the standard of writing being generally 'below average' across the school. Literacy standards were seen to be 'satisfactory' with strengths in listening and reading.

## Extra-curricular activities

The school runs homework, IT, chess and table tennis clubs. Pupils make, maintain and run their own go-karts, and the Footloose Club is available for camping, orienteering and climbing. Roller hockey is popular. There are trips to theatres, concert halls and sporting fixtures. The school has raised funds for Save the Children and the NSPCC.

# Sacred Heart of Mary Girls' School

**St Mary's Lane, Upminster RM14 2QR** 01708 222660 01708 226686 Mrs B Williams MA (Lond); Chair of Governors: Mr Mike O'Riordan Upminster Upminster **Buses:** 346, 348 : Navy blazer with badge, navy skirt, navy V-neck cardigan or pullover, blue blouse and school tie **Demand:** 120 places available in 2002;

oversubscribed **Type:** Voluntary aided Roman Catholic comprehensive for 800 girls, aged 11 to 18 **Submit application form:** End November/early December 2003 **Motto:** *Veritas liberabit vos* (The Truth Will Make You Free) **Mission statement:** The school is founded on concern and respect for each individual members. A commitment to Christ and Gospel values is explicit through development of faith through prayer and training in moral leadership. While cherishing the Catholic tradition, the school seeks to foster tolerance, understanding and respect for other faiths. **School hours:** 8.45am–3.30pm; homework clubs are available **Meals:** Hot and cold available, including breakfast **Strong GCSE subjects:** All relatively strong **London league table position:** 85

## Profile

Founded in 1927 by the Sisters of the Sacred Heart of Mary, the school became a voluntary aided school in 1950 at the request of the then Bishop of Brentwood. The diocese acquired it in 1977. In 1978 it admitted its first comprehensive entry. Facilities include six laboratories, four technology and four language rooms, a performing arts block (the school is a Centre of Excellence in Music), three networked computer rooms and two business studies rooms. The school also has a gymnasium, hard courts for tennis and netball, and playing fields. A-levels focus strongly on science and mathematics but also include home economics and business. Design and technology and childcare and development are offered at GCSE. Project Trident helps arrange two weeks of work experience in Year 10. The school is divided into houses, each of which has its own head and prefects, which form part of the school's strong pastoral care structure. Special-needs pupils are rarely withdrawn from mainstream classes but are provided with classroom support. Progress reports are given regularly, and parents are encouraged to raise any questions or problems with the school directly. There is a strong PTA. School Masses are celebrated on major feast days and house patronal days. There is lunchtime Mass in the convent chapel.

## Admissions and intake

The LEA sets an annual closing date for applications but the governors set the criteria. The family's parish priest must confirm applicants are practising Catholics, living in the Brentwood diocese. If oversubscribed, exceptional need, having a sibling at the school and proximity of home to the school are assessed. Applicants are interviewed to ensure the child will prosper in the religious character of the school. In 1994, Ofsted noted a 'slight skew' towards average and above average pupils. In 2000, there were 39 special needs pupils, one of whom had a statement.

## Achievement

The school's performance is consistently very good. The percentage of pupils gaining five or more GCSE grades A*–C in 2002 was 91, up from 90 per cent in 2001. The average A-level point score was 336.6. The last Ofsted inspection was September 2000 when Inspectors praised the 'good quality teaching'. Pupils' behaviour was described as 'excellent' and their personal development 'outstanding'. Unauthorized absence is low at 0.1 per cent.

## Extra-curricular activities

Music, drama and sport are important to the school. There are also clubs and associations to support the curriculum, such as homework clubs, and to develop other interests outside of the curriculum. Cultural visits and field trips are made in the UK and abroad. There are exchange arrangements with Strasbourg, Rome and Siena. Charitable work is encouraged.

# St Edward's CofE Comprehensive School

**London Road, Romford RM7 9NX** ☎ 01708 730462 📠 01708 731485 ⓔ enquiries@steds.havering.sch.uk 🌐 www.steds.havering.sch.uk Mr GCS Drew BA; Chair of Governors: Mr Richard Fishleigh BA ⇌ Romford **Buses:** 86, 248, 251, 551 Charcoal grey blazer with badge, trousers or skirt, white shirt, school tie **Demand:** 210 places available in 2002; oversubscribed **Type:** Voluntary aided CofE comprehensive for 1077 mixed pupils, aged 11 to 18 **Submit application form:** November 2003 **Mission statement:** To achieve a happy, fulfilled community permeated with lively faith and Christian values, in which the full potential of each individual is realized, and excellence is energetically pursued. **School hours:** 8.50am–3.30pm; homework clubs are available **Meals:** Hot and cold available **Strong GCSE subjects:** English literature, science **London league table position:** 184

## Profile

Founded in 1710 by the Vestry of St Edward's Church in Romford as a charity school, this school has been on its present site since 1965. Facilities include six science laboratories, five computing rooms, technology and music blocks and specialist rooms for all subject needs. Sports are very well provided for, including a 25m indoor heated swimming pool. Pupils have played for England under-18 volleyball and for Essex in hockey and netball teams. The school holds a short act of daily worship and Communion services throughout the year. Design and technology, including business technology and child development, can be taken at GCSE, and RSA and CLAIT examinations are also taken. The standard curriculum for A-level is offered, plus government and politics, accounting and finance and CDT. Project Trident helps arrange two weeks of work experience and the Rotary Club helps with practising job applications and interview techniques. Sixth form and Year 11 pupils are invited to act as prefects and all years have their own councils. Pupils help to produce *Reach-out*, which provides information for parents, and is a platform for pupils' views. Specialist help is available in mainstream teaching and in small groups for assistance with maths and reading or writing difficulties. Exceptionally able pupils take part in the borough's provision for able students. The PTA is very active and has raised substantial funds.

## Admissions and intake

The principal criterion for admission is commitment to and involvement in Christian worship and work. If demand exceeds the 210 places, priority is given to applicants with siblings at the school, followed by other practising Christians. An interview is rarely required although a recommendation from a priest, minister, or the primary head teacher is required. In 2000, there were 94 pupils with special needs, of whom 14 had statements.

## Achievement

The school performs consistently well, above national and borough averages. The number of pupils gaining five or more GCSE grades A*–C was 67 per cent in 2002, down slightly from 71 per cent the previous year. The average A-level point score was 235. The core subjects English, mathematics and science are good, with science fractionally best at the higher-grade end, while geography is poor. In 1998, Ofsted commented: 'This is a good school, with many more strengths than weaknesses, and most of the weaknesses have been identified and plans made to deal with them.'

## Extra-curricular activities

The music department runs concert tours abroad, there is an annual large-cast performance and senior pupils take a play to the Edinburgh Fringe biannually. Competitive sports are encouraged. There are canal holidays in the UK, and in 2000, there were trips to Canada and Russia. The sixth form organizes Christian Union meetings. The school undertakes substantial fund-raising for charity. After-school homework clubs are available.

# The Sanders Draper School

**Suttons Lane, Hornchurch RM12 6RT** ☎ 01708 443068 📠 01708 479005 Mr B Rogers BA, MA, ACP, FcollP, FRSA; Chair of Governors: Mr S Harding Hornchurch **Buses:** 193, 252 Black blazer and badge, black or dark grey trousers or skirt, white shirt or blouse, school tie **Demand:** 452 applications for 192 places in 2002 **Type:** Community comprehensive for 875 mixed pupils, aged 11 to 16 **Submit application form:** End November/early December 2003 **Motto:** Positive Achievement for All **School hours:** 8.50am–3.25pm; homework clubs are available **Meals:** Hot and cold available, including vegetarian options **Strong GCSE subjects:** Art and design, information studies, science **London league table position:** 187

## Profile

Founded in 1938, the school gets its present name from a US pilot serving with the RAF whose engine failed immediately after take-off in 1943. Eyewitnesses (pupils then in their classrooms) believe he deliberately crashed in the playing field to avoid hitting the school. Facilities include six science laboratories, art and technology rooms, three technology workshops with a computer-aided design area, a music suite and a media studies centre. The learning resources centre has Internet access and the three networked computer rooms were updated in 1996. The school also has a sports hall, gymnasium, fitness centre, playing fields for soccer, rugby and hockey, tennis and netball courts. Vocational subjects offered are design and technology textiles, graphics, materials and food technology. Project Trident helps organize two weeks' work experience. There is a school council. Prefects are selected in Year 11 and there is a series of awards and credits. There is a hearing-impaired unit, the only one in the borough, which enables pupils with profound and severe hearing difficulties to continue their education in a mainstream school. Pupils and staff without hearing difficulties have learned to sign and passed examinations in British Sign Language. Support is available in the classroom for special-needs pupils or they can be withdrawn for intensive assistance according to need. The parent-teacher association raises funds. Regular meetings are held and full school reports and briefer progress reports are provided to keep parents informed. Pupils can also join the school council.

## Admissions and intake

The admission process is standard LEA procedure. Oversubscription is dealt with by applying the criteria of: exceptional need; having a sibling at the school; and proximity of home to the school. Pupils have an average level of attainment on entry. In 2000, there were 189 special needs pupils, of whom 45 had statements.

## Achievement

Over the past seven years, the schools GCSE performance has varied wildly, from a low of 34 per cent of pupils gaining five or more GCSE grades A*–C in 1998, to a high of 67 per cent in 2001. This slipped to 65 per cent in 2002, still above borough and national averages. The school was ranked seventh in the borough. Art and design, information studies and science are the best subjects, but PE and English literature are poor. In 1996, Ofsted commented that this was a good school which provided well for its pupils and was well managed.

## Extra-curricular activities

Pupils take responsibility for team selection and training for inter-school and form competitive sports. Drama is strong, and there are brass, percussion and guitar ensembles as well as an orchestra and choir. Clubs include chess, badminton, art and dance. Science, history and geography field trips are organized, along with visits to galleries, exhibitions and theatres. Water sports, language and business studies courses are arranged in France, as well as skiing in Italy and pony-trekking in Wales. There are regular fund-raising activities.

# Hillingdon

**Key**

1. Abbotsfield School
2. American Community School
3. Barnhill Community High School
4. Bishop Ramsey CofE Voluntary Aided School
5. Bishopshalt School
6. The Douay Martyrs RC School
7. Evelyn's Community High School
8. Guru Nanak Sikh Secondary School
9. Harlington Community School
10. Haydon School
11. The Hayes Manor School
12. John Penrose School
13. Mellow Lane School
14. Northwood College
15. Northwood School
16. Queensmead School
17. St Helen's School
18. Swakeleys School
19. Uxbridge High School
20. Vyners School (FD)

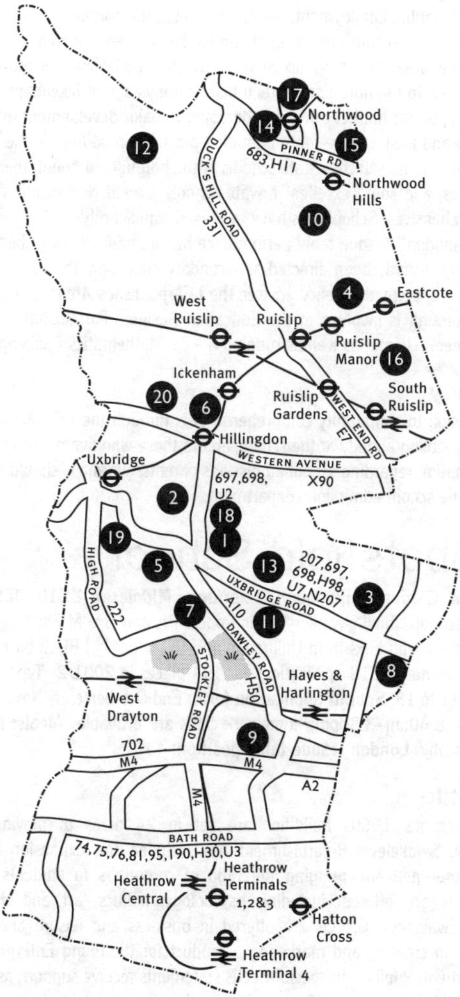


## Factfile

**LEA:** Civic Centre, High Street, Uxbridge UB8 1UW ☎ 01895 250111 🌐 www.hillingdon.gov.uk **Director of Education:** Mr Phillip O'Hear **Political control of council:** Conservative **Percentage of pupils from outside the borough:** 8.5 per cent **Percentage of pupils educated outside the borough:** 8.8 per cent **London league table positions (out of 32 boroughs):** 20th

## Profile

The ancient parish of Hillingdon was first recorded in the Domesday Book of 1086, but it was not until 1965 that several urban districts in north-west (former) Middlesex were amalgamated to form London's second largest borough. Much of the borough still has a semi-rural feel to it, with an abundance of green spaces.

Hillingdon is dominated in the south by the world's biggest airport, Heathrow, which creates traffic and noise but also substantial employment; unemployment in the borough is only 2.8 per cent. Recently, over £21 million has been invested in boosting employment, protecting the environment and cutting crime north of Heathrow. The heavily industrial area stretching up to West Drayton and Hayes is moving its emphasis towards high-tech and retail commerce. To the north, on a green belt, is the village of Ickenham and to the west, Uxbridge. The high street of this once important market town is undergoing a major development to create new shop fronts and a multiplex cinema. Ruislip and Eastcote are more upmarket but the top address in the borough is Northwood.

There are no selective state schools in the borough, although there are Language, Technology and Performing Arts Colleges, and some excellent private schools around Northwood. There are only three independents alongside 17 comprehensives. School rolls have increased significantly.

Hillingdon's league table performance has traditionally been better at primary level, since the council's attention has only recently been directed at secondary education. The LEA is now actively pursuing the raising of standards, and has appointed a policy adviser. The LEA publishes *Arena*, a professional journal showcasing practice and ideas. The borough is involved in the Education Business Partnership, the Youth Award scheme and the Neighbourhood Engineers scheme, as well as running a local Mathematics Challenge.

## Policy

Admission to community comprehensives is through the LEA. Most secondary schools give priority to children who have a sibling already at the school, and to those who live nearest the school measured in a straight line. For further information regarding school admissions parents/guardians should obtain a copy of *Starting Secondary School 2003* from the school admissions department.

# Abbotsfield School

**Clifton Gardens, Hillingdon, Uxbridge, Middlesex UB10 0EX** ☎ 01895 237350 📠 01895 271995 ⓔ Aschool@lbhill.gov.uk ✉ Mr Robert Preston BA, M.Ed; Chair of Governors: Mrs Jill Rhodes ⊖ Hillingdon **Buses:** U2 and links from Hillingdon and Uxbridge 👔 Black blazer, red and black school tie, black trousers, white shirt **Demand:** 318 applications for 194 places in 2001/2 **Type:** Comprehensive foundation school for 628 boys, aged 11 to 18 **Submit application form:** End October/early November 2003 **Motto:** Achieving Excellence **School hours:** 8.40am–3.30pm; homework clubs are available **Meals:** Hot and cold available **Strong GCSE subjects:** Geography **London league table position:** 436

## Profile

The school's 1960s buildings are set in 24 acres of playing fields, shared with the neighbouring girls' school, Swakeleys. Refurbishment has included the expansion of the library and the installation of a large computer network, bringing the ratio of computers to students to 1:5. The sixth form is small, but over 20 A-levels are offered, including psychology, politics, art and theatre studies – an advantage of combining with Swakeleys. GNVQs are offered in business and leisure and tourism. Local businesses provide support for pupils in creating and marketing a product for the Young Enterprise scheme and in the Year 11 work experience placement. Pupils with special-needs statements receive support, as do the large proportion of pupils with English as an additional language. Responsible pupils can become form reps in the school forum or prefects in Year 11. Sixth-formers are involved in paired reading schemes. Parents are kept informed through a regular newsletter, student progress monitoring, consultation evenings and annual written reports. The school's unauthorized absence rate was 3.7 per cent in 1999/2000, well above the national average. The astrologer Russell Grant is a former pupil.

## Admissions and intake

Applications should be made direct to the school. Preference is given, in order of priority, to: those applicants with medical grounds; those with siblings in the school; and those living nearest. There is a wide catchment area and some pupils commute from Ealing and Buckinghamshire.

### Achievement

Abbotsfield's GCSE results have remained fairly constant in the last five years. In 1998, there was a 93 per cent pass rate and 23 per cent of pupils achieving five or more A*–C grades. In 2002, this stood at 26 per cent, down from 30 per cent the previous year. The ranked the school 15th in the borough. In 2001, the average point score for pupils taking two or more A-levels was 191.1. Results in vocational subjects are well above the national average. Over two-thirds of those pupils taking intermediate GNVQ and all of those taking advanced passed in 2000. When Ofsted inspected in 1998, the school was judged to have 'serious weaknesses'. The school's ethos was felt to be 'unsatisfactory', as was behaviour and attitudes to learning and relationships. However, it received a favourable inspection report in July 2000, which recognized that 'standards have improved'.

### Extra-curricular activities

There are many inter-form and inter-school sports competitions. Activities and clubs include sci-fi, art, music, homework clubs and the school magazine. The maths class is involved in masterclasses and the local Maths Challenge, and some pupils have been involved in the Science Roadshow at Reading University. Abbotsfield has reached the Greater London finals for three years running in the Young Enterprise project. Annual trips include regular visits to France, skiing trips and visits to theatres, museums and, in the sixth form, universities. Funds for charities are raised at Christmas and through casual clothes days.

# American Community School

**108 Vine Lane, Hillingdon, Uxbridge, Middlesex UB10 OBE** 01895 259771 01895 256974 hillingdonadmissions@acs-england.co.uk www.acs-england.co.uk Mrs G Apple; Chair of Governors: Mr Malcolm Kay Uxbridge **Buses:** 207; school bus provides transport to and from many local towns None **Demand:** No figures available but highly variable **Type:** Selective independent for 648 mixed pupils, aged 3 to 19 **Fees:** (per semester; 2 semesters per year): £6,575 (Years 9 to 10); £6,600 (Years 11 to 13) **Submit application form:** No cut-off date **Motto:** Passport to the World **School hours:** 8.45am–3.10pm **Meals:** Hot and cold available **Strong GCSE subjects:** Not applicable **London league table position:** Not applicable

### Profile

Housed in Hillingdon Court, a 19th-century aristocrat's home, the ACS Hillingdon has formal gardens and 11 acres of lawns. It is one of three ACS 'campuses' in the area, formed in 1967 to serve the expatriate community. Facilities include an auditorium, gym, libraries, an all-weather floodlit tennis court and playing fields. Nearby are baseball diamonds, a swimming pool and a golf course. The school is accredited by the New England Association of Schools and the Independent Schools Joint Association. It also holds memberships in the International Baccalaureate Diploma Programme, the Advance Placement Programme, the European Council of International Schools, the Near East/South Asia Council of Overseas Schools and the College Board. Qualifications offered include the standard American diploma, and the more challenging Advanced Placement (AP) and International Baccalaureate (IB) diplomas. To graduate, pupils must complete at least 21 credits, including 6 in social studies and foreign languages, 6 in maths and science, 4 in English, 2 in PE, 1 in fine arts and 2 in additional courses. A wide range of subjects are available including world history, drama and word processing. AP and IB courses can include Spanish, US/European history, calculus, physics, psychology and economics. ESL support is offered from kindergarten to grade 10. Parents receive quarterly reports and there are twice-yearly parent-teacher conferences. Pupils can join the school council.

### Admissions and intake

ACS select pupils of average to above average academic ability; applications must be accompanied by school transcripts and teacher recommendations, and pupils are given diagnostic tests. A disproportionately large number of pupils have been identified as gifted by their previous school districts. Most children are from families in business or government on assignment in London, with a third of the community leaving each year. Some 60 per cent are American, but the school enrols from 50 other countries.

### Achievement

Most pupils at the school take the internationally recognized IB diploma. In 2002 there was a 100 per cent pass rate – all 40 pupils who took the diploma passed it – and in the two previous years just two pupils failed, well above the average for all IB schools. Five pupils have gone on to Harvard in the past two years. A proportion of graduates also go on to study at the University of Tokyo, Oxbridge, Yale, Stanford and the London School of Economics.

### Extra-curricular activities

The school is involved in the Center for Talented Youth programme run by John Hopkins University in the US. School teams compete with local American and British schools and international schools in Europe in basketball, cross-country, tennis, volleyball and soccer. There are also boys' rugby and baseball teams and girls' softball and cheerleading teams. In addition to local cultural trips and subject field trips, there are annual language trips and a skiing trip to Europe. All IB pupils undertake community service.

## Barnhill Community High School

**Yeading Lane, Hayes, Middlesex UB4 9LE** 020 8839 0600 020 8839 0661 enquiries@barnhillhigh.com www.barnhillhigh.com Ian Marshall MA, FRSA; Chair of Governors: Cllr J Major Hayes, Harlington Northolt **Buses:** E6, E9, 140 White shirt, black skirt or trousers, dark red jumper, school tie **Demand:** 563 applications for 240 places in 2001/2 **Type:** Comprehensive foundation school for 860 mixed pupils (only Years 7 to 8 so far), aged 11 to 18 **Submit application form:** End October/early November 2003 **Motto:** *Sapere aude* (Dare to Be Wise) **School hours:** 8.35am–3.15pm; homework clubs are available **Meals:** Hot and cold available, including breakfast **Strong GCSE subjects:** Not applicable **London league table position:** Not available

### Profile

Barnhill Community High was the first new school of the millennium and is housed in a smart modern building in the industrial area of Hayes. It is one of only three schools in the country to have public and private funding combined in a new Private Finance Initiative (PFI). It intends to 'develop confident, high achieving individuals with the knowledge and skills to positively contribute to a fast changing world'. The school takes a 'multi-sensory approach to teaching and learning and deliver(s) programmes of study through individual accelerated learning programmes...lessons are structured to suit the unique needs of each child'. A separate subject, called Enrichment, is offered in addition to PSHE and RE as part of an 'innovative curriculum'. The school has established links with the business community. A combination of withdrawal and class support is available for pupils with special needs, and there is a special needs coordinator. The school also has disability access and lift ramps. The prospectus says: 'The students, family and school will enter into a voluntary learning commitment partnership.' Pupils' form tutors communicate directly with parents through meetings, letters and phone calls. There is a school council which pupils can join.

### Admissions and intake

Application is made direct to the school. Preference is given, in order of priority, to: those applicants with siblings at the school; those with proven medical need; and those living closest to the school.

### Achievement

With no Year 11 yet, there are no exam results to compare. The attendance rate looks promising and was 92 per cent in 1999/2000, with only 0.6 per cent unauthorized absences.

### Extra-curricular activities

The usual range of sports are on offer, including netball, football and hockey, and there is a nightly homework club. The school has good links with local community associations and its facilities are made available to community groups. Pupils are offered a range of educational day visits and there is a residential experience.

## Bishop Ramsey CofE Voluntary Aided School

**Eastcote Road, Ruislip, HA4 8DJ** (lower school); **Hume Way, Ruislip, Middlesex HA4 8EE** (upper school) 01895 634506 (lower school); 01895 639227 (upper school); 01895 638868 (lower school); 01895 622429 (upper school) lower@bishopramsey.hillingdon.sch.uk; upper@bishopramsey.hillingdon.sch.uk A Wilcock MA; Chair of Governors: Rev D Coleman West Ruislip West Ruislip, Ruislip Manor **Buses:** H13, J14, 282

Dark brown blazer and jumper or cardigan, dark brown skirt or black trousers, beige shirt, school tie **Demand:** 421 applications for 180 places in 2001/2 **Type:** Voluntary aided Church of England comprehensive for 1155 mixed pupils, aged 11 to 18 **Fees:** £120 per year voluntary contribution **Submit application form:** End October/early November 2003 **School hours:** 8.45am–3.30pm, 8.45am–4pm (Mon, Years 10 to 11) **Meals:** Hot snacks available **Strong GCSE subjects:** English, history, maths **London league table position:** 138

## Profile

Split between two sites in the prosperous area of Ruislip, Bishop Ramsey is a successful church school. The modern buildings and new facilities of the upper school contrast with the older accommodation of the lower school. A recently completed building offers facilities for IT, modern languages, music, sixth form and learning resources, including a new library. Bishop Ramsey offers a broad based curriculum including Spanish, French and German. Some 26 A-levels are offered including drama, IT, law, three varieties of maths, music, theology, philosophy and PE. GNVQs are offered in leisure and tourism, business and finance and art. The school was accredited by the OCR exam board for the quality of its work experience programme. Its links with industry include the Business Council partnership and an annual two-day induction programme, when 70 industrialists prepare Year 10 pupils for their two-week work placements in Year 11. There is also an advanced level 'understanding industry' course, sponsored by a private company. A special-needs coordinator caters for very able students and there is an Oxbridge support group. Pupils can participate in the school council or become year officers and house captains. Parental involvement is through the school's PTA, Friends of Bishop Ramsey and regular consultation evenings.

## Admissions and intake

Application is made direct to the school. Admission criteria are detailed but are based on the family's pattern of regular church attendance. Pupils are drawn from a large number of schools in Hillingdon and neighbouring boroughs.

## Achievement

A total of 81 per cent of pupils gained five or more A*–C grades at GCSE in 2002. This was up on 68 per cent in 2001 and the school was ranked fourth in the borough. The average point score for pupils taking two or more A/AS-levels was 282.5, placing the school third in the borough. The school is particularly strong in maths, English and history. A large proportion of pupils – around 90 per cent – go on to higher education. In 2001, Ofsted described it as a 'very good school' which is 'well led' and pupils' behaviour is '...never less than good'.

## Extra-curricular activities

The school has an annual arts festival, as well as regular school productions and concerts involving the junior and senior orchestra, concert bands and choirs. Pupils have performed in national television and theatre productions. In 1998/9, Bishop Ramsey were the borough champions in cross-country, swimming, athletics and Year 9 and 11 basketball. Other activities include orienteering, dance, gymnastics, cricket and chess. As well as visits and language exchanges to Europe, skiing trips, activity holidays and fieldwork trips are organized. Bishop Ramsey was the first school in the borough to win the Community Award. Pupils have organized a millennium project, linking Bishop Ramsey with Malosa Secondary School in Malawi. The school organizes fund-raising events for charities within the local community.

# Bishopshalt School

**Royal Lane, Hillingdon, Uxbridge, Middlesex UB8 3AF** ☎ 01895 233909 Fax 01985 273102 e admin@bishopshalt.hillingdon.sch.uk www.bishopshalt.hillingdon.sch.uk Mr JF Hodkinson B.Sc Econ; Chair of Governors: Mr Ian Carter ⊖ Uxbridge **Buses:** H98, U7, 207, 607 Up to sixth form: Navy blazer, jumper, navy skirt or charcoal trousers, white shirt, school tie **Demand:** 700 applications for 181 places in 2001/2 **Type:** Comprehensive Arts College foundation school for 1158 mixed pupils, aged 11 to 18 **Submit application form:** December 2003 **Motto:** *Fidelis* (Faithful) **School hours:** 8.45am–3.45pm **Meals:** Hot and cold available, including breakfast **Strong GCSE subject:** Art **London league table position:** 259

## Profile

Bishopshalt School was given Arts College status in performing arts in 1998. It has a new maths suite and a performing arts block, and the main library is very well resourced. In addition to a gym, tennis courts and playing fields, the school has a sunken croquet lawn. Bishopshalt received the Sportsmark Award in 2000 for its facilities and it is affiliated to the Technology Colleges Trust. There is an artist in residence every year. In addition to the National Curriculum, dance is offered as a subject at Key Stage 3 and at GCSE with drama offered as a core subject at Key Stage 3. A-levels available include performing arts, German and French. GNVQ courses are offered in health and social care and business studies, and the school has introduced work-related learning, which includes day-release to attend college courses. Bishopshalt received the West London Quality Award for its career guidance programme. Year 10 receive two weeks' work experience and Years 11 to 12 can have a placement in France or Germany. Sixth-formers can become prefects and library assistants. Pupils with special needs are catered for with smaller class sizes and additional support, and there are also good facilities for the visually impaired. A literacy coordinator has also been appointed. The school works closely with parents through the PTA. Former pupils include Clare Richards, singer with Steps; Lord (Bernard) Miles of Blackfriars, founder of the Mermaid Theatre; and Vernon Bogdanor, fellow and tutor in politics at Brasenose College, Oxford.

### Admissions and intake

Application is made direct to the school. Preference is given, in order of priority, to those applicants with siblings at the school, those with medical grounds and those living nearest to the school.

### Achievement

Ofsted reported in 2000 that Bishophalt's staff care for their pupils well and support their overall development. The standards achieved in Key Stages 3 and 4 are above national averages and rising steadily, and standards in the sixth form are broadly in line with those nationally. In 2002, 52 per cent of pupils achieved five or more A*–C grades at GCSE, above the borough and national averages. The school was ranked ninth in the borough. The average point score of pupils taking two or more A/AS-levels was 242.5, above the borough but below the national average, placing the school ninth in the borough. Particularly good results have been obtained in psychology, art and history in recent years. Pupils have positive attitudes towards their work and their behaviour is very good.

### Extra-curricular activities

Sports available include cricket, athletics, cross-country running, dance, gymnastics, orienteering and swimming. The outstanding Operatic and Dramatic Society has a long tradition of annual productions. The 50-member school orchestra performs regularly, as do the jazz band and string ensembles. Exchanges are organized to France and Germany, in addition to residential trips overseas and in the UK. Pupils run a Charities Committee, which arranges fund-raising events.

## The Douay Martyrs Roman Catholic School

**Edinburgh Drive, Ickenham, Uxbridge, Middlesex UB10 8QY** ☎ 01895 679400 📠 01895 679401 ✉ tdmsickenh@aol.com 🌐 www.douaymartyrs.school.co.uk Mrs Geraldine Davies B.SC (Hons); Chair of Governors: Canon John McDonald West Ruislip Ickenham, West Ruislip **Buses:** U1, U9, U10 Navy school blazer, blue shirt or blouse, grey trousers or navy skirt, blue school tie **Demand:** 363 applications for 240 places in 2001/2 **Type:** Voluntary aided Roman Catholic comprehensive for 1384 mixed pupils, aged 11 to 18 **Submit application form:** End October/early November 2003 **Motto:** *Pro fide petri* (For the Faith of Peter) **School hours:** 9am–3.45pm; homework clubs are available **Meals:** Breakfast and hot snacks available **Strong GCSE subjects:** English literature, maths, science **London league table position:** 352

### Profile

Situated in affluent Ickenham, this school is the only Roman Catholic secondary in Hillingdon. Facilities have been dramatically improved, with a new Year 7 learning centre, upgraded science rooms, media studies suite, music practice rooms, 22 new classrooms, a new sixth-form study centre and a sports hall. There is now a separate site for the sixth form, with IT-equipped learning resources centres on both sites. Douay has had the Charter Mark for excellence in public service since 1996. Although the school has a strong commitment to the Catholic faith, 'the formal and informal curriculum is inclusive of all cultures and traditions' (Ofsted). Subjects outside the national curriculum range from Mandarin to media studies. Year 7 pupils sample French, Spanish and German before choosing which to study. Each year group also has an enrichment programme. A-level provision has been reviewed and now includes computing, psychology and theology, while GNVQs are offered in business, leisure and tourism and a modern language. Work experience receives the support of a number of businesses. Pupils can lead assemblies, mentor younger pupils and become reps on the academic board or pupil council. Special-needs pupils make good progress. Particularly able pupils are offered a teacher mentor. There are parents' evenings, reports and a telephone helpline.

## Admissions and intake

Application is made direct to the school. Entry criteria, in order of priority, are: practising Roman Catholics with a letter from their parish priest; bapstized Roman Catholics who state a first preference; applicants from other Christian denominations; applicants from other faiths.

## Achievement

The school is in the bottom third of the borough league table for GCSE results and has very high percentages when compared to averages for similar schools. In 200s, 42 per cent of pupils gained five or more A*–C grades, down from 46 per cent in 2001. The average point score for pupils taking two or more A/AS-levels was 172.1, below the borough average. Results had been improving up to 1998, when they were above the borough average. Vocational qualifications are strong, with 100 per cent of pupils gaining merit or distinction in 2000. Almost 95 per cent of teaching was judged to be satisfactory by Ofsted in 1999, while nearly a third was very good or excellent. Impressively, Ofsted reported that the school had no 'key weaknesses', commenting that 'parents feel that the school fosters a love of learning and inspectors agree'.

## Extra-curricular activities

Clubs available vary from basketball and football to chess and the Shakespeare Society. The school is visited by theatre groups, temporary resident artists and musicians. The chaplaincy arranges retreats for Catholics. There are theatre and museum visits, and overseas trips. Fund-raising events, such as the Lenten fast, support various charities. Older students take part in community service projects. The school has homework clubs for many subjects.

# Evelyn's Community High School

**Appletree Avenue, Yiewsley, West Drayton, Middlesex UB7 8DA** ☎ 01895 430066 📠 01895 430062 ⓔ ecommuni@lbhill.gov.uk 🏫 Mr F Groom BA, MA; Chair of Governors: Mr P Ryerson 🚉 West Drayton **Buses:** U1, U3, 222 👔 White shirt, school tie, navy or black trousers or skirt, navy school sweatshirt **Demand:** 100 applications for 175 places in 2001/2 **Type:** Community comprehensive for 740 mixed pupils, aged 11 to 19 **Submit application form:** End October/early November 2003 **School hours:** 8.45am–3pm, 8.45am–2.30pm (Fri); homework clubs are available **Meals:** Hot meals and breakfast available **Strong GCSE subjects:** Drama, food technology, office studies **London league table position:** 524

## Profile

There is considerable movement in and out of the school, with almost 20 per cent of 1998's Year 11 having joined after Year 7. In spite of these difficulties, the school is striving hard to achieve its aim of creating 'a friendly school, where students feel safe and happy to learn, enhancing their self worth within a caring environment'. In 2001, Ofsted recommended that the school be put on special measures as it is 'failing to give its pupils an acceptable standard of education'. Facilities include a business and IT suite, art studios, floodlit astroturf, playing fields, a swimming pool, tennis courts and gym. French and German are offered at GCSE. A-levels options include art and design, computer science and drama, with intermediate GNVQs in business and finance and health and social care, among others. Many local businesses provide work experience for these courses and for Year 10 pupils. Evelyn's provides excellent levels of staffing. Class sizes are below the national average and there is good provision for the high proportion (35 per cent), of special-needs pupils. There are three support teachers qualified in ESL and a teacher for the deaf. The PTA is very active. The school's unauthorized absence rate is 1.9 per cent, just above the national average.

## Admissions and intake

Admission is through the LEA (see borough factfile for details). There are no formal entry requirements for Evelyn's.

## Achievement

Evelyn's GCSE results in 2002 were down from those of 2001, with eight per cent of pupils gaining A*–C grades. The school was ranked bottom of the borough league table. The school achieves its best results in vocational subjects. In

1998, 60 per cent of pupils gained a merit in intermediate GNVQ, six achieved RSA distinctions and three had merits in the BTEC National Childhood Studies Course. Ofsted found the school to have significant weaknesses with a low attendance rate and a high number of exclusions. Although GCSE results had improved in recent years, this had only returned to the levels of attainment achieved in 1996. However, GCSE results are amost in line with similar school and Inspectors acknowledged that the pupils' standards of attainment on entry are 'well below national averages'. Teaching was found to be good in over a quarter of lessons but 'unsatisfactory or poor' in three out of 10 lessons. Pupils' behaviour was found to be 'generally satisfactory'.

## Extra-curricular activities

Activities available include drama productions, external art competitions and a mentoring scheme with Hasbro. The hockey and football teams regularly enter borough competitions and sixth-formers compete for a Sports Leadership Award. The school has a choir, string, bass and woodwind ensembles and a recorder group. There are visits to galleries and theatres, field trips and yearly European trips for the upper school. There is good provision for the Youth Award scheme. After-school homework clubs are available.

# Guru Nanak Sikh Secondary School

**Springfield Road, Hayes, Middlesex UB4 0LT** 020 8573 6085 020 8561 6772 vss@gurunanak.tsnet.co.uk RS Sandhu B.Sc (Hons), PGCE; Chair of Governors: Mr Santamaji Babog Southall **Buses:** 207, 607 Royal blue blazer, orange school tie; white shirt, black trousers, grey V-neck jumper (boys); traditional outfit (shalwar kameez), grey cardigan (girls) **Demand:** 262 applications for 120 places in 2001/2 **Type:** Voluntary aided comprehensive for 330 mixed pupils, aged 11 to 18 **Fees:** For day/residential visits, instrumental music, classroom materials and some exams (in exceptional circumstances) **Submit application form:** End October/early November 2003 **Mission statement:** Education for all with a high expectation of discipline **School hours:** 8.30am–4pm **Meals:** Hot and cold available **Strong GCSE subjects:** English, maths, science **London league table position:** 132

## Profile

Situated in the industrial area of Hayes and housed in a modern low-rise building, Guru Nanak Sikh College opened in 1993 as an independent school, with the purpose of providing education with a Sikh cultural and moral aspect. A sixth form was opened in 1995 and the first student gained a place at Oxford in 1998. In the same year, amid a flurry of media attention, the school was reopened by Jack Straw as the first voluntary aided Sikh school in Britain and changed its name to Guru Nanak Secondary School. The school's stated aim is to 'provide a happy and outward-looking school, within which all the pupils work hard to realize their full potential intellectually, morally, physically, personally and socially, and in which the Sikh religion is fostered'. It promotes traditional Sikh values such as respect for others, caring for the elderly and underprivileged, and humility. Classes are taught in mixed-ability groups. Sikh studies is taught in all years and RE and worship form an integral part of school life. Punjabi is offered at GCSE, in addition to the National Curriculum, while Sikh studies is an option for AS-level. The sixth form is also offered A/AS-levels in art, biology, business studies, chemistry, computer science, English, maths, Punjabi and physics. Intermediate and advanced GNVQ science and IT are also on offer, as well as intermediate art. The school plans to increase the number of subjects available, depending on student demand. Sixth-formers are interviewed regarding careers, and visits are organized to institutes of higher education. The school provides for students with special needs by following the five-stage model as outlined in the DfES code of practice. Particularly able and talented pupils are dealt with in the context of special needs, with extension and enrichment built into schemes of work. The PTA is working to promote parent-school relations. These relations are already built on a strong foundation following the support given by parents to the school when it was struggling to survive on private funds. The school has both prefects and a school council.

## Admissions and intake

Applications are made direct to the school. Entry requirements, in order of priority, are: parental adherence to the Sikh faith; siblings at the school; parents' adherence to other faiths; medical needs; and proximity to the school. Guru Nanak takes children from across west London, including Hillingdon, Hounslow and the large Sikh community of Southall. Some pupils commute from Reading and Luton.

### Achievement

In 2002, 75 per cent of pupils achieved A*–C grades at GCSE. This was an increase from 70 per cent in 2001, and the school was ranked third in the borough. At A-level, the average point score was 200, placing the school 10th in the borough. A high proportion of pupils go on to take degree courses at university.

### Extra-curricular activities

Traditional sports are played, such as Kabaddi and wrestling, as well as the National Curriculum. Trips are organized to museums and other places of educational interest, and theme parks. The school regularly engages in fund-raising for the local community and for the building of religious facilities.

## Harlington Community School

**Pinkwell Lane, Hayes, Middlesex UB3 1PB** 020 8569 1610 020 8569 1624 admin@harlington-school.hillingdon.sch.uk www.harlington-school.hillingdon.sch.uk Mr N Sherman; Chair of Governors: Mr GR Tomlin Hayes, Harlington **Buses:** 90B, 98, 140 Black school blazer, black skirt or trousers, white shirt, red jumper, black, yellow and red school tie **Demand:** 450 applications for 224 places in 2001/2 **Type:** Comprehensive foundation school for 1222 mixed pupils, aged 11 to 18 **Submit application form:** End October/early November 2003 **School hours:** 8.10am–2.45pm ('FLEXI' – 2.45–4pm); homework clubs are available **Meals:** Hot and cold available **Strong GCSE subjects:** Art, drama, science **London league table position:** 350

### Profile

Harlington Community School is the result of the amalgamation in 1994 of an upper and lower school originally two miles apart. The extensive building programme has resulted in purpose-built accommodation with a variety of shared facilities including a well-stocked public library with IT facilities and an adult education centre. Outdoor sports facilities include two soccer pitches, an artificial cricket square and space for four tennis courts. Art, dance, drama, Punjabi, Urdu, Japanese and Spanish are amongst the subjects available. The school provides an optional period at the end of each day called 'FLEXI' which offers additional activities, including sports, and support for both those pupils with special needs and high attainers. Harlington is a designated school for the physically disabled with a purpose-built medical centre and an integrated PE programme. A-level subjects include art, computing, information systems, media studies and psychology. There are GNVQs available in manufacturing, leisure and tourism, business and art and design. The school has strong links with the local Education Business Partnership and careers service, which help to organize work experience for pupils in Year 11. Pupils can act as form reps to the school council. Parents receive information on their children's progress. Unauthorized absence was 2.6 per cent in 2000, above the national average.

### Admissions and intake

Applications are made direct to the school. Admissions criteria are detailed but priority is given, in order, to: those applicants with disability; those with a sibling at the school; those with medical grounds; and those having family members with medical grounds. About 41.3 per cent of pupils have English as an additional language.

### Achievement

In 2002, 41 per cent of pupils gained five or more A*–C grades at GCSE. This was well below the national average but slightly up on 2001's results, continuing an upward trend. The school was ranked 11th in the borough league table. The average point score for pupils taking two or more A/AS-levels was 192.8, below the national average. Results in psychology tend to be strong. Boys are further behind girls than in most other schools. In 1999, Ofsted noted that 'the school is a very harmonious community in which relationships...are very positive and productive', and notably caring towards pupils with disabilities. Ofsted added: 'The degree of racial harmony is impressive'.

### Extra-curricular activities

There is an extensive range of sporting activities available, including cricket, tennis, short tennis, trampolining, weight/circuit training and cross-country. Drama productions and musical events are staged, including a Christmas concert, and 'a number of events to celebrate the cultural richness within the surrounding area' (Ofsted). Visiting speakers have included the police, fire service and travelling theatre companies. Homework clubs are available.

# Haydon School

**Wiltshire Lane, Eastcote, Pinner, Middlesex HA5 2LX** ☎ 020 8429 0005 📠 020 8429 9555 ✉ haydonschool@tctrust.net Mr Peter Woods MBA, M.Sc, ARCS; Chair of Governors: Chris Murray Northwood Hills ⊖ Eastcote, Northwood Hills **Buses:** H13, 282 ; Dark blue jumper with yellow trim, dark blue skirt/trousers, white shirt **Demand:** 734 applicants for 250 places in 2001/2 **Type:** Comprehensive Language College foundation school for 1671 mixed pupils, aged 11 to 18 **Submit application form:** End October/early November 2003 **Mission statement**: Committed to individual excellence in a caring community **School hours:** 8.40am–3.40pm, 8.40am–2.40pm (Tues), 8.40am–3pm (Fri) **Meals:** Hot meals and breakfast available **Strong GCSE subjects:** English, French, geography, German, maths **London league table position:** 233

## Profile

Haydon School became a Language College in 1997. A recent building programme has provided a new teaching block for modern languages, sports hall, library, sixth-form centre, science labs and IT facilities. In 1999, the school was awarded the national Sportsmark Award for the quality of its PE and sports provision. In addition to the National Curriculum, drama, expressive arts, classical civilization, sociology and media studies are options at GCSE, as well as a range of modern languages. Vocational courses, with work experience, are offered in business studies, health and social care, IT and leisure and tourism leading to foundation, advanced or intermediate GNVQs. A total of 25 subjects are offered at A-level, including art and design, government and politics, media studies, practical music and theatre studies. Community service is part of the post-16 timetable. Careers education provides job applications advice, work experience and alternatives to work at the age of 16. Sixth-formers can become house prefects and participate in the paired reading scheme, while younger pupils can become school council reps. Pupils with special needs are given specialist group work, one-to-one tuition and in-class support. They are seen to 'make significant progress' (Ofsted). In 1997, pupils raised money to enable easier access to the school for disabled pupils. Parents' involvement is encouraged through the PTA.

## Admissions and intake

Application is made direct to the school, with priority given, in order, to: those applicants with a sibling at the school; those with medical grounds; and those living closest to the school.

## Achievement

In 2002, 56 per cent of pupils gained five or more A*–C grades at GCSE, down from 68 per cent in 2001 but still above the national average. The school came eighth in the borough league table. Pass rates are very good – 98 per cent in 1999 and 2000. The average point score for pupils taking two or more A/AS-levels was 262.2, placing the school fourth in the borough. In 2000, 91 per cent of pupils received their GNVQs, with over three-quarters gaining a merit or distinction. However, in 1997, Ofsted inspectors noted that although 'pupils and adults work together in a generally good and caring climate...little attention is given to preparing pupils for life in a culturally diverse society', which has resulted in 'significant pockets of disruption...and evidence of intolerance'.

## Extra-curricular activities

Haydon has represented Middlesex in a number of sports including football, hockey, rugby and cricket, and the school has competed at national level in boxing, swimming and trampolining. There are three orchestras, a wind band, a jazz band and two choirs. Drama productions, concerts and dance and gymnastic performances are held. Years 8 and 9 have school camps, and foreign visits and exchanges are arranged every year. In 2000, Haydon was awarded the Charter Mark for its service to the wider community and is actively engaged in fund-raising for charity.

# The Hayes Manor School

**Wood End, Green Road, Hayes, Middlesex UB3 2SG** ☎ 020 8573 2097/7103 📠 020 8573 0280 ✉ info@hayesmanorsch.co.uk www.hayesmanorsch.co.uk C Neathey MA; Chair of Governors: Mrs L Wedlock ⊖ Hillingdon, Uxbridge **Buses:** U4 (from Uxbridge), 98, 297 Dark grey or black trousers or black skirt, white shirt or polo-neck, royal blue school sweatshirt **Demand:** 105 applications for 179 places in 2001/2 **Type:** Comprehensive foundation school for 658 mixed pupils, aged 11 to 18 **Submit application form:** End October/early November 2003 **Mission statement**: Our purpose is to realize the ability of each one of us to achieve success.

**School hours:** 8.40am–3.20pm (3.40pm 'extension time') **Meals:** Hot and cold available **Strong GCSE subject:** Media studies **London league table position:** 507

## Profile

Hayes Manor was made subject to 'special measures' in 1996 after Ofsted reported it was failing to give its pupils an acceptable quality of education. Since then, it has improved its standards considerably. Facilities include a sports centre, gym and library with IT facilities. The school aims to offer economic awareness, citizenship and environmental education besides a balanced curriculum. Personal reading is part of the Year 7 timetable and prizes are awarded for good records. The number of pupils entering A-level exams has increased from 15 in 1996 to 75 in 1998. Subjects available include art, biology, business studies, physics and information studies. Vocational courses include a GNVQ in leisure and tourism and a beauty course. Pupils can also participate in the school council. Work experience is offered in Years 11 and 12. Parents are kept informed by signing homework diaries and checking form messages from school. There is also a PTA. Efforts have been made to improve the rate of attendance, with some effect, but the school is still one of the worst in the borough for unauthorized absences, at 3.3 per cent. Greg Dyke, Director of the BBC, is a former pupil.

## Admissions and intake

Application is made direct to the school. Preference is given to pupils with siblings in the school, on medical grounds and those living closest to the school. Over 20 per cent of the school population has entered in the last two years. Some 22 per cent of Years 7 to 11 have designated special education needs.

## Achievement

Although attainment is still well below national average, the quality of teaching at Hayes Manor has improved. In 2001, Ofsted reported that '61 per cent is now good, very good or excellent'. The school was seen to have made 'significant improvements' since the last inspection. In 2002, 20 per cent of pupils achieved five or more A*–C grades at GCSE. This was down on 30 per cent in 2001 and the school was ranked 16th in the borough. The average point score of pupils taking two or more A/AS-levels was 163.5, placing the school 16th out of 18 in the borough league table. Ofsted noted that 'pupils generally display good attitudes to learning'. However, pupils' overall attainment still has to be improved along with their numeracy and ICT skillls. Inspectors also noted the need to improve pupils' punctuality and attendance.

## Extra-curricular activities

Clubs available include science, music and IT. Team sports on offer include basketball and football. Annual trips include a Year 9 residential trip to the Isle of Wight and an ICT trip to Disneyland, Paris. There are also annual exchanges with schools in the US. The school supports the Open Door Church, homeless charities and the Salvation Army.

# John Penrose School

**Northwood Way, Harefield, Middlesex UB9 6ET** 01895 822108 01895 822414 jpenrose@lbhill.gov.uk Anthea Way BA; Chair of Governors: Mrs W Rice-Morley Northwood Northwood; connecting bus (331) needed **Buses:** R1, U9, 331 Black school blazer, black trousers, white shirt, school tie (boys); black V-neck sweater or cardigan and pinafore (girls), optional **Demand:** 215 applications for 150 places in 2001/2 **Type:** Community comprehensive for 600 mixed pupils, aged 11 to 18 **Submit application form:** End October/early November 2003 **Motto:** A Partnership for Success **School hours:** 8.50am–3.30pm; homework clubs are available **Meals:** Hot meals available **Strong GCSE subjects:** Drama, history **London league table position:** 510

## Profile

In 1954, John Penrose replaced the original Harefield village school. It is still small and friendly and its intake is increasing. The 1950s building provides a pleasant learning environment in a rural setting. A recently built teaching block houses a food technology room, drama studio and four classrooms. A new science lab was completed in 2001. The pupil to computer ratio is about 11:1, with plans to improve it further. There is a playing field and tennis courts, and pupils can use the John Penrose Sports Centre. French and Italian are offered at GCSE. The small size of the sixth form (25 to 35 pupils) limits A-level subjects to English literature, maths, biology, IT, sport studies and theatre studies, plus a successful GNVQ in business. Links with the Business Education Partnership are well used and all pupils undertake three weeks' work experience in Year 11. Provision for special needs is very 'good' and special-needs pupils make 'good progress' (Ofsted). Part-time support staff include an educational psychologist, a speech therapist and an advisory teacher on hearing impairment. Pupils can serve on the school council. Parents are positive about the school and value the regular progress reports.

## Admissions and intake

Admission is through the LEA. At least one third of pupils come from Ruislip, Northwood, Hillingdon and Hertfordshire.

## Achievement

GCSE standards had been improving at John Penrose but they saw a slight decline in 2000 with a total of just 15 per cent of pupils achieving five or more A*–C grades. After improving in 2001, 2002 was similar at just 17 per cent. The average point score of pupils taking two or more A/AS-levels was 127.5. These results placed John Penrose 17th in the borough league table. In 2001, Ofsted described John Penrose as giving a 'satisfactory' education to its pupils. Inspectors praised the 'clear direction' of the head teacher and the range of initiatives being developed with the aim of raising standards. Pupils were seen to do well in English, PE, music, history, design and technology and French. Inspectors acknowledged that the small numbers in each Year group makes comparison with national date 'unreliable'. However, attainment was below average in Years 9 and 11 because 'many students have poor basic skills' and despite the school's efforts, attendance is still below average.

## Extra-curricular activities

Ofsted praised the 'good range' of extra-curricular activities that 'enriches the curriculum'. A theatre group performs twice a year and there are homework clubs, music and sports clubs, chess, pottery and computer clubs. Major team sports are available, plus cricket, tennis, trampolining, ice-skating, table tennis and judo. Many pupils participate in the Duke of Edinburgh's Award scheme. There is a range of visits and year group outings, including trips to theatres, museums and TV studios, and geography fieldwork. There are also language and skiing trips abroad.

# Mellow Lane School

**Hewens Road, Hayes, Middlesex UB4 8JP** 020 8573 1039 020 8813 7058 mlschool@rmplc.co.uk www.mellow-lane.hillingdon.sch.uk RC Stafford B.Sc; Chair of Governors: Mr P Scammel Hayes, Harlington **Buses:** 98, 207, 607 Navy school sweater, black or charcoal grey skirt or trousers, white shirt, school tie **Demand:** 846 applications for 224 places in 2001/2 **Type:** Comprehensive foundation school for 1326 mixed pupils, aged 11 to 19 **Submit application form:** End October/early November 2003 **Motto:** *Perseverando vinces* (Perseverence Succeeds) **School hours:** 8.45am–3.20pm **Meals:** Hot and cold available **Strong GCSE subjects:** Art, IT, science **London league table position:** 372

## Profile

One of the first comprehensive schools in England, Mellow Lane serves the Hayes area, Stockley Park and Uxbridge areas. Recent upgrading includes a remodelled library with multimedia resources, facilities for technology, humanities and post-16, and extensive IT networks, increasing the pupil to computer ratio to 5:1. The pupil to teacher ratio is very favourable at 16:1. A/AS-levels available include the sciences, art, economics, German, law and sociology, with GNVQs in business, IT and health and social care. Pupils can also take part in Youth Award projects, the school council, prefect duties and paired reading. Year 10 and post-16 pupils have work experience and mock interviews, as do pupils following the extended Work Related Learning programme. There are good links with both local firms and multinational companies, and there is an Industry Week for Year 10. Support is given to special -needs pupils and there is good provision for able students. The school counsellor gives confidential advice independent of the pastoral team. Parents have frequent newsletters and bi-annual academic review days. The singer/musician Cleo Laine was a former pupil.

## Admissions and intake

Application is made direct to the school. Priority is given, in order, to: those applicants with medical/special needs reasons for attending; those with siblings in the school; and those living closest to the school. The school increased its intake in 1994 from 188 to 224. Feeder primary schools include Wood End and Charleville.

## Achievement

Results have been generally maintained in spite of pupils entering with lower attainment levels and a rising proportion of boys. In 2002, 42 per cent of pupils gained five or more A*–C grades at GCSE, below the borough average. The school was ranked 13th in the borough. The average point score for pupils taking two or more A/AS-levels was 186.5, below the borough average. Advanced GNVQ business studies is consistently successful, with the majority of pupils receiving distinctions or credits. General standards of maths have fallen since 1993 and are currently 'well below national standards', according to Ofsted in 1998. Inspectors noted that 'there is a climate in the school which encourages constant striving for further improvement'. Inter-faith and inter-racial harmony are a feature of the school and behaviour is good.

## Extra-curricular activities

Mellow Lane have been the English Schools Junior Gymnastics Champions. The school has a band and instrument ensembles, and holds drama productions. The school newspaper *Jump Start* is produced entirely by the pupils. Mellow Lane also competes in the Magistrates' Court Competition and National Bar Mock Trial Competition. It was the first English school, and the first comprehensive, to win the Royal Bank of Scotland IT Innovation Award (1998/9). The school provides activity weekends and foreign trips. Many pupils participate in the Duke of Edinburgh's Award scheme.

# Northwood College

**Maxwell Road, Northwood, Middlesex HA6 2YE** ☎ 01923 825446 📠 01923 836526 ⓔ school@northwood-college.hillingdon.sch.uk 🌐 www.northwoodcollege.co.uk Mrs Ruth Mercer; Chair of Governors: Mr G Hudson ⊖ Northwood **Buses:** H11, 282, 331, 347, 348 Navy blue skirt or trousers, light blue jumper, striped blue and white shirt **Demand:** Typically 3:1 applications to places **Type:** Selective independent for 776 girls (460 in senior school), aged 3 to 19 **Fees:** £2,484 per term (senior school/sixth form) **Submit application form:** End of December 2003 **Motto:** *Nisi dominus frustra* (In God we Trust) **School hours:** 8.40am–4pm **Meals:** Hot and cold available **Strong GCSE subjects:** Art, German, Latin, Spanish **London league table position:** 325

## Profile

Founded in 1878, Northwood College aims to 'foster a love of learning, develop creative and sporting talents and promote traditional values'. Its Christian base is non-denominational and welcomes children of other faiths. Situated in the prosperous area of Northwood, the school encompasses pre-prep, junior, senior schools and sixth form. It belongs to the Girls' Schools Association, which regularly checks its members' standards. It has three libraries, art studios, a science and technology centre, a music school, a modern languages centre, a computer centre, a careers room, two assembly halls, a drama studio, indoor swimming pool and sports hall, playing fields and all-weather tennis and netball courts. Classes average 15 pupils. There is a special-needs coordinator. Pupils study drama from the age of 6, French from age 7, separate sciences from 11 and Latin from 12. They are introduced to German, Spanish or classical Greek at 13. Most pupils sit nine GCSEs. Optional subjects include graphic design, RE, classical civilization, home economics, design technology and drama. A-levels offered include art and design, graphic design, classical civilization, drama, business studies, home economics and RE. Girls can become form captains or representatives on the school council. Northwood belongs to the Independent Schools Career Organization and work experience is offered after GCSE. Placements have included BBC Television and the Crown Prosecution Service. Pupils also take part in the Neighbourhood Engineers scheme. Judge Dame Margaret Booth is a former pupil.

## Admissions and intake

Entry to the school is by reference from the candidate's former school head teacher, diagnostic tests in maths and English, informal group assessment and individual interview. For the sixth form, entry is by interview and GCSE results. Academic and musical scholarships are available, for which candidates must sit exams.

## Achievement

Standards at Northwood are almost twice the national average at GCSE and were the second highest in the borough in 2002. A total of 92 per cent of pupils gained five or more A*–C grades. The average point score of pupils taking two or more A/AS-levels was 334.6, comfortably above the national average and keeping pace with the national rise in standards. This placed the school second in the borough.

### Extra-curricular activities

There are two orchestras, a concert band and three choirs. Group and solo concerts as well as major drama productions are held regularly. Instrument, speech and singing tuition is offered, and pupils attend classes in ballet and judo. Clubs include art, craft, computing, debating and drama. The college has a detached flight of the Air Training Corps and girls can participate in the Duke of Edinburgh's Award scheme. There are lessons in a variety of sports and teams compete at borough and county levels. Pupils go on local and overseas trips, theatre and field trips, foreign exchanges to Europe and America and sporting and cultural tours. Each term, girls vote to decide which charity they will support, and charity representatives in each form organize fund-raising events.

## Northwood School

**Potter Street, Northwood, Middlesex HA6 1QG** ☎ 01923 836363 📠 01923 836010 ⓔ office@northwoodschool.biblio.net 🌐 www.northwoodhillingdon.sch.uk 🎓 Mrs C Ketley B.Ed, MA, MBA; Chair of Governors: Mrs Edmonds ⊖ Northwood Hills **Buses:** 282 and Harrow Hopper link with Eastcote, Pinner and Harrow 👔 Navy school blazer, dark grey trousers or navy skirt, navy V-neck jumper, school tie **Demand:** 625 applications for 198 places in 2001/2 **Type:** Comprehensive foundation school for 1225 mixed pupils, aged 11 to 18 **Submit application form:** End October/early November 2003 **Motto:** Achievement through Support **School hours:** 8.50am–3.30pm, 8.50am–2.40pm (Fri, Years 7 to 9) **Meals:** Hot meals and breakfast available **Strong GCSE subjects:** Art, drama, music **London league table position:** 325

### Profile

This school is situated in the affluent district of Northwood Hills. Its large, well-managed site includes a purpose-built technology block, nine refurbished science labs and good facilities for music and drama. A sports hall shared with the borough and off-site facilities enable the full range of sports to be taught. In addition to a language lab and satellite television, the school now has 150 networked computers. It has won the Education Extra Award and the Investors in People Award in 1998/9. A wide range of A-levels are available including business studies, German, government and politics, psychology and theatre studies. GNVQs are offered in business studies and leisure and tourism. Companies support the Young Engineers project, and a national bank has helped pupils run a bank at the school. Work experience placements are provided for Year 10 and the sixth form. Pupils can become form heads and sit on the school council. Very able pupils are offered a programme of academically challenging extension clubs. Special-needs pupils are helped by learning support assistants and through individual and small group teaching. Parents are kept informed through newspapers, booklets and meetings. A weekly 'surgery' is held and there is an active PTA.

### Admissions and intake

Application is made direct to the school. Entry criteria, in order of priority, are: those applicants with medical grounds; those with siblings in the school; and those living closest. Northwood draws pupils from a large geographical area.

### Achievement

Northwood is around the middle of the borough league table for GCSE results, and below the national average. A total of 43 per cent of pupils have gained five or more A*–C grades for 2002. This reversed an upward trend since 1998. The average point score for pupils taking two or more A/AS-levels was 233.1 in 2002, above the borough average. In 2002, Ofsted commented that Northwood is 'a good school with excellent features'. Pupils were seen to enjoy 'very good' pastoral care and become 'confident and secure young people'. Special-needs pupils 'make good progress and achieve well'. The strongest GCSE subjects are art and design, drama, business education and geography. Weaker subjects are English language, maths and modern foreign languages.

### Extra-curricular activities

Over 35 clubs are available, including Amnesty International, bridge, the Duke of Edinburgh's Award scheme, trampolining, gardening and art, as well as choirs and orchestras. A number of school sports teams usually reach, and often win, the borough finals. The school holds a major production and two concerts annually, as well as a creative arts evening. There are visits to theatres and foreign exchanges. Each year group chooses its own charity and raises money throughout the year. Pupils also perform musical events in a local club for the elderly.

# Queensmead School

**Queen's Walk, South Ruislip, Middlesex HA4 0LS** 020 8845 6266 020 8845 8331 qms@queensmead.hillingdon.sch.uk; qmead@aol.com Mr N McLaughlin MA; Chair of Governors: Mr S Rawana South Ruislip **Buses:** 114, 282 Black school blazer, black trousers or skirt, white shirt, school tie for boys **Demand:** 442 applications for 180 places in 2001/2 **Type:** Comprehensive Technology College foundation school for 1067 mixed pupils, aged 11 to 18 **Submit application form:** End October/early November 2003 **Motto:** Endeavour **School hours:** 8.30am–3.15pm, 8.50am–3.15pm (Fri), 8.50am–3.15pm (Thurs, Years 7–11) **Meals:** Hot meals and breakfast available **Strong GCSE subjects:** Business studies, IT **London league table position:** 188

## Profile

Queensmead has served South Ruislip since 1953. It resources are good in PE, design technology and geography. A language block has been added, IT resources have been upgraded and the library is well stocked. The school recently gained Technology College status. A-levels available include art and design, design and technology, German, IT, drama, law, photography and PE. Some subjects are taught jointly with Bishop Ramsey School. Around 50 per cent of pupils take vocational courses, including GNVQs in business, leisure and tourism, and health and social care, plus a BTEC in childhood studies. There is work experience on vocational courses, two weeks' work experience in Year 10 and shadowing in the sixth form. The school has a business link with Rover, which holds a popular after-school engineering club. Pupils can take on extra responsibility as prefects, library monitors and reps on the school forum. The provision for pupils with special needs is good, although facilities for disabled pupils are limited. Pupils receive exceptional support through monitoring, target setting and regular interviews with staff. Parents' consultation meetings are held and there are newsletters and 'very good' end of year reports (Ofsted). The Friends of Queensmead is very active.

## Admissions and intake

Application is made direct to the school. Entry criteria, in order of priority, are: those applicants with medical grounds; those with siblings in the school; and those living closest to the school. A total of 15.4 per cent of pupils have special needs, above the national average.

## Achievement

Queensmead is in the top half of the borough league table for GCSE results. In 2002, 60 per cent of pupils gained five or more A*–C grades, up from 55 per cent in 2001. Pass rates are good, with 95 per cent in 2000 being typical. The average point score of pupils taking two or more A/AS-levels was 249.2 in 2002, placing the school seventh in the borough league table. Business GNVQ courses attain well above national averages – 66 per cent of intermediate and 75 per cent of advanced pupils obtained merit and distinction grades in 2000. Reporting in 1999, Ofsted found 98 per cent of teaching to be satisfactory, 48 per cent to be good and 25 per cent very good, although some dedicated, long-term staff left in 2000. Pupils 'behave well and make a good contribution to the life of the school'.

## Extra-curricular activities

Sports available include gymnastics, dance, aerobics, weights, and self-defence. School teams in soccer, cricket, athletics, cross-country and netball regularly get to the borough finals. The media studies group produces a school newspaper and all pupils can work with the artists in residence. Bi-annual concerts and drama productions involve many pupils. There are history trips and visits to galleries, theatres and museums, as well as language visits to France and Germany. Pupils participate in voluntary community service and charitable events are staged throughout the year.

# St Helen's School

**Eastbury Road, Northwood, Middlesex HA6 3AS** 01923 843210 01923 843211 mail@StHelensNorthwood.co.uk www.StHelensNorthwood.co.uk Mary Morris BA; Chair of Governors: Miss R Faunch Watford Junction (connecting with 348 bus) Northwood **Buses:** H11, 282, 331, 347, 348 Up to sixth form: Bottle green skirt, jumper, tights and school blazer, white and green checked shirt **Demand:** Usually oversubscribed by 4 or 5:1 **Type:** Selective independent for 979 girls, aged 4 to 19 **Fees:** £2,600 per term tuition; boarding is an additional £2,250, plus fees for some extra-curricular activities **Submit**

**application form:** No cut-off date **Motto:** *In hoc vincite velut illi crescite* (As You Grow, So Will You Conquer) **School hours:** 8.30am–3.55pm, 8.30am–3.35pm (Fri) **Meals:** Hot meals available for boarders and day boarders; breakfast for boarders only **Strong GCSE subjects:** Art, chemistry, English literature, French **London league table position:** 25

## Profile

Founded in 1899, St Helen's delivers impressive results for those who can afford the fees. The senior school has a gymnasium, 25-metre swimming pool and IT-equipped library. Golf is also available on a nearby course. In addition to core subjects, all girls study two modern languages and Latin. Science is taught as three separate subjects and IT, music, art, drama and sport are an integral part of school life. Options at GCSE include art and design, child development, design and technology, and religious studies. Over 20 A-levels are on offer including art and design, art history, classical civilization, politics, further maths, Spanish and theatre studies. Girls can supplement their studies with ancient Greek, Italian and Japanese. GNVQs are not offered, but the complementary studies programme offers a diploma accredited by Oxbridge in subjects such as first aid and environmental awareness. St Helen's participates in the 'Take your Daughters to Work' scheme and all pupils undertake work experience. Sixth-formers can become monitors or prefects or help organize the school council. Girls are also trained in listening skills for the peer counselling programme. Individual tutorials are offered for dyslexia and English as a foreign language. There are written reports and consultation evenings for parents, and an active PTA. Actress Patricia Hodge and Dame Barbara Mills are former pupils.

## Admissions and intake

Applications should be made direct to the school. Entry is by exam and interview. A very small percentage of pupils need support with English. Scholarships and bursaries are available.

## Achievement

St Helen's is one of the highest achieving schools in the borough. In 2002, 98 per cent of pupils gained five or more A*–C grades. The school was ranked first in the borough. The average point score for pupils taking two or more A/AS-levels was 376.6, well above the national average and ranking the school first in the borough. Almost all pupils go on to higher education.

## Extra-curricular activities

Many activities are shared with Merchant Taylors' boys school in Northwood, Middlesex. Clubs include bridge, chess, drama, languages and technology. There is an orchestra, swing band, ensemble and drum groups, and concerts and plays are regularly produced. A house arts competition is held annually. Lessons are available in instrumental music, singing, diction, ballet, fencing and horse-riding. Sixth-formers take part in the Global Young Leader's Conference and European Youth Parliament. St Helen's has competed at national level in debating in the Cambridge Union and Observer Mace competitions. Many pupils participate in the Duke of Edinburgh's Award scheme, Young Enterprise and the CCF. The school organizes classics trips to Italy and Greece, skiing trips, European exchanges, adventure holidays, team-building weekends and many cultural and field trips. There is a physically handicapped and able-bodied week and a charity week.

# Swakeleys School

**Clifton Gardens, Hillingdon, Uxbridge, Middlesex UB10 0EJ** ☎ 01895 251962 📠 01895 235027 ⓔ office@swakeleys.hillingdon.sch.uk Mr J Taylor MA; Chair of Governors: Mrs Jill Rhodes ⊖ Uxbridge **Buses:** U2 and links from Hillingdon and Uxbridge White collared T-shirt, green sweatshirt, black trousers or skirt **Demand:** 476 applications for 180 places in 2001/2 **Type:** Comprehensive foundation school for 1008 girls, aged 11 to 18 **Submit application form:** End October/early November 2003 **School hours:** 8.30am–3.30pm, 8.30am–2.25pm (Tues) **Meals:** Hot and cold available, including breakfast **Strong GCSE subjects:** Art, design, drama, languages, music **London league table position:** 229

## Profile

Swakeleys is the only all-girls school in the borough. Recent additions include a new humanities block, further sixth-form provision, a second sports hall and a fully computerized learning resources centre. Class sizes are below average. Year 7 pupils study both French and German, with the option to continue into Year 8. The majority of pupils study 10 GCSEs. Optional subjects include sociology, business education, dance and drama. Although the sixth form is shared with the neighbouring Abbotsfield School, Ofsted found class sizes too small to support discussion and entry criteria too lenient. Options at A-level include sociology, business, government and politics, art and theatre studies. Vocational qualifications include GNVQs in ICT, leisure and tourism and business, an Assessment and Qualifications Alliance (AQA) in child development and an ASDAN Challenge Award. Work experience is offered in Year 10 and the school is part of the Hillingdon Education Business Partnership. Pupils can participate in the school council, while sixth-formers organize their own committee and tuck shop. There is a designated special-needs governor and an able pupils coordinator. Provision is available for disabled pupils and a few are currently attending. Regular newsletters, interim reports and annual consultation evenings are provided for parents. The Friends of Swakeleys organizes fund-raising events.

### Admissions and intake

Application is made direct to the school. Entry criteria, in order of priority, are: those applicants with medical grounds; those with family medical grounds; those with siblings in the school; and those living closest to the school.

### Achievement

Swakeleys' results at GCSE are above average nationally and well above those of similar schools. In 2002, 58 per cent of pupils gained five or more A*–C grades. The school was placed seventh in the borough. Results at A/AS-levels are above the national average. In 2002, the average point score for pupils taking two or more A/AS-levels was 255.5. This ranked the school sixth in the borough. Teaching is good and 60 per cent of lessons observed by Ofsted in 1998 were good or better. Ofsted noted that pupils are well cared for and 'show real enjoyment in their work'. Occasional verbal bullying is combated by the remarkable Swakeleys Against Bullying scheme, which 'gives pupils careful training so that they can provide support for their peers'.

### Extra-curricular activities

Swakeleys competes at borough level in athletics and cross-country, and the gymnastics team were the 2000 national champions. The orchestra, vocal ensembles, choir and guitar groups perform regularly. The dance performance group has twice won Greater London Arts grants and has appeared at the Lillian Baylis Theatre. There are residential trips for year groups, language visits abroad, plus theatre visits, sports trips and educational visits. Sixth-formers participate or help in the Duke of Edinburgh's Award scheme. The annual charities week usually raises over £5,000.

## Uxbridge High School

**The Greenway, Uxbridge, Middlesex UB8 2PR** 01895 234060 01895 256738 uhs@uxbridge.hillingdon.sch.uk Peter Lang MA; Chair of Governors: Mrs S Pritchard Uxbridge **Buses:** U3, U4 Black school blazer, black trousers or skirt, black school jumper, white shirt **Demand:** 490 applicants for 210 places in 2001/2 **Type:** Comprehensive foundation school for 1140 mixed pupils, aged 11 to 18 **Submit application form:** End October/early November 2003 **Motto:** Making Success Happen **School hours:** 8.40am–3.15pm; homework clubs are available **Meals:** Hot and cold available, including breakfast **Strong GCSE subjects:** Art, business, design and technology, drama, music **London league table position:** 399

### Profile

Uxbridge High is situated in the less affluent southern side of the borough. Its numbers have increased from 894 to 1140 and recently it was recognized, by Ofsted, as one of the 50 most improved state sixth forms and colleges. The buildings were extensively refurbished in the 1990s. New facilities include a drama studio, music lab, technology workshops, tennis courts and an extended library. There are specialist rooms for IT. The school makes use of the sports facilities of the adjacent university. Class size is smaller than average nationally. Pupils have a 10-week taster of French, Spanish and German before deciding which language to study. A-levels available include art and design, business, Spanish, German, ICT and technology. GNVQs are offered in business and finance, and health and social care. The Hillingdon Business Partnership supports work experience in Year 10. The language department has an excellent link with British Airways and Glaxo Wellcome organizes a two-day business conference for sixth-formers. Pupils can serve on the school council. Older pupils help younger ones through the paired reading scheme and with languages and PSHE. In 1998, Ofsted found the provision for special needs to be satisfactory, although pupils with

English as an additional language and higher attainers are not always catered for. The school is responsive to parents' queries and produces detailed newsletters, letters and annual reports. Pupils can also join the school council.

## Admissions and intake

Application is made direct to the school. Preference is given to those applicants with siblings in the school, on medical grounds and those living nearest.

## Achievement

Uxbridge High is in the lower third of the borough for GCSE results, with 34 per cent of pupils gaining five or more A*–C grades in 2002. This was down from 37 per cent in 2001. Results have been improving at A-level, with the average point score of pupils taking two or more at 175.3 in 2002. This was still below the borough and national averages. Results in GNVQs are impressive and over 80 per cent of entries achieved merit or distinction in 2000. Ofsted noted that 92 per cent of teaching overall is satisfactory or better and almost half is good or very good. They also found that the school offers a 'caring secure environment in which the rounded development of the whole child is seen as a priority...and pupils' good behaviour, positive attitudes and relationships are a strength'.

## Extra-curricular activities

Clubs available include music, art and design, computing, photography, drama and homework clubs. Tuition in musical instruments is free if parents are in receipt of income support. There are regular fixtures with other schools for most major sports including basketball, football, hockey and netball. Trips are organized to theatres, galleries and museums, and there are annual drama and music productions. Foreign trips, including skiing, are also arranged. Pupils are actively engaged in fund-raising for charities.

# Vyners School (FD)

**Warren Road, Ickenham, Uxbridge, Middlesex UB10 8AB** ☎ 01895 234342 📠 01895 237955 ⓔ office@vyners.hillingdon.sch.uk ✉ Mr BP Houghton MA, Dip.Ed, FRSA; Chair of Governors: Mr T Sellers ⊖ Ickenham **Buses:** U1, U9, U10 👔 Bottle green school blazer, white shirt or blouse, dark grey trousers (boys); bottle green skirt or black trousers (girls); grey V-neck cardigan or jumper, red, green and yellow school tie; Sixth form: Dress code **Demand:** 520 applications for 180 places in 2001/2 **Type:** Comprehensive foundation school for 1100 mixed pupils, aged 11 to 18 **Submit application form:** End October/early November 2003 **Motto:** Abide in Me **School hours:** 8.45am–3.55pm (Mon–Tues, Year 10), 8.45am–3.20pm (Mon–Tues, other years), 8.45am–3.20pm (Wed–Thurs), 8.45am–3pm (Fri) **Meals:** Hot and cold available **Strong GCSE subject:** Business **London league table position:** 172

## Profile

Vyners is a popular school situated on a clean, pleasant site. Its resurfaced playgrounds and new sports hall have earned it the Sportsmark Award. The attractive library has particularly good provision for business and ICT. In addition to the National Curriculum, courses are offered in business, economics, drama and child development at GCSE. A-level numbers are growing and options include the sciences, art, languages, PE, politics, psychology and computers. Numbers opting for GNVQs are declining and science only was offered in 2000. The Year 10 work-experience programme is run in conjunction with Hillingdon Education and Business Partnership. The school also has productive associations with various businesses including Glaxo Wellcome, M&S, BA and local banks. Vyners is a Young Enterprise centre. Sixth-formers can become house captains, support staff in supervision and participate in the paired reading scheme. There are above average numbers of support staff and very good provision for pupils with hearing impairment, although Ofsted found that the special-needs provision needed improvement in 1998. Parents assist with the work experience programme and there is an active Friends of Vyners.

## Admissions and intake

Application is made direct to the school. Entry criteria, in order of priority, are: pupils with siblings in the school; those with medical grounds; and those living closest.

## Achievement

Vyners came fifth in the borough league table for GCSE results in 2002, with 64 per cent of pupils gaining five or more A*–C grades, well above the national average. The average point score for pupils taking two or more A/AS-levels in 2002 was 259.4. This was above the borough and national averages. GNVQ results to date are in line with national averages. Ofsted found teaching to be satisfactory in 95 per cent of lessons, good in 40 per cent and very good or excellent in a further 22 per cent. They also confirmed that 'the school has a very strong ethos and its aim to seek excellence through a caring and cooperative approach permeates much of the work and activities of the school'. Behaviour is generally good.

## Extra-curricular activities

A wide range of activities are on offer. Clubs include bridge, chess, photography and the Duke of Edinburgh's Award scheme. There are choirs, bands, ensemble and drama groups and productions. Vyners is particularly renowned for its swing band, which has toured abroad. Art is also strong and the Royal Academy selected Vyners to contribute to their Year 2000 exhibition. Sports range from athletics to wind surfing, with emphasis on the major games. Visits are arranged to complement subject areas, for example, there are history trips to the Imperial War Museum and Russia. Years 7 and 8 also go on adventure trips.

# Hounslow

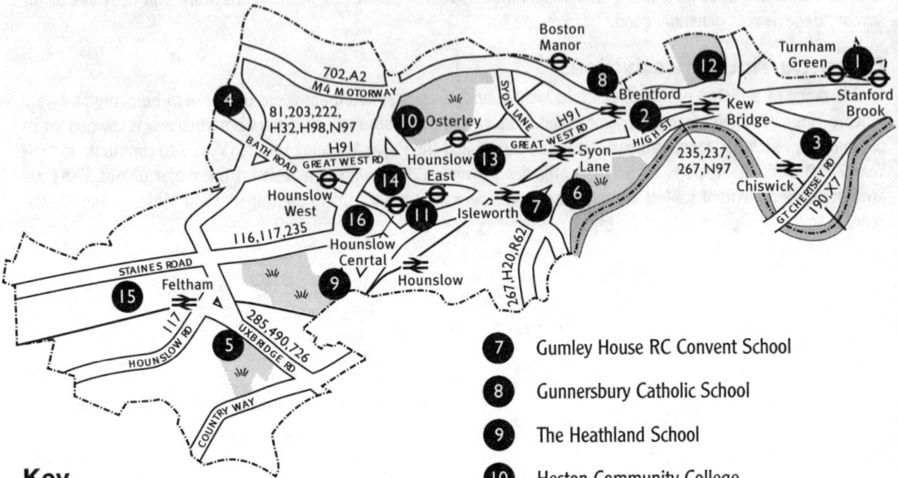


## Key

1. The Arts Educational School
2. Brentford School for Girls
3. Chiswick Community School
4. Cranford Community College
5. Feltham Community College
6. The Green School
7. Gumley House RC Convent School
8. Gunnersbury Catholic School
9. The Heathland School
10. Heston Community College
11. Hounslow Manor School
12. International School of London
13. Isleworth and Syon Boys' School
14. Lampton School
15. Longford Community School
16. St Mark's Catholic School

# Factfile

**LEA: Civic Centre, Hampton Road, Hounslow TW3 3DN** ☎ 020 8583 2000 🌐 www.hounslow.gov.uk **Director of Education:** Bob Garrett **Political control of council:** Labour **Percentage of pupils from outside the borough:** 15.4 per cent, mostly from Ealing **Percentage of pupils educated outside the borough:** 14.3 per cent, mostly in Richmond **London league table position (out of 32 boroughs):** 14th

## Profile

Hounslow is an outer London borough, lying in the west of the capital with the River Thames forming its southern border. It stretches out almost to Heathrow airport in the west, to Chiswick in the east, and is cut through by the M3 and M4 motorways. Like most London boroughs, Hounslow reflects the rich cultural diversity of a capital city, with Asian residents making up almost a quarter of its population. It has a rich diversity of landscape, too, incorporating areas of high-rise, high-density accommodation as well as leafy suburbs, riverside walks and informal parkland. Some of London's most beautiful parks lie within its boundaries, such as Osterley and Syon Parks. There are also museums at Kew Bridge, Gunnersbury Park and Fullers Brewery in Chiswick, to name but a few. The Waterman Arts Centre in Brentford, a leading producer of Asian comedy and theatre, hosts world music events and has a cinema, theatre and art gallery.

Hounslow council has been awarded Beacon status. It spends over 50 per cent of its budget on education. Hounslow's schools perform well. In 2002, 49.5 per cent of pupils gained five or more A*–C grades at GCSE, just below the national average of 51.6 per cent. The average point score for pupils taking two or more A-/AS-levels was 196.7, below the national average of 254.5.

It should be noted that St Thomas More School in Isleworth is a special unit, with only one pupil in the secondary school age group, so it has not been included in this guide.

## Policy

The borough has 16 secondary schools: nine community schools, one voluntary controlled, four voluntary aided and two independents. Should its community schools be oversubscribed, the borough's admissions criteria are as follows: having a sibling currently at the school; medical or social need; and children living nearest to the school. The date for applications to the LEA is mid-November.

# The Arts Educational School

**Cone Ripman House, 14 Bath Road, Chiswick W4 1LY** ☎ 020 8987 6600 ℻ 020 8987 6601 ⓔ head@artsed.co.uk 🌐 www.artsed.co.uk Mr Tom Sampson; Chair of Governors: Mrs John Ind ⊖ Turnham Green **Buses**: 94 Green and white striped shirts, green jumper, green skirt, blazer (girls); black trousers, white shirt, school tie (boys) **Demand:** Places available **Type**: Selective independent for 145 mixed pupils, aged 8 to 16 **Fees:** £7,662 per annum **Submit application form:** No cut-off date **Mission statement**: We aim to give our pupils the confidence, the knowledge and the skills to prepare them for a world of increasing change, as well as an appreciation of the arts which will enrich their adult lives. **School hours**: 8.30am–4pm or 5.30pm (depends on timetable) **Meals:** Hot and cold available **Strong GCSE subjects**: All relatively strong **London league table position**: 130

## Profile

This school occupies the site of the former Chiswick Polytechnic, in London's first garden suburb, Bedford Park. The new head teacher was appointed in June 2000. There is a school council. The school specializes in the arts, dance, music, drama and art, as well as English, English literature, French, maths and science up to GCSE. The school wants pupils to 'participate in as many aspects of the performing arts as is possible. The arts experience is enhanced by cross-curricular themes in music, drama, dance, art and academic subjects'. The school's aim is that pupils 'will have career ambitions as performers and also in the legal, administrative and financial aspects of the arts'. There is a special needs coordinator. The school library holds dance recordings and musical scores as well more conventional stock. There is a fully equipped theatre and a studio theatre. There is no sixth form. The majority of the senior school feed in from their own preparatory department. There is some setting by ability and extra tuition is available for highly gifted pupils. Teaching is supplemented by one-to-one tuition where necessary, and many visiting specialists give master-classes. There is a thriving PTA.

## Admissions and intake

Admission is by entrance test. After the preparatory department, there are some places available in Years 7 and 10, with occasional places in other year groups.

## Achievement

The school's results for GCSE are always very good, and in 2002, 76 per cent of pupils gained A*–C grades. This was up from 75 per cent the previous year and the school came first in the GCSE borough league table. Pupils are also entered for external specialist exams.

## Extra-curricular activities

Art rooms are available on open access at lunchtime and after school. There are dance and drama clubs and performances, recitals and exhibitions are held throughout the year. There are foreign school trips, including trips to Europe and the USA.

# Brentford School for Girls

**5 Boston Manor Road, Brentford, Middlesex TW8 0PG** ☎ 020 8847 4281 ℻ 020 8568 2093 ⓔ BRENTFORD_EDU@classic.msn.com Susan Higgins; Chair of Governors: C Benn (Acting Chair) ⇄ Brentford **Buses**: E2, E8, H91, 16, 17, 65, 237, 267 Dark blue school sweat shirt, black trousers or skirt, cream shirt **Demand:** 152 places available **Type:** Community comprehensive for 750 girls, aged 11 to 18 **Submit application form:** Mid-November 2003 **School hours:** 8.50am–3.20pm; homework clubs are available **Meals:** Hot and cold available **Strong GCSE subjects:** Drama **London league table position:** 365

## Profile

Brentford prides itself on being a multi-ethnic school, developing in its pupils a full understanding of 'the richness of the multicultural society in which we live'. French and German are studied in Years 7 to 9. Maths teaching is tailored around each pupil by use of individual learning schemes. A variety of technology subjects are studied in rotation. At GCSE, Brentford offers modular courses in a range of subjects such as French, German, media studies and IT, completed in nine-week blocks. Brentford is part of the local sixth-form consortium, offering a range of A-levels, including sports studies, physics and media studies. Girls can also study for a BTEC in performing arts. Small group or individual support is available for girls with special needs or high ability. The foundation language centre provides teaching for girls whose first language is not English. A one-year ESL course is run in the sixth form and in the lower school. There is a school council. The Friends of Brentford organizes fund-raising events.

## Admissions and intake

All applications should be made to the LEA on the borough transfer forms. Almost half of new entrants to Year 7 have a reading age of two or more years below their chronological age. In 1998, Ofsted noted that 'the intake of pupils does not reflect the whole ability range, and the attainment of the majority of pupils on entry is below the national expectation for that age'.

## Achievement

In 2002, 46 per cent of pupils achieved five or more GCSEs at A*–C grade, an increase from 31 per cent in 2001. This was below the borough average and Brentford was ranked in 12th place in the borough in its GCSE table. At A-level, the average point score was 160.8, ranking the school 12th in the borough. Ofsted were very pleased with the progress pupils made by the end of Key Stage 3 in 1998. They commented that 'standards in English were in line with the national average. Standards are rising in English and pupil progress is good. All pupils at this school make satisfactory and often good progress. GCSE results are well above those achieved in similar schools.' They also praised the pupils' attitude to work, and the quality of their relationships with peers and staff. Drama at the school was noted to be of a very high quality. IT was deemed 'unsatisfactory', but since then the school has upgraded its IT facilities with the opening of a new IT block. The inspectors judged that 'the school has more strengths than weaknesses,' and they found many improvements since their inspection in 1996.

## Extra-curricular activities

Interests catered for include drama, craft, technologies, music and sports. There is also a science club and a homework club. Years 7 to 9 have an annual extension week, with activities such as museum trips and visits to local factories. The Duke of Edinburgh's Award scheme is available. There is a choir and some pupils have won places on the scheme for talented young musicians, run by the Royal College. Brentford has an excellent reputation for school productions.

# Chiswick Community School

**Burlington Lane, London W4 3UN** ☎ 020 8747 0031 📠 020 8742 2074 Mr D Brockie (acting); Chair of Governors: Mr Robert Alker ⇄ Chiswick **Buses:** E3, 190 Black or grey skirt or trousers, black or grey sweater or cardigan (girls); black or grey trousers, black or grey sweater or cardigan school tie (boys) **Demand:** 210 places available; oversubscribed **Type:** Community comprehensive school for 1200 mixed pupils, aged 11 to 18 **Submit application form:** Mid-November 2003 **School hours:** 8.50am–3.25pm **Meals:** Hot and cold available **Strong GCSE subjects:** English, sciences **London league table position:** 381

## Profile

Chiswick Community School is situated in the eastern end of the borough of Hounslow. There is good provision for IT, and facilities in the library, which is staffed by a professional librarian, include access to the Internet and CD-ROMs. There is also a large conference room. For PE there is a multi-gym and two squash courts. Outdoors, pupils have use of a floodlit area and tennis courts. The school goes rowing from Chiswick Boathouse. The school can make provision for disabled pupils where appropriate. It recently won an Investors in People Award. Communication with parents is highly valued, and takes place through an excellent weekly newsletter as well as termly and annual reports. Parents are automatically members of the PTA, and may join a fund-raising group, The Friends of Chiswick. Famous ex-pupils include Phil Collins.

### Admissions and intake

Admission is through the LEA and applications should be made on the borough transfer forms. The school has a good reputation locally and is heavily oversubscribed, with pupils coming from 30 primary schools in a wide geographical area. The wide intake includes pupils from areas with serious urban deprivation. There is also an increasing number of refugee families at the school, which can mean a high turnover of pupils and late entry into Key Stage 4. On entry, attainment is generally below average.

### Achievement

Attainment at Key Stage 3 is above average for similar schools. The school's GCSE results used to be above the local and national averages but the number of pupils achieving five or more A*–C grades has dipped since 1999. This downward trend continued in 2002 with 38 per cent of pupils gaining five or more A*–C grades. This was below the borough and national averages, and Chiswick was placed 13th in the borough. However, A-level results were better in 2002, with an average point score of 239.3 for pupils taking two or more A-levels. This was up on 2000, ranking the school third in the borough. In 1999, Ofsted's findings were overwhelmingly positive. They praised the 'high quality of teaching', and the 'inspirational leadership of the head teacher and her deputies.' The school was found to provide 'excellent information for parents and good enrichment through links with the community', and continues to make marked improvements. The provision for special-needs pupils was also said to be well managed.

### Extra-curricular activities

The school offers many extra-curricular opportunities, including more than 50 lunchtime clubs, after-school sports such as rowing, judo, trampolining and dance and a Saturday morning music school. School productions are given a high priority and there are regular concerts. Years 7 to 9 take part in a variety of trips and other activities. Trips include skiing, foreign exchanges, water sports and Outward Bound.

## Cranford Community College

**High Street, Cranford, Hounslow TW5 9PD** ☎ 020 8897 2001 📠 020 8759 8073 ⓔ cranford@cranford.hounslow.sch.uk 🌐 www.cranford.hounslow.sch.uk Mr T Masters (acting); Chair of Governors: Mrs Kay Jenkins Hounslow West **Buses:** 81, 98, 105, 110, 111, 222 Maroon V-neck jumpers, white shirt, school tie or maroon polo shirts, black trousers **Demand:** 210 places available **Type:** Community comprehensive Language College for 1252 mixed pupils, aged 11 to 18 **Submit application form:** Mid-November 2003 **Motto:** Achieving Is Believing **School hours:** 8.40am–3.15pm **Meals:** Hot and cold available, including breakfast **Strong GCSE subjects:** All relatively strong **London league table position:** 315

### Profile

Cranford Community School was built in the mid-1970s, and has 29 acres of playing fields. With National Lottery funding, it has added two floodlit astroturf pitches. It also has a double size sports hall, gymnasium, dance studio, squash courts and fitness and weight-training room. Its IT facilities are 'quite outstanding' (Ofsted). There is one computer per three pupils, a learning resources centre open to the community and a language excellence centre with video-conferencing facilities. Cranford has gained the Schools Curriculum Award three times, and has close links with industry. These links are worldwide, as well as local, and consequently the school has won an International Schools Award. The school also has Language College status, and offers 'an outstanding range and quality of modern foreign language courses'. GNVQs are offered in the sixth form as well as 15 A-levels, of which sociology has been very strong. In 1998, Ofsted found that the school kept parents well informed through regular newsletters. However, there is no parent-teacher association.

### Admissions and intake

Admission is through the LEA and applications should be made on the borough transfer forms. Ofsted stated that 'Pupils entering the school cover the full range of ability and attainment but most have poor literacy and numeracy skills. A large proportion of the pupils has special educational needs.' Pupil turnover was 27 per cent in 1997. In 2000, about 23 per cent of pupils had special needs.

## Achievement

Cranford Community College has received 18 national awards for excellence in education. The number of pupils gaining five or more A*–C grades at GCSE tends to be below the national and LEA average and in 2002 it was 44 per cent. This was up from 37 per cent in 2001 and the average point score was 33.6. Cranford was ranked 10th in the borough league table. Ofsted found that standards of attainment observed in sixth-form lessons were generally a little lower than the national average. In 2002, pupils averaged 163.2 points at A-level, below the borough and national averages. This placed the school 10th in the borough league table.

## Extra-curricular activities

Cranford has, according to Ofsted, 'an impressive range of trips, visits, and links with outside agencies, which is a major strength of the school and provides considerable enhancement of the curriculum'. Sports provision 'at both school and club level is outstanding'. Homework clubs are available. Music is another strong tradition at Cranford, with pupils performing in Europe and America, and winning the National Music for Youth Competition.

# Feltham Community College

**Browells Lane, Feltham, Middlesex TW13 7EF** 020 8831 3000 020 8751 3000 Gillian Smith; Chair of Governors: Mr D Snaddon Feltham **Buses:** H25, H26, 90, 117, 237, 285, 417, 490 Dark blue blazer, grey trousers/skirt, blue or white shirt/blouse, tie; navy sweatshirt or pale blue polo shirt (Year 11) **Demand:** 270 places available in 2003 **Type:** Co-educational community comprehensive for 1309 mixed pupils, aged 11 to 18 **Submit application form:** Mid-November 2003 **Motto:** *Carpe Diem* (Seize the Day) **School hours:** 8.30am–3.05pm **Meals:** Hot and cold available **Strong GCSE subjects:** Art, English **London league table position:** 485

## Profile

Built as a community college, Feltham moved to a single site in the 1980s and now occupies very attractive modern buildings on a well laid-out campus. The school has a good range of facilities, which are well used. These include networked computers, a sports centre, gym, 20 acres of playing fields and floodlit all-weather pitches, and a fully equipped music studio, including keyboard rooms. The school has won the Sports Curriculum Award several times. As a community college, Feltham has strong community links. The campus is open during the evening for community use and has more than 2000 people enrolled in adult education classes. Local businesses are also involved with some school activities. From Year 8, pupils are grouped by ability for most subjects. The sixth form offers A-levels as well as vocational courses, including nursery nursing. Pupils may also take some GCSEs in the sixth form, and media studies is a popular option. The Friends is an active PTA, which arranges educational and social events. The school has a special unit catering for the disabled, and all buildings have disabled access and a disabled users sports club. In 1997, Ofsted praised the school's induction programme for new Year 7 pupils.

## Admissions and intake

All applications should be made directly to the LEA.

## Achievement

In 2002, 28 per cent of pupils achieved five GCSEs at grades A*–C. This was 11 per cent up on 2001's results and Feltham came one from of the borough league table. The average points score was 24.4. For A-levels, the average point score for pupils taking two or more was 128.8 and the school was ranked 13th in the borough league table. When Ofsted visited the school in 1997, they praised the outstanding leadership of the head, the dedication and involvement of the governors and the hard work and commitment of teaching and support staff. There are good channels of communication with parents.

## Extra-curricular activities

Feltham has a series of lunchtime clubs, including homework, poetry, revision, art and computers, as well as sports and music clubs. A drama pavilion and a hall are used for large-scale productions, and these are well supported by parents.

# The Green School

**Busch Corner, Isleworth, Middlesex TW7 5BB** 020 8321 8080 020 8321 8081 administrator@green.hounslow.sch.uk green.hounslow.sch.uk Mrs PE Butterfield; Chair of Governors: Mr I Harman Syon Lane **Buses:** H28, H29, 235, 237 Bottle green sweat shirt and skirt, white blouse **Demand:** Oversubscribed for 125 places **Type:** Voluntary aided Church of England comprehensive for 833 girls (mixed sixth form), aged 11 to 18 **Submit application form:** Mid-November 2003 **Motto:** Outstanding Education in a Christian Context **School hours:** 8.30am–3.30pm **Meals:** Hot and cold available **Strong GCSE subjects:** English, history, RE **London league table position:** 163

## Profile

The Green School occupies a 19th-century building close to London's Syon Park. It is one of the first Beacon schools. The school has three dedicated IT rooms, each having networked computers and Internet access, with 'clusters' of computers in other classrooms. A learning resources centre is staffed full time, and also houses computers and multimedia facilities, as well as traditional book materials.The pastoral care system involves a close relationship with a form tutor, a house system with prefects and trained student mentors, a merit system and close relationships with its many feeder primary schools and with parents. Christian values underpin the work of the school.The sixth form is mixed, as part of the local consortium of four schools. Pupils participate in structured tutorial programmes and a personal tutor monitors them.There is a school council. All parents belong to the Green School Society, which runs fund-raising events. Even if a pupil is from another faith, attendance at Christian assemblies is compulsory.

## Admissions and intake

Applications should be made to the governors, on a form available from the school, and supported by a reference from a parish priest, minister of religion or other religious leader. Priority is given under the following criteria: girls with at least one parent who is a committed member of, and regularly worships in an Anglican Church; girls with at least one parent who is a committed member of, and regularly worships in a church or chapel of another Christian denomination; an applicant whose daughter is a committed member of, and regularly worships in an Anglican church; an applicant whose daughter is a committed member of, and regularly worships in a church or chapel of another Christian denomination; an applicant who desires a religious background to education and is an active member of another faith; applicants requesting single sex school; and applicants who live nearest to the school.

## Achievement

In 2002, 65 per cent of pupils gained five or more A*–C grades at GCSE. This was well above the borough and national averages, but down from 73 per cent in 2001.The Green School came fourth in the borough league table. At A-level, pupils scored an average of 226.4 points, which was above the borough average, ranking the school sixth in the borough. Ofsted visited the school in 2001 and described it as 'a good school with many very good features'. It was seen to provide a 'high quality educational experience' with pupils being well taught in all subjects. High standards are achieved in external examinations at Key Stages 3 and 4, and Inspectors praised the school's 'positive ethos' in which all pupils are enabled to achieve.

## Extra-curricular activities

The school has a host of activities, including debating and public speaking, as well as clubs connected with sport and art.There are a variety of musical groups, including a wind band and a guitar group and regular opportunities for performance in music and drama.The pupils go on field trips at home and overseas and there are thriving links with local industries.

# Gumley House RC Convent School

**St. John's Road, Isleworth, Middlesex TW7 6XF** 020 8568 8692 020 8758 2674 general@gumley.hounslow.sch.uk www.gumley.hounslow.sch.uk Sister Brenda Wallace; Chair of Governors: Mr DPA Murphy Isleworth Hounslow East **Buses:** H37, 237, 267 (plus five school buses serving Hanwell, Ealing, Northolt/West Ealing, West Drayton/Hayes and Greenford/Southall) Up to sixth form: Dark brown skirt, cream blouse, a tie (house colour), brown V-neck school pullover; PE: polo or sweatshirt, brown games skirt, black cycling shorts **Demand:** 192 places in 2003; oversubscribed **Type:** Voluntary aided for 1110 girls, aged 11 to 18 **Submit**

**application form:** Mid-November 2003 **Motto:** *Vive Ut Vivas* (Live That You May Have Life) **School hours:** 8.50am–3.40pm **Meals:** Hot and cold available **Strong GCSE subjects:** Geography, history, RE **London league table position:** 148

## Profile

Founded in 1841, Gumley House is set in a beautiful 10-acre site close to Syon Park and the Thames. There are many new buildings on the site, including a prayer centre, media resource centre, seven computer centres and a well-equipped library and learning resources centre. The sixth form has its own common room and private study areas in the library, and students can choose from a wide variety of subjects as part of the West London Catholic Consortium. In 1999, Polish, Italian, and Christian theology were studied, as well as the more usual subjects. The sixth form also offers advanced GNVQs. The school prides itself on sport, and 'many (girls) have won places in national rowing and canoeing teams, and have played netball and hockey for their counties'. Gumley House has a coordinator for pupils with special needs, and girls with exceptional ability are regarded as also having special needs. All parents belong to the parents' association, which organizes social and fund-raising events.

## Admissions and intake

Applications are made directly to the school. The school receives nearly twice as many first choice applications as there are places available and therefore operates a set of strict criteria for entrance: Catholicity with priest support, having a sister in the school, and attendance at a Catholic primary school are the most highly weighted criteria. A priest's reference form is handed out with the application form. In 2001, Ofsted found that the ability of pupils on entry was above the national average, although a wide range of ability is represented.

## Achievement

In 2002, 74 per cent of pupils achieved five or more A*–C grades at GCSE, well above both local and national averages and six per cent up on 2001. The school was ranked third in the borough league table. At A-level, the average point score per pupil was 254.5, above the borough and national averages, and ranking Gumley House second of the borough league table. Ofsted visited the school in 2001 and described it as 'a very good school' where the great majority of pupils achieve high standards at the end of both Key Stages'. Inspectors praised the head teacher's 'excellent leadership' and the school's 'very good' teaching.

## Extra-curricular activities

Sports have a high priority as have music and drama. Many girls learn to play instruments. There is an orchestra and international musical exchanges are arranged. Other school trips take place each year, including a skiing trip. Lunchtime and after-school clubs include chess, computers and science. Pupils are encouraged to take part in community events.

# Gunnersbury Catholic School

**The Ride, Boston Manor Road, Brentford, Middlesex TW8 9LB** ☎ 020 8568 7281 Fax 020 8569 7946 Head: John Heffernan MA; Chair of Governors: Derek Bourn Rail: Brentford Tube: Northfields or Boston Manor **Buses:** E2, E3, E8, H91, 65, 267 Uniform: Black trousers, blazer and shoes, blue shirt, school tie **Demand:** 184 places regularly and heavily oversubscribed **Type:** Voluntary aided Catholic comprehensive for 1049 boys (mixed in sixth form), aged 11 to 19 **Submit application form:** Mid-November 2003 **Motto:** *Ad Altiora* (To Higher Things) **Mission statement:** The school strives to educate all its pupils within an environment where the Catholic traditions of learning, truth, justice, respect and community are promoted. **School hours:** 8.50am–3.25pm; homework clubs are available **Meals:** Hot and cold available **Strong GCSE subjects:** All relatively strong **London league table position:** 240

## Profile

Gunnersbury has a good reputation and in 2000 Ofsted reported that 'This is a successful and improving school where standards of work and behaviour are high. The school is well led by the head teacher and strongly supported by governors and the community it serves.' The sixth form offers 15 different A-levels and 3 AS-levels on-site, with more subjects available through the consortium. Intermediate level GNVQs are also on offer. RE, general studies and games are compulsory for all sixth-formers. Parents and staff are all members of the Gunnersbury Association, which arranges fund-raising events. Parents receive a fortnightly newsletter. Special-needs provision has improved in recent years but Ofsted noted that 'more in-class support is needed and specialist help for the small number of very weak readers. Some large groups at Key Stage 3 make effective support difficult'. There is a school council, chaired by the head boy, with a representative from each year.

## Admissions and intake

The governors are the admissions authority for the school, so all applications should be made to the head. Gunnersbury is oversubscribed and adheres to the following criteria for Catholic pupils with written priest support or without priest support: sibling connection, evidence of Catholic involvement. There is a waiting list for places. In 2000, Ofsted found that attainment on entry to the school is above average. The special-needs register is fairly low, at just 8 per cent.

## Achievement

Ofsted found that in comparison to similar schools, GCSE results at Gunnersbury were well above average and 'in the top five per cent of schools nationally'. The current GCSE and A-level results show great improvement on those of four and five years ago. Gunnersbury's results are above the norm for boys' achievement. In 2002, 59 per cent of pupils achieved five GCSEs at A*–C grades and the school was ranked seventh in the borough for GCSE results. The A-level results for 2002 gave an average point score of 255.5 to those pupils taking two or more A-levels. This was above national and borough averages but Ofsted commented that the school's A-level results are a distortion of the true picture, because pupils are not entered for general studies at A-level. This ranked the school first in the borough for A-level results. Intermediate level GNVQ results tend to be good with some distinctions. Ofsted commented that IT, soft technology and music could all do with extra facilities.

## Extra-curricular activities

Boys have a retreat day each year and there are activities such as computers and chess, field trips, theatre visits and the Duke of Edinburgh's Award scheme. The school competes successfully in borough and county sport fixtures. About 10 per cent of boys have individual instrumental tuition, and there is the opportunity to join the Hounslow School's orchestra. The drama department has regular productions. Pupils are encouraged to participate in community fund-raising activities.

# The Heathland School

**Wellington Road South, Hounslow TW4 5HU** 020 8572 4411 020 8569 5126 heathland.hounslow.sch.uk HS Pattar; Chair of Governors: MJ Nicholls Whitton, Hounslow Hounslow Central **Buses:** H23, H28, R62, 110, 111, 116, 117, 237 Black trousers and blazer, white shirt, school tie **Demand:** Oversubscribed for 270 places in Year 7 **Type:** Community comprehensive for 1842 mixed pupils, aged 11 to 18 **Submit application form:** Mid-November 2003 **Motto:** Committed to Excellence **School hours:** 8.40am–3.20pm; homework clubs are available **Meals:** Hot and cold available **Strong GCSE subjects:** Art **London league table position:** 165

## Profile

The Heathland School is located in modern buildings on a 30-acre site that edges Hounslow Heath. It has 13 fully equipped science labs, 250 IT workstations, with supervised Internet access, and a well stocked and equipped library, which was highly praised during the 1995 Ofsted. The school has recently increased its computer provision with a network of 150 workstations. Computers are also located in the library, which has many CD-ROMs. The excellent sporting facilities include three sports halls, a floodlit playing field, tennis and netball courts, all-weather cricket pitches and a fitness studio. The sixth form is very large and offers more than 25 A- and AS-level courses as well as GNVQs. Ofsted found that 'standards achieved by pupils with special educational needs are predominantly good'. The Heathland has a programme that identifies and monitors potential high-achievers. There is a school council. The PTA is very active and well supported.

## Admissions and intake

Applications should be made directly to the LEA on the borough transfer forms. In 2001, Ofsted noted that attainment on entry, is 'just above the national average'. There is a significant number of pupils who need literacy support when they join the school' due to the large majority of students for whom English is an additional language. In 2001, 4 per cent of pupils were refugees, mainly from Somalia.

## Achievement

In March 2001, the Department for Education and Employment presented Heathland with an Achievement Award for Excellence for gaining better results in 2000 than most schools of similar standards. In 2002, 66 per cent of pupils were awarded five or more GCSEs at A*–C grades. This was above the borough and national averages, and up from 64 per cent in 2001, continuing an upward trend. The school was ranked fifth in the borough league table. At A-level, pupils gained 235.2 points on average in 2002. This was above the borough average. This placed the school fourth in the borough league table for A-level results. The school prospectus notes that 'more than 90 per cent of students secure a place at university, including Oxford and Cambridge'. The school recently gained the Sportsmark Award. It was featured in *The Good State Schools Guide* and had a very good Ofsted report, which ranked it amongst the best 20 per cent of state schools in the country. Inspectors praised the 'outstanding' leadership of the head teacher and noted that: 'Teaching is consistently good and students' attitudes to learning are very good'. Heathland was seen to be a 'very good school' which 'achieves high standards in all its work'.

## Extra-curricular activities

The Heathland has over 80 clubs, activity days, and wide links with the local community, through work experience, sixth-form community work, vocational courses and access to the excellent sporting facilities. The school values its good reputation for music education and has a programme that includes concerts, performances and workshops. There are also regular educational and cultural trips.

# Heston Community School

**Heston Road, Heston, Hounslow TW5 0QR** ☎ 020 8572 1931 Fax 020 8570 2647 ⓔ info@hestoncs.hounslow.sch.uk ✉ Angela Bennett; Chair of Governors: Cllr J Kenna ⇌ Hounslow Central, Hounslow East, Osterley **Buses:** 111, 120 Uniform: Black trousers, black V-neck jumper, white shirt, school tie **Demand:** 190 places availalbe in 2003 **Type:** Community comprehensive for 1168 mixed pupils, aged 11 to 18 **Submit application form:** Mid-November 2003 **Motto:** A Complete Learning Environment **School hours:** 8.40am–3.30pm; homework clubs are available **Meals:** Hot and cold available **Strong GCSE subjects:** All relatively strong **London league table position:** 214

## Profile

This large, purpose-built school opened in the 1930s and has continued to expand. It is situated in 'a definable urban village' in the north of the borough, and has nine acres of fields. There is a sports hall, gymnasium, four grass pitches and an all-weather pitch. There is also a photographic dark room and seven science labs. Heston's avowed purpose is to: 'enable all members of our community to achieve excellence and experience self-worth, to provide high quality educational provision and to provide equality of opportunity. This should be achieved in an atmosphere of respect for individuality, tolerance for difference and commitment to the well being and development of all.' The sixth form is large and offers advanced level GNVQs as well as A-levels. Pupils attend a residential induction course before joining the sixth form. The school houses an area centre for hearing impaired children. There is a school council chaired by a senior pupil and an active PTA.

## Admissions and intake

Applications should be made directly to the LEA on the transfer forms. In 1998, Ofsted noted that 'Pupils enter the school with their overall attainment broadly in line with that of pupils of the same age across the country, although their English language skills are less well developed'.

## Achievement

At Heston, 'expectations are high and achievement at Key Stage 3 is rewarded through the Heston Challenge Award scheme.' In 2002, 57 per cent of pupils gained five or more A*–C grades at GCSE. These results were up by 6 per cent on 2001's results and the school was ranked sixth in the borough league table. Ofsted were delighted with the progress the school had made since their previous inspection, and Heston's results have risen sharply since 1996. In 2002, the average point score for pupils taking two or more A-levels was 207. Heston was placed ninth in the borough league table for A-level results. During the last inspection, particular comment was made on the courteous and polite behaviour of the pupils and the positive ethos of the school. Heston has lower truancy rates than the borough as a whole, with only 0.7 per cent of unauthorized absence.

### Extra-curricular activities

Heston encourages extra-curricular activities and has clubs for drama, music and sport, as well as residential courses for leadership and adventure, and some curricular subjects. The school has links with a professional basketball team, who visit the school to coach. More than 100 pupils have instrumental tuition and many are in the school band or perform in small ensembles. There are trips abroad, including an annual skiing trip.

## Hounslow Manor School

**Prince Regent Road, Hounslow TW3 1NE** 020 8572 4461 020 8577 1605 Richard Shortt; Chair of Governors: Matthew Cavill Hounslow East, Hounslow Central **Buses:** 117, 235, 237 Black sweatshirt with blue logo, black trousers, white shirts, school tie **Demand:** 165 places available **Type:** Community comprehensive for 928 mixed pupils, aged 11 to 18 **Submit application form:** Mid-November 2003 **School hours:** 8.40am–3.35pm (Mon and Wed), 8.40am–3.10pm (Tues, Thurs and Fri); homework clubs are available **Meals:** Hot and cold available **Strong GCSE subjects:** Art, business studies, drama, integrated humanities **London league table position:** 503

### Profile

In 2000, Hounslow Manor School was praised by Ofsted inspectors for the racial harmony in the school and the recognition of the contribution made to the life of the school by pupils from a variety of cultural backgrounds. The sixth form is part of a consortium with three other schools locally. It has a thriving portfolio of GNVQs on offer, including leisure and tourism. Some sixth-formers have spent time on work experience in France. One more unusual A-level on offer is media studies. The school has a parents group, and there is a school council. Approximately 28 per cent of the pupil roll is on the special-needs register.

### Admissions and intake

Applications should be made to the LEA on the borough transfer forms. Ofsted noted that 'the intake of pupils comes from a much wider area with a much higher than average number of disadvantaged people'. At that time, about 46 per cent of pupils came from homes where English is the second language, so that on entry, many had poor levels of literacy and of numeracy. Ofsted added that 'almost 90 per cent of pupils arrive at the school with lower than average verbal reasoning skills. The school has to build educational achievement on this low baseline'.

### Achievement

The proportion of pupils gaining five or more A*–C grades at GCSE in 2002 was 21 per cent, down from 30 per cent the previous year. Hounslow Manor was ranked 16th in the borough league table. At A-level, the average point score for pupils taking two or more A-levels was 134.1 in 2002. This ranked the school 12th in the borough league table for A-level results. Ofsted found that 'Results in art, drama, business studies and integrated humanities were above the national average'. They also praised the 'outstandingly high standards in sixth-form art'. Music is a strong feature of life at Hounslow Manor, and this was heartily praised by the inspectors. The PE department was picked out for particular praise, and the school has topped the borough athletics championships.

### Extra-curricular activities

The school invites many visitors into the school, including local councillors for a forum on democracy and Ken Campbell for a Channel 4 science programme. In a science week, pupils visited the Royal Institution and the Science Museum. The sixth form visited the Foreign Office, and school trips are regularly arranged in England and overseas. Students of music at GCSE have performed alongside the London Philharmonic Orchestra. Pupils can also learn African drumming, Indian music or music from other traditions. There are opportunities to play sports, and girls are encouraged to play rugby. The individual departments arrange homework clubs.

## International School of London

**139 Gunnersbury Avenue W3 8LG** 020 8992 5823 020 8993 7012 ISLondon@dial.pipex.com www.islondon.com Elaine Whelan Acton Town, Gunnersbury **Buses:** Door-to-door bus service No uniform, except shorts and T-shirt for PE **Demand:** 20 places available for Year 7 in 2003 **Type:** Non-selective independent for 264 mixed pupils, aged 3 to 19 **Fees:** £12,250 (Years 7 to 9); £13,000 (Years 10 to 11); £13,750

(Sixth Form) **Submit application form:** No cut-off date **School hours:** 8.30am–3.20pm **Meals:** Hot and cold available **Strong GCSE subjects:** English, maths, science **London league table position:** 293

## Profile

According to its prospectus, 'The International School of London exists to serve the needs of the international community in London. It aims to maximize the achievement of each of its students across the breadth of the curriculum (and to) develop in each student a global outlook which seeks to understand and appreciate the attitudes of others'. The school was founded in 1972 and is accredited by the European Council of International Schools (ECIS). English is the language of instruction throughout the school, and there is special ESL help available, but the school can also offer mother-tongue instruction in Japanese, Italian, Arabic, Spanish and French and 'almost any language' by special arrangement. Afrikaans, Korean and Turkish are just some of the languages offered recently. The school has full multimedia capability, Internet access, a video room and computerized library. After GCSE, sixth-formers are entered for the International Baccalaureate, which ISL has helped to promote. This qualification, accepted at universities worldwide, is less specialized than current A-levels. Pupils are required to study six subjects, as well as the Theory of Knowledge. To encourage research skills they are also required to write an extended 4000-word essay, and take part in a Creative Active and Service Programme. The PTA members play a special role in helping new parents with their move to London and explaining the way the school operates. Classes throughout the school are small, with only 14 to 16 pupils in each. There is a school council.

## Admissions and intake

Admission is based on a personal interview and previous school records. Forms are available from the school and should be returned with a £50 registration fee to the admissions officer.

## Achievement

At GCSE, 73 per cent of pupils gained A*–C grades in 2002. This was animprovement on 63 per cent in 2001 and the school was ranked ninth in the GCSE borough league table. These results were well above the borough and national averages, and the average GCSE points score was 34.7. As most pupils have English as a second language, 'promotion from one year to another is based upon satisfactory overall results'. At sixth form, pupils sit for the International Baccalaureate and 'progress to universities all over the world'. In 2002, of the 15 students who took the IB diploma, 75 per cent were successful. There is virtually no truancy at the school, with only 0.3 per cent of absences being unauthorized.

## Extra-curricular activities

A summer school takes place each year 'to further develop English as a second language and incorporates daily cultural and sporting outings around London. There is an annual skiing trip, an annual activity week for Years 7 to 11 and long weekend trips in the sixth form. Lunchtime clubs include bee keeping, photography and computing, and there is an annual international festival. The ISL enter their football, basketball and volleyball teams for the three-day American and International Schools contest'.

# Isleworth and Syon Boys' School

**Ridgeway Road, Isleworth, Middlesex TW7 5LJ** 020 8568 5791 020 8569 5791 Mr E Ferguson; Chair of Governors: T Tranter Isleworth **Buses:** H91 Black blazer, dark grey or black trousers, white shirt, grey or black V-neck pullover, school tie **Demand:** 165 places available; oversubscribed **Type:** Voluntary controlled comprehensive for 981 boys, aged 11 to 18 **Submit application form:** Mid-November 2003 **Motto:** *Finis Coronat Opus* (Work Crowns the End) **School hours:** 8.35am–3.10pm; homework clubs are available **Meals:** Hot and cold available **Strong GCSE subjects:** English, geography, history, maths **London league table position:** 274

## Profile

Isleworth and Syon, a non-denominational boys' school, has evolved from a grammar school that was established in 1630. The present school dates from 1979, but the main buildings were constructed in 1939. Later additions include art and craft areas and a sports hall. There are extensive playing fields and playground areas, seven science labs, two computer rooms and a suite of music rooms. The library is well stocked and has been involved in research into the use of IT. In the LEA *Admissions to Secondary Schools 2001*, the school characterizes itself thus: 'Isleworth and Syon School's tradition has been built on academic excellence, outstanding sporting achievement and the extensive extra curricular programme.' The school is part of the Central Consortium of sixth forms, offering more than 20 A-levels as well as GNVQs. All parents are members of the PTA, which is very active in fund-raising for the school.The PTA runs a helpline to organize parental help for tasks such as staffing the school bookshop.

## Admissions and intake

Applications should be made to the LEA on the borough transfer forms. In 2002, Ofsted noted that the proportion of pupils with special educational needs is above average but the number of pupils with statements is below average.

## Achievement

In 1998, the DfES identified the school as 'the 42nd most improved school in Britain'. The number of boys gaining five or more GCSEs at A*–C grades was 56 per cent in 2002, up from 46 per cent in 2001.These results were above the borough average and the school was ranked eighth in the borough's GCSE league table. In 2002, pupils taking two or more A-levels scored an average of 219.1 points, placing the school eighth in the borough. Ofsted described Isleworth and Syon as an 'effective school' with standards in Key Stage 3 national tests 'very high' compared to similar schools. GCSE standards are in line with the national average.Teaching was found to be 'satisfactory overall' but greater use of ICT was needed across the curriculum.The school is proud of its reputation for sport, for which it has been awarded the National Sportsmark Award, and for the traditional values of attitude, behaviour and dress, which it upholds.

## Extra-curricular activities

There is a proud emphasis on competitive sport and the school hopes to gain Sports College status.The cross-country team competes nationally. Boys can be entered for the Duke of Edinburgh's Award scheme.There are residential trips and activities weeks. Homework clubs are available.

# Lampton School

**Lampton Avenue, Hounslow TW3 4EP** ☎ 020 8572 1936 📠 020 8572 8500 ✉ Susan E John; Chair of Governors: Mrs M Stuart 🚆 Hounslow Central **Buses:** H20, 91, 110, 111, 120, 237 👔 Black blazer, black trousers, white shirt, school tie, black shoes **Demand:** 210 places available in 2003 **Type:** Co-educational community comprehensive for 1051 mixed pupils, aged 11 to 18 **Submit application form:** Mid-November 2003 **Motto:** *Optima Tenete* (Committed to excellence) **School hours:** 8.40am–3.30pm, 8.50am–3.30pm (Fri) **Meals:** Hot and cold available **Strong GCSE subjects:** All relatively strong **London league table position:** 318

## Profile

Lampton School is located in the west-central area of Hounslow. It has recently undergone a lot of modernization and refurbishment and now has seven science labs, networked IT facilities, a new library and language centres, hard and soft technology workshops and a new business studies suite. The school has many sporting facilities, including a gym, sports hall, netball and tennis courts, pitches for soccer, rounders, rugby and hockey, a running track and athletics area, as well as an all-weather cricket area, The new speech and language centre was deemed 'very good' by Ofsted and there is also a new main hall with 'excellent staging facilities'. Ofsted inspected before the new building work was completed, and was very pleased with the improvements the school was making and found the pupils 'well motivated, keen to learn and interested in their lessons'. The majority of pupils decide to stay on for the sixth form, which offers over 17 A- and AS-level courses, GNVQs, a community service scheme, as well as work-based opportunities. Ofsted found that overall provision for special-needs pupils was good. Brunel University helps to provide enrichment and extension for more able children. The school council is active and influential.The school has a PTA, which organizes many functions.

## Admissions and intake

Applications should be made to the LEA on the borough transfer forms. Ofsted noted that 'a higher than average proportion of students enter the school with weak literacy skills' and that 'the intake is skewed towards the middle/lower ability range'.

### Achievement

Ofsted found that Lampton's results at Key Stage 3 in 1998 were well above average for similar schools. In 2002, 44 per cent of pupils gained five or more A*–C grade passes at GCSE. This was down from 46 per cent in 2001, continuing a downward trend in results. The A-level results for 2002 were above the borough average with an average point score of 223.7. Ofsted noted that the 'very good provision for moral and social development' was one of the strengths of the school, with cultural diversity being celebrated. They also praised the quality of teaching and the good progress made in nearly all subjects, along with pupils' good attitudes to learning. Lampton was found to have an excellent partnership with parents and the community.

### Extra-curricular activities

Ofsted included the 'very good extra-curricular provision' as one of Lampton's strengths. Lunchtime and after-school clubs include music, sports, chess, drama, and technology. In the sixth form, pupils can participate in skiing, skating, swimming, overseas trips and Outward Bound courses.

# Longford Community School

**Tachbrook Road, Feltham, Middlesex TE14 9PE** ☎ 020 8890 0245 📠 020 8844 2441 ⓔ general@longord.hounslow.sch.uk 🌐 www.longford.hounslow.sch.uk Ms A Dalglish; Chair of Governors: Paul Edmonds ⇄ Hounslow West, Hatton Cross, Feltham **Buses:** H25, 116, 117, 235 Black skirt or trousers, black shoes, white shirt, school tie, school V-neck sweat shirt **Demand:** 213 places available in 2003 **Type:** Co-educational community comprehensive for 1111 mixed pupils, aged 11 to 18 **Submit application form:** Mid-November 2003 **School hours:** 8.40am–3.05pm; homework clubs are available **Meals:** Hot and cold available **Strong GCSE subjects:** Information unavailable **London league table position:** 440

### Profile

Longford is a large, culturally diverse school in the west of the borough. There is a lot of new housing development near the school. In 1998, the school was recognized as one of the 50 most improved schools in the country. In January 2000, the former Chief Inspector of Schools Chris Woodhead wrote, 'You are justified in the pride you have in your school and I will certainly add it to our working list of effective schools that are used by HMI to exemplify good practice, particularly in areas of management and evaluation'. The majority of pupils stay on into the sixth form. There were 130 in the sixth form in the year 2000–2001, choosing from at least 14 A- or AS-levels and a range of GNVQs. Longford has strong links with the community 'that support and enrich the curriculum'. There is disabled access to 90 per cent of the school and special-needs support is strong. The prospectus is well designed and informative. Parents are sent a printed school calendar at the start of every year. There is no PTA as such, but each year team leader runs a parents' support group.

### Admissions and intake

Applications should be made to the LEA on the borough transfer forms. In 1999, Ofsted found that attainment on entry fell well below national averages, with 14 per cent of pupils having English as an additional language, and a 'substantial number' having weak literacy skills.

### Achievement

Ofsted were very impressed by the improvements at Longford, and particularly praised the leadership of the head, the 'significant added value' to attainment, good attitudes to learning and the dedication and commitment of teachers. Results at the end of Key Stage 3 have risen steadily over the last four years, in English, maths and science. In the summer of 2002, 34 per cent of pupils scored five or more A*–C grades at GCSE. This was up from 28 per cent in 2001 and the school was ranked 14th out of 16 schools in the borough league table. At A-level, the average point score for pupils taking two or more was 12.8, again ranking the school 14th in the borough.

### Extra-curricular activities

There is both a homework and a success-maker club, and the library opens from 8am to 5pm. There are also many extra-curricular clubs, such as chess and dance, as well as choirs, orchestras and a rock and pop group. Pupils can take part in the Duke of Edinburgh's Award scheme and visits and foreign exchanges also take place.

# St Mark's Catholic School

**106 Bath Road, Hounslow TW3 3EJ** 020 8577 3600 020 8577 0559 staffroom@stmarks.hounslow.sch.uk www.stmarks.hounslow.sch.uk Mr P Enright; Chair of Governors: K Sullivan Hounslow Hounslow Central, Hounslow West **Buses:** H22, H23, H32, H98, 81, 116, 117, 222, 237 Dark blue blazer, blue shirts, school tie, black trousers or skirt **Demand:** 186 places available; oversubscribed **Type:** Voluntary aided Catholic co-educational Technology College for 1146 mixed pupils, aged 11 to 18 **Submit application form:** Mid-November 2003 **Mission statement:** The school is committed to providing the best possible education in a community which sees each of its members as charged with God's presence and every aspect of its life as an opportunity to deepen its knowledge and love of God. The school promotes the Christian faith and the Gospel values given by Christ. **School hours:** 8.40am–3.20pm; homework clubs are available **Meals:** Hot and cold available **Strong GCSE subjects:** All relatively strong **London league table position:** 144

## Profile

This school was awarded Technology College status in 1998. It boasts some superb facilities such as a purpose-built science centre and a well equipped learning resources centre, housing 16 networked computers, all with Internet access. St Mark's also has video-conferencing facilities and the capability to enable children to send in their homework by e-mail. Technology College status has enabled the school to provide 'integrated learning systems' in maths, science and technology. Pupils study the usual curriculum subjects in Years 7 to 9, with drama, art and music and a choice of French or German. Year 7 study ICT as well. Years 10 and 11 take up to 10 GCSEs – the usual core of subjects, plus two from a range that includes business studies, office skills and the Youth Award scheme. The sixth form is joined with the Consortium of Catholic Schools to offer GNVQs, A-and AS-levels. Sixth-formers may also re-sit GCSE maths and English in a one-year course. Famous ex-pupils include musician Elvis Costello.

## Admissions and intake

Applications are made directly to the school. Admission is based on the following criteria, in order of priority: practising Catholic students with written priest support and school given as first preference, and practising Catholic students without written priest support and school given as first preference. As well as the written support of a priest, parents must also submit copies of the child's baptismal certificate.

## Achievement

In 2002, 71 per cent of pupils gained five or more A*–C grades at GCSE. This was up from 65 per cent in 2001 and well above the borough and national averages. The school was ranked second in the borough league table. The average point score for pupils taking two or more A-levels was 227.3 in 2002. This ranked the school fifth in the borough league table.

## Extra-curricular activities

St Mark's has a wide range of activities. Pupils may join basketball, girls' football and cricket clubs. They may also join one of three choirs (including a gospel choir), a woodwind ensemble or a folk group. After-school activities include homework clubs, classics, yoga and oral history. The school stages drama productions every year. There are numerous trips, including an annual skiing trip to Europe. There are also cultural and historical trips.

# Islington

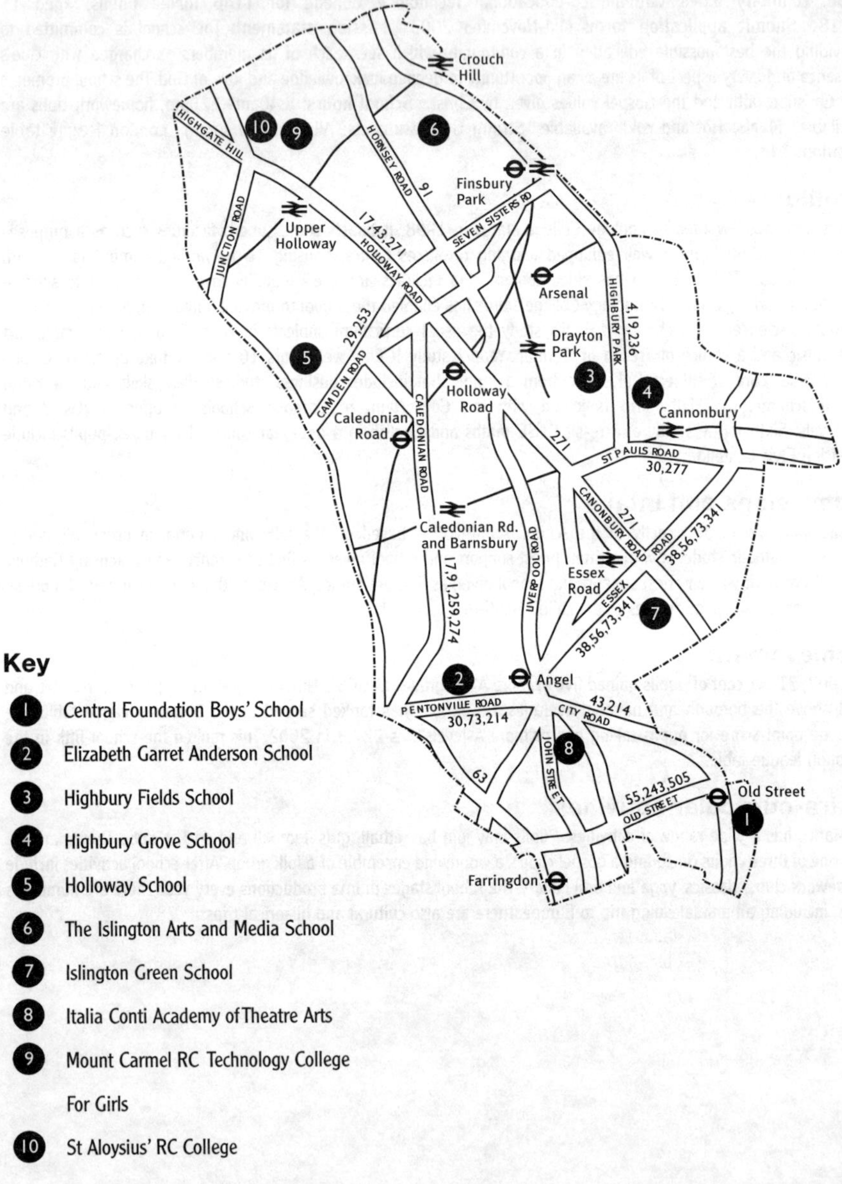
Crouch Hill
HIGHGATE HILL
HORNSEY ROAD
91
Finsbury Park
SEVEN SISTERS RD
JUNCTION ROAD
Upper Holloway
17,43,271
HOLLOWAY ROAD
Arsenal
HIGHBURY PARK
4,19,236
29,253
Drayton Park
CAMDEN ROAD
Holloway Road
CALEDONIAN ROAD
Caledonian Road
Cannonbury
271
ST PAULS ROAD
30,277
Caledonian Rd. and Barnsbury
CANONBURY ROAD
271
38,56,73,341
LIVERPOOL ROAD
Essex Road
ESSEX ROAD
38,56,73,341
17,91,259,274
Angel
PENTONVILLE ROAD
30,73,214
CITY ROAD
43,214
JOHN STREET
63
55,243,505
OLD STREET
Old Street
Farringdon
Key
1 Central Foundation Boys' School
2 Elizabeth Garret Anderson School
3 Highbury Fields School
4 Highbury Grove School
5 Holloway School
6 The Islington Arts and Media School
7 Islington Green School
8 Italia Conti Academy of Theatre Arts
9 Mount Carmel RC Technology College For Girls
10 St Aloysius' RC College

# Factfile

**LEA: Laylock Street, London N1 1TH** 020 7527 2000 www.islington.gov.uk **Director of Regeneration and Education:** Mohammed Mehmet (for the council); Bill Clark (director of school services, Cambridge Education Associates [CEA]) **Political control of council:** Liberal Democrat **Percentage of pupils from outside the borough:** 21.4 per cent (from Hackney and Camden) **Percentage of pupils educated outside the borough:** 23.1 per cent **London league table positions (out of 32 boroughs):** 32nd

## Profile

Islington still conjures up a moneyed 'New Labour' image despite the departure of its most famous family to Downing Street. Such an image certainly fits areas like Canonbury, Islington 'proper' and Barnsbury, which are all known for their fine Victorian streets. Parts of Highbury are also upmarket with Clerkenwell the home of 'loft-living'. Tufnell Park and parts of Archway are not so trendy but their large houses have become popular with the middle classes. But not everyone can afford the smart eateries and exclusive shops of Clerkenwell and Upper Street and the borough is the fourth most deprived in the country. Holloway is an example of this much poorer Islington. In fact, even the borough's most prosperous areas live cheek by jowl with less well-off housing and grim council estates.

Islington is also Arsenal country – there was practically dancing in the streets when the team 'did the double'. Unfortunately when it comes to education, the borough is at the bottom, not the top of the league. Its secondary schools usually produce the worst GCSE results in London. Even the council itself had so little confidence that it could right years of mismanagement that in 2000 it privatized its school services. However, the new managers, Cambridge Education Associates (CEA), were identified as making improvements by Ofsted in its report of March 2001, which concluded that 'the task facing the LEA has been a formidable one but, to a remarkable extent, it has been successfully accomplished. The tide has turned in Islington.' Difficulties that have been faced by the borough include severe problems in the recruitment of both teachers and heads and the disrepair of many schools. Most parents look elsewhere for secondary education if they can. They will also not have been heartened by the fiasco surrounding the 'Fresh Start' school Islington Arts and Media, which after becoming a fresh start school with a 'super head' was put on special measures a year later. It is said to be improving under its new management. The Liberal Democrats, who recently took control of the council, announced results in Islington would improve. Also, a proposal to establish the borough's first CofE secondary school is being considered by the council.

## Policy

Parents should contact Islington council for an application form for Islington's community schools. If a school is oversubscribed, places are first offered to children with a sibling at the school and then to children living nearest the school. Applications to voluntary schools should be made directly to the schools.

# Central Foundation Boys' School

**Cowper Street, City Road, London EC2A 4SH** 020 7253 3741 020 7336 7295 headteacher@cfbs.islinton.sch.uk www.cfbs.islington.sch.uk Ms J Fortune; Chair of Governors: Dr CA Beck Old Street **Buses:** 5, 43, 55, 76, 141, 214, 243, 505 Up to sixth form: Black blazer and trousers, white shirt, blue and white striped school tie **Demand:** 432 first-choice applications for 150 places in 2001/2 **Type:** Voluntary aided comprehensive for 800 boys, aged 11 to 19 **Submit application form:** 28 November 2003 **Motto:** *Spe Labore Fide* (Labour Overcomes All) **School hours:** 8.55am–3.30pm; homework clubs are available **Meals:** Hot and cold available **Strong GCSE subjects:** Art, design technology, French **London league table position:** 392

## Profile

Originally founded as a grammar school 130 years ago, Central Foundation now serves a less academic intake. Its rather grimy site on the edge of the City is cramped but the buildings are well kept. The school has an astroturf pitch and a good gym as well as use of off-site sports facilities. A learning resources centre includes science labs, technology workshops, art, music and language rooms. IT facilities are strong. There is a prefect system and a school council. There is also a PTA with a regular newsletter. The school recently became a member of a government scheme to improve provision for able and gifted children. One weakness is truancy, which at 1.6 per cent is higher than the national average but low for the borough. Ex-pupils include the architect Richard Seifert and author of *The Ascent of Man*, Dr Jacob Bronowski.

## Admissions and intake

Applicants are placed in an ability band following a verbal reasoning test. Equal numbers are taken from each band with priority given to: those with a brother at the school; and those nearest the school by the shortest walking distance. Exceptional priority may be given to those applicants with special medical, social or educational needs. Most pupils live within a mile of the school and about 25 per cent have special needs.

## Achievement

In 2002, 37 per cent of pupils at Central Foundation obtained five or more A*–C grades, continuing an upward trend. The school was ranked fifth in the GCSE borough league table. An Ofsted report in 1997 noted that Central Foundation is 'a caring school which provides a very sound education'. Inspectors found the teaching to be satisfactory overall but had some concerns about lessons in Year 7 and 8, areas the school has since worked to strengthen. Ofsted was especially impressed by the art department, where GCSE results were very good. French and design technology also performed well. At A-level, media studies was especially strong. The sixth form offers 12 A-levels and GNVQs in two subjects. In 2001, the average point score for pupils taking two of more A-levels was 10.0, just below the borough average, ranking the school second in the borough league table. The inspectors found behaviour to be orderly, although there were some problems among Year 8 boys. Relationships between different racial groups were friendly and the school did well by both its more able pupils and those with special needs. Inspectors commented 'pupils feel valued and know staff are willing to help'.

## Extra-curricular activities

Activities on offer include homework, reading and angling clubs and an environmental group. Specialist musical and singing tuition is provided free to talented pupils. A full sporting programme includes basketball and swimming. The school is strong at football, with many district team members and a player in the under-21s national squad. There are exchange visits with other British schools and overseas visits. The school has a good relationship with the City and can offer excellent work experience and a mentoring scheme, as well as helping pupils with later employment.

# Elizabeth Garret Anderson School

**Risinghill Street, Off Penton Street, London N1 9QG** 020 7837 0739 020 7278 9764 admin@egas.org.uk www.egas.islington.sch.uk Jill Coughlan MA; Chair of Governors: Toni Parker King's Cross King's Cross, Angel **Buses:** 4, 19, 30, 38, 43, 43X, 56, 73, 153, 214, 341 Maroon sweatshirt, white blouse **Demand:** 183 first-choice applications for 240 places in 2001/2 **Type:** Community comprehensive Language College for 1150 girls, aged 11 to 16 **Submit application form:** 28 November 2003 **Motto:** Excellence, Achievement, Opportunity, Community **School hours:** 8.45am–3.20pm, 8.45am–3.15pm (Fri); homework clubs are available **Meals:** Hot and cold available **Strong GCSE subjects:** German, music, textiles, Turkish, sociology **London league table position:** 353

## Profile

Elizabeth Garrett Anderson is located near King's Cross and lives up to the pioneering spirit of its namesake, one of the first women doctors. In 2000 it became a Language College, with the aim that all girls be taught two foreign languages. Sponsorship money from *The Guardian* newspaper has been combined with government funding to build on the work of the strong modern languages department. Money is also available to help support gifted and talented children. There is a PTA. Recent refurbishment has improved technology and science facilities and the library. There are three gyms and outdoor pitches, and Years 10 and 11 also use the Sobell Centre sports facilities. The school council has established an anti-bullying policy. Truancy is a problem and, despite efforts by the school, remains very high at 3.3 per cent. Ex-pupils include Susan Tully, who played 'Michelle' in *Eastenders*.

## Admissions and intake

Admission is through the council. If oversubscribed, priority is given to those applicants with siblings at the school and then to those living closest to it. The girls come from 60 feeder primaries and 50 per cent speak English as an additional language. Over half of all girls in Year 7 have a reading ability at least two or more years below their age.

### Achievement

In 2002, 40 per cent of pupils obtained five or more A*–C grades, up from 32 per cent in 2001. The school was ranked fourth in the GCSE borough league table. In 1998, Ofsted described the school as 'an institution in which pupils are happy and confident and staff enjoy working'. Inspectors thought the teaching was good, with special praise for art, music, RE and design technology. Modern languages was 'a very good department with outstanding features'. They were less impressed by the support for special-needs children and those with English as an additional language. Results at GCSE were found to be low overall, but above the national average in German, Turkish, music, textiles and sociology. History results were impressive with nearly a quarter getting A or A* grades. Art, Bengali, drama and PE were on a par with national results. At A-level most girls tend to go on to the Islington Sixth Form Centre, where they have guaranteed places or attend Camden School for Girls. Ofsted found that the attitude of pupils had 'much improved'. Despite 'some rowdy behaviour', girls generally were orderly and calm.

### Extra-curricular activities

Clubs on offer include Shakespeare, science, drama, art and technology, and a wide range of musical activities. There are homework clubs and most GCSE subjects have support groups. Trips abroad for skiing and language-learning take place as well as weekend events away, to which pupils' families are invited. Theatre visits are popular and the dance group has toured local primary schools. There is also a strong community service volunteer programme.

## Highbury Fields School

**Highbury Hill, London N5 1AR** ☎ 020 7288 1888 Fax 020 7288 2121 ✉ highbury.fields@virgin.net 🌐 www.highburyfields.islington.sch.uk Head: Ann Mullins BA, FRSA; Chair of Governors: Anthony Mooney Rail: Drayton Park Tube: Arsenal, Highbury and Islington **Buses:** 4, 19, 30, 43, 43X, 236, 271, 277, 279 Uniform: Up to sixth form: School sweatshirt, pale blue blouse and navy skirt; trousers optional in winter or for religious reasons **Demand:** 351 first-choice applications for 140 places in 2001/2 **Type:** Community comprehensive for 785 girls, aged 11 to 19 **Submit application form:** 28 November 2003 **Motto:** After Battle Tighten Your Helmet Cords **School hours:** 8.45am–3.25pm; homework clubs are available **Meals:** Hot and cold available **Strong GCSE subjects:** Art, design technology, drama, English, music **London league table position:** 317

### Profile

Highbury Fields' popularity reflects a feeling among many parents that it is the best secondary school in the borough. This success was recognized in 2000 when it was made a Beacon school. Its main buildings look out over Highbury Fields although they are near to some of London's busiest roads. Facilities include a new maths block, art and photographic rooms and a mini-TV studio. There is also a technology annex about half a mile away. Year 10 pupils are trained as mediators to support others, and older girls can help the younger ones with reading. Relations with parents are excellent and a regular newsletter is sent home. There is provision for special needs pupils. The home-school association has helped refurbish the maths classrooms and science labs. There is an active school council. Truancy, however, remains above the national average at 1.4 per cent.

### Admissions and intake

Admission is through the LEA. Priority is given to those with siblings at the school, then to those living closest to it, measured by the shortest walking distance. About 30 per cent of pupils speak English as an additional language.

### Achievement

Highbury Fields is one of Islington's better schools, helping its pupils make good progress. In 2002, 45 per cent of pupils obtained five or more A*–C grades at GCSE. This was down from 50 per cent in 2001 and well above the borough average. These results were just below the national average and the school was ranked third in the borough league table. This made Highbury Fields the best performing state school in the borough. Ofsted reported in 1999 that the girls' 'performance is very high in comparison with students from similar backgrounds'. This is especially true in English and there were also good results in drama, art, music and design technology. Inspectors found only 5 per cent of lessons to be unsatisfactory and 24 per cent were very good or better. The sixth form is run in conjunction with Highbury Grove, offering 20 A-levels and 6 choices of GNVQ. Pupils taking two or more subjects at A-level averaged 133.2 points in 2002. The school came second in the borough for A-level results. Ofsted found that the girls were well behaved, although a few younger ones were disruptive. Pastoral care was described as 'sensitive' and inspectors noted the 'very positive attitude of parents'. However, inspectors felt written work and PE needed attention, and were also worried by a small, hard core of truants.

### Extra-curricular activities

A wide range of clubs is on offer, including homework clubs, an ICT group and a maths group, some of whose members go on to Saturday masterclasses at City University. All girls can learn an instrument, such as the violin, saxophone and percussion. There is a school choir and ensembles, as well as regular productions of musicals. Residential field trips and journeys take place to Italy, Spain and France. Sport is strong, with girls representing London at the All England Championships. Good links with employers allow the school to offer varied work experience. Pupils work with local charities.

## Highbury Grove School

**Highbury New Park, London N5 2EG** 020 7288 8900 020 7690 8654 info@staff.higrove.islington.sch.uk www.highburygrove.islington.sch.uk Mrs Truda White; Chair of Governors: Ms M Dawes Canonbury Highbury and Islington **Buses:** 4, 19, 30, 43, 236, 271, 277 Up to sixth form: black skirt or trousers, black shoes, black sweatshirt, white shirt **Demand:** 340 first-choice applications for 210 places in 2001/2 **Type:** Community comprehensive for 1141 mixed pupils, aged 11 to 19 **Submit application form:** 28 November 2003 **School hours:** 8.30am–5pm; homework clubs are available **Meals:** Hot and cold available **Strong GCSE subjects:** ICT, PE and Turkish **London league table position:** 500

### Profile

Highbury Grove has had plenty of media attention over the years, usually focusing on low exam results and bad behaviour. However, it has improved a great deal since the mid-1990s, following the appointment of a dynamic new head. Another big change came in 1998 when girls were admitted. Highbury Grove's current facilities include a swimming pool, and in 2002 the school opened its City Learning Centre for ICT with state-of-the-art IT facilities and teaching. New kitchens and a new music suite are being built with a new library and sixth form facilities to be built in the coming years. The most able pupils are supported by a Gold Group and a new learning support unit is aimed at those for whom normal classes are unsuitable. There is a prefects system and a school council. Truancy has been a real problem. Since an Ofsted report in 1998, the school managed to reduce truancy levels to 1.7 per cent but it rose to 2.2 per cent in 2000, above the borough and national averages. There is a parents' association and provision for special-needs pupils.

### Admissions and intake

Admission is through the LEA. Priority is given to those with siblings at the school and then to those living closest to it, measured by the shortest walking distance. In 2002, Ofsted found that 'the pupils' home backgrounds are very mixed but, overall, they reflect considerable levels of social and financial hardship'.

### Achievement

In 2002, 25 per cent of pupils obtained five or more A*–C grades at GCSE, five per cent down on 2001. The school was placed eighth in the borough. These results represent a considerable achievement, given the school's previous rather dismal record and the fact that the level of social deprivation among its pupils actually increased over the late 1990s. Ofsted described Highbury Grove as an 'effective and improving' school. The head teacher's leadership is 'very good'. GCSE results, though still well below average, show good signs of improvement. Above average results are achieved in ICT, PE, and Turkish. Pupils studying two or more subjects at A-level averaged 190 points in 2002, placing the school first in the borough. The sixth form is run in conjunction with Highbury Fields and offers 15 A-levels and five GNVQs. In the sixth form, GNVQ results were slightly above the national average. Except for a disruptive minority, Inspectors found behaviour to be 'satisfactory' in most lessons.

## Extra-curricular activities

Ofsted found the school's provision for extra-curricular activites to be 'very good'. Activities on offer are boosted by a youth club on site. They include street hockey and photography, and homework, 'bookworm' and other clubs. The drama club puts on regular productions, and members of the environmental club help look after the school grounds. Latin is taught after school. The school has a strong record at sport, especially football and won the Sports Council Sportsmark Award. Other sporting activities include basketball, swimming, dance, netball and girls' football. Tuition is available in a range of instruments, as well as bands and ensembles. There are school trips, both locally and abroad.

# Holloway School

**Hilldrop Road, London N7 OJG** 020 7607 5885 020 7700 3697 Holln7@rmplc.co.uk atschool.eduweb.co.uk Dr John Hudson B.Sc, M.Sc, M.Phil, Ph.D; Chair of Governors: Peter Rees Kentish Town Kentish Town, Tufnell Park, Caledonian Road **Buses:** C11, C12, 4, 10, 17, 27, 29, 43, 253, 259, 279 Black blazer and trousers, white shirt, school tie **Demand:** 111 applications for 180 places in 2001/2 **Type:** Community comprehensive for 690 boys and girls, aged 11 to 16 **Submit application form:** 28 November 2003 **Motto:** *Persequere* (Persevere) **School hours:** 8.40am–3pm; homework clubs are available **Meals:** Hot and cold available **Strong GCSE subjects:** Music, sport **London league table position:** 521

## Profile

'A sink school...now buoyant' was how the local paper described Holloway in 2000, and it has certainly made some remarkable progress since the mid-1990s. Under the new head appointed in 1997, the school has had a makeover both of its culture and facilities. A £4-million building programme is revamping its previously depressing premises. This will provide state-of-the-art IT facilities and a new library as well as upgrading all specialist provision. A new sports hall and all-weather football pitch are also planned. Among its innovations, Holloway is pioneering a web site that allows parents to check pupils' progress online. A Yamaha music school was also opened on the site in 1999. The school runs an ethnic minorities achievement department and has a coordinator for gifted and talented students, as well as an established mentor system. There is a school council and a system 'rather like prefects'. There is provision for special-needs pupils. One sign of how things have improved is the truancy rate, now at 0.7 per cent and below the national average. Perhaps the biggest change for Holloway came in 2002 when girls were admitted. Famous ex-pupils include Jazzie B of the band Soul II Soul.

## Admissions and intake

Admission is through the LEA. At the time of writing, any applicant putting the school as a first choice will be admitted. If that situation changes, priority will then be given to siblings, then to those living closest to the school.

## Achievement

In 1995, Holloway obtained one of the worst GCSE results in Britain, with 9.8 per cent of pupils gaining five A*–C grades. It was notorious for bad behaviour and in 1996 Ofsted put the school under 'special measures'. The following year a new head was appointed and is credited with steering the school towards a more hopeful future. Results are still poor, and the school continues to find it hard to recruit teachers. However, in 1999, Ofsted removed it from its list of failing schools. In 2002, 20 per cent of pupils obtained five or more A*–C grades at GCSE, which was up from 12 per cent in 2001. The school came bottom of the borough league table. Confidence in the school faltered in 2000 when the head was asked to take over temporarily at Islington Arts and Media, but he has since returned. In 2001, Ofsted described Holloway as an 'effective and improving school' with 'much good teaching'. Pupils were seen to make 'satisfactory progress in their learning'. Pupils mostly attend Islington Sixth Form or North London College for sixth-form studies.

## Extra-curricular activities

Extra-curricular activities are boosted by a youth centre on site. A theatre company that stages regular drama productions is based at the school. Holloway won the Islington Public Speaking Contest and the London Debating Competition. Sport includes a very successful basketball team. There are homework and subject clubs and a chess group. Foreign trips include visits to New York, Berlin, Amsterdam and Barcelona.

# The Islington Arts and Media School

**Turle Road, London N4 3LS** 020 7281 5511 020 281 5514 iams@iams.net www.iams.net Richard Ewen B.Sc, MA; Chair of Governors: Richard Reiser / Finsbury Park **Buses:** W3, W7, 4, 19, 29, 91, 106, 168A, 210, 236, 253, 259, 279 Designed in conjunction with pupils and staff **Demand:** 142 first-choice applications for 180 places in 2001/2 **Type:** Community comprehensive for 800 mixed pupils rising to 1100, aged 11 to 18 **Submit application form:** 28 November 2003 **School hours:** 8.45am–3.30pm **Meals:** Hot and cold available **Strong GCSE subjects:** Art, English **London league table position:** 519

## Profile

Islington Arts and Media School was opened in 1999 under the government's 'Fresh Start' scheme to replace the George Orwell comprehensive, and a 'super-head' was appointed. However, the school was in chaos when it opened in September – there was no hot water, no hot food, the toilets failed to work, and there were clashes between pupils. The head resigned and a temporary replacement made some headway in improving things. However, in 2000 Ofsted were still worried by the standard of teaching and behaviour and put the school back onto 'special measures'. It was also revealed that the school had a budget deficit of £250,000. Despite this, £2 million has been spent on refurbishment of the school buildings and a further £3.8 million is being spent on new science, technology, dance, drama and PE facilities. A new, well-regarded head teacher took over in 2000 and when the school reopened in September 2000 it was much more orderly. Inspectors revisted the school in 2002 and recommended it be removed from special measures. The school has provisions for pupils with special needs. There is a PTA.

## Admissions and intake

Admission is through the LEA. Priority is given to those applicants with siblings at the school, then to those living nearest to the school.

## Achievement

IAMS is struggling with the problems of poverty and a transient school population. Even so, its current state is also a result of previous poor management and teaching. In 2002, 23 per cent of pupils achieved five or more A*–C grades at GCSE. This was an increase on 22 per cent in 2001 and the school was ranked ninth in the borough. These improved results were boosted by a more positive Ofsted report which described the school as being 'successful in providing for its pupils in very challenging circumstances'. Standards of attainment were seen to be improving, although still well below average and the quality of teaching was found to be 'satisfactory or better in 40 out of 47 lessons, including 31 where the teaching was good, very good or excellent'. Pupils with special educational needs and those with English as an additional language receive 'effective support' and make 'good, sometimes very good' progress. Inspectors praised the school's distinctive curriculum with its emphasis on the arts and media. It was seen to have developed good links with artists, performers and arts agencies, and to provide 'exciting learning opportunities'. Attendance had improved but is still low at 89 per cent.

## Extra-curricular activities

The school sees these activities as 'an extension programme' for pupils and promises a wide array of clubs, particularly in dance, drama, music and other performing arts. After-school arts and media courses will also be open to the wider community, and trips are organized for theatre shows. There is also a skiing trip. Pupils are involved in fund-raising for charities within the community.

# Islington Green School

**Prebend Street, London N1 8PQ** 020 7226 8611 020 7226 9363 admin@staff.islingtongreen.islington.sch.uk www.islingtongreen.islington.sch.uk Trevor Averre-Beeson; Chair of Governors: Cecilia Darker Essex Road Angel **Buses:** 4, 19, 30, 38, 43, 43X, 56, 73, 76, 141, 171A, 271 White shirt, school tie and sweatshirt, black or grey trousers or skirt **Demand:** 295 first-choice applications for 180 places in 2001/2 **Type:** Community comprehensive for 1050 mixed pupils, aged 11 to 16 **Submit application form:** 28 November 2003 **School hours:** 8.40am–3.10pm; homework clubs are available **Meals:** Hot and cold available **Strong GCSE subjects:** Art, drama **London league table position:** 470

### Profile

Islington Green seems to be bouncing back after some difficult years. In 1998, an Ofsted report slammed the school, saying that 'an unacceptably high proportion of teaching was unsatisfactory or poor'. Bullying was also bad and the school was put on 'special measures'. A 'super-head', Marion Parsons, was appointed the following year and turned the school around. In 2000 it was taken off the list of failing schools. The head's dynamic approach was typified by the immediate introduction of the 'dial-a-dreamer' scheme – teachers and governors gathered at school every morning to put in wake-up calls to those pupils persistently late for class. A new head teacher has now been installed. There is setting in all subjects. IT is used throughout the curriculum with wide access to networked computers. There is a good library and recently upgraded science labs. A weekly newsletter is sent home and a friends of the school association encourages parental involvement. There is a school council. However, truancy is still a problem. In 2000, it was at 3.7 per cent, down from 5.7 per cent but still high. Famous ex-pupils include the actress Pauline Quirke.

### Admissions and intake

Admission is through the LEA. If oversubscribed, priority is given to those with siblings at the school, then to those living closest to it, measured by the shortest walking distance. About 36 per cent of pupils have special educational needs.

### Achievement

In 2000, Ofsted inspectors revisited Islington Green and found 'vast improvements' in behaviour and teaching. The school's new spirit can be seen in its well-designed web site and the optimism of many teachers and pupils. But there is still, as the school itself recognizes, a long way to go. In 2002, 27 per cent of pupils obtained five or more A*–C grades at GCSE, up from 24 per cent in 2001. The school was ranked seventh in the borough league table. Most pupils go on to the Islington Sixth Form Centre, part of City and Islington College, where they are guaranteed places.

### Extra-curricular activities

Activities available include subject and homework clubs, as well as access to computers. There are also revision schemes in the holidays. Football, basketball and tennis are strong on the sports side. Tuition in dance and musical instruments is also available. There are language trips to France, Germany and Italy, in addition to a regular geography field trip. All Year 10 pupils go on work experience and local employers are involved in business studies GCSEs and GNVQs

## Italia Conti Academy of Theatre Arts

**23 Goswell Road, London EC1M 7AJ** ☎ 020 7608 0044 Fax 020 7253 1430 e cliffvote@italiaconti.co.uk www.italia-conti.co.uk Head: CK Vote BA, Dip.Ed; Chair of The Italia Conti Academy of Theatre Arts Ltd: EM Sherwood ⊖ Barbican **Buses:** 4, 5, 55, 243, 277 Uniform: Royal blue blazer, pale blue shirt or blouse, grey trousers or royal blue and white kilt, school tie **Demand:** c.300 children audition for up to 20 places **Type:** Selective independent for 79 mixed pupils, aged 10 to 16, with separate courses offered at ages 16 and 18 **Fees:** £2,370 per term; £3,250 (Age 16+) **Submit application form:** December 2003 **School hours:** 9.15am–4.15pm **Meals:** Hot and cold available **Strong GCSE subjects:** All comparably strong **London league table position:** 115

### Profile

The academy, Britain's first school of performing arts, was founded in 1911 by actress Italia Conti. It is housed in a modern nine-storey block near the Barbican. There is a library and art room but much of the building is dedicated to dance, acting and singing studios. Pupils also use facilities at the school's previous premises in Stockwell. These include a fully equipped modern theatre and a 24-track recording studio of professional quality. There is a prefects system and a head girl and boy. The academy also offers part-time courses to 3- to 18-year-olds. The small size of the school means there is plenty of individual attention and pastoral care. The school has excellent links with all branches of the theatre, cinema and media. Many of its pupils are working professionally even before they leave school and are automatically represented by the Italia Conti Agency. Its famous theatrical ex-pupils include: Noel Coward, Gertrude Lawrence, Sadie Frost, Patsy Kensit, Emily Lloyd, Roy Marsden, Gabrielle Anwar and Julia Sawalha.

## Admissions and intake

Candidates must submit a full-length photograph and previous school reports. At audition they must perform two short acting pieces, three dances and one song. They and their parents will be interviewed and children may also be required to sit a school room test. There are 14 Saturday schools associated with the school that can help candidates prepare for audition. As well as plenty of talent, pupils – and their families – have to have lots of dedication and a disciplined approach to both performing and academic study.

## Achievement

The academy is considered to be in the top three or four performing arts schools in Britain. It grooms pupils for success on the stage, in television, film and pop. Although not all pupils become household names, most go on to become performers, with others involved backstage or behind the camera. However, academic work is taken seriously. Unlike some theatre schools, half of each day is kept clear for class work and there is at least two hours a day of homework. This is in addition to the requirements for practice in the performing arts, 'which is why,' the school says, 'we interview the parents – they will need to be able to support children through it all'. In 2002, 95 per cent of pupils obtained five or more A*–C grades. This was a big increase on 81 per cent in 2001 and the school was ranked at the top of the GCSE borough league table. A few pupils take A-levels and in 2002 the average point score was 105. However, a far larger number take the performing arts course at age 16. Pupils have to re-audition for this course along with any newcomers.

## Extra-curricular activities

The school's full programme of theatre arts and academic study does not allow much time for extra activities. However, pupils may find themselves involved in events outside school. These have included the Royal Variety Performance, the Lord Mayor of London's show and the Children in Need appeal. There are many theatre trips.

# Mount Carmel RC Technology College for Girls

**Holland Walk, Duncombe Road, London N19 3EU** ☎ 020 7281 3536 Fax 020 7281 0420 e office@mountcarmel.islinton.sch.uk Head Christine Eisen MA; Chair of Governors: Paul Smith Rail Upper Holloway Tube Archway **Buses:** C11, C12, 4, 10, 41, 43, 91, 149, 143, 210, 263, 271 Uniform Grey jumper with red piping, pink and white blouse, grey skirt **Demand:** 265 first-choice applications for 140 places in 2001/2 **Type:** Voluntary aided Roman Catholic comprehensive Technology College for 670 girls, aged 11 to 16 **Submit application form:** 28 November 2003 **Motto:** Under the Shadow of Carmel **School hours:** 8.50am–3.30pm **Meals:** Hot and cold available, including breakfast **Strong GCSE subjects:** Art, English, music **London league table position:** 252

## Profile

Mount Carmel is by Islington standards a success story. Under an energetic head it has improved a great deal in recent years. In 2000 it was awarded Technology College status. The school's site is cramped, with its brick buildings hemmed in by council estates and terraced streets. During the 1990s, £3 to £4 million was spent on improving facilities, which include two sports halls and new science labs. IT resources are now being boosted by up to £200,000 of Technology College money. The school likes to see staff and pupils as 'part of an extended family' and pastoral care is a real strength, with good links to outside services. There is an active PTA. Mount Carmel has worked hard at building up links with industry and it provides all Year 10 pupils with two weeks' work experience. There is a prefect system and a school council, as well as 'paired reading' schemes where older girls help younger ones. There is provision for special needs pupils. Regular church services are held and there are good links with a nearby Roman Catholic Church. The school has a truancy rate of only 0.4 per cent. This is a great improvement on previous years and was achieved by a vigorous anti-truancy policy implemented by the staff, with the cooperation of parents.

## Admissions and intake

Priority is given, in order, to: baptized Roman Catholics resident in the Deaneries of Islington, Camden, Hackney and Haringey; those resident elsewhere but for whom Mount Carmel is the nearest RC school with places; other baptized

Roman Catholics; and other Christians whose application is supported by a minister. About 70 per cent of pupils going into Year 7 have a reading age below their actual age.

## Achievement

Mount Carmel is a well-run, well-staffed school that continues to build on the improvements of the late 1990s. In 2002, 58 per cent of pupils obtained five or more A*–C grades, up from 35 per cent in 2001. The school was ranked second in the borough league table. When Ofsted visited the school in 1998, they found almost all lessons were satisfactory and 19 per cent were very good or better. English was especially strong, owing to a strong emphasis on literacy and despite the low reading ages of some pupils on entry. Results in music and art were also above the national average. Inspectors were impressed by the girls' good behaviour and positive attitudes. They commented on the school's racial harmony and the way girls were encouraged to develop a sense of responsibility. Pastoral care and careers advice were described as very good, and praise was given to the links made with parents, the community and industry. Inspectors credited much of this to the 'courage and determination' of an 'outstanding' head, supported by able deputies.

## Extra-curricular activities

Clubs available include sports, aerobics, drama, dance, computer and art and media studies. The school library opens before and after school and in break time. The school also has its own choir. School trips are arranged to Wales and France.

# St Aloysius' RC College

**30 Hornsey Lane, Highgate, London N6 5LY** 020 7263 1391 020 7263 5963 Michael Pittendreigh B.Ed, Cert.Ed; Chair of Governors: Francis Ayers Archway **Buses:** C11, W5, 10, 43, 91, 134, 143, 210, 263, 271 Up to sixth form: Green blazer, grey trousers, white shirt, school tie **Demand:** 294 first-choice applications for 180 places in 2001/2 **Type:** Voluntary aided Roman Catholic comprehensive for 950 boys, aged 11 to 19 **Submit application form:** 28 November 2003 **Motto:** *Beati Mondo Gorge* (Blessed Are the Pure in Heart) **School hours:** 8.45am–3.30pm, 8.45–3pm (Tues); homework clubs are available **Meals:** Hot and cold available **Strong GCSE subjects:** Art, drama, music **London league table position:** 464

## Profile

St Aloysius' College is situated in a prosperous residential street near to Highgate's Waterlow Park. Its buildings are an unprepossessing mixture of brick, concrete and glass but are reasonably well kept. It is a Roman Catholic school whose facilities include a music suite and computer studies centre. There are two gyms on site with 13 acres of playing fields located 10 minutes away from the school. The school is strong at cricket and especially soccer, with 27 ex-pupils signed by professional clubs. Mass is celebrated regularly and there are opportunities to go on retreat. Pastoral care includes a chaplaincy team. Truancy was a problem but has been reduced from 2 per cent in 1999 to 1.2 per cent in 2000. Famous ex-pupils include West Ham football player, Joe Cole. There is a PTA and a school council.

## Admissions and intake

Applicants are interviewed and sit an assessment test, placing them into three ability bands: 45 pupils are admitted from the above average category, 90 pupils from the average category and 45 pupils from the below average category. Within each band priority is given, in order, to those applicants with: evidence of practising Catholicism, evidence of Catholicism, evidence of the practise of another faith, special medical or educational needs and distance from the school. Pupils are drawn from a wide area and tend to come from less affluent homes than those that face directly onto the school.

## Achievement

St Aloysius hit a bad patch in the early and mid-1990s. It has improved following the appointment of a new head, who acted against some poor teachers and brought the school budget back into the black. It is 'an improving school...robustly tackling its weaknesses', according to an Ofsted report in 1997. GCSE results have recovered a good deal, although they are still low. In 2002, 30 per cent of pupils obtained five or more A*–C grades, up two per cent from 2001's results. The school ranked sixth in the GCSE borough league table. Art, music and drama are good with pupils doing better than the national average. Few sixth-formers take A-levels but GNVQ results have been strong. Those pupils taking two or more subjects at A-level averaged 50.8 points, placing the school fifth in the borough league table. More than 12 A-level subjects and GNVQs are offered in the sixth form which also admits girls. Ofsted found lessons at the school were variable; 40 per cent were good or better. There were some weaknesses, especially for lower-attaining pupils, which the school has since tackled. Teaching tended to improve higher up the school. The boys were 'attentive and diligent' and 'enthusiastic'. Inspectors were impressed by the standard of pastoral care and the leadership of the head teacher was considered 'excellent'.

## Extra-curricular activities

Sports available include orienteering, table tennis and gymnastics as well as cricket and football, at which the college has previously won the London championships. There is an annual pilgrimage to Europe and a skiing holiday. There are also homework clubs, drama and music clubs. Pupils work with the local community, for example with the St Vincent de Paul charity.

# Kensington and Chelsea

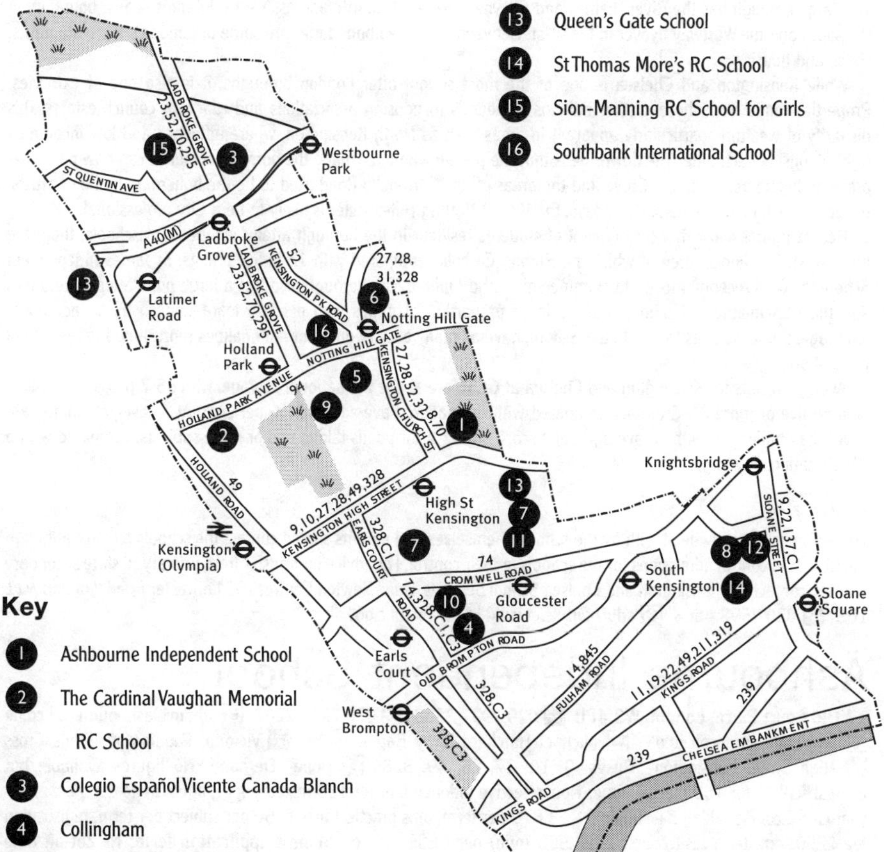


12 More House School
13 Queen's Gate School
14 St Thomas More's RC School
15 Sion-Manning RC School for Girls
16 Southbank International School

**Key**

1 Ashbourne Independent School
2 The Cardinal Vaughan Memorial RC School
3 Colegio Español Vicente Canada Blanch
4 Collingham
5 David Game College
6 Davies Laing and Dick College
7 Duff Miller College
8 Hellenic College of London
9 Holland Park School
10 Lycée Français
11 Mander Portman Woodward School

# Factfile

**LEA: Town Hall, Hornton Street, London W8 7NX** 020 7937 5464 www.rbkc.gov.uk **Director of Education:** Mrs Jackie Griffin **Political control of council:** Conservative **Percentage of pupils from outside the borough:** 38 per cent **Percentage of pupils educated outside the borough:** 27.2 per cent **London league table positions (out of 32 boroughs):** 8th

## Profile

This large borough has the River Thames and Cheyne Walk – a favourite address with celebrities – as a boundary in the south and the Westway flyover in the West. Between these two boundaries are some of London's top restaurants, shops and housing.

While Kensington and Chelsea is one of the most sought-after London boroughs, it is also one of extremes. Properties range from those costing millions of pounds to housing associations and rundown council estates. This disparity of wealth is particularly apparent in areas such as North Kensington, where affluence and low income sit right alongside each other. The downside is that the people who once made the borough colourful can now no longer afford to live there. Ladbroke Grove and the areas off the Portobello Road used to be the bohemian home of artists, musicians, actors and writers. Nowadays, the typical Notting Hill-dweller is likely to be a City professional.

Recent figures show that 52 per cent of students resident in the borough attend independent schools; there are just five state schools, three of which are Roman Catholic, compared with 12 independents. St James Independent School for Girls recently moved to Hammersmith and Fulham. The borough also has a large population of refugees and the LEA-maintained schools have a large proportion of pupils who need to learn English as an additional language. Some, such as Holland Park School, have as many as 100 different nationalities represented in the school population.

Average results for Kensington and Chelsea at GCSE are above the national average, with 55.7 per cent of pupils gaining five or more A*–C grades, compared with the national average of 51.6 per cent. At A-level, standards are lower than nationally, with an average point score of 231.4 for pupils taking two or more subjects, compared with a 254.5 national average.

## Policy

Admissions are mostly dealt with by the schools themselves and parents should contact the schools directly, although the LEA does control admissions for the schools in their control. For advice on transfer from primary to state secondary schools, contact the Kensington and Chelsea School Services, Isaac Newton Centre, 108 Lancaster Road, London W11 1QS 020 7598 4868 educr@rbkc.gov.uk www.rbkc.gov.uk.

# Ashbourne Independent School

**17 Old Court Place, London W8 4PL** 020 7937 3858 020 7937 2207 admin@ashbournecoll.co.uk www.ashbournecoll.co.uk Michael Hatchard-Kirby Bap.Sc, M.Sc Victoria, Paddington, Kings Cross High Street Kensington **Buses:** 9, 10, 27, 28, 49, 328 None **Demand:** No figures available but oversubscribed for 150 places **Type:** Non-selective independent for 138 mixed pupils, aged 14 to 19 **Fees:** Two-year GCSE course taking 5+ subjects – £3,870 per term, plus practical fees £150 per subject per term, registration fee £250; one-term resit course – £2,500 (min) per GCSE subject **Submit application form:** No cut-off date **Mission statement:** To establish strong academic foundations, achieve outstanding examination results and engender a mature and independent attitude, vital for taking advantage of life's opportunities **School hours:** 9am–6pm; homework clubs are available **Meals:** None **Strong GCSE subjects:** Sciences **London league table position:** 454

## Profile

Ashbourne College was established in 1982 and is housed in a shared 1900s Edwardian department store building just off Kensington High Street. It has built up an enviable reputation in preparatory tuition for medicine, law and psychology. Accommodation consists of four student hostels with wardens on call 24 hours a day. Three of the hostels are within walking distance of the college. Rooms are usually doubles, and singles need to be booked well in advance. The hostels also provide laundry facilities. The medical school programme offers specialist help not only in academic study but also in mock interviews and other aspects of applying to medical school. Class sizes are a maximum of 10 and an average of five to six students. This enables tutors to identify weaknesses and act accordingly. Each week, a senior member of staff reviews pastoral care and support, as well as students' performance. The college has special provision for dyslexics but it does not have any wheelchair access. Teachers work closely with parents.

## Admission and intake

Applications are considered case by case. The college actively seeks overseas students. This ensures a lively mix of nationalities and helps engender greater cultural awareness. To encourage overseas students, the University of Nottingham offers an exclusive £750 scholarship to Ashbourne students from selected countries. This goes towards their first year of undergraduate study at the university. Although the school specializes in two-year GCSE courses, they can take younger students on specially arranged programmes.

## Achievement

Ashbourne's GCSE results vary greatly from year to year, and in 2002, 42 per cent of pupils achieved five or more A*–C grades. This was down from 57 per cent in 2001 and below the borough and national averages. The school was ranked 13th in the borough league table. Ashbourne's A-levels results are also below the borough average for two or more A/AS-levels, with an average point score of 231.4 in 2002. These results placed the college 10th in the borough league table. A strength of Ashbourne College is its very wide range of subjects available at A-level, such as classical languages, modern languages including Arabic, Chinese, Japanese and Thai, a wide range of science, sports science, and fine and applied arts, including fashion design. There is also a strong business and finance programme, which offers accountancy, economics and law, as well as business studies. Art and design is another strength, with courses available in fine and applied arts, ranging from sculpture to animation. The medical programme's detailed preparation for applying to medical school appears to pay off as 65 per cent of applicants seeking medical school places have been successful.

## Extra-curricular activities

Pupils are encouraged to organize their own after-school activities, such as homework clubs and basketball. There is a European trip for the lower sixth every year during half term. Trips to the theatre, exhibitions and places of interest are also arranged. Pupils stage a fashion show for charity.

# The Cardinal Vaughan Memorial RC School

**89 Addison Road, London W14 8BZ** 020 7603 8478 020 7602 3124 mail@cvms.co.uk www.cvms.co.uk Mr Michael A Gormally BA, ACP, FRSA; Chair of Governors: Rev Vincent Brady Kensington Olympia Kensington Olympia, Shepherd's Bush, Holland Park **Buses:** 12, 49, 94, 220, 295 Black blazer and trousers, white shirt, grey pullover; Sixth form: Grey suit, white shirt, school tie (boys); maroon blazer, cream blouse, grey skirt (girls) **Demand:** 300 applications for 120 places in 2002 **Type:** Voluntary aided Roman Catholic for 865 boys (220 in mixed sixth form), aged 11 to 18 **Submit application form:** October 2003 **Mission statement:** We believe in the formation of the whole man: his intellect, his heart, his will, his character and his soul. **School hours:** 8.30am–3.30pm; homework clubs are available **Meals:** Hot and cold available **Strong GCSE subjects:** Maths **London league table position:** 89

## Profile

Founded in 1914 as a private school, Cardinal Vaughan is now state-funded and situated in a sought-after residential area. It comprises two sites on opposite sides of Addison Road, one Victorian block and a 1970s block with the new Pellegrini building. The condition and maintenance of the buildings are good but the premises are verging on the cramped side. There are five labs and a three-storey arts and technology centre. The school places a strong emphasis on arts and music, particularly since the establishment of the Vaughan Centre for Young Musicians. Pupils are encouraged to learn musical instruments. There is also a strong vocational education department, which has been made a Centre of Excellence for work-related learning and was awarded a Platinum Award for Excellence in 1999. High-profile companies, including the BBC, HM Customs & Excise, the Isaac Newton Centre and the Kensington Hilton, offer support, advice and work-experience places. Sport is also encouraged – there are six football teams and the school has a reputation for producing outstanding rowers. Former pupils Gary Herbert and Martin Cross both won gold for rowing in the Olympics. Facilities are also offered for athletics, cricket, swimming, fencing and karate. RE is taught throughout the school. Pupils are streamed on entry, but special-needs and gifted students are included in ordinary classroom teaching and given specialized help. Parents are encouraged to participate in the school and receive information on pupils' progress. There is a school council and a prefects system.

### Admissions and intake

The governors seek to admit pupils from across the ability range of above average, average and below average, maintaining a ratio of 2:2:1. They take account of the following criteria: practising Roman Catholic families; children with brothers or sisters attending the school; and, in exceptional circumstances, Catholic applicants with medical or pastoral needs. Up to 10 per cent of places are offered to Catholic children who are musically gifted. Primary school feeders are St Joseph's, St Charles, St Francis of Assisi, Our Lady of Victories and Pope John. The governors propose to admit 50 external pupils, girls and boys, annually to the sixth form, provided they meet the required academic qualifications. Places may also be offered to non-Catholics.

### Achievement

The school's GCSE results are consistently nearly double the national average for five or more A*–C grades, with 89 per cent in 2002. The school was ranked fourth in the borough. Results are above both the borough and national average for pupils taking two or more A/AS-levels, with an average of 301 points in 2002, the third best result locally. In 2002, Ofsted described Cardinal Vaughan as 'a very successful school where pupils attain exceptionally high standards as a result of very good teaching coupled with very good leadership'. Pupils can take GNVQs.

### Extra-curricular activities

Cardinal Vaughan has a variety of choirs, including a barbershop group, and possesses two three-manual Coperman-Hart organs. Every year, a week is devoted to activities such as music, sports, chess and computers. The school also offers a homework centre, with after-school homework clubs. Apart from the regular sports, pupils can learn fencing and participate in the Army Cadet Corps and the Duke of Edinburgh's Award scheme. Skiing trips are also arranged.

## Colegio Español Vicente Canada Blanch

**317 Portobello Road, London W10 5SZ** ☎ 020 8969 2664 Fax 020 8968 9432 Head teacher/Chair of Governors: Albert Vitria ⊖ Ladbroke Grove, Westbourne Park **Buses:** 7, 23, 52, 295 **Demand:** No figures available but oversubscribed **Type:** Non-selective independent for 405 mixed pupils, aged 4 to 19 **Fees:** If pupil has a Spanish passport there is no fee, otherwise it is £800 per term **Submit application form:** Contact school for details **School hours:** 9am–3.30pm; homework clubs are available **Meals:** Hot and cold available **Strong GCSE subjects:** Information not available **London league table position:** Not available

### Profile

The Colegio Español Vicente Canada Blanch was opened in 1972 in Greenwich and was named after its major benefactor, the businessman Vicente Canada Blanch. It is a Spanish state school so there is no fee for pupils with a Spanish passport. In 1982, the college moved into its present premises, a former Dominican convent in the Portobello Road. The former chapel has been converted into a well-stocked library, and other facilities include an IT room, a technical workshop, art and music rooms, two large labs for the natural sciences, physics and chemistry, and a gym. The cloisters and the garden in the centre form a pleasant place for study and relaxation. The school provides education from kindergarten to baccalaureate level, and the majority of pupils are from Spanish families living in the UK. The syllabus comes under the Spanish education system, but there is bilingual (Spanish and English) teaching. The qualifications were validated with effect from 1999–2000 as equivalent to, respectively, GCSE and A-level. They will, therefore, be accepted by universities and other schools in both countries. Teachers are fully accredited in Spain. There is a PTA and provision for special-needs pupils.

### Admissions and intake

Parents submit a completed application form, along with a report from the pupil's former school, plus a photocopy of the pupil's passport.

## Achievement

There was a 100 per cent success rate for the Baccalaureate in 2000, in which pupils are examined by a board from Spanish universities.

## Extra-curricular activities

A wide range of sport is on offer, including badminton, swimming and use of the Kensington and Chelsea athletics club. Pupils have the opportunity of work experience in the City. There are trips both at home and abroad, including two trips a year to Spain. There are after-school homework clubs.

# Collingham

**23 Collingham Gardens, London SW5 OHL** ☎ 020 7244 7414 📠 020 7584 2475 (GCSE dept); 020 7370 7312 (A-level dept) ✉ london@collingham.co.uk 🌐 www.collingham.co.uk 👤 Gerald Hattee MA, Dip.Ed 🚆 Kensington Olympia, Victoria, West Brompton 🚇 Earls Court, Gloucester Road, South Kensington **Buses:** 9, 30, 52, 73, 74 None **Demand:** No figures available but fully subscribed for 60 places at GCSE and 200 places for sixth form **Type:** Selective independent for 189 mixed pupils, aged 14 to 19 **Fees:** £3,660 per term (full-time GCSE); fees for A/AS-levels according to number of subjects taken **Submit application form:** No cut-off date **Mission statement:** Our aim is to enable individuals to discover their strengths, set their own goals and develop their potential and confidence. **School hours:** 9.15am–4pm; 9am–5/6pm three times a week in second year; homework clubs are available **Meals:** Soup and sandwiches in sixth form building **Strong GCSE subjects:** Arts, drama, English, photography **London league table position:** 46

## Profile

Collingham was founded in 1975 and is a co-educational GCSE and sixth-form college. The school's main building at Collingham Gardens is a well-maintained late Victorian brick-built property. It was originally a private house but was converted for use as Gibbs Preparatory School in 1925. Extended and refurbished, it now offers 27 classrooms, a large study room, three well-equipped science labs and a computer lab. There is also a cafeteria in the basement. The GCSE building is located at 17 Queen's Gate Place, close to the Natural History Museum. Facilities there are good, with science labs and a computer lab, a darkroom and a computer/audio-visual resource centre. All pupils have access to the Internet and European cable TV. The school timetable allows non-standard combinations of arts and science subjects. Class sizes are five on average at GCSE and eight, occasionally nine, at A/A-S level. With a staff to student ratio of 1:4, all students have a personal tutor who is in contact with both subject tutors and parents. Homework is an important part of study, and emphasis is placed on exam techniques. Collingham offers dyslexia support and tries to accommodate students with disabilities, but it does not have wheelchair access. English as a foreign language is offered to overseas students.

## Admissions and intake

The catchment area tends to be Central and Greater London. Entry is through a personal interview by the director of studies. Admission at A-level is based upon assessment at interview, GCSE results and previous school records.

## Achievement

From 1997–99, the school had excellent GCSE results, with 100 per cent of pupils obtaining five or more A*–C grades. However, in 2000, this dropped considerably to 58 per cent. In 2001 and 2002, results were back to an impressive 100 per cent. The average point score was 55 and the school was ranked second in the borough. The school offers a remarkable range of subjects at both GCSE and A/AS-levels, with a variety of languages including Arabic and Chinese, as well as photography, arts and theatre studies. Vocational subjects offered include art, psychology, law and chemistry. The average point score for pupils taking two or more A/AS-levels was 230.4 in 2002. Approximately 25 per cent of Collingham pupils go on to Oxbridge or a University of London college, with 40 per cent going on to other prestigious universities. The school has strong links with universities in Europe and the US.

## Extra-curricular activities

A full range of sports is on offer, including aerobics. Field trips take place both in the UK and abroad. These trips make use of the proximity of London's resources, including visits to TV studios, the Houses of Parliament, the Law Courts, art galleries, theatres and the French and German institutes. Involvement with charities is encouraged, with pupils organizing an annual sponsored walk. A pupil from the school won the *Independent's* Young Photographer of the Year Award in 1998 and the Kensington and Chelsea Photographer of the Year Award in 2000.

# David Game College

**David Game House, 69 Notting Hill Gate, London W11 3JS** 020 7221 6665 020 7243 1730 davidgame-group.com www.davidgame-group.com David Game MA (Oxon), M.Phil (London) Paddington Notting Hill Gate **Buses:** 12, 27, 28, 31, 52, 70, 94, 302 None **Demand:** No figures available but oversubscribed for 80 places for GCSE level **Type:** Non-selective independent for 288 mixed pupils, aged 13 to 19 **Fees:** GCSE £1,730–£8,300 depending on the number of subjects studied and the length of course; A-levels £2,660–£8,610 per year; 1 year A-level course £3,470–£9,100; University Foundation course – £6,950 per year **Submit application form:** No cut-off date **School hours:** 9am–6pm, dependent on which subjects taken **Meals:** Hot and cold available **Strong GCSE subjects:** Sciences **London league table position:** Not available

## Profile

David Game College occupies a redesigned and refurbished 1960s building. Set amongst commercial premises in Notting Hill Gate, it is within walking distance of Portobello Road market, Hyde Park and Kensington Gardens. The college was founded in 1974 by David Game, a maths scholar from New College, Oxford University, and part of his collection of contemporary paintings and prints are on display at the school. It has expanded and now has linked colleges throughout the world. David Game House boasts a spacious, well-equipped library, including computer facilities, which is supervised all day, providing a quiet environment conducive to study. The college provides six self-catering residences, each with single or shared rooms, mostly within walking distance. Arrangements can also be made for students to stay with families, who provide breakfast and an evening meal, normally within 30–40 minutes' journey from the college. Overall options at GCSE and A-level are both academic and business-orientated. The GCSE programme comprises of 20–25 hours of tuition each week, with students scheduled to spend a further five hours studying. Attendance is closely monitored and class sizes are no more than 10. The college does not have special-needs provision but it does have wheelchair access. The director of studies provides pastoral care for pupils. There is a prefects system and a school council.

## Admissions and intake

Applicants should contact the school. A deposit is required.

## Achievement

In 2001, 25 per cent of pupils achieved five or more passes at A–C grades. This was an improvement on 2000 where no pupils gained an A–C pass. However, these results were below the borough and national averages, and the school was ranked bottom of the borough league table. David Game's wide interest in languages is reflected in the variety of the school's curriculum, with Arabic to Urdu offered among an extensive range of GCSEs and A-levels. The average point score for pupils taking two or more A/AS-levels was 20.4 in 2001, above the borough and national averages, ranking the school sixth in the borough. The college website boasts favourable comments from former students and a strong list of university achievements. This could be in part attributed to the fast-track-routes-to-university programme. The University Foundation Programme is designed to provide a guaranteed pathway to the first year of most UK degree courses and the University Diploma Programme leads into the second year of various UK degree courses. The college also hopes to offer the International Baccalaureate Diploma in the future.

## Extra-curricular activities

Various outings and trips take place during the year, and these tend not to be included in the fees. Sports are encouraged; there is a football team and the facilities of Imperial College are available for use. Table tennis, pool and chess are on offer in David Game House, along with a cinema club in-house, showing the latest films. The school supports a number of charities and encourages students to become involved in fund-raising activities. There are trips both at home and abroad.

# Davies Laing and Dick College

**10 Pembridge Square, London W2 4ED** 020 7727 2797 020 7792 0730 dld2@dld.org www.dld.org Elizabeth Rickards; Chair of Governors: Sir Angus Fraser Paddington Notting Hill Gate, Bayswater, Queensway **Buses:** 12, 27, 28, 52, 94, 328 None **Demand:** No figures available but oversubscribed **Type:** Selective independent for 307 mixed pupils, aged 14 to 19 **Fees:** £12,225 per annum **Submit application form:** No cut-off date **Mission statement:** Building the confidence of students really makes the difference **School hours:** 9am–5.45pm **Meals:** Sandwiches and snacks are available **Strong GCSE subjects:** Art, English, maths, sciences **London league table position:** 272

## Profile

Founded in 1931 for intensive tuition, Davies Laing and Dick College has developed into a group of 10 schools taking pupils from nursery school to age 18. It was a founder member of the Conference for Independent Education (CIFE) and was re-accredited by the British Accreditation Council in 1999. It is located at 10 Pembridge Square, a beautiful, detached Victorian house in a highly sought-after garden square within five minutes' walking distance of Notting Hill Gate. In September 2001, extra premises (in Pembridge Villas, from which St James Independent Girls School moved), came on stream. This allowed the school to increase its GCSE provision, taking pupils from the age of 14 and adding new science labs. There are also plans to improve the already impressive art, music, drama and IT facilities. The school boasts two large, well-equipped computer rooms. A special feature of the school is its Oxbridge preparation, and entry into medicine, veterinary science and dentistry is encouraged. Class sizes are between six and eight. Tutorials are sometimes as much as two hours long and there is fortnightly testing in all subjects. The staff are chosen as much for their ability to communicate with and enthuse pupils as for their own high standards of achievement in their specialization. All pupils have a personal tutor. Support is available for dyslexia and dyspraxia. Pupils sign a contract when they join to encourage an adult approach to study. Former pupils include the author Martin Amis.

## Admissions and intake

The school draws pupils from a 30-mile radius around the school, with some drawn from elsewhere in the UK and abroad. Applicants require grade C at GCSE to study A-levels.

## Achievement

The college continues to make a feature of retakes and performs above the borough average, with 76 per cent of pupils gaining five or more A*–C grades at GCSE in 2002. This was up on 65 per cent in 2001 and the school was ranked 10th in the borough. In 2002, the average point score of 272.4 for pupils taking two or more subjects at A-level, was above the borough and national averages. This placed the school sixth in the borough. A wide variety of A-levels is on offer, including law, music, psychology and sociology.

## Extra-curricular activities

After-school activities include a philosophy club, art, music, drama, foreign languages and a film unit. In 2000, a horror film was made and a broadsheet newspaper produced. The school has access to nearby recreational sports facilities and offers the opportunity to pursue rock climbing. Numerous trips and outings are provided, including scuba-diving and watersports in Greece. Trips pertaining to courses are included in the fees, others are charged at cost. Pupils are encouraged to become involved in fund-raising events for charity.

# Duff Miller College

**59 Queen's Gate, London SW7 5JP** 020 7225 0577 020 7589 5155 enqs@duffmiller.com www.duffmiller.demon.com Mr Clive Denning Kensington Olympia, Victoria High Street Kensington, Gloucester Road, South Kensington **Buses:** 9, 10, 52, 70, 74 None **Demand:** No figures available **Type:** Selective independent for 163 mixed pupils, aged 13 to 19 **Fees:** £1,175–3,650 per term **Submit application form:** No cut-off date **Motto:** Every young person should be treated as an adult, and an individual, not a child. **School hours:** 9am–6pm; homework clubs are available **Meals:** Hot and cold available **Strong GCSE subject:** Sciences **London league table position:** 426

## Profile

Duff Miller was founded in 1952 by Muriel Duff Miller, the wife of a high court judge and a teacher with 20 years' experience in public schools. By the time she retired in 1972, she had established a school known for its small class sizes and its capacity to enable pupils to achieve their full potential. It now has a flourishing sixth form, with average class sizes of around six and a teacher to pupil ratio of 1:6. The college's premises are ideally placed for access to the museums in South Kensington, such as the Natural History Museum and the Victoria and Albert Museum. The school prides itself on an ethos of old-fashioned insistence on academic discipline and hard work. There are no prefects, monitors or detentions and pupils are encouraged to develop self-discipline. Teaching facilities include an art/drama studio, biology, chemistry and physics labs and a fully equipped computer/IT room. All pupils have access to a supervised study room with computer and Internet facilities. Non-standard subjects or combinations of subjects are possible within the curriculum. The college actively encourages work experience and helps pupils to find suitable placements. Students are assigned a personal tutor who provides pastoral care and also acts as a mentor. Provision is available for dyslexic pupils.

## Admissions and intake

Applicants are required to sit the college's own tests. Pupils are drawn from the top third of the academic ability range.

## Achievement

From 1996 to 1998, the percentage of pupils gaining five or more A*–C grades at GCSE rose from 41 per cent to 73 per cent, well above the borough and national average. Since then results have been variable, reaching 46 per cent in 2002, up from 31 in 2001. This is still below the borough and national averages. The school was ranked 12th in the borough. The average point score of pupils taking two or more A/AS-levels rose steadily over the past five years, reaching 237.4 in 2002, placing the school 12th out of 13 in the borough for A-levels. A wide range of A-levels are offered at the school, including accountancy, film studies, classical civilization, archaeology and government and politics. Special features of the curriculum are very good science modules, humanities and modern languages.

## Extra-curricular activities

Activities available have included science and legal excursions, with visits to the Inns of Court and the Old Bailey. There is a full range of sports on offer. Trips to the European Parliament and EU offices in Brussels are organized for pupils studying social sciences, and outings to West End theatres and fringe activities assist drama and theatre students. Field trips take place throughout the year, some of which are subject-related and others peer- and socially based. There are after-school homework clubs.

# Hellenic College of London

**67 Pont Street, London SW1X 0BD** 020 7581 5044 020 7589 9055 head@hellenic.org.uk www.hellenic.org.uk James Wardrobe MA (Oxon) Victoria Knightsbridge, Sloane Square **Buses:** 19, 22, 137 Navy blue blazer, grey trousers or skirt, shirt, school tie; Sixth form: Smart dress **Demand:** No figures available **Type:** Selective Greek Orthodox independent for 167 mixed pupils, aged 11 to 18 (nursery and primary school starts at age 2) **Fees:** £2,999 per term **Submit application form:** No cut-off date **School hours:** 9am–3.30pm **Meals:** Hot and cold available **Strong GCSE subjects:** Greek **London league table position:** 186

## Profile

Hellenic College was founded in 1980 by prominent members of the Greek community in London. It was established to give children of Greek-speaking origin a first-class British education combined with familiarity with their own language, culture and religion. Housed in an elegant Grade II-listed building in the heart of affluent Knightsbridge, the premises are impressive and well maintained. Teaching facilities include 15 classrooms, three well-equipped science labs, a computer science lab, music room and art studio. Sports are an integral part of the curriculum, including soccer, basketball, badminton, tennis, swimming and athletics. The school makes use of local sports facilities such as the Queen Mother Sports Centre, the Latchmere Leisure Centre and Battersea Park. Post GCSE, a work-experience programme helps pupils to make career and study decisions. Strong links are maintained between the school and London's Greek-speaking community and the Greek Orthodox Church. A comprehensive welfare system is available, including counselling and social activities. There is a prefect system and sixth-formers look after younger pupils. Homework diaries are checked periodically by the school and parents are encouraged to check their children's homework diaries. The PTA organizes the annual college bazaar and various cultural events. There is provision for special-needs pupils.

## Admissions and intake

Students either transfer from the Hellenic Primary School or other primary schools. All entrants must pass the school's own English, maths, Greek and verbal reasoning tests before being accepted into the secondary school. Students entering the sixth form must have passed at least five GCSEs at grade C or higher.

## Achievement

From 100 per cent of pupils gaining five or more A*–C grades at GCSE in 1996 and 1997, the school dropped back to 80 per cent in 1999 and 2000, a result repeated in 2002. The school was ranked sixth in the borough. The average point score of pupils taking two or more A/AS-levels was 275.5 in 2002, placing the school fifth in the borough. A strength of the school is its wide range of A-levels that includes art, biology, business studies, classical civilization and physics.

## Extra-curricular activities

The drama department encourages plays to be performed in both Greek and English , the highlight being the annual Greek play on 25 October. There is also a festival of Greek singing and dancing performed in national costume (the school has a collection of over 130 traditional costumes). Sports, societies and hobbies are on offer, such as chess, judo, debating, yoga, dancing, arts and crafts, and a poetry club. Overseas educational trips include participation in the Round Square Conference, an association of schools that upholds ideals of personal development and responsibility through choice, challenge, adventure and international understanding. Field trips and visits to public lectures and places of interest also take place throughout the year. Pupils are encouraged to participate in charity fund-raising events.

# Holland Park School

**Airlie Gardens, Campden Hill Road, London W8 7AF** ☎ 020 7727 5631 📠 020 7908 1098 🌐 www.rbkc.gov.uk/kcservices/education/Holland.htm Mr Colin Hall; Chair of Governors: Terry Furlong ⇌ Kensington Olympia ⊖ High Street Kensington, Holland Park, Notting Hill Gate **Buses:** C1, 9, 9A, 10, 12, 27, 28, 31, 49, 52, 70, 94 Introduced in 2002 for all new pupils: grey zipped overwear shirt, blue or grey T-shirt, black trousers or skirt **Demand:** 471 applications for 240 places in 2002 **Type:** Community comprehensive for 1555 mixed pupils, aged 11 to 18 **Submit application form:** November 2003 **Mission statement:** We seek to enable all individuals to fulfil their potential in a rich, dynamic, international community, full of life, energy and creativity. We expect high standards of achievement and behaviour, which demonstrate care and concern for others. **School hours:** 8.45am–3.25pm; homework clubs are available **Meals:** Hot and cold available **Strong GCSE subjects:** Art, maths, science **London league table position:** 405

## Profile

Founded in 1958, Holland Park was considered a ground-breaking comprehensive, with new teaching methods, and by the late 1960s it had become a fashionable London school. The Labour MP Tony Benn sent his children here, as did a variety of other high-profile parents. It is the only non-denominational state secondary school in the borough. Situated in one of the most affluent parts of central London, it occupies a utilitarian 1950s building. Extensions were added in the 1970s and in 1990 it was extensively refurbished. It offers well-equipped sports facilities, with a swimming pool on site, specialist studios for art and design, drama workshops complete with good audio, video and lighting systems and music studios with digital recording facilities. Several former pupils have gone on to have successful careers in the music business. Parents, students and staff are members of the Holland Park School Association, which arranges discussions and fund-raising activities. There are annual parents' evenings and the head holds weekly surgeries for parents. A newsletter is published each term. Unauthorized absence is quite high at 4.1 per cent. The school has a computerized records system and works closely with the community to try to reduce absenteeism. There is a school council and provision for special-needs pupils.

### Admissions and intake

Admission is through the LEA. If oversubscribed, priority is given to applicants in the following order: siblings of children on the roll; children who live nearest to the school or, in exceptional circumstances, on the grounds of medical or social need. The sixth form welcomes applications. There are more than 100 nationalities represented at the school and about 20 per cent are from refugee or asylum-seeking families.

### Achievement

In 2002, the percentage of pupils gaining five or more A*–C grades at GCSE was 38 per cent, the same as in 2001. The average point score of pupils taking two or more A/AS-levels was 198.5, below the borough average. The school tends to be above average in maths, science and several GNVQ subjects, and outstandingly high in art. It also offers a good range of A-levels, including business studies, government and politics and psychology, as well as GNVQs in art and design and performing arts. In the last Ofsted report in 1997, the school's strengths were identified as a 'safe, supportive and productive background' and inspectors commented: 'The school clearly has a sense of purpose and commitment to encourage a diverse mix of pupils to achieve.'

### Extra-curricular activities

The performing arts are particularly strong, including drama, music and dance. Sport is also popular, including gymnastics, trampolining and participation in local, London and national competitions. There are after-school homework clubs and involvement with local community schemes. There are trips both at home and abroad.

## Lycée Français

35 Cromwell Road, London SW7 2DG ☎ 020 7584 6322 (main switchboard) 📠 020 7823 7684 ✉ conseduca.lon@dial.pipex.com 🌐 www.cec-spain.org.uk/Vcb Andre Brecherand Victoria ⊖ Gloucester Road **Buses:** 49, 74 None **Demand:** No figures available, but 68 places in the British section oversubscribed **Type:** Selective independent for 206 mixed pupils, aged 13 to 19; aged 14 to 18 in British section **Fees:** £1,346 per term **Submit application form:** No cut-off date, submit 6–12 months in advance **School hours:** 8.40am–5.45pm **Meals:** Hot and cold available; three-course French-style meal, which scored highly in Egon Ronay guide **Strong GCSE subjects:** French, maths **London league table position:** 33

### Profile

The Lycée Français was founded in 1915 by Marie Bohn. It was originally located near to Victoria station and had only 120 pupils. In 1920, it moved to Cromwell Gardens, opposite the Victoria and Albert Museum, but soon moved to larger premises in a site between Cromwell Road, Queensberry Place and Harrington Road. It acquired the title Charles de Gaulle in 1980 and has expanded still further, with premises in Clapham Common and Ealing (l'Ecole André Malraux). The school offers the full French curriculum in French to children from French families living in London. However, it now also has a British section, where GCSE and A-levels can be taken in English. There is a PTA and a school council.

### Admissions and intake

The proportion of pupils is roughly 63 per cent French, 21 per cent British and 16 per cent from some 60 other nationalities. Contact the school for details.

### Achievement

The school's GCSE results are rarely below 80 per cent for pupils achieving five or more A*–C grades, and in 2000, 2001 and 2002 they were was impressive 100 per cent. The average point score was 55.7, placing the school at the top of the borough league table. A-level results are above both the borough and national average. In 2002, the average point score for pupils taking two or more A/AS-levels was 385.8. The school was ranked top of the borough league table.

### Extra-curricular activities

There is a wide range of sports on offer. Pupils can take part in a choir and an orchestra. There are trips abroad for skiing and also a historical trip to Prague. There are also local field trips.

# Mander Portman Woodward School

**91 Queen's Gate, London SW7 5NQ** 020 7835 1335 020 7259 2705 london@mpw.co.uk www.mpw.co.uk James Burnett Victoria Gloucester Road **Buses:** 9, 10, 52, 70 None **Demand:** No figures available for 429 places **Type:** Selective independent for 392 mixed pupils, aged 14 to 19 **Fees** (per term): GCSEs in 6 subjects £4,171; 2-year A-level course with 3 subjects £4,178; 1-year A-level course with 3 subjects £4,486 **Submit application form:** No cut-off date **Mission statement:** We have a relaxed and friendly atmosphere, an environment in which those students who may have lost motivation or confidence are able to rediscover and enjoy the traditional values of hard work and academic discipline. **School hours:** 9am–6pm **Meals:** Hot and cold available **Strong GCSE subjects:** All relatively strong **London league table position:** 221

## Profile

The college was founded in 1973 primarily for those pupils needing to retake A-levels and wanting to gain entrance to Oxbridge. It has since become a popular sixth-form college, and there are new, smaller Mander Portman Wood (MPW) colleges in Birmingham and Cambridge. Based in South Kensington, the college operates from three closely situated buildings. The site at 24 Elvaston Place is the home of the maths, science and social science departments, with five science and two computer labs, while visual and performing arts, the GCSE section and academic administration are based at 3 Elvaston Place. The building at 108 Cromwell Road is primarily for arts and humanities. There are student common rooms in each building and cafeterias at the latter two. Assistance with homework is available and is included in the fees. Extra coaching is also on offer and is open to pupils from other schools. Lower sixth-form pupils can take part in a two-day 'insight into management' programme. Class sizes are six on average. Two trained counsellors are available for pastoral care, and there is special-needs provision for a wide range of disabilities, including dyslexia.

## Admissions and intake

Candidates are assessed through a report from their previous school and an exam and interview at the college. Applicants are attracted not only from Greater London, and the college has its own database of student residences and families which offer accommodation.

## Achievement

The percentage of students achieving five or more GCSEs at grades A*–C varies from year to year, but it is consistently above the borough and national averages. In 2002, it was 73 per cent. At A-level, the average point score of students taking two or more subjects is usually above the borough average. In 2002, it was 242.2, just below the national average. The school offers a wide choice of A-levels and GCSEs along with more unusual options such as environmental studies, and graphical and technical communication. There are also specialist retake courses and short-revision programmes, which allow less traditional combinations of subjects. MPW specializes in preparing students for entrance to medical, dental, veterinary and law schools. Each year the college prepares students for entrance to Oxbridge and approximately one in three is successful. The school was first accredited by the British Accreditation Council in 1988, and reaccredited in 1998, when the inspectors were particularly impressed with the 'sense of genuine excitement shared by students and staff alike'.

## Extra-curricular activities

Extra-curricular activities are voluntary for pupils over age 16. Both the college and pupils agree that the main focus should be on studies, but sports, a debating society, charity fund-raising committee, drama and musical productions are on offer. A newspaper is also produced by the lower sixth. Homework is supervised during the day. There is involvement with the local community and fund-raising for charities such as Medicins sans Frontières. There is an art history trip to Italy and various other field trips.

# More House School

**22–24 Pont Street, Chelsea, London SW1X 0AA** 020 7235 2855 020 7259 6782 office@morehouse.org.uk www.morehouse.org.uk Mrs L Falconer; Chair of Governors: Mr Tom Read Victoria Knightsbridge, Sloane Square **Buses:** 11, 19, 22, 137, 211, 319 Up to sixth form: Navy blue blazer and skirt, navy blue and white top **Demand:** No figures available but oversubscribed **Type:** Selective Roman Catholic independent for 366 girls, aged 11 to 18 **Fees:** £2,975 per term **Submit application form:** First week in December 2003 **Mission statement:** To establish an environment where pupils and staff are valued and supported as individuals and where their rights and dignity are maintained; to foster an ethos of spiritual growth, not only for those within the Roman Catholic Church, but also for those who adhere to other Christian traditions and other faiths; to develop the spiritual, academic and cultural potential of each pupil to the full at every stage of her school career in such a way that this development will continue throughout her life; to encourage intellectual curiosity and pride in achievement. The school expects all its members to act with integrity and to be sensitive to the needs of other people. **School hours:** 8.30am–3.40pm; homework clubs are available **Meals:** Hot and cold available, including vegetarian options **Strong GCSE subjects:** Art, music, sciences **London league table position:**

## Profile

More House School was founded in 1953 when a group of Catholic parents asked the Canonesses of St Augustine to open a London day school for their daughters. It moved to its present home in Pont Street in 1971. It is in a highly desirable part of London, close to Harrods and Belgrave Square. The school is part of a well-appointed terrace of Victorian town houses and it is in excellent condition. It has four science labs, an art room and a gym. The library is well-equipped with reference books and also has computers with CD-ROM and multimedia capabilities. Word processing is taught from an early age, progressing to other useful software packages. Class sizes are kept to a maximum of 20. Special-needs provision is made for pupils with speech defects, the partially sighted and hearing-impaired, those with cystic fibrosis and dyslexia, and delicate children. A counsellor provides pastoral care, and there is a close relationship between the school and parents.

## Admissions and intake

Entry is by interview and is also dependant on applicants successfully passing the London Independent Girls' Schools entrance examination. Pupils are drawn from all over Greater and Central London.

## Achievement

In both 1998 and 1999, 100 per cent of pupils gained five or more A*–C grades at More House. In 2002, this dropped to 82 per cent, down from 97 in 2001. The school was ranked fifth in the borough. The average point score for pupils taking two or more A/AS-levels was 281.4 in 2002, higher than the borough and national averages. In addition to the standard academic curriculum, the school also offers Latin, English as a foreign or second language, government and politics, and life skills.

## Extra-curricular activities

A varied range of activities are available, including a choir, orchestra, and jazz dance group, as well as debating and fencing. An after-school homework assistance club is also provided. Sports on offer include cricket, football, volleyball, hockey and swimming. These take place at various venues and are included in the fees. Frequent educational visits are arranged at no extra cost. Pupils in the second and third forms spend a week at a field centre in different parts of the country. There are skiing holidays and a visit to Florence for those studying history of art in the sixth form. Pupils work with charities in the local community.

# Queen's Gate School

**133 Queen's Gate, Kensington, London SW7 5LE** ☎ 020 7589 3587 📠 020 7584 7691 ⓔ registrar@queensgate.org.uk 🌐 www.queensgate.org.uk Mrs A Holyoak; Chair of Governors: Mr David Hurst Kensington Olympia, Victoria ⊖ Gloucester Road, South Kensington **Buses:** 9, 10, 49, 52, 70, 74 None, except for gym and PE, although girls are expected to wear clothing and shoes suitable for school **Demand:** Oversubscribed **Type:** Selective independent for 384 girls, aged 3 to 18 **Fees:** £2,870 per term **Submit application form:** Early December 2003 **Mission statement:** We offer an education for life in a challenging environment where sound values and individuality are nurtured within a supportive atmosphere. **School hours:** 8.40am–3.30pm **Meals:** Hot and cold available, including vegetarian, kosher, vegan and halal **Strong GCSE subjects:** All relatively strong **London league table position:** 88

### Profile

Established in 1891, Queen's Gate School is an educational trust that occupies three splendid Victorian town houses in Queen's Gate. They are beautifully maintained and within walking distance of the Science, Victoria and Albert, and Natural History museums. The school sets out to provide a challenging and rigorous academic target within a secure and happy environment. In addition to academic provision, there is a strong emphasis on music, art and drama. Girls can join in the sixth form to follow a two-year A-level course, and expectation for entry into universities is high. Particular emphasis is put on awareness of career opportunities and requirements. Computer skills are taught from age 13, and visiting speakers provide insights into their own careers. Vocational guidance tests are taken at the beginning of the GCSE year, and pupils are enrolled in the Independent Schools Career Organization, which offers support and guidance through to the age of 23. The teacher-to-pupil ratio is low at 1:7 and class sizes are between 17 and 24 students. Each girl has a form or year tutor who oversees her general progress and well-being. Special-needs provision is available, with help provided for dyslexics. Close relationships with parents are maintained, and girls from Year 3 upwards are invited to regular meetings between school and parents. There is a prefects system.

### Admissions and intake

Candidates sit the London Day Schools' Consortium examination at 11+, but the school has its own entry exam for Years 8, 9, 10 and 11. All prospective pupils are interviewed.

### Achievement

The school achieves results substantially above the borough average, with 86 per cent of pupils gaining five or more GCSEs at A*–C grades in 2002. The lowest result was 73 per cent in 1997. The average point score was 48.5 and the school was ranked third in the borough league table. The average point score for pupils taking two or more A/AS-levels in 2002 was 353.9. This was the second best result in the borough. These results are consistent with previous years' performance. A strength of the school is its well-balanced curriculum with classics, computing and sociology offered alongside modern languages, current affairs, singing and health and sex education. All girls take English language and literature and maths GCSE, with at least one of the four modern languages offered, and a minimum of one science.

### Extra-curricular activities

A wide range of sports is available, including aerobics, fencing, judo, dance, hockey, netball, basketball and volleyball. Courses on health, hygiene and first aid are also on offer. Pupils work with international, national and local charities. They visit elderly people in their homes and have organized a homework club in a local primary school. Regular trips to museums and art galleries are provided to supplement the daily learning process. Study trips are also arranged to Greece, France and Italy to enhance GCSE and A-level study. The library is open until 5pm daily.

## St Thomas More's RC School

**Cadogan Street, London SW3 2QS** ☎ 020 7589 9734 📠 020 7823 7868 ✉ Mr G Connolly B.Comm, MA, NPQH; Chair of Governors: Canon Vincent Berry ⇌ Victoria ⊖ Victoria, Sloane Square **Buses:** 11, 19, 22, 137, 211 👔 Green and grey for girls, black for boys, with white or grey shirt **Demand:** 295 applications for 120 places in 2001/2 **Type:** Voluntary aided Roman Catholic comprehensive for 623 mixed pupils, aged 11 to 16 **Submit application form:** November 2003 **Mission statement:** The mission of St Thomas More's School is to develop as a community of faith – a community in which the teaching of Jesus Christ is the foundation of all that we undertake. This will be evidenced through the example given by staff, through the delivery of the pastoral and academic curriculum and through the expectations that pupils will strive for in excellence. **School hours:** 8.40am–3.25pm; homework clubs are available **Meals:** Hot and cold available **Strong GCSE subjects:** Foreign languages **London league table position:** 201

### Profile

The Sisters of Mercy have provided education in this school since 1845. The early Victorian building surrounding the Church of St Mary has a new addition in yellow brick to match the original. The school has recently invested in updating its IT centre, which has a total of 22 computers. There are also computers in every classroom, and as well as word-processing and spreadsheets, pupils can take part in multimedia production, image manipulation and have

Internet access. From Year 9 onwards, pupils are in contact with the careers department as part of the PHSE programme, and at the end of Year 11 all students undertake two weeks' work experience. Special-needs provision is very good, with support provided by specialist teachers. In 1999, Ofsted commented on the active support offered by parents, including a 'remarkably affirmative parents' evening'. There is a school council that pupils can sit on and also a prefects system.

### Admissions and intake

Applicants must be practising Catholics, come from Catholic families or be considered by their parish priest to have a pastoral need for education in a Catholic school. Demand for places is high and the intake is drawn from nearly 50 primary schools right across London. A high percentage of pupils have English as an additional language and nearly 25 per cent have special needs.

### Achievement

Ofsted noted that the achievement of high GCSE grades was 'well above the average for similar schools'. In 2002, the percentage of pupils gaining five or more grades A*–C was above the borough average at 61 per cent. These results were down from 62 per cent in 2001 and continue a decline in recent years. The school was ranked seventh in the borough league table. Ofsted noted that the prior attainment of the 1999 year group had been lower than previous years. Inspectors highlighted the leadership and vision of the head as a strength, along with spiritual, moral and social development provision, the very good behaviour of pupils and the high level of good and very good teaching. These strengths 'significantly outweigh the weaknesses', namely some weak teaching and low expectations in maths, and a need to develop line management.

### Extra-curricular activities

A full range of gymnastic and keep-fit activities are on offer, along with badminton, football and netball. After-school clubs include homework clubs, dance, music and art. Each year the art department presents an annual fashion show. School trips and outings, organized by the geography department, take place both in the UK and abroad. There is a strong involvement with the community and charities; a senior citizens' music hall, organized and performed by the pupils, is an annual highlight. Pupils can also participate in the Duke of Edinburgh's Award scheme.

# Sion-Manning RC School for Girls

**St Charles Square, London W10 6EL** 020 8969 7111 020 8969 5119 info@ sionmanning.kingston-chelsea.sch.uk CM Leach MA; Chair of Governors: JM O'Donnell Paddington Ladbroke Grove **Buses:** 7, 23, 52, 70, 295, 302 White shirt, grey skirt and blazer, or white shirt, grey skirt and grey sweater **Demand:** 345 first-choice applications for 120 places in 2001/2 **Type:** Voluntary aided Roman Catholic comprehensive for 597 girls, aged 11 to 16 **Submit application form:** November 2003 **Mission statement:** To give every student an education, which will enable her to develop to her fullest potential, academically, personally and spiritually, the means to become a thinking, confident and creative adult to take an effective and positive place in the world and in the life of the Church, and an orderly and disciplined atmosphere, which supports the learning process and the pursuit of excellence. **School hours:** 7.30am–5.30pm; homework clubs are available **Meals:** Hot and cold available **Strong GCSE subjects:** Art, English, music **London league table position:** 238

### Profile

Sion-Manning was formed in 1968 when the Convent of Our Lady of Sion amalgamated with the Cardinal Manning Girls' School. It is situated in a quiet North Kensington Victorian square with little traffic, but its 1960s building, with later additions, is poorly maintained and the surrounding grounds are overgrown. Security cameras are in evidence and facilities include five science labs and an IT room. In 2002, Sion-Maning gained specialist school status in the visual arts. The curriculum meets the demands of the National Curriculum. Art, drama, science, PE and music are specialities, with peripatetic brass, keyboards, percussion, string and woodwind teachers providing individual and group lessons. Music students are entered for the Trinity College and Associated Board of Music exams. RE is compulsory throughout the school and students of all ages take part in religious retreats and visits. Mass for the whole school is provided on holy days of obligation, in addition to weekly Mass (attendance voluntary), and all assemblies have a religious content. Class sizes are a maximum of 30. Provision for learning

English as a Foreign Language (EFL) is available where necessary, and support is given to pupils with dyslexia. Careers education is given to all students, and pupils are interviewed individually by members of the careers service to help them formulate a career plan. Work placements are arranged and encouraged. These have included working alongside dentists, architects, in primary and nursery schools and at an RSPCA animal hospital. All members of staff are involved in providing pastoral care. Parents are kept informed through regular detailed reports. There are regular PTA and parents' meetings, and parents are asked to take a keen interest in homework assignments. Sion-Manning has Beacon School status. There is a school council and a prefects system.

### Admissions and intake

Practising Roman Catholics resident in the Deanery of North Kensington have first preference, but members of other Christian denominations and other faiths may also be accepted. However, these will not normally jointly exceed 10 per cent of the intake. Documentary evidence that Sion-Manning is the first choice of an applicant will increase the priority of an application within each category. All applicants are interviewed.

### Achievement

The percentage of pupils achieving five or more A*–C grades at GCSE was above the national average in 2002 at 55 per cent and in line with the borough average. This was three per cent up from 2001's results and the school was ranked ninth in the borough league table. Many pupils go to St Charles Sixth Form College. In 2002, Ofsted described Sion-Manning as a 'vibrant and successful multi-ethnic school with many excellent features'. Overall performance at GCSE is above that nationally and represents 'very good progress'. Strong GCSE subjects are English, art and music while mathematics and science are the weaker subjects. Teaching is 'good' and the school provides a 'safe, secure and friendly environment'.

### Extra-curricular activities

The school is renowned for its flourishing orchestra, choir and ensembles. A variety of trips are organized, some of which are free, while others are partially subsidized. Involvement with the local community and charities is encouraged. Homework clubs are also provided. There are trips both locally and abroad. A wide range of sports is on offer, including football.

## Southbank International School

**36–38 Kensington Park Road, London W11 3BU** ☎ 020 7229 8230 📠 020 7229 3784 ⓔ admissions@southbank.org 🌐 www.southbank.org N Hughes ⇌ Paddington ⊖ Notting Hill Gate **Buses:** 52; door-to-door bus service provided by the school None **Demand:** No figures available but fully subscribed **Type:** Selective independent for 263 mixed pupils, aged 3 to 19 **Fees:** £3,500–5,000 per term **Submit application form:** No cut-off date **School hours:** 8.45am–4pm **Meals:** Snacks and breakfast available **London league table position:** Not available

### Profile

Founded in 1979 by a group of British and American educators, the school originally opened on London's South Bank, hence its name, which the school has retained in spite of its move north of the river. It is based in two beautiful and well-maintained Victorian town houses in one of Notting Hill's prestigious residential areas. There is extensive CCTV security. The school is divided into primary, middle years and Diploma programmes. The middle years programme is equivalent to secondary education. It has five themes: effective study skills; community service; health and social education; the environment; and the products of the creative and inventive genius of people. They are followed within eight academic subject groups: two languages, history and geography, sciences, maths, arts, PE and technology. The diploma programme is equivalent to sixth form and adds to a liberal arts curriculum an interdisciplinary study of the 'Theory of Knowledge'. This requires original research in one of 60 subjects. IT underpins all study and the school has a state-of-the-art computer centre equipped with Apple Macintosh computers. Class sizes are a maximum of 16. There is limited special-needs provision and families may be referred to outside institutions for testing or additional remedial help. An experienced counsellor provides pastoral care. There is also an extensive career and college counselling service managed by a qualified specialist who consults both student and parents. Parents are automatically made members of the PTA, which organizes social and fund-raising events. There is a school council.

## Admissions and intake

Southbank accepts applications from students aged 3 to 18. Over 40 different nationalities are represented at the school. Applications are generally dealt with on a first-come, first-served basis. Admission is based on previous records, teacher references, a statement from parents and a self-written pupil profile. Academic achievement, motivation, work habits and behaviour are the factors considered in the admissions process.

## Achievement

The school is one of a thousand in the International Baccalaureate Organization (IBO). All British universities, including Oxford and Cambridge, accept IB Diplomas. GCSE examinations are not required for the IB Diploma, so the school does not feature in the performance tables. In 2002, out of 39 pupils who took the IB diploma, just one failed. Over the past 15 years, the school has achieved a pass rate of more than 94 per cent.

## Extra-curricular activities

Sports on offer range from athletics to lifesaving skills. After-school activities include Scouts, judo, art, an orchestra, a choir, publication clubs, theatre and film-making. The Model United Nations Association allows students to study the issues facing particular countries, to learn about parliamentary debate and to take part in MUNA conferences, one of which is at The Hague. There are compulsory residential trips each year and many visits to museums, theatres and places of historic and cultural interest. There is also an optional skiing trip. Involvement with the community is encouraged; students do a minimum of 50 hours community service during their final two years.

# Kingston upon Thames

## Key

1. Beverley School
2. Canbury School
3. Chessington Community College
4. Coombe Girls' School
5. The Hollyfield School
6. The Holy Cross School
7. Kingston Grammar School
8. Marymount International School
9. Richard Challoner School
10. Southborough School
11. Surbiton High School
12. The Tiffin Girls' School
13. Tiffin School
14. Tolworth Girls' School

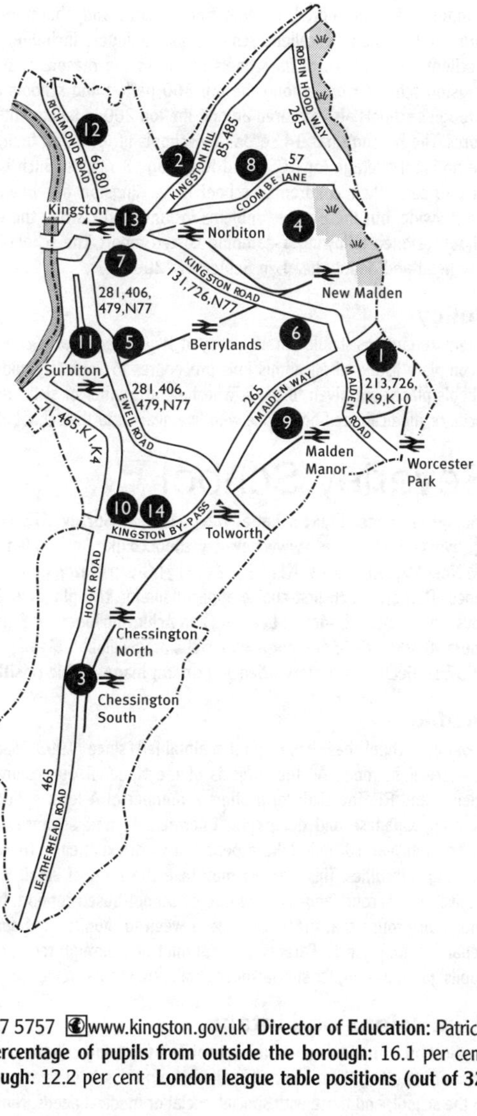


# Factfile

**LEA: Guildhall, Kingston KT1 1EU** ☎ 020 8547 5757 🌐www.kingston.gov.uk **Director of Education:** Patrick Leeson **Political control of council:** Liberal **Percentage of pupils from outside the borough:** 16.1 per cent **Percentage of pupils educated outside the borough:** 12.2 per cent **London league table positions (out of 32 boroughs):** 3rd

## Profile

Kingston upon Thames is one of just four royal boroughs in England and Wales. It is an historic borough and one of the most attractive of the 32 London boroughs. Within its boundaries are a section of Richmond Park and almost three miles of the River Thames; the open countryside is within easy reach and Hampton Court, Bushy Park, Kew Gardens and Wimbledon Common are all nearby. Chessington World of Adventures is one of the borough's major attractions but this brings its own problems of crime. Kingston has been regarded as a place of considerable importance since Saxon times, and today it is well known as one of the main shopping centres of London, which attracts many thousands of visitors to the town each year. The borough is primarily residential, but a wide range of industry is represented, ranging from aircraft and pharmaceutical industries to paint and wine-making. The borough has many excellent schools and colleges, including Kingston College and Kingston University. The excellent performance of its schools is one of the reasons that Kingston is often in the media. In 2000, three Kingston schools were among the top 300 performing schools countrywide for GCSE results, while three of the borough's schools also featured among the top 200 independent schools in London and the South-East for A-level scores. The borough has 14 secondary schools in total and their overall performance continues to be better than the national average for GCSE and Key Stage 3 results. Such is their success, parents come in from outside the area to send their children to school here. Kingston has been consistently near the top of the league tables countrywide, but there were problems in June 2000, when the entire full-time teaching staff at one Chessington school resigned following a damning Ofsted report. The school later reopened with brand new staff, including a new head and deputy head, in September 2000.

## Policy

Parents/guardians should obtain a copy of *Which Secondary School?* from Kingston education and leisure services for a complete listing of all admissions procedures to voluntary, foundation and independent schools. For community schools places are given to those who have a brother or sister attending the same school, pupils with a particular social or medical need and those who live nearest to the school of choice via the shortest safe walking route.

# Beverley School

**College Gardens, Blake's Lane, New Malden, Surrey KT3 6NU** 020 8949 1537 020 8942 6725 bvb@rbksch.org www.beverleyschool.co.uk Paul Templeman-Wright; Chair of Governors: John Heamon New Malden **Buses:** K1, 131, 213 Green blazer, green jacket, black trousers, white shirt, school tie, black shoes **Demand:** 176 first-choice applications for 180 places in 2001/2 **Type:** Foundation comprehensive for 513 boys, aged 11 to 18 **Motto:** Learning and Achieving Together **Submit application form:** Mid-October 2003 **School hours:** 8.40am–3.05pm; homework clubs are available **Meals:** Hot and cold available, including breakfast **Strong GCSE subjects:** Art, history, science **London league table position:** 479

## Profile

Beverley School has been grant-maintained since 1993. Facilities include an excellent sports hall with a fitness/weight room. All the subjects of the National Curriculum are taught, including English, mathematics and science and RE. The sixth form offers a number of A-level options including art and design, photography, biology, German, Japanese and geography. Intermediate and advanced GNVQ in leisure and tourism is also offered. All students in Year 10 undertake a period of work experience. There is a learning support department for pupils with learning difficulties. This support may take the form of small withdrawal groups or in-class support. Pupils with English as a second language are offered school-based support. New students have a programme of primary liaison and tutor groups that meet two days a week to monitor and support pupils. Many pupils can become school and departmental prefects. Parents are kept informed through regular newsletters, annual and interim reports for Year 7, pupils' journals and, for special-needs children, regular reviews.

## Admissions and intake

Application is made direct to the school. The following criteria are used to determine places: those boys who have a brother attending the school; all students from the school's partner schools will be offered places; those living nearest to the school; and those with special, social or medical needs. Nineteen per cent of pupils are on the school's register of special educational needs, which is again above average.

### Achievement

Owing to a significant proportion of selective schools in the area, pupils' achievements are broadly below average on entry to the school. In 2002, the proportion of pupils obtaining five or more A*–C grades at GCSE was 29 per cent, well below the national average, but slightly up from 28 per cent in 2001. This was below the borough average and the school was ranked 13th in the borough league table. However, in comparison with other non-selective schools, Beverley's results compare more favourably and are broadly in line for pupils gaining five or more A*–C grades. The overall points score shows a downward trend, whilst the national trend is rising. Standards in English and mathematics are in line with similar schools and above in science. Standards in art and history are high by national standards for all schools. At A-level, the average point score was 79.4, placing the school at the bottom of the borough. In 1999, Ofsted praised the school's 'orderly community'. Truancy is above average at 1.8 per cent.

### Extra-curricular activities

There is a range of musical groups available, including instrumental ensembles, band, choir and a barbershop group. Beverley has been very strong at sport, particularly football, and Years 8 and 10 were winners in the Kingston district cup. Rugby, athletics and cross-country are also popular. School trips have been organized to Heidelburg, Paris and the Wimbledon All England Lawn Tennis Club. The school actively supports the Macmillan Cancer Relief Fund. Homework clubs are available after school.

# Canbury School

**Kingston Hill, Kingston upon Thames, Surrey KT2 7LN** ☎ 020 8549 8622 Fax 020 8974 6018 ✉ head@canburyschool.co.uk Head: Mr Robin F Metters; Chair of Governors: The Rev Peter Haughton MA Rail: Norbiton and Kingston **Buses:** 85 Uniform: Black skirt or trousers, white shirt, black shoes **Demand:** Waiting list **Type:** Selective independent for 67 mixed pupils, aged 10 to 16 **Fees:** £2,250 per term **Submit application form:** No cut-off date **School hours:** 8.10am–3.45pm **Meals:** Hot and cold available **Strong GCSE subjects:** All relatively strong **London league table position:** 331

### Profile

Canbury School was established by John Wyatt in 1982. It is housed in an Edwardian house, home of Sir Donald Campbell of 'Bluebird' fame. It is a small school and deliberately so. The school aims at high academic standards and largely traditional methods of teaching; its small classes allow it to focus on each child, all the time. It can act on pupils' particular requirements and, when appropriate, call upon trained specialists for still more individual work. The maximum number of pupils in any class is 12. There are good computer facilities, and pupils' IT skills are developed using a suite of computers. Each classroom is equipped with a multi-media workstation. National Curriculum subjects are taught with the addition of subjects such as history, IT, art, drama and music. Physics, chemistry and biology can later be taken as doubly-certified GCSE subjects. Individual arrangements can be made for pupils to prepare for GCSEs in German, Chinese and other languages. There is no sixth form but the majority of pupils go on to the sixth forms of local schools such as Kingston Grammar and Tiffin. Some pupils who have suffered from a learning difficulty have benefited from Canbury's small classes. Assisting staff and a special-needs specialist also work individually with pupils. There is a school council and parents' evenings are held every term.

### Admissions and intake

The following admissions procedure applies: request a prospectus, interview with headmaster, entrance test, and application form. The school has a wide catchment area.

### Achievement

In 2002, 45 per cent of pupils gained five A*–C grades at GCSE and the school came ninth in the borough. The school has had a number of talented instrumentalists who have gone on to musical sixth forms and then to further study.

### Extra-curricular activities

School clubs available include electronics, natural history, cross-stitch embroidery and computing. Sports on offer range from canoeing and sailing on the Thames to mountain biking, basketball and snooker. Trips organized include visits to Sussex University, Sandown dry-ski slopes and Wales. The school supports a different charity each year.

# Chessington Community College

**Garrison Lane, Chessington, Surrey KT9 2JS** 020 8974 1156 0208 974 2603 ccc@rbksch.org Mr D Kemp B.Ed, MA; Chair of Governors: Paul Johnston Chessington South **Buses:** 71, 486 Black skirt or trousers, red V-neck jumper, tie; Sixth form: manner suitable for formal work **Demand:** 263 applications for 150 places in 2001/2 **Type:** Community comprehensive for 660 mixed pupils, aged 11 to 18 **Submit application form:** Mid-October 2003 **Motto:** None higher **School hours:** 8.40am–3.20pm; homework clubs are available **Meals:** Hot and cold available, including breakfast **Strong GCSE subjects:** English language, mathematics, science **London league table position:** 421

## Profile

Chessington Community College provides a sound education for boys and girls of a wide range of abilities. The college occupies an attractive site in the south of Kingston. A new building has been opened for maths, modern languages and special needs. A computer room has also recently opened. The college has a development plan for the next three years, including the building of a new teaching block. A-level subjects offered include art, business studies, history and maths. A week's work experience is offered in Year 12. The college has an excellent reputation for addressing the issues of children with special needs. Pupils with particular needs in literacy and language are taught by specialist teachers, for one lesson a week. Nine pupils with speech and language difficulties receive specialist provision through the open-door speech and language initiative. Pupils also have full access to the curriculum and are well supported. Upper school pupils can become prefects and pupils can also become members of the student council. A good level of pastoral care is provided through the PSHE programme. Newsletters, reports and consultation evenings keep parents informed.

## Admissions and intake

Applications are made direct to the LEA. Places are offered according to the following criteria: those with a brother or sister attending the school at the time of admission; social or medical need; and those living nearest the school. There are 170 pupils on the college's register of special needs, of whom 47 are statemented.

## Achievement

In 2002, 34 per cent of pupils achieved five or more grades A*–C at GCSE, down on 37 per cent in 2001. This was below the borough average of 60 per cent and below the national average of 51.6 per cent. The school was ranked 11th in the borough league table. GCSE results in English language, mathematics and science tend to be well above the national average. At A-level in 2002, the average point score for pupils taking two or more was 106. This was below the local and national averages. The school was ranked 10th in the borough. In 1997, Ofsted reported that 'the spiritual, moral, social and cultural development of pupils is sound.' Such is the improved growth of the college that it was mentioned in Her Majesty's Chief Inspector's 1996 Annual Report to the government as an improved school.

## Extra-curricular activities

Activities available include netball, choir, drama technology, music, fitness training and badminton. More unusual activities include pentathlon, trampolining and orienteering. The college has been participating in a three-year project called the Comensius Project, along with other institutions in Belgium, Finland and the Czech Republic. This has involved pupils producing a video, publicity material and displays. Trips in 1999/2000 included a skiing trip to America, language visits to France and Germany and cultural exchanges to the Czech Republic. The college has one of the largest Duke of Edinburgh's Award scheme programmes in south-west London. After-school homework clubs are available, and pupils work with the elderly in the local community.

# Coombe Girls' School

**Clarence Avenue, New Malden, Surrey KT3 3TU** 020 8942 1242 0208 8942 6385 cmg@rbksch.org www.coombegirlsschool.org Carol Campbell; Chair of Governors: Mr R Burt New Malden **Buses:** 213 Up to sixth form: green cardigan, grey skirt, green/coloured tie **Demand:** 629 first-choice applications for 210 places in 2001/2 **Type:** Community comprehensive for 1335 girls (mixed in sixth form), aged 11 to 18 **Submit application form:** Mid-October 2003 **Motto:** Preparing Today for the Challenges of Tomorrow **School hours:** 8.45am–3.30pm **Meals:** Hot and cold available, including breakfast **Strong GCSE subjects:** All relatively strong **London league table position:** 217

### Profile

Coombe Girls' School was established in 1955. From its inception, it has enjoyed an enviable academic reputation which has continued to the present day. Accommodation has improved significantly with the building of a mathematics and science block. A £2.1-million building project has also provided extra accommodation and new facilities for technology, art, English and media studies. The school has made a lottery bid for a new sports hall. The learning resources centre is well resourced and has access to computers, CD-ROMs and the Internet. The school is also involved in an international video-conferencing project linking with San Francisco and Morocco. Coombe was awarded Beacon School status in 1999. The National Curriculum is taught, along with additional subjects such as German, Spanish and French. At sixth-form, 25 A-level subjects are on offer, including biology, computer studies, government and politics and media studies. A number of GNVQs are also on offer. Coombe has strong links with employers such as BT, Disneyland, Paris, and Granada Studios, who offer work experience. There is a system of prefects, house and school officials. There is excellent provision for special needs. Parents are kept informed through the school diary, annual reports and parents' evenings.

### Admissions and intake

Application is made direct to the LEA. The criteria for placements are as follows: those with a sister attending the school at the time of admission; particular social or medical need; and those living nearest the school. Sixth form pupils apply direct to the school/head of sixth form. Almost 20 per cent of pupils at Coombe have English as an additional language and this is high for an outer London borough. It also has the highest number of refugee pupils in the borough and the percentage from ethnic minority backgrounds is above the national average. There are 220 pupils on the register of special needs, broadly in line with the national average. Eleven pupils had statements in 2000, which is below the national average.

### Achievement

For several years, the percentage of pupils achieving five grades A*–C at GCSE has been well above the national average. In 2002, 60 per cent achieved five A*–C grades. This was an increase from 58 per cent in 2001 and the school was placed seventh in the borough. In 2002, the average point score for pupils taking two or more A-levels was 220.3, ranking Coombe eighth in the borough. Ofsted visited in 1999 and found no weaknesses. It described Coombe as having a 'racially harmonious, effective community'. Unauthorized absence was very low at 0.5 per cent.

### Extra-curricular activities

Ofsted reported that 'there is an excellent, rich and varied programme of extra-curricular activities, with a wide range of clubs and revision courses at lunchtime and after school'. Clubs range from the Duke of Edinburgh's Award scheme and Young Enterprise to flamenco dancing and aerobics. The school sports curriculum follows the national curriculum. There is an annual Outward Bound weekend, plus trips to New York, Washington and Barcelona.

## The Hollyfield School

**Surbiton Hill Road, Surbiton, Surrey KT6 4TU** 020 8547 6800 020 8547 6872 hollyfield@rbksch.org www.hollyfield.kingston.sch.uk Stephen J. Chamberlain B.Ed (hons); Chair of Governors: Dr Michael Morton Surbiton **Buses:** K1, K2, K4, K8, 71, 281, 406, 479 Up to sixth form: black skirt or trousers, black V-neck jumper, blazer, tie **Demand:** 744 applications for 180 places in 2001/2 **Type:** Partially selective foundation school for 961 mixed pupils, aged 11 to 18 **Mission Statement:** Hollyfield promotes high achievement, high standards, high expectations, personal development, moral values, support and care and a sense of community. **Submit application form:** Mid-October 2003 **Motto:** Your Child – Their Future – Our School **School hours:** 8.45am–3.20pm **Meals:** Hot and cold available, including breakfast **Strong GCSE subjects:** All relatively strong **London league table position:** 435

### Profile

Hollyfield School was originally established in Hollyfield Road. It moved to its present site in 1966 and became grant-maintained in 1996, and a foundation school in 1998. Years 10 and 11 receive a broad and balanced education, covering maths, English, sciences, at least one modern language, humanities and arts subjects. The school also offers combined courses in electronics, graphics, fashion and catering. A range of subjects are offered at A- and AS-level. Careers education is provided by experienced teachers and by Search, the local independent careers organization. In

1998, Ofsted reported: 'provision is good for pupils with statements of special educational need'. The special-needs department is headed by a special needs coordinator. Parents are kept well informed through newsletters, a calendar of events, a parents' conference and curriculum, reports and consultation evenings. All parents are automatically members of the Hollyfield PTA. In 1998, the school's rate of unauthorized absence was above the national average at 2.35 per cent and, despite the use of electronic registration, it was up to 2.4 per cent in 2000.

## Admissions and intake

There are 180 places available and they are several times oversubscribed. Places are offered according to the following criteria: sibling attending the school; pupil coming from a partner primary school; particular social or medical needs (with written evidence from a suitably qualified person); and distance from the school.

## Achievement

Hollyfield is the most improved Kingston school at GCSE during 1996–99. It then set a new record in 2000, where 49 per cent of pupils achieved five A*–C grades. In 2001, this dropped slightly to 46 per cent and to 36 per cent in 2002, when the school was ranked 12th in the borough. At A-level, the average point score was 203.4, ranking Hollyfield ninth in the borough. Ofsted reported that the school's results are part of a rising trend over the last seven years. Hollyfield has received the prestigious Schools' Curriculum Award. It has also received an award of £200,000 under the Technology Schools' initiative and an award as a Satellite Centre of Excellence for information technology.

## Extra-curricular activities

After-school clubs include: swing band, philosophy, athletics, theatre and board games. Sport is strong and Hollyfield are Surrey champions at tenpin bowling, the Year 7 football team are district champions, the Year 10 boys' football team were recently joint district champions and the school has had 14 athletes representing the borough in the county schools athletics championships. There are frequent visits to art galleries, with a residential weekend for A-level students in Cornwall.

# The Holy Cross School

**Westbury Road, New Malden, Surrey KT3 5AN** ☎ 020 8395 4225 Fax 020 8395 4234 ✉ HXS@rbksch.org 🌐 www.schoolsite.edex.net.uk/193 Mr Tom Gibson B.Sc (Hons), M.Ed; Chair of Governors: Dr Desmond Fitzpatrick ⇌ New Malden **Buses**: 131, 213 Green blazer, green jumper, white shirt, tartan skirt **Demand:** 623 applications for 150 places in 2001/2 **Type:** Voluntary aided for 847 girls, aged 11 to 18 **Submit application form**: Mid-October 2003 **Mission Statement**: To empower the individual student to develop academically, physically, socially and spiritually as a global citizen of the 21st century. **School hours**: 8.40am–3.20pm; homework clubs are available **Meals:** Cold only **Strong GCSE subjects:** English **London league table position:** 248

## Profile

Holy Cross School was founded in 1931 and is under the trusteeship of the Holy Cross Sisters. The school prides itself on its reputation for the care of the individual student and for high disciplinary standards. It has its own chapel and garden areas have been created in which pupils can sit quietly during breaks. Sports facilities include playing fields, hard court areas, gymnasium and dance studio. All pupils at Key Stage 4 follow a curriculum that includes English, maths, science, French, design and technology, RE, careers and PSE. The school provides a programme for post-16 study in partnership with a neighbouring school for boys (Richard Challoner School). A total of 22 subjects are offered, including a general studies course on the world for women, art, biology, English literature and German. A programme of careers education is taught by specialists and complemented by work experience in Year 10 and in the sixth form. The school ensures provision for pupils with special needs. Some pupils in the upper school act as prefects and there is a school council. Pastoral support is provided by form tutors. Ofsted praised the school's links with parents who are kept well informed about the school through regular reports, the diary system and the school brochure. There is also an active PTA.

## Admissions and intake

From 1995, the school has admitted 20 pupils each year to a grammar school stream. In Years 7 to 11 there is also an 'express' class of pupils who have been successful in an examination administered by the school. The remainder of its pupils are not selected. A total of 11 pupils have a statement of special needs and there are 85 pupils on the school's register of special needs.

### Achievement

In 2002, 55 per cent of pupils achieved five A*–C grades at GCSE. This was down from 65 per cent in 2001 and Holy Cross was ranked eighth in the borough league table. Results at this level have improved steadily over the last four years and at a faster rate than is found nationally. Over the past four years, the average points score of pupils entered for two or more A-levels has been below average. In 2002, the A-level point score was 222.5, below the borough average. This placed the school seventh in the borough league table. In 1997, the Holy Cross tennis club was set up and is run by an LTA qualified coach. In 1998, the school was selected as one of the schools to provide pupils each year to train as Wimbledon ball girls.

### Extra-curricular activities

During lunch times and after school, a wide variety of clubs are available such as karate, dance, tennis, trampolining, poetry and football. There is an orchestra and a choir. Pupils can participate in the Duke of Edinburgh's Award scheme and many girls undertake forms of voluntary service. Field trips and journeys abroad are organized, and the school is twinned with a French school in the Loire Valley. After-school homework clubs are available.

## Kingston Grammar School

**70–72 London Road, Kingston upon Thames, Surrey KT2 6PY** 020 8546 5875 020 8547 1499 head@kingston-grammar.surrey.sch.uk www.kingston-grammar.surrey.sch.uk CD Baxter; Chair of Governors: JA Elvidge Kingston Charcoal grey blazer and black trousers or suit, white shirt or blouse; Sixth form: Smart business wear **Demand:** 7:1 applications for places **Type:** Independent for 596 mixed pupils, aged 10 to 19 **Fees:** £2,855 per term **Submit application form:** December 2003 **Motto:** Excellence and Respect **School hours:** 8.30am–4pm **Meals:** Hot and cold available, including breakfast **Strong GCSE subjects:** All relatively strong **London league table position:** 35

### Profile

Kingston Grammar is an excellent school, achieving very good results. It dates back to the Middle Ages and is fortunate in having acquired and developed a fine sportsground of some 22 acres situated at Thames Ditton and overlooking Hampton Court Palace. Facilities include first class pavilion accommodation and adjoining squash courts. The boathouse has been built on ground nearby. There are art studios, a sixth-form studio, a computer area for graphic design and the Finlay Gallery, which provides excellent facilities for pupils to experiment with a variety of media and equipment. Technology facilities include a workshop for work in wood and plastic, and information technology and micro-electronics areas. At GCSE, English, maths, the three separate sciences and at least one language are taken by all and then three choices from French, German, Spanish, Latin, RS, history, geography, art, design technology and music. Further subjects are added at A-level, such as politics, theatre studies, economics, sports studies, classical civilization and further maths. Pupils undertake work experience and the careers department has good links with local business and industry. Members of staff attend to special-needs pupils, and a teacher is available for special support teaching in English. Parents are kept informed through twice-termly newsletters, a termly letter from the head, the school magazine, an annual parent-teacher meeting, twice-termly grade cards and written reports twice a year. Famous ex-pupils include James Cracknell (Olympic rower), Michael Frayn (playwright) and Edward Gibbon (author).

### Admissions and intake

Application is made direct to the school and all applicants must sit an entrance exam. Candidates wishing to join the sixth form are interviewed by the head of the sixth form. Many scholarships and bursaries are on offer to enable talented pupils to join the school.

### Achievement

Kingston Grammar is a very high-achieving school. In 2002, 100 per cent of pupils achieved five or more A*–C grades at GCSE. This result was well above the borough and national averages and the school was ranked second within the borough league table. At A-level, the average point score was 338.4. This ranked the school fourth in the borough.

### Extra-curricular activities

There are a number of clubs available, including The Gibbon Society, which covers debating, public speaking and theatre visits and the Natural History Club. Pupils can participate in the Duke of Edinburgh's Awards scheme. A variety of trips are organized, including visits to Germany, Switzerland and Belgium. Sports on offer include gymnastics, swimming and athletics. There is an orchestra, a concert band and several choirs.

# Marymount International School

**George Road, Kingston upon Thames, Surrey KT2 7PE** 020 8949 0571 020 8336 2485 info@marymount.kingston.sch.uk www.marymount.kingston.sch.uk Sister Rosaleen Sheridan, RSHM; Board of Regents: Mr Julian Walton Wimbledon, Kingston **Buses**: 57, 85, 213 Navy blue and white blazer, white blouse, navy skirt **Demand:** Rolling system of admission – no suitable applicants turned away **Type**: Independent college-preparatory for 197 girls, aged 11 to 18 **Fees**: Years 7 to 9 – £10,200 per year; Years 10 to 13 – £11,400 per year; Years 7 to 9 – £18,250 per year (7 day boarder); Years 10 to 13 – £19,450 (7 day boarder); Years 7 to 9 – £18,000 (5 day boarder); Years 10 to 13 – £19,250 (5 day boarder) **Submit application form**: No cut-off date **Mission statement**: Marymount seeks to perpetuate the mission and educational purposes of the Religious of the sacred heart of Mary. These purposes are the encouragement of learning, the education of the whole person, service to the community and the promotion of justice. The school is committed to the development of values and to an appreciation of the role of spirituality in a fully integrated life. **School hours**: 8.40am–3.40pm (Mon, Wed, Fri) 8.40am–4.30pm (Tues, Thurs) **Meals**: Hot and cold available **Strong GCSE subjects**: English, French, German, Japanese, Korean, Spanish **London league table position**: Not applicable.

### Profile

Marymount was established in 1955 to meet the educational needs of families in the international business and diplomatic community. It is part of a worldwide system of schools and colleges directed by the Sacred Heart of Mary, a Roman Catholic order. Today, about 40 different nationalities are represented within the student body. An ongoing development plan has borne a series of new buildings: a science centre, sports hall, a humanities-library-computer complex and an additional boarding wing with three student lounges. The middle school and high school syllabuses are based on American curricula. This is integrated in Years 6 to 12 with the International Baccalaureate middle years programme, and in Years 11 to 12 with the IB diploma programme, designed to enable high school graduates to attend major universities in Britain, the US and elsewhere. There are two special needs teachers available and a sister and a chaplain provide pastoral care. Pupils can participate in the running of the school through the national honor society and join the school council. There is an active parent-teacher association and parents are kept informed through parents' evenings, newsletters and a monthly bulletin.

### Admissions and intake

Admissions procedure is listed in the school booklet and is as follows: read all the material carefully, complete the application form, attach student's photograph and the registration fee, sign the request slip for the student's academic records and return the application form to the school's admissions officer.

### Achievement

In 2002, 21 out of the school's 22 IB diploma candidates passed, well above the average for IB schools. The equivalent A-level score would be 63 per cent As and Bs, and one candidate achieved the maximum possible IB score of 45 points. The school is particularly strong in languages, especially those not commonly taught in this country, such as Arabic, Chinese and Japanese, as well as French and German. Most students go on to a university of their choice.

### Extra-curricular activities

Popular after-school activities include aerobics, boating (on the Thames), cycling, gymnastics, golf and ice-skating. Every girl is encouraged to take part in plays and team sports. Each year there are three major concerts, two full-scale theatre productions, Homo Faber Day, the arts and crafts festival and an international day. Marymount girls are also given the chance to meet with other students in Europe: at the Model United Nations in the Hague, interscholastic sports tournaments and drama festivals. Pupils organize fund-raising for local charities.

# Richard Challoner School

**Manor Drive North, New Malden, Surrey KT3 5PE** 020 8330 5947 020 8330 3842 rcb@rbksch.org www.challoner.kingston.sch.uk MrTG Cahill B.Sc (hons); Chair of Governors: Mark Draper Malden Manor **Buses:** K1, 213 Black blazer, black or dark grey trousers, grey pullover, white or blue shirt, tie **Demand:** 345 applications for 120 places in 2001/2 **Type:** Non-selective voluntary aided Roman Catholic school for 700 boys (mixed sixth form), aged 11 to 18 **Submit application form:** Mid-October 2003 **Motto:** Living, Learning and Sharing in a Caring Christian Community **School hours:** 8.45am–3.20pm, 8.45am–2.35pm (Fri): homework clubs are available **Meals:** Hot and cold available **Strong GCSE subjects:** ICT, music, PE **London league table position:** 149

## Profile

Richard Challoner School was opened in 1959. Specialist teaching areas include six modern science laboratories, three design and technology rooms, an electronics workshop, a graphical communication room and three IT rooms, each with 22 workstations. There is also a gymnasium with multi-gym and attached to the school is a large pitch used for rugby, football and athletics. The school aims to provide a broad, balanced and challenging curriculum that meets National Curriculum requirements and at the same time operates within the strong Christian ethos of its mission statement. A well-established federation of the sixth form with a local girls' school results in a wide range of subjects being offered at A-level. Richard Challoner have applied for Technology College status. All Year 11 pupils undertake two-weeks' work experience and careers guidance is an integral part of the curriculum. There is a full-time coordinator of special needs, two full-time specialists and other peripatetic staff. Pupils can become prefects. Parents are kept informed through reports, consultation evenings and homework diaries. There is a hard-working PTA. Famous ex-pupils include Ben Lake (singer), Graham Barber (referee), Steven Reid (footballer) and Jimmy Glass (Carlisle goalkeeper).

## Admissions and intake

A popular choice for parents, the school is regularly oversubscribed. Where there are more applications than positions available, places are offered according to the following criteria: baptized and practising Roman Catholic; baptized and practising non-Roman Catholic Christian; brother of a pupil or former pupil at the school; and special medical grounds. A total of 21.1 per cent of pupils have special needs, of whom 2.5 per cent have statements.

## Achievement

In 2002, 73 per cent of pupils achieved five or more A*–C grades at GCSE. This was up from 62 per cent the previous year and the school was placed sixth in the borough GCSE league table. At A-level, the average point score per pupil was 230.7, placing the school fifth in the borough. Richard Challoner's GCSE results are consistently well above national averages and have improved more rapidly than the national trend over the past five years. However, its A-level results are below national averages. Ofsted last visited the school in 2002 and described it as a 'very good school'. Pupils were seen to achieve very well throughout the school and 'pupils' attitudes and behaviour are a particular strength'. GSCE results are above average in music, ICT and PE but below average in geography and history. Inspectors praised the 'good' leadership and management of the school.

## Extra-curricular activities

School clubs available include chess, design technology, outdoor pursuits, language club and school magazine. Sports played include cricket, squash, tennis, athletics, swimming and basketball. The school has enjoyed a great deal of success over the past years in district, county, London and national competitions. Pupils can join a concert band, brass ensemble, guitar ensemble or percussion ensemble. There are skiing trips as well as trips to Italy and France. Each year the school presents a major drama production, and since 1990 the school play has annually toured Hungary. Pupils are involved within the local community. After-school homework clubs are available.

# Southborough School

**Hook Road, Surbiton, Surrey KT6 5AS** 020 8391 4324 020 8391 0177 southborough@rbksch.org www.southborough.kingston.sch.uk John Rook; Chair of Governors: Mr P Osborne Surbiton **Buses:** K1, 71, 671 Black blazer, school blue and gold badge, blue and gold tie, white shirt, grey trousers **Demand:** 377 applications for 150 places in 2001/2 **Type:** Community comprehensive for 745 boys, aged 11 to 18 **Submit application form:** Mid-October 2003 **School hours:** 8.40am–3.15pm; homework clubs are available **Meals:** Hot and cold available **Strong GCSE subjects:** All relatively strong **London league table position:** 334

## Profile

Southborough School has a rolling schedule of building improvements. The buildings are generally well-maintained and there is a planned programme for extending the use of the school grounds. The school governors are considering whether to become a voluntary aided CofE school in September 2003. Southborough provides a broad and balanced curriculum in both Key Stages and post-16, and almost all boys are able to follow their first choices. At sixth form, the school has established a link with a local girls' school, enabling students to attend courses in either school where numbers are low. A total of 14 A-level subjects are offered, including English, art, music, physical education and modern languages. Pupils in Year 10 participate in two-weeks' work experience. Each department has a member of staff responsible for the provision of special-needs support. There is special emphasis on reading and additional support is available for pupils with particular problems. Each class has a representative on the school council. Parents are kept informed through annual reports, parents' meetings, the *Southborough Journal*, a termly publication by pupils, the termly home-school newsletter *Link* and *Chatline* (edited by the head teacher), the news-sheet for the school and home partnership. Southborough operates the Bentalls Award scheme, a system of prizes for homework, classroom work, punctuality, effort and behaviour. The school says this scheme has led to a dramatic improvement in education standards and behaviour.

## Admissions and intake

Application is made direct to the LEA. Places are offered according to the following criteria: those with a brother or sister attending the school at the time of admission; those with particular social or medical need; and those living nearest the school.

## Achievement

In 2002, 46 per cent of pupils achieved five or more A*–C grades at GCSE, below the borough and national averages. This was up on 34 per cent in 2001 and the school was ranked 10th in the borough league table. In 1998, Ofsted commented: 'Examination results in art, business studies, design technology, French, geography, Spanish, media studies, food studies and music were better than those achieved in all schools on average. Results in English are lower than national averages and those for boys. In mathematics, results were in line with all schools nationally and boys' achievements. When comparing results with boys' schools, achievement in the majority of subjects was better.' At A-level, the average point score was 120 in 2002, placing the school 10th in the borough. Pupils tend to behave well around the school and in classrooms, and are very courteous to adults and respectful towards each other. The truancy rate was only 0.3 per cent in 2000, compared with 1.0 per cent nationally.

## Extra-curricular activities

After-school clubs available include revision classes, SATS classes, chess and drama club. The full range of sports is on offer, including rugby. Year 7 attend an Outward Bound course. Year 9 go to the Docklands/Thames barrier, Year 8 go to Portsmouth and Year 10 travel to Osmington Bay for a week. After-school homework clubs are available. Pupils engage in fund-raising for charities in the local community.

# Surbiton High School

**Surbiton Crescent, Kingston upon Thames KT1 2JT** 020 8546 5245 020 8547 0026 surbiton.high@church-schools.com www.surbitonhigh.com Dr Jennifer Longhurst; Chair of Governors: Mrs M Hicks Surbiton **Buses:** K1, K2, K3, 281, 406, 465, 479, 511, 512 grey skirt, grey jumper, grey tie, white blouse

**Demand:** Fully subscribed **Type:** Selective independent for 1097 girls, aged 4 to 18. The school has four sections: junior girls (4 to 11), senior girls (11 to 18), sixth form (16 to 18) and Surbiton Preparatory School for Boys (4 to 11). **Fees:** £1,680 (Years 1 and 2); £2,290 (Years 3 to 6); senior school and sixth form: £2,790 per term **Submit application form:** 30 November 2003 **Motto:** May Love Always Lead Us **School hours:** 8.30am–3.45pm **Meals:** Hot and cold available, including breakfast **Strong GCSE subjects:** All relatively strong **London league table position:** 50

### Profile

Surbiton High School opened in January 1884. Recent additions have included the new junior girls' building, an imaginative conversion of Surbiton assembly rooms and a new, purpose-built sixth form college. At the end of Year 9, girls make their GCSE choices, consisting of a common core of English, English literature, mathematics, one modern language and sciences, to which three options are added. All girls study the three sciences until the age of 16, either as separate subjects or as a double award GCSE. In the sixth form, a total of 28 A-level choices are offered. Two-weeks' work experience is undertaken by pupils and the school has special-needs provision. Those pupils wanting more responsibility can stand for the committee, the equivalent of a prefect body. Parents are kept informed through parents' evenings and weekly newsletters. There is an active parent-teacher association.

### Admissions and intake

Surbiton High School is selective and all girls sit an entrance exam in the January before entry at the age of 11. Every girl who sits the exam is interviewed. This interview is as important as the written papers as it allows the school to see what interests and motivates the girls. To apply, the registration form should be completed and returned to the head not later than 30 November of the year prior to proposed entry, accompanied by the registration and examination fee of £50, together with a named passport-sized photo.

### Achievement

The school is extremely high achieving at all levels and GCSE results have always been 99 or 100 per cent five A*–C grades. In 2002, 99 per cent of pupils gained five or more A*–C grades. The average point score was 54.2, placing the school fourth in the borough. At A-level, the average point score was 372.1, above the borough and national averages. This placed the school second in the borough league table.

### Extra-curricular activities

There are over 50 after-school clubs on offer including ceramics, design, photography and textiles. There is also a junior and senior choir and several musical groups. Many individual and team titles at national level are currently held by the school for ski-racing. Visits are organized to museums, theatres and sites of historical and geographical interest. There are annual exchanges with schools in France, Germany and Spain. The school also does charity work within the community.

## The Tiffin Girls' School

**Richmond Road, Kingston upon Thames, Surrey KT2 5PL** 020 8546 0773 020 8547 0191 tiffingirls@rbksch.org www.tiffingirls.kingston.sch.uk Mrs P Cox BA, MA; Chair of Governors: Mrs Sandra Holdsworth Kingston **Buses:** 65 Grey skirt, Tiffin blue blazer, striped blouse and Tiffin blue jumper **Demand:** 961 applicants for 122 places in 2001/2 **Type:** Selective grammar for 849 girls, aged 11 to 18 **Submit application form:** Mid-October 2003 **Motto:** *Sapere aude* (Dare to Be Wise) **School hours:** 8.45am–3.40pm **Meals:** Cafe/snacks **Strong GCSE subjects:** All relatively strong **London league table position:** 19

### Profile

This school is very successful and is one of London's 19 remaining grammar schools. It has put in a successful bid to Sport England for over £500,000 of lottery funds to construct a floodlit all-weather pitch for hockey and football, together with resurfacing of netball and tennis courts plus a new floodlit netball court. Two new computer rooms have been built with a third refurbished. An ICT technician, portable laptops and new PCs are also in place. In 2000, Ofsted praised the quality and range of the curriculum. All girls in Years 8 and 9 study Latin. Pupils in Key Stage 3 study subjects such as history, geography, art, music and drama. There are five option blocks in the sixth form and most pupils take three A-levels. There is also a joint general studies programme with Tiffin Boys' School. Year 11 take two-weeks' work experience. Ofsted reported that 'The accomplishment of pupils with special educational needs is very good. People with special educational needs achieve well and speak highly of the support they have received, which has enabled them to reach their full potential.' Each form is represented on the school council. The school's care for its pupils was described as 'very good. Provision for the care and support of pupils makes a major contribution to their development.'

### Admissions and intake

The school's pupils are of much higher than average attainment on entry, reflecting its selective nature. About 1.6 per cent of pupils have special needs, well below the national average. Pupils come predominantly from homes that are socio-economically above average and are from a wide variety of religious, cultural and ethnic backgrounds.

### Achievement

Tiffin came first in the borough league table for GCSE results in 2002. A total of 100 per cent of pupils achieved five or more A*–C grades. This was well above both local and national averages. Ofsted reported that results at GCSE were consistently very high and show a rising trend. At A-level, the average point score was 375, the highest in the borough. Ofsted stated that results at A-level in most subjects are excellent and are well above average for selective schools. They said if current rates can be maintained, almost all pupils will gain A* in all GCSE subjects by 2008 and almost all A-level results will be grade A by 2010. The school was one of the top 50 countrywide state schools for A-level results in 2000. Ofsted also gave the rare accolade that the school provides excellent value for money and that there were no weak subjects. It said 'this is an outstandingly effective school. Pupils achieve excellent standards. Standards achieved in the sixth form are particularly good. The overall quality of teaching and learning is achieved.' The rate of unauthorized absence in 2000 was well below the national average.

### Extra-curricular activities

There is an extensive range of extra-curricular opportunities available. They include over 11 different musical ensembles, numerous sporting activities, media society, book club, art club, creative writing workshop, debating club and Christian Union. The pupils are also involved in many fund-raising events for local charities in the community. Previous trips organized have included Stratford upon Avon, the Isle of Wight, Bruges, China and the US.

## Tiffin School

**Queen Elizabeth Road, Kingston upon Thames, Surrey KT2 6RL** ☎ 020 8546 4638 📠 020 8546 6365 ⓔ office@tiffin.kingston.sch.uk 🌐 www.tiffin.kingston.sch.uk Dr AM Dempsey, B.Sc, Ph.D; Chair of Governors: Mr M Taylor Kingston **Buses:** K9, K10, 213 Blue blazer, grey or white shirt, blue V-neck pullover, grey trousers **Demand:** 1040 applications for 140 places in 2001/2 **Type:** Selective grant-maintained grammar for 1038 boys, aged 11 to 18 **Submit application form:** Mid-October 2003 **Motto:** *Faire sans dire* (To Do Without Saying) **School hours:** 8.45am–4.05pm **Meals:** Hot and cold available **Strong GCSE subjects:** All relatively strong **London league table position:** 37

### Profile

The first Tiffin School opened in 1880 but it has a longer history, having been endowed in 1638 by local merchants, John and Thomas Tiffin. It is one of London's 19 remaining grammar schools. Facilities include up-to-date computers, a technology suite consisting of four multimedia areas, a music suite and a drama studio/workshop. The school also has excellent playing fields at Hampton Court. Ofsted stated: 'the school has worked hard over the last 10 years to make great improvements in the quality of its accommodation'. Tiffin is successful in meeting its stated aim of providing a curriculum that is broad, flexible and relevant to each pupil's needs. Work experience is undertaken by all Year 11 pupils. The requirements of special-needs pupils are generally met by a specialist teacher and the special-needs coordinator. Representatives from forms can be elected to year councils which, with the school council, consider matters raised by pupils. Subject teachers and form tutors know their pupils well and enjoy purposeful relationships with them. Parents are kept informed through regular newsletters and the school's achievements are celebrated in the annual *Tiffinian* magazine. The thriving Tiffin parents' association is involved in fund-raising.

## Admissions and intake

The school is selective and boys gaining the highest aggregate marks in two nationally recognized reasoning tests (one verbal and one non-verbal), will be offered places in order, until 140 have been accepted. The marks will be age-weighted so that the allocation of places to boys who have obtained the same aggregate score will favour the younger applicants. In the sixth form, offers will be made on the basis of at least six GCSE grades A* to B, which must include a) three grade As and b) the intended AS/A-level subjects (note that grade As are required to study maths and, if double science is taken, any science).

## Achievement

Tiffin's standards of achievement are consistently above national expectations in all year groups. In 2002, 99 per cent of pupils achieved five A*–C grades. This was down from 100 per cent in 2001 and Tiffin was the third best performing school in the borough. At A-level, the average point score for pupils taking two or more was 341.7. This ranked the school third in the borough league table. In 1996, Ofsted visted the school and reported that 'Tiffin is a very good school'. Ofsted stated: 'At GCSE A-level, the school has achieved consistently good results over the last four years.'

## Extra-curricular activities

After-school clubs include bridge, chess and photography. Pupils can also participate in the Duke of Edinburgh's Award scheme or Young Enterprise scheme. The school choir sings at many prestigious functions both in England and abroad, and the school is renowned for its drama and theatre. Sport is very popular and the school enjoys great success in cricket, rowing, badminton and tennis. Trips are organized to Wales, Germany, Rome and Athens.

# Tolworth Girls' School

**Fullers Way North, Surbiton, Surrey KT6 7LQ** 020 8397 3854 020 8974 2600 tolworthgirls@rbksch.org www.tolgirls-tcce.kingston.sch.uk Mrs C Williams MA; Chair of Governors: Margaret Turner Tolworth **Buses**: K1, 71, 281; London Country buses 406, 479 White blouse, navy blue skirt, school sweater with logo **Demand:** 551 applications for 210 places in 2001/2 **Type:** Non-selective community comprehensive for 1255 girls (mixed sixth form), aged 11 to 18 **Submit application form:** Mid-October 2003 **Mission Statement:** To ensure that each pupil has an equal opportunity to experience a whole curriculum that is balanced, relevant and broadly based and which will promote the intellectual, cultural, moral, spiritual, aesthetic and physical development of the individual to the benefit of herself, the school and the wider community. **Motto:** Let Your Love So Shine **School hours:** 8.45am–3.20pm **Meals:** Hot and cold available, including breakfast **Strong GCSE subjects:** Art **London league table position:** 127

## Profile

Tolworth has the advantage of sharing its site with Tolworth Recreation Centre, which gives the school priority daytime use of extensive sports facilities and the Croft Theatre. A maths and technology building was opened in 1995 and a new building for the English and media departments recently opened. Other facilities include art studios, multimedia workshops and design studios. At Key Stage 4, English, English literature, maths, PE, PHSE (Personal, Health and Social Education) and single science are taken by all pupils who then choose a further five subjects with a course from each of four curriculum areas. At A-level, pupils can take subjects such as biology, business studies, chemistry, dance, government and politics, law and textiles. Religious studies form part of every pupil's education throughout the school. All Year 10 pupils go on work experience. The learning support department identifies those girls who will benefit from extra help and ensures that all pupils follow the National Curriculum and make progress in their learning. There is a very supportive parent-teacher association, the TGSA. There is also a student council.

## Admissions and intake

Applications are made to the LEA. Places are offered according to the following criteria: those applicants with a brother or sister attending the school at the time of admission; those with social or medical need; and those living nearest the school. The location of the school in a borough where there is a selective system results in the intake on entry being potentially skewed to the lower ability range. However, the school has been oversubscribed for some years and all levels of ability are represented. In 2000, just over 1 per cent of all pupils at Tolworth had a local education authority statement of special needs. The school also has a number of pupils from a range of religious and cultural backgrounds.

## Achievement

In 2002, 75 per cent of pupils achieved five or more A*–C grades at GCSE. This was well above the borough and national averages and the school was ranked fifth in the borough. At A-level, the average point score was 228.6, ranking the school sixth in the borough. Tolworth achieved an Investors in People Award for the professionalism of its staff, and it is a Beacon School. It has also received an Education Extra Award at distinction level for its extra-curricular programme. The school has an excellent reputation for competitive sports.

## Extra-curricular activities

Every night, there is a study club open to all students. Other clubs available include reach-out, environment group, Amnesty International, maths and chess. There are regular trips in the UK and abroad, including visits to France, Spain and Germany. Sports on offer include trampolining, basketball, athletics and cross-country. The school also raises money for local charities.

# Lambeth

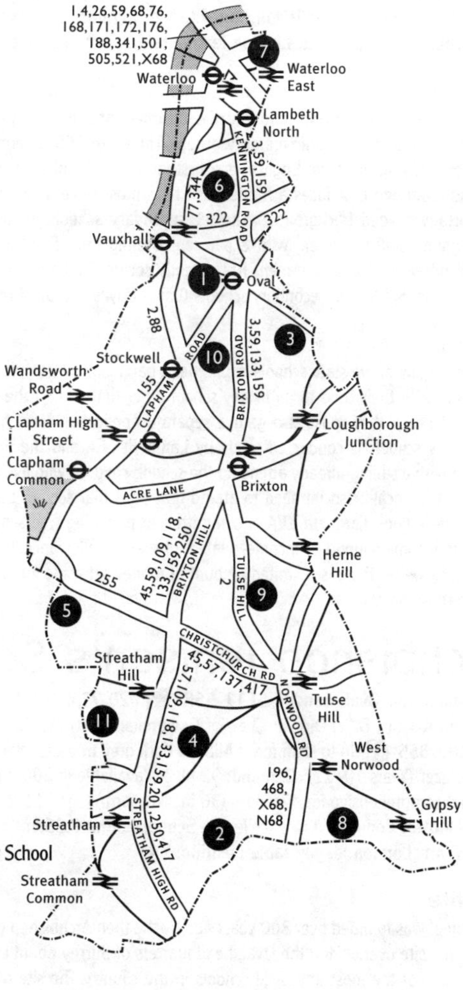


## Key

1. Archbishop Tenison's School
2. Bishop Thomas Grant Catholic Secondary School
3. Charles Edward Brooke School
4. Dunraven School
5. La Retraite RC Girls' School
6. Lilian Baylis School
7. London Nautical School
8. Norwood School
9. St Martin-in-the-Fields High School for Girls
10. Stockwell Park School
11. Streatham and Clapham High School

# Factfile

**LEA: Blue Star House, 234–244 Stockwell Road, London SW9 7QG** 020 7926-1000 www.lambeth.gov.uk **Director of Education:** Phyllis Dunipace (acting) **Political control of council:** Hung: Conservative and Liberal **Percentage of pupils from outside the borough:** 14.4 per cent **Percentage of pupils educated outside the borough:** 32.3 per cent **London league table positions (out of 32 boroughs):** 24th

## Profile

Lambeth is an ethnically and culturally diverse inner London borough. The overall population is around 265,000, with one third belonging to ethnic minority groups. There are 165 different languages spoken in the borough and many of its residents do not have English as a first language. Lambeth is rated the 12th most deprived local authority in England. Lambeth LEA faces a harder task than most since so many of its secondary school age population come from disadvantaged backgrounds. The 11 secondary schools in the borough, including one independent school, serve around 7000 children, with 8 per cent coming from Southwark, 4 per cent from Croydon and 13 per cent from Wandsworth. The government has recently set up the Lambeth EAZ, which consists of two nursery schools, 23 primary schools and two secondary schools (Lilian Baylis and Stockwell Park), and which aims to improve standards.

## Policy

To apply to any of the state schools in Lambeth, parents must complete and submit an application form from the LEA. If parents wish their child to go to any school other than one of the community schools (Lilian Baylis, Norwood and Stockwell Park), they must also gain a separate application form from the relevant school. Allocation of places at community schools is conducted solely by Lambeth LEA and the following criteria are applied in order of priority: children with a sibling already attending the school; children who live nearest to the school; those with a professionally supported medical or social need to attend that particular school; those with an unreasonably difficult journey to an alternative school. Lambeth LEA is committed to providing free school meals for those children whose parents are receiving income support or income-related jobseekers' allowance. The LEA also provides clothing and travel grants if needed. However, there is a limited amount of money set aside for each of these so, even if eligible, not everyone will receive these grants.

# Archbishop Tenison's School

**55 Kennington Oval, London SE11 5SR** 020 7735 3771 020 7793 8519 archtensch@aol.com Brian K Jones B.Sc, Dip.Ed; Chair of Governors: Mr JG Mordue Vauxhall Oval **Buses:** 3, 36, 109, 133, 159, 185, 355 Up to sixth form: Mid- or dark grey trousers, plain white shirt, school tie; blue blazer (Years 7–9); black blazer (Years 10–11) **Demand:** 92 places available in 2003; oversubscribed **Type:** Voluntary aided Church of England comprehensive for 476 boys (36 in sixth form), aged 11 to 18 **Submit application form:** Early November 2003 **Motto:** Committed to Excellence **School hours:** 8.35am–3.20pm **Meals:** Hot and cold available **Strong GCSEs:** Art **London league table position:** 247

## Profile

The school was founded over 300 years ago by the then Archbishop of Canterbury, Thomas Tenison. Today it is situated in a prime site overlooking the Oval, headquarters of Surrey County Cricket Club. In 2000, Archibishop Tenison's was named one of the most improved schools in the country. The site offers excellent facilities, including fully equipped science labs, a computer network giving a ratio of one computer to every two boys, a technology block, music suite, art and craft studios and a fully resourced library. On-site sporting facilities include a multigym and weight-training room, while Motspur Park offers football pitches, cricket nets and an athletics track. The school also enjoys extensive use of the Ken Barrington Centre at the Oval, the Shell Centre for swimming and the National Sports Centre at Crystal Palace. Gifted children are catered for through 'express' classes. After GCSE many boys choose to enter the school's sixth form, which is a consortium with Charles Edward Brooke School offering both A-levels and GNVQs. Sixth-formers act as prefects, school ambassadors on public occasions and assist younger pupils. The school's Christian foundation remains central to the ethos of the school. Each day begins with an act of worship or assembly. Holy Communion is held once a week in the school chapel and the chaplain acts as a counsellor to staff, boys and parents. There is a school council, a parent-teacher association and provision for special-needs pupils.

## Admissions and intake

Parents wishing to apply for a place at Archbishop Tenison's should contact the school for application forms.

## Achievement

In the Ofsted report of May 1999 inspectors considered 97 per cent of lessons to be satisfactory or above. Key Stage 3 results in maths, science and English were viewed favourably compared to similar schools. Music, art and drama are particular strengths. Overall, Ofsted concluded that 'the school's strengths far outweigh its weaknesses'. In 2002, 56 per cent of pupils gained five or more A*–C grades at GCSE. This was an increase on 35 per cent in 2001, continuing an upward trend and above the borough average. The school was ranked fourth in the borough league table. The average point score for pupils taking two or more A/AS-levels was 149.2, ranking the school fourth in Lambeth. Ofsted highlighted the 'support and guidance provided for pupils and the concern shown for individual pupils' as one of the strengths of the school.

## Extra-curricular activities

There is a popular handbell team that often performs at public events. The school also offers a variety of academic study and sporting clubs that run at lunchtimes and after school. Those studying or interested in art benefit from an artist in residence, while drama enthusiasts are able to participate in an annual international evening of cabaret. Pupils work with the charities in the local community.

# Bishop Thomas Grant Catholic Secondary School

**Beltrees Grove, London SW16 2HY** 020 8769 3294 020 8769 4917 info@btg-secondary.lambeth.sch.uk www.btg-secondary.lambeth.sch.uk Mr Louis Desa; Chair of Governors: Rev Canon JP Devane Streatham, Streatham Hill **Buses:** 249, 315, 417, 50, 60, 109, 118, 250 Black blazer, black trousers, white shirt **Demand:** 180 places available in 2003 **Type:** Voluntary aided Roman Catholic comprehensive for 953 mixed pupils, aged 11 to 16 **Submit application form:** Early November 2003 **Motto:** *Instaurare omnia in Christo* (To Unite All Things in Christ, Ephesians 1:10) **Mission statement:** High academic attainment in the context of Catholic spiritual and moral values **School hours:** 8.50am–3.30pm; homework clubs are available **Meals:** Hot and cold available **Strong GCSE subjects:** English, maths, science **London league table position:** 429

## Profile

The school was built in 1959 to serve the Catholic population of South London. It was purpose-built as a comprehensive and is situated in spacious grounds close to Streatham Common. Recently the science labs, business studies area and ceramics room have been refurbished and a new learning resources centre established. Ofsted remarked: 'The curriculum is broad and balanced and is a strength of the school.' With its strong Catholic ethos, assemblies, liturgies and RE play a prominent role in school life. Considerable emphasis is placed on pastoral care; each child has a form tutor who they can go to with questions and problems. There are also school councils in each year where pupils' views on school life can be aired, and older boys are trained as 'mediators' in order to assist younger pupils. There is a prefects system. One staff member, Sister Ella Flynn FMA, offers confidential counselling to students and their families. There is provision for special-needs pupils.

## Admissions and intake

Priority in admissions is given to those who have been baptized into the Catholic Church and who continue to practise along with one parent. If places still remain, the following criteria are used: those with a sibling already attending the school; those baptized into the Catholic faith whose parents desire a Catholic education for them; those whose parents are members of the Christian Orthodox Church and are baptized into the church but who have no access to a school of their own denomination; and baptized children whose parents are non-Catholics but who desire a Christian education for their child. The final two criteria both require the support of a minister. A high proportion of the intake, around 21 per cent, have low levels of numeracy and literacy upon admission.

## Achievement

In 2002, 29 per cent of pupils gained five or more A*–C grades at GCSE. These results were down from 37 per cent in 2001 and below the borough average. The school was ranked ninth in the borough league table overall. Ofsted inspectors considered the school's GCSE results as 'much better than for similar schools nationally'. Despite close monitoring of pupils, Ofsted noted 'management of behaviour and attendance' as a 'significant weakness'. The authorized absence rate for 2000 was above average for the borough at 9.4 per cent, but unauthorized absence at 0.5 per cent was below average nationally and for the borough.

## Extra-curricular activities

Art, drama and music are all encouraged outside of as well as within lessons. Tuition is available in all orchestral instruments. Strong links have been developed with the Young Vic Theatre. Sport is well catered for through non-competitive clubs, such as aerobics and gymnastics, as well as through inter-school competition. After-school homework clubs are offered in many of its subjects.

# Charles Edward Brooke School

**Brooke Site, Langton Rd, London SW9 6UL (upper school); Dennen Site, Cormont Rd, London SE5 9RF (lower school)** 020 7274 6311 020 7735 8132 (upper school); 020 7733 2367 (lower school) heads@cebs-secondary.lambeth.sch.uk Jane Cruse BA; Chair of Governors: Margaret Spooner Oval **Buses**: 3, 36, 159, 185 Navy skirt or dark blue trousers, white blouse, house tie, house belt **Demand**: 150 places in 2003; oversubscribed **Type**: Voluntary controlled Art College for 825 (78 in sixth form) girls, aged 11 to 18 **Submit application form**: Early November 2003 **Mission statement**: We will support each student in developing her talents in a stimulating, secure environment based on Christian principles. As a Media Arts College our mission is to make Charles Edward Brooke School a high achieving school... we will be a beacon locally and nationally, leading the way into the future through the media arts. **School hours**: 8.50am–3.25pm; homework clubs are available **Meals**: Hot and cold available **Strong GCSE subjects:** Art, dance, drama, English, media studies, religious studies
**London league table position**: 407

## Profile

Founded in 1898 by Canon Brooke, vicar at St John the Divine in Vassall Road, the school moved to Langton Road in 1968, taking over the site in Cormont Road in 1983, which now houses the lower school. The school is in one of Lambeth's most deprived areas, with high levels of unemployment. The school was the first in London to gain Media Arts College status in September 1998. Accordingly, it has excellent information and communication facilities and a state-of-the-art multimedia studio with editing suite. The school was awarded the Artsmark Gold Award in 2001. There is a chapel and RE centre, and a high-quality three-storey technology block. The school runs a joint sixth form with Archbishop Tenison's, offering a range of A-levels and GNVQs. It has many links with employers and universities and is part of the Eagle Scheme working with Cambridge University. Staff links with parents are strong and include an annual action-planning day to agree targets for each pupil as well as parents' evenings and reports. There is a school council, prefects system and provision for special-needs pupils. Student responsibility is a focus.

## Admissions and intake

Twenty-five per cent of places are reserved for applicants who are committed regular worshippers at a Christian church or whose families are. A letter of support is required from the church leader, followed by an interview. Admissions criteria in order of priority are: attendance at St John the Divine Church, Kennington; having a sister at the school; having a special need that the school can meet; and proximity of home to the school. Seventy five per cent are 'open' places and allocated according to the latter three criteria.

## Achievement

In 2002, 36 per cent of pupils gained five or more A*-C grades, down from 40 per cent in 2001 and reinstating a downward trend. This was also below the borough average and the school was ranked eighth in the borough league table. These results are a vast improvement on previous years as 10 years ago, results were as low as eight per cent for five or more A*–Cs. Ofsted visted in 2002 and commented that 'this is a good, oversubscribed school, with numerous very good features'. Inspectors praised the 'dynamic, high quality leadership' of the school and GCSE results were seen to be higher than would reasonably be expected. However, Ofsted noted that attendance is 'unsatisfactory' and 'too many students' punctuality is poor'. The average point score for pupils taking two or more A/AS-levels was 117.3, ranking it fifth in the borough. The school has been graded at A and A* in the nationally produced performance and assessment charts (PANDA), which compare schools in similar social circumstances.

## Extra-curricular activities

A variety of clubs and societies are run outside of lesson time, including an Outward Bound challenge scheme and homework clubs. There are extra Saturday morning classes for GCSE students and also holiday schemes/revision classes, which include some to support parents trying to help their children in their studies. The school's ethos and media arts status encourages strong links with the community and pupils have recently participated in supporting charities such as Shelter and the Great Ormond Street Hospital. There is an impressive mentoring scheme, involving the area health authority staff and school staff. Media arts provides masterclasses in many areas and there are a large number of performances for music and dance with prestigious national companies. The school is part of the Excellence in Cities initiative and this includes projects for gifted and talented students. There are parent and community workshops in ICT, together with family worship services. There are also regular school trips, including a trip to France.

# Dunraven School

**94–98 Leigham Court, London SW16 2QB** 020 8677 2431 020 8664 7242 info@dunraven-school.org.uk www.dunraven-school.org.uk Richard Townsend MA (Cantab), PGCE, FRSA; Chair of Governors: Dr Alan Aylward Streatham Hill; **Buses**: 57, 109, 118, 133, 159, 249, 250, 417 Royal blue blazer and pullover, plain dark blue or grey skirt or trousers, white, plain blue or grey shirt or blouse, royal blue and gold school tie **Demand**: 1400 applications for 192 places in 2001/2 **Type**: Foundation comprehensive for 927 mixed pupils, aged 11 to 16 **Submit application form**: Early November 2003 **Motto**: Excellence for All **School hours**: 8.45am–3.30pm; homework clubs are available **Meals**: Hot and cold available **Strong GCSEs**: Performing arts **London league table position**: 237

## Profile

Dunraven is situated on a split site either side of the Leigham Court Road, with the upper school occupying the site of the former Philippa Fawcett College. The location provides extensive grounds, including tennis courts and games areas. Facilities include eight science labs, a technology suite, dance/drama theatre, music suite, art suite, business education centre, home economic facilities, two gymnasia and an excellent computer network, giving both sites access to the Internet. A landscaped garden was opened on the lower school site in 1991 and in 1994 this site received a grant of £500,000 for extensive improvements. The school has been awarded £3 million of government funding to open a new sixth form in 2003. Particular attention is paid to able pupils, with both accelerated and accelerating learning groups, and where possible GCSEs are taken early. Special attention is also paid to those with special educational needs and pupils who have English as an additional language. Parents are kept in touch with their child's progress through parents' evenings, termly assessments and homework organizers, which they must sign. A weekly newsletter is distributed to keep parents and pupils up-to-date with school life. There is a prefects system.

## Admissions and intake

All applicants are required to take a standardized test in verbal reasoning, non-verbal reasoning and numeracy. Applicants are then divided into three ability bands: 40 per cent of places are then filled from each of the top two bands, 20 per cent from the lowest. Priority is given, in order, to those with a sibling at the school; medical and/or social reasons for attending; and proximity to the school. Although there is an option of appeal, few are successful. Just over a quarter of pupils are considered to have special educational needs.

## Achievement

In 2002, 55 per cent of pupils gained five A*–C grades at GCSE, well above the borough average of 40.1 per cent and above the national average of 51.65 per cent. This surpassed the results of 2001 and Dunraven was placed third in the borough league table. The average point score was 31.1. Ofsted commented that the 'majority of pupils, including those with special educational needs, are achieving at levels commensurate with their capability'. Inspectors noted that 'very good relationships exist between teachers and pupils', which are aided by the school council where representatives from each tutor group have a voice. Overall Dunraven was considered to be 'an effectively managed school with many strong features'.

### Extra-curricular activities

Music is strong, with over 200 pupils enjoying individual music lessons. Links have been established with the Centre for Young Musicians and the Royal Opera House. Activities and clubs run at both lunchtimes and after school, and range from homework clubs, chess and pottery to volleyball. The school has access to the Crystal Palace Sports Centre for Years 10–11, which offers specialist equipment for activities such as diving and trampolining. There are fund-raising activities for the local community and trips both at home and abroad.

# La Retraite RC Girls' School

**Atkins Rd, London SW12 0AB** 020 8673 5644 020 8675 8577 schsec.laretraite@rmplc.co.uk Mrs M Howie MA, FRSA; Chair of Governors: Mrs M Arnold MBE Balham Balham, Clapham South **Buses**: 57, 60, 417 Up to sixth form: Blue blazer, tartan plaid kilt, white blouse (long-sleeved with tie in winter; short sleeved, open-neck in summer), navy blue V-neck jumper with gold trim **Demand**: 135 places; ratio of applications to places 3:1 **Type**: Voluntary aided Roman Catholic for 776 girls, aged 11 to 18 **Submit application form**: Early November 2003 **Motto**: *Ad majorem dei gloriam* (To God's Greatest Glory) **Mission statement**: A traditional academic education in a Christian environment **School hours**: 8.40am–3.35pm; homework clubs are available **Meals**: Hot and cold available, including breakfast **Strong GCSEs**: English, music, sciences **London league table position**: 213

### Profile

La Retraite has been providing education for girls in the local area for over 100 years. Situated between two commons, facilities on offer include a new six-lab science block, multi-purpose technology and arts centre, recently refurbished maths, business studies, languages and humanities blocks and excellent computer resources. La Retraite is a designated Beacon School. The school offers a broad curriculum with a strong emphasis on science and is also a specialist music school. Fifty per cent of pupils continue into the recently established sixth form, which offers a wide range of A/AS-levels and GNVQs. The school is currently developing an MA in education with King's College, London. The vast majority go on to university, including Oxbridge, and La Retraite has sponsorship from St John's College, Cambridge. Progress is monitored on a half-termly basis with two sets of exams annually, reports being sent home after each. The Christian ethos gives a strong communal feel; sixth-formers act as role models for the younger girls. Pastoral care is a strength, with a number of classes having assistant form tutors. Links between staff and pupils are built up through year-group councils and the school council. There is a prefects system, a parent-teacher association and provision for special-needs pupils.

### Admissions and intake

Applicants must take aptitude tests and are then divided into three ability bands. Fifty per cent are drawn from the middle band and 25 per cent from each of the first and third. Ten per cent of places are awarded to pupils with particular musical aptitude. Applicants will be prioritized by membership and practice in the Catholic Church, with a priest's religious reference required. In exceptional cases places may be offered on compassionate grounds. If places still remain, applicants from other Christian churches will be considered. If two applications are equal, the decision will rest on accessibility of the school to the home. Fifty two percent of pupils speak English as an additional language.

### Achievement

In 2002, 61 per cent of pupils gained five or more A*–C grades at GCSE, above the national average. This made it the highest-achieving comprehensive in Lambeth for the third year running. The average point score for pupils taking two or more A/AS-levels was 193.8, the second-best results locally.

### Extra-curricular activities

Having won a Lawn Tennis Association grant, the sport has grown in popularity and strong links have been forged with Grafton Lawn Tennis Club. Any girl on a music scholarship is given free tuition upon the instrument of her choice. A music school, open to all, takes place on Wednesday evenings, and there are supervised homework clubs. Two major drama productions are staged annually, with Shakespeare workshops on offer at the Young Vic. A number of trips are arranged in the UK and abroad. Pupils can take part in the Duke of Edinburgh's Award scheme.

# Lilian Baylis School

**Lollard Street, London SE11 6PY** ☎ 020 7735 3105 Fax 020 7820 0159 e school@lilianbaylis.com www.lilian.baylis.com Gary Philips B.Sc (Hons), MA; Chair of Governors: Mr David Smith ⇌ Vauxhall, Waterloo ⊖ Kennington, Lambeth North **Buses:** 3, 10, 12, 53, 77, 109, 155, 159, 344, 507 Dark blazer, navy blue pullover or sweatshirt, dark trousers, white shirt, school tie **Demand:** 210 places available in 2002; oversubscribed **Type:** Community comprehensive for 522 mixed pupils, aged 11 to 16 **Submit application form:** Early November 2003 **Motto:** At Lilian Baylis Children Come First **School hours:** 8.30am–3.05pm; homework clubs are available **Meals:** Hot and cold available **Strong GCSEs:** Drama **London league table position:** 515

## Profile

Lilian Baylis school is situated very near Lambeth Walk in the heart of inner-city London. It lies in an area of mainly local authority housing. The school buildings include a residential centre, a vast all-weather sports hall, an excellent library and five computer suites. In 1999, Lilian Baylis embarked on a two-year plan to become a specialist IT school located in a new purpose-built building. This is part of a regeneration programme for the whole area involving investment of millions of pounds. The project has provided the school with the very best in modern computer facilities. The school operates a career-targeted programme, which includes work experience and mentoring by senior employees such as bankers, journalists and firefighters. It also offers a family learning programme, which includes residential and day courses as well as study trips abroad for both pupils and parents. This has included trips to the Thames Barrier, Oxford University and Gatwick Airport. The school has a special nurturing programme for new entrants in Year 7. There is a school council and provision for special-needs pupils.

## Admissions and intake

Admissions are dealt with by the LEA (see borough factfile). A quarter of admissions each year are casual, often after the age of 11 when new students move into the area. Pupils are drawn largely from an area of high social and economic disadvantage. The Ofsted report of 2000 noted that: 'Nearly half of the pupils have English as an additional language and 10 per cent are at an early stage of learning English'.

## Achievement

Lilian Baylis School has a chequered history with Ofsted. It has been inspected eight times since 1994. However, over recent years the school has made a new start, winning praise from all quarters. *The Times Educational Supplement* described it as 'London's fastest improving school'. The most recent inspection was in 2001 when Inspectors noted that 'the situation is improving with well-focused and determined leadership'. Strategies to improve behaviour, attendance and quality of teaching were seen to be beginning to pay off although 'there is still a long way to go'. In 2002, only six per cent of pupils achieved five or more A*–C grades. This was down from 18 per cent in 2001 and still well below the borough and national averages. The school was ranked bottom of the borough league table. Lilian Bayliss School has a tough approach to discipline and this was described by the *Evening Standard* as 'zero tolerance, getting tough on truancy, attitude, uniform, everything'. In 1999, this approach worked as truancy was just 0.1 per cent but this has since risen to 13.0 per cent in 2000.

## Extra-curricular activities

The school offers after-school homework clubs. A wide range of sports is on offer. There are trips both at home and abroad. Pupils are involved in mentoring schemes with local businesses.

# London Nautical School

**61 Stamford St, Blackfriars, London SE1 9NA** ☎ 020 7928 6801 Fax 020 7261 9408 e admin@nautical.lambeth.sch.uk Mr GH Wilson BA, M.Ed FRSA; Chair of Governors: Mr K Sime ACII ⇌ London Bridge **Buses:** 381 Plain black socks, black beret, black tie, black flannel trousers, plain white shirt, plain black lace-up shoes, lower school jersey (with epaulettes) and watch flashes, black anorak **Demand:** Variable for 90 places in 2001/2 **Type:** Foundation comprehensive secondary for 561 boys, aged 11 to 18 **Submit application form:** Early

November 2003 **Motto**: *Tamesis suos Ubique Feret* (Wherever the Thames May Carry Us) **School hours**: 8.45am–3.40pm, 8.45am–2.50pm (Wed); homework clubs are available **Meals**: Hot and cold available **Strong GCSEs**: Science (double award), nautical studies **London league table position**: 280

## Profile

The London Nautical School was founded in 1915, following the official report into the Titanic disaster. In 1990 the school became one of the first in the country to achieve grant-maintained status and in 1999 assumed foundation status within the borough of Lambeth. The school reflects its maritime origins in both study and ethos, preparing its pupils to meet the 'requirements of society, either at sea or in any other occupation'. The school has excellent sports facilities, including a gymnasium with multi-weights area, a playing field, use of the swimming pool at Guy's Hospital and use of the Tooting Bec Athletics Stadium. All boys are expected to attend a week-long residential course on the River Blackwater in Essex. In 1999, £65,000 was spent upgrading and improving the computer network, which now has 80 computers linked to the Internet. There is a PTA, a prefects system, a school council and provision for pupils with special needs.

## Admissions and Intake

New entrants are admitted without reference to academic ability, the importance being placed upon the boy's subscription to the school's nautical ethos. Preference is given to those boys who fulfil certain criteria, for example: family nautical history, boys' career/ambition choice (maritime preferred) and nautical interest.

## Achievement

The school was awarded a National Sportsmark Award in recognition of its sporting achievements and gained the FA Charter Mark for Excellence in 1999. The school finished sixth in the Lambeth school league for GCSEs in 2002. The school has enjoyed a steady improvement in GCSE results since 1996, with 47 per cent of pupils achieving A–C grades in five or more subjects in 2002. This was up from 45 per cent in 2001. The average A/AS-level grade point score for 16–18 year old pupils in 2002 was 167 (for two or more subjects). Strong A-levels include business studies.

## Extra-curricular activities

The school boasts an impressive extra-curricular sports programme, also offering after-school and lunchtime clubs, judo and tae kwon do. There are after-school homework clubs. The modern languages department organizes trips to Spain and France, including a French nautical week in Biscarosse for Years 7, 8 and 9; a weekend in Paris for Year 10; and a visit to Spain for those taking GCSE Spanish. Pupils work with local charities.

# Norwood School

**Crown Dale, London SE19 3NY** ☎ 020 8670 9382 📠 020 8761 5933 ⓔ post@norwoodschool.com 🌐 www.norwoodschool.com Barbara Williams BA ⇌ West Norwood **Buses**: 2, 68, 196, 249, 417, 468 Bottle green blazer, white school shirt or polo shirt with green stripe on collar, bottle green sweatshirt with school badge **Demand**: 150 places in 2001/2; oversubscribed **Type**: Community comprehensive for 653 girls, aged 11 to 16 **Submit application form**: Early November 2003 **Motto**: Dedication to Learning, Dedication to Achieve **School hours**: 8.50am–3.30pm; homework clubs are available **Meals**: Hot and cold available **Strong GCSE subjects**: Art, design and technology **London league table position**: 374

## Profile

Norwood is located next to Norwood Park, set in attractive grounds, giving plenty of space for relaxation and play. The school itself is well equipped for science, ICT, technology and PE, as well as having provision for the arts with a dance studio, drama studio, art rooms and music centre. The Great Hall is large enough for both whole school assemblies and performances. An ongoing development is the learning resource centre, which gives students access to library facilities and computers. Students are able to voice their opinions on the school council, and various focus groups meet for different year groups. Each year a head girl and a number of deputies are appointed, along with a team of prefects in order to carry out supervisory duties. Parents are kept up-to-date with their child's progress through the recently revised annual report system. There is provision for special-needs pupils.

## Admissions and intake

Admission is dealt with by the LEA (see borough factfile). Thirty-five per cent of pupils have English as an additional language.

## Achievement

In 2002, 33 per cent of entrants gained five or more A*–C grades at GCSE and the school was ranked seventh in the borough league table. This was 14 per cent up on 2001's results but below the borough average. Ofsted reported that 'good teaching occurs in most subject areas, though even in the same subject there is weak alongside good'. Science shows itself to be a weakness of the school, with 25 per cent of entrants not gaining even a G grade in 1999. However, art and design and technology are strengths; 64 per cent of those taking art gained A*–Cs and 97 per cent of those taking design and technology gained A*–Gs in 1999. Ofsted reported that 'Norwood is an improving school'. Furthermore 'pupils with English as a second language are being enabled to achieve in line with their peers due to good support teaching'. Ofsted praised pupils as 'an asset to the school. Their attitude to their work is good; they are conscientious, want to learn and are working towards the school motto'. The racial harmony was considered 'a real strength'. Authorized absence is high at 10.8 per cent, while unauthorized absence is only below the borough and national average at 0.8 per cent.

## Extra-curricular activities

There are clubs both after school and at lunchtime, with a Cyber Club giving girls access to the Internet. Arts are an area of excellence, and music, drama and dance performances are regularly presented at assemblies and to the public. Links have been established with the Ballet Rambert, the Bubble Theatre and the Dulwich Picture Gallery. After-school homework clubs are available. Pupils are involved in mentoring schemes with local businesses and also collect for various charities. A wide range of sports is on offer.

# St Martin-in-the-Fields High School for Girls

**155 Tulse Hill, London SW2 3UP** 020 8674 5594 020 8674 1379 stmartins@stmartins.lambeth.sch.uk www.stmartins.lambeth.sch.uk Mrs Lesley Morrison B.Sc; Chair of Governors: Lady Reid MA Tulse Hill, Brixton Brixton **Buses:** P13, 2, 68, 68A, 196, 201, 322 School blazer, plain dark brown skirt in plain material, plain beige blouse; brown school jumper with red neck stripe (Years 7–8); red with brown neck stripe (Years 9–11) **Demand:** Three applicants for each of 140 places **Type:** Voluntary aided Technology College for 617 girls aged 11 to 16 **Submit application form:** Early November 2003 **Motto:** *Caritate et disciplina* (Affection and Discipline) **Mission statement:** Fostering self-esteem, promoting excellence **School hours:** 8.40am–3.30pm; homework clubs are available **Meals:** Hot and cold available **Strong GCSE subjects:** Art, business, design and technology **London league table position:** 256

## Profile

Over 300 years old, the school's present-day site is in Tulse Hill, but strong links are maintained with its founder church, St Martin-in-the-Fields in Trafalgar Square. While Christian principles remain central to the school, St Martin's welcomes pupils from other denominations and faiths, and is proud to consider itself a multi-ethnic and culturally diverse school. In 1996 it was awarded Technology College status and has benefited considerably from sponsorship by Accord Energy Ltd, totalling £150,000. The school now boasts a state-of-the-art ICT and business centre as well as a new design and technology block, named the Anne Philpott Centre in honour of the previous head teacher, and a new music centre. A broad range of GCSE subjects is offered, including the chance to study single sciences. Speakers from many denominations are invited to the daily assembly. The small size of the school encourages the atmosphere of a close-knit community. This is aided by the school council, with representatives from each class, which meets regularly, and also by the prefects who help support staff and Year 7 pupils. There is provision available for special needs pupils.

## Admissions and intake

Applicants are required to take standardized tests in English and maths from which they are placed into three ability bands. Half of the places are filled from the middle band and 25 per cent from each of the first and third. Half of the places in each ability band are reserved for children of regular worshippers at a Christian church. If there are more applicants than places, priority is given, in order, to: those with a sibling at the school; those with a special need; and those living nearest to the school. The remaining 'open' places are allocated according to the same criteria, but the desire of parents for a religious foundation school and an all-girls environment is also taken into account. The school expects all children to take part in Christian worship and attend RE lessons.

### Achievement

St Martin's has shown considerable academic improvement over recent years. In 2002, 59 per cent of entrants gained five or more A*-C grades at GCSE, up from 54 per cent in 2001. The school was placed fifth in the borough league table. This was above the borough and national averages. In 1999's exams, results were particularly high in art, design and technology and business studies, with 83 per cent, 86 per cent and 91 per cent respectively gaining A*–C grades.

### Extra-curricular activities

The school has become well known for its outstanding gospel choirs. These have been featured on national television and have performed in venues such as the Royal Albert Hall and St Paul's Cathedral. Recently the school won an Outstanding Performance Award at the National Festival of Music for Youth. Sportswomen at the school regularly pit their abilities against rival schools in both athletics and football. Homework clubs are available during the lunch hour and after school. There are many school trips, both at home and abroad.

## Stockwell Park School

**Clapham Road, London SW9 0AL** 020 7733 6156 020 7738 6196 info@stockpark.lambeth.sch.uk Ms J Tapper; Chair of Governors: Mr A Alabi Stockwell **Buses:** 2, 50, 88, 155, 345 Black jacket, black trousers (girls can wear black culottes/skirts), white shirt, black, white or grey socks, black shoes; white T-shirt (summer); black sweatshirt, cardigan or pullover optional **Demand:** Figures unavailable but 180 places are oversubscribed **Type:** Community comprehensive for 807 mixed pupils, aged 11 to 16 **Submit application form:** Early November 2003 **Mission statement:** High Achievement for All **School hours:** 9am–3.30pm; homework clubs are available **Meals:** Hot and cold available **Strong GCSEs:** Art, English, media studies **London league table position:** 457

### Profile

Stockwell Park School is located near the clock tower at Stockwell on a purpose-built site. It has spacious grounds that provide three separate play areas for pupils, two of which are grassed. The buildings include six newly built science labs, enlarged classrooms to aid computer-assisted learning, and three computer suites. In addition, the school has its own swimming pool, boys' and girls' gyms, a students' recreation room and tuck shop. Stockwell Park prides itself on its respect for all racial groups so that different cultures are valued and the self-esteem of pupils nurtured. This attitude is encapsulated by the school badge, which comprises a lion with the word 'Unity' running underneath. A full range of subjects are offered at GCSE. An impressive element of Stockwell Park is its close-knit community. Form tutors see their pupils every morning and afternoon, and help pupils work through difficulties. The school's pastoral team works closely with education social workers for pupils with problems such as attendance, punctuality or general school work. Merit marks are given for good work and certificates are presented in assembly. Pupils have the opportunity to participate in the school council and become prefects, who assist staff in the supervision of the school site. Particular attention is paid to those pupils who have special educational needs, and the bilingual department supports those who do not have English as their first language. There is an active parent-teacher association.

### Admissions and intake

Admissions are dealt with by the LEA (see borough factfile).

### Achievement

GCSE results have improved overall in recent years, with 26 per cent of pupils gaining five or more A*–C grades in 2002, down from 29 per cent in 2001. The school was ranked 10th in the borough league table. Ofsted visited the school in 2002 and described Stockwell Park as 'an improving school which provides a sound education'. GCSE results were seen to be improving and are in line with those of similar schools. Pupils of all levels of attainment and background were seen to 'make good progress as a result of good teaching'. Inspectors praised the school's 'positive atmosphere' and noted that pupils with English as an additional language 'make good progress overall'. Behaviour has improved since the last inspection and provision for pupils with special needs was 'satisfactory overall'. However, improvements need to be made in the scope of the curriculum, the teaching of numeracy and the use of assessment. Attendance was found to be 'unsatisfactory' and authorized absence is high at 8.7 per cent, while unauthorized absence is below the borough and national average at 0.9 per cent.

### Extra-curricular activities

After-school activities range from martial arts to Arabic, and provision is given for pupils to learn a variety of musical instruments. There are after-school homework clubs. Pupils are involved with the local community, working with local charities. There are many local trips.

# Streatham and Clapham High School

**42 Abbotswood Rd, Streatham Hill, London SW16 1AW** 020 8677 8400 020 8677 2001 enquiry@shc.gdst.net www.gdst.net/streathamhigh Mrs S Mitchell MA (Hons) Oxford Streatham Hill, Balham Balham **Buses:** 115; school coach service runs from Clapham and Putney/Wimbledon areas Olive green skirt, white blouse, green sweater; modern black fleece jacket and black tights in winter **Demand:** No figures available but oversubscribed **Type:** Selective independent, part of the Girls' Day School Trust, for 900 girls, aged 3 to 18 (and boys aged 3 to5) **Fees:** £2,385 per term (senior school) **Submit application form:** Mid-November 2003 **School hours:** 8.35am–4.00pm (senior school) **Meals:** Hot and cold available **Strong GCSEs:** Sciences **London league table position:** 75

### Profile

The school dates back to 1894 and is the result of an amalgamation of schools in Clapham and Brixton. Today the senior school is situated next to Tooting Bec Common, with its 3.7 acres of grounds providing a highly attractive, peaceful environment. Facilities include a newly opened Millennium building which houses a sixth form suite, recital room, six modern science labs, a purpose-built IT centre, a large sports hall, library, dance studio, fitness centre, music suite, art studio and pottery room. Girls study nine or 10 GCSE subjects including the option of Latin from Year 7. Most pupils carry on into the sixth form where an extensive choice of A-levels are on offer. Languages are a particular strength and include Spanish, Italian and German. The school has also successfully pioneered distance learning at A-level which includes psychology, sociology and law. Two sixth formers are assigned to each class to support new entrants. Parents are kept in touch with their child's progress through regular feedback. In-depth reports are sent home twice each year and there are regular parents'evenings. Effort and attainment grades are sent to parents four times a year. Prefects and a head girl are elected by the staff and senior school members. The girls' successes are celebrated at daily assemblies. There is a school council and effective provision for special-needs pupils. Famous ex-pupils include the novelist Angela Carter and actresses June Whitfield and Hannah Waddingham.

### Admissions and intake

Admission to the nursery is from the age of three and is made by assessment from the age of four upwards. Applicants aged 11 plus and for the sixth form have to sit an entrance examination. Bursaries are available from age 11 upwards and at sixth form entry. Applications for bursaries at other levels can be made to the head teacher in cases of financial need. These awards are means-tested and all requests are considered in confidence. Scholarships are available to internal and external candidates from age 11 upwards and at sixth form level.

### Achievement

In 2002, 94 per cent of pupils gained five or more A*–C grades at GCSE. These were the top results in the borough league table and in line with the success of previous years. At A-level, the average point score for pupils taking two or more A/AS levels in 2002 was 362.7, again the top result in Lambeth. The school won first prize in the Institution of Civil Engineering national competition in 1998 and 1999, and one pupil was selected in 2000 for the National Youth Theatre.

## Extra-curricular activities

Streatham Hill and Clapham High School offers a wide variety of clubs, numbering around 70 in total, including photography, dance, astronomy and debating. A wide range of sports is also on offer and Years 7 and 10 participate in self-defence classes. Girls can learn a variety of musical instruments and can play in one of the school's several orchestras. There are many school trips on offer to the pupils, which are designed to complement the girls' study. This includes foreign exchanges to France, Germany and Spain as well as visits to galleries, museums and concerts. Pupils also have the opportunity to participate in the Duke of Edinburgh's Award scheme. Pupils have substantial involvement with the local community and regularly raise funds for a number of local charities.

# Lewisham

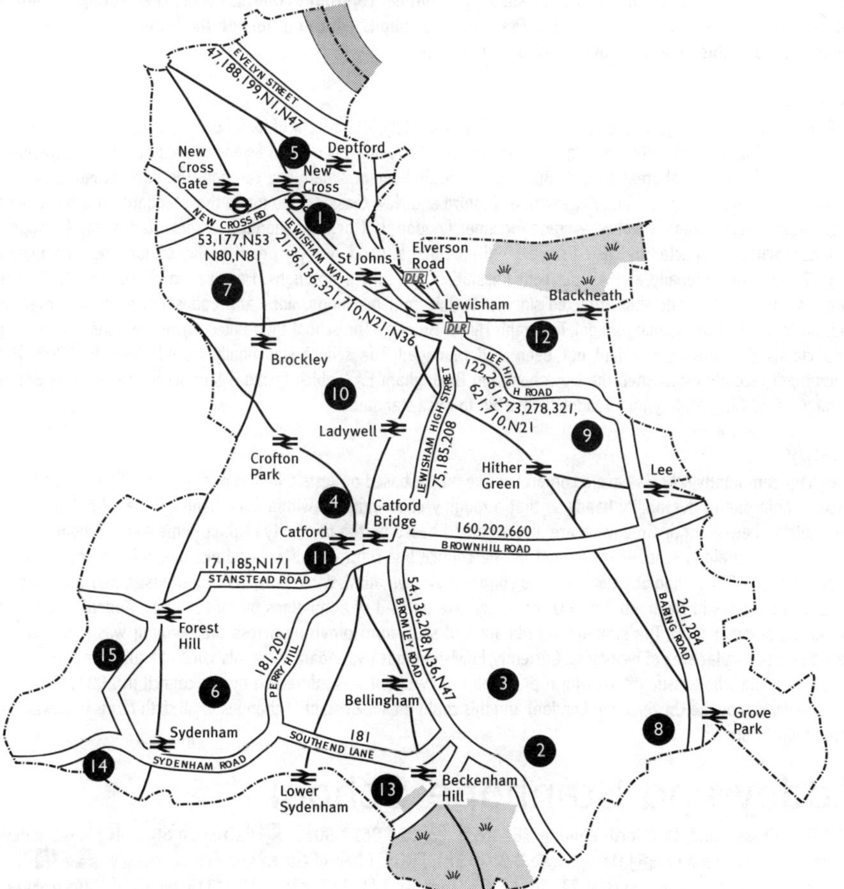


**Key**

1. Addey and Stanhope School
2. Bonus Pastor RC School
3. Catford Girls' School
4. Crofton School
5. Deptford Green School
6. Forest Hill School
7. Haberdashers' Aske's Hatcham College
8. Malory School
9. Northbrook CofE School
10. Prendergast School
11. St Dunstan's College
12. St Joseph's Academy
13. Sedgehill School
14. Sydenham High School
15. Sydenham School

# Factfile

**LEA: Laurence House, 1 Catford Road, London SE6 4SW** ☎ 020 8314 6000 www.lewisham.gov.uk **Director of education and culture:** Ms Frankie Sulke **Political control of council:** Labour **Percentage of pupils from outside the borough:** 10.5 per cent **Percentage of pupils educated outside the borough:** 20.4 per cent **London league table positions (out of 32 boroughs):** 26th

## Profile

Lewisham is the third-largest borough in London. Approximately 50 per cent of its school population are from ethnic minorities and about 121 different languages are spoken. Although it is classed as an inner-city borough, Lewisham has a good mix of genteel areas such as Blackheath and Sydenham, where you can find tree-lined avenues, as well as vibrant enclaves of a typical inner-city such as Catford and New Cross. Ofsted found that standards of achievement in Lewisham were generally above average for inner London, but below national averages. Half of the borough's secondary schools inspected by Ofsted since 1996 provided a 'good' or 'very good' quality of education, compared with 67 per cent nationally and 45 per cent for statistically similar boroughs. However, in September 1999, the council's educational leadership attracted significant flak from teaching unions and opposition politicians over its decision to 'fresh start' a failing school, Telegraph Hill in Brockley. The school then failed again less than a year later amid claims that the change had not been well managed. The school was finally closed down in 2001. The government recently established the Downham and Bellingham EAZ which includes four secondary schools, Bonus Pastor, Catford Girls, Malory and Sedgehill, in a bid to raise standards.

## Policy

Lewisham community schools have a comprehensive intake based on tests taken at primary school level. Pupils are placed within one of five ability bands so that a roughly equal number within each band can be admitted. Pupils from outside Lewisham or Greenwich are also admitted based on the proximity of their home to the school of their choice. Voluntary aided schools are funded by the council but control their own admissions policies. Independent schools and the City Technology Colleges also control their own admissions. Prospective parents should visit schools on scheduled dates in September and October, and are notified of admissions by mid-January. Appeals are heard during the summer term. The strategic coordination of sixth-form provision across the borough was identified by Ofsted as a particular area of weakness. Currently, Lewisham has two separate schools' consortia providing combined sixth forms. The whole issue of sixth-form provision in Lewisham was addressed by the council in 2001, (a review was undertaken by the University of London) and this could mean substantial changes to all sixth forms in Lewisham in the near future.

# Addey and Stanhope School

**472 New Cross Road, Deptford, London SE14 6TJ** ☎ 020 8692 3012 Fax 020 8694 8877 info@addey-stanhope.lewisham.sch.uk David Whyte B.Sc (Hons), FRGS; Chair of Governors: Cliff Hardcastle New Cross; DLR: Deptford Bridge **Buses:** 21, 36, 47, 53, 75, 136, 171, 177, 225, 321 Brown blazer, brown skirt or grey trousers, school tie; Sixth form: Office-style dress in black, white or grey **Demand:** 492 applications for 99 places in 2001/2; 120 places in 2003 **Type:** Voluntary aided comprehensive for 587 mixed pupils, aged 11 to 19 **Submit application form:** Mid-October 2003 **Mission statement:** Learning Together, Achieving Together **School hours:** 8.50am–3.30pm, 8.50am–3pm (Wed); homework clubs are available **Meals:** Hot available **Strong GCSE subjects:** Art, drama, science **London league table position:** 403

## Profile

This school performs well, although it is in an area with recognized indications of high social deprivation. Established in 1715, it is a registered charity. In the late 1990s the school governors opted out of LEA control in order to garner government cash for building upgrades and extensions. There are good facilities, including a new design and technology block, food technology rooms, a music suite and the largest art room in southern England. Thousands of pounds have been spent in overhauling the science labs. There are also plans for a new gym and English centre. Special-needs facilities are available and form teachers are responsible for pastoral care. There are regular meetings between parents and teachers and an active PTA.

### Admissions and intake

Admissions are drawn evenly from all ability groups according to set criteria. Prospective parents must attend an open session in the autumn term. Most pupils entering the school have low levels of literacy and numeracy.The school plans to increase its number of pupils to about 700 over the next few years.

### Achievement

Results at GCSE level were below average for the borough in 2002; 32 per cent of pupils gained five or more A*–C grades, which was down on 40 per cent in 2001 and reinstates a downward trend. Pupils achieve high standards when compared with similar schools, although on leaving school at the age of 16, their achievement level is generally below the national average.The exceptions to this are art, science and drama, which are average or above.The school is also strong in music and PE.The sixth form is provided through a consortium with Deptford Green and is supported by Lewisham College.The average point score for pupils with two or more A-levels in 2002 was 142.5, putting the school eighth in the local league table. When Ofsted inspectors visited Addey and Stanhope in 1999 they wrote: 'Pupils' attainment and progress is rising at a rate close to the national trend.'

### Extra-curricular activities

A wide range of lunchtime and after-school activities is on offer, from a variety of sports, including aerobics and trampolining, to drama.There are geography, history and biology field trips, as well as a school camp site in Sussex. The school also organizes overseas trips to France and the ski club travels to ski resorts. Many sixth-formers take part in community work.

## Bonus Pastor Roman Catholic School

**Winlaton Road, Downham, Bromley, Kent BR1 5PZ** ☎ 020 8695 2100 📠 020 8461 4621 ⓔ info@bonuspastor.lewisham.sch.uk Mr MA Cullinane MA, Dip.Ed; Chair of Governors: Rev M Sheehan ⇌ Beckenham Hill **Buses**: 54, 136, 138, 181, 208 Black blazer, tie, white shirt, grey V-neck pullover and grey trousers or skirt **Demand**: 280 applications for 150 places in 2001/2 **Type**: Voluntary aided Roman Catholic comprehensive for 634 mixed pupils, aged 11 to 16 **Submit application form**: Mid-October 2003 **Motto**: *Auxiliare Non Nocere* (Help Not Hinder) **School hours**: 8.45am–3.25pm; homework clubs are available **Meals**: Hot and cold available **Strong GCSE subjects**: English, history, PE **London league table position**: 271

### Profile

On the border of Lewisham, Bonus Pastor is based at two sites about 400m (440yds) apart. Pupils travel between the two, although younger children (Years 7 to 9), spend most of their time on one site.The school has benefited from a £1-million refurbishment and rebuilding programme, and it now has up-to-date technology studios and workshops, science labs, computer suites, drama and dance studio, textiles workshop, graphics room and a new combined library/resource/computer centre. A £100,000 30-station ICT suite recently opened. There is a school council and extra classes in some subjects are available. As a Catholic school, Bonus Pastor is very strong on pastoral care. It holds regular assemblies, described as 'acts of worship', and there are seasonal Masses and liturgies. There are regular consultations with parents to discuss pupils' progress and an active PTA.

### Admissions and intake

Priority admissions are given to actively practising Roman Catholics. Other practising Christians or non-practising Roman Catholics are considered if places are available. Ability or aptitude is not a factor in the admissions process. Prospective parents are encouraged to visit the school on set dates in late September to early October.

### Achievement

The school performs relatively well when compared with other Lewisham schools. According to Ofsted, GCSE pupils perform well above average compared to statistically similar schools, although only average or below average compared to all schools. Over the last six years, Bonus Pastor's exam results have shown a general upwards trend. In 2002, 49 per cent of pupils gained five or more A*–C GCSE grades, which was down from 57 per cent in 2001. These results were above the borough but below the national average. Bonus Pastor was ranked fifth in the borough in 2002.Within classes pupils are placed in tutor groups to help them get the highest possible GCSE grades.The form tutor is their key contact. Most pupils are encouraged to sit 10 GCSEs and an IT certificate.The strongest subjects are

English, history and PE, while IT, maths and music were found to be the weakest. There are non-exam courses in PE and PSE. The school does not have a sixth form but it is in partnership with Christ the King Sixth Form College. Bonus Pastor pupils have priority entry to the college and are offered places before general enrolment is opened up. In 1998, Ofsted inspectors praised the calm and orderly environment, and found pupils were well behaved in lessons. The inspectors reported that: 'Communication with parents is good and is underpinned by the strong sense of community and common purpose.'

### Extra-curricular activities

A limited range of activities is on offer: homework clubs, music, drama and sports clubs, including gymnastics, table tennis and a canoeing club. Activities vary from year to year, although Ofsted inspectors noted that provision could have been expanded overall. There is a school band, orchestra and choir. Several trips take place both abroad and within Britain, and the school organizes retreats and days of recollection. Pupils are encouraged to become involved in community work, including local charities.

## Catford Girls' School

**Bellingham Road, London SE6 2PS** ☎ 020 8697 8911 📠 020 8461 5758 ✉ info@catford-girls.lewisham.sch.uk 🌐 schoolsite.edex.net.uk/300/index.htm Susan O'Neill MA, B.Ed; Chair of Governors: Andy Hawkins ⇌ Bellingham **Buses**: 47, 54, 136, 138, 181, 199, 208 Navy blue skirt or trousers, navy V-neck jumper or school sweatshirt, white blouse and school tie **Demand**: 62 applications for 209 places in 2001/2 **Type**: Community comprehensive for 900 girls, aged 11 to 19 **Submit application form**: Mid-October 2003 **Motto**: Educating the Women of the Future **School hours**: 8.50am–3.35pm; homework clubs are available **Meals**: Hot and cold available **Strong GCSE subjects**: Art, music **London league table position**: 396

### Profile

Based in the south of the borough, near the border with Bromley, this school draws pupils from a wide range of social backgrounds. It backs on to the borough-run Forester Memorial Park, and on the site are playing fields, tennis courts and a pavilion. In the last six years the school environment has improved dramatically with a new music suite and recording studio, IT and food-technology rooms, refurbished library and a new maths block. A modern languages block was completed in 2001. It is the only school in greater London to have a Scatex lab – a control-systems laboratory. There is a school council and prefects system and provisions for special-needs pupils. The school holds regular parents evenings and two reports are sent home a year. A PTA arranges social, educational and fund-raising events. One weakness is attendance, but attitudes and relationships within the school are generally good.

### Admissions and intake

Admissions are according to the LEA general admissions policy for community comprehensives (see borough factfile). According to Ofsted, nearly half of the pupils come from single-parent families. Roughly a quarter of pupils are from families where English is an additional language. Catford Girls' has a high, and rising, rate of casual admissions, where pupils join during the year.

### Achievement

Catford Girls' is below the average for the borough in terms of GCSE results. In 2002, 36 per cent of pupils gained five or more A*–C GCSE grades, up on 21 per cent in 2001 but also below the national average. The school was ranked in 10th place in the borough league table. According to Ofsted, overall GCSE results are well below national averages and below the average for similar schools. However, when they visited in February 2000, Ofsted inspectors wrote: 'Taking into account the socio-economic context in which it operates, the low attainment of pupils on entry, the progress they make and the quality of education offered, the school is providing satisfactory value for money.' In general, results have been rising over the last few years. Music and art are the school's strengths in exams, followed by design technology and geography. According to Ofsted, curricular provision is good and special-needs provision serves pupils well. Teachers are aware of, and take into account, individual education plans (IEPs). More able girls are put into 'fast track' tutorial groups. In addition to core subjects, pupils can select from a choice of optional subjects, including additional languages, technology and child development. There is a limited sixth form and both A-level and vocational courses are offered.

### Extra-curricular activities

There is a good range of activities available in the areas of sports, music and drama. Art and computer rooms are open at lunchtimes for pupils to do extra work and there is access to extra music lessons. Homework clubs are available for many subjects and there are holiday-revision programmes for Year 7 pupils. There is an annual school concert and dance and drama club productions. There are regular school trips, including trips abroad organized by the modern languages department. The pupils are involved with the local community and raise funds for a range of charities.

## Crofton School

**Manwood Road, Brockley, London SE4 1SA** 020 8690 1114 020 8314 1859 info@crofton.lewisham.sch.uk Monica Duncan B.Ed, M.Ed; Chair of Governors: Pauline Morrison Catford, Catford Bridge **Buses**: 54, 75, 108B, 122, 136, 181, 185, 284 Up to sixth form: Black blazer, shirt, school tie, trousers or skirt and maroon jumper **Demand**: 113 applications for 209 places in 2001/2 **Type**: Community comprehensive for 1017 mixed pupils, aged 11 to 19 **Submit application form**: Mid-October 2003 **Motto**: Striving for Excellence **School hours**: 8.45am–3.30pm; homework clubs are available **Meals**: Hot and cold available **Strong GCSE subjects**: Art **London league table position**: 471

### Profile

Crofton school is one of the weakest schools in the borough, if judged purely on its academic achievement. However, it is privileged to have one of the more pleasant sites in the borough. It is nestled in the green spaces of Ladywell Fields, overlooking Crofton Park. The site has an all-weather sports ground and a leisure centre. The school has a number of specialist facilities, including computing and technology suites, dance, drama and music studios, science labs and a large library. A prefect system and a school council offer pupils the opportunity to take on extra responsibilities. There are mentoring programmes and girls-only conferences run through the support of the Lewisham Young Women's Project. Crofton claims to encourage close links with parents. Pupils must carry a homework diary, where school events and notes are recorded. However, in the last year there have been sporadic reports of some bullying within the school. Ofsted inspectors found attendance to be less than satisfactory, though it has since improved. There are provisions for pupils with special needs.

### Admissions and intake

Admissions to the school are in line with the LEA policy for community comprehensives (see borough factfile). It has a high intake of socially deprived pupils with a large range of abilities and cultural diversity.

### Achievement

Crofton school offers a wide range of subjects, including expressive arts, personal, health and social education (PHSE) and sociology. In 2002, only 22 per cent of pupils gained five or more A*–C GCSE grades, and this was well below the national average of 51.6 per cent. These results were, however, four per cent up on 2001's results and the school was ranked 13th in the borough. Results have fluctuated over the last few years and it is difficult to tell whether they are improving. At A-level, the average point score for two or more A-levels was 101, and the school was ranked bottom of the borough. A purpose-built block caters for the large sixth form of 134 pupils, about half of whom transfer into the school for the sixth-form year. A wide variety of sixth-form subjects is available, including vocational courses such as leisure and tourism, design technology, business and finance and computer studies. A-level courses include science, art, drama and theatre studies. Ofsted inspected the school in 2000 and praised the many improvements along with the 'excellent leadership' of the head teacher.

### Extra-curricular activities

Crofton prides itself on its wealth of lunchtime and after-school clubs, including sports teams, music, drama and homework clubs. There are regular field trips and the school is involved in community and charitable events.

## Deptford Green School

**Amersham Vale, New Cross, London SE14 6LQ** 020 8691 3236 020 8694 1789 deptfordgreen@btconnect.com Keith Ajegbo OBE, MA; Chair of Governors: Mike Brewer New Cross, New Cross Gate **Buses:**

P5, 21, 47, 53, 136, 171, 172, 177, 255 Up to sixth form: Grey or black trousers, navy or black skirt, white school shirt or polo shirt, school sweatshirt and black school shoes **Demand**: 533 applications for 220 places in 2001/2 **Type**: Community comprehensive for 1200 mixed pupils, aged 11 to 19 **Submit application form**: Mid-October 2003 **School hours**: 8.45am–3.25pm; homework clubs are available **Meals**: Hot and cold available **Strong GCSE subjects**: Art, drama, English Literature, food, geography, history ICT statistics, music, textiles **London league table position**: 373

## Profile

Deptford Green school is located in an area that has seen increased investment and regeneration, particularly with the arrival of the Docklands Light Railway. The school was purpose-built in the mid-1970s, and has received more than £5 million for building works over the last six years. There are now new science labs, music and drama suites. The New Cross Sports Arena is on site and a fitness centre is attached to the sports hall. A mentoring programme is in place with two firms, IPC Magazines and Warburg Dillon Read. The learning support unit helps pupils in the classroom and withdraws them where necessary. Although truancy is not a particular problem, two staff members are trained to work with children with attendance problems. There are twice-yearly reports and an annual parents' evening. Regular newsletters are sent home and parents are asked to sign a weekly homework diary. There is a school council.

## Admissions and intake

Entry to the school is based on the LEA admissions policy for community schools (see borough factfile). It has an ethnically diverse intake that is drawn from more than 35 primary schools. About one third of pupils speak English as an additional language but very few are at an early stage of learning English. Pupil numbers have been rising steadily at the school, and it is now heavily over-subscribed.

## Achievement

Deptford Green school has been highlighted by Lewisham council as an example of 'best practice'. In 2002, the school was ranked seventh in the GCSE tables for the borough; 36 per cent of pupils gained five or more A*–C grades, which was a slight fall on 2001's 41 per cent. These results were below the national average. Able pupils are catered for, particularly in maths, where a small group is fast-tracked to sit GCSE a year early. Vocational options include IT and leisure and tourism. The sixth form is currently run through a consortium with Addey and Stanhope School. In 1999, there were more than 100 pupils in the sixth form across the two schools. Sixth-form vocational courses include business administration, catering and construction. At A-level, the average point score was 183.5 in 2002, below national and local averages and near the bottom of the Lewisham table. In 2002, Ofsted visted Deptford Green and commented that: 'this is a good school that has several impressive features'. Inspectors praised the school's 'successful cultural and racial mix' and its 'very good relationships'. Teaching was seen to have improved and there were above average results in GCSE art, food, textiles, drama, English Literature, geography, history, ICT statistics and music. However, standards in GCSE English language and PE needed to be improved as did punctuality and attendance, especially in Years 9 to 11. There was also a 'small percentage' of lessons where the quality of teaching was 'unsatisfactory'.

## Extra-curricular activities

The school offers a wide range of activities including sport, music and drama, as well as homework classes. Many of the clubs and classes are funded through business sponsorships or lottery grants. There is a wide variety of visits to theatres, museums and sporting events. There is a mentoring system in conjunction with local companies and schemes involving pupils with the community.

# Forest Hill School

**Dacres Road, Forest Hill, London SE23 2XN** 020 8699 9343 020 8699 9198 enquiries@foresthill.edu.uk; info@foresthill.lewisham.sch.uk www.foresthill.lewisham.sch.uk Peter Walsh BA (Hons); Chair of Governors: Leslia Thauoos Forest Hill, Sydenham **Buses** 12, 75, 171, 185, 194, 352 Up to sixth form: Black blazer and trousers, school tie, badge and black shoes **Demand**: 504 applications for 227 places in 2001/2; 240 places in 2003 **Type**: County comprehensive for 1260 boys, aged 11 to 18; mixed sixth-form **Submit application form**: Mid-October 2003 **School hours**: 8.50am–3.25pm, 8.50am–3.05pm (Wed); homework clubs are available **Meals**: Hot and cold available **Strong GCSE subjects**: Art, languages, media studies, RE **London league table position**: 385

## Profile

Forest Hill school is one of only two boys-only schools in Lewisham. It is situated in the south-west of the borough, across the road from Mayow Park. There have been some recent refurbishments, including a new art block. The school has applied for funding to build a community sports hall and performance area for drama and music. The pupils are divided into houses and tutor groups and can expect to have the same tutor throughout their time at the school. A school council enables pupils to express their views and increase their responsibility, and there is a monitors and prefects system. There is a learning support department for special-needs boys whose literacy programme was identified by the Ofsted inspectors as 'exemplary'. Each year there is a full school report with shorter reports throughout the year. A parents' meeting is also held each year.

## Admissions and intake

Admissions are according to the LEA community schools admissions policy (see borough factfile). The intake is well balanced in terms of abilities.

## Achievement

Forest Hill was in eighth place in the borough's GCSE tables in 2002. A total of 42 per cent of pupils gained five or more A*–C grades, up from 37 per cent in 2001. When Ofsted visited the school in 1997, they said: 'It has had considerable success in establishing a positive ethos for the school reflecting strong values.' The pupils were found generally to score below the national averages in core subjects, although there were some very able pupils who did score well in these subjects. Exam results in art, media studies, RE, foreign languages and PE were found to be good, while IT and music were found to be the weaker subjects. Forest Hill is also particularly strong in sport and has a long history of success in film-making and video-production. Attendance at the school is in line with national averages. At A-level, the average point score, in 2002, for pupils sitting two or more papers was 182.2, below the borough and national averages. The sixth form is provided through a consortium with Sydenham and Sedgehill schools and a handful of girls are admitted as a result. Pupils have access to a wide range of subjects and vocational courses across the three schools, and Ofsted found that the post-16 vocational education was a particular strength. Sixth-formers have their own study area and teaching rooms. Ofsted inspectors wrote: 'Staff have high expectations about behaviour and conduct, and have established a learning environment where boys are trusting of staff, respectful of differences and treat each other well.'

## Extra-curricular activities

Forest Hill offers lunchtime clubs, including those for homework and after-school clubs. Its musical groups are regularly invited to perform in assemblies. There are regular local field trips as well as trips to a residential field centre in Wales, along with theatre and cultural visits, trips to France and Germany and sports activity holidays. The school has strong links with local businesses and the community, and in Years 10 and 11 pupils utilize these links for work experience.

# Haberdashers' Aske's Hatcham College

**136 Pepys Road, New Cross SE14 5S;, Jerningham Road, New Cross, London SE14** ☎ 020 7652 9500 📠 020 7277 9680 ⓔ reception@ hahc.org.uk 🌐 www.hahc.org.uk Dr Elizabeth Sidwell Ph.D, FRSA, FRGS; Chair of Governors: Mrs DJ Knight 🚆 New Cross Gate, Brockley, Nunhead ⊖ New Cross Gate **Buses**: P3, 484 👔 School blazer and tie, skirt or trousers; Sixth form: Tidy dress code **Demand**: Figures unavailable for 200 places **Type**: City Technology College for 1309 mixed pupils, aged 11 to 19 **Submit application form**: Contact school for details **Motto**: Serve and Obey **School hours**: 8.15am–3.15pm; homework clubs are available **Meals**: Hot and cold available **Strong GCSE subjects**: Art, maths, music, science **London league table position**: 121

## Profile

One of the better-performing schools in the borough, this City Technology College, which is independent of council control, was formed in 1991 through an amalgamation of the boys' and girls' schools. Since 1946 both schools had been funded by the Haberdashers' Company and the combined school is still funded in this way, together with other business sponsorships. Until the sixth form, boys and girls are taught separately on two different sites that are about 1.5 miles apart, with a sports field a short distance from both. The school's facilities are generally good, but there is no sports hall or specialist facility for drama. A well-staffed supported learning department helps pupils who fall behind and those with special needs. There is a structured prefect system and a school council. Reports are sent home each term. A 'day book' is designed for extra communication between home and school.

### Admissions and intake

The school draws pupils from the boroughs of Lewisham, Southwark and Greenwich. Prospective pupils must sit an entrance exam, but despite this, the intake represents all ability levels.

### Achievement

Haberdashers' ranked fourth in the borough league table for GCSE results in 2002; 79 per cent of pupils gained five or more A*–C grades, which was up on 73 per cent the previous year. Although it leans towards technical subjects, it also caters thoroughly for arts-based subjects. All pupils take double science in Years 10 and 11. When Ofsted inspectors visited the school in 1997, they found that the teachers had good relationships with the pupils and a strong command of their subjects, though they did not always have high enough expectations of their pupils. According to Ofsted, pupils perform particularly well in science, maths, music and art at GCSE and A-levels, and also in English at A-level. A wide range of A-level subjects is on offer, including psychology, sociology and media studies. In 2002, the average point score for pupils sitting three or more A-levels was 318.30, placing the school second in the borough league tables. IT has proven a weak point in the last few years but staff are working to address low achievement in this area. Haberdashers' also provides a good variety of work experience opportunities within the community and in Europe. All Year 10 and 12 pupils go on university visits. Ofsted found the school's careers advice to be thorough and effective.

### Extra-curricular activities

Haberdashers' has a strong extra-curricular focus, including a compulsory 'enrichment' programme in which pupils take part in a range of activities, including sports, art, drama music and literature. There is a provision for pupils to do their homework in the library, which is open until 4:30pm, except on Fridays. There is an annual junior drama festival with opera and concerts throughout the year as well as school trips. Pupils are also encouraged to get involved with charities.

# Malory School

**Launcelot Road, Bromley, Kent BR1 5EB** ☎ 020 8698 1025 📠 020 8695 5403 ✉ info@malory.lewisham.sch.uk 🌐 Under development 👤 Margaret Bond BA, MA; Chair of Governors: Donald Stavert 🚆 Grove Park **Buses:** 124, 126, 136, 261, 284, 361 👕: Blue school shirt and tie, trousers or skirt; school polo shirt may be worn in summer **Demand:** 69 applications for 180 places in 2001/2; 180 places in 2003 **Type:** Community comprehensive for 850 mixed pupils, aged 11 to 19 **Submit application form:** Mid-October 2003 **Motto:** We Are Proud of Ourselves, Our Families and Our School **School hours:** 8.40am–3.15pm; homework clubs are available **Meals:** Hot and cold available **Strong GCSE subjects:** Information technology **London league table position:** 514

### Profile

Situated in the southern part of the borough of Lewisham, Malory has a challenging and disadvantaged intake, which is reflected in its low exam results. In 1995 the school was deemed to be failing and put on 'special measures'. However, since then there have been some improvements and when the school was re-inspected in November 1999, the 'special measures' were removed. Malory has also seen an improvement in facilities and it now has a new music suite, an independent learning centre and a sports hall. In response to high demand, the special-needs provision has improved, especially for English as an additional language. There is a peer reading project, where senior pupils can help younger ones, a school council, a prefects system and an anti-bullying project. There is also an active PTA.

### Admissions and intake

Admissions are in line with the LEA's provision for community schools (see borough factfile). The intake is generally from nearby primary schools, but there is a high rate of casual admissions; between a quarter and two-thirds of each year group are admitted during the year. Nearly one-third of pupils have special educational needs which is above average, 24 of whom have statements.

## Achievement

The school benefits from a strong head and increasingly effective management. However, it still has serious weaknesses. In 2002, just 18 per cent of pupils gained five or more A*–C grades at GCSE. This was up from nine per cent in 2001 and the lowest results in the borough. There is a good range of subjects available up to Year 11, including vocational courses. Ofsted visted the school in 2001 and described it as 'an improving school which copes extremely well with its challenging circumstances'. Inspectors saw it as 'a good school' and standards and teaching were seen to have improved since the last inspection. The head teacher was praised for 'steering the school in the right direction'. GCSE results are low but a high percentage of pupils gained A*–C grades in information technology. However, standards are still well below average in most subjects. Truancy remains a problem at the school, although this has been identified and monitored, and does show signs of improving. In 2000, the rate of unauthorized absence was 4.1 per cent, above the borough and national averages.

## Extra-curricular activities

There are regular performances by the school orchestra, choir and bands, and there is an annual school production. Each year a music and dance festival is held with the local primary schools. Lunchtime and after-school clubs offer activities from homework clubs, a comic cartoon club to sports, including judo, and drama. There are regular school trips and pupils can take part in the Duke of Edinburgh's Award scheme. There are schemes involving pupils working with the local community.

# Northbrook Church of England School

**Taunton Road, Lee Green, London SE12 8PD** ☎ 020 8852 3191 📠 020 8463 0201 ⓔ northbrook@freeuk.com 🎓 Mr John Ratcliffe; Chair of Governors: Jack Poole 🚆 Hither Green, Lee **Buses:** 122, 261, 202, 321 👔 Green school blazer, green school jersey, green school tie, trousers or skirt **Demand:** 119 applications for 90 places in 2001/2; 100 places in 2003 **Type:** Voluntary aided Church of England comprehensive for 470 mixed pupils, aged 11 to 16 **Submit application form:** Mid-October 2003 **Motto:** *Probitate et Labore* (Honesty and Hard Work) **School hours:** 8.45am–3.25pm; homework provision available **Meals:** Hot meals available **Strong GCSE subjects:** Art, English, food technology, music, textiles **London league table position:** 409

## Profile

Northbrook is in the east of Lewisham, close to the border of Greenwich and Blackheath, and backing onto the pleasant Manor House gardens. The school has specialist labs for science, technology, computer networks, art and music. It also has a well-equipped gym. In 1997 a new teaching block was opened, including seven new classrooms, a science lab, sixth-form common room and changing rooms. However, there is still some pressure on space at this small school. Pupils with special needs progress well with support through withdrawal classes and in the classroom.

## Admissions and intake

The school draws pupils from outside Lewisham as well as from local primary schools. The governors control admissions but try to accept pupils across the same ability level as the bands set by the LEA for community schools. Of the 90 available places, 55 go to practising Anglicans. Other Christian pupils are considered if supported by a parish priest or minister. Priority is given to families living within a four-mile radius according to specific criteria, followed by families living outside the radius.

## Achievement

Northbrook is a rapidly improving school, recently judged by Ofsted inspectors to have many more strengths than weaknesses. In 2002, it was 11th in the borough league table for GCSE results; 20 per cent of pupils gained five or more A*–C grades, well below the England average of 51.6 per cent, and down on the previous year. Pupils achieve below national averages but perform well in comparison to similar schools, and their levels of attainment in core subjects are improving faster than the national average. Academic standards have risen in the last six years, particularly in English. Northbrook pupils generally perform above average in art, music, textiles, food technology and English. Their performance is weaker in ICT and resistant materials (woodwork and metalwork). There is no sixth form, but pupils are given priority interviews at nearby Christ the King Roman Catholic Sixth Form College. Northbrook also has very strong links with businesses and the community. Ofsted, who inspected the school in late 1999, judged the careers service to be very strong and providing good preparation for employment. Behaviour and attendance are generally good. The inspectors reported: 'Parents speak highly of the school; they appreciate the way good attitudes and standards of behaviour are promoted.' They also wrote: 'The school has a strong commitment to high achievement and high expectations of its pupils. Relationships are good. The inspection team supports the positive view parents have of the school and believes that their confidence is justified.'

## Extra-curricular activities

Extra-curricular activities include music, IT, Christian Union, photography, art and sport. Pupils can work in the library for an hour after school. There are regular cultural performances and inter-form and inter-school sporting events. School excursions have included trips to Europe and Canada.

# Prendergast School

**Hilly Fields, Adelaide Avenue, London SE4 1LE** ☎ 020 8690 3710 📠 020 8690 3155 ⓔ smt@prendergast.lewisham.sch.uk ✉ Miss Erica Pienaar; Chair of Governors: Mrs Margaret Riddel ⇄ Ladywell, Crofton Park, Brockley **Buses:** P4, 122, 284, 484 👔 Navy skirt, white blouse, school tie and blue jumper **Demand:** 579 applications for 95 places in 2001/2 **Type:** Voluntary aided comprehensive for 680 girls, aged 11 to 19 **Submit application form:** Mid-October 2003 **Motto:** Trouthe & Honour Fredom & Curteisye (Truth and Honour, Freedom and Courtesy) **School hours:** 8.50am–3.25pm; homework provision available **Meals:** Hot meals are available **Strong GCSE subjects:** Art and design, modern languages, music, science **London league table position:** 119

## Profile

Founded in 1890, this popular and successful girls' school moved to its present site in the middle of lush Hilly Fields in 1995. Since its founding, the school has been linked with St Mary's Church in Lewisham and, although the school is non-denominational, worship is encouraged. The new site has been completely refurbished, modernized and extended. A new exam hall and fitness suite have also been added. In 1997, Ofsted inspectors praised Prendergast for its early identification and speedy remediation of special-needs pupils by means of its summer school for new entrants. Pupils with English as an additional language also receive extra help. There is a school council, a prefect system is in place and homework is set every night. Parents are invited to an annual parents' evening and are asked to sign a weekly homework diary. Reports are sent home annually.

## Admissions and intake

Admissions are drawn from across the whole ability range and pupils from outside Lewisham have to sit a test to determine their band. Selection is based on the following weighted criteria: sibling at Prendergast (50 points); ease of journey to school (10 points); active worship within a Lewisham church (10 points); the outcome of an interview (30 points). Prospective parents are required to attend open sessions in October and complete an application form.

## Achievement

In mid-2000, Prendergast was awarded Beacon status under the government's scheme to identify schools that are examples of 'good practice'. Pupils perform above national averages at GCSE, although the results are not as good at A-level, according to Ofsted. In 2002, the school was third in the borough for GCSE results; 75 per cent of pupils gained five or more A*–C grades. This was slightly up on 73 per cent in 2001 and well above both the national and borough averages. The average point score was 44.7. In core subjects at GCSE, results are generally better than national averages, particularly in science. Art and design, modern languages and music are also strong subjects. Careers advice and education begins in Year 9. The sixth form is relatively small, which reduces the subject choice when compared to larger schools. However, the year group is growing and Ofsted expects both choice and achievement to improve. A small number of vocational options are offered in addition to A-levels. In 2002, the average points score for pupils taking two or more A-levels was 249.8. This ranked the school fourth in the borough. Ofsted inspectors wrote: 'The atmosphere of calm orderliness helps pupils work in a sustained and productive way'. There is no evidence of bullying. Levels of attendance are good and attendance and punctuality are rewarded through award schemes.

### Extra-curricular activities

A wide range of activities is available, including clubs for drama, art, music, wildlife appreciation and trampolining. There is provision for pupils to do homework at school. There is a school orchestra, wind and steel bands and a variety of other musical groups. Classes enjoy regular field trips. Sports offered include swimming, hockey, netball, cricket, tennis, athletics, dance and health-related fitness. Pupils are encouraged to become involved in charities and each year there is a fund-raising event.

# St Dunstan's College

**Stanstead Road, Catford, London SE6 4TY** 020 8516 7200 020 8516 7300 hm@stdunstans. org.uk www.stdunstans.org.uk Ian Davies MA, FRSA; Chair of Governors: Sir Paul Judge Catford, Catford Bridge **Buses**: 171, 185; the school runs a coach and minibus for south London pupils Navy blazer, school badge, school tie, white shirt or blouse, charcoal grey school trousers or skirt, black shoes **Type**: Selective independent for 941 mixed pupils, aged 4 to 18 (senior school: aged 11 to 18)) **Fees**: £2,895 per term, including lunch **Submit application form**: Contact school for details **Motto**: *Albam exorna* (Adorn the White) **School hours**: Pre-prep: 8.45am–3.15pm, juniors: 8.20am–3.30pm, seniors: 8.20am–3.45pm **Meals**: Hot and cold available **Strong GCSE subjects**: Art, design technology, English literature, history **London league table position**: 98

### Profile

St Dunstan's is one of London's oldest public schools and was founded more than 500 years ago in the parish of St Dunstan in the City. The school became co-educational in the early 1990s. Set on busy Stanstead Road, the college has invested heavily in new buildings. There are three new biology labs, a new sports hall and a drama studio. There is also a large library. The senior school is divided into lower and middle schools and a sixth form. In 1999/2000, only one pupil had a statement of special needs. Work reports are sent home every six weeks, and there are at least two parents' meetings a year. There is a school council and a prefects system. Homework is always set.

### Admissions and intake

To enter the lower school of the senior college, pupils must sit an exam in January and parents should register their children by December. Pupils entering the middle school must also sit exams. Most pupils pass successfully from the St Dunstan's prep school to the senior school. Several scholarships and bursaries are offered based on academic merit, and there are also music and sports scholarships. Foundation places are available for low-income families.

### Achievement

St Dunstan's is consistently in the top two schools in the borough for GCSE results. In 2002, 89 per cent of pupils gained five or more A*–C grades, slightly down on 95 per cent the year before. The school came second in the borough league table. Strong subjects tend to be art, design technology, English literature and history. The pupils sit at least nine GCSEs while in the middle school. Of pupils sitting three or more A-levels, the average point score was 340.5, placing it first in the borough. Strong A-level subjects include geography, art and design, economics, history and sciences. In the sixth form, pupils are grouped into small tutor groups. More than 20 subjects are offered at sixth form and pupils can take almost any combination of subjects. The destination of its graduates is an enviable testimony to St Dunstan's academic success. Almost all pupils go on to university courses (including Oxbridge) or medical schools.

### Extra-curricular activities

St Dunstan's has a high reputation for musical activities and has a large number of musical groups. Drama and music productions are held each year. Pupils can choose from more than 20 sports, from athletics to weight-training. Clubs include bridge, chess and classical studies. There are regular field trips as well as international exchanges with France, Spain and Germany. The school sports teams have toured South Africa, Canada, Australia and Zimbabwe. There is also a contingent of the Combined Cadet Force within the school. There is a well-established community service scheme.

# St Joseph's Academy

**Lee Terrace, Blackheath, London SE3 9TY** 020 8852 7433 020 8318 0103 pat@leeterrace. fsnet.co.uk Mr P Stickings; Chair of Governors: Brother Benedict Foy Blackheath **Buses**: 54, 89, 108 Green blazer and badge, white or grey shirt, dark grey trousers, school tie and grey pullover **Demand**: 38 applications for 120 places in 2001/2; 120 places in 2003 **Type:** Voluntary aided Roman Catholic comprehensive for 483 boys, aged 11 to 16 **Submit application form:** Mid-October 2003 **Mission statement:** Aims to promote 'the Gospel values of Love, Truth, Justice and Toleration' **School hours:** 8.35am–3.25pm; homework clubs available **Meals:** Hot available **Strong GCSE subjects:** Art, design **London league table position:** 494

## Profile

St Joseph's Academy was founded in 1860 by the De La Salle brothers. It is set in a relatively affluent part of the borough, between Lee Terrace and the railway line. In 1992, St Joseph's failed its Ofsted inspection and was placed on 'special measures', but when reinspected in 1998, it was found to have improved and the measures were lifted. The school is close to Blackheath and has on-site rugby and football fields and tennis courts. It has recently benefited from some refurbishment and the science labs have been upgraded. There is a facility for extension work for more able pupils, while pupils with special needs are supported by a dedicated learning support department. There is a school council and a prefects system. Parents are sent an annual report and attend a parents' evening. There is an active PTA.

## Admissions and intake

Admissions are made by the governing body but are based on the LEA's banding system for comprehensives. Interviews are conducted to determine a child's suitability. Parents can appeal against decisions made by the governors. The school's numbers, once declining, have shown a small increase in recent years. The catchment area includes Lewisham, Greenwich, Southwark, Tower Hamlets, Newham and Hackney. The intake is generally below average in ability and about a quarter of the pupils have special needs.

## Achievement

In 2002, St Joseph's Academy was one of the poorer performers in the borough at GCSE level. Only 13 per cent of pupils gained five or more A*–C grades, down on 16 per cent in 2001. Ofsted visited the school in 2001 and noted that it '...did not serve its pupils as well as it should'. The school was seen to 'face many challenges' and its standards were still low. However, inspectors noted that: 'Some teaching is good particularly in Years 10 and 11 where over half the lessons are good or better'. Similarly, the school was seen to give good support to those pupils with special needs. Pupils were seen to do best in art and design but all other subjects were weak, including English, mathematics, science and information technology. Standards were high in art and were improving in history. St Joseph's range of subjects is in line with the National Curriculum, but additional subjects are on offer including art and photography, sociology and business studies. In keeping with the Roman Catholic ethos of the school, religious education is provided and approved by the Archdiocese of Southwark. The school also offers vocational courses, a careers service and work experience opportunities. There is no sixth form and the majority of pupils transfer to nearby Christ the King Sixth Form College.

## Extra-curricular activities

St Joseph's pupils can participate in a variety of sports teams, field trips, language trips, Christian retreats and skiing trips. They can take part in the Duke of Edinburgh's Award and Young Enterprise schemes. There is also a range of lunchtime and after-school clubs and schemes to involve students in the local community.

# Sedgehill School

**Sedgehill Road, London SE6 3QW** ☎ 020 8698 8911 📠 020 8461 4004 ✉ info@sedgehill.lewisham.sch.uk 🌐 schoolsite.edex.net.uk/192/ Ms K Bastick-Styles MA; Chair of Governors: Mr A Jacques 🚉 Beckenham Hill **Buses** 54, 136, 138, 181, 208 Up to sixth form: Black school blazer and badge, school tie, white shirt, black school skirt or trousers, black shoes **Demand:** 583 for 306 places in 2001/2 **Type:** Community comprehensive for 1700 mixed pupils, aged 11 to 18 **Submit application form:** Mid-October 2003 **Motto:** *Dominus Regnat* (Learning Rules) **School hours:** 8.45am–3.30pm; homework provision available **Meals:** Hot and cold available **Strong GCSE subjects:** Business studies, dance and drama, economics, history **London league table position:** 438

## Profile

Sedgehill is the largest and southernmost school in the borough of Lewisham. It is set in a pleasant area, backing onto sports fields and across the road from the expansive Beckenham Place Park. A new performing arts block was built in the mid-1990s, and there is also a good library. The school has six computer rooms, a business centre and a modern languages suite. Strong support is available for special needs pupils, and there is a specialized hearing-impaired unit. The school's head claims that standards of discipline are 'high, but fair'. Grades are monitored and sent home every six to eight weeks. The *Boomerang* newsletter is sent home regularly and there is an active PTA. There is a school council and a prefects system.

## Admissions and intake

Admissions are according to the LEA community schools admissions policy (see borough factfile). The school is popular and has a wide intake but most pupils are drawn from areas close to the school. It has been over-subscribed at all ability levels.

## Achievement

Sedgehill offers a broad and balanced curriculum, which offers subjects beyond those required by the National Curriculum. It has extensive links with local businesses and the community, particularly for sixth-form pupils. Careers lessons begin in Year 9 and pupils plan their subjects based on these. The 2002 GCSE results placed Sedgehill in 12th place in the borough; 30 per cent of pupils gained five or more A*–C grades. This was four per cent up on 2001. The sixth form is provided through a consortium with Sydenham School, Forest Hill School and Sedgehill. Pupils have access to more than 20 A-level subjects and vocational courses across the three schools. In 2001, the average A-level point score was 113.3. This placed the school ninth in the borough. Ofsted have not inspected the school since 1996, but their findings at the time were that the stronger exam performances had been in history, economics, business studies, dance and drama. Inspectors wrote: 'Sedgehill is an improving school with some strong and very good features. Overall standards of attainment were about average when compared to national standards.'

## Extra-curricular activities

Sedgehill has a variety of activities on offer but is particularly strong on music and sport. Approximately 250 pupils receive music lessons and many are in the school orchestra or bands. The school band has toured Russia, Canada and the US. There are regular school trips to Sussex, the Lewisham Mountain Centre in Wales, and exchanges with schools abroad. The sports teams on offer include watersports, football, hockey, netball, rugby, athletics, cricket and tennis. In May 2000, the school was awarded the prestigious Sportsmark Gold Award by Sports England, based on the strength of its sports department and its commitment to PE. Annual charity days are held and pupils are encouraged to become involved in community work. Pupils can work in the library for an hour after school.

# Sydenham High School

**19 Westwood Hill, London SE26 6BL** ☎ 020 8768 8000 📠 020 8768 8002 ✉ info@syd.gdst.net (admissions information) 🌐 www.gdst.net/sydenhamhigh Mrs Kathyrn Pullen; Chair of Governors: Mrs Sarah Hanna 🚉 Sydenham **Buses:** 122, 450; school coach service Up to sixth form: Navy school jersey, pale blue school blouse, navy school skirt **Type:** Selective independent, part of the Girls' Day School Trust, for 689 girls (500 in senior school), aged 4–19 (senior school: aged 11 to 19) **Fees:** £7,155 per annum **Submit application form:** October 2003 **Motto:** *Nyle Ye Drede* (Fear Nothing) **School hours:** 8.40am–3.45pm; homework clubs available **Meals:** Hot and cold available **Strong GCSE subjects:** All equally strong **London league table position:** 57

## Profile

Sydenham High School is based around a large Victorian mansion that forms the school's main building and is set within its own pleasant grounds. It is close to Crystal Palace Park, and is able to take advantage of the swimming and other sports facilities the park has to offer. There are new music, sports and drama facilities on site and a full-sized, all-weather pitch, large sports hall, multi-gym and performing-arts centre. The school caters for special-needs pupils with partial deafness and diabetes. It is non-denominational and aims to respect a wide variety of religions and faiths. Senior pupils can be elected as prefects and there is a school council. There are annual parents' meetings and grade cards are sent home four times a year along with a written annual report. There is an active PTA.

### Admission and intake

Admission is by interview and examination. However, the school says it looks mainly for potential and an enthusiasm for learning. Welcome meetings for prospective parents are held from September to December and there is an open day in November. Entrance exams are held in January.

### Achievement

At GCSE level, Sydenham High School is one of the consistently top-performing schools in the borough. In 2002, 100 per cent of pupils gained five or more A*–C grades. This was in line with 2001's results and the school was ranked top in the borough. The curriculum is based around the National Curriculum, but is extended to include other subjects. At GCSE, in addition to core subjects and options, pupils also study PE, IT and courses in RE, health education and study skills. Careers courses begin in Year 9 and are taught as part of the school's PSHE programme. Pupils also take part in work experience programmes. There is a relatively large sixth form where pupils can choose from 22 subjects, including Greek, Latin and sociology. Teaching is in small groups. More than 95 per cent of the school's A-level pupils go on to higher education. The best A-level performances tend to be in French, German, history, maths and religious studies.. The weaker subjects are home economics, physics and theatre studies. Of pupils sitting two or more A-levels, the average score in 2002 was 282.1. This result was well above the borough and national averages and put Sydenham High third in the Lewisham A-level league table.

### Extra-curricular activities

The school performs well in sporting competitions and a wide range of sports is available, including fencing. Music lessons are offered for many instruments and there are wind and flute groups, a chamber group, jazz band and junior and senior choirs. A major drama production is held each year with smaller productions throughout the year. Other clubs include photography, computing and gymnastics. Cultural visits and field trips take place, while visits are made annually to France, Germany and Spain. There are also skiing holidays and foreign travel linked to language studies. Pupils are encouraged to work with the local community and charities.

## Sydenham School

**Dartmouth Road, London SE26 4RD** ☎ 020 8699 6731 📠 020 8699 7532 Miss Daphne Such; Chair of Governors: Mrs Anne Fahey ⇄ Forest Hill **Buses**: 12, 122, 171, 176, 185, 312 Blue shirts (Years 7–9); White shirts (Years 10–11); all pupils wear school sweatshirts and all other items are navy **Demand**: 439 applications for 280 places in 2001/2 **Type**: Community comprehensive for 1450 girls, aged 11 to 19 **Submit application form**: Mid-October 2003 **Motto**: Aim High **School hours**: 8.50am–3.30pm; homework clubs available **Meals**: Hot and cold available **Strong GCSE subjects**: Art, PE, textiles **London league table position**: 327

### Profile

Not to be confused with nearby Sydenham High, this school attracts girls from a much wider background than its independent namesake. It was founded in 1917 as a girls' grammar school. In 1956, it expanded to become a comprehensive school and additional buildings were added. The original school building houses the English and maths departments as well as classes for business, technology, dance and personal and social education. In 1994, a new sixth-form annex and reception area were opened. There are also three large gyms, a library and a drama studio. Specialized staff identify pupils with special needs and support them. The needs catered for include learning problems, marked aptitude difficulties, physical problems and emotional or behavioural problems. A school council contributes to developing school policies such as an anti-bullying policy. Homework is always set and recorded in a planner for parents to peruse. Parents' evenings are held regularly along with frequent reports and a termly newsletter called *Snippets*. There are also provisions for pupils to complete homework on site.

### Admissions and intake

Entry is according to the LEA admissions policy for community schools (see borough factfile), but the school tends to draw a larger proportion of high-attaining pupils than other Lewisham schools. However, it still admits pupils from many areas with high levels of social deprivation. Ofsted commented that the result of Sydenham's mixed intake was 'a lively and vibrant community with mutual tolerance and respect at the heart of its endeavours.'

## Achievement

A wide range of subjects is taught at all levels. The school performs well compared to the average standard in the borough and exam results have been improving over the last few years. In 2002, 49 per cent of pupils gained five or more A*–C grades at GCSE level, three per cent up on 2001. Sydenham School was ranked sixth in the borough. When Ofsted visited in 1996, art, textiles and PE were seen to be strong subjects, while design technology was considered to be relatively weak. The sixth form is provided through a consortium with Forest Hill and Sedgehill schools, which gives pupils access to a good variety of subjects, including vocational courses, at the three sites. In 2002, those pupils taking two or more A-levels scored an average of 194.9, this was roughly in line with the borough average but below the national average, ranking the school fifth in the borough. Ofsted inspectors noted that: 'There is a positive, supportive ethos and a firm commitment by staff and governors alike to raise standards of achievement further.' They found that pupils were proud to belong to the school.

## Extra-curricular activities

The school has a strong performing-arts department and highly popular musical groups and choirs. Lunchtime clubs range from sports and self-defence to homework and cultural clubs. There is also a variety of local and overseas field trips. Pupils are encouraged to become involved in charity and community work.

# Merton

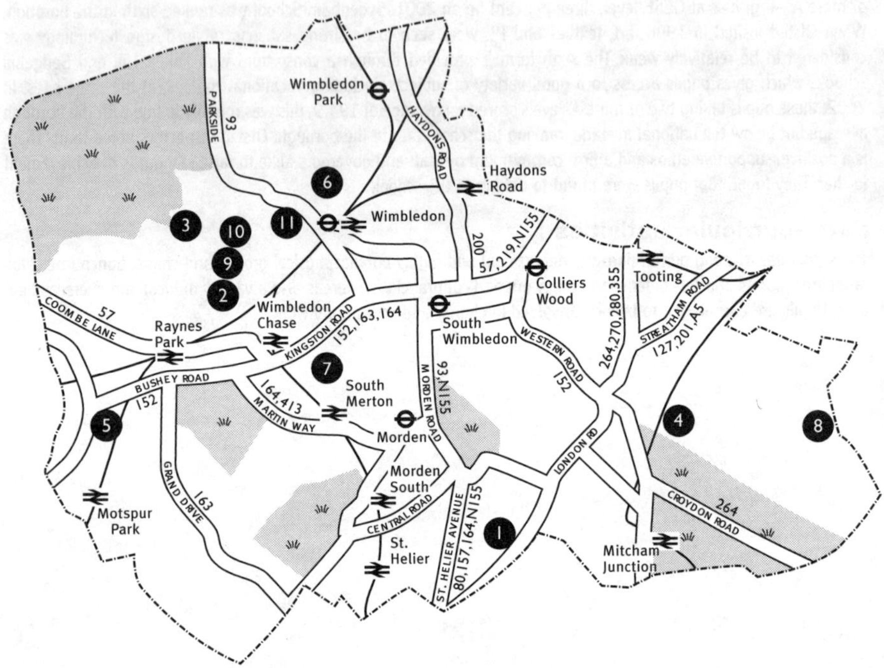


## Key

1. Bishopsford Community School
2. Hall School Wimbledon
3. Kings College School
4. Mitcham Vale
5. Raynes Park High School
6. Ricards Lodge High School
7. Rutlish School
8. Tamworth Manor High School
9. Ursuline High School Wimbledon
10. Wimbledon College
11. Wimbledon High School

# Factfile

**LEA: Civic Centre, Horndon Road, Morden SM4 5DX** ☎ 020 8543 2222 Fax 020 8545 3443 Web www.merton.gov.uk **Director of Education:** Ms Sue Evans **Political control of council:** Labour **Percentage of pupils from outside the borough:** 13.2 per cent **Percentage of pupils educated outside the borough:** 19 per cent **London league table positions (out of 32 boroughs):** 27th

Merton is full of rivers, parks and commons, including Wimbledon, one of the largest sites of special scientific interest, and the National Trust also has several properties in the borough. Merton is small, with a population of 182,300. It has lower than average unemployment and a higher proportion than other boroughs of managerial and professional occupations. There is a higher than average proportion of special-needs pupils.

Possibly the most famous of all Merton connections is the All-England Lawn Tennis Championships at Wimbledon, first held in 1877. Mitcham also has a sporting connection: cricket has been played on the cricket ground for 250 years, predating the MCC and Lords, and the introduction of the third stump in 1775. In September 2002, Merton changed from its old three tier system of first, middle and high schools to a two-tier system of primary and secondary schools, with children changing school only once at age 11. This resulted in the closure of Rowan High School and Eastfields High School in July 2002. Mitcham Vale, a new mixed communinty secondary school on the Eastfields site opened in September 2002. Merton has five community schools, two voluntary aided schools and three independents. According to Ofsted in 2000, Merton has more strengths than weaknesses, but is still below average in its support for IT in schools, absenteeism, building maintenance and the support of ethnic minority pupils. However, a clear commitment to raising standards was evident. In 2002, an average of 40.9 per cent of pupils gained five or more A*–C grades and the average A/AS level score was 229.6 points. Merton has a good interactive page on its web site [www.merton.gov.uk] for the Merton High Schools Citizenship project.

## Policy

Parents should get a copy of the brochure *Merton High Schools Admission Arrangements* from the LEA. If a high school is oversubscribed, the following admissions criteria apply: children who have given the school as a first preference and who have a medical or social need for a place at that school; children who have given the school as first preference and who have a sibling at the school; children who have given the school as a first preference and for whom the preferred school is nearest to their home address; children who have given the school as a first preference but for whom an alternative school is nearer to the home address; and children who have given the school as a second preference. Applications to the Roman Catholic schools should be made directly to the schools themselves. Merton includes The Norwegian School in London, but as this does not offer a GCSE curriculum, it has not been included in this guide.

# Bishopsford Community School

**Lilleshall Road, Morden, Surrey SM4 6DU** 020 8687 1157 020 8687 1158 Paul Harwood B.Ed, Med; Chair of Governors: Fran Hollis Mitcham **Buses:** 80, 280 Black trousers/skirt/culottes, white shirt, tie, black jumper with white polo top (summer) **Demand:** 150 applications for 210 places **Type:** Community comprehensive for 459 mixed pupils, aged 11 to 16; roll will rise to 1,200 by 2005 **Submit application form:** Mid-October 2003 **Mission Statement:** We aim for a calm, stimulating environment with clear purposeful learning objectives where we are 'challenging all to achieve'. **School hours:** 8.45am–2.40pm; homework clubs are available **Meals:** Hot and cold available, including breakfast **Strong GCSE subjects:** Information unavailable **London league table position:** 502

## Profile

Bishopsford Community School opened in September 1999, taking the place of the Garth and Watermead Schools. It was decided to replace both with a new school, a new head and nearly all new staff, to give the pupils the chance of a new start. Building work has been in progress on a further addition to the school building. The school has already benefited from a £2.8-million investment, and a further £2.6 million was allocated for 2000–2. As a result, it has nine science laboratories and purpose-built technology laboratories, food and graphics rooms. It has three networked ICT suites, with a fourth suite and CAD facilities to come. It also has excellent provision for drama, dance and music. The school is also seeking specialist status in the performing arts. The school also has seven acres of land, and a new sports hall is to come in the next phase of building. Vocational subjects offered include GNVQ leisure and tourism. Courses in catering, childcare, engineering and other trades are offered through links with Merton College. The Trident Project helps arrange two weeks' work experience in Year 10. The key stage and year heads are directly involved in the pastoral care of their pupils. There is a prefect system and a strong student council. There is strong provision for special-needs pupils. Two reports are sent to parents each term, and there are tutors' evenings and individual consultations. An active PTA is hoped and planned for.

## Admissions and intake

The LEA sets the procedure and closing date for applications. If oversubscribed, choice is made on the presence of a sibling at the school, exceptional need and distance of home from the school. Bishopsford has a large catchment area, with a mix of social and economic levels, and it seeks a broad range of attainment level on entry.

## Achievement

In 2002, just 18 per cent of pupils gained five or more A*–C grades at GCSE, ranking the school at the bottom of the borough league table. This was, however, eight per cent down on 2001's results. Ofsted inspected the school in both the spring and summer 2000 terms and commented favourably on its progress.

## Extra-curricular activities

Although the school closes its formal lessons at 2.40pm, there is an hour of activities from 3pm to 4pm called the extension programme, on Monday, Wednesday and Thursday. Activities range from sport (including girls' football), drama, poetry and rap to homework support, chess and model-making. The school also produces *Bishopsford News*, with fiction and nightclub reviews, and there is also a wall of fame, showing students of the month. The school has already organized field study weekends in England and trips to France. There is a non-uniform day each term to raise money for charities.

# Hall School Wimbledon

**17 The Downs, Wimbledon, London SW20 8HF** ☎ 020 8879 9200 📠 020 8946 0864 ⓔ enquiries@hallschoolwimbledon.co.uk 🌐 www.hallschoolwimbledon.co.uk Tim Hobbs ⇄ Raynes Park ⊖ Wimbledon **Buses**: 57, 131 Navy sweatshirt, corduroy trousers or skirt, white polo shirt, fleece and waterproof jacket in school colours (navy and emerald green) **Demand:** Oversubscribed **Type:** Non-selective independent for 200 mixed pupils, aged 11 to 16 **Fees:** £2,010–2,558 per term **Submit application form:** No cut-off date **Mission Statement:** We believe in the all-round child, who leaves us with self-esteem and self-confidence intact and resilient, in whom the qualities of loyalty, kindness, honesty, duty, tolerance and consideration are paramount. It is our duty to enable and not hinder, to encourage and not indoctrinate, so that the child's potential may be wholly realized in a happy school. **School hours:** 8.30am–5pm **Meals:** Hot and cold available, including breakfast **Strong GCSE subjects:** All relatively strong **London league table position:** Not available.

## Profile

In 1990 Tim Hobbs established Hall School Wimbledon with just nine pupils. By 1995, he had 240 pupils and had moved to Putney Vale, in Wandsworth LEA. In 1998, the principal of Hazelhurst School for Girls sold the present building to him. The senior school has two science laboratories, a large technical room, hall/gymnasium, library and large computer room with 30 computers. The playing field is in Putney. Each day starts with circuit training and ends with sport, from squash and rugby to athletics and fencing. A-levels will be offered from 2003. Vocational subjects offered include rural science, animal husbandry and gardening, plus GCSE design and technology and ICT. There is currently no work experience but careers guidance is ongoing. Prefects are not seen as necessary as all pupils are regarded as having responsibilities. The school will decline to take a special-needs pupil if it cannot provide him/her with suitable teaching. However, it has built up a team of specialists to identify problems and assist classroom teachers. More able pupils are also set weekly projects, often requiring extensive independent research. There is no formal PTA but parents are part of the school community. An innovative system for homework, called Flints, emphasizes revision and learning. The school sets out to create healthy, well-mannered, ambitious, hard-working and independent individuals.

## Admissions and intake

Applications can be made directly to the school at any time. Pupils are mainly from Wimbledon, Putney, Kingston and Barnes, with some from abroad. The attainment level of pupils on entry is average. In 1999, there were eight special-needs pupils, all without statements.

## Achievement

The GCSE grades for 1999 were for the first year of Hazelhurst as Hall School Wimbledon. A total of 91 per cent of pupils achieved five or more A*–C grades at GCSE. This is an increase on 50 per cent in 1996. Only five pupils were entered for GCSEs in 2000 and these results along with 2002's results were unavailable at the time of writing.

## Extra-curricular activities

Over 150 visits are made annually to farms, museums and places of interest. There are also long walks for bringing history and geography to life. Visiting the exchange school in Provence improves pupils' language and culinary skills. The school believes that learning takes place mainly through experience, backed up with good teaching. The school offers a wide range of sports, including fencing and tennis. The school is also involved in charity work, and sent 150 boxes of gifts collected by the children to Eastern European countries at Christmas 2000.

# King's College School

**Southside, Wimbledon Common, London SW19 4TT** 020 8255 5300 020 8255 5359 jsa admissions@ kcs.org.uk www.kcs.org.uk JA Evans MA, M.Phil, FIL; Chair of Governors: Sir Robert Andrew KCB, MA Raynes Park, Wimbledon Wimbledon **Buses:** 80, 93, 200, 293 (There are also three coach services organized by parent volunteers and provided by commercial coach companies, serving areas from Kew to Hammersmith and Esher.) Dark grey trousers, with navy blue blazer and badge in the upper school (red in the lower school), white shirt and school tie; Sixth form: Dark suit with white shirt **Demand:** Oversubscribed **Type:** Selective independent for 1137 boys, aged 7 to 19 **Fees:** £3,560 per term **Submit application form:** Three years before entry for common entrance, beginning of December of previous year for sixth form entry **Motto:** *Sancte et sapienter* (Health and Wisdom) **School hours:** 8.40am–4pm **Meals:** Hot and cold available, including vegetarian options **Strong GCSE subjects:** All relatively strong **London league table position:** 13

## Profile

In 1829 a royal charter established a junior department of the new King's College, University of London. Originally in the Strand, the school moved to Wimbledon in 1897. In 1905, an Act of Parliament gave the school independence and its own governing body. The school has three laboratories for science, five for languages, an art and design technology centre, a music school with nine practice rooms, chamber music rooms, classrooms, a recital room and the Collyer Hall theatre. All subjects are well served by the school's computer network. The 24 acres of playing fields are in Motspur Park. There is also a boathouse at Putney, sports hall, heated indoor swimming pool, squash courts and small-bore rifle range. A-level subjects offered range from the classics to electronics and religious studies. The International Baccalaureate is also available. Pupils are appointed as prefects and each pupil has a tutor. There are two chaplains and professional counselling services available. Responsibility for special-needs pupils lies with a master and outside consultants provide advice and assistance. There is a school council. Parents and alumni can join the Friends of King's College School.

## Admissions and intake

Entry to the senior school is through the common entrance exam and applicants must be registered at least three years before entry. Applications for entry to the sixth form must be in by the end of the previous November, and requires satisfactory GCSE results, an interview and recommendation from the previous head teacher. Pupils' entry attainment level is generally above average. In 2000, there were 15 special-needs pupils, none with statements.

## Achievement

Kings College has excellent exams results. From 1996–2002, 100 per cent of pupils gained five or more GCSE grades A*–C, with the exception of 2001, when the figure slipped to 99 per cent. The school was ranked first in the borough league table. The average point score for A–levels was 392.1 in 2002, again ranking the school second in the borough. The last independent inspection was in 1999, and its comments were generally favourable. There were a few reservations but inspectors acknowledged that the head teacher had not been in the post long and had not yet had a chance to put his aims fully into practice.

## Extra-curricular activities

All sports are encouraged, including archery and riding. Clubs available range from cooking and engineering to Dante Gabriel Rossetti. The Collyer Hall theatre has its own full-time manager and an artistic director, with performances by professional artists. Pupils can also write and direct their own work, and a production is taken to the Edinburgh

Festival each year. The science club invites distinguished speakers and attends lectures at University College, London and King's College, London. Charity work is encouraged.

# Mitcham Vale High School

**Acacia Road, Mitcham, Surrey CR4 1SF** 020 8648 6627 020 8640 8305 staff@mitchamvale.merton.sch.uk www.merton.gov.uk/schoolreorg/schools/mitchamvale.asp Paullette Braithwaite Chair of Governors: Brian Alexander Mitcham, Streatham Common Morden, Tooting Broadway **Buses:** 60, 118, 152, 255, 463 Black jumper with school logo, lilac tie with different coloured stripe for each year group, white shirt or blouse, black trousers or skirt, black shoes (no trainers) **Demand:** 240 places in 2002 were oversubscribed **Type:** Community comprehensive for 1,200 mixed pupils, aged 11 to 16 **Submit application form:** Mid-October 2003 **School hours:** 8.30am–3pm **Meals:** Hot and cold available including breakfast **Strong GCSE subjects:** Not yet known **London league table position:** Not yet known

## Profile

Mitcham Vale opened in September 2002. The main site is the former Eastfields High School for boys but there are also facilities at the former Rowan High School for girls, in nearby Rowan Road. Pupils from both schools have been accommodated in the new mixed school. New school facilities are being built at the Acacia Road site by means of the Private Finance Initiative (PFI). The school aims to become a specialist Technology College. If successful, it will receive extra funding and be allowed to select up to 10 per cent of its pupils each year on the basis of their aptitude for technology. On entry, each pupil is assigned to a tutor group that they remain with throughout their time at the school. Pupils are taught in tutor groups and ability sets. For the first three years, pupils in Years 7, 8 and 9 are taught English, maths, technology, science, history, geography, religious studies, PE, music, art, dance and drama. They also study two modern foreign languages from French, German and Spanish. Information and communication technology (ICT) is taught across the curriculum and also as a separate subject. Years 10 and 11 take a minimum of nine GCSEs, or equivalent vocational qualifications. Personal, Social and Health Education, careers Education, work related issues and citizenship are also part of the curriculum.

## Admissions and intake

Admission is through the LEA and, if the school is oversubscribed, the authority's criteria apply. Priority is given to children whose parents or carers name the school as their first preference, then to those who have exceptional medical or social need, followed by those with a sibling already at the school and those who live closest, measured by the shortest walking route.

## Achievement

Mitcham Vale pupils will sit Key Stage 3 tests and GCSE exams in summer 2003.

## Extra-curricular activities

Extra-curricular activities are viewed as an essential part of the school's provision for pupils. There are activities before school, at break, lunch times and after school, including a breakfast club plus clubs for art and design, the Internet, music, dance, sports, 'fantasy football' and charity events. There is also a homework club. One major school trip will take place each year and recent destinations include the Isle of Wight, Normandy and skiing in Colorado.

# Raynes Park High School

**Bushey Road, Raynes Park, London SW20 0JL** 020 8946 4112 020 8947 0224 school@raynespark.merton.sch www.raynespark.merton.sch.uk Ian Newman; Chair of Governors: Bob Higgins Raynes Park **Buses:** 72, 131, 152, 163, 265 Blue sweatshirt with school logo, dark-coloured skirts or trousers (girls); dark-coloured trousers, white shirt, school tie (boys) **Demand:** Slightly oversubscribed **Type:** Comprehensive for 811 mixed pupils, aged 11 to 16; roll will increase to 1200 by 2005 **Submit application form:** Mid-October 2003 **Motto:** To Each His Need, From Each His Power **School hours:** 8.45am–3.35pm, 8.45–2.45pm (Fri); homework clubs are available **School meals:** Hot and cold available, including breakfast **Strong GCSE subjects:** All relatively strong **London league table position:** 419

## Profile

Raynes Park dates back to 1935 when it was founded as a boys' grammar school. It became a comprehensive in the 1960s. A change in the age at which pupils transfer to secondary school in 2001 saw sweeping changes to Merton's schools and saw Raynes Park School take over neighbouring Bushey middle school first. The extra space allows for an anticipated 25 per cent growth in intake. The school won an Investors in People Award in 2000 and has also won a Sportsmark Award. It has a high-standard of facilities, from a state-of-the art computer centre and music and drama studios to a new library and floodlit, all-weather tennis courts. The range of courses on offer was described by Ofsted as 'good' when they inspected in 1999, including GNVQ and short courses at Key Stage 4. The school is organized around a tutorial system and has a head of year. It is able to cater for mentally and physically handicapped pupils. Special-needs pupils make satisfactory progress, although Ofsted has shown concern for the 'insufficiently specific' targets set in the educational plans. Parents can join the active PTA. Raynes Park fares badly in attendance with authorized absence at 9 per cent – the fourth worst in the borough – and unauthorized absence at 2.1 per cent However, an ongoing approach to improving attendance has been introduced. Pupils go on to Esher and Merton colleges amongst others. Famous ex-pupils include Robert Robinson from TV show *Ask The Family*.

## Admissions and intake

All entries are dealt with through the LEA (see borough factfile). A total of 50 special-needs pupils have statements, with 167 on the register.

## Achievement

On entry, academic standards are below the national average, with single-sex and selective schools creaming off the upper half of the ability range, but the most recent Ofsted inspection recognized a pattern of attainment which indicates that Raynes Park is an improving school. It was positioned sixth in the borough league table in 2002 with 37 per cent of pupils achieved five or more GCSEs at grades A*–C. This down on 40 per cent in 2001. Ofsted reported a good standard of teaching and learning in English language, art, PE and design technology. However, there was concern over business studies at Year 11, where the teaching was described as ineffective. The school's ethos is positive, which arises from good teamwork, while staff and pupils seem to get on well. Pupils go on to Merton, Kingston and Esher colleges.

## Extra-curricular activities

Sports clubs available include football and tennis. Year 10 pupils are ball girls and boys at Wimbledon Tennis Championships. Mufti days are held for charity. The strong house system offers a debating society and drama and music competitions, including singing. Skiing and other sporting trips as well as academic trips are also on offer. Homework clubs are available but times vary.

# Ricards Lodge High School

**Lake Road, Wimbledon, London SW19 7HB** 020 8946 2208 020 8971 9700 Mrs Sheila Oviatt Ham BA (Hons), MA; Chair of Governors: Mr Alex Youel Wimbledon Wimbledon **Buses:** 57, 93, 131, 155, 156, 163, 164, 200 Navy blue sweatshirt with school logo, white shirt, navy blue skirt **Demand:** Varies **Type:** County comprehensive for 823 girls, aged 11 to 16; roll will increase to 1200 by 2005 **Submit application form:** Early February 2003 **School hours:** 8.45am–3.20pm, 8.45am–2pm (Fri); homework clubs are available **School meals:** Hot and cold available **Strong GCSE subjects:** Art, design and technology, drama, geography, PE, textiles **London league table position:** 319

## Profile

Ricards Lodge shares large sports fields with neighbouring schools. There is a well-equipped computer suite, a music suite with a recording studio and a fully equipped learning resource centre with CD-ROMs and Internet access. The school plans to extend and improve upon its facilities to accommodate its increasing roll of pupils. In the upper years (Years 10 to 11), girls must study the core subjects: English and English literature, maths, science, technology, RE, humanities and languages. Pupils can also choose from arts, a second humanity or language or business studies, child development, media studies and PE. All girls must study IT. Classes are streamed for maths, science and languages only. In Year 10 mock interviews with employers are arranged, and all girls undertake work experience. By the end of Year 11, every pupil will have had an individual interview with a careers adviser. Girls are divided into tutor groups of mixed abilities, friendships and personalities, led by a tutor who will stay with them throughout their school lives. The school council offers a forum for consultation between staff and girls. Pupils and parents sign a code of conduct designed to reward high standards of work and behaviour. Cooperation between parents and the school is encouraged through contacts books, a half-termly newsletter, regular reports, parents' evenings and invitations to performances and events. The school has made efforts to improve attendance. In 2001, Ofsted noted that the school's attendance levels were just below national averages, especially in Years 10 and 11.

## Admissions and intake

Admission is through the LEA (see borough factfile). The school sees its intake as 'reasonably comprehensive, but slightly skewed towards the weak side' (Ofsted). It achieves some top band scores but proportionally more lower band scores. It also admits a high number of pupils with significant reading difficulties. In 2001, the school had 12 pupils with statements and 185 on the special-needs register.

## Achievement

Ricards achieved the fifth best results in the borough in 2002. A total of 52 per cent of pupils gained five or more GCSEs at grades A*–C, 11 per cent down on 2001's results. Since 1996, results have been steady apart from a dip in 1997. Ofsted described Ricards as 'a very good school' where 'attainment is well above average and the progress of students is good'. Good GCSE results are achieved in art, design and technology, drama, geography, PE and textiles. Pupils' behaviour was seen to be good although a 'small minority' of pupils were seen to be 'inattentive and poorly behaved'. Pupils' access to ICT needed to be improved as did levels of attendance. Relationships at the school are good with a high level of harmony. Pupils go on to study at Merton and Esher colleges.

## Extra-curricular activities

Clubs available include dance, football, athletics, rounders and health and fitness units. Girls have been England trialists in athletics, cross country, korfball and swimming. Ricards provides a large number of ball girls for Wimbledon Tennis Championships. They also have links with Wimbledon Football Club and Wandsworth Hurricanes basketball club. There are regular charity events and a community day when pupils work to help the community or the environment. Homework clubs are available.

# Rutlish School

**Watery Lane, Merton Park, London SW20 9AD** ☎ 020 8542 1212 📠 020 8544 0580 Ms Karen Bastick-Styles; Chair of Governors: Elaine McCormack ⇌ Wimbledon Chase **Buses:** 152, 163, 164 Black trousers, white shirt, plain black blazer, black jumper, school tie **Type:** Voluntary controlled comprehensive for 793 boys, aged 11 to 16; roll will increase to 1200 by 2005 **Demand:** Equal demand for places **Submit application form:** Mid-October 2003 **Mission statement:** Where Boys Can Achieve Beyond Their Potential **School hours:** 8.30am–3.10pm; homework clubs are available **School meals:** Hot and cold available, including breakfast **Strong GCSE subjects:** Design and technology, ICT, modern foreign languages **London league table position:** 469

## Profile

Rutlish is a long-established school, having celebrated its centenary in 1995. Recent developments include new IT facilities with a refurbished suite, good football and rugby pitches, access to tennis and squash courts and a learning resources centre stocking CD-ROMs, TV and video and Internet access. More developments are planned to accommodate the increasing number of pupils. By Key Stage 4, boys can choose to continue earlier studies or take on new subjects, including life skills, study support and sports studies. Boys are both streamed and taught in mixed ability groups, depending on the curriculum. They are split into tutor groups in Year 8. Careers guidance is first offered in Year 8, followed up by a Year 9 industry day, a mini-enterprise for Year 10 pupils and a National Record of Achievement Validation in Year 11. Year 10 pupils also undertake work experience. Pupils can become prefects and there is a student council. Rutlish makes good provision for pupils with special needs but lacks the appropriate facilities to admit boys with disabilities. Close relationships are promoted with parents through study planners, monthly newsletters, regular reports on pupil progress and information evenings and events. Famous ex-pupils include: John Major (ex-Prime Minister) and Raymond Briggs (author).

### Admissions and intake

Admission is first and foremost handled by the LEA. Wimbledon Chase, Dundonald, Mitcham, Cranmer and Bushey are the main feeder schools. Where Rutlish is first preference, the order of priority for admission is medical or social need, siblings, then proximity of home to school. Reading abilities on entry are lower than the national average.

### Achievement

Rutlish appears in the bottom half of the borough GCSE league table for overall performance and is below the national average. In 2002, 27 per cent of pupils gained five or more A*–C grades at GCSE. This was slightly down on 32 per cent in 2001. The past five years has seen results hover below the borough average. Ofsted visted the school in 2001 and commented that: 'Rutlish is a good school with some significant strengths'. Inspectors praised the head teacher's 'outstanding leadership' and said 'students make good progress, achieve well and have an enthusiasm for learning'. GCSE results are below average but are in line with similar schools. Pupils do well in English language and literature, drama, history and mathematics. Inspectors noted that the school needs to continue to raise standards of attainment overall. Unauthorized absence is 1.7 per cent, above the national average.

### Extra-curricular activities

Competitive sports are popular at Rutlish, with fixtures in the Surrey and Rosslyn Park Rugby seven-a-side tournaments and the national schools' fives championships. Seasonal sports include rugby, football, cross country, swimming, dance and tennis. There are foreign exchanges, skiing trips, science trips and outings to theatres and art galleries. Boys can also join the Combined Cadet Force. Homework clubs are available, and the school raises money for local charities such as the Red Cross.

## Tamworth Manor High School

**Wide Way, Mitcham, Surrey CR4 1BP** ☎ 020 8764 5112 📠 020 8764 7655 ✉ tamworth@btconnect.com 🌐 www.freespace.virgin.net\n.shami\tamworth Ms Sue Williamson BA (Hons); Chair of Governors: Mr Lionel Cartlidge Streatham Common **Buses:** 60, 118, 152 Navy blue jumper with school logo, shirt, navy blue skirt or trousers, tie **Demand:** Oversubscribed **Type:** Comprehensive for 826 mixed pupils, aged 11 to 16; roll will increase to 1200 by 2005 **Submit application form:** Mid-October 2003 **Mission statement:** To bring about effective learning and maximize the achievement of each of our students and enable them to discover the power of knowledge and acquire the values needed for a worthwhile future. **School hours:** 8.45am–3.15pm (Tues and Fri), 8.45am–3.40pm (other days); homework clubs available **School meals:** Hot and cold available **Strong GCSE subjects:** Media studies **London league table position:** 476

### Profile

This school has already undergone major change in 1990 when it switched from a 13 to 18 age range to 12 to 16, before changing again to become an 11 to 16 comprehensive in 2002. Recent improvements include new design and technology areas, two temporary classrooms and a meeting room for parents. The school has nearly 90 computers. Curriculum at Key Stage 4 allows pupils to take two GCSEs in science as an extension option. Others choose a second modern language from Italian, French and German. GVNQs on offer include health and social care, and leisure and tourism. Sound links have been built with the community, including work experience with local employers, undertaken in Year 10. Year coordinators oversee pupils' academic progress. A school council and buddying of senior pupils with younger ones encourages responsibility. Pupils with special educational needs are well served. Due to a high prevalence of asthma, the school has a relevant policy and all staff are fully trained. Good links with parents are maintained through a student journal, parents' evenings, letters and phone calls. There is a special-needs teacher available to give support. Parents are all automatic members of the Tamworth Manor Association. Attendance is poor (below 90 per cent), but rigorous procedures have helped bring about a small improvement.

### Admissions and intake

Admission is through the LEA (see borough factfile). On entry, standards are below the national average.

### Achievement

The school's achievement is below average when compared with similar schools, but the staff and governors are fully committed to raising standards, and this is proven by an upward trend since 1999's results. In 2002, Tamworth was ranked eighth in the borough and below the national average. A total of 25 per cent of pupils achieved five or more at grades A*–C. This was four per cent below 2001's results. In 1999, Ofsted reported that the school is strong at monitoring progress and provides very good support for pupils with English as an additional language, as well as good guidance and support for all the youngsters. The school falls down though in basic writing skills and presentation, which is below national expectations. The school performs above the national average in media studies and below in English and maths. The school has been awarded an Investors in People accolade twice. Pupils go on to Croydon and Carshalton Colleges.

### Extra-curricular activities

There is a good range of activities available, including drama, Scrabble, ICT club and art clubs. An activity centre stocked with pool tables and table tennis is open at lunchtimes and from 6pm to 8pm for junior school members at 50p per night. Pupils train to be ball boys and girls at Wimbledon. After-school homework clubs are available. Pupils have visited the Clothes Show Live in Birmingham, and have been skiing in Italy.

# Ursuline High School Wimbledon

**Crescent Road, Wimbledon SW20 8HA** 020 8255 2688 020 8255 2687 106540.357@compuserve.com Dr Calvert; Chair of Governors: Mr Snalune Raynes Park, Wimbledon **Buses:** 57, 131, 200 Blue and white striped shirt, navy blue skirt, navy jumper **Demand:** 180 places each year **Type:** Voluntary aided Roman Catholic for 975 girls, aged 11 to 18 **Submit application form:** Mid-October 2003 **School hours:** 8.30am–3.30pm **School meals:** Hot and cold available **Strong GCSE subjects:** All relatively strong **London league table position:** 174

### Profile

This school is run by Ursuline sisters, an international religious order. The buildings, set in extensive grounds, mainly date back to the 1930s but there is also a new two-storey block. Existing IT facilities, which were criticized by Ofsted in 1997 as having a serious deficiency in up-to-date equipment, have recently been upgraded and improved. A £1.1 million building programme is underway which will include eight new classrooms and two new labs. The curriculum is broad and balanced. The 224-strong sixth form (224 pupils) is a consortium with a neighbouring Catholic boys' school, Wimbledon College, about five-minutes' walk away. A good range of subjects is on offer, including GNVQs in business and leisure and tourism. Authorized absence was 7.1 per cent in 2000, below the national average. The school has a special-needs coordinator. There is an active PTA.

### Admissions and intake

Application is made direct to the school. Non-Catholics are admitted. The school's intake is from the full ability range and from a wide catchment area. The main feeder schools are St Thomas's, St Catherine's and Ursuline Preparatory School.

### Achievement

Ursuline is positioned third in the LEA table for 2002. A total of 71 per cent of pupils gained GCSEs at grades A*–C. This is well above the national and local averages. In 2002, the average point score for pupils taking two or more A-levels was 280, which shows a significant improvement over the last five years. These results placed St Ursuline fourth in the borough. In 1997, Ofsted reported that Ursuline is 'a good school with significant strengths' with 'a high quality of teaching' and that it 'makes a very strong contribution to pupils' spiritual, moral, social and cultural development.' Attainment was in line or above national expectations in 90 per cent of lessons observed by Ofsted inspectors. The school's distinctive Christian community is supportive and caring. Ofsted observed that behaviour was very good and pupils have 'very positive attitudes'. Its level of unauthorized absence is very low for the borough.

### Extra-curricular activities

The school is strong in sport, particularly hockey and netball. Drama is also popular. There is an annual pilgrimage to Lake Garda in Italy, as well as skiing trips and adventure holidays. There are also regular visits to art galleries, museums and exhibitions. The school undertakes extensive charity work.

# Wimbledon College

**Edge Hill, London SW19 4NS** 020 8946 2533 020 8947 6513 enquiries@wimbledoncollege.org.uk www.wimbledoncollege.fsnet.co.uk Rev Michael Holman SJ, BA, M.Sc, M.Div; Chair of Governors: Mr Andrew Kennedy Wimbledon, Wimbledon Chase Wimbledon **Buses:** 57, 93, 131, 152, 155, 156, 163, 164, 200 Up to sixth form: Dark navy or black blazer, badge and house colours, dark grey trousers, college or prefect or sports tie, white or grey shirts, black, grey or navy V-neck pullover **Demand:** 180 places available; oversubscribed **Type:** Voluntary aided Roman Catholic comprehensive for 1066 boys, aged 11 to 18 **Submit application form:** Mid-October 2003 **Motto:** For the Greater Glory of God **School hours:** 8.45am–3.30pm **Meals:** Hot and cold available, including breakfast and vegetarian options **Strong GCSE subjects:** English Literature, IT **London league table position:** 180

## Profile

Founded in 1892, Wimbledon College is one of many Jesuit establishments throughout the world. Its excellent science and technology laboratories enabled two pupils to win silver and bronze medals in the national Physics Challenge. There is a large library and resource centre, a music block, theatre and art rooms. In 2002, a new library, IT centre, dining room and sixth form area opened. A sports/multi-purpose assembly and examination hall is also being built. The choice of subjects at A-level has a strong emphasis on academic courses, but includes business and theatre studies as well as theology. Since 1988, the school has run a joint sixth form with Ursuline High School, enabling more subject choice. Vocational courses available include leisure and tourism, health and social care, and art and design. Pupils undertake two weeks' work experience. The special-needs department assesses new pupils and plans suitable assistance. Academically gifted pupils are placed on the brighter pupil programme. Two chaplains provide pastoral care and a counselling service. The Friends of Wimbledon College raise funds. There are regular reports to parents and annual parents' evenings. There is also a termly newsletter and an annual college magazine.

## Admissions and intake

Applications must be in by the LEA's closing date. The school sets the admissions criteria, with active Catholic faith as the main criterion (a recommendation is required from a parish priest), but other applicants are accepted if they will participate in the school's Christian activities. Exceptional need, a sibling at the school or the Ursuline High School, and distance from the school are also considered. In 2001, one-fifth of pupils had special educational needs pupils and nearly two per cent had statements of special-needs. These proportions are near the average for schools.

## Achievement

Wimbledon College performs consistently well. In 2002, 65 per cent of pupils gained five or more GCSE grades A*–C. This was up from 56 per cent in 2001. The average A-level point score in 2002 was 281. English literature and IT are good subjects, but design and technology are poor. In 2001 Ofsted described Wimbledon College as 'a good school' where 'students achieve above average standards'. Unauthorized absence was low at 0.3 per cent in 2000.

## Extra-curricular activities

Competitive sport at the national level is strongly supported. Music, judo, Latin, board games, and the Young Engineers are also popular. Pupils take part in exchanges with a school in St Petersburg. Volunteers help with a weekly soup run for the homeless and there are pilgrimages to Lourdes. Senior pupils help mentor younger pupils and organize charity events.

# Wimbledon High School

**Mansel Road, London SW19 4AB** 020 8971 0900 020 8971 0901 info@wim.gdst.net www.gdst.net/wimbledon Mrs Pamela Wilkes; Chair of Governors: Dame Angela Rumbold Wimbledon Wimbledon **Buses:** 57, 93, 131, 155, 156, 163, 164, 200 Navy or black coat, navy gored or kilt style skirt (plain green or blue skirt as an alternative in summer), or navy trousers, navy jumper with school colours, white blouse **Demand:** Information unavailable **Type:** Selective independent, part of the Girls' Day School Trust, for 881 girls, aged 4 to 19 **Fees:** £2,385 per term **Submit application form:** First week of December 2003 **Mission statement:** We set out to educate girls so that their intellectual, creative, aesthetic, practical, physical and spiritual qualities and talents will be fully realized, they develop a sense of social justice and compassion, become enthusiastic, assured individuals who wish to lead and influence society, and acquire the appropriate qualifications and character to do so. **Motto:** *Ex humilibus ad excelsa* (From the humble roots up to the heights) **School hours:** 8.30am–4pm, 8.30am–3.25pm (Fri) **Meals:** Hot and cold available, including vegetarian options **Strong GCSE subjects:** All relatively strong **London league table position:** 18

## Profile

Wimbledon High is one of the 25 Girls' Day School Trust schools in the UK. The school joined the state-funded Direct Grant scheme in 1944 but reverted to independence in 1976 when the scheme was discontinued. Wimbledon High itself was founded in 1880. Facilities on-site include a modern block for the three sciences, design and technology rooms, a theatre, music and art centres. There is one computer per four pupils and laptops in the labs. In addition to the playing fields, there is a sports hall and a 25m covered swimming pool. The classics, theology and philosophy of religion are among subjects offered at A-level. Liberal studies, a wide-ranging programme offered jointly with King's College School sixth form, encourages thinking, without the pressure of an examination. Vocational subjects include ICT and design and technology. There is good careers advice and two weeks' work experience, for which high quality placements are sought. The school has no prefects, but all sixth formers are expected to take on responsibilities. There are also elections to the sixth-form committee. Teachers are assisted by specialists to devise teaching strategies for special-needs individuals, who may also have impaired hearing, temporary physical disability or dyslexia. There is a thriving PTA and a school council.

## Admissions and intake

Applications can be made directly to the school any time. There are several entry points and the school sets practical and academic tests. Sixth form entry requires at least seven GCSE C grades or an IQ test and written papers if coming from outside the UK education system. All applicants are interviewed. The attainment level of pupils on entry is above average. In 2000, there were 59 special-needs pupils, none with statements.

## Achievement

In 2002, 100 per cent of pupils achieved five or more GCSE grades A*–C. This was one per cent above 2001's results and the school came second in the borough. Wimbledon High pupils scored an average A-level point score of 427.4 for taking two or more A-levels, well above borough and national averages. This ranked the school top of the borough. The last independent school inspection was in 1998.

## Extra-curricular activities

Karate and engineering, poetry, the Young Enterprise scheme and debating are just some of the clubs available. A number of trips abroad are organized. Pupils are encouraged to raise funds for charities and to undertake community service for the handicapped and the elderly. Sporting clubs include trampolining, badminton and dance.

# Newham

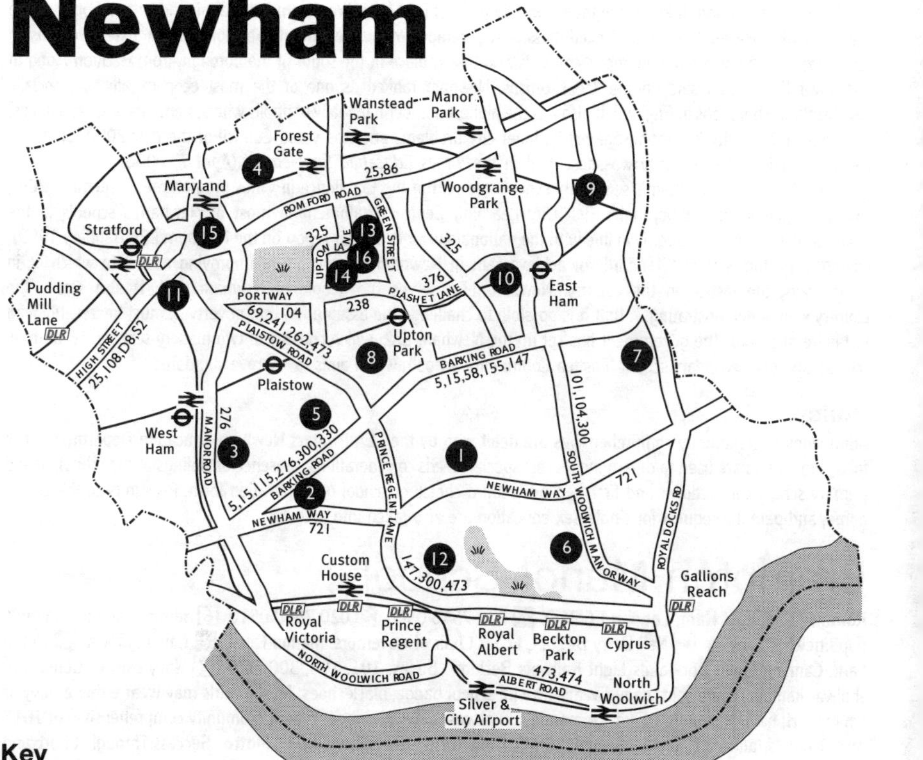


## Key

| | | | |
|---|---|---|---|
| 1 | Brampton Manor School | 9 | Little Ilford School |
| 2 | Cumberland School | 10 | Plashet School |
| 3 | Eastlea Community School | 11 | Rokeby School |
| 4 | Forest Gate Community School | 12 | The Royal Docks Community School |
| 5 | Jamia Ramania Islamic Institute | 13 | St Angela's Ursuline Convent School |
| 6 | Kingsford Community School | 14 | St Bonaventure's RC School |
| 7 | Langdon School | 15 | Sarah Bonnell School |
| 8 | Lister Community School | 16 | Stratford School |

# Factfile

**LEA: Broadway House, 322 High Street, London E15 1EP** ☎ **020 8472 1430** www.newham.gov.uk **Director of Education:** Pauline Maddison **Political control of council:** Labour **Percentage of pupils from outside the borough:** 3 per cent **Percentage of pupils educated outside the borough:** 5.6 per cent **London league table positions (out of 32 boroughs):** 19th

The borough of Newham takes in the three constituencies of East Ham, West Ham and Canning Town and Poplar. Since the late 1980s, Newham has experienced massive regeneration of the area around Stratford station. Extensive housing regeneration and environmental improvement is also taking place in the south of the borough, from Beckton along to the Royal Docks. That said, in the 1991 census, Newham ranked as one of the most economically and socially disadvantaged boroughs in England. It also has the highest number nationally of pupils with statements of special needs.

The local authority is fighting against its inner-city problems and was voted Council of the Year 2000. Similarly, Newham's education authority was described in the *Times Education Supplement* (April 7, 2000) as 'an icon of good practice'. All of Newham's secondary schools are part of the Excellence in Cities programme. September 2000 saw the opening of the borough's first City Learning Centre. Attainment in most of Newham's schools in the lower grades at GCSE is roughly in line with the national average. In their report on the Newham LEA (January 1999), Ofsted inspectors stated: 'Standards of achievement in Newham schools ... are improving at a rate which is, in some ways, the fastest in the country...Newham LEA serves the people of Newham well. It also serves the country well in demonstrating ... that it is possible to challenge the assumption that poverty ... must necessarily lead to failure at school.' The government has set up the Newham EAZ, which consists of two nursery schools, 16 primary schools and one secondary school (Eastlea Community School), which aims to improve standards.

## Policy

Admissions to community comprehensives are dealt with by the LEA (contact Newham Education Department). The following criteria are used to determine places: special-needs considerations; presence of siblings at the school; linked primary school connections; and first, second or third choice of school on application form. Proximity to the child's home, and parental request for single-sex education are also taken into account.

# Brampton Manor School

**Roman Road, East Ham, London E6 3SQ** ☎ 020 7540 0500 📠 020 7540 0510 ⓔ admin.bramptonmanor@pop3.newham.gov.uk ✉ Neil Berry BA, MA, FCST; Chair of Governors: Marion Faust ⇄ Canning Town ⊖ Upton Park, Canning Town; Docklands Light Railway: Beckton **Buses**: 101, 104, 300, 376 👔 Navy skirt or trousers or shalwar kameez, white shirt, navy sweatshirt with school badge, black shoes; Muslim girls may wear either a navy or white scarf; navy and white PE kit **Demand**: 330 places; oversubscribed **Type**: Community comprehensive for 1612 mixed pupils, aged 11 to 16 **Submit application form**: November 2003 **Motto**: Success Through Effort and Determination **School hours**: 8.40am–3.20pm; homework clubs are available **Meals**: Hot and cold available **Strong GCSE subjects**: Drama, history, music, RE **London league table position**: 424

## Profile

Brampton Manor is the second largest school in Newham, and although its academic standards are low compared to the national picture, it nevertheless attempts to provide a caring environment in which pupils are encouraged to achieve their best. Established in 1972, the school is undergoing redevelopment. The new buildings are state-of-the-art, with excellent facilities. Pupils are put into forms of around 30 and there is some streaming in maths, science and modern languages. Pupils study up to 12 subjects at Key Stage 4, including French or German, drama and IT, as well as social and ethical studies and vocational subjects. All pupils take part in work experience. Sports include canoeing and rowing, which are taught at the Royal Docks. The school also has two gymnasia and on-site playing fields. Brampton Manor operates an equal opportunities policy and prides itself on promoting its pupils' respect for the many faiths and cultures within the school and local community. Seven staff provide support (usually inclusive), for pupils with special needs, and two full-time teachers help pupils who have English as an additional language. There are year councils and an active school council. Parents are kept informed through annual parents' evenings, reports and a fund-raising friends' group. Truancy remains a problem and unauthorized absence is above the national average at 3.2 per cent.

## Admissions and intake

Admissions are dealt with by Newham LEA (see borough factfile). Brampton Manor has five linked primary schools: Brampton, Central Park, New City, Roman Road and Tollgate. A large number of pupils, higher than the national average have special needs.

## Achievement

Ofsted visited the school in 2001 and described it as 'an improving and a much more effective school' than it was at the time of their last report in 1999. Inspectors praised the head teacher's 'determined and purposeful' leadership and noted that 'improved teaching has led to better attitudes to learning and higher achievement'. The school was no longer judged to have serious weaknesses. Although GCSE results are below average nationally, the average point score is comparable with similar schools. Clear improvements were seen in pupils' attainment in modern foreign languages, sociology, media studies, business studies and PE studies. At GCSE, 30 per cent of pupils gained five or more A*–C grades in 2002 and the school was ranked 13th in the borough. Ofsted noted that pupils' speaking and reading skills need to be improved as does the provision for pupils with English as an additional language.

## Extra-curricular activities

Lunchtime and after-school activities include sports clubs, music clubs and learning-support groups. Pupils publish their own paper, *Brampton News*. The school's resource-based learning centre, which houses the library, is open at lunchtime and after school for independent study. There are trips both at home and abroad.

# Cumberland School

**Barking Road, Canning Town, London E16 4DD** ☎ 020 7474 0231 📠 020 7511 2510 ⓔ admin.cumberland@pop3.newham.gov.uk; admin@se002516.dialnet.com Ms Jane V Noble BA (Hons); Chair of Governors: Mrs Sharon Higgins Docklands Light Railway: Canning Town **Buses**: 5, 15, 69, 115, 241, 276, 330 Navy jumper, trousers or skirt and red or white shirt **Demand**: 180 places available **Type**: Community comprehensive for 894 mixed pupils, aged 11 to 16 **Submit application form**: November 2003 **Motto**: Working for and Celebrating Achievement **School hours**: 8.55am–3.20pm **Meals**: Hot and cold available, including breakfast; homework clubs are available **Strong GCSE subjects**: English, maths **London league table position**: 408

## Profile

The Cumberland School offers a welcoming environment to pupils of all abilities. In 1997, Ofsted praised the head as offering 'clear and good leadership', but social and economic difficulties have had a serious impact on overall attainment. Facilities are mostly good, especially the school's library, which has excellent computer facilities, and spacious art rooms. There is a gym, weights room, hard-surface play area and dance studio, and the facilities at Newham Leisure Centre are also used for sports. At Key Stage 4, pupils study English, maths, double science, PE, RE, focusing on Christianity, Judaism and Islam (unless parents specify otherwise), IT and PSE, plus a number of optional subjects. There are around 22 pupils in each class and there is streaming in French and maths. Form tutors are responsible for pastoral care. All pupils undertake work experience. Parents are kept informed through the *Cumberland Chronicle* and the PTA, and they also help to monitor homework using planners. There is provision for pupils with special needs.

## Admissions and intake

Admissions are dealt with by Newham LEA (see borough factfile). Pupils come from five local wards and five main feeder primary schools including three linked primaries: Hallsville, Keir Hardie and Ravenscroft. Open days and evenings and interviews are organized for prospective pupils and their parents.

## Achievement

In 2002, 27 per cent of pupils gained five or more A*–C grades at GCSE. This was up on the previous year and the school was ranked 11th in the borough. Attainment in almost all subjects is very low compared with the national average, principally because of poor levels of literacy throughout the school. In 2001, Ofsted recognised that the school serves a community with 'multiple challenges' and has a very high rate of pupils joining or leaving the school at various times. Despite these problems, Cumberland was seen to be 'improving at a good rate' and to offer its pupils 'very good educational opportunities'. Most pupils make good progress over time and achieve well. Although the school's standards are generally below the national average, standards achieved in tests in English and mathematics at the end of Year 9 are average compared to similar schools. Pupils with special educational needs make good progress as do pupils with English as an additional language. However, despite some improvements, the school's attendance levels are persistently well below average and punctuality is also a problem. Ofsted wanted to see improvements in literacy levels throughout the school and a better rate of progress for pupils in Years 7, 8 and 9.

## Extra-curricular activities

Cumberland performs well in sport, especially in inter-school football and netball competitions. Sports 'taster sessions' allow pupils to try their hand at sports such as archery, canoeing, fencing and sailing. Other activities include a gospel choir, recorder group and annual staged production. Instrumental lessons are offered by Newham Music Academy. Pupils are able to voice their opinions at the annual 'put it to your MP day'. Support groups include a homework club at the learning resource base, a summer literacy school, English-language support classes and an after-school numeracy project. There are trips both at home and abroad.

# Eastlea Community School

**Hilda Road, Canning Town, London E16 4NP** 020 7540 0400 020 7540 0410 admin.eastlea@pop3.newham.gov.uk Ms Linda Powell M.Sc; Chair of Governors: Mr R Benton Canning Town, West Ham Canning Town, West Ham; Docklands Light Railway: Canning Town **Buses**: 5, 69, 276 Black skirt or trousers, white school polo shirt featuring school badge, school sweatshirt with badge, black blazer **Demand**: 240 places available; oversubscribed **Type**: Community comprehensive Technology College for 1058 mixed pupils, aged 11 to 16 **Submit application form**: November 2003 **Motto**: Learning Together and Building on Our Success **School hours**: 9am–3.35pm; homework clubs are available **School meals**: Hot and cold available **Strong GCSE subjects**: Art, drama, English literature, graphics **London league table position**: 416

## Profile

Eastlea is the only school in the borough to be within the Education Action Zone, which means that it promotes alternative approaches to learning, new methods of school management and new investment in the school site. It emphasizes its links with local businesses and has a wide range of vocational and business-linked courses. The school recently achieved Technology College status. Eastlea's buildings include a modern science block, sports hall, a well-equipped gym and IT suites. In September 2000, the language and literacy department moved into refurbished classrooms. A new area for maths opened in January 2001 and there are plans to refurbish facilities for drama, music and sport. Work experience for pupils is arranged through Project Trident in Years 10 or 11. Pupils are placed in tutor groups, and tutors, along with student support officers, are responsible for welfare. Special-needs pupils are taught mostly inclusively and there is provision for pupils with physical difficulties and complex medical conditions. There is a prefects system and a parent-teacher association. Pupils with learning difficulties are given extra support, and some gifted pupils may sit exams early. Parents are kept informed through parents' evenings, reports and homework diaries.

## Admissions and intake

Admissions are dealt with by Newham LEA (see borough factfile). Most pupils at the school come from the local south Newham area and local Newham primary schools. There are five linked primaries: Curwen, Gainsborough, Manor, St Luke's and Star.

## Achievement

In 2000, Ofsted highlighted the disadvantaged intake of the school as many pupils arrive with 'low levels of skill in numeracy, reading and writing'. A total of 486 pupils have English as an additional language and 60 different languages are spoken in the school. Inspectors found Eastlea to provide 'acceptable standards of education' and teaching was 'excellent, very good or good in nearly two out of three of the lessons'. The strongest subjects at GCSE were found to include English, graphics, art and drama. Weaker subjects were French, textiles, business education and information technology. In 2002, 36 per cent of pupils earned five or more A*–C grades, an increase on 35 per cent in 2001 but below the borough and national averages. The school was ranked 12th in the borough. Eastlea has an extremely high level of exclusions which also reflects negatively on results. The school does, however, employ a code of behaviour and detentions are used as a disciplinary measure.

## Extra-curricular activities

Sports available include football, rugby, badminton, dance and athletics. There are also skiing trips abroad. Arts activities include trips to galleries and theatres and the production of plays at the school's own theatre. Some pupils attend workshops at Newham's Educational Arts Centre and take music lessons from the borough's peripatetic teachers. Eastlea is hoping to establish an artist in residence.

# Forest Gate Community School

**Forest Street, London E7 0HR** 020 8534 8666 020 8519 8702 admin.forestgate@pop3.newham.gov.uk www.angliacampus.com/schools/org2619/ Margaret Wheeler BA (Hons), Dip.Ed (Adv), FRSA; Chair of Governors: Mr R Wenborne Forest Gate, Wanstead **Buses:** 58, 308, 330, 678 Black trousers or skirt, black jumper with school logo, white shirt, striped school tie **Demand:** 210 places available **Type:** Community comprehensive for 1031 mixed pupils, aged 11 to 16 **Submit application form:** November 2003 **School hours:** 9am–3.30pm **Meals:** Hot and cold available **Strong GCSE subjects:** Bengali, drama, music, Urdu **London league table position:** 389

## Profile

Forest Gate has a policy of enabling each pupil to attain their best and develop a strong set of values and positive attitudes within a friendly, happy environment. The school has been given a Sportsmark Award and it is also a centre of excellence for Essex County Cricket Club. It has excellent sports facilities including a fine astroturf pitch. At Key Stage 4, pupils study core subjects such as English, maths, science, a modern language, design technology and IT, plus two other GCSEs from subjects such as French, history, religious studies, art, music and GNVQ in IT. English language support is given in the form of an additional course. On entry, pupils are placed in mixed-ability tutor groups and have the same form tutor throughout their school life. Tutor periods, assemblies and PSHE classes help to establish good relations between pupils and their tutors. There is a school council. Homework is recorded in homework diaries, which are signed by parents. A regular newsletter, written reports and parents' evenings help maintain good links with parents. Behaviour is fairly good at the school, although the unauthorized absence rate of 5.1 per cent in 2000 is relatively high.

## Admissions and intake

Admissions are dealt with by Newham LEA (see borough factfile). Linked primary schools are Colegrave (girls only), Earlham (girls only), Godwin, Maryland (girls only), Monega, St James's and Sandringham. There is a very high number of pupils speaking English as an additional language and 91 of them are at an early stage of learning English.

## Achievement

In 2002, Ofsted praised the school for creating a 'positive learning environment in which students feel valued'. Teaching was seen to be 'satisfactory in all subjects and good in some'. The most effective teaching is in Years 9, 10 and 11 while the weakest teaching is in Year 7. Attainment is generally below the borough's average on entry. In 2002, 33 per cent of pupils earned five or more A*–C grades at GCSE. This result was down on 34 per cent in 2001 but below the borough average. The school was placed ninth in the borough league table. Pupils do well in drama, music, Bengali and Urdu. Ofsted found pupils to have 'postive attitudes to learning' and to 'generally behave well, both in and outside lessons'. Inspectors praised the 'good leadership' of the head teacher. However, they wanted to see the school develop a wider range of ways in which to help pupils learn to read and write well, and to improve standards in modern foreign languages and ICT.

## Extra-curricular activities

Ofsted praised the school's 'very good' provision for extra-curricular activities. A wide range of sport, music and drama activities and homework-support sessions are organized at lunchtime and after school. Productions are put on at the school, notably fund-raising fashion shows. Ofsted praised the Forest Gate Celebration, which was designed to raise awareness of the many cultural traditions represented at the school. All Year 7 pupils may spend a week at Newham's outdoor centre in Essex.

# Jamia Ramania Islamic Institute

**163–165 Balaam Street, Plaistow, London E13 8AA** 020 8472 9911 020 8472 9911 M Torik Ullah (principal); Chair of Governors: Mumtaz Ali Plaistow **Buses:** 241, 325 All white, appropriate Muslim dress **Demand:** 25 applications for 20 places **Type:** Selective Islamic independent for 75 boys, aged 11 to 23 (no sixth form; exams up to GCSE only) **Fees:** Prospective parents should contact the school for details **Submit application form:** No cut-off date **Mission statement:** To educate Muslim children in Islam, good morals and manners and to make them good citizens. **School hours:** 9am–4.45pm **Meals:** Hot and cold available **Strong GCSE subjects:** English, maths **London league table position:** Not available.

## Profile

The Jamia Ramania Islamic Institute is situated opposite a small playing ground on Balaam Street, a fairly quiet throughway 15 minutes away from Plaistow tube station. The school is located in an area of high social and economic deprivation. It was originally established with around 10 to 12 pupils in 1996 and housed in a small building in Manor Park. The school has grown considerably since then and moved to its present site, a former 19th-century warehouse that appears in need of renovation, in May 1999. Boys are divided into four classes (Years 7, 8, 9 and 10/11), and grouped according to age, then ability, with some mixed-ability groups also. All teachers are responsible for pastoral care. Islamic education is studied every morning, with secondary education courses – a range of GCSEs in line with the national curriculum – taught in the afternoons. Subjects studied include Arabic, Bengali, and Urdu. Homework is monitored in homework books and parents are also kept informed of their sons' progress through reports and parents' evenings. Since the Institute is small, there is no school council and there are no prefects at present. There are currently two special-needs pupils at the school.

## Admissions and intake

Parents of boys wishing to apply to the school should contact the school for an application form and further details. Candidates for places are called to attend interviews. Boys must be Muslim to attend. About 75 to 80 per cent of pupils come from within Newham, remaining pupils are drawn mostly from across London with about five boys from outside the capital.

## Achievement

Boys sit SATs exams and follow GCSE courses. The majority achieve passes, although typically at grades C–F. In 2001, no boys gained an A–C pass but the average point score was 4.5. Half of the school's teaching time is spent on following Islamic studies and the Institute is highly noted for its Islamic theology course. Since the school is small, it is ideally suited to providing a caring, intimate environment. Boys are encouraged to develop a deeper understanding of the Islamic faith, to learn good morals and manners and enjoy a healthy social life in accordance with its mission statement. As class sizes are small, good relations are easily established between boys and their teachers

## Extra-curricular activities

Sport takes the form of football lessons, which are held every Friday afternoon on the playing ground opposite the school. There are regular school trips.

# Kingsford Community School

**Woodside Road, London E13 8RX** ☎ 020 7473 5867 📠 020 7476 7451 ✉ admin.kingsford@pop3.newham.gov.uk 🌐 www.kingsford.school.org.uk ✉ Paul Regan; Chair of Governors: Quentin Peppiat ⊖ Plaistow **Buses:** 276 👕 White polo shirt, navy sweatshirt, black trousers/skirt **Demand:** 360 places available **Type:** Community comprehensive for 1200 mixed pupils, aged 11 to 16 **Submit application form:** November 2003 **School hours:** 8.30am–3.30pm; homework clubs are available **Meals:** Hot and cold available **Strong GCSE subjects:** Information unavailable **London league table position:** Not yet available

## Profile

Kingsford is a brand-new school that opened in September 2000. Built with private funds, its curriculum includes Mandarin and Japanese. It offers one computer between every two pupils. The school had 300 pupils in 2000, but is designed to accommodate 1200.

## Achievement

No results available yet as the school only opened in September 2000.

## Extra-curricular activities

Trips are planned for both at home and abroad. There is also a range of sports is on offer along with a variety of breakfast and after-school clubs.

# Langdon School

**Sussex Road, East Ham London E6 2PS** 020 8471 2411 020 8470 7436 admin@sse002514.dialnet.com; admin.langdon@pop3.newham.gov.uk Ms Vanessa Wiseman BA, MA (Ed), Adv.Dip.Ed; Chair of Governors: Mr D Benn Barking Barking, East Ham **Buses**: 5, 238, 300, 325 Maroon jacket, school tie, jumper with school badge, black skirt or trousers **Demand**: 390 places available; oversubscribed **Type**: Community comprehensive Sports College for 1922 mixed pupils, aged 11 to 16 **Submit application form**: November 2003 **Motto**: *Progresso Cumpopulo* (Learning Together) **School hours**: 8.45am–3.30pm; homework clubs are available **Meals**: Hot and cold available **Strong GCSE subjects**: Geography, history, science **London league table position**: 321

## Profile

Langdon was awarded Sports College status in 1998 and is now one of three Beacon Schools in the borough. Set in a 42-acre campus, Langdon has an athletics track, tennis courts and three gymnasia. Indoor facilities include three large assembly halls, five computer rooms, six art rooms and 15 science labs. The school has its own language lab and a well-equipped geography department with two Meteosat weather satellite systems and two automatic weather stations. Special-needs pupils are serviced by a learning support department, which organizes a lunchtime club to provide extra help with homework. There is also a department to help pupils with English as an additional language. Langdon has a careers department and arranges work experience in Years 10 to 11. There is also an active school council. Links with parents are commended by Ofsted as 'a strength of the school'. Homework is recorded in a homework diary, and there is an active PTA. Weekly surgeries and evening meetings are held for parents. Each pupil has a Record of Achievement.

## Admissions and intake

Admissions are dealt with by Newham LEA (see borough factfile). The school has strong links with its feeder primary schools: Hartley, Kensington, Lathom, Nelsom and Vicarage.

## Achievement

Ofsted noted that Langdon 'meets the needs of pupils, parents and the community extremly well'. The school's exam results are in the highest five per cent of similar schools and have continued to improve consistently since 1996. In 2002, 41 per cent of pupils gained five or more GCSEs at A*–C grades, slightly down on 2001. This percentage is below the borough and national averages. Langdon ranks sixth in the borough. Inspectors praised the school's 'can do' attitude and its 'strong and visionary leadership'. Langdon's forté is sport. Its football and cricket teams regularly achieve honours in matches in the borough and the Essex cup, and past pupils have represented their county and gone on to pursue professional sports careers. Football connections with the local team, West Ham, are strong, with some pupils having access to IT learning facilities at the club's ground. The school tennis scene is also thriving – new courts are being built in conjunction with the Lawn Tennis Association.

## Extra-curricular activities

Notable activities include Saturday school, modern language clubs, prayer groups, speaker meetings and Langdon Summer University. The usual range of sports is on offer. There are musical concerts, links with the Saturday Newham Orchestra, school productions, cultural visits in London and abroad and Book Week and Bookworms Club. The geography department organizes field trips and there are exchange schemes with France and Germany. Langdon is one of six schools in England to be involved in a European project on school effectiveness, and one of 16 European 'health-promoting' schools.

# Lister Community School

**St Mary's Road, Plaistow, London E13 9AE** 020 8471 3311 020 8472 1027 admin.lister@pop3.newham.gov.uk Martin Buck MA; Chair of Governors: Cllr W Brown Plaistow **Buses**: 69, 241, 262, 325, 473, 678 Purple sweatshirt with school badge, white shirt or blouse, black skirt or trousers, black V-neck sweater with purple inlay or black cardigan, school tie (optional), plain black footwear; black kameez, shalwar and scarf also allowed **Demand**: 270 places available; oversubscribed **Type**: Community comprehensive for 1311 mixed pupils, aged 11 to 16 **Submit application form**: November 2003 **Mission statement**: Our purpose is to ensure an education, as an inclusive school, which promotes and achieves excellence and continues to nurture the values, confidence and skills of students, staff and community in order that they can meet the emerging opportunities of the 21st century. **School hours**: 8.45am–3.30pm; homework clubs are available **Meals**: Hot and cold available, including breakfast **Strong GCSE subjects**: Art, design and technology, music, PE **London league table position**: 368

## Profile

In 1998, Ofsted described this school's pupils as motivated and polite and the school environment was portrayed as conducive to learning. Lister offers its pupils good opportunities in drama, dance and music and has applied for Performing Arts Specialist School status. A new block houses a dining room, kitchen, library, IT rooms and science labs. Pupils follow the National Curriculum, plus drama and PSE. In Years 10 to 11, optional subjects include sociology, media studies and business studies, plus GNVQ in performing arts. Extra classes in literacy and ICT are also available. Homework planners are monitored by form tutors. Careers advice is given by an external careers officer and work experience is undertaken at Key Stage 4. Governors and parents receive newsletters and reports and may attend open evenings and weekly parents' surgeries with the head. There is a school code of conduct.

## Admissions and intake

Admissions are dealt with by Newham LEA (see borough factfile). The school is linked with the following primaries: Carpenters, Selwyn, Southern Road and Upton Cross (all mixed), and Cleves, Portway, Ranelagh and West Ham Church (girls only). About one-third of pupils has special needs.

## Achievement

In spite of many pupils showing poor levels of literacy and numeracy in Year 7, GCSE results show that the rate of progress at Lister is good compared with schools with a similar intake. In 2002, 37 per cent of pupils earned five or more A*–C grades. This was up from 30 per cent in 2001 and Lister was ranked seventh in the borough. Subjects in which attainment is in line with national expectations include art, design and technology, music and PE; weaker subjects include English, maths, science, geography, history, modern languages and RE. Pupils are given what Ofsted describe as 'good support and guidance'. Especially notable is the support given to pupils with hearing impairments by their peers, several of whom learn to sign. Although the school's attitude towards special-needs' pupils is very positive, the number of learning-support staff and the special needs facilities were found to be insufficient.

## Extra-curricular activities

Extra-curricular activities are a strength of the school. Lister has a good reputation in sport – notable successes include the boys' cricket team progressing to the semi final of the London Cup and one pupil competed in the London Youth Trampoline team. Some pupils are involved in the West Ham United Football Club coaching programme. There is a Saturday school, summer literacy programmes and a breakfast learning club. The learning resource centre is open before school and at lunchtime.

# Little Ilford School

**Browning Road, Manor Park, London E12 6ET** ☎ 020 8478 8024 📠 020 8478 5954 Ⓔ admin.littleilford@pop3.newham.gov.uk Pam Belmour B.Ed (Hons); Chair of Governors: Mr I Powell Manor Park **Buses**: 25, 86, 147 White shirt or blouse, school tie, red V-neck jumper with embroidered school badge or, from Key Stage 4, black cardigan (girls), black trousers or culottes or skirt; black shalwar kameez and black or white scarf; school PE kit **Demand**: 270 places available; oversubscribed **Type**: Community comprehensive for 1312 mixed pupils, aged 11 to 16 **Submit application form**: November 2003 **Motto**: Learning Together, Achieving Together, Succeeding Together **School hours**: 8.50am–3.25pm **Meals**: Hot and cold available **Strong GCSE subjects**: Art, business studies, drama **London league table position**: 404

## Profile

Little Ilford forms part of a multi-use site, shared with a youth centre and adult-learning facilities. The school has a self-contained technology department, a well-equipped media resources room, new science facilities, a well-equipped library, drama studios and an environmental garden. It is an equal-opportunities school, which claims to provide a challenging environment for all pupils. Students follow a broad, balanced curriculum. In Years 10 to 11, they study for GCSEs in subjects such as English (literature) and media studies, maths, a modern foreign language and a vocational course. Additional options include art, drama, music and sports studies. All pupils are given careers guidance and Year 10 undertake work experience. Representatives from each year group are elected to a school council. Pupils are grouped in mixed-ability forms, and form tutors along with heads of year are responsible for welfare. Homework is monitored in homework diaries. There is provision for pupils with special needs, although not for disabled pupils. The school operates a code of conduct. Parents' evenings and written reports keep parents informed, and parents are encouraged to join school trips, partake in family literacy schemes and become school governors.

### Admissions and intake

Admissions are dealt with by Newham LEA (see borough factfile). Little Ilford has four linked primary schools: Avenue, Essex, Salisbury and Sheringham.

### Achievement

In 1995, the standard of education at Little Ilford was deemed unsatisfactory and the school was made subject to 'special measures'. In 1997, it was judged to no longer require special measures. Ofsted inspectors visited in 2000 and found that standards had continued to improve. There are still, however, points to address across the school. These issues are mainly due to its unstable population (17 per cent of pupils typically leave or join the school in any one academic year) and because about 90 per cent of pupils have poor levels of literacy in English when they enter the school. More positively, good progress is made in art, drama, geography, history, PE and science and in all subjects at Key Stage 4. Attainment in art, business studies and drama is in line with the national average; attainment in English, maths, science, French and German is below the national average. In 2002, 32 per cent of pupils gained five or more A*–C grades at GCSE. This was up from 27 per cent in 2001 and the school was ranked 10th in the borough. Ofsted described pupils as showing 'a significant improvement in attitudes' since the last inspection.

### Extra-curricular activities

A wide selection of activities are available in sport, art, foreign languages and drama. Homework support groups are also held. There are trips to the theatre and museums, talks by artists and poets and an annual 'celebrating achievement' event for each year group. There are also trips abroad.

## Plashet School

**Plashet Grove, East Ham, London E6 1DG** 020 8471 2418 020 8471 3029 admin.plashet@pop3.newham.gov.uk www.angliacampus.com/schools/org2625 Mrs Bushra Nasir B.Sc (Hons); Chair of Governors: Ms Dona Henriques East Ham **Buses:** 101, 104, 147, 238, 300, 325, 376 Navy skirt or trousers, white blouse, navy or white sweater or navy shalwar kameez; Muslim girls may wear blue or white headscarves **Demand:** 421 for 270 places in 2000/1 **Type:** Community comprehensive for 1344 girls, aged 11 to 16 **Submit application form:** November 2003 **Motto:** Working Together to Promote and Celebrate Achievement **School hours:** 8.50am–3.35pm; homework clubs are available **Meals:** Hot and cold available **Strong GCSE subjects:** Art, English **London league table position:** 218

### Profile

Plashet offers a positive environment in which its pupils thrive both personally and academically. It is one of three schools in the borough to have Beacon status. Established in the middle of the last century, the school is split between two sites. For the large number of pupils, accommodation is cramped, although in the late 1990s several science labs were built to alleviate the lack of space. The library was described by Ofsted in 1999 as offering 'exemplary provision'. The school's curriculum is balanced, with Key Stage 4 pupils able to sit GCSEs in subjects such as English language and literature, maths, science, a language (French, Urdu or Bengali), a humanities subject and an arts subject. Girls are streamed in maths and languages in the upper school. Form tutors work with year coordinators to provide pastoral care and advice on curriculum choices and post-16 education. Pupils can join the school council. Work experience is undertaken in Year 10. Parents are kept informed through annual reports, parents' evenings and newsletters; information is usually provided in English, Urdu and Bengali.

### Admissions and intake

Admissions are dealt with by Newham LEA (see borough factfile).The school is heavily oversubscribed. In 1998, pupils entering the school in Year 7 came from 28 primary schools (none linked).

### Achievement

Despite levels of attainment on entry being well below the national average, Plashet's GCSE results are well above the national average. In 2002, 56 per cent of pupils gained five or more A*–C grades, down from 59 per cent in 2001. Pupils' progress has been improving faster than the average rate for England for the past five years and this looks set to continue. Attainment tends to be well above the national average in art, where 90 per cent of pupils earn grades A*–C, and English; above average in science, history, sociology, some short RE courses, Bengali and Urdu and in line with the national average in maths. Achievement is below the national averages in IT, music, geography and German. The school operates a policy of inclusivity for pupils with special needs and these girls progress well within the school. Pupils show high levels of motivation and enjoy what Ofsted inspectors describe as 'excellent' relationships with their teachers. There is a high degree of racial harmony. The level of attendance is well above the national average and pupils adhere to the school's code of behaviour.

### Extra-curricular activities

Ofsted reported that Plashet had an 'outstanding scheme of out-of-school activities' which earned the school a certificate of distinction from Education Extra in 1998. These activities include lunchtime and after-school language clubs, drama groups, music clubs and homework clubs. Extra teaching and help with homework is also available. The school organizes geography field trips, cultural visits and overseas trips.

# Rokeby School

**Pitchford Street, Stratford, London E15 4RZ** ☎ 020 8534 8946 Fax 020 8519 5239 Email admin.rokeby@pop3.newham.gov.uk Head Richard Jarman BA (Hons); Chair of Governors: Mr G Hill Rail / Underground Docklands Light Railway: Stratford **Buses**: 25, 69, 86 Uniform Black trousers, white shirt, V-neck black jumper, black blazer with school badge, school tie **Demand**: 240 places available **Type**: Community comprehensive for 1060 boys, aged 11 to 16 **Submit application form**: November 2003 **School hours**: 9.45am–3.20pm; homework clubs are available **Meals**: Hot and cold available **Strong GCSE subject**: Technology **London league table position**: 447

### Profile

Although Rokeby's academic results are low for the borough, the school aims to provide good opportunities for its pupils' all-round moral and social education, and prides itself on offering an environment in which everyone feels valued and supported. A financial injection from the Stratford City Challenge youth project facilitated the refurbishment of science and technology areas. Boys follow a range of subjects in line with the National Curriculum. All pupils may take part in work experience during Year 10. A school council and the head's 'suggestion box' enables pupils to voice their concerns. From Year 7, boys are grouped in forms under a tutor who, together with a head of year, is responsible for their welfare. Boys with special needs are given support from a special education department. The school also has a pastoral centre, which has connections with a local youth worker and local careers offices. Boys are encouraged to maintain good levels of attendance and behaviour by means of reward schemes. A record of achievement for both inside and outside school is maintained, to be presented to an admissions tutor or employer on leaving Rokeby. Parents are kept informed through written reports and parents' evenings. Homework is monitored in a home diary. School literature is available in several community languages and home visits can be made if parents are unable to visit the school themselves.

### Admissions and intake

Admissions are dealt with by Newham LEA (see borough factfile). Rokeby has eight linked primaries: Carpenters, Colegrave, Earlham, Maryland, Park, Portway, Ranelagh and West Ham Church.

### Achievement

On entry, most pupils have poor levels of both literacy and numeracy and levels of attainment are generally much lower than the national average. Attainment in the majority of subjects at the end of Key Stage 4, including English, maths and science, is lower than national expectancy levels. However, at the time of the last Ofsted inspection in 1997, the rate of progress made by pupils was faster than the national average rate. In 2002, GCSE results for those gaining five or more A*–C grades was 23 per cent. This was up from 21 per cent in 2001 and Rokeby ranked 14th in the borough. Ofsted found that pupils show an 'obvious pride' and are generally well behaved in lessons. However, many find sustained concentration difficult but demonstrate good abilities to interact with one another.

## Extra-curricular activities

The school offers an eclectic range of sports, from football and hockey, to skiing, canoeing and sailing. In recent years, school teams have become county champions in basketball and swimming. Less adequate provision is made for performing arts, although cultural trips are organized to the theatre, cinema and overseas. There are after-school homework clubs. Some pupils take part in the Duke of Edinburgh's Award scheme.

# The Royal Docks Community School

**Prince Regent Lane, London E16 3HS** ☎ 020 7540 2700 📠 020 7540 2701 ⓔ admin.theroyaldocks@pop3.newham.gov.uk 👤 Pat Bagshawe MA (Ed), FRSA; Chair of Governors: Cllr N Wilson 🚆 Custom House; Docklands Light Railway: Custom House, Prince Regent **Buses**: 147, 276, 325, 473 👕 Royal blue or bottle green sweatshirt with school badge, black skirt or trousers, white, sky blue or emerald green polo shirt **Demand**: 365 for 240 places in 2000/1 **Type**: Community comprehensive for 1202 mixed pupils, aged 11 to 16 **Submit application form**: November 2003 **School hours**: 8.30am–3pm; homework clubs are available **Meals**: Hot and cold available **Strong GCSE subjects**: Information not available **London league table position**: 370

## Profile

The Royal Docks School opened during the 1998/9 academic year and offers a state-of-the-art learning environment, wonderful facilities and a dynamic new approach to the curriculum for all pupils, regardless of ability. Its facilities are based on one of the largest school sites in Newham and include teaching rooms, offices, labs, studios, a theatre, sports hall and gym, music and dance areas, learning resource facilities and a library and a training area. The school also has its own grass playing field and hard courts for sport. Its location by the Prince Regent Canal makes it ideally placed for watersports. The school's alternative approach to the curriculum involves dividing subjects into four main categories: communications (covering English, modern languages, British Sign Language, ICT, English as an additional language and media studies); arts (drama, art, PE, dance and music); investigations (maths, science and design technology); and humanities (RE, PSE, history, GNVQ courses in health and social care, business studies, and travel and tourism). At Key Stage 4, pupils study English, maths, design technology, RE, science and a humanities subject, plus a choice from the above. Careers advice and counselling is also available. Extra support is given to pupils with learning difficulties, and an intensive reading scheme is organized for those pupils with poor levels of literacy in Year 7. This school also offers provision for pupils with profound and multiple learning difficulties. All pupils in Years 10 or 11 are encouraged to undertake work experience. There is also a school council.

Pupils are placed in form groups, with form tutors, Key Stage staff and a mentor for each pupil being responsible for pastoral care. Records of achievement are kept for all Year 11 pupils, to present to future admissions tutors or employers. Parents are sent a regular newsletter and annual reports on their child's progress. Annual parents' evenings are also held.

## Admissions and intake

Admissions are dealt with by Newham LEA (see borough factfile). The school has five linked primaries: Britannia Village, Calverton, Drew, Rosetta and Scott Wilkie.

## Achievement

In 2002, 40 per cent of pupils gained five or more A*–C grades at GCSE. The school was ranked eighth in the borough. Ofsted visited in 2001 and commented that the school 'provides satisfactory standards of education' and 'teaching is good overall'. However, inspectors noted that attainment needs to be improved throughout the school.

## Extra-curricular activities

The school's excellent facilities are ideally suited to an impressive range of extra-curricular activities in the performing arts and sport. The school is developing possibilities for outdoor activities, such as camping, skiing and canoeing. Exchange links are also being established with schools in France and Germany. There are after-school homework clubs.

# St Angela's Ursuline Convent School

**St George's Road, Forest Gate, London E7 8HU** 020 8472 6022 020 8475 0245 admin.stangelas@pop3.newham.gov.uk www.st-angelas.newham.sch.uk./newsite/ Mrs Delia A Smith BA, M.Sc; Chair of Governors: Sister Frances Oakley Forest Gate Upton Park **Buses**: 325, 678 Up to sixth form: Brown kilt, cream blouse (Years 7 to 8), or gold blouse (Years 9 to 11), dark brown jumper, brown, black or navy shoes, plain coat in brown, black or navy; PE kit: black shorts or tracksuit bottoms, yellow shirt, school sweatshirt **Demand**: 180 places available; oversubscribed **Type**: Voluntary aided comprehensive Technology College for 1130 girls (mixed in sixth form), aged 11 to 18 **Submit application form**: November 2003 **Motto**: *Serviam* (Let Me Serve) **School hours**: 8.45am–3.25pm; homework clubs are available **Meals**: Hot and cold available, including breakfast **Strong GCSE subjects**: Art, drama, English, French, German, science, sociology **London league table position**: 136

## Profile

St Angela's is the only Roman Catholic girls' school in the borough and was established in 1862 by Ursuline sisters. It combines a tradition of excellence with a modern Catholic environment. St Angela's was awarded Technology College status in 1995 and recognized as a phase II Technology College in 1998, enabling it to receive funding to raise standards in maths, design technology, science and computer studies. It has also earned a Sportsmark Award, and in 2000 it achieved Beacon status. Notable facilities include a library with over 10,000 books, a chapel, music suites, a drama studio, seven science labs, an art suite with a dark room and two newly equipped design technology rooms. Sports facilities include a gym, five-a-side football pitch, basketball courts and an athletics ground. Pupils also use facilities at West Ham Park and Newham Leisure Centre. Pupils can study up to 10 subjects at GCSE. The sixth form is run in conjunction with St Bonaventure's RC (boys') School. There is a school council, and all pupils take part in work experience. There is an active PTA and homework is monitored in student planners. There is provision for pupils with special needs.

## Admissions and intake

Applications are only invited from parents wishing a Catholic education for their children, and priority is given to girls who are baptized, practising Catholics and whose parents make St Angela's a first choice. Application forms are available from the school.

## Achievement

In 2000, Ofsted stated that 'the school achieves very high standards in most aspects of its work'. In 2002, 74 per cent of pupils gained five or more GCSEs at grades A*–C. This continued an upward trend and was well above the borough and national averages. St Angela's came top of the borough league table in 2002. The average point score earned by pupils taking two or more A/AS-levels in 2002 was 243.4, ranking the school top of the borough. GCSE results are well above the national average in most subjects, notably in English, science, French, German, art, drama and sociology. Ofsted described the teaching as 'consistently good with much that is very good' and the head teacher was praised for her strong leadership. A-level results have continued to improve since 1997 and are now roughly in line with the national average, most notably in English, art, sociology and media studies. Pupils can also take GNVQs. The school provides good pastoral care and is highly supportive of its pupils.

## Extra-curricular activities

There have been visits to galleries and theatres with guest workshops (notably by the Royal Opera and National Theatre). A range of activities, from drama and music clubs to computer studies and an extra-curricular study support programme, are also available. The usual range of sports is on offer. Past excursions include trips to the Body Shop headquarters and French and German exchanges.

# St Bonaventure's Roman Catholic School

**Boleyn Road, Forest Gate, London E7 9QD** 020 8472 3844 020 8471 2749 admin.stbonaventures @pop3.newham.gov.uk Sir Michael Wilshaw BA; Chair of Governors: Father J Clifford

Upton Park **Buses**: 104, 238, 325, 678 Up to sixth form: Black trousers, white shirt, school tie and blazer with badge (brown in lower school, black with gold trim from Year 9) **Demand**: 180 places available; oversubscribed **Type**: Comprehensive Roman Catholic voluntary aided Technology College for 1164 boys (mixed sixth form), aged 11 to 18 **Submit application form**: November 2003 **Motto**: In Holiness and Learning **School hours**: 8.45am–3.25pm **Meals**: Hot and cold meals **Strong GCSE subjects**: All relatively strong **London league table position**: 145

## Profile

St Bonaventure's is one of the borough's two single-sex Roman Catholic schools, the other being St Angela's Ursuline Convent School with which St Bonaventure's shares a sixth-form centre. St Bonaventure's featured in the *Evening Standard* in September 2000 as the first school in Newham to send a pupil to Eton College. Bobby José won a £32,000 scholarship place after passing Eton's internal exam and obtaining excellent GCSE grades. Recent additions to the school include two new science labs, a business centre, new changing rooms and a three-storey state-of-the-art technology block. The school was awarded Technology College status in 1996. The broad curriculum has a distinct emphasis on RE and IT. Years 10 to 11 study English, maths, double science, religious studies, French or German, design and technology, IT, PE and PSE. Additional options include history, art and GNVQ IT. Around 24 A/AS-level subjects are offered, along with vocational qualifications. Boys are taught in mixed-ability forms in their first year but are then streamed in most subjects. Special-needs pupils are given inclusive help, although those pupils with severe difficulties are taught separately in Year 7. Collective worship takes place during daily assemblies. Work experience is available for each boy and the school attracts invaluable sponsorship through its strong business links. Pastoral teams are responsible for welfare. Parents are kept informed through homework diaries and annual parents' evenings. There is a parent, teacher and friends association.

## Admissions and intake

Applications are made direct to the school. Priority is given according to the following criteria: baptized boys; practising Catholics; and election of the school as first choice. Parents must support the ethos and Catholic nature of the school as outlined in its mission statement. Catholic applicants must support their application with documentation from their parish priest. Open evenings are held for students wishing to join the sixth form. Many pupils have low reading standards on entry.

## Achievement

The rate of progress made by pupils at St Bonaventure's and the average GCSE results attained in all subjects are well above the national average. In 2002, 74 per cent of pupils earned five or more A*–C grades, equalling the results of the previous year. The school came second in the borough. Performance tends to be especially strong in maths, science and technology. The average point score for pupils taking two or more A/AS-levels was 233.5, below the national average, ranking the school second in the borough league table. Pupils can also take GNVQs. Ofsted reported in 2000 that it was an 'outstandingly effective school' with 'remarkable leadership' by the head teacher. Inspectors noted that: 'Behaviour, personal development and relationships are all excellent'.

## Extra-curricular activities

A range of technology and sports clubs are offered and the school also runs a Catholic Youth Club. Lunchtime homework clubs and extra tuition are available. Field trips and foreign exchange trips are also organized. Pupils raise funds for local charities.

# Sarah Bonnell School

**Deanery Road, London E15 4LP** 020 8534 6791 020 8555 3793 admin.sarahbonnell@pop3.newham.gov.uk Cauthar Tooley; Chair of Governors: Mr Ian Campbell Maryland, Stratford Stratford; Docklands Light Railway: Stratford **Buses**: 25, 86, 308 Navy sweatshirt with school badge, pale-blue polo shirt, navy trousers, skirt or shalwar kameez **Demand**: 240 places available; oversubscribed **Type**: Community comprehensive for 1197 girls, aged 11 to 16 **Submit application form**: November 2003 **Motto**: Learning for Life **School hours**: 8.45am–3.20pm; homework clubs are available **Meals**: Hot and cold available **Strong GCSE subjects**: Art, history **London league table position**: 261

### Profile

Sarah Bonnell has a positive ethos of striving towards excellence and motivated, culturally aware pupils. In 1997, it was named as one of the most improved schools in England by Ofsted and awarded a Sportsmark Award. In 1999, it was appointed a Beacon School. Established in 1769, on a different site, it is one of the oldest girls' schools in the country. Good facilities include the library, a technology 'village' and a science/modern languages wing. The school has a sports hall, but no sports grounds. Pupils are taught in mixed-ability forms and offered a balanced curriculum in line with national recommendations. Modern languages include French, Spanish, Italian, Bengali and Urdu. Morning assemblies based on universal religious themes are held daily but parents may excuse their children from these (and RE classes), if they wish. A PSHRE course covers personal, social and health issues, RE and, in Year 11, further education and career options. Work experience is undertaken in Year 10. All girls maintain a portfolio of achievements. Special-needs pupils are well supported in conjunction with a team of learning support staff. Some parents help run lunchtime study clubs and the school's book shop. All parents are kept informed through a termly newspaper, an annual governors' report and annual parents' evenings. Translation services are available.

### Admissions and intake

Admissions are dealt with by Newham LEA (see borough factfile). Sarah Bonnell is a popular, oversubscribed school, which receives applications for places from around 30 primary schools in Newham and neighbouring boroughs. Parents and prospective pupils attend open evenings and an interview at the school; follow-up parents' evenings take place during the child's first term at the school.

### Achievement

Although attainment on entry is well below the national average, principally because of the English-language barrier, progress is made at a much faster rate than the national average. In 2002, 46 per cent of pupils gained five or more A*–C grades at GCSE. This was slightly up on 43 per cent in 2001 and the school was ranked fourth in the borough league table. Attainment at GCSE in English language, maths and science tends to be much better than in similar schools and GCSE results are higher than the England average in art and history, in line with drama, French, music, PE and design and technology, but below in geography, RE and Spanish. Behaviour at the school was commended by Ofsted in 1998.

### Extra-curricular activities

A wide range of activities includes homework clubs, subject clubs, a school choir, instrumental ensemble, drama group, poetry club, writers' group and sports clubs. Cultural visits, field trips and excursions overseas are also organized. The school is the only girls' school to be involved in the UK Prince's Trust scheme and is also a member of a European Health Initiative.

## Stratford School

**Upton Lane, Forest Gate, London E7 9PR** ☎ 020 8471 2415 Fax 020 8471 4684 ✉ stratford@stratford.rmplc.co.uk Head: Mr Keith Holt B.Sc; Chair of Governors: Mr Yajub Umer Rail: Forest Gate Tube: Upton Park **Buses:** 325, 678 Uniform: Purple blazer, white shirt, black trousers or skirt **Demand:** 180 places available; oversubscribed **Type:** Comprehensive foundation school for 855 mixed pupils (33 in sixth form), aged 11 to 18 **Submit application form:** November 2003 **School hours:** 8.30am–3pm; 8.30am–3.15pm (Mon); homework clubs are available **Meals:** Hot and cold available **Strong GCSE subjects:** Art, Bengali, Maths, music, PE, Urdu **London league table position:** 262

### Profile

Stratford School was established in 1906 and is now the only foundation school in the borough. Recent additions to the school include several design and technology workshops and some well-equipped science labs. The school has been granted an Investor in People Award in recognition of its high-quality staff training. At Key Stages 3 and 4, all pupils follow a balanced curriculum; at Key Stage 4, they study English language and literature, maths, double science, a modern language (Bengali, French or Urdu), RE, PE, IT, plus one technology subject and two other subjects of their choice. Pupils also follow a PSHE course. There is a small sixth form, which offers GNVQ courses in engineering and business studies. All pupils spend one day each week at the school's business and technology college. Pupils are organized into tutor groups, with tutors responsible for monitoring welfare. Homework diaries are monitored by parents. The school organizes careers advice and work experience at the end of Year 10. Certificates are given in reward for good levels of attendance and behaviour.

## Admissions and intake

Parents of children attending a linked primary school in Newham (Elmhurst, Park, Shafesbury, William Davies and St Stephen's) should sign the application form given to their child and return it to the head teacher of the primary school within the application deadline. Otherwise, contact Newham Education Department. If oversubscribed, priority is given as follows: sibling at the school; preference for mixed education; and proximity of home to school. One in five pupils are on the school's register of special needs with about 2 per cent of pupils having special needs statements.

## Achievement

Following an Ofsted inspection in 1993, the school was judged to require 'special measures', but many improvements have since been made. Although the level of attainment on entry has dropped since 1993, with this level generally very low compared with the national average, pupils are making increasingly good progress, especially at Key Stage 4. In 2002, 46 per cent of pupils gained five or more A*–C grades at GCSE. This was up on 40 per cent in 2002 and the school was placed fifth in the borough. Attainment in maths, Urdu, Bengali, art, PE and music are all now in line with national averages, although English and science is below average. In the sixth form, attainment is generally below the national average, although progress made in business studies is very good. Pupils' attitudes towards the school and learning were described by Ofsted as 'very good'.

## Extra-curricular activities

There is a limited range of clubs available, including those for sport, music, drama and computer studies. Extra lessons are on offer in many subjects and those on Saturday mornings are well attended. Cultural trips are organized, for example, to France and to theatres.

# Redbridge

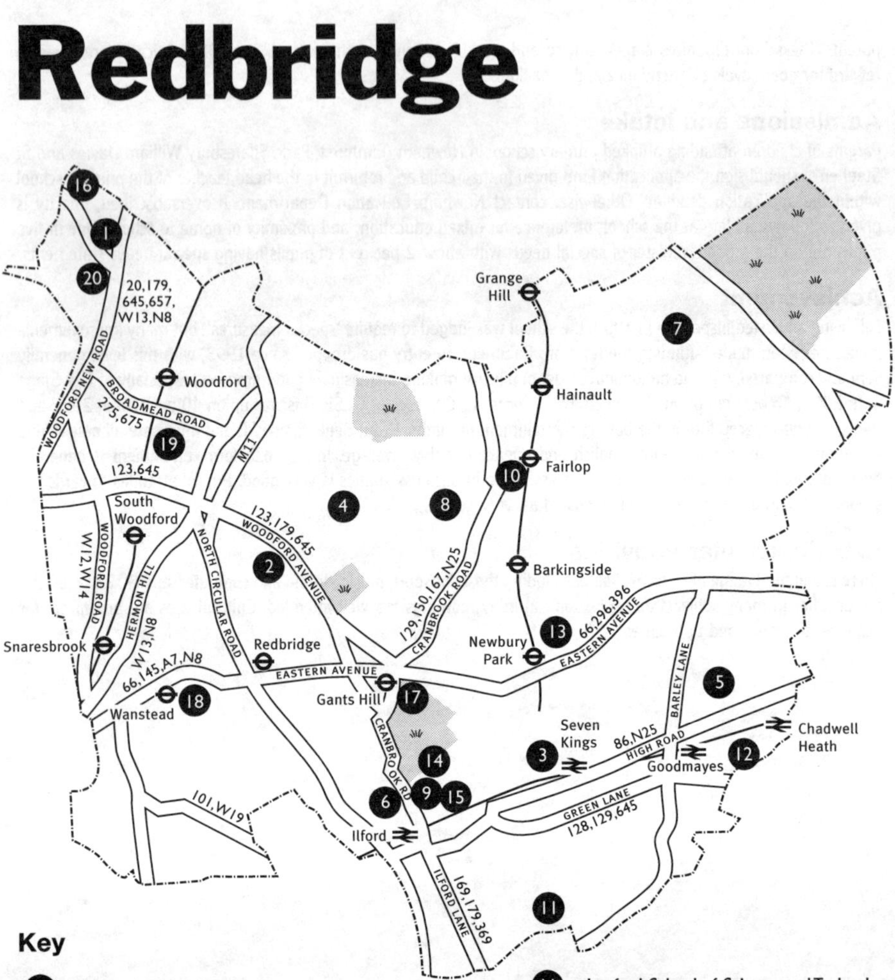


## Key

1. Bancrofts School
2. Beal High School
3. Canon Palmer Catholic School
4. Caterham High School
5. The Chadwell Heath Foundation School
6. Cranbrook College
7. Hainault Forest High School
8. Ilford County High School
9. Ilford Ursuline High School
10. King Solomon High School
11. Loxford School of Science and Technology
12. Mayfield School and College
13. Oaks Park High School
14. Park School for Girls
15. Seven Kings High School
16. Trinity Catholic High School
17. Valentines High School
18. Wanstead High School
19. Woodbridge High School
20. Woodford County High School

# Factfile

**LEA: Town Hall, High Road, Ilford, Essex IG1 1DD** ☎ 020 8478 3020 🌐 www.redbridge.gov.uk **Director of Education, Leisure and Libraries:** Edwina Grant **Political control of council:** Hung council with Labour administration **Percentage of pupils from outside the borough:** 11.8 per cent **Percentage of pupils educated outside the borough:** 7.9 per cent **London league table positions (out of 32 boroughs):** 2nd

Situated on the boundary between East London and Essex, Redbridge offers both rural village life in the north of the borough juxtaposed with a hectic, and often run-down, suburbia to the south. Woodford Green and Wanstead, a borough in itself until the 70s, are both affluent, quiet, leafy and spacious. With no major shopping centre, this area depends upon local shopping and small high streets. To the south is Ilford, the administrative centre, with high density shopping areas and extensive public transport centring around Ilford mainline station.

Redbridge is a particularly strong education authority, which celebrated coming in sixth place in the national league tables for 2000. It features a number of high performing independent schools alongside two strong grammar schools and comprehensives with a range of success. However, in a recent Ofsted report, Redbridge Council was praised for raising standards but it also received strong criticism for a lack of support for its schools. Fundamental weaknesses were found with a severe deterioration in relationships between the schools and LEA. Elected members were seen to have given poor leadership and unearthed a legacy of mistrust. The authority pledged to improve, and it had the second best results of the London LEAs in 2002.

Pride of place for the authority are its flagship and strongly protected grammar schools. There has been some controversy over whether they will maintain their selective status, but there are no real signs it may change in the foreseeable future. Grammar schools Ilford County High and Woodford County High scored highly in 2002, averaging 323.7 and 357.9 A-level scores respectively. As for non-selective state schools, Ilford Ursuline High School for girls fared the best with 294.6, while Seven Kings High School averaged 296.4. Despite some problems with the local authority, Redbridge remains in a strong position academically and with good, borough-wide extra-curricular facilities, particularly sport and music.

## Policy

Parents should get a copy of the brochure *Transfer to Secondary School* from the LEA. The criteria used when a community school is oversubscribed are: children resident in catchment area after 1 September 2003; children resident in linked school's catchment area after 1 September 2003; children who live outside of the catchment area with a sibling present at the school; and other first preference applicants who live outside of the catchment area. Applications to foundation schools and grammar schools should be made directly to the schools themselves.

# Bancrofts School

**Woodford Green IG8 ORF** ☎ 020 8505 4821 📠 020 8559 0032 ✉ admissions@bancrofts-essex.sch.uk 🌐 www. bancrofts.essex.sch.uk Dr PR Scott ⊖ Woodford **Buses:** 275 Dark grey suit, navy blue blazer, tartan skirt, cream shirt **Demand:** Highly subscribed **Type:** Independent for 991 mixed pupils, aged 7 to 18 **Fees:** £2,823 a term **Submit application form:** End of December 2003 **Motto:** Unto God only be Honour and Glory **School hours:** 8.40am–4.00pm **School meals:** Hot and cold available **Strong GCSE subjects:** All relatively strong **London league table position:** 20

## Profile

Bancrofts is a well established school with preparatory and senior school departments. It is a very high-performing school with excellent facilities and it demands high standards from its pupils. It was first established in 1737 and moved to its present location in 1889. It became fully independent in 1977, with boarders until 1981. Set in Edwardian buildings, the site is imposing but comfortable with a strong sense of history. Yet the school is modern looking and stresses strong links with the community. The buildings are well-kept, with recent improvements including a fine library, strong sports centre, swimming pool and creative arts centre. More recently, work has been done on re-roofing and refurbishment. A separate sixth form offers a range of subjects including compulsory general studies. Subjects available at A-level include art, biology, classical civilization, economics, Greek, history and technology. Other subjects available at AS level include design technology, electronics, French, German and music. A supportive pastoral care system is organized through a house system, with a teacher taking on the role of tutor. Sixth-formers take on important roles supervising and guiding younger pupils and sport, drama and music are emphasized at this stage. The school does not cater for special-needs pupils. Parents are kept informed of what happens at the school and there is an emphasis on 'preparation for life in the contemporary world'.

## Admissions and intake

Admission at ages 7, 11, 13 and 16 is selective through an entrance exam, with some scholarships given occasionally following an interview.

## Achievement

Bancrofts is an extremely high-performing school with a large number of Oxbridge-bound sixth formers produced each year. It is always high in the borough's tables and high in the list of London's independent schools. In 2002, 100 per cent of pupils gained five or more A*–C grades at GCSE. The average point score was 57.9, ranking the school first in the borough league table. These results repeated the sucess of the last five years. At A-level, the average point score for pupils taking two or more A-levels was 394.3, ranking the school first in the borough. A government inspection in 1999 said the school had a 'high level of academic attainment with an atmosphere of scholarly endeavour in which pupils take a pride in their performance'. Much of the teaching was found to be 'very good' and all staff 'show great commitment to the welfare and all round development of the pupils'. They also commented that 'the mutual respect and friendship in a community with a broad mix of religious, racial and cultural backgrounds are particularly noble'. However, the school was criticized for its resources for drama, science and music at a junior level, and because IT needed developing. The school was also told that its sixth-form facilities needed improving to give a greater sense of identity.

## Extra-curricular activities

Sports, music and drama are well catered for and there is a community service part of this programme. Many foreign trips are planned from language exchanges to sports tours. Within the country, field trips are organized and pupils can also attend lectures at Cambridge. The school also provides homework clubs for the pupils.

# Beal High School

**Woodford Bridge Road, Ilford, Essex IG4 5LP** 020 8551 4954 020 8551 4421 Ms S Snowden; Chair of Governors: Mrs R Giemajner Ilford Redbridge **Buses:** 123, 179 Tan blazer, black trousers or skirt, white shirt or blouse, tie for boys (Years 7 to 11); Sixth form: Navy blue blazer, navy blue or black trousers, a plain white or blue shirt, special sixth-form tie (optional for girls) **Demand:** Oversubscribed **Type:** Comprehensive for 1462 mixed pupils, aged 11 to 18 **Submit application form:** Mid-October 2003 **Mission statement:** We aim to equip this school to challenge you: to make the best of yourself, to learn all you can and to use it to help yourself and give service to others. **School hours:** 8.25am–3.15pm; homework clubs are available **School meals:** Hot and cold available **Strong GCSE subjects:** Art, English, modern languages, sociology **London league table position:** 152

## Profile

Beal High is an ex-grammar school. As a result of a high demand for school places in Redbridge, the school has expanded. New classrooms have been built, including a drama studio, science laboratories, a library resource centre, information technology rooms and sixth-form facilities. The school emphasizes self-discovery, befitting its mission statement. All pupils from Years 9 to 13 receive careers guidance and work experience takes place in Year 10. Placements are carried out in a two-week period throughout the area and the City of London. In Year 11, guidance is given on interview techniques and CV writing. In line with its policy to draw the best out of its pupils, the school opened a special autistic unit in 2002. It is based in the new building and provides an education for up to 30 pupils. In terms of pastoral care, the school assigns pupils to eight tutor groups in each year. The work of these groups is overseen by the head of year and the head teacher. A code of conduct has been set up where the aim 'is to make the school an orderly, safe, calm and effective environment for students and adults to work in'. Homework has been described as an integral part of learning at Beal High. A work diary is issued to all pupils and must be signed by parents or guardians at the end of the week. The school also has a school council.

## Admissions and intake

As a Redbridge community comprehensive, the school gives priority to those applicants living in the catchment area or near the school prior to the start of the academic year (1 September). Preference is also given to those applicants who have named the school as their number one choice or who have brothers and sisters already studying there.

## Achievement

The school has consistently produced good GCSE results. In 2002, 72 per cent of pupils attained five or more A–C grades. This was down on 76 per cent in 2001 and the school was ranked ninth in the borough. In 1995, the figure was just 47 per cent. However, the school's A-level results are below national standards and the average point score was 235 in 2002. The majority of pupils stay on at the school and complete the sixth form.

## Extra-curricular activities

While the school offers a range of academic opportunities, it also provides a host of sporting and extra-curricular activities. The pupils take part in a range of community projects, and raise funds for local charities. There is a school radio club, chess club, science club and homework club. The school also has a good sports record. Last year, the boys' Year 11 football team were cup semi-finalists and the school came second in the Essex schools' league for basketball.

# Canon Palmer Catholic School

**Aldborough Road South, Seven Kings, Ilford, Essex IG3 8EU** 020 8590 3808 020 8597 5119 canpalmer@aol.com www.canonpalmer.school.co.uk Frank Maguire; Chair of Governors: Mr D Lillis Seven Kings **Buses:** 86 Navy jumper, white or grey shirt, dark grey trousers or navy skirt, navy blazer (boys only), black shoes **Demand:** Oversubscribed **Type:** Roman Catholic for 1171 mixed pupils, aged 11 to 18 **Submit application form:** November 2003 **Mission statement:** We, as a Catholic school, believe all have a divine origin and an eternal destiny. We promote the development and care of each individual, both pupils and staff, serving Christ in each of them. We follow the example of our founder, Canon Patrick Palmer, to do all things to the glory of God and the service of all. **School hours:** 8.45am–3.30pm; homework clubs are available **School meals:** Hot and cold available **Strong GCSE subjects:** All relatively strong **London league table position:** 245

## Profile

Canon Palmer school was founded in 1961. It took the name of a much-loved and respected priest who laid the foundations of the Catholic community in and around Ilford. The school boasts spacious classroom accommodation, a science laboratory and IT rooms. There is a sports hall on-site, which can cater for most indoor sports, including cricket. It can accommodate a full-sized basketball court or three badminton courts. There is also a separate gym/dance studio and an outdoor floodlit multi-sports area with two tennis courts, basketball and netball courts. The school also uses playing fields at Seven Kings Park. Swimming allocations are given to the school at the nearby public baths. The school is also given access to the Cricklefield Athletics Track. The curriculum at Canon Palmer reflects both the National Curriculum and the Catholic nature of the school. In Year 7, the curriculum consists of the core subjects, English, maths, French, science and technology, together with history, geography, religious education, music, drama, art, information technology, personal, social and health education, physical education and games. In Years 8 and 9, pupils are also expected to take a second modern language chosen from German and Spanish. In the sixth form, pupils can opt to take a two-year course of up to four AS Levels or a two-year secretarial course, leading to RSA and Pitman certificates. GNVQs, validated by City and Guilds in business and in leisure and tourism, are available at intermediate level. The students also participate in the school council. All pupils are sent on a two-week work-experience placement in Years 10 or 12. A homework club, handwriting club and spelling club meet under the guidance of the learning support team to assist special-needs pupils. Subject reports and pastoral reports are prepared twice a year, there is an active home-school association.

## Admissions and intake

The school admits Catholic pupils of all abilities who attend local parish churches. If the school has free places when it has met its obligations to the Catholic community, non-Catholic pupils may be admitted. This usually makes up to 10 per cent of the school roll.

### Achievement

In 2002, 62 per cent of pupils gained five or more A*–C grades at GCSE and the school was ranked 13th in the borough. At A-level, the average point score was 227.2, below the borough and national averages. Ofsted visited the school in 2001 and described it as 'a good and effective school' with high standards compared to similar schools.

### Extra-curricular activities

Activities occur at lunchtimes and after school, including choirs, orchestras, recorder groups, maths clubs, sixth form debating society, computer clubs and homework clubs. Pupils take part in a large amount of trips and outings, and participate in the normal array of sporting activities. There is also sixth-form community service with the physically and mentally handicapped and many other local groups, as well as work with the Catholic Children's Society.

## Caterham High School

**Caterham Avenue, Ilford, Essex IG5 0QW** 020 8551 4321 020 8551 1933 welcome@caterham.redbridge.school.uk www.caterham.redbridge.sch.uk Alan J Atkins; Chair of Governors: Councillor John Tyne **Buses:** 129, 169, 275 Black blazer, white shirt, black trousers or skirt, black shoes **Demand:** Fully subscribed **Type:** Comprehensive for 1097 mixed pupils, aged 11 to 18 **Submit application form:** Mid-October 2003 **Mission statement:** Caring attitude, academic excellence, tolerance, education for life, responsibility, home/school/links, all-round personality, modern technology **School hours:** 8.30am–3.15pm **School meals:** Hot and cold available **Strong GCSE subjects:** All relatively strong **London league table position:** 290

### Profile

Caterham High School has a modern school building and has extensive playing fields just a few minutes' walk away. An increasing number of students are applying to the school's sixth form and, because of this, the sixth-form suite was enlarged in 1994. The school boasts some impressive sports facilities. A new sports hall has been erected, and the school also has its own heated swimming pool, gymnasium, and an all-weather play area and tennis courts. It has a number of academic facilities, including five computer rooms, eight science laboratories and a media studies suite. Further new developments include a drama studio, a new art extension and an improved suite for design and technology. The sixth form offers a range of A-levels, as well as vocational GNVQs. Staff are available to listen to pupils at all times and senior staff monitor their progress. Year groups have their own school councils and coordinate charity events and social functions. Special-needs coordinators are also on hand to provide for any pupils that may need special attention. There is a thriving parents' association, which has provided the school with a new minibus.

### Admissions and intake

Parents should contact the LEA regarding admissions procedure.

### Achievement

In 2002, 49 per cent of pupils gained five or more A*–C grades at GCSE, down from 53 per cent in 2001. The average A-level point score was 211, ranking the school fourth in the borough. In 2001, Ofsted described it as 'a good school, and improving'. Teaching was found to be good overall. Unauthorized half-day absences from September 1999 to May 2000 were low at 0.6 per cent.

### Extra-curricular activities

Activities available include orchestras, choirs and music productions. The school is noted for its drama productions, which have included *Daisy Pulls it Off* and *Bugsy Malone*. The school also provides homework clubs and offers a regular choice of sporting activities. Pupils take part in community projects and fund-raising for various local charities.

## The Chadwell Heath Foundation School

**Christie Gardens, Chadwell Heath, Romford, Essex RM6 4RS** 0208 252 5151 0208 252 5152 chadwell@learnfree.co.uk Mr KE Wilkinson; Chair of Governors: Mr L Herbert Romford **Buses:** 86 Navy blazer, blue shirt, and navy trousers or skirt **Demand:** Increasingly subscribed **Type:** Grant maintained comprehensive for 1223 mixed pupils, aged 11 to 18 **Submit application form:** Mid-October 2003 **Mission statement:** The school aims to provide the environment and resources that will enable our pupils to develop their potential to the full and be equipped to play their part in the adult world. **School hours:** 8.50 am–3.20pm **School meals:** Hot and cold available **Strong GCSE subjects:** All relatively strong **London league table position:** 210

## Profile

Chadwell Heath School has been building a good reputation in recent years. Standards across the board are now above average and places are now in demand. The school is modern and well maintained and it has a long-term building programme in place. A new media and drama block was completed and work is underway on further technology facilities. A music and science department has also been added. These developments have helped to address issues of class size and the school has successfully kept these within reasonable limits. A sports hall, playground and tennis court provide extra-curricular activities. Limited library facilities are also available. The curriculum is wide-ranging and includes business and technology. Work experience is organized through local businesses for Year 10 pupils and the sixth form, and the school works closely with the careers service. There is a prefect system run by sixth-formers and a sixth-form committee, chaired and run by pupils. The pastoral system is well established, with a history of close relations between teachers and pupils. Good facilities and teaching is on offer for special-needs pupils. Parents attend a special meeting for Year 7 entrants and parents sign pupils' organizers on a weekly basis to keep in touch with their child's progress.

## Admissions and intake

A total of 15 per cent of the school's intake is based on selection through an attainment test.

## Achievement

Chadwell Heath has improved in the past six years. For GCSE results in 2002, 65 per cent of pupils achieved five or more A*–C grades, below the borough average. This was the same percentage as 2001 and the school came 12th in the borough. For A-level, the school has been below average for some years due to its open sixth-form policy. In 2002, the average point score was 187.3. GNVQs are also offered. The school's strengths lie in English literature and language and mathematics but science is less strong. In 1998, Ofsted stated that: 'Chadwell Heath is a much improved school. The most significant improvement had been in the standards achieved by its pupils. The head teacher, governing body, senior management team and all the staff at the school are now poised to improve the school further and improve the quality of education for all its pupils.' Key weaknesses have been in the science facilities and underdeveloped information technology. Modern languages were also seen as lacking. Unauthorized attendance is 0.2 per cent. Discipline, according to Ofsted, is excellent.

## Extra-curricular activities

A full sporting programme is offered, and music covers choral and orchestral opportunities. Local sports clubs are also used and pupils enter events such as the Redbridge Show. Homework clubs are organized, as well as theatre trips and away-days. The pupils also take part regularly in community-based events, organizing fund-raising activities to help local charities.

# Cranbrook College

**Mansfield Road, Ilford, Essex IG1 3BD** ☎ 020 8554 1757 Fax 020 8518 0317 Head Mr CP Lacey; Chair of Governors: Brian Hill ⇌ Ilford Uniform Blue and gold – navy blue blazer with grey trousers **Demand:** Heavily subscribed **Type:** Independent for 207 boys, aged 4 to 16 **Fees:** £1,722 per term (aged 7 to 13), £1,877 per term (aged 14 and over) **Submit application form:** No cut-off date **Motto:** *Per Laberem as Honerem* (Through Hard Work to Honour) **School hours:** 9am–3.30pm **School meals:** Hot and cold available **Strong GCSE subjects:** All relatively strong **London league table position:** 129

## Profile

Cranbrook College has a long history, being founded in 1896 by WH Carte. The school became an educational trust, a non-profit-making body, in 1960. The current building was built in 1922, with extensions added in 1939 and 1991. Facilities include a hall, library, art room, computer room, laboratory, classrooms and two playgrounds. The school prides itself on a 'family' atmosphere and there are no classes larger than 26 pupils. At the lower end of the school, class sizes are often less than 20. There is not a sudden break at the age of 11 because pupils can stay at the school from ages 4 to 16. The school does not have a sixth form and typically pupils go on to Bancrofts, Ilford County High and Seven Kings High School. There is also a strong PTA.

### Admissions and intake

Pupils come to the school from north-east London and Essex, although there is no explicit catchment area.

### Achievement

In 2002, 88 per cent of pupils gained five or more GCSEs at grades A*–C. This was well above borough and national averages, and the school was ranked seventh in the borough. Cranbrook was subject to an Independent Schools' Information Service (ISIS report) in 1997.

### Extra-curricular activities

Clubs available include chess, choir, public speaking, skiing, Duke of Edinburgh's Award scheme and drama. Sports on offer include athletics, basketball, badminton, cricket, cross-country, football, hockey, swimming and sailing.

## Hainault Forest High School

**Harbourer Road, Hainault, Ilford, Essex IG6 3TN** ☎ 020 8500 4266 Fax 020 8500 0036 e hforest@leonet.co.uk www.hainaultforest.com Mr G Deery; Chair of Governors: Mrs Bleet ⊖ Hainault **Buses:** 150, 247, 362, 511 Black skirt/trousers, black blazer, off-white shirt, black V-neck jumper **Demand:** Spaces available **Type:** Comprehensive for 964 mixed pupils, aged 11 to 18 **Submit application form:** Mid-October 2003 **Motto:** Working Together to Achieve High Standards **School hours:** 8.45am–3.25pm; homework clubs are available (Mon, Wed and Fri) **School meals:** Hot and cold available **Strong GCSE subjects:** All relatively strong **London league table position:** 358

### Profile

Hainault Forest High School is the amalgamation of two secondary modern schools, which merged in 1976. The main building is situated near Hainault Forest. Facilities include a sports hall and specialist facilities in English, science, drama, art, technology, humanities and music. There is a youth club linked to the school. Reports on pupils' progress are sent home six times a year and there is at least one parents' evening per year. There is an anti-bullying campaign and 'buddies' scheme. There is a student council and a home-school association. Provision for pupils with special needs is available.

### Admissions and intake

Parents should contact the LEA for information on admissions.

### Achievement

In 1998, Ofsted said that Hainault Forest had improved significantly since the last inspection in 1994, especially at GCSE level. Boys are not as far behind the national average as girls. In 2002, 37 per cent of pupils gained five or more A*–C grades at GCSE. This was down on 41 per cent in 2001 and the school came bottom of the borough. At A-level, the average point score was 194.5. This placed the school near the bottom of the borough league table. However, it should be noted that the school is a comprehensive in a borough with grammar schools and in one of the most deprived parts of Redbridge. The Ofsted report said behaviour was generally good and highlighted the art department as being particularly strong.

### Extra-curricular activities

There are clubs available for art, badminton, gymnastics, Christian Fellowship, history, maths, music, athletics, trampolining, football, basketball, cricket, tennis, weight training and singing. Each year, groups go to an outdoor education centre at Glasbury-on-Wye. There are regular trips to London galleries. Pupils are encouraged to take part in community work, and recent events include a Christmas collection of food for local pensioners and a sponsored skip in aid of the British Heart Foundation. After-school homework clubs are available.

# Ilford County High School

**Fremantle Road, Barkingside, Ilford IG6 2JB** 020 8551 6496 020 8503 9960 enquiries@ichs.org.uk Mr S Devereux; Chair of Governors: Cllr M Hickey Barkingside and Fairlop **Buses:** 129 Purple blazer, grey trousers, white shirt **Demand:** Oversubscribed **Type:** Grammar school for 834 boys, aged 11 to 18 **Submit application form:** Contact school for information **School hours:** 9am–3.30pm; homework clubs are available **School meals:** Hot and cold available **Strong GCSE subjects:** Chemistry, economics, maths **London league table position:** 66

## Profile

Ilford County High School is one of the leading grammar schools in the country and one of the 19 remaining grammar schools in London. It is the borough's only remaining boys' grammar school and is committed to maintaining high standards. It also aims to oversee the emotional and social development of its pupils. With its strong sporting emphasis and opportunities for studying music, the school provides one of the best environments for all-round education in the borough. It was founded in 1902 as Park Higher Grade School and moved onto its present location in 1934 when it was renamed. From Year 7, pupils are taught a wide syllabus, including personal and social education, design and technology and classics. A second modern language (after French) is offered atYear 8. All pupils are expected to take 10 GCSE subjects, including English language, English literature, maths, chemistry, physics, biology, and a modern language, and three options, which can include a second language. A wide range of A-levels is also on offer, including accounting, art and design, business studies, computing, electronics and Latin. A wide range of foreign languages, for example, Urdu and modern Greek, can also be taken. Tutor groups form an important part of school life, where form tutors keep a close eye on individual pupils, and a head of year follows each year group throughout their school life. Pupils with special educational needs are catered for. Parents are also expected to contribute by signing a home-school agreement to ensure homework is done and to maintain pupils' progress. The parents' association is a strong fund-raising body. A highly active old boy's society retains the school's original name.

## Admissions and intake

Admission is via the national 11+ examination available for Redbridge residents. Admission to applicants living outside the borough is only possible after requests from within the catchment area have been met. An average of 10 pupils apply for each place. Normally admission is only at Year 7, but direct entry to the sixth form is possible by special arrangement.

## Achievement

The school's results fair extremely well against some of the top private schools in the annual league tables. In 2002, 98 per cent of pupils achieved five or more grades A*–C at GCSE.The school was ranked third in the borough. The average A-level score for pupils taking two or more A-levels in 2002 was 323.7 This placed the school third in the borough league table. Nationally, the school was placed 50th best grammar school in 1999. There was no unauthorized absence in 2000.

## Extra-curricular activities

The school's activities are wide-ranging and include competitive sports aimed at all levels of ability and a sailing club based at Fairlop Waters. A strong musical tradition also offers a range of performing groups, and an annual musical stage production is organized. Drama and other clubs and societies are popular and the school organizes trips and visits across the country and beyond. There are after-school homework clubs. Pupils can also take part in fund-raising events and volunteer at a nearby sheltered housing estate for senior citizens.

# Ilford Ursuline High School

**Morland Road, Ilford IG1 4JU** 020 8554 1995 020 8554 9537 Miss Jackie Reddington; Chair of Governors: Sister Maureen Moloney OSU Ilford Gants Hill **Buses:** 123, 129, 150, 179, 364, 366 Navy blue skirt and blazer, white blouse, black shoes; Sixth form: Office-style skirts and jackets **Demand:** 90 places available in 2002; oversubscribed **Type:** Voluntary aided Roman Catholic school for 477 girls, aged 4–18 **Submit application form:** Mid-October 2003 **Motto:** *Serviam* (I Serve) **School hours:** **School meals:** Hot and cold available, including breakfast **Strong GCSE subjects:** All relatively strong **London league table position:** 104

### Profile

Ilford Ursuline High School is a girl's voluntary aided Catholic secondary school, centrally located 10 minutes' walk from Ilford train station. It was founded in 1903 and, although there are no Catholic sisters on the teaching body, the school maintains a strong religious focus. It was a direct grant grammar school for many years and more recently an independent school, but returned to the state sector in 1999. Teaching is carried out on a single site, where building work was recently completed. A sixth form and music centre were finished in 1999 and there is a fully completed school library. The school's motto is *Serviam*, Latin for 'I Serve', which reflects the school's emphasis on involvement with the community, demonstrated by the voluntary work done by all pupils. A broad curriculum encompasses religious and physical education, art, music, IT, design technology, music and German, as well as traditional core subjects and a weekly personal and social education lesson. All pupils are expected to do two weeks of work experience at the end of Year 10. The school has a strong tradition of sixth-form prefects. First year intake students (Year 7) have pastoral tutors, who spend time with pupils. Family evenings are arranged by an active parents' association. An emphasis on dialogue between staff and parents is maintained. At GCSE level, pupils study English language and literature, maths, combined science, religious education, French, technology and business studies. They also have the choice of two additional subjects from art, geography, German, history, music and PE. In the lower sixth form, students take AS courses in four subjects, as well as general studies and preparing for key skills qualifications in communications, numeracy and information and communication technology. In the upper sixth, only three subjects are pursued to A-level standard.

### Admissions and intake

With 431 pupils, Ilford Ursuline is a large school that admits both Catholic and non-Catholic girls, provided parents accept the broad ethos of the school. When the school is oversubscribed, priority is given to: children with a sister currently attending the school; and baptized practising Roman Catholics from a Redbridge parish, supported by a letter from the parish priest. Twenty pupils are expected to be non-Roman Catholics. Parents should contact the school to obtain an application form.

### Achievement

The school's GCSE results in 2002 placed it fifth in the borough with 82 per cent of pupils achieving five or more A*-C grade results. This was five per cent up on 2001 and well above the borough and national averages. At A-level, pupils taking two or more subjects averaged 294.6 points, ranking the school fifth in the borough.

### Extra-curricular activities

The school encourages development in music, art and drama and has many extra-curricular activities, including an orchestra, ensembles and choirs. There is also a strong tradition of theatre, with students engaging in all aspects of its production. Pupils practise the regular range of sports. There are school trips both at home and abroad.

## King Solomon High School

**Forest Road, Barkingside, Ilford, Essex IG6 3HB** 020 8501 2083 020 8559 9445 Mr Alastair Falk; Chair of Governors: Mrs Pat Stanton Fairlop **Buses:** 167, 169 Grey skirt or trousers, white shirt or blouse, navy sweatshirt **Demand:** Some places available **Type:** Voluntary aided Jewish Technology College for 912 mixed pupils, aged 11 to 18 **Fees:** Suggested contribution of £190 per term or £570 per year **Submit application form:** End November 2003 **Mission Statement:** Our aim is to produce young Jewish people who are caring, tolerant and knowledgeable – at home in the traditions of the past but able and willing to contribute to the world of tomorrow. **School hours:** 8.30am–4pm, 8.30am–1.30pm (Fri) **School meals:** Hot and cold available – all kosher **Strong GCSE subjects:** Art **London league table position:** 161

### Profile

King Solomon High School serves the Jewish community and has grown rapidly to a roll of 915 in seven years. It is not a private school, but there is a suggested financial contribution. It opened in 1993 with 85 pupils and in a new, well-designed building. It has gained status as a Technology College and has an Amstrad Technology Wing, which is one of the finest in the country. There is one computer for every seven pupils. The school offers French, Spanish and Ivrit (modern Hebrew). All students are issued with a responsibility code, which outlines the pupils' rights, and their responsibilities to take pride in themselves, treat each other respectfully and take care of the environment. The code states: 'You have the right to come to school without facing rudeness, insults or bullying of any kind. You must treat students and adults in a respectful, friendly manner and respect the opinions of others.' The school also provides a special-needs coordinator.

### Admissions and intake

Parents should apply directly to the school. Admission is only open to children who are recognized as being Jewish by the Office of the Chief Rabbi of the United Hebrew Congregation of the Commonwealth.

### Achievement

The school's GCSE results in 2002 placed it 10th in Redbridge. A total of 68 per cent of pupils gained five or more A*–C grades at GCSE. At A-level, the average point score was 249.1, placing the school seventh in the borough. In 1997, Ofsted reported: 'In the short time the school has been in existence, it has been very successful in creating a vibrant, positive and flourishing institution for learning where pupils are happy and sociable.' There was an unauthorized absence of 1.2 per cent in 2000, above the borough and national averages.

### Extra-curricular activities

There are clubs available in aerobics, athletics, basketball, cricket, dry-slope skiing, football, netball, sailing and swimming. A number of teams compete in local leagues and against other Jewish schools. There is close involvement with the Jewish community and students are encouraged to raise money for charity. There have been recent trips to Gibraltar, Spain, France and Israel.

## Loxford School of Science and Technology

**Loxford House, Ilford, Essex IG1 2UT** ☎ 020 8514 4666 📠 020 8514 6257 ⓔ lssp@loxford. redbridge.sch.uk 🌐 www.redbridge.gov.uk Ms H Farrow; Chair of Governors: Peter Ballard Up to sixth form: Navy blue blazer trousers or skirt, red or green crest, black/green tie **Demand:** Annual intake of 240 **Type:** Technology College for 1482 mixed pupils, aged 11 to 19 **Submit application form:** Mid-October 2003 **Mission Statement:** Teamwork – achievement **School hours:** 9.00am–3.25pm **School meals:** Hot and cold available **Strong GCSE subjects:** IT, sciences **London league table position:** 257

### Profile

Loxford provides specialist education in science, technology, mathematics and information technology, while still being committed to a broad and balanced curriculum for all. Built in 1971, the school is modern in appearance and its new science labs are said to be the best in London. In 1996, it was named as the first Technology College in Greater London. This accreditation resulted in a cash injection of £475,000 from the government. The school's library facilities have recently been updated. A multi-resource centre gives pupils access to information on computers in a variety of formats, including CD-ROM, video, audiotape and books. There is also a large indoor heated swimming pool, sports hall and playing fields. It also houses a music suite complete with individual practice rooms. Most lessons are taught in mixed-ability tutor groups. Pupils are taught in smaller groups for technology, art and IT. Streaming by ability is introduced in Year 9. The school's A-level courses include accounting, business studies, computer science, design realization, drama, economics, law, media studies and sociology. Loxford is keen to promote links with employers and pupils are expected to complete two weeks of work experience in Years 10 and 11, and again in the sixth form. The school is also a member of the Redbridge Compact Scheme, which gives pupils access to companies and higher-education establishments. Pupils are given responsibility in all years. In Year 11, some pupils serve as prefects. Each year group has a students committee for matters of concern. Loxford is supportive to pupils with special needs both with and without a statement and operates a register based on staged procedures as administered by Redbridge council. The heads of year have set times when they are available to see parents, but individual appointments can be made. Each pupil has a formal interview with the college's senior management team before making choices at age 14 and in the sixth form. The college has an active parent-teacher association.

## Admissions and intake

Most students are drawn from primary schools in Redbridge, but Loxford also attracts pupils from neighbouring boroughs. Selection procedure was undergoing change at the time the book was going to press, so please contact the school for further information.

## Achievement

In 2002, 52 per cent of pupils gained five or more A*–C grades at GCSE, up from 51 per cent in 2001, and showing steady improvement each year since 1996. The average point score at A-level was 213.3, ranking the school 13th in the borough. Unauthorized absence was 0.4 per cent.

## Extra-curricular activities

Exam revision classes are held at Easter and half-terms. The students participate in normal, curriculum sporting activities.

# Mayfield School and College

**Mayfield Road, Dagenham, Essex RM8 1X5** 020 8590 5211 020 8597 5729 mayfld1@ aol.com www.redbridge.gov.uk/education/secondary/core/mayfield.html Mr Trevor Averre-Beeson; Chair of Governors: Mr D Backhouse Goodmayes, Chadwell Heath **Buses:** 128, 129 between Ilford and Becontree heath Up to sixth form: Black blazer, white shirt/blouse, school tie, black shoes **Demand:** 240 places in 2002 **Type:** Comprehensive Foundation School for 1292 mixed pupils, aged 11–18 **Submit application form:** Mid-October 2003 **School hours:** 8.55am–3.40pm (Mon), 8.55am–3.15pm (Tues, Wed, Thurs), 8.55am–2.15pm (Fri); homework clubs are available **Meals:** Hot and cold available **Strong GCSE subjects:** All relatively strong **London league table position:** 333

## Profile

Mayfield School is located in a busy residential area of Ilford between Goodmayes and Chadwell Heath, to the far south of the borough. It is a highly residential, outer London urban area with few green areas of recreation. It is a large school with a wide academic syllabus but the school tends to have disappointing results at GCSE level, both for within the borough and on a national level.

Mayfield has seen considerable investment in its facilities in past years, with a £2.5-million re-building project providing a range of new facilities (in particular £200,000 of IT equipment). It also boasts a music suite, extensive playing fields, sports hall, gymnasium and fitness room. It recently acquired Foundation School status. All Year 11 pupils take two weeks' work experience and a school careers library is offered to all students. Pastoral care is left in the hands of a form teacher, who follows the class from Years 7 to 11 and parents receive a regular progress report. A big breakfast club is run at 8.15am three days a week, where students can do homework in return for a free breakfast. There is a school council. Famous ex-pupils include the footballer Paul Ince.

## Admissions and intake

The school admits 240 pupils a term, with priority given to those within the immediate catchment area and those with siblings attending. An above average number of pupils out of the catchment area find a place at the school.

## Achievement

A wide school curriculum covers GCSE English language, English literature, mathematics and science as core subjects, with a wide range of extra subjects, including food technology, graphic products and resistant materials. In 2002, 46 per cent of pupils gained five or more A*–C grades at GCSE, up from 44 per cent in 2001. This was below the borough average and the school was placed 18th in the borough. A sixth form college is located in separate buildings and the college is gradually growing. There are 22 subjects offered at A-level, including Urdu, sports studies and accounting. In 2002, the average point score for pupils taking two or more A-levels, was 206.3, below the borough and national averages. These results ranked the school 15th in the borough league table. There was 0.1 per cent unauthorized absence in 2000.

### Extra-curricular activities

A wide range of clubs and activities includes careers, computer work, drama club and IT. Choirs and a range of orchestras are available and sports, including badminton, table tennis and netball, are on offer. Mayfield has won awards for producing educational and social videos. School field trips are organized by the geography and history departments and modern languages departments arrange trips abroad. Pupils raise funds for local charities.

# Oaks Park High School

**45–46 Oaks Lane, Newbury Park, Ilford, Essex 1G2 7PQ** 020 8590 2245 020 8590 2246 office@oakspark.redbridge.sch.uk www.oakspark.redbridge.sch.uk Steve Wilks; Chair of Governors: Cllr Roy Brunnen Newbury Park Buses: 66, 296, 396 Green blazer and black trousers or skirt, white shirt, school tie, black shoes. **Demand:** 240 places available in 2002 **Type:** Community comprehensive for 1500 mixed pupils, aged 11 to 18 **Submit application form:** Mid-October 2003 **Motto:** Learning Together, Achieving Together **School hours:** 8.30am–3.10pm **School meals:** Cafeteria-style hot and cold available **Strong GCSE subjects:** Not applicable, no pupils will sit GCSEs until 2006 **London league table position:** Not applicable

### Profile

Oaks Park High School opened in September 2001. It was deliberately sited in the centre of Redbridge, on a former sports field, to cater for pupils who were unable to get into a local school and were having to travel eight or 10 miles a day across the borough to get to an alternative school. The school was built at a cost of £17 million under the Private Finance Initiative (PFI), in a partnership between Redbridge council and Norwich Union. However, a delay in signing the contract meant that it wasn't actually built until 2002. In the meantime, 180 first-year students were housed in 59 temporary buildings next to the main school building site. A partnership with Canon means that the school will have state-of-the-art computer facilities.

### Admissions and intake

Despite the less than ideal circumstances surrounding its opening, and the fact that it has no exam record for parents to judge its performance by, the school was slightly oversubscribed in 2001 with more than 200 applications for 180 places. Head teacher Steve Wilkes confidently expects to fill the 240 places available in 2002 and subsequent years. Eventually the school will have 1200 pupils, aged 11 to 16 and a sixth form with a further 250 pupils. At the present rate the school will not be full until 2007, although the sixth form may open before the lower school is full. The school uses criteria laid down by Redbridge council to decide who to admit if the school is over-subscribed. This is based on the schools catchment area, whether an applicant has siblings already at the school, and the distance they live from the school, measured as the shortest reasonable walking route.

### Achievement

Pupils at the school will not sit GCSEs until summer 2006. They will sit Key Stage 3 tests in 2004, and the government has said it will publish these results nationally. The school is not eligible to become a specialist college until it has GCSE results, but it has a particularly strong emphasis on information technology.

### Extra-curricular activities

The school already has football, netball, chess and table tennis teams. There is an after-school information technology club, which is working on a project to create links with a school in the United States. Art, music and drama are also strong, and the school had a well-received Christmas show in 2001.

# Park School for Girls

**20–22 Park Avenue, Ilford, Essex IG1 4RS** 0208 554 2466 020 8554 3003 Mrs N O'Brien; Company Secretary: Rev D Bament Ilford Grants Hill Up to sixth form: Brown skirt, brown blazer, brown jumper, turquoise blouse (summer), same for winter except striped blouse; Sixth form: Smart office dress **Demand:** Heavily subscribed **Type:** Independent for 231 girls, aged 6 to 18 **Fees:** £1,430–1,772 per term **Submit application form:** No cut-off date **Motto:** Youth Strive Through Adversity **School hours:** 8.50am–3pm **School meals:** Not provided **Strong GCSE subjects:** Information technology **London league table position:** 102

## Profile

Park School is located in central Ilford. It was founded in 1974 when the school's previous owners closed the premises, which were then bought and re-opened by a parents' body before the end of the same academic year. As part of that legacy, all parents are expected to pay a small bond in addition to the fees of the school. The school buildings are smart and modern with many recent alterations and extensions. Laboratories and classrooms are well equipped, with a separate sixth-form common room, a music practice room and PE lessons for the preparatory school on-site. Excellent sports facilities are also offered at the nearby Redbridge Sports Centre and Fairlop Sailing Club. The school prides itself on a high teacher-to-pupil ratio, with small classes and an awareness of the importance of 'good manners and correct speech'. Up to the age of 11, pupils can take speech lessons, and at GCSE pupils study the core subjects of English literature, English language, maths, French and IT. In addition, art and design/textiles, economics, geography, history, Latin, religious studies, Spanish, biology, chemistry, physics and combined sciences are also offered. A strong emphasis is placed on homework. Many of the students participate in the school council. A special-needs coordinator is also on hand to provide any additional care to pupils who should need it.

## Admissions and intake

Admission is by written examination and interview. A formal application should be made to the head teacher.

## Achievement

In 2002, 86 per cent of pupils gained five or more grades A*–C at GCSE. This was six per cent down on 2001's results and the school was ranked fourth in the borough league table. Particular strengths at GCSE include information technology, and at A-level the strongest subject tends to be economics. At A-level, pupils taking two or more scored an average of 240.7 points in 2002, making it the eighth-best school in the borough.

## Extra-curricular activities

Tuition is available in piano, woodwind instruments and violin. Other activities on offer include choirs, drama, dance and musical productions and a number of school clubs, for example a homework club. Participation in the Duke of Edinburgh's Award scheme is encouraged. A wide range of sports includes netball, hockey, rounders, badminton and aerobics. Educational and cultural trips are arranged, including visits abroad.

# Seven Kings High School

**Ley Street, Ilford, Essex IG2 7BT** 020 8554 8935 020 8518 2975 email@sksh.ssne.co.uk www.sevenkings.redbridge.sch.uk Mr AW Steer; Chair of Governors: Mrs P Green Seven Kings Gants Hill, Newbury Park **Buses:** 69 Up to sixth form: Navy blue **Demand:** 180 places in 2002 **Type:** Secondary comprehensive Technology College for 1304 pupils, aged 11 to 18 **Submit application form:** Mid-October 2003 **Motto:** Friendship, Excellence and Opportunity **School hours:** 8.30am–3.00pm **School meals:** Hot and cold available, including breakfast **Strong GCSE subjects:** All relatively strong **London league table position:** 133

## Profile

Seven Kings High School is a large, dynamic school with excellent facilities for sport. The school offers a solid, all round education and it recently acquired Technology College status. The school buildings are mostly modern and a building programme completed in 1990 added a range of extra facilities. These included new classrooms and corridors, designed to create a quiet working environment. There is also a well-stocked school library, computer rooms, a giant outdoor chessboard and an ecology garden, which is home to a host of birds and insects. A private study area and separate library is available to sixth-formers, as well as a common room and media studio. The curriculum at GCSE includes art design, business studies, CDT, drama, product design, English, French, food studies, geography, history, information studies, maths, music, Punjabi, sociology and Spanish. Additional subjects at A-level include accounting, biology, chemistry, design technology, economics, government politics and media studies. AS-levels can also be taken. Work experience in places such as hospitals, university laboratories and legal and financial institutions is offered to Year 10 and 11 pupils. A well thought-out pastoral system involves a team of tutors who look after new arrivals and monitor their work and general progress. Year heads, academic coordinators and tutors then continue this work and careers officers are on hand for pupils choosing GCSE courses and beyond. Student councils give pupils an active voice at each key stage. A small number of physically disabled pupils are catered for. There is an active PTA.

## Admissions and intake

A total of 183 pupils are admitted each year from within a strict catchment area and a small number of out-of-catchment children are also admitted each year.

## Achievement

The school's results for 2002 saw 80 per cent of pupils at GCSE scoring five or more passes at A*–C grade. The average point score was 43.5 and this ranked the school eighth in the borough league table. At A-level, the average points score for pupils entered for two or more A-levels was 296.4. These results again placed the school fourth in the borough. A glowing Ofsted report in 2002 noted that Seven Kings 'provides its pupils with an excellent education'. Standards of attainment were seen to be high and 'pupils' achievements are excellent across the whole range of ability in comparison with similar schools'. Inspectors praised the head teacher's 'outstanding' leadership and the 'excellent' behaviour of the pupils. Attendance is well above average and Inspectors could find no significant areas for improvement.

## Extra-curricular activities

Activities available include a wide range of music lessons, dramatic productions and clubs including chess, sailing and biology. All other normal curriculum sports are also available to the students. Trips are organized within England, to Wales and Europe. The school has won awards for its community work with pupils regularly visiting day centres, junior schools and hospitals. The school also provides a homework club for students to attend.

# Trinity Catholic High School

**Mornington Road, Woodford Green, Essex 1G8 0TP** 020 8504 3419 (lower school); 020 8504 8946 (upper school) 020 8505 7546 Paul Doherty; Chair of Governors: Mr CA Carter Woodford **Buses:** W13, 20, 179, 645 Black leather shoes, no make-up or jewellery, long hair tied back (girls); no dyed or tinted hair, no very long or short hair (boys); navy blazer with school badge, navy tie with white and red stripes, grey trousers, or navy skirt; Sixth form: Dark suits, or black skirts, white blouse, black pullover and cardigan **Demand:** Demand for places varies **Type:** Roman Catholic comprehensive for 1688 mixed pupils, aged 11 to 18 **Submit application form:** Mid-October 2003 **School hours:** 8.50am–3.45pm; homework clubs are available **School meals:** Hot and cold available **Strong GCSE subjects:** Art, drama, maths, media studies, science **London league table position:** 116

## Profile

Set within the exclusive surroundings of Woodford Green, Trinity Catholic High School was formed in 1976 through an amalgamation of Holy Family Convent School and St Paul's Catholic Secondary School. Its history means the school is based on two sites – a lower school in Sydney Road, catering for Years 7 to 9 students, and an upper site, housing Years 10 to 11, plus a sixth form in Mornington Road. There is a wide range of facilities in both schools, with a textiles room in the lower site and fully equipped IT rooms in the upper site. Although the school is maintained by the London Borough of Redbridge, as it is a Catholic voluntary aided school it comes under the jurisdiction of the Bishop of Brentwood. As such, the school lays heavy emphasis on Catholic values and teachings. The school offers a wide range of A- and AS-level subjects, including psychology, economics and theatre studies. Homework is set every day. The school's pastoral care has a strong religious influence and aims to 'reinforce and develop the uniqueness of each individual in his/her relationship to Christ and his or her neighbour'. Emphasis is placed on discipline and there were no unauthorized absences in 2000. However the head teacher stresses 'punishment is balanced by praise and rewards'. The school has a strong PTA and there is a special-needs coordinator.

## Admissions and intake

Parents should apply directly to the school.

## Achievement

Educationally, the school achieves high results compared to many comprehensives in London. In 2002, 81 per cent of pupils gained five or more GCSEs grades A–C, down on 85 per cent in 2001. The school came sixth in the borough. At A-level, the average point score was 258.2, ranking the school sixth in the borough league table.

### Extra-curricular activities

There are plenty of sporting opportunities for pupils, and pony trekking, canoeing and climbing is offered. A homework club is available. The school also organizes trips both at home and abroad, that are both recreational and educational, for example, skiing trips and museum tours. The students participate in many fund-raising activities to encourage their awareness of the community and to raise money for local charities.

# Valentines High School

**Cranbrook Road, Gants Hill, Ilford, Essex IG2 6HX** 020 8554 3608 020 8518 2621 mail@valentines-sch.co.uk www.valentines-sch.org.uk Mr Daniel Moynihan; Chair of Governors: Cllr Keith Axon Ilford Gants Hill **Buses:** 123, 150, 251, 296, 645 Navy jumper with school badge, white shirt, black trousers or skirt school tie **Demand:** Oversubscribed **Type:** Comprehensive Technology College for 1222 mixed pupils, aged 11 to 18 **Submit application form:** Mid-October 2003 **School hours:** 8.30am–3.20pm, 8.30am–3.05pm (Fri) **School meals:** Hot and cold available **Strong GCSE subjects:** Art, drama **London league table position:** 176

### Profile

The school was founded in 1977 and has a specially designed block for 300 sixth formers. The outdoor pitches need improvements, but there is a large modern sports hall and four all-weather tennis courts. The school has an anti-bullying policy in place and many of the students participate in the school council. Spanish, French and Urdu are some of the subjects on offer. It recently acquired Technology College status. Ofsted congratulated the school on its pastoral care. A special-needs coordinator is available. There is a school council and a parent-teacher association.

### Admissions and intake

See borough factfile for details of admissions.

### Achievement

Children enter the school with skills in English, maths and science that are well below average, but they achieve GCSEs at the national average or above. In 2002, 67 per cent of pupils achieved five or more grades A*–C up 11 per cent on 2001. The school came 11th in the borough. At A-level, the average point score was 237.6, ranking the school ninth in the borough. The Ofsted report said 'the majority of pupils make good progress'. It described the school as a 'well disciplined community where the relationships are good'. However, Ofsted identified information technology as a key weakness of the school.

### Extra-curricular activities

Sports on offer include trampolining, football and basketball. There are clubs for pupils interested in computers, animals, chess, art, drama and photography. There is a high level of participation in the school clubs. Trips are also regularly organized, both at home and abroad. The school encourages pupils to participate in community projects, raising funds for various local charities.

# Wanstead High School

**Redbridge Lane West, Wanstead, London E11 2JZ** 020 8989 2791 020 8530 8879 Mr George Ferris; Chair of Governors: Mr G Wombwell Wanstead Black trousers/skirt, white shirt, school jumper and tie **Demand:** Oversubscribed **Type:** Comprehensive for 1,521 mixed pupils, aged 11 to 18 **Submit application form:** Mid-October 2003 **Motto:** *Abeunt Studia in Mores* (Studies Become Morals) **School hours:** 8.40am–3.25pm; homework clubs are available **School meals:** Hot and cold available **Strong GCSE subjects:** Art, drama, English, geography, history, informational studies, languages, music, RE, sociology, technology **London league table position:** 273

### Profile

Wanstead High was founded in 1924 and has seen a number of physical changes over the years. The buildings are a mixture of Victorian-style brick and 1960–70s additions along with a new science block. It also has a purpose-built theatre and music suite, with seven practice rooms. New computer suites have been installed, with 10 well-equipped laboratories, and the school runs Wanstead Leisure Centre – a huge multi-use area for indoor sports along with hard-paved pitches. A wide range of subjects is offered at Key Stage 4 and the school offers 22 A-levels, GNVQs and other vocational qualifications. A specialist team of teachers and classroom assistants support pupils both with special-needs and also more able pupils. Wanstead High prides itself on its use of pastoral care to support pupils' education, and each year group is led by an experienced team, with tutors who closely monitor the progress of each pupil. Strong links are maintained between teachers and pupils through curriculum events and functions. Homework is set according to a published timetable. The PTA is very active.

## Admissions and intake

Admissions are strictly from the LEA's defined catchment area, with preference for pupils with siblings at the school. Some out-catchment pupils are taken in each year. In 2000, there were 10 pupils with special needs.

## Achievement

In 2002, 51 per cent of pupils received five or more A*–C grades at GCSE, a repeat of 2001's results. This was in line with the national average of 51.6 per cent but below the borough average of 63.7 per cent. The average point score was 36, ranking the school joint 15th in the borough. Pupils gained 219.5 points on average at A-level. The school's most recent Ofsted report, in 1996, reported that: 'This is a welcoming school which provides a secure and often good education for the majority of its pupils'. There was found to be 'sound and sometimes high standards' attained in many areas, but academic achievements 'vary across the school, closely related to the quality of teaching provided'. There was 0.2 per cent unauthorized absence in 2000.

## Extra-curricular activities

A wide range of clubs are available at lunchtimes, with particular strengths in sports and the performing arts. Academic clubs to support aspects of the curriculum are also offered, such as homework clubs. Wanstead is well known for its colourful and popular dramatic performances, which are supported by teachers specializing in this area. The students also organize many community fund-raising activities for local charities. School trips are regularly organized, whether as field trips within the UK or as language excursions abroad.

# Woodbridge High School

**St Barnabas Road, Woodford Green, Essex IG88 7DH** ☎ 020 8504 9618 📠 020 8559 0487 ✉ Barbara Haigh; Chair of Governors: Cllr Richard Hoskins ⊖ Woodford **Buses:** 14, 28 👔 Black trousers and blazer, black jumper, white shirt or blouse, tie; trainers are not allowed **Demand:** Demand varies **Type:** Comprehensive Language College for 1365 mixed pupils, aged 11 to 18 **Submit application form:** Mid-October 2003 **Motto:** Pride in Achievement **School hours:** 8.50am–3.20pm; homework clubs are available **School meals:** Hot and cold available **Strong GCSE subjects:** Expressive arts, modern languages **London league table position:** 276

## Profile

Woodbridge High is a school whose academic prowess has led to high demand from parents. The school places great stress on high academic standards but it is not elitist in a regressive sense, aiming to give 'all children the chance to succeed'. Woodbridge High offers a range of academic and sporting facilities, and it recently acquired Language College status. It built a new wing at the cost of £1.1 million. This building houses a library and resources centre, four new rooms for the maths department, a laboratory, a media studies room and a large sixth-form area. There are also three computer suites on the school site and a drama studio. A multi-purpose sports hall caters for badminton, basketball, netball, tennis and volleyball. There are also facilities for indoor cricket, plus a fully equipped gymnasium. The school offers a wide range of A-level subjects including maths, biology, chemistry, art and design, Russian, music and economics and business. All pupils from Years 7 to 13 receive careers guidance. Work experience takes place in Year 10 and is arranged in conjunction with the borough's careers officers. Consistent with its aim to educate all, the school places great importance on special needs. It provides support teachers and assistants who work alongside teachers in the classroom to help pupils make progress. There is also a reading club during lunchtime and booster groups are provided to offer support for pupils with learning difficulties. Pastoral care is handled initially within the tutor group. There is also a year group coordinator who is supported by the school's management team, which consists of four elected parent governors, two elected teacher governors, five co-opted members and the head teacher. An anti-bullying programme has been established and the school has a 'Trust and Tell' drop-in centre, where pupils can confide in a third-party in confidence. The school has a keen sense of discipline. It has drawn up its own code of conduct and demands pupils conform to its high dress standards. There is a strong PTA, and pupils participate in the school council.

### Admissions and intake

As a Redbridge county comprehensive, the school gives priority to those applicants living in the catchment area. Preference is also given to those who have named the school as their number one choice or who have siblings already studying there.

### Achievement

Woodbridge High's educational qualities are impressive. In 2002, 53 per cent of pupils gained five or more A*–C grades. This was slightly down on 55 per cent in 2001 and the school was ranked 16th in the borough league table. The school also boasts the only ever pupil in the borough to attain 11 A* grade GCSEs. In 2002, the average A-level point score was 205.1, ranking the school 16th in the borough league table.

### Extra-curricular activities

Sport is popular and the school regularly sends teams out to compete in football, basketball, rugby, netball and hockey. Ex-pupil David Holdsworth, the Bolton footballer, runs a number of soccer courses during the year. The school also arranges a number of trips both at home and abroad, including skiing trips. The school provides pupils with the opportunity to attend homework clubs after school.

## Woodford County High School

**High Road, Woodford Green, Essex IG8 9LA** ☎ 020 8504 0611 Fax 020 8506 1880 e woodford@leonet.co.uk www.woodford.redbridge.sch.uk Ms H Cleland; Chair of Governors: Mr W Brock ⊖ Woodford **Buses:** W13, 275, 531, 645 Compulsory up to sixth form: navy skirt, blazer, white blouse, white socks **Demand:** Demand varies **Type:** Grammar for 838 girls, aged 11 to 18 **Submit application form:** Mid-October 2003 **Motto:** *Laeti Gratias Deo Agimus* (We Give Thanks to God) **School hours:** 8.30am–3.25pm **School meals:** Hot and cold available **Strong GCSE subjects:** All relatively strong **London league table position:** 21

### Profile

Woodford County High School is a prestigious school which opened in 1919. It is one of London's 19 remaining grammar schools. It is situated in Highams Manor, which was built in 1768, complete with landscaped gardens. Italian, Latin, French, German are just some of the subjects on offer.

### Admissions and intake

Pupils need to live in the catchment area and sit the school's test. There are 120 places available. At the time of going to press, none of the pupils had special needs.

### Achievement

Woodford County High is consistently in the top five per cent of schools nationwide, and often top in the Redbridge league tables. In 2002, it had an impressive 99 per cent pass rate for grades A*–C at GCSE, with an average point score of 57.2. This placed the school second in the borough league table. These results were down on 100 per cent in 2001. The average A-level point score was 357.9 ranking the school second in the borough. Ofsted visited Woodford County High in 2000 and noted that: 'This is a very good school with some exceptional features'. Standards were seen to be 'very high' and there was an 'extremely good quality of teaching'. Inspectors praised the head teacher and senior staff for providing 'outstanding direction'. However, Ofsted felt reports sent to parents should give education targets and there needed to be better provision for ICT.

### Extra-curricular activities

There are many clubs and societies available, including: Amnesty International, art club, basketball, badminton, choir, Christian Union, debating society, Muslim Society, table tennis and others. Pupils can participate in the Duke of Edinburgh's Award scheme and the Young Enterprise scheme. Many girls take part in the Redbridge Symphony Orchestra.

# Richmond upon Thames

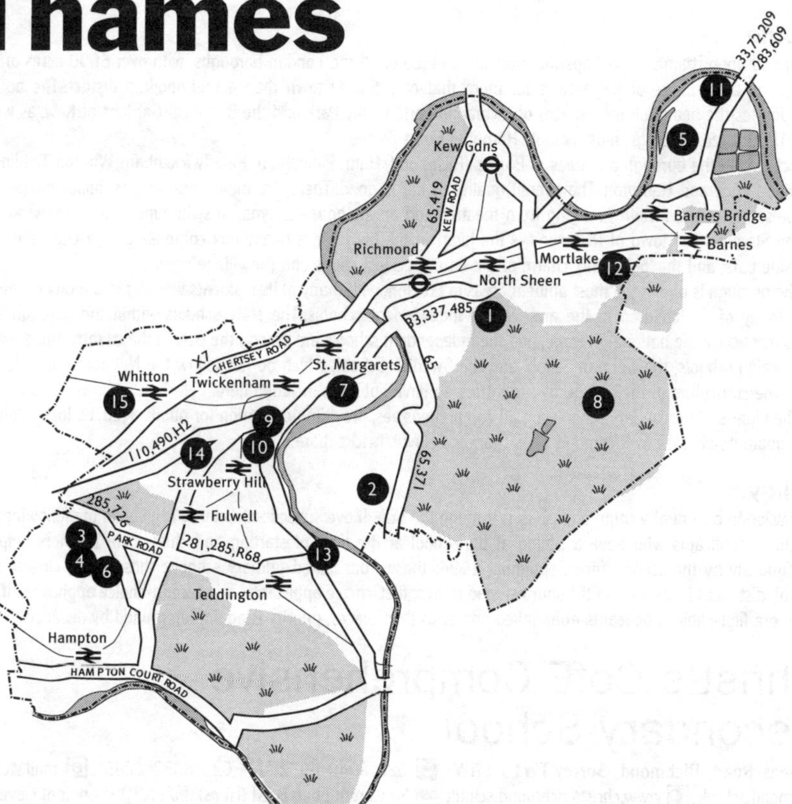


**Key**

1. Christ's CofE Comprehensive Secondary School
2. Grey Court School
3. Hampton Community College
4. Hampton School
5. The Harrodian School
6. The Lady Eleanor Holles School
7. Orleans Park School
8. The Royal Ballet School
9. St Catherine's School
10. St James Independent School for Boys
11. St Paul's School
12. Shene School
13. Teddington School
14. Waldegrave School
15. Whitton School

# Factfile

**LEA: Regal House, 1st floor, London Road, Twickenham TW1 3QB** 020 8891 1411 www.richmond.gov.uk **Chief Education Officer:** Anji Phillips **Political control of council:** Conservative **Percentage of pupils from outside the borough:** 22.8 per cent **Percentage of pupils educated outside the borough:** 10.7 per cent **London league table positions (out of 32 boroughs):** 10th

## Profile

Richmond upon Thames is perhaps the most picturesque of all the London boroughs, with over 5000 acres of open space. The atmosphere of the area is far more that of a Surrey town than a metropolitan district. The borough incorporates the beautiful open spaces of Richmond Park, Bushy Park and the Botanical Gardens at Kew, as well as over 1000 listed buildings, most notably Hampton Court Palace.

Included in the borough are areas of Barnes, Richmond, Ham, Petersham, Kew, Twickenham, Whitton, Teddington, Hampton Wick and Hampton. The overall quality of life is good. There are many local events, including fairs and festivals, and public facilities ranging from theatres and an art-house cinema, to swimming pools and Twickenham Rugby Stadium. The town of Richmond is the heart of the borough, a heady mix comprising high-class shops and riverside bars, and the 'old-world' charm of the little specialist shops and the village green.

The borough is one of the most affluent areas of London, with many of its residents working in the City or the West End. Many of the children in the area attend independent schools. The state schools within the borough attain standards above the national average, and the independent schools are among the best in the country. There are also two foreign schools, the German School and the Swedish School, which do not follow the National Curriculum but study the curriculum of their respective countries, so have not been included here.

The eight state secondary schools are all comprehensives, providing education for pupils aged 11 to 16, followed by a guaranteed place at Richmond upon Thames College, Twickenham.

## Policy

Admission to community comprehensives is through the LEA. If oversubscribed, priority is given in the following order to: those applicants who have a sibling at the school at the time of starting and children of teachers employed continuously by the school since September 1996; those from linked primary schools; those living closest to the school; distances judged along the shortest road routes; first-choice applicants; and second-choice applicants. If there are more first-choice applicants from linked primaries than places, priority is again determined by distance.

# Christ's CofE Comprehensive Secondary School

**Queens Road, Richmond, Surrey TW10 6HW** 020 8940 6982 020 8332 6085 mail@christs.richmond.sch.uk www.christs.richmond.sch.uk Mr Gareth Long B.Ed (Hons), MA, NPQH; Chair of Governors: Rev Lee Francis Dehqani Richmond, North Sheen **Buses:** 33, 337, 371 Blue blazer with school badge, black trousers or skirt, white shirt, school tie **Demand:** No figures available but 120 places (max) in 2001 **Type:** Voluntary aided comprehensive for 202 mixed pupils, aged 11 to 16 **Submit application form:** 10 November 2003 **Mission statement:** Within a Christian and equal-opportunities context, our purpose is to challenge all pupils to the highest standards of achievement. **School hours:** 8.30am–3pm **Meals:** Hot and cold available **Strong GCSE subjects:** History, mathematics **London league table position:** 397

## Profile

Christ's School has a long tradition, dating back to 1713. It is the designated Church of England secondary school for Richmond. The school is close to Richmond Park, which includes over 16 acres of playing fields. It has had a major rebuilding programme, funded by the DfES, the LEA and the school's trustees. This included a new entrance, new classrooms, offices, an extension to the library and a computer network with a dedicated ICT suite, as well as computer access in classrooms and the learning resource centre. The school has used this rebuilding as a chance to re-launch itself. A further multi-million pound building programme has begun to create a school of completely new or refurbished buildings. There have been widespread changes to the curriculum. Pupils at Key Stage 3 now follow a broad, National Curriculum-based timetable, which also includes drama, dance and Spanish. For GCSEs, all pupils study design technology, double-award science, English, English literature, French, Spanish and maths, together with non-exam courses in PRSE, PE and RE. Pupils can also choose a further three GCSEs from a range that includes food technology, history and drama. The school has a special-needs coordinator. Pupils can join the school council.

## Admissions and intake

The school's intake will now be centred on Richmond. Of the 120 places available, 70 will be available first to families from the local Church of England diocese, and then to families of other Christian denominations. The remaining 50 will be 'open' places with priority given to families living within a four-mile radius of the school in the following order: children attending church primary schools at the time of application; children with siblings at the school; and others in order of proximity along the safest travelling route.

## Achievement

In 1998, Ofsted found that, despite the fact that the attainment of most pupils was below the national average on entry, the majority make sound progress. Teaching in history, maths, dance and music was identified as largely of a good standard, and the school was seen to have 'made significant improvements since the last (1993) inspection'. However, attainment at both Key Stage 3 and GCSE was still below the national average. In 2002, 36 per cent of pupils gained five or more A*–C grades at GCSE, up from 19 per cent in 2001. The school was successfully relaunched in 2000 with a full intake of Year 7 pupils. Pupils are able to take a GNVQ in ICT, linked via the Internet to Thomas Telford School, the highest achieving state school in the country.

## Extra-curricular activities

The school is part of the OASIS (Organizing After School in School), scheme, developed in conjunction with the Prince's Trust and the West London Training and Enterprise Council. Activities available include ceramics, a choir, dance, homework study groups, Latin and poetry. The school competes locally in athletics, football, rugby and tennis. Gymnastics, volleyball and badminton are also available. There are organized day trips to museums and other places of interest, and longer trips to other European countries. Pupils are involved in fund-raising within the local community.

# Grey Court School

**Ham Street, Ham, Richmond, Surrey TW10 7HN** ☎ 020 8948 1173/020 8940 3848 Fax 020 8332 2428 e info@greycourt.richmond.sch.uk www.greycourt.richmond.sch.uk Mr T Haveland-Smith, B.Ed, MA; Chair of Governors: Mrs Barbara Adams ⇄ Richmond **Buses:** 65, 371 Navy school sweatshirt, black trousers or skirt, white shirt **Demand:** 291 first-choice applicants for 200 places in 2001/2 **Type:** Community comprehensive for 1018 mixed pupils, aged 11 to 16 **Submit application form:** 10 November 2003 **School hours:** 8.30am–3pm **Meals:** Hot and cold available, including breakfast **Strong GCSE subjects:** Art, business studies, information studies, statistics **London league table position:** 190

## Profile

Grey Court School is situated in a residential area on a 19-acre site adjoining Ham Common. The grounds even include a wildlife sanctuary. Science labs and technology workshops are well equipped and there are both IBM PC and Apple Mac computer facilities. A purpose-built arts complex houses a dance and drama studio, art rooms and a suite of music rooms. Sports facilities include on-site playing fields, tennis courts, a fully-equipped gym and a large sports hall. The library has been converted into a state-of-the-art learning resource centre. The school was chosen as the site for the 'Classroom of the Future' in conjunction with the University of the First Age, and this opened in 2003. Subjects offered cover the full basic range of the national curriculum, with additional options such as drama and classical studies and Latin. Further new subjects are available at GCSE level, such as media studies and statistics. All pupils undertake two weeks' work-experience in Year 11. Pupils can participate in the school council and special-needs pupils are well catered for. There are regular parents' evenings and the parents' association functions both as a forum for dialogue and as a source of practical and financial support. Grey Court has Beacon School status.

## Admissions and intake

Admission is through the LEA (see borough factfile). The school draws pupils from a linear catchment area extending from North Kingston to Kew. Pupils of all abilities and a wide range of backgrounds are admitted to the school. About 75 per cent of entrants were considered to be of average ability by Ofsted inspectors.

## Achievement

Sustained academic achievement is one of the school's hallmarks. Results for GCSEs prior to the last Ofsted inspection in 1998 were mostly well above the national average, with art, business studies and statistics praised as 'outstanding'. The quality of teaching was rated by inspectors as good or very good in seven out of every 10 lessons, and this was also singled out as a major strength of the school. In 2002, 63 per cent of pupils gained five or more GCSEs at grades A*–C, six per cent up on 2001, and above the borough average.

## Extra-curricular activities

The school's hobby clubs cover subjects as diverse as debating and hovercraft. There is a junior band and a music school that operates at weekends. Sport is a strength, with pupils achieving national recognition in skiing, basketball and canoeing. They have also won county championships in tennis (for which coaching is available), table tennis, athletics and badminton. Other pupils have represented Surrey in girls' football, netball, cross-country and athletics. In July the normal timetable is suspended so that all pupils can take part in a curriculum extension week. In Year 7 this involves two days studying modern languages and a day trip to St Omer in France, followed by three days of outdoor pursuits. In Year 8, pupils go on a resident history and geography field trip to Swanage, and for older pupils there are language exchange trips to France and Germany. Other school activities include a school production for Year 10 and skiing trips to Austria.

# Hampton Community College

**Hanworth Road, Hampton, Middlesex TW12 3HB** 020 8979 3399 020 8783 0086 info@hamptoncommunitycollege-hcc.richmond.sch.uk Mr J Flintoff; Chair of Governors: Mrs Rosemary Samuel Hampton Station Richmond **Buses** 111 Navy school sweatshirt, dark trousers or skirt, white shirt, school tie, black shoes **Demand:** 191 first-choice applications for 200 places ion 2001/2 **Type:** Community comprehensive for 986 mixed pupils, aged 11 to 16 **Submit application form:** 10 November 2003 **School hours:** 8.35am–2.50pm (Year 7); homework clubs are available **Meals:** Hot and cold available **Strong GCSE subjects:** All relatively strong **London league table position:** 320

## Profile

Hampton Community College, formerly the rectory school, is situated in an area called 'the Hamptons'. Its policy is to 'build on pupils' talents and strengths, to support any weaknesses and to respond to individual needs'. The school has opened a new sports and expressive arts centre, which includes four studios for two- and three-dimensional art, a music suite and a recording studio, practice rooms, an auditorium, a sports hall and a fitness suite. This was in response to increasing accommodation needs and as a supplement to its existing facilities, which include extensive playing fields. In Year 7, teaching for most subjects is within the tutor group, but ability sets are introduced in English, mathematics, languages and science. Practical subjects may be taught in smaller units than tutor groups. At the end of Year 9, pupils are prepared for 10 GCSEs. They are organized into new tutor and teaching groups on the basis of their previous achievements, overall attitude and their personal feelings plus those of their parents. Their choices are organized around the core subjects: English language and literature, maths and double-award science. Each pupil also follows at least one further course from each of the creative arts, humanities, modern languages and technology. There is the opportunity to gain certificates of competence in IT, and non-exam courses in religion, PE and careers education are also included in the timetable. Pupils are encouraged to take on responsibilities. There is a regular school council and senior representatives from Years 10 and 11 supervise some areas of the school. Form tutors supervise the secure storage of pupils' bags during breaks if they do not have a locker. Currently, all Key Stage 4 students are offered lockers and further installation is planned for Key Stage 3. There is an active parent-teacher association.

## Admissions and intake

Admission is through the LEA (see borough factfile). The school is oversubscribed and serves a diverse population, with pupils travelling from Hounslow and other boroughs. About 25 per cent of pupils are identified as having special needs.

## Achievement

Hampton Community College fosters improvement in pupils. In 2002, 46 per cent of pupils achieved five or more A*–C grades, below the national average and slightly up from 45 per cent in 2001. The 1999 Ofsted inspection identified the quality of teaching at the school as a particular strength. This was reflected in the fact that although

National Curriculum test results on entry tend to be below the national average, results at GCSE are better than most similar schools.

### Extra-curricular activities

The community role of the college is well established. It runs a nursery, an after-school club and a study support centre for Year 6 children upwards. Other activities available include participation in competitive sports for the school, a choir and orchestra, theatrical productions and subject-based clubs. Pupils also have the chance to help out in the school's print room. Lessons are supplemented with visits to theatres, museums and galleries. There are day trips and annual excursions to France. Homework clubs after school are available.

## Hampton School

**Hanworth Road, Hampton, Middlesex TW12 3HD** ☎ 020 8979 5526 📠 020 8941 7368 ⓔ admissions@hampton.richmond.sch.uk 🌐 www.hampton.richmond.sch.uk BR Martin; Chair of Governors: Peter Baker ⇌ Hampton **Buses:** R62, R68, R70, 111, 216, 285, 290, 490 (stop in walking distance); joint coach system with Lady Eleanor Holles girls' school Black blazer with school badge, dark grey trousers, white shirt, school tie, black shoes, dark socks **Demand:** No figures available **Type:** Selective independent for 1069 boys, aged 11 to 18 **Fees:** £2,755 per term, plus £151 lunch charge **Submit application form:** Mid-December 2003 **Motto:** *Praestat opes sapientia* (Wisdom Surpasses Wealth) **School hours:** 8.40am–3.10pm **Meals:** Hot and cold available **Strong GCSE subjects:** Double-award science, French, mathematics **London league table position:** 36

### Profile

Hampton School was endowed by the will of Robert Hammond in 1557. It became Hampton Grammar School in 1910 before switching to voluntary aided status in 1952. In 1975, it became fully independent once more. The school stands in a 27-acre site containing rugby and football pitches, four cricket squares, hard tennis courts and a climbing wall. A new ICT lab, with 30 workstations, and a computerized modern languages lab, were added in 1999. A new boathouse has also been built. In their first two years, pupils take all academic subjects. At GCSE, they take a core of English language and literature, maths, a modern language, chemistry and physics (or double-award science), together with three further options ranging from RE to Russian. The school has a special-needs coordinator and a PTA. There is a prefects system and a school council.

### Admissions and intake

There are different points of admission. The first is through an 11+ entrance exam, a report from the head of the applicant's current school and an interview. The second is via the Common Entrance Examination, taken at 13+. Candidates must be registered at least two years before the intended first term. A pre-test will also be administered at age 11. Common Entrance scores of 65 per cent or more, as well as another satisfactory report from the current head and a good interview, are all required. In both cases, there is a £40 registration fee and a £500 committal fee, which is refundable when the pupil finishes at the school. The final point is in the sixth form. Candidates are assessed at interview and on a report from their current school. Good all-round results and A/A* GCSE grades in the subjects intended for A-level are required. The school has a number of scholarships for music, art and academic subjects, as well as a bursary scheme.

### Achievement

Hampton has an extremely good academic record. In 2002, 98 per cent pupils gained five or more at grades A*–C. This was equal to the result of 2001 and the school was ranked third in the borough league tables. The average point score was 55.5. Results over the last few years indicate that, for both GCSE and A-level, maths and science subjects are by far the strongest. The school's A-level results in 2002 were the second best in the borough with an average point score of 464.3 for pupils taking two or more A/A-S levels. This was well above the borough and national averages.

### Extra-curricular activities

Activities range from the school newspaper, *The Lion*, to the full orchestra and choral society. There is a strong sporting tradition, with teams for rugby, football, cricket, tennis, athletics and rowing. Other school clubs include debating, Christian Union, chess and bridge. School visits are organized to France, Germany and Spain. The school's theatre company also took a play, *The London Thing*, to the 2000 Edinburgh Festival.

# The Harrodian School

**Lonsdale Road, London SW13 9QN** 020 8748 6117 020 8563 7327 James Hooke; Chair of Governors: Sir Alford Houstoun-Boswall Barnes, Barnes Bridge Grey skirt or trousers, shirt (of own choice), navy-blue jumper; games kit with school badge **Demand:** No figures available **Type:** Selective independent for 455 mixed pupils, aged 4 to 18 **Fees:** £2,450–3,450 per term, plus £170 (pre-prep)–£190 (prep & senior) **Submit application form:** Contact school for details **School hours:** 8.40am–4.20pm (end times vary according to syllabus); homework clubs are available **Meals:** Hot and cold available **Strong GCSE subjects:** All relatively strong **London league table position:** 153

## Profile

The Harrodian school is a very new school. It opened in 1993 with 65 pupils. It is co-educational from the age of 5 to GCSE level. The school has fine buildings and grounds with a traditional style library, theatre, outdoor heated swimming pool and four new, all-weather tennis courts.

## Admissions and intake

Children must be registered with the school prior to their year of entry, and there is a £50 registration fee. Pre-prep candidates have an interview with the head. Those applicants aged 7 to 9 sit a series of short tests in English, maths and science, and have an interview with the head. Senior pupils, depending on age group, take the Common Entrance Examination, and also have an interview. If places are offered, they must be secured with a £1,500 deposit.

## Achievement

The school's second GCSE results in 2002 saw 70 per cent of pupils gain five or more A*–C grades at GCSE, just down from 71 per cent the previous year. The average point score was 41.9 and this ranked the school seventh in the borough.

## Extra-curricular activities

All age groups have the opportunity to visit museums, exhibitions, theatres and concerts, and go on field trips. There is a wide variety of after-school optional activities, including art, chess, choir, drama and a homework club. The school also offers an annual skiing trip, sports day and swimming gala.

# The Lady Eleanor Holles School

**Hanworth Road, Hampton, Middlesex TW12 3HF** 020 8979 1601 020 8941 8291 office@ladyeleanorholles.richmond.sch.uk www.ladyeleanorholles.richmond.sch.uk Miss Elizabeth Candy; Chair of Governors: Mrs J Ross Hampton **Buses:** R70, 111, 285; joint coach system with Hampton School Dark grey skirt, white shirt, light grey sweatshirt or jumper, red and white school tie **Demand:** No figures available but number of places variable **Type:** Selective independent for 884 girls, aged 6 to 19 **Fees:** £2,791 per term, plus extra fees for music, speech and drama, and chess **Submit application form:** December 2003 **Mission statement:** To produce young women of grace and integrity **School hours:** 8.50am–4pm **Meals:** Hot and cold available **Strong GCSE subjects:** All relatively strong **London league table position:** 9

## Profile

LEH dates back to 1711 when a trust for its endowment was established under the will of the eponymous lady, the daughter of the 2nd Earl of Clare. Its original site was in the Cripplegate Ward of the City of London, but it moved to Hackney in 1878 and became a new middle school. The present accommodation was opened in 1936. The school stands on a 30-acre site, which includes playing fields and school gardens. Various additions have been made to the original buildings, including the dining hall and chapel, a gym and heated indoor swimming pool, extra science labs, the Ruth Garwood-Scott Art and Design Centre, a sixth-form library and common rooms and sports hall. The school also has very good IT facilities. Additional curriculum options include home economics, specialist areas of art and design, such as needlecraft, and music – one of the school's strengths. Assemblies are held three times a week.

## Admissions and intake

There are two points of entry into the senior school. The first is at 11+. Applications must be made to the head and include the relevant registration and exam fee by the beginning of December of the year prior to proposed entry.

Exams are held in January for entrance the following September. The second point of entry is in the sixth form, for which applications must be received by 1 November of the year prior to proposed entry. Acceptance is decided on GCSE results, a report from the candidate's previous school and an entrance exam sat in the autumn term. All candidates are considered on the merits of their entrance exam results for the year of proposed entry, so there is no advantage in early registration (although for administration reasons, registering one year in advance is suggested). Some entrance bursaries are made available by the Cripplegate Schools Foundation, and there are also some non-income-related scholarships for excellence in academic subjects and music.

## Achievement

The school's academic standards are some of the best in the borough. In 2002, 100 per cent of pupils received five or more A*–C grades at GCSE, a repeat of 2001's results, and the school came second in the borough. A-level results were the best in Richmond, with an average point score of 492.7. The school takes pride in its ability to nurture pupils in a wider sense, encouraging their continued growth into adults.

## Extra-curricular activities

Various sporting activities are offered including hockey, netball, swimming and gymnastics. Musical activities include junior and senior madrigal choirs, full and string orchestras and instrumental groups. An annual choral and orchestral concert is held jointly with Hampton School as well as a drama festival. A range of clubs are available, from Amnesty International to Scrabble. School trips include skiing for both juniors and seniors, weeks in France or Germany for Year 8 students and GCSE language exchanges with schools in Germany and France.

# Orleans Park School

**Richmond Road, Twickenham TW1 3BB** ☎ 020 8891 0187 📠 020 8744 0312 ✉ info@orleanspark.richmond.sch.uk 👤 Mr David Talbot BA, MA; Chair of Governors: Mr L Mann 🚉 Twickenham, St Margarets **Buses:** H22, R68, R70, 33, 290, 490 👕 Burgundy sweatshirt, white polo shirt, dark grey trousers or skirt; PE kit **Demand:** 310 first-choice applications for 200 places in 2001/2 **Type:** Community comprehensive for 1028 mixed pupils, aged 11 to 16 **Submit application form:** 10 November 2003 **Motto:** Looking Forward **School hours:** 8.40am–3.15pm; homework clubs are available **Meals:** Hot and cold available **Strong GCSE subjects:** Art, drama, English literature, history, maths **London league table position:** 225

## Profile

Orleans Park School consists of a series of purpose-designed buildings, situated on the edge of Twickenham and Richmond on a secluded 16-acre site. The original accommodation was built in the 1970s and includes seven science labs, seven technology studios, the art and music departments, a drama studio, sports hall and gym. In 1993, the school opened a new library and resource centre, an IT suite and a teaching block for the modern languages, maths, learning support, RE and social education departments. Pupils are organized into tutor groups for registration, and each year group has an assembly once a week. The school aims to teach a broad and balanced curriculum with all the core National Curriculum subjects available for both Key Stage 3 and 4. Class prefects are selected in Year 11 from volunteers. Their job is to help staff with the organization and supervision of younger pupils. Students mainly go onto sixth-form studies at Richmond, Kingston and Esher Colleges. The school has a PTA and a special-needs coordinator.

## Admissions and intake

Admission is through the LEA (see borough factfile). Orleans Park has been increasingly heavily oversubscribed since 1989. In 2001, it received 357 first-choice applications for the 200 places available for the following September. About 28 per cent of pupils are drawn from outside the borough, mainly from the Hounslow area.

## Achievement

The school's GCSE results for 1993–2002 show that the proportion of pupils attaining five or more A*–C grades was above the national average. In 2002, 64 per cent of pupils gained five or more A*–C grades. This was up from 59 per cent in 2001, and above the borough average. The results were above the national average and the school was ranked 10th in the borough league table. Particularly strong subjects are seen to be English literature, drama, history and art. The 1997 Ofsted inspection also identified English, drama, RE, maths, music and IT as being the best-taught subjects.

## Extra-curricular activities

Clubs are on offer for a variety of interests, from science to French films. These clubs operate at lunchtime and after school. Sporting activities are strongly supported, particularly athletics and rugby, although there is also a significant musical and dramatic presence, and several subject-based clubs also exist. The library and resource centre is open from 8.15am until after school, and there is an organized homework club system run by different year groups. Trips to concerts and the theatre are organized each year, together with more ambitious events such as skiing, watersports and camping holidays, language exchanges, field trips and sports tours.

# The Royal Ballet School

**White Lodge, Richmond Park, Richmond, Surrey TW10 5HR** 020 8392 8000 020 8563 0649 Miss Gailene Stock (Director); Chair of Governors: Mr David Norman Richmond **Buses:** 57, 65, 85, 213 (outside park) Grey skirt, red cardigan (girls); blue jumper and blazer, grey trousers (boys) **Demand:** No figures available but number of places variable **Type:** Selective independent for 217 mixed pupils, aged 11 to 16 **Fees:** £15,930 per year (day); £21,516 per year (boarder) **Submit application form:** Early December 2003 **Mission statement:** To train and educate outstanding classical ballet dancers for The Royal Ballet, Birmingham Royal Ballet and other top international dance companies, and in doing so to set the standard for dance training, nationally and internationally **School hours:** 8.30am–4pm, 4pm–6.30pm (evening dance classes) **Meals:** Hot and cold available **Strong GCSE subjects:** English, expressive arts, French, science **London league table position:** 164

## Profile

The Royal Ballet School was first set up in its present form in Talgarth Road in 1947. In 1955 the school moved to White Lodge, a former royal hunting lodge in the centre of Richmond Park. It has a swimming pool and well-equipped dance studios, and although the teaching rooms are compact, the class sizes are similarly small. There is a well-kept hard court for team games, a small but satisfactory ICT room and a well-stocked library. At GCSE, all pupils follow core courses in English language, maths, sciences, French, dance and expressive arts. Pupils can also select two further GCSE courses from English literature, art, history, music and geography. There is a specially timetabled session for PHSE. At age 16, pupils can move to the upper school based in Covent Garden to study A-levels. However, the A-level curriculum is rather narrow – pupils take two, one each year – and there is less evidence of careers advice than in other schools.

## Admissions and intake

Candidates are selected on their ability to dance, rather than academic ability. However, according to Ofsted in 1999, the standardized tests given in Year 7 show that the school has an academically strong intake. Competition for places is extremely fierce. There is an international audition procedure to seek out potential pupils. Candidates have preliminary auditions in centres worldwide, although overseas pupils may submit their initial audition on video. The short-listed candidates are later invited to attend a final audition in London. Academic tests are also taken, but have no bearing on the entrance application.

## Achievement

In addition to the excellent standards of dance teaching, results at both Key Stage 3 and GCSE are well above the national average. In 2002, 88 per cent of pupils gained five or more GCSEs at A*–C grades, equalling the results of 2001. The school was ranked eighth in the borough. The average A-level point score was 97.4, ranking the school fifth out of five schools in the borough. French, expressive arts, science and English were singled out by Ofsted as particular strengths. Inspectors also noted that pupils from abroad made quick progress towards fluency in English. Despite the rigours of their schedule, pupils' attitudes and behaviour are exemplary.

## Extra-curricular activities

There are historical visits to the Imperial War Museum and Hampton Court Palace. Geography fieldwork takes place, and there are trips to drama, music and – of course – ballet performances. Pupils can participate in the annual drama production, music concerts and a 'summer fayre'. Workshop sessions are held by visiting groups, such as African drumming groups, and pupils can compete in dance competitions. Fund-raising concerts are performed for charities within the local community.

# St Catherine's School

**Cross Deep, Twickenham TW1 4QJ** 020 8891 2898 020 8744 9629 admissions@stcatherineschool.co.uk www.stcatherineschool.co.uk Mrs T Barganza; Chair of Governors: Mrs B Lane Twickenham **Buses:** Coach service to and from Fulham Black blazer and jumper with white edging, black skirt and shoes, white shirt and socks, school tie **Demand:** No figures available but number of places variable **Type:** Selective independent for 355 girls, aged 3 to 17 **Fees** (per term): £1,680 (pre-primary), £2,200 (Years 10 to 11) **Submit application form:** No cut-off date **Motto:** *Non verba sed facta* (Not Words but Deeds) **School hours:** 8.40am–3.30pm (prep), 8.40am–3.55pm (senior) **Meals:** Hot and cold available **Strong GCSE subjects:** All relatively strong **London league table position:** 122

## Profile

St Catherine's has been educating girls in Twickenham since 1914. It was established by the Sisters of Mercy and is the only Catholic independent school for girls in West London. The school occupies a site which was once part of the gardens of the poet Alexander Pope's riverside villa. RE is a strong feature of the timetable, with assemblies and school Masses held daily. Classrooms, particularly the science labs, are well-equipped. There is a school library and a variety of IT facilities. The art department is also well-maintained and features a ceramics workshop and photography studio. There are extensive sports facilities, including a heated indoor swimming pool, hockey pitch, running track and tennis and netball courts. The school's teaching meets the demands of the National Curriculum, while allowing for a greater range and flexibility of study. Additional subjects include classical civilization, ceramics (for pre-GCSE pupils only), and home economics. At GCSE, all girls study a core group of subjects: English, English literature, maths, science (double-award), RE and a modern language. They can then choose three further GCSE subjects from history, geography, drama, German, classical civilization, art, music and home economics. Pupils' progress is constantly monitored to ensure the highest standards. The majority of pupils continue their studies to A-levels and university, and the school's careers office takes an active role in advising pupils. The school has a special-needs coordinator. Although the school does not have a formal PTA, it does have Fast Friends of St Catherine's.

## Admissions and intake

The small size and good reputation of St Catherine's makes for fierce competition for the limited number of places it has available. The admissions system varies according to the age at which the candidate hopes to enter. For the prep school, an assessment is made of their current performance and they undergo an interview. Candidates for the senior school sit an entrance exam, taken in January for entry the following September. In both cases, there is a non-refundable £35 registration fee and an entrance deposit of either £250 (for the prep) or £500 (for the senior school, of which half goes towards the first term's fees and half is refunded on leaving the school). Scholarships of up to 50 per cent of fees are available at the head's discretion. Pupils go on to a variety of sixth forms.

## Achievement

The school has a very high academic standard and consistently performs above the borough average. In 2002, 85 per cent of pupils gained five or more GCSEs at grades A*–C, up from 81 per cent in 2001. The school was ranked fifth in the borough league table.

## Extra-curricular activities

There are many clubs on offer during lunchtimes and after school. Drama activities include plays and musicals. There is a junior orchestra and choir, as well as a senior choir, wind band and string group. The school has sports teams in all age groups for netball, hockey, swimming and athletics, and there are clubs for badminton, aerobics and tennis. A range of travel opportunities is organized, such as skiing and annual trips to Germany and France.

# St James Independent School for Boys

**Pope's Villa, 19 Cross Deep, Twickenham TW1 4QG** 020 8892 2002 020 8892 4442 stjames@boysschool.co.uk www.stjamesschools.co.uk Mr Nicholas Debenham; Chair of Governors: Mr RJ Pincham Strawberry Hill **Buses:** R68, 33 and daily school bus from Victoria Station via South Kensington and Hammersmith Blue blazer, light blue shirt, grey trousers, house tie, black shoes; grey suit may be worn after 16th birthday **Demand:** No figures available but c.20 places oversubscribed **Type:** Selective independent for 262 boys, aged 10 to 19 **Fees:** £2,400–2,480 per term, plus £820 for weekday boarders (discounts for families with multiple children) **Submit application form:** No cut-off date **School hours:** 8.10am–4.15pm **Meals:** Hot and cold available **Strong GCSE subjects:** Mathematics, science **London league table position:** 106

## Profile

The St James Schools were first founded in 1975 to provide continual education for boys and girls aged 4½ to 18. They were set up on the initiative of a group of parents and others who shared a common philosophical attitude. The senior boys' school stands on the one-time site of the riverside residence of the poet Alexander Pope. It occupies buildings which date back to 1844 and offers comprehensive facilities. The school considers itself to have 'a radical approach to education'. The stated belief is that pupils will benefit from studying the best that civilization has produced: 'Give them the King James Bible, Shakespeare, Mozart, Homer, Plato...Latin, Greek and Sanskrit...real insight into mathematics and science... Knowledge sets free, and ignorance binds. This is the essence.' Accordingly, the timetable for each year group includes non-exam subjects such as philosophy and the British constitution. Boys in the lower and upper fourth and fifth forms are required to attend school on some Saturday mornings for coursework. The school has a special-needs coordinator.

## Admissions and intake

Boys can enter the school at the ages of 11, 13 and 16. At 11+, there are entrance exams held in January for entry in the following September and an interview. Pupils entering at 13+ will have passed the Common Entrance Examination prior to their acceptance. Admittance to the sixth form is decided on the basis of an interview, together with the applicant's GCSE results; As or Bs are required in any subject being studied at A-level, with a good range of passes needed in others. Parents who wish to enter boys at other ages should contact the head. The school offers some bursaries and there are a number of scholarships for entrants who display particular promise in any field, not necessarily academic. The majority of pupils travel daily from their homes, but there are facilities for those who wish to board during the week.

## Achievement

Although the school states that it 'caters for a wide range of ability, from Oxbridge entrants to those whose talents are less academic', exam results and teaching at St James School for Boys are of a consistently high quality. In 2002, 83 per cent of pupils gained five or more GCSEs at grades A*–C . This was down from 96 per cent in 2001 and the school was ranked fourth in the borough. The average A-level point score for pupils was 271.3, ranking St James fourth in the borough. Scientific subjects and maths appear to be particular strengths.

## Extra-curricular activities

Additional activities and sports clubs available include sailing, basketball, climbing, fencing and squash. Sport is compulsory – rugby, cross-country and swimming in winter and cricket, rowing and athletics in summer. Pupils can take part in the Duke of Edinburgh's Award scheme and the Army Cadet Force Unit. There are also dramatic productions and concerts performed by the school. Trips are regularly organized, including skiing trips to France.

# St Paul's School

**Lonsdale Road, Barnes, London SW13 9JT** ☎ 020 8748 9162 Fax 020 8748 9557 e HMSec@stpaulsschool.org.uk 🌐 www.stpaulsschool.org.uk Head RS Baldock; Chair of Governors: David Tate Rail Barnes Tube Hammersmith **Buses:** 33, 67, 72, 209; a school bus also runs daily from Henley's Corner via Finchley Road, Swiss Cottage and Baker Street, and from Walton via Kingston Uniform Dark grey or black trousers, tie **Demand:** No figures available but c.200 places oversubscribed **Type:** Selective independent for 814 boys, aged 7 to 19 **Fees** (per term): Colet Court prep school – £3,065 (day); senior school – £3,915 (day), plus £1,910 (boarder) **Submit application form:** Contact school for details **Motto:** *Fide et literis* (Faith and Knowledge) **School hours:** 8.40am–4.15pm **Meals:** Hot and cold available **Strong GCSE subjects:** All relatively strong **London league table position:** 7

## Profile

St Paul's was founded in 1509 by John Colet, Dean of St Paul's Cathedral. In 1968, the school was transferred from its old site in the City to the present 40-acre site on the south bank of the Thames. Facilities are nothing if not luxurious. A large, well-stocked library offers over 20,000 books, CD-ROMs and Internet access. There is a new technology block and a large sports centre includes a swimming pool, squash courts and gym. Playing fields and tennis courts are also on-site. There is even a 300-seat theatre and a school boathouse on the bank of the Thames. Anglican services are held daily in the school chapel, although boys of all faiths are welcome and attendance is voluntary. For GCSEs, all pupils take English, French, maths, chemistry, physics and biology, plus one creative or technical subject and three humanities. At A-level, the choice is much more flexible with options ranging from ancient history to Japanese. According to the prospectus 'every effort is made to meet the needs of the individual boy and to encourage him to work to the best level of which he is capable'. Progress is closely monitored and parents can meet teachers to discuss their sons' development. The school has both a PTA and a school council. There are two special-needs coordinators. Former pupils include John Milton, the Duke of Marlborough, GK Chesterton and Field Marshal Montgomery.

### Admissions and intake

Admission to St Paul's is a long-term consideration. The first step is registration on the waiting list (£100 fee), as early as the child's birth. A reference is subsequently required from the head of the candidate's current school. Boys entering the prep school at age 7+ or 8+ sit a competitive entrance exam during the spring term. Boys entering the senior school usually do so at 13+, after taking the Common Entrance Examination at their prep school and an interview. Boys may sometimes enter at later stages subject to assessment of their GCSE progress. The school also offers 20–30 foundation scholarships in a variety of subjects/areas each year.

### Achievement

The school has a long tradition of excellence. Academic standards are high, with the vast majority of pupils continuing their education to A-level and university. In 2002, 99 per cent of pupils achieved five or more GCSEs at grades A*–C and the school came top of the borough. A-level results were third best in the borough, with an average point score for pupils taking two or more A/AS-levels of 429.4.

### Extra-curricular activities

Sports available include rugby, cricket, rowing and fives. There are more than 30 extra-curricular societies at the school, from an orchestra to a film-making club. There is a Duke of Edinburgh's Award scheme and a Christian Union. Regular school trips are organized, including mountaineering, skiing parties and exchange trips.

## Shene School

**Park Avenue, East Sheen, London SW14 8RG** ☎ 020 8876 8891 📠 020 8392 9694 ⓔ general@shene.richmond.sch.uk 🌐 www.shene.richmond.sch.uk ✉ Mrs Judith Gavars; Chair of Governors: Mr Michael Lumley 🚉 Barnes, Mortlake **Buses:** 33, 337 👔 Navy sweatshirt with school logo, black skirt or trousers, white shirt, school tie **Demand:** 399 first-choice applications for 200 places in 2001/2 **Type:** Community comprehensive Language College for 1038 mixed pupils, aged 11 to 16 **Submit application form:** 10 November 2003 **Mission statement:** We will work together towards excellence for all at Shene School. **School hours:** 8.30am–3.15pm; homework clubs are available **Meals:** Hot and cold available **Strong GCSE subjects:** Art, history, RE **London league table position:** 449

### Profile

Shene School is set in attractive grounds close to Richmond Park and recently gained Technology College status. It enjoys good facilities, which are well-decorated and cared for. These include a purpose-built art centre and IT suite. There is an all-weather sports pitch on-site along with a well-equipped sports hall, and the school has a new gym and dance studio. The teaching facilities have also been recently updated, with a new maths building completed in 1999. The large numbers of pupils can make the facilities seem rather crowded. In 1999, Ofsted noted that it was necessary for one year group to finish lessons 10 minutes early before lunch, in order to control the flow of pupils through the canteen and get everyone served within the break period. Shene has a broad and balanced curriculum, and classes are organized according to ability. Pupils with special needs are well supported. There is a school council, through which pupils are encouraged to put forward their ideas. The school has an educational philosophy centred around its four core values: self-reliance, teamwork, improvement and achievement. One way in which these values are upheld is in the home-school agreement, which all parents and children are asked to sign before joining the school. Parents are kept informed through termly grade sheets, an annual report and a parent-teacher consultation evening held each year. In 1999, the school arranged for a number of pupils to attend GNVQ part 1 courses at Richmond Tertiary Education College.

### Admissions and intake

Admission is through the LEA (see borough factfile). Only 26 per cent of pupils are actually from the borough, the rest coming from neighbouring boroughs. Some pupils travel considerable distances.

### Achievement

According to Ofsted, Shene School has 'significantly more strengths than weaknesses'. Despite the fact that on entry, pupils' results were 'somewhat below' the national average, results for both Key Stage 3 and GCSE were well above average when compared to similar comprehensives across the country. In 2002, 30 per cent of pupils gained five or more A*–C grades, below the national average. This was 12 per cent down on 2001's results and the school was placed 15th in the borough league table. In recent years, the best results have been for history, RE, drama and art. Geography, art, modern languages and RE were singled out by Ofsted as the best-taught subjects. Inspectors noted that, overall, the atmosphere at the school was good. There is a high level of mutual respect and cooperation between staff and pupils. Pupils go to a variety of sixth forms.

### Extra-curricular activities

A variety of activities on offer at lunchtime and after school include sports, drama, music, IT, chess and a homework club. Trips are arranged to museums and other places of interest, in order to enhance the teaching of certain subjects. There are also excursions abroad. The school holds an annual programme of art exhibitions, concerts and plays.

# Teddington School

**Broom Road, Teddington Middlesex TW11 9PJ** 020 8943 0033 020 8943 2999 info@teddington.richmond.sch.uk Mr RT Weeks; Chair of Governors: Mr J Stephen Teddington, Hampton Wick **Buses:** 281 Black blazer, black trousers or skirt, white shirt, red and black school tie **Demand:** 382 first-choice applications for 225 places in 2001/2 **Type:** Community comprehensive for 1160 mixed pupils, aged 11 to 16 **Submit application form:** 10 November 2003 **Motto:** *Merit qui laborat* (He Who Works is Rewarded) **School hours:** 8.45am–3.15pm **Meals:** Hot and cold available **Strong GCSE subjects:** Arts subjects, English, humanities **London league table position:** 241

### Profile

Teddington School stands in a beautiful location, its grounds extending to the River Thames opposite Trowlock Island. There are good facilities for all subjects, particularly practical and technical subjects such as science, for which there are 10 labs. The school's most outstanding features are the 1985 music and drama block, including extensive rehearsal and production facilities, and its resource centre, with a very well-equipped television and film studio. Sporting facilities include a gym and sports hall, as well as an artificial grass sports area. Most pupils study for 10 GCSEs, including more unusual subjects such as Latin, which are studied outside of lesson time. In 1999/2000, about 40 pupils in Year 10 were able to take foundation courses leading to GNVQs at the Richmond Tertiary Education College. Pupils are encouraged to exercise responsibility within the 'buddy' system, which aims to help new pupils adapt to life at the school. There is reasonable support for those pupils with special needs, although most help is provided outside classes. Parents are automatically made members of the PTA, which organizes a number of events.

### Admissions and intake

Admission is through the LEA (see borough factfile). The school is popular and oversubscribed, and has good links with a number of feeder primary schools, some of which are outside Richmond LEA. Tests administered at primary schools prior to entry show that pupils' attainment is already above the national average. The school has twice as many boys as girls, and a small minority of pupils (2.2 per cent), have English as their second language.

### Achievement

Standards of attainment at the Teddington School are generally high, though the results dipped in 2002, as 55 per cent of pupils obtained five or more grades A*–C at GCSE, down from 72 per cent in 2001, but still above the national average. The school was ranked 11th in the borough. According to the 2000 Ofsted report, teachers work hard to maintain and improve standards. Inspectors noted that history, geography and RE were particular strengths at GCSE, achieving 'very good' standards, and the school's results and standards overall were considered above the national average for both Key Stage 3 and GCSE, and well above the results of similar schools elsewhere. However, Ofsted highlighted some issues in the provision of IT and RE, which are being addressed by the school. Most pupils were considered well-motivated and well-behaved.

### Extra-curricular activities

There are many lunchtime clubs available, often related to subjects studied, including a girls-only computer club. The school makes good provision for a variety of dance, drama and musical events. Coaching is available for cricket, football and netball. Approximately 45 per cent of all pupils take part in extra-curricular sporting activities in some way. Visits are arranged in relation to subject areas, for example, theatre trips in English or fieldwork in geography. There is also an annual exchange visit to France for over 60 pupils in Year 8.

## Waldegrave School

**Fifth Cross Road, Twickenham TW2 5LH** 020 8894 3244 020 8893 3670 info@waldegrave.richmond.sch.uk www.waldegrave.richmond.sch.uk Ms Heather Flint MA, B.Soc.Sc; Chair of Governors: Mrs J Fellows Fullwell, Strawberry Hill **Buses:** H22, R70, 33, 110, 267, 281, 290, 490 Royal blue V-neck sweater with school logo, black kilt, white blouse with collar, black shoes **Demand:** 426 first-choice applicants for 200 places in 2001/2 **Type:** Community comprehensive for 1034 girls, aged 11 to 16 **Submit application form:** 10 November 2003 **Mission statement:** For girls and staff to enjoy learning, experience success and to develop their full potential **School hours:** 8.45am–3.10pm; homework clubs are available **Meals:** Hot and cold available **Strong GCSE subjects:** English, mathematics, science **London league table position:** 134

### Profile

Waldegrave is the only single-sex state school in the borough. It is set within a compact yet attractive 14.5 acre site with its own playing fields. Facilities include a well-stocked library and resource centre, a drama studio, gym, specialist food technology and textiles rooms and a photographic darkroom. There are also seven science labs, technology workshops, music rooms and two dedicated IT rooms, as well as clusters of computers in some teaching rooms. The school has been awarded the prestigious Investors in People Award. It is also designated a Beacon School, running workshops and seminars and offering advice on curriculum issues for other schools. Pupils are usually entered for at least nine GCSEs, including English, maths, double-award science and technology, plus a choice of a modern language and a mix of creative arts and humanities subjects. Parents are kept informed through written profiles, interim monitoring sheets and consultation evenings. The school has a special-needs coordinator.

### Admissions and intake

Admission is through the LEA. Priority for places is determined, in order, by: girls with a sister at the school at the time of entry; daughters of teachers employed by the school since before September 1996; girls whose parents expressed a preference for single-sex education and who live in a rectangular area based around link primary schools (boundaries set by the John Betts School in Hammersmith to the north, St John's School in Kingston to the south, St Faith's School in Wandsworth to the east and Forge Lane in Hounslow to the west); and those girls whose parents did not express a preference and who live in the same rectangular area. The school is heavily oversubscribed.

### Achievement

Waldegrave is the highest achieving state school in the borough. In 2002, 75 per cent of pupils gained five or more GCSEs at A*–C grades and the school was ranked sixth in the borough. Ofsted visted the school in 2002 and described it as 'a very good school that provides a high quality education for its pupils'. GCSE results are well above average and higher than would be expected given the pupils' attainment on entry. Very good results are achieved in English, mathematics and science. Over 80 per cent of Waldegrave's pupils go on to further education.

### Extra-curricular activities

After school, a homework club, spelling and handwriting clubs all supplement the basic curriculum. Sports also have a strong presence, with rugby, football, cricket, jazz dance and gymnastics on offer in addition to the traditional hockey and netball. There is an orchestra, a choir and instrumental groups. All tutor groups organize charity events, and there are school trips linked to most subjects, including exchange visits to France and Germany, and holiday and study tours in Britain and abroad.

# Whitton School

**Percy Road, Twickenham TW2 6JW** ☎ 020 8894 4503 ℻ 020 8894 0690 ✉ info@whitton.richmond.sch.uk Head: Ms S Raynor B.Ed, MA; Chair of Governors: Mrs Anne Rogers ⇌ Whitton **Buses:** H22, 110 Uniform: Black trousers or skirt, black school sweatshirt, grey school polo shirt **Demand:** 131 first-choice applications for 200 places in 2001/2 **Type:** Community comprehensive Sports College for 1007 mixed pupils, aged 11 to 16 **Submit application form:** 10 November 2003 **Motto:** High Expectations, Achieving Success **School hours:** 8.40am–3.10pm; homework clubs are available **Meals:** Hot and cold available **Strong GCSE subjects:** Leisure and tourism, PE, RE **London league table position:** 423

## Profile

Whitton School was opened in 1959 and enjoys attractive, purpose-built accommodation set in pleasant grounds. There are particularly good facilities for science, business and information studies, English, art and music, including a fully equipped food technology suite. The sports facilities are also particularly good, and include the Whitton Sports Centre, the local community fitness centre, which has a state-of-the-art fitness studio and recently refurbished changing rooms. The school recently gained Sports College status. According to the LEA website, there has also been investment in the development of the library and resource centre. Whitton has received the Investors in People Award, reflecting its commitment to the professional development of all its staff. The school offers a broad curriculum, covering all the National Curriculum subjects. At GCSE, pupils take the core subjects of English, English literature, maths and double-award science, plus non-exam classes in PSHE and PE. In addition, they also study French or German, a technology subject and two subjects from art and design, drama, music, PE (GCSE), geography, history, RE and information studies. As an alternative to studying the two subjects, they can take a GNVQ in leisure and tourism. NVQ link courses are also offered by Richmond College, as well as extended work experience to selected pupils in Year 11. Twice a year, parents are invited to attend an individual 'tutor review' meeting as well as the traditional parents' evening. The Whitton School newsletter is sent home once a month. Truancy is a problem at the school, and its rate of unauthorized absence was high in 2000 at 3.5 per cent, compared with the national average of 1.0 per cent. The school has a school council and a PTA. There is a special-needs coordinator and a coordinator for gifted and talented pupils.

## Admissions and intake

Admission is through the LEA (see borough factfile). The school is regularly oversubscribed. Most pupils live locally in Whitton, Twickenham or Hounslow and have attended primary schools in the borough.

## Achievement

The school has a good reputation in its surrounding area and with the community it serves. In 2001, 31 per cent of pupils gained five or more GCSEs at A*–C grades, below the national average and five per cent down on 2001. The school was ranked 14th in the borough. The most recent Ofsted report was in 2002 when the school was described as 'effective overall'. Standards of attainment were seen to be improving, particularly in the lower school where they are in line with the national average. Standards are lower in the upper school and below average in comparison with similar schools. However, average pupils were seen to attain well. Strong GCSE subjects include RE, leisure and tourism and PE. Inspectors praised the 'very good leadership' of the head teacher and the school was seen to have tackled almost all of the areas for improvement identified in the last Ofsted report in 1996. However, attendance was seen to be 'very poor' which contributes to below average attainment in Key Stage 4. A large majority of pupils continue their studies after leaving at age 16.

## Extra-curricular activities

The range of extra-curricular activities offered at Whitton is outstanding, with one of the most impressive aspects being dance. The annual dance show is a major performance in which dozens of pupils take part. Pupils from Years 8 and 10 have the opportunity to go on a French exchange with children in Issy-les-Moulineaux, near Paris, and several other trips take place both at home and abroad, including the popular Whitton ski course. A number of lunchtime and evening clubs are available, including chess, Latin, hockey, an after-school homework club and breakfast clubs.

# Southwark

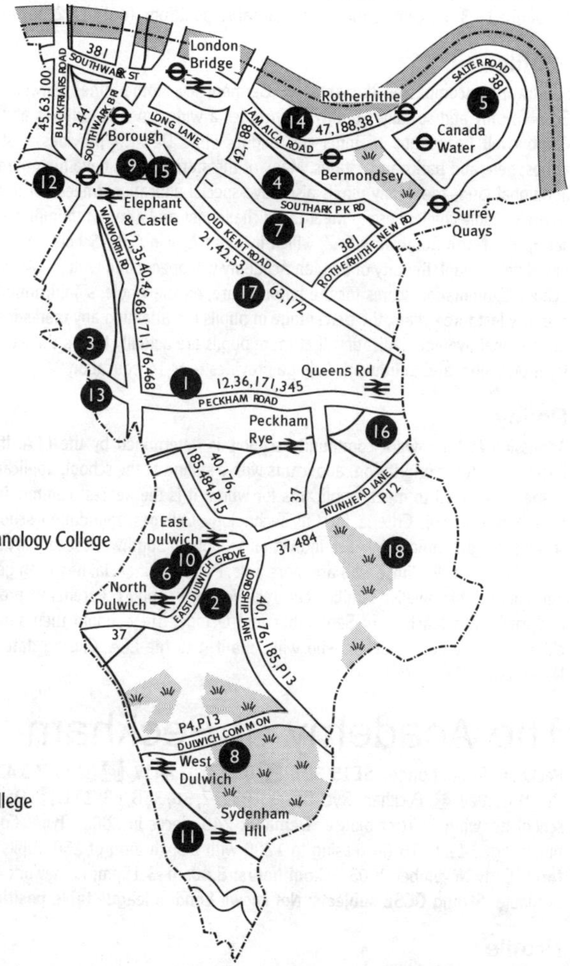


**Key**

1 The Academy at Peckham
2 Alleyn's School
3 Archbishop Michael Ramsey Technology College
4 Aylwin Girls' School
5 Bacon's College
6 Charter School
7 City of London Academy
8 Dulwich College
9 Geoffrey Chaucer Technology College
10 James Allen's Girls' School
11 Kingsdale Secondary School
12 Notre Dame RC Girls' School
13 Sacred Heart RC Secondary School
14 St Michael's RC School
15 St Saviour's and St Olave's CofE School
16 The St Thomas the Apostle College
17 Walworth School
18 Waverley School

# Factfile

**LEA: Education Department, John Smith House, Walworth Road, London SE17 1JL** 020 7525 5000 www.southwark.gov.uk **Director of Education:** Dr Roger Smith **Political control of council:** Liberal **Percentage of pupils from outside the borough:** 15.3 per cent **Percentage of pupils educated outside the borough:** 15.3 per cent **London league table positions (out of 32 boroughs):** 28th

## Profile

Southwark encompasses the areas of Bermondsey, Rotherhithe, Walworth, Peckham, Dulwich and Camberwell. Economically and socially, Southwark includes a wide range of cultures and ethnicities. Peckham, Bermondsey and Camberwell bear signs of inner-city blight, while Dulwich provides a stark contrast, with its affluent, village atmosphere and parks and estates. Many of the state schools have high numbers of pupils who speak English as an additional language. Many pupils also have special educational needs or qualify for free school meals. These factors create sizeable challenges. To meet these challenges and attempt to improve standards, the government has recently set up the North Southwark EAZ, which includes Aylwin Girls' School and Geoffrey Chaucer. In September 2003, a brand new school, the City of London Academy will open along with The Academy at Peckham, formerly Warwick Park School. Examination scores for the borough are, on the whole, significantly lower than national averages. However, over the last three years, the percentage of pupils not attaining any marks in GCSEs and GNVQs has also been below the national average, indicating that more pupils are actually taking the exams. Six of the schools have on-site sixth form provision, and Southwark College provides over-16 education.

## Policy

Admission to Southwark community schools is determined by the LEA. If oversubscribed, admission criteria are based, in order of priority, on: applicants with a sibling at the school; applicants having specific needs that the school is specially suited to meet; applicants for whom it is the nearest community school; and applicants for whom it is the nearest school. Criteria for City Technology Colleges, foundation schools, independents and voluntary aided schools, are determined by each individual school. All Southwark secondary schools have provisions for children with special needs or for those who are more able. Pupils in financial need can get free school meals and clothing grants, and children of traveller families can receive extra support. Parents of prospective applicants should visit schools and meet with teachers in September and October. They should then submit the secondary transfer form to the child's primary head teacher, who will submit it to the LEA. Closing dates for applications are generally in early November.

# The Academy at Peckham

**Peckham Road, London SE15 5DZ** 020 7703 4417 020 7703 4305 Peter Crook; Chair of Governors: Rev D Hartley Peckham Rye **Buses:** P3, 12, 36, 36B, 63, 171, Dark grey trousers or skirt, navy blue blazer, school tie, white shirt or blouse **Demand:** 240 places in 2003 **Type:** Community comprehensive for 850 mixed pupils, aged 11 to 16 (increasing to 1200 with a sixth form of 250 pupils opening in 2004) **Submit application form:** Early November 2003 **School hours:** 8.40am–3.15pm; homework clubs are available **Meals:** Hot and cold available **Strong GCSE subjects:** Not known **London league table position:** Not yet known

## Profile

The Academy at Peckham opens in September 2003 and was formerly Warwick Park School. When the school opens it will have a new all-weather pitch and a TV/radio studio. Current facilities include a music block, drama studio and computer suites. Over the next three years £20 million will be spent on creating brand new teaching areas with a strong emphasis on technology. A sixth form will open in 2004. The full National Curriculum will be taught and pupils can also choose from GCSEs in subjects such as dance, technology and drama. GNVQs and City and Guilds courses will also be available. Parents will be kept informed through end of year reports and parents' evenings. Support will be provided for pupils with special educational needs and for those who speak English as an additional language.

## Admissions and intake

Applications should be made direct to the school. If oversubscribed, priority is given to applicants with statements of special educational need. Other applicants will be required to take a non-verbal reasoning test and will then be placed in one of five ability bands. Within each band, priority will be given in order to applicants with siblings at the school; applicants attending one of the EAZ primary schools; applicants not attending an EAZ primary school.

### Achievement

As The Academy is a new school, no exams have been taken yet.

### Extra-curricular activities

Departments such as drama, geography, art and PE will offer after-school clubs, study trips and visits to perfomances and exhibitions.

## Alleyn's School

**Townley Road, Dulwich, London SE22 8SU** 020 8557 1478/1500 020 8557 1462 enquiries@alleyns.org.uk www.alleyns.org.uk Colin Diggory; Chair of Governors: Mr R Cousins East Dulwich, Brixton Brixton **Buses:** P13, P15, 37, 484; for an additional fee, coach services run by the Dulwich Foundation bring in pupils who live further out Dark grey trousers or skirt, navy blue blazer with school badge, school tie, white shirt, black shoes **Demand:** 500–600 applications for 135 places **Type:** Selective independent for 1128 mixed pupils, aged 5 to 18 **Fees:** Contact school for details **Submit application form:** Contact school for details **Motto:** God's Gift **School hours:** 9am–3.45pm, 9am–3.25pm (Thurs); homework clubs available **Meals:** Hot and cold available **Strong GCSE subjects:** All relatively strong **London league table position:** 40

### Profile

Established as a boys' school in 1882, Alleyn's School is descended from founder Edward Alleyn's College of God's Gift, founded in 1620. The school became South London's first co-ed independent school in 1976. It has been developing continuously since the 1970s, with recent additions including a new sports hall, indoor swimming pool, technology complex, music school, maths and computer suites, seminar building, pavilion and all-weather pitch. The school also has facilities for drama and art. Due to the selective intake, there is no streaming, although maths setting is introduced in Year 8. Pupils study two languages by the end of Year 9 and at least one for GCSE. French, Spanish, Latin and German are on offer. The sixth form can choose from 24 subjects, including business studies, design technology and theatre studies. Careers tutors offer careers and A-level advice and a work-experience programme follows GCSEs. Pastoral and academic guidance is provided by housemasters, school heads and form tutors. The school has a written policy on behaviour, which includes bullying. Parents are kept informed by way of bi-annual progress reports, homework diaries, parents' evenings and separate meetings if necessary. The school does not provide remedial teaching for special-needs pupils, although time allowances may be made on examinations. Former pupils include the writers CS Forester and VS Pritchett; wartime scientific genius Prof R V Jones; Dr Stuart Blanch, Archbishop of York; Sir Ronald Leach, Chairman of KPMG; and the actors Julian Glover and Simon Ward.

### Admissions and intake

Most of Alleyn's applicants come from state primary and private preparatory schools, while 35 per cent continue on from Alleyn's Junior School. Main entry is through an exam. There is a limited number of fee-paying places, bursaries and scholarships, for which the school takes into account exam performance, interview impressions and reports from previous schools. Twelve scholarships are awarded for music, art and sports, contingent on exceptional aptitude and potential. Up to 10 half-fee bursaries are also available. Entry into the upper school is conditional upon good GCSE results along with an interview, recommendation by the pupil's previous school, and a general paper.

### Achievement

Alleyn's has a very strong record for GCSEs and A-levels, scoring well above both national and borough averages. In 2002, 99 per cent of pupils scored five or more A*–C grades and the school was ranked second in the borough. At A-level, the average point score per pupil was 437.9, again placing the school top of the borough.

### Extra-curricular activities

Clubs and societies available include homework clubs, a Christian Union and a club that runs the school telephone system. Holiday activities have included trips to Greece and Italy and a modern language exchange programme. The school's musical groups perform throughout the term, and a number of plays and musicals are staged each year. Sports activities include fives for boys and badminton, football and cricket for girls. All pupils join either the CCF, the Duke of Edinburgh's Award scheme or community service in Year 10.

# Archbishop Michael Ramsey Technology College

**Farmers Road, Camberwell, London SE5 0UB** 020 7701 4166 020 7701 8461 info@amrtc.southwark.sch.uk www.amrtc.southwark.sch.uk Mrs WDC Parmley B.Ed (Hons), Dip.TEFL, LTCL; Chair of Governors: Mr M Seaton Elephant and Castle Oval, Elephant and Castle, Kennington **Buses**: 12, 35, 36, 40, 42, 45, 68, 68A, 171, 176, 185 Up to sixth form: Grey, black, and maroon with yellow and black tie and badge, black blazers with school badge **Demand:** 240 applications for 160 places in 2001/2 **Type:** Comprehensive Church of England voluntary aided Technology College for 900 mixed pupils, aged 11 to 19 **Submit application form:** Early November 2003 **Motto:** *Omnibus reverentia* (Respect for All) **School hours:** 8.45am–3.20pm; homework clubs are available **Meals:** Hot and cold available **Strong GCSE subjects:** RE, textiles **London league table position:** 491

## Profile

This school became a Technology College in 1997. As a Church of England school, AMRTC seeks to foster Christian values, while its technology status prepares pupils for adult life and employment. The college is a member of the Central London Technology and Enterprise Council and spent half a million pounds in 1997 on improving facilities. The curriculum includes core subjects as well as expressive arts, IT, French and German. The sixth form offers a wide range of A-level subjects. GNVQ courses and National Curriculum requirements are met at all key stages. Pupils leave the school with a National Record of Achievement (NRA). Pupils can become prefects and monitors in Year 11. There are daily prayers and regular assemblies. Year 11 and sixth-form pupils undertake work experience. There are homework diaries, regular written reports and parents' meetings. Friends of AMRTC organizes events. Pupils with special needs are attended to by specialized teachers. The 2000 unauthorized absence rate was 3.0 per cent, higher than national and borough averages.

## Admissions and intake

Criteria for admission, in order of priority, are: children whose parents regularly attend an Anglican Church, whose parents attend churches of other Christian denominations or are members of other recognized religions, with siblings at AMRTC, attending Church primary schools, living close to the school, and who have other established pastoral reasons for why they would benefit from attending AMRTC. The sixth-form college has an open admissions policy, with more than half the entrants coming from other schools. All prospective pupils and their parents are interviewed prior to admission.

## Achievement

In 1998, Ofsted recommended 'special measures'. However, following a 2000 inspection, these measures were lifted. Ofsted revisited the school in 2002 and noted that the school is 'improving and has made good progress since its last inspection'. Standards were seen to be 'broadly in average in relation to similar schools'. The school's 2002 GCSE scores were below borough and national averages, with 22 per cent of pupils gaining five or more A*–C grades. This was four per cent down on 2001's results and the school was placed 15th in the borough. The average point score for pupils taking two or more A-levels in 2002 was 171.4. This ranked the school fifth in the borough.

## Extra-curricular activities

Activities include music, sports, homework clubs, chess clubs and a girls' club. Senior pupils can attend Saturday schools. Sports include football and basketball, and one former pupil competed in the 2000 Olympics. There are annual theatrical productions and regular cultural outings. The school band and choir compete nationally. Students are given the opportunity, under the Woodward Corporation, to attend other types of schools, including those in the independent sector. Pupils regularly organize fund-raising events for charities within the local community.

# Aylwin Girls' School

**55 Southwark Park Road, London SE16 3TZ** 020 7237 9316 020 7237 9204 headteacher@aylwings.biblia.net Mrs Catharine Loxton; Chair of Governors: Mr Malcolm Lowe South Bermondsey, Elephant and Castle Elephant and Castle **Buses:** P11, P13, 1, 78, 199 New uniform in 2001: light blue blouse, navy blue jumper with red and white piping, navy blue skirt/trousers, black/brown shoes; religious head scarves should be white, navy or white and navy **Demand:** 414 applications for 182 places in 2001/2 **Type:** Community comprehensive for 850 girls, aged 11 to 16 **Submit application form:** Early November 2003 **Motto:** I Care (Integrity, Confidence, Achievement, Respect, Enjoyment) **School hours:** 8.00am–3.25pm; homework clubs are available **Meals:** Hot and cold available **Strong GCSE subjects:** Drama, food technology, French **London league table position:** 413

## Profile

Aylwin Girls' School was named after Aylwin Childe, who founded Bermondsey Abbey some 1000 years ago. The school was established at its present site in 1936. Brand new school facilities have been built to house a new dining/assembly hall. Other facilities include a library with computers, sports hall/gym and tennis courts. The curriculum includes art, English, history and other core subjects. Languages include French and Spanish. Year 10 to 11 pupils take a GNVQ, choosing from subjects such as health and social care, performing arts and IT. Pupils can also take GCSEs in their mother tongues, including Bengali and Urdu. Free music tuition is provided and the school has applied to become a performing arts college. The school has strong ties with industry and the community and provides work experience and careers-education programmes. Support is provided for pupils with learning disabilities. Pastoral care is provided by heads of year. The school has a code of conduct, which condemns prejudice and discrimination. Christian and Jehovah's Witnesses groups meet regularly and there is a Muslim prayer room. Homework diaries are checked regularly by parents. There is a special-needs coordinator at the school.

## Admissions and intake

The school's intake is comprehensive and all Year 7 applicants are interviewed. Criteria for admission are the same as for other community schools (see borough factfile). If oversubscribed, places are allocated on a 'first-come, first-served' basis.

## Achievement

Upon entering the school, most pupils have below average literacy and numeracy skills, although some have very high rates of attainment. The number of pupils attaining five or more A*–C grades at GCSE in 2002 was 29 per cent, below both national and borough averages but one per cent up on 2001. The school was ranked 10th in the borough. In 2001, Ofsted noted that pupils achieve well in design and technology, dance, English, science, geography, history, modern foreign languages and vocational courses. Results match the national averages in drama, food technology and French. Inspectors praised the 'purposeful' leadership of the head teacher and described Aylwin Girl's as an 'effective school' where 'teaching is satisfactory overall'. The school no longer has serious weaknesses.

## Extra-curricular activities

The school has a wide range of clubs, including talent festivals, women's week activities, a Black History Month programme, Shakespeare performances, homework clubs and poetry workshops. Sports include netball, volleyball, football and hockey. The sports department has close ties to Millwall Football Club, Southwark Sports Department Team and the London Coaching Foundation. Musical activities include an orchestra and choir.

# Bacon's College

**Timberpond Road, Rotherhithe, London SE16 1AG** 020 7237 1928 020 7237 4501 correspondence@baconsctc.co.uk www.baconsctc.co.uk Mr Tony Perry; Chair of Governors: Mr Eugene O'Keeffe Rotherhithe, Canada Water **Buses:** N381, P13, 47, 188, 225, 381, 395, College blazer and tie, black or grey trousers, white shirt for boys; college kilt, blazer and tie, white shirt and white socks or tights for girls; Sixth form: Pupils are expected to dress smartly **Demand:** 6 first-choice applications for every 1 Year 7 place in 2001/2 **Type:** Comprehensive City Technology College for 1057 mixed pupils, aged 11 to 18 **Submit application form:** Contact school for information **Motto:** *Gloria in Excelsis Deo* (Glory to God in the Highest) **School hours:**

8.40am–3.20pm; homework clubs are available **Meals:** Hot and cold available, including breakfast **Strong GCSE subjects:** Mathematics, RE **London league table position:** 239

## Profile

Bacon's College opened in 1991. Its aim was to raise education standards and increase opportunities within a Christian framework while using an inclusive approach to a diverse population. It has a library, science labs, computer/multimedia facilities, a recording studio, dance and drama studios and a radio station. Sports facilities include a weight training/fitness centre, football pitch, and indoor cricket nets. The curriculum includes National Curriculum subjects, as well as health and sex education, religion, PE and vocational and IT skills. Sixth-form subjects include physics, maths, fashion, theology and media. Work experience placement is required for all Year 11 pupils and is incorporated into all GNVQ programmes for Key Stage 4 and post-16 pupils. Students have access to a careers suite and participate in careers-related activities. Special needs are provided for with the intention of giving all pupils access to a comprehensive curriculum. All pupils participate in daily worship. Parents receive half-termly and annual reports with at least one consultation evening per year group.

## Admissions and intake

Criteria for admission to Bacon's are technological aptitude and commitment to learning and post-16 education and training. Prospective candidates submit an application form, which is followed by oral assessment and testing, intake selection and a review procedure. Incoming Year 7 pupils are given baseline tests as an indicator of general abilities and the sixth-form intake is based on GCSE and GNVQ scores, good attendance/punctuality and evidence of commitment and motivation.

## Achievement

In 2002, Ofsted described Bacon's College as ' a good and improving school' where the GCSE results have improved every year since the college opened. There was a dramatic improvement in GCSE marks from 1996 to 2001. A total of 54 per cent of pupils achieved five or more A*–C grades in 2002, however, down from 72 per cent in 2001. These results were still above national and local averages and made the school the second best performing non-independent in the borough. The average score per pupil for A-levels was 209.3 in 2002, above the borough average, placing the school fourth in the borough. The rate of unauthorized absences was just 0.6 per cent, well below local and national averages.

## Extra-curricular activities

Activities include a performing arts club, homework clubs, a debating society, a theatre and cinema club, visiting speakers and charity events. Pupils can have musical tuition on request. The sixth form claims a tradition of excelling in computer-based technologies, and the football team has won several awards. Sixth-form students have recently been on trips to the US, Italy and Greece.

# Charter School

**Red Post Hill, London SE24 9JN** ☎ 020 7346 6600 📠 020 7346 6601 ⓔ admin@charter.southwark.sch.uk ✉ Pam Bowmaker OBE, MA; Chair of Governors: Jan Barden 🚉 North Dulwich, Herne Hill **Buses:** P4, 2, 3, 37, 40, 42, 68, 196 👔 Navy blue with light-weight fleece jacket carrying school logo in gold **Demand:** 1,039 applications for 180 places in 2001/2 **Type:** Community comprehensive for 450 mixed pupils, aged 11 to 19 **Submit application form:** Early November 2003 **School hours:** 8am–4pm; homework clubs available **Meals:** Hot and cold available **Strong GCSE subjects:** Not applicable **London league table position:** Not yet known

## Profile

The Charter School opened its doors to its first class of 150 Year 7 pupils in 2000. Located on a five-acre site in the prosperous Dulwich area, the school was founded in response to a parents' campaign for a non-selective, mixed secondary school with a sixth form. More than £15 million will be spent on new school buildings and the school places strong emphasis on technological development, with IT networking in every classroom and a school intranet. A brand new four-storey teaching block opened in September 2002. The buildings have been planned with environmental concerns in mind, incorporating energy-saving measures into their designs. Facilities include a library, music, art and design rooms, a sixth-form centre, an all-weather pitch, a gym and a hall for theatrical productions. The curriculum follows National Curriculum guidelines, with English language and literature, maths, science and technology as core subjects, including at least one modern foreign language. Personal and social education focuses on developing good relationships, and sex education is taught at the school. The sixth form, which is scheduled to open in 2005 at the latest, will include A- and AS-level courses as well as GNVQs. Arts courses available include visual arts, dance and drama, and every pupil has the opportunity to learn a musical instrument. Learning support is provided for pupils with special needs. The school is working on forming liaisons with arts organizations, sports clubs, the business community and commercial organizations. The school day is longer than usual, leading to a 20 per cent increase in learning time. Form tutors meet children individually to review progress and set targets. All modules are clearly differentiated, and pupils are grouped according to their aptitudes for individual subjects, not streamed. Class sizes vary, with basic groups of less than 30. The school has a special-needs coordinator.

### Admissions and intake

Admission is non-selective, with the process identical to that for other Southwark community schools (see borough factfile). Candidates should submit applications to the Southwark admissions department. The catchment areas include Southwark and Lambeth.

### Achievement

As Charter School has only just opened, it has no exam results as yet.

### Extra-curricular activities

The school has a number of activities available from university-style classes on subjects such as philosophy to extra music, drama, sports, crafts, computer training and additional languages, including Spanish and Latin. It is also working to create links with various London music colleges and the London Symphony Orchestra, as well as theatres, arts organizations and galleries, such as the nearby Dulwich Picture Gallery. There are also plans for an annual community arts festival and excursions. After-school homework clubs are available in many subjects.

## City of London Academy

**Temporary accommodation at Peckham Rye, London SE22 0AT** ☎ Interim enquiries: 020 7332 3998 📠 020 7231 6899 ⓔ city-Academy@corpoflondon ✉ Martin Coles MA; Chair of Governors: Mr William Fraser ⇌ South Bermondsey ⊖ Bermondsey **Buses:** P13, 1, 78, 381 👔 Purple blazer, grey skirt or trousers, grey pullover, white shirt, purple and silver tie **Demand:** Not known **Type:** Community City Academy for 180 mixed pupils, aged 11 to 16 (growing to 900 pupils in 2007 plus a sixth form of 300) **Submit application form:** Early November 2003 **School hours:** 8.30am-4.10pm **Meals:** Hot and cold available **Strong GCSE subjects:** Not yet known **London league table position:** Not yet known

### Profile

The City of London Academy is a brand new school, due to open in September 2003. It will be the first completely new City Academy in the country. The school will be housed in temporary specialist educational buildings on site for the first year while the permanent school is being built. The site is in North Bermondsey between the Old Kent and Southwark Park Roads. The Academy is sponsored by the Corporation of London. It aims to provide state-of-the-art facilities with a high level of computer and technology equipment. The school will create close links with business and commerce, particularly the City and financial services, to provide work experience opportunities for pupils. The Academy intends to become a local centre of excellence and allow its facilities to be used by the community.

### Admissions and intake

Applications should be made direct to the school.

### Achievement

As the school will only open this year, no exams have been taken yet.

### Extra-curricular activities

Not known at present.

# Dulwich College

**Dulwich, London SE21 7LD** 020 8693 3601 020 8693 6319 registrar@dulwich.org.uk www.dulwich.org.uk Mr Graham Able MA West Dulwich, Sydenham Hill, Gipsy Hill **Buses:** 3, N3; for an additional fee, coach services run by the Dulwich Foundation bring in students who live further out Black blazer and shoes, grey trousers, white shirt, tie in college colours **Demand:** No figures available but 60 places for middle school and up to 40 for upper school (sixth form) **Type:** Selective independent for 1448 boys, aged 7 to 19 **Fees:** £3,110 per term for tuition plus registration fee; additional £3,040 per term for full boarders, £2,795 for weekly boarders **Submit Application Form:** Contact registrar's office for details **Motto:** God's Gift **School hours:** 8.45am–4pm **Meals:** Hot and cold available **Strong GCSE subjects:** All relatively strong **London league table position:** 52

## Profile

Dulwich College is one of the three Southwark schools descended from Edward Alleyn's original 1620 foundation, God's Gift. The school has extensive sports facilities, including two astroturf pitches, a swimming pool, a boathouse on the Thames and 60 acres of playing fields. It also has three libraries, all equipped with networked computers and Internet service; a college shop; three dining areas; a music complex; a theatre with a drama library; a medical centre and a college counsellor. In Year 9 pupils begin preparation for GCSE courses, most of them studying 10 GCSE subjects. In the upper school, pupils study four AS-levels. For A-level preparation, pupils study five subjects, general studies plus four of their own choice. Subjects range from classics, religious studies and the sciences to business studies and IT. Languages include French, German and Italian. A careers department provides details of work-experience opportunities. The school is divided into four sections, each with a pupil as its head, as well as deputies and form tutors. These teams oversee pupils' pastoral and academic welfare. Regular competitions take place between the houses. There is a special-needs coordinator.

## Admissions and intake

Admission to Dulwich is determined on the basis of an entry exam, an interview and a confidential report from the head of the candidate's previous school and is subject to the school's standard terms and conditions. Initial approach is through submission of a registration form. Sixth-formers also need satisfactory GCSE results and agreement from the head of their previous school. Scholarships are available for pupils of high academic potential, as well as for music, art and design and technology. Bursaries are also available.

## Achievement

In 2002, Dulwich ranked third in the borough for GCSE scores and, with 97 per cent of pupils earning five or more A*–C grades, far above local and national averages. For A-levels, the school ranked second in the borough, with an average point score of 393.1 for pupils taking more than two A-levels. This was well over the national average.

## Extra-curricular activities

Activities include trips to a Dulwich property in South Wales, where pupils engage in environmental studies and outdoor pursuits. Pupils can also go on educational exchanges to Dulwich International College in Thailand. Drama students can travel abroad to perform, and modern language pupils may travel to France, Italy, Germany and Spain. Pupils are encouraged to participate in community activities such as the Combined Cadet Force and Scouts. The school offers sport in keeping with the national curriculum as well as sub-aqua, shooting, martial arts and riding. In recent years, Dulwich pupils have played in the National Youth Orchestra, performed at the National Theatre and been highly placed in the British Mathematical Olympian.

# Geoffrey Chaucer Technology College

**Harper Road, London, SE1 6AG** 020 7407 6877 020 7403 8922 gchaucerschool@rmplc.co.uk Ms S Yardon-Pinder Bed, MBA (Ed); Chair of Governors: Mrs J Bell, Ms E Okoli, Mr M Willbourn Elephant and Castle Elephant and Castle, Borough **Buses:** P3, 1, 21, 53, 63, 172, 188, 199 Black blazer, white shirt, grey trousers or skirt, red pullover; black trousers or skirt for the upper school **Demand:** 417 applications for 180 places in 2001/2 **Type:** Community comprehensive Technology College for 940 mixed pupils, aged 11 to 16 **Submit application form:** Early November 2003 **School hours:** 8.30am–3.20pm: homework clubs are available **Meals:** Hot and cold available **Strong GCSE subjects:** Art, English, history **London league table position:** 434

## Profile

The Geoffrey Chaucer School does its best to address the needs of a multiracial community, offering pupils the chance to study and take exams in their mother tongue, including Bengali, Turkish and Spanish. The school emphasizes the need for intercultural understanding and has written policies on bullying and discrimination. The staff use a variety of teaching methods, including group discussion, role play, CD-ROMs and audio-visual aids. The library is networked with computers and multimedia and has books in a number of different languages. The school recently acquired Technology College status. GCSE subjects available include traditional ones as well as art and design, IT and modern foreign languages. GNVQ choices include manufacturing (food science) and health and community care. The more able pupils are regularly entered early for exams. Year 11 pupils undertake two weeks' work experience. The learning support faculty provides support for special-needs pupils and English lessons for pupils with English as an additional language. Parents help guide their children by seeing that homework is completed, signing off weekly diaries, ensuring that they wear the school uniform and by attending annual parents' meetings. There is a special-needs coordinator and pupils can join the school council.

## Admissions and intake

All applicants are entitled to an interview, and cognitive ability tests are the initial means of evaluation for new pupils. Results of these are then used to devise individual learning plans and targets for each pupil. Upon acceptance, pupils are assessed and placed in mixed-ability tutor groups. Emphasis in the lower school is on preparation for Standard Attainment Tests (SATs) and in the upper school on exam preparation.

## Achievement

Although the school performs below national and borough averages on GCSEs, the percentage of pupils taking them has risen sharply and the school claims an increase in the number of pupils gaining high exam grades. In 2002, a total of 22 per cent of pupils gained five or more A*–C grades at GCSE. These results were three per cent up on 2001, and the school was placed 11th in the borough. In 2000, Ofsted revisited Chaucer and found that the school no longer needed 'special measures' and that it provided an 'acceptable standard of education for its pupils', noting that 'the number of pupils who leave with no qualification has been sharply reduced'. However, Chaucer had an unauthorized absence rate of 3.8 per cent in 1999, above both national and local averages.

## Extra-curricular activities

Activities include piano, drama, computers, choir and chess. The school has a link with the African and Caribbean Finance Forum, which provides mentors and helps develop study skills. Through this, pupils can also attend a summer school session at Oxford and a conference in the US that provides guidance for African and Caribbean pupils. There are also homework clubs. Pupils can also attend an army camp, take driving lessons and help to establish a school radio station. Participation in the arts and sports is encouraged – pupils have worked with the London Philharmonic and TV broadcasting, and the cricket team has won prizes and competitions.

# James Allen's Girls' School

**East Dulwich Grove, London SE22 8TE** 020 8693 1181 020 8693 7842 postmaster@jags.demon.co.uk www.jags.org.uk Mrs Marion Gibbs BA (Hons), M.Litt (Bristol), FRSA; Chair of Governors: Lord McColl of Dulwich MS, FRCS, FACS, FRCSE, CBE North Dulwich, Herne Hill **Buses:** 3, 12, 37, 68, 176, 184, 185; for an additional fee, coach services run by the Dulwich Foundation bring in pupils who live further out Navy blue skirt, navy blazer with school logo, white blouse, black shoes **Demand:** 350–400 applications for 112 places **Type:** Selective independent for 1038 girls, aged 4 to 19 **Fees:** £2,810 per term (Years 11 to 18), £35 registration fee **Submit application form:** Contact school for details **School hours:** 8.25am–3.45pm; homework clubs are available **Meals:** Hot and cold available **Strong GCSE subjects:** All relatively strong **London league table position:** 14

## Profile

JAGS was founded in 1741 by James Allen. It became a girls' school in 1857. Facilities include design and production workshops, computer rooms, art studios, sports pitches and tennis courts. The curriculum includes traditional subjects as well as courses in classical civilization, art history and IT. Languages available include French, Greek and Latin. The sixth form offers 26 A-level subjects and a liberal studies course run jointly with Dulwich College. Sixth-formers can study languages such as Japanese and Arabic. Sports include hockey, tennis, rounders and dance and a self-awareness/self-defence course is compulsory. Form teachers are responsible for pastoral care. University open days are on offer, and a careers centre gives talks and individual guidance. There is a parents' guild, which arranges social events. Special-needs provisions are given for pupils with conditions such as dyslexia and hearing loss. Pupils can become involved in the school council.

### Admissions and intake

Entry into the middle school is determined by school examination placement (verbal reasoning, mathematics, English), a subsequent interview and recommendation from the pupil's primary school. The exam for 13+ applicants also includes a foreign language paper. Sixth-form entrance depends on an entrance exam, GCSE results, recommendation from the previous school and an interview. One of the school's primary aims is to provide a large number of scholarships, ensuring acceptance is based on merit rather than the ability to pay. Up to 20 scholarships are available, with one for art and one for music. Additional sixth-form scholarships may also be available.

### Achievement

The school's rate of achievement is very high, with JAGS attaining some of the borough's highest GCSE and A-level results. In 2002, 100 per cent of pupils taking GCSEs achieved five of more A*–C grades. The average point score was 59.4 and the school came top of the borough. A-level results were above national and local averages at 387.2. Scores were consistently strong over the years, with slightly lower marks in AS maths, history and geography. The school aims to 'promote excellence in academic, creative and athletic endeavours' and stresses 'morality, integrity and a concern for others'. Pupils have had success in young writers' competitions and in the National Mathematics Challenge.

### Extra-curricular activities

Activities include a number of clubs and societies, such as homework clubs, the Political Society, the Black History Society, the Debating Society and the Christian Union, as well as regular visits to museums, theatres and lectures. Pupils spend a week in an outdoor pursuits centre in Cumbria, and weekend and holiday activities include pony trekking, scuba diving, and climbing. There are exchange programmes with schools in France, Italy, Germany, Spain, Russia and Jordan as well as programmes in the US and South Africa. Drama productions are held each term. Pupils contribute to the community through charitable activities and community service.

# Kingsdale Secondary School

**Alleyn Park, Dulwich, London SE21 8SQ** ☎ 020 8670 7575 📠 020 8766 7051 Mr SH Morrison MA (Oxon), F.Coll.P; Chair of Governors: Councillor N Gibbes ⇌ Sydenham Hill, Gypsy Hill, Crystal Palace **Buses:** 2, 2B, 3, 63, 122, 137, 157, 202, 227, 249, 306, 322 Black blazer, black or grey trousers or black skirt, navy or black pullover, school tie, white shirt or blouse **Demand:** 173 applications for 240 places in 2001/2 **Type:** Community comprehensive for 1150 mixed pupils, aged 11 to 16 **Submit application form:** Early November 2003 **Motto:** *Fac omnia ad dei gloriam* (In the Glory of God) **School hours:** 8.30am–3.25pm **Meals:** Hot and cold available **Strong GCSE subjects:** Drama, music **London league table position:** 460

### Profile

Kingsdale School has a 'fully international and comprehensive intake' – an indication of the diversity of its local community. Its performance level is an indication of the difficulties that staff and pupils face, although significant improvements have been made. The school's facilities include four gyms, football and rugby pitches, a cricket pitch, a running track and tennis courts. More than £12.5 million is to be spent on transforming the school buildings. New facilities will include a modern theatre and conference area, a multi-million pound sports hall and an all-weather pitch. Strong points include the art and music departments, and the multimedia programme, which has been strengthened by a £1-million grant. The school recenty became a Centre of Excellence for the teaching of music, art and drama. Pupils can take GNVQ as well as GCSE courses. All pupils attend a weekly Personal, Social and Health Education (PSHE) lesson to receive guidance on careers, health and moral, political and social education. Local businesses provide support through work-experience placements. Special-needs pupils are allocated key teachers and special programmes according to their needs, with an emphasis on the development of literacy skills. Upon entrance to the school, pupils are placed into tutor groups, staying with the same tutor throughout their stay at the school.

Selected Year 11 pupils become mentors to new intakes. Parents are kept informed through diaries, grades, annual reports, newsletters, consultation evenings and parent forums. The school does have a PTA.

## Admissions and intake

Applicants should complete the borough's application form (see borough factfile). Parents of Kingsdale pupils are required to sign the 'Kingsdale Charter', itemizing responsibilities of school, parent and child.

## Achievement

In 2002, 41 per cent of pupils received five A*–C grades, well below both the England and borough averages. However, this was up from just 16 per cent in 2001 and the school was ranked 13th out of 16 in the borough. After Ofsted's 1998 inspection, the school was put on 'special measures' but these measures were lifted in 2000. Ofsted revisited the school in 2002 and praised the head teacher's 'excellent leadership' which has created a 'rapidly improving school that is more than usually effective'. The school was judged to no longer have any serious weaknesses. In 2001, 'outstanding' GCSE results were achieved in music and drama. However, Ofsted noted that attendance levels remain below the national average and too many pupils are late at the start of lessons. Some pupils have taken A-level classes early in art and music. A number of the school's music pupils have also gained high marks in the Royal Schools of Music exams. Pupils go on to a variety of sixth forms.

## Extra-curricular activities

Activities available include a number of sports clubs such as football, cricket, trampolining and basketball. The music department includes a jazz band, steel band and saxophone quartet. These groups perform regularly in the local community, contributing to the Dulwich Festival and performing in the South Bank. The school works with other schools to produce the Kingsdale music, dance and drama festival. There are also science- and academic-related activities and facilities for girls-only activities. Pupils have the opportunity to go on educational visits and school trips, including a skiing trip and a planned Himalayan trek. Extra classes are offered on Saturdays for those pupils who require extra tuition.

# Notre Dame RC Girls' School

**118 St George's Road, London SE1 6EX** ☎ 020 7261 1121 📠 020 7620 2922 ⓔ admin@notredame.southwark.sch.uk Sister Anne Marie Niblock B.Sc; Chair of Governors: Mrs C Bruggemeyer / Elephant and Castle **Buses:** N11, 53, 63, 100, 155, 168, 172, 188, 322 Dark brown blazer, skirt and jumper; each year group has its blouse colour, which it retains for the five years **Demand:** 313 applications for 124 places in 2001/2 **Type:** Voluntary aided Roman Catholic comprehensive for 600 girls, aged 11 to 16 **Submit application form:** Early November 2003 **Motto:** Educating Girls for Success **School hours:** 8.55am–3.20pm; homework clubs are available **Meals:** Hot and cold available **Strong GCSE subjects:** Drama, English literature, history **London league table position:** 167

## Profile

Notre Dame School was founded in 1855 by the Sisters of Notre Dame. It became a voluntary aided comprehensive school in 1999. Apart from the core curriculum, subjects studied include IT and media studies and the school is one of the few schools in England with Irish language studies. Sports activities, including netball, football, kwik cricket and dance, take place in the school gym and in a neighbouring park. Pupils have the option to attend a work-experience summer session in Year 10. The school places strong emphasis on group worship with weekly assemblies, daily prayer, services on holy days and a Mass to begin each academic year. Pupils are grouped into two bands of ability, starting in mixed ability classes and subsequently placed in specific ability sets. There is a special-needs department and form tutors teach personal and social education. Pastoral heads oversee each of these groups, with deputy heads, a senior teacher and the head teacher having overall charge of pastoral needs. Parents are kept informed by way of a pupil planner. The school has a PTA and special-needs coordinator. Pupils can join the school council.

## Admissions and intake

The primary factor in gaining admission to the school is proof of a firm commitment to the Roman Catholic Church, determined by frequency of Mass attendance and evidence of baptism and communion. Applicants must have a priest's reference. If candidates are equal in this respect, further criteria, in order of priority, are the applicant's having a sister at the school and the applicant living close to the school. Due to the high volume of Roman Catholic applicants, those of other faiths are unlikely to be accepted. Pupils go on to a variety of sixth forms.

### Achievement

One of the aims of Notre Dame is the 'development of Christian women who are confident, can think for themselves, who understand the concepts of equality and justice and can play a full and responsible part in a changing and multicultural society'. The school has consistently achieved the highest percentage of five or more A*–C GCSE grades of voluntary aided and state schools in Southwark. This was 66 per cent in 2002, above the borough and national averages. The school was ranked fourth in the borough. Strong subjects include English literature, drama and history. In 2000, the school achieved Beacon status. That same year, Ofsted commended the 'very high' standards of attainment in GCSEs and the 'very good' ethos that 'permeates all aspects of the school's life'. Ofsted cited the lack of satisfactory accommodation for extra-curricular activities as one of the school's main weaknesses. The unauthorized absence rate was very low at only 0.1 per cent.

### Extra-curricular activities

Activities include drama, homework clubs, music, PE and computer skills. Each July, students can participate in a week of activities, including journeys abroad. Past trips have included Manchester, Spain and Devon. Certain days are set aside for fund-raising activities. Sport activities follow the national curriculum.

## Sacred Heart RC Secondary School

**Camberwell New Road, London SE5 0RP** 020 7274 6844 020 7737 1713 Mr CM Garvey MA; Chair of Governors: Rev Michael Gould Vauxhall Vauxhall, Oval **Buses:** 12, 36, 36A, 36B, 40, 45, 45A, 68, 171, 185 Grey skirt or trousers, white blouse or shirt, school tie, black blazer and badge; red sweatshirt with school badge optional **Demand:** 120 places in 2003 **Type:** Voluntary aided Roman Catholic for 1600 mixed pupils, aged 11 to 16 **Submit application form:** Early November 2003 **Motto:** *In hoc signo vinces* (Under This Sign You Will Succeed) **School hours:** 8.45am–3.00pm; homework clubs are available **Meals:** Hot and cold available **Strong GCSE subjects:** English Literature, French **London league table position:** 250

### Profile

Sacred Heart has invested up to £1.3 million in new facilities including a library, IT suite, science laboratories and a drama suite. Neighbourhood fields and facilities are used for sports, including football, basketball, canoeing and cross country. The school emphasizes the development of Christian principles of care and RE is taught in all years. Prayers are said daily and Masses take place regularly at the Sacred Heart Church. The curriculum includes core subjects as well as IT, French and personal and social education (PSE). GCSE subjects include design and technology, food technology and options such as information systems and sports studies. Musical tuition is available. A PSE programme provides careers guidance and includes a two-week work placement in Year 10. Pupils are set in ability bands and frequent evaluations allow for appropriate placement. Parents receive two reports per year and regularly check homework diaries. Pupils with special needs and English as an additional language are assigned extra teachers or individual tuition. Pastoral care is given by form tutors, pastoral heads and departmental teams. There is a strong PTA.

### Admissions and intake

The school's admissions policy is non-selective. When oversubscribed, criteria for entry are, in order of priority: the applicant being a baptized Roman Catholic with Catholic parents and written reference from a priest; having parents who are members of other Christian churches and who want a Catholic education for their children; being someone who would benefit from Catholic education; and all other applicants. Further selection is based on a siblings presence at the school, the applicant being at a Catholic primary and proximity to the school. Prospective applicants should read the admission policy and submit an application form. Interviews take place in November and December.

### Achievement

Sacred Heart's 2002 GCSE scores were strong, with 56 per cent of pupils attaining five or more A*–Cs, above the borough and national averages. This was down seven per cent on 2001. The school has also won accolades in the London press. In 2002, Ofsted described Sacred Heart as 'a highly effective school 'where 'pupils make very good progress due to consistently good teaching, strong leadership and management'. GCSE results were particulary high in 2001 in English Literature and French but lower than average in art and design and PE. The 2000 unauthorized absence rate was 1.0 per cent, below the local average and in line with the national average. Pupils go to a variety of sixth forms.

### Extra-curricular activities

Activities include a band and choir, homework clubs, regular music and drama productions; sports teams and competitions with other schools. School trips include skiing trips to Andorra, visits to France and the Isle of Wight and day trips to museums, galleries and sporting events around London. After-school and Saturday classes are on offer to help prepare for exams. Pupils regularly participate in fund-raising activities for charity.

# St Michael's RC School

**John Felton Road, Bermondsey, London SE16 4UN** ☎ 020 7237 6432 📠 020 7252 2411 ✉ Mr M Tissot MA, MBA; Chair of Governors: Mr E Kings ⇌ London Bridge, Bermondsey ⊖ London Bridge, Rotherhithe, Bermondsey **Buses:** P11, P13, 47, 188, 225 👔 Dark grey or navy blue trousers, navy blue blazer with school badge, white shirt, school tie, black shoes **Demand:** No figures available but 120 pupils admitted in Year 7 **Type:** Voluntary aided for 600 mixed pupils, aged 11 to 16 **Submit application form:** Early November 2003 **Motto:** *Vince in bono malum* (Good Over Evil) **School hours:** 9.00am–3.30pm; homework clubs are available **Meals:** Hot and cold available **Strong GCSE subjects:** English **London league table position:** 351

### Profile

St Michael's School was established in 1959 by the Roman Catholic Archdiocese, and all pupils are practising Catholics. The school was described by Ofsted as being 'led and managed with wisdom and compassion'. The school was awarded Beacon status in 2000. Facilities include a library, a chapel, computer rooms, design and technology workshops and a science suite. The curriculum includes National Curriculum subjects as well as food technology, personal and social education, IT and modular science. French, Spanish and Irish languages are also offered. Most upper-school pupils take nine GCSE subjects and most pupils take a technology subject. Sports on offer include football, rugby, sailing, canoeing and cricket. Careers guidance is offered from Year 9 onwards, and pupils do a two-week work-experience placement in Year 10. Assemblies take place daily. Teaching groups are banded according to ability. Special-needs pupils and those of high potential are given specialized help and in-class support. Parents' involvement is encouraged through the use of a homework journal, parents' evenings and individual interviews. Bullying, racist and sexist behaviour are officially forbidden.

### Admissions and intake

The school's principal catchment area includes 13 Catholic primary schools in the areas of Southwark, Lewisham, Lambeth and Tower Hamlets. If oversubscribed, criteria for admission, in order of priority, are: Roman Catholic applicants with a strong commitment and endorsement from a Catholic priest; presence of a committed Catholic sibling at the school; and being committed members of other Christian churches.

### Achievement

St Michael's has fared very well in exams over recent years, scoring significantly higher than borough averages and often close to national averages on GCSEs. In 2002, 39 per cent of pupils achieved five or more A*–Cs, above the borough but below the national average. The school was ranked ninth in the borough. In 1997, Ofsted described St Michael's as a 'good school with many strengths'. Its strengths were in English, with maths and science being weaker areas. Pupils were described as generally making good progress, many of them having entered the school with below average attainments. Pupils with special needs were well-supported. Unauthorized absences in 2000 were just 0.1 per cent, very low both in national and local terms. Pupils attend a variety of sixth forms.

### Extra-curricular activities

Activities include clubs for homework, computers, drama and sports. Some of these form part of the Adventure Service Challenge and the Duke of Edinburgh's Award schemes. Lunchtime activities include choir and Irish classes. Organized trips go regularly to France and Spain, as well as excursions within Britain. The school has a residential annexe in Alverstoke, Hampshire, which is used for educational trips and prayer and leadership weekends, as well as for water sports. Year 7 to 9 pupils can join a youth club, which involves sporting activities, games, dramatic performances and theatre visits. Pupils are encouraged to participate in charitable causes.

# St Saviour's and St Olave's CofE School

**New Kent Road, London SE1 4AN** 020 7407 1843 020 7403 9163 deperini@ssso.southwark.sch.uk Mrs Irene Bishop MA, Bed (Hons), CPP; Chair of Governors: Professor MB Naylor RDDL, B.Sc, Ph.D, BDS, FDS Elephant and Castle, London Bridge Elephant and Castle, London Bridge, Borough **Buses:** P3, 1, 21, 42, 53, 63, 78, 172, 177, 188, 199 Navy blue skirt, cardigan or jumper, blazer with school badge, pin-striped blouse **Demand:** 700 applications for 120 places in 2001/2 **Type:** Voluntary aided Church of England for 659 girls, aged 11 to 18 **Submit application form:** End of October 2003 **Motto:** Heirs of the Past, Children of the Present, Makers of the Future **School hours:** 8.45am–3.30pm; homework clubs are available **Meals:** Hot and cold available **Strong GCSE subjects:** Art and design, double science, drama **London league table position:** 196

## Profile

St Saviour's and St Olave's School was founded as a girls' grammar school in 1903. It has been a voluntary aided school since 1951, and in 1990 it came under the authority of Southwark. It was awarded Beacon status in 1999. Facilities include a library, photographic darkrooms, music and IT suites, besides a sports hall, gym and playground. The curriculum follows National Curriculum guidelines, with art, drama, electronics and textiles also on offer. Languages include French and German. The 16 A-level courses include art and design, chemistry and psychology. There is a careers library and work-experience programme forYear 10. Provisions are made for special needs pupils. Assemblies are held weekly and pastoral care is provided by all staff members. Day books are used to record homework and are signed weekly by parents. Progress reports are sent home annually and there are regular parents' evenings. Pupils can join the school council.

## Admissions and intake

The school admits girls of all abilities with three categories for applicants.The first category is for those applicants of high academic ability, determined by a test, for which there are 18 places. Second is for foundation places, with a maximum of 70 places.The criteria is active membership in the Church of England or other Christian faiths; reference from a priest or minister is also necessary.The third category is open places, with a minimum of 32 spots, for which the criteria are, in order of priority: girls whose sister(s) attend the school; whose mothers have attended; who attend Church of England primary schools; and who live close to the school. After application, parents and their daughters will be invited to an interview.

## Achievement

The school's 2002 GCSE scores were above the borough and national averages, with 59 per cent of pupils gaining five or more A*–Cs.This reversed a downward trend since 1999. A-level students attained an average point score of 162.This placed the school fifth in the borough for A-levels. Results in science, art and drama were strong while the weaker subjects were ICT, design and technology, French and history. The art and design department was commissioned by the Pool of London Partnership to design an illustrated tourist guide. In 2002, Ofsted described the school as providing 'a good standard of education' with a 'powerfully caring environment, which encourages each girl to strive to reach her full potential'. Standards at the end of Year 11 were seen to be very good in comparison with similar schools.Teaching was 'good overall and very good in the sixth form'. However, Inspectors wanted to see improvements in the use of ICT across the curriculum.

## Extra-curricular activities

Ofsted praised an 'outstanding range of extra-curricular activities', which includes sports, arts and crafts, photography and homework clubs. The school has links with Millwall Football Club and the British Sports Association for the disabled, and it holds an annual sports day. Musical groups perform at venues such as the Globe and Southbank Centre. School journeys include skiing trips to Austria and visits to museums and theatres.

# The St Thomas the Apostle College

**Hollydale Road, London SE15 2EB** 020 7639 0106 020 7277 5471 admin@stac.southwark.sch.uk www.stac.southwark.sch.uk Eric Tope B.Sc, M.Ed, MBA, FRSA; Chair of Governors: Mrs Eileen Doran Queen's Road Peckham, Nunhead, New Cross Gate New Cross Gate **Buses:** P12, P13, 36, 136, 171, 177 Compulsory: maroon blazer with school badge, grey trousers, white shirt, college jumper, house tie, college scarf; strict haircut policy **Demand:** Figures not available but 152 places **Type:** Voluntary aided Roman Catholic for 750 boys, aged 11 to 16 **Submit application form:** Early November 2003 **Motto:** Achieving Excellence with Care **School hours:** 8.50am–3.30pm **Meals:** Hot and cold available **Strong GCSE subjects:** Art, English literature, music, PE **London league table position:** 243

## Profile

St Thomas the Apostle was built in 1965 and retains the chapel of the convent previously built on the site. Facilities include a gym, swimming pool and cricket nets with additional sports being played at Crystal Palace and nearby sports centres. There is a library, careers library, food technology and drama suites, and IT suites with Internet access. The school is strong in sports and music. Pupils going on to sixth form can take GNVQ business studies courses or transfer to independent or Catholic sixth forms. The school's five forms are divided into four houses. Setting of pupils occurs in the first year, with high-ability pupils placed into two streamed classes in each year group. The school has extra provisions for special-needs and gifted pupils. School heads and curriculum coordinators are responsible for pastoral care, and pupils keep homework diaries that are checked weekly by parents. Parents' evenings take place each term and there is a PTA.

## Admissions and intake

The school, described by Ofsted as 'popular and successful', is comprehensive in its intake, but gives first priority to pupils with a proven commitment to the Roman Catholic Church. This commitment must be certified by a priest. Further positions go only to committed Christians. After application, candidates will be interviewed for admission.

## Achievement

The school has a strong record of achievement and was granted Beacon status in 2000. Its ethos places strong emphasis on producing 'self-disciplined Christian citizens'. In 2002, 53 per cent of pupils achieved five or more A*–Cs in GCSEs. This was above the national average and above the borough average. The school was ranked sixth in the borough. In 1998, Ofsted found that Key Stage 3 overall results ranged from 'above average' to 'very high' compared to similar schools. Overall weaknesses identified by Ofsted included excessive variance in standards between subjects and disruption caused by the withdrawal of special needs pupils. However, the school was described as having 'many more strengths than weaknesses' and as having shown significant improvement in education standards, attendance and staff training. The school performs strongly in music and sports, having won several football trophies and has had successes in swimming, rugby and athletics. Truancy is very low, at 0.1 per cent.

## Extra-curricular activities

Many activities are related to sports and music. The school orchestra, choir and band perform regularly and pupils are encouraged to play instruments. St Thomas was chosen as the Centre for Young Musicians for Southwark. There are field trips and theatre visits plus trips to Cornwall, Belgium and Italy. Pupils organize fund-raising events.

# Walworth School

**Shorncliffe Road, London SE1 5UJ** 020 7450 9570 020 7450 9571 school@walworth.southwark.sch.uk www.walworth.southwark.sch.uk Miss EV Hanham; Chair of Governors: Mr T Eckersley / Elephant and Castle **Buses:** P3, 21, 42, 53, 63, 141, 177 Maroon, black and white **Demand:** 412 applications for 241 places in 2001/2 **Type:** Community comprehensive for 1200 mixed pupils, aged 11 to 16 **Submit application form:** Early November 2003 **School hours:** 8.35am–3.25pm; homework clubs are available **Meals:** Hot and cold available **Strong GCSE subjects:** Art, music **London league table position:** 499

## Profile

Walworth School is divided into an upper and lower school, the two separated by a 15-minute walk. Overall test scores for both schools have been low, although some improvement has been seen recently. The school library is well equipped with computer equipment. National Curriculum subjects are taught at all levels. The personal health and social curriculum includes sex education and work experience. Sports available include football, hockey, netball, volleyball and basketball. Christian, multi-faith and 'moral precept' assemblies take place daily, either for the whole school or for tutor/year groups. Lower school classes are taught in mixed-ability groups and pupils are put into groups according to their appropriate levels as they progress. Walworth recognizes pupils who exhibit outstanding effort with regular 'achievement assemblies'. Pupils are given homework for all subjects and homework diaries are used to monitor work, with parents/carers expected to check them regularly. Parents are kept informed of pupils' progress through written reports, which are sent out at least once a year, plus consultation evenings and by appointment with staff. Form tutors are led by year heads, who assume most of the pastoral and disciplinary duties. The school strongly reprimands pupils for bullying and racist or sexist behaviour, sometimes resorting to exclusion. The school has a council that pupils can join.

## Admissions and intake

The school's intake is comprehensive, and the abilities of incoming pupils vary widely, with their overall attainment well below the national average. The number of pupils with special educational needs is higher than average, while nearly one third speak English as an additional language, a percentage far above the national average.

## Achievement

Walworth's achievements have been consistently below both national and borough averages, most likely reflecting the social and economic difficulties experienced by many of its pupils. In 2002, just 14 per cent of pupils achieved A*–Cs at GCSE, up on 12 per cent in 2001. The school was ranked bottom of the borough. Although GCSE results are low, they were noted by Ofsted in 1999, to be 'in line with results obtained by schools in similar circumstances'. The strongest GCSE subjects were art and music, while modern languages were cited as weak areas, partly due to insufficient staffing. Despite low scores, pupils were seen as making 'satisfactory progress in relation to their prior attainment'. Weaknesses identified included poor attendance, 4.4 per cent of half-days were missed due to unauthorized absences, as well as insufficient support for special needs and pupils with English as an additional language and a poorly maintained environment. However, Ofsted recognized the staff's 'commitment to improvement' as well as a 'good standard of teaching'. Efforts have been made towards improving literacy, such as equipping the library with new computer software and a summer literacy scheme for new pupils.

## Extra-curricular activities

Activities include sports teams and events, recreational and theatre visits and various clubs, including homework clubs. Pupils can also go on trips at home and abroad. There is a new Saturday morning activities programme. Ofsted commended the school on its 'good range of extra-curricular activities, including weekend sport'.

# Waverley School

**Homestall Road, London SE22 0NR** 020 7732 2276 020 7277 7785 info@waverleyschool.org www.waverleyschool.org Lesley Day; Chair of Governors: Trevor Hall Honor Oak Park, Nunhead, Peckham Rye **Buses:** P3, 184 Navy skirt or trousers, red school sweatshirt, white blouse; any religious headwear must be white, black or navy **Demand:** 357 applications for 180 places in 2001/2 **Type:** Community comprehensive for 900 girls, aged 11 to 16 **Submit application form:** Early November 2003 **School hours:** 8.45am–3.25pm; homework clubs are available **Meals:** Hot and cold available **Strong GCSE subjects:** Art and design, English, geography, history, mathematics **London league table position:** 443

## Profile

Waverley is one of the better-performing Southwark community schools and maintains a healthy and supportive atmosphere. Its facilities include a sports hall, music school, film studio and computer and multimedia facilities. A total of £7 million is being spent on new projects including an open-air theatre, floodlit sports pitches, a maths suite and an arts and humanities block. In addition to National Curriculum subjects, pupils follow courses in the arts, humanities, IT and vocational studies. Languages studied include French and Spanish. Sports on offer include rowing, judo, dance, basketball and sailing and there are plans to introduce new sports such as water polo. Older pupils can take vocational courses and receive vocational advice. The school has links with many London businesses, offering a two-week work placement in Year 10. Ofsted reported 'a good range of curricular opportunities' for special needs and English as an additional language pupils. Pupils can participate in the school council. Form tutors and pastoral staff work closely to offer support and advice, and there is a full-time youth worker and a 'peer mentoring' scheme. School diaries are used for recording homework and for communication between parents and the school. Parents receive termly progress assessments and can attend annual parents' evenings or make separate appointments. Pupils can join the school council.

## Admissions and intake

As a comprehensive school, Waverley's admissions procedure is non-selective and is through the LEA.

## Achievement

On the whole, Waverley's GCSE results have been below average, both nationally and for the borough. In 2002, 26 per cent of pupils achieved A*–C grades at GCSE, up from 23 per cent in 2001, continuing an upward trend. The school was placed 12th in the borough. However, Ofsted concluded in 2000, that 'results have improved since the previous inspection at a rate better than the trend nationally'. The best results were in art and design, English, maths, geography and history, the weaker areas being science, design and technology, French and Spanish. Other weaknesses cited by Ofsted included the level of attendance and poor music provisions, but their overall impression was of 'a caring school where staff have good relationships with pupils'. The school had an unauthorized absence rate of 2.0 per cent, which is below the local average but above the national average.

## Extra-curricular activities

Activities include concerts, performances and field trips to support studies. A programme of 'enrichment activities' includes art, IT and dance. There are weekly study clubs and holiday revision classes, and professional actors and musicians visit regularly. Trips to France, Spain and Denmark are organized to supplement language studies and to help develop an understanding of European issues. The school regularly participates in charity fund-raising and community initiatives. Performing arts pupils have performed at the Royal, National and Globe Theatres and the Year 7 to 8 basketball team has enjoyed a number of successes. Homework clubs are also on offer.

# Sutton

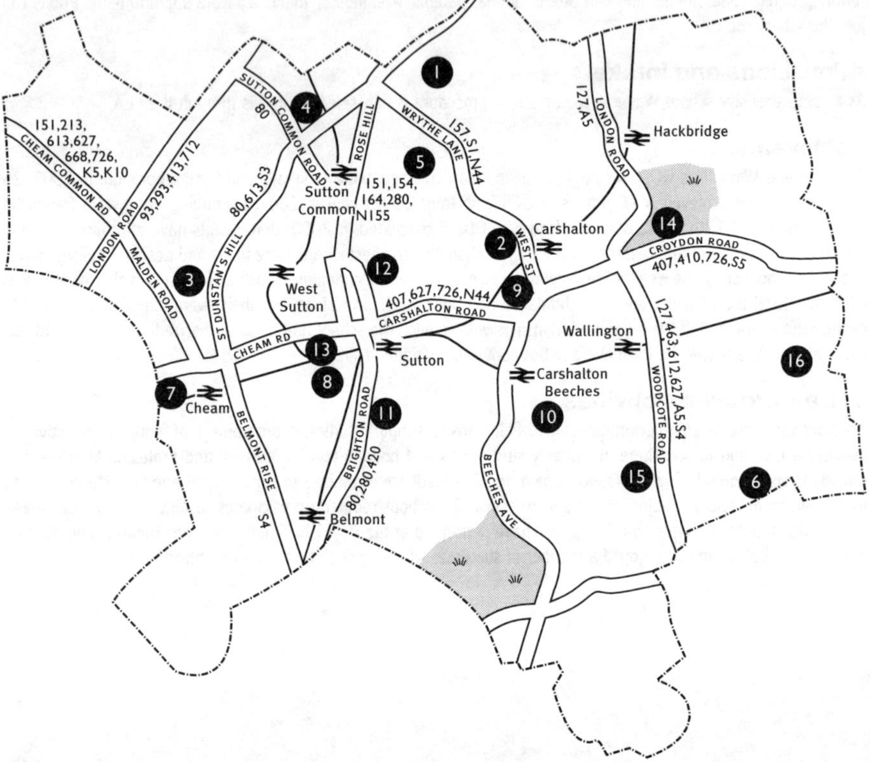


**Key**

1. Carshalton High School for Boys
2. Carshalton High School for Girls
3. Cheam High School
4. Glenthorne High School
5. Greenshaw High School
6. The John Fisher School
7. Nonsuch High School for Girls
8. Overton Grange School
9. St Philomena's School
10. Stanley Park High School
11. Stowford College
12. Sutton Grammar School for Boys
13. Sutton High School
14. Wallington County Grammar School
15. Wallington High School for Girls
16. Wilson's School

# Factfile

**LEA: Civic Offices, St Nicholas Way, Sutton SM1 1EA** 020 8770 5000 www.sutton.gov.uk **Director of Education:** Ian Birnbaum **Political control of council:** Liberal Democrats **Percentage of pupils from outside the borough:** 8.3 per cent **Percentage of pupils educated outside the borough:** 14.1 per cent **London league table positions (out of 32 boroughs):** 1st

## Profile

Sutton is a pleasant suburb situated on London's southern border with Surrey. With the exception of pockets of socio-economic disadvantage to its north, it is dominated by wealthy suburban estates.

The borough is served by a total of 16 schools, of which only two are independents. Despite the selective system in Sutton, standards are high across the board. There is, for example, no school that has been listed on the government's list of failing schools. Instead, many of Sutton's schools have been praised by education officials. The borough consistently outstrips national expectations at both Key Stage 4 and beyond. In 2002, an average of 64.8 per cent of pupils gained five or more GCSEs at the higher grades. This compares favourably to the national average of 51.6 per cent. Similarly, the average point score at GCSE in Sutton was 41.1, again higher than the national average of 34.7 points. The average score for Sutton's sixth form pupils sitting two or more A-levels was 300.6 points, higher than the national average of 254.5.

## Policy

Unusually, Sutton operates a grammar school system, with five of its state-funded schools selecting their pupils on the basis of ability. While this allows the selective schools to offer its pupils the best standards of education that can be found in the state sector, it also has profound implications for the borough's comprehensive schools. For although these continue to have comprehensive status, the success of the grammar schools in attracting the most able 25 per cent of the school population ensures that the remaining state schools have an intake consisting of pupils in the lower-ability bands.

Sutton LEA operates a strict equal-opportunities policy to determine admissions to each of its community comprehensives. Unless it is clearly stated otherwise, priority is always given to prospective pupils whose applications are supported by special medical reasons, followed by those who have an elder sibling at the school at the time of admission. Any remaining places are then determined by proximity to the school as measured in a straight line.

# Carshalton High School for Boys

**Winchcombe Road, Carshalton, Surrey SM5 1RW** 020 8644 7325 020 8641 8721 carboys@suttonlea.org Mr S Barber; Chair of Governors: Mr J Munt Carshalton **Buses:** 151, 154, 157, 164, 280, 407, 408, 726 Dark navy blazer, black trousers, white shirt, school tie; Sixth form: Jacket and tie **Demand:** 365 applications for 180 places in 2001/2 **Type:** Community comprehensive for 1,060 boys, aged 11 to 18 **Submit application form:** Mid-October 2003 **Motto:** Building on Success **School hours:** 8.30am–3.15pm; homework clubs are available **Meals:** Hot and cold available, including breakfast **Strong GCSE subjects:** Drama, PE **London league table position:** 428

## Profile

Situated in a residential area, Carshalton High School for Boys is the school that most obviously suffers from the competition presented by the local grammar schools. Add to this a lack of resources, and it is understandable why its exam results have traditionally been among the lowest in the borough. Staff and pupils, however, have been working hard to combat this trend, aided by a recent improvement in the school's facilities. In 1996, a new science block was opened and its sports, maths, IT, business studies, food technology and textile capabilities have recently been upgraded. The school has also gained the prestigious Sportsmark Award in recognition of the high standards of its sports provision. Average class sizes are just under 20. Beyond the requirements of the National Curriculum, Carshalton High offers courses in food studies, textiles, rural science, engineering, dance and both media and pre-vocational studies. In the sixth form, GNVQs are proving more popular than traditional A-levels, with engineering and leisure and tourism among those on offer. All pupils have a two-week work placement in Year 10. They also have the opportunity to assume various responsibilities around the school, such as staffing the reception desk. There is a school council, parent-teacher association and provision for pupils with special needs.

### Admissions and intake

Admission is through the LEA (see borough factfile). The four selective state schools continue to attract the most able students, with the result that most of Carshalton's intake is in the lower-ability bands. The majority of pupils are drawn from the immediate locality, an area of high socio-economic disadvantage.

### Achievement

Carshalton's performance at GCSE level remains poor. In 2002, 28 per cent of pupils who sat GCSEs obtained five or more A*–C grades. This was up from 25 per cent in 2001 and the school was ranked 14th in the borough overall. Standards at Key Stage 4 have improved dramatically in recent years as have A-level standards. A-level results have more than doubled between 1996 and 1999. However, they still fail to meet national expectations and in 2001, those pupils who sat two or more A/AS-levels gained an average of just 121.9 points. This was well below the national average. This placed the school 14th in the borough. When Ofsted inspected the school in 1999, they particularly praised the school for its high standards in drama and PE. In general, Carshalton's pupils are well behaved and show a respect for their learning environment.

### Extra-curricular activities

The scope and popularity of the activities available is a strength of the school. Pupils of all abilities regularly engage in competitive and non-competitive football, rugby, athletics, tennis and golf matches, with the school recently reaching the final of the All England Golf Championship. Lunchtime and after-school clubs cater for interests as diverse as sailing, horticulture and archery. There is also a Duke of Edinburgh's Award group, which has achieved 400 awards in the past 15 years, and is the strongest group of its kind in Sutton. After-school homework clubs are available in many subjects. There is a skiing trip and a trip to France. Pupils do fund-raising for local charities.

# Carshalton High School for Girls

**West Street, Carshalton, Surrey SM5 2QX** ☎ 020 8647 8294 📠 020 8773 8931 ⓔ office@chsg.sutton.sch.uk ✉ Mrs E Coate BA; Chair of Governors: Mr T Bennett ⇄ Carshalton **Buses:** S3, S1, 127, 154, 157, 407, 408, 726 👔 Pale blue and white checked blouse, navy skirt; Sixth form: Smart clothes **Demand:** 493 first-choice applications for 210 places in 2001/2 **Type:** Community comprehensive for 1100 girls, aged 11 to 18 **Submit application form:** Mid-October 2003 **School hours:** 8.30am–3.15pm; homework clubs are available **Meals:** Hot and cold available **Strong GCSE subjects:** Art, drama **London league table position:** 310

### Profile

Carshalton High School for Girls opened in 1931. Formerly a secondary modern, it was granted comprehensive status in 1992. The school has increased in numbers over the past few years, reflecting its growing popularity. The site is fairly pleasant, but its buildings are too small to cope with its expanding numbers. As a result, much of the teaching takes place in temporary accommodation or prefabricated buildings. This has also limited the amount of open outdoor space available to just one grass pitch. Carshalton High does, however, have some good art facilities, helping it to achieve high standards in the subject. In 1999, 52 per cent of pupils who took their Key Stage 4 exams decided to stay at the school, and a further 16 per cent continued in education at another institution. Those pupils who remain at Carshalton are presented with a wide range of A-level, GCSE, GNVQ and City and Guild qualifications from which to choose. Most study in small classes of approximately 10, and pupils stay with the same form tutor up to Year 11. All girls have the opportunity to participate in a work-experience programme. A prefects system allows older girls to play a part in the running of the school. There is a parent-teacher association and provision for pupils with special needs.

### Admissions and intake

Admission is through the LEA (see borough factfile). Applications are mainly from parents living within the immediate locality.

### Achievement

Pupils seem to make good progress at Carshalton High despite their relative disadvantages. The most recent Ofsted inspection in 2002 found that pupils 'attain standards that are better than would normally be expected given their attainment on entry'. This was seen to be due to 'good teaching' and pupils' 'good attitudes'. In 2002, 48 per cent of pupils gained five or more grades A*–C at GCSE. The school was placed 12th in the borough. A strength of the school is its broad and flexible curriculum, including opportunities for studying sociology, life skills, child development and home economics. All pupils follow nine full and two short GCSE courses. While most students do not opt to study two or more A/AS-levels, those who do gained an average score of 220.6 points. This placed the school 10th in the borough. This was below the national average. Standards for those pupils who sit additional GCSEs or GNVQ courses tend to be higher.

### Extra-curricular activities

There is a wide range of activities on offer. Sports available include netball, football, trampolining, gymnastics, basketball and badminton. There is also a host of drama and music groups as well as after-school homework clubs. The school participates in the Young Enterprise, Agenda 21 – a UN-run project focused on environmentally sustainable development – and Sports Leadership Award schemes. There are skiing trips to the US and residential trips to France and Germany, in addition to visits to theatres, museums and other places of interest.

## Cheam High School

**Chatsworth Road, Cheam, Surrey SM3 8PW** 020 8644 5790 020 8641 8611 secretary @cheam.sutton.sch.uk www.cheam.sutton.sch.uk Ms RJ Allott; Chair of Governors: Dr RS Satchell West Sutton, Cheam **Buses:** 93, 151, 213, 408 Black blazer, grey or black trousers, white shirt, school tie (boys); medium length navy skirt, white blouse, navy school jumper (girls); Sixth form: Formal dress **Demand:** 763 applications for 270 places in 2001/2 **Type:** Comprehensive foundation school for 1490 mixed pupils (247 in sixth form), aged 11 to 18 **Submit application form:** Mid-October 2003 **Motto:** Undaunted **School hours:** 8.35am–3.30pm; homework clubs are available **Meals:** Hot and cold available **Strong GCSE subjects:** Drama, German, Spanish **London league table position:** 269

### Profile

Cheam High is Sutton's largest school. In 1996, Ofsted noted that 'the school has barely sufficient accommodation to meet its present curricular needs'. This has been partially resolved through a recent building programme, with the addition of several new labs and a learning resources centre. Excellent sports facilities include a sports hall, netball courts and two grass pitches. The school also makes use of external facilities such as the Cheam swimming baths and Raynes Park, to which pupils are transported by the school's minibus if necessary. Cheam High has gained the Sportsmark Award in recognition of its contribution to PE. A choice of 20 A-levels are on offer in the sixth form, as well as vocational courses in art and design, business and finance, leisure and tourism, manufacturing, IT and science. To aid pastoral care, pupils generally stay with the same form tutor up to Year 11. The school aims wherever possible to keep children with special needs within the classroom. There is a parent-teacher association and a school council.

### Admissions and intake

Application is made directly to the school. Priority in admissions is given to those applicants who have a sibling at the school at the time of application, followed by those who have medical or special reasons for wanting to attend. Any remaining places are awarded first of all to those living closest to the school.

### Achievement

Standards have risen significantly at Cheam High over the past few years. In 2002, 50 per cent of pupils gained five or more A*–C grades at GCSE. This was up from 47 per cent in 2001 but below the borough and national averages. The school was placed 11th in the borough league table. However, these results are commendable given the presence of a large number of selective schools locally, which tend to draw the most able pupils. Ofsted visited the school in 2001 and described it as a 'good school with some significant strengths'. Teaching was seen to be 'good overall' and Inspectors gave particular praise to the school's 'outstanding' provision for modern languages. At present, 86 per cent of Year 11 students choose to continue their education in one form or another. The average point score for pupils taking two or more A/AS-levels was 176.4. This was below the national average, placing the school 12th in the borough league table. However, results for GNVQs tend to be far closer to the national norm. In 1999, a total of 23 per cent of pupils went on to places of further education, with another 38 per cent proceeding to higher education.

### Extra-curricular activities

Sport is strong at the school, with successful teams for football, basketball, rugby, cricket, athletics and netball. There is also a wide variety of clubs catering for all interests, ranging from homework clubs, debating and drama to photography and the RSPCA. In addition to theatre and museum visits in the UK, the school organizes residential trips to France and an annual watersports trip to Spain or France. Students raise funds for local charities.

## Glenthorne High School

**Sutton Common Road, Sutton, Surrey SM3 9PS** ☎ 020 8644 6307 📠 020 8641 8725 ⓔ glenthorne @rmplc.co.uk ▶ Mr S Hulme; Chair of Governors: Mrs L Wiggins ⇄ Sutton Common **Buses**: 80, 93, 154, 293, 613 👕 Blue school sweatshirt, dark trousers or skirt, white or light blue polo shirt; Sixth form: Smart casual dress **Demand**: 504 applications for 210 places in 2001/2 **Type**: Community comprehensive Arts College for 1100 mixed pupils (123 in sixth form), aged 11 to 18 **Submit application form**: Mid-October 2003 **Motto**: Achievement for All **School hours**: 8.30–3.10pm; homework clubs are available **Meals**: Hot and cold available **Strong GCSE subjects**: English, maths **London league table position**: 378

### Profile

An Ofsted inspection of Glenthorne High in 1997 described its resources and buildings as 'barely adequate'. This is especially true in the provision of rooms for music and to a lesser degree the sports facilities; outdoor recreational areas and dining space are too small for the number of pupils. The appearance of the school is also marred by litter and the occasional marks of graffiti. However, some significant improvements have been made, including the addition of a new learning resources centre with eight extra classrooms for the teaching of modern languages, English and humanities. A new science building with purpose-built facilities and a new music area have also been constructed, greatly easing the pressures of space that concerned the Ofsted inspectors. The school offers 19 GCSE subjects, including business studies, fashion and food technology. There is also a wide range of GNVQ courses available, including art and design, health and social care, IT, leisure and tourism and business, together with 14 A-levels. The school recently acquired Arts College status. There is a strong school council and prefect system in place. Many sixth-formers are involved in the 'paired' reading scheme with Year 7 pupils. There is a parent-teacher association and provision for pupils with special needs.

### Admissions and intake

Admission is through the LEA (see borough factfile). The presence of four grammar schools in the borough means that although the school has been classified as a comprehensive, it predominantly draws its students from lower-ability ranges. Most of Glenthorne's pupils are drawn from the immediate locality.

### Achievement

Ofsted revisited Glenthorne High in 2002 and noted that it had made considerable improvements since the last inspection. Standards were seen to be improving in many subjects and the 'quality of teaching and learning is good'. However, standards still needed to be improved and Inspectors again expressed concern regarding the limitations of the school's facilities. There has been a steady decline in GCSE results. In 2002, the proportion of pupils achieving at least five A*–C grades rose to 35 per cent, five per cent up on 2001. At A-level, the average point score of pupils taking two or more A/AS-levels was 202.1, placing the school 11th in the borough.

### Extra-curricular activities

A wide range of lunchtime and after-school activities includes a number of choirs and music groups, a computer club, an electronic music workshop, a strong Christian Union and a homework club. Sports available include basketball, football, trampolining, netball and rugby. The school organizes visits to museums and other places of interest in the UK, as well as French trips as part of an activity week and a German exchange. Pupils raise funds for local charities.

# Greenshaw High School

**Grennell Road, Sutton, Surrey SM1 3DY** 020 8715 1001 020 8641 7335 lindawelch@suttonlea.org www.greenshaw.sutton.sch.uk Mr JK Fuller B.Sc; Chair of Governors: D Hammond Sutton Common **Buses**: S1, S3, S4, 70D, 151, 154, 157, 164, 280, 420, 440 Dark green school sweatshirt, dark trousers or skirt, white shirt or blouse, house tie; Sixth form: Smart dress **Demand**: 1103 applications for 244 places in 2001/2 **Type**: Community comprehensive for 1340 mixed pupils, aged 11 to 18 **Submit application form**: Mid-October 2003 **School hours**: 8.30am–3.20pm, 8.30am–2.55pm (Wed); homework clubs are available **Meals**: Hot and cold available **Strong GCSE subjects**: Business studies, design and technology, history, mathematics **London league table position**: 234

## Profile

Greenshaw opened as a purpose-built comprehensive in 1968 and is among Sutton's largest schools. The past few years have seen a £1.5-million redevelopment of the school, which has done much to improve its facilities. In 1996, a new music block was opened, followed by a new learning resources centre and extended sixth-form accommodation. In 1999, further specialist rooms for IT, science and a new drama studio were also constructed. Unfortunately, Greenshaw does not have proper access to playing fields for team sports, such as football, rugby and cricket. Class sizes average 22 pupils. A number of interesting options are available at Key Stage 4, including child development, computer graphics and electronic music. Those pupils who continue into the sixth form are offered a choice of 20 A-levels and GNVQs in business studies, IT and leisure and tourism. The majority of pupils take two or more A-levels. All Year 11 pupils take part in a compulsory work-experience programme. Pupils are also given the opportunity to become involved in the house council and sixth-form committee, which meet on a regular basis. The PTA raises significant funds for the school. There is provision for pupils with special needs and a school council.

## Admissions and intake

Up to 60 places each year are offered on the basis of ability, as determined by verbal and non-verbal reasoning tests held at the school in late November preceding the September start. The remaining places are allocated according to the council's equal opportunities policy (see borough factfile). The school has consistently attracted pupils from a wide range of socio-economic backgrounds.

## Achievement

In 2002, 52 per cent of pupils gained five or more A*–C grades at GCSE. This was up on 2001's result of 51 per cent and the school came 10th in the borough. In 1999, 51 per cent stayed on into the school's sixth form, while another 35 per cent continued their learning at a further education institution. The average point score for pupils taking two or more A/AS-levels in 2002 was 223, again ranking the school ninth in the borough. In 2001, Ofsted described Greenshaw as 'a successful school with very good and excellent features'. Pupils 'achieve well' and 'teaching is good overall'. Two-thirds of pupils go on to higher education.

## Extra-curricular activities

There is an impressive range of lunchtime and after-school clubs and activities, including homework clubs, chess and Scrabble clubs and an active environmental group. The school also has a strong sporting tradition, with an outstanding reputation for basketball, having won the national championships on two past occasions. Greenshaw consistently performs well at the Borough Athletics Championship, and in 1999, it won the Midland Bank shield for the seventh time. Regular adventure holidays are arranged to Cornwall, Spain and the South of France, in addition to museum, theatre and art gallery visits.

# The John Fisher School

**Peaks Hill, Purley, Surrey CR8 3YP** 020 8660 4555 020 8763 1837 johnfisherschool@suttonlea.org Mr R Gregory BA, MA; Chair of Governors: Mrs T Hobbs Purley **Buses**: 127, 289 Royal blue blazer, dark grey trousers, grey shirt, house tie **Demand**: 280 applications for 150 places in 2001/2 **Type**: Voluntary aided

Roman Catholic comprehensive for 894 boys, aged 11 to 18 **Submit application form**: Mid-October 2003 **School hours**: 8.45am–3.25pm **Meals**: Hot and cold available **Strong GCSE subjects**: English language and literature, German, Latin **London league table position**: 147

## Profile

The school was founded in 1929 by the Archbishop of Southwark, John Fisher, and continues to have a strong Catholic ethos. Its elegant red-brick building, featuring a fine chapel, has been supplemented by an array of facilities, including 12 new classrooms, a sixth-form centre and an art block. The immediate school grounds provide two rugby pitches, but most of the sporting activities take place on the 'New Fields' which are located just a short distance from the school complex. The sixth-form curriculum has been enriched by the inclusion of A-levels in business studies and IT, as well as a GNVQ business course and an advanced BTEC Diploma in sports science. Careers education is a compulsory part of the curriculum in Year 10. The John Fisher Association (PTA) organizes an annual fund-raising fete. There is a prefects system for pupils to be able to take on extra responsibilities and provision for pupils with special needs.

## Admissions and intake

The demand for places is such that only first-choice Catholic applicants are likely to be successful. Applications should be supported in writing by the family's local Catholic priest. Priority is given, in order, to: those applicants with either a sibling or a direct family connection with the school; those with a medical or special reason supporting their application; and those living closest to the school, measured in a straight line. The school's catchment area is very wide, covering the whole of Sutton and much of Croydon.

## Achievement

In 2002, 76 per cent of boys obtained five or more A*–C grades at GCSE. This was significantly higher than the national average and also above the borough average. The school was placed eighth in Sutton. A total of 62 per cent of pupils stay on into the sixth form, where unfortunately achievement drops from well above national averages at Key Stage 4 to marginally below. In 2002, the average point score for pupils taking two or more A/AS-levels was 236.1, below the national average. However, these results are still sufficient to place the school eighth in the borough and compare very favourably with those of many schools in neighbouring Croydon. Results have also been rising over the last six years. The most recent Ofsted inspection in 1998 largely praised the standard of education offered at John Fisher, albeit with some minor reservations. The design and technology department in particular came in for strong criticism in terms of its teaching and facilities. Ofsted described the school as a 'fine example of an orderly community', which produces many fine exam results.

## Extra-curricular activities

Rugby tends to dominate the sporting calendar, with the school winning the National Schools' Rugby 7-a-side competition in 1997 and 1998, and again reaching the finals in 1999. There is a popular choir, which has made visits to Vienna, Venice, Rome, New York and Ireland. There are also music groups, and the school regularly puts on drama productions in conjunction with St Philomena's. The school also organizes a geography field trip, a residential trip to Aylesford, skiing holidays and outdoor activity weeks in the Lake District.

# Nonsuch High School for Girls

**Ewell Road, Cheam, Sutton, Surrey SM3 8AB** ☎ 020 8394 1308 📠 020 8393 2307 ⓔ email@nonsuch.sutton.sch.uk 🌐 www.nonsuch.sutton.sch.uk Mrs G Espejo BA, FRSA; Chair of Governors: Mr BW Doonar ⇄ Cheam **Buses**: 408 Blue school jumper, dark and light blue checked school skirt, blue blouse; Sixth form: Smart clothes **Demand**: 1,063 applications for 180 places in 2001/2 **Type**: Grammar school for 1130 girls, aged 11 to 18 **Submit application form**: Mid-October 2003 **Motto**: Serve God and Be Cheerful **School hours**: 8.30am–3pm (Mon,Wed), 8.30am–3.35pm (Tues, Thurs, Fri); homework clubs available **Meals**: Hot and cold available **Strong GCSE subjects**: All relatively strong **London league table position**: 31

## Profile

Opened in 1938 on the edge of Nonsuch Park, this school provides a fine example of the best education available in the state sector. It is also attractive, with its stately red-brick buildings set within 22 acres of landscaped grounds. It is therefore hardly surprising that the school continues to be a very popular choice amongst parents. It is one of London's 19 remaining grammar schools. Facilities at the school include a new technology wing and the Barkey Music Suite, opened in 1995. During the course of 2000 the school underwent a major redevelopment programme to provide it with more space. For those pupils who wish to assume responsibilities around the school, Nonsuch has a sixth-form prefect system and a school council.There is also a parent-teacher association and provision for pupils with special needs.

## Admissions and intake

Admissions are based primarily upon success at the school's own selective exam held in November, with 40 places each year being offered purely on merit. Priority is subsequently given to those applicants who have sisters at the school at the time of allocation, and then to those whose applications are supported by medical reasons. A complicated system based upon the distance prospective pupils live from the school is then used to allocate the remaining places.

## Achievement

In 2002, an impressive 98 per cent of pupils gained five or more A*–C grades at GCSE. This was well above the national average and the continuation of a consistently high performance over recent years.The school came second in the borough. Nonsuch offers its pupils a wide range of subjects, including food technology, Latin, Spanish, theatre studies and textiles, in addition to the requirements of the National Curriculum. Most girls take 10 GCSEs, with a high proportion achieving top standards. Given the school's great success at Key Stage 4, it is hardly surprising that the overwhelming majority of pupils decide to continue into the sixth form. In 2002, the average point score of pupils taking two or more A/AS-levels was 435.4.This result was well above the national average, placing the school in first place in Sutton and making it the highest-performing girls' state school in the borough.The school offers a choice of 27 A-level options, including business studies, government and politics, social biology, sociology and theatre studies. However, no vocational courses are available. In 1998, Ofsted stated that 'the school nurtures excellent attitudes to learning', and that it 'achieves very high standards in nearly all subjects'. Pupils are courteous, friendly and help to make the school a supportive and caring community.

## Extra-curricular activities

Nonsuch has particularly strong traditions in sport and music. Sports on offer include swimming, gymnastics, netball and tennis, while there are three orchestras and several instrumental groups and choirs. Pupils can take advantage of after-school homework clubs. In addition, pupils can join Amnesty International and Duke of Edinburgh's Award groups and do fund-raising for local charities. The school organizes regular visits to London's museums and other places of interest and also arranges residential exchanges to France and Germany.

# Overton Grange School

**Stanley Road, Sutton, Surrey SM2 6TQ** ☎ 020 8239 2383 📠 020 8239 2382 Mr KJ Osbourne B.Soc.Sci, MA; Chair of Governors: Mrs B Morley Cheam, Sutton **Buses:** S4, 70D, 80, 280, 420, 440 Green school blazer, mid-grey trousers or skirt, white shirt or blouse, school tie **Demand:** 1117 applications for 210 places in 2001/2 **Type:** Community comprehensive for 1200 mixed pupils, aged 11 to 18 **Submit application form:** Mid-October 2003 **School hours:** 8.25am–3.05pm; homework clubs are available **Meals:** Hot and cold available **Strong GCSE subjects:** Information not available **London league table position:** 177

## Profile

Overton Grange is Sutton's newest school. Its purpose-built facilities welcomed their first 180 Year 7 pupils in September 1997.The school initially had just 606 pupils but the roll has since risen to over 1000 pupils, aged 11 to 18, following the completion of the third phase of building in 2002. Overton Grange has a well-planned, modern environment. It enjoys the benefits of purpose-built science labs, technology and computing suites, dance and drama studios and a fully equipped sports hall. However, the dining hall is rather cramped, and there is a lack of small practice rooms for music. Facilities for football, athletics, cross-country, rounders, cricket and other team sports are provided by the playing fields located next to the school.The school offers a balanced curriculum at GCSE level. All pupils follow courses in English, maths, science, languages, design and technology, RE, IT and PE. They may then choose further options from history, geography, art, music, dance, business studies and a second language. Pupils are set according to their ability in maths, science, IT and modern languages. Overton Grange is not due to accept its first sixth-form entry until 2002, and as a result the curriculum, to be worked out in conjunction with Carshalton College, has not yet been established. The school is particularly well resourced to deal with those pupils with hearing difficulties. There is a prefects system, a school council and a parent-teacher association.

## Admissions and intake

Admission is through the LEA (see borough factfile).

## Achievement

As yet, no student from Overton Grange has taken formal GCSE exams. The school received a positive Ofsted report when it was inspected in 1999, which concluded that 'pupils and teachers share a commitment to work and strive to reach high standards'. Of the lessons that were observed, the inspectors rated teaching as satisfactory in 92 per cent of cases, and very good or better in around 38 per cent of classes. Both of these conclusions bode well for the school's future.

## Extra-curricular activities

Pupils are encouraged to engage in at least one extra-curricular activity each week, and there is a commendable range to choose from. Although music and sports groups have taken prominence, drama and the school newspaper are also popular options. Curriculum-enriching societies include those for science and computers, and there is also a homework club.

# St Philomena's School

**Pound Street, Carshalton, Surrey SM5 3PS** ☎ 020 8642 2025 📠 020 8643 7925 Mrs J Johnson BA (Hons), M.Ed; Chair of Governors: Sister Damian Carshalton, Carshalton Beeches **Buses**: 154, 407, 408, 726 Up to sixth form: Brown school blazer, school kilt, white blouse **Demand**: 320 applications for 184 places in 2001/2 **Type**: Voluntary aided Roman Catholic Technology College for 1120 girls, aged 11 to 18 **Submit application form**: Mid-October 2003 **Motto**: Unless the Lord builds this house, they labour in vain who build it. (Ps:127:1) **School hours**: 8.45am–3.35pm; homework clubs are available **Meals**: Hot and cold available **Strong GCSE subjects**: Art, English language and literature, geography, music, PE, RE **London league table position**: 109

## Profile

St Philomena's has been meeting the educational needs of Catholic girls predominantly in the Sutton and Croydon areas since it was first founded by the Daughters of the Cross in 1893. The school has a strong Catholic ethos. It gained Technical College status in 1997, allowing it dramatically to improve its IT, science and technology facilities. Despite having a population of 1120, St Philomena's retains an air of intimacy and offers a welcoming and pleasant community. It is one of Sutton's more attractive schools and is situated in 25 acres of grounds. A beautiful Queen Anne mansion houses the school offices and sixth-form centre. St Philomena's also enjoys very good accommodation for design and technology, with good facilities for science, history, geography, music and an indoor swimming pool. In addition, there is a new dining hall and a new school hall has been built. Pupils are encouraged to become involved in the running of the school, especially in the sixth-form council. There is a parent-teacher association and provision for pupils with special needs.

## Admissions and intake

Application is made directly to the school. Priority is given, in order, to: practising Catholics living within a 6km (3.75 mile) radius of the school; practising Catholics living outside this limit; and those who have a link with another faith; and can show that they would benefit from a Catholic education.

## Achievement

St Philomena's 2002 GCSE exam results were well above the national average, with 84 per cent of pupils obtaining five or more A*–C grades. This was up from 74 per cent in 2001 and an improvement on recent years, when results have consistently hovered between 61 and 65 per cent. The average point score was 45.3 and the school was ranked seventh in the borough. Over 95 per cent of pupils decide to remain in education following GCSEs, most choosing to stay at St Philomena's. Most pupils sit 10 GCSEs. There are 18 A-levels on offer, including unusual options such as sociology, psychology, human biology and theatre studies. These have been augmented by the introduction of vocational courses in business studies, health and social care and a nursery nursing course. Standards have risen sharply in recent years, and in 2002 the average point score for pupils taking two or more A/AS-levels was 252.7, just below the national average. This placed the school seventh in the borough league table and these results represent a standard far exceeding that of many similar schools in neighbouring boroughs. According to the 1999 Ofsted report, 'pupils show a mature and positive approach to their work'. A total of 79 per cent of pupils continue into higher education.

### Extra-curricular activities

Societies on offer include those for music, art, drama, gardening, debating and public-speaking. Gymnastics, netball, dance, tennis, athletics, volleyball, rounders, lacrosse and swimming are among the various sports available. The school also has homework clubs after school hours in many of its subjects. Visits are arranged to local museums, galleries, theatres and lectures. Residential skiing and canoeing trips are also organized, as well as language visits to France and Germany. Pupils raise funds for local charities.

# Stanley Park High School

**Stanley Park Road, Carshalton, Surrey SM5 3HP** ☎ 020 8647 5842 📠 020 8669 0151 ⓔ actsphs@rmplc.co.uk Mr MG Dunman; Chair of Governors: Mrs S Norris ⇌ Wallington, Carshalton **Buses**: 154 Navy blue sweatshirt, white or blue shirt or blouse; school tie for boys; Sixth form: Smart casual dress **Demand**: 362 applications for 180 places in 2001/2 **Type**: Community comprehensive for 1000 mixed pupils, aged 11 to 18 **Submit application form**: Mid-October 2003 **School hours**: 8.30am–3.10pm, 8.30am–4.10pm (Friday, Years 10/11); homework clubs are available **Meals**: Hot and cold available **Strong GCSE subjects**: Drama **London league table position**: 490

## Profile

Stanley Park is an improving school, with a pleasant residential setting. It is also expanding, having welcomed its first sixth-form students in 1997. The attractive main building is well complemented by modern additions, providing the school with up-to-date IT units, science labs, art studios, a purpose-built learning resources centre and a number of classrooms in recent years. Pupils are streamed according to ability from Year 8 in many subjects. The curriculum has been enhanced by the addition of GNVQs in art and design, IT and a basic skills course in leisure and tourism. Around 70 per cent of Stanley Park's Year 11 pupils decide to remain in education beyond the age of 16. Those that remain at Stanley Park have a wide choice of traditional A- and AS-levels as well as GNVQ courses. All pupils in Year 10 or 11 have a work-experience placement. Pupils also have a one-to-one discussion about progress with their form tutor each term. The school encourages pupils to participate in the school council, where all year groups are able to voice their opinions. There is a parent-teacher association and provision for pupils with special needs. Truancy is a problem and although the truancy rate is just above the national average at 1.6 per cent, it is high for the borough.

## Admissions and intake

Admission is through the LEA (see borough factfile). The school suffers from the proximity of four selective schools, which regularly succeed in attracting the most able students. As a result, many of Stanley Park's pupils have have low levels of attainment on entry, with about a quarter of the annual intake having reading and writing difficulties. Most pupils are drawn from the Wallington and Beddington wards, which are characterized by comparatively high levels of social and economic disadvantage.

## Achievement

Considering the school's difficulties, the progress that pupils make while at Stanley Park is commendable. Results have improved markedly over the past few years, with the proportion of pupils gaining five or more A*–C grades at GCSE more than doubling between 1997 and 1999. They were, however, starting from a low base and in 2002 reached 26 per cent, well below the national average. The school came one from the bottom of the borough league table. In 2002, the average point score for those pupils taking two or more A-levels was 172.2 This was below the borough and national averages. These results again placed the school near the bottom of the borough league table for A-levels. Ofsted visited the school in 2001 and noted that it provides its pupils with 'a satisfactory quality of education whilst operating within a very challenging context'. Pupils were seen to make progress at the rate expected, given their attainment when they enter the school. Inspectors found the quality of teaching and learning overall to be 'satisfactory' and good in the sixth form. However, behaviour was seen to be 'variable' with standards of attainment needing to be improved throughout the school. Attendance levels also need to be raised and authorized absence is the highest in the borough at 10.5 per cent.

### Extra-curricular activities

The school's main emphasis is on sport and drama. Sports on offer include football, rugby, athletics, cricket and tennis. Drama productions are regularly staged at the school. After-school homework clubs are organized at the school. There are trips both at home and abroad. Pupils are involved with the local community and undertake community service.

## Stowford College

**95 Brighton Road, Sutton, Surrey SM2 5SJ** ☎ 020 8661 9444 Fax 020 8661 6136 RJ Shakespeare BA (Hons), MA Sutton **Buses:** 80, 280, 420 Dark trousers or blue skirt, blue shirt or blouse, school tie, royal blue blazer (boys); blue V-neck jumper (girls) **Demand:** No figures available but intake variable **Type:** Selective independent for 87 mixed pupils, aged 7 to 17 **Fees** (per term): From £1,700 in Year 7 to £2,180 in Year 11 **Submit application form:** No cut-off date **Motto:** To Love and Learn **School hours:** 8.40am–3.35pm, 8.40am–3pm (Fri); homework clubs are available **Meals:** Not provided **Strong GCSE subjects:** All relatively strong **London league table position:** 513

### Profile

Founded in 1975, this small independent day school has found considerable success in dealing with pupils who have had learning difficulties in more conventional secondary schools. It is an attractive school, set in two acres of landscaped grounds that include a playground, lawns and woodland. Playing fields are within a few minutes' walk from the school. For more specialist sporting needs, local facilities such as the Westcroft Sports Centre are used. Given its size, the school offers a remarkably broad curriculum. It guarantees a teacher-to-pupil ratio of less than 10:1, enabling it to provide a family atmosphere and unique levels of personal attention throughout a pupil's school life. As a result, the school achieves well with pupils who have found it hard to settle or perform at larger, more amorphous institutions. Stowford also offers a comprehensive dyslexia programme, which is taught by a team of qualified dyslexia tutors throughout the school.

### Admissions and intake

Applications are made directly to the school. All prospective pupils and their parents are interviewed.

### Achievement

In 2002, just eight per cent of pupils gained five or more A*–C grades at GCSE. This was down from 29 per cent in 2001. The average point score was 21.3 and the school was placed bottom of the borough league table. With such small numbers of pupils each year, results are highly variable, but there is a definite upward trend. Considering the difficulties that its pupils face, the majority of students make good progress in its intimate environment.

### Extra-curricular activities

Given the size of the school, the range of activities on offer is understandably limited. However, Friday afternoons are set aside for arts and crafts, drama, computers, stamp collecting, chess and discussion groups, as well as various sporting activities. The main competitive sports are football, athletics and hockey. Drama productions of a high standard are staged annually, some of which have gained several merit awards at ISA drama competitions. Many trips are organized, including geography field trips to Dorset, history trips to York and science trips to Bath. A one-week trip to Israel, a weekend in Cologne and longer trips to France and Italy are among those that have been arranged overseas. Homework clubs are available.

# Sutton Grammar School for Boys

**Manor Lane, Sutton, Surrey SM1 4AS** 020 8642 3821 020 8770 9070 info-sgs@suttonlea.org www.suttongrammar.sutton.sch.uk Mr GD Ironside MA, C.Math, FIMA; Chair of Governors: Mr C Townsend Sutton **Buses**: S1, S3, 80, 151, 164, 213, 280, 407, 413 Red school blazer, dark trousers, white shirt, school tie; Sixth form: Jacket and tie **Demand**: 1054 applications for 120 places in 2001/2 **Type**: Grammar school for 790 boys, aged 11 to 18 **Submit application form**: Mid-October 2003 **Motto**: Keep Faith **School hours**: 8.35am–3.45pm; homework clubs are available **Meals**: Hot and cold available **Strong GCSE subjects**: English, mathematics, science **London league table position**: 48

## Profile

Sutton Grammar has been providing an excellent standard of education for its pupils since it was founded in 1899. It is one of London's 19 remaining grammar schools. Its central Sutton site is somewhat restricted, with no outside sports facilities, but the school does own 27 acres at Northey Avenue in Cheam, access to which is provided by the school's own coach. The buildings are dominated by the original 1928 structure, but an indoor heated swimming pool was added in 1970. Similarly, a major new teaching block and an up-to-date music centre were built in the 1990s. All boys in Year 11 undertake work experience, and pupils are able to participate in the school council. There is a parent-teacher association and provision for pupils with special needs.

## Admissions and intake

Application is made directly to the school. Priority in admissions is given firstly to those boys whose applications are supported by appropriate medical reasons, and secondly to those who gain the 30 highest results in the school's own entrance exam, held in mid-November, and irrespective of where they live. Places are then given to those applicants who live within a 9km (5.5 mile) radius of the Sutton civic offices, in rank order according to the entrance exam, followed by those beyond this limit, again in rank order. About half of the pupils come from Sutton, with the rest coming from surrounding boroughs.

## Achievement

In 2000, Ofsted visited the school and noted that 'students' attitudes to work and their behaviour are excellent'. Sutton Grammar is a 'successful school' where the teaching is 'good or better in just over three-quarters of lessons'. Standards are high in many subjects but especially in English, mathematics and science. In 2002, 95 per cent of pupils gained five or more A*–C grades at GCSE. This was well above the national average but down from 99 per cent in 2001. The average point score was 54.5 and the school was placed sixth in the borough. Sutton Grammar also consistently performs well at A-level. In 2002, it finished joint second in the borough league table, with pupils taking two or more subjects gaining an average of 425.8 points. This was significantly above the national and local averages.

## Extra-curricular activities

The school has a fine tradition of sporting success, with football, athletics, cricket and basketball dominating the sporting calendar. It also has a Combined Cadet Force, with both Army and RAF sections, as well as a Duke of Edinburgh's Award group. The school also offers chess and its chess club has won the London Championship in recent years. Clubs available include those for electronics, art, debating, computers and radio-controlled cars, as well as after-school homework clubs. *The Suttonian* magazine, along with drama and music productions, provide further opportunities for pupils' creative talents. There is an activities week in July when Years 7 to 9 enjoy a variety of special outings and events. The school also organizes exchanges to France and Germany, geography and history trips and an annual skiing trip.

# Sutton High School

**55 Cheam Road, Sutton, Surrey SM1 2AX** 020 8642 0594 020 8642 2014 office@sut.gdst.net Mr S Callaghan; Chair of Governors: Mr EB Totman Sutton **Buses**: 151, 420, 613 Up to sixth form: Lilac blazer, white blouse, grey skirt **Demand**: No figures available but 60 places **Type**: Selective independent girls' day school trust for 689 girls, aged 4 to 18 **Fees**: £2,385 per term **Submit application form**: End of November 2003 **Motto**: Faithfully, Bravely, Cheerfully **School hours**: 8.30am–3.45pm **Meals**: Not provided **Strong GCSE subjects**: All relatively strong **London league table position**: 38

## Profile

Sutton High School was founded in 1884, and currently occupies a five-acre site near to the centre of Sutton. Although the school has an impressive range of modern facilities, the main site itself is somewhat cramped. The school's playing fields are located off-site in Cheam. The buildings comprise six adjacent houses on Cheam and Grove Roads, supplemented by modern additions such as the recently refurbished swimming pool and new sixth-form centre. At Key Stage 4, pupils are presented with a wide range of options, all of which are taught to the highest standards. The vast majority of students continue their education at the school, joined by a handful of pupils from neighbouring schools. Girls can choose from 21 A-levels, with most pupils studying at least three subjects. The school council provides pupils of all ages with the chance to contribute to the running of the school. There is provision for pupils with special needs.

## Admissions and intake

The school has its own entrance exam held in early January. In keeping with the founding principles of the Girls' Day School Trust of providing affordable independent schooling, a generous system of bursaries is available, depending on financial need. The school also runs a separate system of scholarships, but these are awarded solely on the grounds of academic merit. Pupils are drawn from across Sutton and large parts of the surrounding areas of Surrey.

## Achievement

In 2002, 97 per cent of pupils gained five or more A*–C grades at GCSE. This was three per cent down on 2001 and well above the national average. The average point score was 55.3 and this placed the school third in the borough league table. At A-level, the average point score for pupils taking two or more subjects was 360, placing it fifth in the borough for A-level results. The school has also worked hard to develop good links with universities – successfully sending 90 per cent of its students on to them, with a significant number each year going on to Oxford and Cambridge.

## Extra-curricular activities

The lack of playing fields at the main site does not appear to have hindered pupils' appetite for sports, and there are many competitive and non-competitive opportunities to play hockey, netball, tennis and rounders. Pupils can also enjoy swimming, gymnastics, badminton, volleyball and aerobics. The school has a thriving Duke of Edinburgh's Award group. Drama and music activities are strong, with a wide range of orchestras, bands and string groups. Girls are encouraged to engage in community service. The school organizes a variety of trips, including visits to London's museums, theatres and other places of interest. It also arranges French and German exchanges.

# Wallington County Grammar School

**Croydon Road, Wallington, Surrey SM6 7PH** ☎ 020 8254 7921 📠 020 8669 8190 ⓔ wcgs@suttonlea.org Dr JM Haworth; Chair of Governors: Mr FL Townsend ⇌ Wallington **Buses**: S5, 151, 407, 408, 410, 726 School blazer, dark grey trousers, white shirt, school tie; Sixth form: Jacket and tie **Demand**: 1163 applications for 120 places in 2001/2 **Type**: Grammar school for 800 boys (mixed in sixth form), aged 11 to 18 **Submit application form**: Mid-October 2003 **School hours**: 8.30am–2.40pm (Mon, Thurs, Fri, Year 11), 8.30am–3.15pm (Mon, Thurs, Fri, Sixth form), 8.30am–2.55pm (Tues, Wed; all Years); homework clubs are available **Meals**: Hot and cold available **Strong GCSE subjects**: All relatively strong **London league table position**: 43

## Profile

The school was founded in 1927 and moved to its current location in 1935. It is one of London's 19 remaining grammar schools. The attractive buildings are well complemented by the nine acres of landscaped grounds in which they are set. In 1996, the school's facilities were enhanced with the construction of a new science block, allowing accommodation for music, IT and geography to be expanded. The school has sufficient on-site playing fields to cover most of its sporting needs, with additional pitches and an all-weather, floodlit hockey pitch at the Old Walcountians' Association at Woodmansterne. However, the sports hall and design and technology facilities have some serious deficiencies. In 1999, Ofsted suggested that these deficiencies impaired the education available in these departments. A total of 81 per cent of boys stay on into the sixth form and are joined by a small number of girls. Pupils can assume extra responsibilities through the prefect system for sixth-formers and house committees, which are open to all years. There is an active PTA, which is successful in raising funds for the school.

### Admissions and intake

Admissions are based on the school's own entrance exam, held in the November preceding the start of the academic year. Of the 686 boys who took the selective test in 1999, 221 were successful, all of whom were offered a place. In the event of applications from pupils deemed of selective ability, priority will be given to those with a direct family link to the school, or those with medical reasons supporting their application. Remaining places will be given in rank order as determined by the selective tests to those who live within a 9km (5.5 mile) radius of the school, and then in rank order to those living beyond this limit.

### Achievement

Ofsted found that 'pupils show very positive attitudes to learning; they are highly motivated, conscientious and demonstrate a very good work ethos'. These attitudes are reflected in the school's very high levels of achievement over the past few years. In 2002, 100 per cent of pupils gained five or more A*–C grades at GCSE, well above the national average. The school was placed fourth in the borough. A strength of the school is its broad choice of subjects with Latin and economics available on the pre-sixth form curriculum. Most pupils take 10 or more GCSEs. The average point score for pupils taking two or more A/AS-levels was 388.4. This placed the school fourth in the borough. The pupils currently studying for A-level exams have the choice of 23 subjects and numerous AS-level courses.

### Extra-curricular activities

Lunchtime and after-school clubs available include bridge, chess, history of art, public speaking, the Christian Union and pottery. A strong emphasis is also placed on competitive sports, with rugby, hockey, cricket and athletics having the highest profile. Music and drama groups are also popular. The school organizes annual French and German exchanges. School trips have included a history visit to the battlefields of World War I, a skiing trip and a number of sports tours.

## Wallington High School for Girls

**Woodcote Road, Wallington, Surrey SM6 0PH** 020 8647 2380 020 8773 9884 Miss MJ Edwards B.Sc; Chair of Governors: Mr P Stockwell Wallington **Buses:** S4, S5, 127 151, 410, 455, 463 Up to sixth form: Blue checked skirt, green school jumper, blue blouse **Demand:** 1015 applications for 180 places in 2001/2 **Type:** Grammar school for 1100 girls, aged 11 to 18 **Submit application form:** Mid-October 2003 **Motto:** Heirs of the Past, Makers of the Future **School hours:** 8.30am–2.40pm (Mon, Thurs), 8.30am–3.05pm (Tues, Fri) **Meals:** Hot and cold available **Strong GCSE subjects:** All relatively strong **London league table position:** 23

### Profile

Wallington High is a grant-maintained grammar school situated in pleasant surroundings on the edge of London's green belt. Originally established in Carshalton in 1888, the school moved to its present, purpose-built site in 1965. It is one of London's 19 remaining grammar schools. Most pupils select nine or 10 GCSEs from a broad range on offer. A total of 91 per cent then choose to remain at the school beyond Key Stage 4, and it is also a popular choice with pupils from other schools. All pupils in Year 10 have a work experience placement. There is a school council and a parent-teacher association. There is provision for pupils with special needs.

### Admissions and intake

The school selects its pupils from the top 20 per cent of the ability range via a selective exam held in November. Priority amongst those who are deemed to be of selective ability is given to those applicants who have either siblings at the school or special medical reasons supporting their application. A total of 40 places are then awarded solely on the basis of academic merit, with the remaining places being determined by a complex formula involving the distance that prospective pupils live from the school.

### Achievement

In 2002, 99 per cent of pupils gained five or more A*–C grades at GCSE. This was consistent with previous years, and the school was placed top of the borough GCSE league table. Results at A/AS-level were also impressive. Pupils taking two or more subjects gained an average point score of 323.5, above the borough and national averages. This placed the school sixth in the borough league table. The curriculum is extensive in the sixth form, with a choice of 31 A-levels and 18 AS-levels. GNVQs, however, are not on offer. In 1999, 77 per cent of pupils went on to institutions of higher education. Wallington High provides an orderly, well-disciplined and attractive environment in which pupils can excel. Indeed, the 1999 Ofsted report could find 'no significant weaknesses' in the school, describing it as an institution that 'nourishes and sustains the excellent personal development of its pupils'.

### Extra-curricular activities

Pupils enjoy a wide range of activities, from masterclasses in maths and Royal Institute of Science seminars, to theatre visits and drama, Christian Union and Amnesty International groups. Additional certificated courses are also available through the Young Enterprise, Foreign Languages at Work and Community Sports Leadership schemes. Sports on offer include netball, hockey, tennis, rounders, cricket and badminton. Pupils raise funds for local charities. There are trips both at home and abroad, including a skiing trip to the US and an art trip to Italy.

## Wilson's School

**Mollison Drive, Wallington, Surrey SM6 9JW** ☎ 020 8773 2931 📠 020 8773 4972 ⓔ adminoffice@wilsonschool.sutton.sch.uk Mr DM Charnock BD Mth; Chair of Governors: Mr RE McAlister Waddon **Buses:** S4, 154, 157, 445 Black school blazer, dark trousers, white shirt, school tie **Demand:** 1042 applications for 120 places in 2001/2 **Type:** Voluntary aided Church of England grammar school for 890 boys, aged 11 to 18 **Submit application form:** Mid-October 2003 **School hours:** 8.40am–3.40pm **Meals:** Hot and cold available **Strong GCSE subjects:** English, history **London league table position:** 42

### Profile

Wilson's School was originally founded in 1615 and located in Camberwell. It is one of London's 19 remaining grammar schools and was recently designated a specialist college in mathematics and computing. It moved to its current, more spacious location on the edge of Sutton in 1975. The school benefits from a pleasant setting and an outstanding range of facilities. The striking yellow-brick school building was purpose built during the mid-1970s. However, the building has had recent additions, all of which are in keeping with the school's original design. A new sixth-form block was opened in 1997. It has also upgraded its IT resources, constructed a well-equipped technology and creative arts block and added a science lab. The classrooms are generally well maintained and spacious. Sports facilities include a large indoor swimming pool, squash courts and extensive on-site playing fields. All Year 11 pupils have a work experience placement. The school is keen to develop a sense of responsibility, and there is a strong system of prefects in the sixth form and a school council open to all year groups. All but a small minority of pupils stay on into the sixth form. There is a parent-teacher association and provision for pupils with special needs.

### Admissions and intake

While the school maintains its traditional links with the Church of England, it does welcome all faiths. Admissions are based solely on academic ability as determined by the school's selective exam held in November. Pupils are drawn from all over Sutton and Croydon.

### Achievement

The school has a long tradition of providing its pupils with the best educational opportunities, as well as producing outstanding results and well-rounded individuals. In 2002, 100 per cent of pupils gained five or more A*–C grades at GCSE, four per cent up on the previous year. This result was well above the national average and the school was ranked fifth in the borough. Wilson's offers a selection of interesting GCSE choices beyond the requirements of the National Curriculum. Business studies, economics, IT, Latin, Greek and sports studies may all be taken as options at Key Stage 4. The average point score of pupils taking two or more A/AS-levels in 2002 was 418.1, well above the national and local averages, ranking the school third in the borough. The school also offers a strong choice of A-levels, including classical studies, economics, music technology and further maths, plus an AS-level in psychology. Ofsted noted that 'Wilson's is a very good school in which an ethos of learning and high achievement is promoted in the context of a caring and supportive environment.' Moreover, 'pupils learn to take responsibility for their actions and have well-developed values and principles'.

## Extra-curricular activities

A wide range of extra-curricular activities are on offer at Wilson's. There are regular competitive events for Wilson's strong football, athletics, cricket, cross-country and water-polo teams. An impressive range of lunchtime and after-school clubs cater for almost all interests. Pupils are also given the opportunity to make use of a field centre in Wales for biology and geography field trips, as well as trips abroad. Pupils raise funds for local charities.

# Tower Hamlets

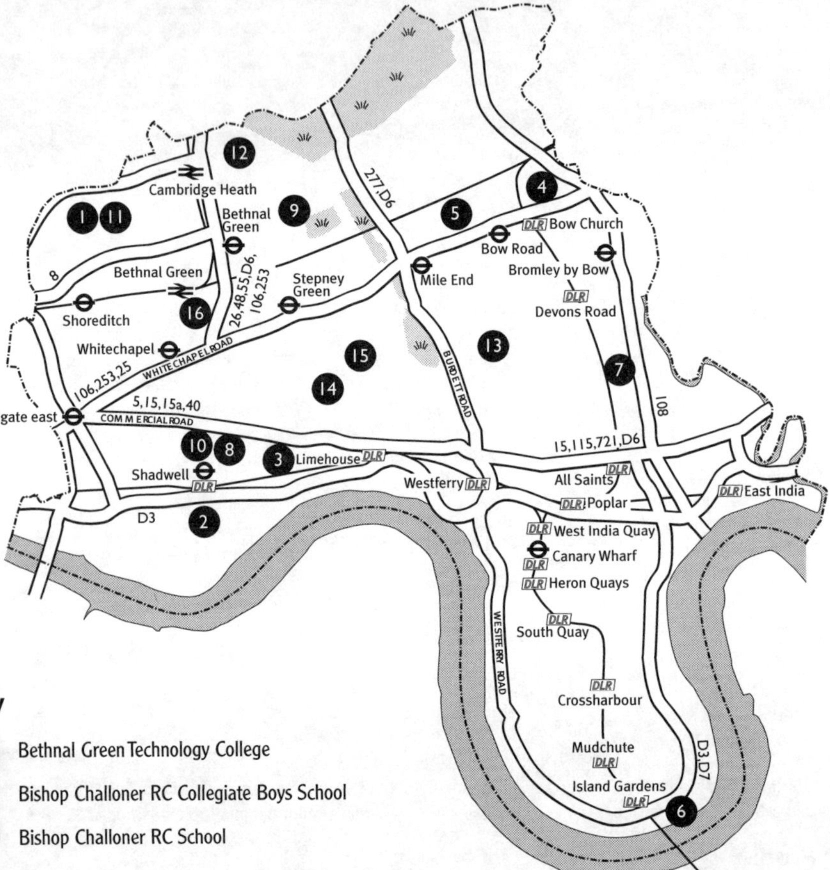


## Key

1. Bethnal Green Technology College
2. Bishop Challoner RC Collegiate Boys School
3. Bishop Challoner RC School
4. Bow School
5. Central Foundation Girls' School
6. George Green's School
7. Langdon Park Community School
8. Madni Secondary Girls' School
9. Morpeth School
10. Mulberry School for Girls
11. Oaklands School
12. Raine's Foundation School
13. St Paul's Way Community School
14. Sir John Cass Foundation & Redcoat CofE School
15. Stepney Green School
16. Swanlea School

# Factfile

**LEA: Mulberry Place, 5 Clove Crescent, London E14 2BG** 020 7364 5000 www.towerhamlets.gov.uk **Director of Education:** Stephen Grix **Political control of council:** Labour **Percentage of pupils from outside the borough:** 7.6 per cent **Percentage of pupils educated outside the borough:** 4.3 per cent **London league table positions (out of 32 boroughs):** 22nd

## Profile

Tower Hamlets is Britain's poorest borough, but is also the most improved borough in London, despite its high level of social disadvantage. The rate of improvement between 1995–7 was generally at or above the national rate, and data for 1998–9 shows a continuation of this trend. Since 1989, those pupils achieving five or more GCSEs at A*–C grades has risen from 8 per cent to 43.6 per cent in 2002. The number of pupils gaining two A-levels has more than trebled since 1991. An Ofsted inspection in 1998 found serious weaknesses in management and strategic planning. A new director has since been appointed and a second inspection in 2000 described the progress made as a 'success story for the LEA'.

## Policy

The council's admissions policy applies to all community and voluntary controlled schools and Sir John Cass. A quarter of the places available at each school are allocated to each of the four reading bands. If any of these schools are oversubscribed in any reading band, the following criteria, in order of priority, is used: pupils with a statement of special educational needs; pupils who have a medical or social reason to attend the school; pupils living nearest the school who are the first born of their sex for single-sex schools or the eldest child for mixed schools; pupils with a sibling currently at the school; and pupils who live nearest to the school by the shortest walking route. In the last three categories, a higher priority will be given to pupils who live in the geographical areas of south Wapping applying to Mulberry, Stepney Green and Sir John Cass, or those who live in west Bethnal Green and are applying to Swanlea and Sir John Cass.

# Bethnal Green Technology College

**Gosset Street, Bethnal Green, London E2 6NW** 020 7920 7900 020 7920 7999 info@bgtc.t-hamlets.sch.uk Mr Allen Wadsworth B.Sc, MA; Chair of Governors: Mr Ian Hastings Liverpool Street Bethnal Green, Liverpool Street **Buses:** 5, 6, 8, 55 Green blazer, black trousers or skirt, yellow and green striped school tie, black shoes **Demand:** 284 applications for 180 places in 2001/2 **Type:** Community comprehensive Technology College for 773 mixed pupils, aged 11 to 16 **Submit application form:** 28 November 2003 **Mission statement:** To give our students the broadest educational opportunities in a college committed to harnessing the practical and motivational benefits of modern technology in science, technology and maths, so they can achieve their highest standards across the curriculum, and leave the college well prepared to earn their living in a technologically advanced society. **School hours:** 8.45am–3.15pm; homework clubs are available **Meals:** Hot and cold available **Strong GCSE subjects:** Bengali, drama, IT, PE **London league table position:** 401

## Profile

Bethnal Green Technology College became mixed in 1995, having previously been a boys' school. It was built 100 years ago and merged with nearby Mansford school in 1964 to become the Daneford School for Boys. In 1996, it became a Technology College, specializing in ICT. Over recent years, the school has invested heavily in Apple Macintosh computer hardware and has become an 'Apple college', with a fibre-optic network running 200 stations in seven ICT rooms. ICT is also becoming an integral part of science, maths, English, technology, music and art. In 1998, a new sports hall was built with lottery money, funded by the Sports Council. There are now two new squash courts, badminton courts, indoor hockey and two multi-gyms with weight-lifting equipment. The school is open in the evenings and at weekends and is well used by members of the community. It has a strong special-needs department. There is a parent-teacher association and a school council.

## Admissions and intake

Admission is through the LEA (see borough factfile). Boys still outnumber girls; there are twice as many boys than girls and they are taught separately.

## Achievement

The Ofsted report in 2000 found that the school does well for its pupils and by the end of Year 11 they achieve high standards in comparison to similar schools. Results for humanities are the most disappointing but are showing signs of improvement. The best-performing subjects are languages and the creative arts. Ofsted found that pupils achieve high standards in Bengali, PE, drama and GNVQ IT. It also noted that determined, effective and well-organized teaching in Years 10 and 11 has led to a steady improvement in pupils' achievement. However, the weaknesses mentioned included low standards of literacy and numeracy and slow pupils' learning. Achievements in Years 7 to 9 were also deemed to be too low, particularly for boys, pupils with special educational needs and in maths. However, Ofsted noted that GCSE results have greatly improved since the last inspection in 1996, although they were still below the national average. In 2002, 42 per cent of pupils gained five or more A*–C grades, below the borough average. This was up from 24 per cent in 2001 and the school was placed 13th in the borough. Inspectors commented that lateness to lessons and uneven attendance, together with the attitudes and behaviour of some boys, could mean some pupils do not learn as well as they could. A large proportion of pupils go on to further education.

## Extra-curricular activities

Hockey is one area of sport in which pupils excel, regularly representing Middlesex and England at college-student level. Five years ago, the under-14 hockey team became national champions after winning the Middlesex and South of England titles. Pupils also compete in weightlifting. There are after-school homework clubs and trips both at home and abroad.

# Bishop Challoner Roman Catholic Collegiate Boys' School

455 The Highway, London E1W 9HT ☎ 020 7364 5742 Fax 020 7364 5029 ✉ donben@bishopchalloner.thamlets.sch.uk Head: Mrs Catherine Myers BA, Dip.Ed; Chair of Governors: Mr Dan Regan ⊖ Shadwell, Docklands Light Railway: Limehouse **Buses**: D3, 5, 15, 40, 100, 156, 215 Uniform: Green blazer and pullover, school tie, black shoes, the required shirt colour changes with each year group **Demand**: 212 applications for 90 places in 2001/2 **Type**: Voluntary aided Catholic boys school for 450 pupils, aged 11 to 16 **Submit application form**: December 2003 **Motto**: Thy Kingdom Come **School hours**: 8.30am–3.05pm **Meals**: Hot and cold available **Strong GCSE subjects**: Not applicable (no pupils will sit GCSEs until 2006) **London league table position**: Not applicable

## Profile

Bishop Challoner boys school opened in September 2001 as the country's first collegiate school. It shares a governing body and teaching staff with the established girls school in Commercial Road but they are on different sites and funded separately. The arrangement is so unusual that the school needed special legislation before it could open. The diocese and LEA are working to provide a site on which to build the new boys' school. Until then, lessons are held in one half of the Shadwell Centre, a former school and adult education centre.

## Admissions and intake

The opening of Bishop Challoner boys' school coincides with the closure of The Blessed John Roche school in Upper North Street, Poplar, to new applications. Bishop Challoner will not be full until 2005, at which time The Blessed John Roche will close for good. Bishop Challoner has a relatively small intake and this is deliberate. There were 150 applications for 93 places in 2000/1, and 10 of those who failed to get in then appealed. Applications are invited from practising Catholics, but will be considered from practising Christians of any denomination. As a voluntary aided school, it is its own admissions authority, so applications should be made directly to the school.

## Achievement

Pupils at the school will not sit GCSEs until summer 2006. They will sit Key Stage 3 tests in 2004, and the government has said it will publish these results nationally.

## Extra curricular activities

There are after-school football, basketball, art and information technology clubs.

# Bishop Challoner Roman Catholic School

**Hardinge Street, London E1 0EB** 020 7790 3634 020 7702 7398 Mrs Catherine Myers; Chair of Governors: Mr Dan Regan Aldgate East, Shadwell, Whitechapel; Docklands Light Railway: Limehouse **Buses:** D3, 5, 15B, 25, 40, 215 Up to sixth form: Navy blue skirt and blazer; each year group has a different-coloured shirt collar **Demand:** 235 applications for 180 places in 2001/2 **Type:** Voluntary aided comprehensive for 1020 girls (mixed in sixth form), aged 11 to 18 **Submit application form:** 28 November 2003 **Mission statement:** Bishop Challoner is a community for teaching and learning, where each individual's distinctive talents are recognized and nurtured within a Catholic framework. **School hours:** 8.40am–3.05pm; homework clubs are available **Meals:** Hot and cold available **Strong GCSE subjects:** Art, English **London league table position:** 339

## Profile

Bishop Challoner School was founded by the Sisters of Mercy in the early 1930s, and was run by nuns until the current lay head was appointed. The oldest building dates from 1972, with recent additions including the sixth-form building, an extension with 19 new classrooms, new admin and computer rooms, a new library and Olympic-standard sports hall. The school's computer facilities are very good and include a multimedia suite with 30 Apple Macs. There is also a dance studio, a music recording studio and a theatre. The performing arts are one of the school's strengths. Pupils can participate in the school council, and older students act as mentors towards the younger girls. There is a parent-teacher association. In 2000, unauthorized absence was at 4.7 per cent, above the national average.

## Admissions and intake

Application is through the school. When oversubscribed, the following order of priority is applied: practising baptized Roman Catholic children, supported by evidence from their parish priest; other practising Christians; and children of other parents/guardians who fully support the school's Catholic aims and ethos. Those applicants living closest to the school, measured in a straight line, are given preference if there is oversubscription. In all instances, siblings have first priority. Around 40 pupils have statements of special needs.

## Achievement

In 1999, Bishop Challoner was deemed one of the most improved schools in the country. Ofsted's report praised the school's focus on teaching and learning as well as its strong leadership. In 2002, 48 per cent of pupils achieved five or more A*–C grades at GCSE, this was up from 38 per cent the previous year. The school was placed 10th in the borough. Ofsted commended the school's strengths in English and art. However, inspectors also commented that there were low standards in three areas where National Curriculum requirements were not met: few students study modern languages at Key Stage 4, provision for games is insufficient in PE at Key Stage 3 and little work on control is done in design and technology. They also noted that results at A-level are much lower than results of sixth-form vocational courses. In 2002, the average point score for pupils taking two or more A/AS-levels was 152.7, ranking the school fourth out of six in the borough. Results at GNVQ tend to be in line with or better than the national average. Similarly, progress on GNVQ courses is found to be generally good.

## Extra curricular activities

Activities available include gymnastics, athletics, cricket and horse riding, as well as drama and dance. There are homework and revision classes. School trips have included visits to Lithuania to do volunteer work with orphans, and Disneyland Paris. Year 8 spend a week at a Catholic boarding school in Surrey, where they take part in outdoor activities. Pupils do fund-raising for local charities.

# Bow School

**Paton Close, Fairfield Road, London E3 2QD** 020 8980 0118 020 8980 1556 bs@bow-school.org.uk Ms Beverly Dobson; Chair of Governors: Mr Charles Teale Bow Road; Docklands Light Railway: Bow Church **Buses:** D8, S2, 10, 25, 86, 225 Grey trousers and sweater, green school tie **Demand:** 148 applications for 150 places in 2001/2 **Type:** Community comprehensive for 669 boys, aged 11 to 16 **Submit application form:** 28 November 2003 **Motto:** Educating the Whole Child **School hours:** 9am–3.35pm, 9am–2.45pm (Fri) **Meals:** Hot and cold available **Strong GCSE subjects:** Art, Bengali, drama, statistics **London league table position:** 487

## Profile

Bow School has three very distinct main buildings, two of which were refurbished in 1995. All teaching areas are now linked by a computer network, and there are five new science labs, an entire floor for technology, graphics and art, and a modern language faculty that includes a language lab. The third building houses the Bow Family Centre, which is used by pupils and their families, and provides counselling and support for the local community. The school also has a state-of-the-art drama studio, recording studio and fitness suite. Additional land is being acquired through a compulsory purchase order for recreational use. ICT provision will also be expanded, and three ICT suites are due to be built. The school has a new head with an impressive track record, who aims to inspire confidence amongst all pupils and raise levels of achievement across the school. A new, revised curriculum was launched in 2001. Tutors and heads of year provide pastoral care. Pupils are encouraged to assist with the running of the library or production of the half-termly newsletter. They can also care for the school plants and act as guides for visitors. The Friends of Bow School promotes the partnership between home and school, and its activities include arranging parents' evenings, organizing fund-raising events for the school and running the school shop. There is a school council. Ashley Cole, football player for Arsenal, is a former pupil.

## Admission and intake

Admission is through the LEA (see borough factfile). In 2001, 24 per cent of pupils had special needs with six per cent having statements of special needs.

## Achievement

In 2002, 18 per cent of pupils achieved A*–C grades at GCSE. These were the worst results in the borough but an increase on 16 per cent in 2001. Ofsted visited the school in 2001 and commented: 'Though the school has many strengths, and improvement has been rapid in the last year, results are lower than they should be and behaviour and attendance are unsatisfactory'. However, Inspectors praised the 'very good' leadership of the head teacher, and teaching, learning and pupils' progress overall were seen to be 'satisfactory'. Over half the teaching was seen to be good. Strong GCSE subjects are art, drama, Bengali and statistics, but overall the school's GCSE performance was in the lowest five per cent of schools nationally. Provisional figures for unauthorized absence in 1999–2000 show a welcome improvement from 5.2 per cent in 1998–9 to 3.5 per cent. Many students go on to further education.

## Extra-curricular activities

There is a wide range of activities on offer, including homework clubs, reading clubs, creative arts clubs and a breakfast club. Sport is a particular strength at the school. One pupil runs for England, while another trains for the under-15 England football team. Bow School has represented the county at rugby and pupils have also played at county level in basketball. The school is also successful in cross-country. Boys regularly stage drama productions and musicals. There are visits to art galleries, museums and theatres, and pupils have the opportunity to go on sailing trips.

# Central Foundation Girls' School

**Harley Grove, Bow, London E3 2AT (upper school); College Road, Bow, London E3 5AW (lower school)** ☎ 020 8981 1131 📠 020 8983 0188 ⓔ welcome@central.towerhamlets.sch.uk ✉ Miss Pat Hull BA, M.Sc, FCP; Chair of Governors: Dr Keith Sales ⊖ Mile End, Bow Road; Docklands Light Railway: Bow Church **Buses:** D5, D6, D7, 25, 277 👔 Royal blue jumper with crest, grey skirt or trousers, or shalwar khameez; Sixth form: Smart office dress **Demand**: 436 applications for 240 in 2001/2 **Type**: Voluntary controlled comprehensive Performing Arts College for 1307 girls, aged 11 to 18 **Submit application form**: 28 November 2003 **Motto**: Educating Tomorrow's Women **School hours**: 8.45am–3.30pm, 8.45am–3.10pm (Fri); homework clubs are available **Meals**: Hot and cold available **Strong GCSE subjects**: English, geography, maths **London league table position**: 305

## Profile

Central Foundation Girls' School, one of the oldest schools in London, was founded in 1726 around Liverpool Street station. It is now on two sites, with an eight-minute walk in-between. In 2001, it became a Perfoming Arts College. Sixth-formers and Year 11 pupils study in a listed 1800s building and younger pupils study in one modern and three Victorian buildings. The new building has state-of-the-art facilities for English, maths, art and IT and a split-level library/learning resources centre. There are also new music rooms, science labs, graphics, textiles and food technology rooms. New dining facilities and a sports hall are planned for the upper school. The school gates are locked during the day and pupils are not allowed out of school at lunchtime. The school is keen to offer a broad curriculum and aims to ensure that girls have the confidence to pursue their goals. Music, sport and the arts play an important part in school life and pupils can learn to play an instrument or take singing lessons. The school also has links with the Guildhall School of Music. Work shadowing is arranged and most students are mentored by Unilever personnel, with whom the school has developed business links, as well as by the school governors. Parents are encouraged to take an active interest in their daughters' education. There is a school council and a prefects system.

### Admissions and intake

Admission is through the LEA (see borough factfile). Six months before pupils join, they are invited with their parents to visit the school. There are 31 students with statements of special needs.

### Achievement

In 2000, Ofsted described the school as a 'sound and improving school' where 'standards overall are rising'. The school usually performs well in relation to other secondary schools in the borough league table. In 2002, 42 per cent of pupils gained five or more A*–C grades – down from 46 per cent in 2001. The school was ranked seventh in the borough league table with an average point score of 34.2. The school came third in the borough for A-level results. The average point score for pupils taking two or more subjects was 162.6 in 2002, below the national and borough averages.

### Extra-curricular activities

There is a wide choice of clubs available, from homework and reading to sports. More unusual activities on offer include go-karting, canoeing, caving and orienteering. Girls take part in both borough and national sports competitions and have won the Tower Hamlets Youth Games, netball and football tournaments and athletics championships. One pupil went on to become an international gymnast. Activity trips are organized in the UK and abroad. The school has an annual arts festival, and there are frequent trips to the theatre, museums and galleries. Sixth-formers visit universities, enjoy residential weekends and also take part in volunteer work in the community.

## George Green's School

**100 Manchester Road, London E14 3DW** ☎ 020 7987 6032 📠 020 7538 2316 🌐 www.georgegreens.towerhamlets.sch.uk ✉ Mrs Kenny Frederick; Chair of Governors: Mrs Linda Williams ⊖ Docklands Light Railway: Island Gardens **Buses:** D7 👕 Navy blue sweatshirt with school logo, white polo shirt with school logo, dark trousers or skirt or shalwar khameez **Demand:** 335 applications for 210 places in 2001/2 **Type:** Voluntary controlled comprehensive for 930 mixed pupils, aged 11 to 19 **Submit application form:** 28 November 2003 **Motto:** Fidelity **School hours:** 8.45am–3.15pm; homework clubs are available **Meals:** Hot and cold available, including breakfast **Strong GCSE subjects:** Drama, performing arts, science **London league table position:** 363

### Profile

George Green's School was founded 160 years ago by a successful shipbuilder from Poplar. The present building was built in 1976 to resemble a ship and overlooks the Greenwich Maritime Museum. A new block houses eight science labs and all the IT areas have been refurbished. CCTV cameras protect the site and there is an electronic register. George Green's prides itself on meeting the needs of every one of its pupils, and it has earned an Investors in People Award. Many pupils have disabilities and learning difficulties, and the school is renowned for its inclusive educational policy. However, it does not offer wheelchair access. All pupils undertake work experience in Year 11, and there is a good deal of involvement from local businesses through the Tower Hamlets Education Business Partnership. Older pupils participate in a training programme and work alongside younger pupils to support them. They can also take part in peer counselling. Despite the school's very thorough approach towards attendance, an Ofsted inspection in 1998 found that unauthorized absence and punctuality were still unsatisfactory. There is a school council.

### Admissions and intake

Admission is through the LEA (see borough factfile). Some 45 pupils had special-needs statements in 2000.

### Achievement

In 1998, Ofsted commented on the dramatic improvements made since the last inspection and noted that the school had the understanding, motivation, systems and strategies to maintain this improvement. The rise in achievement in GCSEs was found to be higher than the national average. In 2002, 35 per cent of pupils gained five or more A*–C grades. This was below the borough and national averages, but up from 30 per cent in 2001. The school was placed 12th in the borough league table. Science is emerging as a strong subject, as are the performing arts and music. The school has applied for specialist status in the performing arts and drama. Weaknesses mentioned by Ofsted included the curriculum in IT and RE, and in PE in Years 10 and 11. At A-level, pupils taking two or more subjects achieved an average point score of 135.4 in 2002. This was below the borough average. The school was placed fifth out of six in the borough for A-levels.

### Extra-curricular activities

There is a wide variety of after-school clubs and activities on offer, one of the more unusual being cheerleading. Rugby and rowing are popular with both girls and boys and a school band performs regular concerts and shows. There is a breakfast club before school, the learning resource centre is open early in the morning and there are after-school homework clubs. During the summer holidays, a five-week programme is organized for gifted and talented pupils. There are weekend residential events along with trips to Europe. Sixth-formers are involved in the Young Enterprise programme, which includes setting up their own businesses. The school supports a different charity every year.

## Langdon Park Community School

**Byron Street, Poplar, London E14 ORY** 020 7987 4811 020 7537 7282 langdonpark.towerhamlets.sch.uk Mr Chris Dunne; Chair of Governors: Peter Wright Bromley-by-Bow; Docklands Light Railway: All Saints **Buses**: D6, D8, 309, 5, 15, 40 Black trousers or skirt, white shirt, black school tie with a yellow stripe **Demand**: 259 applications for 180 places in 2001/2 **Type**: Community comprehensive for 889 mixed pupils, aged 11 to 16 **Submit application form**: 28 November 2003 **School hours**: 8.50am–3.15pm; homework clubs are available **Meals**: Hot and cold available **Strong GCSE subjects**: Art, PE **London league table position**: 414

### Profile

Langdon Park School was established in 1965 on the same site as a former Victorian boarding school. An £8-million redevelopment programme has been drawn up, which will see the addition of new sports facilities, including a purpose-built gymnasium and a dance studio, and three large IT rooms. Some classrooms will be expanded. The tennis courts and playing fields currently used by pupils, and which belong to the Langdon Park Community Centre, will also be redeveloped, so that the facilities become joint. CCTV cameras are installed and there is a residential site manager. Arts are popular at the school, and drama and music are growth areas. Dance is also on the curriculum. Pupils are encouraged to take an online GNVQ in IT, which is designed by a school in Shropshire. Bilingual pupils are supported in their studies by qualified teachers of English as a second language. The school takes pride in its strong learning support facility, which helps not only those pupils with special-needs statements but also those who are very able. A partnership agreement is signed by all pupils, parents and the school, and outlines what is expected of everyone. Parental support is encouraged and there are three progress review days throughout the year. The school also has a parent support advice group that helps pupils to settle in. Any other concerns are dealt with by either the home-school support worker, an education social worker or the team of 'Learning Mentors'. There is a school council.

### Admissions and intake

Admission is through the LEA (see borough factfile). Some 54 pupils have statements of special needs.

### Achievement

Langdon Park was 14th in the borough league table for GCSE performance in 2002, with 29 per cent of pupils gaining five or more A*–C grades. This was one per cent up on 2001's results and the average point score was 29.1. An Ofsted report in 1997 noted that GCSE results were well below the national average in all subjects. They recognized that this was due to the fact that pupils on entry have unusually low levels of skill in reading, writing and numbers, and many lack confidence in speaking. However, by the end of Key Stage 3, most pupils were seen to have made notable progress in most basic skills. Strengths highlighted by Ofsted included the high level of support provided by the pastoral care system and the good opportunities for pupils to take responsibility in the school and to work with adults in making policy. Good management and dynamic leadership from the head were also noted as strengths. Another success is the unauthorized absence level, which has fallen from 4.4 per cent in 1999 to 3.7 per cent in 2000.

### Extra curricular activities

All subjects have their own club and there are also computer and homework clubs. Coaches from Leyton Orient football team visit the school to train younger pupils. Many school trips take place, including skiing trips and visits to France and Spain, as well as residential study weekends.

## Madni Secondary Girls' School

**15–17 Rampart Street, London E1 2LA** 020 7791 3531 020 7791 3531 Mrs Fatima Liyawdeen; Chair of Governors: Mr Habibur Rahman Whitechapel and Shadwell **Buses:** D3, 15, 100, 115 Green shalwar kameez, white scarf **Demand:** Over subscribed in Year 7, seven on waiting list **Type:** Independent for 91 girls, aged 11 to 16 **Fees:** £800 a year **Submit application form:** No cut-off date **School hours:** 8.55am–3.15pm; homework clubs are available **Meals:** Hot and cold available **Strong GCSE subjects:** Bengali, science **London league table position:** 3

### Profile

Madani School was opened in 1991 by a group of parents who felt a need to create an Islamic girls' school in their community. The aim was to provide a school where Muslim girls could be educated in an environment conducive to the development of the Islamic character. In 1991, just 30 pupils attended Madani, but within two years, a demand for places led to the school moving to larger accommodation in a converted factory. The school committee is negotiating with the council for a move to yet larger and more suitable accommodation in the borough. The current building is considerably lacking in resources and a move to new premises is needed to ensure pupils have access to more facilities (at present there is only one science lab). In spite of poor accommodation, Madani pupils benefit from a committed staff and strong support from parents and different community groups, that also make donations to the school. Class sizes are between 25 and 27, and extra support is given to both less able and more able pupils. Vocational courses are not offered, and there is no provision for disabled pupils.

### Admissions and intake

Applications are made directly to the school and pupils will be expected to attend an interview.

### Achievement

In 2002, an impressive 100 per cent of pupils gained five or more A*–C grades at GCSE, maintaining the standard of the previous year. The school was the best-performing school in the borough league table. Since opening, the school has been inspected twice by an independent governor from the DfES. The inspection highlighted that the school's accommodation fell short of expected standards but noted that lesson planning and teaching methods were good. In 1999, the percentage for authorized absence was 5.0 per cent and for unauthorized absence, it was an impressive 0 per cent.

### Extra-curricular activities

The school offers after-school homework classes and the normal range of sports. There are several school trips within the UK.

## Morpeth School

**Portland Place, Bethnal Green, London E2 OPX** 020 8981 0921 020 8981 0139 morpethsmt@aol.com Mr Alasdair Macdonald MA; Chair of Governors: Chris Hull Cambridge Heath Bethnal Green, Stepney Green **Buses:** D6, D7, S2, 8, 25, 106, 253, 277, 309 White blouse with school badge, black round-neck jumper with school badge, black trousers or skirt, or shalwar khameez (girls, Years 7 to 11); blazer, white shirt, black V-neck jumper, school tie, optional black trousers (boys, Years 7 to 9); white shirt, school tie or white shirt no tie with black jumper and school badge; outdoor jackets plain and dark (boys, Years 10 to 11); school sports shirt with school badge in summer (boys and girls) **Demand**: 648 applications for 240 places in 2001/2 **Type**: Community comprehensive for 1108 mixed pupils, aged 11 to 16 **Submit application form**: 28 November 2003 **Mission statement**: Committed to learning and achievement based on friendship and respect where everyone is valued **School hours**: 8.55am–3.30pm; homework clubs are available **Meals**: Hot and cold meals available, including breakfast **Strong GCSE subjects**: Drama, history, PE **London league table position**: 258

## Profile

Morpeth School has stood on its present site for the last 100 years. A total of £7–8 million has been spent on a major building programme, including a new library, dining room and kitchen, four science labs, art rooms and IT facilities. Art and IT are strong areas, and there is a flourishing performing arts and music department. In 2000, the poet laureate, Andrew Motion, along with the then Secretary of State for Education, David Blunkett, paid a visit to Morpeth to launch a poetry initiative. Pupils take part in the National Poetry Competition and last year scooped three of the 10 top prizes. Morpeth has close links with the City and support is given by linked companies. In 1997, Ofsted noted the strength of communications between home and school, which are conducted in English and Bengali. They also highlighted the need for improving academic standards at Key Stage 3. Morpeth has a conflict-resolution programme and peer mediation scheme, involving pupils of different ages working together. There is also a 'seniors' programme whereby older pupils organize events for the younger pupils and act as their guides. They also act as interpreters at parents' evenings. There is coordinator for pupils with special needs.

## Admissions and intake

Admission is through the LEA (see borough factfile). Morpeth was the first school in the borough to form a mini Education Action Zone, which strengthens ties with its feeder primaries.

## Achievement

In 1999, Morpeth won the first *Evening Standard* London School Award for Outstanding Achievement. Targets are set for all abilities, and the percentage of pupils who score five or more A*–G GCSEs and one A*–G GCSE are above national averages. In 2002, 54 per cent of pupils achieved five or more A*–C grades. This was well over the borough average of 43.6 and above the national average of 51.6 per cent. The school was fourth in the borough. Inspectors described pupils' cultural development as having made great strides as a result of cultural visits, and opportunities to hear speakers, work with artists and meet outside groups. The school also had good cross-cultural relationships.

## Extra-curricular activities

Activities available include basketball, cricket, athletics and photography. Pupils can join the school orchestra, the jazz band, a concert band, steel bands and a Bengali music group. Residential trips are organized, and pupils attend a poetry study week in Yorkshire, in addition to trips to France and Spain. There is also an exchange programme with a school in New York sponsored by Citibank. A study centre is open before and after school.

# Mulberry School for Girls

**Richard Street, Commercial Road, London E1 2JP** ☎ 020 7790 6327 Fax 020 7265 9882 Web www.mulfe.org.uk Head Dame Marlene Robottom B.Ed, M.Sc; Chair of Governors: Dr Walter Ross ⊖ Whitechapel, Shadwell **Buses**: 5, 15, 40 Uniform Mulberry-coloured trousers, skirt or shalwar kameez; Sixth form: Smart casual wear **Demand**: 457 applications for 210 places in 2001/2 **Type**: Community comprehensive for 1360 girls (350 in sixth form), aged 11 to 18 **Submit application form**: 28 November 2003 **School hours**: 9am–3.30pm; homework clubs are available **Meals**: Hot and cold available **Strong GCSE subjects**: Bengali, education, expressive and perfoming arts, French, history, ICT, PE, RE, Spanish, sociology **London league table position**: 244

## Profile

Mulberry school was established in 1964 and currently has a split site: a modern main site and a Victorian sixth-form building. The school is currently undergoing extensive building and refurbishment works as part of a £19.3 million project that will be completed in 2004. Facilities will also be expanded for out-of-school use to encourage greater participation from the community, especially women, and there will be improved access for disabled pupils. Existing facilities include dance and drama studios, a music suite, 10 science labs, five computer rooms, a multi-gym, a newly equipped technology wing, two libraries and a hard court sports area. Mulberry aims to offer a broad, balanced curriculum so that all pupils can study a range of subjects throughout their secondary education. The school recently achieved Beacon School status. Mulberry boasts strong links with local businesses, whose employees are encouraged to come and work alongside pupils. The school operates an induction scheme called 'headstart' during the first week of the summer holidays to help new entrants settle into the school. There is a strong system of pastoral care and a tutorial programme to support the personal and academic success of each pupil. Many pupils have hearing and visual impairment, and Mulberry has an inclusive education policy where every effort is made to facilitate access to all areas for pupils with physical needs. There is also a strong learning and language support team and a programme for gifted and talented pupils. Alison Limerick, actress and musician of *Starlight Express* fame, is a former pupil. There is a school council and a prefects system.

## Admissions and intake

Admission is through the LEA (see borough factfile). In Years 7–11, just over 23 per cent of pupils have special educational needs and two per cent have statements.

## Achievement

Mulberry is the second best performing secondary school in the borough and its results have continued to improve since 1995. This is a significant achievement given the high proportion of pupils with English as a second language. In 2002, 52 per cent of pupils achieved five or more A*–C grades at GCSE. Mulberry was the second best in the borough for A-levels, with an average point score of 167.2 for pupils taking two or more A/AS-levels. Art is a particular strength of the school. In 2002, Ofsted described it as a 'very good school' where 'pupils make good progress'.

## Extra-curricular activities

Sports on offer include cricket, rugby, canoeing and rock climbing. Many trips are organized throughout the school year, including cultural trips to France and Spain. During the summer holidays, pupils can attend a literacy and numeracy programme. There are opportunities to participate in voluntary work, including working at the Royal London Hospital in Whitechapel. The school has after-school homework clubs.

# Oaklands School

**Old Bethnal Green Road, London E2 6PR** ☎ 020 7613 1014 📠 020 7729 3756 🌐 www.oaklands.towerhamlets.sch 🎓 Ms Jo Dibb; Chair of Governors: Kim Fletcher 🚆 Bethnal Green, Cambridge Heath ⊖ Bethnal Green **Buses**: D6, 6, 8, 35, 55, 253 👔 Black trousers, skirt and shoes, white shirt, green school sweater, school tie **Demand**: 406 applications for 120 places in 2001/2 **Type**: Community comprehensive for 600 mixed pupils, aged 11 to 16 **Submit application form**: 28 November 2003 **Motto**: A Learning Community **School hours**: 8.45am–3.30pm; homework clubs are available **Meals**: Hot and cold available, including breakfast **Strong GCSE subjects**: Art, Bengali, English literature, IT **London league table position**: 253

## Profile

Oaklands was built in 1991 to answer the demand for school places in the Bethnal Green area. The building was purpose-built to meet the needs of the National Curriculum. It has excellent ICT facilities, a good sports hall and gym and a very good drama studio. There is a strong climate of learning at Oaklands and achievements are celebrated with certificates, assemblies and displays of work. Pupils take on responsibility through the 'seniors' programme, working as library assistants and technicians or being a receptionist for the day. Two representatives from each tutor group sit on the school council. A flourishing partnership with an American investment bank gives pupils the opportunity to spend time with City workers. Oaklands' learning support department closely monitors pupils who need extra help. There is specialist help for those pupils whose first language is not English and support for gifted pupils. Parents are asked to sign a contract supporting the school to ensure that pupils are well behaved and well organized.

## Admissions and intake

Admission is through the LEA (see borough factfile). Thirty-six pupils have statements of special needs.

## Achievement

Oaklands is one of the most improved schools in the country and its pupils are exceeding expectations, with boys performing as well as girls. An Ofsted report in 1998 noted how GCSE results and test results at the age of 14 had improved at a faster rate than the national trend. In 2002, 57 per cent of pupils gained five or more A*–C grades at GCSE. This was 16 per cent up on 2001's results and the school was placed third in the borough league table. Results in English literature, IT, art and Bengali tend to be above average compared to similar schools, and standards in IT are in line with national averages and often above. Ofsted commended the strong leadership at the school, the good range of well-attended clubs and study-support activities. They also praised the school's productive links with business and the community. The report saw ICT emerging as a strength. Weaknesses included the lack of high expectations for achievement in Years 10 to 11 and the teaching of PSE for 14 to 16 year olds. Improvements made by Oaklands since the last inspection have included the absence rate, which was above the national average at 1.8 per cent in 2000.

## Extra-curricular activities

A wide range of extra-curricular activities are on offer. There are a number of short courses, such as mosaic making, Greek cooking and dress designing, as well as the traditional sports. Drama and music enjoy a high profile, and pupils are currently working alongside professionals on their own production of *Guys and Dolls*. There is an ICT club at lunchtime and a breakfast club in the school's cyber café. After-school homework clubs are available.

# Raine's Foundation School

**Approach Road, Bethnal Green, London E2 9RQ** ☎ 020 8981 1231 Fax 020 8983 0153 e success@raines.t-hamlets.sch.uk www.raines.t-hamlets.sch.uk Mr Paul Hollingum; Chair of Governors: Dr Gavin Gardiner ⊖ Bethnal Green **Buses**: D6, 106, 253, 309 Up to sixth form: French blue skirt or trousers and jumper (girls); black trousers, navy blazer and navy and French blue school tie (boys) **Demand**: 549 applications for 150 places in 2001/2 **Type**: Voluntary aided Church of England comprehensive for 899 mixed pupils, aged 11 to 18 **Submit application form**: 28 November 2003 **Motto**: Come in and Learn Your Duty to God and Man **School hours**: 8.35am–3.35pm; homework clubs are available **Meals**: Hot and cold available **Strong GCSE subjects**: Art, English, German, maths, science, Spanish **London league table position**: 275

## Profile

This school dates back to 1719 when wealthy East End benefactor Henry Raine established a hostel for the poor children of St George's in the East parish. Years 7 to 8 are now housed in a 1960s building in Old Bethnal Green Road, and Years 9 to 13 study in a listed Victorian building in leafy Approach Road. Raine's has strong links with local churches and holds a daily act of collective worship. A post-16 arts facility is being developed, and the school is now linked to a national video-conferencing system that enables pupils to experience nationwide learning opportunities. Raine's can offer very able students a variety of extra study sessions out of school hours, including Latin. It also supports further education for former pupils, providing bursaries and apprenticeships. There is a PTA. Famous ex-pupils include the actor/director Stephen Berkoff.

## Admissions and intake

The school's application forms must be completed in addition to the borough's transfer form. About 75 per cent of the annual intake and of each ability band are designated foundation places, for which priority is given first to pupils whose families are active members of the Church of England, then to other Christian denominations. Any remaining foundation places will be given to children whose parents wish them to be educated in the Christian tradition and who would benefit from the general aims of the school. In all cases, consideration is given first to those with siblings at the school, then to those with special medical or social needs. A total of 29 pupils had statements of special needs in 2000.

## Achievement

Raine's was the highest performing school in the borough in 2002, with 48 per cent of pupils achieved five or more A*–C grades. This was nine per cent up on 2001's results. Raine's held first position in Tower Hamlets for A-level results with an average point score of 253.9. This was above the borough average. An Ofsted inspection in 1999 praised the school's caring and supportive environment. However, weaknesses mentioned included the lack of long-term priorities in the school's development plan and lack of provision for developing ICT skills at Key Stage 4. The report did note, however, that progress since the last inspection had been inhibited by the illness and death of the previous head, two different acting heads and successive losses of leadership in the governing body.

## Extra-curricular activities

Raines offers excellent provision for sports, with pupils representing the school in basketball at national level. Drama is popular and pupils can participate in the school choir and orchestra. A wide range of study-support activities are on offer before and after school, including homework clubs. Regular school trips are also organized throughout the year. A thriving Old Rainians Association organizes a variety of events, including an annual Christmas social.

# St Paul's Way Community School

**Shelmerdine Close, Poplar, London E3 4AN** ☎ 020 7987 1883 📠 020 7537 4529 ⓔ school@spwcs.freeserve.co.uk 🌐 www.st-paulsway.towerhamlets.sch.uk Mr Martyn Coles MA; Chair of Governors: Cllr Helal Abbas ⊖ Mile End; Docklands Light Railway: Devons Road **Buses:** D5, D6, D7, 86, 277, 309 Navy blue sweatshirt, black trousers, white shirt and school tie (boys); navy blue shalwar kameez (Muslim girls) or sweatshirt (supplied by school), white blouse, black trousers or black skirt **Demand:** 358 applications for 240 places in 2001/2 **Type:** Community comprehensive Arts College for 1,007 mixed pupils, aged 11 to 16 **Submit application form:** 28 November 2003 **Motto:** Education for Success **School hours:** 9am–3.40pm, 9am–2.45pm (Fri): homework clubs are available **Meals:** Hot and cold available **Strong GCSE subjects:** Geography **London league table position:** 340

## Profile

St Paul's Way Community School occupies a modern, six-storey building. It plays a central role in the community since, unlike many other schools, it is not surrounded by shops or facilities. The school has Arts College status, specializing in the visual arts. More than £250,000 has been spent on arts facilities, and in 1998, the arts and textiles department underwent a complete refurbishment. There are separate wings for each different subject. A new science wing was built in 1993, the IT block was refurbished in 1996 and the maths and technology suites are only six years old. The PE department boasts two gyms, a swimming pool and recently renovated, floodlit outdoor areas. The curriculum is slightly skewed towards art in the lower school, with pupils being entered a year early for GCSE art. The upper school offers a wide range of arts subjects, including textiles, art and design and sculpture. The school also works with Bow Arts Trust, a community organization, and welcomes artists-in-residence to work with pupils. It is currently bidding for an extra four years of Arts College funding to incorporate dance and drama in the curriculum. There is a hearing impaired unit, four full-time special-needs teachers and language-support assistants. There is a school council and a parent-teacher association.

## Admissions and intake

Admission is through the LEA (see borough factfile). Some 32 pupils have statements of special needs.

## Achievement

Out of the 500 specialist colleges in England, St Paul's Way was the fifth most improved school in 1999. In 2002, 41 per cent of pupils gained five or more A*–C grades, compared to 23 per cent in 2001. In an Ofsted report in 2000, the best teaching was to be found in art, drama, geography, history, music and PE. Geography GCSE results are 5 per cent above the national average and for history they are in line with the national average. Weaker subjects include maths, modern foreign languages, IT and design and technology at Key Stage 3. Ofsted described the school's ethos as warm and positive, which fostered good relations. Curricular provision, however, did not fully meet legal requirements, being narrow and not as relevant as it should be at Key Stage 4.

## Extra-curricular activities

Pupils excel in sports, with national and international success in volleyball, and the school has been a regular winner of the Tower Hamlets Youth Games. It also has a formidable cricket team, which reached the London Schools Cricket Final, and an under-17s team, which plays for Middlesex. Other activities include a public-speaking club, choir and bands – over a third of pupils learn how to play instruments. Homework classes take place several nights a week.

# Sir John Cass Foundation and Red Coat CofE School

**Stepney Way, London E1 ORH** ☎ 020 7790 6712 📠 020 7790 0499 🌐 www.sjcass.t-hamlets.sch.uk Mr Haydn Evans MA, M.Sc; Chair of Governors: Mrs Celia Swan ⊖ Stepney Green; Docklands Light Railway: Limehouse **Buses**: 15, 25, 253, 277, 309 Navy blue blazer, trousers or skirt, white shirt; navy blue school tie with a white stripe in lower school, sweatshirts in place of blazers in upper school; Sixth form: Smart office dress **Demand**: 442 applications for 180 places in 2001/2 **Type**: Comprehensive voluntary aided Language College for 795 mixed pupils, aged 11 to 19 **Submit application form**: 28 November 2003 **School hours**: 8.40am–3.05pm: homework clubs are available **Meals**: Hot and cold available **Strong GCSE subjects**: Art, drama, history, PE **London league table position**: 297

## Profile

Sir John Cass school was formed in 1720 when City businessman Sir John Cass established a charitable trust to meet the educational needs of youngsters in the East End. It is located in the heart of Stepney in a 1960s building, and has recently undergone a major building programme. New facilities include a modern languages and an IT centre, and the sixth-form block has been expanded to double its original size. The school was awarded Language College status, and a multimedia centre has been built to support study. A City Learning Centre is also being housed at the school as part of the government's Excellence in Cities initiative. An extra 40 computers have been installed in addition to the existing 300. The school also boasts a new video-conferencing facility, a state-of-the-art learning centre for pupils and a facility to attract local businesses. A wide range of specialist languages are on offer including Turkish, Arabic, Urdu, Chinese and Russian. The sixth form has grown from 70 students in 1997 to 160. Pupils are encouraged to take on extra responsibilities, such as library duty and reading with younger pupils. There is a good special-needs department and disabled pupils are welcomed. There is a parent-teacher association.

## Admissions and intake

Application is made direct to the school and through the LEA (see borough factfile). Twenty-six pupils have statements of special needs.

## Achievement

Sir John Cass was in the top 4 per cent of improved secondary schools in the country in 2000. The percentage of pupils gaining five or more A*–C grades at GCSE has increased from 14 per cent in 1996 to 69 per cent in 2002. In 1999, Ofsted noted that the school raises pupils' levels of attainment at a much faster rate than the national trend. It also noted that GCSE results are very high when compared to similar schools, and in history, drama, art and PE, the standards achieved are in line with national expectations. Weaknesses included English at Key Stage 3 and Bengali at Key Stage 4, along with the teaching of science throughout the school. Low standards of literacy, oracy and numeracy were also noted. At A-level, the average point score was 126, ranking the school bottom of the borough. Ofsted praised the impressive improvement made in virtually all areas since the previous inspection reports, and in spite of disruption from the school's major building programme.

## Extra-curricular activities

Ofsted identified the wide range of activities on offer as a strength of the school. Clubs include homework clubs, drama, IT, chess, swimming and a book and breakfast club. There is a steel band, string ensemble and the school has some gifted musicians, including a concert pianist. A number of trips include skiing, residential visits to the Norfolk Broads and educational trips in the UK. There are also school trips to Spain and France as well as weekend residential trips. A number of visits are arranged to art galleries and museums.

# Stepney Green School

**Ben Jonson Road, London E1 4SD** ☎ 020 7790 6361 📠 020 7265 9766 Mr Sean McGrath; Chair of Governors: Belayeth Hussein ⊖ Stepney Green; Docklands Light Railway: Limehouse **Buses**: 5, 15, 25, 40, 309 Black trousers, black blazer, black school tie with red stripe **Demand**: 362 applications for 210 places in 2001/2 **Type**: Community comprehensive for 932 boys, aged 11 to 16 **Submit application form**: 28 November 2003

**School hours**: 8.45am–3.30pm: homework clubs are available **Meals**: Hot and cold available **Strong GCSE subjects**: Art, PE **London league table position**: 307

## Profile

Stepney Green School was opened in the 1960s by Harold Wilson. The building was only meant to stand for 25 years, but because of its success in the community, it continues to operate. Pupils are accommodated in an eight-storey building and the classrooms are small. Unlike other schools in the borough, the condition of the building is poor and in need of refurbishment. The school is due to be upgraded as part of the Private Finance Initiative. However, Stepney Green can boast of its library, which has been completely gutted and reconstructed in close consultation with the librarian. There is also a new learning support centre with 30 new computers. The site is secure and the gates are locked during the school day. The school's ethos is positive and pupils are encouraged to do their best. Extra responsibilities on offer to the boys include a number of youth initiatives, such as removing graffiti from housing estates to taking part in a workshop to become peer mediators. As part of the Excellence in Cities initiative, there is a programme of learning opportunities and extra-curricular activities for gifted and talented pupils. The learning support centre supports pupils in their language skills. Pastoral support is strong and pupils are looked after by their tutors and heads of year. There is also an education social worker and home-liaison worker. Parents are encouraged to take an interest in their children's education and support them throughout their schooling. They are provided with regular reports and are expected to check that homework is done.

## Admissions and intake

Admission is through the LEA (see borough factfile). Twenty-two pupils have statements of special needs.

## Achievement

The school was put on special measures in 2000 after an Ofsted inspection in May. Despite being the most successful boys' school in the borough in terms of GCSE results in 1999, attainment is still well below the national norm and there is too much 'unsatisfactory or poor teaching'. In 2002, 49 per cent of boys achieved five or more A*–C grades, up from 37 per cent in 2001. Stepney Green was placed ninth in the borough in 2001. The school has also managed to reverse the national trend in boys having lower levels of attainment than girls.

## Extra-curricular activities

The school is rich in sports facilities. The football team competes every Saturday and pupils are successful in athletics – one former pupil, Monu Miah, is the England under-16s champion in the 100m, although he left the school in 2000 after successfully completing his GCSEs. School trips are regularly organized, from residential study weekends for exam preparation to trips to Disneyland, Paris for Year 10. The library is open at lunchtime and after school, and the computer suites are also available every day after school.

# Swanlea School

**31 Brady Street, Bethnal Green, London E1 5DJ** ☎ 020 7375 3267 Fax 020 7375 3567 ✉ swanlea.school@virgin.net 🌐 www.swanlea.towerhamlets.sch.uk Ms Linda Austin; Chair of Governors: Mr MD Habib Rahman 🚆 Cambridge Heath, Bethnal Green ⊖ Whitechapel, Bethnal Green **Buses**: 25, 106, 253 Red blazer, red and white striped school tie; grey skirt or trousers in lower school and black sweatshirt with school badge in upper school **Demand**: 503 applications for 210 places in 2001/2 **Type**: Community comprehensive for 1031 mixed pupils, aged 11 to 16 **Submit application form**: 28 November 2003 **Motto**: Learning for Excellence and Achievement in Partnership (LEAP) **School hours**: 8.45am–3.30pm; homework clubs are available **Meals**: Hot and cold available **Strong GCSE subjects**: Creative arts, drama, German, media studies **London league table position**: 309

## Profile

Swanlea opened in 1992. The school building is modern, spacious and light, and was one of the buildings of architectural interest open to the public during the Open Buildings weekend in 2000. It is one of the most secure schools in the borough, with CCTV cameras and high walls. There are exciting future prospects at Swanlea, with the school playing host to a City Learning Centre. Pupils who attend will have access to one of the most up-to-date ICT systems in the borough, which is also on offer to the community as a whole. The school has been designated one of the first Business and Enterprise Schools in the country and will receive extra funding for the development of business studies, ICT and mathematics. Swanlea offers a broad curriculum and pupils are expected to reach as high a level as they can. There is very good provision in ICT and languages – Latin is one of the languages on offer – and pupils are fortunate to have access to video-conferencing to broaden their educational experience. Older pupils can take part in peer mentoring and conflict-resolution programmes in which they assume a caring role towards the younger pupils. There is a strong special-needs department, with two teachers in classes to offer support for pupils with special educational and language needs. Swanlea is also the lead cluster school for gifted and talented pupils in its area. There is a parent-teacher association.

## Admissions and intake

Admission is through the LEA (see borough factfile). Some 38 pupils have statements of special needs.

## Achievement

Exam results have continued to improve at Swanlea since it opened, and pupils score very highly in comparison with the national average for similar schools. In 2002, Swanlea came ninth in the borough for GCSEs. A total of 44 per cent of pupils gained five or more A*–C grades compared to 38 per cent in 2001. Pupils do very well in the creative arts, media studies and drama. In 1999, Ofsted highlighted the good support for bilingual pupils across the school. Inspectors also noted the school's good leadership and management, its strong ethos for learning and the good links with parents and the community. Weaknesses were found in the low levels of literacy across the school, but inspectors added that significant improvements had been made since the last inspection. However, the failure to provide a daily act of collective worship had still not been effectively addressed.

## Extra-curricular activities

Some of the more interesting activities on offer include photography, ceramics, a rocket club organized by the science faculty and a joke club. There are also public-speaking sessions to inspire confidence in all youngsters. Sports on offer include cross-country, gymnastics (some pupils are part of the Tower Hamlets gymnastics team), trampolining and hockey, with one pupil on the under-16s England hockey team. Pupils are involved with fund-raising for the local community.

# Waltham Forest

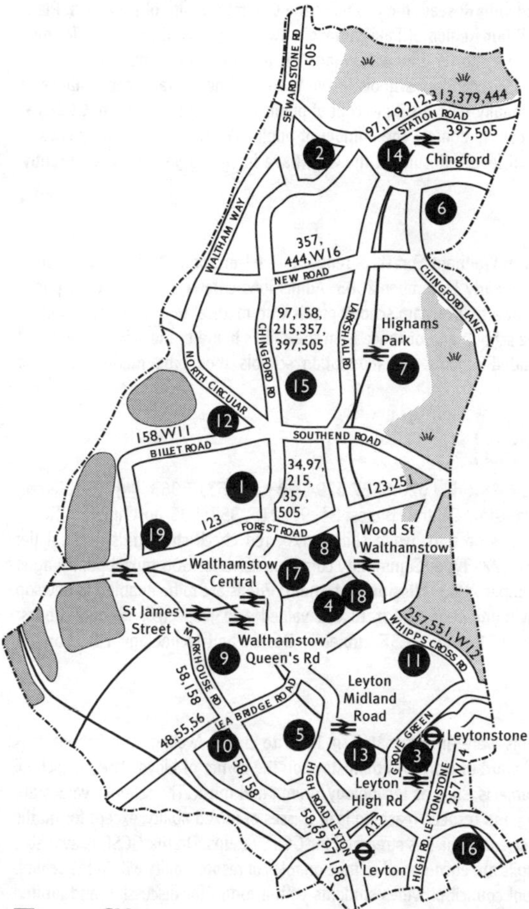


**Key**

1. Aveling Park School
2. Chingford Foundation School
3. Connaught School for Girls
4. Forest School
5. George Mitchell Community School
6. Heathcote School
7. Highams Park School
8. The Holy Family Catholic College
9. Kelmscott School
10. Lammas School
11. Leytonstone School
12. The McEntee School
13. Norlington School for Boys
14. Normanhurst School
15. Rush Croft School
16. Tom Hood School
17. Walthamstow School for Girls
18. Warwick School for Boys
19. Willowfield School

## Factfile

**LEA: Education Office, Leyton Municipal Offices, High Road Leyton, London E10 6QJ** ☎ 020 8527 5544 🌐 www.lbwf.gov.uk **Director of Education:** Stephen Hay **Political control of council:** Labour **Percentage of pupils from outside the borough:** 4.4 per cent **Percentage of pupils educated outside the borough:** 7.9 per cent **London league table positions (out of 32 boroughs):** 18th

### Profile

Waltham Forest has a population of 221,000 living in its three areas of Leyton, Walthamstow and Chingford. Almost a third of the working population are employed in managerial or technical occupations with over 40 per cent employed as manual workers and 5 per cent as professionals. The unemployment rate was 6.7 per cent in 1999, significantly higher than the average for other areas of outer London. However, unemployment has been falling, as it has nationally, from a peak of 16.1 per cent in 1993. Over a fifth of the borough is green land, with residents enjoying generous access to landscaped parks, playing fields and open green spaces. Brooks Farm can be found in Leyton, giving city residents the opportunity to experience rural activities in their own neighbourhood. Walthamstow boasts its famous greyhound stadium, which attracts visitors from all over London and the south. The borough is also home to the William Morris Gallery, dedicated to the great Pre-Raphaelite designer and artist. The borough has established friendship links with towns across the world, as an adjunct to its rich cultural diversity, for example with St John's, the capital town of Antigua in the Caribbean, and with Roseau, the capital of the Commonwealth of Dominica. Plans are in the pipeline to establish a link with the Mirpur Region of Pakistan, while twinning links have existed for over 40 years with the St Mande region of Paris and for a shorter time with Wandsbek, a suburb of Hamburg in Germany. There are only two independent schools out of 19 secondary schools in the borough. The average performance at GCSE in Waltham Forest is below that found nationally, with 44.3 per cent of pupils obtaining five or more GCSEs at grades A*–C in 2002, compared with 51.6 per cent nationally. The number of pupils gaining five or more passes at grades A*–G tends to be much closer to national levels. Results in the area have improved year-on-year recently, matching the national trend.

## Policy

To apply to any of the state secondary schools in Waltham Forest, parents must fill in and submit an application form from the LEA. Forms must be submitted by early December 2003. Admissions criteria are as follows: pupils with statements specifying designated provision at a mainstream school; pupils with medical reasons to be admitted to a particular school; pupils with a sibling at the school; and distance from the child's home to the school, measured in a straight line. Applications to voluntary aided schools and foundation schools should be made directly to the schools themselves.

# Aveling Park School

**Aveling Park Road, Walthamstow, London E17 4NR** 020 8527 5794 020 8531 5063 Mrs K Terrell; Chair of Governors: Mrs B Miller / Walthamstow Central **Buses**: 34, 97, 215, 357, 505 (to Chingford Road) Black blazer with school badge, black trousers or skirt, white shirt (boys); red check shirt (girls), school tie; **Demand**: 115 applications for 120 places in 2001/2 **Type**: Community comprehensive for 600 mixed pupils, aged 11 to 16 **Submit application form**: Early December 2003 **Mission statement**: Pupils are to be enabled to develop their academic and social potential in an environment in which all are valued and respected **School hours**: 8.30am–3.20pm **Meals**: Hot and cold available **Strong GCSE subjects**: Design and technology, PE **London league table position**: 362

## Profile

William Fitt and Chapel End Junior High Schools were amalgamated in 1986 to create Aveling Park School. It is situated in a residential area in the Chapel End ward of North Walthamstow, on the corner of Lloyd Park. The school has good specialist accommodation for some subjects, such as technology, drama and music. The school's values are traditional, and include tolerance, understanding and respect. Teaching is in classes of mixed ability, except for maths and French which are banded from Year 8, and science which is streamed for GCSE groups. Drama GCSE is available as an option, as are media studies and Urdu. Pupils are encouraged to take on roles of responsibility within the school. Older children can become prefects and a school council provides students with a forum for discussion and limited decision-making. The PTA was founded in 1986. There is support for students with special needs.

## Admissions and intake

Admission is through the LEA. There are over a dozen primary schools feeding into Aveling Park, the two major contributors being local. Prior attainment of the typical Year 7 intake is below the local average.

## Achievement

In 2002, 37 per cent of pupils obtained five or more grades A*–C at GCSE. This equalled the results of 2001 and the school was placed 13th in the borough league table. This was below the borough and national averages. Aveling Park was inspected by Ofsted in 2001 and was seen to have 'serious weaknesses in teaching, attendance and pupils' attitudes that affect achievement'. The current head teacher joined in September 2000 and has '...established a pattern for improvement' but has had 'insufficient time to turn the school around'. Inspectors praised the head's 'clear educational direction' and found that some improvements had been made to the school but overall, 'unsatisfactory progress' had been made since their last inspection in 1996. Standards had 'improved at a slower rate than nationally and are below average in comparison with similar schools'. Pupils perform above average in design and technology and PE but improvement is needed in achievement overall, especially in geography, ICT, modern foreign languages and music. The school has had some problems with attendance, often falling below the required 90 per cent for certain year groups. In 1999, it was 89.5 per cent, although unauthorized absences were below the local and national averages at just 0.9 per cent. However, unauthorized absences increased to 3.9 per cent in 2000, well above the national average. A large proportion of pupils go on to further education, mostly to St George Monoux.

### Extra-curricular activities

Provision for sport is good and includes the opportunity for pupils to participate in outdoor pursuits. HSBC Bank operates a school bank at Aveling Park, which allows pupils to gain business experience.

## Chingford Foundation School

**Nevin Drive, Chingford, London E4 7LT** 020 8529 1853 020 8559 4329 admin@chingford-school.co.uk www.chingford-school.co.uk Mr C Moore; Chair of Governors: Mr D Maxim Chingford **Buses:** 97 (to the Ridgeway), 215 (to Mansfield Hill) Up to sixth form: Black blazer, maroon V-neck sweater with school emblem, white shirt, grey trousers or skirt **Demand:** 489 applications for 210 places in 2001/2 **Type:** Comprehensive foundation school for 1196 mixed pupils, aged 11 to 18 **Submit application form:** Early December 2003 **Mission statement:** To provide for children of all backgrounds and abilities a high-calibre education within a comprehensive system that ensures a secure, caring, learning environment with an expert teaching force so that all pupils achieve their potential and are equipped with the skills, knowledge and understanding to become responsible adults **School hours:** 8.40am–3.25pm **Meals:** Hot and cold available **Strong GCSE subjects:** English language and literature **London league table position:** 202

### Profile

Chingford School is situated in a pleasant residential area to the north of Chingford, near to the William Girling reservoir. The site is spacious, extending to full-size grass sports pitches, tennis courts and an athletics track. The modern building is well kept. Recent developments include a new sixth-form centre and a new block of nine science labs. A learning resource centre was opened in September 1998, as was a completely refurbished maths block. IT has also been significantly upgraded for all levels of the school. The recently established sixth form offers courses at GNVQ and A-level. The school has had problems with truancy but in 2000 it had fallen to 0.8 per cent, below the borough and national averages.

### Admissions and intake

Applications should be made through the school. The school's intake displays broadly average attainment on entry, representing the full range of ability, though with slightly more able pupils than at a typical comprehensive. The number of pupils with special educational needs is low.

### Achievement

The school's results at Key Stage 3 and GCSE have risen and are well above the local average. In 2002, 58 per cent of pupils obtained five or more A*–C grades. This was also above the national average and the school was placed fifth in the borough. This was up four per cent from 2001's results. Pupils' attainment in English language and literature has often been well above the national average. In 1998, Ofsted found that 'standards are improving in most subjects', especially maths, science and modern languages. Attainment by pupils in relation to previous attainment was found to be encouraging, while 'pupils have generally positive attitudes to learning'. The A-level results at the school in 2002 placed it fourth in the borough league table, with an average point score for pupils taking two or more of 202.6. Ofsted noted that 'the quality of teaching is at least satisfactory in almost nine tenths of the lessons overall and good or very good in half of these', and that the school provides 'a friendly and welcoming atmosphere for its pupils'.

### Extra-curricular activities

A full range of sporting activities is offered to all pupils, while the sixth form can enjoy activities such as mountain walking expeditions. The school also runs a skiing trip to the Swiss resort of Chateaux d'Oex. Pupils participate in the Duke of Edinburgh's Award scheme. Concerts and dramatic productions are regularly staged.

# Connaught School for Girls

**Connaught Road, Leytonstone, London E11 4AB** 020 8539 3029 020 8558 3827 mail@connaught-school.com members.aol.com/cschoolfg Miss P Barford BA, MA; Chair of Governors: Nigel Patterson Leytonstone High Road Leytonstone **Buses**: W15, W16 (to Green Road) Navy skirt, white blouse, blue sweatshirt or cardigan with school logo **Demand**: 210 applications for 120 places in 2001/2 **Type**: Community comprehensive for 600 girls, aged 11 to 16 **Submit application form**: Early December 2003 **Mission statement**: The school has set itself nine aims; to foster: a sense of mutual respect; a facility for self-discipline; a sense of responsibility for others and the environment; self-confidence; a sense of achievement; positive attitudes to all racial groups; positive attitudes to women; the best possible achievement; a desire for further education. **School hours**: 8.40am–3.30pm; homework clubs are available **Meals**: Hot and cold available **Strong GCSE subjects**: All relatively strong **London league table position**: 155

## Profile

Connaught School was built in 1932 as a primary school before becoming a secondary in 1948. It is a Beacon school. Latin is on offer, and apart from maths, science and French, all teaching is in mixed-ability groups. The school has specialist teachers of English as an additional language. The learning support department provides assistance to those pupils with extra needs, who sometimes receive one-to-one tuition. There is a well-resourced careers room and specialist teachers to provide pupils with advice on post-GCSE options. Girls can assume official roles as prefects, captains or representatives on the school council. The school values its relationship with parents, and new parents are expected to sign a 'contract' detailing what should be expected of the school and themselves.

## Admissions and intake

Applications should be made through the LEA. Key Stage 2 and reading test results show attainment of the yearly intake to be below the local average. The number of pupils on the register of special educational needs is above average, at 128 at the time of the last Ofsted inspection in 1998. A high proportion of pupils speak English as an additional language. The socio-economic background of the school's catchment area is one of relative deprivation.

## Achievement

Connaught's GCSE results have improved rapidly in recent years. In 2002, 64 per cent of pupils gained five or more A*–C grades. This was above the national average and an increase on 59 per cent in 2001. The school was placed second in the borough. The number failing to gain a GCSE is always very low – at just 2 per cent in 2000. When Ofsted inspected in 1998, it found many aspects of the school to be praiseworthy. Particularly encouraging have been the results achieved by pupils from ethnic minority backgrounds, which have been favourable in comparison with those at other schools in Waltham. The report also highlighted 'the high-quality support for pupils' spiritual and moral development, and the outstanding contribution to broadening their cultural interests and understanding' which the school provides in a 'very caring community which values individuals and provides very good guidance'. About 82 per cent of 1999 leavers continued into further education.

## Extra-curricular activities

Competitive sports available include athletics, football and gymnastics, with many PE clubs run at lunchtime and after school. There are also after-school homework clubs. Other clubs include gardening, public speaking and music. Annual visits and residential trips are made to countries across Europe, while the classical studies department organizes a field trip to Greece. Tuition in musical instruments is also available.

# Forest School

**College Place, Snaresbrook, London E17 3PY** 020 8520 1744 020 8520 3656 warden@forest.org.uk www.forest.org.uk AG Boggis (Warden); Chair of Governors: JW Matthews Wood Street Snaresbrook, Wanstead **Buses:** W12 (to Snaresbrook Road), 2A, 20 (to Woodford New Road); school bus service currently extends south to Islington, north to Ongar Black blazer, trousers, shoes, house tie (boys); black blazer, skirt, white blouse (girls) **Demand**: 60 to 70 places in Year 7; c.200 applications for 20 to 25 places available **Type**: Selective independent Church of England school for 1166 mixed pupils (including 16 male boarders), aged 7 to 18 **Fees** (per term): £2,916 (day), £4,567 (boarder) **Submit application form**: Contact school for details **Motto**:

*In pectore robur* (Hearts of Oak) **School hours**: 8.30am–4pm **Meals**: Hot and cold available **Strong GCSE subjects**: All relatively strong **London league table position**: 65

## Profile

Dating back to 1834 when it had 22 pupils, Forest School now has a student population of around 1166. The school is divided into three separate sections: a junior school, girls' school and boys' school. The genders are reunited in the sixth form where 240 students share a centre and common room in the girls' school. Shared facilities include a heated swimming pool and cricket pavilion, drama, music, IT and science. The school aims to combine the benefits of the facilities provided by being part of a large school with the pastoral care and familiarity of belonging to a smaller unit. Three libraries are provided across the school, while the computer centre houses 72 networked PCs. A design studio and workshops provide accommodation for science and technology. A purpose-built music school is run by a full-time director of music and art is spread across three studios. The school has its own television studio, funded by money raised by the parents' association. Drama benefits from the in-school Deaton Theatre which is put to multiple uses. All pupils are grouped into houses. Many pupils are weekly boarders, who live in the boarding house where sixth-formers have individual study bedrooms. Other pupils live in self-contained living areas. Latin is offered at A-level but GNVQs are not available. There is a school council.

## Admissions and intake

Prospective pupils must sit the Common Entrance Examination after undergoing an interview. Application forms are available from the school and should be returned along with a registration fee.

## Achievement

The number of pupils gaining five or more grades A*–C at GCSE was 97 per cent in 2002, the same as in 2001. These were the top results in the borough. The school is also ranked first in A-level performance, with an average point score of 357.6 in 2002, reversing a downward trend over the last four years. More than 90 per cent of pupils go on to university, with about 10 pupils a year going to Oxford or Cambridge.

## Extra-curricular activities

Pupils participate in fencing and in hockey festivals held in Bath and Oxford. Pupils can play football for the only school side ever to have played in the FA Cup. The school's 1997 football captain played for England at U19 level. The Deaton Theatre plays host to the annual Shakespeare play, a tradition dating back to 1860. Three orchestras provide opportunities for the 300 pupils learning an instrument to demonstrate their skills. The chapel choir has performed at Southwark and Chelmsford cathedrals. Pupils have the opportunity to take part in exchange visits to the US, Australia, Europe and Russia, with other trips arranged to China. Pupils do fund-raising for local charities.

# George Mitchell Community School

**Farmer Road, Leyton, London E10 5DN** ☎ 020 8539 6198 📠 020 8532 8766 Colin Ravden MA; Chair of Governors: Mr V Scantlebury 🚆 Leyton Midland Road, Walthamstow Central ⊖ Leyton **Buses**: 69, 97 Pupils can wear any clothes that are black or white, except jeans, immodest clothes and clothes with logos; any flat shoes or trainers are allowed **Demand**: 73 applications for 120 places in 2001/2 **Type**: Community comprehensive for 600 mixed pupils, aged 11 to 16 **Submit application form**: Early December 2003 **Motto**: More Is in Me **School hours**: 8.40am–3.40pm; homework clubs are available **Meals**: Hot and cold available **Strong GCSE subjects**: All relatively strong **London league table position**: 448

## Profile

George Mitchell School can trace its roots back to 1903 when it was established as Farmer Road School. The school was renamed in honour of a former pupil who was awarded the Victoria Cross while serving in World War II. It is housed in a three-storey Edwardian building, now extended to include a gym, science block, library and design and technology facilities. The arts centre was opened in 1994 and is shared with Leyton Youth Centre. It is of an especially high quality, which Ofsted claimed in 1999 'makes a very strong contribution to standards of achievement and the quality of education'. Teaching is in mixed-ability classes until Year 10, when it is setted for some subjects, and arranged in a fortnightly timetable. Urdu is taught and there is a language support department for pupils who speak English as a second language. A parent-teacher association organizes fund-raising activities.

### Admissions and intake

Applications should be made through the LEA. Applicants are admitted in order of priority to: children with a statement of special needs, which specifies George Mitchell School; children who have strong medical reasons for coming to George Mitchell; children with a brother or sister at George Mitchell at the proposed time of entry; and children who live closest to the school. A large number of pupils are from refugee families from Eastern Europe and Africa. Half of the school is Muslim, and their religious needs are well catered for. Attainment on entry is below average.

### Achievement

In 1999, Ofsted found that: 'Standards are above the average for schools with similar intakes.' The report praised the school's 'welcoming and inclusive ethos'. It was found to deal well with its challenging and diverse intake, giving good support to those pupils who speak English as an additional language and to those with special needs, who are seen to make good progress. However, the school's commitment to educating such a diverse intake was not having such a positive effect on the performances of the most able. By the time they leave, pupils' attainment is not as high as at the average school in the country. However, in comparison with schools with similar intakes, performances are much higher and results are above average overall. In 2002, 20 per cent of pupils gained five or more GCSEs at grades A*–C, which was a fall from 24 per cent in 2001. The school was ranked second from last in the borough league table. This was also well below borough and national averages. The average point score was 27.1. Ofsted found the provision for cultural development, especially multicultural development, outstanding.

### Extra-curricular activities

Lunchtime homework clubs are held and pupils can stay behind for an extra lesson after school, when staff are available to give them support. Tuition is provided in musical instruments. There is a wide range of track and field sports on offer, including gymnastics and athletics. There are good links with Leyton Orient Football Club, as well as with local rugby clubs.

## Heathcote School

**Normanton Park, Chingford, London E4 6ES** ☎ 020 8529 5953 Fax 020 8529 3935 Head: Mr Barry Hersom; Chair of Governors: Mr I Moyes Rail: Chingford Tube: Woodford **Buses**: 179, 397 (Whitehall Road) Uniform: Black trousers or skirt, sweatshirt with school logo, white shirt, black shoes **Demand**: 190 applications for 180 places in 2001/2 **Type**: Community comprehensive for 670 mixed pupils, aged 11 to 16 **Submit application form**: Early December 2003 **Motto**: Committed to Quality **School hours**: 8.30am–3.10pm; homework clubs are available **Meals**: Hot and cold available **Strong GCSE subjects**: English, maths, science **London league table position**: 346

### Profile

Heathcote is situated on a large and fairly modern site, with recently improved accommodation including a music suite, counselling suite and year group common rooms. A tennis dome is shared with the local community. Sporting activity is enhanced by two gymnasia, outdoor fields and all-weather playing surfaces. Pupils can also take advantage of year-round access to the adjacent Chingford Sports Centre. Music is one of the school's strongest areas, with all Year 7 pupils learning an instrument and others having the opportunity to use a BBC-standard recording studio as part of the curriculum. There is a parent-teacher association.

### Admissions and intake

Applications should be made through the LEA. A total of 28 primary schools feed into Heathcote, with an extensive visiting programme in place for the years leading up to Year 7. The school gains a large proportion of its intake from relatively deprived areas in the borough. Recently, the proportion of lower achievers among pupils starting Year 7 has been greater than in most schools. There are 144 pupils on the register of special educational needs. Many pupils enter the school in years other than Year 7, some having been excluded from other local schools.

### Achievement

In 2002, 39 per cent of pupils obtained five or more grades A*–C at GCSE. This was below the borough and national averages but up from 33 per cent in 2001, continuing an upward trend. The school was ranked 11th in the borough. Following an Ofsted inspection, the school was placed on 'special measures' in 1998. However, Inspectors revisited the school in 2001 and these measures were removed. Ofsted noted that 'standards are improving across the school' and the quality of teaching had improved and is 'sound or better in nine out of 10 lessons and good or very good in four out of 10 lessons'. Inspectors praised the head teacher's 'good understanding of the school's strengths and weaknesses'. The pupils' behaviour had also improved and was 'good in six out of 10 lessons'. Standards of literacy and numeracy still need improving. The truancy rate has been high but has improved and was 0.9 per cent in 2000, below borough and national averages.

### Extra-curricular activities

The school holds regular dance and drama clubs as well as theatrical productions. Its strong musical tradition includes two steel bands. Visits take place to France and Germany and the work experience scheme takes advantage of established links with local businesses and the community. The normal range of sports is on offer.

# Highams Park School

**Handsworth Avenue, Highams Park, London E4 9PJ** 020 8527 4051 020 8503 3349 enquiries@highamspark.waltham.sch.uk www.highamspark.sch.uk Mr Anthony Perrett B.Sc; Chair of Governors: Mr S Carter Highams Park **Buses**: W16 (to Winchester Road), 212, 275 (to the Avenue) Black blazer with school badge, trousers or grey skirt, plain white shirt, grey V-neck pullover (optional), black socks or dark tights and shoes, house tie; Sixth form: Smart attire **Demand**: 436 applications for 215 places in 2001/2 **Type**: Voluntary aided comprehensive Technology College for 1343 mixed pupils, aged 11 to 18 **Submit application form**: Early December 2003 **School hours**: 8.35am–3.25pm; homework clubs are available **Meals**: Hot and cold available **Strong GCSE subjects**: All relatively strong **London league table position**: 173

### Profile

This popular school is housed in pleasant, modern accommodation close to Epping Forest. As a Technology College, it receives extra funding to promote the education of science, maths, technology and IT. The school has a unique partnership with Arsenal Football Club and many of their younger players attend the school. A-levels and GNVQs are offered in the sixth form, where the 230 pupils must also spend four hours a week in PE or community service. Each year, eight members of the sixth form make up a student committee, which is established as an agent of responsible decision-making. All pupils are divided into four houses, which increases opportunities for them to get involved in additional activities, such as setting up house web sites. The 'home-school agreement' establishes the responsibilities of students, parents, governors and staff. Strong parental support is enjoyed by the school. There is provision for pupils with special needs.

### Admissions and intake

Applications are made direct to the school, and are dealt with by its governing body.

### Achievement

Attainment at the school is high compared locally and nationally, and the school is rightly proud of its good standards. In 2002, 62 per cent of pupils achieved five or more A*–C grades at GCSE. This was a fall on 66 per cent in 2001, which was the school's best results in recent years. These results were higher than the borough and national averages, and the school came third in the borough league table overall. Highams Park was the best performing state school in the borough. The average point score for pupils taking two or more A/AS-levels was 219.8, the third best results in the borough, and just below the national average. Ofsted visited the school in 2000 and noted that: 'Highams Park school is a good and vibrant school with many strengths and relatively few weaknesses'. A high percentage of lessons were seen to have 'good or very good teaching' and there is 'clear and effective leadership' from the head teacher and senior management team. Good progress is made at Key Stages 3 and 4 and in the sixth form.

### Extra-curricular activities

Pupils benefit from access to a wide range of clubs and activities, including a wind ensemble and dance club. Theatre trips are regularly organized by the English department. Arsenal manager Arsene Wenger has visited pupils to give a talk about languages. The normal range of sports is on offer. Pupils do fund-raising for local charities.

# The Holy Family Catholic College

**1 Shernhall Street, Walthamstow, London E17 3EA (Walthamstow site); Shernhall Street, Walthamstow, London E17 9RT (Wiseman site)** 020 8520 0482 (Walthamstow site); 020 8520 3587 (Wiseman site) 020 8521 0364 holywstow@hotmail.com www.holyfamily.sch.uk Mr EG Breen BA, M.Ed; Chair of Governors: Mrs Sheila Hutchinson Wood Street Walthamstow, Walthamstow Central Walthamstow Central **Buses:** W12, W16, 123, 275, 251, 212 Up to sixth form: Black trousers, black jumper with school logo, white shirt, red and black school tie, black socks, black shoes (boys); black and white kilt, black jumper or cardigan with school logo, white blouse, black shoes, black or white socks or black or skin-coloured tights (girls) **Demand:** 353 applications for 180 places in 2001/2 **Type:** Voluntary aided Roman Catholic comprehensive Technology College for 975 mixed pupils, aged 11 to 18 **Submit application form:** 4 December 2003 **Mission statement:** The Holy Family College is a Catholic community embracing the clear Christian values of respect, service and justice. We are a family of many cultures sharing one faith. We exist to educate young people towards excellence in all dimensions of their lives, recognizing the uniqueness of each and quality of all. **School hours:** 8.45am–3.30pm **Meals:** Hot and cold available **Strong GCSE subjects:** Art, English language and literature, RE **London league table position:** 289

## Profile

Holy Family is an improving school with many good features. It is based on two sites 400m (440yds), apart on Shernhall Street. The Walthamstow site (Years 7 to 8 and sixth form) is a three-storey, Grade II-listed building, while Wiseman House is a modern building. The school recenty acquired Technology College status. Parents and others can join the friends of the school. There is provision for pupils with special needs.

## Admissions and intake

The school deals with its own admissions. It regards its primary purpose as serving the needs of the Roman Catholic community by educating baptized Roman Catholic children. The governors will, however, admit other children where there is evidence of a desire for a Catholic education. As a denominational school, its catchment area is wide, extending into boroughs such as Hackney and Newham.

## Achievement

Compared nationally, fewer Holy Family pupils leave school without a qualification than at similar schools. In 2002, 51 per cent of pupils gained five or more A*–C grades at GCSE, down from 52 per cent in 2001. This was above the borough and national averages, and the school was ranked seventh in the borough league table. Results have improved considerably since 1997, when only 27 per cent gained five or more A*–Cs. The school does very well in the sixth form, with pupils achieving surprisingly high results; in 2002 they attained an average point score of 228.7, the second highest results in the borough. Ofsted noted that provision and performance in some subjects was 'very good', such as in English. Also praised was the 'positive ethos' and 'good relationships' found among pupils and staff. The inspection team did find, however, an irregular amount of unsatisfactory teaching, particularly at Key Stage 3.

## Extra-curricular activities

A computer club, chess club and an Amnesty International group meet every week. The school's computer rooms are open to pupils at lunchtime and after school, as is the library, which also opens on Friday evenings for GCSE students. Year 7 pupils can attend an educational activity weekend on the Isle of Wight. Pupils do fund-raising for local charities. The normal range of sports is on offer.

# Kelmscott School

**Markhouse Road, Walthamstow, London E17 8DN** 020 8521 2115 020 8521 2115 Michael Whitworth; Chair of Governors: Mr Morrall St James's Street Walthamstow, Walthamstow Queens Road, Walthamstow Central Walthamstow Central **Buses:** 58, 158 Navy sweatshirt with school logo, navy trousers/skirt **Demand:** 210 applications for 180 places in 2001/2 **Type:** Community comprehensive for 900 mixed pupils, aged 11 to 16 **Submit application form:** 4 December 2003 **Motto:** Putting Learning First **School hours:** 8.40am–3.30pm; homework clubs are available **Meals:** Hot and cold available **Strong GCSE subjects:** English, design and technology, geography, history, RE **London league table position:** 376

## Profile

Kelmscott School is located in a relatively densely populated, urban environment. It is housed in high-quality, new accommodation. Most of the intake at the school is local and is drawn from about 30 primary schools with which good links are established. The local population is ethnically diverse and this is reflected in the profile of the school population. About 10 per cent of pupils receive financial support from the Home Office to learn English as an additional language. Truancy has been higher than the school would like, at 2.6 per cent in 1999 but this fell to 1.7 per cent in 2000. There is a school council and a parent-teacher association. There is provision for pupils with special educational needs.

## Admissions and intake

Applications should be made through the LEA. At the time of the last Ofsted inspection in 2002, the number of pupils with special educational needs was well above average.

## Achievement

In 2002, 37 per cent of pupils obtained five or more A*–C grades at GCSE. This was up from 29 per cent in 2001 and the school was placed 14th in the borough league table. This was below the borough and national averages. Ofsted noted that: 'pupils achieve well and make good progress during their time at Kelmscott School because much of the teaching is of a high quality, particularly in Years 10 and 11'. GCSE results are above those of similar schools. Inspectors praised the school's 'strong leadership and management', noting the 'good attitudes' of pupils who 'mostly behave well'. The provision for pupils with special educational needs was 'satisfactory overall' with 'good' provision for pupils with English as an additional language. Pupils were seen to do well in English, design and technology, history, geography and RE. However, pupils do not achieve as well as they should in mathematics, science and Urdu, and Inspectors wanted to see improvements in the settting of homework and the management of PE. The curriculum in Years 10 and 11 does not fulfill National Curriculum requirements.

## Extra-curricular activities

Sports played at the school include netball, football, cricket, rounders, basketball, baseball, tennis, badminton, volleyball and athletics, with regular sporting fixtures held against other schools. There are after-school homework clubs. Visits are organized to France and a summer camp. The school provides financial support for families of pupils who would otherwise be unable to participate in extra-curricular activities because of economic constraints.

# The Lammas School

**150 Seymour Road, Leytonstone, London E10 7LX** 020 8988 5860 020 8988 5861 Josephine Beaton; Chair of Governors: Paul Redcliffe Leyton, Walthamstow Central **Buses:** 48, 55, 56, 58, 158 White polo shirt, navy blue sweatshirt and fleece jacket with school crest, navy blue trousers or skirt, flat black shoes **Demand:** 250 applications for 180 places in 2001/2 **Type:** Community comprehensive for 900 mixed pupils, aged 11 to 16 (when the school is full in 2005) **Submit application form:** 4 December 2003 **School hours:** 8.40am–3.30pm, 8.30am–2.30pm (Thurs) **Meals:** Hot and cold available **Strong GCSE subjects:** N/A (no pupils will sit GCSEs until 2006) **London league table position:** Not applicable

## Profile

Waltham Forest's newest secondary school opened in September 2001 in the south of the borough, near to the border with Hackney. It was built at a cost of £15 million under the Private Finance Initiative (PFI), in a partnership between Waltham Forest council and New Schools (Leyton) Ltd (a consortium including the construction company Wates and management firm WS Atkins). As a newly built school, on the site of a former factory, it has full disabled access and state-of-the-art computing and sports facilities. The area the school serves is socially deprived - more than half the pupils are eligible for free school meals – and ethnically diverse – 45 per cent of pupils have black African or Afro-Caribbean roots and, after English, the main languages spoken are Urdu, Bengali and Turkish.

## Admissions and intake

The Lammas School is filling up one year at a time. The first 180 pupils joined in September 2001 and when it is full in 2005 it will have 900 pupils. The school was built in response to longstanding local demand for school places and, despite not having a GCSE track record, there were 320 first-choice applications for the first year of intake. The school uses criteria laid down by Waltham Forest council to decide who to admit if the school is over-subscribed, taking into account special educational needs, whether pupils have siblings at the school and the distance they live from the school (measured as the crow flies). As a result most places are taken by local children, despite huge demand from parents keen to get their children out of schools in neighbouring Hackney.

### Achievement

Pupils at the school will not sit GCSEs until summer 2006. They will sit Key Stage 3 tests in 2004, which the government has said it will publish. The school is not eligible to become a specialist college until it has GCSE results but has a particularly strong focus on information technology and sport.

### Extra-curricular activities

The school already has after-school clubs for maths, art and computing. It also has separate boys' and girls' soccer and basketball teams and a girls' netball team. There are two musical groups, one for keyboard players and one for percussion instruments. The school is next to a large area of common land on which horses graze (the mediaeval lammas land from which the school takes its name), which can also be used for sports.

## Leytonstone School

**Colworth Road, Leytonstone, London E11 1JD** 020 8496 2800 020 8496 2801 leytonstone@school.lbwf.govf.co.uk Mrs Joan McVittie; Chair of Governors: Miranda Smith Leytonstone High Road Snaresbrook, Leytonstone **Buses:** W12, W15, 97A, 257, 551 Black trousers or skirt, green V-neck pullover with school badge, school tie, black shoes **Demand**: 296 applicaitons for 180 places in 2001/2 **Type**: Community comprehensive for 902 mixed pupils, aged 11 to 16 **Submit application form**: 4 December 2003 **Mission statement**: For Leytonstone to be: a happy and well-disciplined school which promotes self-esteem; a caring school which values everybody equally; a school which promotes the benefits of a multicultural, co-educational population; a welcoming environment for children of all abilities; a school which focuses on student achievement; a school determined to achieve the highest standards; a school which values and celebrates learning, success and achievement; a school which works in partnership with the community; a school of warmth and excellence **School hours**: 8.45am–3.25pm, 8.45am–3.10pm (Fri); homework clubs are available **Meals**: Hot and cold available **Strong GCSE subjects**: History, maths, PE **London league table position**: 316

### Profile

Leytonstone School is situated on a small and compact site in the Forest Ward which has areas of considerable social deprivation. The Duchess of Argyll established the main building in 1911, with extensions having been made since. The limited size of the site means that accommodation is fairly cramped both indoors and out. Urdu is offered as an alternative modern language, and options available at GCSE include environmental studies. The work experience programme for GCSE pupils is well supported by local industry and commerce, including newspapers, hospitals and theatres. A broad section of the community also gets involved in helping with industry days and careers conventions at Leytonstone. There is a school council and pupils can be trained as library assistants. There is also a parent-teacher association. The school makes a high number of exclusions (139 in 1999), and unauthorized absence is slightly above the high local average at 2.0 per cent.

### Admissions and intake:

Applications should be made through the LEA. Almost a third of pupils have special educational needs, 33 of whom are statemented, and this is well above local and national averages. Attainment on entry is below average for each intake, though pupils 'demonstrate a broad spectrum of social skills and behaviour' (Ofsted 1998).

### Achievement

In 2002, 48 per cent of pupils gained five or more A*–C grades at GCSE. This was above the borough average of 44.3 per cent but below the national average of 51.6 per cent. The school was placed eighth in the borough league table with Willowfield School. This was a rise on 47 per cent in 2001 and the average point score was 33.5. In comparison with schools with pupils from similar backgrounds, pupils' attainment at age 16 is very high. The findings of Ofsted in 1998 were encouraging. Standards of attainment were said to be improving throughout, while teaching in nearly six out of 10 observed lessons was of a 'good' quality. At GCSE level, a high percentage of teaching was found to be 'very good'. Ofsted further recognized that 'The partnership between the school, parents, carers and the community is strong.'

### Extra-curricular activities

RE trips are made to churches, cathedrals, mosques, temples and synagogues. The art department arranges regular visits to London's art galleries, while the drama department has organized visits to the school from theatre groups. Residential trips are held both in the UK and overseas. Exchange visits are held with a French school. There are after-school homework clubs and the normal range of sports is on offer.

## The McEntee School

**Billet Road, Walthamstow, London E17 5DP** 020 8527 3750 020 8527 3603 admin@mcentee.waltham.sch.uk www.mcentee.sch.waltham.uk G Levitt (interim); Chair of Governors: Rick Eutener Walthamstow Central **Buses:** W11, 34, 97, 97A, 158, 215 (to Chingford Road, A112) Black trousers or skirt, sweatshirt with school badge, white shirt, black shoes **Demand:** 42 applications for 180 places in 2001/2 **Type:** Community comprehensive for 767 mixed pupils, aged 11 to 16 **Submit application form:** 4 December 2003 **Motto:** The Pathway to Success **School hours:** 8.50am–3.50pm (Mon–Wed), 8.50am–3.20pm (Thurs–Fri); homework clubs are available **Meals:** Hot and cold available **Strong GCSE subjects:** Geography, PE **London league table position:** 477

### Profile

McEntee School is housed in a modern building near to the Banbury Reservoir. It has sports facilities for indoor and outdoor activities, and boasts its own outdoor heated swimming pool. There is a school council and a parent-teacher association. The school faces the problem of high levels of mobility, with a growing number of refugees at the school. Attendance at the school has been a problem, hence the special Ofsted report (see 'Achievement'). In 2000, truancy was high at 3.4 per cent.

### Admissions and intake

Applications should be made through the LEA. Links are established with primary schools, by staff visiting them throughout the year, and primary pupils are able to use the school's facilities to get a feel for the place. Almost a fifth of pupils are registered as having special educational needs, which is above average. On entry, the majority of pupils have low attainment.

### Achievement

GCSE results at the school are considerably below average for schools in the area, but the school faces greater problems in its intake than many of its neighbours. In 2002, 20 per cent of pupils obtained five or more A*–C grades at GCSE. This was seven per cent up on 2001's results and the lowest in the borough. McEntee was inspected in 1998 with special regard to the management of behaviour and attendance. This followed a request from the secretary of state that certain schools with disproportionately high levels of truancy or exclusion undergo special inspections. Osted revisited the school in 2002 and noted that McEntee is 'improving under the strong leadership of the interim head teacher'. However, it still has serious weaknesses. Inspectors found the overall quality of teaching in Years 7 to 9 to be 'unsatisfactory' and as a result, many pupils do not achieve as well as they should. However, Ofsted recognised that the school's low exam results are 'adversly affected' by the low attainment of pupils on entry to the school. Inspectors praised the 'considerable progress' that has been made in improving pupils' behaviour and attendance. In 1999, 37 fixed-term exclusions and 7 permanent exclusions were made, a rate fairly close to the national average.

### Extra-curricular activities

Ofsted gave special mention to the school's 'wide and varied' range of extra-curricular activities. Teams exist for a range of sports from football to athletics, competing with teams across the capital. Many sports can be played to a less competitive level, including table tennis and swimming. Pupils can stay on after school to study in the learning resources centre, and the school also provides a homework club. There are trips both at home and abroad.

# Norlington School for Boys

**Norlington Road, Leytonstone, London E10 6JZ** 020 8539 3055 020 8556 4657 quickthinkers@norlingtonschool.co.uk www.norlingtonschool.co.uk Mr N Primrose; Chair of Governors: Stephen Pierpoint Leyton Midland Road Leytonston **Buses**: W16 (Hainault Road) Black trousers, black sweatshirt, white shirt, black trainers **Demand**: 130 applications for 120 places in 2001/2 **Type**: Community comprehensive for 600 boys, aged 11 to 16 **Submit application form**: 4 December 2003 **Motto**: Wisdom Is Strength **Mission statement**: Our aim is to build on our distinctive family atmosphere to achieve high levels of academic and social success. Norlington boys should develop into well-educated, balanced and happy young men, who are equipped to make a confident and responsible contribution to their community. **School hours**: 8.45am–3.20pm **Meals**: Hot and cold available **Strong GCSE subjects**: Geography, history, PE **London league table position**: 343

## Profile

Norlington is a successful boys' school situated in an area of relative economic deprivation in Leytonstone. The school building was extended in 1990 to create specialist teaching areas for science, music, design technology and PE. The school has received the Investors in People Award. Bengali, Punjabi and Urdu are taught to some of the high numbers of Asian pupils at Norlington. Further options available include product design, electronics and graphics. A GNVQ in ICT is also on offer. Parents are very supportive of the school and enjoy a good relationship with staff.

## Admissions and intake

Applications should be made through the LEA. The school is popular and oversubscribed. Pupils are drawn from the immediate locality and the school has developed strong links with its feeder primaries. On entry, reading skills are generally poor and attainment overall is below average. A total of 27 per cent of pupils are recognized as having special educational needs.

## Achievement

Given the disadvantaged nature of its intake, Norlington has done well to achieve GCSE results above the LEA average. However, in 2002, 44 per cent of pupils obtained five or more GCSEs at grades A*–C, 10 per cent up on the year before and in line with the local average. The school was ranked 10th in the borough. Attainment at Key Stage 3 and GCSE is well above average for similar schools. Ofsted made many encouraging findings in 1999, including 'the support and guidance offered to pupils are very good', as is 'provision for pupils' social, moral and cultural education'. The report stated that 'the school has an excellent school policy for the managing of behaviour and discipline'. Ofsted found the quality of teaching to have 'improved greatly' over three years. There were a high number of fixed-term exclusions in 1999, over 200.

## Extra-curricular activities

A full range of sporting activities is on offer, and a number of school teams have won various district tournaments and leagues. The rugby team participated in an international tournament which involved Paris St Germain. Visits are organized to France and the Netherlands and skiing trips are also arranged. The school takes advantage of its London location and takes pupils on educational visits to museums. Year 11 pupils can better their GCSE prospects by attending after-school revision sessions.

# Normanhurst School

**68–74 Station Road, Chingford, London E4 7BA** 020 8529 4307 020 8524 7737 pwilliams@normahurst school.co.uk www.oaktreeschools.co.uk Mr Peter Williams; Principal: Nicholas Hagger; Chair of Governors: Mr M Kendall-Torry Chingford **Buses**: 97, 179, 212, 313, 397, 444, 505 Black blazer and trousers or skirt, white shirt, school tie **Demand**: No figures available but c.50 pupils sit the entrance exam at Year 7 **Type**: Non-selective independent for 233 mixed pupils, aged 2 to 16 **Fees** (per term): £1,650–2,430 **Submit application form**: No cut-off date **Motto**: *Filius viri pater est* (The Child Is the Father of the Man) **School hours**: 8.30am–3.30pm **Meals**: Hot and cold available **Strong GCSE subjects**: All relatively strong **London league table position**: 287

## Profile

Normanhurst School is a small independent school with just over 200 pupils running through nursery, pre-prep, prep and senior age groups. The boys outnumber the girls 3:2. It was founded in 1923 by Miss Rudge and Miss Rawson at a site on the Ridgeway. Today it is housed in four large converted Victorian houses, set back from the tree-lined Station Road. It is close to Epping Forest and Queen Elizabeth I's hunting lodge. Senior school facilities include a computer suite and science lab. On-site there is a heated covered swimming pool, while sports facilities available to pupils off-site include an all-weather pitch, athletics track and sports hall. The school is non-denominational and pupils do not board. Normanhurst was bought by the current principal and his wife, and is now a member of the Oak Tree group of local independent schools. A full range of subjects is taught including commerce, computing and IT and drama and theatre studies. The school emphasizes subjects such as drama, music, sport and art, which it believes make a contribution to pupils' self-confidence. Class sizes are very small and the school operates a policy of setting by ability for some classes. There is a dyslexia unit, and all pupils are given work especially suited to their individual needs. A parents' association with an elected committee raises funds for the school.

## Admissions and intake

Applications should be made directly to the school. Candidates are required to sit an exam and undergo an interview. There are currently 34 pupils with special educational needs.

## Achievement

Normanhurst's exam results at GCSE have fluctuated greatly over five years, from 18 per cent of pupils gaining five or more A*–C grades in 1996 to 71 per cent in 2001; in 2002 this fell to 50 per cent. The school was ranked sixth in the borough, and was above the borough average. This degree of variation reflects the fact that the number of pupils in each year is very small, making such statistics less useful. Attendance is high at over 93 per cent in 1999, with truancies negligible at 0.3 per cent in 2000.

## Extra-curricular activities

A wide range of sports is on offer. Racquet sports enthusiasts can play badminton, squash and tennis; outdoor sports include football, rugby and hockey. A range of less common activities can be pursued including cross-country, gymnastics and martial arts. Pupils can also participate in ballet, a drama club and a French club. The school also offers instrumental tuition. England cricket captain Nasser Hussain visited the school on founders' day. Pupils do fund-raising for local charities.

# Rush Croft School

**Rushcroft Road, Chingford, London E4 8SG** ☎ 020 8531 9231 📠 020 8523 4779 ⓔ rushcroft@hotmail.com 🌐 www.rushcroft.waltham.sch.uk Ms P Cutler B.Ed; Chair of Governors: Ms A Encinas ⇌ Highams Park, Leyton Midland Road, Walthamstow Central ⊖ Walthamstow Central, Blackhorse Road **Buses:** 34, 69, 97, 97A, 158, 215 Green polo shirt with school logo, navy blue trousers (for girls or boys), skirt or shalwar kameez and navy blue school sweatshirt with school logo, black trainers **Demand:** 239 applications for 180 places in 2001/2 **Type:** Community comprehensive for 840 mixed pupils, aged 11 to 16 **Submit application form:** 4 December 2003 **Mission statement:** To ensure that pupils are: really proud to be part of Rush Croft; understanding of others; secure and welcomed; high achieving **School hours:** 8.45am–3.20pm **Meals:** Hot and cold available **Strong GCSE subjects:** English, IT, maths **London league table position:** 382

## Profile

Since 1997, Rush Croft has undergone extensive rebuilding as the school has expanded, and its facilities now include a new sports hall, music suite, ICT suite and library. The school faces the difficulties of an intake that has low levels of attainment and tends to come from areas of high socio-economic disadvantage. A large number of pupils have behavioural difficulties and the staff turnover is high. Some Year 10 pupils act as reading mentors to those in Year 7, while others run an advice centre as peer group counsellors. Pupils can volunteer to assist in the library, and each year has its own student council. There is provision for pupils with special needs and a parent-teacher association.

## Admissions and intake

Admission is through the LEA. The school's intake is generally below, and often well below, average levels of attainment. Pupils reflect the entire range of academic ability, but testing indicates that the majority have below average standards of attainment compared nationally.

## Achievement

In 2002, 36 per cent of pupils obtained five or more A*–C grades at GCSE, up from 35 per cent in 2001. The average points score gained per pupil shows a rising trend, and at a much faster rate than the national average. It is now in above those for similar schools. In 2002, the average point score was 30.2, below the national average of 34.7 points. In 2001, Ofsted noted that: 'Students make satisfactory or better progress in almost all subjects, but not in information and communication technology throughout the school and music in Years 7 to 9'. Teaching is 'satisfactory in most subjects and good or better in several, including English'. Inspectors praised the school's provision for those pupils with special educational needs. The school has faced some behavioural problems, which have led to a large number of exclusions. Attendance has also been a problem but is now rising, with truancy falling.

## Extra-curricular activities

The Year 11 boys' basketball team won the Waltham Forest Cup and the prestigious Essex Cup competition. Other sports available include football, netball and hockey. Pupils sing in a community gospel choir and do fund-raising for local charities. There is good provision for complementing lessons with extra study including an Easter revision course, extra classes at lunchtime for GCSE and a literacy summer school. There is also a revision club held for maths and an after-school supported study centre in the library. There are trips organized to France and Spain.

# Tom Hood School

**Terling Close, Leytonstone, London E11 3NT** ☎ 020 8534 3425 📠 020 8534 3317 ⓔ tomhoodschool@hotmail.com ✉ Mrs Candice Dwight; Chair of Governors: Clyde Kitson ⇄ Leytonstone High Road ⊖ Leytonstone **Buses**: 58 (Cann Hall Road), 257 (Leytonstone High Road) 👔 Black skirt or trousers, black jumper with school logo, white shirt, black shoes **Demand**: 155 applications for 180 places in 2001/2 **Type**: Community comprehensive for 900 mixed pupils, aged 11 to 16 **Submit application form**: 4 December 2003 **Mission statement**: To provide a quality learning experience for all our pupils. This can be broken down into four key areas: learning, achievement, partnership, responsibility **School hours**: 8.35am–3.20pm; homework clubs are available **Meals**: Hot and cold available **Strong GCSE subjects**: History, science **London league table position**: 355

## Profile

Tom Hood School is situated opposite the expansive open area of Wanstead Flats, close to Newham. Accommodation includes a new science block and reception area. Pupils benefit from all-weather pitches, tennis courts, a sports hall and gym. There is also a drama studio. The school buildings have been significantly refurbished and generally improved over recent years. IT resources have been well-funded and the school is now well-equipped with computers. GCSE options available include drama and resistant materials. Each year group has an elected council, which provides a forum for discussion. Within the school there is a centre for pupils with moderate learning difficulties. Good support is also given to pupils speaking English as an additional language. The school operates an open policy towards parents, allowing direct contact with teachers and senior members of staff, including the head. There is a strong PTA. Specialist bilingual staff are available to allow non-English-speaking parents to articulate their views. Truancy was 1.7 per cent in 2000, down from a high of 2.5 per cent in 1999.

## Admissions and intake

Applications should be made through the LEA. The ability of the intake is skewed towards the lower end of the spectrum. Half of 11-year-olds have reading ages below their actual age on entry. Many of the school's intake are from refugee families, which means a high turnover of pupils in each year group.

## Achievement

The proportion of pupils obtaining five or more GCSEs at grades A*– C was 45 per cent in 2002, up on 2001 and continuing an upward trend. The school was placed 12th in the borough league table. The average points score was 31.4, below the borough and national averages. In 2001, Ofsted described Tom Hood as a 'good school where pupils achieve well'. Pupils do 'very well' when compared with similar schools. Teaching is seen to be 'very good or excellent' in a third of the lessons observed. The school has problems with pooor attendance and 'unsatisfactory or poor' teaching was seen in a few lessons, particularly in Years 7, 8 and 9.

## Extra-curricular activities

The school fields teams in a range of sports, including football, basketball, table tennis, hockey and athletics. There is a school choir and pupils may learn to play instruments and join orchestral groups. An annual school play is held and London's galleries and other educational attractions are patronized. The Prince's Trust has given money to the school to help finance study weekends. There is a skiing trip and a trip to France.

# Walthamstow School for Girls

**Church Hill, Walthamstow, London E17 9RZ** 020 8509 9446 020 8509 9445 walthamstow.school@sch.lbwf.gov.uk sol.ultralab.anglia.ac.uk/pages/school_onLine/schools/Walthamstow Jane Quigley; Chair of Governors: Mrs Carmen Edwards Walthamstow Queen's Road, Walthamstow Central Walthamstow Central **Buses**: 212 Green trousers or skirt, green jumper, white shirt; school tie and blazer optional **Demand**: 330 applications for 180 places in 2001/2 **Type**: Community comprehensive for 900 girls, aged 11 to 16 **Submit application form**: 4 December 2003 **Motto**: Quality Education for All Girls **School hours**: 8.45am–3.30pm; homework clubs are available **Meals**: Hot and cold available **Strong GCSE subjects**: Art, history **London league table position**: 183

## Profile

Known as 'the Green School' because of its distinctive uniform, Walthamstow School has been educating girls for over 100 years. It was opened in 1890, and moved to its present site in 1924. The grounds have beautiful gardens, which include a flowering cherry tree that has a preservation order. Playing fields and hard courts provide ample opportunity for the girls to participate in a range of sports. In 1930, the Greek Theatre was built, where to this day the Greek Theatre Players still stage shows. A recent addition is the technology block, while an old vicarage known as 'the House' is used for office and classroom space. In 1993, the school put in a successful bid for a £200,000 funding from the Technology College initiative, and has been on-line since 1995. It takes seriously its commitment to equality of opportunity and lives up to its comprehensive status. There is a parents' association, Friends of Walthamstow, and a school council. There is provision for pupils with special needs.

## Admissions and intake

Applications should be made through the LEA. Most pupils are admitted from eight feeder schools: Barclay, Thomas Gamuel, St Mary's, Mission Grove, Henry Maynard, Greenleaf, Edinburgh and Chapel End primaries.

## Achievement

Results at the school have been rising in line with the national trend. In 2002, 61 per cent of pupils gained five or more A*–C grades at GCSE, above the national average. This was down from 63 per cent in 2001 and the school was placed fourth in the borough league table. Candidates averaged 40.2 points. The findings of the latest Ofsted inspection in 1996 were overwhelmingly positive. The report stated that Walthamstow is a 'good school with many outstanding features', including a 'positive ethos', which makes 'a significant contribution to the quality of education'. The school was said to have had 'much success in building self-esteem and respect for others'. The strong leadership was said to be a major strength. The report added that there is an 'atmosphere of racial harmony' and that the school provides a 'very good range of high quality extra-curricular activities'. Unauthorized absences were below the local average at 1.1 per cent in 2000.

## Extra-curricular activities

The school has an environmental club, which ensures that it lives up to its 'Green' nickname in more ways than one. The school collaborates with schools in Finland and Sweden as part of its European project, and arranges a trip to Italy and a foreign skiing expedition. Girls can play a wide range of sports including netball, tennis, football and basketball, and many go on to represent the school at local level. Other pupils are involved in the steel band. There are after-school homework clubs.

# Warwick School for Boys

**Barrett Road, Walthamstow, London E17 3ND** 020 8520 4173 020 8509 9949 warwick.school@sch.lbwf.gov.uk Mrs Ruth Woodward; Chair of Governors: Mrs Elizabeth Phillips Wood Street Walthamstow, Walthamstow Central Walthamstow Central **Buses:** W16, 230 Black trousers, school sweatshirt, white shirt, school tie **Demand:** 93 applications for 180 places in 2001/2 **Type:** Community comprehensive for 900 boys, aged 11 to 16 **Submit application form:** 4 December 2003 **School hours:** 8.40am–3.20pm; homework clubs are available **Meals:** Hot and cold available **Strong GCSE subjects:** Business, English, maths **London league table position:** 461

## Profile

Warwick School is split across two sites, which are very close to each other. The school has improved dramatically since the appointment of a new head in 1997, following a poor Ofsted report in 1995, and is now considered to provide a much higher standard of education for its pupils. However, exam results are still well below the local and national averages. The school's design technology area has been completely re-equipped. Warwick responds to the particular needs of its unusual intake, for instance offering Polish and Urdu as subject options. Of the 1998 leavers, 67 per cent continued in education. The truancy rate (2.2 per cent for 2000), is high and overall attendance is below the average. There is a school council and a parent-teacher association.

## Admissions and intake

Applications should be made through the LEA. The school has a very challenging intake. The families of pupils face economic disadvantage and many live in very crowded households. Pupils have low literacy standards on entry. There is a high turnover of children at the school, with each year group accepting new pupils, many of whom come from refugee families or have troubled backgrounds in other schools. Over half of pupils live in homes where English is not spoken as the first language. Well over a third of pupils are recognized to have special needs, more than double the national average.

## Achievement

In 2002, 30 per cent of pupils obtained five or more GCSEs at grades A*–C, up one per cent on 2001's results. The school was ranked 17th in the borough. When Ofsted visited the school in 1999, it found some praiseworthy aspects, for instance the 'very strong leadership with excellent whole school development work' and the 'very good arrangements for the assessment on entry of the large number of pupils who join the school'. Overall, it was found that attainment at both Key Stages is average or above average for similar schools and that teaching was at least satisfactory in 86 per cent of lessons, and good or better in almost half of these. The school has suffered from under-staffing but its results still show a high quality of 'value-added' by its teaching.

## Extra-curricular activities

The school provides a wide range of sporting activities, with teams and practice sessions being run by enthusiastic members of staff. Sports include badminton, squash, climbing, cricket and canoeing. The school cricket team has won the London Cup and the Essex Cup. Music activities include a steel band, a keyboard club and instrumental tuition. Some pupils join a film club and others go on London theatre trips. There is a residential course at the Gilwell Park Centre for Scouting, which is offered to Year 7. Summer careers days are held for Year 11, before they decide on their work experience placements. Homework and revision clubs are also on offer.

# Willowfield School

**Clifton Avenue, Walthamstow, London E17 6HL** 020 8527 4065 020 8523 4939 Eve Wilson; Chair of Governors: Maureen Chadwick Blackhorse Road, St James's Street, Walthamstow Blackhorse Road **Buses:** 123 (Forest Road), 158 (Blackhorse Lane) Royal blue sweatshirt with school logo or royal blue kameez; black skirt, trousers or shalwar and plain black or brown shoes **Demand:** 180 applications for 120 places in 2001/2 **Type:** Community comprehensive for 596 mixed pupils, aged 11 to 16 **Submit application form:** 4 December 2003 **Mission statement:** The promotion of a safe and secure environment in which children of all abilities from a diversity of cultural and social backgrounds are enabled and encouraged to achieve their full potential **School hours:**

8.50am–3.35pm; homework clubs are available **Meals:** Hot and cold available **Strong GCSE subjects:** ICT, RE, Urdu **London league table position:** 322

## Profile

Willowfield is a well-respected school. On site it has netball, volleyball and tennis courts, as well as a small hockey pitch and sizeable gym. It also uses grass pitches at the off-site Douglas Eyre Playing Fields. A 'life skills' course is taught in Years 10 to 11 for pupils for whom GCSEs are considered too demanding. Teaching is in mixed-ability classes, except for maths and science at Key Stage 4. There are three full-time special needs teachers and three assistants, and a counsellor is employed one day a week. The ethnic minority achievement department has two full-time teachers who collaborate with mainstream teaching staff.

## Admissions and intake

Applications should be made through the LEA. The school draws its intake from the full ability range, but almost a third of all pupils have special educational needs and a large number have statements.

## Achievement

Willowfield's exam results are very impressive when the challenging intake of the school is taken into account. In 2002, the proportion of pupils gaining five or more GCSEs at grades A*–C was 41 per cent, nearly up to the borough average, though down from 42 per cent in 2001. The school was placed ninth in the borough. In 2001, Ofsted noted that: 'Willowfield is an effective school that does well for its pupils and is continuing to improve'. At GCSE, above average results are achieved in ICT, RE and Urdu. Pupils also achieve well in mathematics, art and science. Pupils are 'happy and secure' and the school does well in comparison to similar schools. Some teaching still needs improving as does standards in some subject areas, especially music.

## Extra-curricular activities

Pupils can join art and drama clubs or the choir. There is also a drama and a literary/poetry club for Urdu. The ethnic minorities achievement department runs a weekly homework club. Volunteers from across the year groups created a Millennium Garden. Team sports include football, hockey, rugby, cricket, basketball and netball. Pupils may also take part in activities organized by local groups including Leyton Orient Football Club, London Towers Basketball Club and the London Schools Cricket Association. The art department organizes trips to galleries, while the drama department arranges theatre visits.

# Wandsworth

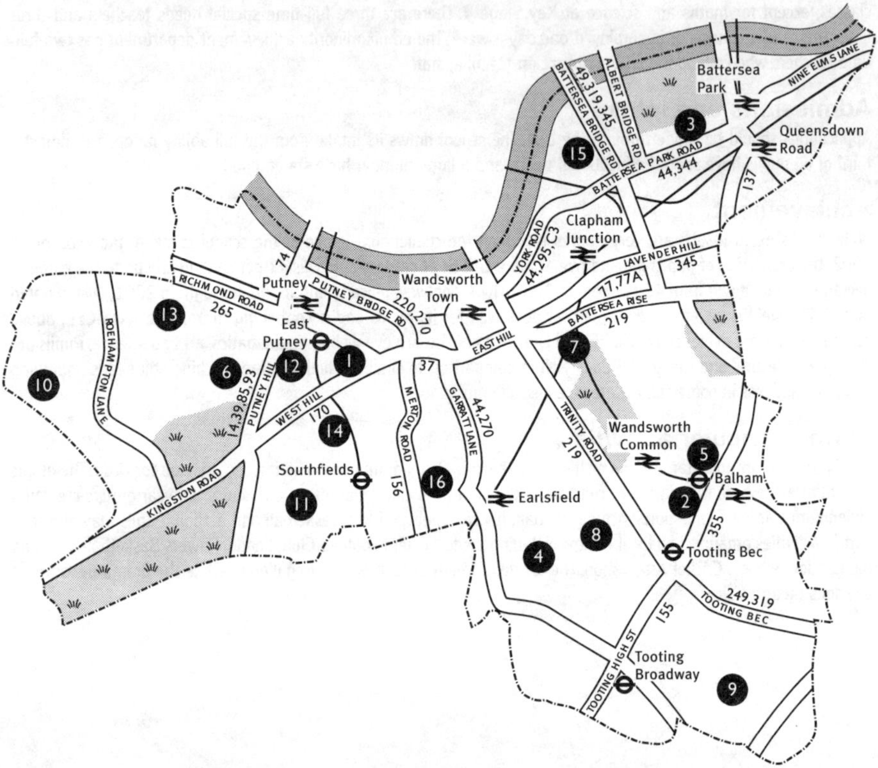


## Key

1 ADT College
2 Balham Preparatory School
3 Battersea Technology College
4 Burntwood School
5 Chestnut Grove School
6 Elliott School
7 Emanuel School
8 Ernest Bevin College
9 Graveney School
10 Ibstock Place
11 John Paul II School
12 Putney High School
13 Putney Park School
14 Saint Cecilia's Wandsworth School
15 Salesian College
16 Southfields Community College

# Factfile

**LEA: Town Hall, Wandsworth High Street, London SW18 2PU** ☎ 020 8871 6000 🌐 www.wandsworth.gov.uk **Director of Education:** Paul Robinson **Political control of council:** Conservative **Percentage of pupils from outside the borough:** 23.4 per cent **Percentage of pupils educated outside the borough:** 14.8 per cent **London league table positions (out of 32 boroughs):** 21st

## Profile

The borough of Wandsworth contains extremes of affluence and poverty. It is significantly more disadvantaged than most areas in England. Wandsworth is surrounded by Clapham, Balham, Tooting and Putney, and the borough is bounded to the north by 8km of waterfront.

In 2002, the borough average for pupils gaining five or more A*–C grades at GCSE was 48.6 per cent. The average point score for A/AS levels was 182.7. The borough council has an enviable record of gaining funds for regeneration and cooperation from developers. The government has set up the East Battersea EAZ, which includes one secondary school, Battersea Technology College, with an aim to improve standards. Ofsted's report on the borough in May 2000 was complimentary about its commitment to raising standards for a high proportion of pupils for whom English is an additional language. It also mentioned BEST (Business and Education Succeeding Together), with approval, and noted that the borough's priority is to provide information to its schools to enable them to manage themselves and to monitor their performance rigorously to ensure they do well.

## Policy

There is no comprehensive borough-wide policy on entrance. Wandsworth's criteria for entry to its three community schools (Battersea Technology College, Ernest Bevin College and Southfields Community College) gives priority to siblings at the school and proximity of the family home to the school. There is also a Year 6 test for entrance to Ernest Bevin school, which is a partially selective community school. The borough-wide date for application for Wandsworth LEA controlled schools is November of the preceding year of entry.

# ADT College

**100 West Hill, Wandsworth, London SW15 2UT** ☎ 020 8877 0357 📠 020 8877 0617 ✉ info@adtcollege.org.uk 🌐 www.adt.tcnet.org.uk Mr David D Durban; Chair of Governors: Mr RE Painter OBE ⇄ Putney ⊖ East Putney **Buses:** 14, 39, 77A, 77C, 85, 93, 170, 270, 337 **Demand:** 1160 applications for 180 places in 2001/2 **Type:** Comprehensive City Technology College for 986 mixed pupils, aged 11 to 18 **Submit application form:** October 2003 **Mission statement:** ADT college will prepare children for living and working in the 21st century by: providing technology-rich education; a partnership between students, parents, industry and college; high expectations; a business-like ethos; quality spiritual, moral, social and cultural development and professional development for staff. **School hours:** 8.30am–4.45pm (Tues–Thurs); 8.30am–3.20pm (Mon, Fri) **Meals:** Hot and cold available **Strong GCSE subjects:** Science **London league table position:** 137

## Profile

ADT College is sponsored, which allows for an above-average income (although not necessarily more than other CTCs), ensuring that the school is well-equipped and fully refurbished. Its involvement with the business world directs the school towards a vocational, entrepreneurial focus. The curriculum is broad and balanced for all pupils, but science and technology are the main focus. Years 7, 8 and 9 follow an extension programme, which focuses on 'understanding industry' and extends the normal National Curriculum. At Key stage 4 pupils study maths, English, double-certificate science, design and technology and a modern language, as well as optional subjects and a part 1 GNVQ. In the sixth form, there is a strong commitment to GNVQ. Pupils can become monitors and take part in the year council. Two weeks' work experience is offered in Year 10. Pastoral care is via a tutorial system and a head of year.

## Admissions and intake

Applications are direct to the college trustees. To ensure applicants are suited to this type of specialist education, they are asked to take part in a structured discussion at the college. Only where children show an aptitude will priority be given to siblings and children of staff members. If the sibling criteria does not apply, a child will be given priority on the basis of distance from the school. If oversubscribed, a short non-verbal reasoning test is taken. Priority is given to children with mathematical, scientific and technological leanings.

### Achievement

The school is achieving above average results with prior attainment levels close to the national average. In 2002, 86 per cent of pupils gained grades A*–C in five or more GCSEs. This was up from 71 per cent in 2001 and the school was ranked fifth in the borough league table. The school has made a good improvement over recent years, and has consistently had 99–100 per cent of pupils gain at least one GCSE at grades A–G. The strongest subject tends to be science, but it has also improved at English and maths. Other subjects are generally in line or better than the national average. In 2002, A-level pupils taking two or more subjects gained an average point score of 212.4. This was above the borough average and performance has been steady since 1997. Ofsted visited the school in 1997 and found the teaching to be strong in the sixth form with 93 per cent of lessons judged as 'satisfactory or better'. Attendance is better than the national average with unauthorized absence low at 0.6 per cent.

### Extra-curricular activities

Music and drama are very popular. The college makes good use of the local careers service and the local police. Regular visits are organized from religious leaders and youth groups. The college is also involved in fund-raising for charity, volunteer work and the Duke of Edinburgh's Award scheme.

# Balham Preparatory School

**47a Balham High Road, Balham, London SW12 9AW** ☎ 020 8767 6057 📠 020 8682 4272 Mr Maksud Gangat; Chair of Governors: Mr Karim ⇌ Balham ⊖ Balham, Tooting Bec **Buses:** T55, 155 Grey trousers, white shirt and navy blue jumper (boys); white shirt, blue long dress, white scarf (girls) **Demand:** Fully subscribed **Type:** Non-selective independent for 266 mixed pupils, aged 3 to 16 **Fees:** £1,450 per year **Submit application form:** Contact school for details **Mission statement:** To serve the children of the Muslim community in Southwest London in a safe protected environment where they can excel in education **School hours:** 8.15am–3.45pm **Meals:** Not provided **Strong GCSE subjects:** Information not available **London league table position:** 112

### Profile

The school is housed in a converted mosque, but there are plans to develop a purpose-built school. Most of the pupils are Muslim but admission is open to other religions. It was first established in 1993 and is growing in numbers. As the school expands, there are plans to introduce a sixth form. The curriculum is broad and balanced, and a 90-minute lesson in Islamic studies is delivered daily. Arabic and Urdu are offered as optional subjects. Pupils also have the opportunity to take on the responsibility of being a monitor. Aided by the limited size of the school and classes –15 pupils per class on average – relationships between teachers and pupils are good. The school maintains close contact with parents through newsletters, parents' evenings and reports.

### Admissions and intake

Most of the secondary school pupils come up through the primary school. The remaining pupils come from a catchment area that includes Streatham, Battersea, Balham, Wandsworth and Croydon. An entrance test in maths and English is taken before a place is offered.

### Achievement

In 2002, 88 per cent of pupils achieved five or more A*-C grades at GCSE, up from 46 per cent in 2001. There is no Ofsted report available, but the school is evidently close-knit and the atmosphere is one of caring and warmth with a strong religious ethos. Authorized absence stood at 5.3 per cent and unauthorized absence at 1.2 per cent in 2000, above the borough and national averages.

### Extra-curricular activities

Children play football on Saturdays. Both day and week trips are offered to pupils and there are plenty of prayer facilities at the school. There are plans to develop the range of activities offered once the school expands.

# Battersea Technology College

**401 Battersea Park Road, London SW11 5AP** ☎ 020 7622 0026 📠 020 7978 2683 info@batterseatech.wandsworth.sch.uk Mr G Keller; Chair of Governors: Mr Anthony Cole ⇌ Battersea Park Road

**Buses:** 44, 49, 319, 344, 345 Up to sixth form: Navy blue jumper, black trousers or skirt and white shirt **Demand:** All applicants for September 2001/2 were offered places **Type:** Comprehensive community college for 675 mixed pupils, aged 11 to 18 **Submit application form:** 7 November 2003 **Mission statement:** Building a community where learning is for everyone **School hours:** 8.30am–3.30pm; homework clubs are available **Meals:** Hot and cold available **Strong GCSE subjects:** French, performing arts **London league table position:** 518

## Profile

The school has successfully turned around since it was placed on 'special measures' due to failing standards in 1993. This came about thanks to committed leadership, which helped change the school's culture. New computer suites, food studies, textiles, art and design, and drama facilities have boosted the school's growing appeal. The school has made a bid for Arts College status. The curriculum is broad and balanced, and has been developed by adding work-related and enrichment studies. In the sixth form, pupils can take A-levels, AS-levels, BTEC Nationals, GNVQs and mature GCSEs. Pupils can become prefects or representatives on a student council. The school is part of an Education Zone Partnership, which helps improve standards in numeracy and literacy. The school has an Investors in People Award. Special-needs provision is very comprehensive. A learning mentor programme offers one-to-one mentoring and help with attendance or family difficulties. The school holds parents' evenings, performance review days and is hoping to set up a PTA. Heads of year and tutors are responsible for pastoral care.

## Admissions and intake

Admissions are dealt with by the council, but an application is available from the secretary or from the child's primary head teacher at the transfer interview. Open days are held in October. If oversubscribed, places are offered, in order of priority, to those with siblings already at the school and those who are closest geographically. On entry, pupils' attainment levels range from average to below the national average.

## Achievement

Since coming off 'special measures' in 1998, there has been an upward turn in the school's attainment reflected by the increase in the number of pupils achieving at least one GCSE pass. In 1996, 25 per cent had no passes but by 2000, no pupil failed to achieve a pass. Poor admissions and variable standards during 'special measures' meant that there were fewer children capable of achieving five or more GCSEs. However, the school is looking to improve these figures. In 1999, only 4 per cent achieved five or more A*–C grades but this increased to 6 per cent in 2000 and 17 per cent in 2001, dropping to 14 per cent in 2002. At A-level, the average point score was 81 in 2002, ranking the school bottom of the borough league table. In 2001, Ofsted noted that the school had 'improved in many areas in recent years'. Inspectors observed that: 'In almost all lessons teaching is satisfactory or better and in the majority of lessons it is good or better'. However, there is still a need to improve attendance, punctuality and special-needs provision. Unauthorized absence has dropped from 15 per cent in 1994–5 to 1.3 per cent in 2000.

## Extra-curricular activities

The school holds regular drama productions and is often used by film companies, for example, for the TV drama, *The Last of the Blonde Bombshells.* The school was without sports clubs in 1996, but now there is a successful basketball team, which reached the London and regional finals, and a girls' football team, besides others. The school hosts the Panathalon Sports Challenge and an activities week. There are geography field trips and other trips abroad. Pupils are encouraged to participate in charity work and recently took part in the *Blue Peter* incubators for babies appeal. Hour-long homework clubs are available.

# Burntwood School

**Burntwood Lane, Tooting, London SW17 OAQ** 020 8946 6201 020 8944 6592 info@burntwood.wandsworth.school.uk www.burntwoodschool.com Mrs H Dorfman BA, B.Sc, MA; Chair of Governors: Ms Kathy Hooper Earlsfield Tooting Broadway **Buses:** G1, 44, 77, 219, 249, 270, 689, 690 Grey skirt or trousers, white shirt, tie, red sweatshirt **Demand:** 964 applications for 283 places in 2001/2 **Type:** Partially selective foundation school for 1,680 girls (mixed in sixth form), aged 11 to 18 **Submit application form:** 7 November 2003 **Motto:** The Best Education for Women of Tomorrow **School hours:** 8.35am–3.30pm, 8.35am–3.00pm (Wed); homework clubs are available **Meals:** Hot and cold available, including breakfast **Strong GCSE subjects:** English, geography, history, RE **London league table position:** 228

## Profile

Burntwood is a Beacon School set on a large campus with 13 acres of grounds including playing fields, tennis and netball courts and a large indoor swimming pool. There are also good drama facilities and a well-equipped library and media resource unit. The school is well-maintained and has a rolling programme of refurbishment, with plenty of subject-dedicated classrooms. The curriculum was described in the 1997 Ofsted report as 'rich and varied'. In the sixth form pupils study A- and AS-levels in over 20 subjects. They also have the option of studying GNVQs in art and design, business studies and health and social care. Work experience is undertaken for two weeks in Year 10 and Year 12 in connection with GNVQs. There is a student council and prefects. Special-needs pupils and those who have English as an additional language make good progress. There are tutorial groups and a year system. Parent forums deal with school issues. Parents' evenings, annual reports and mid-year grade sheets keep parents informed.

## Admissions and intake

Partial selection operates whereby 90 out of 283 pupils are selected. The other 193 places are given priority in this order: siblings, special medical or social grounds and proximity. Parents apply in the autumn term directly to Burntwood, and open days are held in October and November. A total of 20 pupils have statements of educational needs and 404 are on the special needs register.

## Achievement

In 2002, 62 per cent of pupils achieved five or more GCSEs at grades A*–C, well above the borough and national averages. This was up two per cent on 2001's results and the school was ranked seventh in the borough. Exam results have generally improved steadily since 1996. The average point score per pupil for those pupils taking two or more A-levels was 223.6. This ranked the school fourth in the borough league table and was above the borough average. In 1997, Ofsted reported that standards of attainment are satisfactory and sometimes good, with students making good progress through the school. The quality of teaching was described as a strength. The strongest subjects are English, history, geography and RE, while maths, IT and PE tend to be better in Key Stage 3 than in Key Stage 4. Inspectors called Burntwood 'an outstanding school'. It has created a 'harmonious and supportive community characterized by good relationships and well-motivated students'. Attendance at Burntwood is on the whole good.

## Extra-curricular activities

After-school extension lessons are offered, allowing pupils to take a second or third language from Latin and Urdu. Homework clubs are also available. The school is big on water sports – the school has been the dragon boat-racing champion. Regular trips are arranged at home and abroad, including foreign exchanges and visits to art galleries. Pupils are encouraged to take part in charity fund-raising activities.

# Chestnut Grove School

**Chestnut Grove, Balham, London SW12 8JZ** ☎ 020 8673 8737 📠 020 8675 1190 🌐 www.chestnutgrove.wandsworth.sch.uk ✉ Ms Margaret Peacock; Chair of Governors: John O'Malley ⇌ Balham ⊖ Balham; **Buses** 155, 315, 355 👕 Bottle green sweatshirt, black trousers or skirt **Demand:** 450 applicants for 156 places in 2001/2 **Type:** Partially selective community comprehensive for 889 mixed pupils, aged 11 to 18 **Submit application form:** 7 November 2003 **Motto:** A Creative Learning Community **School hours:** 8.35am–3.00pm; homework clubs are available **Meals:** Hot and cold available **Strong GCSE subjects:** All comparable **London league table position:** 390

## Profile

Chestnut Grove occupies a crowded and complex site. It is a well-maintained, clean school with very good sports facilities and two sports halls. In 1995 a redevelopment programme was completed, which included new labs and three art pavilions to add to the already good specialist facilities. The school doubles up as an adult education centre. The school has good local links with industry and commerce. Work experience is offered to senior pupils, as well as a mentoring scheme linked to industry. Pupils can assume wider responsibility through the school council. Special learning needs provision is generally sound. Pupils are organized into tutor groups and homework diaries are a focal point for informal guidance. Parents are kept informed through parents' evenings and reports. A PTA is developing.

## Admissions and intake

A total of 30 pupils are selected for their abilities in art and design and another 30 for foreign languages. A total of 96 places are offered across the full range of abilities to siblings, and then to those living nearest the school. On entry, there is a wide range of abilities. The school, which is on the border of Lambeth and Wandsworth, takes pupils from a large catchment area reaching beyond the LEA. This means there are a number of feeder primary schools, which have close links with the school. At the time of writing there were 42 special-needs pupils with statements and 262 on the register.

## Achievement

In 2002, 32 per cent of pupils achieved grades A*–C in five or more GCSEs, which was below the borough and national averages. The school was ranked 12th in the borough league table with an average point score of 30. There have been significant improvements in results over the years. Back in 1996, just 16 per cent were getting grades A*–C and 17 per cent left without any passes. In 2002, those pupils taking two or more A-levels achieved an average point score of 144.8. This ranked the school ninth in the borough. Results have been varied over the last five years, peaking in 1996.

## Extra-curricular activities

There is a varied programme of activities on offer at Chestnut Grove, including trips to the theatre, museums, a European week and educational trips to Europe and around Britain. There is a variety of sports, including football, hockey and netball clubs. Dance and drama reflect the cultural diversity of the school; in 2000 the head of PE, Mr John Brooks, won the 'Working with Parents and the Community' Award at the National Teaching Awards for his work with the school's Chestnut Grove Lindy Hoppers dance troupe. Pupils are encouraged to participate in community fund-raising events.

# Elliott School

**Pullman Gardens, Putney, London SW15 3DG** ☎ 020 8788 3421 📠 020 8789 8280 ⓔ elliottschool@elliott-school.org.uk ✉ Mr A Willis M.Ed; Chair of Governors: Mrs Carol Crane ⇌ Putney ⊖ East Putney **Buses:** 14, 37, 39, 85, 93, 170, 270, 337 👕 Sweatshirt with school name **Demand:** 877 applicants for 233 places in 2001/2 **Type:** Foundation school for 1432 mixed pupils, aged 11 to 18 **Submit application form:** 7 November 2001/2 **School hours:** 8.30am–3.15pm; homework clubs are available **Meals:** Hot and cold available **Strong GCSE subjects:** Modern languages **London league table position:** 314

## Profile

Elliott is a large comprehensive situated in an economically mixed, residential part of Putney. The school has developed a specialist language college which has led to an increase in pupil numbers and has had a significant impact on the curriculum. Other facilities include science, IT blocks and a library. While facilities are good, the games fields are some distance from the school. The curriculum is broad, particularly in languages. Options include French, German, Spanish and from Year 9, Italian and Japanese. After school, pupils can learn Hebrew, Japanese, Latin and Arabic. For the most able linguists, there is a GCSE fast-track and for talented newcomers there are masterclasses. European projects are being developed, for example a joint study of war by Years 10 and 12 with a German school and a 'Science in Europe' project in Year 9. A total of 20 A-levels are on offer in the sixth form, including more unusual options such as philosophy. Year 10 are offered two weeks of work experience and the school runs a Challenge of Industry programme. There is good provision for pupils with special needs. In 2000, Elliott won the *Evening Standard* London Schools Award for Outstanding Achievement.

## Admissions and intake

Admission is through the LEA (see borough factfile). Pupils enter with a range of abilities, overall, below the national average, but they make good progress and reach standards above or better than the national average by the time they leave. Currently, there are 38 special-needs pupils with statements and 265 on the register.

## Achievement

Elliott performs roughly in line with the LEA average for average GCSE point scores. In 2002, 46 per cent of pupils passed with five or more GCSEs at grades A*–C. This was down on 47 per cent in 2001. It has performed steadily since 1996, with a previous peak in 1998 with 43 per cent gaining five or more grades A*–C. In 1998, Ofsted described the school as 'outstandingly well led'. The teaching is good (92 per cent is satisfactory or better), and pupils are looked after well. Strong subjects at end of Key Stage 4 are science, French, design and technology, textiles and food science and music. All other subjects are average, except for English, which is weak, although the school has started to tackle this weakness. Sixth-form provision is very good. The strongest subjects at A-level tend to be history, art and modern foreign languages, with high standards in English, maths, science, design and technology, geography and music. In 2002, the school achieved fifth highest results in the LEA for pupils gaining two or more A-levels, with an average point score of 223.5, which is below the national average. Unauthorized absence was high at 3 per cent in 1999 but this was reduced to 0.7 per cent in 2000.

### Extra-curricular activities

An association with a French college brings post-16 pupils together in England and France to study French and English drama. There is a varied array of sports, including basketball and rowing. Homework clubs area available. The school has good links with the local community from businesses to residents' associations.

## Emanuel School

**Battersea Rise, Battersea, London SW11 1HS** ☎ 020 8870 4171 📠 020 8877 1424 ⓔ asp@emanuel.org.uk 🌐 www.emanuel.org.uk Mrs Anne-Marie Sutcliffe; Chair of Governors: The Right Hon Viscount Hampden DL Clapham Junction **Buses:** 35, 37, 39, 49, 77, 77A, 156, 170, 219, 295, 319, 344, 345 Navy blue, grey and black **Demand:** Oversubscribed **Type:** Selective independent for 719 mixed pupils, aged 10 to 18 years **Fees:** £2,753 (Age 10), £2,853 (Rest of school) **Submit application form:** Contact school for details **Motto:** *Per ben desirer* (Do Your Best) **School hours:** 8.45am–4pm **Meals:** Hot meals, plus cold snacks **Strong GCSE subjects:** Sciences **London league table position:** 108

### Profile

The school dates back to 1594, when it was erected on the command of Lady Dacre in Westminster. In 1883, the pupils moved into an orphanage built after the Crimean War. The school is set in 12 acres of land. The school has a continous development of new facilities including a sports hall, sixth-form centre and upgraded science laboratories. The sixth form consists of 175 pupils, and A-level options are broad including classical civilisation, history of art, Latin and Russian. AS-levels include general studies, French, German, Italian, Russian, Spanish and psychology, if the demand is great enough. A new video-conference facility enables the school to offer a wider range of A-levels. No vocational qualifications are offered. A form tutor system is in place and parents are kept informed with reports and parents' evenings. There is a school council in the lower sixth.

### Admissions and intake

Pupils come from a wide catchment area, reaching to the M25 as far north as Northwood and as far east as Bromley. Open days are held in October and November. Normal points of entry are at 10+, 11+, 13+ and the sixth form. Every child needs to be registered on the official registration form which is available from the school. Entrance examinations take place in January for the lower school. Entry at 16+ is on the basis of academic reference and interview. Some scholarships and bursaries are available. All things being equal, preference will be given to children from St Luke's, Chelsea and St Stephen and St John's, Westminster primary schools. Currently, there no pupils with a special-needs statement and 15 on the special-needs register.

### Achievement

Emanuel achieved the third highest GCSE results in the borough in 2002, which were well above the national average. A total of 87 per cent of pupils gained five or more GCSEs at grades A*–C. These good results were even down on 93 per cent the previous year. At A-level, Emanuel achieved the joint second best performance in the borough, achieving an average point score of 293.6 among pupils taking two or more A-levels. Authorized attendance for 2000 was 5.0 per cent, which is below the LEA and national average. There was no unauthorized absence.

### Extra-curricular activities

There are inter-house competitions including tug-of-war, chess and maths, and a school play is performed in December. Other groups include the chapel choir, school choir and orchestra, and an opera or musical is produced each year. Visiting teachers offer lessons in instruments, including strings, woodwind and brass. Sports include rugby,

Eton fives, hockey, swimming, rowing and sub-aqua.The school has been the winner of the School's Head of the River 11 times and has won gold medals in the rowing National Championships. It is also winner of the Surrey Cricket Cup and is the London Schools Champion in athletics. Exchanges are organized to France, Germany and Spain.The school is also involved in the Duke of Edinburgh's Award scheme and a programme for the charity Help the Aged.

# Ernest Bevin College

**Beechcroft Road, Tooting, London SW17 7DF** ☎ 020 8672 8582 📠 020 8767 5502 Mr Naz Bokhari OBE; Chair of Governors: Dr D Lewis ⇌ Wandsworth Common ⊖ Tooting Bec **Buses:** 155, 189, 219, 249, 349, 355 Up to sixth form: black blazer, year tie, black trousers, white shirt, V-neck black jumper **Demand:** 425 applicants for 209 places in 2001/2; 180 places in 2003 **Type:** Partially selective community college for 1080 boys (mixed sixth form), aged 11 to 18 **Submit application form:** 7 November 2003 **Mission statement:** To provide all pupils with the equal opportunities to achieve their full academic potential and social development; to maintain a stimulating educational community with which all pupils' individual needs are known, identified and met and which enables staff and students to work in a cooperative way **School hours:** 8.50am–3.30pm **Meals:** Hot and cold available **Strong GCSE subjects:** Art, design and technology, English literature **London league table position:** 384

## Profile

This school was described by Ofsted inspectors as 'very good and exceptionally good in some areas'. There is a swimming pool, judo area and two gyms.The curriculum is broad and balanced through Key Stages 3 and 4.Top band language students can study German as an additional language. At Key Stage 4, pupils study integrated humanities including RE, GNVQ courses in business and manufacturing, direct teaching of IT and classes in Urdu. GCSE options include business studies and media studies. Classes are streamed, although for the first three years most classes are taught in tutor groups. High-achievers can take GCSEs early.The sixth form offers a range of A-level and vocational courses. Work experience is offered in Year 10 and Year 12. Special-needs requirements are met and pupils progress well.There is a school council and a prefect system. Unauthorized absence in Year 10 and 11 is high due to truancy and parents failing to offer reasons for absence. Parents can join the Friends of Ernest Bevin.

## Admissions and intake

A total of 60 places a year are offered to boys who attain the highest scores in the Wandsworth Year 6 Test. A total of 120 places are offered to siblings and then to those who live nearest the college. On accepting a place, pupils are interviewed in September, before the start of the school year. Around 60 per cent of pupils were on the special needs register and 21 had statements in 2000.

## Achievement

In 2002, 54 per cent of pupils gained five or more GCSEs at grades A*–C. These results were 25 per cent up on 2001's results and above the borough and national averages.The school was ranked 11th in the borough league table. Standards have been steady over the last six years. Not all boys are entered for five or more GCSE, and therefore the number who gain grades A*–G is higher. Sixth-formers taking two or more A-levels came below the LEA average with an average point score of 159.5 and the school was ranked seventh in the borough league table. In 1997, Ofsted commended the school as being led with 'compassion and understanding', providing a 'sound education'. At Key Stage 4 and GCSE, history standards are good, English literature, design and technology and art are in line with the national average and progress is sound, but below the national average is maths, English language, science, IT and music.

## Extra-curricular activities

Sports are competitive, with the Year 8 football team winning the South London Cup in 1999, and other students reaching regional and national levels in judo and athletics. Drama and music activities include a locally renowned African drumming group. One pupil represented the school in the Young Scientist of the Year final. Skiing trips, geography fields trips and visits to museums and art galleries are all on offer. Pupils are encouraged to raise funds for local charities such as Trinity Hospice.

# Graveney School

**Welham Road, Tooting, London SW17 9BU** ☎ 020 8682 7000 Fax 020 8682 7075 Email info@graveney.wandsworth.sch.uk Web www.graveney.wandsworth.sch.uk Head Mr GE Stapleton MA (Cantab); Chair of Governors: Mr D Atkins Rail Mitcham Junction, Tooting Tube Tooting Broadway **Buses:** G1, 44, 57, 77, 127, 133, 201, 249, 270, 280, 355 Uniform Black blazer with badge, white shirt, school tie, back or grey trousers or skirt **Demand:** 1725 applications for 250 places in 2001/2 **Type:** Partially selective foundation for 1745 mixed pupils, aged 11 to 18 **Submit application form:** 7 November 2003 **Mission Statement:** Committed to excellence, committed to developing the talents of all pupils to the full **School hours:** 8.30am–4.50pm (Mon), 8.30am–3.25pm (Tues–Thurs), 8.30am–3.05pm (Fri); homework clubs available **Meals:** Hot and cold available, including breakfast and vegetarian options **Strong GCSE subjects:** English language and literature, mathematics, science **London league table position:** 139

## Profile

Graveney is one of the second wave of 300 Beacon Schools. In 1986, Battersea and Rosa Bassett Grammar Schools, Furzedown and Ensham Schools were amalgamated as Graveney. In 1991, it achieved grant-maintained status. ICT college status was achieved in 1995 and confirmed in 1998. In May 1999, it was designated a centre for training teachers in ICT. Facilities include a learning resource centre, 12 science labs, 10 technology rooms, six art rooms, four music rooms and nine ICT suites. There are 350 networked computers. The school has a new sports hall and all-weather facility offering athletics, table tennis, football and korfball, plus two gymnasiums and a multigym. The London Cricket Project enables county standard cricket coaching to be offered. Classical civilization, economics, law and psychology are offered at A-level as well as standard subjects. As an ICT college, this is the mainstay of vocational education, with design and technology, careers advice and two weeks' work experience offered. Gifted pupils are placed on the fast track to achieve their potential. Special-needs pupils are taught in support classes. There are prefects and a school council. Parents receive two reports and can attend parents' evening twice a year. The PTA is active.

## Admissions and intake

The application process is the standard LEA procedure (see borough factfile), but the governors set the criteria. A total of 75 places are offered to applicants with the highest scores in the Wandsworth Year 6 test, and the remaining 175 depending on exceptional need, siblings at the school and distance from the school. Entry level attainment is average and pupils make good progress. In 2000 there were 577 special-needs pupils, of whom 19 have statements,

## Achievement

The school's performance is improving faster than average. In 2002, 76 per cent of pupils gained five or more GCSE grades A*–C. This was up on 2001. A-level point scores are more variable, dropping to 228.5 in 2002. This was higher than the borough but lower than the national average. English language and literature, mathematics, science tend to have good results, and there are no poor subjects. In 1997, Ofsted commented that it is 'a very good school, with many outstanding features'. Unauthorized absence is low at 0.6 per cent.

## Extra-curricular activities

On offer to the sixth form is a university access programme, guest speakers from a wide range of organizations and a debating society. Creative writing is encouraged at all levels, with *Zephyr* magazine produced by the sixth form each term, and *Blaze* produced by the lower school. Poetry writing and public performance is encouraged. Various music ensembles perform regularly. There are history and social science links with Milan and the Ukraine and trips abroad, including an annual skiing trip. Homework clubs are available. Fund-raising for charity is encouraged.

# Ibstock Place

**Clarence Lane, Roehampton, London SW15 5PY** ☎ 020 8876 9991 Fax 020 8878 4897 Email office@ibstockplaceschool.co.uk Web www.ibstockplaceschool.co.uk Head Mrs A Sylvester-Johnson; Chair of Governors: Mr McIntyre Rail Barnes, Putney Tube East Putney **Buses:** 72, 255, 485 Uniform Navy blue skirt or trousers, grey or navy sweatshirt, white shirt with tan and navy stripes, and tie for the boys **Demand:** Oversubscribed **Type:** Selective independent for 650 mixed pupils, aged 3 to 16 **Fees:** £3,017 per term including lunch **Submit application form:** Beginning of December 2003 **School hours:** 8.40am–3.40pm **Meals:** Hot and cold meals available, including vegetarian options **Strong GCSE subjects:** All relatively strong **London league table position:** 72

## Profile

Friedrich Froebel (1782–1852), pioneered the kindergarten with an emphasis on early development through play. His ideas were expanded to cover the whole of a child's schooling, and training centres were established for teachers using the method. One was at Roehampton. In 1894, Ibstock Place was opened in Kensington as its demonstration school. After the Second World War, it moved back to take over the Roehampton Institute, and continues to offer education at all ages. Facilities include two science laboratories, a technical workshop, specialist art and craft rooms, a library and the Roberts Hall. There are also four networked IT suites with 26 computers, and all technical rooms and the library have computers. There is a gym and swimming pool as well as the playing fields. Vocational subjects offered are design and technology, office and secretarial skills. There is career guidance, and two weeks' work experience. There is no prefect system, but both a head and deputy head boy and girl. The school seeks to develop the whole child, entrusting each with various tasks to increase personal responsibility. There is also no provision to deal with severe learning difficulties. The school will be sympathetic and try to help to find a more suitable school for any pupil experiencing problems. The PTA is active. Parents are encouraged to contact the school with any problems.

## Admissions and intake

Pupils from the lower school normally progress to the senior school, but all applicants have to take the school's English, mathematics and science tests, and will also be interviewed. A reference from the previous school is required. Entry level attainment is average, but the Froebel method puts as much emphasis on personal qualities as on academic achievement, and improvement is quite striking.

## Achievement

The school achieves excellent results. The number of pupils gaining five or more GCSE grades A*–C increased from 90 per cent in 2000 to 97 per cent in 2001 and 2002, reversing a downward trend. This is well above the national and borough averages and the school was ranked second in the borough league table. The last independent school inspection was in 1998.

## Extra-curricular activities

Pupils can join clubs for life saving, first aid, the Duke of Edinburgh's Award scheme, photography, dance, chess and various musical activities. As well as trips to London and other UK sites for cultural and curricular purposes, the school sends a party of pupils, bi-annually, to an African or Third World school, where they undertake building projects to help the destination school. In turn the destination schools come to the UK to undertake environmental projects. There is an annual sponsored walk around Richmond Park.

# John Paul II School

**Princes Way, Wimbledon, London SW19 6QE** ☎ 020 8788 8142 📠 020 8780 1393 Mr J King BA; Chair of Governors: Mr NM Fitzsimons ⇄ Wimbledon ⊖ Southfields **Buses:** 39, 93, 77C, 170 Navy blazer with school badge, light grey trousers or skirt, blue shirt or blouse, navy V-neck sweater with school colours, school tie **Demand:** 247 applications for 120 places in 2001/2 **Type:** Voluntary aided comprehensive Roman Catholic school for 597 mixed pupils, aged 11 to 16 **Submit application form:** 7 November 2003 **Motto:** Seek the Truth. A Catholic School Guided by Gospel Values **School hours:** 8.45am–3.20pm, 3.15pm (Fri) **Meals:** Hot and cold available, including breakfast **Strong GCSE subjects:** English literature, RE **London league table position:** 411

## Profile

In 1985, John Griffiths School (for boys) and Notre Dame School (for girls) were amalgamated as a comprehensive. It achieved grant maintained status in 1993, and then became a voluntary aided school. There are sufficient science and technology laboratories to meet curriculum demands, good specialist music and art rooms, and theatre facilities. The learning resources centre was recently upgraded. There are three computer rooms, computers in several classrooms and two computers running special mathematics software for special-needs support. The school has two gyms, and playgrounds, but there are no playing fields on-site. For ball and team games it has to hire facilities within the neighbourhood. Statistics, IT, art and design, leisure and tourism are offered as vocational subjects as well as design and technology. Years 9–11 have visits from careers advisers, leading to two weeks' work experience. GNVQ business studies are now being offered. Prefects are appointed at the end of Year 10 by the school and there is a school council. The special-needs coordinator and department work well together. In 1999 Ofsted noted that there is a 'sound whole school initiative' to improve literacy skills. A friends' association raises funds and there are regular and good reports, including the 'excellent school journals'.

## Admissions and intake

The LEA sets the closing date for applications (mid-November) but the governors set the criteria for admissions. It is necessary to have active or at least partial commitment to the Catholic faith or to churches belonging to Churches Together in England, or a willingness to accept the Catholic ethos of the school. Recommendation from a parish priest is also needed. Thereafter, choice is on exceptional need, sibling at the school and distance from the school. In 2000, there were 161 special-needs pupils, of whom 13 had statements.

## Achievement

The school's performance is consistently at or just below the borough average and below the national average, though in 2002 the number of pupils gaining five or more GCSE grades A*–C was 32 per cent. This is well below both the borough and national averages. English literature and religious studies tend to be good subjects, but geography is poor. Ofsted commented favourably on improvements in the quality of teaching, staff-pupil relations and good ethnic integration. Unauthorized absence was low at 0.7 per cent.

## Extra-curricular activities

There is a computer club, which is open before school and during the lunch break, various musical ensembles, and several sports activities. The school works with national sports organizations, Fulham Football Club and the local authority sports development team. There are regular field trips and visits. The orchestra plays for local elderly people, and charity fund-raising is encouraged.

# Putney High School

**35 Putney Hill, London SW15 6BH** ☎ 020 8788 4886 📠 020 8789 8068 ✉ putneyhigh@put.gdst.net 🌐 www.gdst.net/putneyhigh Head: Dr Denise Lodge; Chair of Governors: Christopher Rochier ⇄ Putney ⊖ East Putney **Buses:** 14, 37, 39, 74, 85, 93, 270, 337 Uniform: Up to sixth form: Grey skirt or trousers, white blouse, purple V-neck pullover, cardigan or grey or purple sweatshirt, black or grey blazer or coat. **Demand:** Figures not available; oversubscribed **Type:** Selective independent, part of the Girls' day School Trust, for 796 girls, aged 4 to 18 **Fees:** £2,385 per term **Submit application form:** 4 December 2003 **Mission Statement:** We provide a school environment which is rigorous but supportive, where each student is valued as an individual and develops independent learning skills, an awareness of the wider world, and the skills needed for the 21st century. **School hours:** 8.30am–3.50pm; homework clubs are available **Meals:** Hot and cold available, including vegetarian options and sometimes breakfast **Strong GCSE subjects:** All strong **London league table position:** 249

## Profile

Putney High is one of 25 schools in England and Wales (12 in London) in the Girls' Day Schools Trust, which was founded in 1872 to provide high quality education for girls at the lowest possible cost. In 1976, it reverted to independence in order to remain academically selective. After the Assisted Places Scheme was phased out in 1998, the Trust set up its own bursary scheme to ensure that talented girls are not excluded through financial considerations. Facilities include seven science laboratories, the Lockley Centre for Design and Technology and soundproofed rooms in the music department. Five further ICT rooms contain 130 Microsoft NT4 networked computers, all with Internet access. There is a new sports hall and the school has boats at the Thames Rowing Club and strong links with Belgrave Harriers Athletics Club. Past pupils have competed at Olympic level. To the standard range of A-levels are added economics, Latin, Greek and government and politics. Careers education and two weeks' work experience are offered as part of the GCSE curriculum. Pastoral care is primarily through form tutors. There is a school council and prefects. There is an active PTA and parents are encouraged to contact the form tutors with questions.

## Admissions and intake

Applications for admission at age 11 should be made before the end of November. The school sets entry tests in English and mathematics. The applicant pupil is also interviewed. Entry to the sixth form is conditional on GCSE results and an interview. Demand is extremely high, and the entry attainment level is above average.

## Achievement

The school achieves remarkable results at GCSE and A-level. In 2002, the proportion of pupils gaining five or more GCSE grades A*–C was 99 per cent and the school came top of the borough. At A-level, the school has consistently achieved the highest point score in the borough, with 375.4 in 2002. The last independent school inspection, in 2000, commented that this is an 'outstanding school, which lives its aims. It has many strengths, and no major weaknesses.'

## Extra-curricular activities

Clubs and societies may be curriculum-based or focus on different interests. Pupils have played in the National Youth Orchestra, and the senior choir has toured Canada and South Africa. Sport, especially rowing, is actively pursued. The Duke of Edinburgh's Award scheme is a great success. The RNLI and Royal British Legion are supported and carol singing at Christmas and a summer party for senior citizens strengthen ties with the community.

# Putney Park School

**Woodborough Road, London SW15 6PY** ☎ 020 8788 8316 📠 020 8780 2376 ✉ office@putneypark.london.sch.uk 🌐 www.putneypark.london.sch.uk Mrs J Irving ⇌ Barnes, Putney ⊖ East Putney **Buses:** 33, 74, 337; a school bus transports a limited number of pupils between Wimbledon and Barnes and the school Grey and gold blazer, grey skirt, yellow short sleeved blouse **Demand:** 20 places available **Type:** Non-selective (up to 11) independent for 365 mixed pupils (girls only from 11), aged 4 to 16 **Fees** : £2,400 per term **Submit application form:** No cut-off date **Motto:** *E labore praemia manant* (From Work Comes Reward) **School hours:** 8.45am–3.35pm; homework clubs are available **Meals:** Hot and cold meals available, including breakfast and vegetarian option **Strong GCSE subjects:** Drama, music **London league table position:** 249

## Profile

Miss Tweedie-Smith opened the school in a private house in 1953. Since then it has grown, and further houses have been acquired. There are four science laboratories, a home economics room, library, art, music and drama rooms. There is also a computer suite, with 12 computers. The school has its own gymnasium, but also uses the Bank of England sports ground for ball games, swimming and athletics. Rowing is also offered. Despite its lack of facilities, the school competes with some success in inter-school matches and also arranges inter-house games. The school is able to meet the demands of the National Curriculum, including science and mathematics, and to exceed it in some areas, (though work experience is not offered). French is taught from reception class, and German from Year 8. English as a foreign or second language is taught to pupils from overseas. The vocational subjects are design and technology, but pupils can be prepared for instrumental and vocal examinations for the Associated Board of Music, and for Royal Academy of Dancing and London Academy of Music and Dramatic Art examinations. Sympathetic assistance is offered to dyslexic pupils. The school acknowledges its Christian affiliation and builds on it to provide 'a sound education in a happy atmosphere'. The school operates a house system, which enables parents to receive good and valuable reports. Parents are also welcome to contact the school directly, but are requested to make an appointment if wishing to meet the head teacher. There is also a school council in the upper school. The Friends of Putney Park arranges fund-raising activities.

## Admissions and intake

Application should be made to the school for procedure details and dates of entry tests. Applicants and parents are interviewed, and a report is required from the previous school where applicable. Although its own primary school is non-selective, to pass into the senior school pupils must pass the same tests as applicants from elsewhere. In 2000, there was one special-needs and statemented pupil, who received personal attention.

### Achievement

The school achieves high grades for its pupils. The number of pupils gaining five or more GCSE grades A*–C is usually above 80 or 90 per cent, though this dipped to 60 per cent in 2002. This was still above the local average and the school was ranked third in the borough league table. The school is a member of the Independent Schools Association, and the last inspection was in 1996.

### Extra-curricular activities

The school arranges visits to places of interest in and around London. There are also trips abroad. Various clubs are available, including computer, sports, technology and embroidery. Charity fund-raising is encouraged, with the recipient organizations varying from year to year. Homework clubs are available.

## Saint Cecilia's, Wandsworth School

Sutherland Grove, London SW18 5JR 020 8871 6455 020 8871 7202 st-cecilias@wandsworth.gov.uk www.wandsworth.gov.uk/st-cecilias Mr JE Risbridger BA; Chair of Governors: Rev Cannon Peter Clark Putney, Wimbledon Southfields **Buses:** 39, 93, 156, 170 Not known **Demand:** 150 places available in 2003 **Type:** Voluntary aided comprehensive for 150 mixed pupils, aged 11 to 18; increasing to 900 pupils by 2009 **Submit application form:** 7 November 2003 **Motto:** Not known **School hours:** 8.25am–2.30pm with extra-curricular activities in the afternoon **Meals:** Hot and cold meals available **Strong GCSE subjects:** Not yet known **London league table position:** Not available

### Profile

Saint Cecilia's, Wandsworth School will is a brand new school which will open in September 2003. It will be a Church of England, voluntary-aided comprehensive. The school's emphasis is on music. It offers 15 places for music scholars each year.

### Admissions and intake

The LEA sets the closing date for applications, but the governors set the criteria for acceptance. A total of 100 places are offered to applicants who themselves or their families are practising members of a Christian church; 50 places are then offered to applicants irrespective of their religious background but with priority given to applicants with special needs and those living nearest the school; 10 foundation and five open places are then offered to applicants who demonstrate that they have the aptitude to benefit from a specialist course in music by means of an assessment test in October. Open evenings are held in September.

### Achievement

As the school only opens in 2003, no exams have been taken to date.

### Extra-curricular activities

A large number of activities will focus on music. Details have not yet been finalized.

## Salesian College

Surrey Lane, Battersea, London SW11 3PB 020 7228 2857 020 7223 4921 info@salesiancollege.co.uk www.salesiancollege.co.uk Mr S McCann M.Phil, BA; Chair of Governors: Mr N Potter Clapham Junction Sloane Square **Buses:** 19, 49, 239, 249, 295, 319, 344, 345 Maroon blazer with badge (Years 7 to 10); black blazer with badge, grey trousers, grey V-neck pullover, white shirt, school tie (Year 11) **Demand:** 305 applications for 150 places in 2001/2; 139 places available in 2003 **Type:** Voluntary aided comprehensive for 643 boys, aged 11 to 16 **Submit application form:** 7 November 2003 **Motto:** Reason, Religion and Kindness **Mission statement:** We aim to enable each pupil to become a good Christian, an honest citizen, able to earn his bread. **School hours:** 8.30am–3pm (Mon, Fri), 8.30am–3.30pm (Tues–Thurs); homework clubs are available **Meals:** Hot and cold available, including breakfast and vegetarian options **Strong GCSE subjects:** History, information studies, languages **London league table position:** 288

## Profile

The Salesian Community was founded in Italy in the mid-1800s by St John Bosco, to help boys left abandoned in Turin. There are now Salesian communities all over the world. Battersea was the last one founded by the saint, in 1888 and opened in 1895. The arts are well provided for and there are six science laboratories and the technology rooms have been re-equipped. The school playing fields are at Ewell. The five Salesian Schools in the UK take turns hosting an athletics championship and football teams undertake annual inter-school tours. Design and technology, IT and electronics are offered as vocational subjects. Two weeks' work experience is arranged. There are prefects in Years 10 and 11 and the school council is active. The chaplains and tutors provide pastoral care. There is an on-site learning support unit for special-needs pupils and the LEA recently obtained funds from the Excellence in Cities initiative for a programme to stretch high achievers. Written reports are sent to parents twice yearly, and there are regular consultation evenings. The parents' association is active in fund-raising.

## Admissions and intake

The LEA sets the closing date for applications, but the governors set the criteria for acceptance. Priority is given to children of families committed to the Roman Catholic Church. Other criteria are: exceptional need; sibling presence or family connection; and distance from the school. A recommendation from a parish priest is required. In 2001, over over a third of pupils had special educational needs, which is very high, but the percentage of pupils with statements was average.

## Achievement

The school's performance is inconsistent. In 1996, 34 per cent of pupils gained five or more GCSE grades A*–C, but by 1999, it was 26 per cent. In 2000, it increased to 33 per cent of pupils and in 2002, it went up again to 45 per cent. Modern languages, history and information studies tend to be good; music, design and technology and religious studies are poor. In 2001, Ofsted described Salesian College as 'effective' and 'developing into a good school'. It was seen to be 'well led' with 'many strengths'. GCSE results were above average when compared to similar schools. The rate of attendance is satisfactory and broadly in line with the national average for boys' schools.

## Extra-curricular activities

Clubs range from rambling to science and Latin. Homework clubs are available. There is a poetry magazine and the choir is regularly invited to sing in St George's Cathedral, Southwark. Opera, musicals and exhibitions are visited. The exchange school is in Moscow and trips are made to France, Spain and Italy. Each tutor group adopts its own charity, and food parcels are delivered to needy pensioners.

# Southfields Community College

**333 Merton Road, London SW18 5JU** 020 8875 2600 020 8874 9949 info@southfields.wandsworth.sch.uk www.southfields.wandsworth.sch.uk Ms Jacqueline Valin; Chair of Governors: Mr Girvan Thompson Earlsfield Southfields **Buses:** 39, 44, 77, 220, 270 Black trousers, royal blue sweaters and white shirts **Demand:** 527 applications for 269 places in 2001/2; 249 places in 2003 **Type:** Comprehensive foundation Sports College for 1260 mixed pupils, aged 11 to 18 **Submit application form:** 7 November 2003 **Mission Statement:** An achievement focused college. The aim of Southfields Community College is for students and staff to accept the challenges of learning so that students leave with the knowledge, skills and maturity to take up their adult roles. **School hours:** 8.20am–3.05 (Mon), 8.20am–2.40pm (Tues–Fri) **Meals:** Hot and cold meals available, including vegetarian options **Strong GCSE subjects:** Art. music, RE **London league table position:** 417

## Profile

A pre-war school on the site changed its name to Southfields post war, becoming a community college in the 1990s, and a sports college and accredited sports teacher training institution in September 2000. A new building, the Wandsworth City Learning Centre, opened in 2000 and offers specialized training to primary school pupils, to adults and the local community generally. Facilities include a library, eight science laboratories, nine technology workshops, with computer controlled robotics, and a soundproof recording and electronic music centre. The school has two gymnasiums, a swimming pool, playing fields and tennis and netball courts. In 1999, the school won a Sportsmark Award from Sport England. It subsequently became a Sports College through a DfES initiative. It also has a Sportsmark Award from the Youth Sport Trust for its commitment to sport.

A-levels range from art and design to economics and business. Business and industry representatives visit the school, and there is a range of opportunities for work experience. Pupils are taught in both ability and mixed ability sets. The school has a hearing-impaired unit (the only one in south-west London for secondary pupils), and there is a learning support team and two specialist IT suites for special-needs pupils. The more able are put in fast track groups. There is an active school council. There is no PTA but the school makes every effort to keep parents informed about the school and their children's progress.

## Admissions and intake

The LEA sets the closing date for applications, but the governors set the intake criteria. The first 25 places are for pupils with a special aptitude for sport: they take practical tests and an interview. The remaining 224 places are non-selective. In 2001, there were 244 general places. When the school is oversubscribed the criteria is: exceptional need; sibling at the school; and distance from the school. In 2001, over half the school's pupils had special educational needs, which is very high, with two per cent having statements.

## Achievement

In 2002, 27 per cent of pupils gained five or more GCSE grades A*–C, compared to 17 per cent in 2001. The school was ranked 14th in the borough. A-level point scores have been reasonably consistent and were 202 in 2002. This ranked the school seventh in the borough. In 2001, Ofsted visited the school and described it as a 'good and improving college'. Inspectors praised the 'positive ethos and strong leadership' of the school. GCSE results are well above average for similar schools with good results in music, art and RE. Behaviour was seen to be 'good'. Attendance levels need to be raised as Ofsted noted low attendance in some lessons. However, attendance is broadly in line with the national average and unauthorised attendance is below the national average.

## Extra-curricular activities

A wide variety of extra-curricular activities are on offer. Clubs include chess, performing arts and study clinics. After-school homework clubs are available. Pupils have made visits and field trips to Kew Gardens, the Body Shop's factory, the Bank of England and Arsenal Football Club. The school premises are available for use by the community outside school hours. The school holds regular charity days.

# Westminster

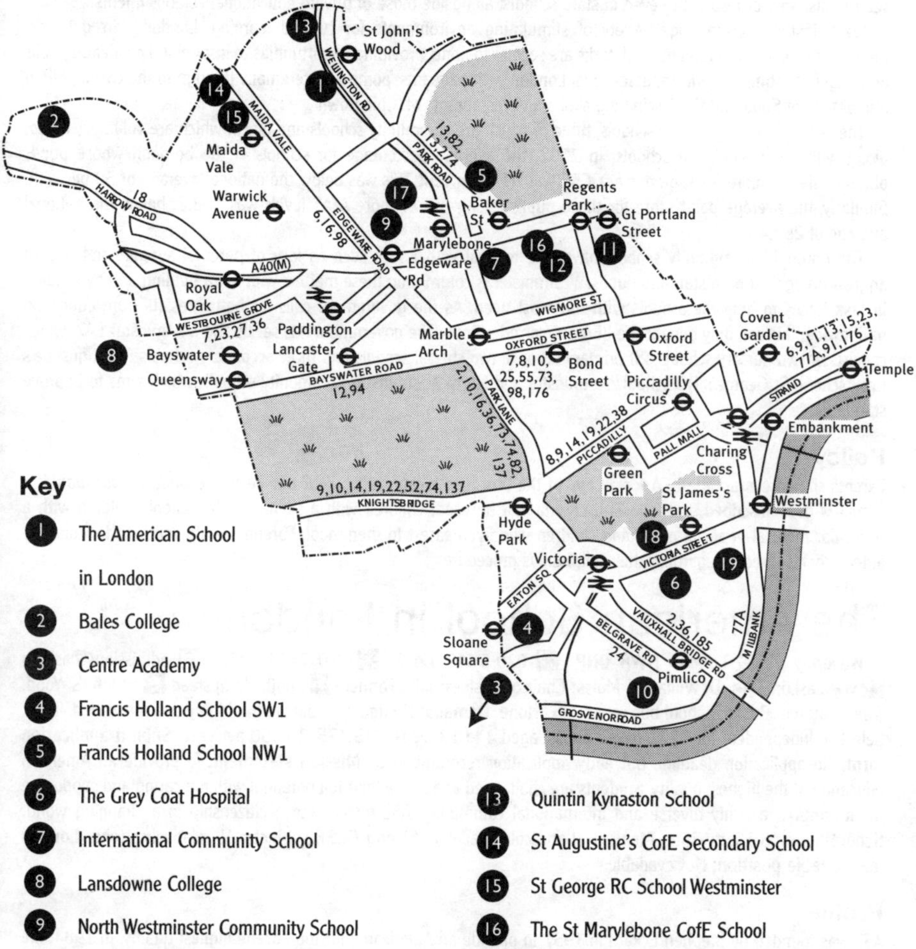


## Key

1. The American School in London
2. Bales College
3. Centre Academy
4. Francis Holland School SW1
5. Francis Holland School NW1
6. The Grey Coat Hospital
7. International Community School
8. Lansdowne College
9. North Westminster Community School
10. Pimlico School
11. Portland Place School
12. Queen's College London
13. Quintin Kynaston School
14. St Augustine's CofE Secondary School
15. St George RC School Westminster
16. The St Marylebone CofE School
17. Sylvia Young Theatre School
18. Westminster City School
19. Westminster School

# Factfile

**LEA: Westminster City Hall, Victoria Street, London SW1E 6QP** ☎ 020 7641 6000 www.westminster.gov.uk **Director of Education:** John Harris **Political control of council:** Conservative **Percentage of pupils from outside the borough:** 37.5 per cent **Percentage of pupils educated outside the borough:** 20.6 per cent **London league table positions (out of 32 boroughs):** 25th

## Profile

Westminster is a borough typical of an inner-city area, with extremes of affluence and deprivation. Some of the most wealthy areas in London are in Westminster, alongside rundown housing estates. It therefore comes as no surprise to see the disparity of results achieved in state schools, alongside those of private educational establishments.

Westminster offers a huge variety of stimulating environments for cultural learning. London's art galleries, theatres, museums, monuments and parks are second to none, providing opportunities to inspire and challenge pupils of all ages. Westminster encompasses royal London with pageants, pomp and ceremony through to the cosmopolitan inhabitants of Soho and the fascinating shops and restaurants of 'Chinatown'.

The borough has eight state schools, three of which are community schools and five of which are voluntary aided, along with 12 independent schools. In 2002, the average percentage for schools in the borough whose pupils obtained five or more A*–C grades at GCSE was 41.5 per cent. This was below the national average of 50 per cent. Similarly, the average point score for those pupils taking two or more A/AS levels was 183.2, below the national average of 254.4.

The borough's community schools have had to deal with issues such as lack of parental support and acts of aggression against both staff and pupils. Westminster is confronting these matters with extra funding and by sending in task forces to help the schools with the most need. As the government calls for better results from education nationwide, this can only benefit the LEA-supported schools. The government has set up the Westminster EAZ, which consists of two nursery schools, 20 primary schools, two special schools and three secondary schools (St Augustine's CofE school, St George's RC School Westminster and North Westminster Community school), which aims to improve standards.

## Policy

Parents should contact the LEA for a copy of the brochure *Westminster: Your Choice for Secondary Education.* If a school is oversubscribed, the following criteria will be used: children with a sibling at the school; children with a particular medical or social need; and children who live nearest to the school. Parents should contact the voluntary aided schools directly regarding their admissions procedure.

# The American School in London

**1 Waverley Place, London NW8 0NP** 020 7449 1200 020 7449 1350 admissions@asl.org www.asl.org Dr William C Mules; Chair of Trustees: John Farmer South Hampstead St John's Wood, Swiss Cottage **Buses**: School bus service None **Demand**: No figures available but highly oversubscribed **Type**: Selective independent for 1272 mixed pupils, aged 4 to 18 **Fees**: £13,175–15,350 per year **Submit application form**: No application deadline but early application recommended **Mission statement**: To provide an American education of the highest quality. Students are challenged to achieve their full potential within a caring and supportive framework. As a richly diverse and international community, ASL fosters active citizenship in a changing world. **School hours**: 8.15am–3pm **Meals**: Hot and cold available **Strong GCSE subjects**: All relatively strong **London league table position**: Not available

## Profile

ASL was founded by Stephen Eckard in 1951 to provide an American education of the highest quality. In 1984, the school became an Educational Trust. About 50 different nationalities are represented and 30 per cent of students hold non-USA passports. Its present buildings date from 1971. Facilities are excellent and include the Anenburg Theatre and two libraries with extensive book, video and CD-ROM collections. There are seven computer labs. ASL has its own sports fields at Canons Park, and the Loudoun Road campus has a large recreational area and gym/fitness facility. A major programme of renovation and expansion began in 1999, and will add 20 per cent more space for classrooms, arts centres and another gym. The school's curriculum is American. Students are successful in gaining admission to universities internationally and in the UK, including Oxbridge. Extensive career counselling with students and parents is provided, and college recruiters visit the school regularly. There is a school council and a prefects system. The parent-teacher organization is active, with its own web site and regular newsletters. Parents are very involved.

## Admissions and intake

Places are offered to pupils considered likely to succeed in the school's programmes. Past school records, teacher recommendations and the results of standardized tests are considered. There are no deadlines or interviews, but parents are encouraged to request a tour of the school to learn more about its ethos and aims. A limited amount of financial aid is available.

### Achievement

The school is accredited by the Middle States Association of Colleges and Schools and the European Council of Independent Schools. The last independent school inspection date was 1997; to retain accreditation, schools must be inspected, and pass, every 10 years. There is a standard procedure for unauthorized absence from any lesson, starting with referral to the dean of students, but the incidence is low.

### Extra-curricular activities

There is a range of language, sports and study clubs available, including an AIDS awareness club. Sports played include baseball, tennis, rowing, soccer (for boys and girls) and golf. Competitive sports and public music performance have been important in the school's development. The ASL swimming team won competitions in Brussels in 2000 and defended their title in Cairo in 2001, while the ASL concert band played for President Reagan at Winfield House. ASL field trips have included Hampton Court, Canterbury, the National Gallery and the Lake District. The school is involved in the Model United Nations project. Pupils can help produce a student newspaper and take part in a Battle of the Bands and the all-school annual family picnic, a gathering of 2200 students, staff and parents. Community service activities include cooking and serving at the soup kitchen in the American Church in London.

# Bales College

**21 Kilburn Lane, London W10 4AA** 020 8960 5899 020 8960 8269 enquiries@cife.org.uk www.cife.org.uk/bales WB Moore B.Sc Queens Park Kensal Green **Buses:** 18, 52, 316 None **Demand:** No figures available **Type:** Non-selective independent for 69 mixed pupils, aged 13 to 19 **Fees:** £1,790 per term (full-time) **Submit application form:** No cut-off date **Mission statement:** To raise pupils' expectations of their own potential, to provide energy and commitment in teaching and to enable pupils to gain academic qualifications for entry into degree courses at university **School hours:** 9am–4pm (science practicals may continue to 5pm) **Meals:** Hot and cold meals available, including vegetarian options **Strong GCSE subjects:** Art, science **London league table position:** 523

### Profile

The school's prime focus is on helping pupils to recover from loss of motivation. Accordingly, it adapts the style and quantity of tuition to the needs of the individual pupil. It was founded in 1966 as a tutorial college, offering one- and two-year courses for re-takes of GCSE and A-levels. It has since expanded. For older pupils, it offers a sixth-form college, but it is taking an increasing number of younger pupils. The school has three labs on site, one for each of the sciences and a computer/IT room. The site is too small to provide sports facilities but the school uses a sports centre and swimming pool nearby. Bales College is not formally structured, but there are weekly meetings with groups of pupils, where problems can be resolved. Class sizes are a maximum of six, and are not age-based. A range of A-levels are available, including government and politics, law and sociology. Special-needs provision is available for dyslexia and learning disabilities. Extra tuition and support is available as necessary. Although there is no formal PTA, parents are encouraged to be involved with the school.

### Admissions and intake

Applicants are assessed for their ability to fit in with the ethos of the school and for their willingness to apply themselves. For applications, contact the school at any time: the timetable will be adapted to accommodate the pupil's needs if at all possible. There is no entrance exam: prospective students are interviewed. A formal recommendation is not required, but previous school reports and examination results may be taken into consideration. The school places more emphasis on the interview and its own assessment of the present or potential commitment of the student. Some bursaries are available.

### Achievement

Bales College claims to improve performance by two grades at least, and has on occasion achieved a turn around from grade E on entry to grade A. At GCSE, the school has remarkable variation from year to year in the percentage of pupils achieving five or more A*–C grades, with zero per cent in 1996, 1998 and 2001, 44 per cent in 1997, 25 per cent in 1999 and 50 per cent in 2000. In 2002, 18 per cent of pupils gained GCSEs at A*–C grades and the average point score was 17.5. The average A-level point score for two or more was 169.6 in 2002, ranking the school 13th in the borough. This is below the national average. BAC accredits the school and unauthorized absence is low at 0.4 per cent.

### Extra-curricular activities

The drama club and contemporary dance clubs are a favourite with students. There are also fieldwork trips for geography and biology, and court visits for law students. Visits are organized to museums, theatres and galleries. The school is too small for any corporate involvement with charity or community work.

## Centre Academy

**92 St John's Hill, Battersea, London SW11 1SH** ☎ 020 7738 2344 Fax 020 7738 9862 ✉ ukadmin@centreacademy.com 🌐 www.centreacademy.com Head: Miss C Hakim; Chair of Governors: Dr M Hicks (founder) Rail: Clapham Junction **Buses**: 37, 39, 77A, 156, 170, 337 Uniform: None **Demand**: 60 applications for 25 places in 2000/1 **Type**: Selective independent for 44 mixed pupils, aged 8 to 19 **Fees**: £9,000–15,000 per year **Submit application form**: No cut-off date **Mission statement**: Learning to learn: we get the motivation back into your child's education **School hours**: 8.30am–3pm **Meals**: Hot and cold available **Strong GCSE subjects**: Arts, geography, science **London league table position**: Not available

### Profile

The Centre Academy was founded in1968 by Dr M Hicks and was originally for the American ex-patriate community. It now offers both the US curriculum and UK curriculum to GCSE level. The main building is a 1920s neo-Georgian building, which is well maintained. There is a computer room, with 16 computers, science laboratories, technical and art rooms and five classrooms. Sports are encouraged and the Academy uses two local sports centres and a local playing field. The basketball and football teams are successful in competitions. The school specializes in individual tuition, designed specifically for each pupil in mathematics and English, and joint learning takes place in classes with eight pupils. It has specialized in the diagnosis of dyslexia and ADHD (Attention Deficiency), since it opened. Pupils following the UK curriculum go on to sixth forms elsewhere. Parents are asked to be actively involved with the school, to ensure the pupils' success. A bi-weekly written report is provided on progress, and there are conferences and special meetings. All pupils are assigned a staff mentor who works with them on academic and personal growth and liaises with their parents. In conjunction with college placement advice and careers services, the school helps pupils to find the right sixth form or American university placement to ensure success. Work experience and career guidance are also offered.

### Admissions and intake

The Academy takes dyslexic and ADD/ADHD pupils only. Applicants may contact the school at any time. Prospective candidates are interviewed, and their previous work and reports discussed. Bursaries are available.

### Achievement

In recent years, the Academy's GCSE achievement has been rising steadily and substantially. However, in 2000, just 9 per cent of pupils gained five or more A*–C grades at GCSE, down from 33 per cent in 1999. In 2001, the downward trend continued with no pupils gaining a pass with an A*–C grade. The average point score was 5.1 and the school was ranked bottom of the borough league table.

### Extra-curricular activities

The school organizes skiing trips, foreign visits and field trips both in London and to activity centres throughout the UK. There is an annual science fair, talent show, school play, sports day and student newspaper. The school is associated with a local children's charity and club for the elderly, for which it arranges a Christmas party.

## Francis Holland School NW1

**Clarence Gate, Ivor Place, London NW1 6XR** ☎ 020 7723 0176 Fax 020 7706 1522 ✉ admin@fhs-nw1.org.uk 🌐 www.fhs-nw1.org.uk Head: Mrs G Low MA (Oxon); Chair of Governors: Lady V France OBE, MA Rail: Marylebone Underground: Baker Street, Marylebone **Buses**: 13, 82, 113, 274 Uniform: Black coat of regulation length, grey skirt, school shirt, deep red sweatshirt, dark tights (winter); short-sleeved blouse (summer); Sixth form: Sensible clothes **Demand**: Figures unavailable; oversubscribed **Type**: Selective Church of England independent for 380 girls, aged 11 to 18 **Fees**: £2,900 per term, including lunch **Submit application form**: 28 November 2003 **Motto**: That Our Daughters May Be As the Polished Corners of the Temple **School hours**: 8.30am–4pm; homework clubs are available **Meals**: Hot and cold available, including vegetarian, vegan, kosher and halal options **Strong GCSE subjects**: Art, music, PE **London league table position**: 54

## Profile

The Reverend Francis Holland, Canon of Canterbury, founded two schools for girls in 1878. One (in Graham Terrace), was to serve south London, the other north London. This school was originally in Baker Street, but moved to the Clarence Gate site in 1915. The school's emphasis is on encouraging study and developing the talents of pupils. There is an extensive library with CD-ROM resources, Internet access and connection to the school computer network, with both Apple Macs and PCs. There is also a specially designed computer suite. The school uses the sports facilities in Regents Park for hockey, rounders, netball, and tennis. It has also built an indoor swimming pool and has a gym on site, allowing gymnastics, volleyball and self-defence classes. A-level subjects offered include the humanities and sciences, with government and politics and statistics. GNVQs are not available but subjects taught include electronics, computing and life skills. Career education is introduced in the third year, and periodical careers conventions take place. The school uses the services of Cambridge Occupational Analysts. Some special needs can be accommodated, but not dyslexia. There is a prefect system and a parents' association, with regular open days. Famous ex-pupils include EH Shepard, illustrator of *Winnie the Pooh* and *The Wind in the Willows*.

## Admissions and intake

Application is made directly to the school. Admission is dependent upon passing the entrance examination, which includes English and mathematics. Prospective students and parents are interviewed, and a recommendation from the previous school is required. Bursaries are available.

## Achievement

The school performs well and places are much sought after. In 2002, 97 per cent of pupils gained five or more A*–C grades at GCSE. This was well above the borough and national averages. Results are always in the upper 90 per cent. The school was ranked third in the borough league table. At A-level, there is also steady achievement, with a point score of 375.5, substantially above the borough average, gained in 2002. This is also above the national average and ranked the school second in the borough league table. There were no unauthorized absences in 2000.

## Extra-curricular activities

The school offers a wide range of activities, including chess club, debating, astronomy, ornithology and pottery. There is a variety of sports, including fencing, football and swimming. Homework clubs are available. Field trips and visits have included the USA, India, Italy, France and Greece. Field trips in the UK for practical scientific work are also arranged. Pupils are encouraged to raise money for charities.

# Francis Holland School SW1

**39 Graham Terrace, London SW1W 8JF** 020 7730 2971 020 7823 4066 education@fhs-sw1.org.uk www.fhs-sw1.org.uk Miss SJ Pattenden B.Sc (Durham); Chair of Council: Lady V France OBE, MA Victoria Sloane Square **Buses**: 11 Black coat of regulation length, grey skirt, school shirt, deep red sweatshirt, dark tights (winter); short-sleeved blouse (summer); Sixth form: Sensible clothes **Demand**: Figures unavailable; oversubscribed **Type**: Selective Church of England independent for 450 girls, aged 4 to 19 **Fees**: £2,460–2,900 per term, including lunch **Submit application form**: 28 November 2003 **Motto**: That our Daughters May Be As the Polished Corners of the Temple **School hours**: 8.30am–4pm; homework clubs are available **Meals**: Hot and cold available, including vegetarian, vegan, kosher and halal options **Strong GCSE subjects**: All relatively strong **London league table position**: 26

## Profile

This is the second of the schools founded by the Reverend Francis Holland, Canon of Canterbury. The first, now in Clarence Gate, serves north London; this school serves south London. It has been on its present site since 1884. A new science and technology block, with gym and art rooms, was added in 2000. The school has also enlarged its library space, and it has a full-time chartered librarian, who is able to offer advice on research resources. There is an IT department and all subject classrooms are provided with computers. Pupils use facilities at Battersea for outdoor sports. The PE programme includes ice skating, golf, cricket and rock climbing. A range of A-level subjects is offered including the humanities and sciences, government and politics and statistics. Career counselling is available and pupils have two weeks' work experience. There is a prefects system, a school council, and the head teacher and head girl meet weekly. A school counsellor provides pastoral care. Severe asthma, coeliac disease and diabetes are specifically catered for, and the school offers 'sympathetic support' for dyslexics. There is no PTA as such, but parents are automatically enrolled in the Friends of Francis Holland.

## Admissions and intake

Academic standards are part of the admissions criteria, but also compatibility with the school's ethos. Applications should be made direct to the school. Applicants take an entry exam and attend an interview with their parents; there are open sessions during which applicants have sample lessons. From this, the school can assess 'the whole girl' and make a more informed decision, whilst the applicant herself learns about the school. A report from the previous school is sought if a place is to be offered.

## Achievement

The school performs well and places are much sought after. The number of pupils gaining five or more A*–C grades at GCSE remains steadily at the top end, and well above the borough average. In 2002, it was 98 per cent, up from 83 per cent in 2001. The school was ranked second in the borough. A-level achievements are more variable, but are again well above the borough average, with 340 points in 2002. This placed the school in third place for A-level results in the borough.

## Extra-curricular activities

The school encourages public speaking and debating is seen as a particular strength. The lower sixth takes part in the Mini-Enterprise scheme run in conjunction with the local branch of Nat West bank. Other activities include chess, drama, fencing, life saving and first aid as well as a range of sports. The Duke of Edinburgh's Award scheme is encouraged. The school visits museums and galleries. Students choose two or three charities to support each term. Homework clubs are available.

# The Grey Coat Hospital

**98 Regency Street, London SW1P 4GH (St Michael's, upper school); Grey Coat Place, London SW1P 2DY (St Andrew's, lower school, and office)** ☎ 020 7969 1950 (upper school); 020 7969 1998 (lower school) 📠 020 7592 9633 (upper school); 020 7828 2697 (lower school) ⓔ info@thegreycoathospital.org.uk 🌐 www.thegreycoathospital.org.uk Mrs R Allard; Chair of Governors: Lady Laws ⇌ Victoria ⊖ Pimlico, Victoria **Buses**: C10, 2, 24, 36, 77A, 88, 185, 507 Up to sixth form: Grey skirt and blazer, maroon or grey sweatshirt, white blouse **Demand**: 806 applications for 150 places in 2001/2 **Type**: Voluntary aided Church of England for 1017 girls (mixed in sixth form), aged 11 to 18 **Submit application form**: 2 December 2003 **Motto**: God Give the Increase **School hours**: 8.30am–3.30pm; homework clubs are available **Meals**: Hot and cold available (St Andrew's only) **Strong GCSE subjects**: English, maths, science **London league table position**: 124

## Profile

In 1698, eight parishioners of St Margaret's Westminster each contributed 12 shillings and persuaded others to join them to form The Grey Coat Hospital, a boarding school for 40 boys and girls. The school became a local authority school in 1871 and gave up boarding, becoming a day school for girls only in 1874. The school is in the second wave of 300 schools to be confirmed as Beacon Schools. In 1998, an £11-million building was completed in Regency Street. Called St Michael's, it houses the upper school, leaving St Andrew's in Grey Coat Place as home to the lower school. Both premises have gyms and libraries, as well as laboratories and classrooms. There are two fully equipped computer rooms in the lower school, and one in the upper school. Sports are played in the yard within the school grounds and on recreation grounds in Battersea. The Queen Mother Sports Centre is used for swimming. The standard selection of A-level subjects is offered, including design and technology, law, psychology and theatre studies. Work experience is available in Year 10. There is a head of special needs, and a separate project for gifted pupils through the Excellence in Schools initiative. Parents can join the Parents' Guild.

### Admissions and intake

Priority is given to girls from practising CofE families from the London and Southwark dioceses, after which the standard LEA criteria apply. Students take an examination for streaming purposes but not for entrance. Pupils and parents attend an interview. The attainment level of pupils on entry varies. In 2000, Ofsted observed that overall attainment on entry is 'around average'.

### Achievement

The school is committed to improve its pupils' abilities and, according to Ofsted, this is borne out by its GCSE results. Results have been moving steadily upwards. In 2002, 81 per cent of pupils gained five or more A*–C grades at GCSE, up from 79 per cent in 2001. This was well above the borough and national averages. A-level students attained an average of 255 points in 2002. This was above the borough but below the national average. Ofsted commented that" 'This is a very good school where the students are excellently guided and supported in achieving very high standards of attainment'. Inspectors praised the school's 'exciting and varied' curriculum. Attainment is well above average in English, mathematics and science.

### Extra-curricular activities

The school has a number of clubs including debating, computing, history, science and mathematics. Homework clubs are available. Various trips abroad are organized including exchange visits with other schools. There is an annual activities week at the end of summer term. The school and pupils contribute extensively to charity. Participation in the Duke of Edinburgh's Award scheme is encouraged.

## International Community School

**21 Star Street, London W2 1QB (senior school); 4 York Terrace East, Regent's Park, London NW1 4PT (primary school and office)** 020 7298 8877 020 7706 8171 skola@easynet.co.uk www.skola.co.uk Megan Mitchell; Marylebone, Euston Marylebone **Buses:** Door-to-door school bus service None, except sports kit **Demand:** No figures available but matched supply in 2000/1 **Type:** Non-selective independent for 150 mixed pupils, aged 3 to 19 **Fees** (per term): £3,075 (Years 7 to 9); £3,451 (Years 10 to 11/sixth form) plus charges for accommodation, welfare and transport **Submit application form:** No cut-off date **School hours:** 8.45am–3.20pm **Meals:** Hot and cold available, mainly vegetarian **Strong GCSE subjects:** English, maths **London league table position:** 520

### Profile

In 1979 Niels Toettcher established an English Language School, from which has developed the Skola Group of schools. This school is situated in the west wing of a mid-Victorian, purpose-built community education centre. Facilities include science laboratories, art and design rooms and a computer/IT department. There is a gymnasium and the school also uses Regent's Park and the YMCA sports facilities. Activities include football, volleyball, tennis, aerobics, trampolining and climbing. The school operates a three-term year for GCSE and A-levels, but is open all year round for intensive English courses. All pupils have individually tailored learning programmes. A-level subjects offered are dependent upon pupils' requirements. No vocational subjects are offered. Pupils undertake an induction programme as preparation for university or going into a full-time career. This includes study skills, careers advice, interview preparation and application support. A special-needs team helps pupils with learning difficulties. Class sizes are an average of 10. The school is quite informal and there are no prefects. A parent-teacher association was formed in October 2000. There was no unauthorized absence in 2000.

### Admissions and intake

Application can be made directly to the school at any time: the procedure is an interview with parents and pupil. The criteria for acceptance are preparedness to work and ability to pay the fees. Recommendation is not required. Only after a pupil is accepted will the previous school be asked to comment (except in the case of special-needs pupils).

## Achievement

In 2002, just 21 per cent of pupils gained five or more A*–C grades at GCSE. This was a rise from 12 per cent in 2001 and the school was ranked 10th in the borough league table. This result was well below the borough and national averages but it must be remembered that this school does not base its selection process on academic testing. Results for previous years have fluctuated from 29 per cent in 1996 to 14 per cent in 1997 and 40 per cent in 1998 and 1999. In 2002, the average point score for pupils taking two or more A-levels was 216.7, ranking the school 10th in the borough. The school is accredited by the British Council.

## Extra-curricular activities

There are sports clubs, a Model United Nations, and language clubs available. Regular trips, both educational and recreational, are organized each year to a variety of foreign countries. Field study trips are also made to a sister school in Norfolk, where there is riding and outdoor pursuits.

# Lansdowne College

**40–44 Bark Place, Bayswater, London W2 4AT** 020 7616 4400 020 7606 4401 enquiries@lansdownecollege.com www.lansdownecollege.com Hugh Templeton Paddington Bayswater, Queensway **Buses:** 12, 70, 94 None **Demand:** No figures available **Type:** Non-selective independent for 202 mixed pupils, aged 15 to 19 **Fees:** £1,110–3,500 per term, depending upon choice of subjects **Submit application form:** Contact school for details **Motto:** First, One Must Learn How to Learn. In Order to Learn One Must Enjoy **School hours:** 9am–5pm **Meals:** Hot and cold available **Strong GCSE subjects:** Languages, maths **London league table position:** 131

## Profile

Lansdowne College is situated in a quiet residential road one minute's walk from Hyde Park and Kensington Palace, and close to the South Kensington museums. The college is housed in a purpose-built 1970s building with excellent facilities. There are 20 classrooms, three science labs, a computer room and a language lab. It also has a large art studio and a photographic darkroom. Pupils have access to a study area, library and computer and Internet facilities. A 250-seat hall is fully equipped for use as a theatre and special events centre. Residential accommodation is within easy reach and there are facilities to accommodate pupils within flats as well as host family accommodation for pupils under 18. Lansdowne focuses on students achieving their personal best, as expressed in its catchphrase of 'I can is as important as IQ'. According to the college, the majority of pupils attend Lansdowne as an alternative to school, taking the opportunity it offers to study unusual combinations of subjects in a less restrictive atmosphere. Pupils must pass the 'learning to learn' course, which leads to a Diploma of Achievement. This is recognized and accredited by the Oxford and Cambridge Schools Examining Boards and is supported by the CBI. It is designed to give pupils the opportunity to discover how they learn best and to go on to develop study skills that match their preferred way of learning. With the support of their tutors, pupils are shown how to set personal and academic goals, and much attention is paid to time management. All pupils have a personal log-book, which provides a good reference point for parents. They must also follow 'Project K', requiring them to produce case studies on issues and individuals within their specialization, thus relating study to real life. There is special provision for students with dyslexia.

## Admissions and intake

The school should be contacted with regard to admissions.

## Achievement

The DfES statistics for GCSE results at Lansdowne may be misleading. Only in 1999 did attainment of five or more A*–C grades rise above zero per cent, but it rose spectacularly to 60 per cent, well above both borough and national averages. In 2002, 75 per cent of pupils gained five or more A*–C grades and the school was ranked joint eighth in the borough. For those pupils attaining two or more A/AS-levels, the average score was 286.1, ranking the school fifth in the borough. These results may reflect the fact that the school is non-selective. The strong curriculum includes all core subjects, but also offers a wide range of maths, science and social science courses.

### Extra-curricular activities

Sports are encouraged at Lansdowne and include college tennis, cricket, football and netball teams. For a nominal sum pupils are able to use the sports facilities at Imperial College, including the gym, squash courts and swimming pool. There are some school trips.

# North Westminster Community School

**Marylebone Lower House, Penfold Street, London NW1 6RX** 020 7641 7700 020 7641 7788 nwcs@rmplc.co.uk www.nwc.school.co.uk Mrs Jan Woodhead; Chair of Governors: Mr Richard Simmons Marylebone, Paddington Edgware Road, Paddington, Warwick Avenue **Buses**: 15, 18, 23, 27 Up to sixth form: Black blazer, black trousers/skirt **Demand**: 451 applications for 336 places in 2001/2 **Type**: Community comprehensive for 1920 mixed pupils, aged 11 to 18 **Submit application form**: 2 December 2003 **Mission statement**: To enable its pupils to develop personally, intellectually, morally, physically, aesthetically and socially to the highest possible level, so that they may be best placed to shape their own lives and to develop an understanding and sympathy for others **School hours**: 9am–3.35pm; homework clubs are available **Meals**: Hot and cold available **Strong GCSE subjects**: Art, Bengali, dance, drama **London league table position**: 468

### Profile

North Westminster Community School was established as St Marylebone's in 1980 when three existing schools were amalgamated to form one unit. Marylebone Lower House and the upper school are close neighbours. The upper school has a studio theatre, which is well used by the pupils. All sites have gyms, laboratories and art rooms. There are fully equipped IT rooms, and computers in subject rooms. Good sports facilities are on site and playing fields and sports centres elsewhere are also used. The National Curriculum is taught with Arabic, Bengali, Portuguese and Spanish as additional language choices, and there is strong science provision. Vocational subjects include art and design, business studies, engineering and leisure and tourism. There is carefully planned work experience and employers visit the school. Special-needs provision is available. There is a PTA.

### Admissions and intake

Standard LEA admissions procedures apply. If oversubscribed, the additional criteria, in order of priority, are: a sibling at the school, exceptional need and distance from the school. The school's catchment area contains a number of wards with significant levels of social deprivation. More than 25 per cent of pupils have special needs, above the average.

### Achievement

In 2002, 27 per cent of pupils achieved five or more A*–C grades at GCSE, the same as 2001. This was below the borough average and well below the national average. Points awarded at A/AS-level have tended to be at or above the borough average since 1996, although point scores were 160.7 in 2001, below the borough average. The school excels at drama, but is poor in mathematics, science, and English. Ofsted visited the school in 2001 and praised its 'inclusive, harmonious and tolerant multicultural community'. Standards in national tests and exams are low but are seen to be improving. Although well below the national average, the school's GCSE results are above average for similar schools. Inspectors gave special praise to the school's 'very good' social, personal and community education programme, known as SPACE. Unauthorized absence fell to 4.7 per cent in 2000.

### Extra-curricular activities

A good range of activities is provided, especially in theatre, with visits to the Japanese Theatre, the Africa Centre and Battersea Arts Centre. Pupils also take part in productions at the Studio Youth Theatre. There is a well-supported Saturday music school. Both boys and girls play football, cricket (the more able receiving coaching at Lords), basketball and table tennis. There are homework clubs. Sixth-formers are encouraged to be involved in charity projects.

# Pimlico School

**Lupus Street, London SW1V 3AT** 020 7828 0881 020 7931 0549 Mr Philip Barnard; Chair of Governors: Europe Singh Victoria Victoria **Buses**: C10, 24, There is a dress code but details are unavailable **Demand**: 543 applications for 240 places in 2001/2 **Type**: Community comprehensive for 1361 mixed pupils, aged 11 to 19 **Submit application form**: 2 December 2003 **Mission statement**: To educate each child to the very best of her or his ability, to enable all students to achieve academic and social excellence, to value every student's worth **School hours**: 8.55am–3.30pm **Meals**: Hot and cold available, including vegetarian options **Strong GCSE subjects**: Art, drama, music, RE **London league table position**: 445

## Profile

Pimlico School was founded in 1970. Facilities at the school include a library, laboratories and a swimming pool. A new computer/IT suite was added in 1999. The governors have been locked in disagreement with the LEA for some years over improvements to the building through a private funding initiative. The governors are refusing to agree to the LEA's plans, which include disposing of part of the site for housing, and the demolition and rebuilding, to a superior standard, of the school. This would result in a further 130 places and increase the sixth-form capacity to 250. At the time of writing, these extra places have yet to be achieved. A wide range of A-level subjects is offered. The school offers the unique provision of a special music course for up to 15 pupils with ability in every year. In the vocational field, business studies is offered, and there is a work experience coordinator. Careers advice and guidance is also provided. The school has a dedicated special-needs department. The parent-school association produces a newsletter and organizes parents' evenings, school functions and educational events, which are well attended. Non-English speaking parents are helped with written and spoken material.

## Admissions and intake

Standard LEA applications procedures apply. If oversubscribed, criteria, in order of priority, are: a sibling at the school, exceptional need and distance from the school. Interviews and entrance exams are not required. A third of pupils have special needs, some with statements.

## Achievement

The Ofsted inspection in 1997 reported that, after a period of some staff and financial turbulence, the school was beginning to 'move forward vigorously'. In 2002, 27 per cent of pupils achieved five or more A*–C grades at GCSE. This was down from 33 per cent in 2001 and below the borough and national averages. For A/AS levels, the average point score in 2002 was 233.9, ranking the school ninth in the borough. About 50 per cent of pupils have low reading ages on entry but the school improves attainment to being in line with national averages by the end of Key Stage 5. Ofsted were cautiously complimentary, with hopes for future improvement. IT was stated to be below standard but a new centre has since been added.

## Extra-curricular activities

After-school clubs are run by different departments to support the curriculum. A wide range of sporting activities is available, including athletics, basketball, cricket, gymnastics and tennis, and good use is made of the indoor swimming pool. Field trips are organized in Britain, including Outward Bound courses. Both the art and the languages departments arrange trips, and there are exchanges with German students.

# Portland Place School

**56–58 Portland Place, London W1N 3DG** ☎ 020 7307 8700 Fax 020 7436 2676 ✉ admin@portland-place.co.uk 🌐 www.portland-place.co.uk Head: Richard Walker B.Sc, Chem, MRSC, PGCE; Chair of Governors: John Dalby ⇌ Euston, Marylebone ⊖ Regent's Park **Buses**: 135 Uniform: Up to sixth form: Navy and burgundy sweaters, dark grey or blue skirts or trousers, white polo shirts, burgundy PE kit **Demand**: No figures available but there is a waiting list **Type**: Selective independent for 223 mixed pupils, aged 10 to 18 **Fees**: £2,825–3,050 per term **Submit application form**: No cut-off date **Mission statement**: We aim to maximize the academic potential of each child, and to allow his or her voice to be heard in the classroom. **School hours**: 8.50am–3.40pm **Meals**: Hot and cold available, including vegetarian, vegan, kosher and halal options **Strong GCSE subjects**: Science **London league table position**: 267

## Profile

This school is part of the Davies Laing and Dick Education Group, which was formed in 1931 to provide high quality teaching and facilities in its associated schools. Portland Place was opened in 1996 and claims to be the first independent secondary school to be founded in central London for over a century. The buildings are Grade II listed

James Adam town houses, refurbished and adapted to educational use. Facilities include specialist laboratories plus rooms for drama, design and technology, photography and computing. All teaching rooms are wired for computers and all pupils have their own e-mail address. Pupils take part in physical education with activities such as keep-fit, fencing and self-defence, going outdoors to Regent's Park for ball games, cross-country and athletics. Other sports, including swimming, are available at a local sports centre, and the sixth form is encouraged to join the University of Westminster gymnasium in Baker Street. A wide choice of A-level subjects is offered, including science, mathematics, languages, humanities, theatre studies, art and photography. There is a school council. Careers and educational guidance is available and the school uses the services of Capital Careers. Class sizes are a maximum of 16. The sixth form is on-site and has around 50 pupils. A new special-needs tutor has been appointed to support students where required. There is no PTA. Parents are sent reports at half term and term end. They are also expected to countersign the homework book weekly.

### Admissions and intake

The school has only been open since 1996, but demand is growing steadily. Applications are made directly to the school. The procedure includes an appointment with the head teacher, an entrance exam in English and mathematics, interviews with the applicant pupils and parents, and a reference from the previous school. One scholarship is available each year.

### Achievement

Achievement at GCSE has more than doubled in recent years, with 72 per cent of pupils achieving five or more A*–C grades in 2000, compared to 68 per cent in 1999, 60 per cent in 1998, 52 per cent in 1997 and 25 per cent in 1996. However, in 2002, it dropped to 61 per cent. This was still above the borough and national averages. A-level points per candidate in 2002 were 243.1. This was above the borough but below the national average. In 2000, pupils studying science achieved 100 per cent success.

### Extra-curricular activities

All pupils must take part in a non-academic activity at lunchtime, from fencing to board games and gardening. Music is compulsory in Years 1 to 3, and all pupils are encouraged to take up an instrument. There are trips to Paris, Madrid and skiing. Study tours to the battlefields of Belgium and Northern France have been arranged.

## Queen's College London

**43–49 Harley Street, London W1N 8BT** ☎ 020 7291 7000 📠 020 7291 7099 ⓔ queens@qcl.org.uk 🌐 www.qcl.org.uk Miss Margaret Connell; Chair of Governors: Dr Somerville ⇌ Euston ⊖ Regent's Park, Bond Street **Buses**: 10, 12, 73 and 94 along Oxford Street; 135 along Portland Place None **Demand**: Figures unavailable; oversubscribed **Type**: Selective independent for 510 girls, aged 10 to 19 **Fees**: Contact school for details **Submit application form**: Contact school for details **Mission statement**: The pursuit of academic excellence and the fostering of independence of mind in an informal and relaxed atmosphere **School hours**: 9am–4pm **Meals**: Hot and cold available, including vegetarian options **Strong GCSE subjects**: All relatively strong **London league table position**: 87

### Profile

The school was founded in 1848, through the efforts of the Governesses' Benevolent Institution and Professor Frederick Maurice, one of the great Victorian social and educational reformers and founder of the Christian Socialist movement. Queen's College was the first school to provide academic qualifications for women. In 1853, it was granted the first Royal Charter for women's education. Facilities include four large and two small laboratories, recently refurbished and re-equipped, and two computer rooms. There is a full-time librarian and the senior library has 17,000 volumes, which are scrupulously kept up-to-date. There is also a bookshop as the school seeks to inculcate the habit of reading from the start of a pupil's school life. A broad range of A-level subjects are offered, including the classics and humanities, plus a good range of modern languages (including Japanese), science and mathematics, together with arts, politics and economics. Career counselling and work experience is available. There is a special-needs department and a school council. The parents association is highly supportive and the school produces a weekly newsletter for parents called *Queen's News*. The school states that it values academic excellence for its own sake, rather than the sterile pursuit of marks, and measures success by the development of individuals, and valuing personal integrity and ability to deal responsibly with others. Famous ex-pupils include the first English-educated woman doctor, Sophia Jex Blake, Gertrude Bell and the author, Katherine Mansfield.

## Admissions and intake

A form should be requested from the admission secretary, and returned with a deposit, photo and copy of daughter's birth certificate. Examinations are held in early January, and interviews take place before then. A report from previous school is required. Bursaries are available.

## Achievement

The school's GCSE results are consistently high, nearly twice the borough and national averages. In 2002, 93 per cent of pupils achieved five or more A*–C grades at GCSE, two per cent down on 2001's results. A-level results are consistently above the borough average, with a 317.9 points average gained in 2002. This was also above the national average. The school was last inspected in 1994, when inspectors remarked on the relaxation and confidence of the pupils, the friendly atmosphere, good facilities and good staff/pupil relations. Unauthorized absence is only 0.2 per cent.

## Extra-curricular activities

Sport is a particular strength and there are two teams for every year in all sports. The hockey and gymnastic teams are consistently successful in competitions with other London schools. The wide range of sports and physical activity includes netball, athletics, fencing and dance. There is a choir and musical ensembles, as well as debating, life saving and first aid clubs on offer, amongst others. Around 90 trips are arranged each year to a number of destinations.

# Quintin Kynaston School

**Marlborough Hill, St John's Wood, London NW8 0NL** 020 7722 8141 020 7586 8473 www.qkschool.org.uk Mr N Elliott-Kemp BA, DHRM; Chair of Governors: Patrick Lees South Hampstead St John's Wood, Swiss Cottage **Buses:** 13, 46, 82, 113, 187 Up to sixth form: Grey T-shirt/polo shirt with school logo, any skirt, trousers, shorts or tracksuit bottoms (jeans and trainers are acceptable, but must be suitable for school) **Demand:** 341 applications for 210 places in 2001/2 **Type:** Community comprehensive Technology College for 1050 mixed pupils, aged 11 to 18 **Submit application form:** 2 December 2003 **Mission statement:** To deliver rigorous, high-quality education to enable students to leave school with their best possible examination results, knowing how to learn in continuing education and as an adult, and with clear moral values to guide their behaviour throughout life **School hours:** 8.45am–3.30pm; homework clubs are available **Meals:** Hot and cold available **Strong GCSE subjects:** Ceramics, drama, drawing, IT, painting **London league table position:** 406

## Profile

Quintin Kynaston School was created in 1969. The school is faced with an unusual set of challenges, with 63 per cent of its intake having English as an additional language and 49 languages other than English being spoken. There is a high turnover of pupils at each Key Stage. Facilities include a well-resourced library, five new computer workrooms, a satellite weather station, six new science labs, media resources and a drama centre and studio. The school has extensive grounds, a sports hall, three gymnasia and a weights room. It also receives support from sports coaches, including Arsenal Ladies' Football Club. The school has emerged from serious weakness status, on the recommendation of the last Ofsted inspection in 1999, and recently gained Technology College status. A-levels are offered in a range of subjects, from fine art to design technology. A work experience programme is supported by Capital Careers. The school has gained extra financial help from the LEA for special needs students. and there is a special-needs coordinator. Parents are kept informed through newsletters, homework diaries, progress review days and an annual report. There is a school council.

## Admissions and intake

The standard LEA application procedure applies. There is a waiting list for places in most years. Since the school emerged from serious weakness status, its popularity has grown.

## Achievement

The school has been through troubled times, but it seems to be emerging into a more dynamic future, with parents (and pupils) commenting favourably on the ethos of the school and its recent progress. In 1999, Ofsted remarked that 'it is clearly focused on enabling all students to achieve well for their futures.' Ofsted expressed the hope that the GCSE results would improve. In 2000, 24 per cent of pupils gained five or more A*–C grades and this rose to 33 per cent in 2001 and 38 per cent in 2002, suggesting Ofsted's hopes are being realised. However, the school is still below the borough average and substantially below the national average. For A-levels, the school's 189.9 points average was above the borough average but below the national average. Ofsted were generally complimentary about the standard of teaching and about the good personal development in this multi-ethnic school.

## Extra-curricular activities

A local theatre company has a base on the site and works with students, who take part in youth arts projects arranged by the borough. There are gospel choirs and drumming and steel bands. The school has a number of links with the community, and lets space to a Saturday Iranian school and Neti Neti theatre.

# St Augustine's CofE Secondary School

**Oxford Road, London NW6 5SN** 020 7328 3434 020 7328 3435 admin@st_augustines_scho.dialnet.com atschool.eduweb.co.uk/staug Mr R Cooper; Chair of Governors: Father R Bushau Kilburn High Road Kilburn Park **Buses:** 31, 32, 206, 316, 328 Up to sixth form: Black blazer and trousers, white shirt, grey jumper, school tie (boys); black blazer, blue trousers or skirt, white shirt, royal blue jumper, school tie (girls) **Demand:** 233 applications for 120 places in 2001/2 **Type:** Voluntary aided Church of England comprehensive for 674 mixed pupils, aged 11 to 18 **Submit application form:** 2 December 2003 **School hours:** 9am–3.30pm; homework clubs are available **Meals:** Hot and cold available, including breakfast **Strong GCSE subjects:** Business studies, English language and literature, French **London league table position:** 452

## Profile

St Augustine's has been in existence since 1884, when it began life as an all boys' secondary school on the site of its current playground. In 1969, the present buildings were opened on an enlarged site and the school became a mixed comprehensive. The school facilities include a library, computer/IT department, gym and laboratories. Sports are important and the school claims an excellent reputation for athletics, cricket, swimming and tennis, even though it has to use off-site recreational facilities. The standard range of A-level subjects are offered along with vocational subjects such as ceramics, fine art and design and technology. A career guidance program begins in Year 9. Work experience is arranged and encouraged for all pupils. There is a school council and pupils in Year 8 can become monitors. In year 9, pupils may be selected to mentor Year 7 students. Sixth-formers help primary school students with reading. Support is provided for those pupils who have special educational needs and those with English as an additional language.

## Admissions and intake

Standard LEA admissions criteria apply. About a fifth of pupils have special educational needs and 18 have statements. Both of these figures are above average.

## Achievement

The attainment level of pupils on entry is very low. Ofsted has reported success in raising standards, but not to an extent which brings pupils generally up to average. In 2002, 28 per cent of pupils achieved five or more A*–Cs at GCSE, up from 25 per cent in 2001. This was below the borough and national averages. The average point score was 72 for those pupils taking two or more A-levels. The school was ranked 15th in the borough league table. In 2001, Ofsted described the school as 'an improved and improving school, with notable strengths'. Leadership and management were seen to be 'very good' and the quality of the teaching a strength of the school. Almost all lessons observed had 'satisfactory or better' teaching and teaching was 'good and often very good' in a high proportion of lessons. Occasionally it was seen to be 'excellent'. Many pupils with special educational needs or English as an additional language were seen to do well and Inspectors praised the school's 'orderly community'. However, standards still need to improve in the National Curriculum tests at 14 and at GCSE level. Overall attendance was seen to be satisfactory but sixth form attendance needs to be improved.

### Extra-curricular activities

There are some clubs available, and the school supports participation in the Duke of Edinburgh's Award scheme. Every year, a group of pupils spend a week at Tyn-y-Berth Mountain Centre in the Snowdonia National Park. After-school homework clubs are available. Pupils are involved with fund-raising for local charities.

# St George RC School Westminster

**Lanark Road, Maida Vale, London W9 1RB** 020 7328 0904 020 7624 6083 stgeorgesmv1@netscapeonline.co.uk www.stgeorges_maidavale.org.uk Phil Jakszta; Chair of Governors: Canon John MacDonald Kilburn High Road Maida Vale **Buses**: 16, 46, 98 Black blazer, black trousers or skirt, white shirt, school tie **Demand**: 212 applications for 120 places in 2001/2 **Type**: Voluntary aided Roman Catholic comprehensive for 550 mixed pupils, aged 11 to 16 **Submit application form**: 2 December 2003 **Mission statement**: To enable all pupils to acquire skills, knowledge and Catholic values which will help them to develop both as individuals, members of their parishes and members of the wider community **School hours**: 9am–3.30pm **Meals**: Hot and cold available **Strong GCSE subjects**: English, ICT, maths **London league table position**: 501

### Profile

An Ofsted inspection of St George in 1994 identified serious weaknesses, and this was exacerbated when head teacher Philip Lawrence was murdered at the school gates by pupils from outside the school in 1995. The school's reputation as one of serious violence led to major difficulties in attracting and keeping staff. When Ofsted inspected again, in 1998, it was decided that insufficient progress had been made, and an LEA task force was sent in. Under the new and charismatic head teacher a great deal of effort is now being put into turning the school around. It aims to be 'committed to excellence, challenging students to be academically successful and responsible citizens'. Its facilities include excellent technical rooms, well-equipped science laboratories, computing facilities in the learning resource centre and business studies suite. Paddington playing fields are used for sport. Careers education is part of the curriculum and two weeks' work experience is offered in Year 11.

### Admissions and intake

First choice is given to children baptized into and practising the Roman Catholic faith, whose parents make St George their first choice with priestly support. Other considerations are: Roman Catholic children baptized into the faith; those who have a sibling at the school; or children whose parents make St George's their first choice. If oversubscribed, the standard comprehensive school criteria, including exceptional need and distance from the school, apply. Over 30 per cent of pupils have special-needs statements.

### Achievement

In 2002, the percentage of pupils who achieved five or more A*–Cs at GCSE was just 20 per cent, substantially below the borough and national averages. This was six per cent up on 2001's results. The school had been placed on special measures in 1998 but following an Ofsted visit in 2001, these measures were removed. Inspectors found that 'pupils' rate of progress is now satisfactory overall'. Ofsted noted that the teaching is 'satisfactory with many strengths' and there are 'positive relationships' between teachers and pupils. Standards of literacy and numeracy need improvement.

### Extra-curricular activities

Activities include sports, drama, a choir and an orchestra. There is a distinguished visitor programme through which pupils are able to meet successful people in law, medicine, sport and the arts. Visits to the theatre are organized, along with geography field trips and visits to France. Homework clubs are available. Pupils raise money for local charities.

# The St Marylebone CofE School

**64 Marylebone High Street, London W1M 4BA** 020 7935 4704 020 7935 4005 Mrs E Phillips BA, MA, AKC; Chair of Governors: Mr Michael Bithell Marylebone Baker Street, Regent's Park **Buses**: 18, 27, 30 Bottle green with gold logo; Sixth form: Smart office dress **Demand**: 824 applications for 120 places in 2001/2 **Type**: Voluntary aided Church of England comprehensive Arts College for 802 girls (mixed in sixth form), aged 11 to 18 **Submit application form**: 2 December 2003 **School hours**: 8.30am–3.30pm; homework clubs are available **Meals:** Hot and cold available **Strong GCSE subjects:** Science, technology **London league table position:** 91

## Profile

Originally opened in 1791 as a church school for poor girls of the parish, St Marylebone was taken into LEA control under the 1871 Local Government Act. The main school building is classical late Georgian/early Victorian with more modern additions. The neighbourhood is an affluent residential area, close to shops in Marylebone High Street. The school has six new science labs, two large computer rooms, two design and technology departments and designated areas for performing arts. Classrooms also have computers. Pupils can make use of Seymour Place swimming pool and Regent's Park playing fields. CCTV and security measures are in place. The school is one of the second wave of 300 Beacon Schools. The school has Arts College status for the performing arts, with dance and drama added to the standard curriculum. There are also very popular and successful IT courses at two GNVQ levels. The 160-strong sixth form currently comprises 25 per cent boys, and demand is growing. Career counselling is provided and work experience is offered and encouraged. There is a prefect system with a head girl and a school council. Pupils with disabilities not dependent on wheelchairs are accommodated. There is also a dyslexia unit. The school encourages involvement with and support from parents, and there is an active PTA.

## Admissions and intake

Applications are through the LEA. A total of 60 foundation places go to CofE children within the diocese of London; 44 open places go to those of other faiths; 12 places go to applicants with a talent in art, music or drama; and four places are given for special consideration. Proximity is also taken into account.

## Achievement

In 2002, 93 per cent of pupils achieved five or more A*–C grades at GCSE. This continues a rising trend and the school was ranked fifth in the borough. The average point score for pupils taking two or more A/AS-levels was 242.1. In 2001, Ofsted described it as 'a very good school with many outstanding features'. Since 1999, the rate of improvement at GCSE has been faster than the national trend, with 'spectacular gains' in some years. St Marylebone took part in EXSCTEC99, part of the CREST project celebrating science and technology at Loughborough University, and won the bronze award in the Environmental Research Challenge for their wind turbine.

## Extra-curricular activities

There are plenty of opportunities available in the performing arts, a natural reflection of the school's speciality, with two orchestras, ensembles and choirs. A street performance of five mystery plays was recently staged by pupils in Marylebone with the help of the English National Opera, the Wigmore Hall and the Wallace Collection. Clubs include chess, bridge, a homework club and Latin classes. Trips are arranged to theatres and galleries, as well as Outward Bound trips and a World Team Challenge trip to Malaysia. Pupils also participate in the the Duke of Edinburgh's Award scheme. Charity work and community service is encouraged.

# Sylvia Young Theatre School

**Rossmore Road, Marylebone, London NW1 6NJ** ☎ 020 7402 0673 📠 020 7723 1040 ⓔ sylviayoung@freeuk.com ✉ Colin Townsend B.Sc, H.Sc, PGCE ⇄ Marylebone ⊖ Marylebone **Buses:** 13, 82, 113, 139, 189, 274 👔 Full uniform worn on academic days; school tracksuit and T-shirt worn on vocational days **Demand:** No figures available **Type:** Selective independent for 146 mixed pupils, aged 8 to 16 **Fees:** £1,475–2,100 per term **Submit application form:** No cut-off date **School hours:** Variable – depends on pupil's timetable **Meals:** Hot and cold available **Strong GCSE subjects:** Drama and theatre arts, expressive arts, English and foreign languages **London league table position:** 114

## Profile

The Sylvia Young Theatre School opened in 1981 in Drury Lane. In 1983, due to increased demand, it moved to its present premises in a quaint mid-Victorian church hall and vicarage. It has since been adapted to include a library, a studio, a theatre and rehearsal rooms. The building is reasonably well maintained and has security entry systems. The site is located between council flats on one side and a private development of well-maintained modern flats on the other. As a school for the performing arts, it has an enviable reputation. Many of its former students have gone on to become television personalities and familiar faces in soap operas. Class sizes vary according to subject and the vocational studies offered include music, drama and dance. Work experience is provided through the school and most pupils appear in commercials, TV dramas and plays, as well as West End productions. The school has its own agency, which represents the pupils throughout their education. The agency also liaises closely with parents and provides tutor chaperones when pupils are working professionally. The school has a very active PTA, which is involved in fund-raising and organizes evenings where parents and staff can meet informally.

## Admissions and intake

Entry is by audition, interview and written test. Detailed information will be sent on receipt of a completed application form. Applicants are required to prepare a song and a dance routine as well as a dramatic piece. The school also requires recent school reports and examples of pupils' work. Bursaries are available.

## Achievement

The school's levels of achievement in gaining five or more A*–Cs at GCSE has been above the borough average since 1996, with a peak of 96 per cent in 2001 and 2002. This was up from 79 per cent in 2000, continuing an upward trend. This result took the school substantially above the national average and it was ranked sixth in the borough with an average point score of 44.8.

## Extra-curricular activities

Outings are arranged to complement the pupils' studies, and full use is made of the many facilities London has to offer. Visits are organized to museums, galleries, places of historic interest and, of course, the theatre. Concerts and plays are performed regularly.

# Westminster City School

**55 Palace Street, Victoria, London SW1E 5HJ** ☎ 020 7641 8760 📠 020 7641 8761 ✉ David Maloney; Chair of Governors: Prof Lisa Jardine ⇌ Victoria ⊖ Victoria **Buses:** 11, 24, 211 👔 Grey blazer, dark grey trousers, grey shirt, grey V-neck jersey for winter **Demand:** 447 applications for 130 places in 2001/2 **Type:** Voluntary aided Church of England comprehensive for 756 boys, aged 11 to 18 **Submit application form:** 2 December 2003 **Motto:** *Unitate fortior* (Together We Stand) **School hours:** 8.50am–3.35pm **Meals:** Hot and cold available **Strong GCSE subjects:** English, history, RE **London league table position:** 303

## Profile

Built in 1876, the Westminster City School is located in pleasant, if small, grounds. Class sizes average 25 pupils. There is a well-stocked library, three laboratories, and a well-equipped computer room. The school plans to install computers in all teaching rooms. An extension to the main school building has been completed and a new science block is to be completed for the 2003/4 school year. Pupils have to go to Mitcham for its playing fields but football is still popular. The school offers A-levels in the standard subjects. Vocational subjects include design and technology and business studies. Two weeks' work experience is arranged for Year 10, along with placements for Year 12 and career counselling. There is a school council with representation from each year, and the sixth form act as prefects. A full-time special-needs coordinator was appointed from September 1999. The Westminster City School Association is the equivalent of a PTA, but since many pupils live a considerable distance from the school, the school assumes that the rather limited participation by parents is due to travel disadvantages.

## Admissions and intake

Of the 130 annual intake, the school takes 105 boys from church-going families in the London and Southwark diocese (confirmed by a form signed by the minister concerned), and 25 from families practising other faiths but prepared to support the school's ethos. No examination is set, but recommendation from the applicant's minister is mandatory. Choice outside these criteria is dictated by the standard LEA process of sibling at the school, exceptional need and distance from the school. The proportion of pupils with special educational needs is average but the number of pupils with statements is above average.

## Achievement

The school was put on special measures in 1997, but following an Ofsted inspection in 1999 it was withdrawn from these as inspectors felt the educational standard was now acceptable.Ofsted revisited the school in 2001 and noted that it provides a 'good education for all pupils as a result of the clear direction and firm leadership provided by the head teacher and governors'. Pupils achieve well and make good progress due to 'high quality' teaching. The achievement of five or more A*–Cs at GCSE has varied over the years, reaching 47 per cent of pupils in 2002, up from 35 per cent the previous year.This placed the school tenth in the borough. At A-level, the 2002 point score was 181.4, below borough and national averages. Ofsted wanted to see improvements in standards of ICT and criticized the 'poor' accommodation which is in a 'poor state of repair'.

## Extra-curricular activities

Extra-curricular activities are not very popular, due possibly to the fact that pupils travel quite a long distance to school. However, football is available. A skiing trip to France has taken place for a number of years and in 2000 the art group went to Barcelona. There are regular geography field trips made to Abergavenny and Shropshire.

# Westminster School

**17 Dean's Yard, Westminster, London SW1 3PB** 020 7963 1003 020 7943 1006 headmaster@Westminster.org.uk www.westminster.org.uk Mr Tristram Jones-Parry; Chair of Governors: The Dean of Westminster Victoria Westminster, St James' Park **Buses**: 3, 11, 24, 159 Plain grey suit with no badges, white shirt; girls in the sixth form are given guidance as to what would be acceptable **Demand**: No figures available but oversubscribed **Type**: Selective independent for 680 boys (mixed in sixth form), aged 13 to 19 **Fees (per term)**: from £4,089 (day), from £5,904 (boarder), from £4,435 (sixth form day boarder), from £5,904 (sixth-form boarder) **Submit application form**: Annually, but entrance exams in May/June 2002 **Motto**: *Dat Deus Incrementum* (God Gives Growth) **School hours**: 9am–4pm, 9am–1pm (Sat) **Meals**: Hot and cold available, including vegetarian, kosher and halal options **Strong GCSE subjects**: All relatively strong **London league table position**: 6

## Profile

In 1179, the Benedictine monks of the Abbey of St Peter in Westminster were required by Pope Alexander III to provide a small charity school. This is considered to be the school's forerunner and it can trace a continuous existence from the early 14th century. The main building is a listed Georgian building with 19th- and 20th-century additions. Facilities include a science block, the Robert Hooke Centre near Smith Square, and the Sutcliffe, in Great College Street, which contains the art and design and technology departments. There is also a chapel and a theatre. The computer/IT department is constantly under review and expanding. Games are played on the green in the centre of Vincent Square. There is also a gym within the school site, and the school has its own boathouse at Putney. A-level subjects offered include classical and modern languages, the humanities and sciences, including electronics. Career counselling is provided by the careers department, enabling students to make informed choices. There is an embryonic school council, and a structure of monitors. The parents' committee is very active. There is provision for pupils with physical disabilities. Famous ex-pupils include John Dryden, Christopher Wren, Edward Gibbon, AA Milne and Andrew Lloyd Webber.

## Admissions and intake

Contact should be made with the registrar. Boys may be registered for entry at any time up to the age of 10, on payment of a fee. Registered candidates are invited for an informal interview and oral test after they reach the age of 10. A place may then be offered conditional on achieving the required standard in the Challenge or Common Entrance Exam. There is a reserve list designed to permit late developers. Girls wishing to join the sixth form take written tests and an interview in the November before the year of entry. Registrations are accepted from June until the closing date in mid-October. The head teacher of the previous school is always consulted. About 40 per cent of the intake comes from the school's own Under School, with the remainder from preparatory schools throughout London and the home counties, and a few from abroad.

## Achievement

The school has a very high achievement rate and pupils tend to achieve in the upper 90 percentages. In 2002, 100 per cent of pupils achieved five or more A*–Cs at GCSE. This was two per cent up on 2001's results and well above the borough and national averages. The school was the best performing in the borough. The average point score for pupils taking two or more A/AS levels was 451.1. This again was well above national and borough averages, ranking the school in first place in the borough league table. The rate of unauthorized absence is low at 0.1 per cent.

## Extra-curricular activities

A broad range of activities is available from book-binding to practical engineering and outdoor pursuits. Sports offered include martial arts, rowing, fencing, shooting and Eton fives. There have been trips to the Arctic, Rocky Mountains and the Himalayas, as well as short field trips for practical science work. There is a thriving community service programme.

## BOROUGH LEAGUE TABLES

### KEY TO SCHOOL ABBREVIATIONS

**CTC** City Technology College.
**CY** Community. State school controlled by a Local Education Authority (LEA).
**FD** Foundation. State school (often formerly grant-maintained) with a foundation that appoints some of the governors. School controls its own admissions.
**IN** Independent. Fee-paying private school that controls its own admissions.
**VA** Voluntary Aided. State school with a foundation (usually religious) that appoints most of the governors. School controls its own admissions.
**VC** Voluntary Controlled. State school with a foundation (usually religious) that appoints some of the governors. LEA controls admissions.
**C** Comprehensive. State school that admits pupils regardless of academic ability.
**N** Non-selective independent school.
**S** Selective. State or independent school that selects pupils for their academic ability.
**B** Boys. Single-sex boys' school.
**G** Girls. Single-sex girls' school.
**M** Mixed. Mixed school.

### UNDERSTANDING THE PERFORMANCE TABLES

The following tables show results for all 33 inner and outer London boroughs. The tables start with a 'value added' measure for each school. Schools are then ranked by pupils' average GCSE point score in 2002, the percentage of pupils who achieved five or more GCSE grades A*-C in 2002 and the average A-Level point score per student in 2002.

VALUE ADDED: The value added measure for each school is based on the progress made by individual pupils between Key Stage 3 tests (at age 14) and GCSE/GNVQ exams. Each pupil's score is calculated by comparing their performance with that of pupils of similar ability. Individual pupil scores are averaged to give a score for the school, based around 100. A higher figure than 100 indicates that a school 'adds value' to children's education, a lower figure suggests that value has been reduced. The value added measure only applies to state schools.

GCSE POINTS: Each pupil's best eight GCSE/GNVQ results are used to calculate their point score. Eight points are awarded for an A* grade down to one for a G. Individual pupil scores are averaged to give a score for the school.

GCSE %5A*-C: The percentage of pupils who achieved five or more GCSE grades A*-C in 2002.

A-LEVEL POINTS: A new UCAS tariff allows many different qualifications to be combined to produce a point score that students can use to apply for higher education. For full A-Level results: 120 points are awarded for an A grade, 100 for a B, 80 for a C, 60 for a D and 40 for an E. Half as many points are awarded for each AS exam grade. Individual student scores are averaged to give a point score per student for the school.

| SCHOOL | VALUE ADDED 02 | GCSE 02 POINTS | GCSE 01 POINTS | GCSE 02 %5 A*-C | GCSE 01 %5 A*-C | A-LEVEL 02 POINTS |
|---|---|---|---|---|---|---|
| **BARKING AND DAGENHAM** | | | | | | |
| All Saints Catholic School & Technology College (VA/C/M) | 103.1 | 39.0 | 42.8 | 68% | 51% | 203.5 |
| Barking Abbey Comprehensive School (CY/C/M) | 99.9 | 35.2 | 44.5 | 54% | 64% | 218.3 |
| Robert Clack School (CY/C/M) | 101.5 | 34.3 | 34.6 | 47% | 39% | 253.5 |
| The Warren School (CY/C/M) | 96.7 | 32.1 | 37.6 | 44% | 41% | 205.3 |
| Eastbrook Comprehensive School (CY/C/M) | 99.6 | 30.5 | 32.8 | 38% | 29% | 200 |
| Eastbury Comprehensive School (CY/C/M) | 96.3 | 28.1 | 31.6 | 38% | 27% | 216.7 |
| The Sydney Russell School (CY/C/M) | 97.1 | 26.8 | 29.4 | 27% | 24% | 162.8 |
| Dagenham Priory Comprehensive School (CY/C/M) | 93.0 | 24.8 | 26.8 | 20% | 29% | 114.1 |
| **BARNET** | | | | | | |
| Pardes House Grammar School (IN/N/B) | | 64.0 | 143.3 | 100% | 100% | |
| The Henrietta Barnett School (VA/S/G) | 100.5 | 58.9 | 79.3 | 100% | 100% | 371.9 |
| Queen Elizabeth's School (FD/S/B) | 99.1 | 55.2 | 60.5 | 99% | 99% | 387.8 |
| St Michael's Catholic Grammar School (VA/S/G) | 103.6 | 54.8 | 73.3 | 96% | 100% | 347.3 |
| Hasmonean High School (VA/C/M) | 104.3 | 49.1 | 56.3 | 87% | 84% | 311.1 |
| Mill Hill High School (FD/C/M) | 103.3 | 47.7 | 53.8 | 84% | 71% | 296.7 |
| St Martha's Senior School (IN/N/G) | | 47.1 | 53.9 | 94% | 91% | 337.1 |
| King Alfred School (IN/N/M) | | 47.0 | 47.2 | 87% | 81% | 345.7 |
| Beth Jacob Grammar School for Girls (IN/N/G) | | 47.0 | 48.0 | 83% | 87% | 229.6 |
| Menorah Grammar School (IN/S/B) | | 46.5 | 41.2 | 89% | 71% | 331.7 |
| The Mount School (IN/S/G) | | 42.8 | 58.0 | 84% | 97% | 308.5 |
| Copthall School (CY/C/G) | 100.3 | 41.3 | 46.1 | 71% | 66% | 308 |
| Ashmole School (FD/C/M) | 102.7 | 41.2 | 45.8 | 69% | 65% | 252.3 |
| Mill Hill School Foundation (IN/S/M) | | 40.4 | 43.7 | 81% | 80% | 307.9 |
| Queen Elizabeth's Girls' School (CY/C/G) | 99.4 | 39.3 | 47.7 | 66% | 75% | 266.8 |
| Finchley Catholic High School (VA/C/B) | 100.0 | 38.5 | 42.5 | 68% | 60% | 200 |
| Christ's College (CY/C/B) | 102.3 | 38.3 | 39.8 | 55% | 57% | 213.7 |

| SCHOOL | VALUE ADDED 02 | GCSE 02 POINTS | GCSE 01 POINTS | GCSE 02 %5 A*-C | GCSE 01 %5 A*-C | A-LEVEL 02 POINTS |
|---|---|---|---|---|---|---|
| Hendon School (FD/C/M) | 97.3 | 37.6 | 42.3 | 58% | 57% | 247.7 |
| The Compton School (CY/C/M) | 102.1 | 37.6 | 38.1 | 57% | 53% | |
| East Barnet School (CY/C/M) | 98.1 | 37.2 | 40.2 | 58% | 51% | 225.3 |
| Woodside Park International School (IN/S/M) | | 36.1 | 37.8 | 53% | 50% | |
| St James' Catholic High School (VA/C/M) | 97.5 | 34.8 | 40.4 | 48% | 52% | 269.4 |
| Christ Church CofE Secondary School (VA/C/M) | 99.8 | 32.3 | 34.0 | 38% | 34% | |
| St Mary's CofE High School (VA/C/M) | 96.8 | 31.2 | 36.1 | 39% | 40% | 185.7 |
| Friern Barnet School (CY/C/M) | 96.8 | 30.1 | 31.9 | 37% | 36% | |
| Bishop Douglass RC High School (VA/C/M) | 96.5 | 30.0 | 36.0 | 37% | 42% | 199.1 |
| The Albany College (IN/S/M) | | 29.6 | 34.3 | 56% | 67% | 221.4 |
| The Ravenscroft School (CY/C/M) | 98.0 | 29.4 | 25.8 | 34% | 20% | 116.7 |
| The Edgware School (CY/C/M) | 103.0 | 27.5 | 27.4 | 28% | 21% | 150 |
| Whitefield School (CY/C/M) | 99.3 | 20.7 | 24.1 | 24% | 21% | 86.5 |
| **BEXLEY** | | | | | | |
| Townley Grammar School for Girls (CY/S/G) | 99.8 | 53.0 | 62.8 | 100% | 100% | 354.8 |
| Bexley Grammar School (CY/S/M) | 99.8 | 51.8 | 51.4 | 100% | 95% | 371.1 |
| Chislehurst & Sidcup Grammar School (CY/S/M) | 99.3 | 50.7 | 60.3 | 96% | 97% | 300.6 |
| Beths Grammar School for Boys (FD/S/B) | 96.9 | 47.7 | 65.8 | 95% | 100% | 337.9 |
| St Catherine's RC School for Girls (VA/C/G) | 101.7 | 40.6 | 45.1 | 66% | 64% | 244.5 |
| Blackfen School for Girls (CY/C/G) | 101.9 | 39.2 | 40.5 | 61% | 61% | 198.4 |
| Hurstmere Foundation School for Boys (FD/C/B) | 99.3 | 34.4 | 32.9 | 52% | 35% | |
| St Columba's Catholic Boys' School (VA/C/B) | 98.7 | 33.6 | 37.4 | 57% | 42% | 195.9 |
| Trinity School , Belvedere (VA/C/M) | 100.4 | 32.9 | 36.2 | 43% | 33% | 220 |
| Cleeve Park School (CY/C/M) | 99.1 | 31.3 | 34.3 | 42% | 35% | 142.2 |
| St Mary & St Joseph's Catholic School (VA/C/M) | 95.4 | 31.0 | 38.9 | 38% | 49% | 170.8 |
| Welling School (CY/C/M) | 98.0 | 30.4 | 31.4 | 42% | 30% | 200.3 |
| Erith School (CY/C/M) | 99.3 | 30.4 | 31.0 | 28% | 29% | 155.2 |
| Bexleyheath School (CY/C/M) | 96.3 | 30.3 | 30.9 | 34% | 28% | 162.5 |
| Westwood College (CY/C/M) | 100.3 | 28.2 | 30.1 | 29% | 26% | |
| **BRENT** | | | | | | |
| Al-Sadiq & Al-Zahra Schools (IN/N/M) | 100.8 | 51.1 | 57.3 | 86% | 82% | |
| Islamia Girls' High School (IN/S/G) | 100.1 | 49.9 | 70.2 | 95% | 100% | |
| The Swaminarayan School (IN/S/M) | 106.3 | 49.6 | 55.0 | 92% | 81% | 216.9 |
| JFS (VA/C/M) | 104.8 | 44.7 | 49.8 | 75% | 75% | 299.2 |
| Claremont High School (FD/C/M) | 102.8 | 41.4 | 47.3 | 69% | 62% | 257.2 |
| Preston Manor High School (FD/C/M) | 99.5 | 40.2 | 44.0 | 65% | 68% | 238.5 |
| Kingsbury High School (FD/C/M) | 101.9 | 39.2 | 41.3 | 63% | 55% | 230 |
| Convent of Jesus & Mary Language College (VA/C/G) | 102.4 | 38.6 | 43.8 | 65% | 63% | 205.8 |
| St Gregory's RC High School (VA/C/M) | 97.7 | 36.8 | 42.9 | 61% | 55% | 214 |
| Alperton Community School (FD/C/M) | 100.5 | 32.1 | 35.9 | 43% | 38% | 183.9 |
| Queens Park Community School (FD/C/M) | 101.1 | 31.9 | 35.5 | 42% | 41% | 172.7 |
| Copland Community School & Technology Centre (FD/C/M) | 97.1 | 31.3 | 36.4 | 41% | 42% | 232.3 |
| John Kelly Girls' Technology College (FD/C/G) | 100.8 | 30.8 | 36.4 | 41% | 46% | 203.3 |
| Wembley High School (CY/C/M) | 97.8 | 28.9 | 31.0 | 34% | 32% | 192.2 |
| John Kelly Boys' Technology College (FD/C/B) | 101.1 | 26.4 | 27.2 | 31% | 24% | 152.9 |
| Cardinal Hinsley High School (VA/C/B) | 96.0 | 24.6 | 24.4 | 21% | 25% | 138.7 |
| Willesden High School (CY/C/M) | 100.4 | 15.5 | 17.4 | 14% | 13% | 135 |
| **BROMLEY** | | | | | | |
| Newstead Wood School for Girls (FD/S/G) | 100.5 | 58.4 | 75.0 | 100% | 99% | 383 |
| Bromley High School (IN/S/G) | | 57.0 | 61.0 | 100% | 100% | 350.3 |
| St Olave's & St Saviour's Grammar School (VA/S/B) | 98.1 | 56.2 | 60.8 | 98% | 100% | 385 |
| Eltham College (IN/S/B) | | 55.9 | 70.2 | 99% | 100% | 404.6 |
| Babington House School (IN/N/G) | | 49.7 | 46.5 | 100% | 82% | |
| Holy Trinity College (IN/N/G) | | 47.2 | 58.8 | 92% | 88% | 270 |
| Bishop Challoner School (IN/N/M) | 99.7 | 46.9 | 41.7 | 89% | 46% | 266 |
| Bullers Wood School (FD/C/G) | 100.5 | 46.3 | 47.7 | 84% | 73% | 341.2 |
| Langley Park School for Girls (FD/C/G) | 101.3 | 44.6 | 52.2 | 79% | 81% | 239.9 |
| Langley Park School for Boys (FD/C/B) | 99.2 | 43.3 | 49.8 | 81% | 68% | 282.8 |
| Farringtons & Stratford House(IN/N/G) | | 40.6 | 46.8 | 69% | 62% | 257.6 |

| SCHOOL | VALUE ADDED 02 | GCSE 02 POINTS | GCSE 01 POINTS | GCSE 02 %5 A*-C | GCSE 01 %5 A*-C | A-LEVEL 02 POINTS |
|---|---|---|---|---|---|---|
| Darrick Wood School (FD/C/M) | 99.6 | 40.2 | 47.1 | 66% | 63% | 240.5 |
| Ravens Wood School (FD/C/B) | 98.3 | 39.3 | 45.6 | 72% | 56% | 270.8 |
| Hayes School (FD/C/M) | 97.4 | 39.0 | 43.8 | 62% | 65% | 237.9 |
| Beaverwood School for Girls (FD/C/G) | 100.9 | 38.7 | 40.2 | 64% | 55% | 191.7 |
| Coopers School (FD/C/M) | 96.5 | 36.2 | 41.8 | 53% | 55% | 234.5 |
| Charles Darwin School (FD/C/M) | 99.7 | 35.5 | 40.5 | 58% | 56% | 220.3 |
| Kemnal Technology College (FD/C/B) | 102.7 | 34.3 | 37.5 | 56% | 37% | 151 |
| Baston School (IN/N/G) | 103.1 | 33.7 | 55.0 | 60% | 89% | |
| St John Rigby Catholic College (VA/C/M) | 93.1 | 32.5 | 33.8 | 39% | 32% | 138.8 |
| The Ravensbourne School (FD/C/M) | 100.0 | 32.4 | 35.6 | 43% | 39% | 174.9 |
| The Priory School (FD/C/M) | 99.2 | 31.5 | 38.8 | 39% | 41% | 211.9 |
| Kelsey Park School (FD/C/B) | 95.1 | 27.8 | 29.2 | 30% | 23% | 125 |
| Cator Park School for Girls (CY/C/G) | 94.6 | 27.2 | 30.1 | 31% | 32% | 189.3 |
| Darul Uloom London (IN/S/B) | | 22.1 | 27.6 | 6% | 46% | |
| **CAMDEN** | | | | | | |
| South Hampstead High School (IN/S/G) | | 60.2 | 69.3 | 100% | 99% | 382.3 |
| University College School (IN/S/B) | | 55.1 | 61.3 | 98% | 98% | 382.3 |
| North Bridge House School (IN/S/M) | | 48.8 | 52.1 | 92% | 85% | |
| Royal School Hampstead (IN/S/G) | 105.1 | 45.7 | 55.6 | 74% | 92% | 243 |
| La Sainte Union Catholic Secondary School (VA/C/G) | 102.1 | 42.8 | 47.9 | 79% | 70% | 248.8 |
| St Margaret's School (IN/S/G) | 106.7 | 41.8 | 48.2 | 85% | 83% | |
| The Camden School for Girls (VA/C/G) | 103.6 | 40.7 | 52.8 | 61% | 74% | 282 |
| Parliament Hill School (CY/C/G) | 100.3 | 36.3 | 36.1 | 53% | 47% | 282.8 |
| William Ellis School (VA/C/B) | 98.1 | 35.3 | 38.5 | 51% | 47% | 245.7 |
| Hampstead School (CY/C/M) | 98.5 | 34.6 | 37.2 | 50% | 44% | 234 |
| Acland Burghley School (CY/C/M) | 101.4 | 33.9 | 37.0 | 48% | 49% | 251 |
| Maria Fidelis RC Convent School (VA/C/G) | 99.2 | 32.8 | 39.4 | 43% | 41% | 197.9 |
| South Camden Community School (CY/C/M) | 104.0 | 30.2 | 29.8 | 32% | 30% | 165.7 |
| Haverstock School (CY/C/M) | 98.2 | 24.7 | 28.5 | 28% | 27% | 180 |
| Fine Arts College (IN/N/M) | | 24.3 | 46.3 | 55% | 83% | 261.8 |
| **CORPORATION OF LONDON** | | | | | | |
| City of London School for Girls (IN/S/G) | | 60.9 | 68.9 | 100% | 100% | 407.6 |
| City of London School (IN/S/B) | | 54.2 | 67.7 | 96% | 96% | 384.5 |
| **CROYDON** | | | | | | |
| Old Palace School of John Whitgift (IN/S/G) | | 56.7 | 65.1 | 97% | 99% | 403.5 |
| Croydon High School (IN/S/G) | | 55.6 | 61.5 | 100% | 100% | 366.8 |
| Whitgift School (IN/S/B) | | 55.3 | 72.1 | 96% | 99% | 378.3 |
| Trinity School (IN/S/B) | | 55.1 | 63.5 | 100% | 98% | 355.8 |
| Croham Hurst School (IN/S/G) | | 51.0 | 57.1 | 95% | 91% | 266.8 |
| Coloma Convent Girls' School (VA/C/G) | 100.6 | 49.6 | 58.0 | 89% | 91% | 305.8 |
| Harris City Technology College (CTC/C/M) | 99.6 | 45.4 | 53.1 | 91% | 88% | 208 |
| Archbishop Tenison's CofE High School (VA/C/M) | 99.2 | 44.2 | 46.2 | 80% | 68% | 280.5 |
| BRIT School for Performing Arts & Technology (CTC/C/M) | 107.5 | 44.0 | 40.0 | 87% | 53% | 118.6 |
| St Andrew's CofE Voluntary Aided High School (VA/C/M) | 98.6 | 43.7 | 45.8 | 75% | 64% | |
| Virgo Fidelis Convent Senior School (VA/C/G) | 99.5 | 40.9 | 41.7 | 66% | 66% | 164.4 |
| Norbury Manor High School for Girls (FD/C/G) | 103.0 | 39.8 | 44.8 | 53% | 58% | |
| Riddlesdown High School (VA/C/M) | 100.1 | 39.2 | 47.8 | 65% | 60% | |
| Lodge School (IN/N/G) | 106.4 | 38.7 | 52.5 | 72% | 85% | 238.3 |
| Woodcote High School (CY/C/M) | 99.1 | 38.1 | 40.9 | 57% | 56% | |
| Shirley High School (FD/C/M) | 98.8 | 38.0 | 41.9 | 56% | 53% | |
| St Joseph's College (VA/C/B) | 99.1 | 37.7 | 41.5 | 58% | 53% | 177.7 |
| Edenham High School (FD/C/M) | 98.8 | 35.2 | 42.1 | 52% | 60% | |
| Royal Russell School (IN/S/M) | | 34.8 | 34.6 | 64% | 59% | 259.3 |
| Coulsdon High School (FD/C/M) | 98.2 | 33.0 | 37.8 | 44% | 42% | |
| Thomas More School (VA/C/M) | 99.4 | 32.4 | 32.1 | 36% | 28% | |
| The Archbishop Lanfranc School (FD/C/M) | 100.1 | 32.1 | 34.0 | 37% | 33% | |
| Westwood High School (CY/C/G) | 99.6 | 31.3 | 33.7 | 32% | 36% | |
| St Mary's High School (VA/C/M) | 102.2 | 31.2 | 33.5 | 37% | 30% | |
| Ashburton Community School (CY/C/M) | 102.0 | 29.6 | 28.4 | 31% | 22% | |

| SCHOOL | VALUE ADDED 02 | GCSE 02 POINTS | GCSE 01 POINTS | GCSE 02 %5 A*-C | GCSE 01 %5 A*-C | A-LEVEL 02 POINTS |
|---|---|---|---|---|---|---|
| Selsdon High School (CY/C/M) | 96.3 | 25.6 | 26.9 | 28% | 22% | |
| Addington High School (CY/C/M) | 96.4 | 24.0 | 23.9 | 18% | 10% | |
| Stanley Technical High School for Boys (VA/C/B) | 94.3 | 23.5 | 27.5 | 14% | 16% | |
| The Selhurst High School for Boys (CY/C/B) | 95.2 | 23.4 | 23.2 | 25% | 12% | |
| Haling Manor High School (CY/C/M) | 98.9 | 21.6 | 25.4 | 16% | 15% | |

## EALING

| SCHOOL | VALUE ADDED 02 | GCSE 02 POINTS | GCSE 01 POINTS | GCSE 02 %5 A*-C | GCSE 01 %5 A*-C | A-LEVEL 02 POINTS |
|---|---|---|---|---|---|---|
| Notting Hill & Ealing High School (IN/S/G) | | 54.3 | 60.6 | 98% | 96% | 373.5 |
| St Augustine's Priory (IN/S/G) | | 52.6 | 57.9 | 100% | 92% | 300.3 |
| St Benedict's School (IN/S/B) | 100.9 | 49.2 | 51.4 | 92% | 87% | 303.3 |
| Harvington School (IN/S/G) | 99.3 | 44.3 | 48.4 | 83% | 77% | |
| The Cardinal Wiseman RC School (VA/C/M) | 104.0 | 42.7 | 44.2 | 76% | 60% | 214.6 |
| Twyford CofE High School (VA/C/M) | 103.0 | 42.1 | 49.2 | 72% | 68% | 296.2 |
| The Ellen Wilkinson School for Girls (FD/C/G) | 101.7 | 41.5 | 47.2 | 70% | 63% | 231.3 |
| Drayton Manor High School (FD/C/M) | 98.9 | 39.1 | 43.5 | 65% | 55% | 212.5 |
| Ealing College Upper School (IN/N/B) | 102.9 | 38.6 | 42.8 | 65% | 63% | 219.4 |
| Barbara Speake Stage School (IN/S/M) | 97.7 | 38.4 | 36.0 | 43% | 69% | |
| Greenford High School (FD/C/M) | 101.9 | 37.8 | 43.7 | 56% | 60% | 223 |
| Villiers High School (CY/C/M) | 104.7 | 36.7 | 41.7 | 54% | 48% | |
| Northolt High School (FD/C/M) | 97.3 | 33.3 | 37.8 | 47% | 38% | 229.2 |
| Featherstone High School (CY/C/M) | 105.6 | 32.4 | 43.7 | 39% | 50% | |
| Dormers Wells High School (CY/C/M) | 104.5 | 29.8 | 35.4 | 36% | 31% | |
| Brentside High School (FD/C/M) | 100.4 | 28.8 | 35.3 | 32% | 38% | 202.7 |
| Acton High School (CY/C/M) | 98.3 | 24.8 | 28.4 | 26% | 28% | |
| The Compton High School & Sports College (CY/C/M) | 94.0 | 22.0 | 28.1 | 13% | 20% | 164.2 |

## ENFIELD

| SCHOOL | VALUE ADDED 02 | GCSE 02 POINTS | GCSE 01 POINTS | GCSE 02 %5 A*-C | GCSE 01 %5 A*-C | A-LEVEL 02 POINTS |
|---|---|---|---|---|---|---|
| The Latymer School (VA/S/M) | 105.7 | 58.4 | 66.9 | 99% | 98% | 367.5 |
| St John's Preparatory & Senior School (IN/S/M) | 104.2 | 53.2 | 54.3 | 100% | 100% | |
| Palmers Green High School (IN/S/G) | 102.3 | 52.5 | 58.9 | 100% | 100% | |
| Enfield County School (CY/C/G) | 100.9 | 40.5 | 47.5 | 68% | 77% | 219.4 |
| Southgate School (CY/C/M) | 102.1 | 40.4 | 44.3 | 64% | 69% | 205.9 |
| St Ignatius College (VA/C/B) | 100.7 | 39.6 | 47.0 | 63% | 67% | 246.5 |
| Enfield Grammar School (FD/C/B) | 97.6 | 38.2 | 44.6 | 60% | 53% | 227.1 |
| St Anne's Catholic High School for Girls (VA/C/G) | 102.0 | 38.0 | 41.3 | 63% | 58% | 252.7 |
| Winchmore School (CY/C/M) | 101.9 | 34.4 | 38.8 | 47% | 48% | 184 |
| Broomfield School (FD/C/M) | 101.0 | 34.3 | 42.6 | 50% | 54% | 191.8 |
| Edmonton County School (CY/C/M) | 99.9 | 34.1 | 36.9 | 45% | 40% | 178.7 |
| Bishop Stopford's School (VA/C/M) | 97.3 | 33.2 | 43.3 | 45% | 48% | 185 |
| Kingsmead School (CY/C/M) | 99.2 | 30.7 | 28.6 | 38% | 33% | 157 |
| Chace Community School (CY/C/M) | 97.5 | 29.1 | 34.9 | 33% | 35% | 208.4 |
| Salisbury School (CY/C/M) | 102.1 | 26.9 | 25.5 | 22% | 19% | 81.3 |
| Albany School (FD/C/M) | 98.0 | 26.1 | 29.2 | 28% | 22% | 137.2 |
| Aylward School (CY/C/M) | 97.6 | 24.5 | 31.3 | 19% | 28% | 182.9 |
| Lea Valley High School (CY/C/M) | 97.6 | 24.1 | 31.6 | 25% | 26% | 115.7 |

## GREENWICH

| SCHOOL | VALUE ADDED 02 | GCSE 02 POINTS | GCSE 01 POINTS | GCSE 02 %5 A*-C | GCSE 01 %5 A*-C | A-LEVEL 02 POINTS |
|---|---|---|---|---|---|---|
| Blackheath High School (IN/S/G) | | 49.1 | 59.4 | 92% | 94% | 294.6 |
| Colfes School (IN/S/M) | | 48.7 | 57.1 | 92% | 93% | 380.2 |
| St Thomas More RC Comprehensive School (VA/C/M) | 100.5 | 41.5 | 50.5 | 67% | 69% | |
| St Ursula's Convent School (VA/C/G) | 99.1 | 38.1 | 47.4 | 50% | 66% | |
| St Paul's Catholic School (VA/C/M) | 101.6 | 36.4 | 41.3 | 46% | 52% | |
| Thomas Tallis School (CY/C/M) | 102.7 | 34.5 | 44.1 | 41% | 48% | 233.6 |
| Eltham Hill Technology College for Girls (CY/C/G) | 102.4 | 32.9 | 34.8 | 42% | 41% | 172.2 |
| The John Roan School (VC/C/M) | 99.2 | 30.1 | 35.9 | 37% | 35% | 147.6 |
| Crown Woods School (CY/C/M) | 98.0 | 29.0 | 34.3 | 39% | 33% | 166.8 |
| BLA Theatre School (IN/S/M) | | 27.7 | 22.8 | 11% | 0% | |
| Woolwich Polytechnic School for Boys (CY/C/B) | 96.7 | 27.3 | 32.3 | 27% | 31% | 200 |
| Plumstead Manor School (CY/C/G) | 99.8 | 27.1 | 34.3 | 26% | 35% | 168.5 |
| Blackheath Bluecoat CofE Secondary School (VA/C/M) | 96.2 | 26.6 | 27.7 | 27% | 20% | 115.4 |
| Eltham Green School (CY/C/M) | 101.6 | 26.3 | 25.7 | 17% | 16% | |
| Kidbrooke School (CY/C/M) | 101.1 | 25.6 | 27.5 | 29% | 27% | 157.9 |

| SCHOOL | VALUE ADDED 02 | GCSE 02 POINTS | GCSE 01 POINTS | GCSE 02 %5 A*-C | GCSE 01 %5 A*-C | A-LEVEL 02 POINTS |
|---|---|---|---|---|---|---|
| Riverston School (IN/N/M) | | 25.3 | 28.0 | 42% | 39% | |
| Abbey Wood School (CY/C/M) | 92.7 | 21.6 | 27.5 | 12% | 19% | |
| **HACKNEY** | | | | | | |
| Tayyibah Girls' School (IN/N/G) | 102.6 | 63.8 | 59.8 | 100% | 100% | 325 |
| Yesodey Hatorah School (IN/N/M) | 104.9 | 55.9 | 56.6 | 84% | 80% | |
| Our Lady's Convent RC High School (VA/C/G) | 98.0 | 38.4 | 51.5 | 54% | 63% | 233.9 |
| Beis Malka Girls' School (IN/N/G) | | 36.1 | 32.6 | 65% | 58% | |
| Haggerston School (CY/C/G) | 106.9 | 35.2 | 33.4 | 41% | 35% | |
| Cardinal Pole RC School (VA/C/M) | 101.8 | 34.3 | 39.4 | 40% | 46% | 163.2 |
| Stoke Newington School Media Arts College (CY/C/M) | 101.7 | 32.3 | 41.3 | 40% | 49% | |
| Clapton Girls' Technology College (CY/C/G) | 107.1 | 31.2 | 33.0 | 34% | 29% | |
| Beis Chinuch Lebonos Girls School (IN/N/G) | | 29.9 | 34.4 | 68% | 67% | |
| The Skinners' Company's School for Girls (VA/C/G) | 105.3 | 28.6 | 31.5 | 34% | 30% | 116.6 |
| Homerton College of Technology (CY/C/B) | 102.5 | 25.3 | 27.2 | 22% | 27% | |
| Hackney Free & Parochial CofE Secondary School (VA/C/M) | 94.1 | 20.1 | 27.6 | 18% | 21% | |
| Beis Rochel d'Satmar Girls' School (IN/S/G) | 97.5 | 18.8 | 19.4 | 8% | 9% | |
| **HAMMERSMITH AND FULHAM** | | | | | | |
| St Paul's Girls' School (IN/S/G) | | 61.2 | 69.9 | 99% | 99% | 438.7 |
| The Godolphin & Latymer School (IN/S/G) | | 59.7 | 66.5 | 100% | 99% | 401.4 |
| Latymer Upper School (IN/S/B) | | 53.9 | 65.2 | 97% | 99% | 360.1 |
| St James Independent School for Girls (IN/N/G) | | 52.1 | 58.7 | 100% | 100% | 387.7 |
| Lady Margaret School (VA/C/G) | 105.2 | 50.6 | 58.0 | 90% | 91% | 330.2 |
| Sacred Heart High School (VA/C/G) | 103.7 | 47.7 | 56.6 | 88% | 84% | |
| The London Oratory School (VA/C/B) | 99.7 | 47.4 | 57.2 | 88% | 89% | 305.8 |
| Holborn College (IN/S/M) | 105.8 | 41.4 | 34.3 | 70% | 50% | 370 |
| Fulham Cross Secondary School (CY/C/G) | 101.2 | 31.1 | 29.9 | 43% | 35% | |
| Burlington Danes CofE School (VA/C/M) | 94.6 | 28.0 | 34.8 | 26% | 40% | |
| Phoenix High School (CY/C/M) | 101.3 | 26.2 | 21.1 | 25% | 11% | |
| Hurlingham & Chelsea Secondary School (CY/C/M) | 97.0 | 25.9 | 30.6 | 23% | 34% | |
| Ravenscourt Theatre School (IN/S/M) | 99.6 | 25.7 | 34.8 | 14% | 33% | |
| Henry Compton Secondary School (CY/C/B) | 100.1 | 25.1 | 29.8 | 29% | 29% | |
| **HARINGEY** | | | | | | |
| Channing School (IN/S/G) | | 56.1 | 62.3 | 98% | 98% | 372.4 |
| Highgate School (IN/S/B) | | 53.7 | 57.7 | 96% | 95% | 348.5 |
| Fortismere School (CY/C/M) | 99.5 | 40.6 | 48.2 | 67% | 69% | 275.8 |
| Hornsey Secondary School for Girls (CY/C/G) | 101.9 | 35.2 | 39.4 | 52% | 44% | 164.9 |
| St Thomas More RC School (VA/C/M) | 97.6 | 29.5 | 33.7 | 33% | 31% | 130.9 |
| Highgate Wood Secondary School (CY/C/M) | 95.5 | 28.9 | 32.4 | 41% | 41% | 139.1 |
| Northumberland Park Community School (CY/C/M) | 103.4 | 28.3 | 27.3 | 19% | 18% | 108 |
| Gladesmore Community School (CY/C/M) | 100.2 | 25.2 | 23.9 | 30% | 16% | 80 |
| The John Loughborough School (VA/C/M) | 91.9 | 23.2 | 26.7 | 24% | 24% | |
| White Hart Lane Secondary School (CY/C/M) | 100.5 | 21.4 | 19.3 | 24% | 10% | 94.2 |
| Park View Academy (CY/C/M) | 99.3 | 21.4 | 26.0 | 16% | 15% | 165 |
| **HARROW** | | | | | | |
| North London Collegiate School (IN/S/G) | | 60.7 | 71.8 | 100% | 97% | 419.1 |
| The John Lyon School (IN/S/B) | | 53.3 | 61.5 | 98% | 97% | 323 |
| Heathfield School Pinner (IN/S/G) | | 51.1 | 58.9 | 91% | 93% | 342.1 |
| Harrow School (IN/S/B) | | 50.0 | 55.0 | 88% | 85% | 379.6 |
| Peterborough & St Margaret's School (IN/S/G) | | 48.1 | 54.5 | 89% | 88% | |
| Buckingham College School (IN/S/B) | | 44.8 | 48.5 | 73% | 75% | 277.9 |
| Park High School (CY/C/M) | 103.8 | 42.2 | 47.1 | 74% | 66% | |
| Nower Hill High School (CY/C/M) | 100.2 | 40.0 | 46.0 | 66% | 64% | |
| Hatch End High School (CY/C/M) | 100.4 | 39.8 | 46.3 | 68% | 63% | |
| Whitmore High School (CY/C/M) | 103.9 | 39.0 | 43.5 | 66% | 57% | |
| The Sacred Heart RC High School (VA/C/G) | 96.7 | 38.5 | 45.3 | 64% | 56% | |
| Salvatorian RC College (VA/C/B) | 96.2 | 36.8 | 40.0 | 51% | 58% | |
| Bentley Wood High School (CY/C/G) | 101.1 | 35.6 | 44.0 | 56% | 66% | |
| Canons High School (CY/C/M) | 102.5 | 34.7 | 38.1 | 48% | 43% | |

| SCHOOL | VALUE ADDED 02 | GCSE 02 POINTS | GCSE 01 POINTS | GCSE 02 %5 A*-C | GCSE 01 %5 A*-C | A-LEVEL 02 POINTS |
|---|---|---|---|---|---|---|
| Rooks Heath High School (CY/C/M) | 101.8 | 33.7 | 39.0 | 49% | 53% | |
| Harrow High School (CY/C/M) | 95.0 | 29.6 | 33.8 | 37% | 33% | |
| **HAVERING** | | | | | | |
| Raphael Independent School (IN/S/M) | 101.6 | 62.7 | 41.3 | 100% | 55% | |
| The Coopers' Company & Coborn School (VA/C/M) | 100.8 | 52.9 | 63.8 | 99% | 100% | 372 |
| Sacred Heart of Mary Girls' School (VA/C/G) | 100.3 | 48.8 | 57.5 | 91% | 90% | 336.6 |
| Hall Mead School (CY/C/M) | 104.1 | 42.8 | 52.2 | 80% | 75% | |
| The Campion School (VA/C/B) | 99.9 | 42.0 | 54.9 | 73% | 83% | 280.3 |
| St Edward's CofE Comprehensive School (VA/C/M) | 100.0 | 40.0 | 51.5 | 67% | 71% | 235 |
| The Sanders Draper School (CY/C/M) | 102.5 | 39.9 | 47.2 | 65% | 67% | |
| Gaynes School (CY/C/M) | 97.4 | 38.1 | 43.0 | 59% | 60% | |
| The Frances Bardsley School for Girls (FD/C/G) | 98.1 | 37.8 | 47.4 | 58% | 64% | 263.9 |
| The Albany School (CY/C/M) | 99.8 | 37.0 | 47.4 | 59% | 54% | |
| Immanuel School (IN/N/M) | | 36.3 | 43.3 | 58% | 63% | |
| Abbs Cross School (FD/C/M) | 100.6 | 36.1 | 44.0 | 49% | 60% | |
| The Chafford School (CY/C/M) | 99.8 | 35.7 | 34.2 | 53% | 42% | |
| Brittons School & Technology College (CY/C/M) | 99.0 | 35.2 | 38.2 | 49% | 48% | |
| Marshalls Park School (CY/C/M) | 94.4 | 32.5 | 32.0 | 53% | 29% | |
| Emerson Park School (CY/C/M) | 98.5 | 32.0 | 37.4 | 39% | 45% | |
| Bower Park School (CY/C/M) | 96.9 | 29.2 | 33.0 | 39% | 33% | |
| The Royal Liberty School (CY/C/B) | 99.3 | 28.5 | 28.2 | 32% | 25% | |
| King's Wood School (CY/C/M) | 95.4 | 24.0 | 23.0 | 16% | 16% | |
| Redden Court School (CY/C/M) | 96.6 | 23.5 | 29.7 | 26% | 28% | |
| **HILLINGDON** | | | | | | |
| St Helen's School (IN/S/G) | 102.1 | 56.5 | 63.4 | 98% | 99% | 376.6 |
| Northwood College (IN/S/G) | | 52.9 | 63.4 | 92% | 97% | 334.6 |
| Guru Nanak Sikh Secondary School (VA/C/M) | 102.6 | 43.6 | 45.2 | 75% | 70% | 200 |
| Bishop Ramsey CofE Voluntary Aided Secondary (VA/C/M) | 99.5 | 43.1 | 45.7 | 81% | 68% | 282.5 |
| Vyners School (FD/C/M) | 97.7 | 40.6 | 46.9 | 64% | 61% | 259.4 |
| Queensmead School (FD/C/M) | 102.7 | 39.9 | 43.4 | 60% | 55% | 249.7 |
| Swakeleys School (FD/C/G) | 100.2 | 37.9 | 42.5 | 58% | 62% | 255.5 |
| Haydon School (FD/C/M) | 99.2 | 37.7 | 47.8 | 56% | 68% | 262.2 |
| Bishopshalt School (FD/C/M) | 99.9 | 36.4 | 40.4 | 52% | 58% | 242.5 |
| Northwood School (FD/C/M) | 95.7 | 33.2 | 38.6 | 43% | 43% | 233.1 |
| Harlington Community School (FD/C/M) | 99.5 | 31.8 | 32.9 | 41% | 38% | 192.8 |
| The Douay Martyrs RC School (VA/C/M) | 95.9 | 31.7 | 39.1 | 42% | 46% | 172.1 |
| Mellow Lane School (FD/C/M) | 98.3 | 30.6 | 34.9 | 42% | 40% | 186.5 |
| Uxbridge High School (FD/C/M) | 99.0 | 29.5 | 34.8 | 34% | 37% | 175.3 |
| Abbotsfield School (FD/C/B) | 94.1 | 27.9 | 32.2 | 26% | 30% | 191.1 |
| The Hayes Manor School (FD/C/M) | 93.6 | 21.8 | 29.9 | 20% | 30% | 163.5 |
| John Penrose School (CY/C/M) | 92.6 | 21.5 | 27.4 | 17% | 23% | 127.5 |
| Evelyns Community School (CY/C/M) | 92.5 | 17.5 | 21.8 | 8% | 17% | 0 |
| **HOUNSLOW** | | | | | | |
| The Arts Educational School (IN/S/M) | 105.1 | 43.6 | 49.8 | 76% | 75% | |
| St Mark's Catholic School (VA/C/M) | 101.1 | 42.6 | 49.0 | 71% | 65% | 227.3 |
| Gumley House RC Convent School (VA/C/G) | 100.5 | 42.1 | 47.8 | 74% | 68% | 254.5 |
| The Green School (VA/C/G) | 101.1 | 41.2 | 50.2 | 65% | 73% | 226.4 |
| The Heathland School (CY/C/M) | 102.7 | 41.0 | 49.5 | 66% | 64% | 235.2 |
| Heston Community School (CY/C/M) | 102.0 | 38.4 | 38.9 | 57% | 51% | 207 |
| Gunnersbury Catholic School (VA/C/B) | 96.5 | 37.4 | 40.3 | 59% | 58% | 255.5 |
| Isleworth & Syon School for Boys (VC/C/B) | 97.6 | 35.9 | 36.6 | 56% | 46% | 219.1 |
| International School of London (IN/N/M) | | 34.7 | 41.9 | 73% | 63% | |
| Cranford Community College (CY/C/M) | 99.1 | 33.6 | 34.2 | 44% | 37% | 163.2 |
| Lampton School (CY/C/M) | 101.1 | 33.5 | 37.8 | 44% | 46% | 223.7 |
| Brentford School for Girls (CY/C/G) | 103.0 | 31.1 | 35.9 | 46% | 31% | 160.8 |
| Chiswick Community School (CY/C/M) | 95.8 | 30.2 | 33.9 | 38% | 36% | 239.3 |
| Longford Community School (CY/C/M) | 94.7 | 27.5 | 26.5 | 34% | 28% | 126.8 |
| Feltham Community College (CY/C/M) | 95.0 | 24.4 | 23.2 | 28% | 17% | 128.8 |
| Hounslow Manor School (CY/C/M) | 98.3 | 22.1 | 30.6 | 21% | 30% | 134.1 |

| SCHOOL | VALUE ADDED 02 | GCSE 02 POINTS | GCSE 01 POINTS | GCSE 02 %5 A*-C | GCSE 01 %5 A*-C | A-LEVEL 02 POINTS |
|---|---|---|---|---|---|---|
| **ISLINGTON** | | | | | | |
| Italia Conti Academy of Theatre Arts (IN/S/M) | 105.7 | 44.8 | 47.0 | 95% | 81% | 105 |
| Mount Carmel RC Technology College for Girls (VA/C/G) | 104.7 | 36.8 | 35.2 | 58% | 35% | |
| Highbury Fields School (CY/C/G) | 102.4 | 33.5 | 38.6 | 45% | 50% | 133.2 |
| Elizabeth Garrett Anderson School (CY/C/G) | 101.1 | 31.5 | 31.6 | 40% | 32% | |
| Central Foundation Boys' School (VA/C/B) | 101.3 | 29.9 | 29.6 | 37% | 27% | |
| St Aloysius RC College (VA/C/B) | 96.3 | 25.7 | 27.2 | 30% | 28% | 50.8 |
| Islington Green School (CY/C/M) | 100.3 | 25.5 | 24.4 | 27% | 24% | |
| Highbury Grove School (CY/C/M) | 94.5 | 22.9 | 25.9 | 25% | 30% | 190 |
| Islington Arts & Media School (CY/C/M) | 99.6 | 19.3 | 27.6 | 23% | 22% | 80 |
| Holloway School (CY/C/B) | 96.8 | 18.8 | 20.4 | 20% | 12% | |
| **KENSINGTON AND CHELSEA** | | | | | | |
| Lycee Francais (IN/S/M) | | 55.7 | 75.8 | 100% | 100% | 385.8 |
| Collingham (IN/S/M) | | 55.0 | 52.8 | 100% | 100% | 230.9 |
| Queen's Gate School (IN/S/G) | | 48.5 | 52.0 | 86% | 94% | 353.9 |
| The Cardinal Vaughan Memorial RC School (VA/C/B) | 101.2 | 48.4 | 58.5 | 89% | 86% | 301.2 |
| More House School (IN/S/G) | | 46.0 | 57.0 | 82% | 97% | 281.4 |
| Hellenic College of London (IN/S/M) | | 39.9 | 65.6 | 80% | 100% | 275.5 |
| Saint Thomas More RC School (VA/C/M) | 102.7 | 39.1 | 45.1 | 61% | 62% | |
| Mander Portman Woodward School (IN/S/M) | | 38.1 | 43.8 | 73% | 69% | 242.2 |
| Sion-Manning RC School for Girls (VA/C/G) | 103.6 | 37.5 | 42.4 | 55% | 52% | |
| Davies Laing & Dick College (IN/S/M) | | 36.0 | 34.0 | 76% | 65% | 272.4 |
| Holland Park School (CY/C/M) | 98.9 | 29.3 | 32.7 | 38% | 38% | 198.5 |
| Duff Miller College (IN/S/M) | | 28.5 | 26.9 | 46% | 31% | 237.4 |
| Ashbourne Independent School (IN/N/M) | | 26.4 | 32.7 | 42% | 57% | 216.7 |
| **KINGSTON** | | | | | | |
| The Tiffin Girls' School (CY/S/G) | 102.3 | 58.0 | 67.9 | 100% | 99% | 375 |
| Kingston Grammar School (IN/S/M) | | 55.5 | 66.9 | 100% | 98% | 338.4 |
| Tiffin School (VA/S/B) | 99.2 | 55.4 | 72.0 | 99% | 100% | 341.7 |
| Surbiton High School (IN/S/G) | 103.9 | 54.2 | 65.1 | 99% | 100% | 372.1 |
| Tolworth Girls' School (CY/C/G) | 101.4 | 43.9 | 44.4 | 75% | 73% | 228.6 |
| Richard Challoner School (VA/C/B) | 104.3 | 42.1 | 48.1 | 73% | 62% | 230.7 |
| Coombe Girls' School (CY/C/G) | 100.9 | 38.3 | 45.0 | 60% | 58% | 220.3 |
| The Holy Cross School (VA/C/G) | 99.1 | 37.0 | 48.8 | 55% | 65% | 222.5 |
| Canbury School (IN/S/M) | | 32.7 | 28.3 | 45% | 38% | |
| Southborough School (CY/C/B) | 98.0 | 32.5 | 31.2 | 46% | 34% | 120 |
| Chessington Community College (CY/C/M) | 96.8 | 28.8 | 33.5 | 34% | 37% | 106 |
| The Hollyfield School (FD/C/M) | 96.3 | 27.9 | 34.2 | 36% | 46% | 203.4 |
| Beverley School (FD/C/B) | 93.9 | 24.9 | 30.8 | 29% | 38% | 79.4 |
| **LAMBETH** | | | | | | |
| Streatham & Clapham High School (IN/S/G) | | 50.1 | 61.4 | 94% | 92% | 362.7 |
| La Retraite RC Girls' School (VA/C/G) | 103.7 | 38.4 | 45.8 | 61% | 55% | 193.8 |
| Dunraven School (FD/C/M) | 99.6 | 37.6 | 39.5 | 55% | 43% | |
| Archbishop Tenison's School (VA/C/B) | 104.1 | 37.0 | 35.5 | 56% | 35% | 149.2 |
| St Martin in the Fields High School for Girls (VA/C/G) | 103.1 | 36.5 | 41.0 | 59% | 54% | |
| London Nautical School (FD/C/B) | 94.8 | 35.5 | 35.8 | 47% | 45% | 167 |
| Norwood School (CY/C/G) | 104.8 | 30.6 | 31.1 | 33% | 19% | |
| Charles Edward Brooke School (VC/C/G) | 103.8 | 29.3 | 37.4 | 36% | 40% | 117.3 |
| Bishop Thomas Grant Catholic Secondary School (VA/C/M) | 99.0 | 28.3 | 33.4 | 29% | 37% | |
| Stockwell Park School (CY/C/M) | 105.3 | 26.2 | 25.1 | 26% | 29% | |
| Lilian Baylis School (CY/C/M) | 104.1 | 21.0 | 23.0 | 6% | 18% | |
| **LEWISHAM** | | | | | | |
| Sydenham High School GDST (IN/S/G) | | 53.4 | 55.9 | 100% | 96% | 282.1 |
| St Dunstan's College (IN/S/M) | | 47.0 | 56.4 | 89% | 95% | 340.5 |
| Prendergast School (VA/C/G) | 104.6 | 44.7 | 49.0 | 75% | 72% | 249.8 |
| Haberdashers' Aske's Hatcham College (CTC/C/M) | 99.3 | 44.5 | 49.6 | 79% | 73% | 318.3 |
| Bonus Pastor RC School (VA/C/M) | 103.5 | 36.1 | 41.8 | 49% | 57% | |
| Sydenham School (CY/C/G) | 102.7 | 32.9 | 38.2 | 49% | 47% | 194.9 |

| SCHOOL | VALUE ADDED 02 | GCSE 02 POINTS | GCSE 01 POINTS | GCSE 02 %5 A*-C | GCSE 01 %5 A*-C | A-LEVEL 02 POINTS |
|---|---|---|---|---|---|---|
| Deptford Green School (CY/C/M) | 102.2 | 30.6 | 34.8 | 36% | 41% | 183.5 |
| Forest Hill School (CY/C/B) | 99.8 | 30.1 | 34.7 | 42% | 37% | 182.2 |
| Catford Girls' School (CY/C/G) | 101.0 | 29.6 | 30.5 | 36% | 21% | |
| Addey & Stanhope School (VA/C/M) | 99.1 | 29.4 | 36.2 | 32% | 40% | 142.5 |
| Northbrook CofE School (VA/C/M) | 99.7 | 29.3 | 29.1 | 20% | 26% | |
| Sedgehill School (CY/C/M) | 96.9 | 27.7 | 29.3 | 30% | 26% | 113.3 |
| Crofton School (CY/C/M) | 101.8 | 25.5 | 27.5 | 22% | 18% | 101 |
| St Joseph's Academy (VA/C/B) | 99.3 | 23.7 | 24.4 | 13% | 16% | |
| Malory School (CY/C/M) | 98.3 | 21.0 | 19.7 | 18% | 9% | |
| **MERTON** | | | | | | |
| King's College School (IN/S/B) | | 59.5 | 67.7 | 100% | 99% | 392.1 |
| Wimbledon High School (IN/S/G) | | 58.3 | 74.7 | 100% | 99% | 427.4 |
| Ursuline High School Wimbledon (VA/C/G) | 102.5 | 40.5 | 44.4 | 71% | 64% | 280 |
| Wimbledon College (VA/C/B) | 101.2 | 40.3 | 42.1 | 65% | 56% | 281 |
| Ricards Lodge High School (CY/C/G) | 101.2 | 33.4 | 45.2 | 52% | 63% | |
| Raynes Park High School (CY/C/M) | 100.4 | 28.9 | 34.3 | 37% | 40% | |
| Rutlish School (VC/C/B) | 95.1 | 25.6 | 33.6 | 27% | 32% | |
| Tamworth Manor High School (CY/C/M) | 96.2 | 25.2 | 31.1 | 25% | 29% | |
| Bishopsford Community School (CY/C/M) | 100.9 | 22.8 | 20.1 | 18% | 10% | |
| **NEWHAM** | | | | | | |
| St Angela's Ursuline Convent School (VA/C/G) | 103.5 | 43.2 | 49.4 | 74% | 69% | 243.4 |
| St Bonaventure's RC School (VA/C/B) | 104.2 | 42.3 | 49.5 | 74% | 74% | 233.5 |
| Plashet School (CY/C/G) | 106.9 | 38.3 | 45.8 | 56% | 59% | |
| Sarah Bonnell School (CY/C/G) | 104.2 | 36.4 | 37.5 | 46% | 43% | |
| Stratford School (FD/C/M) | 103.5 | 36.4 | 38.5 | 46% | 40% | |
| Langdon School (CY/C/M) | 102.4 | 33.4 | 42.7 | 41% | 43% | |
| Lister Community School (CY/C/M) | 100.6 | 31.0 | 30.7 | 37% | 29% | |
| The Royal Docks Community School (CY/C/M) | 105.5 | 30.8 | 26.5 | 40% | 22% | |
| Forest Gate Community School (CY/C/M) | 103.3 | 30.0 | 32.0 | 34% | 33% | |
| Little Ilford School (CY/C/M) | 101.9 | 29.4 | 31.9 | 32% | 27% | |
| Cumberland School (CY/C/M) | 103.1 | 29.3 | 28.9 | 27% | 26% | |
| Eastlea Community School (CY/C/M) | 101.0 | 29.0 | 32.4 | 36% | 35% | |
| Brampton Manor School (CY/C/M) | 103.1 | 28.7 | 29.5 | 30% | 28% | |
| Rokeby School (CY/C/B) | 99.1 | 27.1 | 29.9 | 23% | 21% | |
| **REDBRIDGE** | | | | | | |
| Bancrofts School (IN/S/M) | | 57.9 | 62.5 | 100% | 100% | 394.3 |
| Woodford County High School (CY/S/G) | 101.0 | 57.2 | 66.8 | 99% | 100% | 357.9 |
| Ilford County High School (CY/S/B) | 99.2 | 52.4 | 66.4 | 98% | 98% | 323.7 |
| Park School for Girls (IN/S/G) | | 46.8 | 48.1 | 86% | 92% | 240.7 |
| Ilford Ursuline High School (VA/C/G) | 103.1 | 46.5 | 54.9 | 82% | 77% | 294.6 |
| Trinity Catholic High School (VA/C/M) | 104.4 | 44.8 | 49.9 | 81% | 85% | 258.2 |
| Cranbrook College (IN/S/B) | 101.7 | 43.6 | 50.8 | 88% | 91% | |
| Seven Kings High School (CY/C/M) | 101.8 | 43.5 | 53.8 | 80% | 81% | 296.4 |
| Beal High School (CY/C/M) | 102.0 | 42.0 | 51.4 | 72% | 76% | 235 |
| King Solomon High School (VA/C/M) | 102.2 | 41.3 | 53.1 | 68% | 76% | 249.1 |
| Valentines High School (CY/C/M) | 104.8 | 40.5 | 43.9 | 67% | 56% | 237.6 |
| The Chadwell Heath Foundation School (FD/C/M) | 103.4 | 38.6 | 42.5 | 65% | 65% | 187.3 |
| Canon Palmer Catholic School (VA/C/M) | 100.1 | 37.0 | 43.8 | 62% | 56% | 227.2 |
| Loxford School of Science & Technology (CY/C/M) | 107.1 | 36.5 | 41.5 | 52% | 51% | 213.3 |
| Wanstead High School (CY/C/M) | 101.5 | 36.0 | 37.3 | 51% | 51% | 219.5 |
| Woodbridge High School (CY/C/M) | 103.2 | 35.7 | 42.7 | 53% | 55% | 205.1 |
| Caterham High School (CY/C/M) | 101.2 | 35.0 | 42.0 | 49% | 53% | 211 |
| Mayfield School & College (CY/C/M) | 102.1 | 32.5 | 38.1 | 46% | 44% | 206.3 |
| Hainault Forest High School (CY/C/M) | 100.2 | 31.3 | 33.9 | 37% | 41% | 194.5 |
| **RICHMOND** | | | | | | |
| St Paul's School (IN/S/B) | | 61.0 | 76.0 | 99% | 100% | 429.4 |
| The Lady Eleanor Holles School (IN/S/G) | | 60.7 | 74.6 | 100% | 100% | 492.7 |
| Hampton School (IN/S/B) | | 55.5 | 64.3 | 98% | 98% | 464.3 |

| SCHOOL | VALUE ADDED 02 | GCSE 02 POINTS | GCSE 01 POINTS | GCSE 02 %5 A*-C | GCSE 01 %5 A*-C | A-LEVEL 02 POINTS |
|---|---|---|---|---|---|---|
| St James Independent School for Boys (IN/S/B) | | 46.1 | 56.7 | 83% | 96% | 271.3 |
| St Catherine's School (IN/S/G) | 44.4 | 52.2 | 85% | 81% | | |
| Waldegrave School (CY/C/G) | 101.8 | 43.4 | 51.2 | 75% | 75% | |
| The Harrodian School (IN/S/M) | | 41.9 | 34.0 | 70% | 71% | |
| The Royal Ballet School (IN/S/M) | 94.3 | 41.1 | 45.4 | 88% | 88% | 97.4 |
| Grey Court School (CY/C/M) | 99.9 | 39.8 | 44.3 | 63% | 57% | |
| Orleans Park School (CY/C/M) | 100.2 | 38.0 | 40.2 | 64% | 59% | |
| Teddington School (CY/C/M) | 97.6 | 37.4 | 46.2 | 55% | 72% | |
| Hampton Community College (CY/C/M) | 100.6 | 33.4 | 38.1 | 46% | 45% | |
| Christ's CofE Comprehensive Secondary School (VA/C/M) | 100.7 | 29.6 | 28.4 | 36% | 19% | |
| Whitton School (CY/C/M) | 95.8 | 28.8 | 32.1 | 31% | 36% | |
| Shene School (CY/C/M) | 96.2 | 27.0 | 35.1 | 30% | 42% | |
| **SOUTHWARK** | | | | | | |
| James Allen's Girls' School (IN/S/G) | 102.1 | 59.4 | 69.2 | 100% | 99% | 387.2 |
| Alleyn's School (IN/S/M) | | 55.2 | 64.9 | 99% | 99% | 437.9 |
| Dulwich College (IN/S/B) | | 53.9 | 64.2 | 97% | 96% | 393.1 |
| Notre Dame RC Girls' School (VA/C/G) | 102.8 | 40.7 | 44.7 | 66% | 55% | |
| St Saviour's & St Olave's CofE School (VA/C/G) | 101.5 | 39.3 | 38.4 | 59% | 40% | 167.1 |
| Bacon's College (CTC/C/M) | 99.9 | 37.5 | 47.1 | 54% | 72% | 209.3 |
| The St Thomas the Apostle College (VA/C/B) | 100.4 | 37.1 | 42.8 | 53% | 53% | |
| Sacred Heart RC Secondary School (VA/C/M) | 99.4 | 36.9 | 40.9 | 56% | 63% | |
| St Michael's RC School (VA/C/M) | 98.0 | 31.8 | 39.9 | 39% | 43% | |
| Aylwin Girls' School (CY/C/G) | 103.8 | 29.1 | 30.7 | 29% | 28% | |
| Geoffrey Chaucer Technology College (CY/C/M) | 101.2 | 28.0 | 31.2 | 22% | 19% | |
| Waverley School (CY/C/G) | 101.8 | 27.3 | 27.0 | 26% | 23% | |
| Kingsdale Secondary School (CY/C/M) | 101.3 | 26.0 | 23.0 | 41% | 16% | |
| Archbishop Michael Ramsey Technology College (VA/C/M) | 104.2 | 24.0 | 25.5 | 22% | 26% | 171.4 |
| Walworth School (CY/C/M) | 96.2 | 23.1 | 21.0 | 14% | 12% | |
| **SUTTON** | | | | | | |
| Wallington High School for Girls (FD/S/G) | 102.1 | 56.9 | 68.0 | 99% | 99% | 323.5 |
| Nonsuch High School for Girls (FD/S/G) | 100.0 | 55.9 | 70.8 | 98% | 100% | 435.4 |
| Sutton High School (IN/S/G) | | 55.3 | 68.2 | 97% | 100% | 360 |
| Wallington County Grammar School (FD/S/B) | 99.6 | 55.1 | 64.8 | 100% | 98% | 388.4 |
| Wilson's School (VA/S/B) | 99.0 | 55.1 | 63.5 | 100% | 96% | 418.1 |
| Sutton Grammar School for Boys (FD/S/B) | 98.9 | 54.5 | 62.9 | 95% | 99% | 425.8 |
| St Philomena's School (VA/C/G) | 104.5 | 45.9 | 53.4 | 84% | 75% | 252.7 |
| The John Fisher School (VA/C/B) | 98.3 | 42.1 | 51.2 | 76% | 74% | 236.1 |
| Overton Grange School (CY/C/M) | 99.7 | 40.5 | | 66% | | |
| Greenshaw High School (CY/C/M) | 99.3 | 37.7 | 43.6 | 52% | 51% | 223 |
| Cheam High School (FD/C/M) | 100.4 | 36.1 | 40.1 | 50% | 47% | 176.4 |
| Carshalton High School for Girls (CY/C/G) | 97.6 | 33.8 | 40.0 | 48% | 48% | 220.6 |
| Glenthorne High School (CY/C/M) | 98.5 | 30.4 | 32.3 | 35% | 30% | 202.1 |
| Carshalton High School for Boys (CY/C/B) | 96.7 | 28.5 | 27.1 | 28% | 25% | 121.9 |
| Stanley Park High School (CY/C/M) | 92.5 | 24.0 | 25.6 | 26% | 22% | 172.2 |
| Stowford College (IN/S/M) | 95.3 | 21.3 | 25.8 | 8% | 29% | |
| **TOWER HAMLETS** | | | | | | |
| Madni Secondary Girls' School (IN/S/G) | 101.3 | 63.5 | 64.1 | 100% | 100% | |
| Mulberry School for Girls (CY/C/G) | 108.5 | 37.1 | 44.1 | 52% | 54% | 167.2 |
| Oaklands School (CY/C/M) | 106.1 | 36.8 | 37.9 | 57% | 41% | |
| Morpeth School (CY/C/M) | 107.9 | 36.4 | 42.4 | 54% | 50% | |
| Raine's Foundation School (VA/C/M) | 99.3 | 35.9 | 36.6 | 48% | 39% | 253.9 |
| Sir John Cass Foundation & Redcoat CofE (VA/C/M) | 109.8 | 34.4 | 36.4 | 69% | 36% | 126 |
| Central Foundation Girls' School (VC/C/G) | 104.8 | 34.2 | 39.1 | 42% | 46% | 162.6 |
| Stepney Green School (CY/C/B) | 104.7 | 34.0 | 33.5 | 49% | 37% | |
| Swanlea School (CY/C/M) | 105.0 | 33.9 | 36.1 | 44% | 38% | |
| Bishop Challoner RC School (VA/C/G) | 100.9 | 32.3 | 36.4 | 48% | 38% | 152.7 |
| St Paul's Way Community School (CY/C/M) | 107.5 | 32.3 | 32.1 | 41% | 23% | |
| George Green's School (VC/C/M) | 99.0 | 31.2 | 32.5 | 35% | 30% | 135.4 |
| Bethnal Green Technology College (CY/C/M) | 104.2 | 29.4 | 30.0 | 42% | 24% | |

| SCHOOL | VALUE ADDED 02 | GCSE 02 POINTS | GCSE 01 POINTS | GCSE 02 %5 A*-C | GCSE 01 %5 A*-C | A-LEVEL 02 POINTS |
|---|---|---|---|---|---|---|
| Langdon Park Community School (CY/C/M) | 105.8 | 29.1 | 30.1 | 29% | 28% | |
| Bow School (CY/C/B) | 99.0 | 24.3 | 18.7 | 18% | 16% | |
| **WALTHAM FOREST** | | | | | | |
| Forest School (IN/S/M) | 101.8 | 52.5 | 60.5 | 97% | 97% | 357.6 |
| Connaught School for Girls (CY/C/G) | 104.2 | 41.8 | 46.1 | 64% | 59% | |
| Highams Park School (VA/C/M) | 101.0 | 40.6 | 46.6 | 62% | 66% | 219.8 |
| Walthamstow School for Girls (CY/C/G) | 106.1 | 40.2 | 45.3 | 61% | 63% | |
| Chingford Foundation School (FD/C/M) | 101.5 | 39.1 | 40.6 | 58% | 54% | 202.6 |
| Normanhurst School (IN/N/M) | 100.8 | 35.1 | 38.5 | 50% | 71% | |
| The Holy Family Catholic College (VA/C/M) | 101.9 | 35.0 | 41.9 | 51% | 52% | 228.7 |
| Leytonstone School (CY/C/M) | 101.6 | 33.5 | 37.7 | 48% | 47% | |
| Willowfield School (CY/C/M) | 102.8 | 33.4 | 37.7 | 41% | 42% | |
| Norlington School for Boys (CY/C/B) | 101.6 | 32.2 | 33.2 | 44% | 34% | |
| Heathcote School (CY/C/M) | 100.2 | 32.1 | 31.1 | 39% | 33% | |
| Tom Hood School (CY/C/M) | 101.4 | 31.4 | 31.5 | 45% | 42% | |
| Aveling Park School (CY/C/M) | 101.0 | 31.2 | 33.9 | 37% | 37% | |
| Kelmscott School (CY/C/M) | 100.0 | 30.5 | 30.0 | 37% | 29% | |
| Rush Croft School (CY/C/M) | 99.2 | 30.2 | 34.2 | 36% | 35% | |
| George Mitchell Community School (CY/C/M) | 100.4 | 27.1 | 27.1 | 20% | 24% | |
| Warwick School for Boys (CY/C/B) | 100.2 | 26.0 | 29.3 | 30% | 29% | |
| The McEntee School (CY/C/M) | 99.5 | 25.2 | 17.0 | 20% | 13% | |
| **WANDSWORTH** | | | | | | |
| Putney High School (IN/S/G) | | 56.2 | 62.2 | 99% | 98% | 375.4 |
| Ibstock Place (IN/S/M) | | 50.8 | 56.0 | 97% | 97% | |
| Emanuel School (IN/S/M) | | 45.9 | 53.0 | 87% | 93% | 293.6 |
| Balham Preparatory School (IN/N/M) | 105.7 | 45.0 | 25.1 | 88% | 46% | |
| ADT College (CTC/C/M) | 101.6 | 43.1 | 54.8 | 86% | 71% | 212.4 |
| Graveney School (FD/C/M) | 99.2 | 42.9 | 47.0 | 76% | 72% | 228.5 |
| Burntwood School (FD/C/G) | 99.0 | 37.9 | 44.8 | 62% | 60% | 223.6 |
| Putney Park School (IN/S/M) | 105.8 | 36.9 | 55.2 | 60% | 92% | |
| Salesian College (VA/C/B) | 103.2 | 35.1 | 39.0 | 45% | 42% | |
| Elliott School (FD/C/M) | 98.1 | 33.6 | 37.0 | 46% | 47% | 223.5 |
| Ernest Bevin College (CY/C/B) | 99.9 | 30.1 | 32.7 | 54% | 29% | 159.5 |
| Chestnut Grove School (CY/C/M) | 100.8 | 30.0 | 32.6 | 32% | 34% | 144.8 |
| John Paul II School (VA/C/M) | 101.6 | 29.2 | 32.7 | 32% | 27% | |
| Southfields Community College (FD/C/M) | 101.2 | 29.0 | 28.1 | 27% | 17% | 202 |
| Battersea Technology College (CY/C/M) | 97.5 | 20.0 | 20.4 | 14% | 17% | 81 |
| **WESTMINSTER** | | | | | | |
| Westminster School (IN/S/B) | | 61.1 | 73.8 | 100% | 98% | 451.1 |
| Francis Holland School SW1 (IN/S/G) | | 56.5 | 55.9 | 98% | 83% | 340 |
| Francis Holland School NW1 (IN/S/G) | | 53.8 | 60.6 | 97% | 97% | 375.5 |
| Queen's College London (IN/S/G) | | 48.6 | 57.0 | 93% | 95% | 317.9 |
| The St Marylebone CofE School (VA/C/G) | 103.2 | 48.0 | 56.9 | 93% | 91% | 242.1 |
| Sylvia Young Theatre School (IN/S/M) | 106.9 | 44.8 | 51.6 | 96% | 96% | |
| The Grey Coat Hospital (VA/C/G) | 99.8 | 44.3 | 52.2 | 81% | 79% | 255 |
| Lansdowne College (IN/N/M) | 98.8 | 43.6 | 27.7 | 75% | 44% | 286.1 |
| Portland Place School (IN/S/M) | 36.1 | 34.7 | 61% | 57% | 243.1 | |
| Westminster City School (VA/C/B) | 94.6 | 34.3 | 32.8 | 47% | 35% | 181.4 |
| Quintin Kynaston School (CY/C/M) | 100.9 | 29.3 | 33.1 | 38% | 33% | 189.8 |
| Pimlico School (CY/C/M) | 97.3 | 27.2 | 31.9 | 27% | 33% | 233.9 |
| St Augustine's CofE Secondary School (VA/C/M) | 99.2 | 26.6 | 27.7 | 28% | 25% | 72 |
| North Westminster Community School (CY/C/M) | 100.5 | 25.6 | 27.4 | 27% | 27% | 160.7 |
| St George RC School (VA/C/M) | 97.9 | 22.9 | 22.0 | 20% | 14% | |
| International Community School (IN/N/M) | | 19.1 | 12.9 | 21% | 12% | 216.7 |
| Bales College (IN/N/M) | | 17.5 | 23.3 | 18% | 0% | 169.6 |

## LONDON-WIDE LEAGUE TABLE

### KEY TO BOROUGH ABBREVIATIONS

| | | | | | |
|---|---|---|---|---|---|
| Barking & Dagenham | BD | Hackney | HK | Lewisham | LE |
| Barnet | BA | Hammersmith & Fulham | HS | Merton | ME |
| Bexley | BE | Haringey | HG | Newham | NE |
| Brent | BR | Harrow | HA | Redbridge | RE |
| Bromley | BO | Havering | HV | Richmond | RI |
| Camden | CA | Hillingdon | HI | Southwark | SW |
| Corporation of London | CL | Hounslow | HW | Sutton | SU |
| Croydon | CR | Islington | IS | Tower Hamlets | TH |
| Ealing | EA | Kensington & Chelsea | KE | Waltham Forest | WF |
| Enfield | EN | Kingston | KI | Wandsworth | WA |
| Greenwich | GR | Lambeth | LA | Westminister | WM |

| | BOROUGH/SCHOOL | | VALUE ADDED 02 | GCSE 02 POINTS | GCSE 01 POINTS | GCSE 02 %5 A*-C | GCSE 01 %5 A*-C | A-LEVEL 02 POINTS |
|---|---|---|---|---|---|---|---|---|
| 1 | BA | Pardes House Grammar School (IN/N/B) | 64.0 | 143.3 | 100% | 100% | | |
| 2 | HK | Tayyibah Girls' School (IN/N/G) | 102.6 | 63.8 | 59.8 | 100% | 100% | 325 |
| 3 | TH | Madni Secondary Girls' School (IN/S/G) | 101.3 | 63.5 | 64.1 | 100% | 100% | |
| 4 | HV | Raphael Independent School (IN/S/M) | 101.6 | 62.7 | 41.3 | 100% | 55% | |
| 5 | HS | St Paul's Girls' School (IN/S/G) | | 61.2 | 69.9 | 99% | 99% | 438.7 |
| 6 | WE | Westminster School (IN/S/B) | | 61.1 | 73.8 | 100% | 98% | 451.1 |
| 7 | RI | St Paul's School (IN/S/B) | | 61.0 | 76.0 | 99% | 100% | 429.4 |
| 8 | CL | City of London School for Girls (IN/S/G) | | 60.9 | 68.9 | 100% | 100% | 407.6 |
| 9 | RI | The Lady Eleanor Holles School (IN/S/G) | 60.7 | 74.6 | 100% | 100% | 492.7 | |
| 10 | HA | North London Collegiate School (IN/S/G) | 60.7 | 71.8 | 100% | 97% | 419.1 | |
| 11 | CA | South Hampstead High School (IN/S/G) | | 60.2 | 69.3 | 100% | 99% | 382.3 |
| 12 | HS | The Godolphin & Latymer School (IN/S/G) | 59.7 | 66.5 | 100% | 99% | 401.4 | |
| 13 | ME | King's College School (IN/S/B) | | 59.5 | 67.7 | 100% | 99% | 392.1 |
| 14 | SW | James Allen's Girls' School (IN/S/G) | 102.1 | 59.4 | 69.2 | 100% | 99% | 387.2 |
| 15 | BA | The Henrietta Barnett School (VA/S/G) | 100.5 | 58.9 | 79.3 | 100% | 100% | 371.9 |
| 16 | BO | Newstead Wood School for Girls (FD/S/G) | 100.5 | 58.4 | 75.0 | 100% | 99% | 383 |
| 17 | EN | The Latymer School (VA/S/M) | 105.7 | 58.4 | 66.9 | 99% | 98% | 367.5 |
| 18 | ME | Wimbledon High School (IN/S/G) | | 58.3 | 74.7 | 100% | 99% | 427.4 |
| 19 | KI | The Tiffin Girls' School (CY/S/G) | 102.3 | 58.0 | 67.9 | 100% | 99% | 375 |
| 20 | RE | Bancrofts School (IN/S/M) | | 57.9 | 62.5 | 100% | 100% | 394.3 |
| 21 | RE | Woodford County High School (CY/S/G) | 101.0 | 57.2 | 66.8 | 99% | 100% | 357.9 |
| 22 | BO | Bromley High School (IN/S/G) | | 57.0 | 61.0 | 100% | 100% | 350.3 |
| 23 | SU | Wallington High School for Girls (FD/S/G) | 102.1 | 56.9 | 68.0 | 99% | 99% | 323.5 |
| 24 | CR | Old Palace School of John Whitgift (IN/S/G) | | 56.7 | 65.1 | 97% | 99% | 403.5 |
| 25 | HI | St Helen's School (IN/S/G) | 102.1 | 56.5 | 63.4 | 98% | 99% | 376.6 |
| 26 | WE | Francis Holland School SW1 (IN/S/G) | | 56.5 | 55.9 | 98% | 83% | 340 |
| 27 | WA | Putney High School (IN/S/G) | | 56.2 | 62.2 | 99% | 98% | 375.4 |
| 28 | BO | St Olave's & St Saviour's Grammar (VA/S/B) | 98.1 | 56.2 | 60.8 | 98% | 100% | 385 |
| 29 | HG | Channing School (IN/S/G) | | 56.1 | 62.3 | 98% | 98% | 372.4 |
| 30 | BO | Eltham College (IN/S/B) | | 55.9 | 70.2 | 99% | 100% | 404.6 |
| 31 | SU | Nonsuch High School for Girls (FD/S/G) | 100.0 | 55.9 | 70.8 | 98% | 100% | 435.4 |
| 32 | HK | Yesodey Hatorah School (IN/N/M) | 104.9 | 55.9 | 56.6 | 84% | 80% | |
| 33 | KE | Lycee Francais (IN/S/M) | | 55.7 | 75.8 | 100% | 100% | 385.8 |
| 34 | CR | Croydon High School (IN/S/G) | | 55.6 | 61.5 | 100% | 100% | 366.8 |
| 35 | KI | Kingston Grammar School (IN/S/M) | | 55.5 | 66.9 | 100% | 98% | 338.4 |
| 36 | RI | Hampton School (IN/S/B) | | 55.5 | 64.3 | 98% | 98% | 464.3 |
| 37 | KI | Tiffin School (VA/S/B) | 99.2 | 55.4 | 72.0 | 99% | 100% | 341.7 |
| 38 | SU | Sutton High School (IN/S/G) | | 55.3 | 68.2 | 97% | 100% | 360 |
| 39 | CR | Whitgift School (IN/S/B) | | 55.3 | 72.1 | 96% | 99% | 378.3 |
| 40 | SW | Alleyn's School (IN/S/M) | | 55.2 | 64.9 | 99% | 99% | 437.9 |
| 41 | BA | Queen Elizabeth's School (FD/S/B) | 99.1 | 55.2 | 60.5 | 99% | 99% | 387.8 |
| 42 | SU | Wilson's School (VA/S/B) | 99.0 | 55.1 | 63.5 | 100% | 96% | 418.1 |

| | BOROUGH/SCHOOL | | VALUE ADDED 02 | GCSE 02 POINTS | GCSE 01 POINTS | GCSE 02 %5 A*-C | GCSE 01 %5 A*-C | A-LEVEL 02 POINTS |
|---|---|---|---|---|---|---|---|---|
| 43 | SU | Wallington County Grammar School (FD/S/B) | 99.6 | 55.1 | 64.8 | 100% | 98% | 388.4 |
| 44 | CR | Trinity School (IN/S/B) | | 55.1 | 63.5 | 100% | 98% | 355.8 |
| 45 | CA | University College School (IN/S/B) | | 55.1 | 61.3 | 98% | 98% | 382.3 |
| 46 | KE | Collingham (IN/S/M) | | 55.0 | 52.8 | 100% | 100% | 230.9 |
| 47 | BA | St Michael's Catholic Grammar (VA/S/G) | 103.6 | 54.8 | 73.3 | 96% | 100% | 347.3 |
| 48 | SU | Sutton Grammar School for Boys (FD/S/B) | 98.9 | 54.5 | 62.9 | 95% | 99% | 425.8 |
| 49 | EA | Notting Hill & Ealing High School (IN/S/G) | | 54.3 | 60.6 | 98% | 96% | 373.5 |
| 50 | KI | Surbiton High School (IN/S/G) | 103.9 | 54.2 | 65.1 | 99% | 100% | 372.1 |
| 51 | CL | City of London School (IN/S/B) | | 54.2 | 67.7 | 96% | 96% | 384.5 |
| 52 | SW | Dulwich College (IN/S/B) | | 53.9 | 64.2 | 97% | 96% | 393.1 |
| 53 | HS | Latymer Upper School (IN/S/B) | | 53.9 | 65.2 | 97% | 99% | 360.1 |
| 54 | WE | Francis Holland School NW1 (IN/S/G) | | 53.8 | 60.6 | 97% | 97% | 375.5 |
| 55 | BR | Brondesbury College for Boys (IN/S/B) | 101.1 | 53.7 | 49.4 | 100% | 85% | |
| 56 | HG | Highgate School (IN/S/B) | | 53.7 | 57.7 | 96% | 95% | 348.5 |
| 57 | LE | Sydenham High School GDST(IN/S/G) | | 53.4 | 55.9 | 100% | 96% | 282.1 |
| 58 | HA | The John Lyon School (IN/S/B) | | 53.3 | 61.5 | 98% | 97% | 323 |
| 59 | EN | St John's Preparatory & Senior (IN/S/M) | 104.2 | 53.2 | 54.3 | 100% | 100% | |
| 60 | BE | Townley Grammar School (CY/S/G) | 99.8 | 53.0 | 62.8 | 100% | 100% | 354.8 |
| 61 | HV | The Coopers' Company & Coborn (VA/C/M) | 100.8 | 52.9 | 63.8 | 99% | 100% | 372 |
| 62 | HI | Northwood College (IN/S/G) | | 52.9 | 63.4 | 92% | 97% | 334.6 |
| 63 | EA | St Augustine's Priory(IN/S/G) | | 52.6 | 57.9 | 100% | 92% | 300.3 |
| 64 | EN | Palmers Green High School (IN/S/G) | 102.3 | 52.5 | 58.9 | 100% | 100% | |
| 65 | WF | Forest School (IN/S/M) | 101.8 | 52.5 | 60.5 | 97% | 97% | 357.6 |
| 66 | RE | Ilford County High School (CY/S/B) | 99.2 | 52.4 | 66.4 | 98% | 98% | 323.7 |
| 67 | HS | St James Independent School (IN/N/G) | | 52.1 | 58.7 | 100% | 100% | 387.7 |
| 68 | BE | Bexley Grammar School (CY/S/M) | 99.8 | 51.8 | 51.4 | 100% | 95% | 371.1 |
| 69 | HA | Heathfield School Pinner (IN/S/G) | | 51.1 | 58.9 | 91% | 93% | 342.1 |
| 70 | BR | Al-Sadiq & Al-Zahra Schools (IN/N/M) | 100.8 | 51.1 | 57.3 | 86% | 82% | |
| 71 | CR | Croham Hurst School (IN/S/G) | | 51.0 | 57.1 | 95% | 91% | 266.8 |
| 72 | WA | Ibstock Place (IN/S/M) | | 50.8 | 56.0 | 97% | 97% | |
| 73 | BE | Chislehurst & Sidcup Grammar (CY/S/M) | 99.3 | 50.7 | 60.3 | 96% | 97% | 300.6 |
| 74 | HS | Lady Margaret School (VA/C/G) | 105.2 | 50.6 | 58.0 | 90% | 91% | 330.2 |
| 75 | LA | Streatham & Clapham High (IN/S/G) | | 50.1 | 61.4 | 94% | 92% | 362.7 |
| 76 | HA | Harrow School (IN/S/B) | | 50.0 | 55.0 | 88% | 85% | 379.6 |
| 77 | BR | Islamia Girls' High School (IN/S/G) | 100.1 | 49.9 | 70.2 | 95% | 100% | |
| 78 | BO | Babington House School (IN/N/G) | | 49.7 | 46.5 | 100% | 82% | |
| 79 | BR | The Swaminarayan School (IN/S/M) | 106.3 | 49.6 | 55.0 | 92% | 81% | 216.9 |
| 80 | CR | Coloma Convent Girls' School (VA/C/G) | 100.6 | 49.6 | 58.0 | 89% | 91% | 305.8 |
| 81 | EA | St Benedict's School (IN/S/B) | 100.9 | 49.2 | 51.4 | 92% | 87% | 303.3 |
| 82 | GR | Blackheath High School (IN/S/G) | | 49.1 | 59.4 | 92% | 94% | 294.6 |
| 83 | BA | Hasmonean High School (VA/C/M) | 104.3 | 49.1 | 56.3 | 87% | 84% | 311.1 |
| 84 | CA | North Bridge House School (IN/S/M) | | 48.8 | 52.1 | 92% | 85% | |
| 85 | HV | Sacred Heart of Mary Girls' School (VA/C/G) | 100.3 | 48.8 | 57.5 | 91% | 90% | 336.6 |
| 86 | GR | Colfes School (IN/S/M) | | 48.7 | 57.1 | 92% | 93% | 380.2 |
| 87 | WE | Queen's College London (IN/S/G) | | 48.6 | 57.0 | 93% | 95% | 317.9 |
| 88 | KE | Queen's Gate School (IN/S/G) | | 48.5 | 52.0 | 86% | 94% | 353.9 |
| 89 | KE | The Cardinal Vaughan Memorial RC (VA/C/B) | 101.2 | 48.4 | 58.5 | 89% | 86% | 301.2 |
| 90 | HA | Peterborough & St Margaret's (IN/S/G) | 48.1 | 54.5 | 89% | 88% | | |
| 91 | WE | The St Marylebone CofE School (VA/C/G) | 103.2 | 48.0 | 56.9 | 93% | 91% | 242.1 |
| 92 | BE | Beths Grammar School for Boys (FD/S/B) | 96.9 | 47.7 | 65.8 | 95% | 100% | 337.9 |
| 93 | HS | Sacred Heart High School (VA/C/G) | 103.7 | 47.7 | 56.6 | 88% | 84% | |
| 94 | BA | Mill Hill High School (FD/C/M) | 103.3 | 47.7 | 53.8 | 84% | 71% | 296.7 |
| 95 | HS | The London Oratory School (VA/C/B) | 99.7 | 47.4 | 57.2 | 88% | 89% | 305.8 |
| 96 | BO | Holy Trinity College (IN/N/G) | | 47.2 | 58.8 | 92% | 88% | 270 |
| 97 | BA | St Martha's Senior School (IN/N/G) | | 47.1 | 53.9 | 94% | 91% | 337.1 |
| 98 | LE | St Dunstan's College (IN/S/M) | | 47.0 | 56.4 | 89% | 95% | 340.5 |
| 99 | BA | King Alfred School (IN/N/M) | | 47.0 | 47.2 | 87% | 81% | 345.7 |
| 100 | BA | Beth Jacob Grammar School (IN/N/G) | | 47.0 | 48.0 | 83% | 87% | 229.6 |
| 101 | BO | Bishop Challoner School (IN/N/M) | 99.7 | 46.9 | 41.7 | 89% | 46% | 266 |

| | | BOROUGH/SCHOOL | VALUE ADDED 02 | GCSE 02 POINTS | GCSE 01 POINTS | GCSE 02 %5 A*-C | GCSE 01 %5 A*-C | A-LEVEL 02 POINTS |
|---|---|---|---|---|---|---|---|---|
| 102 | RE | Park School for Girls (IN/S/G) | | 46.8 | 48.1 | 86% | 92% | 240.7 |
| 103 | BA | Menorah Grammar School (IN/S/B) | | 46.5 | 41.2 | 89% | 71% | 331.7 |
| 104 | RE | Ilford Ursuline High School (VA/C/G) | 103.1 | 46.5 | 54.9 | 82% | 77% | 294.6 |
| 105 | BO | Bullers Wood School (FD/C/G) | 100.5 | 46.3 | 47.7 | 84% | 73% | 341.2 |
| 106 | RI | St James Independent School (IN/S/B) | | 46.1 | 56.7 | 83% | 96% | 271.3 |
| 107 | KE | More House School (IN/S/G) | | 46.0 | 57.0 | 82% | 97% | 281.4 |
| 108 | WA | Emanuel School (IN/S/M) | | 45.9 | 53.0 | 87% | 93% | 293.6 |
| 109 | SU | St Philomena's School (VA/C/G) | 104.5 | 45.9 | 53.4 | 84% | 75% | 252.7 |
| 110 | CA | Royal School Hampstead (IN/S/G) | 105.1 | 45.7 | 55.6 | 74% | 92% | 243 |
| 111 | CR | Harris City Technology College (CTC/C/M) | 99.6 | 45.4 | 53.1 | 91% | 88% | 208 |
| 112 | WA | Balham Preparatory School (IN/N/M) | 105.7 | 45.0 | 25.1 | 88% | 46% | |
| 113 | EA | Tutorial College of West London (IN/N/M) | 106.1 | 44.9 | 52.2 | 100% | 100% | 277.8 |
| 114 | WE | Sylvia Young Theatre School (IN/S/M) | 106.9 | 44.8 | 51.6 | 96% | 96% | |
| 115 | IS | Italia Conti Academy of Theatre Arts (IN/S/M) | 105.7 | 44.8 | 47.0 | 95% | 81% | 105 |
| 116 | RE | Trinity Catholic High School (VA/C/M) | 104.4 | 44.8 | 49.9 | 81% | 85% | 258.2 |
| 117 | HA | Buckingham College School (IN/S/B) | | 44.8 | 48.5 | 73% | 75% | 277.9 |
| 118 | BR | JFS (VA/C/M) | 104.8 | 44.7 | 49.8 | 75% | 75% | 299.2 |
| 119 | LE | Prendergast School (VA/C/G) | 104.6 | 44.7 | 49.0 | 75% | 72% | 249.8 |
| 120 | BO | Langley Park School for Girls (FD/C/G) | 101.3 | 44.6 | 52.2 | 79% | 81% | 239.9 |
| 121 | LE | Haberdashers' Aske's Hatcham (CTC/C/M) | 99.3 | 44.5 | 49.6 | 79% | 73% | 318.3 |
| 122 | RI | St Catherine's School (IN/S/G) | | 44.4 | 52.2 | 85% | 81% | |
| 123 | EA | Harvington School (IN/S/G) | 99.3 | 44.3 | 48.4 | 83% | 77% | |
| 124 | WE | The Grey Coat Hospital (VA/C/G) | 99.8 | 44.3 | 52.2 | 81% | 79% | 255 |
| 125 | CR | Archbishop Tenison's CofE High (VA/C/M) | 99.2 | 44.2 | 46.2 | 80% | 68% | 280.5 |
| 126 | CR | BRIT School for Performing Arts (CTC/C/M) | 107.5 | 44.0 | 40.0 | 87% | 53% | 118.6 |
| 127 | KI | Tolworth Girls' School (CY/C/G) | 101.4 | 43.9 | 44.4 | 75% | 73% | 228.6 |
| 128 | CR | St Andrew's CofE Voluntary Aided (VA/C/M) | 98.6 | 43.7 | 45.8 | 75% | 64% | |
| 129 | RE | Cranbrook College (IN/S/B) | 101.7 | 43.6 | 50.8 | 88% | 91% | |
| 130 | HW | The Arts Educational School (IN/S/M) | 105.1 | 43.6 | 49.8 | 76% | 75% | |
| 131 | WE | Lansdowne College (IN/N/M) | 98.8 | 43.6 | 27.7 | 75% | 44% | 286.1 |
| 132 | HI | Guru Nanak Sikh Secondary (VA/C/M) | 102.6 | 43.6 | 45.2 | 75% | 70% | 200 |
| 133 | RE | Seven Kings High School (CY/C/M) | 101.8 | 43.5 | 53.8 | 80% | 81% | 296.4 |
| 134 | RI | Waldegrave School (CY/C/G) | 101.8 | 43.4 | 51.2 | 75% | 75% | |
| 135 | BO | Langley Park School for Boys (FD/C/B) | 99.2 | 43.3 | 49.8 | 81% | 68% | 282.8 |
| 136 | NE | St Angela's Ursuline Convent (VA/C/G) | 103.5 | 43.2 | 49.4 | 74% | 69% | 243.4 |
| 137 | WA | ADT College (CTC/C/M) | 101.6 | 43.1 | 54.8 | 86% | 71% | 212.4 |
| 138 | HI | Bishop Ramsey CofE VA (VA/C/M) | 99.5 | 43.1 | 45.7 | 81% | 68% | 282.5 |
| 139 | WA | Graveney School (FD/C/M) | 99.2 | 42.9 | 47.0 | 76% | 72% | 228.5 |
| 140 | BA | The Mount School (IN/S/G) | | 42.8 | 58.0 | 84% | 97% | 308.5 |
| 141 | HV | Hall Mead School (CY/C/M) | 104.1 | 42.8 | 52.2 | 80% | 75% | |
| 142 | CA | La Sainte Union Catholic (VA/C/G) | 102.1 | 42.8 | 47.9 | 79% | 70% | 248.8 |
| 143 | EA | The Cardinal Wiseman RC School (VA/C/M) | 104.0 | 42.7 | 44.2 | 76% | 60% | 214.6 |
| 144 | HW | St Mark's Catholic School (VA/C/M) | 101.1 | 42.6 | 49.0 | 71% | 65% | 227.3 |
| 145 | NE | St Bonaventure's RC School (VA/C/B) | 104.2 | 42.3 | 49.5 | 74% | 74% | 233.5 |
| 146 | HA | Park High School (CY/C/M) | 103.8 | 42.2 | 47.1 | 74% | 66% | |
| 147 | SU | The John Fisher School (VA/C/B) | 98.3 | 42.1 | 51.2 | 76% | 74% | 236.1 |
| 148 | HW | Gumley House RC Convent (VA/C/G) | 100.5 | 42.1 | 47.8 | 74% | 68% | 254.5 |
| 149 | KI | Richard Challoner School (VA/C/B) | 104.3 | 42.1 | 48.1 | 73% | 62% | 230.7 |
| 150 | EA | Twyford CofE High School (VA/C/M) | 103.0 | 42.1 | 49.2 | 72% | 68% | 296.2 |
| 151 | HV | The Campion School (VA/C/B) | 99.9 | 42.0 | 54.9 | 73% | 83% | 280.3 |
| 152 | RE | Beal High School (CY/C/M) | 102.0 | 42.0 | 51.4 | 72% | 76% | 235 |
| 153 | RI | The Harrodian School (IN/S/M) | | 41.9 | 34.0 | 70% | 71% | |
| 154 | CA | St Margaret's School (IN/S/G) | 106.7 | 41.8 | 48.2 | 85% | 83% | |
| 155 | WF | Connaught School for Girls (CY/C/G) | 104.2 | 41.8 | 46.1 | 64% | 59% | |
| 156 | EA | The Ellen Wilkinson School (FD/C/G) | 101.7 | 41.5 | 47.2 | 70% | 63% | 231.3 |
| 157 | GR | St Thomas More RC (VA/C/M) | 100.5 | 41.5 | 50.5 | 67% | 69% | |
| 158 | HS | Holborn College (IN/S/M) | 105.8 | 41.4 | 34.3 | 70% | 50% | 370 |
| 159 | BR | Claremont High School (FD/C/M) | 102.8 | 41.4 | 47.3 | 69% | 62% | 257.2 |
| 160 | BA | Copthall School (CY/C/G) | 100.3 | 41.3 | 46.1 | 71% | 66% | 308 |

| | BOROUGH/SCHOOL | | VALUE ADDED 02 | GCSE 02 POINTS | GCSE 01 POINTS | GCSE 02 %5 A*-C | GCSE 01 %5 A*-C | A-LEVEL 02 POINTS |
|---|---|---|---|---|---|---|---|---|
| 161 | RE | King Solomon High School (VA/C/M) | 102.2 | 41.3 | 53.1 | 68% | 76% | 249.1 |
| 162 | BA | Ashmole School (FD/C/M) | 102.7 | 41.2 | 45.8 | 69% | 65% | 252.3 |
| 163 | HW | The Green School (VA/C/G) | 101.1 | 41.2 | 50.2 | 65% | 73% | 226.4 |
| 164 | RI | The Royal Ballet School (IN/S/M) | 94.3 | 41.1 | 45.4 | 88% | 88% | 97.4 |
| 165 | HW | The Heathland School (CY/C/M) | 102.7 | 41.0 | 49.5 | 66% | 64% | 235.2 |
| 166 | CR | Virgo Fidelis Convent Senior School (VA/C/G) | 99.5 | 40.9 | 41.7 | 66% | 66% | 164.4 |
| 167 | SW | Notre Dame RC Girls' School (VA/C/G) | 102.8 | 40.7 | 44.7 | 66% | 55% | |
| 168 | CA | The Camden School for Girls (VA/C/G) | 103.6 | 40.7 | 52.8 | 61% | 74% | 282 |
| 169 | BO | Farringtons & Stratford House (IN/N/G) | | 40.6 | 46.8 | 69% | 62% | 257.6 |
| 170 | HG | Fortismere School (CY/C/M) | 99.5 | 40.6 | 48.2 | 67% | 69% | 275.8 |
| 171 | BE | St Catherine's RC School for Girls (VA/C/G) | 101.7 | 40.6 | 45.1 | 66% | 64% | 244.5 |
| 172 | HI | Vyners School (FD/C/M) | 97.7 | 40.6 | 46.9 | 64% | 61% | 259.4 |
| 173 | WF | Highams Park School (VA/C/M) | 101.0 | 40.6 | 46.6 | 62% | 66% | 219.8 |
| 174 | ME | Ursuline High School Wimbledon (VA/C/G) | 102.5 | 40.5 | 44.4 | 71% | 64% | 280 |
| 175 | EN | Enfield County School (CY/C/G) | 100.9 | 40.5 | 47.5 | 68% | 77% | 219.4 |
| 176 | RE | Valentines High School (CY/C/M) | 104.8 | 40.5 | 43.9 | 67% | 56% | 237.6 |
| 177 | SU | Overton Grange School (CY/C/M) | 99.7 | 40.5 | | 66% | | |
| 178 | BA | Mill Hill School Foundation (IN/S/M) | | 40.4 | 43.7 | 81% | 80% | 307.9 |
| 179 | EN | Southgate School (CY/C/M) | 102.1 | 40.4 | 44.3 | 64% | 69% | 205.9 |
| 180 | ME | Wimbledon College (VA/C/B) | 101.2 | 40.3 | 42.1 | 65% | 56% | 281 |
| 181 | BO | Darrick Wood School (FD/C/M) | 99.6 | 40.2 | 47.1 | 66% | 63% | 240.5 |
| 182 | BR | Preston Manor High School (FD/C/M) | 99.5 | 40.2 | 44.0 | 65% | 68% | 238.5 |
| 183 | WF | Walthamstow School for Girls (CY/C/G) | 106.1 | 40.2 | 45.3 | 61% | 63% | |
| 184 | HV | St Edward's CofE Comprehensive (VA/C/M) | 100.0 | 40.0 | 51.5 | 67% | 71% | 235 |
| 185 | HA | Nower Hill High School (CY/C/M) | 100.2 | 40.0 | 46.0 | 66% | 64% | |
| 186 | KE | Hellenic College of London (IN/S/M) | | 39.9 | 65.6 | 80% | 100% | 275.5 |
| 187 | HV | The Sanders Draper School (CY/C/M) | 102.5 | 39.9 | 47.2 | 65% | 67% | |
| 188 | HI | Queensmead School (FD/C/M) | 102.7 | 39.9 | 43.4 | 60% | 55% | 249.7 |
| 189 | HA | Hatch End High School (CY/C/M) | 100.4 | 39.8 | 46.3 | 68% | 63% | |
| 190 | RI | Grey Court School (CY/C/M) | 99.9 | 39.8 | 44.3 | 63% | 57% | |
| 191 | CR | Norbury Manor High School (FD/C/G) | 103.0 | 39.8 | 44.8 | 53% | 58% | |
| 192 | EN | St Ignatius College (VA/C/B) | 100.7 | 39.6 | 47.0 | 63% | 67% | 246.5 |
| 193 | EA | King Fahad Academy (IN/N/M) | 98.1 | 39.5 | 42.4 | 62% | 63% | 234.8 |
| 194 | BO | Ravens Wood School (FD/C/B) | 98.3 | 39.3 | 45.6 | 72% | 56% | 270.8 |
| 195 | BA | Queen Elizabeth's Girls' School (CY/C/G) | 99.4 | 39.3 | 47.7 | 66% | 75% | 266.8 |
| 196 | SW | St Saviour's & St Olave's CofE (VA/C/G) | 101.5 | 39.3 | 38.4 | 59% | 40% | 167.1 |
| 197 | CR | Riddlesdown High School (VA/C/M) | 100.1 | 39.2 | 47.8 | 65% | 60% | |
| 198 | BR | Kingsbury High School (FD/C/M) | 101.9 | 39.2 | 41.3 | 63% | 55% | 230 |
| 199 | BE | Blackfen School for Girls (CY/C/G) | 101.9 | 39.2 | 40.5 | 61% | 61% | 198.4 |
| 200 | EA | Drayton Manor High School (FD/C/M) | 98.9 | 39.1 | 43.5 | 65% | 55% | 212.5 |
| 201 | KE | Saint Thomas More RC School (VA/C/M) | 102.7 | 39.1 | 45.1 | 61% | 62% | |
| 202 | WF | Chingford Foundation School (FD/C/M) | 101.5 | 39.1 | 40.6 | 58% | 54% | 202.6 |
| 203 | BD | All Saints Catholic School & Tech (VA/C/M) | 103.1 | 39.0 | 42.8 | 68% | 51% | 203.5 |
| 204 | HA | Whitmore High School (CY/C/M) | 103.9 | 39.0 | 43.5 | 66% | 57% | |
| 205 | BO | Hayes School (FD/C/M) | 97.4 | 39.0 | 43.8 | 62% | 65% | 237.9 |
| 206 | CR | Lodge School (IN/N/G) | 106.4 | 38.7 | 52.5 | 72% | 85% | 238.3 |
| 207 | BO | Beaverwood School for Girls (FD/C/G) | 100.9 | 38.7 | 40.2 | 64% | 55% | 191.7 |
| 208 | EA | Ealing College Upper School (IN/N/B) | 102.9 | 38.6 | 42.8 | 65% | 63% | 219.4 |
| 209 | BR | Convent of Jesus & Mary Language (VA/C/G) | 102.4 | 38.6 | 43.8 | 65% | 63% | 205.8 |
| 210 | RE | The Chadwell Heath Foundation (FD/C/M) | 103.4 | 38.6 | 42.5 | 65% | 65% | 187.3 |
| 211 | BA | Finchley Catholic High School (VA/C/B) | 100.0 | 38.5 | 42.5 | 68% | 60% | 200 |
| 212 | HA | The Sacred Heart RC High School (VA/C/G) | 96.7 | 38.5 | 45.3 | 64% | 56% | |
| 213 | LA | La Retraite RC Girls' School (VA/C/G) | 103.7 | 38.4 | 45.8 | 61% | 55% | 193.8 |
| 214 | HW | Heston Community School (CY/C/M) | 102.0 | 38.4 | 38.9 | 57% | 51% | 207 |
| 215 | HK | Our Lady's Convent RC High (VA/C/G) | 98.0 | 38.4 | 51.5 | 54% | 63% | 233.9 |
| 216 | EA | Barbara Speake Stage School (IN/S/M) | 97.7 | 38.4 | 36.0 | 43% | 69% | |
| 217 | KI | Coombe Girls' School (CY/C/G) | 100.9 | 38.3 | 45.0 | 60% | 58% | 220.3 |
| 218 | NE | Plashet School (CY/C/G) | 106.9 | 38.3 | 45.8 | 56% | 59% | |
| 219 | BA | Christ's College (CY/C/B) | 102.3 | 38.3 | 39.8 | 55% | 57% | 213.7 |

| | BOROUGH/SCHOOL | VALUE ADDED 02 | GCSE 02 POINTS | GCSE 01 POINTS | GCSE 02 %5 A*-C | GCSE 01 %5 A*-C | A-LEVEL 02 POINTS |
|---|---|---|---|---|---|---|---|
| 220 EN | Enfield Grammar School (FD/C/B) | 97.6 | 38.2 | 44.6 | 60% | 53% | 227.1 |
| 221 KE | Mander Portman Woodward (IN/S/M) | | 38.1 | 43.8 | 73% | 69% | 242.2 |
| 222 HV | Gaynes School (CY/C/M) | 97.4 | 38.1 | 43.0 | 59% | 60% | |
| 223 CR | Woodcote High School (CY/C/M) | 99.1 | 38.1 | 40.9 | 57% | 56% | |
| 224 GR | St Ursula's Convent School (VA/C/G) | 99.1 | 38.1 | 47.4 | 50% | 66% | |
| 225 RI | Orleans Park School (CY/C/M) | 100.2 | 38.0 | 40.2 | 64% | 59% | |
| 226 EN | St Anne's Catholic High School (VA/C/G) | 102.0 | 38.0 | 41.3 | 63% | 58% | 252.7 |
| 227 CR | Shirley High School (FD/C/M) | 98.8 | 38.0 | 41.9 | 56% | 53% | |
| 228 WA | Burntwood School (FD/C/G) | 99.0 | 37.9 | 44.8 | 62% | 60% | 223.6 |
| 229 HI | Swakeleys School (FD/C/G) | 100.2 | 37.9 | 42.5 | 58% | 62% | 255.5 |
| 230 HV | The Frances Bardsley School (FD/C/G) | 98.1 | 37.8 | 47.4 | 58% | 64% | 263.9 |
| 231 EA | Greenford High School (FD/C/M) | 101.9 | 37.8 | 43.7 | 56% | 60% | 223 |
| 232 CR | St Joseph's College (VA/C/B) | 99.1 | 37.7 | 41.5 | 58% | 53% | 177.7 |
| 233 HI | Haydon School (FD/C/M) | 99.2 | 37.7 | 47.8 | 56% | 68% | 262.2 |
| 234 SU | Greenshaw High School (CY/C/M) | 99.3 | 37.7 | 43.6 | 52% | 51% | 223 |
| 235 BA | Hendon School (FD/C/M) | 97.3 | 37.6 | 42.3 | 58% | 57% | 247.7 |
| 236 BA | The Compton School (CY/C/M) | 102.1 | 37.6 | 38.1 | 57% | 53% | |
| 237 LA | Dunraven School (FD/C/M) | 99.6 | 37.6 | 39.5 | 55% | 43% | |
| 238 KE | Sion-Manning RC School for Girls (VA/C/G) | 103.6 | 37.5 | 42.4 | 55% | 52% | |
| 239 SW | Bacon's College (CTC/C/M) | 99.9 | 37.5 | 47.1 | 54% | 72% | 209.3 |
| 240 HW | Gunnersbury Catholic School (VA/C/B) | 96.5 | 37.4 | 40.3 | 59% | 58% | 255.5 |
| 241 RI | Teddington School (CY/C/M) | 97.6 | 37.4 | 46.2 | 55% | 72% | |
| 242 BA | East Barnet School (CY/C/M) | 98.1 | 37.2 | 40.2 | 58% | 51% | 225.3 |
| 243 SW | The St Thomas the Apostle College (VA/C/B) | 100.4 | 37.1 | 42.8 | 53% | 53% | |
| 244 TH | Mulberry School for Girls (CY/C/G) | 108.5 | 37.1 | 44.1 | 52% | 54% | 167.2 |
| 245 RE | Canon Palmer Catholic School (VA/C/M) | 100.1 | 37.0 | 43.8 | 62% | 56% | 227.2 |
| 246 HV | The Albany School (CY/C/M) | 99.8 | 37.0 | 47.4 | 59% | 54% | |
| 247 LA | Archbishop Tenison's School (VA/C/B) | 104.1 | 37.0 | 35.5 | 56% | 35% | 149.2 |
| 248 KI | The Holy Cross School (VA/C/G) | 99.1 | 37.0 | 48.8 | 55% | 65% | 222.5 |
| 249 WA | Putney Park School (IN/S/M) | 105.8 | 36.9 | 55.2 | 60% | 92% | |
| 250 SW | Sacred Heart RC Secondary (VA/C/M) | 99.4 | 36.9 | 40.9 | 56% | 63% | |
| 251 BR | St Gregory's RC High School (VA/C/M) | 97.7 | 36.8 | 42.9 | 61% | 55% | 214 |
| 252 IS | Mount Carmel RC Technology (VA/C/G) | 104.7 | 36.8 | 35.2 | 58% | 35% | |
| 253 TH | Oaklands School (CY/C/M) | 106.1 | 36.8 | 37.9 | 57% | 41% | |
| 254 HA | Salvatorian RC College (VA/C/B) | 96.2 | 36.8 | 40.0 | 51% | 58% | |
| 255 EA | Villiers High School (CY/C/M) | 104.7 | 36.7 | 41.7 | 54% | 48% | |
| 256 LA | St Martin in the Fields High School (VA/C/G) | 103.1 | 36.5 | 41.0 | 59% | 54% | |
| 257 RE | Loxford School of Science & Tech (CY/C/M) | 107.1 | 36.5 | 41.5 | 52% | 51% | 213.3 |
| 258 TH | Morpeth School (CY/C/M) | 107.9 | 36.4 | 42.4 | 54% | 50% | |
| 259 HI | Bishopshalt School (FD/C/M) | 99.9 | 36.4 | 40.4 | 52% | 58% | 242.5 |
| 260 GR | St Paul's Catholic School (VA/C/M) | 101.6 | 36.4 | 41.3 | 46% | 52% | |
| 261 NE | Sarah Bonnell School (CY/C/G) | 104.2 | 36.4 | 37.5 | 46% | 43% | |
| 262 NE | Stratford School (FD/C/M) | 103.5 | 36.4 | 38.5 | 46% | 40% | |
| 263 HV | Immanuel School (IN/N/M) | | 36.3 | 43.3 | 58% | 63% | |
| 264 CA | Parliament Hill School (CY/C/G) | 100.3 | 36.3 | 36.1 | 53% | 47% | 282.8 |
| 265 BO | Coopers School (FD/C/M) | 96.5 | 36.2 | 41.8 | 53% | 55% | 234.5 |
| 266 HK | Beis Malka Girls' School (IN/N/G) | | 36.1 | 32.6 | 65% | 58% | |
| 267 WE | Portland Place School (IN/S/M) | | 36.1 | 34.7 | 61% | 57% | 243.1 |
| 268 BA | Woodside Park International School (IN/S/M) | | 36.1 | 37.8 | 53% | 50% | |
| 269 SU | Cheam High School (FD/C/M) | 100.4 | 36.1 | 40.1 | 50% | 47% | 176.4 |
| 270 HV | Abbs Cross School (FD/C/M) | 100.6 | 36.1 | 44.0 | 49% | 60% | |
| 271 LE | Bonus Pastor RC School (VA/C/M) | 103.5 | 36.1 | 41.8 | 49% | 57% | |
| 272 KE | Davies Laing & Dick College (IN/S/M) | | 36.0 | 34.0 | 76% | 65% | 272.4 |
| 273 RE | Wanstead High School (CY/C/M) | 101.5 | 36.0 | 37.3 | 51% | 51% | 219.5 |
| 274 HW | Isleworth & Syon School for Boys (VC/C/B) | 97.6 | 35.9 | 36.6 | 56% | 46% | 219.1 |
| 275 TH | Raine's Foundation School (VA/C/M) | 99.3 | 35.9 | 36.6 | 48% | 39% | 253.9 |
| 276 RE | Woodbridge High School (CY/C/M) | 103.2 | 35.7 | 42.7 | 53% | 55% | 205.1 |
| 277 HV | The Chafford School (CY/C/M) | 99.8 | 35.7 | 34.2 | 53% | 42% | |
| 278 HA | Bentley Wood High School (CY/C/G) | 101.1 | 35.6 | 44.0 | 56% | 66% | |

| | BOROUGH/SCHOOL | | VALUE ADDED 02 | GCSE 02 POINTS | GCSE 01 POINTS | GCSE 02 %5 A*-C | GCSE 01 %5 A*-C | A-LEVEL 02 POINTS |
|---|---|---|---|---|---|---|---|---|
| 279 | BO | Charles Darwin School (FD/C/M) | 99.7 | 35.5 | 40.5 | 58% | 56% | 220.3 |
| 280 | LA | London Nautical School (FD/C/B) | 94.8 | 35.5 | 35.8 | 47% | 45% | 167 |
| 281 | CA | William Ellis School (VA/C/B) | 98.1 | 35.3 | 38.5 | 51% | 47% | 245.7 |
| 282 | BD | Barking Abbey Comprehensive (CY/C/M) | 99.9 | 35.2 | 44.5 | 54% | 64% | 218.3 |
| 283 | HG | Hornsey Secondary School (CY/C/G) | 101.9 | 35.2 | 39.4 | 52% | 44% | 164.9 |
| 284 | CR | Edenham High School (FD/C/M) | 98.8 | 35.2 | 42.1 | 52% | 60% | |
| 285 | HV | Brittons School & Technology College (CY/C/M) | 99.0 | 35.2 | 38.2 | 49% | 48% | |
| 286 | HK | Haggerston School (CY/C/G) | 106.9 | 35.2 | 33.4 | 41% | 35% | |
| 287 | WF | Normanhurst School (IN/N/M) | 100.8 | 35.1 | 38.5 | 50% | 71% | |
| 288 | WA | Salesian College (VA/C/B) | 103.2 | 35.1 | 39.0 | 45% | 42% | |
| 289 | WF | The Holy Family Catholic College (VA/C/M) | 101.9 | 35.0 | 41.9 | 51% | 52% | 228.7 |
| 290 | RE | Caterham High School (CY/C/M) | 101.2 | 35.0 | 42.0 | 49% | 53% | 211 |
| 291 | CR | Royal Russell School (IN/S/M) | | 34.8 | 34.6 | 64% | 59% | 259.3 |
| 292 | BA | St James' Catholic High School (VA/C/M) | 97.5 | 34.8 | 40.4 | 48% | 52% | 269.4 |
| 293 | HW | International School of London (IN/N/M) | | 34.7 | 41.9 | 73% | 63% | |
| 294 | HA | Canons High School (CY/C/M) | 102.5 | 34.7 | 38.1 | 48% | 43% | |
| 295 | CA | Hampstead School (CY/C/M) | 98.5 | 34.6 | 37.2 | 50% | 44% | 234 |
| 296 | GR | Thomas Tallis School (CY/C/M) | 102.7 | 34.5 | 44.1 | 41% | 48% | 233.6 |
| 297 | TH | Sir John Cass Foundation (VA/C/M) | 109.8 | 34.4 | 36.4 | 69% | 36% | 126 |
| 298 | BE | Hurstmere Foundation School (FD/C/B) | 99.3 | 34.4 | 32.9 | 52% | 35% | |
| 299 | EN | Winchmore School (CY/C/M) | 101.9 | 34.4 | 38.8 | 47% | 48% | 184 |
| 300 | BO | Kemnal Technology College (FD/C/B) | 102.7 | 34.3 | 37.5 | 56% | 37% | 151 |
| 301 | EN | Broomfield School (FD/C/M) | 101.0 | 34.3 | 42.6 | 50% | 54% | 191.8 |
| 302 | BD | Robert Clack School (CY/C/M) | 101.5 | 34.3 | 34.6 | 47% | 39% | 253.5 |
| 303 | WE | Westminster City School (VA/C/B) | 94.6 | 34.3 | 32.8 | 47% | 35% | 181.4 |
| 304 | HK | Cardinal Pole RC School (VA/C/M) | 101.8 | 34.3 | 39.4 | 40% | 46% | 163.2 |
| 305 | TH | Central Foundation Girls' School (VC/C/G) | 104.8 | 34.2 | 39.1 | 42% | 46% | 162.6 |
| 306 | EN | Edmonton County School (CY/C/M) | 99.9 | 34.1 | 36.9 | 45% | 40% | 178.7 |
| 307 | TH | Stepney Green School (CY/C/B) | 104.7 | 34.0 | 33.5 | 49% | 37% | |
| 308 | CA | Acland Burghley School (CY/C/M) | 101.4 | 33.9 | 37.0 | 48% | 49% | 251 |
| 309 | TH | Swanlea School (CY/C/M) | 105.0 | 33.9 | 36.1 | 44% | 38% | |
| 310 | SU | Carshalton High School for Girls (CY/C/G) | 97.6 | 33.8 | 40.0 | 48% | 48% | 220.6 |
| 311 | BO | Baston School (IN/N/G) | 103.1 | 33.7 | 55.0 | 60% | 89% | |
| 312 | HA | Rooks Heath High School (CY/C/M) | 101.8 | 33.7 | 39.0 | 49% | 53% | |
| 313 | BE | St Columba's Catholic Boys' (VA/C/B) | 98.7 | 33.6 | 37.4 | 57% | 42% | 195.9 |
| 314 | WA | Elliott School (FD/C/M) | 98.1 | 33.6 | 37.0 | 46% | 47% | 223.5 |
| 315 | HW | Cranford Community College (CY/C/M) | 99.1 | 33.6 | 34.2 | 44% | 37% | 163.2 |
| 316 | WF | Leytonstone School (CY/C/M) | 101.6 | 33.5 | 37.7 | 48% | 47% | |
| 317 | IS | Highbury Fields School (CY/C/G) | 102.4 | 33.5 | 38.6 | 45% | 50% | 133.2 |
| 318 | HW | Lampton School (CY/C/M) | 101.1 | 33.5 | 37.8 | 44% | 46% | 223.7 |
| 319 | ME | Ricards Lodge High School (CY/C/G) | 101.2 | 33.4 | 45.2 | 52% | 63% | |
| 320 | RI | Hampton Community College (CY/C/M) | 100.6 | 33.4 | 38.1 | 46% | 45% | |
| 321 | NE | Langdon School (CY/C/M) | 102.4 | 33.4 | 42.7 | 41% | 43% | |
| 322 | WF | Willowfield School (CY/C/M) | 102.8 | 33.4 | 37.7 | 41% | 42% | |
| 323 | EA | Northolt High School (FD/C/M) | 97.3 | 33.3 | 37.8 | 47% | 38% | 229.2 |
| 324 | EN | Bishop Stopford's School (VA/C/M) | 97.3 | 33.2 | 43.3 | 45% | 48% | 185 |
| 325 | HI | Northwood School (FD/C/M) | 95.7 | 33.2 | 38.6 | 43% | 43% | 233.1 |
| 326 | CR | Coulsdon High School (FD/C/M) | 98.2 | 33.0 | 37.8 | 44% | 42% | |
| 327 | LE | Sydenham School (CY/C/G) | 102.7 | 32.9 | 38.2 | 49% | 47% | 194.9 |
| 328 | BE | Trinity School, Belvedere (VA/C/M) | 100.4 | 32.9 | 36.2 | 43% | 33% | 220 |
| 329 | GR | Eltham Hill Technology College (CY/C/G) | 102.4 | 32.9 | 34.8 | 42% | 41% | 172.2 |
| 330 | CA | Maria Fidelis RC Convent School (VA/C/G) | 99.2 | 32.8 | 39.4 | 43% | 41% | 197.9 |
| 331 | KI | Canbury School (IN/S/M) | | 32.7 | 28.3 | 45% | 38% | |
| 332 | HV | Marshalls Park School (CY/C/M) | 94.4 | 32.5 | 32.0 | 53% | 29% | |
| 333 | RE | Mayfield School & College (CY/C/M) | 102.1 | 32.5 | 38.1 | 46% | 44% | 206.3 |
| 334 | KI | Southborough School (CY/C/B) | 98.0 | 32.5 | 31.2 | 46% | 34% | 120 |
| 335 | BO | St John Rigby Catholic College (VA/C/M) | 93.1 | 32.5 | 33.8 | 39% | 32% | 138.8 |
| 336 | BO | The Ravensbourne School (FD/C/M) | 100.0 | 32.4 | 35.6 | 43% | 39% | 174.9 |
| 337 | EA | Featherstone High School (CY/C/M) | 105.6 | 32.4 | 43.7 | 39% | 50% | |

| | BOROUGH/SCHOOL | | VALUE ADDED 02 | GCSE 02 POINTS | GCSE 01 POINTS | GCSE 02 %5 A*-C | GCSE 01 %5 A*-C | A-LEVEL 02 POINTS |
|---|---|---|---|---|---|---|---|---|
| 338 | CR | Thomas More School (VA/C/M) | 99.4 | 32.4 | 32.1 | 36% | 28% | |
| 339 | TH | Bishop Challoner RC School (VA/C/G) | 100.9 | 32.3 | 36.4 | 48% | 38% | 152.7 |
| 340 | TH | St Paul's Way Community School (CY/C/M) | 107.5 | 32.3 | 32.1 | 41% | 23% | |
| 341 | HK | Stoke Newington School Media (CY/C/M) | 101.7 | 32.3 | 41.3 | 40% | 49% | |
| 342 | BA | Christ Church CofE Secondary (VA/C/M) | 99.8 | 32.3 | 34.0 | 38% | 34% | |
| 343 | WF | Norlington School for Boys (CY/C/B) | 101.6 | 32.2 | 33.2 | 44% | 34% | |
| 344 | BD | The Warren School (CY/C/M) | 96.7 | 32.1 | 37.6 | 44% | 41% | 205.3 |
| 345 | BR | Alperton Community School (FD/C/M) | 100.5 | 32.1 | 35.9 | 43% | 38% | 183.9 |
| 346 | WF | Heathcote School (CY/C/M) | 100.2 | 32.1 | 31.1 | 39% | 33% | |
| 347 | CR | The Archbishop Lanfranc School (FD/C/M) | 100.1 | 32.1 | 34.0 | 37% | 33% | |
| 348 | HV | Emerson Park School (CY/C/M) | 98.5 | 32.0 | 37.4 | 39% | 45% | |
| 349 | BR | Queens Park Community School (FD/C/M) | 101.1 | 31.9 | 35.5 | 42% | 41% | 172.7 |
| 350 | HI | Harlington Community School (FD/C/M) | 99.5 | 31.8 | 32.9 | 41% | 38% | 192.8 |
| 351 | SW | St Michael's RC School (VA/C/M) | 98.0 | 31.8 | 39.9 | 39% | 43% | |
| 352 | HI | The Douay Martyrs RC School (VA/C/M) | 95.9 | 31.7 | 39.1 | 42% | 46% | 172.1 |
| 353 | IS | Elizabeth Garrett Anderson School (CY/C/G) | 101.1 | 31.5 | 31.6 | 40% | 32% | |
| 354 | BO | The Priory School (FD/C/M) | 99.2 | 31.5 | 38.8 | 39% | 41% | 211.9 |
| 355 | WF | Tom Hood School (CY/C/M) | 101.4 | 31.4 | 31.5 | 45% | 42% | |
| 356 | BE | Cleeve Park School (CY/C/M) | 99.1 | 31.3 | 34.3 | 42% | 35% | 142.2 |
| 357 | BR | Copland Community School & Tech (FD/C/M) | 97.1 | 31.3 | 36.4 | 41% | 42% | 232.3 |
| 358 | RE | Hainault Forest High School (CY/C/M) | 100.2 | 31.3 | 33.9 | 37% | 41% | 194.5 |
| 359 | CR | Westwood High School (CY/C/G) | 99.6 | 31.3 | 33.7 | 32% | 36% | |
| 360 | BA | St Mary's CofE High School (VA/C/M) | 96.8 | 31.2 | 36.1 | 39% | 40% | 185.7 |
| 361 | CR | St Mary's High School (VA/C/M) | 102.2 | 31.2 | 33.5 | 37% | 30% | |
| 362 | WF | Aveling Park School (CY/C/M) | 101.0 | 31.2 | 33.9 | 37% | 37% | |
| 363 | TH | George Green's School (VC/C/M) | 99.0 | 31.2 | 32.5 | 35% | 30% | 135.4 |
| 364 | HK | Clapton Girls' Technology College (CY/C/G) | 107.1 | 31.2 | 33.0 | 34% | 29% | |
| 365 | HW | Brentford School for Girls (CY/C/G) | 103.0 | 31.1 | 35.9 | 46% | 31% | 160.8 |
| 366 | HS | Fulham Cross Secondary School (CY/C/G) | 101.2 | 31.1 | 29.9 | 43% | 35% | |
| 367 | BE | St Mary & St Joseph's Catholic (VA/C/M) | 95.4 | 31.0 | 38.9 | 38% | 49% | 170.8 |
| 368 | NE | Lister Community School (CY/C/M) | 100.6 | 31.0 | 30.7 | 37% | 29% | |
| 369 | BR | John Kelly Girls' Technology (FD/C/G) | 100.8 | 30.8 | 36.4 | 41% | 46% | 203.3 |
| 370 | NE | The Royal Docks Community (CY/C/M) | 105.5 | 30.8 | 26.5 | 40% | 22% | |
| 371 | EN | Kingsmead School (CY/C/M) | 99.2 | 30.7 | 28.6 | 38% | 33% | 157 |
| 372 | HI | Mellow Lane School (FD/C/M) | 98.3 | 30.6 | 34.9 | 42% | 40% | 186.5 |
| 373 | LE | Deptford Green School (CY/C/M) | 102.2 | 30.6 | 34.8 | 36% | 41% | 183.5 |
| 374 | LA | Norwood School (CY/C/G) | 104.8 | 30.6 | 31.1 | 33% | 19% | |
| 375 | BD | Eastbrook Comprehensive School (CY/C/M) | 99.6 | 30.5 | 32.8 | 38% | 29% | 200 |
| 376 | WF | Kelmscott School (CY/C/M) | 100.0 | 30.5 | 30.0 | 37% | 29% | |
| 377 | BE | Welling School (CY/C/M) | 98.0 | 30.4 | 31.4 | 42% | 30% | 200.3 |
| 378 | SU | Glenthorne High School (CY/C/M) | 98.5 | 30.4 | 32.3 | 35% | 30% | 202.1 |
| 379 | BE | Erith School (CY/C/M) | 99.3 | 30.4 | 31.0 | 28% | 29% | 155.2 |
| 380 | BE | Bexleyheath School (CY/C/M) | 96.3 | 30.3 | 30.9 | 34% | 28% | 162.5 |
| 381 | HW | Chiswick Community School (CY/C/M) | 95.8 | 30.2 | 33.9 | 38% | 36% | 239.3 |
| 382 | WF | Rush Croft School (CY/C/M) | 99.2 | 30.2 | 34.2 | 36% | 35% | |
| 383 | CA | South Camden Community School (CY/C/M) | 104.0 | 30.2 | 29.8 | 32% | 30% | 165.7 |
| 384 | WA | Ernest Bevin College (CY/C/B) | 99.9 | 30.1 | 32.7 | 54% | 29% | 159.5 |
| 385 | LE | Forest Hill School (CY/C/B) | 99.8 | 30.1 | 34.7 | 42% | 37% | 182.2 |
| 386 | GR | The John Roan School (VC/C/M) | 99.2 | 30.1 | 35.9 | 37% | 35% | 147.6 |
| 387 | BA | Friern Barnet School (CY/C/M) | 96.8 | 30.1 | 31.9 | 37% | 36% | |
| 388 | BA | Bishop Douglass RC High School (VA/C/M) | 96.5 | 30.0 | 36.0 | 37% | 42% | 199.1 |
| 389 | NE | Forest Gate Community School (CY/C/M) | 103.3 | 30.0 | 32.0 | 34% | 33% | |
| 390 | WA | Chestnut Grove School (CY/C/M) | 100.8 | 30.0 | 32.6 | 32% | 34% | 144.8 |
| 391 | HK | Beis Chinuch Lebonos Girls School (IN/N/G) | | 29.9 | 34.4 | 68% | 67% | |
| 392 | IS | Central Foundation Boys' School (VA/C/B) | 101.3 | 29.9 | 29.6 | 37% | 27% | |
| 393 | EA | Dormers Wells High School (CY/C/M) | 104.5 | 29.8 | 35.4 | 36% | 31% | |
| 394 | BA | The Albany College (IN/S/M) | | 29.6 | 34.3 | 56% | 67% | 221.4 |
| 395 | HA | Harrow High School (CY/C/M) | 95.0 | 29.6 | 33.8 | 37% | 33% | |
| 396 | LE | Catford Girls' School (CY/C/G) | 101.0 | 29.6 | 30.5 | 36% | 21% | |

| | BOROUGH/SCHOOL | | VALUE ADDED 02 | GCSE 02 POINTS | GCSE 01 POINTS | GCSE 02 %5 A*-C | GCSE 01 %5 A*-C | A-LEVEL 02 POINTS |
|---|---|---|---|---|---|---|---|---|
| 397 | RI | Christ's CofE Comprehensive (VA/C/M) | 100.7 | 29.6 | 28.4 | 36% | 19% | |
| 398 | CR | Ashburton Community School (CY/C/M) | 102.0 | 29.6 | 28.4 | 31% | 22% | |
| 399 | HI | Uxbridge High School (FD/C/M) | 99.0 | 29.5 | 34.8 | 34% | 37% | 175.3 |
| 400 | HG | St Thomas More RC School (VA/C/M) | 97.6 | 29.5 | 33.7 | 33% | 31% | 130.9 |
| 401 | TH | Bethnal Green Technology College (CY/C/M) | 104.2 | 29.4 | 30.0 | 42% | 24% | |
| 402 | BA | The Ravenscroft School (CY/C/M) | 98.0 | 29.4 | 25.8 | 34% | 20% | 116.7 |
| 403 | LE | Addey & Stanhope School (VA/C/M) | 99.1 | 29.4 | 36.2 | 32% | 40% | 142.5 |
| 404 | NE | Little Ilford School (CY/C/M) | 101.9 | 29.4 | 31.9 | 32% | 27% | |
| 405 | KE | Holland Park School (CY/C/M) | 98.9 | 29.3 | 32.7 | 38% | 38% | 198.5 |
| 406 | WE | Quintin Kynaston School (CY/C/M) | 100.9 | 29.3 | 33.1 | 38% | 33% | 189.8 |
| 407 | LA | Charles Edward Brooke School (VC/C/G) | 103.8 | 29.3 | 37.4 | 36% | 40% | 117.3 |
| 408 | NE | Cumberland School (CY/C/M) | 103.1 | 29.3 | 28.9 | 27% | 26% | |
| 409 | LE | Northbrook CofE School (VA/C/M) | 99.7 | 29.3 | 29.1 | 20% | 26% | |
| 410 | HV | Bower Park School (CY/C/M) | 96.9 | 29.2 | 33.0 | 39% | 33% | |
| 411 | WA | John Paul II School (VA/C/M) | 101.6 | 29.2 | 32.7 | 32% | 27% | |
| 412 | EN | Chace Community School (CY/C/M) | 97.5 | 29.1 | 34.9 | 33% | 35% | 208.4 |
| 413 | SW | Aylwin Girls' School (CY/C/G) | 103.8 | 29.1 | 30.7 | 29% | 28% | |
| 414 | TH | Langdon Park Community School (CY/C/M) | 105.8 | 29.1 | 30.1 | 29% | 28% | |
| 415 | GR | Crown Woods School (CY/C/M) | 98.0 | 29.0 | 34.3 | 39% | 33% | 166.8 |
| 416 | NE | Eastlea Community School (CY/C/M) | 101.0 | 29.0 | 32.4 | 36% | 35% | |
| 417 | WA | Southfields Community College (FD/C/M) | 101.2 | 29.0 | 28.1 | 27% | 17% | 202 |
| 418 | HG | Highgate Wood Secondary School (CY/C/M) | 95.5 | 28.9 | 32.4 | 41% | 41% | 139.1 |
| 419 | ME | Raynes Park High School (CY/C/M) | 100.4 | 28.9 | 34.3 | 37% | 40% | |
| 420 | BR | Wembley High School (CY/C/M) | 97.8 | 28.9 | 31.0 | 34% | 32% | 192.2 |
| 421 | KI | Chessington Community College (CY/C/M) | 96.8 | 28.8 | 33.5 | 34% | 37% | 106 |
| 422 | EA | Brentside High School (FD/C/M) | 100.4 | 28.8 | 35.3 | 32% | 38% | 202.7 |
| 423 | RI | Whitton School (CY/C/M) | 95.8 | 28.8 | 32.1 | 31% | 36% | |
| 424 | NE | Brampton Manor School (CY/C/M) | 103.1 | 28.7 | 29.5 | 30% | 28% | |
| 425 | HK | The Skinners' Company's School (VA/C/G) | 105.3 | 28.6 | 31.5 | 34% | 30% | 116.6 |
| 426 | KE | Duff Miller College (IN/S/M) | | 28.5 | 26.9 | 46% | 31% | 237.4 |
| 427 | HV | The Royal Liberty School (CY/C/B) | 99.3 | 28.5 | 28.2 | 32% | 25% | |
| 428 | SU | Carshalton High School for Boys (CY/C/B) | 96.7 | 28.5 | 27.1 | 28% | 25% | 121.9 |
| 429 | LA | Bishop Thomas Grant Catholic (VA/C/M) | 99.0 | 28.3 | 33.4 | 29% | 37% | |
| 430 | HG | Northumberland Park Community (CY/C/M) | 103.4 | 28.3 | 27.3 | 19% | 18% | 108 |
| 431 | BE | Westwood College (CY/C/M) | 100.3 | 28.2 | 30.1 | 29% | 26% | |
| 432 | BD | Eastbury Comprehensive School (CY/C/M) | 96.3 | 28.1 | 31.6 | 38% | 27% | 216.7 |
| 433 | HS | Burlington Danes CofE School (VA/C/M) | 94.6 | 28.0 | 34.8 | 26% | 40% | |
| 434 | SW | Geoffrey Chaucer Technology (CY/C/M) | 101.2 | 28.0 | 31.2 | 22% | 19% | |
| 435 | KI | The Hollyfield School (FD/C/M) | 96.3 | 27.9 | 34.2 | 36% | 46% | 203.4 |
| 436 | HI | Abbotsfield School (FD/C/B) | 94.1 | 27.9 | 32.2 | 26% | 30% | 191.1 |
| 437 | BO | Kelsey Park School (FD/C/B) | 95.1 | 27.8 | 29.2 | 30% | 23% | 125 |
| 438 | LE | Sedgehill School (CY/C/M) | 96.9 | 27.7 | 29.3 | 30% | 26% | 113.3 |
| 439 | GR | BLA Theatre School (IN/S/M) | | 27.7 | 22.8 | 11% | 0% | |
| 440 | HW | Longford Community School (CY/C/M) | 94.7 | 27.5 | 26.5 | 34% | 28% | 126.8 |
| 441 | BA | The Edgware School (CY/C/M) | 103.0 | 27.5 | 27.4 | 28% | 21% | 150 |
| 442 | GR | Woolwich Polytechnic School (CY/C/B) | 96.7 | 27.3 | 32.3 | 27% | 31% | 200 |
| 443 | SW | Waverley School (CY/C/G) | 101.8 | 27.3 | 27.0 | 26% | 23% | |
| 444 | BO | Cator Park School for Girls (CY/C/G) | 94.6 | 27.2 | 30.1 | 31% | 32% | 189.3 |
| 445 | WE | Pimlico School (CY/C/M) | 97.3 | 27.2 | 31.9 | 27% | 33% | 233.9 |
| 446 | GR | Plumstead Manor School (CY/C/G) | 99.8 | 27.1 | 34.3 | 26% | 35% | 168.5 |
| 447 | NE | Rokeby School (CY/C/B) | 99.1 | 27.1 | 29.9 | 23% | 21% | |
| 448 | WF | George Mitchell Community (CY/C/M) | 100.4 | 27.1 | 27.1 | 20% | 24% | |
| 449 | RI | Shene School (CY/C/M) | 96.2 | 27.0 | 35.1 | 30% | 42% | |
| 450 | EN | Salisbury School (CY/C/M) | 102.1 | 26.9 | 25.5 | 22% | 19% | 81.3 |
| 451 | BD | The Sydney Russell School (CY/C/M) | 97.1 | 26.8 | 29.4 | 27% | 24% | 162.8 |
| 452 | WE | St Augustine's CofE Secondary (VA/C/M) | 99.2 | 26.6 | 27.7 | 28% | 25% | 72 |
| 453 | GR | Blackheath Bluecoat CofE (VA/C/M) | 96.2 | 26.6 | 27.7 | 27% | 20% | 115.4 |
| 454 | KE | Ashbourne Independent School (IN/N/M) | | 26.4 | 32.7 | 42% | 57% | 216.7 |
| 455 | BR | John Kelly Boys' Technology College (FD/C/B) | 101.1 | 26.4 | 27.2 | 31% | 24% | 152.9 |

| | BOROUGH/SCHOOL | | VALUE ADDED 02 | GCSE 02 POINTS | GCSE 01 POINTS | GCSE 02 %5 A*-C | GCSE 01 %5 A*-C | A-LEVEL 02 POINTS |
|---|---|---|---|---|---|---|---|---|
| 456 | GR | Eltham Green School (CY/C/M) | 101.6 | 26.3 | 25.7 | 17% | 16% | |
| 457 | LA | Stockwell Park School (CY/C/M) | 105.3 | 26.2 | 25.1 | 26% | 29% | |
| 458 | HS | Phoenix High School (CY/C/M) | 101.3 | 26.2 | 21.1 | 25% | 11% | |
| 459 | EN | Albany School (FD/C/M) | 98.0 | 26.1 | 29.2 | 28% | 22% | 137.2 |
| 460 | SW | Kingsdale Secondary School (CY/C/M) | 101.3 | 26.0 | 23.0 | 41% | 16% | |
| 461 | WF | Warwick School for Boys (CY/C/B) | 100.2 | 26.0 | 29.3 | 30% | 29% | |
| 462 | TH | The Blessed John Roche RC (VA/C/B) | 101.0 | 25.9 | 24.5 | 31% | 23% | |
| 463 | HS | Hurlingham & Chelsea Secondary (CY/C/M) | 97.0 | 25.9 | 30.6 | 23% | 34% | |
| 464 | IS | St Aloysius RC College (VA/C/B) | 96.3 | 25.7 | 27.2 | 30% | 28% | 50.8 |
| 465 | HS | Ravenscourt Theatre School (IN/S/M) | 99.6 | 25.7 | 34.8 | 14% | 33% | |
| 466 | GR | Kidbrooke School (CY/C/M) | 101.1 | 25.6 | 27.5 | 29% | 27% | 157.9 |
| 467 | CR | Selsdon High School (CY/C/M) | 96.3 | 25.6 | 26.9 | 28% | 22% | |
| 468 | WE | North Westminster Community (CY/C/M) | 100.5 | 25.6 | 27.4 | 27% | 27% | 160.7 |
| 469 | ME | Rutlish School (VC/C/B) | 95.1 | 25.6 | 33.6 | 27% | 32% | |
| 470 | IS | Islington Green School (CY/C/M) | 100.3 | 25.5 | 24.4 | 27% | 24% | |
| 471 | LE | Crofton School (CY/C/M) | 101.8 | 25.5 | 27.5 | 22% | 18% | 101 |
| 472 | SW | Warwick Park School (CY/C/M) | 103.8 | 25.4 | 26.6 | 26% | 19% | |
| 473 | GR | Riverston School (IN/N/M) | | 25.3 | 28.0 | 42% | 39% | |
| 474 | HK | Homerton College of Technology (CY/C/B) | 102.5 | 25.3 | 27.2 | 22% | 27% | |
| 475 | HG | Gladesmore Community School (CY/C/M) | 100.2 | 25.2 | 23.9 | 30% | 16% | 80 |
| 476 | ME | Tamworth Manor High School (CY/C/M) | 96.2 | 25.2 | 31.1 | 25% | 29% | |
| 477 | WF | The McEntee School (CY/C/M) | 99.5 | 25.2 | 17.0 | 20% | 13% | |
| 478 | HS | Henry Compton Secondary School (CY/C/B) | 100.1 | 25.1 | 29.8 | 29% | 29% | |
| 479 | KI | Beverley School (FD/C/B) | 93.9 | 24.9 | 30.8 | 29% | 38% | 79.4 |
| 480 | EA | Acton High School (CY/C/M) | 98.3 | 24.8 | 28.4 | 26% | 28% | |
| 481 | BD | Dagenham Priory Comprehensive (CY/C/M) | 93.0 | 24.8 | 26.8 | 20% | 29% | 114.1 |
| 482 | CA | Haverstock School (CY/C/M) | 98.2 | 24.7 | 28.5 | 28% | 27% | 180 |
| 483 | BR | Cardinal Hinsley High School (VA/C/B) | 96.0 | 24.6 | 24.4 | 21% | 25% | 138.7 |
| 484 | EN | Aylward School (CY/C/M) | 97.6 | 24.5 | 31.3 | 19% | 28% | 182.9 |
| 485 | HW | Feltham Community College (CY/C/M) | 95.0 | 24.4 | 23.2 | 28% | 17% | 128.8 |
| 486 | CA | Fine Arts College (IN/N/M) | | 24.3 | 46.3 | 55% | 83% | 261.8 |
| 487 | TH | Bow School (CY/C/B) | 99.0 | 24.3 | 18.7 | 18% | 16% | |
| 488 | EN | Lea Valley High School (CY/C/M) | 97.6 | 24.1 | 31.6 | 25% | 26% | 115.7 |
| 489 | GR | Eaglesfield School (CY/C/B) | 96.0 | 24.1 | 24.7 | 25% | 19% | 109.7 |
| 490 | SU | Stanley Park High School (CY/C/M) | 92.5 | 24.0 | 25.6 | 26% | 22% | 172.2 |
| 491 | SW | Archbishop Michael Ramsey Tech (VA/C/M) | 104.2 | 24.0 | 25.5 | 22% | 26% | 171.4 |
| 492 | CR | Addington High School (CY/C/M) | 96.4 | 24.0 | 23.9 | 18% | 10% | |
| 493 | HV | King's Wood School (CY/C/M) | 95.4 | 24.0 | 23.0 | 16% | 16% | |
| 494 | LE | St Joseph's Academy (VA/C/B) | 99.3 | 23.7 | 24.4 | 13% | 16% | |
| 495 | HV | Redden Court School (CY/C/M) | 96.6 | 23.5 | 29.7 | 26% | 28% | |
| 496 | CR | Stanley Technical High School (VA/C/B) | 94.3 | 23.5 | 27.5 | 14% | 16% | |
| 497 | CR | The Selhurst High School (CY/C/B) | 95.2 | 23.4 | 23.2 | 25% | 12% | |
| 498 | HG | The John Loughborough School (VA/C/M) | 91.9 | 23.2 | 26.7 | 24% | 24% | |
| 499 | SW | Walworth School (CY/C/M) | 96.2 | 23.1 | 21.0 | 14% | 12% | |
| 500 | IS | Highbury Grove School (CY/C/M) | 94.5 | 22.9 | 25.9 | 25% | 30% | 190 |
| 501 | WE | St George RC School (VA/C/M) | 97.9 | 22.9 | 22.0 | 20% | 14% | |
| 502 | ME | Bishopsford Community School (CY/C/M) | 100.9 | 22.8 | 20.1 | 18% | 10% | |
| 503 | HW | Hounslow Manor School (CY/C/M) | 98.3 | 22.1 | 30.6 | 21% | 30% | 134.1 |
| 504 | BO | Darul Uloom London (IN/S/B) | | 22.1 | 27.6 | 6% | 46% | |
| 505 | HK | Kingsland School (CY/C/M) | 98.1 | 22.0 | 24.6 | 20% | 20% | |
| 506 | EA | The Compton High School (CY/C/M) | 94.0 | 22.0 | 28.1 | 13% | 20% | 164.2 |
| 507 | HI | The Hayes Manor School (FD/C/M) | 93.6 | 21.8 | 29.9 | 20% | 30% | 163.5 |
| 508 | CR | Haling Manor High School (CY/C/M) | 98.9 | 21.6 | 25.4 | 16% | 15% | |
| 509 | GR | Abbey Wood School (CY/C/M) | 92.7 | 21.6 | 27.5 | 12% | 19% | |
| 510 | HI | John Penrose School (CY/C/M) | 92.6 | 21.5 | 27.4 | 17% | 23% | 127.5 |
| 511 | HG | White Hart Lane Secondary (CY/C/M) | 100.5 | 21.4 | 19.3 | 24% | 10% | 94.2 |
| 512 | HG | Park View Academy (CY/C/M) | 99.3 | 21.4 | 26.0 | 16% | 15% | 165 |
| 513 | SU | Stowford College (IN/S/M) | 95.3 | 21.3 | 25.8 | 8% | 29% | |
| 514 | LE | Malory School (CY/C/M) | 98.3 | 21.0 | 19.7 | 18% | 9% | |

| | BOROUGH/SCHOOL | | VALUE ADDED 02 | GCSE 02 POINTS | GCSE 01 POINTS | GCSE 02 %5 A*-C | GCSE 01 %5 A*-C | A-LEVEL 02 POINTS |
|---|---|---|---|---|---|---|---|---|
| 515 | LA | Lilian Baylis School (CY/C/M) | 104.1 | 21.0 | 23.0 | 6% | 18% | |
| 516 | BA | Whitefield School (CY/C/M) | 99.3 | 20.7 | 24.1 | 24% | 21% | 86.5 |
| 517 | HK | Hackney Free & Parochial CofE (VA/C/M) | 94.1 | 20.1 | 27.6 | 18% | 21% | |
| 518 | WA | Battersea Technology College (CY/C/M) | 97.5 | 20.0 | 20.4 | 14% | 17% | 81 |
| 519 | IS | Islington Arts & Media School (CY/C/M) | 99.6 | 19.3 | 27.6 | 23% | 22% | 80 |
| 520 | WE | International Community School (IN/N/M) | | 19.1 | 12.9 | 21% | 12% | 216.7 |
| 521 | IS | Holloway School (CY/C/B) | 96.8 | 18.8 | 20.4 | 20% | 12% | |
| 522 | HK | Beis Rochel d'Satmar Girls' School (IN/S/G) | 97.5 | 18.8 | 19.4 | 8% | 9% | |
| 523 | WE | Bales College (IN/N/M) | | 17.5 | 23.3 | 18% | 0% | 169.6 |
| 524 | HI | Evelyns Community School (CY/C/M) | 92.5 | 17.5 | 21.8 | 8% | 17% | 0 |
| 525 | BA | Wentworth Tutorial College (IN/N/M) | | 17.0 | 20.9 | 27% | 17% | 247.1 |
| 526 | BR | Willesden High School (CY/C/M) | 100.4 | 15.5 | 17.4 | 14% | 13% | 135 |

# Glossary

**ABRSM** Associated Board of the Royal Schools of Music
**ADT** Art, design and technology
**AICE** Advanced International Certificate of Education
**A-level** Advanced level examination
**APT** Advanced Placement Test
**ASDAN** Awards Scheme Development and Accreditation Network
**AS-level** Advanced Subsidiary level
**ATC** Air Training Corps
**AQA** Assessment and Qualifications Alliance
**BA** Bachelor of Arts degree
**B.Ed** Bachelor of Education degree
**B.Sc** Bachelor of Science degree
**BTEC** Business and Technical Education Council
**CCF** Combined Cadet Force
**CDT** Craft, design and technology
**Cert Ed** Certificate of Education
**CofE** Church of England
**CPVE** Certificate of Pre-vocational Education
**CREST** Creativity in Science and Technology
DfES Department for Education and Skills
**DipEd** Diploma of Education
**DPVE** Diploma in Pre-vocational Education
**DT** Design technology
**EAL** English as an additional language
**EAZ** Education Action Zone
**EFL** English as a foreign language
**ESL** English as a second language
**FRSA** Fellow of the Royal Society of Arts
**GCSE** General Certificate of Secondary Education
**GDST** Girls' Day School Trust
**GNVQ** General National Vocational Qualification
**HMI** Her Majesty's Inspectorate
**Hons** Honours degree
**IB** International Baccalaureate
**ICT** Information and communication technology
**ISTD** Imperial Society of Teachers of Dance
**IT** Information technology
**LAMDA** London Academy of Music and Dramatic Art
**LEA** Local Education Authority
**MA** Master of Arts
**M.Ed** Master of Education
**NVQ** National Vocational Qualification
**Ofsted** Office for Standards in Education
**PE** Physical education
**PHSE/PSHE** Personal, health and social education
**PRSE** Personal, religious and social education
**PSD** Personal and social development
**PSE** Personal and social education
**PSHRE** Personal, social, health and religious education
**PTA** Parent–teacher association
**RAD** Royal Academy of Dance
**RADA** Royal Academy of Dramatic Art
**RAM** Royal Academy of Music
**RC** Roman Catholic
**RCM** Royal College of Music
**RE** Religious Education
**RSA** Royal Society of Arts
**SATs** Standard Assessment Tests
**SEN** Special Educational Needs
**TEFL** Teaching English as a Foreign Language
**UCAS** Universities and Colleges Admissions Service

# Index

## Subject index

## Schools index

## R



## S



## T